# HANDBOOK OF EDUCATIONAL PSYCHOLOGY

The third edition of the *Handbook of Educational Psychology* is sponsored by Division 15 of the American Psychological Association. In this volume, 30 chapters address new developments in theory and research methods while honoring the legacy of the field's past. A diverse group of recognized scholars within and outside the United States provide integrative reviews and critical syntheses of developments in the substantive areas of psychological inquiry in education, functional processes for learning, learner readiness and development, building knowledge and subject matter expertise, and the learning and task environment. New chapters in this edition cover topics such as learning sciences research; latent variable models; data analytics; neuropsychology; relations between emotion, motivation, and volition (EMOVO); scientific literacy; sociocultural perspectives on learning; dialogic instruction; and networked learning. Expanded treatment has been given to relevant individual differences, underlying processes, and new research on subject matter acquisition.

The *Handbook of Educational Psychology*, Third Edition, provides an indispensable reference volume for scholars in education and the learning sciences, broadly conceived, as well as for teacher educators, practicing teachers, policy makers, and the academic libraries serving these audiences. It is also appropriate for graduate-level courses in educational psychology, human learning and motivation, the learning sciences, and psychological research methods in education and psychology.

**Lyn Corno** is former Professor of Education and Psychology (retired) at Teachers College, Columbia University, USA, and co-Editor of *Teachers College Record* and the National Society for the Study of Education *Yearbooks*.

**Eric M. Anderman** is Professor of Educational Psychology and Chair of the Department of Educational Studies at The Ohio State University, USA.

# HANDBOOK OF EDUCATIONAL PSYCHOLOGY

## Third Edition

Edited by

## Lyn Corno and Eric M. Anderman

Routledge
Taylor & Francis Group

NEW YORK AND LONDON

Third edition published 2016
by Routledge
711 Third Avenue, New York, NY 10017

and by Routledge
2 Park Square, Milton Park, Abingdon, Oxon, OX14 4RN

*Routledge is an imprint of the Taylor & Francis Group, an informa business*

First edition published by Routledge 1996
Second edition published by Routledge 2006

*Library of Congress Cataloging in Publication Data*
A catalog record has been requested

ISBN: 978-0-415-89481-4 (hbk)
ISBN: 978-0-415-89482-1 (pbk)
ISBN: 978-1-315-68824-4 (ebk)

Typeset in Times
by Swales & Willis Ltd, Exeter, Devon, UK

*With gratitude for his gracious guidance over many years, we dedicate this volume to the memory of Robert C. Calfee.*

# Contents

# Foreword

## Capturing the Landscape of Educational Psychology Today

*Lyn Corno*
Teachers College, Columbia University

*Eric M. Anderman*
The Ohio State University

With this third edition of the *Handbook of Educational Psychology,* we hope to move the field forward at the same time that we honor its history and legacy of years past. Today the field is not being redefined by individual scholars studying general tendencies within groups or current movements in educational research and policy, but by a growing understanding of what underlies learning and development through education. Over time, conducting meticulously planned studies of pointed research questions that build on one another has provided the recipe for growth, changing even some historic markers in the field. For example, in some areas of educational psychology, there is now an established relationship between data and theory that is leading to a new practice of science marked by modeling and visualization rather than hypothesis testing. In other areas, the data–theory relationship is informed by biography or narrative-experiential history. A third *Handbook of Educational Psychology* needs to support this changing landscape. The field no longer offers a limited menu; today it is more like a fully sustaining farm.

## Structure of the Volume

To shape the volume, we conducted a content analysis of the two previous editions of this *Handbook* (Alexander & Winne, 2006; Berliner & Calfee, 1996), alongside the table of contents for the three-volume *Educational Psychology Handbook* published by the American Psychological Association (Harris, Graham, & Urdan, 2012). This analysis led to a structure aligned with the previous editions of Division 15's *Handbook*, and some similar sections. It also allowed us to assess potential problems with overlapping content across the several different volumes.

We formed an advisory board to help us to think about topic coverage for the third edition. The advisory board members included a range of scholars representing diversity in expertise. These advisors helped us to identify salient topics, controversial issues, and new trends in the field. In addition, they assisted us in identifying scholars who might provide innovative perspectives and voices.

Prior editions of this *Handbook* included chapters on the history of educational psychology along with its underlying theory, research foci, and traditional methods of investigation. The authors of those chapters discussed central topics in learning and teaching within and across subject matter areas, as well as different types of students and educational contexts. For the present volume, we needed to make sense of the fact that a revolution is occurring in learning science and technology at the same time that educational research is more strongly than ever embracing the gold standards of longitudinal and experimental design, buttressed by systematic reviews of such trials. Herein, we sought to feature cutting-edge research across a wide range of conceptual approaches and topics.

We felt the need for fresh thinking in this *Handbook*, and so we decided to invite chapter authors who had made limited or no contributions to previous Division *Handbooks*. We also purposely invited some authors whose expertise is in disciplines other than educational psychology, because they are doing work that is becoming critical to our field. In addition, our publishing contract for this volume required relatively short chapters, so we requested that authors keep the number of co-authors to a maximum of two, and asked that they select co-authors who were established scholars. We reasoned that fewer, more experienced authors could produce timely chapters of good density and breadth given the page length constraints. Thus, we chose authors and topics, hoping to produce a volume that spoke to the factors making this era in our field such an exciting one.

## Five Research Domains

What seems clear from the chapters that comprise this volume is that each reworking of a research domain serves a particular function. Accordingly, the five domains included in the third edition illustrate: (a) new ways that we conduct our work and the assumptions that underlie them; (b) growing understandings of the fundamental processes that drive outcomes; (c) how best to conceptualize the critical qualities of learners and their development; (d) the combinations and sequences of instructional activities that lead to acquisition of subject matter knowledge and skill; and (e) the key role of contextual factors in education as a human cultural practice.

***Psychological inquiry in education.*** The first seeds, presented in our section on inquiry, generate an explication of some philosophically deep issues at the heart of education as a cooperative endeavor of humans and their environment. Neuroscience now shows that brain activity and circuits actually change with repeated situational transactions, providing justification for an evolutionary account of human reflective behavior driven in part by education. The chapters in this section illustrate the sharp research questions and corresponding methods of investigation that underlie dynamic, process-level theories and complex procedures for analyzing nested evidence. These chapters also address key measurement issues; they reflect the richness that is obtained through qualitative description; and they illustrate how disaggregation can be enhanced by modern digital technologies and data analytics. Finally, the value of multivariate and multimeasure longitudinal studies, which permit efficient assessment of change over a number of spaced occasions, is made clear; these methods also allow for the assessment of individual differences in change.

***Functional processes for learning.*** The second section of the volume, on functional processes, provides a modern perspective on the ancient triumvirate of cognition, affection, and conation (Hilgard, 1980). These mental processes all interplay with the tasks and events of learning and teaching. The chapter on cognition emphasizes the role of coordination in student learning and decision making, including involuntary processes and functional changes being studied using neuroimaging techniques. It shows how the human attention system helps to regulate and transform learner perceptions into short- and long-term cognitive-intellectual resources.

The three chapters on emotion, motivation, and volition together capture qualities that we might call *EMOVO*, for short. These are qualities that students bring into educational situations, but that also *arise during completion* of tasks and activities to either threaten or invigorate learning and productive follow-through. Studies of emotions, moods, attitudes, and physiological factors such as stress and flow states have led to important self-regulation interventions across school and other life experiences (e.g., relationships, addictive behavior). In the long run, the study of EMOVO promises an integrated path to understanding a variety of psychological phenomena that have historically been examined in isolation from one another. EMOVO qualities are proving to be: (a) reliably measured with innovative indices; (b) influenced in some cases through relatively simple, priming-based interventions or curriculum-embedded instruction; and (c) demonstrably important to successful

learning and engagement. Like some critical intellectual abilities, EMOVO sensibilities can also be fostered or wither, depending on social opportunities and student abilities to modulate them. Increasingly, researchers are also gaining insight into the neural basis of how habitual actions such as goal commitment or procrastination can alter an individual's EMOVO for better or worse.

***Learner readiness and development.*** The group of chapters under the section on readiness and development examines general cognitive and language abilities and disabilities, as well as beliefs, personality, and biographical characteristics of students, to inform how all of these variables influence motivational, linguistic, and moral development in schools. Person–environment interactions and modes of assessment contribute to individual differences in cognitive functioning, as well as to moral and identity trajectories, but so do differences in brain memory processes and sensitivities to cues. Studies of developmental-relational systems provide strong evidence that many of the readiness qualities, including those initially conceived as trait-like, are best conceptualized as dynamically malleable within specific ecologies. Carefully designed intervention environments offer trusting affordances for skill or habit development as well as behavior change in even very young children. Targeted and multicomponent programs can lead to demonstrable payoffs that grow over time.

***Building knowledge and subject matter expertise.*** The fourth part on knowledge and subject matter acquisition presents six chapters addressing the content areas of academic and social literacy, mathematics, science, history, and civics, respectively. Each of these chapters discusses new questions and methods for teaching practice and subject matter instruction that are informed by cognitive and sociocultural theory. Literacy interventions conducted in schools and classrooms can improve student knowledge in K-12 reading, writing, and use of oral language. Informal experiences in early childhood set the stage for thinking and learning in mathematics and science tasks that increasingly benefit from computer-guided inquiry. With controversial topics, such as scientific debates, there are new techniques for influencing student attitudes and conceptual understandings. Likewise, an understanding of history can grow from reflection on students' own experiences as well as their interpretations of the past. Many subject matter gains reflect domain-dependent individual practice, such as prompts for students to self-explain. These chapters show that deliberate practice is afforded by structured interventions designed to promote and accelerate complex learning.

***The learning and task environment.*** Finally, Part V's chapters consider the environment for learning in the larger sense. These chapters discuss spaces where children actually live and work, both in and beyond school. Digital learning communities and after-school programs now supplement and complement projects in school settings. The chapters bring us back to the critical importance of context by capturing the movement away from the narrow focus on learning tasks in classrooms and labs that used to be routine in educational psychology. After the methodological controversies of recent decades, the landscape today reflects important sociocultural principles. These authors are reworking the assumptions guiding earlier investigations, and suggesting ways to address and embrace more appropriate theory for subsequent generations.

To take one example, this shifting paradigm is present in modern research on academic discourse in classrooms where instruction is considered as dialogue, argumentation, and problem-based learning. New technology also offers affordances for fixing problems (e.g., how teachers can reach all students in a class; how researchers can collect real-time data to assess student learning). The internet can advantage learning if students are using it for web-mediated knowledge synthesis. Students can profitably use the internet as well in ways that make them think differently about educational communities, or for social purposes and fun that can increase engagement with academic content. Counter-narrative, qualitative cultural studies add a critical layer into this soil, calling into question untenable assumptions and methodological arrogance. Cultural values and practices that surround learners during their development become enmeshed in brain activity that affects behavior. If poverty at home subverts school learning, then other factors in the system need to change.

In addition to heightening awareness of subtle stereotypes and other unintentional behavior hovering beneath the surface, cultural studies in education highlight the important role of social perspective taking in teacher–student relationships. They illustrate how cultivating an understanding of difference among the scholarly community further benefits the system. Only with deeper plantings like this does a research terrain finally become loaded with the requisite resources needed for knowledge to grow.

## An Ever-Changing Ground

As much as people may like to cling to established research principles and routines, we find it noteworthy that our authors in this *Handbook* do not. Following on what their experiences produce, these scholars roll out entirely different prototypes for future work. If there is a problem with evidence in the field, then a new generation of research will investigate how to tighten or calibrate it, followed by how to extend and then catalog it. Theory built from interpretive analyses of large quantities of catalogued databases now at the fingertips of research scientists is in fact among the current trends. The technological revolution makes it possible for psychologists to capture some broader outcomes of education from the details of millions of individual students. Once again, the landscape is ready for new growth.

To edit of course is to collect and organize, as well as to gauge and guide the writing of others. It is also, we have realized, to make material more readable and, one hopes, engaging. We have to offer what the science shows, even if this is not always material that translates easily to practical circumstances in education settings. Additionally, instead of including a conventional chapter on the history of educational psychology at the beginning of our volume, we invited veteran educational psychologist Frank Farley to be innovative and craft a forward-looking chapter on its history that would appear at the end. This chapter, presented in the Afterword, provides a compilation of reflective commentaries from eight outstanding leaders of Division 15 and our field more broadly. In these essays, the authors consider the harvest: what are the most important accomplishments and major failures of educational psychology during their own careers? These leaders also comment on the current status of educational psychology and where they feel we are and should be headed in the future.

We are particularly pleased to include the essay by Robert C. Calfee, entitled "Back to the Future: Learning and Transfer Redux," which is being published posthumously; Bob passed away on October 24, 2014. We have dedicated this *Handbook* to his memory—he was and will continue to be a revered mentor to many of us writing in these pages. Knowing Bob, we feel he would concur with our final hope—that, overall, this volume of the *Handbook* conveys a deep respect for our complex and varied, never self-satisfied field.

## References

Alexander, P.A., & Winne, P. H. (Eds.) (2006). *Handbook of Educational Psychology* (2nd Ed.). Mahwah, NJ: Lawrence Erlbaum Associates.

Berliner, D.C., & Calfee, R. C. (Eds.) (1996). *Handbook of Educational Psychology.* New York, NY: Macmillan.

Harris, K. R., Graham, S., & Urdan, T. (Eds.) (2012). *Educational Psychology Handbook, Vols. 1-3.* Washington, D.C.: American Psychological Association.

Hilgard, E. R. (1980). The trilogy of the mind: Cognition, affection, and conation. *Journal of the History of Behavioral Sciences, 16,* 107–117.

# Acknowledgments

To say thank you for the fine counsel and dedicated time provided by our board of advisors is insufficient but heartfelt.

## Advisory Board Members

Philip Ackerman, Georgia Institute of Technology

Carole Ames, Michigan State University

Mimi Bong, Korea University, South Korea

Eric Bredo, University of Toronto, Canada

Martha Carr, University of Georgia

Robert Floden, Michigan State University

Donna Y. Ford, Vanderbilt University

John Hattie, University of Auckland, New Zealand

Robert Klassen, University of Alberta, Canada

Jonna M. Kulikowich, Pennsylvania State University

Susanne P. Lajoie, McGill University, Canada

Marcia C. Linn, University of California, Berkeley

Richard E. Mayer, University of California, Santa Barbara

Mary M. McCaslin, University of Arizona

P. David Pearson, University of California, Berkeley

Reinhard Pekrun, University of Munich, Germany

Gale M. Sinatra, University of Southern California

Sam Wineberg, Stanford University

We are also indebted to Trevor Gori, Rebecca Novak, Lane Akers, and the production editing team at Taylor & Francis/ Routledge who worked closely with us to ensure quality in publication.

In the end, the authors and reviewers are what make a *Handbook* what it is and can be for posterity. Those writing in the pages that follow, as well as the reviewers who graciously read their work and gave feedback, are not only among the finest scholars in the field, but also the kind of people who make editing satisfying as well as worthwhile.

## List of Reviewers

Philip Ackerman, Georgia Institute of Technology

Donna E. Alvermann, The University of Georgia

Terry Au, University of Hong Kong, Hong Kong

Jürgen Baumert, Max Planck Institute for Human Development, Germany

Daphne Bevalier, University of Rochester

Bronwyn Bevan, Exploratorium

Derek Briggs, University of Colorado

Bertram (Chip) Bruce, University of Illinois, Urbana-Champaign

Michelle M. Buehl, George Mason University

Brian Carolan, Montclair State University

Clark A. Chinn, Rutgers University

Julie Coiro, University of Rhode Island

Carol Connor, Arizona State University

Heather A. Davis, North Carolina State College of Education

Angela L. Duckworth, University of Pennsylvania

Richard Duschl, Pennsylvania State University

Jacquelynne Eccles, University of California Irvine

Christina E. Erneling, Lund University, Sweden

Constance Flanagan, University of Wisconsin Madison

Kimberley Freeman, Howard University

Richard Gilman, Cincinnati Children's Hospital

Christine Greenhow, Michigan State University

Jan-Eric Gustafsson, University of Gothenberg, Sweden

Geneva Haertal, SRI International

Rogers Hall, Vanderbilt University

Karen Harris, Arizona State University

Joan Herman, University of California, Los Angeles

Avi Kaplan, Temple University

A. Eamonn Kelly, George Mason University

Kenneth R. Koedinger, Carnegie Mellon University

Richard Lerner, Tufts University

Tzu-Jung Lin, The Ohio State University

David Lubinski, Vanderbilt University

Andrew Martin, University of Sydney, Australia

Lucia Mason, University of Padova, Italy

Allison McCabe, University of Massachusetts Lowell

Carolyn MacCann, The University of Sydney, Australia

Debra Meyer, Elmhurst College

James Moore, The Ohio State University

Karen Murphy, Pennsylvania State University

Darcia F. Narvaez, University of Notre Dame

Harry O'Neil, University of Southern California

David R. Olson, University of Toronto, Canada

Allison Ryan, The University of Michigan

Leona Schauble, Vanderbilt University

Dale H. Schunk, University of North Carolina at Greensboro

Simone Schweber, University of Wisconsin Madison

Peter Sexias, University of British Columbia, Canada

Finbarr (Barry) Sloane, National Science Foundation

John Sweller, University of New South Wales, Australia

Nicole Patton Terry, Georgia State University

Sharon Tettegah, University of Illinois, Urbana-Champaign

Tim Urdan, Santa Clara University

Lieven Verschaffel, Katholieke Universiteit Leuven, Belgium

Noreen M. Webb, University of California, Los Angeles

Allan Wigfield, University of Maryland

Louise Wilkinson, Syracuse University

Philip H. Winne, Simon Fraser University

Frank Worrell, University of California Berkeley

Jonathan Zaff, Tufts University and Center for Promise

Moshe Zeidner, University of Haifa, Israel

# Part I

## Psychological Inquiry in Education

# 1

# Philosophical Perspectives on Mind, Nature, and Educational Psychology

*Eric Bredo*[1]
University of Toronto, Canada

This chapter opens the *Handbook*, and provides a reflective, philosophical discussion intended to inform the educational psychology emerging today. To gain perspective on current theory and research in the field it is helpful to consider some of the basic ways that human nature and conduct are conceived. Since the most basic images of human nature and conduct often have earlier historical origins as parts of larger visions of mind and nature that were first articulated by philosophers, perspective on present and emerging thought can often be gained by considering it in the context of earlier ways of thinking.

The sections that follow begin with a discussion of what a philosophical perspective might mean to psychological research in education, and why an educational psychologist should care about a philosophical consideration of the field. Three different ways of thinking about mind and nature that address this issue are discussed and related to vitalistic, mechanistic, and evolutionary ways of thinking represented, iconically, in the work of Aristotle, Newton, and Darwin. The perspectives toward mind and nature that these three great revolutions in thought introduced bear on how contemporary educational psychologists conceptualize human nature and conduct. Some implications of these different conceptions for education are considered in the conclusions.

## Philosophical Perspectives

The way an issue is conceptualized is usually the most important step in dealing with it. The first stroke on the canvas, or the first cut of the marble, affects everything that comes later. The same is true of an initial choice of conception, model, metaphor, or image in psychology. As William James wrote:

> It is astonishing what havoc is wrought in psychology by admitting at the outset apparently innocent suppositions, that nevertheless contain a flaw. The bad consequences

> develop . . . and are irremediable, being woven through the whole texture of the work. (James 1890/1952, p. 146)

Despite the importance of the way an issue is first conceived, it is often difficult to correct poor conceptualizations because the basic distinctions involved in them are so familiar that they are not recognized as choices that are open to revision (Wittgenstein, 1958). One of the aims of philosophy is to make these basic concepts or distinctions more visible and open to conscious choice so that we do not become trapped in intellectual cages of our own construction.[2] Isaiah Berlin articulated this task well:

> The task of philosophy . . . is to extricate and bring to light the hidden categories and models in terms of which human beings think (that is, their use of words, images and other symbols), to reveal what is obscure or contradictory in them, to discern the conflicts between them that prevent - the construction of more adequate ways of organizing and describing and explaining . . . and then, at a still "higher" level, to examine the nature of this activity itself . . . and to bring to light the concealed models that operate in this second-order, philosophical, activity itself. (Berlin, 1939/1999, p. 10)

As this description suggests, there are both critical and constructive aspects of this effort, philosophy attempting to critically appraise different conceptualizations, and to suggest better, less problematic ones. In doing so the aim is to develop "as unified, consistent, and complete an outlook upon experience as is possible" (Dewey, 1916b, p. 378). Let me begin with the critical aspect.

## Prior Criticisms

In the first edition of this *Handbook*, written now 20 years ago, Denis Phillips noted three lines of philosophical criticism of then prominent thinking in educational psychology. These criticisms suggested that educational psychologists had a tendency: (a) to derive recommendations for educational practice too directly from psychological theories or generalizations; (b) for conceptual confusion and lack of conceptual clarity; and (c) to adopt psychological conceptions that fail to "do justice to human experience," and depict "people as being, in some ways, sub-human" (Phillips, 1996, p. 1010). My own chapter in the second edition of the *Handbook*, written ten years later, elaborated on the second of these issues (Bredo, 2006a).

The first criticism was directed against the notion that educational practice can be directly deduced from psychological laws or generalizations. The notion that finding "what works" will tell us how to educate, or that "education science" will do the same, are examples. The popular notion that knowledge of the brain will tell one how to teach is another. There are at least two problems with this notion. First, knowledge of what may be effective does not speak to what is desirable, just as a street map does not determine where it is good to go. Second, theory is general but practical situations are unique. As a result the practical consequences of acting on a theory depend on many considerations that can never be fully stated in the theory. Theoretical knowledge is not the same as practical wisdom.

The second line of criticism points to instances of conceptual confusion or lack of conceptual clarity. One form of conceptual confusion involves misplaced concreteness or reification (Ryle, 1949). The fact that the word "mind" is a noun often leads to thinking of it as a thing. Conceived this way, the inquirer naturally wants to know where it is located, leading to the effort to locate the mind in the brain (for a critique, see Bakhurst, 2008). Since it is impossible to find the mind as a whole in the brain as a whole, the effort then shifts to finding specific mental functions in specific brain regions, as in the notion that there are different mental "modules" located in different brain regions (see Chapter 5, this volume). Such attempts at spatial localization inevitably fail, however, because functions are relationships, and relationships have no location.[3] To take a less mystified example, the heart is vital to pumping blood and oxygen to other organs, but a heart beating without regard to the state of these other organs results in death, not proper functioning. Functioning is not *in* the heart since functioning involves coordination and coordination is not "in" anything. This issue is practically important because improperly locating a cause can lead to misguided treatment, such as focusing on an organ or individual in isolation, while ignoring the relationships in which they participate (e.g., Watzlawick, Beavin, & Jackson, 1967).

Another form of conceptual error occurring in educational psychology and other fields is the tendency to treat a name for a form of behavior as its cause. Viewing a person's angry behavior as *caused* by "anger," or inattention as *caused* by "attention deficit hyperactivity disorder," are examples. When terms for a pattern of behavior are treated as causal explanations of the same behavior, they clearly fail to explain anything. A closely related problem occurs when psychological concepts useful for understanding or explaining behavior, such as cognitive rules, schemata, and structures, are imputed to the individuals themselves, as though the individuals used the same rules or structures as the psychologist does in accounting for their behavior (Phillips, 1987c). This tendency has been so common in psychology that James termed it the "psychologist's fallacy" (James, 1890/1952, p. 128). Yet another conceptual error involves confusing a representation with reality. Stated more carefully, this involves confusing *a* representation with *the* representation (Goodman, 1972). Dewey termed this the "philosophical fallacy" (Dewey, 1929/1958), but it is also common in other fields, including educational psychology. The notion that nature is basically or essentially mechanical is an example, of which more will be said later.

This brings us to Phillips' third point: that psychological models are frequently dehumanizing. Simplification or idealization is necessary for explanation and empirical endeavor, which cannot attend to everything, but every model biases attention in a certain way, highlighting some things and obscuring others (March, 1972). As Bandura noted:

> What we believe man [*sic*] to be affects which aspects of human functioning we study most thoroughly and which we disregard. Premises thus delimit research and are, in turn, shaped by it. As knowledge gained through study is put into practice, the images of man [*sic*] on which social practices are based have even vaster implications. (Bandura, 1974, p. 859)

Among the "vaster consequences" of the models adopted in educational psychology are effects on schools, whose structures and practices are often built around psychological concepts (McDermott & Hood, 1982; Ramirez & Boli-Bennett, 1982), ultimately affecting students. These considerations imply that a choice of psychological model involves ethical as well as descriptive concerns, since how we think of ourselves is not only about who we are, but, when acted upon, also about who we want to become (see Chapter 12, this volume).

## The Paradox of Self-Knowledge

These points begin to suggest a paradox implicit in the attempt to gain self-knowledge. Can we ever really grasp ourselves intellectually when every conception is necessarily partial, in both senses? This question applies with some force to psychology, the science of the *psyche*. Since the Greek word *"psyche"* is commonly translated as "soul," the whole notion of *"psych*ology," a science of the *psyche,* appears to be a contradiction in terms (the soul not being recognized as an object of scientific inquiry). As a result, psychology apparently faces a choice between being either scientific and soulless, or soulful and unscientific.

This point may seem facile since it merely plays on the word *"psyche,"* and psychology long ago got over the embarrassment of its name and chose science over the soul. Nevertheless, tensions remain between the aim of understanding ourselves in a more definite scientific sense, and the aim of understanding ourselves more holistically and sympathetically. This tension was evident in psychology's formative years in Wilhelm Wundt's the "two psychologies," one physiological and positivistic, and the other cultural and interpretive (Cole, 1996). Similar tensions continue today, reflected in the continuing methodology wars in education, among others (see Chapter 2, this volume). It would seem that the attempt to grasp ourselves involves a paradox, like the notion of a hand grasping itself, in which only parts can be grasped firmly, leaving the whole only felt or vaguely known.

The philosopher Wilfred Sellars depicted this tension as arising from a conflict between two images of ourselves that have different historical origins (Sellars, 1963). The "manifest image" is the way we conceive of ourselves in everyday life, such as understanding our own behavior and that of others as resulting from motives or desires associated with an inner self. Sellars suggested that this image, which is the default theory that we use in understanding our own and others' conduct, is largely Aristotelian in origin. [4] This first image conflicts with a second, "scientific image" that derives largely from seventeenth-century mechanics. When people, and particularly scholars and researchers, seek to explain behavior "objectively" or "scientifically," they are likely to appeal to this second image, explaining behavior in terms of external forces or material entities, such as the brain.

These two images conflict in theory, one basing explanation on purposes or aims and the other on external forces. They also conflict in practice, creating dilemmas about how to respond to conduct that can be interpreted either as willed or as caused (Olson, 2011). The manifest image also appears to be relatively complete, but untrue, while the scientific image appears to be relatively true, but incomplete (Sellars, 1963). As a result, we are left with something like an M. C. Escher drawing in which one interpretation ends up contradicting itself, suggesting another interpretation that also ends up contradicting itself. Sellars suggested that the philosophical task in such situations is to attempt to find an approach in which these "differing perspectives on a landscape are fused into one coherent experience" (Sellars, 1963, p. 4) (For further reflections on the need for conceptual double vision, see Bateson, 1988.)

## Three Images of Mind and Nature

Given this tension, it may be helpful to consider three, rather than two, perspectives on mind, nature, and ourselves. A first approach considered here is a vitalistic one, for which Aristotle is the iconic thinker. Since Aristotle might also be considered the first psychologist—the first to study the *psyche* naturalistically—this view has historical priority and has been enormously influential in Western thought. The second approach is a mechanistic one, for which Newton is the iconic scientist or natural philosopher, and Descartes a key philosopher/psychologist. Since Descartes is often considered the first modern psychologist, we might view him as representative of a "modern" view of human nature and conduct. Finally, a third image derives from nineteenth-century evolutionary thought, for which Darwin is the iconic

scientist, and Charles Sanders Peirce, perhaps, the most prescient philosopher. Peirce may seem an odd choice here, and one could appeal to Dewey instead; however, Peirce laid the groundwork for a statistical and non-linear approach to science, helped to found the science of semiotics, and developed a semiotic conception of mind and self, and as such is sometimes considered the first "post-modern" philosopher. The fact that his work is gaining new consideration today provides another reason for reconsidering it in the context of an emerging educational psychology.

While I have introduced these three approaches in historical terms, one can also consider them more analytically, and I will in fact do a bit of both. Perhaps the closest parallel to the set of distinctions I am drawing is Dewey and Bentley's comparison of explanations based on "self-action," "interaction," and "transaction" (Dewey & Bentley, 1949). In "self-action" the cause of behavior is viewed as internal to the object, such as in its intrinsic character, quality, or potential. In "interaction" (as Dewey and Bentley used the term) the cause of behavior is an interaction between two things that affect one another externally, like interacting billiard balls. Finally, in a "transaction" the relationship changes the interacting objects themselves.

An example closer to educational psychology occurs in Cronbach's comparison of different paradigms of scientific psychology. Cronbach (1957) first compared two paradigms: the psychology of human individual differences (characterized by its use of correlational methods), and behavioral psychology (characterized by the use of experimental methods). As he noted, these paradigms are mirror opposites, the first focusing on the effects of individual differences on behavior in the same environment, and the second on the effects of environmental differences on the behavior of the same individuals. As such, each represented only half of a more general approach that could consider the interactive effects of individual and environmental differences on behavior (task performance). In a later paper Cronbach argued for this more general approach, represented by aptitude × treatment interaction research (Cronbach, 1975). This discussion is important because it represents another way of highlighting a third form of relationship that is not reducible to simpler ones, at least when interactions are actually present.

A number of other approaches to psychology and education adopt similar comparisons involving three kinds of relationships. Bandura's (1985) comparison of internal theories (psychodynamic and trait theories), external theories (radical behaviorism), and interactional accounts (his own social-cognitive theory) is an example. In the last approach three factors interact—personality factors, environmental factors, and behavior—while the first and second approaches are simpler.

In education, Kohlberg and Mayer's (1972) comparison of "romantic," "cultural transmission," and "progressive" approaches to educational aims is also similar, although here the focus is on educational aims rather than on causes for changes in behavior. "Romantic" approaches to education base their aims on the inner desires or potentials of individuals, while "cultural transmission" approaches base aims on external demands. Kohlberg and Mayer's preferred approach, a "progressive" one based primarily on Piagetian theory (which they claim, incorrectly in my view, also represents Deweyan theory), adapts educational aims to universal stages of development that are viewed as integrating individual and cultural concerns. Finally, a similar contrast between internalist, externalist, and interactional/evolutionary approaches informed my own discussion of the way the concept of "learning" has evolved in psychology (Bredo, 1997), and contrasting methodological orientations in educational research (Bredo, 2006b). While these analytic comparisons may be helpful in clarifying the contrasts to be drawn here, I believe it is also helpful to consider educational psychology in the wider context of the historical development of ideas—beginning with Aristotle.

## The Manifest Image—Vitalism

As noted previously, the "manifest image" is the everyday or common-sense way in which people tend to envision themselves, inherited in fair part from Aristotle. Aristotle's approach has been characterized as a form of "vitalism" (Royce, 1914/1951) or "natural teleology" (Bambrough, 1963/2003) because he considered all of nature to be purposive or end-directed. As he put it, "Nature does nothing in vain. For all things that exist by Nature are means to an end, or will be concomitants of means to an end" (McKeon, 1941, p. 600). Aristotle's approach was also typological, as many sciences are in their early phases. Adopting the Greek conception of nature, *physis*, in which a thing's nature is what it tends to develop into under ideal conditions, he sought to categorize things in terms of the ends essential to their being that kind of thing. As one Aristotle scholar put it:

> The character of a substance—what it is to be a substance of the kind to which it belongs—is comprehensible only in terms of the condition in which the substance reaches its proper fulfillment . . . To know what something is is to know what it is *for*; to know what something is for, we must learn what is its nature, its character, its *form.* (Bambrough, 1963/2003, p. xxxii)

Aristotle faced a version of the mind/body problem in his day since earlier materialists, like Democritus, had argued that everything is made of minute atoms whose interactions result in an object's properties, while idealists, like Plato, believed that patterns or forms are primary, and that particular things are imperfect appearances of ideal types which constitute reality. Aristotle attempted to soften this matter/form dichotomy by introducing a series of steps or gradations between matter and mind. In this view even inert matter is driven by ends, since it has inherent potentials that it tends to actualize, heavy things, like earth and water, tending to move down toward the center of the earth, if unconstrained, and light things, like air and fire, up towards the heavens. Living things also have their characteristic ends, all acting to reproduce themselves and "partake of the eternal and divine" by making their forms eternal, so far as possible. This was the "goal towards which all things strive" and "for the sake

of which they do whatsoever their nature renders possible" (McKeon, 1941, p. 561).

What makes life possible, in this conception, is having a *psyche*, "the form of a natural body having life potentially within it" (McKeon, 1941, p. 555). The psyche was what enabled living things to move themselves as they do. While all living things have a "nutritive" *psyche* enabling them to grow and reproduce, growth being considered a form of movement (see Darwin, 1881), animals have a "sensitive" *psyche*, in addition, enabling them to move away from threatening or toward beneficial conditions before they occur. Finally, human beings have a "rational" *psyche* (in addition to nutritive and sensitive *psyches*), a social or discursive ability allowing them to select responses on the basis of "forechoice" (Randall, 1960). Considered in this way, the rational mental abilities of human beings are a subset of life functions possessed by all animals, which are a subset of those possessed by all living things, including plants. Mind was a subset of nature, rather than something opposed to it.

In a related analysis, Aristotle also distinguished between four types of cause—material, efficient, formal, and final. As with the analysis of the *psyche,* there are levels or types of cause that help relate crude material beginnings to final ideal endings. The material cause is the effect of the matter of which an object is formed, the efficient cause the effect of action on the object, the formal cause the effect of the form being sought, and the final cause the ultimate end or function of the object. This analysis enabled Aristotle to account for a wide range of phenomena, including human action, which is not well explained by efficient or mechanical causation alone (Juarrero, 1999).

Aristotle's analysis of the human *psyche* suggested that it was hierarchically layered, the rational *psyche* on top, regulating the sensitive and nutritive *psyches*. Since the essential or defining characteristic of human beings is to be rational, the end or *telos* of human life was understood to involve becoming a rationally self-regulated and self-realizing person (Aristotle, 1980). If we understand our own natures properly, he suggested, the goal of human life, *eudaimonia* (translated as "happiness" or "self-realization") can be understood to be to use reason to form our own characters, shaping our habits and desires so that we tend to behave in ever more virtuous ways.

This model of the *psyche* mirrored Aristotle's hierarchical view of nature, in which inanimate things, living things, animals, and human beings are related in a ladder leading toward the divine, the unmoved mover, or God, who accounted for motion and was viewed as pure mind or pure reflection. One can see this orderly model of the cosmos as also mirroring a hierarchical conception of social order in which the reasoning classes are on top, and other classes below. As Ferry comments,

> The Greek world was fundamentally an aristocratic world, a universe organized as a hierarchy in which those most endowed by nature should in principle be "at the top," while the less endowed saw themselves occupying inferior ranks. And we should not forget that the Greek city-state was founded on slavery. (Ferry, 2002, p. 72)

Aristotle's hierarchical conception of nature, social life, and the *psyche* served as a link between the Platonic conception of values and the "great chain of being" of the Middle with its feudal social order based on fixed, inherited classes and functions (Lovejoy, 1936).

This sketch may suggest some of what we have also inherited from Aristotelian thought (especially as mediated by Christian scholastics). Perhaps the most important is the tendency to explain change in terms of inner drives or desires, representing latent potentials that are actualized under appropriate conditions. Conceiving of individuals (and biological species) as falling into fixed, essential types is another inheritance, the first study of character types being conducted by a Roman follower of Aristotle (Bambrough, 1963/2003). An emphasis on the use of reason to train one's character toward virtue is a third inheritance, of which current work on student self-regulation can be seen as an outgrowth (see Chapter 12, this volume). Finally, the value hierarchy implicit in Aristotelian (and Platonic) thought also remains important. We continue—in both everyday and scholarly life—to value mind over body, theory over practice, reason over emotion or habit, "higher" humans over other "lower" organisms. We are more Aristotelian than we realize.

## The Scientific Image—Mechanism

The second image of mind, nature, and ourselves is based on mechanistic thought deriving from the scientific revolution of the seventeenth century. Mechanistic ideas developed, in part, in reaction to Aristotelian thought, which had become associated with religious dogmatism under the scholastics (Alexander, 2014). With the development of the Copernican view of the heavens, supported by Galileo's telescopic observations and Newton's equations, the earth became one bit of matter revolving around other bits, displacing human beings from the center of the cosmos. The development of an experimental approach to science also displaced passive Aristotelian observation with a more directly manipulative approach, providing the basis for quantitative laws of motion that better accorded with the movement of matter than Aristotle's categories and potentials.

To be clear about what a classical "mechanistic" account means for contemporary theory and research it may be helpful to summarize its basic assumptions and assertions, drawing on Newton (1686/1952).

1. Matter is composed of simple particles, without inner structure, whose properties do not change with changes in their movement (Newton's idealized point-masses).
2. Changes in motion (acceleration) only occur as a result of external forces (Newton's first law).
3. Changes in motion are related to their cause (force) by a universal, deterministic law (Newton's second law, $F = ma$).
4. The force exerted by interacting particles on one another is equal and opposite (Newton's third law).

These four statements help highlight the contrast between Newtonian and Aristotelian assumptions. First, if movement can be understood in terms of the interaction of idealized *particles,* then form plays no role in nature. Bits of matter attract one another throughout the universe regardless of the ways in which they happen to be clumped (although their distance from one another matters). Second, if changes in movement only occur as a result of external forces, then matter has no internal drives or tendencies. It isn't "trying" to go anywhere and has no "potential" it seeks to actualize. If it has no inherent direction of change then time is also purely extrinsic (Prigogine, 1980) and nature has no "consummations" (Dewey, 1929/1958). Third, Newton's quantitative, deterministic laws also differed from Aristotle's qualitative categorizations and potentials. Finally, the fact that interacting masses affect one another means there can be no "unmoved mover," unlike Aristotle's conception of God and the rational *psyche*, which were viewed as causing movement but as not being moved themselves (Juarrero, 1999).

The puzzling feature of a mechanistic account is what to make of the observer. The observer has to care about form, such as the size and shape of the earth or moon. The observer also has to act intentionally and care about beginnings and endings, such as by performing an experiment and noting the results. In a Newtonian analysis the observer also has to be separable from the interactions being studied, which is not possible if everything is affected in equal and opposite ways. Making nature a purposeless machine created a gap between observer and observed, subject and object, mind and nature, ends and means that became difficult—if not impossible—to resolve.

Descartes at least faced this issue directly. Noting that some behaviors, like reflexes, are mechanical in nature, he considered the body to be a complex machine or automaton, not unlike the reflex-arc conception of the nineteenth century (Huxley, 1870/1893). Subtle "animal spirits" flowed "from the heart to the brain, and from there . . . through the nerves into the muscles . . . [giving] movement to all the members, without the need for imagining any other reason" (Descartes, 1637/1969, p. 29). This flow was regulated by sensory impressions, internal passions, and memory, with the result that, "the members of this body move in as many different ways . . . as our own bodies can move, without the intervention of our will" (Descartes, 1637/1969, p. 30).

Other aspects of human behavior appeared to be decidedly non-mechanical, such as the ability to put words and signs together "to tell our thoughts to others" and arrange them "differently in order to answer to the sense of all that is said" (Descartes, 1637/1969, p. 30). The ability to solve novel problems also differentiated human beings from machines, which "inevitably fail" because they "do not act through knowledge but only through the disposition of their organs" (Descartes, 1637/1969, p. 30). Observing that if his conscious thought stopped he would have no idea if he existed, Descartes concluded that he must be, "a substance the whole essence or nature of which was merely to think, and which, in order to exist, needed no place and depended on no material thing" (Descartes, 1637/1969, p. 18).

In dividing human conduct in this way, Descartes split Aristotle's more continuous levels of the *psyche* in two. The rational *psyche* was placed in the soul, while the nutritive and sensitive *psyches* were allocated to the body (Lowry, 1971). Aristotle's types of causation were similarly divided, the material and efficient causes being represented in bodily behavior, and formal and final causes in the soul (Juarrero, 1999). In conceiving of human behavior in this way, Descartes took thought back to the categorical division between the material and ideal worlds that Christianity inherited from Plato, while rejecting Aristotle's more continuous, naturalistic scheme.

Cartesian dualism was extraordinarily influential (Huxley, 1870/1893), perhaps because it allowed science and religion to go their separate ways without too much entanglement. Science could focus on means, while religion could focus on ends. However, conceiving of mind and matter as different substances, located in categorically different realms (the extensional realm of space and time and the intentional realm of ideas), created insuperable problems for understanding how the two could interact:

> If thoughts and sensations belong to an immaterial or non-physical portion of reality . . . how can they have effects in the physical world? How, for example, can a decision or act of will cause a movement of a human body? How, for that matter, can changes in the physical world have effects in the non-physical part of reality? If one's feeling pain is a non-physical event, how can a physical injury to one's body cause one to feel pain? (van Inwagen, 2007)

Since these questions appear to have no adequate answers, metaphysical dualism has often been rejected in favor of either its materialistic or idealistic half. Either everything is matter (conceived mechanistically), and mind, soul, and consciousness are illusions or, if everything is an idea, pattern, or form, then matter is an illusion. Contemporary "eliminative materialists" adopt the first position, arguing, "there is nothing more to the mind than what occurs in the brain. The reason mental states are irreducible is not because they are non-physical" but because "they do not really exist" (Ramsey, 2013). But if mind is just the functioning of a particularly complicated machine it becomes difficult to explain the non-mechanical aspects of behavior that Descartes outlined, such as the ability to respond to hypothetical events that have not yet occurred or may never occur. As Deacon argues, phenomena like life and mind involve responses to "incomplete" or "unfinished" events that are part of a process that has its own internal development, while matter, mechanistically construed, has no intrinsic development and is moved only by actual events (Deacon, 2012).

The other alternative, idealism, conceives of material objects as really or essentially ideas, like Platonic forms. Today's "radical constructivists" come close to this idea, suggesting that "objects" are mental constructs (Glasersfeld, 1995). The sense of this notion clearly depends on how one defines an "object," but if matter is just an idea, it becomes difficult to explain events like walking into a door accidentally, which has a decidedly non-ideal quality. As a result all three of these choices—metaphysical dualism, materialism, and idealism—have tended to be problematic, raising

suspicions that the whole line of thinking has gone wrong—undoubtedly at its conception.

Related disputes, important to educational psychology, derive from epistemological rather than metaphysical dualism. Here the issue is not a metaphysical question, such as whether the soul or mind is real or imaginary, but an epistemological question about whether knowledge is founded in mental or material events. Descartes' followers started on the mental side, viewing knowledge as based on clear and distinct *a priori* ideas, while Newton's followers, like Locke, started from the material side, viewing knowledge as based on elementary sensations caused by external objects (Feingold, 2004). This tension has been represented in differing approaches to learning theory as well as in methodological disputes between rationalists and empiricists. Debate between "configurationist" and "associationist" approaches to learning theory is one example, the former holding that learning is shaped by preexisting mental patterns, while the latter views learning as the association of elementary stimuli or sensory impressions (Bruner, 2004; Hilgard & Bower, 1966). Each approach had its successes, but associationists found it difficult to account for one-trial and illusory learning, while configurationists had difficulty accounting for gradual and veridical learning (Hilgard & Bower, 1966). Later divisions between behavioral and cognitive learning theories repeated a similar pattern. Behaviorists (influenced by Hume's skepticism about knowing other minds) focused on the association of externally observable stimuli and responses, while cognitivists focused on inferred internal rules or representations, and symbol-manipulating operations (Newell & Simon, 1972). Each tended to oppose the other's foundations—directly observed external changes versus inferred internal rules and procedures—but I believe it is fair to say that each was, again, able to account for phenomena the other found difficult to explain (see, e.g. Catania, 1984).

The principal source of these difficulties appears to lie in the original notion that nature is inherently mechanistic. Once nature is viewed as a machine, and this model confounded with nature itself (an instance of the philosophical fallacy), there is no place for purposes, goals, values, ends, functions, or meanings, since these all depend on intrinsic relations between beginnings and endings. As a result, it appears that we have written ourselves out of our own story of nature (Deacon, 2012). And, what is particularly relevant for educational psychology, the resulting conception of mind as rationalistic and "out of it," emotionally, practically, and socially, is dysfunctional if taken seriously (Damasio, 1994; Lave & Wenger, 1991; Suchman, 1987). A strong division between mind and body may also align with the contemporary system of social classes and educational tracks, to the detriment of all.

## The Evolutionary Image

This brings us to the third image of mind, nature, and ourselves—an evolutionary one. Evolutionary ideas came into vogue in the nineteenth century, affecting most scholarly fields (Prigogine & Stengers, 1984). In the United

States the dominant influences were Darwinian ideas about the evolution of biological species and neo-Hegelian ideas about the evolution of culture (Miller, 1968). While stimulated by technological changes, as well as by social changes, such as the American and French revolutions, evolutionary ideas also grew out of developments within science, such as the adoption of statistical thinking (Gigerenzer & Swijtink, 1989; Maxwell, 1859/1965; Menand, 2001), and interest in self-governing machines, like the Watt steam engine (Maxwell, 1868). These developments began to lead to a third conception of science in which a statistical approach was adopted (Royce, 1914/1951), as well as a dynamically recursive, non-linear one.

Since there is continuing dispute about the merits of different ways of understanding evolution, it may be helpful to refer to Darwin's original submission to the Linnean Society (Darwin & Wallace, 1858), which is lucid and at least somewhat authoritative. As Darwin noted, the fact that different species of organisms can reproduce at geometric rates yet often have fairly stable populations in a region suggests that they continually "check" one another's growth through competition. When a relatively stable relationship has developed and is then disturbed by a novel event, like a change in climate or invasion by a new species:

> Some of its inhabitants will be exterminated; and the remainder will be exposed to the mutual action of a different set of inhabitants, which I believe to be far more important to the life of each being than mere climate . . . I cannot doubt that during millions of generations individuals . . . will be occasionally born with some slight variation, profitable to some part of their economy. Such individuals will have a better chance of surviving, and of propagating their new and slightly different structure, and the modification may be slowly increased by the accumulative action of natural selection to any profitable extent . . . An organic being . . . may thus come to be adapted to a score of contingencies—natural selection accumulating those slight variations in all parts of its structure, which are in any way useful to it during any part of its life. (Darwin, in Darwin & Wallace, 1858, pp. 3–4)

This process, elaborated as specialized niches develop, was understood to be the principal cause of the "classification and affinities of organic beings," that "seem to branch, and sub-branch like the limbs of a tree from a common trunk" (Darwin & Wallace, 1858, p. 4).

Darwin's model differs interestingly from the others we have been considering. It attends to differing species and forms, like Aristotle, but views them as changing, and rejects the notion that they have essences (since they are populations of unique, interbreeding individuals having common descent). It also involves quantitative relationships, like those emphasized in Newtonian theory, but they are statistical and non-linear (growth of a population at one time increases its rate of growth in the next, while growth of its competitors decreases it), unlike the linear, deterministic relationships of Newtonian theory (e.g., $F = ma$). Third, explanation is neither in terms of fixed ends nor deterministic means, but

in terms of cycles of implicitly risky, experimental action that may or may not work out to reproduce itself. Finally, Darwin's suggestion that the "mutual action" of organisms is far more important than exogenous events, like a change in climate, introduces a social or co-evolutionary aspect to his account that is often overlooked.

While Darwin focused on the evolution of biological life, philosophers, other scholars, and scientists generalized his approach to all of nature and the universe more generally (Dewey, 1910/1997; Mead, 1964). As Karl Popper put it more recently, "science suggests to us (tentatively of course) a picture of the universe that is inventive or even creative; of a universe in which *new things* emerge on *new levels*" (Popper, 1978, p. 341). Among these emergent phenomena is mind. To restore greater continuity between mind and nature, and do so scientifically, all three categories needed to be rethought.

The scholar who most presciently and carefully, rethought all three of these categories was Charles Sanders Peirce. For those unfamiliar with him, Peirce was an amazing polymath who contributed to many fields. He viewed himself primarily as a logician, and contributed to the development of modern relational logic, originated pragmatism as a school of philosophy, was one of the principal originators of semiotics, the science of signs, and made contributions to a number of other fields, such as mathematics, physics, and geography. Bertrand Russell described him as "beyond doubt . . . one of the most original minds of the later nineteenth century, and certainly the greatest American thinker ever," and Popper as "one of the greatest philosophers of all time" (Popper, 1972). The fact that he influenced important philosopher/psychologists, such as William James, Josiah Royce, John Dewey, and George Herbert Mead, and laid the groundwork for a new approach to psychology, makes his approach important for this discussion, even though he did not influence many others until recently, since much of his work was unpublished and is only becoming available today.

The key to Peirce's approach lies in an abstract distinction that he drew between three kinds of relationships and their objects, which he termed "firsts," "seconds," and "thirds" (Peirce, 1878/1992b). "Firsts" are characterized by their participation in unary relationships. They are essentially qualities before they have been described or categorized as such. The psychological equivalent would be a feeling before it has been recognized or become a stimulus to a response. "Seconds" are objects or events that are defined by their participation in binary relationships, like stimulus and response, cause and effect, blow and pain, subject and object. In this case each term is only meaningful in relation to the other. For example, a stimulus that makes no difference to a response is not a "stimulus," just as a force that has no effect is not a "force." Finally, "thirds" are defined by their participation in trinary relationships. An example would be the act of "giving," which requires a giver, a recipient, and a gift. None of which makes sense if it is not related to the other two. The concept of "reinforcement" in psychology is an example, since it involves an initial stimulus, a response, and a reinforcing stimulus that alters the relationship between the first two. Without all three terms the concept of "reinforcement" makes no sense.

While I have used psychological examples, this set of distinctions was applied far beyond psychology—to everything. Since these distinctions were drawn initially from logic, and the contrast between logical terms, propositions, and arguments, Peirce argued that they are the basic kinds of relationships involved in everything we can possibly know. In other words, they constitute a minimalistic metaphysics, a "guess at the riddle" of the universe (Peirce, 1878/1992b). The point of the analysis was to argue that all three of these kinds of events or processes are needed to account for change, and that one cannot reduce the set by doing away with "firsts," which are essentially novel or random events, or by doing away with "thirds," which are mediated events. The need for all three kinds of relationships in making sense of the universe, and their irreducibility to a smaller set, was Peirce's way of defending the reality of all three against the tendency to reduce or absorb them.

These points apply to evolution because it involves three similar elements—qualitatively unique events, such as random variants (firsts), relatively stable ongoing relationships (seconds), and mediated processes in which unique forms and established relationships are altered contingently, resulting in the new forms and relationships. In some situations random changes may predominate, such as when a new organism appears in an environment with few competitors. In others habitual or mechanical relationships dominate, such as when organisms are well adapted to one another in sufficient numbers so that variants are quickly overwhelmed. And in a third class of situations there is an interaction between random qualitative differences and "habitual" quantitative processes that results in the more gradual evolution of new forms. The parallel with Cronbach's analysis of three approaches to psychology, discussed earlier, may be evident, except now everything is interpreted in cyclical, evolutionary terms.

Peirce applied this approach to reconceptualizing nature in evolutionary and statistical terms, rather than mechanistic ones (Houser & Kloesel, 1992, pp. 99–199). Since Newtonian laws make such precise claims that they can never truly be tested, he argued that we are free to conjecture that they are approximations to relationships that have an element of randomness or looseness in them. On the other hand, recurrent processes, like those involved in canalization (e.g., rainfall making a gulley deeper so that future rainfall will likely be channeled to the same place) also result in the formation of "habits," or structures whose components interact in highly predictable, tightly coupled ways (for processes of canalization in biology and psychology, see Waddington, 1975, and Scarr, 1983). As Popper noted, using a metaphorical contrast between loosely related, non-deterministic "clouds" and tightly related, deterministic "clocks," "Peirce was the first post-Newtonian physicist and philosopher who . . . dared to adopt the view that to some degree *all clocks are clouds*; or in other words that *only clouds exist*, though . . . of . . . different degrees of cloudiness" (Popper, 1972). Given this view, the universe is neither chaotic nor tightly ordered, but partially ordered and evolving.

Peirce also applied an evolutionary approach to understanding the way beliefs change, especially beliefs in science. In effect, his was one of the first evolutionary epistemologies (see, e.g., Campbell, 1974). To understand Peirce's approach one needs to understand his conceptions of "belief," "doubt," and "inquiry." Peirce borrowed his conception of belief, "that on which a man is prepared to act," from Alexander Bain. Believing in a proposition means that you will act *as if* the outcome it suggests is certain to occur, like betting everything on a horse without a moment's hesitation. Doubt, on the other hand, involves conflict between such beliefs or habits (generalized beliefs). If new information suggests that the horse is ill you might hesitate or freeze. Conceived in this way, belief and doubt are not subjective feelings or propositions in the head, but action tendencies. Nonetheless, both may cause feelings. Doubt causes the "irritation of doubt," a sense of loss, puzzlement, or uncertainty (Peirce, 1877/1923) which stimulates a "struggle" to reduce the doubt. Peirce termed this struggle "inquiry." While inquiry seems to mean "thinking," it includes a wider set of actions than are usually included in this concept, such as overt manipulation, observation, and experimentation. In other words, inquiry is also not internal or located in the head, but is a form of activity. Peirce argued that we have no way of knowing if a belief is true, aside from having no doubts about it, so the aim of inquiry is to eliminate doubt: "With the doubt, therefore, the struggle begins, and with the cessation of doubt, it ends. Hence the sole object of inquiry is the settlement of opinion" (Peirce, 1877/1923, p. 16).

Since belief is a way of acting, it cannot be changed voluntarily or by willing it to be different, but only by experience based on acting on the belief. Here Peirce outlined three social methods for resolving conflicts between entrenched beliefs—the methods of authority, *a priori* reasoning, and scientific experimentation (Peirce, 1877/1923). While beliefs have evolved, so have methods of resolving conflicts between beliefs, the latter methods being more refined and general than the earlier ones since they can resolve conflicts the earlier cannot. However, even with methods of scientific experimentation one can never determine that a generalization is true, since the next case may always disprove it. "Truth" then becomes a kind of ideal, reached only at the end of an evolutionary process of inquiry when a belief is found that will never cause further doubts, just as "reality" consists of the objects described by those ideal beliefs. As Peirce put it:

> The opinion which is fated to be ultimately agreed to by all who investigate, is what we mean by the truth, and the object represented in this opinion is the real. That is the way I would explain reality. (Peirce, 1877/1923, pp. 56–57)

As part of his effort to rethink science, Peirce also reconsidered logical inference. The point is important here because it has fairly direct implications for learning theory, analogous to those mentioned earlier in the discussion of Cartesian dualism. As noted, traditional epistemological debate has tended to divide deductive rationalists, like the followers of Descartes, and inductive empiricists, like the followers of Newton or Locke. Learning theory has tended to divide similarly. In contrast to this division, Peirce reasoned that since there are three statements in the simplest logical argument, a syllogism, there must also be three basic forms of inference (Peirce, 1878/1992a). In *deduction* one reasons "forwards" from an antecedent and a rule to a conclusion; in *induction* one reasons "upwards" from antecedent and consequent events to a rule describing the universe from which they were sampled; and in *retroduction* (which Peirce also called "abduction" and "hypothesis") one reasons "backwards" from a consequent and a rule to an antecedent. Given three statements, one can use a guess at any two to make an inference about the third. One can develop a hypothesis about an initial cause, using retroduction, deduce some implications of that hypothesis and perform an experiment to see if the results are as suggested, and then use the new facts generated by the experiment to inductively alter beliefs about the rule (for Peirce's use of this cycle, see Fisch, 1986). A cyclical, experimental approach in which each element can change gets one out of the conflict between rationalist and empiricist foundationalism (see Dewey, 1922/1984).

This analysis suggests that there is a third approach to "learning" that traditional approaches ignore (Wojcikiewicz, 2010). The common denominator in the traditional approaches is that the task remains fixed (Newman, Griffin, & Cole, 1989). For behavioristic learning theory this means that environmental contingencies have to remain stable, while for cognitive theories the inner symbolic problem representation must also remain constant. The task cannot change in either case because it would then be unclear if one were observing "learning," this being defined as a change in performance on the same task or class of tasks. Yet people and animals leave environments when they can, change environments so that they present different contingencies (such as by building houses), and reconceptualize the situations facing them. As a result it would seem that one can also "learn" to change the task or problem. More generally, Peirce's interactive approach to inquiry (like Dewey's) suggests that inquiry proceeds by changing the situation, and not merely the individual or the environment alone, doubt being resolved by changing the person/environment situation or relationship. To neglect this kind of "learning" seriously limits one's conception of human abilities—a point consistent with current work on situated learning (Lave & Wenger, 1991), and Snow's transactional approach to aptitude, which views it as a property of person-in-situation (Corno et al., 2002) and with analyses of the way teachers and students learn to modify common activities cooperatively (see Chapter 5, this volume).

Peirce's later work on semiotics, the science of signs, generalized this approach, resulting in a broad evolutionary conception of mind applicable to a wide range of natural phenomena. Here again, conventional scholarship has tended to be dualistic, distinguishing between "sign" and "object," or "signifier" and "signified." This results in familiar problems of dualistic schemes, such as disputes over which determines the other, or how such different things can relate to one another. In contrast, Peirce distinguished three phases of a semiotic process: "object," "sign," and "interpretant." As an example, an "object" might be a fire, smoke a "sign" of the fire, and someone's running away after seeing the smoke an "interpretant" of the sign, as having indicated a fire. Needless to say. given Peirce's penchant for triples, this threesome is related to Peirce's distinction between "firsts," "seconds," and "thirds," the object being a first, the relation between object and interpretant a second, and the three-way relationship between object, sign, and interpretant a "third."

The point of introducing three (rather than two) functions is, again, to make the analysis more interactive and evolutionary. With three differences in play, meanings may change and evolve, yet may also be corrected when what is signaled does not arrive. In effect, one gets the benefits of both subjectivism (novelty) and objectivism (correction). Introducing three phases to the process of "semiosis" also makes it possible to understand how social meanings develop and are used in interaction, which is the basis for human reflective thought. To see this point it may help to turn to George Herbert Mead's social interactional account of the evolution of mind and self, which was based on Peirce's semiotic distinctions (Mead, 1934/1967).

Using the concept of a "gesture," borrowed from Darwin (1889/1904), Mead suggested that organisms frequently learn from the beginnings of each other's acts (a gesture), responding to them as though they meant, or were signs of, a completed act to come. If one boxer begins to pull an arm back, that beginning may be responded to by a second by beginning to duck, as though the original arm movement was the beginning of a "blow." In this case the initial gesture functions as a "sign" of a completed act (the "object") as interpreted by a response (the "interpretant"). Each boxer may respond to the other's gestures, in a continuing series or set of cycles, implicating giving each a meaning, although the process may be largely unconscious, at least until after the fact.

Mead viewed this interactive behavior as the basis for social meaning, since each gesture's meaning is worked out in the interaction itself. Meaning is then neither in anyone's head nor determined outside of the interaction. What a gesture comes to mean—what it signals is coming—depends on how it is interpreted by a response, and whether that interpretation is itself confirmed or disconfirmed by subsequent responses.

The point of this analysis is that human reflective thought can be considered to be a kind of "conversation of gestures" that one carries on with oneself. Insofar as one participates in joint action with others in which signaling is important to coordination, and can learn to "take the role of the other" by responding to one's own signs or gestures as another would, one can respond to the beginning of one's own acts in terms of their meaning. Responding to the meaning of a latent or emerging act is what is involved in reflective thought, as opposed to the non-reflective thought of animals, or at least of animals incapable of this kind of behavior. Similarly, responding to oneself as a meaningful object, as others would, is what it means to have a "self" (Mead, 1934/1967). Considered in this way, reflective thought is a social process in which one works out the meaning of one's own latent or potential acts over time, first taking one perspective then another in an effort to find a sequence of acts that resolves an issue. This may involve manipulating propositions in the form of aural statements, or written inscriptions, or other signs, to which one responds, and then responding to the response. Thinking evolves, like the other processes we have considered. And, just as cognitive psychologists have argued that there are no images in the head, one can also argue similarly that there are also no propositions in the head, mind being a social/interactional process, and not a thing.

This brief account neglects many very important things, such as the difference between gestures and linguistic signs, whose meaning is at least partly determined by convention. The present point has only been to suggest how Peircean semiotics can form the basis for a theory of meaning and reflective thought. One can also extend a similar analysis of semiosis "downwards" to consider meaningful communication between plants or other organisms, where there is no possibility of reflective thought, and no sensing of the meaning of gestures at a distance, only direct sensing, over time, of gradients or differences. As this suggests, Peirce's semiotics can be used to lay the groundwork for a very general approach to "mind" applicable across a wide range of natural phenomena. The field of biosemiotics has adopted Peircean ideas to analyze meaningful signaling in biological systems (Kull, Deacon, Emmeche, Hoffmeyer, & Stjernfelt, 2009), just as anthropologists have also adopted them in considering human symbolic communication in all of its varied forms (Danesi, 2004).

The idea of an evolutionary approach to mind and nature that involves an interplay of randomness, regularity, and corrective adjustment appears to be extremely valuable, yet still underappreciated, although many of its wider ramifications were worked out by Dewey in his evolutionary conceptions of education, democracy, and science. In each case there is an evolving, self-corrective process that builds on its own previous results (except when they, too, are corrected). There is no certainty, either internal or external, only a continued effort to build experimentally, based on what has worked in the past and what appears likely to work in the future. The price is loss of certainty and centeredness balanced by a gain in life.

## Conclusions

This chapter represents an attempt to gain philosophical perspective on educational psychology by considering the origins of psychological conceptions of human nature and conduct in wider and longer-run movements of thought. Since the dominant way of thinking in educational research arguably continues to be mechanistic or externalist, the news is that there is more to an Aristotelian approach than one might imagine, and that we may still not have caught up with the implications of a Darwinian evolutionary approach.

In fleshing out some further implications for educational psychology and educational practice I would like to return to

three streams of educational psychology that were strongly influenced by evolutionary ideas (Boring, 1963) but failed to fully incorporate the wider meaning of a Darwinian approach, at least as frequently interpreted. Two of these were considered earlier, differential or trait psychology and behavioristic psychology. The third consists of hierarchical stage theories of development. Differential or trait psychology emerged from the work of Darwin's cousin, Francis Galton, on hereditary genius in English families (Galton, 1869/1892). Behaviorism emerged from experimental work comparing the mental functioning of different animals. Stage theories of development emerged, in turn, from Ernst Haeckel's notion that "ontogeny recapitulates phylogeny," as represented in the work of G. Stanley Hall, among others.

These three traditions of educational psychology have been enormously influential in educational theory and practice. They point to phenomena that are extremely important in schooling—what students bring to the classroom, the kinds of knowledge and skills they are expected to learn, and their long-run patterns of development. From both teacher and student perspectives these represent the beginnings, middles, and ends of an educational experience that should be related to one another. However, divisions between these traditions tended to fragment educational psychology into concerns for beginnings, middles, and endings that were unrelated, as suggested by Cronbach's analysis of the first two. The third, hierarchical-stage theories of development, can also be seen as unrelated since the ends of development, such as formal or post-conventional reasoning, are considered to be already known, independent of knowledge of student aptitudes and school tasks.

One of the reasons that these approaches violated an evolutionary attitude, despite claiming to be consistent with one, is that they tended to base research on external norms that were presumed to be universal. That is, research was based on situations where it was clear what the "right" or "good" answer was. In IQ testing, for example, "intelligence" was assumed to be universal among human beings—and could be judged by getting more right answers than other individuals on school-like tasks (normed, of course). In learning theory fixed external tasks created a norm defining a "correct" (reinforced) answer, the laws of learning to get there being presumed to be universal. And in hierarchical theories of development, the highest stage of development defined the end of development, also presumed to be universal across all cultures.

All three of these approaches have been criticized extensively. Criticism of trait psychology (of which IQ testing is a branch) is long-standing, as indicated by Allport's defense of it, originally written in 1929 (Allport, 1968). The notion that "latent traits" express themselves in different forms of behavior, or performance, like Aristotelian potentials, fails to recognize that people tend to be more diverse in their ways of responding than this suggests, and that responses may be interpreted or "taken" in different ways, resulting potentially in the development of different patterns of interaction. An analogy would be the notion that oxygen has the "latent trait" to become water, when it clearly has the potential to become many different things depending on the other elements with which it interacts.

Shifting to learning theory, the notion that one learns from external task contingencies depends on how the task is conceived, as cognitive theorists pointed out (e.g., Chomsky, 1959). Students approaching a school task in order to get a good grade or to please the teacher have made those activities the "task" to which they attempt to learn answers (Dewey, 1916a). Beyond the notion that tasks may be conceived differently lies the point that they may also be modified and negotiated in interaction. Newman, Griffin, and Cole's (1989) analysis of the way teachers and students may appropriate one another's conceptions or approaches to a task into their own conceptions or approaches is an example.

Similar points apply to hierarchical-stage theories of development. The notion that cognitive development proceeds through a linear sequence of stages leading toward a predefined "highest" stage, such as formal operations, has been criticized extensively. Intellectual problems or puzzles do not necessarily have only one solution or equilibrium, and while steps may build on one another, there need not be a single set of hierarchical stages (Phillips, 1987a, 1987b). As in other evolutionary or developmental processes, the end is not predetermined at the beginning. Rather, it seems that developmental trajectories get worked out in interaction with others, certain paths becoming relatively irreversible or closed off, canalizing likely futures in certain directions while making others highly unlikely (Werthman, 1970). At the populational level there also appear to be interactions between differences in early trauma and vulnerability and the degree to which the social environment is structured to create unequal opportunities and contingencies (Keating & Hertzman, 1999).

In each of these cases the suggestion is that an interactional/evolutionary approach—in which similar student beginnings can evolve in different ways, present task environments can be renegotiated, and long-run futures may develop in diverse ways in accord with different values— may be helpful. This may be so in particular when considering the simplifications of an externalist approach (like the mechanistic attitude suggested earlier) or an internalist one (like the vitalistic approach also discussed). An interactional/evolutionary approach may also make it possible to unite the three streams of traditional educational psychology by suggesting how what a student brings to school, how tasks are understood and mutually negotiated, and how development occurs in long-run directions are related over time, in a semiotic process, rather than remaining unrelated phases of life. Adopting an interactional/evolutionary approach would then relate educational psychology to Dewey's (1938) criteria of an educative experience as involving "interaction" and "continuity," rather than building educational psychology in a way that interrupts these very processes.

Another implication of this discussion is that the models of human nature and conduct adopted in educational psychology need to be considered in the light of their wider social and ethical consequences. What Bruner suggested of psychological models of the learner applies to the other areas of educational psychology as well:

> The best approach to models of the learner is a reflective one that permits you to "go meta," in enquire whether the script being imposed on the learner is there for the reason that was intended or for some other reason . . . You cannot improve education without a model of the learner. Yet the model of the learner is not fixed, but various. A choice of one reflects many political, practical, and cultural issues. Perhaps the best choice is not a choice of one, but an appreciation of the variety that is possible. (Bruner, 1985, p. 8)

I would only add that such models may not only be chosen in the light of wider aims but can also be evaluated in terms of their observed consequences. These points apply to the present discussion as well, which also needs to be assessed in the light of its consequences, intended and unintended. At the very least I hope it serves to introduce some of the concepts, issues, and debates in the educational psychology emerging today.

## Notes

1. I would like to acknowledge helpful comments and suggestions from Ramsey Affifi. I am grateful for many helpful comments and suggestions from Christina Erneling, Walter Feinberg, Sarah Cashmore, Lyn Corno, Ray McDermott, David Olson, and Denis Phillips. With colleagues like these the source of remaining difficulties is clear.
2. When I use the pronouns "we" or "us" or "ourselves," it is meant to refer to the reflexivity practiced by all human beings and not to any particular person or group.
3. As an example, try to identify the location of the difference or similarity between two things.
4. As Newman wrote, "We cannot help, to a great extent, being Aristotelians, for the great Master does but analyze the thoughts, feelings, views, and opinions of human kind. He has told us the meaning of our own words and ideas, before we were born. In many subject matters, to think correctly, is to think like Aristotle, and we are his disciples whether we will or no, though we may not know it" (Newman, 1854/1976, pp. 165–166). I am grateful to Trystan Goetze for this quotation.

## References

Alexander, A. (2014). *Infinitesimal: How a dangerous mathematical theory shaped the modern world.* New York: Scientific American.

Allport, G. W. (1968). Traits revisited. In G. W. Allport (Ed.), *The person in psychology: Selected essays.* Boston, MA: Beacon Press.

Aristotle. (1980). *Nicomachean ethics.* Oxford: Oxford University Press.

Bakhurst, D. (2008). Minds, brains, and education. *Journal of Philosophy of Education, 42* (3–4), 415–432.

Bambrough, R. (1963/2003). Introduction. In R. Bambrough (Ed.), *The philosophy of Aristotle* (pp. xi–xxxv). New York: Penguin.

Bandura, A. (1974). Behavior theory and the models of man. *American Psychologist* December, 859–869.

Bandura, A. (1985). Models of human nature and causality. In *Social foundations of thought and action: A social cognitive theory* (pp. 1–46). New York: Prentice Hall.

Bateson, G. (1988). *Mind and nature: A necessary unity.* New York: Bantam.

Berlin, I. (1939/1999). The purpose of philosophy. In *Concepts and categories: Philosophical essays* (pp. 1–11). London: Pimlico.

Boring, E. G. (1963). The influence of evolutionary theory upon American psychological thought. In R. I. Watson & D. T. Campbell (Eds.), *History, psychology, and science: Selected papers* (pp. 159–184). New York: John Wiley.

Bredo, E. (1997). The social construction of learning. In G. Phye (Ed.), *Handbook of academic learning: The construction of knowledge* (pp. 3–43). New York: Academic Press.

Bredo, E. (2006a). Conceptual confusion and educational psychology. In P. Winne, P. Alexander, & G. Phye (Eds.), *Handbook of educational psychology* (pp. 43–57). Fairfax, VA: Techbooks.

Bredo, E. (2006b). Philosophies of educational research. In J. Green, G. Camilli, & P. Elmore (Eds.), *Complementary methods in educational research* (pp. 3–31). Washington, DC: American Educational Research Association.

Bruner, J. (1985). Models of the learner. *Educational Researcher, 14*(6), 5–8.

Bruner, J. (2004). A short history of psychological theories of learning. *Daedalus, Winter,* 13–20.

Campbell, D. T. (1974). Evolutionary epistemology. In P. Schlipp (Ed.), *The philosophy of Karl Popper.* La Salle, IL: Open Court.

Catania, C. A. (1984). *Learning.* Englewood Cliffs, NJ: Prentice-Hall.

Chomsky, N. (1959). A review of B. F. Skinner's *Verbal Behavior. Language 35,* 1–58.

Cole, M. (1996). *Cultural psychology: A once and future discipline.* Cambridge, MA: Harvard University Press.

Corno, L., Cronbach, L. J., Kupermintz, H., Lohman, D. F., Mandinach, E. B., Porteus, A. W. . . . et al. (2002). *Remaking the concept of aptitude: Extending the legacy of Richard E. Snow.* Mahwah, NJ: Lawrence, Erlbaum Associates.

Cronbach, L. J. (1957). The two disciplines of scientific psychology. *American Psychologist, 12,* 671–684.

Cronbach, L. J. (1975). Beyond the two disciplines of scientific psychology. *American Psychologist, 30,* 116–127.

Damasio, A. R. (1994). *Descartes' error: Emotion, reason, and the human brain.* New York: G. P. Putnam's Sons.

Danesi, M. (2004). *Messages, signs, and meanings: A basic textbook in semiotics and communication.* Toronto: Canadian Scholars Press.

Darwin, C. (1881). *The power of movement in plants.* New York: D. Appleton.

Darwin, C. (1889/1904). *The expression of the emotions in man and animals.* London: John Murray.

Darwin, C., & Wallace, A. R. (1858). On the tendency of species to form varieties; and on the perpetuation of varieties and species by natural means of selection. In P. H. Barrett (Ed.), *The collected papers of Charles Darwin* (Vol. 2, pp. 3–19). Chicago, IL: University of Chicago Press.

Deacon, T. W. (2012). *Incomplete nature: How mind emerged from matter.* New York: W. W. Norton.

Descartes, R. (1637/1969). Discourse on the method of rightly conducting one's reason and seeking truth in the sciences. In M. D. Wilson (Ed.), *The essential Descartes* (pp. 1–42). New York: Mentor.

Dewey, J. (1910/1997). The influence of Darwinism on philosophy. In *The influence of Darwin on philosophy and other essays* (pp. 1–19). Amherst, NY: Prometheus.

Dewey, J. (1916a). *Democracy and education.* New York: Macmillan.

Dewey, J. (1916b). Philosophy of education. In *Democracy and education* (pp. 375–387). New York: Macmillan.

Dewey, J. (1922/1984). Experimentalism, answer to the conflict between empiricism and rationalism. In *Types of thinking* (pp. 111–119). New York: Philosophical Library.

Dewey, J. (1929/1958). *Experience and nature.* New York: Dover Publications.

Dewey, J. (1938). *Experience and education.* New York: Collier-Macmillan.

Dewey, J., & Bentley, A. (1949). *Knowing and the known.* Boston, MA: Beacon Press.

Feingold, M. (2004). *The Newtonian moment.* Oxford: Oxford University Press.

Ferry, L. (2003). *A brief history of thought.* New York: Harper.

Fisch, M. H. (1986). *Peirce, semiotic, and pragmatism.* Bloomington, IN: Indiana University Press.

Galton, F. (1869/1892). *Hereditary genius: An inquiry into its laws and consequences.* London: Macmillan.

Gigerenzer, G., & Swijtink, Z. (1989). *The empire of chance: How probability changed science.* Cambridge, UK: Cambridge University Press.

Glasersfeld, E. v. (1995). *Radical constructivism: A way of knowing and learning.* Washington, DC: Falmer Press.

Goodman, N. (1972). The way the world is. In *Problems and projects* (pp. 24–32). Indianapolis, IN: Hackett Publishing.

Hilgard, E. R., & Bower, G. (1966). *Theories of learning.* New York: Appleton-Century-Crofts.

Houser, N., & Kloesel, C. (Eds.) (1992). *The essential Peirce* (Vol. 1). Bloomington, IN: Indiana University Press.

Huxley, T. H. (1870/1893). Descartes' discourse on method. In T. H. Huxley (Ed.), *Collected essays* (pp. 166–198). London: Macmillan.

James, W. (1890/1952). The principles of psychology. In R. M. Hutchins (Ed.), *Great books of the western world* (Vol. 53). Chicago, IL: Encyclopedia Britannica.

Juarrero, A. (1999). *Dynamics in action: Intentional behavior as a complex system.* Cambridge, MA: MIT Press.

Keating, D., & Hertzman, P. (1999). *Developmental health and the wealth of nations: Social, biological, and educational dynamics.* New York: Guilford Press.

Kohlberg, L., & Mayer, R. (1972). Development as the aim of education. *Harvard Educational Review, 42*(4), 449–496.

Kull, K., Deacon, T., Emmeche, C., Hoffmeyer, J., & Stjernfelt, F. (2009). Theses on biosemiotics: Prolegomena to a theoretical biology. *Biological Theory, 4*(2), 167–173.

Lave, J., & Wenger, E. (1991). *Situated learning: Legitimate peripheral participation.* Cambridge, UK: Cambridge University Press.

Lovejoy, A. O. (1936). *The great chain of being.* Cambridge, MA: Harvard University Press.

Lowry, R. (1971). *The evolution of psychological theory: 1650 to the present.* Chicago, IL: Aldine.

March, J. G. (1972). Model bias in social action. *Review of Educational Research, 42*(4), 413–429.

Maxwell, J. C. (1859/1965). Illustrations of the dynamical theory of gases. In W. D. Niven (Ed.), *The scientific papers of James Clerk Maxwell* (Vol. 1, pp. 377–409). New York: Dover Press.

Maxwell, J. C. (1868). On governors. *Proceedings of the Royal Society of London, 16,* 270–283.

McDermott, R., & Hood, L. (1982). Institutionalized psychology and the ethnography of schooling. In P. Gilmore & A. Gladthorn (Eds.), *Children in and out of school.* Washington, DC: Center for Applied Linguistics.

McKeon, R. (1941). *The basic works of Aristotle.* New York: Random House.

Mead, G. H. (1934/1967). *Mind, self, and society: From the standpoint of a social behaviorist.* Chicago, IL: University of Chicago Press.

Mead, G. H. (1964). Evolution becomes a general idea. In A. Strauss (Ed.), *George Herbert Mead: On social psychology* (pp. 3–18). Chicago, IL: University of Chicago Press.

Menand, L. (2001). *The metaphysical club.* New York: Farrar, Straus & Giroux.

Miller, P. (1968). *American thought: Civil War to World War I.* New York: Holt, Rinehart and Winston.

Newell, A., & Simon, H. (1972). *Human problem solving.* Englewood Cliffs, NY: Prentice-Hall.

Newman, J. H. (1854/1976). *The idea of a university, defined and illustrated.* Oxford, UK: Clarendon Press.

Newman, D., Griffin, P., & Cole, M. (1989). *The construction zone: Working for cognitive change in schools.* Cambridge, UK: Cambridge University Press.

Olson, D. R. (2011). Agency and intentionality in pedagogy: Where the accountability train left the tracks. Paper presented at the workshop Building Learning Cultures through Genre Practice, New York, USA. Retrieved from http://www.learningcultures.net/journal/archive/agency-and-intentionality-in-pedagogy-where-the-accountability-train-left-the-tracks.

Peirce, C. S. (1877/1923). The fixation of belief. In M. R. Cohen (Ed.), *Love, chance, and logic* (pp. 7–31). New York: Harcourt, Brace and Co.

Peirce, C. S. (1878/1992a). Deduction, induction, and hypothesis. In N. Hauser & C. Kloesel (Eds.), *The essential Peirce: Selected philosophical writings* (Vol. 1, pp. 186–199). Bloomington, IN: Indiana University Press.

Peirce, C. S. (1878/1992b). A guess at the riddle. In N. Hauser & C. Kloesel (Eds.), *The essential Peirce: Selected philosophical writings* (Vol. 1, pp. 247–279).

Phillips, D. C. (1987a). Change and development of cognitive structures: Piaget as theorist. *Philosophy, science, and social inquiry* (pp. 158–168). Elmsford, NY: Pergamon Press.

Phillips, D. C. (1987b). Kohlberg's stages of moral development: A Lakatosian critique. In *Philosophy, science, and social inquiry*. New York: Pergamon.

Phillips, D. C. (1987c). Describing a student's cognitive structure. *Philosophy, science, and social inquiry*. New York: Pergamon.

Phillips, D. C. (1996). Philosophical perspectives. In D. C. Berliner & R. C. Calfee (Eds.), *Handbook of educational psychology* (pp. 1005–1019). New York: Macmillan.

Popper, K. (1972). Of clouds and clocks. *Objective knowledge: An evolutionary approach* (pp. 206–255). Oxford: Clarendon Press.

Popper, K. (1978). Natural selection and the emergence of mind. *Dialectica, 34*(3–4), 339–355.

Prigogine, I. (1980). *From being to becoming: Time and complexity in the physical sciences.* San Francisco: W. H. Freeman.

Prigogine, I., & Stengers, I. (1984). *Order out of chaos: Man's new dialogue with nature.* New York: Bantam.

Ramirez, F., & Boli-Bennett, J. (1982). Global patterns of educational institutionalization. In P. G. Altbach, R. F. Arnov, & G. P. Kelley (Eds.). *Comparative Education.* New York: Macmillan.

Ramsey, W. (2013). Eliminative materialism. In E. N. Zalta (Ed.), *The Stanford Encyclopedia of Philosophy* (summer ed.). Retrieved from http://plato.stanford.edu/archives/sum2013/entries/materialism-eliminative/ (accessed 13 March 2015).

Randall, J. H. (1960). *Aristotle.* New York: Columbia University Press.

Royce, J. (1914/1951). The mechanical, the historical and the statistical. In D. S. Robinson (Ed.), *Royce's logical essays: Collected logical essays of Josiah Royce* (pp. 35–62). Dubuque, IA: Wm. C. Brown.

Russell, B. (1959). *Wisdom of the west* (p. 276). Garden City, NY: Doubleday.

Ryle, G. (1949). *The concept of mind.* Chicago, IL: University of Chicago Press.

Scarr, S. (1983). An evolutionary perspective on infant intelligence. In M. Lewis (Ed.), *Origins of intelligence: Infancy and early childhood* (pp. 191–223). New York: Plenum Press.

Sellars, W. (1963). Philosophy and the scientific image of man. In R. Colodny (Ed.), *Frontiers of science and philosophy* (pp. 35–78). Pittsburgh: University of Pittsburgh Press.

Suchman, L. A. (1987). *Plans and situated actions: The problem of human–machine communication.* Cambridge, U.K.: Cambridge University Press.

van Inwagen, P. (2007). Metaphysics. *Stanford Encyclopedia of Philosophy.* Retrieved from http://plato.stanford.edu/archives/win2014/entries/metaphysics/ (accessed 13 March 2015).

Waddington, C. H. (1975). *The evolution of an evolutionist.* Ithaca, NY: Cornell University Press.

Watzlawick, P., Beavin, J. H., & Jackson, D. D. (1967). *Pragmatics of human communication.* New York: W. W. Norton.

Werthman, C. (1970). The function of social definitions in the development of delinquent careers. In P. Garabedian & D. Gibbons (Eds.), *Becoming delinquent: Young offenders and the correctional process.* Chicago, IL: Aldine.

Wittgenstein, L. (1958). *Philosophical investigations.* New York: Macmillan.

Wojcikiewicz, S. K. (2010). Dewey, Peirce, and the categories of learning. *Education and Culture, 26*(2), 65–82.

# 2

# Modes of Inquiry in Educational Psychology and Learning Sciences Research

*William R. Penuel*
University of Colorado Boulder

*Kenneth A. Frank*
Michigan State University

Educational psychologists and learning scientists rely on multiple *modes of inquiry* to answer different kinds of research questions. Modes of inquiry refer to more than just methods and sources of data. They refer to distinct approaches to the study of learning and development in educational settings that draw from different disciplines. Moreover, modes of inquiry employ different standards of evidence for making judgments about the validity and reliability of claims, and make different kinds of value commitments (Eisenhart & Towne, 2003). In this chapter, we take up four questions for six different contemporary and emerging modes of inquiry within the field:

1. What kinds of claims can the mode of inquiry support?
2. Who are the audiences for these claims?
3. What is the form and substance of arguments in this mode of inquiry?
4. What are the scope and some limitations of this mode of inquiry?

Each of these questions frames educational psychology or learning sciences research as a form of humanistic inquiry grounded in argument from evidence. This perspective on educational psychology is grounded in Toulmin's (1958) model of practical arguments, particularly as elaborated within House's (1977, 1979) notion of evaluative arguments in educational research. In both Toulmin's and House's frameworks, investigators begin with a *claim* or conclusion to be elaborated, refined, or tested through empirical research. Such claims are framed always in terms of specific goals for research, and they are informed by values about desired ends for education (Kelly & Yin, 2007). An example of a claim investigated by educational psychologists is, "Schools can play an active role in the provision of opportunities for social mobility or in the exacerbation of social inequality, depending on how they are structured" (Muller, Riegle-Crumb, Schiller, Wilkinson, & Frank, 2010, p. 1039). This claim is framed relative to a specific purpose—to explore whether racially diverse high schools provide equality of opportunity to students of different racial backgrounds. The claim is also informed by presumed shared values of the audience, especially equality of opportunity and social mobility. Implicit in the claim are some implications for policy and practice, particularly with respect to how resources should be allocated, in this case to schools and organizations that support schools to structure more equitable opportunities for student learning. Each of these aspects of claims highlights the significance and consequentiality of evaluative arguments.

***Different modes of inquiry are well suited for some kinds of claims but not others.*** Modes of inquiry are central to argumentation, in that the credibility of the warrant for linking claims and data is based on the particular methods used, which must be backed by a "shared and appropriate methodology" (Kelly & Yin, 2007, p. 134). As such, different modes of inquiry are well suited for making certain kinds of claims, but not others. An ethnographic study of how a young person encounters mathematics at home and school may be useful for investigating claims about how young people recruit family members to assist with homework (Jackson, 2011). Further following young people as they move across contexts of learning may help to account for why some school-based interventions succeed or fail, but such a study cannot address a claim about the comparative benefits of different interventions, such as the claim that "providing students with extra homework help at school is better than providing parents with guidance about how to help their children." Such a claim might better be addressed with a series of comparison studies, explored across a range of contexts that are informed by findings from ethnographic studies.

***Arguments are made to persuade particular audiences.*** The task of research, from the perspective we develop here, is persuasion and not proof (House, 1977). As such, adjectives such as "credible" and "plausible" are more appropriate for describing and evaluating arguments than are terms like "definitive" or "unassailable." What is credible or plausible, moreover, is always at least partly relative to a particular audience, and the audiences of educational research are varied. They include other researchers, teachers, educational leaders, and policy makers, each of whom bring different concerns, intentions for using research, as well as different approaches to deliberation about how research findings should be used (Asen, Gurke, Solomon, Conners, & Gumm, 2011). Even among researchers, there is considerable contestation about what modes of inquiry are appropriate for what purposes (e.g., Eisenhart & Towne, 2003), and the uses of even a single research finding or study are often varied. These differences are not to be overcome, but they are a reminder that research yields knowledge that is both uncertain and contestable.

***Different modes of inquiry can be distinguished by the form and substance of arguments.*** Kelly (2004) calls the form that arguments take for a particular mode of inquiry that mode's *argumentative grammar*. He defines an argumentative grammar as "the logic that guides the use of a method and that supports reasoning about its data" (Kelly, 2004, p. 118). An argumentative grammar is not peculiar to a particular study, and it is analytically separable from the substance of a particular study's focus, claims, and conclusions. It should provide researchers who regularly employ a different mode of inquiry—in the case of this chapter, educational psychologists and learning scientists—a framework for evaluating the strength of the argument advanced in a particular study within a different mode of inquiry.

The substance of arguments is also an important consideration for judging the quality of individual studies. A study may faithfully adhere to the argumentative grammar of a particular mode of inquiry, but its argument may not be persuasive to others. The substance of the claims may be judged to be neither important nor relevant to the audiences for the research, or audiences may challenge the credibility of the components of the argument or links among those components (Cronbach, 1988). Audiences may also judge arguments to be either incomplete or biased toward a particular point of view (House, 1977).

***Scope and limitations of forms of inquiry.*** Judging the degree to which a particular mode of inquiry provides an adequate backing for a warrant linking claim and evidence depends upon the *reproducibility* and *generalizability* of findings (Cronbach, 1982). Judgments about reproducibility answer the question of whether another investigation would hypothetically have generated the same conclusions. Sources of variation that could condition claims and reduce reproducibility include changes to the sample, a change in investigators, or choice of different sources of evidence (Cronbach, 1982).

Even though such thought experiments about reproducibility inevitably involve qualitative judgments about what kinds of differences might lead investigators to draw different conclusions from a particular study, it is possible to quantify certain aspects of the situation, such as how large an unmeasured variable's relation to an outcome would have to be to invalidate an inference (e.g., Frank, 2000). Insofar as claims developed in research are intended to apply to other contexts, populations, and actions, research aims at some form of *generalizability*. Particular modes of inquiry seek to generalize to other kinds of objects: for example, case study (Yin, 2003) and ethnographic research (Goetz & LeCompte, 1984) both aim principally to generalize to theory rather than to populations. Just as claims to reproducibility are contested on qualitative grounds, so, too, are claims about generalizability. Here as well, efforts to quantify generalizability can inform such arguments (Hedges, 2013).

## Organization of this Review

In this chapter, we review several different modes of inquiry and describe their use in studies published in educational psychology journals between 2006 and 2013. To help us organize the chapter, we initially reviewed abstracts of articles published in five major English-language journals in educational psychology: *Educational Psychologist, Journal of Educational Psychology, Educational Psychology, British Journal of Educational Psychology*, and *Contemporary Educational Psychology*. To broaden our reach, we also reviewed abstracts from the *Journal of the Learning Sciences*, the *American Journal of Evaluation,* and the Teaching, Learning, and Human Development section of the *American Educational Research Journal*. We illustrate the typology of different modes of inquiry reviewed below with selected articles from this initial search that we believe are paradigmatic—meaning useful studies for explicating the mode of inquiry to someone less familiar with it. The typology includes both methods that are widely used within educational psychology today, as well as some that are still emerging and developing. Ours is certainly a selective approach with respect to emerging areas of inquiry, but our selection was guided by considerations of areas of increased interest among both researchers and policy makers in education who make funding decisions about educational research.

For each mode of inquiry, we present answers to the four key questions posed in the introduction. In addition, to illustrate the substance of argumentation within each mode of inquiry, we describe a research study that is an example of the approach. Each example was selected carefully to be paradigmatic of the approach, and because other investigators have—in some way or another—taken the interventions, theories, or design principles from the study, and applied them to other contexts. Table 2.1 identifies the modes of inquiry reviewed in this chapter and the kinds of claims each type seeks to support with evidence from research.

**Table 2.1    Typology of Modes of Inquiry in Educational Psychology and Learning Sciences**

| Type of Research | Description |
|---|---|
| *Intervention Research* | |
| Randomized controlled trials | A type of intervention research in which the principal aim is to investigate the impact of programs and policies. Researchers use random assignment to treatment and comparison groups to reduce threats to internal validity of findings |
| Design-based research | A type of intervention research in which the principal aims are to develop theories, principles for the design of learning environments, or new interventions that can be refined and tested in subsequent studies. Researchers both engineer and study the learning environments in iterative cycles |
| *Studies of Development over Longer Periods of Time and Across Settings* | |
| Longitudinal observation studies | A type of research that analyzes relationships among psychological processes and outcomes over time. Researchers use these studies both to describe and develop causal explanations for growth or decline on focal measures of outcomes |
| Learning trajectories or learning progressions research | A type of developmental research that analyzes viable routes to learning in disciplines over time. Researchers generate and empirically test these routes using a range of cross-sectional and longitudinal designs |
| *Emerging Forms of Learning Sciences and Educational Psychology Research* | |
| Research on learning as a cross-setting phenomenon | A type of research that focuses on learning that takes place as people move across varied sociocultural contexts and practices. Researchers use ethnographic methods to document what individuals bring from one setting to another and the social supports they rely on in and across settings |
| Educational data mining and learning analytics | A type of research that uses large datasets from digital learning environments to discover emergent patterns of learning and to develop insight into theoretically informed learning processes. Researchers use techniques for investigating online interactions with peers and content to draw inferences about learning |

## Intervention Research in Educational Psychology

Intervention research has long been an important mode of inquiry within educational psychology. It is a form of applied psychological research that overlaps closely with concerns and methods of both policy and evaluation researchers. Intervention research in educational psychology has often sought to investigate claims related to the efficacy and effectiveness of particular interventions in group or cluster randomized controlled trials. Another kind of intervention research, design-based research, is aimed not at testing the efficacy of interventions, but rather at developing new hypotheses about how to support learning. Below, we review both of these modes of inquiry into interventions.

### Cluster Randomized Controlled Trials of Educational Interventions

Randomized controlled trials can be used to obtain unbiased estimates of the impacts of interventions. Because participants are randomly assigned to treatments, estimates are not expected to be biased by differences between students or teachers opting into programs or other factors that are unrelated to the intervention but that could shape outcomes (Shadish, Cook, & Campbell, 2002). Such trials may be focused on establishing the *efficacy* of an intervention, under conditions in which researchers try to optimize conditions for successful implementation, or for testing the *effectiveness* of an intervention under more typical conditions of implementation (Flay et al., 2005). Regardless, a defining feature of such studies is random assignment to treatment and comparison conditions or to alternate treatment conditions.

Today, most randomized controlled trials in education are field trials because they occur in real educational settings, rather than in laboratories. In addition, while some involve random assignment of individuals to treatment and comparison conditions, many involve random assignment of *clusters* of students within classrooms and schools, whichever is appropriate given the purpose and scope of the intervention. In the past decade, software programs like *Optimal Design* (Spybrook, Raudenbush, Liu, Congdon, & Martinez, 2009) have been developed to help researchers estimate the necessary sample size for intervention research, given assumptions about the level of treatment assignment (i.e., whether assignment is at the level of an individual student or teacher, or at the level of classroom or school), the likely magnitude of effects, the size of groups or clusters such as classrooms, and the estimated variance in outcomes associated with groups. In addition, a variety of statistical software packages exist today that permit researchers to analyze the results of cluster randomized trials using multi-level modeling techniques.

***Claims cluster randomized controlled trials can support.***   The results of randomized controlled trials are intended to support causal inferences about the impacts of programs, that is, claims about whether a program causes an increase in an outcome of interest (Shadish et al., 2002). In educational psychology in the past decade, randomized controlled trials have focused, for example, on the efficacy of interventions to improve academic performance (Vadasy, Sanders, & Peyton, 2006) and citizenship outcomes (Schultema, Veugelers, Rijlaarsdam, & ten Dam, 2009). In addition, randomized controlled trials have been conducted of professional development interventions that aim to improve teaching and learning outcomes (Powell, Diamond, Burchinal, & Koehler, 2010).

When trials focus on programs, it is possible to investigate whether and how the implementation of certain program features correlate with outcomes (MacKinnon, Lockwood, Hoffman, West, & Sheets, 2002). Some researchers question whether supporting causal inferences about the contribution of specific features to outcomes is possible when there is no random assignment to different versions of a treatment (Green, Ha, & Bullock, 2010). Occasionally, cluster randomized controlled trials assign schools or classrooms to alternate versions of a treatment, which can support more robust causal inferences about the efficacy of specific design features of the treatment (e.g., Penuel, Gallagher, & Moorthy, 2011).

*Audiences for cluster randomized controlled trials.* Key audiences for results of studies of the efficacy and effectiveness of interventions are policy makers and educational leaders. Both of these sets of actors make decisions about programs, curriculum materials, and interventions to support struggling students. They always face constrained resources, and under such circumstances, policy makers and educational leaders benefit from guidance that allows them to choose more effective programs over less effective ones (Dynarski, 2008). There are now databases of summaries of research findings from randomized controlled trials in education, such as the What Works Clearinghouse (http://www.whatworks.ed.gov/), that are intended to help policy makers and educational leaders select programs with the best and most credible evidence of effectiveness.

*Form and substance of arguments in cluster randomized controlled trials.* Many intervention researchers embrace random assignment as the best approach to eliminate bias from estimates of program impact, because it is the best procedure for eliminating or significantly reducing threats to internal validity of claims. Common threats to internal validity include selection processes, in which certain kinds of people are more likely to choose to be part of an intervention; maturation, in which natural growth accounts for changes in outcomes instead of the treatment; and attrition. True experiments that employ random assignment are still subject to some threats to internal validity and potentially biased results, such as attrition. However, if participants have an equal probability of being assigned to each of the conditions and one participant's outcomes are not affected by any other participant's assignment, then researchers can use randomized experiments to obtain unbiased estimates of any differences in outcomes between those in different treatment conditions (Rubin, 1974).

An evidentiary argument that supports claims about program impact requires more than appeals to the logic of causal inference. The persuasiveness of claims depends in part on the strength of the argument about the mechanism by which the treatment is expected to produce the desired outcome (Cordray & Pion, 2006). In addition, the outcome must measure student behavior that the intervention is intended to develop and must be sensitive to a range of interventions focused on changing those behaviors (Ruiz-Primo, Shavelson, Hamilton, & Klein, 2002). The argument's persuasiveness also depends on the nature and appropriateness of the control condition to the potential users of evaluation results (Morgan & Winship, 2007) and the quality of implementation, or the achieved relative strength of the intervention (Cordray & Pion, 2006). Finally, a compelling argument considers possible counterarguments that would lead to different claims about program impact. For example, perhaps students in a treatment performed better on an outcome measure than students in a comparison group, but treatment students learned more simply because they had been more time on task than comparison group students had and not because the treatment engaged students in a more effective, efficient manner.

Intervention research on a program called *SimCalc Mathworlds* illustrates how one team of researchers designed a series of studies that built toward a well-designed cluster randomized field trial. *SimCalc* is a technology-supported intervention intended to democratize access to the mathematics of change and that employs graphical visualizations of mathematical phenomena to facilitate student understanding (Roschelle, Kaput, & Stroup, 2000). The team that developed *SimCalc* wanted to test the claim that the intervention could be implemented in a wide variety of classrooms and effective with a range of student subpopulations. Prior to conducting a large cluster randomized controlled trial of *SimCalc,* the team pursued three preliminary studies to reduce uncertainty and aid in the design of the larger study. First, the team developed and tested a set of assessments that measured the kinds of complex mathematics problem-solving skills taught in *SimCalc* but that are rarely included as part of standardized tests used by states for accountability purposes. Second, the team developed what they called a "curricular activity system," that is, an integrated set of curriculum materials for teachers, student activities, and professional development designs that could support implementation (Roschelle et al., 2010b). Third, the team undertook a set of pilot studies, so that they could use the results to estimate potential effect sizes, as well as variance in outcomes associated with classrooms and students, in order to estimate the sample size they would need for a larger study (Tatar et al., 2008).

The cluster randomized controlled trial that the *SimCalc* team conducted provided supporting evidence for the claim that *SimCalc* could have a positive impact on student learning in a wide variety of contexts (Roschelle et al., 2010b). In that trial, 88 eighth-grade teachers who volunteered for the study were assigned to one of two conditions, a treatment condition or a comparison condition. Teachers in both conditions received professional development in the mathematics content that was the focus of the *SimCalc* curricular activity system; teachers in the treatment condition also received the *SimCalc* materials and professional development in the use of those materials. The researchers used logs or diaries of instruction to assess implementation fidelity. Pre- and posttest differences on the *SimCalc*-designed assessments were analyzed to support inferences about differences between the two conditions with respect to an overall average treatment effect, and results were also disaggregated by ethnicity (Roschelle et al., 2010a). A subsequent analysis of the same data provided evidence that these impacts might be generalizable to most school districts in the state where the study was conducted, districts that include significant racial, ethnic, and socioeconomic diversity (Hedges, 2013).

*Scope and limitation of cluster randomized controlled trials.* Field-based randomized controlled trials are a difficult undertaking, and they are more easily conducted when interventions are well defined, brief, and not too difficult to implement well (Cook, 2002). It is possible to test the efficacy of interventions in earlier stages of development using randomized controlled trials, but, because of smaller samples, they may not have adequate statistical power to detect statistically significant effects (Osborne, 2008). In addition, randomized controlled trials often include supportive conditions for implementation that may not be continued when studies end, such as more intensive professional development or technology support. As a consequence, the program may be discontinued following the trial, especially when implementers perceive that the program does not meet the needs of participants or support the goals of their organization (Fishman, Penuel, Hegedus, & Roschelle, 2011). Finally, although cluster randomized controlled trials of programs may be useful in determining *whether* programs work, few are designed to investigate how to *make* programs work for a wide variety of participants, or to explain why they do not (Bryk, Gomez, & Grunow, 2011).

### Design-Based Research

Educational psychologists who identify as learning scientists, an interdisciplinary group of researchers focused on the study of learning processes, employ methods that are more akin to those used by engineers than by psychologists. *Design-based research* aims to create or engineer new supports for learning in order to study how children learn (Cobb, Confrey, diSessa, Lehrer, & Schauble, 2003; Sandoval, 2004; Sandoval & Bell, 2004). Design-based research is perhaps best described as a "family of approaches" to research—rather than a methodology—because its proponents do not yet share a common argumentative grammar or logic for argumentation (Kelly, 2004; Reimann, 2011). Indeed, proponents employ a variety of terms to describe the kind of design-based research they do. These terms, which share common characteristics but have different roots, include *design experiments* (Brown, 1992), *formative experiments* (Reinking & Bradley, 2008), and *development research* (van den Akker, 1999).

*Claims design-based research can support.* A key aim of design experiments is to specify how people learn to engage in practices of disciplines (e.g., argumentation in science) and to gather research evidence to identify ways to support their learning successfully (Cobb et al., 2003). The particular goals for disciplinary learning draw from multiple sources, including studies of expert practice as well as tradition (Gravemeijer & Cobb, 2006). The claims design-based research generates pertain to conjectures about how people learn, principles for designing learning environments, and educational design practice (Edelson, 2002).

The particular conjectures for which design-based research develops claims are sometimes called "local instruction theories" (Gravemeijer & Cobb, 2006), because they pertain to learning goals that pertain to a few disciplinary core ideas and practices, and because they specify ways that teaching can support learning these ideas and practices. Here, teaching encompasses the skillful sequencing and orchestration of tasks and classroom discourse to promote learning, as well as the use of tools (including technology) that enable students to construct and assess their own understanding of subject matter. Guiding the teacher's decision making in design research is a hypothetical learning trajectory that specifies one or more pathways from an instructional beginning point to the learning goal (Simon, 1995).

In other design-based research in which the goal is to develop new software or learning environments to explore new possibilities for learning, claims are developed with the support of a *conjecture map* (Sandoval, 2014). A conjecture map is a graphical depiction—accompanied by text with supporting theory and evidence—of key features of a learning environment hypothesized to support learning in a particular domain. Design-based research that uses conjecture mapping has as its main aim the refinement and revision of conjectures related to how particular tools and materials, task structures, participant structures, and discourse practices can support learning when used in concert in a particular learning environment.

*Audiences and uses for design-based research.* The proponents of design-based research argue that research on interventions developed, refined, and tested in the crucible of classrooms can play an important role in developing theories of learning and producing practical, usable interventions for teachers and students (Edelson, 2002). In fact, few products of design-based research have had a broad impact on practice, in part because the supports needed to organize learning environments on a small scale by learning scientists require capacities and resources many schools do not have (Fishman & Krajcik, 2003). Moreover, design-based researchers do not typically engage directly in policy debate, and so the impacts on policy have been more limited than with some of the other modes of inquiry (Penuel & Spillane, in press).

Design-based research has had its greatest influence on other researchers and on curriculum developers, through the articulation of design principles. Design principles are statements intended to inform the development of new learning environments and innovative curriculum materials warranted by evidence from design research studies (Bell, Hoadley, & Linn, 2004). Design principles may be focused on how to support learning along specific learning trajectories, or on how to design technology-based learning environments.

*Form and substance of arguments in design-based research.* Unlike experimental research that develops claims about the efficacy of particular interventions, the goal of design-based research is to develop process-oriented explanations of learning (Reimann, 2011). Design-based research puts local instruction theories and conjectures "in harm's way" by implementing designs in real classrooms, gathering evidence of student learning processes and outcomes, and then iteratively refining those theories and conjectures. The logic of design research is distinct from formal hypothesis testing, and is more akin to the goal of grounded theory (Charmaz, 2000), in which a central aim of research is the generation of theory. When specific conjectures are embodied in designs, implementation can lead either to a refinement of the conjecture or to an iterative improvement of some aspect of the design itself (Sandoval, 2014).

In design-based research, iteration unfolds both as the research unfolds and retrospectively, after a cycle of classroom-based research is complete (Gravemeijer & Cobb, 2006). In the course of a single design experiment, researchers typically debrief with classroom teachers and members of the research team after each day's activities. In these debriefings, the team relies on a combination of informal observations, notes about student interactions, and artifacts from the classroom to make decisions about how the learning trajectory might need to be altered the next day, or to identify some specific ways that the conjectured means of support did or did not help students learn that day. In a retrospective analysis, the research team reviews video recordings of classroom activities, artifacts of student work, and formal and informal assessments of student thinking (often in the form of pre- and post-tests, administered as interviews with students). The aim in retrospective analysis is to refine, revise, or even challenge particular aspects of a local instructional theory, using evidence from these different sources. The retrospective analysis may lead to a new local instructional theory, a new set of conjectures or design, or a new cycle of design-based research. It can also lead to the specification of an intervention whose efficacy may be tested using a different mode of inquiry (such as an efficacy trial).

An example of design-based research from mathematics is reported by Jurow, Hall, and Ma (2008), who developed and studied an adaptation to the materials of the middle school Mathematics through Applications Project (MMAP). MMAP was a project-based, technology-supported curriculum in mathematics aligned to standards developed in the 1990s (Greeno & Middle School Mathematics through Applications Project Group, 1998). The adaptation that Jurow and colleagues made was to incorporate professional design reviews of student work at the end of individual units. As part of these design reviews for one such unit on population ecology, graduate students in biology served as expert reviewers of students' models of predator–prey system dynamics. The idea for design reviews came from an earlier set of studies of the mathematical practices of professional architects, who worked in a field where design reviews were an integral part of their practice (Stevens & Hall, 1998).

The organization of the research project was typical of many design-based research projects in most respects. The team worked in close partnership with a single teacher in a school near the researchers' home institution over the course of a school year. The team jointly discussed and planned the adaptations to the unit, and conducted weekly research meetings that included the teacher. At these meetings, the team discussed the classroom activities and analyzed classroom interactions captured on videotape. For most of the unit, the teacher taught the activities, but for the new activities—the

design reviews—the researchers assisted and were more involved in supporting implementation.

Also, as is typical of design-based research, the research team had as a primary aim to generate design principles that could inform future research on learning. To that end, their analyses focused on variation in the unfolding and effects of what they termed "recontextualization exchanges" between the graduate student biologists and students in design reviews. By this term, the researchers called attention to contingent interactions in which students were positioned much as professional biologists might be in situations where they are asked to defend, justify, or revise their systems models. Their research drew on a rich tradition of study of recontextualization from interactional sociolinguistics, particularly with respect to the development of professional vision (Goodwin & Goodwin, 1996).

***Scope and limitations of design-based research.*** The products of design-based research—local instruction theories, design principles, learning environments—may be most useful to other researchers exploring new and emerging areas of learning, in that design-based research can guide what to look for, suggest important kinds of evidence to gather, and provide interpretive frameworks for analysis (Kelly, 2004). From the perspective of its proponents, being of use to other researchers is not enough, because design-based research aims to yield practical solutions that can be implemented in real classrooms. To that end, a number of scholars are engaged in efforts to extend design-based research to problems of implementation (Bryk et al., 2011; Donovan, 2013; Penuel, Fishman, Cheng, & Sabelli, 2011). The aim of these forms of design-based research is to increase the reproducibility of research in practice settings by developing and testing conjectures about how best to support the implementation of innovations.

Critics of design-based research sometimes question the generalizability of findings from smaller-scale design-based research. For one, they question whether or not design-based research is the best mode of inquiry for testing whether observed learning is causally related to specific learning designs (Shavelson, Phillips, Towne, & Feuer, 2003). Design-based researchers might counter that the aim of their research is not to estimate causal impacts, but rather to identify causes of learning evident from analysis of interactions of students with materials, peers, and their teacher in classrooms (e.g., Gravemeijer & Cobb, 2006). Even so, there are not yet agreed-upon standards for selecting classroom episodes for analysis or deciding how to triangulate among different sources of evidence that may point to competing explanations for learning (Kelly, 2004).

## Studies of Development Over Longer Periods of Time and Across Settings

A second mode of inquiry in educational psychology aims to document and analyze changes to learning and development over time and conditions that account for those changes. Its methods are principally observational, though in some cases, researchers may intervene to promote and observe certain psychological phenomena, forms of problem solving and reasoning, or subject matter understandings. In addition, researchers may, as part of their work, attempt to develop validity evidence for the use of particular measures of learning over time.

### Longitudinal Observation Studies Using Large-scale Databases

Many observational studies today make use of the large-scale databases that have been developed in recent decades to address research questions of fundamental interest to educational psychologists. The power of these databases for inquiry is multifold. Most draw random samples of subjects that represent well-defined populations, reducing concerns about external validity (Shadish et al., 2002). In addition, most include multiple waves of data, which allow researchers to estimate the effects of educational or other experiences on change over time. Third, many are interoperable, meaning they can be linked to other datasets. This property is especially useful for conducting analyses that cross societal sectors, such as education and social services (McLaughlin & O'Brien-Strain, 2008).

**Claims longitudinal observation studies can support.** Observational studies carried out longitudinally using large-scale databases can support descriptive or causal claims. For example, studies using the Wisconsin Longitudinal Study have documented the educational and occupational aspirations and trajectories of those graduating from high school in Wisconsin since the 1950s (e.g., Sewell, Hauser, Springer, & Hauser, 2003). Some longitudinal studies develop causal inferences about the relation of psychological processes to outcomes. For example, Chan and Moore (2006) developed evidence for claims about the causal influence of students' beliefs about reasons for school success or failure and use of learning strategies on achievement. Other longitudinal studies aim for accurate prediction of future outcomes. For example, Balfanz and colleagues (Balfanz, Herzog, & Mac Iver, 2007) sought to develop "early warning indicators" for high-school dropout from middle-school administrative datasets that could accurately target young people who are off track for graduation.

**Audiences for longitudinal observation studies.** The results of observational studies can be useful to policy makers at a range of levels in educational systems. For example, analyses of longitudinal databases can help identify new issues and concerns and investigate the plausibility of theories of change associated with particular interventions (Penuel & Means, 2011). Longitudinal observation studies (e.g., Burstein, 1993) have also been influential in developing and supporting the adoption of new standards for core subject areas in American schools (McDonnell & Weatherford, 2013). In addition, a number of districts have developed "on track" and "early warning systems" on the basis of longitudinal analyses showing the promise of early

identification of students for dropout (Kemple, Segeritz, & Stephenson, 2013).

**Form and substance of arguments in longitudinal observation studies.** The basic form of argument in a longitudinal observation study is that the changes people exhibit between two time periods are a function of different measured experiences between those two time points. Inferences from longitudinal observation studies depend on the capacity of the study to account for alternative explanations of the inferred phenomenon. In the absence of random assignment of subjects to treatments, others may challenge inferences on the basis of confounding variables not accounted for in the analysis. To inform debate about such challenges, analysts of longitudinal observation datasets can use techniques that allow one to estimate how large of an effect a confounding variable would have to be to invalidate an inference about a relationship between two variables.

As an example, consider the study by Hong and Raudenbush (2005) that examined effects of grade retention in kindergarten on 11,843 children's achievement. They found that children who were retained in kindergarten learned less in the following year than those who had been promoted. On the basis of observational data, Hong and Raudenbush (2005) inferred that "children who were retained would have learned more had they been promoted" (p. 200). They accounted for alternative explanations by matching retained and promoted students for their propensity to be retained based on 207 covariates, including family background, emotional disposition, and multiple pretests. Such statistical controls, especially for pretests, have been shown to account for 84–94% of bias in an observational study compared to an analogous randomized experiment (e.g., Shadish, Clark, & Steiner, 2008).

Although Hong and Raudenbush employed extensive statistical controls, in the absence of random assignment of subjects to treatments, their inference may still be challenged based on alternative explanations not accounted for. Frank and colleagues (Frank, Maroulis, Duong, & Kelcey, 2013) respond to such concerns by quantifying how much an estimated effect would have to be due to bias to invalidate a causal inference. In particular, 85% of Hong and Raudenbush's estimate would have to have been due to bias to invalidate their inference. As a basis of comparison, controlling for family background, including mother's education, altered the estimated effect by less than 1% (once controlling for pretests). Therefore any omitted variable(s) would have to be 85 times more important than family background to invalidate Hong and Raudenbush's (2005) inference that kindergarten retention reduces achievement. While Frank et al.'s analyses do not change the inference, they contribute to scientific discourse in a research or policy community by quantifying the conditions that would invalidate the inference.

**Scope and limitations of observational studies.** In recent years, educational psychologists have used a range of longitudinal databases to study children's learning and development. For example, McCoach, O'Connell, Reis, and Levitt (2006) employed the Early Childhood Longitudinal Study Kindergarten cohort (ECLS-K) data to study children's reading growth over the course of kindergarten and first grade. Their analyses focused on between-school differences in instruction, resource allocation, and student composition; their findings underscored the significance of initial differences in reading ability and summer learning loss in accounting for achievement gaps between low-income and more advantaged children. Other databases used by educational psychologists include the High School and Beyond Database (e.g., Marsh, 1992), the National Educational Longitudinal Study (e.g., Jordan & Nettles, 2000; Lan & Lanthier, 2003), the Educational Longitudinal Study of 2002 (e.g., Fan & Williams, 2010; Fan, Williams, & Corkin, 2011), and the High School Longitudinal Study of 2009 (Willoughby, Adachi, & Good, 2012).

While large-scale longitudinal databases can contribute to policy formation and choices, they have considerable limitations. For one, estimates of effects from observational studies are not theoretically unbiased as they are from randomized experiments. Second, observational studies rarely provide the close, iterative contact with practitioners leveraged in design-based research. One must carefully consider the political and scientific contexts in which potentially alternative explanations are conceptualized and measured in observational studies (e.g., Altonji, Elder, & Taber, 2005). Finally, it may be important to know trajectories of behavior or learning prior to receiving a treatment, as well as participants' state at baseline. For example, Hong and Raudenbush use multiple lagged measurements to control for growth rates prior to the end of kindergarten. Interrupted time series analyses (Shadish et al., 2002) take this to its logical conclusion, estimating effects based on trajectories leading up to and then after experimental conditions.

### Research on Learning Trajectories or Learning Progressions

Another mode of inquiry within educational psychology that analyzes learning over time focuses on developing evidence for *learning trajectories* (the term used by those studying mathematics) or *learning progressions* (a synonymous term used by those studying science) research. A learning trajectory or progression is a set of testable, empirically supported hypotheses about how students' understanding develops toward specific disciplinary goals for learning (Smith, Wiser, Anderson, & Krajcik, 2006). Some researchers trace this line of research to Piaget's constructivism (e.g., Simon, 1995), but learning trajectories researchers argue that one way that their hypotheses differ from traditional stage theories of development is that a trajectory represents one of many possible viable pathways of learning.

***Claims learning trajectories and progressions research can support.*** The claims made in learning trajectories or progressions are hypotheses pertaining to how student understandings of particular core disciplinary ideas and practices develop over time (Duncan & Hmelo-Silver, 2009).

Each level in a trajectory or progression is described in qualitative terms, relative to some ideal understanding of an idea or mastery of a practice. Levels on a trajectory are ordered developmentally, in two senses of that term. First, higher levels of a trajectory represent more differentiated and hierarchically integrated (e.g., Werner, 1957) understandings and skills. Second, higher levels are imagined as building upon the foundation of levels below, suggesting a possible way that understanding and skills might emerge over the course of a few weeks, months, or years. For most learning trajectories researchers, movement along the trajectory requires encounters with instruction intentionally designed to support learning (Lehrer & Schauble, 2011). At the same time, many also emphasize the importance of basic developmental capacities for enabling movement along a hypothetical trajectory, particularly at the entry points of that trajectory (Clements & Sarama, 2004).

***Audiences and uses for learning trajectories and progressions research.*** Learning trajectories or progressions research aims to be of use to educational policy makers, curriculum developers, and teachers. For educational policy makers, a key aim is to inform and guide the development of standards and assessments (National Research Council, 2006). Hypothetical learning trajectories are intended to guide the design of standards around a small number of core ideas and practices in the disciplines that can be developed across grade levels and assessed in greater depth. Learning trajectories are also intended to guide curriculum developers in organizing materials so that they support the development of understanding of these core ideas and skills in practice over time (Wiser, Smith, & Doubler, 2012). Some researchers intend hypothetical learning trajectories to be of use to teachers to interpret what students say and do when they engage with tasks intended to support their learning along the trajectory (Lehrer & Petrosino, 2013).

***Form and substance of arguments in learning progressions research.*** Developing evidence to support a hypothetical learning trajectory typically requires many different kinds of studies conducted over many years (Clements, 2007; Lehrer & Schauble, 2011). The process begins with the specification of an initial hypothetical trajectory that draws from past research on learning of the focal core ideas and practices. Some learning trajectories researchers then proceed to develop and test their hypothetical trajectories through a series of teaching or design experiments, in which they develop instructional sequences that are designed to support student development along the trajectory (e.g., Ni & Zhou, 2005). In this approach, researchers conduct studies to test whether exposure to designed supports does in fact enable students to display the kinds of thinking at the highest levels of the trajectory (e.g., Songer, Kelcey, & Gotwals, 2009). Other researchers develop evidence related to an initial trajectory by devising and implementing measures of the trajectory, and then analyzing the fit of student responses to assessments to the hypothetical trajectory (e.g., Mohan, Chen, & Anderson, 2009). In this approach, when student responses do not fit the pattern predicted by the trajectories, researchers may revise their hypothetical trajectory and test the revised trajectory in a subsequent study (Shea & Duncan, 2013).

A good example of a well-developed learning progression in science focuses on children's developing understanding of *how to model phenomena in biological and ecological systems*. It focuses on how children develop proficiency in the practice of developing and using models to develop and test theories that address particular scientific questions (Lehrer & Schauble, 2006). The researchers developed their hypothetical learning trajectories over the course of several years and in collaboration with classroom teachers through a series of teaching experiments, in which the researchers and teachers sought to promote the development of students' scientific modeling practice. The researchers were testing the validity of their approach to cultivating students' scientific modeling practice in a large-scale randomized controlled trial. They compared performance of students in a treatment group to that of students in a coherent, alternative approach to instruction. Outcomes were measures specially developed to assess learning along the hypothetical progression.

As other progressions do, this progression articulates entry points, intermediate levels of understanding, and target understandings related to the practice of modeling. One dimension of the progression is focused on how children develop and use displays of data to model phenomena. In that dimension, the team has posited that an entry point into displaying data is to construct displays of data without reference to the question being posed. Children might group values they obtain from observing or measuring phenomena according to schemes of their own invention (e.g., "We grouped odd and even numbers together"). Over time and with guidance from instruction, students begin to notice or group cases of observation based on similar values and in relation to specific questions they pose. Students whose modeling practice has become sophisticated are able to quantify properties of displays (e.g., through ratios, percentages), recognize that displays provide information about a collective or sample of cases, and discuss how general patterns or trends are either exemplified by or missing from subsets of cases.

*Scope and limitations of research on learning trajectories.* Research within this mode of inquiry currently focuses on a few areas of mathematics and science learning. Standards developers have had to posit many trajectories for areas that do not yet have empirical support. To date, though some assessments of trajectories have strong validity evidence (e.g., Gunckel, Covitt, Salinas, & Anderson, 2012), no large-scale assessments used in states yet employ these trajectories. There are many potential limitations to using learning progressions to guide the development of large-scale assessments, because they require significant departure from the way traditional test items are designed and scored (Alonzo, Neidorf, & Anderson, 2012). Moreover, the design of trajectories-based assessments often requires the development of interventions to help students engage in forms of reasoning and problem-solving characteristic of the highest hypothesized levels of a trajectory

(Penuel, Confrey, Maloney, & Rupp, 2014). In addition, when confronting disconfirming evidence, researchers must grapple with uncertainty as to whether or not their hypothetical trajectories are incorrectly specified or their assessment tasks are not effective in eliciting student thinking and reasoning (Shea & Duncan, 2013).

### Emerging Forms of Educational Psychology and Learning Sciences Research

In this section, we briefly note two emerging areas of inquiry being led by educational psychologists and learning scientists: in both of these cases, evaluative arguments are still under development. These emerging areas point to expanding conceptions of how and where learning happens. They also underscore the potential for new technological tools that can advance understandings of learning and development.

#### Research on Learning as a Cross-setting Phenomenon

One emerging form of research is the study of how learning takes place across different settings (see Chapter 24, this volume). This perspective draws on sociocultural and social practice theories that frame learning and development as transformations in the ways that people participate in and appropriate the resources of culturally valued practices (Gutiérrez & Rogoff, 2003; Holland & Lave, 2009; Lave & Wenger, 1991; Rogoff, 2003). Educational psychologists and learning scientists who pursue this line of work principally use ethnographic methods for "following the person" across different contexts (Jackson, 2011). They focus both on the agency that people exercise within particular settings of practice and on the social supports learners rely upon for guidance and for brokering access to other (Barron, 2006, 2010; Cooper, Cooper, Azmitia, Chavira, & Gullatt, 2002; Cooper, Denner, & Lopez, 1999; Stevens, O'Connor, Garrison, Jocuns, & Amos, 2008). These researchers also document how different institutions restrict access to learning opportunities by limiting participation in particular practices and by valuing some forms of learning over others (Baines, 2012; Bang & Medin, 2010). Other research investigates how groups of people are remaking places in ways that draw on or leverage familiar cultural repertoires for participating in social practices. The hope is that these repertoires can extend access to disciplinary practices taught in schools (Gutiérrez, 2008; Hand, Penuel, & Gutiérrez, 2012).

#### Educational Data Mining and Learning Analytics

Many new digital learning environments provide researchers with opportunities to make use of student "clicks" or keystrokes both to study basic learning processes and to test interventions. A new field called *educational data mining* is emerging that is elaborating and testing methodologies for using large datasets to discover patterns in learning and find associations between forms of learner engagement in particular interventions and learning outcomes (Baker & Yacef, 2009;

Bienkowski, Feng, & Means, 2012). Researchers have used data-mining techniques to study learning processes when students learn mathematics through intelligent tutoring systems (Baker, Goldstein, & Heffernan, 2011) and when students learn science as part of virtual learning environments, including game-like environments (Gobert, Sao Pedro, Baker, Toto, & Montalvo, 2012).

A mode of inquiry closely related to educational data mining that is emerging is *learning analytics* (see Chapter 29, this volume). In contrast to educational data mining, a central focus of learning analytics is developing insight into learning from computer-mediated peer interaction and student–teacher interaction during learning activities (Buckingham Shum & Ferguson, 2012; Wise & Chiu, 2011). Scholars in this area are also developing methods for studying the emergence of new connections students make among ideas and ways of thinking they encounter in digitally mediated learning activities. For example, Shaffer and colleagues (2009) have been using a technique they call Epistemic Network Analysis (ENA) to study how students come to adopt epistemic frames characteristic of social participation in disciplinary practices of urban planners in the context of a game in which learners develop a plan for addressing issues facing a city.

## Looking to the Future of Educational Psychology Research

In coming decades, educational psychology and learning sciences research is likely to continue to embrace a wide range of modes of inquiry, as it has in the past. At the same time, there will continue to be contest and controversy over methods, goals, and strategies of interventions. In this chapter, we have sought to frame differences in modes of inquiry in terms of different evaluative arguments they can and cannot support. In the previous section, we introduced new or emerging methodologies, ones that will require and undoubtedly see development over the coming decade.

In future debates over modes of inquiry, the dialogue must move beyond aphorism and simple dichotomies. The methods researchers use should always "match the question at hand," but such an aphorism diminishes the importance of a fully articulated evaluative argument in designing and judging the quality of research studies. Moreover, we must go beyond House (1977) and others who dichotomized "qualitative" and "qualitative" forms of reasoning. There are multiple modes of inquiry to consider, including some in which argumentation relies on an integration of qualitative and quantitative evidence (Johnson & Onwuegbuzie, 2004). Third, we must pay closer attention to different conceptions of *cause* employed by researchers committed to different modes of inquiry. Some modes of inquiry reviewed in this chapter emphasize the need for causal inferences about interventions' impacts (e.g., Shadish et al., 2002), while others focus on identification of causes of learning evident from analysis of microprocesses in classrooms (e.g., Gravemeijer & Cobb, 2006). These different notions of cause imply the need for a nuanced evaluation of what kinds of claims are suitable for what modes of inquiry.

Finally, we anticipate that, in the coming decade, dialogue will continue over how best to reconcile goals for rigor and goals for relevance. Although these two goals need not be opposed, in actuality, rigorous research can yield empirical results that are not useful for improving practice, and relevant research can produce findings that are not trustworthy guides to decision making. A potential way forward is to promote more long-term partnerships between researchers and practitioners that can address persistent problems of practice (Coburn, Penuel, & Geil, 2013; Donovan, 2013). In our view, research policies are needed that embrace evidence standards that call for both rigor and relevance to practice (Gutiérrez & Penuel, 2014). Such policies have the best potential for supporting the design and conduct of educational psychology research that might broadly impact society.

## References

Alonzo, A. C., Neidorf, T., & Anderson, C. W. (2012). Using learning progressions to inform large-scale assessment. In A. C. Alonzo & A. W. Gotwals (Eds.), *Learning progressions in science: Current challenges and future directions* (pp. 211–240). Rotterdam, the Netherlands: Sense Publishers.

Altonji, J. G., Elder, T. E., & Taber, C. R. (2005). An evaluation of instrumental variable strategies for estimating the effects of Catholic schooling. *Journal of Human Resources, 40*(4), 791–821.

Asen, R., Gurke, D., Solomon, R., Conners, P., & Gumm, E. (2011). "The research says": Definitions and uses of a key policy term in federal law and local school board deliberations. *Argumentation and Advocacy, 47*, 195–213.

Baines, A. D. (2012). Positioning, strategizing, and charming: How students with autism construct identities in relation to disability. *Disability and Society, 27*, 547–561.

Baker, R. S. J. d., Goldstein, A. B., & Heffernan, N. T. (2011). Detecting learning moment-by-moment. *International Journal of Artificial Intelligence in Education, 21*(1–2), 5–25.

Baker, R. S. J. d., & Yacef, K. (2009). The state of educational data mining in 2009: A review and future visions. *Journal of Educational Data Mining, 1*(1), 3–17.

Balfanz, R., Herzog, L., & Mac Iver, D. J. (2007). Preventing student disengagement and keeping students on the graduation path in urban middle-grades schools: Early identification and effective interventions. *Educational Psychologist, 42*(4), 223–235.

Bang, M., & Medin, D. (2010). Cultural processes in science education: Supporting the navigation of multiple epistemologies. *Science Education, 94*(6), 1008–1026.

Barron, B. (2006). Interest and self-sustained learning as catalysts of development: A learning ecology perspective. *Human Development, 49*(4), 193–224.

Barron, B. (2010). Conceptualizing and tracing learning pathways over time and setting. In W. R. Penuel & K. O'Connor (Eds.) *Learning research as a human science. National Society for the Study of Education Yearbook, 109*(1), 113–127.

Bell, P., Hoadley, C., & Linn, M. C. (2004). Design-based research in education. In M. C. Linn, E. A. Davis, & P. Bell (Eds.), *Internet environments for science education* (pp. 73–88). Mahwah, NJ: Erlbaum.

Bienkowski, M., Feng, M., & Means, B. (2012). Enhancing teaching and learning through educational data mining and learning analytics. Draft for public comment. Menlo Park, CA: SRI International.

Brown, A. L. (1992). Design experiments: Theoretical and methodological challenges in creating complex interventions in classroom settings. *Journal of the Learning Sciences, 2*(2), 141–178.

Bryk, A. S., Gomez, L. M., & Grunow, A. (2011). Getting ideas into action: Building networked improvement communities in education. In M. Hallinan (Ed.), *Frontiers in sociology of education* (pp. 127–162). Dordrecht, the Netherlands: Verlag.

Buckingham Shum, S., & Ferguson, R. (2012). Social learning analytics. *Educational Technology & Society, 15*(3), 3–26.

Burstein, L. (1993). *The IEA study of mathematics III: Student growth and classroom processes* (Vol. 3). New York, NY: Pergamon.

Chan, L. K., & Moore, P. J. (2006). Development of attributional beliefs and strategic knowledge in years 5–9: A longitudinal analysis. *Educational Psychology, 26*(2), 161–185.

Charmaz, K. (2000). Grounded theory: Objectivist and constructivist methods. In N. K. Denzin & Y. S. Lincoln (Eds.), *Handbook of qualitative research* (pp. 509–535). Thousand Oaks, CA: Sage.

Clements, D. H. (2007). Curriculum research: Toward a framework for "research-based curricula". *Journal for Research in Mathematics Education, 38*(1), 35–70.

Clements, D. H., & Sarama, J. (2004). Learning trajectories in mathematics education. *Mathematical Thinking and Learning, 6*(2), 81–90.

Cobb, P. A., Confrey, J., diSessa, A. A., Lehrer, R., & Schauble, L. (2003). Design experiments in educational research. *Educational Researcher, 32*(1), 9–13.

Coburn, C. E., Penuel, W. R., & Geil, K. (2013). *Research–practice partnerships at the district level: A new strategy for leveraging research for educational improvement.* Berkeley, CA and Boulder, CO: University of California and University of Colorado.

Cook, T. D. (2002). Randomized experiments in education: Why are they so rare? *Educational Evaluation and Policy Analysis, 24*(3), 175–199.

Cooper, C. R., Cooper, R., Azmitia, M., Chavira, G., & Gullatt, Y. (2002). Bridging multiple worlds: How African American and Latino youth in academic outreach programs navigate math pathways to college. *Applied Developmental Science, 6*(2), 73–87.

Cooper, C. R., Denner, J., & Lopez, E. M. (1999). Cultural brokers: Helping Latino children on pathways toward success. *The Future of Children, 9*, 51–57.

Cordray, D. S., & Pion, G. M. (2006). Treatment strength and integrity: Models and methods. In R. R. Bootzin & P. E. McKnight (Eds.), *Strengthening research methodology: Psychological measurement and evaluation* (pp. 103–124). Washington, DC: American Psychological Association.

Cronbach, L. J. (1982). *Designing evaluations of educational and social programs.* San Francisco, CA: Jossey-Bass.

Cronbach, L. J. (1988). Five perspectives on validation argument. In H. Wainer & H. Braun (Eds.), *Test validity* (pp. 3–17). Hillsdale, NJ: Erlbaum.

Donovan, M. S. (2013). Generating improvement through research and development in educational systems. *Science, 340*, 317–319.

Duncan, R. G., & Hmelo-Silver, C. E. (2009). Learning progressions: Aligning curriculum, instruction, and assessment. *Journal of Research in Science Teaching, 46*(6), 606–609.

Dynarski, M. (2008). Bringing answers to educators: Guiding principles for research syntheses. *Educational Researcher, 37*(1), 27–29.

Edelson, D. C. (2002). Design research: What we learn when we engage in design. *Journal of the Learning Sciences, 11*(1), 105–121.

Eisenhart, M., & Towne, L. (2003). Contestation and change in national policy on "scientifically based" education research. *Educational Researcher, 32*(7), 31–38.

Fan, W., & Williams, C. M. (2010). The effects of parental involvement on students' academic self-efficacy, engagement and intrinsic motivation. *Educational Psychology, 30*(1), 54–74.

Fan, W., Williams, C. M., & Corkin, D. M. (2011). A multilevel analysis of student perceptions of school climate: The effect of social and academic risk factors. *Psychology in the Schools, 48*(6), 632–647.

Fishman, B. J., & Krajcik, J. (2003). What does it mean to create sustainable science curriculum innovations? A commentary. *Science Education, 87*(4), 564–573.

Fishman, B. J., Penuel, W. R., Hegedus, S., & Roschelle, J. (2011). What happens when the research ends? Factors related to the sustainability of a technology-infused mathematics curriculum. *Journal of Computers in Mathematics and Science Teaching, 30*(4), 329–353.

Flay, B. R., Biglan, A., Boruch, R. F., Castro, F. G., Gottfredson, D., Kellam, S., . . . Ji, P. (2005). Standards of evidence: Criteria for efficacy, effectiveness, and dissemination. *Prevention Science, 6*(3), 151–175.

Frank, K. A. (2000). Impact of a confounding variable on a regression coefficient. *Sociological Methods and Research, 29*, 147–194.

Frank, K. A., Maroulis, S. J., Duong, M. Q., & Kelcey, B. M. (2013). What would it take to change an inference? Using Rubin's causal model to interpret the robustness of causal inferences. *Educational Evaluation and Policy Analysis, 35*(4), 437–460.

Gobert, J. D., Sao Pedro, M. A., Baker, R. S. J. d., Toto, E., & Montalvo, O. (2012). Leveraging educational data mining for real-time performance assessment of scientific inquiry skills within microworlds. *Journal of Educational Data Mining, 4*(1), 111–143.

Goetz, J. P., & LeCompte, M. D. (1984). *Ethnography and qualitative design in educational research.* Orlando, FL: Academic Press.

Goodwin, C., & Goodwin, M. H. (1996). Seeing as situated activity: Formulating planes. In Y. Engestrom & D. Middleton (Eds.), *Cognition and communication at work* (pp. 61–95). New York: Cambridge University Press.

Gravemeijer, K., & Cobb, P. (2006). Design research from a learning design perspective. In J. van den Akker, K. Gravemeijer, S. E. McKenney & N. Nieveen (Eds.), *Educational design research* (pp. 17–51). New York, NY: Routledge.

Green, D. P., Ha, S. E., & Bullock, J. G. (2010). Enough already about "black box" experiments: Studying mediation is more difficult than most scholars suppose. *Annals of the American Academy of Political and Social Science, 628*, 200–208.

Greeno, J. G., & Middle School Mathematics through Applications Project Group. (1998). The situativity of knowing, learning, and research. *American Psychologist, 53*(1), 5–26.

Gunckel, K. L., Covitt, B. A., Salinas, I., & Anderson, C. W. (2012). A learning progression for water in socio-ecological systems. *Journal of Research in Science Teaching, 49*(7), 843–868.

Gutiérrez, K. D. (2008). Developing sociocritical literacy in the third space. *Reading Research Quarterly, 43*(2), 148–164.

Gutiérrez, K. D., & Penuel, W. R. (2014). Relevance to practice as a criterion for rigor. *Educational Researcher, 43*(1), 19–23.

Gutiérrez, K. D., & Rogoff, B. (2003). Cultural ways of learning: Individual traits or repertoires of practice. *Educational Researcher, 32*(5), 19–25.

Hand, V., Penuel, W. R., & Gutiérrez, K. D. (2012). (Re)framing educational possibility: Attending to power and equity in shaping access to and within learning opportunities. *Human Development, 55*, 250–268.

Hedges, L. V. (2013). Recommendations for practice: Justifying claims of generalizability. *Educational Psychology Review, 25*(3), 331–337.

Holland, D., & Lave, J. (2009). Social practice theory and the historical production of persons. *Actio: An International Journal of Human Activity Theory, 2*, 1–15.

Hong, G., & Raudenbush, S. W. (2005). Effects of kindergarten retention policy on children's cognitive growth in reading and mathematics. *Educational Evaluation and Policy Analysis, 27*(3), 205–224.

House, E. R. (1977). *The logic of evaluative argument. Center for Study of Evaluation Monograph Series in Evaluation.* Los Angeles, CA: Center for the Study of Evaluation, University of California.

House, E. R. (1979). Coherence and credibility: The aesthetics of evaluation. *Educational Evaluation and Policy Analysis, 1*(5), 5–17.

Jackson, K. (2011). Approaching participation in school-based mathematics as a cross-setting phenomenon. *Journal of the Learning Sciences, 20*(1), 111–150.

Johnson, R. B., & Onwuegbuzie, A. J. (2004). Mixed methods research: A research paradigm whose time has come. *Educational Researcher, 33*(7), 14–26.

Jordan, W. J., & Nettles, S. M. (2000). How students invest their time outside of school: Effects on school-related outcomes. *Social Psychology of Education, 3*, 217–243.

Jurow, A. S., Hall, R., & Ma, J. Y. (2008). Expanding the disciplinary expertise of a middle school mathematics classroom: Re-contextualizing student models in conversations with visiting specialists. *Journal of the Learning Sciences, 17*(3), 338–380.

Kelly, A. E. (2004). Design research in education: Yes, but is it methodological? *Journal of the Learning Sciences, 13*(1), 113–128.

Kelly, A. E., & Yin, R. K. (2007). Strengthening structured abstracts for education research: The need for claim-based structured abstracts. *Educational Researcher, 36*(3), 133–138.

Kemple, J. J., Segeritz, M. D., & Stephenson, N. (2013). Building on-track indicators for high school graduation and college readiness: Evidence from New York City. *Journal of Education for Students Placed at Risk (JESPAR), 18*(1), 7–28.

Lan, W., & Lanthier, R. (2003). Changes in students' academic performance and perceptions of school and self before dropping out of school. *Journal of Education for Students Placed at Risk, 8*(3), 309–332.

Lave, J., & Wenger, E. (1991). *Situated learning: Legitimate peripheral participation.* Cambridge, MA: Harvard University Press.

Lehrer, R., & Petrosino, A. (2013). *A learning progression in data modeling emerges in a trading zone of professional community and identity.* Paper presented at the Waterbury Summit, Pennsylvania State University, State College, PA.

Lehrer, R., & Schauble, L. (2006). Cultivating model-based reasoning in science education. In R. K. Sawyer (Ed.), *Cambridge handbook of the learning sciences* (pp. 371–388). Cambridge, MA: Cambridge University Press.

Lehrer, R., & Schauble, L. (2011). Designing to support long-term growth and development. In T. Koschmann (Ed.), *Theories of learning and studies of instructional practice* (pp. 19–38). New York: Springer.

MacKinnon, D. P., Lockwood, C. M., Hoffman, J. M., West, S. G., & Sheets, V. (2002). A comparison of methods to test mediation and other intervening variable effects. *Psychological Methods, 7*(1), 83–104.

Marsh, H. W. (1992). Extracurricular activities: Beneficial extension of the traditional curriculum or subversion of academic goals. *Journal of Educational Psychology, 84*(4), 553–562.

McCoach, D. B., O'Connell, A. A., Reis, S. M., & Levitt, H. A. (2006). Growing readers: A hierarchical linear model of children's reading growth during the first 2 years of school. *Journal of Educational Psychology, 98*(1), 14–28.

McDonnell, L. M., & Weatherford, M. S. (2013). Evidence use and the Common Core State Standards Movement: From problem definition to policy adoption. *American Journal of Education, 120*(1), 1–25.

McLaughlin, M. W., & O'Brien-Strain, M. (2008). The Youth Data Archive: Integrating data to assess social settings in a societal sector framework. In M. Shinn & H. Yoshikawa (Eds.), *Toward positive youth development: Transforming schools and community programs* (pp. 313–332). New York: Oxford University Press.

Mohan, L., Chen, J., & Anderson, C. W. (2009). Developing a multi-year learning progression for carbon cycling. *Journal of Research in Science Teaching, 46*(6), 675–698.

Morgan, S. L., & Winship, C. (2007). *Counterfactuals and causal inference.* London, UK: Cambridge University Press.

Muller, C., Riegle-Crumb, C., Schiller, K. S., Wilkinson, L., & Frank, K. A. (2010). Race and academic achievement in racially diverse high schools: Opportunity and stratification. *Teachers College Record, 112*(4), 1038–1063.

National Research Council. (2006). *Systems for state science assessment.* Washington, DC: National Academies Press.

Ni, Y., & Zhou, Y.-D. (2005). Teaching and learning fraction and rational numbers: The origins and implications of whole number bias. *Educational Psychologist, 40*(1), 27–52.

Osborne, J. W. (Ed.). (2008). *Best practices in quantitative methods.* Thousand Oaks, CA: Sage.

Penuel, W. R., Confrey, J., Maloney, A., & Rupp, A. A. (2014). Design decisions in developing assessments of learning trajectories: A case study. *Journal of the Learning Sciences, 23*(1), 47–95.

Penuel, W. R., Fishman, B. J., Cheng, B., & Sabelli, N. (2011). Organizing research and development at the intersection of learning, implementation, and design. *Educational Researcher, 40*(7), 331–337.

Penuel, W. R., Gallagher, L. P., & Moorthy, S. (2011). Preparing teachers to design sequences of instruction in Earth science: A comparison of three professional development programs. *American Educational Research Journal, 48*(4), 996–1025.

Penuel, W. R., & Means, B. (2011). Using large-scale databases in evaluation: Advances, opportunities, and challenges. *American Journal of Evaluation, 32*(1), 118–133.

Penuel, W. R., & Spillane, J. P. (in press). Learning sciences and policy design and implementation: Key concepts and tools for collaborative engagement. In R. K. Sawyer (Ed.), *Cambridge handbook of the learning sciences* (2nd ed.). Cambridge, UK: Cambridge University Press.

Powell, D. R., Diamond, K. E., Burchinal, M. R., & Koehler, M. J. (2010). Effects of early literacy professional development intervention on Head Start teachers and children. *Journal of Educational Psychology, 102*(2), 299–312.

Reimann, P. (2011). Design-based research. *Methodological Choice and Design, 9*(2), 37–50.

Reinking, D., & Bradley, B. A. (2008). *Formative and design experiments: Approaches to language and literacy research.* New York, NY: Teachers College Press.

Rogoff, B. (2003). *The cultural nature of human development.* New York: Oxford University Press.

Roschelle, J., Kaput, J., & Stroup, W. (2000). SimCalc: Accelerating students' engagement with the mathematics of change. In M. Jacobson & R. Kozma (Eds.), *Innovations in science and mathematics education: Advanced designs for technologies of learning* (pp. 47–75). Hillsdale, NJ: Earlbaum.

Roschelle, J., Pierson, J., Empson, S., Shechtman, N., Dunn, M., & Tatar, D. (2010a). Equity in scaling up SimCalc: Investigating differences in student learning and classroom implementation. In K. Gomez, L. Lyons & J. Radinsky (Eds.), *Learning in the disciplines: Proceedings of the 9th International Conference of the Learning Sciences* (Vol. 1, pp. 333–340). Chicago, IL: International Society of the Learning Sciences.

Roschelle, J., Shechtman, N., Tatar, D., Hegedus, S., Hopkins, B., Empson, S., . . . Gallagher, L. P. (2010b). Integration of technology, curriculum, and professional development for advancing middle school mathematics: Three large-scale studies. *American Educational Research Journal, 47*(4), 833–878.

Rubin, D. B. (1974). Estimating causal effects of treatments in randomized and nonrandomized studies. *Journal of Educational Psychology, 66*(5), 688–701.

Ruiz-Primo, M. A., Shavelson, R. J., Hamilton, L. S., & Klein, S. (2002). On the evaluation of systemic science education reform: Searching for instructional sensitivity. *Journal of Research in Science Teaching, 39*(5), 369–393.

Sandoval, W. A. (2004). Developing learning theory by refining conjectures embodied in educational designs. *Educational Psychologist, 39*(4), 213–223.

Sandoval, W. A. (2014). Conjecture mapping: An approach to systematic educational design research. *Journal of the Learning Sciences, 23*(1), 18–36.

Sandoval, W. A., & Bell, P. (2004). Design-based research methods for studying learning in context: Introduction. *Educational Psychologist, 39*(4), 199–201.

Schultema, J., Veugelers, W., Rijlaarsdam, G., & ten Dam, G. (2009). Two instructional designs for dialogic citizenship education: An effect study. *British Journal of Educational Psychology, 79*(3), 439–461.

Sewell, W. H., Hauser, R. M., Springer, K. W., & Hauser, T. S. (2003). As we age: A review of the Wisconsin Longitudinal Study, 1957–2001. *Research in Social Stratification and Mobility, 20*, 3–111.

Shadish, W. R., Clark, M. H., & Steiner, P. M. (2008). Can nonrandomized experiments yield accurate answers? A randomized experiment comparing random and nonrandom assignments. *Journal of the American Statistical Association, 103*(484), 1334–1344.

Shadish, W. R., Cook, T. D., & Campbell, D. T. (2002). *Experimental and quasi-experimental designs for generalized causal inference.* Boston, MA: Houghton-Mifflin.

Shaffer, D. W., Hatfield, D., Svarovsky, G. N., Nash, P., Nulty, A., Bagley, E., . . . Mislevy, R. J. (2009). Epistemic network analysis: A prototype for 21st century assessment of learning. *International Journal of Learning and Media, 1*(2), 33–53.

Shavelson, R. J., Phillips, D. C., Towne, L., & Feuer, M. J. (2003). On the science of education design studies. *Educational Researcher, 32*(1), 25–28.

Shea, N. A., & Duncan, R. G. (2013). From theory to data: The process of refining learning progressions. *Journal of the Learning Sciences, 22*(1), 7–32.

Simon, M. A. (1995). Reconstructing mathematics pedagogy from a constructivist perspective. *Journal for Research in Mathematics Education, 26*, 114–145.

Smith, C. L., Wiser, M., Anderson, C. W., & Krajcik, J. (2006). Implications of research on children's learning for standards and assessment: A proposed learning progression for matter and the atomic-molecular theory. *Measurement: Interdisciplinary Research & Perspective, 4*(1&2), 1–98.

Songer, N. B., Kelcey, B., & Gotwals, A. W. (2009). How and when does complex reasoning occur? Empirically driven development of a learning progression focused on complex reasoning about biodiversity. *Journal of Research in Science Teaching, 46*(6), 610–631.

Spybrook, J. K., Raudenbush, S. W., Liu, X., Congdon, R., & Martinez, A. (2009). Optimal design for longitudinal and multilevel research: Documentation for the "Optimal Design" software. New York: William T. Grant Foundation.

Stevens, R., & Hall, R. (1998). Disciplined perception: Learning to see in technoscience. In M. Lampert & M. L. Blunk (Eds.), *Talking mathematics in school: Studies of teaching and learning* (pp. 107–149). Cambridge: Cambridge University Press.

Stevens, R., O'Connor, K., Garrison, L., Jocuns, A., & Amos, D. M. (2008). Becoming an engineer: Toward a three dimensional view of engineering learning. *Journal of Engineering Education, 97*(3), 355–368.

Tatar, D., Roschelle, J., Knudsen, J., Schectman, N., Kaput, K., & Hopkins, B. (2008). Scaling up innovative technology-based mathematics. *Journal of the Learning Sciences, 17*(2), 248–286.

Toulmin, S. (1958). *The uses of argument.* New York: Cambridge University Press.

Vadasy, P. F., Sanders, E. A., & Peyton, J. A. (2006). Code-oriented instruction for kindergarten students at risk for reading difficulties: A randomized field trial with paraeducator implementers. *Journal of Educational Psychology, 98*(3), 508–528.

van den Akker, J. (1999). Principles and methods of development research. In J. van den Akker, K. Branch, K. Gustafson, N. Nieveen & T. Plomp (Eds.), *Design approaches and tools in education and training* (pp. 1–14). Dordrecht: Kluwer.

Werner, H. (1957). *The concept of development from a comparative and organismic point of view.* Minneapolis, MN: University of Minnesota Press.

Willoughby, T., Adachi, P. J., & Good, M. (2012). A longitudinal study of the association between violent video game play and aggression among adolescents. *Developmental Psychology, 48*(4), 1044–1057.

Wise, A. F., & Chiu, M. M. (2011). Analyzing temporal patterns of knowledge construction in a role-based online discussion. *International Journal of Computer-Supported Collaborative Learning, 6*(3), 445–470.

Wiser, M., Smith, C. L., & Doubler, S. (2012). Learnng progressions as tools for curriculum development: Lessons from the Inquiry Project. In A. C. Alonzo & A. W. Gotwals (Eds.), *Learning progressions in science: Current challenges and future directions* (pp. 359–404). Rotterdam, the Netherlands: Sense Publishers.

Yin, R. K. (2003). *Case study research: Design and methods* (3rd ed.). Thousand Oaks, CA: Sage.

# 3

# The Work of Educational Psychologists in a Digitally Networked World

*Punya Mishra*[1]
*Matthew J. Koehler*
*Christine Greenhow*
Michigan State University

New digital technologies have had a dramatic effect on all arenas of human work, and the work of educational psychologists is no exception. There are many ways in which we can think about the role that technologies play in what we do as scholars and researchers of educational psychology. Technology, for instance, has changed how we think about teaching and learning in two key ways. First, it has influenced the kinds of models and theories we have of the mind (from clay tablets to digital computers). Second, technology has changed the ecology or contexts within which learning occurs to include several intersecting spaces (temporal, spatial, home, community, online, etc.).

A close examination of the relationship between technology and the work of educational psychologists reveals changes in nearly every aspect of the work that educational psychologists do. Thus, we have organized this chapter according to the role that technology has played in the everyday activities of educational psychologists, grouped into eight general categories, briefly described below.

1. **Study phenomena.** Educational psychologists study phenomena and contexts where teaching and learning occur. New technologies provide new phenomena and contexts for teaching and learning through the advent of social media, games, and virtual learning environments. These new learning environments also provide new kinds of data and new techniques for data analysis.
2. **Design studies.** Technology affords new forms of research designs allowing, for example, researchers to track individual behavior through online environments, provide tailor-made inputs to individual students (or groups of students), and develop new models of simulation and modeling of virtual learners.
3. **Collect data.** New technologies have afforded new types of data to researchers (including data from educational neuroscience, simulated data, eye-tracking data, video data, and social network data), leading to changes in data collection.

4. **Assess learning.** Digital technologies offer new possibilities and opportunities for assessment of learning through the design of new assessment tasks and the power of large-scale assessment through automated scoring, immediate reporting, and improved feedback.
5. **Analyze data.** New technologies lead to new forms of data analysis—offering tools that provide greater power and efficiency in how quantitative and qualitative analyses are conducted.
6. **Develop theories.** The development of sound, predictable, data-driven theories is paramount to the conduct of research in educational psychology. Some of the consequences of the inclusion of digital technologies are design-based research, testing boundary conditions for the application of theories, and questioning the value of theory itself.
7. **Read, write, publish, and disseminate ideas.** Today's educational psychologists must consider how new technologies have contributed to changes in publishing, accessibility, and scholarship.
8. **Confront ethical issues.** As in all research, new technologies have brought about a new range of ethical issues that educational psychologists have to contend with (such as those related to data security and new regulations concerning institutional review).

We explore the changes occurring at the intersection of educational psychology and technology in the sections below, which correspond with the eight general categories of activity of educational psychologists. Some of these categories are more specific to the work of educational psychology scholars than others. For instance, under "Study phenomena," we explore phenomena now available for investigation by educational psychologists due to technological change, but, under "Read, write, publish, and disseminate ideas," the changes we discuss apply more generally to scholars in many, if not all, disciplines. That said, we focus attention on issues specifically impacting the work of educational psychology researchers, paying less attention to issues that have broader implications across all fields of study. We limit our discussion of the collaborative work educational psychologists do facilitated by technological tools, and refrain from discussing new technology-based sources of data such as electroencephalograms (EEGs), functional magnetic resonance imaging (fMRI), and positron emission tomography (PET) scans in the burgeoning subfield of educational neuroscience. Although these are valuable for educational psychology research, we have not addressed these issues in the present chapter for reasons of space as well as the fact that these topics are addressed in other chapters in this handbook (see Chapters 5, 25, and 26 in this volume).

## Study Phenomena

New technologies have significantly impacted the phenomena we study as researchers in two primary ways. First, technology has introduced a host of new phenomena worthy of research through the advent of social media, games, and virtual learning environments. Second, it has shifted traditional dichotomies, such as informal versus formal, and created new ones, such as virtual versus physical and online versus offline. By introducing new phenomena, technology has often shifted the landscape of these "boundaries," thus complicating what on the surface may appear to be somewhat simplistic dichotomies.

### Social Networks

Technological advancements have contributed increasingly to people's adoption of *social media*, a term often used to refer to online technologies and applications which promote people, their interconnections, and user-generated content (Cormode & Krishnamurthy, 2008). Among the many different kinds of social media, of particular interest to educational psychologists are *social network sites,* including Facebook, LinkedIn, Google Plus, and Twitter, which are dominant in the early decades of the twenty-first century. Such social network sites typically feature the ability to consume, produce, or interact with streams of user-generated content provided by one's connections (Ellison & boyd, 2013).

Social networks offer educational psychologists the opportunity to study a wide range of empirical questions such as how these networks factor into, shape, and are shaped by the learning ecology of their participants (Barron, 2006). Social networks are increasingly being used in virtually all areas of pedagogy (Manca & Ranieri, 2013; Ranieri, Manca, & Fini, 2012). For instance, scholars have studied how online social networking can facilitate new forms of collaboration not feasible with traditional communication technologies (Greenhow & Li, 2013) and the use of social media for teachers' professional development (Ranieri, Manca, & Fini, 2012). This work suggests possibilities for educational designs powered by social media within a variety of learning and teaching contexts as well as a revisiting of conventional learning theories as they play out in such contexts. For instance, in studying social networks, scholars have found that social links indicated in automatically generated and dynamically updated network graphs (e.g., Facebook visualizations) are not valid indicators of real user connection as previous research using social graphs from physical observations of in-person interactions would suggest (Wilson, Sala, Puttaswamy, & Zhao, 2012). Other scholars have examined how aspects of computer-supported collaborative learning theory, generated in other collaborative spaces, are contradicted in social network sites (Judele, Tsovaltzi, Puhl, & Weinberger, 2014). Such studies suggest how educational psychology research may shift, requiring more accurate modeling to evaluate social network phenomena in light of new technologies (see Chapter 25 in this volume).

### Games

Although the educational possibilities of learning from games have been conjectured and studied throughout history, the advent of digital games is a relatively recent phenomenon with tremendous economic, cultural, and social implications (Squire, 2006). Educational psychologists have studied the cognitive, social, and emotional impacts (both positive and negative) of game playing under various conditions. On the positive side, research has shown playing computer games can enhance cognitive processes such as perception, attention, and cognition (Anderson & Bavelier, 2011); reaction time (Karle, Watter, & Shedden, 2010); and mental rotation (Sims & Mayer, 2002). Games have also been shown to have some success in transferring learners' skills to "real-world" situations, including flight training, the training of surgeons, the care of diabetes, and the development of prosocial behavior (Tobias, Fletcher, & Wind, 2014). On the other end of the spectrum are concerns that game play is often associated with lower school achievement (Gentile, 2011) and negative behaviors such as aggression (Tobias et al., 2014).

The important issue for educational psychologists is that these game interactions can have significant psychological consequences because they occur in environments characterized by pretense, virtuality, distance, and mediation. Learning in these networked, digital spaces often occurs through active participation in the game's virtual social structures (Salen & Zimmerman, 2004) and is evaluated through actual performance—a different manner of engaging in learning than in a traditional learning environment such as the classroom.

### Virtual Environments

*Virtual environments* are systems where individuals interact with simulated objects, people, or environments. *Virtual worlds* represent one type of virtual environment. In virtual worlds users are often identified by two- or three-dimensional representations called *avatars* and communicate with each other using text, visual gestures, and sound. Educational psychologists can explore how such environments integrate with, intensify, or contradict learning and teaching in physical environments and explore learners' negotiation of identities within and between these spaces (Tettegah & Calongne, 2009). Moreover, virtual environments form an integral component of the growing contemporary use of online education.

### Online Education

Online education is fast becoming an alternative mode of teaching and learning and a supplement to traditional face-to-face education (Picciano & Seaman, 2009). Online education may consist of wholly online courses or *hybrid* or *blended* courses that combine online components with traditional face-to-face components. Most recently, online education has seen the rise of massive open online courses (MOOC), a term referring to online courses targeting large-scale interactive participation and open access via the internet. Regardless of format (wholly online, blended, or MOOC), online courses may consist of traditional course resources such as readings, videos, tools to facilitate synchronous and asynchronous participation, and course management systems.

The rise of online education offers new phenomena for educational researchers to examine. Researchers have examined issues such as the effectiveness of online instruction compared to face-to-face instruction, practices associated with effective online learning, and factors that influence the effectiveness of online learning (Means, Toyama, Murphy, Bakia, & Jones, 2010). Additionally, approaches in online education (particularly MOOCs) have the potential to generate large datasets—through both the content people upload and the behavioral traces (such as log files) they leave behind—which can be mined for patterns and used to test learning and teaching theories at a scale not previously seen.

### Design Studies

In many ways, how we design studies is at the heart of what research is and of what we do as educational psychologists, academics and scholars; this issue therefore drives the central issues in each of the eight categories of work that educational psychologists do. In this section, however, we focus on three new contexts that digital and networking technologies have created for designing new studies and two important research design strategies that digital environments provide.

#### Studies in Virtual Worlds

One new context that networking technologies have provided is the online virtual world—digital environments where people can work and interact in a somewhat realistic manner. Research contexts include existing recreational, multi-user, virtual worlds that have been adopted for educational purposes (e.g., Active Worlds or Second Life) or worlds designed specifically for educational purposes, such as River City (Clarke, Dede, Ketelhut, & Nelson, 2006). Virtual worlds make attractive research environments because they can be designed to automatically generate data as users interact with the world (e.g., activities most performed, time on task, content generated by users). Designed studies of virtual worlds can examine how well pedagogical approaches used in other settings function in these worlds. They can also test prominent learning

theories, such as theories of self-directed learning and motivation; compare learning and teaching processes and outcomes in-world and out; and explore the co-evolution (or contradiction) of learning and design (De Lucia, Francese, Passero, & Tortora, 2009). Virtual worlds designed for education can be studied in terms of how well they help learners understand disciplinary concepts (e.g., scientific reasoning: see Chapter 24 in this volume), to test theories of how people learn and teach (Bransford, Brown, & Cocking, 2000), and to explore how learning, pedagogical, and design theories co-evolve and shape one another over successive iterations of virtual-world participation and design revisions.

#### Simulations and Modeling as Experimentation

A second related context that can provide expanded sites for research are simulations and other forms of computer-generated modeling. *Simulations* are constructed worlds that are a close representation of the physical world governed by the same rules. Simulations and simulated labs (e.g., virtual frog dissections in science education) may be useful where repeated practice is required or where the actual physical experiment would be too costly, time consuming, or otherwise impractical to enact in real life. Simulations have been used to illustrate key principles in disciplines such as biology, chemistry, physics, and earth and space science. Studies can be designed to examine whether and how simulations help learners understand disciplinary concepts. For example, studies of the simulation environment NetLogo have investigated middle- and high-school students' derivation of the ideal gas law from microlevel interactions among gas particles in a box (Wilensky, 2003); creating and testing models of predator–prey interactions (Wilensky & Reisman, 2006); and exploring the rates and directions of chemical reactions for individual molecules (Stieff & Wilensky, 2003). Studies can also be designed to compare learners' outcomes following simulations versus hands-on lab experiences (Ma & Nickerson, 2006). As technology improves, so does the fidelity of the simulations, providing ever-greater opportunities for future research (see Chapter 20 in this volume).

#### Online Education and Massive Open Online Courses

The rise of online education and MOOCs targeting large-scale interactive student participation, open access via the internet, interorganizational collaboration, and the generation of big datasets provides opportunities for interdisciplinary, intercultural research on a scale not previously seen.

Though relatively new, the potential for research on MOOCs is immense. MOOCs allow for the development of learning analytics that can be used for adaptation and personalization of curriculum through predictive modeling and forecasting of learner behavior and/or achievement or for the application of social network analysis techniques to optimize learner interactions. Insights generated from such studies may contribute to new theoretical models, such as models of self- and peer-assessment, as well as to the design of automated mechanisms to support and augment students' learning goals and processes.

### Designing Studies with Big Data

What is common to all of the technological contexts described above is that users leave complex traces of their interaction with the environment, the content, and with each other and thus generate large and complex datasets. By employing a combination of modern artificial intelligence, machine learning, and statistical techniques, these datasets can be examined in a variety of ways to reveal relationships, patterns, and insights not easily discoverable through standard database management tools or data-processing applications. Coinciding with the rise of big data, learning analytics is a recent area of scholarship that seeks to collect, analyze, and report data "about learners and their contexts, for purposes of understanding and optimizing learning and the environments in which it occurs" (Siemens & Long, 2011, p. 4).

However, designing studies involving big datasets can also be problematic. Designed studies can oversimplify complex human actions and motivations, magnify data errors when multiple datasets are combined, and create divides between those who have access to big data and those who do not (boyd & Crawford, 2011). Additional challenges include establishing norms for collaborating across big data projects, creating ways to measure and reward individual contributions, and defining the most pressing problems; that is, distinguishing the needle from the big data haystack.

### Studies in which Every Participant gets a Tailor-made Condition

Newer digital technologies also enable educational psychologists to design studies in which each subject is assigned a custom experimental condition. For instance, diagnostic educational gaming environments that unlock levels of game play based on how and how well individuals progress through the game can provide each subject with a tailor-made condition. Similarly, different versions of an online course that are randomly assigned to learners can allow for true experiments to test different interventions or theoretical frameworks. Such technologies suggest the promise of tailoring research conditions for individual participants.

### Collect Data

With new technologies come new types of data. Changes in the available types of data also bring about changes in the focus of researchers' attention, the methods they use to study these phenomena, and the types of questions they ask. Key possibilities for new types of data afforded to educational psychologists by technological advances are highlighted in the sections that follow.

### Data from the World Wide Web

Since the advent of the first widely available web browser (Mosaic) in 1993, the internet had grown to over 2.3 billion users by the year 2014. Along with the explosion in the number of users, websites, domain names, and sophisticated designs, the types of data available as tools have also dramatically increased for businesses, marketers, and, more recently, researchers.

*Web analytics* are the data collected automatically by web servers to track visitors' interactions and behaviors with websites. When combined with data from other websites and browser tracking (via cookies and session data), information can be generated about the visitor to a website, including the visitor's prior browsing history, likes and dislikes, sex, age, income, ethnicity, and purchasing history. Another source of data from the internet comes from a technique called *web content mining* or *web scraping* (Bharanipriya & Prasad, 2011). In this approach, data are gathered or extracted from websites via automated processes. These techniques of generating big data have the same strengths and weaknesses described above.

### Simulated Data

Not all data come from direct observation of phenomena or derived measures. The rise of computing technology has driven increased use of *simulated data*, data generated by computing processes that simulate data that might be otherwise difficult to obtain. This technique has been commonly used in statistics to test the properties of many statistical procedures. For example, in simple statistical analyses such as the *t-test*, the statistical power (type II error) can be computed exactly from formulas if all statistical assumptions are met. Other procedures, like non-parametric statistical analyses, do not have easily computed type II values, because the procedure depends so heavily on the type of data to be analyzed. In these cases, *Monte Carlo techniques* (Kalos & Whitlock, 2009), a type of simulated approach, can be used to generate many samples of the kind of data expected. The statistical procedure is then run on these simulated data, repeatedly, in order to establish the rate at which the null hypothesis is rejected. This rate is an estimate of the type II error rate (for examples of this, see Mumby, 2002; Muthén & Muthén, 2002).

Given recent advances in computing power, Monte Carlo techniques will soon become more commonplace in other arenas of social science. Bakker, van Dijk, and Wicherts (2012) explored how researchers have found statistically significant results 96% of the time, when on the surface there is insufficient statistical power to support rejecting the null hypothesis at such a high rate. Generating data for multiple studies under varying effect sizes, sample sizes, and research practices (analyzing more than one variable, sequential testing, splitting studies, and removing outliers), these researchers found that true type I error rate may be as high as 0.40 using such practices and may explain why 96% of studies report significant results.

### User Data Capture

Traditional methods of research in the educational sciences, such as think-aloud protocols, interviews, surveys, and observations, rely on second-hand or indirect data. Technology is increasingly providing opportunities for researchers to collect first-hand data from participants. For example, a tool like Morae allows researchers to simultaneously record screen captures, audio and video data (typically of users interacting with the system), and mouse and keyboard clicks. Morae also has built-in analyses that detect patterns in the massive amounts of data that such recordings can generate.

The challenge with data generated from seamlessly recording participants' interactions with systems is that, even when built-in analyses detect patterns in the massive amount of data captured, researchers must decipher what such patterns mean. It is one thing to know that at a particular moment in time a user clicked on a particular portion of the screen; it is another matter completely to figure out why the user did so and what that interaction means. More research is needed to help uncover patterns in the data and ascribe meaning to data.

### Eye-Tracking Data

One type of user data capture, eye-tracking data, is particularly noteworthy. The previously mentioned forms of user data capture all record what participants do—where they click, what they say, and what they are doing. By recording the movements of the human eye, researchers can gain insight into what participants pay attention to, whether or not that attention is brief or extended, and what may be interesting to participants (Duchowski, 2007). For example, Galesic, Tourangeau, Couper, and Conrad (2008) used eye-tracking data to investigate possible causes for response order effects (i.e., that survey responses tend to be skewed in favor of responses presented earlier in the list of choices). They found that participants often take cognitive shortcuts. The most salient of these is that participants tend to devote more attention to earlier choices and less (sometimes none) to later choices.

The cost of procedures for eye tracking is consistently declining, increasing access of these data to researchers. This newfound access to eye-tracking data has fueled the development of new analysis tools and, in many cases, add-ons to existing data analysis tools. For example, *Morae* offers several plugins and extensions to seamlessly integrate eye-tracking data with key-logging data, allowing for researchers to synchronize participants' actions with their perceptions (Alves, Pagano, & da Silva, 2010).

### Video Data

Dramatic changes in affordability, availability, storage, and quality of video have led researchers to routinely use it as research data. Tools such as Transanna, Morae, DIVER, and ATLAS have been developed to help researchers organize, code, analyze, and connect video data to other data (e.g., transcripts, interviews, qualitative analyses).

The new affordances that video data offer to researchers bring new challenges. Derry et al. (2010) identified four challenges to researchers using video data: (a) how to *select* specific elements to focus study on within complex settings or large corpuses of video; (b) choosing what analytic

frameworks to guide the *analysis* of video; (c) choosing the appropriate *technology* to organize, store, and analyze the video; and (d) adhering to appropriate *ethics* involving consent and use of video data while at the same time promoting sharing and collaboration.

### Data from Social Networks

Online social networks present a number of novel types of data available to researchers. These include the "network" or community itself as a representation of connections between individuals, which can be depicted as a network graph summarizing the "degrees of separation" between people in a community. Types of data available from these networks include the content of the interaction (their messages or photos) and social tagging (short descriptions or signifiers of content) that occurs (Aggarwal, 2011). Other types of data that emerge from social networks include *reputation* systems, *badge* systems, and *influence scores*. These measures capture and reward useful user behavior—such as completing a task, helping others, and so on. Clearly these "reward" structures are important to researchers in that they provide meaningful information about user behavior and interactions (see Chapter 25 in this volume).

### Assess Learning

Digital technologies also offer new possibilities and opportunities for the assessment of learning, primarily through the design of new assessment tasks as well as the power of large-scale assessment through automated scoring, immediate reporting, and improved feedback. One fundamental challenge, however, faced by all assessment techniques (irrespective of the use of technology) is making the assessment tasks valid and reliable, even while making them amenable to computational analysis. For instance, computers are good at evaluating responses to tightly constrained questions, such as multiple-choice questions, and less effective when evaluating open-ended, constructed responses, such as the traditional essay. Though the nature of multiple-choice questions does not preclude the measurement of higher-order thinking skills, there is a general belief that such constrained questions typically focus on measuring lower-order skills. The demand for alternative assessments comes from both a skepticism toward multiple-choice assessments as well as the push towards more authentic, performance-based assessments (see Chapter 29, this volume).

Scalise and Gifford (2006) offered a taxonomy that may be useful in computer-based assessment consisting of 28 item types "based on 7 categories of ordering involving successively decreasing response constraints from fully selected to fully constructed," (p. 3). At the most constrained end of the spectrum are multiple-choice questions, while at the other end are assessment types that seek to measure student performance under simulated or real conditions. The five intermediate categories fall along this dimension and are classified as: (a) selection/identification; (b) reordering/

rearrangement; (c) substitution/correction; (d) completion; and (e) construction types. They also suggest that the 28 types of assessment they describe within these seven broad categories are not necessarily comprehensive in that a variety of other item formats can be designed by combining some of the types listed or through including new media formats such as video, audio, and interactive graphics (e.g. animations or simulations). Two areas (from opposite ends of the constraint spectrum) that have received significant attention are computer-adaptive testing (CAT) and automated text analysis.

### Computer-adaptive Testing

CAT is the computer-based extension of the adaptive testing started with Binet in 1905 (Linacre, 2000). The term encompasses a wide range of assessment approaches administered on a computer, where the test difficulty is adaptively targeted to match the proficiency of the test taker in order to provide the best and most efficient assessment of abilities (Luecht, 2005). Behind the scenes, item response theory (IRT) is typically used to judge the relative difficulty of items, select the next items for test takers to receive, and equate items across test takers.

As CAT approaches become more commonplace, especially in the context of high-stakes testing, there are implications for educational psychologists. CAT approaches are generally considered to be more accurate assessments of skill (Thissen & Mislevy, 2000) but at the same time do not produce tests that can be strictly equated across test takers. CAT approaches offer possibilities for fast or immediate test results for test takers and can easily scale up to large participant pools. Developing the test, however, can be a time-consuming and costly endeavor as CAT approaches require the development of many more items that require large amounts of pilot data to be properly equated using IRT models.

### Automated Text Analysis

Automated essay evaluation, which is derived from automated essay scoring, is the "process of evaluating and scoring written prose via computer programs" (Shermis & Burstein, 2003, p. 7). The approach uses advances in natural language processing, applied mathematics, machine learning, and computational linguistics to analyze syntax, word usage, discourse structure, and higher-level meaning such as thematic analysis. For example, latent semantic analysis (LSA) is an early approach that performed statistical computations on the similarity of all the meanings in a large text, which was then used to approximate writing coherence and the quantity and quality of the writer's knowledge (Landauer, Foltz, & Laham, 1998). More recent and sophisticated approaches include the *E-Rater* system employed by the Educational Testing Service in many of its high-stakes tests; *Coh-Metrix* (Graesser, McNamara, & Kulikowich, 2011), which provides multiple-level indices of text coherence; and *LightSIDE* (Mayfield & Rosé, 2013), which provides open-source machine learning software customizable to many different evaluation purposes. These more advanced approaches merge combinations of LSA, feature extraction (word occurrences, word dyads and triads, parts of speech), machine learning to train underlying models, and multi-level evaluation. For example, *Coh-Metrix* can generate over 100 indices (features) from a given text, which are in turn used in formulae to compute various metrics of text coherence, which some researchers have used to make direct judgments about the quality of written texts.

The growing popularity of such approaches has important implications for educational psychologists. On one hand, there are clear-cut advantages in terms of efficient data analyses that are increasingly becoming as reliable as (and less opaque than) human raters (Shermis & Burstein, 2013). On the other hand, there are legitimate concerns about an undue emphasis on product over process, a focus on the wrong qualities of writing (e.g., its function as expression), and a philosophical concern about the equivalence between how human raters and machine raters make judgments.

### Analyze Data

Data in educational psychology are often used in two ways that need to be carefully delineated (Behrens & Smith, 1996). Behrens and Smith call the first level the "data of phenomena"—the recordings of sense experiences that are then transformed into a second representational level, the "data of the analysis." The data of analysis consist of records of experience, which may include field notes, survey responses, video recordings, software usage characteristics, and tally marks that count particular user behaviors. In quantitative analysis, the recording of experience emphasizes measurement and precision while qualitative analysis emphasizes interpretation. The goal in both cases is to reduce large amounts of data to representations that are comprehensible, allowing researchers to develop a deeper understanding of the original phenomena under study. Both approaches require navigating and managing a series of tradeoffs between the precision and richness of description and the validity of the inferences we can make from the data and subsequent analysis.

### Quantitative Analysis

A powerful impetus for new approaches to quantitative data analysis and representation has come from the world of business and commerce, which is focused on using large datasets and user-generated data to improve decision making, managerial practices, and quality control processes. Examples include the recommendation engines of Amazon, Netflix, iTunes, Google, and Facebook, which provide users with targeted advertisements based upon past behavior.

Accordingly, it is not surprising that the use of student data for educational improvement has also seen increased prominence in education. Learners are increasingly leaving behind sophisticated and detailed traces of their actions as they work in technologically mediated environments, a form of big data then available to educational psychologists. Moreover, educational policies, such as Race to the Top and

No Child Left Behind, have added pressure to the need to collect and analyze large amounts of student data.

Technology has influenced how quantitative data analyses are conducted. At a basic level, statistical analysis packages that offer comprehensive tools for computing descriptive statistics, hypothesis testing, and drawing inferential conclusions have made statistical analyses increasingly assessable, user friendly, commonplace, and powerful. These include standard statistical analysis packages (such as SPSS, SAS, and R) as well as some more specialized packages, such as LISREL, which is used for confirmatory factor analysis and structural equation modeling.

One of the most important areas where computational power has changed educational research is in the area of data mining and visualization. *Data mining* is the process of examining large sets of data with multiple variables to uncover trends and patterns. These data-mining techniques can be combined with the capabilities of digital technologies to represent and present data in rich, visual, and intuitively recognizable formats. Standard statistical packages, such as Excel and SPSS, have increasingly powerful tools for data representation. Beyond this, there are other software programs, such as the interactive environment for data analysis and visualization MATLAB, the computational knowledge engine Wolfram Alpha, and the algebraic and symbolic mathematics package Mathematica, that specialize in the construction and display of complex and sophisticated graphical displays. As Knezek and Christensen (2014) wrote, "the distinction between analysis, modeling, and display tools is beginning to blur as 'math packages' are being routinely employed to produce elegant summaries and visual displays of findings from traditional research" (p. 219). Free web-based software applications, such as Google Fusion Tables and Many Eyes from IBM, allow researchers to upload large datasets and display the data in multiple formats, such as graphs, maps, intensity maps, timelines, and story lines.

### Qualitative Data Analysis

Qualitative research has generally been defined as "any kind of research that produces findings not arrived at by means of statistical procedures or other means of quantification" (Strauss & Corbin, 1990, p. 17). Thus, qualitative researchers require technologies that assist in gathering and coding data to uncover phenomena and make meaning through analyzing patterns in stories, common ideas, and emergent themes. Organization and interpretation are important fundamentals of this work, and new technologies can assist with this (Anfara, Brown, & Mangione, 2002; Creswell, 1998). While the foundational elements of qualitative research—the guiding principles, determinants of reliability, validity, and so forth—remain in place, new technologies have shifted aspects of methodology, and in some ways have changed the way we "see" or interpret qualitative data (Brown, 2002).

Digitalized qualitative processes allow researchers to store and access a variety of types of qualitative data, including text, audio, video, and graphics files. One of the most basic

and critical newer uses of technology involves the use of digital audio or video recording for field studies or interview sessions. At a surface level, such digital recordings are a way to preserve a clearer record of events and conversations, but, at another level, digital recordings afford new ways of thinking about how analysis develops out of the data and how data support it (Gibbs, Friese, & Mangabeira, 2002).

Educational researchers can now attend to small-scale and detail-oriented content in teaching and learning scenarios such as characteristics of speech, movements, or body language (see Chapter 28 in this volume). Examinations of such focused minutiae can be undertaken quickly, putting increased analytical power to work on observed data. While digital media has allowed researchers to home in on visual and audio data at a smaller scale, it has also opened up possibilities for much larger-scale studies because multiple researchers and analysts can connect and collaborate via qualitative coding software.

Computer-assisted qualitative data analysis software (CAQDAS), such as NVivo, Atlas.ti, or HyperRESEARCH, makes the core processes of organizing and coding data from observations, interviews, field research, or ethnography easier and more efficient (Lewins & Silver, 2009). By facilitating organization and categorization of data, such programs facilitate the process of meaning making (Fielding & Lee, 2002). One of the common experiences of qualitative research has always been the challenge of careful and complex management of large amounts of texts, codes, memos, field notes, and observations (Moustakas, 1994). CAQDAS options allow for greater efficiency and consistency in systematic data management.

Such software programs typically provide flexible code trees (or code books), which allow for a more sophisticated categorization and increased ease of complex data searches. A range of group codes, individual codes, and subcodes can allow new and unique visualizations of the themes within a study for a specific look at the building blocks of the study. This allows the coding process—a foundational process in qualitative work—to be not only more systematic in approaching data but also more dynamic and responsive to emergent interpretations.

As noted, many CAQDAS programs today offer coding and organizational techniques for working with video and more traditional text and/or audio transcription. Digital video has unique properties that allow researchers to capture, observe, and reobserve complex phenomena visually and then code or notate behaviors, themes, comments, or anything else of interest (Spiers, 2004). Such affordances can bring the traditional thematic organization of qualitative work to video data and allow researchers to incorporate video vignettes—another powerful addition to the story-telling tradition of qualitative research (Creswell, 1998; Patton, 2002).

## Develop Theories

The development of sound, predictable, data-driven theories is paramount to the conduct of research in educational psychology. Theories provide us with concepts, terminologies, and classification schemes to describe phenomena accurately, highlighting relevant issues and ignoring irrelevant ones. Theories also allow us to make inferences and predict the consequences of an intervention or change. Finally, theories have a pragmatic function, informing how we can apply ideas to the real world by helping us design better learning contexts and systems and by bridging the gap between description and design.

Digital technologies have changed the phenomena being studied, the kinds of data that can be collected (which ground the theory-making process), and the data analyses that are possible. Altogether, these changes in phenomena, data, and analyses have resulted in strong tests of theories not possible before. Theory generation, however, remains outside the scope of even the most intelligent computer programs. That said, technology and theory building have interacted in three significant ways. First, educational design-based research (EDBR) methodologies have allowed researchers to study the effects of technological interventions in educational settings iteratively. Second, technological contexts have provided testing grounds for the boundary conditions of psychological theories and ideas, which have typically been based on studies conducted in face-to-face conditions. Third, the rise of "big data" has potential impacts for the role of theory in educational psychology.

### Educational Design-Based Research

EDBR is a type of research methodology in which educational interventions are conceptualized and then implemented iteratively in natural settings to both test the validity of existing theories and generate new theories for conceptualizing learning, instruction, design processes, and educational reform. A more detailed description of EDBR (and its variations) can be found in Chapter 2 in this volume. Our emphasis here is on two key aspects of EDBR. The first is an emphasis on the development of theory and the second is that many EDBR studies have focused on innovation driven by technology.

One of the main goals of EDBR is the development of theory—to not only use theory to provide a rationale for the intervention or to interpret findings but also help "develop a class of theories about both the process of learning and the means that are designed to support learning" (Cobb, Confrey, diSessa, Lehrer, & Schauble, 2003, p. 9). Also, though EDBR does not necessarily require the use of technology, it is frequently driven by the urge to integrate new psychological conceptions with technological possibilities. An example of EDBR and the twin emphasis on theory generation and technology-related contexts can be seen in the development of the Technological Pedagogical Content Knowledge (TPACK) framework. This framework explicates the knowledge teachers need to know in order to teach effectively with technology by extending Shulman's (1986) idea of pedagogical content knowledge to include technological knowledge (Mishra & Koehler, 2006). This framework emerged from over seven years of multiple studies aimed at understanding the development of teachers' knowledge for effective technology integration while simultaneously helping teachers (through courses, workshops, and other interventions) to develop their teaching with technology. Overall, this work led to a number of smaller studies (or EDBR "iterations") and publications that stood on their own as well as a larger framework (Mishra & Koehler, 2006) that emerged through synthesizing across the iterations.

### Technological Contexts as Providing Boundary Conditions

Most long-standing psychological theories—such as theories of transfer, motivation, and mindfulness—were developed based on research conducted in traditional face-to-face situations. New technologies provide new contexts for studying human interaction and can serve as important tests of the boundary conditions under which such theories can succeed or fail. As Walther (2009) argues, "Boundaries are being foisted upon us by technological developments that may limit (or maybe revise) the scope of our extant theoretical frameworks. There are implicit boundaries that have always been there but which we have ignored, misapprehended, or failed to investigate" (p. 750). At the heart of the issue is the question of fidelity of representation or the correspondence between the virtual and the physical world and our psychological responses to these differences.

For example, consider how studies in human computer interaction show that people often treat computer respondents just as they treat humans. The computers as social actors (CASA) paradigm argues that people may unconsciously perceive interactive media as being "intentional social agents" and read personality, beliefs, and attitudes into them; more importantly, the CASA paradigm argues that people often act on these perceptions. There is a strong body of empirical evidence to support this position: People are polite to machines (Nass, Moon, & Carney, 1999), read gender and personalities into machines (Nass, Moon, & Green, 1997), are flattered by machines (Fogg & Nass, 1997), treat machines as team mates (Nass, Fogg, & Moon, 1996), and get angry and punish them (Ferdig & Mishra, 2004). Technology, however, also illustrates the boundary conditions under which such attributions fail. For instance, Mishra (2006) found that participants respond differently to praise and blame feedback from computer evaluators than they do from human evaluators, suggesting the need for a more complicated theory of interaction.

### Do We Need Theories in the Age of Big Data?

The rise of "big data" has caused some to argue that theories are becoming obsolete (e.g., Anderson, 2008) and will be replaced by large amounts of data, powerful analyses, and pattern recognition. For example, Google Translate works not by "understanding" any of the texts it translates but rather by tracking patterns across a large corpus of texts in multiple languages and associating inputs with outputs. This has led some computer scientists and other researchers using big data to argue that there will be no need for theory or models of phenomena when we have enough data and patterns to process. Although this discourse has not entered the realm of education, it may soon do so. Whether or not this "data deluge" brings about the strong version of "the end of theory," educational psychologists cannot ignore the future impacts of big data on theory building.

## Read, Write, Publish, and Disseminate Ideas

The processes of reading, writing, publishing, and dissemination have seen radical changes brought about by the advent of new digital and networking technologies. First, as in other academic disciplines, educational psychologists read and survey the field to conceptualize broader frames or perspectives in which to situate existing and new research. As has been explained in the scholarship on academic work life (Fry & Talja, 2007), and as touched on here, technology-driven changes in reading have an overall impact on the world of academia (Palmer & Cragin, 2008).

Reading, for example, has become increasingly on the screen (National Endowment for the Arts, 2007). This move towards more online and on-screen reading places "large demands on individuals' literacy skills" (RAND Reading Study Group, 2002, p. 4) and requires new *literacies, skills, strategies, dispositions,* and *social practices* (Coiro, Knobel, Lankshear, & Leu, 2008). Surveying the field, too, has been transformed by new digital and networking technologies, as new databases and citation indexes (Kousha & Thelwall, 2007; Meho & Yang, 2007) offer both qualitative and quantitative changes to how scholars access prior research and scholarship. Such tools can make it easier to gather resources from a wider range of sources and speed up the rate at which new findings can be presented and shared. This can lead to too much cognitive load but also to the creation of fresh connections to related information or to citations that would not otherwise have been possible.

Several important themes also underlie changes in the writing, dissemination, and publishing processes brought about by the advent of new digital and networking technologies. The first is the move towards *open publishing,* producing and distributing data in the "public domain" or with Creative Commons (creativecommons.org) licenses that allow public consumption and comment through open-access journals or self-publishing. More radical still are trends in how research is shared and disseminated that emphasizes *social scholarship,* sharing published or in-progress work via social media outlets. Such scholarship changes research dissemination routes, peer review, and potential audiences for work (Greenhow & Gleason, 2014; Greenhow, Robelia, & Hughes, 2009). A second influence of technology has been to change the tools available for academic collaborative writing. Today's technologies for writing can transform everything from project and bibliographic organization to the nature and process of collaborative writing. A third influence of technology has been the rise of manuscript platforms that can alter how we review and publish our work. Authors now submit their manuscripts online and can track the progress of their manuscripts throughout the review process. Because authors, reviewers, and editors record and archive information within the same online system, editors can track patterns in online activities, and these patterns can then be used to improve the journal's overall review and publishing process.

## Confront Ethical Issues

Technology integration into educational psychologists' contemporary work practices raises a host of ethical issues, such as data security and human subjects issues (Moore & Ellsworth, 2014).

### Data Security

In an increasingly digital and networked data environment, issues of data security have become more prominent. For example, cloud computing is frequently cited as an appealing data protection option because of many obvious affordances—ease of use, scalability, shareability, easy access to data, and built in backups. Researchers' use of cloud storage solutions, however, also raises ethical concerns associated with entrusting third-party vendors with confidential subject data (Newton, 2010).

### Unknowing Participants

Technology has introduced new ways of automatically recording data about people, behaviors, and patterns of interaction that considerably impact potential participants in a research study. First, technology has introduced video recording in many facets of everyday life, including through the widespread use of security cameras, mobile device cameras, and webcams (Koeppel, 2011). Second, people's behaviors online are being recorded, both knowingly and unknowingly, through the use of session variables (e.g., "cookies"), monitoring of behavior on websites, and studies of interactions that occur online. All of this automatically recorded data has ethical implications for would-be researchers. For example, researchers studying individuals in social networking sites may inadvertently access data from individuals in their participants' network that they do not have permission to access. Many studies using data from these auto-recorded sources are determined "IRB-exempt" (see below) because the behavior is "publicly observable" and therefore does not require the consent of any participants in the research. That said, the very idea of what is (or is not) "publicly observable" in a networked, connected world is contentious and open to scholarly and legal debate.

### Instructional Review Board (IRB) Issues Related to Technology

Internet-based research also raises complex issues concerning human subject protections. Topics such as confidentiality, recruitment, and informed consent become complicated when research is conducted online. For example, authentication of identity in online worlds is an issue and may inadvertently lead to conducting research on minors or vulnerable populations. Another potential issue with internet-based research is that requesting consent should not disrupt normal group activity; however, the very act of entering online communities or chat rooms to request consent can be perceived as disruptive. Finally, even apparently anonymous data can be mined to identify geographical location, and as data analytics tools become more intelligent, personal variables (such as age and gender) may be used to identify participants.

## Conclusion

Clearly, the work we do as educational psychologists has changed and will continue to evolve due to the advent of new technologies. An important caveat, given this rapid rate of change, is that much of what we have written here will appear outdated by the time this volume is published, not to mention five years after its publication. What this means is that we have to approach all that we have written with a critical eye and also attempt, even while focusing on the latest tools and techniques, to keep our focus on key ideas that will stand the test of time. It was this concern with relevance that led us to structure this chapter along the eight categories of work. Although the manner in which we go about our business may change, these eight categories will remain important parts of what educational psychologists do.

Looking beyond the eight categories of work, we emphasize three key perspectives on the current literature on technology and its specific role in what we do as educational psychologists. First, among these perspectives is what Salomon and Almog (1998) called the "reciprocal relationship" between technology and educational psychology:

> Technologies and prevailing psychological conceptions of learning, thinking, and instruction have always served and inspired each other in reciprocal ways. On the one hand, technologies in education have served to facilitate and realize the kinds of pedagogies that emanated from the changing zeitgeists and from prevailing psychological conceptions. On the other hand, and possibly only recently, technologies have been imported into education, challenging it and requiring novel psychological explanation and pedagogical justifications. (p. 222)

In other words, Salomon and Almog argue that there is a transactional, dialogic relationship between the psychology of learning and the affordances and constraints of technologies, where each helps define the other (what they have described as "an ongoing duet"). Thus the pedagogical meaning of a technology emerges not just from the tool (and its properties) but rather from its deep integration into the matrix of subject matter, learners, and classroom environments. As Bruce (1997) says, "A technology is a system of people, texts, artifacts, activities, ideology, and cultural meanings" (p. 5).

The second perspective highlights the ways in which technologies and theories of mind have co-evolved over time—either to instantiate our current understandings of learning or, just as importantly, to seek models for thinking about thinking. Our understanding of the human brain and its activity has been consistently influenced by metaphors of the current technology. These include pneumatic/hydraulic metaphors, such as those used by Galen and Descartes, wherein the brain was considered a site for the mixing, storing, and redirection of "spirits" throughout the body to determine behavior and action. With the rise of the Industrial Revolution, new machine metaphors came to be used where the brain was now considered a complex mechanical apparatus with levers, gears, and pulleys. In the early part of the twentieth century, with the rise of telephone networks, the brain came to be seen as a switchboard with inputs, outputs, and signals. More recently, the advent of the digital computer led to the brain being viewed as a device for information processing. The advent of the internet has paralleled visions of the brain as being a networked computer.

The third perspective illuminates how technologies provide important "boundary conditions" to test educational and psychological theories. This involves providing new methodologies and new sources of data to test our theories as well as providing new tools to develop theory and to share our work with others. Technology can also provide novel pedagogical opportunities that offer a new "zone of possibility" (Kereluik, Mishra, Fahnoe, & Terry, 2013, p. 128) beyond our current psychological understandings, explanations, and justifications. Because technologies develop so rapidly, often outpacing developments of our psychological conceptions, technology can pose important conceptual and theoretical challenges for educational psychologists. Suddenly, old and partly dormant issues, such as transfer, intentionality, and mindfulness, can be brought again to the forefront as we develop novel conceptions and understandings of human behavior, learning, and instruction (Salomon & Almog, 1998).

These are truly exciting times for education—in large part distinguished by rapid changes in technology that are changing almost all aspects of our professional lives as educators and educational scholars. We believe that this ongoing duet will continue into the future.

## Note

1. The authors would like to thank Spencer Greenhalgh, Dr. Danah Henriksen, Dr. Michelle Hagerman, Rohit Mehta, and Joshua Rosenberg for their assistance in writing this chapter.

## References

Aggarwal, C. C. (Ed.). (2011). *Social network data analytics.* New York, NY: Springer.

Alves, F., Pagano, A., & da Silva, I. (2010). A new window on translators' cognitive activity: Methodological issues in the combined use of eye tracking, key logging and retrospective protocols. *Copenhagen Studies in Language, 38*, 267–291.

Anderson, A. F., & Bavelier, D. (2011). Action game play as a tool to enhance perception, attention and cognition. In S. Tobias & D. Bavelier (Eds.), *Computer games and instruction* (pp. 307–330). Charlotte, NC: Information Age Publishing.

Anderson, C. (2008). The end of theory: The data deluge makes the scientific method obsolete. *Wired Magazine, 16*(7). Retrieved from http://archive.wired.com/science/discoveries/magazine/16-07/pb_theory (accessed February 18, 2015).

Anfara, V. A., Jr., Brown, K. M., & Mangione, T. L. (2002). Qualitative analysis on stage: Making the research process more public. *Educational Researcher, 31*(7), 28–38.

Bakker, M., van Dijk, A., & Wicherts, J. M. (2012). The rules of the game called psychological science. *Perspectives on Psychological Science, 7,* 543–554.

Barron, B. (2006). Interest and self-sustained learning as catalysts of development: A learning ecology perspective. *Human Development, 49,* 193–224.

Behrens, J. T., & Smith, M. L. (1996). Data and data analysis. In D. C. Berliner & R. C. Calfee (Eds.), *Handbook of educational psychology* (pp. 949–989). New York: Macmillan.

Bharanipriya, V., & Prasad, V. K. (2011). Web content mining tools: A comparative study. *International Journal of Information Technology and Knowledge Management, 4*(1), 211–215.

boyd, d., & Crawford, C. (2011). Six provocations for big data. In B. Dutton, B. Loader, V. Nash, & B. Wellman, *A decade in Internet time: Symposium on the dynamics of the Internet and society, September 2011.* Symposium conducted at the meeting of the Oxford Internet Institute, Oxford, England, UK.

Bransford, J. D., Brown, A. L., & Cocking, R. R. (Eds.). (2000). *How people learn: Brain, mind, experience, and school.* Washington, DC: National Academy Press.

Brown, D. (2002). Going digital and staying qualitative: Some alternative strategies for digitizing the qualitative research process. *Forum: Qualitative Social Research, 3*(2). Retrieved from http://www.qualitative-research.net/index.php/fqs/index (accessed 18 February, 2015).

Bruce, B. C. (1997). *Technology in social practice: Returning to Dewey's conception of learning.* Paper presented at the NSF/ARL/BI (NAB) workshop, Alexandria, VA.

Clarke, J., Dede, C., Ketelhut, D. J., & Nelson, B. (2006). A design-based research strategy to promote scalability for educational innovations. *Educational Technology, 46*(3), 27–36.

Cobb, P., Confrey, J., diSessa, A., Lehrer, R., & Schauble, L. (2003). Design experiments in educational research. *Educational Researcher, 32*(1), 9–13.

Coiro, J., Knobel, M., Lankshear, C., & Leu, D. (2008). Central issues in new literacies and new literacies research. In J. Coiro, M. Knobel, C. Lankshear, & D. Leu (Eds.), *Handbook of research on new literacies* (pp. 1–21). New York, NY: Lawrence Erlbaum Associates.

Cormode, G., & Krishnamurthy, B. (2008). Key differences between Web 1.0 and Web 2.0. *First Monday, 13*(6).

Creswell, J. W. (1998). *Qualitative inquiry and research design: Choosing among five traditions.* Thousand Oaks, CA: Sage.

De Lucia, A., Francese, R., Passero, I., & Tortora, G. (2009). Development and evaluation of a system enhancing Second Life to support synchronous role-based collaborative learning. *Software: Practice and Experience, 39,* 1025–1054.

Derry, S. J., Pea, R. D., Barron, B., Engle, R. A., Erickson, F., Goldman, R., . . . Sherin, B. L. (2010). Conducting video research in the learning sciences: Guidance on selection, analysis, technology, and ethics. *Journal of the Learning Sciences, 19*(1), 3–53.

Duchowski, A. (2007). *Eye tracking methodology: Theory and practice* (Vol. 373). London, UK: Springer.

Ellison, N. B., & boyd, d. m. (2013). Sociality through social network sites. In W. H. Dutton (Ed.), *The Oxford handbook of Internet studies* (pp. 151–172). Oxford, England: Oxford University Press.

Ferdig, R. E., & Mishra, P. (2004). Emotional responses to computers: Experiences in unfairness, anger, and spite. *Journal of Educational Multimedia and Hypermedia, 13,* 143–161.

Fielding, N. G., & Lee, R. M. (2002). New patterns in the adoption and use of qualitative software. *Field Methods, 14,* 190–196.

Fogg, B. J., & Nass, C. (1997). Silicon sycophants: The effects of computers that flatter. *International Journal of Human-Computer Studies, 46,* 551–561.

Fry, J, & Talja, S. (2007). The intellectual and social organization of academic fields and the shaping of digital resources. *Journal of Information Science, 33,* 115–133.

Galesic, M., Tourangeau, R., Couper, M. P., & Conrad, F. G. (2008). Eye-tracking data: New insights on response order effects and other cognitive shortcuts in survey responding. *Public Opinion Quarterly, 72,* 892–913.

Gentile, D. A. (2011). The multiple dimensions of video game effects. *Child Development Perspectives, 5,* 75–81.

Gibbs, G. R., Friese, S., & Mangabeira, W. C. (2002). The use of new technology in qualitative research. Introduction to Issue 3(2) of FQS. *Forum: Qualitative Social Research, 3*(2).

Graesser, A. C., McNamara, D. S., & Kulikowich, J. M. (2011). Coh-Metrix: Providing multilevel analyses of text characteristics. *Educational Researcher, 40,* 223–234.

Greenhow, C., & Gleason, B. (2014). Social scholarship: Reconsidering scholarly practices in the age of social media. *British Journal of Educational Technology, 45,* 309–402.

Greenhow, C., & Li, J. (2013). Like, comment, share: Collaboration and civic engagement within social network sites. In C. Mouza & N. Lavigne (Eds.), *Emerging technologies for the classroom* (pp. 127–141). New York, NY: Springer.

Greenhow, C., Robelia, E., & Hughes, J. (2009). Web 2.0 and classroom research: What path should we take now? *Educational Researcher, 38,* 246–259.

Judele, R., Tsovaltzi, D., Puhl, T., & Weinberger, A. (2014). Collaborative learning in Facebook: Adverse effects of individual preparation. In *Proceedings of the Forty-Seventh Annual Hawaii International Conference on System Sciences* (pp. 1616–1624). Washington, DC: IEEE.

Kalos, M. H., & Whitlock, P. A. (2009). *Monte Carlo methods.* Weinheim, Germany: Wiley-VCH.

Karle, J. W., Watter, S., & Shedden, J. M. (2010). Task switching in video game players: Benefits of selective attention but not resistance to proactive interference. *Acta Psychologica, 134,* 70–78.

Kereluik, K., Mishra, P., Fahnoe, C., & Terry, L. (2013). What knowledge is of most worth: Teacher knowledge for 21st century learning. *Journal of Digital Learning in Teacher Education, 29*(4), 127–140.

Knezek, G. A., & Christensen, R. (2014). Tools for analyzing quantitative data. In J. M. Spector, M. D. Merrill, J. Elen, & M. J. Bishop (Eds.), *Handbook of research on educational communications and technology* (4th ed., pp. 203–220). New York, NY: Springer.

Koeppel, D. (2011). More people are using smartphones to secretly record office conversations (web blog post). Retrieved from http://www.businessinsider.com/smartphones-spying-devices-2011-7 (accessed February 18, 2015).

Kousha, K., & Thelwall, M. (2007). Google Scholar citations and Google web/URL citations: A multi-discipline exploratory analysis. *Journal of the American Society for Information Science and Technology, 58,* 1055–1065.

Landauer, T. K., Foltz, P. W., & Laham, D. (1998). An introduction to latent semantic analysis. *Discourse Processes, 2–3,* 259–284.

Lewins, A., & Silver, C. (2009). *Choosing a CAQDAS package: A working paper* (6th ed.). Surrey: University of Surrey.

Linacre, J. M. (2000). Computer-adaptive testing: A methodology whose time has come. In S. Chae, U. Kang, E. Jeon, & J. M. Linacre (Eds.), *Development of computerized middle school achievement test* (in Korean). Seoul, South Korea: Komesa Press.

Luecht, R. M. (2005). Computer-adaptive testing. In B. S. Everitt, & D. Howell (Eds.), *Encyclopedia of statistics in behavioral science.* Hoboken, NJ: John Wiley.

Ma, J. & Nickerson, J. V. (2006). Hands-on, simulated, and remote laboratories: A comparative literature review. *ACM Computing Surveys, 38*(3).

Manca, S., & Ranieri, M. (2013). Is it a tool suitable for learning? A critical review of the literature on Facebook as a technology-enhanced learning environment. *Journal of Computer Assisted Learning, 29,* 487–504.

Mayfield, E., & Rosé, C. P. (2013). LightSIDE: Open source machine learning for text. In M. D. Shermis & J. Burstein (Eds.), *Handbook of automated essay evaluation: Current applications and new directions* (pp. 124–135). New York, NY: Routledge.

Means, B., Toyama, Y., Murphy, R., Bakia, M., & Jones, K. (2010). *Evaluation of evidence-based practices in online learning: A meta-analysis and review of online learning studies.* Washington, DC: U.S. Department of Education, Office of Planning, Evaluation, and Policy Development.

Meho, L. I., & Yang, K. (2007). Impact of data sources on citation counts and rankings of LIS faculty: Web of Science versus Scopus and Google Scholar. *Journal of the American Society for Information Science and Technology, 58,* 2105–2125.

Mishra, P. (2006). Affective feedback from computers and its effect on perceived ability and affect: A test of the computers as social actor hypothesis. *Journal of Educational Multimedia and Hypermedia, 15,* 107–131.

Mishra, P., & Koehler, M. J. (2006). Technological pedagogical content knowledge: A framework for teacher knowledge. *Teachers College Record, 108,* 1017–1054.

Moore, S. L., & Ellsworth, J. B. (2014). Ethics of educational technology. In J. M. Spector, M. D. Merrill, J. Elen, & M. J. Bishop (Eds.), *Handbook of research on educational communications and technology* (4th ed., pp. 113–128). New York, NY: Springer.

Moustakas, C. (1994). *Phenomenological research methods.* Thousand Oaks, CA: Sage.

Mumby, P. J. (2002). Statistical power of non-parametric tests: A quick guide for designing sampling strategies. *Marine Pollution Bulletin, 44,* 85–87.

Muthén, L. K., & Muthén, B. O. (2002). How to use a Monte Carlo study to decide on sample size and determine power. *Structural Equation Modeling, 9,* 599–620.

Nass, C., Fogg, B. J., & Moon, Y. (1996). Can computers be teammates? *Journal of International Human-Computer Studies, 45,* 669–678.

Nass, C., Moon, Y., & Carney, P. (1999). Are people polite to computers? Responses to computer-based interviewing systems. *Journal of Applied Social Psychology, 29,* 1093–1109.

Nass, C., Moon, Y., & Green, N. (1997). Are machines gender neutral? Gender-stereotypic responses to computers with voices. *Journal of Applied Social Psychology, 27,* 864–876.

National Endowment for the Arts (NEA). (2007). *To read or not to read: A question of national consequence* (Research report #47). Washington, DC: NEA.

Newton, J. (2010). *The ethics and security of cloud computing.* Austin, TX: International Legal Technology Association.

Palmer, C. L. & Cragin, M. H. (2008). Scholarship and disciplinary practices. In B. Cronin (Ed.), *Annual review of information science and technology* (Vol. 42, pp. 165–212). Medford, NJ: Information Today.

Patton, M. Q. (2002). *Qualitative research and evaluation methods* (3rd ed.). Thousand Oaks, CA: Sage Publications.

Picciano, A. G., & Seaman, J. (2009). *K-12 online learning: A 2008 follow-up of the survey of U.S. school district administrators.* New York, NY: The Sloan Consortium.

RAND Reading Study Group. (2002). *Reading for understanding: Toward an R&D program in reading comprehension.* Santa Monica, CA: RAND.

Ranieri, M., Manca, S., & Fini, A. (2012). Why (and how) do teachers engage in social networks? An exploratory study of professional use of Facebook and its implications for lifelong learning. *British Journal of Educational Technology, 43,* 754–769.

Salen, K., & Zimmerman, E. (2004). *Rules of play: Game design fundamentals.* Cambridge, MA: The MIT Press.

Salomon, G., & Almog, T. (1998). Educational psychology and technology: A matter of reciprocal relations. *Teachers College Record, 100*(1), 222–241.

Scalise, K., & Gifford, B. (2006). Computer-based assessment in e-learning: A framework for constructing "intermediate constraint" questions and tasks for technology platforms. *Journal of Technology, Learning, and Assessment, 4*(6), 3–30.

Shermis, M. D., & Burstein, J. C. (Eds.) (2003). *Automated essay scoring: A cross-disciplinary perspective.* Mahwah, NJ: Lawrence Erlbaum Associates.

Shermis, M. D., & Burstein, J. (Eds.) (2013). *Handbook of automated essay evaluation: Current applications and new directions.* New York, NY: Routledge.

Shulman, L. S. (1986). Those who understand: Knowledge growth in teaching. *Educational Researcher, 15*(2), 4–14.

Siemens, G., & Long, P. (2011). Penetrating the fog: Analytics in learning and education. *Educause Review, 46*(5), 30–32.

Sims, V. K., & Mayer, R. E. (2002). Domain specificity of spatial exercise: The case of video game players. *Applied Cognitive Psychology, 16,* 97–115.

Spiers, J. A. (2004). Tech tips: Using video management/analysis technology in qualitative research. *International Journal of Qualitative Methods, 3*(1), 57–61.

Squire, K. (2006). From content to context: Videogames as designed experience. *Educational Researcher, 35*(8), 19–29.

Stieff, M. & Wilensky, U. (2003). Connected chemistry: Incorporating interactive simulations into the chemistry classroom. *Journal of Science Education and Technology, 12,* 285–302.

Strauss, A., & Corbin, J. (1990). *Basics of qualitative research: Grounded theory procedures and techniques.* Newbury Park, CA: Sage.

Tettegah, S., & Calongne, C. (2009). *Identity, learning and support in virtual environments.* Rotterdam, Netherlands: Sense Publishers.

Thissen, D., & Mislevy, R. J. (2000). Testing algorithms. In H. Wainer, N. J. Dorans, D. Eignor, R. Flaugher, B. F. Green, R. J. Mislevy, L. Steinberg, & D. Thissen (Eds.), *Computerized adaptive testing: A primer* (2nd ed., pp. 101–134). Mahwah, NJ: Lawrence Erlbaum Associates.

Tobias, S., Fletcher, J. D., & Wind, A. P. (2014). Game-based learning. In J. M. Spector, M. D. Merrill, J. Elen, & M. J. Bishop (Eds.), *Handbook of research on educational communications and technology* (4th ed., pp. 485–503). New York, NY: Springer.

Walther, J. B. (2009). Theories, boundaries, and all of the above. *Journal of Computer-Mediated Communication, 14,* 748–752.

Wilensky, U. (2003). Statistical mechanics for secondary school: The GasLab modeling toolkit. *International Journal of Computers for Mathematical Learning, 8,* 1–41.

Wilensky, U., & Reisman, K. (2006). Thinking like a wolf, a sheep or a firefly: Learning biology through constructing and testing computational theories—an embodied modeling approach. *Cognition & Instruction, 24,* 171–209.

Wilson, C., Sala, A., Puttaswamy, K. P. N., & Zhao, B. Y. (2012). Beyond social graphs: User interactions in online social networks and their implications. *ACM Transactions on the Web, 6*(4), Article 17.

# 4

# The Prospects and Limitations of Latent Variable Models in Educational Psychology

*Benjamin Nagengast*
*Ulrich Trautwein*[1]
University of Tübingen, Germany

Latent variable models, in particular, structural equation modeling (SEM), are a staple of research in educational psychology. SEM combines measurement models, which provide links between observed responses to items and unobserved latent variables, and structural models, which represent the multivariate relations between latent variables and manifest variables (Jöreskog, 1970; see Matsueda, 2012, for an overview of the history of SEM). The main application of latent variable models in educational psychology lies in the development and validation of measures of core constructs. Second, SEM is used to study and test relations between latent variables in structural models. Often, these structural relations are not only used descriptively but are also given a causal interpretation (e.g., in mediation analyses). There have been many methodological advances with respect to measurement models, structural models, and causal inference that have the potential to impact the ways in which researchers in educational psychology use SEM to analyze their data. In this chapter, we critically review the scope and limitations of applications of SEM in educational psychology and highlight the challenges that researchers will face in the upcoming decade.

Recent numbers show that such a review is timely. In the last decade, researchers in educational psychology have taken advantage of the increased availability of large datasets, which have allowed researchers to apply complex modeling techniques such as path analysis, hierarchical linear modeling, or SEM to questions in educational psychology. A recent review (Reinhart, Haring, Levin, Patall, & Robinson, 2013) showed that, in 2000, only 12 out of 134 (or 9.0%) of all articles published in five leading educational journals had used such modeling techniques. These numbers increased to 57 out of 141 (or 40.4%) in 2010. This increase was at least partly driven by significant advances in latent variable modeling. The emergence of generalized latent variable

modeling (Muthén, 2002; Skrondal & Rabe-Hesketh, 2004) as a unifying framework for many previously unrelated methods has significantly increased the scope of problems that can be addressed. An additional reason for the growing popularity of latent variable modeling techniques is their greatly increased availability. During the first decade of the new century, software implementations of SEM became more accessible and easier to use. This development has considerably lowered the threshold for the adoption of SEM in applied research.

The increased use of latent variable techniques, however, is also a challenge for the field of educational psychology. In order to be able to take full advantage of emerging methodological advances (Marsh & Hau, 2007), researchers must stay current with the rapidly evolving methodology, its opportunities, and its limitations. At the same time, reviews suggest that the methodological standards in modern educational psychology often exceed what is being taught in graduate and postgraduate training programs (e.g., Aiken, West, & Millsap, 2008) and that the "collective quantitative proficiency" (Henson, Hull, & Williams, 2010, p. 233) in the field is rather low. Indeed, this leads to many applications of latent variable models that do not fully exploit their strengths, but also to unjustified conclusions that are based on the results of these models (Foster, 2010a; Reinhart et al., 2013). In particular, the uncritical causal interpretation of path coefficients derived from latent variable models has repeatedly been pointed out as problematic (Foster, 2010a; Freedman, 1987; Reinhart et al., 2013). Researchers in educational psychology appear to be slow at adopting the notion that research design matters more for the validity of causal inferences than a specific statistical method (Cook, Steiner, & Pohl, 2009; Rubin, 2008). All too often, latent variable models are used in research designs that are too weak to support the intended conclusions.

In this chapter, we will focus on developments in latent variable modeling and methodology over the course of the last 10 years. We will begin by reviewing developments in measurement models, focusing on generalized latent variable modeling, measurement invariance, and exploratory measurement models. Next, we will discuss advances in structural models (multilevel SEMs and non-linear models). Finally, we will focus on causal inference in quasi-experimental designs and mediation modeling. Our discussion will be illustrated with examples from educational psychology that highlight methodological challenges and demonstrate the contributions and limitations of latent variable models in addressing such challenges. We have attempted to limit the technical details of our presentation and to point interested readers toward accessible and relevant sources whenever possible.

## Measurement Models

Most constructs in educational psychology cannot be directly observed but rather have to be inferred on the basis of indicators that are often imperfect or unreliable (Lord & Novick, 1968; Steyer & Eid, 2001). For example, students' math competencies have to be inferred on the basis of math problems; academic self-concept, the self-perception of academic abilities (Marsh & Shavelson, 1985), has to be inferred from answers to questionnaire items; and instructional quality has to be inferred from student ratings of their teachers' behavior (e.g., Kunter et al., 2013; Wagner, Göllner, Helmke, Trautwein, & Lüdtke, 2013). Researchers in educational psychology (often implicitly) invoke the latent variable theory of measurement (Markus & Borsboom, 2013; see Michell, 1997, for a discussion of other definitions of measurement), which "rests on the specification of a functional relation between the latent variable and its indicators" (p. 63) in order to locate a person within the latent space. The observed items are not deterministically influenced by the construct but are affected by a wide range of unsystematic influences that are subsumed under measurement error (Lord & Novick, 1968). Thus, educational psychologists often are faced with the challenge of separating measurement error and true score variance (Lord & Novick, 1968).

Confirmatory factor analysis (CFA) as implemented in SEM measurement models has proven to be a versatile tool for this purpose. It assumes that the covariances between observed item responses can be attributed to an underlying set of latent variables (e.g., Jöreskog, 1969). Parameters such as the factor loadings, variances, and covariances of latent variables and residual variances can then be obtained. Figure 4.1a illustrates a confirmatory factor model with three correlated factors. Influential applications of CFA in educational psychology include, for example, the assessment of goal orientations (Elliott & McGregor, 2001; Elliott, Murayama, & Pekrun, 2011; Midgley et al., 1998), integrative models of educational motivation (e.g., Martin, 2007), and academic self-concept (e.g., Marsh & Hocevar, 1985).

In the following section, we will review three methodological advances in SEM measurement models that have

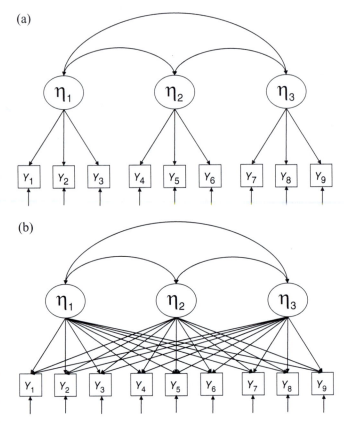

(a)

(b)

**Figure 4.1** Path diagrams of a confirmatory factor model (a) and an exploratory factor model (b) with nine indicators variables ($Y_1$ to $Y_9$) and three correlated latent factors ($\eta_1$ to $\eta_3$).

significantly affected (or have the potential to significantly affect) the way educational psychologists analyze their data: (a) the emergence of generalized latent variable modeling; (b) the stronger focus on establishing measurement invariance; and (c) exploratory structural equation modeling (ESEM).

### Generalized Latent Variable Modeling

Historically, CFA required the indicator variables (e.g., responses to questionnaire items) to be continuous variables with normally distributed residuals (e.g., Bollen, 1989; Jöreskog, 1970). Obviously, this assumption is often violated in measures in educational psychology. Achievement tests typically employ items scored as right or wrong, thus yielding dichotomous indicators, and questionnaire studies typically employ Likert scales, which yield ordered-categorical indicators. For a long time, researchers had two options for dealing with these violations of distributional assumptions. They could ignore them and treat indicator variables as continuous, leading to potential biases in parameter estimates and fit statistics, particularly for data with a limited number of categories and non-symmetric distributions (e.g., DiStefano, 2002; Muthén & Kaplan, 1985, 1992; Olsson, 1979); alternatively, they could construct item parcels (e.g., parallel test versions) that satisfied distributional assumptions but potentially masked important misfit (Bandalos & Finney, 2001; Little, Rhemtulla, Gibson, & Schoemann, 2013; Marsh, Lüdtke, Nagengast, Morin, & Davier, 2013).

Software implementations of models for categorical data were often restricted to a single dimension, thus limiting their usefulness for validating multiple constructs at the same time (e.g., Reckase, 1997; Wirth & Edwards, 2007).

The development of so-called generalized latent variable models allows researchers to take the nature of indicator variables into account systematically. Generalized latent variable models (Muthén, 2002; Rabe-Hesketh, Skrondal, & Pickles, 2004; Skrondal & Rabe-Hesketh, 2004) can incorporate a wider range of indicator variables (e.g., dichotomous, ordered-categorical, unordered-categorical, censored, and count indicators) in measurement models. Thus, these models present a major advance in latent variable methodology. These extensions allow a variety of other latent variable traditions to be subsumed under the umbrella of SEM, including item response theory models that are prominent in educational assessment and measurement (e.g., van der Linden & Hambleton, 1997). Thus, relations between latent variables that have multiple types of indicators can be modeled. Conceptually, generalized latent variable models include link functions in the measurement model. They link a normally distributed latent response variable to the actual responses on the indicators.

Generalized latent variable models are now available in several software programs. One often-used estimator for models with ordered-categorical and dichotomous indicator variables, the robust weighted least-squares estimator (denoted WLSMV in Mplus) (Muthén, du Toit, & Spisic, 1997), has demonstrated flexibility and efficiency even with moderate sample sizes (e.g., Flora & Curran, 2004). Consequently, applications in educational psychology are beginning to appear (e.g., Bulotsky-Shearer, Dominguez, & Bell, 2012; Guay, Morin, Litalien, Valois, & Vallerand, 2015; Waasdorp, Bradshaw, & Duong, 2011).

### Measurement Invariance

After establishing the factor structure of an instrument, it is important to establish its invariance across groups or time points (in longitudinal studies). Differences in measurement models between groups suggest that the instrument functions differently across groups: people with the same value on the latent variable but who are from different groups will show different response behaviors (e.g., see Millsap, 2011, for an overview). In this case, comparisons of observed scale scores and latent variable means will be significantly complicated. Consider the example of gender differences in motivational constructs that are discussed in educational psychology (e.g., Jacobs, Lanza, Osgood, Eccles, & Wigfield, 2002; Watt et al., 2012). In order to interpret such differences substantively, it is necessary that equivalent levels in the latent motivational constructs are manifested similarly in the item responses for girls and boys. If there were items that boys might answer more favorably due to reasons unrelated to their motivational beliefs (e.g., because the item taps typical male self-stereotypes), mean differences in the scale scores could be inflated. In a similar way, items could be related to the latent variable in different ways in each group, further complicating

comparisons. It is thus critical to establish measurement invariance as a precondition for group comparisons.

Measurement invariance is tested by implementing increasingly more restrictive multiple-group SEMs (e.g., gender, experimental groups, countries; see e.g., Millsap, 2011). Taxonomies of measurement invariance are given by Widaman and Reise (1997), Meredith (1993), and Marsh et al. (2009). Similar taxonomies could also be applied when repeatedly measuring the same respondents at multiple time points (e.g., Vandenberg & Lance, 2000).

The *configural invariance model* (Widaman & Reise, 1997) assumes that the factor structure is equal across groups. It is implemented as a multigroup SEM with the same measurement structure in each group. However, the values of the factor loadings, intercepts, residual variances, factor variances, and covariances are not restricted to equality across groups. If this model does not fit the data, there are fundamental differences in the factor structure across groups that make comparisons of the latent variables difficult or impossible. In fact, finding such discrepancies (e.g., between experimental groups) might be an interesting research finding in itself as it points to substantive differences in the ways in which the items are related to underlying constructs.

If the configural invariance model as described above fits the data well, the next step is to test for *weak measurement invariance* (Meredith, 1993). In this model, all factor loadings are constrained to equality across groups. If the model holds, a change in the latent variable affects the expected answers to the indicators in the same way in all groups. Weak measurement invariance is required for meaningful comparisons of variance–covariance matrices of factors across the groups. A comparison of factor means (e.g., for calculating mean differences in experimental designs) is appropriate only if *strong measurement invariance* (Meredith, 1993) holds. In this model, item intercepts are constrained to be equal across groups in addition to the factor loadings. If this restriction holds, there will be no systematic differences in average item responses between the groups that are not due to differences in the latent variables. Finally, it is often of interest to test for *strict measurement invariance* (Meredith, 1993). In this model, the residual variances of items are fixed to equality across groups in addition to the factor loadings and item intercepts. Comparisons of raw scale scores are possible only if strict measurement invariance holds.

In general, researchers in educational psychology have started to acknowledge the importance of measurement invariance facilitated by its increased availability in software packages. Examples include research on academic motivation (e.g., Grouzet, Otis, & Pelletier, 2006; Guay et al., 2015), student engagement (e.g., Wang, Willett, & Eccles, 2011), or the cross-cultural invariance of core constructs in educational psychology (e.g., Nagengast & Marsh, 2013) and academic self-concept (e.g., Brunner, Keller, Hornung, Reichert, & Martin, 2009). However, in applications, the assumptions of measurement invariance are not always explicitly spelled out and often go untested, in cross-cultural studies in particular (e.g., Chen, 2008). In Box 4.1, we present an example of tests of measurement invariance of school engagement across gender and race/ethnicity (Wang et al., 2011).

**Box 4.1    Testing the measurement invariance of school engagement across gender and race/ethnicity (Wang et al., 2011)**

**Research question**

School engagement has been discussed as an important precondition for academic success. Theoretical models (e.g., Fredricks, Blumenfeld, & Paris, 2004) posit three components of engagement (behavior, emotion, and cognition). Can these dimensions (and further subfacets) be empirically identified? Is the structure of engagement invariant with respect to gender and ethnic groups, thus allowing for comparisons between these groups?

**Methodological challenge**

Comparisons across different gender and ethnic groups require that strong measurement invariance holds (i.e., that factor loadings and item intercepts are not influenced by the respective groups).

**Method**

Multigroup SEM was applied to test for measurement invariance separately for gender and race/ethnicity using data from 1,103 ninth-grade students (52% girls; 56% African American, 32% European American, 12% biracial or from other ethnic minorities) from 23 public schools in Maryland. Students were assessed on six scales intended to measure school engagement. Each component of engagement was represented by two scales, leading to a hierarchical factor model with three higher-order factors (behavioral, emotional, and cognitive engagement), with two first-order factors each.

**Results**

The CFA model with six first-order and three second-order factors fit the data well and generalized across the gender and race groups (configural invariance). In addition, there was evidence of strong measurement invariance (invariance of the factor loadings of the first- and second-order factor loadings and intercepts of indicators and first-order factors) permitting mean comparisons on the second-order factors.

**Interpretation**

Boys had lower scores in behavioral and emotional engagement. European Americans scored lower on emotional engagement but reported higher behavioral engagement compared with African Americans. There were no group differences on cognitive engagement. These comparisons were possible only because the strong invariance model held for the second-order factors.

## *Exploratory Structural Equation Modeling*

CFA often relies on the independent cluster model (Thurstone, 1947): each indicator is allowed to load on one and only one latent variable. Cross-loadings (i.e., when an indicator loads substantially on more than one latent variable) are typically not included. In addition, a loading structure needs to be specified *a priori* in CFA. Researchers have to indicate which latent variable underlies which indicators. Thus, the measurement model formally encodes prior assumptions about the factor structure. These assumptions can turn out to be incompatible with the observed data, requiring changes to the measurement model. Also, at the beginning of the scale construction process, the underlying dimensionality of the manifest variables is unknown. In these cases, CFA falls short.

Exploratory measurement models (Browne, 2001) have recently been re-examined as alternatives to CFA (Asparouhov & Muthén, 2009). An exploratory measurement model posits a factor model that restricts only the dimensionality of the indicators but freely estimates all cross-loadings (Figure 4.1b). For a long time, exploratory measurement models could not be easily included in structural models

and lacked many of the advantages of SEM, such as tests of model fit, standard errors for loadings, or the ability to include correlated residuals. Recent developments in ESEM (Asparouhov & Muthén, 2009; Dolan, Oort, Stoel, & Wicherts, 2009) have integrated exploratory measurement models into a broader SEM framework. Introductions to ESEM are given by Asparouhov and Muthén (2009) and Morin, Marsh, and Nagengast (2013).

Measurement models in ESEM (Asparouhov & Muthén, 2009) require only the specification of the hypothesized number of factors. An initial solution is obtained by fitting an unconstrained factor model (Jöreskog, 1969). As in exploratory factor analysis, this solution is then rotated to one of many possible alternative equivalent loading patterns. Most popular rotation algorithms (see Browne, 2001) operationalize Thurstone's (1947) simple structure criterion and try to obtain a solution where most items have high loadings on a single factor. As an alternative, target rotation (Browne, 2001) can be used to rotate the factors as closely as possible to a pre-specified arbitrary loading pattern (Asparouhov & Muthén, 2009; Dolan et al., 2009). As in exploratory factor analysis, it is possible to use both orthogonal (i.e., uncorrelated factors) and oblique (i.e., correlated factors) rotation procedures.

The most important strengths of ESEM are two extensions of exploratory factor analysis: ESEM factors can be used in the structural models as dependent or predictor variables and can be related to manifest covariates and latent factors established in other exploratory or confirmatory measurement models. All parameters in the structural model depend on the rotation algorithm and change when a different rotation is chosen (Asparouhov & Muthén, 2009). Second, ESEM can be used to jointly rotate different sets of exploratory factors and to test the invariance of exploratory measurement models across multiple groups and multiple time points (Asparouhov & Muthén, 2009; Dolan et al., 2009) by including constraints in the rotation process. In Box 4.2, we present an example of tests of measurement invariance across two groups of raters (students and teachers) using ESEM. The most important shortcoming of ESEM is rotational indeterminacy: When using exploratory measurement models, there is an indefinite number of rotated factor solutions that fit the data equally well (e.g., Browne, 2001). In ESEM, this not only affects parameters in the measurement model such as factor loadings and factor correlations, but also influences parameters in the structural model (see Asparouhov & Muthén, 2009). As a result, conclusions about structural relations depend on the chosen rotation algorithm, and more complex ESEM models are often difficult to fit.

Morin et al. (2013) distinguished two uses of ESEM. First, the ESEM framework can be used in an *exploratory* way to establish the dimensionality of a set of manifest variables without firm knowledge of the factor structure. In this context, a series of models with an increasing number of factors is estimated and compared according to model fit indices and the likelihood ratio test (e.g., Jöreskog, 1969) or traditional approaches for establishing the number of factors (e.g., Cattell, 1966; Horn, 1965; Kaiser, 1960). After establishing the factor structure, its invariance across groups and its stability across time points can be tested. Second, the ESEM framework can be used in a *confirmatory* way to analyze existing instruments that have a known (simple) factor structure but that do not fit a confirmatory measurement model very well (see e.g., Marsh et al., 2009, 2010). Here, the use of ESEM is justified if the exploratory measurement model fits considerably better than the more restrictive confirmatory measurement model.

---

**Box 4.2    Agreement between students' and teachers' perspectives of self-regulated learning and math competence—an exploratory use of ESEM (Friedrich, Jonkmann, Nagengast, Schmitz, & Trautwein, 2013)**

**Research question**

Being able to correctly diagnose students' abilities and motivational states is an important skill for teachers who want to adapt their instruction to their students' needs. Can teachers correctly infer their students' abilities for self-regulated learning, or are their perceptions colored by the perceived competency levels of their students? How do teachers' and students' perceptions of students' self-regulated learning ability and competency compare?

**Methodological challenge**

The dimensionality of teachers' ratings of students' self-regulated ability and competency is unclear. Meaningful comparisons of teacher and student ratings require measurement invariance across the two sets.

**Method**

ESEM (Asparouhov & Muthén, 2009) was applied with separate measurement models for teacher and student ratings controlling for negatively worded items with correlated residuals using data from 73 math teachers and their 1,289 fifth-grade students from German lower-track schools. Students and teachers rated competencies on sets of similar items.

**Results**

A three-factor solution differentiating *pre-actional self-regulated learning*, *actional self-regulated learning*, and *perceived math competence* supported the prediction that teachers can in principle differentiate students' abilities to self-regulate from perceptions of competence. The joint model with students' responses (that showed a similar loading structure) revealed relatively low agreement between students and teachers, in particular for self-regulated behavior.

**Interpretation**

ESEM allowed comparisons to be made with regard to the dimensionality and invariance of the exploratory factor structure of the self-regulation and perceived competence scales across teachers and students. A CFA would not have been warranted due to uncertainties about the dimensionality of the items. The use of ESEM highlighted the exploratory nature of the data analysis but nevertheless allowed for strong tests of the congruence of the factor structure of student and teacher ratings.

The options for exploratory and confirmatory uses of ESEM in educational psychology are manifold. Many scales in educational psychology do not follow the independent cluster model (e.g., the Academic Motivation Scale, Guay et al., 2015; the NEO-Five-Factor Inventory, Marsh et al., 2010; the Motivation and Engagement Wheel, Marsh, Liem, Martin, Morin, & Nagengast, 2011a) and cannot be fit adequately using conventional CFA. Cross-loadings are a common occurrence, and ignoring (or removing) them can lead to substantial changes in the interpretation of constructs (e.g., Guay et al., 2015; Marsh et al., 2009, 2010, 2011a, 2011b). By placing exploratory measurement models in a broader SEM framework that includes tests of measurement invariance, correlated residuals, and tests of model fit, ESEM provides a principled way of dealing with these issues.

### Conclusion

SEMs are well entrenched in scale construction and validation in educational psychology. The advances we discussed in measurement models have made their way into educational psychology to varying degrees. Whereas tests for measurement invariance that are based on confirmatory—and to a lesser extent, exploratory—measurement models are being taken more seriously, generalized latent variable models for dichotomous and ordered-categorical indicators have yet to find widespread use in educational psychology. An increased exposition of these methods will likely add to their adoption. ESEM promises to provide a useful alternative when confirmatory measurement models yield unsatisfactory fit and when instruments of unknown dimensionality are included in larger SEMs.

### Structural Models

Conventionally, the SEM structural model consists of multiple linear regression models that describe the regressive dependencies between latent variables and covariates (see e.g., Jöreskog, 1970). However, simple multiple regression is not appropriate for some research questions in educational psychology. In particular, many theoretically important questions involve the interplay of multiple levels, such as influences of classroom climate on learning outcomes and motivation (e.g., Murayama & Elliot, 2009). Similarly, many theories in educational psychology include moderation effects or non-linear relations between constructs. In the following section, we present multilevel SEMs and SEMs with non-linear effects that address these issues.

### Multilevel Structure—How do We Account for the Clustered Structure of Educational Data?

Research in educational psychology is often conducted in a multilevel context: Students are clustered within classrooms and schools. This structure presents two important challenges. Substantively, research questions are often tied to the interplay of different levels of nesting, for example, when studying the effect of instructional quality on student outcomes (e.g., Kunter et al., 2013), the effect of classroom composition on achievement and motivation (e.g., Marsh & Hau, 2003), or

the effects of classroom goal structures and individual goals (e.g., Murayama & Elliot, 2009). Methodologically, the clustering structure can violate the assumption of independent residuals, leading to biased standard errors (for an accessible introduction, see Snijders & Bosker, 2011).

Multilevel models have been used for more than 20 years to address these substantive research questions and to obtain correct standard errors. However, measurement error in the dependent and predictor variables cannot be easily controlled in conventional multilevel models, potentially biasing regression coefficients (e.g., Harker & Tymms, 2004). In addition, conventional multilevel models are restricted to one outcome variable, making it difficult to test complex structural models (see e.g., Bauer, Preacher, & Gil, 2006). Over the course of the last decade, easy-to-use implementations of multilevel SEMs have become increasingly available (e.g., Muthén & Muthén, 1998–2012; Rabe-Hesketh et al., 2004). A good and concise introduction to different modeling frameworks for multilevel SEM is given by Rabe-Hesketh, Skrondal, and Zheng (2012).

Statistically, multilevel SEMs decompose the total variance–covariance matrix of the indicators into level-specific components (Mehta & Neale, 2005). This allows the simultaneous specification of measurement and structural models at different levels. Thus, multilevel SEM has particular strengths for the analysis of effects of learning environments whose properties are often difficult to assess directly. Instead, student ratings are used to assess constructs such as instructional quality (e.g., Fauth, Decristan, Rieser, Klieme, & Büttner, 2014; Wagner et al., 2013) or classroom climate (e.g., Mainhard, Brekelmans, & Wubbels, 2011). These ratings are then aggregated at the classroom level and interpreted as properties of the teacher or classroom. It is quite common to find that the factor structure differs between the student and the classroom level (e.g., Schweig, 2014).

Substantively, the effects of aggregated variables on other measures are often of great interest (e.g., Marsh & Hau, 2003). For this purpose, two possible effects can be distinguished (e.g., Enders & Tofighi, 2007; Lüdtke et al., 2008; Snijders & Bosker, 2011). Contextual effects are effects of the aggregated variable when individual differences in this variable are controlled (Enders & Tofighi, 2007; Marsh et al., 2012a). Climate effects (or between effects) are the effects of the aggregated variable without controlling for individual differences (Enders & Tofighi, 2007; Marsh et al., 2012a). The estimation of contextual and climate effects is fraught with difficulties. When individual measures are unreliable, contextual effects can be spuriously inflated (Harker & Tymms, 2004). Additional unreliability arises when the students are only a sample of all students in a classroom or when student ratings are intended to measure a construct at a higher level, such as classroom climate (Lüdtke et al., 2008; Marsh et al., 2012a).

Although contextual and climate effects are highly relevant in educational psychology, the correct analytical strategy in multilevel SEMs has only recently been conceptually clarified. Lüdtke et al. (Lüdtke, Marsh, Robitzsch, & Trautwein, 2011; Marsh et al., 2009, 2012a) introduced a taxonomy that classifies multilevel SEMs with aggregated variables according to two dimensions: whether they control measurement error by employing multiple indicators and whether they control sampling error by using a latent aggregation procedure to correct the covariance matrix at the classroom level. The conventional multilevel model can be classified as a *doubly manifest* model: It does not control measurement error as it is based on single items (or scale scores), and it does not control sampling error in the aggregation of individual responses as it uses the observed cluster means as predictors. The *doubly latent* model represents the other extreme: It uses multiple indicators to identify latent predictor variables and controls for sampling error in the cluster means by correcting the upper-level covariance matrix. The *latent manifest* and the *manifest latent* model control only one source of error at a time, either measurement error in the constructs or sampling error in the aggregation of variables to the upper level.

What models are most appropriate in applications? Marsh et al. (2012a) argued that the appropriate model specification depends on the nature of the construct. When the effect of classroom composition is of primary interest and the construct has a clear meaning at the individual level (e.g., when average prior achievement is used to characterize a learning environment), the conventional analytical strategy of using the observed cluster means as predictors is appropriate. If all students in a classroom have been assessed, there is no sampling error, and the observed cluster means reflect the learning environments appropriately. However, when individual ratings are used to assess a property of a higher-order unit (e.g., when students rate characteristics of their teacher), correcting for sampling error is the most appropriate analytical strategy. In this case, the student ratings are indicators of a latent characteristic: Each individual rating will be an imperfect reflection of the construct at the higher level, and this source of error will need to be controlled to obtain unbiased effects.

Marsh et al. (2012a) further argued that the two different types of variables require the interpretation of different coefficients in multilevel models. The effects of classroom composition are best represented by contextual effects as they represent the effect of the context over and above individual differences. We present an example of an application of a multilevel SEM for the analysis of the big-fish-little-pond effect (Marsh & Hau, 2003), a prime example of a contextual effect, in Box 4.3. The effects of climate variables, characteristics of the higher-level unit assessed with individual ratings, are represented with climate or between effects. Individual differences in the perception of the higher-level unit do not represent true score variance but rather unique person differences and interactions of the individuals and the higher-level unit. Hence, the effects of the aggregated ratings should not be controlled for these individual differences (Marsh et al., 2012a).

---

**Box 4.3   Studying the big-fish-little-pond effect (BFLPE) with multilevel SEM (Nagengast and Marsh, 2012)**

**Research question**

How are academic self-concept and scientific career aspirations of 15-year-old students affected by school-average achievement, a contextual variable in a multilevel system? Research on the BFLPE predicts negative effects of school-average achievement after controlling for individual achievement differences. Do these findings generalize across 56 culturally diverse countries?

**Methodological challenge**

- *Measurement error*: How to take multiple indicators of the outcome variables (academic self-concept and career aspirations) into account?
- *Sampling error*: How to account for unreliability in the school-average achievement scores due to assessing only a limited sample of students per school?

**Method**

A doubly latent multilevel SEM (Lüdtke et al., 2011; Marsh et al., 2009) with multiple outcome-variable indicators and latent aggregation of the individual achievement measures was applied at the school level using data from 398,750 students assessed as part of Programme for International Student Assessment (PISA) 2006.

**Results**

Clear negative contextual effects of school-average achievement were found on academic self-concept and career aspirations in science, generalizing across the 56 countries.

**Interpretation**

Multilevel SEM helped to statistically control for the impact of the nesting of students within schools. In contrast to conventional multilevel models, it was possible to control for measurement error in the dependent variable and to take into account unreliability in school-average achievement due to sampling error, thus leading to a more precise estimate of the BFLPE for academic self-concept and career aspirations in science.

Multilevel SEM has begun to be picked up by researchers in educational psychology. Examples include studies of instructional quality (Fauth et al., 2014; Wagner et al., 2013), the frame-of-reference effects on academic self-concept (Marsh et al., 2014; Nagengast & Marsh, 2012), and of teachers' professional competencies (Kunter et al., 2013). However, it is not a panacea and will not be appropriate and applicable in all contexts. One of its main problems is the large sample size requirement at the higher level of nesting. The doubly latent model in particular can be run reliably only with samples of over 50 classrooms (Lüdtke et al., 2011). Even then, partial correction models provide more efficient, less variable parameter estimates (Lüdtke et al., 2011). The sample size requirements also limit the number of indicator variables and the complexity of structural models that can be implemented. In addition, there is still some need to clarify rules for assessing model fit in multilevel SEM (see Ryu & West, 2009) and an ongoing debate about the importance of cross-level measurement invariance (Jak, Oort, & Dolan, 2013; Wagner et al., 2013). Alternatives to using the multilevel decomposition of variables such as the design-based correction of standard errors and fit statistics (Muthén & Satorra, 1995, cf., Gardiner, Luo & Roman, 2009; Subramanian & O'Malley, 2010) might be more suitable in some situations. Hence, although the potential for applications of multilevel SEM in educational psychology is high, the future will show how widespread the use of this model will be.

### The Issue of Non-linearity—How do We Address Moderation Effects?

Moderation effects feature prominently in many theories in educational psychology. For example, theoretical accounts that postulate aptitude–treatment interactions (Cronbach & Snow, 1977) assume that the effects of educational interventions vary with aptitude levels. Classical models of expectancy-value theory assume that expectancy and value multiplicatively determine motivation (for a review, see Feather, 1982). Control-value theory of achievement emotions assumes that control and value beliefs determine achievement emotions in complex non-linear patterns (Pekrun, 2006). However, moderation effects are notoriously difficult to establish empirically.

To illustrate this problem, we consider an influential modern version of expectancy-value theory as developed by Eccles (see Eccles (Parsons), 1983). Eccles' expectancy-value theory assumes that academic choices, engagement, and ultimately achievement are influenced by two kinds of subjective beliefs: the *expectancy of success* on a task and the *subjective value* ascribed to a task (Eccles (Parsons), 1983; Wigfield & Eccles, 2000). Since its initial formulation (Eccles (Parsons), 1983), the expectancy-value framework has been empirically validated in many subjects and for many outcome variables (see Wigfield & Eccles, 2000, for a review). However, there is one specific theoretical assumption that sets the modern expectancy-value theory apart from most of its historic predecessors (e.g., Atkinson, 1957; Tolman, 1938, 1955). Interestingly, neither theoretical accounts nor empirical tests of modern expectancy value seem to have tested interaction effects to account for the non-compensatory relation of expectancy and value in predicting achievement and motivation (see Feather, 1982, for the prominence of this assumption in classical expectancy-value models). For the highest motivation, both task value and expectancy of success should be high.

Nagengast et al. (2011) argued that the main reason for the disappearance of the non-compensatory, multiplicative relation of expectancy and value was methodological. Traditionally, expectancy and value had been manipulated in experimental designs (e.g., Atkinson, 1957; Tolman, 1955). In recent tests, however, both beliefs are typically assessed using multi-item questionnaires. This resulted in a change in the statistical methodology: Instead of analysis of variance, researchers have relied on multiple regression models (e.g., Eccles (Parsons), 1983) or have used SEM to control for measurement error (e.g., Meece, Wigfield, & Eccles, 1990). However, measurement error in the predictor variables will lead to biased regression weights particularly affecting the product variables used to test interaction effects (Blanton & Jaccard, 2006; Busemeyer & Jones, 1983). Hence, interaction effects of unreliable variables will be severely underestimated in multiple regression models and easily discarded. Conventional SEMs, on the other hand, allow for linear effects only in the structural model (e.g., Bollen, 1989), making it impossible to estimate interactions between latent variables and limiting their use for testing interactions between grouping variables and latent variables in multigroup models (Mayer, Nagengast, Fletcher, & Steyer, 2014; Sörbom, 1974).

Latent variable models with non-linear effects can be used to test for interactions between latent variables. However, it is very challenging to identify and estimate the effects of latent product variables, and this is the main reason why these models have only recently become available to applied researchers (Kenny & Judd, 1984; Klein & Moosbrugger, 2000). Conceptually, there are two approaches for estimating structural equation models with latent interactions and latent quadratic effects. *Product-indicator* approaches identify the latent product variables by creating products of indicators and can be specified in conventional SEMs. *Distribution-analytic* approaches use the implications of interaction and quadratic effects in the structural model for the distributions of the observed variables (Kelava et al., 2011) and require specialized software.

The first product-indicator approach (Kenny & Judd, 1984) required the specification of a large number of non-linear constraints—a rather cumbersome and error-prone exercise. In addition, there were only a few SEM frameworks that allowed such constraints to be implemented at that time. Further developments stayed true to the original principle of using products of indicators but introduced considerable simplifications to the actual model specifications. The extended unconstrained approach (Kelava & Brandt, 2009; Marsh, Wen, & Hau, 2004), the current state of the art, requires only a single constraint in an interaction model and can be specified in most conventional SEM software packages. Technical advice for specifying latent interaction models with this approach was given by Marsh, Wen, Nagengast, and Hau et al. (2012b) and Marsh, Wen, Hau, and Nagengast (2013). In Box 4.4, we present an example of the use of SEMs with latent interactions based on the product-indicator approach applied to expectancy-value theory.

---

**Box 4.4    Analyzing expectancy-value interactions with non-linear structural equation models (Nagengast et al., 2011)**

**Research question**

How do the *expectancy* of success in science-related fields and the degree to which a person believes that science has *value* interact to predict career aspirations and engagement in extracurricular activities? Is there evidence for a synergistic relation, that is, are the effects of expectancy and value particularly strong when both constructs are high? How do these effects generalize across a set of 57 culturally diverse countries?

**Methodological challenges**

Measurement error in scale scores attenuates estimates of interaction effects in moderated multiple regression models. Conventional SEMs cannot estimate interaction effects between latent variables. Latent interaction models allow for unbiased estimates of the interaction between expectancy and value.

**Method**

The unconstrained product-indicator approach (Marsh et al., 2004) to latent interactions was used to model the regression of career aspirations and extracurricular activities on expectancy of success, value of science, and their interaction (all measured with multiple items). Data were drawn from the background questionnaires from PISA 2006.

**Results**

Clear evidence for an interaction of expectancy of success in science and the intrinsic value of science was found for both career aspirations and engagement in extracurricular activities. Multigroup analyses showed that these effects generalized across the 57 countries that participated in PISA 2006.

**Interpretation**

The latent interaction analyses revealed synergistic effects of value and expectancy of success. For students who attributed low levels of intrinsic value to science, expectancy of success did not predict engagement in extracurricular activities and had only a weak relation to career aspirations. For students who attributed high levels of intrinsic value to science, academic self-concept was a strong predictor of both the engagement in extracurricular activities and career aspirations. The latent interaction model made it possible to obtain unbiased estimates of the interaction effects.

---

Despite their flexibility, product-indicator approaches have some statistical limitations. The formation of product-indicators violates the assumption of normality and makes the interpretation of model fit statistics and fit indices difficult (Jöreskog & Yang, 1996). Distribution-analytic approaches provide a principled alternative by modeling the implied non-normality of the indicators of the latent dependent variable (Kelava et al., 2011). The latent moderated structural equations approach (Klein & Moosbrugger, 2000) is the most popular distribution-analytic approach and is included in commercial SEM software (Muthén & Muthén, 1998–2012). Other distribution-analytic approaches (e.g., Klein & Muthén, 2007) are more robust but also less efficient (Kelava et al., 2011).

SEMs with latent interactions carry great potential for researchers in educational psychology, as many theories include moderation effects and rely on latent variables to operationalize core constructs. Despite their potential, there have been only a few applications in educational psychology (e.g., Holzberger, Philipp, & Kunter, 2014; Nagengast et al., 2011; Trautwein et al., 2012). It is likely that the next few years will bring an increased application of these models.

*Conclusion*

Advances in the structural model of SEMs have considerably broadened their scope for addressing research questions in educational psychology in recent years. However, many of these advances have yet to make a broader impact in applied research. Our examples illustrate the scope of potential applications of multilevel SEM and SEMs with non-linear structural models. However, we note that conventional applications of these models are mostly for descriptive purposes. Causal interpretations of SEMs are much harder to justify, as we will discuss in the next section.

**Causal Inference**

Large-scale research in educational psychology is often confronted with "real-world data" from observational studies or quasi-experiments in which students self-select to different conditions. Whereas this increases external validity, the internal validity of conclusions is severely in doubt (Shadish, Cook, & Campbell, 2002). The "gold standard" (e.g., Rubin, 2008, p. 1350) for increasing internal validity, the randomized experiment, is often very difficult or impossible to implement (e.g., in the case of differential effects of learning environments; Becker, Lüdtke, Trautwein, Köller, & Baumert, 2012) or would be outright unethical (e.g., in the case of grade retention; Hong & Raudenbush, 2006). In addition, uncovering the (causal) mechanism that links an experimental manipulation to an outcome variable (i.e., analyses of mediation effects) is often of great interest and constitutes one of the main uses of latent variable models in educational psychology.

Indeed, latent variable models are often uncritically used as tools for causal inference and prescriptive statements in educational psychology. Reinhart et al. (2013) noted that the proportion of causal interpretations and prescriptive policy recommendations based on latent variable models increased substantially between 2000 and 2010. However, when it comes to causal inference, latent variable models have several limitations that require cautious interpretations. Foster (2010a) argued rightfully that the implementation of a complex model does not imply that the parameters of this model also have a causal interpretation. However, it is not the use of latent variable models per se that is problematic; it is the use of research designs such as observational studies and quasi-experimental designs that limit justifiable conclusions. However, when it comes to the analyses of mediation effects, even a randomized design does not guarantee that indirect effects obtained from a path analytic model have a causal interpretation. In the following section, we will review the counterfactual model of causality (Rubin, 1973, 1974, 1977) and describe how it informs the treatment of selection effects in quasi-experimental designs. We will then discuss the limits and assumptions of causal interpretations in mediation models.

### Uncovering Causal Effects from Quasi-experimental Designs

In non-experimental research designs, a large number of variables are often related to the selection of students to treatment conditions, making it difficult to distinguish selection processes from treatment effects (Rubin, 1973, 1974, 1977). For example, single-sex schooling is often hypothesized to have a positive impact on academic achievement and aspirations (e.g., Lee & Bryk, 1986). Yet, students attending single-sex schools are very different from students attending coeducational schools. Typically, they come from more affluent backgrounds and have higher achievement even before entering a single-sex school. These selection differences have to be taken into account if the efficacy of single-sex education is to be fairly evaluated. Typically, researchers in educational psychology deal with selection effects by including large sets of potential confounders in multiple regression models (e.g., Lee & Bryk, 1986; Marsh, 1989; in studies of single-sex education). However, regression-based adjustment techniques have some severe shortcomings when used as tools for causal inference (e.g., Schafer & Kang, 2008). These shortcomings become apparent when they are considered within formal theories of causal inference, such as the counterfactual model of causality (Neyman, 1923/1990; Rubin, 1973, 1974, 1978).

Typically, the counterfactual model of causality is introduced in the context of two distinct treatment groups (e.g., Morgan & Winship, 2007; Rubin, 1977; Schafer & Kang, 2008), referred to as the treatment group and the control group. The treatment has to be manipulable at least in principle (Rosenbaum & Rubin, 1983). The following thought experiment illustrates the model (e.g., Rubin, 1974; Rosenbaum & Rubin, 1983): Each subject is assumed to have two potential outcomes, $Y_0$ and $Y_1$. The potential outcome $Y_1$ indicates the value of the outcome variable that would be observed if a participant was assigned to the control condition. The potential outcome indicates the value of the outcome variable that would be observed if the participant was assigned to the treatment condition. The difference between the two potential outcomes $Y_1 - Y_0$ is the individual causal effect, the relative effect of the treatment on the individual. In many contexts, it would be highly desirable to know the individual causal effect, for example, for assigning students to the most effective remedial training program or for adapting learning arrangements to the specific strengths of a student. However, only one of the potential outcomes can ever be observed, creating the "fundamental problem of causal inference" (Holland, 1986, p. 947).

Within the counterfactual model of causality, various average causal effects in the total population, in subpopulations, or in treatment groups can be derived as expected values of the individual causal effects (Rosenbaum & Rubin, 1983; Rubin, 1973, 1974, 1977; Schafer & Kang, 2008). In a completely randomized experiment where all subjects have the same probability of being assigned to the treatment group, the average causal effect is identified by the observed mean difference between the treatment and the control group (Rubin, 1974). However, if there are systematic selection processes, the simple mean difference, the prima facie effect (Holland, 1986; Steyer, Gabler, von Davier, Nachtigall, & Buhl, 2000), does not identify the average causal effect.

In this case, the assumption of strong ignorability (Rosenbaum & Rubin, 1983; Rubin, 1978) is commonly invoked to identify the average causal effect. Technically, strong ignorability is the assumption of stochastic independence of the potential outcome variables and the treatment variable conditional on the covariates (Rosenbaum & Rubin, 1983). Strong ignorability will be justifiable when all variables that influence the assignment of subjects to treatment groups and the outcome are observed. If this is the case, it is possible to implement adjustment methods that are based on modeling the outcome variable (e.g., analysis of covariance: ANCOVA) or on modeling the probability of being assigned to the treatment condition, the propensity score (Rosenbaum & Rubin, 1983; Schafer & Kang, 2008).

In principle, both ANCOVA and propensity score methods are appropriate adjustment techniques as long as all relevant covariates are considered (Rosenbaum & Rubin, 1983) and the model is correctly specified (Cochran & Rubin, 1973; Schafer & Kang, 2008). However, propensity score methods have a number of advantages over conventional regression-based estimators. Similar to randomized experiments, they separate the design stage and the analysis stage in causal inference for observational studies (Rubin, 2005). The propensity score approach allows researchers to come up with an optimal model for treatment assignment—the design—without having access to the outcome variable (Rubin, 2001). Furthermore, the specification of this model can be optimized with respect to the criterion of covariate balance that is grounded in the counterfactual model of causality (Rosenbaum & Rubin, 1983). A correctly specified propensity score model balances the distributions of observed covariates between the treatment conditions. Imbalance (i.e., the differential distribution of covariates between the treatment and the control group) is indicative of misspecifications of the model for treatment assignment (see Stuart, 2010; Thoemmes & Kim, 2011). In addition, methods based on the propensity score also allow tests of overlap of the propensity score distributions to assess the assumption of common support, which is a precondition for meaningful comparisons of subjects in the control and the treatment group (Stuart, 2010; Thoemmes & Kim, 2011). Educational psychology has been comparatively slow in adopting the counterfactual model of causality as a conceptual and analytical framework (see Foster, 2010a; Thoemmes & Kim,

2011). Recently however, several high-impact publications have used propensity score approaches to study, for example, the causal effects of kindergarten retention (e.g., Hong & Raudenbush, 2006; Hughes, Chen, Thoemmes, & Kwok, 2010), high-intensity instruction (Hong & Raudenbush, 2008), differential learning environments (e.g., Becker et al., 2012), or the effects of working part-time during high school (e.g., Bachman, Staff, O'Malley, Schulenberg, & Freedman-Doan, 2011; Monahan, Lee, & Steinberg, 2011; Nagengast, Marsh, Chiorri, & Hau, 2014). Box 4.5 presents an example.

What is the potential of latent variable models when it comes to causal inference from observational studies and quasi-experiments? It should be obvious from the discussion above that using SEM to analyze data from quasi-experiments and observational studies will not per se solve the problems of causal inference (see also Martin, 2011). "Design trumps analysis" (Rubin, 2008, p. 808) for observational studies, and a careful account of selection processes is required. Nevertheless, SEMs have the potential to contribute to some of the issues that affect causal inference. Within-study comparisons (Cook et al., 2009) suggest that measurement error in the covariates is an important impediment to causal

---

**Box 4.5    Studying the effects of early ability grouping on students' psychosocial development (Becker et al., 2014)**

**Research question**

How does early transition into academically selective schools affect the development of academic self-concept, peer relations, school satisfaction, and school anxiety?

**Methodological challenge**

Students who stay in primary school longer (for a total of 6 years) differ from students who move to a selective academic track school after Grade 4 with respect to their achievement and the core dependent variables. This selection effect needs to be adequately controlled to investigate the institutional effect of academically selective schools.

**Method**

Propensity score matching that controlled for group differences in the four outcome variables (academic self-concept, peer relations, school satisfaction, and school anxiety) and 20 background variables, including standardized achievement tests, grades, and socioeconomic status, were applied in a sample of 155 early-entry and 3,169 regular students. Pretests and background variables were assessed at the end of Grade 4. Outcome measures were taken at the end of Grade 5.

**Results**

There were large selection effects. At the end of Grade 4, students who entered academically selective schools reported a higher academic self-concept, better peer relations, and less school anxiety. In addition, they also had better test scores, better grades, and came from a more affluent socioeconomic background. After controlling for selection effects with propensity score matching, there were substantial negative effects of early entry into selective schools on academic self-concept, peer relations, and school anxiety.

**Interpretation**

Propensity score matching allowed baseline differences to be controlled between students who entered selective schools early and those who stayed in primary schools longer. The results converged across three different matching approaches that provided a comparable balance of the covariates.

inference. If covariates are unreliable, adjustment techniques such as ANCOVA and propensity score matching will yield biased estimates of average effects. Multigroup SEMs can be used to control for measurement error in covariates that biases effect estimates in regression-based adjustment. Within educational psychology, multigroup multilevel SEM is particularly useful as it also allows contextual covariates to be incorporated with appropriate controls for both sampling error and measurement error (Mayer et al., 2014; Nagengast, 2009). Controlling for measurement error in propensity score models is more challenging, but some first SEM-based approaches are starting to appear (Raykov, 2012). SEMs are also useful tools for data analysis after participants have been matched on the basis of the propensity score, for example, in growth curve analyses (e.g., Goos, Van Damme, Onghena, Petry, & de Bilde, 2013).

### Mediation—How do We Test Hypotheses About Processes?

Mediation analysis is one of the main applications of path models in educational psychology. For example, in the second issue of *Journal of Educational Psychology* in 2014 (volume 106, the current issue at the time this chapter was written), nine out of 18 articles included a mediation analysis (De Meyer et al., 2014; Dicke et al., 2014; Fuchs, Geary, Fuchs, Compton, & Hamlett., 2014a, Fuchs, Schumacher, et al., 2014b; Harackiewicz et al., 2014; Liem, Martin, Anderson, Gibson, & Sudmalis, 2014; Orkibi, Ronen, & Assoulin, 2014; Reeve & Lee, 2014; Stieff, Dixon, Ryu, Kumi, & Hegarty, 2014). Researchers use mediation analyses to uncover the processes that underlie the effect of a predictor on an outcome. Researchers in educational psychology are often interested in studying the effects of learning environments on student outcomes. The identification of mediating processes is of special interest in this area as it could lead to a better understanding of the phenomenon and suggest how interventions can be implemented. For example, grades have been discussed as an important mediator of frame-of-reference effects such as the BFLPE (e.g., Trautwein & Baeriswyl, 2007). The explicit (or implicit) goal is to obtain a causal interpretation of the resulting "mediating effects." For this purpose, the predictor is ideally a treatment to which students have been randomly assigned. Nevertheless, in large-scale applications, researchers also often use mediation analyses that are based on quasi-experimental designs or observed predictor variables such as achievement (e.g., Nagengast & Marsh, 2012). However, the causal interpretation of parameters in mediation models rests on strong assumptions that are often not easily fulfilled, even in randomized experiments, let alone in quasi-experimental designs or observational studies (e.g., Imai, Keele, & Tingley, 2010; Sobel, 2008; Valeri & VanderWeele, 2013; VanderWeele, 2010; VanderWeele & Vansteelandt, 2009).

Let us first consider how a typical mediation analysis proceeds. Figure 4.2 shows a path diagram for a mediation analysis (cf. Baron & Kenny, 1986). The total effect of the predictor variable (denoted as *X* in Figure 4.2) on the outcome variable (denoted as *Y* in Figure 4.2) is decomposed

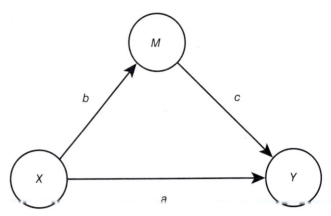

**Figure 4.2** Path diagram of a mediation analysis. *X* = predictor variable; *Y* = outcome variable; *M* = mediator; *a*, *b*, *c* = path coefficients.

into a direct effect (represented by the arrow *a*) and an indirect effect transmitted by the mediator variable *M*. In a linear SEM, the indirect effect is the product of the path coefficients *b*, which links the predictor variable to the mediator, and *c*, which links the mediator to the outcome variable. A reduction in the coefficient of the direct path from the predictor to the outcome variable after including the mediator is interpreted as evidence of a mediation effect (e.g., MacKinnon, 2008). Of course, researchers in educational psychology often have to deal with a multilevel structure, which adds another layer of complexity to mediation analyses. Although multilevel SEM has emerged as a joint framework for multilevel mediation analysis, the best way of testing and interpreting a multilevel mediation hypothesis involving higher-level variables has yet to be determined (see e.g., Pituch & Stapleton, 2011, 2012; Preacher, Zyphur, & Zhang, 2010; Preacher, Zhang, & Zyphur, 2011; VanderWeele, 2010).

In the last decade, methodological research has shown that causal interpretations of direct and indirect effects in both single-level and multilevel mediation analyses are seldom defensible (e.g., Imai et al., 2010; Sobel, 2008; VanderWeele & Vansteelandt, 2009). Although these findings challenge the validity of conclusions from conventional and multilevel mediation analyses, they have not led to a substantial change in how educational psychologists analyze and interpret their data. As a formal presentation of causal mediation analyses is beyond the scope of this chapter, we will provide a brief introduction to the main problems in the remainder. Interested readers are directed to Sobel (2008) and VanderWeele and Vansteelandt (2009), who present excellent discussions of causal mediation analysis.

VanderWeele and Vansteelandt (2009) use the counterfactual model of causality to distinguish three potential causal effects that are to be estimated in mediation analysis. The *controlled direct effect* represents the expected effect of the treatment variable if the mediator was held constant at a specific value in the population. The *natural direct effect* reflects the effect of the treatment if the mediator was held at its value in the control group (i.e., if the effect of the treatment on the mediator was blocked). The *natural indirect effect* reflects the effect of a change in the mediator if the treatment was held constant in the treatment group. Without further assumptions, none of these effects could be identified by the parameters of a linear mediation model.

The direct path from predictor to outcome (path *a* in Figure 4.2) has a causal interpretation only if there are no unmeasured confounders of the treatment–outcome relation and no unmeasured confounders of the mediator–outcome relation (Valeri & VanderWeele, 2013; VanderWeele & Vansteelandt, 2009). An intuitive way to understand this proposition is that, although subjects can be randomized to treatment conditions, the values of the mediator will obviously not be randomly assigned. Including the mediator as a predictor of the outcome variable can also open up the door for new confounders of the treatment–outcome relation similar to suppression effects so that a causal interpretation of this direct path would also be questionable (Steyer, Mayer, & Fiege, in press). Hence, causal interpretations of the direct effect in a mediation analysis require the control of all potential confounders of the treatment–outcome relation conditional on the mediator and of all confounders of the mediator–outcome relation (VanderWeele & Vansteelandt, 2009). In addition, a causal interpretation of the direct effect rests on the assumption that there are no unmodeled interactions or quadratic effects between the predictor and the mediator (Valeri & VanderWeele, 2013; VanderWeele & Vansteelandt, 2009). On the basis of these assumptions, it is possible to estimate the *controlled direct effect*. However, this effect is seldom of interest in applications.

The causal identification of natural direct and indirect effects requires additional assumptions, specifically that there are no unmeasured confounders of the treatment–mediation relation and that there are no additional mediators that could be affected by the treatment (VanderWeele & Vansteelandt, 2009). Such additional mediators would be manifested as confounders of the mediator–outcome relation. Whereas randomization guarantees that there are no confounders of the treatment–mediator relation, it is very difficult to guarantee that there are no confounders of the mediator–outcome relation. Even in simple linear mediation models with continuous outcomes, an unbiased estimation of the indirect effect will require the inclusion of confounders of the mediator–outcome relation. Things get even more complicated in designs without random assignment to treatment conditions when confounders of the treatment–mediator relation have to be controlled. Furthermore, the statistical implementation of a mediation analysis and the causal interpretation of mediation effects need to go beyond conventional SEM when mediator variables are not continuous and when there are moderation effects (e.g., when the treatment–outcome relation is moderated by the mediator or when the treatment affects the mediator–outcome relation). Although some approaches to causal mediation analysis (e.g., Imai et al., 2010; Muthén, 2011; Valeri & VanderWeele, 2013) address some of the issues introduced above, there is currently no consensus on the most appropriate method and the assumptions required to make it work (see e.g., Imai et al., 2010; Valeri & VanderWeele, 2013). Even the definition of causal mediation effects has not been decisively clarified and remains contested between researchers (e.g., Pearl, 2012).

*Conclusion.* Structural parameters in latent variable models are all too often given a causal interpretation and used to justify policy implications (Reinhart et al., 2013). As a field, educational psychology would be well served to fully embrace formal frameworks for causal inference (e.g., Rubin's causal model) and to use the insights derived from these theories to strengthen research design and data analysis. Employing good research designs would imply that randomized designs be embraced in field settings as well (see e.g., Harackiewicz, Rozek, Hulleman, & Hyde, 2012; Hulleman & Harackiewicz, 2009, for examples from motivational research) but also that other techniques be applied in field studies such as regression discontinuity designs (Imbens & Lemieux, 2008), instrumental variable techniques (Heckman & Vytlacil, 2007), or propensity score methods, as discussed above, all of which are prominent in other social sciences. Uncritically relying on a causal interpretation of structural model parameters in SEM, however, will not be sufficient for moving the field forward.

## Outlook: Prospects of Latent Variable Models in Educational Psychology

In this chapter, we reviewed the actual and potential uses of advances in latent variable modeling in educational psychology. In doing so, we focused on measurement models, structural models, and causal inference. Unsurprisingly, latent variable models are not a panacea for all data analytic challenges, and particular caution is needed when causal inference instead of mere descriptive analyses is desired. In this outlook, we discuss some of the prospects and future directions for the use of latent variable models in educational psychology.

Latent variable models are popular tools for scale construction and scale development in educational psychology. Tests of *measurement invariance* are well-entrenched research practices in educational psychology, although there seems to be the potential for a greater use of measurement models that are based on *generalized latent variable modeling*, particularly for psychosocial constructs. *ESEM* offers a viable alternative to confirmatory measurement models when the dimensionality of indicators is unclear or when cross-loadings need to be taken into account. However, it also comes with limitations regarding the interpretability of factors. Future developments, such as Bayesian SEM (Muthén & Asparouhov, 2012), promise to further expand analytical options but also demand that users have a high level of statistical sophistication. Furthermore, discussions about the fundamentals of validity theory and measurement (e.g., Markus & Borsboom, 2013) have the potential to fundamentally affect the way educational psychologists think about developing and validating their measures.

With respect to advances in the structural model, *multilevel SEM* carries great promise for researchers in educational psychology. However, the sample requirements make it unlikely that doubly latent models will be implemented as a standard procedure. Studying the tradeoff between the accuracy and variability of the estimates (Lüdtke et al., 2011) and finding ways to deal with small sample sizes at higher levels of analysis will be important methodological research topics. Further work is needed on computational simplifications for estimating cross-level interactions between latent variables and random effects on factor loadings. In addition, conceptual clarifications as to when and whether it is appropriate to decompose variances and observations in a full-blown multilevel SEM are needed (see e.g., Rabe-Hesketh et al., 2012).

*Non-linear SEMs* can be directly employed to test moderation hypotheses, which are central in educational psychological theories. They promise stronger tests of interaction effects and the chance to better align theoretical predictions and data analytic methods. Future developments will extend the flexibility of these models through semiparametric approaches (Bauer, 2005) and corrections for non-normally distributed variables (Kelava & Nagengast, 2012; Kelava, Nagengast, & Brandt, 2014).

When it comes to *causal inference* in quasi-experimental designs and observational studies, the choice of a research design that accounts for selection effects is more important than the choice of a specific analytical technique. Causal inference, first and foremost, requires that all relevant confounders be measured and modeled. Latent variable models have their role in modeling (e.g., by controlling for measurement error and alleviating assumptions of conventional statistical models such as the heterogeneity of residual variances).

The causal interpretation of path coefficients, particularly in *mediation* models, requires even stronger assumptions that often remain implicit. Even in randomized experiments, a causal interpretation of direct and indirect effects is problematic. In non-experimental settings and in cross-sectional studies in particular, causal interpretation will almost always be unwarranted. Longitudinal designs alone do not guarantee that a causal interpretation of parameters is possible (Foster, 2010b). Mediation analyses and path analysis are so well entrenched as methods for establishing causal processes that the fundamental critique of existing approaches should lead to changes in the way data are collected, analyzed, and interpreted if the field does not want to lose credibility compared with fields such as economics or sociology, which take causal inference more seriously (see e.g., Foster, 2010a, 2010b). However, a consensus about the most appropriate framework and methods for causal mediation analysis has yet to be reached.

Future trends in educational psychology are likely to increase the need for an informed use of latent variable models. Increasingly, large datasets from panel studies, international large-scale assessments, and state-wide assessments include measures that are relevant for research in educational psychology. However, bringing them to fruition for addressing research questions requires that issues of measurement, multilevel structure, and causality be addressed in an informed way. Otherwise, educational psychology easily runs the risk of overstating the potential implications while not using the available information in the data to its full potential. Large-scale randomized designs are also likely to be used more frequently for the evaluation of intervention effects in classrooms or schools. Standards set by institutions such as the What Works Clearinghouse (2008) make randomized studies, potentially with randomization at the classroom level, a requirement for achieving the highest standards of evidence. Obviously, questions of causal

inference and research design will thus have a new bearing on educational psychology, but well-constructed measures and their invariance across treatment groups and classrooms will also be required. Finally, there will likely be a desire to study the processes underlying intervention effects, and this issue ties back to the problems of causal mediation analysis. Measurement issues (e.g., invariance, unidimensionality) are also likely to become more relevant in small-scale experimental work on learning and teaching. In addition, it is this part of educational psychology that most often uses mediation analysis to test process hypotheses in experimental designs. Thus, issues of the causal interpretation of mediation effects will likely impact researchers significantly and might lead to a reconsideration of research designs and analytical methods. Finally, the emergence of intensive longitudinal data (e.g., in experience-based sampling studies; Hektner, Schmidt, & Csikszentmihalyi, 2006) and behavioral measures obtained from computerized learning environments pose new challenges for measurement and causal inference that will likely bring an increased use of modeling techniques.

The challenge for educational psychologists is to keep abreast of methodological developments in order to be able to identify the most appropriate research design and statistical approach for addressing a substantive research question (Marsh & Hau, 2007). Substantive research ideas and knowledge need to be combined with a sound methodological understanding to advance the field as a whole (Marsh & Hau, 2007). The warnings against the limited quantitative proficiency of the field (Henson et al., 2010) should be taken seriously and should inspire educational psychologists to recognize the value of carefully designed research over advanced modeling techniques (Foster, 2010a). This emphasis should be applied in the editing and reviewing of papers as well. On the other hand, choosing a statistical model will always involve compromises. In realistically complex settings, it will almost never be possible to represent all aspects of the data collection process (e.g., the multilevel structure, violations of distributional assumptions) in a statistical model. The challenge for educational psychology as a field is to select strong and informative research designs, assess constructs with psychometrically sound measures, choose statistical models that represent the specificities of the design, but carefully consider the limitations of the research design and the analytical approaches chosen in order to advance knowledge of learning, teaching, and education.

### Note

1. We thank Eric Anderman, Derek Briggs, Andrew Martin, and Norman Rose for comments on earlier versions of the chapter.

### References

Aiken, L. S., West, S. G., & Millsap, R. E. (2008). Doctoral training in statistics, measurement, and methodology in psychology: Replication and extension of Aiken, West, Sechrest, and Reno's (1990) survey of PhD programs in North America. *American Psychologist, 63*, 32–50.

Asparouhov, T., & Muthén, B. O. (2009). Exploratory structural equation modeling. *Structural Equation Modeling: A Multidisciplinary Journal, 16*, 397–438.

Atkinson, J. W. (1957). Motivational determinants of risk-taking behavior. *Psychological Review, 64*, 359–372.

Bachman, J. G., Staff, J., O'Malley, P. M., Schulenberg, J. E., & Freedman-Doan, P. (2011). Twelfth-grade student work intensity linked to later educational attainment and substance use: New longitudinal evidence. *Developmental Psychology, 47*, 344–363.

Bandalos, D. L., & Finney, S. J. (2001). Item parceling issues in structural equation modeling. In G. A. Marcoulides & R. E. Schumacker (Eds.), *New developments and techniques in structural equation modeling* (pp. 269–296). Mahwah, NJ: Erlbaum.

Baron, R. M., & Kenny, D. A. (1986) The moderator-mediator variable distinction in social psychological research: conceptual, strategic and statistical considerations. *Journal of Personality and Social Psychology, 51*, 1173–1182.

Bauer, D. J. (2005). A semiparametric approach to modeling nonlinear relations among latent variables. *Structural Equation Modeling, 12*, 513–535.

Bauer, D. J., Preacher, K. J., & Gil, K. M. (2006). Conceptualizing and testing random indirect effects and moderated mediation in multilevel models: New procedures and recommendations. *Psychological Methods, 11*, 142–163.

Becker, M., Lüdtke, O., Trautwein, U., Köller, O., & Baumert, J. (2012). The differential effects of school tracking: Do academic-track schools make students smarter? *Journal of Educational Psychology, 104*, 682–699.

Becker, M., Neumann, M., Tetzner, J., Böse, S., Knoppick, H., Maaz, K., . . . Lehmann, R. (2014). Is early ability grouping good for high-achieving students' psychosocial development? Effects of the transition into academically selective schools. *Journal of Educational Psychology, 106, 555–568.

Blanton, H., & Jaccard, J. (2006). Tests of multiplicative models in psychology: A case study using the unified theory of implicit attitudes, stereotypes, self-esteem, and self-concept. *Psychological Review, 113*, 155–166.

Bollen, K. A. (1989). *Structural equations with latent variables*. New York: Wiley.

Browne, M. W. (2001). An overview of analytic rotation in exploratory factor analysis. *Multivariate Behavioral Research, 36*, 111–150.

Brunner, M., Keller, U., Hornung, C., Reichert, M., & Martin, R. (2009). The cross-cultural generalizability of a new structural model of academic self-concepts. *Learning and Individual Differences, 19*, 387–403.

Bulotsky-Shearer, R. J., Dominguez, X., & Bell, E. R. (2012). Preschool classroom behavioral context and school readiness outcomes for low-income children: A multilevel examination of child- and classroom-level influences. *Journal of Educational Psychology, 104*, 421.

Busemeyer, J. R., & Jones, L. E. (1983). Analysis of multiplicative combination rules when the causal variables are measured with error. *Psychological Bulletin, 93*, 549–562.

Cattell, R. B. (1966). The scree test for the number of factors. *Multivariate Behavioral Research, 1*, 245–276.

Chen, F. F. (2008). What happens if we compare chopsticks with forks? The impact of making inappropriate comparisons in cross-cultural research. *Journal of Personality and Social Psychology, 95*, 1005–1018.

Cochran, W. G., & Rubin, D. B. (1973). Controlling bias in observational studies: A review. *Sankhya-A, 35*, 417–446.

Cook, T. D., Steiner, P., & Pohl, S. (2009). How bias reduction is affected by covariate choice, unreliability, and mode of data analysis: Results from two types of within-study comparisons. *Multivariate Behavioral Research, 44*, 828–847.

Cronbach, L. J., & Snow, R. E. (1977). *Aptitudes and instructional methods: A handbook for research on interactions.* Oxford, UK: Irvington.

De Meyer, J., Tallir, I. B., Soenens, B., Vansteenkiste, M., Aelterman, N., Van den Berghe, L., . . . & Haerens, L. (2014). Does observed controlling teaching behavior relate to students' motivation in physical education? *Journal of Educational Psychology, 106*, 541–554.

Dicke, T., Parker, P. D., Marsh, H. W., Kunter, M., Schmeck, A., & Leutner, D. (2014). Self-efficacy in classroom management, classroom disturbances, and emotional exhaustion: A moderated mediation analysis of teacher candidates. *Journal of Educational Psychology, 106*, 569–583.

DiStefano, C. (2002). The impact of categorization with confirmatory factor analysis. *Structural Equation Modeling, 9*, 327–346.

Dolan, C. V., Oort, F. J., Stoel, R. D., & Wicherts, J. M. (2009). Testing measurement invariance in the target rotated multigroup exploratory factor model. *Structural Equation Modeling: A Multidisciplinary Journal, 16*, 295–314.

Eccles (Parsons), J. S. (1983). Expectancies, values, and academic behaviours. In J. T. Spence (Ed.), *Achievement and achievement motivation* (pp. 75–146). San Francisco, CA: W. H. Freeman.

Elliot, A. J., & McGregor, H. A. (2001). A 2×2 achievement goal framework. *Journal of Personality and Social Psychology, 80*, 501–519.

Elliot, A. J., Murayama, K., & Pekrun, R. (2011). A 3×2 achievement goal model. *Journal of Educational Psychology, 103*, 632.

Enders, C., & Tofighi, D. (2007). Centering predictor variables in cross-sectional multilevel models: A new look at an old issue. *Psychological Methods, 12*, 121–138.

Fauth, B., Decristan, J., Rieser, S., Klieme, E., & Büttner, G. (2014). Student ratings of teaching quality in primary school: Dimensions and prediction of student outcomes. *Learning and Instruction, 29*, 1-9.

Feather, N. T. (1982). Expectancy-value approaches: Present status and future directions. In N. T. Feather (Ed.), *Expectations and actions: Expectancy-value models in psychology* (pp. 395–420). Hillsdale, NJ: Erlbaum.

Flora, D. B., & Curran, P. J. (2004). An empirical evaluation of alternative methods of estimation for confirmatory factor analysis with ordinal data. *Psychological Methods, 9*, 466–491.

Foster, E. M. (2010a). The U-shaped relationship between complexity and usefulness: A commentary. *Developmental Psychology, 46*, 1760–1766.

Foster, E. M. (2010b). Causal inference and developmental psychology. *Developmental Psychology, 46*, 1454–1480.

Freedman, D. A. (1987). As others see us—a case-study in path-analysis. *Journal of Educational Statistics, 12*, 101–128.

Fredricks, J. A., Blumenfeld, P. C., & Paris, A. H. (2004). School engagement: Potential of the concept, state of the evidence. *Review of Educational Research, 74*, 59–109.

Friedrich, A., Jonkmann, K., Nagengast, B., Schmitz, B., & Trautwein, U. (2013). Teachers' and students' perceptions of self-regulated learning and math competence: Differentiation and agreement. *Learning and Individual Differences, 27*, 26–34.

Fuchs, L. S., Geary, D. C., Fuchs, D., Compton, D. L., & Hamlett, C. L. (2014a). Sources of individual differences in emerging competence with numeration understanding versus multidigit calculation skill. *Journal of Educational Psychology, 106*, 482–498.

Fuchs, L. S., Schumacher, R. F., Sterba, S. K., Long, J., Namkung, J., Malone, A., . . . & Changas, P. (2014b). Does working memory moderate the effects of fraction intervention? An aptitude–treatment interaction. *Journal of Educational Psychology, 106*, 499–514.

Gardiner, J. C., Luo, Z. & Roman, L. A. (2009). Fixed effects, random effects and GEE: What are the differences. *Statistics and Medicine, 28*, 221–239.

Goos, M., Van Damme, J., Onghena, P., Petry, K., & de Bilde, J. (2013). First-grade retention in the Flemish educational context: Effects on children's academic growth, psychosocial growth, and school career throughout primary education. *Journal of School Psychology, 51*, 323–347.

Grouzet, F. M., Otis, N., & Pelletier, L. G. (2006). Longitudinal cross-gender factorial invariance of the Academic Motivation Scale. *Structural Equation Modeling, 13*, 73–98.

Guay, F., Morin, A. J. S., Litalien, D., Valois, P., & Vallerand, R. J. (2015). Application of exploratory structural equation modeling to evaluate the Academic Motivation Scale. *Journal of Experimental Education, 83*, 51–82.

Harackiewicz, J. M., Canning, E. A., Tibbetts, Y., Giffen, C. J., Blair, S. S., Rouse, D. I., & Hyde, J. S. (2014). Closing the social class achievement gap for first-generation students in undergraduate biology. *Journal of Educational Psychology, 106*, 375–389.

Harackiewicz, J. M., Rozek, C. S., Hulleman, C. S., & Hyde, J. S. (2012). Helping parents to motivate adolescents in mathematics and science: An experimental test of a utility–value intervention. *Psychological Science, 23*, 899–906.

Harker, R., & Tymms, P. (2004). The effects of student composition on school outcomes. *School Effectiveness and School Improvement, 15*, 177–199.

Heckman, J. J., & Vytlacil, E. J. (2007). Econometric evaluation of social programs, part I: Causal models, structural models and econometric policy evaluation. In J. J. Heckman & E. E. Leamer (Eds.), *Handbook of econometrics* (Vol. 6, pt. 2, pp. 4779–4874). Amsterdam, the Netherlands: North-Holland.

Hektner, J. M., Schmidt, J. A., & Csikszentmihalyi, M. (2006). *Experience sampling method: Measuring the quality of everyday life.* Thousand Oaks, CA: Sage.

Henson, R. K., Hull, D. M., & Williams, C. S. (2010). Methodology in our education research culture. *Educational Researcher, 39,* 229–240.

Holland, P. (1986). Statistics and causal inference. *Journal of the American Statistical Association, 81,* 945–960.

Holzberger, D., Philipp, A., & Kunter, M. (2014). Predicting teachers' instructional behaviors: The interplay between self-efficacy and intrinsic needs. *Contemporary Educational Psychology, 39,* 100–111.

Hong, G., & Raudenbush, S. W. (2006). Evaluating kindergarten retention policy. *Journal of the American Statistical Association, 101,* 901–910.

Hong, G., & Raudenbush, S. (2008). Causal inference for time-varying instructional treatments. *Journal of Educational and Behavioral Statistics, 33,* 333–362.

Horn, J. L. (1965). A rationale and test for the number of factors in factor analysis. *Psychometrika, 30,* 179–185.

Hughes, J., Chen, Q., Thoemmes, F., & Kwok, O. (2010). An investigation of the relationship between retention in first grade and performance on high stakes tests in 3rd grade. *Educational Evaluation and Policy Analysis, 32,* 166–182.

Hulleman, C. S., & Harackiewicz, J. M. (2009). Promoting interest and performance in high school science classes. *Science, 326,* 1410–1412.

Imai, K., Keele, L., & Tingley, D. (2010). A general approach to causal mediation analysis. *Psychological Methods, 15,* 309–334.

Imbens, G., & Lemieux, T. (2008). Regression discontinuity designs: A guide to practice. *Journal of Econometrics, 142,* 615–635.

Jacobs, J. E., Lanza, S., Osgood, D. W., Eccles, J. S., & Wigfield, A. (2002). Changes in children's self-competence and values: Gender and domain differences across grades one through twelve. *Child Development, 73,* 509–527.

Jak, S., Oort, F. J., & Dolan, C. V. (2013). A test for cluster bias: Detecting violations of measurement invariance across clusters in multilevel data. *Structural Equation Modeling, 20,* 265–282.

Jöreskog, K. G. (1969). A general approach to confirmatory maximum likelihood factor analysis. *Psychometrika, 34,* 183–202.

Jöreskog, K. G. (1970). A general method for analysis of covariance structures. *Biometrika, 57,* 239–251.

Jöreskog, K. G., & Yang, F. (1996). Nonlinear structural equation models: The Kenny-Judd model with interaction effects. In G. Markoulides & R. Schumacker (Eds.), *Advanced structural equation modeling* (pp. 57–87). Mahwah, NJ: Erlbaum.

Kaiser, H.F. (1960). The application of electronic computers to factor analysis. *Educational and Psychological Measurement, 20,* 141–151.

Kelava, A., & Brandt, H. (2009). Estimation of nonlinear latent structural equation models using the extended unconstrained approach. *Review of Psychology, 16,* 123–131.

Kelava, A., & Nagengast, B. (2012). A bayesian model for the estimation of latent interaction and quadratic effects when latent variables are non-normally distributed. *Multivariate Behavioral Research, 47,* 717–742.

Kelava, A., Nagengast, B., & Brandt, H. (2014). A nonlinear structural equation mixture modeling approach for non-normally distributed latent predictor variables. *Structural Equation Modeling, 21,* 468–481.

Kelava, A., Werner, C. S., Schermelleh-Engel, K., Moosbrugger, H., Zapf, D., Ma, Y., Cham, H., Aiken, L., & West, S. G. (2011). Advanced nonlinear latent variable modeling: Distribution analytic LMS and QML estimators of interaction and quadratic effects. *Structural Equation Modeling: A Multidisciplinary Journal, 18,* 465–491.

Kenny, D. A., & Judd, C. M. (1984). Estimating the nonlinear and interactive effects of latent variables. *Psychological Bulletin, 96,* 201–210.

Klein, A. G., & Moosbrugger, H. (2000). Maximum likelihood estimation of latent interaction effects with the LMS method. *Psychometrika, 65,* 457–474.

Klein, A. G., & Muthén, B. O. (2007). Quasi maximum likelihood estimation of structural equation models with multiple interaction and quadratic effects. *Multivariate Behavioral Research, 42,* 647–674.

Kunter, M., Klusmann, U., Baumert, J., Richter, D., Voss, T., & Hachfeld, A. (2013). Professional competence of teachers: Effects on instructional quality and student development. *Journal of Educational Psychology, 105,* 805–820.

Lee, V., & Bryk, A. (1986). Effects of single-sex secondary schools on student achievement and attitudes. *Journal of Educational Psychology, 78,* 381–395.

Liem, G. A. D., Martin, A. J., Anderson, M., Gibson, R., & Sudmalis, D. (2014). The role of arts-related information and communication technology use in problem solving and achievement: findings from the programme for international student assessment. *Journal of Educational Psychology, 106,* 348–363.

Little, T. D., Rhemtulla, M., Gibson, K., & Schoemann, A. M. (2013). Why the items versus parcels controversy needn't be one. *Psychological Methods, 18,* 285–300.

Lord, F. M., & Novick, M. R. (1968). *Statistical theories of mental test scores.* Oxford, UK: Addison-Wesley.

Lüdtke, O., Marsh, H. W., Robitzsch, A., & Trautwein, U. (2011). A 2x2 taxonomy of multilevel latent contextual models: Accuracy and bias tradeoffs in full and partial error-correction models. *Psychological Methods, 16,* 444–467.

Lüdtke, O., Marsh, H. W., Robitzsch, A., Trautwein, U., Asparouhov, T., & Muthén, B. (2008). The multilevel latent covariate model: A new, more reliable approach to group-level effects in contextual studies. *Psychological Methods, 13,* 203–229.

MacKinnon, D. P. (2008). *Introduction to statistical mediation analysis.* New York: Erlbaum.

Mainhard, M. T., Brekelmans, M., & Wubbels, T. (2011). Coercive and supportive teacher behaviour: Within- and across-lesson associations with the classroom social climate. *Learning and Instruction, 21,* 345–354.

Markus, K. A., & Borsboom, D. (2013). *Frontiers of test validity theory: Measurement, causation, and meaning.* New York: Routledge.

Marsh, H. W. (1989). Effects of attending single-sex and coeducational high schools on achievement, attitudes, behaviors, and sex differences. *Journal of Educational Psychology, 81,* 70–85.

Marsh, H. W., Abduljabbar, A. S., Parker, P. D., Morin, A. J. S., Abdelfattah, F., & Nagengast, B. (2014). The big-fish-little-pond effect in mathematics: A cross-cultural comparison of U.S. and Saudi Arabian TIMSS responses. *Journal of Cross-Cultural Psychology, 45,* 777–804.

Marsh, H. W., & Hau, K. (2003). Big-fish-little-pond effect on academic self-concept. A cross-cultural (26-country) test of the negative effects of academically selective schools. *American Psychologist, 58,* 364–376.

Marsh, H. W., & Hau, K.-T. (2007). Applications of latent-variable models in educational psychology: The need for methodological-substantive synergies. *Contemporary Educational Psychology, 32,* 151–170.

Marsh, H. W., & Hocevar, D. (1985). Application of confirmatory factor analysis to the study of self-concept: First-and higher order factor models and their invariance across groups. *Psychological Bulletin, 97,* 562–582.

Marsh, H. W., Liem, G. A. D., Martin, A. J., Morin, A. J. S., & Nagengast, B. (2011). Methodological measurement fruitfulness of exploratory structural equation modeling (ESEM): New approaches to key substantive issues in motivation and engagement. *Journal of Psychoeducational Assessment, 29,* 322–346.

Marsh, H. W., Lüdtke, O., Muthén, B., Asparouhov, T., Morin, A. J. S., Trautwein, U., & Nagengast, B. (2010). A new look at the Big Five factor structure through exploratory structural equation modeling. *Psychological Assessment, 22,* 471–491.

Marsh, H. W., Lüdtke, O., Nagengast, B., Trautwein, U., Morin, A. J. S., Abduljabbar, A. S. & Köller, O. (2012a). Classroom climate and contextual effects: Conceptual and methodological issues in the evaluation of group-level effects. *Educational Psychologist, 47*(2), 106–124.

Marsh, H. W., Lüdtke, O., Nagengast, B., Morin, A. J. S., & Davier, Von, M. (2013). Why item parcels are (almost) never appropriate: Two wrongs do not make a right—camouflaging misspecification with item parcels in CFA models. *Psychological Methods, 18,* 257–284.

Marsh, H. W., Muthén, B. O., Asparouhov, T., Lüdtke, O., Robitzsch, A., Morin, A. J. S., & Trautwein, U. (2009). Exploratory structural equation modeling, integrating CFA and EFA: Application to students' evaluations of university teaching. *Structural Equation Modeling, 16,* 439–476.

Marsh, H. W., Nagengast, B., Morin, A. J. S., Parada, R. H., Craven, R. G., & Hamilton, L. R. (2011b). Construct validity of the multidimensional structure of bullying and victimization: An application of exploratory structural equation modeling. *Journal of Educational Psychology, 103,* 701–732.

Marsh, H.W., & Shavelson, R. (1985). Self-concept: Its multifaceted, hierarchical structure. *Educational Psychologist, 20,* 107–125.

Marsh, H. W., Wen, Z., & Hau, K.-T. (2004). Structural equation models of latent interactions: Evaluation of alternative estimation strategies and indicator construction. *Psychological Methods, 9,* 275–300.

Marsh, H.W., Wen, Z., Hau, K.-T., & Nagengast, B. (2013). Structural equation models of latent interaction and quadratic effects. In G. R. Hancock & R. O. Mueller (Eds.), *Structural equation modeling. A second course* (2nd ed., pp. 395–438). Greenwich, CT: Information Age.

Marsh, H.W., Wen, Z., Nagengast, B., & Hau, K.-T. (2012b). Structural equation models of latent interactions. In R.D. Hoyle (Ed.), *Handbook of structural equation modeling* (pp. 436–458). New York: Guilford Press.

Martin, A. J. (2007). Examining a multidimensional model of student motivation and engagement using a construct validation approach. *British Journal of Educational Psychology, 77,* 413–440.

Martin, A. J. (2011). Prescriptive statements and educational practice: What can structural equation modeling (SEM) offer? *Educational Psychology Review, 23,* 235–244.

Matsueda, R. L. (2012). Key advances in the history of structural equation modeling. In R. D. Hoyle (Ed.), *Handbook of structural equation modeling* (pp. 17–42). New York: Guilford Press.

Mayer, A., Nagengast, B., Fletcher, J., & Steyer, R. (2014). Analyzing average and conditional effects with multigroup multilevel structural equation models. *Frontiers in Psychology, 5,* 304.

Meece, J. L., Wigfield, A., & Eccles, J. S. (1990). Predictors of math anxiety and its influence on young adolescents course enrolment intentions and performance in mathematics. *Journal of Educational Psychology, 82,* 60–70.

Mehta, P. D., & Neale, M. C. (2005). People are variables too: Multilevel structural equations modeling. *Psychological Methods, 10,* 259–284.

Meredith, W. (1993). Measurement invariance, factor analysis and factorial invariance. *Psychometrika, 58,* 525–543.

Michell, J. (1997). Quantitative science and the definition of measurement in psychology. *British Journal of Psychology, 88,* 355–383.

Midgley, C., Kaplan, A., Middleton, M., Maehr, M. L., Urdan, T., Anderman, L. H., et al. (1998). The development and validation of scales assessing students' achievement goal orientations. *Contemporary Educational Psychology, 23,* 113–131.

Millsap, R.E. (2011). *Statistical approaches to measurement invariance.* New York: Routledge.

Monahan, K. C., Lee, J. M., & Steinberg, L. (2011). Revisiting the impact of part-time work on adolescent adjustment: Distinguishing between selection and socialization using propensity score matching. *Child Development, 82,* 96–112.

Morgan, S. L., & Winship, C. (2007). *Counterfactuals and causal inference: Methods and principles for social research.* Cambridge: Cambridge University Press.

Morin, A.J.S., Marsh, H.W., & Nagengast, B. (2013). Exploratory structural equation modeling: An introduction. In G. R. Hancock & R. O. Mueller (Eds.), *Structural equation modeling: A second course*, 2nd ed. Greenwich, CT: IAP.

Murayama, K., & Elliot, A. (2009). The joint influence of personal achievement goals and classroom goal structures on achievement-relevant outcomes. *Journal of Educational Psychology, 101,* 432–447.

Muthén, B. O. (2002). Beyond SEM: General latent variable modeling. *Behaviormetrika, 29,* 81–117.

Muthén, B. O. (2011). *Applications of causally defined direct and indirect effects in mediation analysis using SEM in Mplus.* Retrieved from http://www.statmodel.com/papers.shtml (accessed February 18, 2015).

Muthén, B. O., & Asparouhov, T. (2012). Bayesian structural equation modeling: A more flexible representation of substantive theory. *Psychological Methods, 17,* 313–335.

Muthén, B. O., & Kaplan, D. (1985). A comparison of some methodologies for the factor analysis of non-normal Likert variables. *British Journal of Mathematical and Statistical Psychology, 38,* 171–189.

Muthén, B. O., & Kaplan, D. (1992). A comparison of some methodologies for the factor analysis of non-normal Likert variables: A note on the size of the model. *British Journal of Mathematical and Statistical Psychology, 45,* 19–30.

Muthén, L. K., & Muthén, B. O. (1998–2012). *Mplus user's guide* (7th ed.). Los Angeles, CA: Muthén & Muthén.

Muthén, B. O., & Satorra, A. (1995). Complex sample data in structural equation modeling. *Sociological Methodology, 25,* 267–316.

Muthén, B. O., du Toit, S. H. C., & Spisic, D. (1997). *Robust inference using weighted least squares and quadratic estimating equations in latent variable modeling with categorical and continuous outcomes.* Retrieved from http://www.gseis.ucla.edu/faculty/muthen/articles/Article_075.pdf (accessed February 18, 2015).

Nagengast, B. (2009). *Causal inference in multilevel designs.* Unpublished doctoral dissertation. Jena: Friedrich-Schiller-Universität, Faculty of Social and Behavioral Sciences.

Nagengast, B., & Marsh, H. W. (2012). Big fish in little ponds aspire more: Mediation and cross-cultural generalizability of school-average ability effects on self-concept and career aspirations in science. *Journal of Educational Psychology, 104,* 1033–1053.

Nagengast, B., & Marsh, H.W. (2013). Motivation and engagement in science around the globe: Testing measurement invariance with multigroup structural equation models across 57 countries using PISA 2006. In L. Rutkowski, M. von Davier, & D. Rutkowski (Eds.), *Analysis of international large-scale assessment data.* New York: Taylor & Francis.

Nagengast, B., Marsh, H.W., Chiorri, C., & Hau, K.-T. (2014). Character building or subversive consequences of employment during high school: Causal effects based on propensity score models for categorical treatments. *Journal of Educational Psychology, 106,* 584–603.

Nagengast, B., Marsh, H. W., Scalas, L. F., Xu, M. K., Hau, K.-T., & Trautwein, U. (2011). Who took the "x" out of expectancy-value theory? A psychological mystery, a substantive-methodological synergy, and a cross-national generalization. *Psychological Science, 22,* 1058–1066.

Neyman, J. (1923/1990). On the application of probability theory to agricultural experiments. Essay on principles. *Statistical Science, 5,* 465–480.

Olsson, U. (1979). Maximum likelihood estimation of the polychoric correlation coefficient. *Psychometrika, 44,* 443–460.

Orkibi, H., Ronen, T., & Assoulin, N. (2014). The subjective well-being of Israeli adolescents attending specialized school classes. *Journal of Educational Psychology, 106,* 515–526.

Pearl, J. (2012). The mediation formula: A guide to the assessment of causal pathways in non-linear models. *Prevention Science, 13,* 426–436.

Pekrun, R. (2006). The control-value theory of achievement emotions: Assumptions, corollaries, and implications for educational research and practice. *Educational Psychology Review, 18,* 315–341.

Pituch, K. A., & Stapleton, L. M. (2011). Hierarchical linear and structural equation modeling approaches to mediation analysis in randomized field experiments. In M. Williams & P. Vogt (Eds.), *The SAGE handbook of innovation in social research methods* (pp. 590–619). Thousand Oaks, CA: SAGE.

Pituch, K. A., & Stapleton, L. M. (2012). Distinguishing between cross- and cluster-level mediation processes in the cluster randomized trial. *Sociological Methods & Research, 41,* 630–670.

Preacher, K. J., Zhang, Z., & Zyphur, M. J. (2011). Alternative methods for assessing mediation in multilevel data: the advantages of multilevel SEM. *Structural Equation Modeling, 18,* 161–182.

Preacher, K. J., Zyphur, M. J., & Zhang, Z. (2010). A general multilevel SEM framework for assessing multilevel mediation. *Psychological Methods, 15,* 209–233.

Rabe-Hesketh, S., Skrondal, A., & Pickles, A. (2004). Generalized multilevel structural equation modelling. *Psychometrika, 69,* 167–190.

Rabe-Hesketh, S., Skrondal, A. & Zheng, X. (2012). Multilevel structural equation modeling. In R. D. Hoyle (Ed.), *Handbook of structural equation modeling* (pp. 512–531). New York: Guilford Press.

Raykov, T. (2012). Propensity score analysis with fallible covariates: A note on a latent variable modeling approach. *Educational and Psychological Measurement, 72,* 715–733.

Reckase, M. D. (1997). The past and future of multidimensional item response theory. *Applied Psychological Measurement, 21,* 25–36.

Reeve, J., & Lee, W. (2014). Students' classroom engagement produces longitudinal changes in classroom motivation. *Journal of Educational Psychology, 106*, 527–540.

Reinhart, A. L., Haring, S. H., Levin, J. R., Patall, E. A., & Robinson, D. H. (2013). Models of not-so-good behavior: Yet another way to squeeze causality and recommendations for practice out of correlational data. *Journal of Educational Psychology, 105*, 241–247.

Rosenbaum, P. R., & Rubin, D. B. (1983). The central role of the propensity score in observational studies for causal effects. *Biometrika, 70*, 41.

Rubin, D. B. (1973). The use of matching and regression adjustment to remove bias in observational studies. *Biometrics, 29*, 185–203.

Rubin, D. B. (1974). Estimating causal effects of treatments in randomized and non-randomized studies. *Journal of Educational Psychology, 66*, 688–701.

Rubin, D. B. (1977). Assignment to treatment group on the basis of a covariate. *Journal of Educational Statistics, 2*, 1–26.

Rubin, D. B. (1978). Bayesian-inference for causal effects: The role of randomization. *Annals of Statistics, 6*, 34–58.

Rubin, D. B. (2001). Using propensity scores to help design observational studies: Application to the tobacco litigation. *Health Services & Outcomes Research Methodology, 2*, 169–188.

Rubin, D. B. (2005). Causal inference using potential outcomes: Design, modeling, decisions. *Journal of the American Statistical Association, 100*, 322–331.

Rubin, D. B. (2008). For objective causal inference, design trumps analysis. *The Annals of Applied Statistics, 2*, 808–840.

Ryu, E., & West, S. G. (2009). Level-specific evaluation of model fit in multilevel structural equation modeling. *Structural Equation Modeling, 16*, 583–601.

Schafer, J. L., & Kang, J. (2008). Average causal effects from nonrandomized studies: A practical guide and simulated example. *Psychological Methods, 13*, 279–313.

Schweig, J. (2014). Cross-level measurement invariance in school and classroom environment surveys. *Educational Evaluation and Policy Analysis, 36*, 259–280.

Shadish, W. R., Cook, T. D., & Campbell, D. T. (2002). *Experimental and quasi-experimental design for generalized causal inference.* Boston: Houghton Mifflin.

Skrondal, A., & Rabe-Hesketh, S. (2004). *Generalized latent variable modeling: Multilevel, longitudinal and structural equation models.* Boca Raton, FL: Chapman & Hall/CRC.

Snijders, T.A.B., & Bosker, R.J. (2011). *Multilevel analysis: An introduction to basic and advanced multilevel modeling* (2nd ed.). Thousand Oaks, CA: Sage.

Sobel, M. (2008). Identification of causal parameters in randomized studies with mediating variables. *Journal of Educational and Behavioral Statistics, 33*, 230–251.

Sörbom, D. (1974). A general method for studying differences in factor means and factor structure between groups. *British Journal of Mathematical and Statistical Psychology, 27*, 229–239.

Steyer, R., & Eid, M. (2001). *Messen und Testen* (2. Aufl.). Berlin: Springer.

Steyer, R., Gabler, S., von Davier, A. A., Nachtigall, C., & Buhl, T. (2000). Causal regression models I: Individual and average causal effects. *Methods of Psychological Research Online, 5*, 39–71.

Steyer, R., Mayer, A. & Fiege, C. (in press). Causal inference on total, direct, and indirect effects. In A. C. Michalos (Ed.), *Encyclopedia of quality of life and well-being research.* New York: Springer.

Stieff, M., Dixon, B. L., Ryu, M., Kumi, B. C., & Hegarty, M. (2014). Strategy training eliminates sex differences in spatial problem solving in a STEM domain. *Journal of Educational Psychology, 106*, 390–402.

Stuart, E. (2010). Matching methods for causal inference: A review and a look forward. *Statistical Science, 25*, 1–21.

Subramanian, S. V., & O'Malley, A. J. (2010). Modeling neighborhood effects: The futility of comparing mixed and marginal approaches. *Epidemiology, 21*, 475–478.

Thoemmes, F., & Kim, E. S. (2011). A systematic review of propensity score methods in the social sciences. *Multivariate Behavioral Research, 46*, 90–118.

Thurstone, L. L. (1947). *Multiple factor analysis.* Chicago, IL: University of Chicago.

Tolman, E. C. (1938). The determiners of behavior at a choice point. *Psychological Review, 45*, 1–35.

Tolman, E. C. (1955). Principles of performance. *Psychological Review, 62*, 315–326.

Trautwein, U., & Baeriswyl, F. (2007). Wenn leistungsstarke Klassenkameraden ein Nachteil sind: Referenzgruppeneffekte bei Übergangsentscheidungen [When high-achieving classmates put students at a disadvantage: Reference group effects at the transition to secondary schooling]. *Zeitschrift für Pädagogische Psychologie, 21*, 119–133.

Trautwein, U., Marsh, H. W., Nagengast, B., Lüdtke, O., Nagy, G., & Jonkmann, K. (2012). Probing for the multiplicative term in modern expectancy–value theory: A latent interaction modeling study. *Journal of Educational Psychology, 104*, 763–777.

Valeri, L., & VanderWeele, T. J. (2013). Mediation analysis allowing for exposure-mediator interactions and causal interpretation: Theoretical assumptions and implementation with SAS and SPSS macros. *Psychological Methods, 18*, 137–150.

Vandenberg, R. J., & Lance, C. E. (2000). A review and synthesis of the measurement invariance literature: Suggestions, practices, and recommendations for organizational research. *Organizational Research Methods, 3*, 4–70.

van der Linden, W. J., & Hambleton, R. K. (Eds.). (1997). *Handbook of modern item response theory.* New York: Springer.

VanderWeele, T. J. (2010). Direct and indirect effects for neighbourhood-based clustered and longitudinal data. *Sociological Methods & Research, 38*, 515–544.

VanderWeele, T. J., & Vansteelandt, S. (2009). Conceptual issues concerning mediation, interventions and composition. *Statistics and its Interface, 2*, 457–468.

Waasdorp, T. E., Bradshaw, C. P., & Duong, J. (2011). The link between parents' perceptions of the school and their responses to school bullying: Variation by child characteristics and the forms of victimization. *Journal of Educational Psychology, 103*, 324–335.

Wagner, W., Göllner, R., Helmke, A., Trautwein, U., & Lüdtke, O. (2013). Construct validity of student perceptions of instructional quality is high, but not perfect: Dimensionality and generalizability of domain-independent assessments. *Learning and Instruction, 28*, 1–11.

Wang, M.-T., Willett, J. B., & Eccles, J. S. (2011). The assessment of school engagement: Examining dimensionality and measurement invariance by gender and race/ethnicity. *Journal of School Psychology, 49*, 465–480.

Watt, H. M., Shapka, J. D., Morris, Z. A., Durik, A. M., Keating, D. P., & Eccles, J. S. (2012). Gendered motivational processes affecting high school mathematics participation, educational aspirations, and career plans: a comparison of samples from Australia, Canada, and the United States. *Developmental Psychology, 48*, 1594–1611.

What Works Clearinghouse (2008). *Evidence standards for reviewing studies (version 1.0).* Washington, DC: What Works Clearinghouse.

Widaman, K.F., & Reise, S.P. (1997). Exploring the measurement invariance of psychological instruments: Applications in the substance use domain. In K. J. Bryant, M. Windle & S. G. West (Eds.), *The science of prevention: Methodological advances from alcohol and substance abuse research* (pp. 281–324). Washington, DC: American Psychological Association.

Wigfield, A., & Eccles, J. S. (2000). Expectancy-value theory of achievement motivation. *Contemporary Educational Psychology, 25*, 68–81.

Wirth, R. J., & Edwards, M. C. (2007). Item factor analysis: Current approaches and future directions. *Psychological Methods, 12*, 58–79.

# Part II

**Functional Processes for Learning**

# 5

# Learning as Coordination

## Cognitive Psychology and Education

*Daniel L. Schwartz*
Stanford University

*Robert Goldstone*
Indiana University

It is human nature to create dichotomies—mine versus yours, hot versus cold. Dichotomies usefully structure and simplify the world. They can also lead people astray. Aesop's fable of *The Satyr and the Man* captures this risk:

A Man was walking in the woods on a very cold night. A Satyr came up to him. The Man raised both hands to his mouth and kept on blowing at them.

"What do you do that for?" asked the Satyr.

"My hands are numb with the cold," said the Man, "and my breath warms them."

Later, the Satyr saw the Man again. The Man had a bowl of steaming soup. The Man raised a spoon of soup to his mouth. He began blowing upon it.

"And what do you do that for?" asked the Satyr.

The Man said, "The soup is too hot, and my breath will cool it."

The Satyr shouted, "The Man blows hot and cold with the same breath!"

The Satyr ran away. He was afraid the Man was a demon.

Each pole of the dichotomy contains a truth—the man's breath warmed his hands and cooled his soup. The problem is that the satyr treated the categories of hot and cold as mutually exclusive and did not seek a deeper analysis. Instead, he became agitated and fled the possibility of a unifying explanation.

Education has produced its share of dichotomies: abstract versus concrete, memorizing versus understanding, teacher-centered versus student-centered, authentic tasks versus decomposed practice, efficiency versus innovation, and many more. Often the categories of such dichotomies become mutually exclusive alternatives, and people advocate for one versus the other. Since at least the behaviorism of

B. F. Skinner (1986), scholars have argued whether discovery or entrainment is better for learning (e.g., Kirschner, Sweller, & Clark, 2006; Tobias & Duffy, 2009). The so-called math and reading wars are strong examples of heated polarization in education.

More prevalent and less extreme than heated debates, people simply accept the definition of one category as the negation of another, as in the case of active versus passive learning. People do not flee like the satyr, but they do not seek a deeper analysis either. On deeper analysis, familiar categories of learning, often taken as mutually exclusive, have underlying mechanisms that can make them complementary. So rather than choosing one or the other, the best strategy is to choose both.

The chapter follows a central thesis: A major task of teaching and instruction is to help learners coordinate categories of cognitive processes, capabilities, and representations. While nature confers basic abilities, education synthesizes them to suit the demands of contemporary culture. So, rather than treating categories of learning and instruction as an either–or problem, the problem is how to coordinate learning processes so they can do more together than they can alone. This thesis, which proposes a systems level analysis, is not the norm when thinking about teaching and learning. More common is the belief that learning involves strengthening select cognitive processes rather than coordination across processes. Our chapter, therefore, needs to develop the argument for learning as coordination. To do so, we introduce findings from the field of cognitive psychology.

Cognitive psychology focuses on the mechanisms of mind and brain that determine when and how people solve problems, make decisions, interpret situations, remember, learn, and adapt. There are many reviews of cognitive psychology as it relates to education (e.g., Koedinger, Booth, & Klahr, 2013; Pashler et al., 2007). There are also cognitively minded books for education (Bransford, Brown, & Cocking, 2000; Mayer, 1987), cognitive psychology textbooks (Anderson, 2000), and excellent free online resources (www.learnlab.org/research/wiki/index.php/Main_Page). These all introduce the central constructs of cognitive psychology, including attention, different forms of memory, expertise, problem-solving strategies, schemas, and more. Many topics originally investigated by cognitive psychology have matured to the point that they now have their own chapters in this *Handbook* and do not need further coverage here (e.g., see Chapters 9 and 15). Therefore, the goal of the present chapter is not to provide an encyclopedic review. Instead, the primary goal is to provide framing and examples for how to view learning from a cognitive perspective that is relevant to questions of teaching and instruction ranging from reading to math. A second goal is to introduce cognitive neuroscience, which is increasingly a part of the cognitive psychology tool kit. We show where neuroscience can complement behavioral analyses.

The first section of the chapter considers the natural human tendency towards categorization with a special focus on reconsidering one of the most influential categorical frameworks in education—Bloom's taxonomy. The next section presents a view of the mind and brain that helps to indicate why mutually exclusive categories of learning are problematic. The third section presents the heart of the thesis: A major goal of school-based instruction is to help learners coordinate different cognitive processes in the service of cultural goals such as being able to read. The section is populated with examples from research on the teaching and learning of math and reading. The remaining sections provide two examples of common dichotomies, including memorization versus understanding and concreteness versus abstraction. The examples provide a glimpse into how cognitive processes that putatively occupy the poles of a dichotomy can work in concert. The conclusion considers *dichotomania* more generally and offers a tentative prescription.

## Categorical Thinking and Education

Before developing our alternative to dichotomous thinking, it is worth understanding the power of categories and boundaries, which make dichotomies possible. Boundaries appear throughout cognition. At the lowest levels, vision has dedicated neural circuitry that detects the edges that separate one object from another. Rainbows present to us a continuous range of wavelengths, yet we tend to see rainbows as consisting of seven distinct bands of color. At the highest levels, people intentionally impose boundaries. Political systems depend on fabricated social boundaries that often become physical ones. Creating boundaries is fundamental to the human experience (Medin, Lynch, & Solomon, 2000) and reaches from basic perception to cultural organization.

Categories follow from boundaries; they collect those things that fall within a physical or conceptual boundary. Categories simplify and stabilize an otherwise ever-changing world.

The category of "self" applies during dinner and when waking up, even though one is quite different at those two time points. Without categories, experience would be a flow of inchoate sensations without organizational structure. Once categories are fixed mentally, people de-emphasize differences among members of a category, and accentuate differences across categories (Goldstone & Hendrickson, 2010; Harnad, 1997).

Language is an important contributor to category formation (Boroditsky, 2001; Lupyan, 2008). When speaking, it is impossible to convey the totality of experience and all the subtle variations one might be experiencing right now at this very second. Language fixes the flow of experience into categories. Through language, people can reflect upon and communicate categories. Lawyers' carefully worded statements, political platforms, and the movement toward non-sexist and non-discriminatory language are all motivated by the realization that the words we use do not just label our experiences, but also shape and warp these experiences. Being labeled as a member of a category, by a stereotype for instance, can have large effects on how people experience and perform in the world (Steele, 1997). Humans create categories, and categories create humans (McDermott, 1993).

Given their centrality in human thought, categorization schemes can be extremely powerful. An important goal of education is to help students learn cultural and scientific categorization schemes (e.g., republics, taxonomies). Categories, even imperfect ones, can advance science. They offer initial hypotheses that drive research that may even eventually replace the original categories. On the negative side, once a categorization scheme is in place, it can be difficult to displace. It took over a thousand years to overhaul the categories of Aristotelian physics with the modern conception of force. People still spontaneously develop Aristotelian categories to understand physical phenomena, and it takes substantial instruction to displace those naïve misconceptions (Hestenes, Wells, & Swackhamer, 1992).

Bloom's taxonomy of educational outcomes (Figure 5.1) provides an example of the strengths and weaknesses of categorization schemes (Bloom, Engelhart, Furst, Hill, & Krathwohl, 1956). On the positive side, the taxonomy was a brilliant effort to create an assessment framework. It helped educators focus on a more differentiated set of outcomes than the coarse observation that a student "learned." The taxonomy describes a pyramid of the following order, going from bottom to top: memory (called "knowledge" back then), comprehension, application, analysis, synthesis, and evaluation. More recently, some scholars have put in a new top layer, labeled creativity. The pyramid was seminal in pointing out that there are learning outcomes that go beyond the repetition of behavior, which was the prevailing behaviorist perspective at the time.

On the negative side, many people interpret the categories as forming a prerequisite structure. Students must first learn the lower-order skills at the bottom of the pyramid (memory), before engaging in the skills at the top of the pyramid (evaluation). This interpretation fuels a back-to-basics mentality, so that students should memorize before trying to apply their learning usefully. However, the science

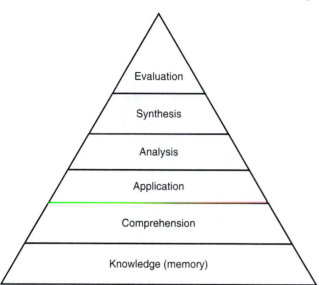

**Figure 5.1** Bloom's taxonomy of cognitive outcomes is a framework for analyzing learning outcomes from 70 years ago (Bloom et al., 1956). Contemporary research does not support the implied ordering that people should learn the bottom of the pyramid before engaging the top of the pyramid.

of learning does not support this interpretation. For example, comprehension occurs above memory in the taxonomy, but people can remember ideas better when they comprehend them (Bransford & Johnson, 1972). Making memories a prerequisite for comprehension does not work very well. Similarly, having students learn a new topic in an application context is a useful way to help them simultaneously learn the facts and evaluate their applications (Barron et al., 1998).

Bloom's taxonomy neatly captures the strengths and weaknesses of categorizations in education. It is a compelling and intuitive categorization scheme, and as such, it has had tremendous influence on practitioners and scientists alike. At the same time, it has been difficult to change, despite 70 years of subsequent research that challenges the pyramidal structure. Moreover, people use the categories in ways that violate their intent. Bloom's taxonomy is an assessment framework for evaluating instructional outcomes. It is not a framework for learning or designing instruction, but people still use it that way.

### The Distributed Nature of Cognition

One of the important qualities of cognition is that different categories of thinking comprise distributed and overlapping subprocesses at another lower level of description (Rumelhart, McClelland, & the PDP Research Group, 1986). For instance, subtraction and multiplication are separate categories of mathematical operation, and each requires its own set of mental steps to compute an answer. It seems safe to say that when people are doing subtraction, they have "shut off" multiplication. However, at a lower level of analysis, they are engaging many of the same underlying processes for both types of computation. What appears to be different at one

level of analysis is not so different at another. We provide an example by introducing brain research that uses functional magnetic resonance imaging (fMRI).

Brain cells are alive and therefore always active to some degree. If one simply looked at the activation of the brain for any category of thought, all the cells would be active. The constant activation of the brain makes for an interesting methodological problem, because it is not possible to say that one cognitive process (set of cells) is on, and another cognitive process is off. To solve this problem, brain research examines relative changes to levels of activation.

The MRI machine used for brain research is the same machine that doctors can use to collect images of soft tissues, such as a torn knee cartilage. For knee injuries, the machine records structural data on the shape and density of tissue. When used for fMRI, the scanner can detect changes in blood flow within the brain. When people complete a task, some of the brain cells do more work than others do. These working cells need to be replenished with oxygenated blood, and the fMRI picks up the changes in the blood flow. fMRI does not capture the firing of the neurons when people are completing the task, but rather the increase in blood flow after the task (about 2 seconds later).

fMRI research depends on comparing the amount of local blood flow for different tasks. When a region of the brain receives more blood, scientists infer it has been more active. A study by Lee (2000) demonstrates a typical research strategy. People completed subtraction tasks and multiplication tasks. The fMRI recorded brain activity during the two tasks. The investigators studied the average activation patterns across the brain for the subtraction tasks, as well as the activation patterns for the multiplication task. The whole brain is active for both tasks, but the researcher wanted to find out which brain regions are selectively more active for one task versus the other. To find out, the investigator took the activation patterns for subtraction and removed the activation patterns in common with multiplication. In other words, the scientist statistically removed all the activation for subtraction that was common with multiplication. The leftover activation indicates which parts of the brain are involved preferentially in subtraction compared to multiplication. The researchers then flipped the comparison. They took the brain activity for the multiplication task, and removed activity that was in common with the subtraction task. Figure 5.2 shows the results. The black regions indicate areas that are more active for multiplication than subtraction, and the white areas show the areas that are more active for subtraction than multiplication.

The circled intraparietal sulcus (IPS) region was more active for subtraction. The IPS is also involved in various spatial attention tasks and judgments about the size of things (Uddin et al., 2010). One interpretation is that people are consulting some form of spatial representation—a mental number line—when doing subtraction (Dehaene, Piazza, Pinel, & Cohen, 2003). They are making sense of the relative magnitudes of the numbers while completing the subtraction on symbolic digits. In contrast, the area indicated as AG (angular gyrus) is more active for multiplication. This region

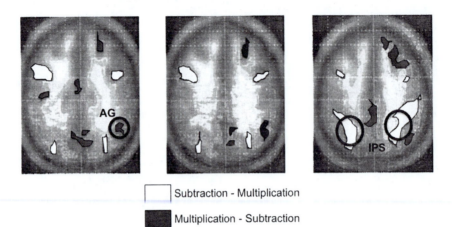

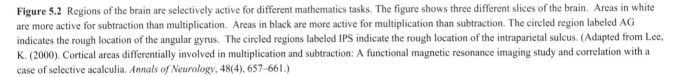

**Figure 5.2** Regions of the brain are selectively active for different mathematics tasks. The figure shows three different slices of the brain. Areas in white are more active for subtraction than multiplication. Areas in black are more active for multiplication than subtraction. The circled region labeled AG indicates the rough location of the angular gyrus. The circled regions labeled IPS indicate the rough location of the intraparietal sulcus. (Adapted from Lee, K. (2000). Cortical areas differentially involved in multiplication and subtraction: A functional magnetic resonance imaging study and correlation with a case of selective acalculia. *Annals of Neurology*, 48(4), 657–661.)

is also involved in the retrieval of factual, verbal memories. Thus, people seem to rely on the semantics of quantity (e.g., size and order) for subtraction, and they appear to rely on rote memory for multiplication, consistent with the idea they are consulting memorized multiplication tables.

Given these results, it may be easy to feel the pull of dichotomous thinking. For instance, one might want to conclude that when people are doing multiplication, their sense of magnitude (the IPS) is shut down. One might even go further to make the reckless conclusion that the proper method of multiplication instruction is to emphasize the memorization of verbal math facts without regard for a sense of magnitude. We take a closer look at IPS activation to see why these are mistaken conclusions.

Cochon, Cohen, van de Moortele, & Dehaene (1999) compared brain activation during multiplication with activation when staring at a small cross on the screen. Figure 5.3 indicates the IPS is very active for multiplication compared to doing a non-mathematical task. When interpreting this new result, one might now conclude that it is important for multiplication facts to be tightly connected with one's sense of magnitude. This is a very different conclusion from a dichotomous interpretation of the results in Figure 5.2.

In summary, cognitive processes are always "on" to some degree. It is a mistake to view them as dichotomous, where one process excludes another. It is tempting to do so, because dichotomous categories simplify the world. On closer inspection, however, exclusive categories often hide a deeper truth about cognition, much as the satyr's assumptions about hot and cold hid a deeper truth.

### Nature Confers Cognitive Processes; Education Coordinates Them

A major goal of typical education is to coordinate evolutionarily conferred abilities into ensembles that can achieve culturally relevant goals. Whereas most everyone learns to speak and interpret language, education coordinates our evolutionarily bestowed linguistic capacity with the visual system so that people can also read language. Similarly, education coordinates the IPS, largely implicated in spatial attention, so it can contribute to mathematical thinking. Evolution bestowed humans with the ability to coordinate and re-coordinate cognitive and neural processes.

A nice example comes from a study by Mackey, Miller Singley, and Bunge (2013). The authors compared brain changes among students who did or did not take a course that provided training for the Law School Admission Test (LSAT) exam (the entrance test for law schools). The LSAT is rich in hypothetical thinking, which requires one to set aside the facts that one knows, and instead, draw logical conclusions based on the stated premises in the problem. That is why it is called "hypothetical reasoning." The effect of the LSAT training was to coordinate the prefrontal and parietal regions. One interpretation is that the prefrontal regions learned to suppress spontaneous memory intrusions from the parietal regions, so people would rely on the premises and logic rather than their memories. Learning to deactivate memory retrieval is useful for doing the types of tasks that appear in the LSAT, a cultural invention.

The reader may have entertained the analogy that learning is like strengthening a muscle. A better analogy would be learning to dance. Dancing requires the coordination of many muscles, as well as the strengthening of the muscles in response to one another. Strengthening without coordination is ineffective. Woltz, Gardner, and Bell (2000), for instance, found that if people already know how to do one set of computation steps very well, they may display more errors when performing a new, related computation compared to a person who has less initial experience. Even though the seasoned subjects had strengthened some relevant computation "cognitive muscles," the coordination was wrong.

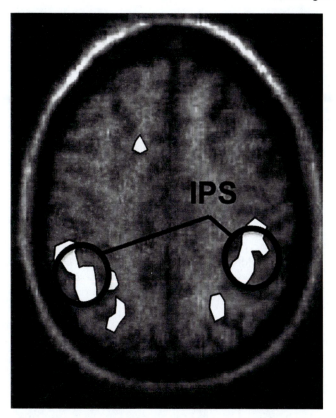

**Figure 5.3** The intraparietal sulcus (IPS) is active for multiplication tasks relative to staring at a fixation cross. (Adapted from Cochon, F., Cohen, L., van de Moortele, P. F., & Dehaene, S. (1999). Differential contributions of the left and right inferior parietal lobules to number processing. *Journal of Cognitive Neuroscience, 11*(6), 617–630. Reprinted by permission of MIT Press Journals. Copyright 1999 Massachusetts Institute of Technology.)

and therefore, instruction should match a person's favored cognitive ability. To be sure, there are individual differences in some foundational capacities. For instance, some people are better at mentally manipulating spatial information than others (Hegarty & Waller, 2005), and there are researchers who work on strengthening these very specific skills (Feng, Spence, & Pratt, 2007). However, this does not support the claim that, therefore, people with high spatial ability should receive instruction spatially, which is the immediate implication of some of the research on learning styles. Despite a thriving belief in learning styles, their effects must be small, because there is surprisingly little evidence to support the idea that people with different native strengths should receive different types of instruction (Pashler, McDaniel, Rohrer, & Bjork, 2009). When people claim they are visual learners, they may be claiming that they can interpret spatial information more easily, or perhaps, they are saying that they do not like to read very much, which is a motivation issue. Regardless, when one thinks of learning the important content taught in schools, it often depends on the coordination of the linguistic, spatial, conceptual, attention, memory, and other systems.

## Examples of Learning as Coordination

Learning to coordinate is foundational to the biology of the brain as it adapts to new information. At the cellular level, brain cells "learn" to coordinate their signals with one another. All learning requires coordination at the cellular level. The neurons need to communicate to accomplish work. Learning comprises an increase and decrease in the number and strength of connections among neurons, so they can coordinate their communication more effectively for specific tasks. Of course, knowing this fact does not get one very far in thinking about the macro-level of learning that teachers handle in classroom instruction. Therefore, in this section we provide some examples of coordination for the types of tasks and learning found in schools. The examples come from reading, mathematics, and conceptual change.

### Learning to Read

A crisp example of the role of learning as coordination involves reading. By the time that children are learning to read, they have extensive vocabularies. They can detect words in sound, and they can use these sound-based words to retrieve their meanings from memory. Arrow 1 in Figure 5.4 indicates this coordination of hearing and memory. With reading, children now have the challenge of hooking up their visual system to their auditory system, as indicated by arrow 2. They need to learn that the look of a set of letters (a written word) corresponds to a sound. Establishing this coordination takes time, because the children need to learn how to see and hear the letters. Over time and with many hundreds of hours of practice, people begin to establish coordination between sight and meaning. They develop a link directly between the look of a word and its meaning, as indicated by arrow 3.

Consider the case of learning to type. One approach might be to have people strike a key faster and faster when they see the relevant letter. For instance, one sees the letter "t" appear on a screen and then types the letter "t" as quickly as possible. It is not hard to imagine a fun little computer game that could train this kind of response. It fits the muscle analogy, where one emphasizes the strengthening of an isolated skill. Typing programs, however, do not take this approach. Instead of helping people learn how to type each letter as quickly as possible, these programs help people coordinate multiple keystrokes. The bottleneck in typing is how well people can coordinate their fingers to handle collections of letters (i.e., words). Moreover, people also need to coordinate the movements of their eyes with their hands, if they are typing from a document. They need to look ahead by just the right amount to anticipate how to coordinate their fingers for the transition from one word to the next. This fits the dance analogy, where one emphasizes the coordination of activity. *Education is more about teaching the brain to dance than teaching it to lift weights.*

Dichotomous thinking brings with it a focus on single cognitive processes, often to the exclusion of others. This can lead to tenacious misconceptions. One major misconception may be the belief in learning styles. The belief is that different people have different favored cognitive abilities,

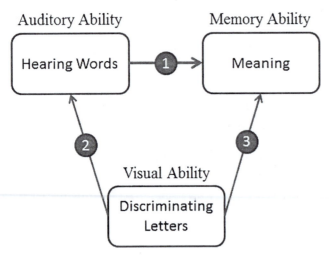

Figure 5.4 Circuits that enable reading. Evolutionarily conferred language circuits map between word sounds and meaning. It requires explicit education to coordinate the activity of the visual system so that reading language also becomes possible.

The link between vision and word meaning becomes automatic with practice. When seeing a word, it is hard to ignore its meaning, as shown by the Stroop task (Stroop, 1935) in Figure 5.5. Moreover, people can read without having to sound out words, which enables them to read much faster. An interesting fact is that once sight and meaning have been coordinated, people do not lose the coordination between sight and sound. For instance, if you run into a word that you do not know immediately, you may notice that you sub-vocalize that word—you are sounding it out in your head in the hopes that arrow 1 will help find the meaning, because you cannot find the direct link from sight to meaning. It is informative to note that population variability in the ability to speak language is much lower than the variability found in reading. This is because reading depends on the special coordinating arrangements of culture and school, whereas speaking and understanding oral language are conferred by nature.

### Approximate Addition

The significance of well-coordinated processes also appears in mathematics tasks. Tsang, Dougherty, Deutsch, Wandell,

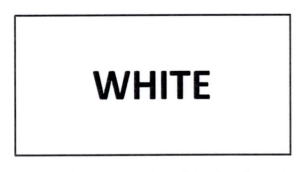

What is the color of the font?

Figure 5.5 The Stroop effect. The task is to say the color of the word (black), but people automatically read and retrieve the meaning of the word (white), which slows down their time to complete the task of saying black.

and Ben-Shachar (2009) investigated children's abilities to do approximate addition. In approximate addition, people receive an addition problem and have to choose which of two answers is closer without computing the answer exactly. Given 27 + 14, is 40 or 60 closer to the answer? The task is an experimental version of the standard "estimate the answer" assignment in school. Tsang had children complete numerous problems and found that there were reliable individual differences in children's performance.

The researchers then took measures of the brain's white matter using MRI. The white matter consists of fibers or tracts that connect regions of gray matter that reside on the surface of the brain. The gray matter is responsible for different types of computations, whereas the white matter helps distal brain regions communicate. Figure 5.6 shows the brains of two children and the white-matter tract of interest (anterior superior longitudinal fasciculus: aSLF) for the approximate addition task. Children who had a more coherent tract connecting the two areas of the brain were also the ones who did better on the approximate addition task. The implication is that they were better able to coordinate the computations between different brain regions.

At this fine level of granularity, the coordination of different processes appears as biological, and one can ask whether and what types of educational experiences might improve the structure of these specific biological pathways. The researchers did not address this question. A likely hypothesis is that the children need to engage in tasks that co-activate and force the coordination of the two areas of gray matter to drive changes in the connective white matter (see Scholz, Klein, Behrens, & Johansen-Berg, 2009).

### Conceptual Change in Mathematics

Conceptual change refers to major shifts in how people think of a situation or problem (see also Chapter 18, this volume). For instance, young children change from a conception of a flat earth to a round one (Vosniadou & Brewer, 1992). Conceptual change in mathematics provides a strong example of learning as coordination. To an adult, the digit "5" coordinates multiple quantitative meanings seamlessly. For instance, 5 can refer to cardinality—five total things. It can refer to ordinality—fifth in a series. It can also refer to magnitude—5 is bigger than 3. Infants, and many animals, have innate abilities for each of these separate meanings of number. They can differentiate between two and three objects at a rapid glance; they can tell whether something comes before or after something else; and they can judge larger and smaller. The task of instruction is to coordinate these different abilities to make an integrated concept of number. For instance, Griffin, Case, and Siegler (1994) created a kindergarten curriculum that involved board games where students had to translate between the different meanings. They might roll a die and count the total number of dots (cardinality). They would then move their character on the game board the same number of spaces forward, thereby translating between cardinality and ordinality. They might then have to decide who has more total spaces so far, translating between

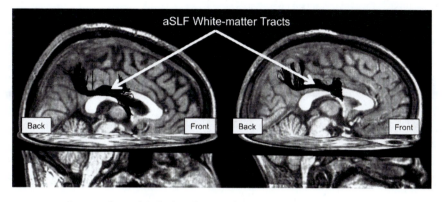

**Figure 5.6** White-matter tracts connect distant surfaces of the brain. These two brains show differences in the anterior superior longitudinal fasciculus (aSLF) white-matter tracts that connect two regions of the brain that coordinate to complete approximate addition tasks. (For visual clarity, the aSLF tracts are shown in black and the many other white-matter tracts of the brain have been removed from the image.) (Courtesy of Dr. Jessica Tsang, based on data collected in Tsang et al., 2009.)

magnitude and ordinality. These researchers found that children who played the coordinating games did better in first grade the following year compared to children who played games that tried to improve each sense of quantity independently (e.g., just counting dots to find cardinality without translating the results into ordinal position or to make a magnitude comparison).

When people learn fundamentally new concepts, they need to re-coordinate the relations between evolutionarily old neural circuits. Dehaene and Cohen (2007) proposed that people "exapt" neural circuits for cultural purposes through a process of cortical recycling. Exapt means that a structure originally evolved to serve one function is borrowed to serve another. For example, the visual circuits responsible for fine discrimination of natural phenomena become repurposed to identify symbolic letters. Blair, Tsang, and Schwartz (2013) looked for evidence of borrowing primitive perceptual computations in the context of a mathematical conceptual change; namely, learning the integers.

The integers introduce the negative numbers and zero to the natural numbers. The understanding of negative numbers is unlikely to have been conferred by nature, given that they are a recent invention (Varma & Schwartz, 2011). The integers also depend on the introduction of new mathematical structure in the form of the additive inverse: $X + -X = 0$. The authors asked what innate abilities were exapted to handle the additional structure of the negative numbers. Adults had to decide the mid-point of two digits, for instance, 2 and 10 (answer: 6), –6 and 2 (answer: –2). As the digits became more symmetric about zero, people answered more quickly. For instance, people could solve –5 and 7 faster than –3 and 9. This was true even if people heard the digits rather than seeing them on a screen. Interestingly, they also found that brain regions associated with detecting visual symmetry (e.g., visual area V5) became more active for the more conceptually symmetric problems. Based on this evidence, it appears that people exapt their abilities to detect symmetry to help make sense of the integers, which can be conceptualized as symmetric about zero.

The authors went a step further to determine if this finding had implications for instruction. They created a curriculum

for fourth graders that emphasized symmetry (Figure 5.7) so that students could coordinate their innate abilities with symmetric structures to understand the negative numbers. They found that this curriculum led to superior abilities to solve novel integer problems compared to current instructional models, which do not help students coordinate their knowledge of natural numbers and symmetry to build an understanding of integers.

## Memory and Understanding

We now turn to the discussion of dichotomies that may be familiar to the reader. The poles of these dichotomies reflect important cognitive processes and outcomes. The risk is that people treat the poles as mutually exclusive and argue for one over the other. We begin with the distinction between memory and understanding. These processes need each other. For instance, a common technique in classrooms around

**Figure 5.7** Hands-on materials created to emphasize the symmetry of positive and negative materials. Children received integer addition problems (e.g., 5 + –6) that they modeled by setting out positive and negative blocks about the zero point. To find the answer, they clapped the blocks together, folding up from the zero point. The number of extra blocks on either side gives the answer.

the world is to have students activate their prior knowledge before a lesson. "Do you remember hugging your dog? Did you notice the warmth? That is because a dog is a mammal, and mammals are warm-blooded." Activating prior knowledge is an example of retrieving memories to help one understand new ideas better. In this case, understanding depends on memory. A second common instructional technique is to ask people to make sentences out of new words. Making a meaningful sentence with a new word will help people remember the word. In this case, memory depends on understanding. Despite the obvious interdependence of memory and understanding, they are often placed into the following exaggerated opposition:

Rote memorization ↔ Deep understanding

People need to memorize important recurrent facts. Knowing the fact families in math is a great asset for solving problems that depend on factoring. Remembering is faster than problem solving, and for many problems, speed matters. Being able to remember an answer also frees up cognitive resources useful for understanding broader aspects of a problem. Similarly, people need understanding. If one truly understands, then one can recreate what may be forgotten. There are important differences between memorization and understanding, but as fits our argument, they work better in coordination than in isolation. We begin with a brief review of the memory literature, and then the literature on understanding. We then consider why the coordination of memory and understanding is important for the transfer of learning from one setting to another.

### Memory

Memory is one of the most intensely studied and theorized domains within cognitive psychology. How can people gain memories without limit, yet still remember the right memory at the right time and at blazing speeds? For example, here is a random word—"peach." You probably recalled the right fruit in about 0.6–0.75 seconds. Given how many memories you have about so many different things, it is a stunning achievement.

Humans have many distinct memory systems, each specializing in a different type of information. At an extreme, one can consider the immune system to be a type of memory. When people receive bone marrow transplants, doctors kill the existing marrow and then replace it. As a result, the immune system "forgets" all the diseases it has encountered and it needs to relearn. For cognitive phenomena, there are multiple memory systems, and recent evidence suggests that each requires separate sleep cycles to help consolidate the memories of the day (Stickgold, 2005). For instance, given a typing lesson, people will type faster after sleeping on the lesson than they did at the end of the typing lesson. If people's sleep is interrupted during the specific cycle associated with this form of procedural memory, they will not perform better in the morning.

Gaining a memory depends on two processes. One is encoding the memory, or "getting it in there." The other is retrieval, or "getting it back out." We consider each briefly.

Encoding involves laying down the initial trace of a memory. Ideally, the way one encodes a memory will improve the chances of remembering it later, and this is an important emphasis of good instruction. There are a number of study techniques for improving memory. One class of strategies relies on the meaning of what one is trying to learn. For instance, connecting a new idea to a pre-existing idea improves encoding. If you are trying to learn a new phone number, it helps to find familiar mathematical patterns. Given 422-8888, one might improve the encoding of the phone number by thinking, "4 divided by 2 makes 2, and adding them up makes 8 of which there are 4 again." This works much better than just repeating the phone number, which is a recipe for forgetting as soon as one stops repeating the digits. In general, the depth of processing (Craik & Lockhart, 1972) and the relevance of elaboration (Stein & Bransford, 1979) predict the success of memory encoding. The more you think about a new idea and relate it to other ideas in meaningful ways, the better the chances of remembering it. It is as if you are laying down lots of neural roads, so it is easier to get back to the idea from other ideas. A second class of general encoding strategy—spaced practice—works regardless of the content of what one is learning (Cepeda et al., 2009). If one plans to work on memorizing words for a total of 10 minutes, it is better to use five separate sessions of 2 minutes each rather than one big session of 10 minutes. Cramming for a test is a bad way to create memories for a lifetime.

The second process of memory is retrieval, which involves bringing the memory back out. Retrieving a memory increases the chances of being able to retrieve it again later. A seminal demonstration comes from the "generation" effect (Slamecka & Graf, 1978). People received word pairs in one of two conditions. In the read condition, the words were presented completely, for instance, FAST : RAPID. In the generate condition, the words were presented as FAST: R_P_D. People knew the words had to be synonyms, and they could easily generate the missing letters to generate "rapid." People read or generated very many words. A short time later, they recalled as many of the words as possible. The generate condition remembered more of the words. One possible explanation is that the generate task required working a little harder to remember the word "rapid" during the task, which made subsequent retrieval a little easier. The importance of retrieval practice has resurfaced recently as the testing effect (Karpicke & Blunt, 2011). Taking a test, which requires retrieving memories, improves the chances of retrieving those memories later, for example, on a future test. Of course, the implication is not necessarily that students should take repeated tests, but rather, they should practice remembering what they know. If one wants to learn using flashcards, it is better to try to remember what is on the other side of the flashcard than just turning it over to see the answer.

With practice, the neural coordination of memories changes (McClelland, McNaughton, & O'Reilly, 1995). An example comes from children solving simple mental addition and subtraction problems. Behaviorally, children are very accurate at all ages, but they answer more quickly as they develop more experience with math facts. Figure 5.8 shows changes in brain activity with development (Rivera, Reiss, Eckert, & Menon, 2005).

The bottom panel highlights areas that decrease activity. As children gain experience, they do not rely on the prefrontal areas of the brain as much. Among other things, the prefrontal area is responsible for the deliberate control of processing. With experience, the children do not need to do as much deliberate control to help them put their memories together to come up with the answer. The top panel shows areas of the brain that become more active for the arithmetic tasks as children gain more experience. With experience, these parietal areas become responsible for holding the relevant memories, and children can access them directly with little deliberate effort. Tasks that once required flexible but cognitively costly executive control come to be executed by quickly retrieving stored memories (see also Chapter 19, this volume).

At the behavioral level, a clear case of memory transformation involves skill acquisition (Anderson, 1982). Acquiring skills involves a transition from declarative to procedural memory. Declarative memory refers to things you can say, and procedural memory refers to things that you do. Imagine that you are learning to change lanes while driving. At first, you followed declarative instructions—"check your blind spot, turn on your blinker, check your blind spot, turn the wheel . . . " With practice, you no longer needed to

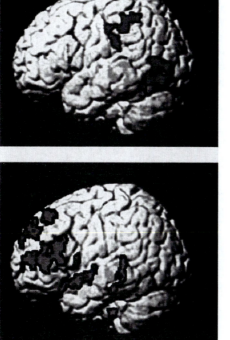

Increasing with development

Decreasing with development

**Figure 5.8** Changes in how the brain solves mental addition problems as children develop. The top panel shows that children increasingly rely on parietal regions to solve addition problems, and the bottom panel shows that they decreasingly rely on executive control from the prefrontal cortex to accomplish the tasks. (Adapted from Rivera, S. M., Reiss, A. L., Eckert, M. A., & Menon, V. (2005). Developmental changes in mental arithmetic: Evidence for increased functional specialization in the left inferior parietal cortex. *Cerebral Cortex*, *15*(11), 1779–1790. By permission of Oxford University Press.)

rely on these verbal memories. Instead, you developed procedural memory. You can tell because you do not need to talk to guide yourself through the steps. Instead, you can just execute them. After even more practice, these skills become automated. They require very little cognitive control or attention to execute. For instance, you can change lanes while also talking to your passenger. Because you do not need to pay attention to the skill execution, you can pay attention to talking. The way this works is that all the steps become "chunked" together so that one quickly leads to the next, and it requires little cognitive control to coordinate the transition from one step to another. They become one big step.

The transition from declarative to procedural memory has been an important guide for the design of many curricula. One of the most notable involves computerized "cognitive tutors" (Anderson, Corbett, Koedinger, & Pelletier, 1995). These intelligent computer programs track a student's progress. By monitoring how well the learner is performing on various tasks, it can infer whether the child has developed chunked procedural knowledge. If not, the program can back up to provide the student with relevant practice.

### Understanding and Analogy

A common objection to memory-focused models of instruction is that students may learn to recall or execute a skill, but they may not understand it. For instance, students who memorize math steps may not really *understand* what those math steps mean. But, what counts as "understanding?"

The definition of "understanding" has been a subject of philosophical investigation since at least the time of Socrates. In cognitive psychology, different investigators choose different ways to operationalize understanding that are most relevant to their topic of study. (The term "operationalize" means that one indicates which measureable behaviors provide evidence for a given mental state or process.) For instance, a researcher who studies mathematics learning may operationalize understanding as the ability to verbally justify the generality of a particular claim (does the operation of addition always make a greater total quantity?). A person who studies language acquisition may operationalize understanding as the ability to identify the referent of a word (given the word dog, point to the right thing). Thus, there is no single definition of understanding. Nevertheless, it has been possible to make important empirical advances.

One major advance has been the distinction between surface features and deep structures. A deep structure is a set of necessary relations that characterize what is the same across many instances (e.g., mammal: warm-blooded, hair). A surface feature is a property that may or may not be important (e.g., red hair). A classic example comes from Chi, Feltovich, and Glaser (1981). They had novices and experts categorize physics problems. Experts grouped spring and inclined-plane problems together, whereas novices did not. The experts identified that the problems shared the deep structure of being about potential energy. To the novices, these situations seemed completely different, because one involved springs and one involved inclined planes, which do not look alike.

In mathematics and science education, helping students learn the deep structure is important. A phenomenon's deep structure is typically what verbal principles and formulas describe.

Oftentimes, people rely on surface features while learning, and this causes them to miss the deep structure. In a telling study, students learned the probability formulas for computing combinations and permutations (Ross, 1987). (As a reminder, imagine pulling two chips from a bag of red and blue chips. There are three possible combinations: two reds, two blues, or one red and one blue. Permutations further consider the possible orderings: red → red, blue → blue, red → blue, blue → red.) In the study, the students learned to compute the number of combinations using marbles as the example, and they learned permutations using cars as the example. On the posttest, students received combination and permutation problems. They used the combination formula for problems about marbles—regardless of whether the problem called for finding combinations or permutations of marbles. Similarly, if a problem involved cars, the students used the permutation formula whether it was appropriate or not. The students had memorized the formulas just fine. The problem was that they relied on the surface features of the problems (e.g., cars or marbles) to decide which formula to use. They did not learn to recognize the deep structure of combinations and permutations, which holds up regardless of cars or marbles.

Analogies capitalize on the distinction between deep structure and surface features. Consider the abbreviated test question:

Deluge is to Droplet as:

(a) Landslide is to Pebble
(b) Cloudburst is to Puddle

Many people choose (b) as the answer, because it shares the surface feature of being about water. Answer (a) can be construed as a better answer because it shares the same deep structure as the prompt, which might be summarized as "many harmless events can accumulate into a disaster." Being able to work with the deep structure of a situation is one useful operationalization of understanding.

### Transfer and Induction—Where Understanding and Memory Work Together

Research on transfer highlights the importance of coordinating memory and understanding. Transfer refers to the use of prior learning in a new situation. Liberal education is predicated on the notion of transfer, because students learn in school, but they need to use this learning outside of school. In contrast, training-oriented instruction often does not need to consider issues of transfer. The application context typically shares the same surface and deep features as the original learning conditions. Training airline pilots in a simulator does not raise large transfer challenges, because the simulated cockpit is very similar to the cockpit of the plane; they share the same surface and deep features.

Transfer depends on the coordination of memory and understanding. For instance, in the preceding study, the students remembered the procedures for computing permutations and combinations. This was insufficient for effective transfer, however. They did not understand the deep structure of situations that call for the use of one or the other formula. Of course, had the students never memorized the procedures, they would not have had a formula to transfer either. How can we help students both memorize and understand?

One solution is to rely on inductive learning (Holland, Holyoak, Nisbett, & Thagard, 1986). Induction refers to the process by which people use multiple instances to create a new category or rule. (It contrasts with deduction, where people start with a rule or category, and determine what instances are possible.) Through induction, people may find the deep structure that unifies discrete memories and generalizes to new situations.

Discrete memories do not transfer well, because they typically apply to a single situation. For instance, memorizing $3 + 1 = 4$ will not help solve $4 + 1$. However, if people memorize that $3 + 1 = 4$, $4 + 1 = 5$, $5 + 1 = 6$, and so forth, they might induce the rule that "any number plus 1 equals the next number in order." Induction is an important way that people generalize from the instances they have encountered and go beyond the information given (Bruner, 1957).

People are always inducing patterns from their memories and experience. However, they may not induce what we consider most important. For instance, given the series of +1 problems above, a student might correctly but inappropriately induce, "this teacher really likes to give problems with a 1 in them." Through education, we want people to induce particular patterns that generalize well, not idiosyncratic ones. Learning through analogy is a powerful way to help people induce targeted understanding from a set of instances.

A classic study on learning from analogy clarifies the role of induction in coordinating memory and understanding for transfer. Gick and Holyoak (1983) tried to determine what would help people solve Duncker's radiation problem, short of giving them the answer. Here is the problem:

A patient has a tumor that needs to be irradiated. If the doctor uses a beam that is powerful enough to kill the tumor, it will kill healthy cells as it passes on the way to the tumor. If the doctor uses a radiation beam that is weak enough that it will not hurt healthy cells, then it will not kill the tumor. What can the doctor do?

*The answer: The doctor can use multiple weak beams from different angles that simultaneously converge on the tumor.*

To see what would help people solve this problem, the researchers constructed several analogs to the radiation problem. For example, in one analog, a general wanted to attack a fortress and had to split up his troops to converge from different angles so they would not be too heavy for any one bridge. In another, firefighters needed to use multiple bucket brigades to douse a fire. In some cases, the researchers also described the general principle, "Split up forces to converge on a central target." Given these elements, the researchers tried different combinations to see which ones would support transfer to the radiation problem.

**Table 5.1    The Effects of Induction and Explanation on
Transfer**

| Percent who Solved the Radiation Problem | Read Principle | Did not Read Principle |
|---|---|---|
| Received no analog | 28% | 18% |
| One analog | 32% | 29% |
| Two analogs | 62% | 52% |

Data from Gick and Holyoak (1983)

College students were randomly assigned to one of several conditions. One factor was the number of analogies included in the packet: zero, one, or two of the analogs (fortress and fire problems). A second factor was whether or not the packet included a statement of the principle. On the last page of all the packets was the radiation problem. Table 5.1 shows the percentage of students who solved the radiation problem at the end of the packet. (Students who received neither the analogs nor the principle received filler materials in their packet and served as the control condition.)

The most notable findings involve the first column. Students who were told the correct principle without receiving any examples did not transfer very well. One interpretation of this result might be that the students did not understand the principle without an example. However, students who received one analog (an example) plus the statement of the principle did not do much better. Why would a single example with a principle be ineffective for transfer? The principle indicated the deep structure of the problem, and the students had an example to help make sense of the principle. It cannot simply be that the students did not know the deep structure.

The students who received two examples (analogs) did much better, with or without a statement of the principle. (The students who received the two examples without the principle were often able to induce the principle from the two analogs, so they did not need to read the principle.) One possible reason that the single analog and the principle did not work very well is that students did not learn the range of variation that might appear for this particular principle. For example, those students who only learned about the story of attacking the fortress from multiple bridges, even with the statement of the principle, had no way of knowing that it can apply to lots of situations. The surface features, while incidental to the deep structure, are still important for transfer. Remembering variability of the surface features allows people to appreciate that the deep structure they understand can apply to many situations. Thus, memory of several instances and understanding work together, and one without the other does not work very well for transfer.

The value of coordinating memory and understanding for transfer yields some simple instructional prescriptions. Loewenstein, Thompson, and Gentner (2003) describe a study where they found that asking business students to find the analogous structure between case studies led to superior learning compared to a condition where students handled each case separately without looking for the common structure. Providing two analogous examples works well for transfer, but students need encouragement to induce the common deep structure that unifies otherwise discrete examples (Schwartz, Chase, Oppezzo, & Chin, 2011).

Despite the simplicity of helping students induce the deep structure across instances, there is an instructional tendency to use single examples plus a statement of the rule. Felder and Silverman (1988) noted that almost all engineering professors claim to use deductive instruction methods when teaching others—going from general rule statements to specific instantiations—even though they often themselves use inductive learning methods, proceeding from particulars to generalities. Additionally, people may neglect the potential of using analogies to support induction. In a review that compared instruction cross-nationally, Richland, Zur, and Holyoak (2007) found that U.S. teachers tended not to capitalize on the use of analogy compared to teachers in Hong Kong and Japan. Perhaps, by understanding how memory and understanding coordinate, educators will take more advantage of analogical induction.

## Concrete and Abstract

A long-standing distinction, at least since the time of Plato, is the dichotomy between concrete and abstract mental representations. The idea is that concrete thinking is tied to the perceptual-motor particulars of a situation, whereas abstract operations rise above immediate experience to use logical relations and hypothetical thinking. The dichotomy is relevant to instruction, because people often favor one over the other mode of operation. For example, in California, the state's science curriculum commission proposed legislation that would limit hands-on learning to "no more than 20 to 25 percent" of instructional time. This resulted in an outcry from educators and business people, and the final legislation reversed the proposal to "at least 20 to 25 percent" of science instruction using hands-on material (2004, www.cascience.org/csta/leg_criteria.asp).

A similar distinction between perception and abstraction occurs in intuitive frameworks for thinking about the brain: The brain is an information-processing system that takes in information from the senses and transforms it in different ways along a series of processing stages. The early stages of information processing are "low-level." For vision, these early stages would include extracting edges from a scene, creating contours for objects, determining stable colors not influenced by lighting conditions, and segregating objects from their backgrounds. "High-level" stages are further "downstream" in the flow of information processing, executed only after a considerable amount of sensory and perceptual processing has completed. High-level processes would involve cognitive actions such as inferring likely career choices of a friend, deciding where to search for an answer, and creating a new diagram for representing relations among cognitive functions.

The intuitive separation of low-level and high-level operations fuels many of the dichotomies found in education, such as Bloom's taxonomy. One key dichotomy might be represented as follows:

Perception ↔ Conception

As with all dichotomies, there is some truth to it. The brain is not a homogeneous lump. It is organized into spatially distinct modules with specialized functions. Some of the best-articulated modules are those dealing with perception, and these perceptual modules are often the first to be activated in response to a stimulus. In contrast, concepts do not need to be stimulus-driven. One can bring to mind the concept of "dog" without seeing or hearing a dog. Moreover, concepts have abstract and logical relations to other concepts, such as "not a cat."

Despite the important distinctions between concepts and percepts, they are not dichotomous. Gross anatomical considerations indicate a high degree of coordination between low-level perceptual processes and high-level conceptual processes. First, there are strong down-stream connections from perception to conception, so that stimulation of the perceptual system gives rise to relevant concepts. Second, there are also reciprocal up-stream connections from conceptual levels of analysis to the perceptual system (Lamme & Roelfsema, 2000). The tight integration is manifest when considering the time course of identifying an object such as a dog's tail. As stimulus information arrives from the senses, populations of neurons complete low-level analysis, such as edge detection, to extract important perceptual features. At 120 milliseconds, these neural populations operate similarly, regardless of whether one is explicitly paying attention to the object, and whether one has knowledge that there is a dog attached to the object. In this time window, the neurons are engaged in pre-attentive, unconscious perceptual processing. Yet, at 160 milliseconds, the same neural populations will respond to high-level information about where to pay attention and the knowledge of the context of the object (it is a dog). It is this latter activity that people consciously experience—"it is the tail of a dog" (Fahrenfort, Scholte, & Lamme, 2007). Thus, if one wants to know whether a neuron is "strictly perceptual," the answer depends on when one asks the question as much as it depends on which neuron is involved.

These broad considerations of neural architecture echo in the functional behavior of people. People adjust the processing of lower-level regions so that they are better adapted to the needs of higher-level cognition. Our perceptual systems are surprisingly adaptive, even late in life, and they typically adapt so that we can perform high-demand tasks more effectively (Fahle & Poggio, 2002).

The renowned philosopher Quine (1977) argued that advanced scientific thought must dispense with notions of perceptual similarity as the basis for its categories (see also Chapter 1, this volume). The argument seems plausible at first sight, and it has some similarity to the idea that understanding depends on finding deep relational structures rather than relying on surface features. Our perceptual systems might mislead us into believing that samples of fool's gold (pyrite) are true gold. Better to rely on the periodic table and the physical chemistry of the elements. There is a good deal of appeal to this argument. However, if one used the possibility of error as a reason to discard perception from scientific thinking, one would also have to throw out conception, because people's concepts are frequently wrong as well (e.g., McCloskey & Kohl, 1983). *It is the possibility of error that creates the possibility of learning and discovery.*

Fittingly, people can learn to perceive. Learning is not confined to abstract matters such as $F = ma$. Perception can be educated and augmented so it complements conceptual thinking. People can look for subtle properties that distinguish fool's gold from the real thing. People can supplement their biological perceptual apparatus with tools such as microscopes, hardness scales, and quantitative measurements of malleability.

Education and experience change the processing of the perceptual system (Goldstone, 1998). Some of these changes can occur in perceptual areas relatively early in the brain's information-processing stream. For instance, consider expert perception. Researchers measured the electrophysiological activity of dog and bird experts while they looked at pictures of dogs and birds (Gauthier, Tarr, & Bubb, 2010). For dog experts, enhanced electrical activity occurred 164 milliseconds after the presentation of dog, but not for a bird. Reciprocally, bird experts showed quick activation for bird pictures but not for photographs of dogs. This is an impressively fast processing effect of expertise given that transmitting a simple electrical signal from one end of a neuron to the other requires about 10 milliseconds. For brain evidence of experience-driven changes to perception, Furmanski, Schluppeck, and Engel (2004) used fMRI to measure brain activity before and after 1 month of practice with detecting hard-to-see lines. Practice increased responses in the primary visual cortex (area V1) and the degree of change correlated with detection performance. Bao, Yang, Rios, and Engel (2010) found changes in electrical activity as fast as 50–70 milliseconds after stimulus onset. Perception, even at the first stages of information uptake, can be educated. In fact, there is evidence that auditory training can produce differential responses in sensory receptors, such as the cochlea (Puel, Bonfils, & Pujol 1988), a sensory organ just inside of the eardrum. Perceptual changes are found at many different neural loci and a general rule seems to be that brain regions associated with early perceptual analysis are implicated in finer, more detailed, and generally less transferable knowledge (Ahissar & Hochstein, 1997).

Even learning abstract topics such as algebra can be improved by harnessing perceptual learning in instruction. A nice example comes from Kellman, Massey, and Son's (2010) perceptual learning modules. The algebra learning modules have high feedback and minimal explicit instruction. They try to develop students' sensitivity at noticing preserved structures in equations across algebraic transformations. For example, students are given trials on which they must determine that $6y - 17 = 32 - 5x$ is a valid transformation of $6y + 5x - 17 = 32$, but that neither $6y - 17 = 32 + 5x$ nor $6y - 17 = 32 - x - 5$ are. Although this kind of training might seem like "mere symbol pushing," the argument from perceptual learning is that by training students to see contrasts between valid and invalid algebraic transformations, they come to naturally perceive or induce the underlying structure of algebra.

Lawrence Barsalou has presented a particularly influential account of the grounding of conception in perception in the form of perceptual symbols theory (Barsalou, 1999).

By this account, conceptual knowledge involves activating brain areas dedicated for perceptual processing. When a concept is brought to mind, sensorimotor areas of the brain are reactivated. Even abstract concepts, such as truth and negation, may be grounded in complex perceptual simulations of combined physical and introspective events. Interestingly, Barsalou's research shows that when people engage in perceptual simulations, their understandings of a concept are likely to be richer and more flexible compared to when they do not. Reasoning based on perception is the "smart," not "stupid" stuff. This result is echoed by studies showing that students who show greater mathematical competence are more, not less, likely to engage in perceptual solutions to algebraic tasks (Goldstone, Landy, & Son, 2010). For example, students who exhibit relatively good mastery of mathematics are more likely to solve problems such as $x - 2 = 7$, by imagining the 2 moving from the left side of the equation to the right side, turning into a +2 as it does so. Rather than viewing perceptual processes as antagonistic to proper formal thought, it is precisely by properly executing these perceptual processes that formally sanctioned reasoning is achieved effectively.

A major challenge of school-based instruction is helping students coordinate the abstract, symbolic representations of culture with the perceptual world of experience. Glenberg, Gutierrez, Japuntich, and Kaschak (2004), for instance, noted that young readers often do not construct a mental model of what they are reading, but instead, they are just saying the words aloud. To help, the researchers had young children manipulate figurines to correspond with each sentence they read (e.g., "the man went into the barn"). They then told the children they should do this in their head when reading. This improved reading comprehension later, even when the children no longer manipulated figurines physically. An important challenge for an educationally relevant cognitive psychology is to develop new theories and evidence that helps guide fresh instructional efforts to coordinate perception, action, and conception (Goldin-Meadow & Beilock, 2010). Simply juxtaposing a concrete and abstract representation may not be sufficient for people to learn to coordinate their perceptual-motor abilities with their symbolic ones.

## Dichotomania

We have sampled a pair of familiar dichotomies. There are others. For instance, a common dichotomy is the distinction between passive versus active learning, which appears in the college instruction literature (e.g., Prince, 2004). Passive learning largely refers to sitting in a large lecture listening to a professor's exposition, whereas active learning refers to being engaged in problem solving during class. Dichotomies with family resemblances include learning by doing versus being told, as well as discovery learning versus direct instruction. The intuition that students can learn more effectively when they are experientially engaged, or at least not being crushed by tedious exposition, is worthwhile. At the same time, a tremendous amount of learning occurs through reading and hearing explanations, for example through mass media, the internet, and books. Experience and explanation each has its place. So again, the task is how to coordinate these different types of learning. Experiential activities can provide direct engagement of a phenomenon or problem, whereas lectures and readings can provide explanations of those experiences in ways that students are unlikely to discover on their own. On this model, one way to coordinate active and passive learning is to use active experience to create a time for telling (Schwartz & Bransford, 1998). For instance, Arena and Schwartz (2014) had students play a modified version of the arcade game Space Invaders that prepared them to then learn a formal treatment on statistical distributions. By itself, the game showed little direct benefit for learning, but when combined with a formal exposition, students learned more from the exposition than otherwise equivalent students who had not played the game.

What can we do about all these dichotomies? It may be useful to notice that many of the dichotomies make one of the poles of the dichotomy something construable as "true understanding." Rote memorization was contrasted with conceptual understanding. Attention to surface features was contrasted with attention to deep principles. Low-level perception was contrasted with high-level abstract reasoning. It is a recurrent motif to contrast the upper reaches of human thought with the lower capabilities shared by animals.

Overcoming dichotomania requires a more humble mindset. First, as we have proposed, what separates humans from animals is the ability to coordinate cognitive processes in concert with cultural demands and opportunities. Through this process of coordination, both the "bottom" and the "top" of cognition refashion one another. Humans are adaptive, and this should be the emphasis of our thinking about learning, not how one type of thinking is superior to another.

Second, it is important to appreciate that even true understandings are always partial and fragmentary. A noteworthy attitude shared by many accomplished scholars is their insistence on how much they, and we, do not yet understand. The dichotomous endpoint of "true understanding" is illusory, and a realization of this may yield a less disparaging attitude toward the purported opposite pole. True and complete understanding certainly has its attractions over more brittle and biologically constrained forms of intelligence, but the latter have the distinct advantage of actually existing.

As part of a more humble attitude towards posing dichotomies, one also needs an attitude towards becoming more knowledgeable. The acceptance of dichotomies presupposes fixed poles, when they may not be fixed but rather grow with respect to one another. Creating dichotomous categories may be an important first step in making intellectual advances; it is native to human thought (Smith & Sera, 1992). Nevertheless, one should avoid becoming a satyr and running away from opportunities to grow beyond the opposition.

In an analogous case, Carol Dweck (2012) has observed that people differ in their implicit views—their mindsets— about the origins of human ability. Some people with a "fixed" theory believe that ability is largely innate. In contrast, those with a "growth" theory believe that ability results from hard work. A "fixed" mindset has an analogous structure to dichotomania. A fixed mindset presupposes there are poles of "smart" and "not-so-smart" people, and there is no path from one to another. For dichotomania, one may feel that there are mutually exclusive cognitive processes, some being better than others, and with no bridge between.

Just as people who adopt a "growth" theory are more likely to achieve actual success, so our understanding of learning may be more successful if we adopt a growth theory. Such a perspective does not focus on the wide gap between the endpoints of putative dichotomies, but rather considers how different processes can be placed into productive relations. The point is to reflect not only on our lofty positions as intelligences capable of infinite flexibility, but also on how we can get to that point using finite means. By this account, properly harnessed and coordinated memory, perception, action, habit formation, and attention processes can grow into a well-organized system that we take as showing improved educational outcomes.

## Acknowledgment

The writing of this chapter was supported by the National Science Foundation under grant nos. SMA-0835854, EHR-0910218, as well as the Institute of Education Sciences, U.S. Department of Education R305A1100060. Any opinions, findings, and conclusions or recommendations expressed in this material are those of the authors and do not necessarily reflect the views of the granting agencies.

## References

Ahissar, M., & Hochstein, S. (1997). Task difficulty and the specificity of perceptual learning. *Nature, 387*, 401–406.

Anderson, J. R. (1982). Acquisition of cognitive skill. *Psychological Review, 89*, 369–406.

Anderson, J. R. (2000). *Cognitive psychology and its implications* (5th ed.). New York: Worth.

Anderson, J. R., Corbett, A. T., Koedinger, K., & Pelletier, R. (1995). Cognitive tutors: Lessons learned. *Journal of Learning Sciences, 4*, 167–207.

Arena, D. A., & Schwartz, D. L. (2014). Experience and explanation: Using videogames to prepare students for formal instruction in statistics. *Journal of Science Education and Technology, 23*, 538–548.

Bao, M., Yang, L., Rios, C., and Engel, S. A. (2010). Perceptual learning increases the strength of the earliest signals in visual cortex. *Journal of Neuroscience, 30*, 15080–15084.

Barron, B. J., Schwartz, D. L., Vye, N. J., Moore, A., Petrosino, A., Zech, L., Bransford, J. D., & CTGV. (1998). Doing with understanding: Lessons from research on problem- and project-based learning. *Journal of the Learning Sciences, 7*, 271–312.

Barsalou, L. W. (1999). Perceptual symbol systems. *Behavioral and Brain Sciences, 22*, 577–660.

Blair, K. P., Tsang, J. M., & Schwartz, D. L. (2013). The bundling hypothesis: How perception and culture give rise to abstract mathematical concepts in individuals. In S. Vosniadou (Ed.), *International handbook of research on conceptual change II* (pp. 322–340). New York: Taylor & Francis.

Bloom, B. S., Engelhart, M. D., Furst, E. J., Hill, W. H., & Krathwohl, D. R. (1956). *Taxonomy of educational objectives: Handbook I: Cognitive domain.* New York: David McKay.

Boroditsky, L. (2001). Does language shape thought? Mandarin and English speakers' conceptions of time. *Cognitive Psychology, 43*, 1–22.

Bransford, J. D., Brown, A. L., & Cocking, R. R. (2000). *How people learn: Brain, mind, experience, and school.* Washington, DC: National Academy Press.

Bransford, J. D., & Johnson, M. K. (1972). Contextual prerequisites for understanding: Some investigations of comprehension and recall. *Journal of Verbal Learning & Verbal Behavior, 11*, 717–726.

Bruner, J. S. (1957). Going beyond the information given. In H. Gruber, G. Terrell, & M. Wertheimer (Eds.), *Contemporary approaches to cognition* (pp. 258–290). Cambridge, MA: Harvard University Press.

Cepeda, N. J., Coburn, N., Rohrer, D., Wixted, J. T., Mozer, M. C., & Pashler, H. (2009). Optimizing distributed practice. *Experimental Psychology, 56*(4), 236–246.

Chi, M. T. H., Feltovich, P., & Glaser, R. (1981). Categorization and representation of physics problems by experts and novices. *Cognitive Science, 3*, 121–152.

Cochon, F., Cohen, L, van de Moortele, P. F., & Dehaene, S. (1999). Differential contributions of the left and right inferior parietal lobules to number processing. *Journal of Cognitive Neuroscience, 11*(6), 617–630.

Craik, F. I., & Lockhart, R. S. (1972). Levels of processing: A framework for memory research. *Journal of Verbal Learning and Verbal Behavior, 11*(6), 671–684.

Dehaene, S., & Cohen, L. (2007). Cultural recycling of cortical maps. *Neuron, 56*(2), 384–398.

Dehaene, S., Piazza, M., Pinel, P., & Cohen, L. (2003). Three parietal circuits for number processing. *Cognitive Neuropsychology, 20*(3/4/5/6), 487–506.

Dweck, C. S. (2012). *Mindset: How you can fulfill your potential.* London: Constable & Robinson.

Fahle, M., & Poggio, T. A. (2002). *Perceptual learning.* Cambridge, MA: MIT Press.

Fahrenfort, J., Scholte, H., & Lamme, V. (2007). Masking disrupts reentrant processing in human visual cortex. *Journal of Cognitive Neuroscience, 19*(9), 1488–1497.

Felder, R. M., & Silverman, L. K. (1988). Learning and teaching styles in engineering education. *Engineering Education, 78*, 674–681.

Feng, J., Spence, I., & Pratt, J. (2007). Playing an action video game reduces gender differences in spatial cognition. *Psychological Science, 18*(10), 850–855.

Furmanski, C. S., Schluppeck, D., and Engel, S. A. (2004). Learning strengthens the response of primary visual cortex to simple patterns. *Current Biology, 14*, 573–578.

Gauthier, I., Tarr, M. J., and Bubb, D. (Eds.) (2010). *Perceptual expertise: Bridging brain and behavior.* Oxford: Oxford University Press.

Gick, M. L., & Holyoak, K. J. (1983). Schema induction and analogical transfer. *Cognitive Psychology, 15*, 1–38.

Glenberg, A. M., Gutierrez, T., Levin, J. R., Japuntich, S., & Kaschak, M. P. (2004). Activity and imagined activity can enhance young children's reading comprehension. *Journal of Educational Psychology, 96*, 424–436.

Goldin-Meadow, S., & Beilock, S. L. (2010). Action's influence on thought: The case of gesture. *Perspectives on Psychological Science, 5*, 664–674.

Goldstone, R. L. (1998). Perceptual learning. *Annual Review of Psychology, 49*, 585–612.

Goldstone, R. L., & Hendrickson, A. T. (2010). Categorical perception. *Interdisciplinary Reviews: Cognitive Science, 1*, 65–78.

Goldstone, R. L., Landy, D. H., & Son, J. Y. (2010). The education of perception. *Topics in Cognitive Science, 2*, 265–284.

Griffin, S. A., Case, R., & Siegler, R. S. (1994). Rightstart: Providing the central conceptual prerequisites for first formal learning of arithmetic to students at risk for school failure. In K. McGilly (Ed.), *Classroom lessons: Integrating cognitive theory and classroom practice* (pp. 25–49). Cambridge, MA: MIT Press.

Harnad, S. (1997). *Categorical perception.* Cambridge: Cambridge University Press.

Hegarty, M., & Waller, D. (2005). Individual differences in spatial abilities. *The Cambridge handbook of visuospatial thinking* (pp. 121–169). New York: Cambridge University Press.

Hestenes, D., Wells, M., & Swackhamer, G. (1992). Force concept inventory. *The Physics Teacher, 30*(3), 141–158.

Holland, J. H., Holyoak, K. J., Nisbett, R. E., & Thagard, P. (1986). *Induction: Processes of inference, learning, and discovery.* Cambridge, MA: MIT Press.

Karpicke, J. D. & Blunt, J. R. (2011). Retrieval practice produces more learning than elaborate studying with concept mapping. *Science, 331,* 772–775.

Kellman, P. J., Massey, C. M., & Son, J. (2010). Perceptual learning modules in mathematics: Enhancing students' pattern recognition, structure extraction, and fluency. *Topics in Cognitive Science, 2,* 285–305.

Kirschner, P. A., Sweller, J., & Clark, R. E. (2006). Why minimal guidance during instruction does not work: An analysis of the failure of constructivist, discovery, problem-based, experiential, and inquiry-based teaching. *Educational Psychologist, 41*(2), 75–86.

Koedinger, K., Booth, J., & Klahr, D. (2013). Instructional complexity and the science to constrain it. *Science, 342* (6161), 935–937.

Lamme, V. A. F., & Roelfsema, P. R. (2000). The distinct modes of vision offered by feedforward and recurrent processing. *Trends in Neuroscience, 23,* 571–579.

Lee, K. (2000). Cortical areas differentially involved in multiplication and subtraction: A functional magnetic resonance imaging study and correlation with a case of selective acalculia. *Annals of Neurology, 48*(4), 657–661.

Loewenstein, J., Thompson, L., & Gentner, D. (2003). Analogical learning in negotiation teams: Comparing cases promotes learning and transfer. *Academy of Management Learning and Education, 2*(2), 119–127.

Lupyan, G. (2008). From chair to "Chair": a representational shift account of object labeling effects on memory. *Journal of Experimental Psychology: General, 137,* 348–369.

Mackey, A. P., Miller Singley, A. T., & Bunge, S. A. (2013). Intensive reasoning training alters patterns of brain connectivity at rest. *Journal of Neuroscience, 33*(11), 4796–4803.

Mayer, R. E. (1987). *Educational psychology: A cognitive approach.* Boston, MA: Little, Brown.

McClelland, J. L., McNaughton, B. L., & O'Reilly, R. C. (1995). Why there are complementary learning systems in the hippocampus and neocortex: Insights from the successes and failures of connectionist models of learning and memory. *Psychological Review, 102*(3), 419.

McCloskey, M., & Kohl, D. (1983). Naive physics: The curvilinear impetus principle and its role in interactions with moving objects. *Journal of Experimental Psychology: Learning, Memory, and Cognition, 9*(1), 146.

McDermott, R. (1993). Acquisition of a child by a Learning Disability. In S. Chaiklin & J. Lave (Eds.), *Understanding practice* (pp. 269–305). London: Cambridge University Press.

Medin, D. L., Lynch, E. B., & Solomon, K. O. (2000). Are there kinds of concepts? *Annual Review of Psychology, 51,* 121–147.

Pashler, H., Bain, P., Bottge, B., Graesser, A., Koedinger, K., McDaniel, M., & Metcalfe, J. (2007). *Organizing instruction and study to improve student learning (NCER 2007-2004).* Washington, DC: National Center for Education Research, Institute of Education Sciences, and U.S. Department of Education.

Pashler, H., McDaniel, M., Rohrer, D., & Bjork, R. (2009). Learning styles. *Psychological Science in the Public Interest, 9,* 105–119.

Prince, M. (2004). Does active learning work? A review of the research. *Journal of Engineering Education, 93*(3), 223–231.

Puel, J. L., Bonfils, P., & Pujol, R. (1988). Selective attention modifies the active micromechanical properties of the cochlea. *Brain Research, 447,* 380–383.

Quine, W. V. (1977). Natural kinds. In S. P. Schwartz (Ed.), *Naming, necessity, and natural kinds* (pp. 155–175). Ithaca, NY: Cornell University Press.

Richland, L. E., Zur, O., & Holyoak, K. J. (2007). Cognitive supports for analogies in the mathematics classroom. *Science, 316,* 1128–1129.

Rivera, S. M., Reiss, A. L., Eckert, M. A., & Menon, V. (2005). Developmental changes in mental arithmetic: Evidence for increased specialization in the left inferior parietal cortex. *Cerebral Cortex, 15*(5), 1779–1790.

Ross, B. H. (1987). This is like that: The use of earlier problems and the separation of similarity effects. *Journal of Experimental Psychology: Learning, Memory, and Cognition, 13,* 629–639.

Rumelhart, D. E., McClelland, J. L., & the PDP Research Group (Eds.) (1986). *Parallel distributed computing: Explorations in the microstructure of cognition. Volume 1: Foundations.* Cambridge, MA: MIT Press.

Scholz, J., Klein, M. C., Behrens, T. E., & Johansen-Berg, H. (2009). Training induces changes in white-matter architecture. *Nature Neuroscience, 12*(11), 1370–1371.

Schwartz, D. L., & Bransford, J. D. (1998). A time for telling. *Cognition & Instruction, 16,* 475–522.

Schwartz, D. L., Chase, C. C., Oppezzo, M. A., & Chin, D. B. (2011). Practicing versus inventing with contrasting cases: The effects of telling first on learning and transfer. *Journal of Educational Psychology, 103*(4), 759–775.

Skinner, B. F. (1986). Programmed instruction revisited. *Phi Delta Kappan, 68,* 103–110.

Slamecka, N. J., & Graf, P. (1978). The generation effect: Delineation of a phenomenon. *Journal of Experimental Psychology: Human Learning and Memory, 6,* 592–604.

Smith, L. B., & Sera, M. D. (1992). A developmental analysis of the polar structure of dimensions. *Cognitive Psychology, 24,* 99–142.

Steele, C. M. (1997). A threat in the air: How stereotypes shape intellectual identity and performance. *American Psychologist, 52*(6), 613–629.

Stein, B. S., & Bransford, J. D. (1979). Constraints on effective elaboration: Effects of precision and subject generation. *Journal of Verbal Learning and Verbal Behavior, 18*(6), 769–777.

Stickgold, R. (2005). Sleep dependent memory consolidation. *Nature, 437,* 1272–1278.

Stroop, J. R. (1935). Studies of interference in serial verbal reactions. *Journal of Experimental Psychology, 18*(6), 643–662.

Tobias, S., & Duffy, T. (Eds.) (2009). *Constructivist instruction: Success or failure.* New York: Routledge, Taylor & Francis.

Tsang, J. M., Dougherty, R. F., Deutsch, G. K., Wandell, B. A., & Ben-Shachar, M. (2009). Frontoparietal white matter diffusion properties predict mental arithmetic skills in children. *Proceedings of the National Academy of Science, 106,* 22546–22551.

Uddin, L. Q., Supekar, K., Amin, H., Rykhlevskaia, E., Nguyen, D. A., Greicius, M. D., & Menon, V. (2010). Dissociable connectivity within human angular gyrus and intraparietal sulcus: Evidence from functional and structural connectivity. *Cerebral Cortex, 20*(11), 2636–2646.

Varma, S., & Schwartz, D. L. (2011). The mental representation of integers: An abstract-to-concrete shift in the understanding of mathematical concepts. *Cognition, 121,* 363–385.

Vosniadou, S., & Brewer, W. F. (1992). Mental models of the earth: A study of conceptual change in childhood. *Cognitive Psychology, 24,* 535–585.

Woltz, D. J., Gardner, M. K., & Bell, B. G. (2000). Negative transfer errors in sequential cognitive skills: Strong-but-wrong sequence application. *Journal of Experimental Psychology: Learning, Memory, and Cognition, 26*(3), 601.

# 6

# Emotions and Emotion Regulation in Academic Settings

*Monique Boekaerts*
Leiden University, The Netherlands

*Reinhard Pekrun*
University of Munich, Germany

The classroom is an emotional place. Students frequently experience emotions such as enjoyment of learning, hope for success, pride in accomplishments, anger about task demands, fear of failing an exam, or boredom in academic settings. Research has shown that both traditional classroom instruction and advanced technology-based learning environments can induce a great variety of such emotions (D'Mello, 2013; Pekrun, Goetz, Titz, & Perry, 2002). Furthermore, the available evidence implies that these emotions are instrumental for achievement and personal growth. Experiencing positive emotions can help a student envision goals, promote creative problem solving, and support self-regulation (Clore & Huntsinger, 2009; Fredrickson, 2001). On the other hand, experiencing excessive negative emotions about studying and taking exams can impede academic performance, prompt school dropout, and negatively influence health (Zeidner, 1998, 2014). The far-reaching consequences of emotional experiences are also likely reflected in the tragic numbers of suicides related to school or college each year (Westefeld et al., 2005).

Despite the clear relevance of emotions for education and the dramatic increase of attention to emotion in other scientific disciplines, for a long time emotions have been neglected by educational psychology. Exceptions were studies on test anxiety (Zeidner, 1998) and on the role of causal attributions for achievement emotions (Weiner, 1985). Since the beginning of the 2000s, however, there has been growing recognition that emotions are central to academic achievement strivings as well as students' and teachers' personality development. Emotions are no longer viewed as incidental phenomena lacking in function or purpose. Rather, in this nascent research, emotions are recognized as being of critical importance for both students' and teachers' productivity (see Pekrun & Linnenbrink-Garcia, 2014; Schutz & Pekrun, 2007).

In this chapter, we consider such emotions. While the principles of emotion discussed in the chapter pertain to both students and teachers, the focus is on students' emotions (for teacher emotions, see Schutz & Zembylas, 2009). To begin, we define emotion and outline concepts of academic emotions. Next, we review research on the functions and origins of academic emotions. This review highlights the importance of emotions for students' learning. In the fourth section, we address emotion regulation (ER) and the role of emotional intelligence. In conclusion, implications for practice and suggestions for future research are discussed.

## Concepts of Academic Emotions

Emotions are typically defined as multifaceted phenomena involving sets of coordinated psychological processes, including affective, cognitive, physiological, motivational, and expressive components (Shuman & Scherer, 2014). For example, a student's anxiety before an exam can be comprised of nervous, uneasy feelings (affective); worries about failing (cognitive); increased heart rate (physiological); impulses to escape the situation (motivation); and an anxious facial expression (expressive). Emotion is part of the superordinate category of affect that is used for a variety of states, including emotion, moods, and metacognitive feelings. In comparison to intense emotions, *moods* are less intense and lack a specific object of reference. *Metacognitive feelings* such as feeling of knowing and feeling of confidence are judgments about one's progress in learning (Efklides, 2006).

### Valence, Activation, and Object Focus

Emotions can be grouped according to their *valence* and to their degree of *activation* (Table 6.1). In terms of valence, positive emotions can be distinguished from negative emotions, such as pleasant enjoyment versus unpleasant anxiety. In terms of activation, physiologically activating emotions can be distinguished from deactivating emotions, such as activating excitement versus deactivating relaxation. These two dimensions are used to arrange affective states in a two-dimensional space ("circumplex models" of affect; Barrett & Russell, 1998).

As addressed in Pekrun's (2006; Pekrun et al., 2002) three-dimensional taxonomy of emotions, another important dimension of emotions is their *object focus* (Table 6.1). In terms of object focus, the following groups of academic emotions can be distinguished.

*Achievement emotions.*    These emotions are tied to achievement activities (e.g., studying) or achievement outcomes (success and failure), resulting in two groups of achievement emotions: activity emotions and outcome emotions. Activity emotions include the ongoing emotions students experience while engaging in an achievement activity. Outcome emotions include both prospective emotions related to upcoming success and failure, and retrospective emotions related to past success and failure. Most emotions pertaining to studying, attending class, and taking tests or exams are considered achievement emotions, because they relate to activities and outcomes that are judged according to competence-based standards of quality.

*Epistemic emotions.*    Epistemic emotions pertain to the knowledge-generating qualities of cognitive tasks and activities. These emotions are triggered when students are engaged in novel, non-routine tasks, such as problem solving and research projects, and are promoted by unexpected information and cognitive incongruity. Examples are surprise, curiosity, excitement, confusion, wonder, frustration at unsolved problems, and joy of confirmation.

*Topic emotions.*    Topic emotions border on epistemic emotions, yet they are different in the sense that they do not refer to the comprehension process per se, but to the appealing effect that the learning material can have. Topic emotions allude to the themes that are dealt with in the learning material. For example, when the topic is the Middle Ages, some students may enjoy the stories of the fighting knights and sympathize with their cause, whereas others may feel disgusted by the blood-thirsty stories.

*Social emotions.*    Educational psychologists have long focused on individual performance rather than on collaborative learning. This narrow research focus may explain why social emotions in the classroom have been neglected. With the advent of social constructivist theories of learning, social emotions have been upgraded. Social emotions are particularly important in teacher–student and student–student interaction. Examples are love, sympathy, empathy, gratitude, compassion, anger, and social anxiety. Social and achievement emotions overlap in emotions that relate to the success and failure of others, such as admiration, envy, and contempt.

## Functions for Learning and Performance

In experimental research, moods and emotions have been found to influence a range of cognitive processes that are relevant to academic learning, such as attention, memory storage and retrieval, and problem solving (Lewis, Haviland-Jones, & Feldman Barrett, 2008). Much of this research, however, has focused on the effects of positive versus negative mood without drawing distinctions between specific, discrete mood states and emotions. This implies that it may be difficult and potentially misleading to use the findings to explain students' emotions and learning in real-world academic contexts. Specifically, as argued in Pekrun's (2006) cognitive/motivational model of emotion effects, it is not sufficient to differentiate positive from negative affective states, but imperative to also attend to the degree of activation implied. As such, the minimum necessary is to distinguish between four groups of emotions: positive activating, positive deactivating, negative activating, and negative deactivating (Table 6.1). For example, both anxiety and hopelessness are negative emotions; however, their effects on students' engagement can differ dramatically, as anxiety can motivate a student to invest effort in order to avoid failure, whereas hopelessness likely undermines any kind of engagement.

In the following sections, we first summarize research on the relation of emotions to different cognitive and motivational processes that are relevant to learning. We then outline implications for the effects of different emotions on students' academic achievement.

### Attention and Flow

Research has shown that both positive and negative emotional states consume attentional resources by focusing attention on the object of emotion (Ellis & Ashbrook, 1988). Consumption of attentional resources implies that fewer resources are available for task completion, thereby negatively impacting performance (Meinhardt & Pekrun, 2003). For example, while preparing for an exam, a student may worry about failure, which in turn may distract her attention

**Table 6.1    A Three-Dimensional Taxonomy of Academic Achievement Emotions**

| Object Focus | Positive[a] | | Negative[b] | |
| --- | --- | --- | --- | --- |
| | Activating | Deactivating | Activating | Deactivating |
| *Activity* | Enjoyment | Relaxation | Anger | Boredom |
| *Outcome* | Joy | Contentment | Anxiety | Sadness |
| | Hope | Relief | Shame | Hopelessness |
| | Gratitude | Pride | Anger | Disappointment |

[a] Positive = pleasant emotion.
[b] Negative = unpleasant emotion.

Adapted from Pekrun (2006).

away from the task. However, the resource consumption effect likely is bound to emotions that have task-extraneous objects and produce task-irrelevant thinking. By contrast, in positive task-related emotions such as curiosity and enjoyment of learning, the task is the object of emotion. In these emotions, attention is focused on the task, working-memory resources can be used for task completion, and experiences of flow are promoted. Corroborating these expectations, empirical studies with K-12 and university students found that negative emotions such as anger, anxiety, shame, boredom, and hopelessness were associated with task-irrelevant thinking and reduced flow, whereas enjoyment related negatively to irrelevant thinking and positively to flow (e.g., Pekrun, Goetz, Frenzel, Barchfeld, & Perry, 2011; Zeidner, 1998). These findings suggest that students' emotions have profound effects on their attentional engagement with academic tasks.

### Motivation to Learn

Emotions prepare us for doing something. For example, negative emotions such as fear are warning signals that arise in response to events that can have negative consequences. Each of the major negative emotions is thought to be associated with distinct action impulses and serves to prepare the organism for action (or non-action), such as fight, flight, and behavioral passivity in anger, anxiety, and hopelessness, respectively. For positive emotions, motivational consequences are less specific. Likely, one of the functions of positive emotions such as joy and interest is to motivate exploratory behavior and an enlargement of one's action repertoire, as addressed in Fredrickson's (2001) broaden-and-build metaphor of positive emotions. By implication, emotions can profoundly influence students' motivational engagement. Supporting this view, positive academic emotions such as enjoyment of learning, hope, and pride have been shown to relate positively to students' interest and intrinsic motivation, whereas negative emotions such as anger, anxiety, shame, hopelessness, and boredom related negatively to these motivational variables (Helmke, 1993; Pekrun et al., 2002, 2011; Zeidner, 1998, 2014).

However, as addressed in Pekrun's (2006) cognitive/motivational model of emotion effects, motivational effects may be different for different types of positive and negative emotions. The model posits that activating positive emotions (e.g., joy, hope, and pride) strengthen motivation, whereas deactivating negative emotions (e.g., hopelessness, boredom) undermine motivation (Pekrun, Goetz, Daniels, Stupinsky, & Perry, 2010). By contrast, effects are posited to be more complex for deactivating positive emotions (e.g., relief, relaxation) and activating negative emotions (e.g., anger, anxiety). For example, relaxed contentment following success can be expected to reduce immediate motivation to re-engage with learning contents but strengthen long-term motivation to do so. Regarding activating negative emotions, anger, anxiety, and shame have been found to reduce intrinsic motivation, but these emotions can strengthen extrinsic motivation to invest effort in order to avoid failure, especially so when

expectations to prevent failure and attain success are favorable (Turner & Schallert, 2001). Due to these variable effects, the impact of these emotions on students' overall motivation to learn can be variable as well.

### Memory Processes

Emotions influence storage and retrieval of information. Two effects that are especially important for the academic context are mood-congruent memory recall and retrieval-induced forgetting and facilitation. Mood-congruent recall (Parrott & Spackman, 2000) implies that mood facilitates the retrieval of like-valenced material, with positive mood facilitating the retrieval of positive self- and task-related information, and negative mood facilitating the retrieval of negative information. Mood-congruent recall can impact students' motivation. For example, positive mood can foster positive self-appraisals and thus benefit motivation to learn; by contrast, negative mood can promote negative-self appraisals and thus hamper motivation.

Retrieval-induced forgetting implies that practicing some learning material impedes later retrieval of related material that was not practiced, presumably so because of inhibitory processes in memory networks. Such forgetting occurs with learning material consisting of disconnected elements. For example, after learning a list of foreign-language words, practicing half of the list can impede students' memory for the other half. By contrast, retrieval-induced facilitation implies that practicing enhances memory for material that was not practiced (Chan, McDermott, & Roediger, 2006). Facilitation has been found to occur for connected materials consisting of elements that show strong interrelations. For example, after learning coherent text material, practicing half of the material leads to better memory for the non-practiced half.

Negative emotions can undo retrieval-induced forgetting, likely because they can inhibit spreading activation in memory networks which underlie such forgetting. Conversely, positive emotions can promote retrieval-induced facilitation since they promote the relational processing of information underlying such facilitation (Kuhbandner & Pekrun, 2013). This suggests that negative emotions can be helpful for learning lists of unrelated material, such as lists of foreign-language vocabulary, whereas positive emotions should promote learning of coherent material.

### Problem Solving, Learning Strategies, and Self-Regulation of Learning

Mood has been shown to influence cognitive problem solving, with positive mood promoting flexible and creative ways of solving problems, and negative mood promoting more rigid, detail-oriented, and analytical ways of thinking (Clore & Huntsinger, 2009; Fredrickson, 2001). Mood-as-information approaches (Clore & Huntsinger, 2009) explain this finding by assuming that positive affective states signal that "all is well," implying safety and the discretion to engage in creative exploration, broaden one's cognitive horizon, and build new actions. By contrast, negative states are thought to indicate that something is going wrong, making it necessary to focus on problems in more cautious, analytical ways.

Judging from the experimental evidence, positive activating emotions such as enjoyment of learning should facilitate use of flexible, holistic learning strategies like elaboration and organization of learning material or critical thinking. Negative emotions, on the other hand, should sustain more rigid, detail-oriented learning, like simple rehearsal of learning material. Correlational evidence from studies with university students generally supports this view (Pekrun et al., 2002, 2011). However, for deactivating positive and negative emotions, these effects may be less pronounced. Deactivating emotions, like relaxation or boredom, may produce shallow information processing rather than any more intensive use of strategies (Pekrun et al., 2010).

Furthermore, given that self-regulation of learning requires cognitive flexibility, positive emotions can foster self-regulation, whereas negative emotions can motivate the individual to rely on external guidance. Correlational evidence is generally in line with these propositions (Linnenbrink & Pintrich, 2002; Pekrun et al., 2002, 2010, 2011). However, the reverse causal direction may also play a role in producing such correlations—self-regulated learning may instigate enjoyment, and external directions for learning may trigger anxiety.

### Academic Achievement

Since many different cognitive and motivational mechanisms can contribute to the functional effects of emotions, the overall effects on students' academic achievement are inevitably complex and may depend on the interplay between different mechanisms. Nevertheless, it seems possible to derive inferences from the existing evidence.

***Positive emotions.*** Traditionally it was assumed that positive emotions, notwithstanding their potential to foster creativity, are often maladaptive for achievement due to inducing unrealistically positive appraisals, fostering non-analytical information processing, and making effort expenditure seem unnecessary by signaling that everything is going well. From this perspective, "our primary goal is to feel good, and feeling good makes us lazy thinkers who are oblivious to potentially useful negative information and unresponsive to meaningful variations in information and situation" (Aspinwall, 1998, p. 7).

However, as noted, positive mood has typically been regarded as a unitary construct in experimental research. As argued earlier, such a view is inadequate because it fails to distinguish between activating versus deactivating moods and emotions. As detailed in Pekrun's (2006) cognitive/motivational model, *deactivating* positive emotions, like relief or relaxation, may well have the negative performance effects described for positive mood, whereas *activating* positive emotions, such as task-related enjoyment, should have positive effects. The evidence cited above suggests that activating enjoyment focuses attention on the task; induces intrinsic motivation; promotes relational memory processing; and facilitates use of flexible learning strategies and

self-regulation, thus likely exerting positive effects on overall performance under many task conditions. By contrast, deactivating positive emotions, such as relief and relaxation, can reduce task attention; can have variable motivational effects; and can lead to superficial information processing, thus likely making effects on overall achievement more variable.

The available evidence supports the view that activating positive emotions can enhance achievement. Specifically, enjoyment of learning was found to correlate moderately positively with K-12 and college students' academic performance (Helmke, 1993; Pekrun et al., 2002, 2011). Furthermore, students' enjoyment, hope, and pride correlated positively with college students' interest, effort invested in studying, elaboration of learning material, and self-regulation of learning, in line with the view that these activating positive emotions can be beneficial for students' academic agency. Consistent with evidence on discrete emotions, general positive affect has also been found to correlate positively with students' cognitive engagement (Linnenbrink, 2007). However, some studies have found null relations between activating positive emotions (or affect) and achievement (Linnenbrink, 2007; Pekrun, Elliot, & Maier, 2009). Also, caution should be exercised in interpreting the reported correlations. Linkages between emotions and achievement are likely due not only to performance effects of emotions, but also to effects of performance attainment on emotions, implying reciprocal rather than unidirectional causation (Pekrun, Hall, Goetz, & Perry, 2014).

***Negative activating emotions.*** Emotions such as anger, anxiety, and shame produce task-irrelevant thinking, thus reducing cognitive resources available for task purposes, and they undermine students' intrinsic motivation. On the other hand, these emotions can induce motivation to avoid failure and facilitate the use of more rigid learning strategies. By implication, the effects on resulting academic performance depend on task conditions and may well be variable, similar to the proposed effects of positive deactivating emotions. The available evidence supports this position.

Specifically, it has been shown that anxiety impairs performance on complex or difficult tasks that demand cognitive resources, such as difficult intelligence test items, whereas performance on easy and less complex tasks may not suffer or is even enhanced (Zeidner, 1998). In line with experimental findings, field studies have shown that test anxiety correlates moderately negatively with students' performance. Typically, 5–10% of the variance in students' achievement scores is explained by self-reported anxiety (Hembree, 1988; Zeidner, 1998). Again, in explaining the correlational evidence, reciprocal causation of emotion and performance has to be considered. Linkages between test anxiety and achievement may be caused by effects of success and failure on the development of test anxiety, in addition to effects of anxiety on achievement. The scarce longitudinal evidence available suggests that test anxiety and students' achievement are in fact linked by reciprocal causation across school years (Meece, Wigfield, & Eccles, 1990; Pekrun, 1992). Furthermore, zero and positive correlations have sometimes been found, in line with our view that anxiety can exert ambiguous effects. Anxiety likely has deleterious effects in many students, but it may facilitate overall performance in those who are more resilient and can productively use the motivational energy provided by anxiety.

Similar to anxiety, shame related to failure showed negative overall correlations with college students' academic achievement and negatively predicted their exam performance (Pekrun et al., 2002, 2011). However, as with anxiety, shame likely exerts variable effects (Turner & Schallert, 2001). Similarly, while achievement-related anger correlated negatively with academic performance in a few studies (Boekaerts, 1993; Pekrun et al., 2011), the underlying mechanisms may imply more than just negative effects. In a study by Lane, Whyte, Terry, and Nevill (2005), depressed mood interacted with anger occurring before an academic exam, such that anger was related to improved performance in students who reported no depressive mood symptoms—presumably because they were able to maintain motivation and invest effort. In sum, the findings for anxiety, shame, and anger support the notion that performance effects of negative activating emotions are complex, although relationships with overall performance are negative for many task conditions and students.

***Negative deactivating emotions.*** In contrast to negative activating emotions, negative deactivating emotions, such as boredom and hopelessness, are posited to uniformly impair performance by reducing cognitive resources, undermining both intrinsic and extrinsic motivation, and promoting superficial information processing (Pekrun, 2006). The little evidence available corroborates that boredom and hopelessness relate uniformly negatively to students' achievement, in line with theoretical expectations (Ahmed, van der Werf, Kuyper, & Minnaert, 2013; Pekrun et al., 2010, 2011, 2014).

In sum, theoretical expectations, the evidence produced by experimental studies, and findings from field studies imply that students' emotions have profound effects on their engagement and academic achievement. As such, administrators and educators should pay attention to the emotions experienced by students. Most likely, the effects of students' enjoyment of learning are beneficial, whereas hopelessness and boredom are detrimental for engagement. The effects of emotions like anger, anxiety, or shame are more complex, but for the average student, these emotions also have negative overall effects.

## Origins and Development of Emotions

Given that emotions affect students' learning and achievement, it is important to acquire knowledge about their antecedents. The emotions that students experience in the classroom are affected by a multitude of factors, including genetic dispositions, gender, early socialization, cognitive appraisals, achievement goals, personality traits (e.g., temperament, achievement motives), and the learning environment (Pekrun & Linnenbrink-Garcia, 2014). Herein, we focus on cognitive appraisals and academic environments as

antecedents and summarize evidence on the development of students' emotions over the school years.

### Cognitive Appraisals

***Test anxiety.*** In research on test anxiety, appraisals concerning threat of failure have been addressed as causing anxiety. Using R. S. Lazarus's transactional stress model (Lazarus & Folkman, 1984) to explain test anxiety, threat in a given achievement setting is evaluated in a primary appraisal related to the likelihood and subjective importance of failure. If failure is appraised as possible and subjectively important, ways to cope with the situation are evaluated in a *secondary appraisal*. A student may experience anxiety when his primary appraisal indicates that failure on an important test is likely, and when his secondary appraisal indicates that this threat is not sufficiently controllable. Empirical research confirms that test anxiety is closely related to perceived lack of control over performance. Specifically, numerous studies have shown that K-12 and postsecondary students' self-concept of ability, self-efficacy expectations, and academic control beliefs correlate negatively with their test anxiety (Zeidner, 1998, 2014).

***Attributional theory.*** Extending the perspective beyond test anxiety, B. Weiner (1985; Graham & Taylor, 2014) proposed an attributional approach to the appraisal antecedents of emotions related to success and failure. In Weiner's theory, causal achievement attributions—explanations about the causes of success and failure (e.g., ability, effort, task difficulty, luck)—are considered primary determinants of these emotions. More specifically, it is assumed that achievement outcomes are first subjectively evaluated as success or failure. This outcome appraisal immediately leads to cognitively less elaborated, "attribution-independent" emotions, namely, happiness following success, and frustration and sadness following failure. Following the outcome appraisal and immediate emotional reaction, causal ascriptions are sought that lead to differentiated, attribution-dependent emotions.

Three dimensions of causal attributions are assumed to play key roles in determining attribution-dependent emotions: the perceived locus of causality differentiating internal versus external causes of achievement (e.g., ability and effort vs. environmental circumstances or chance); the perceived controllability of causes (e.g., subjectively controllable effort vs. uncontrollable ability); and the perceived stability of causes (e.g., stable ability vs. unstable chance). Weiner posits that pride should be experienced when success is attributed to internal causes (e.g., effort or ability); that shame should be experienced when failure is attributed to uncontrollable, internal causes (e.g., lack of ability); and that gratitude and anger should be experienced when success or failure, respectively, is attributed to external, other-controlled causes. Consistent with the retrospective nature of causal attributions for success and failure, Weiner's theory focuses primarily on retrospective emotions following success and failure. However, some predictions for prospective, future-related emotions are also put forward. Specifically, hopefulness and hopelessness are expected to be experienced when past success and failure are attributed to stable causes (e.g., stable ability). Empirical research has generally supported these propositions (Graham & Taylor, 2014).

***Control-value theory.*** While test anxiety theories and attributional theories have addressed emotions pertaining to success and failure outcomes, they have neglected activity-related achievement emotions. In Pekrun's (2006; Pekrun & Perry, 2014) control-value theory of achievement emotions, propositions of the transactional stress model (Lazarus & Folkman, 1984), expectancy-value approaches (Pekrun, 1992; Turner & Schaller, 2001), and attributional theories are expanded to explain a broader variety of achievement emotions, including both outcome emotions and activity emotions. The theory posits that achievement emotions are induced when an individual feels in control of, or out of control of, activities and outcomes that are subjectively important—implying that appraisals of control (i.e., perceived controllability) and value (i.e., perceived importance) are the proximal determinants of these emotions.

Different kinds of control and value appraisals are posited to instigate different kinds of achievement emotions (Table 6.1). *Prospective, anticipatory joy and hopelessness* are expected to be triggered when there is high perceived control (joy) or a complete lack of perceived control (hopelessness). For example, a student who believes she has the necessary resources to get an A on an important exam may feel joyous about the prospect of seeing this grade becoming reality. Conversely, a student who believes he is incapable of preventing failure on a final exam may experience hopelessness. *Prospective hope and anxiety* are instigated when there is uncertainty about control, the attentional focus being on anticipated success in the case of hope and on anticipated failure in the case of anxiety. For example, a student who is unsure about being able to succeed may hope for success, fear failure, or both. *Retrospective joy and sadness* are considered control-independent emotions that immediately follow success and failure (in line with Weiner's, 1985, propositions). *Disappointment and relief* are thought to depend on the perceived match between expectations and the actual outcome: disappointment arises when anticipated success does not occur, and relief when anticipated failure does not occur. Finally, *pride, shame, gratitude, and anger* are assumed to be instigated by causal attributions of success and failure to oneself or others, respectively.

Furthermore, the control-value theory proposes that these outcome-related emotions also depend on the subjective importance of achievement outcomes, implying that they are a joint function of perceived control and value. For instance, a student should feel worried if she judges herself incapable of preparing for an exam (low controllability) that is important (high value). By contrast, if she feels that she is able to prepare successfully (high controllability) or is indifferent about the exam (low value), her anxiety should be low.

Regarding activity emotions, *enjoyment of achievement activities* is proposed to depend on a combination of positive competence appraisals and positive appraisals of the intrinsic value of the action (e.g., studying) and its reference object (e.g., learning material). For example, a student is expected to enjoy learning if she feels competent to meet the demands of the learning task and values the learning material. If she feels incompetent, or is uninterested in the material, studying is not enjoyable. *Anger and frustration* are aroused when the intrinsic value of the activity is negative (e.g., when working on a difficult project is perceived as taking too much effort which is experienced as aversive). Finally, *boredom* is experienced when the activity lacks any intrinsic incentive value (Pekrun et al., 2010).

Empirical studies have confirmed that perceived control over achievement relates positively to achievement-related enjoyment, hope, and pride, and negatively to anger, anxiety, shame, hopelessness, and boredom, in university students (e.g., Pekrun et al., 2002, 2011; Turner & Schallert, 2001) and middle- and high-school students (e.g., Buff, 2014). Similar links have been observed for emotions in online learning environments (Daniels & Stupnisky, 2012). Furthermore, several of these studies have shown that the perceived value of achievement related positively to both positive and negative achievement emotions except boredom, indicating that the importance of success and failure amplifies these emotions. For boredom, negative links with perceived value have been found, suggesting that boredom is reduced when individuals value achievement (Pekrun et al., 2010). Finally, recent research has confirmed that control and value interact in the arousal of achievement emotions, with positive emotions being especially pronounced when both control and value are high, and negative emotions being pronounced when value is high but control is lacking (e.g., Goetz, Frenzel, Stoeger, & Hall, 2010).

## The Influence of Academic Environments

The impact of learning environments on students' emotions is largely unexplored, except research on the antecedents of test anxiety (Zeidner, 1998, 2014). Classroom composition, the design of classroom instruction and exams, as well as goal structures, expectancies, and reactions in students' social environments have been found to play a significant role in students' anxiety.

***Classroom composition.*** The ability level of the classroom determines the likelihood of performing well relative to one's classmates. All things being equal, chances for performing well in the classroom are higher in low-ability classrooms, thus students' self-concepts of ability tend to be higher in low-ability classrooms. By implication, it may be preferable to be a "big fish in a little pond" rather than being a member of a classroom of gifted students (Marsh, 1987). Since negative self-evaluations of competence can trigger anxiety of failure, the "big-fish-little-pond" effect of classroom ability level on self-concept can prompt similar effects on students' anxiety. In fact, students' test anxiety has been found to be higher in high-ability classrooms than in low-ability classrooms (e.g., Preckel, Zeidner, Goetz, & Schleyer, 2008).

*Classroom instruction and exams.* Lack of structure and clarity in classroom instruction as well as excessive task demands are associated with students' elevated test anxiety (Zeidner, 1998, 2014). These links are likely mediated by students' expectancies of low control and failure (Pekrun, 1992). This also applies to exams, whereby lack of structure and transparency has been shown to contribute to students' anxiety (e.g., lack of information regarding demands, materials, and grading practices). Furthermore, the format of test items has been found to be relevant (Zeidner, 1998). For instance, open-ended formats (e.g., essay questions) induce more anxiety than multiple-choice formats, because open-ended formats require more attentional resources. As noted, these resources may be compromised as a result of anxiety-induced worrying, resulting in more experienced threat and debilitating performance in anxious students. The use of multiple-choice formats can reduce these effects. In addition, practices such as permitting students to choose between test items, relaxing time constraints, and giving second chances in terms of opportunities to retake a test have been found to reduce test anxiety, presumably so because perceived control and achievement expectancies are enhanced under these conditions.

Beyond anxiety, a handful of studies have investigated relationships between classroom instruction and students' positive emotions. For example, teacher-centered instruction that emphasizes rigid drilling and exercise has been found to relate negatively to students' positive emotional attitudes toward school and enjoyment of task accomplishment (e.g., Valeski & Stipek, 2001). In contrast, the cognitive quality of instruction in terms of structure and clarity, and tasks oriented towards creative mental modeling as opposed to algorithmic routine procedures, have been found to correlate positively with students' enjoyment of learning mathematics (Pekrun et al., 2007). In addition, support for students' learning-related autonomy correlated positively with students' enjoyment in this study. Finally, teachers' own enjoyment and enthusiasm during teaching have been found to relate positively to students' enjoyment, suggesting transmission of positive emotions from teachers to students (Frenzel, Goetz, Lüdtke, Pekrun, & Sutton, 2009).

*Goal structures and social expectations.* Different standards for defining achievement can imply individualistic (mastery), competitive (normative), or cooperative goal structures in the classroom (Johnson & Johnson, 1974). The goal structures provided in achievement settings conceivably influence emotions in two ways. First, to the extent that students adopt these structures, they influence individual achievement goals and any emotions mediated by these goals (e.g., Roeser, Midgley, & Urdan, 1996). Second, goal structures determine relative opportunities for experiencing success and perceiving control, thus influencing control-dependent emotions. Specifically, competitive goal structures imply that some students have to experience failure, thus inducing negative outcome emotions such as anxiety in these students. In line with this reasoning, empirical research has shown that competition in classrooms is positively related

to students' test anxiety (Zeidner, 1998). Similarly, teachers' and parents' excessively high expectations for achievement can reduce students' sense of control, thus also contributing to negative emotions such as anxiety, shame, and hopelessness (Pekrun, 1992).

By contrast, a cooperative classroom climate and social support provided by parents and teachers often fail to correlate with students' test anxiety scores (Hembree, 1988). This surprising lack of correlation may result from well-meaning teachers and parents whose attempts to support students actually increase pressure to perform, thus counteracting any beneficial effects of support. Alternatively, there may be negative-feedback loops between support and anxiety, with social support alleviating anxiety (negative effect of support on anxiety), but anxiety provoking support in the first place (positive effect of anxiety on demanding support), thus negating any correlation between the two variables.

*Feedback and consequences of achievement.* Cumulative success can strengthen perceived control, and cumulative failure can undermine control. In environments involving frequent assessments, performance feedback is likely of primary importance for the arousal of achievement emotions (Pekrun, Cusack, Murayama, Elliot, & Thomas, 2014). In addition, the perceived consequences of success and failure are important, because these consequences affect the value of achievement outcomes. Positive outcome emotions (e.g., hope for success) can be increased if success produces beneficial long-term outcomes (e.g., acceptance to an esteemed university), provided there is sufficient contingency between one's own efforts, success, and these outcomes. Negative consequences of failure (e.g., unemployment), on the other hand, may increase achievement-related anxiety and hopelessness (Pekrun, 1992).

### Development Across the School Years

Emotions related to achievement evolve early and show continuous development across the life span. Between 2–3 years of age, children are able to express pride and shame when successfully solving tasks or failing to do so, suggesting that they are able to differentiate internal versus external causation of success and failure. During the early elementary school years, children additionally acquire capabilities to distinguish between different types of internal and external causes, such as ability and effort, to develop related causal expectancies, and to cognitively combine expectancies, attributions, and value-related information (Heckhausen, 1991). By implication, students have developed the cognitive competencies to experience all major types of academic emotions early in their educational career.

Empirical evidence on the development of these emotions in school is scarce. Again, test anxiety studies are an exception. These studies have shown that average scores for test anxiety are low at the beginning of elementary school, but increase dramatically during the elementary-school years (Hembree, 1988). This development is congruent with the decline in academic self-concepts and intrinsic motivation during this period, and is likely due to increasing realism in academic self-perceptions and to the cumulative failure feedback students may receive across the school years. After elementary school, average anxiety scores stabilize and remain at high levels throughout middle school, high school, and college. However, stability at the group level notwithstanding, anxiety can change in individual students, for example, when there are transitions between schools and classrooms (Zeidner, 1998).

Whereas anxiety increases in the average student, positive emotions such as enjoyment of learning seem to decrease across the elementary-school years (Helmke, 1993). The decrease of enjoyment can continue through the middle-school years (Pekrun et al., 2007), which is consistent with the decline of average scores for subject matter interest and general attitudes toward school (e.g., Fredricks & Eccles, 2002). Important factors responsible for this development may be an increase of teacher-centered instruction and academic demands in middle school, competition between academic and non-academic interests in adolescence, and the stronger selectivity of subject matter interest that is part of adolescent identity formation.

## Emotion Regulation and Emotional Intelligence

ER involves goal-directed processes aiming to influence the intensity, duration, and type of emotion experienced (Jacobs & Gross, 2014). It allows the individual to respond in flexible ways to situational demands while taking account of short-term and long-term goals and concerns. Boekaerts (2011) defined ER in the context of the classroom as students' capacity to use their emotions as a source of energy, yet modify aspects of the emotional experience when it interferes with the pursuit of important goals. She emphasized that the inability to temper the intensity and duration of one's emotional arousal in the classroom not only hinders learning but social functioning as well. Having access to adequate ER strategies helps students to feel self-efficacious and view the learning process as constructive, and the classroom environment as supportive. As such, ER is based on individual competencies to manage and use one's emotions. "Emotional intelligence" is a summary term often used to denote these competencies. In this section, we address ER, the link between ER and self-regulated learning, and emotional intelligence.

### Emotion Regulation

Research has indicated that emotions can be regulated in a variety of ways. We will use the distinction of problem-focused versus emotion-focused coping as well as Gross's process model of ER to describe different strategies to regulate emotions.

### Emotion-focused versus problem-focused coping. Coping researchers (e.g., Lazarus & Folkman, 1984) have distinguished between problem-focused strategies which involve attempts to alter a stressor, and emotion-focused strategies which attempt to directly change the emotion. Examples of problem-focused coping in educational settings include situation selection, working hard, and seeking help; examples of emotion-focused coping include reappraisal, self-talk, using humor, distraction, relaxation, wishful thinking, self-blame, acting up, distancing, suppression, withdrawal, and self-handicapping (Boekaerts & Röder, 1999).

Boekaerts (1999) reported that students made use of both problem-oriented and emotion-oriented coping in response to interpersonal stressors such as being bullied, whereas they primarily selected problem-focused strategies in relation to academic stressors. Compas, Malcarne, and Fondacaro (1988) reported that adolescent girls used more emotion-focused strategies in response to academic stressors than boys. They showed that both problem-focused and emotion-focused coping strategies reduced negative emotions, provided that there was a match between the students' perception of control over the situation and the selected coping strategy. Perception of control matched with problem-focused strategies, and perception of low control with emotion-focused strategies. This finding suggests that students need to pick up cues informing them whether an academic task or an interpersonal conflict is controllable or not. Next, they should select a strategy from their coping repertoire that is compatible with the degree of control they experience. Pekrun et al. (2002) confirmed that both coping strategies may successfully diminish emotional stress. Students' anxiety during an important exam was positively related to cortisol levels indicating stress-related activation; problem-focused as well as emotion-focused coping during the exam reduced the level of cortisol.

Selecting a coping strategy is not a one-shot process (Boekaerts, 2011). In stressful situations, students may experience an urgent need to feel better right away, even though they may also have the intention to resolve the problem. This goal ambivalence will be reflected in the succession of coping strategies that are used. For example, Boekaerts (1999) reported that students who experienced intense stress in relation to interpersonal stressors, such as being called names by peers, used a double-focused coping strategy. The students realized that it is important to use problem-focused coping (e.g., confronting the aggressor), yet they felt a desire to opt out of the situation to protect their ego (walking away, mental distraction). In other words, problem-oriented and emotion-oriented regulatory goals competed for dominance in the coping process.

### Gross's process model of emotion regulation. Gross (Gross and John, 2002; Jacobs & Gross, 2014) proposed a process model of ER that highlights the time course of regulation. The model is based on a sequence of processes that are involved in an emotion episode (situation, attention, appraisal, and response: Figure 6.1). Each of these processes is a potential target for ER. Gross identified five families of ER strategies, namely situation selection, situation modification, attentional deployment, cognitive change, and response modulation. The first four of these categories apply before the individual has appraised the situation, hence before the

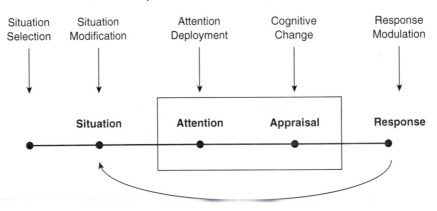

**Figure 6.1** Gross's process model of emotion regulation.

full-blown emotional response occurs, which can make these strategies especially adaptive. Herein we address strategies that are particularly relevant for academic settings, including situation selection and modification, cognitive change, and response modulation (for an extension of Gross's model also considering competence-oriented strategies, see Pekrun, 2006).

*Situation selection.* Situation selection involves choosing situations that minimize the risk to be confronted with an emotional stressor (e.g., failure, threat, loss) and maximize the chances to strengthen one's positive emotions. In the classroom, students may not always be able to select learning situations. Yet, if they understand what the antecedents of their emotions are, they may try to organize their learning in such a way that they have the best chances for mastery and protect their ego at the same time. For example, if teachers allow their students to decide on different types of instruction (e.g., teacher-regulated learning vs. self-regulated learning) or different task assignment (e.g., easy versus difficult exercises), students can make choices that promote their adaptive emotions.

*Situation modification.* This group of strategies involves efforts to intervene in the physical, social, and instructional environment so as to change its emotional impact. Situation modification is an important strategy in the classroom because it may allow students to solicit social and instructional support. For example, a student may ask his teacher to change the seating arrangement so that he sits next to a friendlier peer, or to supply extra exercises that will allow him to practice deficient skills.

Students need metacognitive, metaemotional, and metainterpersonal knowledge to select and modify situations (Boekaerts, 2011). Lack of such knowledge is one barrier to effective selection and modification. Another barrier is weighing short-term benefits of situation selection versus longer-term costs. For example, students may feel better if they can postpone a difficult situation (e.g., preparing for a test) and abandon strategies that take effort, and may be ignorant that such short-term benefits come at the cost of failing an exam.

*Cognitive change.* Cognitive change refers to modifying one's appraisal of the situation so that it changes its emotional impact (reappraisal). For example, Gross and John (2002) described how athletes and musical performers interpret their physiological arousal prior to going on stage. Some performers interpreted the arousal as stage fright, which may have a debilitating effect, whereas others viewed it as getting pumped up, which may have a performance-enhancing effect. Lazarus and Folkman (1984) described reappraisal as changing perceptions of the significance of the situation or one's ability to manage situational demands (e.g., "Is it really such a problem as I originally thought it was?"; "I was able to stand my ground last time, why would I not be able to do it this time?"). Another way to achieve cognitive change is by comparing one's own skills with those of relevant peers (e.g., "If I fail, more than half of the class should fail too"). Gross and John (2002) asserted that reappraisal is positively linked to self-efficacy, positive mood, sharing emotions, and negatively to negative affect, implying that it can be advantageous for learning.

*Response modulation.* Emotions can be regulated by influencing the psychological, physiological, and behavioral responses that are part of emotion. Response modulation occurs late in the emotion episode, after response tendencies have been initiated. For example, students who experience tension and bodily symptoms before taking an important test may try to tone down the physiological aspects of anxiety (e.g., increased heart rate, trembling hands) and its psychological symptoms (e.g., worry, feelings of uncertainty) by taking drugs, smoking, drinking, or by practicing relaxation techniques.

Expressive suppression is a response-focused strategy that aims to prevent the emotional response from being observed. Gross and Thompson (2007) reported that instructions to suppress one's emotions while viewing emotion-arousing videos successfully decreased expressive behavior, but increased rather than decreased sympathetic arousal. Baumeister (2005) explained that suppression requires continuous monitoring, which taxes cognitive resources. Students who were requested to control their emotions gave up faster on a successive task than those who were not requested to do so. Suppression impeded task engagement and persistence unless the spent energy was restored. Gross and John (2003) compared ER strategies and confirmed that habitual use of reappraisal is linked to greater positive affect, better interpersonal functioning, and higher well-being, whereas suppression is associated with a less beneficial profile of emotional functioning.

Rather than hiding emotions, students may express them verbally or non-verbally. The advantage of emotion expression is that attention is called to what one feels, which may contribute to modifying the situation by changing the behavior of others. For example, peers may become more mindful to what a student feels when she shows her disappointment.

*Explicit versus implicit emotion regulation.* Explicit ER requires conscious effort for initiation, demands monitoring during implementation, and is associated with some level of insight and awareness, whereas implicit ER is evoked automatically by the stimulus itself, runs to completion without monitoring, and can happen without insight and awareness (Gyurak, Gross, & Etkin, 2011). The strategies people use to regulate their emotions vary in explicitness over time and across situations. For example, a student who gets upset when the physics teacher makes a cynical remark about his performance may remind himself that on Mondays the teacher resents coming to work. This reappraisal may automatically reduce his irritation on Mondays. Gyurak et al. (2011) maintained that, through repeated use, explicit if-then implementation plans for ER strategies become habitual, involuntary responses that are used with little awareness, similar to the routinization of cognitive appraisals described earlier.

Gross and Thompson (2007) argued that it is the interplay between explicit and implicit processing that makes ER adaptive. Explicit ER can successfully change emotional responses, but it requires extensive monitoring and hence uses considerable resources. Under conditions of high cognitive load, explicit ER and task-related information processing may compete for the same limited processing resources. Specifically, down-regulating negative emotions requires resources that may be depleted when the emotions to be regulated are frequent and intense (Baumeister, Zell, & Tice, 2007). By contrast, implicit regulation involves less load and is often more reliable (Bargh & Williams, 2007).

### Emotion Regulation and Self-regulated Learning: Boekaerts' Dual Processing Model of Self-regulation

Successful ER is an essential aspect of self-regulated learning. Students often experience a dilemma between doing what is expected and will lead to positive learning outcomes in the long term and satisfying immediate needs in order to feel good right away. This dilemma is at the heart of self-regulation: it illustrates that the interaction between top-down and bottom-up self-regulation does not always run smoothly. Boekaerts and colleagues (e.g., Boekaerts & Niemivirta, 2000) described top-down self-regulation as behavior that is driven by the students' own values and goals. It is contrasted with bottom-up self-regulation, which refers to data-driven

processing of environmental cues in the actual situation that may create a mismatch with the students' own goals and trigger emotions.

The adaptable learning model, which later evolved into the dual processing self-regulation model, describes the dynamic aspects of self-regulated learning and offers a theoretical scaffold for understanding the findings from diverse psychological frameworks, including motivation, emotion, and learning (Figure 6.2). The critical features of Boekaerts' self-regulation model are non-stop cognitive appraisals and their concomitant emotions. The model posits that students try to achieve a balance between two main goal priorities, namely mastery strivings (activity in the mastery pathway, symbolized by broken lines in Figure 6.2) and keeping their well-being within reasonable bounds (well-being pathway: dotted lines). The model postulates further that cognitive appraisals—based on actual perceptions and activated cognitive and affective domain-specific information brought into working memory—are triggered when students are first confronted with a learning activity (see top half of Figure 6.2) and that these cognitions are the proximal determinants of prospective, anticipatory positive and negative emotions, learning intention, and coping intention.

Seegers and Boekaerts (1996) tested these assumptions in the mathematics domain. They provided empirical support that the effects of domain-specific beliefs on learning

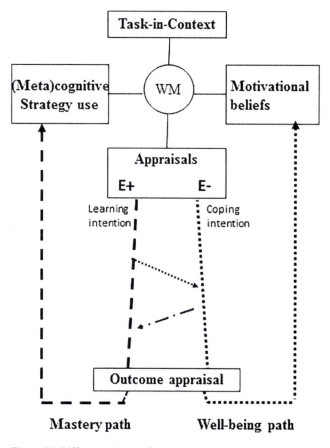

**Figure 6.2** Different pathways of Boekaerts' dual processing self-regulation model: activity in the mastery pathway (– –), activity in the well-being pathway ( . . . ) and connecting pathways using emotion regulation strategies ( . . . ) and volitional strategies (–.. –.. –).

intention, emotions, and actual task performance are mediated by prospective anticipatory appraisals (subjective competence, success expectation, perception of difficulty, personal relevance, and task attraction). Using confirmatory factor analysis, Crombach, Boekaerts, and Voeten (2003) substantiated these findings for mathematics and other subject matter domains and showed that the tested model was stable over a half-year period.

Boekaerts (2006) described how appraisals and emotions direct and redirect the focus of attention in the self-regulation system. Attention is directed to the learning activity itself (mastery pathway) when appraisals and emotions are dominantly positive (implying that working memory capacity as well as (meta)cognitive strategies are used to improve learning outcomes). By contrast, attention is directed away from the task when appraisals and emotions are dominantly negative. At that point, students are more concerned with well-being than with learning, and task-irrelevant scenarios are activated from long-term memory to regulate emotions (coping).

Boekaerts and Corno (2005) described two types of bottom-up self-regulation strategies that students use to stay on task, namely ER strategies and volition strategies. The former strategies, which are called for when students experience emotions that interfere with the learning task, dampen the emotional arousal and make switches between the pathways more probable. The latter strategies, also called good work habits, help students to protect their learning intention when difficult work must be completed, and to re-route activities from the well-being to the mastery route.

The dual processing self-regulation model posits that students who know how to deal with emotions during the learning process will have higher achievement than students who do not have access to ER strategies. Punmongkol (2009) tested this assumption. She asked math teachers to train senior primary-school students in the use of ER strategies and found that these students were better able to reduce their negative emotions. In addition, their mathematics course grades improved significantly, especially when this training was given in concert with metacognitive training in mathematics. Boekaerts (2010) argued that accessible ER and volition strategies act in tandem and function something like the switching track of a railway system. They turn all other lights to red to keep students on the mastery track or re-route them toward goals that make striving for mastery more feasible.

### Emotional Intelligence

The generation and regulation of emotions depend on individual competencies to produce, recognize, evaluate, increase or decrease, and make use of one's own emotions. As such, a broad variety of cognitive and non-cognitive abilities comprise an individual's emotional competencies. The term "emotional intelligence" is often used to denote these diverse abilities (Allen, MacCann, Matthews, & Roberts, 2014). This may imply an overinclusive use of the term "intelligence," which is commonly used to denote cognitive rather than non-cognitive abilities. Further adding to

conceptual ambiguity, authors such as Goleman (1995) and Bar-On (1997) used the term to denote an even broader array of individual dispositions, including various kinds of trait-like variables that can relate to an individual's emotional agency, such as assertiveness, self-regard, empathy, social responsibility, happiness, and optimism (for a critique, see Matthews, Zeidner, & Roberts, 2002). Conceptions of this kind seem more similar to concepts of personality than to a circumscribed set of competencies related specifically to emotion.

Given that emotions affect students' performance, and that the regulation of these emotions depends on emotional competencies, measures of emotional intelligence should be able to predict academic achievement over and above IQ or prior achievement. The existing evidence only partially supports this expectation (e.g., Amelang & Steinmayr, 2006; Di Fabio & Palazzeschi, 2009).

### Recommendations for Practice

What can teachers and parents do to foster students' adaptive emotions and prevent maladaptive emotions? As noted, research on academic emotions is clearly at a nascent stage. In deriving practical recommendations, it should be kept in mind that cumulative evidence exists for students' test anxiety, whereas the evidence for academic emotions other than anxiety is still quite limited. By necessity, evidence-based recommendations to date primarily pertain to influencing students' anxiety, whereas recommendations for emotions other than anxiety are less firmly based on empirical findings. Nevertheless, a number of implications for psychological and educational practice can be derived. Specifically, students' emotions can be influenced by shaping tasks and learning environments in adequate ways and by using principles of social and emotional learning programs. Furthermore, in the case of more severe individual problems, therapy can be used to improve students' academic well-being (Zeidner, 1998).

### Task Design, Teacher Behavior, and Learning Environments

It is the responsibility of educators and administrators to shape school environments to foster students' academic development and health, including their emotional approaches to learning. The following groups of factors may be especially important to consider.

***Cognitive quality of instruction and task assignments.*** Raising the cognitive quality of instruction in terms of clarity, structure, and high-quality examples should promote students' learning and sense of control, thus positively influencing their emotions. The same applies to task assignments. For example, from an affective perspective, cognitively activating material is preferable to less activating material (e.g., mathematical modeling tasks versus algorithmic tasks involving technical routine procedures). Furthermore, the level of task demands is important as well. Task demands influence students' chances for mastery and resulting emotions. Moreover, the relative match between demands and individual capabilities can influence students' valuing of the material. If demands are too high or too low, perceived value can be reduced to the extent that boredom is experienced (Pekrun, 2006).

Cognitive quality and task demands are also critically important to instigate epistemic emotions. Tasks should imply demands that can ultimately be met by students, yet simultaneously challenge their existing cognitive schemas. This should result in the arousal of surprise, curiosity, and productive confusion, possibly prompting conceptual change (D'Mello, Lehman, Pekrun, & Graesser, 2014).

***Motivational quality of instruction and task assignments.*** The control-value theory (Pekrun, 2006) proposes that positive values of academic engagement and achievement should be fostered, and negative values should be prevented, in order to facilitate adaptive emotions. Teachers, parents, and peers deliver direct, verbal messages about academic values, as well as more indirect messages conveyed by their behavior. Two important ways to foster students' academic values include the following. First, the development of values can be promoted by shaping instructional material, assigned tasks, and classroom interaction such that they meet students' needs (Deci & Ryan, 1987). Examples are authentic learning tasks and classroom discourse that engage all students such that needs for social relatedness are met. Second, by way of observational learning and emotional contagion, teachers' own enthusiasm in dealing with academic material likely facilitates students' absorption of values and positive emotions (Frenzel et al., 2009; Turner, Meyer, Midgley, & Patrick, 2003). However, to be effective, it likely is important that enthusiasm is openly displayed, and that displayed enthusiasm is congruent with experienced emotion rather than just being enacted in superficial ways. Apart from value appraisals, competence appraisals that coincide with positive emotions will promote effort investment and positive outcome appraisals (Boekaerts, 2010).

***Autonomy support and self-regulation.*** Learning environments that create demands to engage in self-regulated learning can also promote positive emotions. Self-regulation can take place at the individual or group level (individual vs. cooperative learning). As argued earlier, when the learning environment affords opportunities for self-regulated learning, and when students perceive themselves as capable of regulating their learning, positive emotions (e.g., enjoyment) should be increased for at least two reasons. First, students can fulfill their need for autonomy and increase their sense of personal control (Deci & Ryan, 1987). As compared to individual learning, cooperative self-regulated learning has the additional advantage of serving students' social needs, which may also contribute to their appreciation of academic engagement. Second, students can select and organize learning material to meet their individual interests, thus increasing the subjective value of the course and course material.

However, an important requirement for self-regulated learning to be emotionally effective is that students are in fact competent to self-direct their learning. If students are unable to regulate their learning, negative emotions may be promoted due to perceived loss of control, thus highlighting the need to fine-tune the affordances and constraints of these learning environments to students' regulatory capabilities.

***Goal structures, grading practices, and achievement expectations.*** The goal structures of the classroom define students' opportunities to attain success and avoid failure (Johnson & Johnson, 1974). In *individualistic* goal structures, achievement is defined by individual competence gain (individual standard of evaluation) or by mastery of the learning material (absolute standard). Under such structures, individual achievement is independent of other students' attainment, meaning that all students can attain success provided that sufficient progress is made. By contrast, in *competitive* goal structures, achievement is defined by normative social comparison standards, making individual achievement dependent on the relative attainment of others. In competitive structures, the achievement of different students is negatively linked, because success of some students implies failure of others. By implication, only some students may expect success, while others must expect failure. *Cooperative* goal structures imply that achievement is defined by the performance of the group, meaning that attainment is positively linked across individuals.

Different goal structures give students different opportunities to experience success. For the average student, opportunities for perceived control may be higher under individualistic and cooperative goal structures, as compared with competitive structures. By implication, although competitive structures can be enjoyable for high-achieving students (Frenzel, Pekrun, & Goetz, 2007), their average emotional effects are likely less beneficial. Accordingly, teachers should refrain from using social comparison standards to assess student achievement. Specifically, this applies to high-stakes assessments that can have dramatic emotional consequences due to making important consequences contingent on achievement. Grading based on social comparison may be necessary for purposes of placement and selection, implying that the goals of fostering students' emotions and gathering information on their performance may conflict. However, to the extent that assessments aim to serve teaching and learning rather than selection purposes, criterion-oriented grading pertaining to mastery of the learning material is likely more recommendable.

Teachers', parents', and peers' individual *achievement expectations* can operate in similar ways as the overall goal structures applied to the classroom. These expectations provide definitions of success and failure, thus influencing students' perceived control and their emotions. To promote perceptions of control and positively impact the resulting emotions, expectations should not exceed students' capabilities.

***Design of tests and exams.*** Drawing on test anxiety research, measures that increase perceived control and decrease the importance of failure can be beneficial. These measures include: (a) providing structure and transparency regarding task demands, materials, exam procedures, and grading practices; (b) avoiding excessively high task demands; (c) relaxing time constraints; (d) giving students a choice between tasks; (e) giving students second chances in terms of retaking tests; (f) providing external aids, such as access to lecture notes, text books, or computers; and (g) using closed-item formats to ease working memory load (Zeidner, 1998, 2014). Naturally, some of these measures also have disadvantages. For example, using only multiple-choice items may reduce anxiety, but may preclude the use of item formats better suited to assess deep-level thinking and creative problem solving. As such, educational measures to reduce students' anxiety should be counterbalanced in the context of multiple educational goals.

***Consequences of performance.*** Regarding the value of academic success and failure for future outcomes (e.g., career opportunities), it should prove helpful to highlight connections between students' academic effort and the attainment of future prospects. Effort–outcome associations of this type can increase students' perceived control and interest (Hulleman & Harackiewicz, 2009), thus strengthening positive and reducing negative future-related emotions (Pekrun, 2006). To the contrary, should future desired outcomes not be contingent upon students' effort, then students may experience reduced perceived subjective control and increased negative prospective emotions like anxiety or hopelessness.

***Emotional scaffolding, social and emotional learning, and treatment.*** Students may experience negative emotions or a lack of positive emotions in class and may find it difficult to regulate them. At such a point support from their teacher in terms of external ER and emotional scaffolding can be helpful. Yet, Hyson, Copple, and Jones (2006) observed that only one-third of preschool teachers spent time talking about feelings. As argued by Boekaerts (2010), it may be difficult for the teacher to provide appropriate emotional support. Students may differ in the type of emotional support they expect, and teachers may lack knowledge of how to provide such support. For improving the situation, using principles of SEL programs may be helpful. These programs have been developed to support students' ER skills more generally but could be used to also improve their emotional situation at school (see Brackett & Rivers, 2014). Teaching students how to anticipate emotionally challenging situations and how to prepare for regulating these situations may be especially important in this respect (Punmongkol, 2009).

## Directions for Future Research

As outlined in this chapter, research on students' emotions in academic settings has been slow to emerge. During the past 15 years, however, there has been an increase of studies examining the nature of students' emotions (Pekrun & Linnenbrink-Garcia, 2014). These studies have produced new insights demonstrating that emotions profoundly affect students' engagement, achievement, and identity, which also

implies that they are of critical importance for the agency of educational institutions and of society at large. At the same time, however, the studies conducted thus far seem to pose more new, challenging questions than they can answer. Theories, strategies, and measures for analyzing these emotions have yet to be fully developed. Also, to date studies are too scarce to allow any meta-analytic synthesis based on cumulative evidence, or any firm conclusions informing practitioners in validated ways how to deal with emotions, evidence on test anxiety being an exception. The progress made so far is promising, but much more has to be done if research on academic emotions is to evolve over the next years in ways benefiting education and society. Important challenges include the need for more cross-cultural research, the need to integrate perspectives from affective neuroscience into emotion research in educational psychology, and the need to set up intervention studies that examine how students can acquire ER strategies. We also need a more fine-grained analysis of the interactions between discrete emotions in the classroom as well as longitudinal studies to document the development of students' theory of emotion in connection with their evolving theory of ER and the impact of these theories on student's engagement and learning.

## Acknowledgment

The writing of this chapter was supported by a Ludwig Maximilian University Research Chair grant awarded to Reinhard Pekrun by the University of Munich.

## References

Ahmed, W., van der Werf, G., Kuyper, H., & Minnaert, A. (2013). Emotions, self-regulated learning, and achievement in mathematics: A growth curve analysis. *Journal of Educational Psychology, 105,* 150–161.

Allen, V., MacCann, C., Matthews, G., & Roberts, R. D. (2014). Emotional intelligence in education: From pop to emerging science. In R. Pekrun & L. Linnenbrink-Garcia (Eds.), *International handbook of emotions in education* (pp. 162–182). New York: Taylor & Francis.

Amelang, M., & Steinmayr, R. (2006). Is there a validity increment for tests of emotional intelligence in explaining the variance of performance criteria? *Intelligence, 34,* 459–468.

Aspinwall, L. (1998). Rethinking the role of positive affect in self-regulation. *Motivation and Emotion, 22,* 1–32.

Bargh, J. A., & Williams, L. E. (2007). The nonconscious regulation of emotion. In J. J. Gross (Ed.), *Handbook of emotion regulation* (pp. 429–445). New York: Guilford Press.

Bar-On, R. (1997). *The Emotional Intelligence Inventory (EQ-I): Technical manual.* Toronto, Canada: Multi-Health Systems.

Barrett, L. F., & Russell, J. A. (1998). Independence and bipolarity in the structure of current affect. *Journal of Personality and Social Psychology, 74,* 967-984.

Baumeister, R. F. (2005). *The cultural animal: Human nature, meaning, and social life.* New York: Oxford University Press.

Baumeister, R. F., Zell, A. L., & Tice, D. M. (2007). How emotions facilitate and impair self-regulation. In J. J. Gross (Ed.), *Handbook of emotion regulation* (pp. 408–427). New York: Guilford Press.

Boekaerts, M. (1993). Anger in relation to school learning. *Learning and Instruction, 3,* 269–280.

Boekaerts, M. (1999). Coping in context: Goal frustration and goal ambivalence in relation to academic and interpersonal goals. In E. Frydenberg (Ed.). *Learning to cope: Developing as a person in complex societies* (pp. 175–197). Oxford: Oxford University Press.

Boekaerts, M. (2006). Self-regulation and effort investment. In E. Sigel & K. A. Renninger (Vol. Eds), *Handbook of child psychology* (Vol. 4, pp. 345–377). New York: Wiley.

Boekaerts, M. (2010). Motivation and self-regulation: Two close friends. In T. C. Urdan & S. A. Karabenick (Eds.), *The decade ahead: Applications of motivation and achievement. Advances in motivation and achievement* (Vol. 16b, pp. 69–108). Bingley, UK: Emerald.

Boekaerts, M. (2011). Emotions, emotion regulation, and self-regulation of learning. In B. Zimmerman & D. Schunk (Eds.), *Handbook of self-regulation of learning and performance* (pp. 408–425). London: Routledge.

Boekaerts, M., & Corno, L. (2005). Self-regulation in the classroom: A perspective on assessment and intervention. *Applied Psychology: An International Review, 54,* 199–231.

Boekaerts, M., & Niemivirta, M. (2000). Self-regulated learning: Finding a balance between learning goals and ego-protective goals. In M. Boekaerts, P. R. Pintrich, & M. Zeidner (Eds.), *Handbook of self-regulation* (pp. 417–450). San Diego, CA: Academic Press.

Boekaerts, M., & Röder, I. (1999). Stress, coping, and adjustment in children with a chronic disease: A review of the literature. *Disability and Rehabilitation, 21,* 311–337.

Brackett, M. A., & Rivers, S. E. (2014). Transforming students' lives with social and emotional learning. In R. Pekrun & L. Linnenbrink-Garcia (Eds.), *International handbook of emotions in education* (pp. 368–388). New York: Taylor & Francis.

Buff, A. (2014). Enjoyment of learning and its personal antecedents: Testing the change–change assumption of the control-value theory of achievement emotions. *Learning and Individual Differences, 31,* 21–29.

Chan, C. K., McDermott, K. B., & Roediger, H. L. (2006). Retrieval induced facilitation: Initially nontested material can benefit from prior testing. *Journal of Experimental Psychology: General, 135,* 533–571.

Clore, G. L., & Huntsinger, J. R. (2009). How the object of affect guides its impact. *Emotion Review, 1,* 39–54.

Compas, B. E., Malcarne, V. L., & Fondacaro, K. (1988). Coping with stressful events in older children and adolescents. In L. A. Bond & B. E. Compas (Eds.), *Primary prevention and promotion in the schools* (pp. 319–340). Newbury Park: Sage.

Crombach, M. J., Boekaerts, M., & Voeten, M. J. M. (2003). Online measurement of appraisals of students faced with curricular tasks. *Educational and Psychological Measurement, 63*(1), 96–111.

Daniels, L. M., & Stupnisky, R. H. (2012). Not that different in theory: Discussing the control-value theory of emotions in online learning environments. *Internet and Higher Education, 15,* 222–226.

Deci, E. L., & Ryan, R. M. (1987). The support of autonomy and the control of behavior. *Journal of Personality and Social Psychology, 53,* 1024–1037.

Di Fabio, A., & Palazzeschi, L. (2009). An in-depth look at scholastic success: Fluid intelligence, personality traits or emotional intelligence? *Personality and Individual Differences, 46,* 581–585.

D'Mello, S. (2013). A selective meta-analysis on the relative incidence of discrete affective states during learning with technology. *Journal of Educational Psychology, 105,* 1082–1099.

D'Mello, S., Lehman, B., Pekrun, R., & Graesser, A. (2014). Confusion can be beneficial for learning. *Learning and Instruction, 29,* 153–170.

Efklides, A. (2006). Metacognition and affect: What can metacognitive experiences tell us about the learning process? *Educational Research Review, 1,* 3–14.

Ellis, H. C., & Ashbrook, P. W. (1988). Resource allocation model of the effect of depressed mood states on memory. In K. Fiedler & J. Forgas (Eds.), *Affect, cognition, and social behavior* (pp. 25–43). Toronto: Hogrefe International.

Fredricks, J. A., & Eccles, J. (2002). Children's competence and value beliefs from childhood through adolescence: Growth trajectories in two male-sex-typed domains. *Developmental Psychology, 38,* 519–533.

Fredrickson, B. L. (2001). The role of positive emotions in positive psychology: The broaden-and-build theory of positive emotions. *American Psychologist, 56,* 218–226.

Frenzel, A. C., Goetz, T., Lüdtke, O., Pekrun, R., & Sutton, R. E. (2009). Emotional transmission in the classroom: Exploring the relationship between teacher and student enjoyment. *Journal of Educational Psychology, 101,* 705–716.

Frenzel, A. C., Pekrun, R., & Goetz, T. (2007). Perceived learning environment and students' emotional experiences: A multi-level analysis of mathematics classrooms. *Learning and Instruction, 17,* 478–493.

Goetz, T., Frenzel, A. C., Stoeger, H., & Hall, N. C. (2010). Antecedents of everyday positive emotions: An experience sampling analysis. *Motivation and Emotion, 34,* 49–62.

Goleman, D. (1995). *Emotional intelligence.* New York: Bantam.

Graham, S., & Taylor, A. Z. (2014). An attributional approach to emotional life in the classroom. In R. Pekrun & L. Linnenbrink-Garcia (Eds.), *International handbook of emotions in education* (pp. 96–119). New York: Routledge.

Gross, J. J., & John, O. P. (2002). Wise emotion regulation. In L. F. Barrett & P. Salovey (Eds.), *The wisdom of feelings: Psychological processes in emotional intelligence* (pp. 297–318). New York, NY: Guilford Press.

Gross, J. J., & John, O. P. (2003). Individual differences in two emotion regulation processes: Implications for affect, relationships, and well-being. *Journal of Personality and Social Psychology, 85,* 348–362.

Gross, J. J., & Thompson, R. A. (2007). Emotion regulation: Conceptual foundations. In J. J. Gross (Ed.), *Handbook of emotion regulation* (pp. 3–26). New York, NY: Guilford Press.

Gyurak, A., Gross, J. J., and Etkin, A. (2011). Explicit and implicit emotion regulation: A dual-process framework. *Cognition and Emotion, 25,* 400–412.

Heckhausen, H. (1991). *Motivation and action.* New York: Springer.

Helmke, A. (1993). Die Entwicklung der Lernfreude vom Kindergarten bis zur 5. Klassenstufe [Development of enjoyment of learning from kindergarten to grade 5]. *Zeitschrift für Pädagogische Psychologie, 7,* 77–86.

Hembree, R. (1988). Correlates, causes, effects, and treatment of test anxiety. *Review of Educational Research, 58,* 47–77.

Hulleman, C. S., & Harackiewicz, J. M. (2009). Promoting interest and performance in high school science classes. *Science, 326*(5958), 1410–1412.

Hyson, M., Copple, C., & Jones, J. (2006). Early child development and education. In K. A. Renninger & I. E. Sigel (Eds.), *Handbook of child psychology* (6th ed., pp. 3–47). New York: Wiley.

Jacobs, S. E., & Gross, J. J. (2014). Emotion regulation in education: Conceptual foundations, current applications, and future directions. In R. Pekrun & L. Linnenbrink-Garcia (Eds.), *International handbook of emotions in education* (pp. 183–201). New York: Taylor & Francis.

Johnson, D. W., & Johnson, R. T. (1974). Instructional goal structure: Cooperative, competitive or individualistic. *Review of Educational Research, 4,* 213–240.

Kuhbandner, C., & Pekrun, R. (2013). Affective state influences retrieval-induced forgetting for integrated knowledge. *PloS ONE, 8*(2), e56617.

Lane, A. M., Whyte, G. P., Terry, P. C., & Nevill, A. M. (2005). Mood, self-set goals and examination performance: The moderating effect of depressed mood. *Personality and Individual Differences, 39,* 143–153.

Lazarus, R. S., & Folkman, S. (1984). *Stress, appraisal, and coping.* New York: Springer.

Lewis, M., Haviland-Jones, J. M., & Feldman Barrett, L. (Eds.). (2008). *Handbook of emotions* (3rd ed.). New York: Guilford.

Linnenbrink, E. A. (2007). The role of affect in student learning: A multidimensional approach to considering the interaction of affect, motivation, and engagement. In P. A. Schutz & R. Pekrun (Eds.), *Emotion in education* (pp. 107–124). Amsterdam: Academic Press.

Linnenbrink, E. A., & Pintrich, P. R. (2002). Achievement goal theory and affect: An asymmetrical bidirectional model. *Educational Psychologist, 37,* 69–78.

Marsh, H. W. (1987). The big-fish-little-pond effect on academic self-concept. *Journal of Educational Psychology, 79,* 280–295.

Matthews, G., Zeidner, M., & Roberts, R. D. (2002). *Emotional intelligence: Science and myth.* Cambridge, MA: MIT Press.

Meece, J.L., Wigfield, A., & Eccles, J. S. (1990). Predictors of math anxiety and its influence on young adolescents course enrollment intentions and performance in mathematics. *Journal of Educational Psychology, 82,* 60–70.

Meinhardt, J., & Pekrun, R. (2003). Attentional resource allocation to emotional events: An ERP study. *Cognition and Emotion, 17,* 477–500.

Parrott, W. G., & Spackman, M. P. (2000). Emotion and memory. In M. Lewis & J. M. Haviland-Jones (Eds.), *Handbook of emotions* (2nd ed., pp. 476–490). New York: Guilford Press.

Pekrun, R. (1992). Expectancy-value theory of anxiety. In D. G. Forgays, T. Sosnowski, & K. Wrzesniewski (Eds.), *Anxiety: Recent developments in self-appraisal, psychophysiological and health research* (pp. 23–41). Washington, DC: Hemisphere.

Pekrun, R. (2006). The control-value theory of achievement emotions: Assumptions, corollaries, and implications for educational research and practice. *Educational Psychology Review, 18,* 315–341.

Pekrun, R., Cusack, A., Murayama, K., Elliot, A. J., & Thomas, K. (2014). The power of anticipated feedback: Effects on students' achievement goals and achievement emotions. *Learning and Instruction, 29,* 115–124.

Pekrun, R., Elliot, A. J., & Maier, M. A. (2009). Achievement goals and achievement emotions: Testing a model of their joint relations with academic performance. *Journal of Educational Psychology, 101,* 115–135.

Pekrun, R., Goetz, T., Daniels, L. M., Stupnisky, R. H., & Perry, R. P. (2010). Boredom in achievement settings: Control-value antecedents and performance outcomes of a neglected emotion. *Journal of Educational Psychology, 102,* 531–549.

Pekrun, R., Goetz, T., Frenzel, A. C., Barchfeld, P., & Perry, R. P. (2011). Measuring emotions in students' learning and performance: The Achievement Emotions Questionnaire (AEQ). *Contemporary Educational Psychology, 36,* 36–48.

Pekrun, R., Goetz, T., Titz, W., & Perry, R. P. (2002). Academic emotions in students' self-regulated learning and achievement: A program of quantitative and qualitative research. *Educational Psychologist, 37,* 91–106.

Pekrun, R., Hall, N. C., Goetz, T., & Perry, R. P. (2014). Boredom and academic achievement: Testing a model of reciprocal causation. *Journal of Educational Psychology 106,* 696–710.

Pekrun, R., & Linnenbrink-Garcia, L. (Eds.). (2014). *International handbook of emotions in education.* New York: Taylor & Francis.

Pekrun, R., & Perry, R. P. (2014). Control-value theory of achievement emotions. In R. Pekrun & L. Linnenbrink-Garcia (Eds.), *International handbook of emotions in education* (pp. 120–141). New York: Taylor & Francis.

Pekrun, R., vom Hofe, R., Blum, W., Frenzel, A. C., Goetz, T., & Wartha, S. (2007). Development of mathematical competencies in adolescence. In M. Prenzel (Ed.), *Studies on the educational quality of schools* (pp. 17–37). Münster: Waxmann.

Preckel, F., Zeidner, M., Goetz, T., & Schleyer, E. (2008). Female 'big fish' swimming against the tide: The 'big-fish-little-pond effect' and gender ratio in special gifted classes. *Contemporary Educational Psychology, 33,* 78–96.

Punmongkol, P. (2009). *The regulation of academic emotions* (unpublished doctoral dissertation). Sydney, Australia: University of Sydney.

Roeser, R. W., Midgley, C., & Urdan, T. C. (1996). Perceptions of the school psychological environment and early adolescents' psychological and behavioral functioning in school: The mediating role of goals and belonging. *Journal of Educational Psychology, 88,* 408–422.

Schutz, P. A., & Pekrun, R. (Eds.). (2007). *Emotion in education.* San Diego, CA: Academic Press.

Schutz, P. A., & Zembylas, M. (Eds.). (2009). *Advances in teacher emotion research. The impact on teachers' lives.* New York: Springer.

Seegers, G., & Boekaerts, M. (1990). Gender-related differences in self referenced cognitions in relation to mathematics. *Journal for Research in Mathematics Education, 27*(2), 215–240.

Shuman, V., & Scherer, K. R. (2014). Concepts and structures of emotions. In R. Pekrun & L. Linnenbrink-Garcia (Eds.), *International handbook of emotions in education* (pp. 13–35). New York: Taylor & Francis.

Turner, J. C., Meyer, D. K., Midgley, C., & Patrick, H. (2003). Teacher discourse and sixth graders' reported affect and achievement behaviors in two high-mastery/high-performance mathematics classrooms. *Elementary School Journal, 103,* 357.

Turner, J. E., & Schallert, D. L. (2001). Expectancy-value relationships of shame reactions and shame resiliency. *Journal of Educational Psychology, 93,* 320–329.

Valeski, T. N., & Stipek, D. J. (2001). Young children's feelings about school. *Child Development, 72,* 1198–1213.

Weiner, B. (1985). An attributional theory of achievement motivation and emotion. *Psychological Review, 92,* 548–573.

Westefeld, J. S., Homaifar, B., Spotts, J., Furr, S., Range, L., & Werth, J. L. (2005). Perceptions concerning college student suicide: Data from four universities. *Suicide & Life-Threatening Behavior, 35,* 640–645.

Zeidner, M. (1998). *Test anxiety: The state of the art.* New York: Plenum.

Zeidner, M. (2014). Anxiety in education. In R. Pekrun & L. Linnenbrink-Garcia (Eds.), *International handbook of emotions in education* (pp. 265–288). New York: Taylor & Francis.

# 7

# Motivation

LISA LINNENBRINK-GARCIA
Michigan State University

ERIKA A. PATALL
University of Texas, Austin

What is motivation? As you read this chapter, you may have your own ideas about what constitutes motivation and motivated behavior in the classroom. While definitions vary, a working definition consistent with the theoretical frameworks described in this chapter is that motivation refers to the processes of both *initiating* and *sustaining behavior* (Schunk, Meece, & Pintrich, 2014). Moreover, the study of motivation in educational psychology goes beyond thinking of students as motivated or unmotivated to examine how their self-related beliefs, cognitions, goals, and experiences shape engagement and learning. Importantly, these self-related motivational beliefs are thought to be "cognitive, conscious, affective, and often under control of the individual" (Wigfield, Eccles, Schiefele, Roeser, & Davis-Kean, 2006, p. 933).

We begin this chapter with a focus on six major theoretical frameworks from which much of the motivation research in education is currently conducted. Our aim in describing these theories is to provide a short introduction and description of how motivation relates to learning and engagement within each theory, noting recent theoretical and empirical advances since the publication of the last *Handbook of Educational Psychology*. Next, we consider recent empirical and theoretical work that integrates across theoretical perspectives. We close by suggesting several avenues for future research.

## Major Theoretical Approaches to the Study of Motivation in Education

### Social Cognitive Theory

***Theoretical overview.*** Bandura's (1986) social cognitive theory is one of the major modern theories of motivation, both because it has contributed broad ideas about social cognition and for its theorizing regarding academic self-efficacy. Indeed, the major motivational theories reviewed in this chapter all emphasize reciprocal determinism or the interplay among the person, behavior, and the environment, a key concept within social cognitive theory. Moreover, the concept of agency, that individuals are "self-organizing, proactive, self-regulating, and self-reflecting" (Bandura, 2006, p. 164), underlies modern research on motivation.

Within social cognitive theory, the construct of self-efficacy is most relevant to the current chapter. *Self-efficacy* refers to individuals' beliefs about their capacity to execute behaviors at particular levels (Bandura, 1997). Applied to education, academic self-efficacy refers to students' beliefs about their ability to learn, develop skills, or master material. Self-efficacy is distinct from outcome expectations (e.g., belief that a given behavior will lead to a certain outcome) and self-concept (e.g., cognitive evaluations of ability: Bong & Skaalvik, 2003; Schunk & Pajares, 2005). Below, we briefly describe the construct of self-efficacy and current trends regarding its relations with academic outcomes (see Chapter 11, this volume, for more on self-efficacy).

***Research related to engagement, learning, and achievement.*** Self-efficacy beliefs are related to students' course and career choices, putting forth greater effort and task persistence even in the face of failure, increased use of adaptive self-regulatory strategies, more positive and less negative emotions, and enhanced academic achievement (Bandura, 1986, 1997; Pajares, 1996; see also Klassen & Usher, 2010; Schunk & Pajares, 2005; and Chapter 11, this volume). In the past decade, many studies have further documented how students' self-efficacy beliefs shape affective, behavioral, and cognitive engagement as well as noted group differences based on gender and ethnicity (see Klassen & Usher, 2010; and Chapter 11, this volume). At the intersection of self-regulation and self-efficacy, researchers have also considered calibration (e.g., the congruency between efficacy judgments and actual performance), although this remains understudied.

For instance, Chen (2003) found that both calibration and self-efficacy had independent, positive effects on adolescents' math performance. Klassen (2007) found that learning-disabled students had lower self-efficacy, as expected, but that they were also less calibrated (more overconfident) than non-learning-disabled students, which may partially explain achievement differences between these groups.

There is also a growing body of research focused on collective self-efficacy beliefs. Research on the collective efficacy of teachers for supporting students' learning suggests that this construct is predictive of school-wide achievement and student behavior (see Chapter 30, this volume; Klassen, Tze, Betts, & Gordon, 2011). There is also emerging research on students' collective efficacy in small groups, indicating that it too predicts performance (Klassen & Krawchuk, 2009). Researchers have also sought to clarify how self-efficacy is supported in educational settings (see Usher & Pajares, 2008). For instance, using latent profile analysis, Chen and Usher (2013) found that adolescents who drew from multiple sources of self-efficacy (mastery experience, vicarious experience, social persuasion, and affective/physiological states) simultaneously had the highest science self-efficacy and achievement, which was significantly higher than students who derived their self-efficacy primarily from mastery experiences alone. Those most at risk appeared particularly sensitive to physiological arousal information.

### Expectancy-Value Theory

***Theoretical overview.*** Expectancy-value conceptualizations of behavior have a long history in psychology (e.g., Atkinson, 1964). Similar to predecessors, modern expectancy-value theory (Eccles et al., 1983) assumes that individuals' expectations for success and subjective value for tasks are the most proximal predictors of their academic choices, achievement-related behaviors, and ultimately, learning and achievement, and are themselves predicted by a variety of psychological, social, and cultural influences (for recent reviews, see Eccles, 2005; Wigfield, Tonks, & Klauda, 2009). *Expectancies* refer to individuals' beliefs about how well they will do on upcoming tasks and are distinct conceptually, but not empirically, from *beliefs about ability* (evaluations of competence, Eccles & Wigfield, 1995; see Chapter 11, this volume). Four categories of task value exist: *utility value* (task perceived as useful to other aspects of the person's life), *attainment value* (personal importance or self-relevance of doing well on a task), *intrinsic value* (perceiving the task as interesting, enjoyable, or fun), and *cost* (negative aspects of engaging in the task). Research indicates that students can distinguish between competence and value beliefs in early elementary school and can differentiate among types of value by fifth grade (e.g., Eccles & Wigfield, 1995).

***Research related to engagement, learning, and achievement.*** Much research within the United States and across countries suggests that expectancies and value[1] predict achievement outcomes, including persistence, performance, and choice of activities (e.g., Chow, Eccles, & Salmela-Aro,

2012; Durik, Vida, & Eccles, 2006; Nagengast et al., 2011) among children as young as first grade, and the relations gain strength with age (Denissen, Zarrett, & Eccles, 2007; Eccles et al., 1983). Expectancies for success most strongly predict performance, even when previous performance is controlled, and generally precede and predict students' values (e.g., Jacobs, Lanza, Osgood, Eccles, & Wigfield, 2002), though possibly less so for females (Denissen et al., 2007). In contrast, students' task values most strongly predict activity choices and enrollment decisions, even having long-term consequences. For example, values in elementary years predict activity choice and course enrollment in high school (e.g., Durik et al., 2006). Interestingly, expectancies and values may not simply work to additively and independently predict academic outcomes. Rather, recent research conducted with adolescents suggests that the effect of expectancies on academic choices and achievement is stronger when value is higher and vice versa, but neither high expectancies nor values can compensate for when the other is low (Nagengast et al., 2011; Trautwein et al., 2012).

Given the clear links of expectancies and task value to important academic outcomes, research demonstrating that students experience age-related declines in expectancies (see Chapter 11, this volume) and values in the United States (e.g., Archambault, Eccles, & Vida, 2010; Jacobs et al., 2002) and other countries (e.g., Henderson, Marx, & Kim, 1999; Watt, 2004) is of great concern to educators. Recent advances in this area include the use of growth mixture modeling and other sophisticated techniques to investigate heterogeneity in developmental trajectories across individuals and domains over time (e.g., Archambault et al., 2010). Declines seem to occur particularly for language arts in early elementary years and for math during high school. Likewise, gender-stereotypic differences in competence beliefs and task values are of particular practical interest, given links between these beliefs and career trajectories. For instance, girls express higher expectancies and task value for language arts domains and boys express higher beliefs for math, sports, science, and engineering (e.g., Durik et al., 2006; Jacobs et al., 2002; Watt, 2004; see Chapter 11, this volume; Wigfield, Battle, Keller, & Eccles, 2002 for reviews).

One area of research with particular growth in the last decade is the cost component of task value. Though most empirical examinations of task values have overlooked cost, recent research suggests that cost may help to differentiate levels of academic success. For example, cost negatively predicted undergraduates' intentions to enter graduate school, controlling for other forms of value (Battle & Wigfield, 2003). Similarly, cost differentiated individuals in terms of their motivational profiles, affect, and achievement outcomes, with students in high-cost profiles experiencing less adaptive outcomes overall (Conley, 2012). Recent research further suggests that cost, like other forms of value, is multidimensional. Perez, Cromley, and Kaplan (2014) reported varying results based on type of cost, with effort cost followed by opportunity cost as the strongest predictors of students' intentions to leave science, technology, engineering, and mathematics majors; psychological cost was unrelated to intentions. Finally, there is some limited evidence that costs may be a particularly powerful predictor of women's occupational choices. For example, concerns about job flexibility and high time demands in the context of balancing work and family life, along with lower intrinsic value of physical science, were the best predictors of women changing their occupational aspirations out of male-dominated fields (Frome, Alfeld, Eccles, & Barber, 2006).

## Interest

***Theoretical overview.*** Psychologists have been studying interest for more than a century (e.g., Dewey, 1913; James, 1890). Despite such strong roots, it has been relatively neglected, but has benefited from a surge of research in the past few decades. While there are varying views on interest, much of the current research differentiates between two forms: individual and situational (see Renninger, Hidi, & Krapp, 1992; Renninger & Hidi, 2011). Individual interest (a.k.a. personal interest) is relatively stable and resides within the individual; it includes a deep personal connection to the domain and a willingness to re-engage in the domain over time (Schiefele, 2009). *Individual interest* is characterized by positive feelings (e.g., enjoyment) as well as value for and personal importance of the domain. Additionally, Renninger and colleagues (Hidi & Renninger, 2006) propose that knowledge is a key component and that individual interest can be differentiated into emerging and well-developed forms, with deeper levels of stored knowledge serving as a catalyst for shifts from emerging to well-developed individual interest. *Situational interest* refers to interest that emerges from and is supported by the context (Schiefele, 2009). As with individual interest, there are several different views of situational interest (see Hidi & Renninger, 2006; Krapp, 2002, Krapp & Prenzel, 2011; Mitchell, 1993; Schiefele, 2009; Silvia, 2005), but most of them include at least two primary forms. One form, triggered situational interest,[2] is a relatively short, heightened affective state that is initiated by contextual supports. The other form, maintained situational interest,[3] refers to situational support of more focused involvement, attention, and persistence in a domain, including finding meaning and personal connections to the domain content. With maintained situational interest, students are likely to experience positive feelings (e.g., enjoyment), but are also developing deeper value for and knowledge of the content.

***Research related to engagement, learning, and achievement.***
Much research focused on text-based interest suggests that situational interest or actualized individual interest supports increased attention, cognitive processing, and persistence on reading tasks (Hidi, 2001; Schiefele, 2009; Schraw & Lehman, 2001). Recently, researchers have extended beyond text-based work to examine the role of interest in predicting engagement and learning more broadly. For instance, using multiple assessments within a single daylong problem-based learning session for undergraduates, Rotgans and Schmidt (2011) found that situational interest predicted academic engagement and in turn achievement. In several

classroom and lab-based correlational and experimental studies conducted by Harackiewicz and colleagues, situational interest was positively related to task involvement (Durik & Harackiewicz, 2007) and course grades (e.g., Harackiewicz, Durik, Barron, Linnenbrink-Garcia, & Tauer, 2008; Hulleman & Harackiewicz, 2009), but was a stronger predictor of course choice than achievement several years later (e.g., Harackiewicz et al., 2008). Notably, the observed effects are not always straightforward and at times vary based on perceived competence, initial interest, prior achievement, or type of situational interest. For instance, Durik and Harackiewicz (2007) found that triggered situational interest supported task involvement for undergraduates with low individual interest, but undermined involvement for those with high interest; maintained situational interest was related to higher task involvement for undergraduates with high initial individual interest only.

In the past decade, interest researchers have also developed more detailed theoretical accounts regarding the development of interest (Hidi & Renninger, 2006) and provided empirical evidence documenting shifts from situational to individual interest (e.g., Harackiewicz et al., 2008; Linnenbrink-Garcia, Patall, & Messersmith, 2013; Renninger & Hidi, 2002). Relatedly, there is a growing body of research aimed at understanding contextual supports for situational interest. This work suggests that several contextual factors, including autonomy support, instructor approachability and friendliness, opportunities for involvement, and relevance of course material, support situational interest and may in turn support individual interest (e.g., Hulleman & Harackiewicz, 2009; Linnenbrink-Garcia et al., 2013; Palmer, 2009; Rotgans & Schmidt, 2011).

## Self-determination Theory

***Theoretical overview.*** Self-determination theory (Deci & Ryan, 1985; Ryan & Deci, 2000) is a macro theory of motivation and development that has particular relevance to education. Self-determination theory distinguishes among types of motivation based on reasons for action. In line with a long history in psychology (Berlyne, 1960; White, 1959), the most basic distinction is between *intrinsic motivation*, doing something for the inherent satisfaction that engaging in the activity provides, and *extrinsic motivation*, doing something because it leads to a separable outcome (e.g., praise or money; Ryan & Deci, 2000). Further, extrinsic motivation may itself vary in the degree to which it is internalized and experienced as autonomous versus controlled (Ryan & Connell, 1989). In addition to fully extrinsic versus intrinsic forms, motivation for action may emerge from feelings of obligation, guilt, or pride (*introjected*), because a behavior is perceived to have utility or importance for accomplishing personal goals (*identified*), or because it is fully internalized and representative of one's central values (*integrated*).

Self-determination theory proposes that innate psychological needs for *autonomy* (e.g., feeling that actions emanate from the self*), competence,* and *relatedness* underlie people's natural growth tendencies, optimal psychological functioning, and productivity (e.g., Jang, Reeve, Ryan, &

Kim, 2009; Ryan & Deci, 2000). Satisfaction of or support for these needs enhances intrinsic motivation as well as *internalization* (e.g., moving from more external to internal forms of regulation: Ryan & Deci, 2000). Further, a growing body of evidence has demonstrated the importance of these basic needs for supporting psychological functioning across individualistic (Western) and collectivistic (Eastern) cultures (e.g., Ferguson, Kasser, & Jahng, 2010; Jang et al., 2009).

***Research related to engagement, learning, and achievement.*** Extensive research relates students' intrinsic motivation and other autonomous forms of motivation to adaptive academic outcomes, including creativity, academic engagement, deep conceptual learning strategies, and academic achievement (e.g., Corpus, McClintic-Gilbert, & Hayenga, 2009; Lepper, Corpus, & Iyengar, 2005; Otis, Grouzet, & Pelletier, 2005; Walker, Greene, & Mansell, 2006). In contrast, many studies suggest that more extrinsic forms of motivation predict negative outcomes, such as maladaptive learning strategies and attitudes, anxiety, poorer ability to cope with challenges, poor academic achievement, and even school dropout (e.g., Lepper et al., 2005; Ryan & Connell, 1989; Vansteenkiste, Zhou, Lens, & Soenens, 2005; Walker et al., 2006), though a few studies suggest that extrinsic motivation may at times be beneficial for outcomes such as self-regulation and academic adjustment (Miller, Greene, Montalvo, Ravindran, & Nichols, 1996; Otis et al., 2005). Given these patterns, documented declines in both intrinsic and extrinsic motivation within and across school years (e.g. Corpus et al., 2009; Lepper et al., 2005) are a concern. For example, in a longitudinal study with third- through eighth-graders, intrinsic motivation and classroom grades mutually influenced one another positively and reciprocally over the academic year (Corpus et al., 2009). In contrast, extrinsic motivation was unrelated to grades, but poor academic performance predicted higher extrinsic motivation. Both extrinsic and intrinsic motivation declined within the school year and across grade levels.

Person-centered approaches exploring profiles of intrinsic and extrinsic motivation have led to similar conclusions, with some studies suggesting that high autonomous motivation and low controlled motivation are most adaptive (e.g., Hayenga & Corpus, 2010; Ratelle, Guay, Vallerand, Larose, & Senecal, 2007; Vansteenkiste, Sierens, Soenens, Luyckx, & Lens, 2009), and other studies suggesting that high levels of both forms of motivation can also be beneficial (Wormington, Corpus, & Anderson, 2012). Some of this debate may be resolved by assessing the differential effects of various forms of motivation across outcomes. For example, in one study with elementary-school students, intrinsic motivation was most strongly linked with psychological well-being, while identified motivation was most strongly linked with academic achievement (e.g., Burton, Lydon, D'Alessandro, & Koestner, 2006).

Within the past decade, extensive research suggests that psychological needs, and in turn engagement and achievement, can be supported by the environment through teaching practices such as providing meaningful choices, emphasizing personal relevance, using non-controlling informational language, allowing students to express opinions and negative affect, and providing feedback and structure (see Reeve, 2009; Reeve & Jang, 2006; Stroet, Opdenakker, & Minnaert, 2013 for reviews). Conversely, directly controlling teacher behaviors (e.g., intentional suppression of perspectives, commands, and surveillance) may have maladaptive consequences for motivation, engagement, and learning (e.g., Assor, Kaplan, Kanat-Maymon, & Roth, 2005; Reeve & Jang, 2006). However, the effects of these practices are complex; they seem to interact with one another and with a variety of personal and situational factors to shape students' outcomes. For example, the strategy of providing choices in the classroom may be optimally effective when choices are administered without pressure and allow students to self-regulate, are not overwhelming in number or complexity, and are administered to individuals who feel competent or interested in the task or who ascribe to an upper-class Western cultural sensibility (Patall, 2013; Patall, Dacy, & Han, 2014; see Patall, 2012 for review). Along similar lines, research suggests that competence and autonomy work synergistically such that motivation and learning are optimized when both are supported, despite lay views that autonomy-support and competence-support (i.e., structure) are incompatible (e.g., Jang, Reeve & Deci, 2010; Reeve, 2009; Vansteenkiste et al., 2012). Finally, recent research focuses on the previously neglected need of relatedness, showing that non-controlling relatedness support and satisfaction are linked with engagement, learning, and achievement (e.g., Furrer & Skinner, 2003; Roorda, Koomen, Spilt, & Ooart, 2011; Ryan & Patrick, 2001).

### Achievement Goal Theory

***Theoretical overview.*** Achievement goal theory remains one of the most prominent motivation theories in educational psychology. Achievement goal theory proposes that there are two primary reasons or underlying purposes related to individuals' engagement in achievement-related activities: *mastery*, with a focus on developing competence, and *performance*, with a focus on demonstrating competence (Ames, 1992; Dweck & Leggett, 1988; Maehr & Midgley, 1991; Nicholls, 1984). The trichotomous model (Elliot, 1999) further differentiates performance goals into approach goals, with a focus on appearing competent, and avoidance goals, with a focus on avoiding appearing incompetent. The $2 \times 2$ model (Elliot & McGregor, 2001) extends the approach-avoidance distinction to mastery, such that one can approach the goal to develop competence (mastery-approach) or avoid declining competence or not fulfilling one's potential (mastery-avoidance), although mastery-avoidance goals have not been widely studied.

Goal orientations represent a general framework through which students interpret and react to achievement settings, resulting in varying patterns of affect, cognitions, and behaviors (Dweck & Leggett, 1988). Goal orientations are shaped both by the context, such as underlying goal structure of the classroom or school (Ames, 1992; Maehr & Midgley, 1991;

see Urdan, 2010 for a review), as well as by personal anteced-ents, such as motives (Elliot, 1999) and theories of intelligence (Cury, Elliot, Da Fonseca, & Moller, 2006; Dweck, 1999).

***Research related to engagement, learning, and achieve-ment.*** Research has established the benefits of mastery-approach goals and detriments of performance-avoidance goals across educational outcomes, whereas the findings for performance-approach goals remain mixed and controver-sial (see Anderman & Wolters, 2006). While still relatively understudied, research on mastery-avoidance has increased. Mastery-avoidance goals are related to negative outcomes such as negative affect, poor study strategies, avoidant behaviors, and lower achievement (e.g., Bong, 2009; Elliot & McGregor, 2001; Lovejoy & Durik, 2010; see Huang, 2011, 2012; Hulleman, Schrager, Bodmann, & Harackiewicz, 2010 for meta-analyses), though some studies suggest null or adaptive links to learning strategies (Bong, 2009; Elliot & McGregor, 2001; Madjar, Kaplan, & Weinstock, 2011). Meta-analyses indicate that mastery-avoidance goals are unrelated to positive affect and interest (Huang, 2011; Hulleman et al., 2010).

An ongoing controversy remains regarding how achieve-ment goals relate to achievement, especially mastery-approach and performance-approach goals. Several recent reviews and meta-analyses sought to clarify this pattern (Huang, 2012; Hulleman et al., 2010; Linnenbrink-Garcia, Tyson, & Patall, 2008). For example, Hulleman and colleagues (2010) found small significant positive correlations with achievement for mastery-approach ($\hat{r} = 0.11$) and performance-approach ($\hat{r} = 0.06$) goals and negative correlations for mastery-avoid-ance ($\hat{r} = -0.12$) and performance-avoidance ($\hat{r} = -0.13$) goals. These results were qualified by several significant mod-erators. For instance, when primarily normative items (e.g., outperforming others) were used to measure performance-ap-proach goals, the correlation was larger and positive ($\hat{r} = 0.14$); however, when the majority of items focused on appearance (e.g., looking smart) and/or evaluation (e.g., demonstrating ability), the correlation was negative ($\hat{r} = -0.14$). This suggests that framing performance goals as normative standards (see Elliot, Murayama, & Pekrun, 2011; Elliot & Thrash, 2001; Senko, Hulleman, & Harackiewicz, 2011) versus broader orientations related to demonstrating competence (Dweck & Leggett, 1988; Kaplan & Maehr, 2007) may yield very differ-ent patterns, especially for performance goals. Indeed, this dis-tinction between standards and orientations is part of a larger ongoing discussion of what constitutes a performance goal, how it should be measured, whether approach and avoidance forms are distinct, and how likely performance goals are to emerge in classrooms (see Brophy, 2005; Linnenbrink-Garcia et al., 2012; Senko et al., 2011; Urdan & Mestas, 2006).

Moving beyond variable-centered approaches, recent research has utilized a person-centered approach (e.g., Daniels et al., 2008; Luo, Paris, Hogan, & Luo, 2011; Tuominen-Soini, Salmela-Aro, & Niemivirta, 2012). This extends earlier work examining interactions among multiple goals (e.g., Pintrich, 2000) to identify naturally occurring combinations of goals and their relations to achievement. For

instance, Luo and colleagues (2011) found that a profile with at least moderate mastery, high performance-approach, but low performance-avoidance goals was most beneficial across a variety of outcomes. This research suggests that it is critical to consider the relative levels of multiple goals, as doing so may help to further clarify the observed complexity in find-ings, especially for performance-approach goals.

There is also research examining how the educational context shapes students' goals (see Urdan, 2010, for a review). Recent work seeks to clarify the interplay between goal structures and social-relational components (e.g., Patrick, Kaplan, & Ryan, 2011; Turner, Gray, Anderman, Dawson, & Anderman, 2013), interactions between goal structures and personal goals in shaping academic out-comes (Lau & Nie, 2008; Linnenbrink, 2005; Murayama & Elliot, 2009; Wolters, 2004), the role of teachers' moti-vation in shaping the goal structures they create (Butler, 2012), the relative influence of individual versus shared perceptions of goal structures on academic outcomes (Karabenick, 2004; Urdan, 2004), as well as goal stability and change both within a single context (Fryer & Elliot, 2007; Muis & Edwards, 2009; Senko & Harackiewicz, 2005) and across contexts, particularly school transitions (e.g., Paulick, Watermann, & Nückles, 2013; Tuominen-Soini et al., 2012). This research highlights the importance of considering personal goal orientations embedded in classroom contexts and the need to examine how personal goal orientations change based on both objective features of the classroom as well as students' perceptions of these features. For instance, while personal goals are generally stable over time, they may shift as a function of feedback or exam performance (Muis & Edwards, 2009; Senko & Harackiewicz, 2005). Moreover, there is some evidence that the goal context may magnify the relations between personal goals and academic outcomes (Lau & Nie, 2008; Murayama & Elliot, 2009), although this is not consistent across all studies (Linnenbrink, 2005; Wolters, 2004).

Finally, researchers have expanded achievement goals to focus on the social domain, examining how social goal ori-entations relate to both social and academic outcomes (e.g., Rodkin, Ryan, Jamieson & Wilson, 2013; Ryan & Shim, 2006, 2008). For instance, Ryan and Shim (2006) developed and val-idated measures of social goals focused on developing versus demonstrating social competence and found that social devel-opment goals were associated with social adjustment while social demonstration-avoidance goals were associated with maladjustment. Social demonstration-approach goals were generally unrelated to social adjustment, although more recent research suggests that there may be both benefits and detri-ments of these goals (e.g., Rodkin et al., 2013). This expansion to the social realm is one potential way to more fully capture the nature and function of goals in school settings.

## Attribution Theory

***Theoretical overview.*** Building on early expectancy-value theories and conceptualizations of attributions (e.g., Atkinson,

1964; Heider, 1958; Rotter, 1966), Weiner's attribution theory of achievement (e.g., Weiner, 1985, 2011; for a review see Graham & Williams, 2009) assumes that people are motivated to understand outcomes they experience, especially when outcomes are unexpected or negative. In their search to explain an outcome, students may arrive at many possible causal attributions (i.e., ability, effort, luck, or task difficulty) that are themselves influenced by a variety of factors. These attributions are organized along three underlying dimensions: locus or the extent to which the cause is internal to the individual (e.g., ability, effort) or external (e.g., luck, task difficulty); stability or the extent that the cause will persist in the future (e.g., aptitude) or is transient (e.g., effort); and *controllability* or the extent of perceived influence an individual has on the cause (e.g., effort is controllable, luck is uncontrollable). These dimensions are theorized to have differential implications for expectancies, values and emotions, and subsequent achievement behavior, with stability relating most directly to expectancies for success and failure, a more internal locus to affective reactions to success and failure (i.e., pride or self-esteem), and controllability to hopefulness, social emotions (i.e., shame, guilt) and help giving (Weiner, 2011).

***Research related to engagement, learning, and achievement.*** Research is generally consistent with hypothesized patterns such that attributions are associated with varying emotions, expectancies, and academic functioning (e.g., Liu, Cheng, Chen, & Wu, 2009; Perry, Stupnisky, Daniels, & Haynes, 2008; Shell & Husman, 2008; Wolters, Fan, & Daugherty, 2013), though effort attributions are not consistently more beneficial relative to ability attributions, as attribution theorists often predict (e.g., Hsieh & Schallert, 2008; Vispoel & Austin, 1995). Current research integrates causal attributions, particularly ability and effort attributions, into various theoretical explanations of motivation and achievement. Attributions have an important place in achievement goal theory and implicit theories about the nature of intelligence (e.g., Blackwell, Trzesniewski, & Dweck, 2007; Haynes, Daniels, Stupnisky, Perry, & Hladkyj, 2008; Shell & Husman, 2008; Wolters et al., 2013). This research generally suggests a bidirectional relation between adopting performance goals or a fixed view of intelligence and using more helpless attributions (i.e., more internal, stable, and uncontrollable causes after failure), versus endorsing mastery goals or a malleable view of intelligence and using more adaptive attributions (i.e., controllable causes of success and unstable causes for failure). Current research also focuses on the links between causal attributions and constructs prominent in other motivation theories such as interest and self-regulation (e.g., Fulmer & Fritjers, 2011; Soric & Palekčic, 2009; Wolters et al., 2013). For example, Fulmer and Fritjers (2011) found that high topic interest for a reading passage buffered adolescents from the negative effects of excessive challenge, sustaining engagement and preventing attributions regarding the source of difficulty.

An additional focus of current attribution research is on how attribution training interventions may be used to promote a variety of student outcomes, with many intervention studies demonstrating that training students to think about academic successes as controllable and academic failures as unstable has beneficial effects (e.g., Good, Aronson, & Inzlicht, 2003; Haynes et al., 2008; Perry, Stupnisky, Hall, Chipperfield, & Weiner, 2010). Given links between implicit theories of intelligence and attributions, interventions that train students to adopt a mindset emphasizing the malleable or controllable nature of intelligence seem to have similar beneficial effects (e.g., Blackwell et al., 2007; Good et al., 2003).

Finally, research on attributions has taken several new directions. Current research explores multiple attributions (e.g., Perry et al., 2008, 2010), attributions with a social focus (e.g., Liu et al., 2009; McClure et al., 2011), and the correlates of attributions in new educational contexts or previously unexamined domains (e.g., Hsieh & Schallert, 2008; Perry et al., 2008, 2010), including interpersonal interactions (e.g., Natale, Viljaranta, Lerkkanen, Poikkeus, & Nurmi, 2009; Peterson & Schreiber, 2006, 2012). For example, Peterson and Schreiber (2006) found that college students' outcome expectations and emotions were more strongly related to effort than ability attributions in the context of a collaborative project. Using a person-centered approach, Perry and colleagues (2008) found that compared to students who used other combinations of attributions for poor performance in college, students using a combination of modifiable internal controllable attributions (low effort, bad strategy) and external uncontrollable attributions that protect self-worth (test difficulty, poor teaching) demonstrated the most adaptive motivation and goal striving when transitioning from high school to college.

## Other Theoretical Perspectives

We end this overview of key theories by noting that there are a number of important and influential constructs and theories that are not given adequate attention in our review. While we could not possibly review the tenets and findings of every fruitful motivation theory applicable to achievement contexts, there are many additional theories that make meaningful contributions to our understanding of students' motivation, engagement, and achievement. Many of these theories share and extend ideas and constructs central to those theories summarized above. For example, a number of theories related to personal control (e.g., Connell & Wellborn, 1991; Perry, 2003; Skinner, 1995) share commonalities with social cognitive theory, self-determination theory, and attribution theory. Control-value theory (Pekrun, 2006) focuses on the role of perceived control and value appraisals in achievement emotions and performance, highlighting constructs and ideas that overlap with expectancy-value theory, attribution theory, and achievement goal theory.

Many researchers study self-processes, including possible selves (e.g., Oyserman, Bybee, & Terry, 2006), self-concept (e.g., Harter, 1998; Marsh & O'Mara, 2008), self-worth (e.g., Covington, 1992), and beliefs about ability and intelligence (e.g., Dweck, 2006), that guide, direct, and motivate behaviors in achievement contexts and overlap with competence, control, and goal-related concepts central to many of the theories described in this chapter. In particular, and as alluded to previously, a great deal of research on self-theories or mindsets (see Dweck & Grant, 2008 for a review) suggests that self-theories about the malleability of personal attributes, including personality and intelligence, may underlie several of the motivation constructs previously discussed. Research suggests that those with a more malleable versus fixed theory of self-attributes are more likely to adopt mastery goals, maintain intrinsic interest, persist in the face of challenge, demonstrate higher academic performance, make more adaptive attributions for outcomes, and have greater overall psychological well-being.

Some theorists have studied similar constructs from different time perspectives. For example, flow theory (Shernoff & Csikszentmihalyi, 2009) focuses on in-the-moment or transient subjective flow experiences that are much like the intrinsic motivation or interest constructs. Research on future time perspectives (e.g., Husman & Lens, 1999) focuses on value for educational activities in the future rather than in the present.

Finally, while the theories we reviewed assume people consciously engage in goal-directed action and then evaluate subsequent affective, cognitive, and performance consequences, there is substantial evidence that much motivation is unconscious and people are often unaware of what guides their moods, thoughts, and behavior (see Aarts & Custers, 2012; Chartrand & Bargh, 2002). For example, Bargh, Gollwitzer, Lee Chai, Barndollar, and Trotschel (2001) found participants who were primed with an achievement goal by being unobtrusively exposed to words such as "strive" and "succeed" outperformed and persisted longer on an anagram task compared to those not primed with achievement words. While educational research has not typically included unconscious motivation, the last two decades of psychological research suggest it may provide powerful explanations in educational contexts.

## Integrating Across Theoretical Perspectives

A clear strength of the theory-driven research conducted in the second half of the twentieth century is that it provided the groundwork for many advances in our understanding of motivational functioning in the classroom. However, with this emphasis on theory building came a tendency to conduct research based within a single theoretical tradition. For more than the past decade, however, this trend has been changing. Researchers are now considering, both empirically and theoretically, how multiple forms of motivation from multiple theories combine to shape engagement and learning. This shift is quite important and reflects the common understanding that educational outcomes, including achievement, may be multiply determined. Below, we highlight three complementary approaches to theory integration.

First, researchers have examined the contribution of multiple motivational constructs to students' engagement and learning using a traditional variable-centered approach (e.g., Ciani, Sheldon, Hilpert, & Easter, 2011; Hulleman, Durik,

Schweigert, & Harackiewicz, 2008; Liem, Lau, & Nie, 2008; Wolters et al., 2013). In these studies, researchers often explore the relative or unique contribution of each variable, after controlling for other forms of motivation, and consider interactions among personal and contextual motivational variables in relation to educational outcomes. For example, Ciani and colleagues (2011) explored concepts from self-determination and achievement goal theories; they found that psychological need satisfaction in life was linked with adopting academic mastery goals via autonomous motivation in class, and autonomy support slowed the decline in mastery goals over the course of a semester among undergraduate students. In an integration of expectancy-value, interest, and goal orientation theories, Hulleman and colleagues (2008) found that college and high-school students' intrinsic and utility value for a course or activity mediated the effects of mastery-approach goals on both subsequent interest in the course and final grade; performance-approach goals and utility value also predicted final grades, though values did not mediate these effects.

Going further, researchers also consider the joint and interactive effects of motivation, emotion, and cognitive variables in a multidisciplinary fashion to create more complete models of learning and engagement. For example, in their model of domain learning, Alexander and colleagues (e.g., Alexander, Murphy, Woods, Duhon, & Parker, 1997; Murphy & Alexander, 2002) explored the interplay between knowledge, interest, and strategic processing in students' paths to developing domain expertise. Likewise, research conducted by Pekrun and others (see Pekrun & Perry, 2014) has examined the links among emotion, motivation, self-regulation and learning strategies, cognitive resources, and academic achievement. In general, this variable-centered approach is useful for providing a more complete picture of the function of motivation in school, sometimes in the context of non-motivational factors.

Second, in the past decade, researchers have attempted to integrate motivation theories by examining motivational profiles of individuals across multiple forms of motivation (e.g., Braten & Olaussen, 2005; Conley, 2012; Lau & Roeser, 2008; Shell & Husman, 2008). Rather than focusing on how one particular variable functions, presumably across all individuals and in isolation, this person-centered approach allows researchers to identify particularly adaptive (or maladaptive) combinations of motivation and explore how these profiles function in the classroom. For instance, Conley (2012) created motivational profiles using constructs from achievement goal and expectancy-value theories. She found that combining variables from multiple theories in seven profiles was critical for predicting affect and achievement; neither achievement goals nor subjective task value explained the pattern of findings alone.

In one of the most comprehensive approaches to date, Shell and Husman (2008) examined constructs from social cognitive, expectancy-value, attribution, and achievement goal theories, as well as affect and self-regulatory behaviors, to identify five distinct groupings of variables along three canonical dimensions. For instance, they identified a highly motivated and strategic learner dimension. The motivation coefficients included high competence beliefs, positive affect, attributions to effort, and mastery and performance-approach goals and were linked with highly strategic self-regulatory behavior coefficients. Another dimension reflected more of an intrinsically motivated, mastery, high-competency focus tied with the use of knowledge-building strategies, but not general cognitive and metacognitive strategies or high study effort. These dimensions, along with others they identified, suggest that there may be multiple adaptive and maladaptive groupings of motivational and self-regulatory behaviors.

Third, motivation researchers are integrating across theories to consider how multiple forms of motivation emerge from and are supported by the educational context (e.g., Guthrie, Klauda, & Ho, 2013; Nolen, 2007; Turner, Warzon, & Christensen, 2011). For instance, Turner and colleagues (2011) synthesized motivation theories to identify and implement "best practices" designed to support multiple forms of adaptive motivation. The concept-oriented reading program developed by Guthrie and Wigfield goes further by examining how an intervention based on multiple motivational theories shapes patterns of motivation and engagement (e.g., Guthrie et al., 2013). Other research takes a more situated approach to investigate how multiple forms of motivation develop. For example, Nolen (2007) used a grounded-theory approach to examine the development of elementary students' motivation to read and write in a mixed-methods longitudinal study. While Nolen's primary focus was interest development, she identified shifts in multiple forms of reading and writing motivation (e.g., interest, mastery, ego concerns, reading to learn) and considered how the educational context related to varying motivational patterns. Integrated approaches such as these are critical in the translation of motivation research into coherent and useful recommendations for classroom practice.

## Future Directions

We close this chapter by highlighting several important or promising avenues for future research. First, our overview of the major theoretical models highlights the breadth of motivation constructs; however there is also a great deal of similarity among constructs such as those related to value (e.g., intrinsic motivation, task value, interest) and competence (e.g., self-concept, self-efficacy, expectancies), and the field suffers from the variety of terms used for seemingly similar constructs (Murphy & Alexander, 2000). Thus, it is critical that researchers not only carefully align conceptual definitions with measurement instruments, but also assess where constructs can be combined and where nuanced differences are needed. Likewise, readers should pay special attention to conceptual and operational definitions when interpreting results.

Second, current research integrating motivation perspectives is particularly promising, both for understanding how motivation relates to engagement and learning and for supporting multiple adaptive forms of motivation in school settings (see also Chapter 12, this volume). In pursuing this work, we urge researchers to reflect upon what it means

theoretically to integrate constructs and whether a more unified, cohesive theoretical approach is possible (see Ford, 1992). However, in doing so, there is a need for parsimony, as complex theories will be unlikely to be widely adopted and have limited utility for informing practice.

Third, we urge researchers to continue to investigate underlying psychological processes and mechanisms and to more carefully consider how and why classroom contexts shape motivation. For instance, while research on situational interest has progressed in understanding contextual supports for situational interest and in using situational interest to predict individual interest, we know very little about the processes through which situational interest develops into individual interest. Similarly, within achievement goal theory, a clearer understanding of the psychological processes that shift as a function of goal structures is needed (see O'Keefe, Ben-Eliyahu, & Linnenbrink-Garcia, 2013). Similar suggestions can be made regarding the role of psychological needs in research on the links between external events and academic outcomes or the mechanisms by which attribution retraining influences achievement.

Fourth, motivation researchers may need to look beyond social cognitive theories to consider sociocultural and situated approaches, which place a greater emphasis on understanding the person in the context (for reviews, see Nolen & Ward, 2008; Perry, Turner, & Meyer, 2006). Sociocultural and situated approaches may be especially useful in understanding how motivation develops and functions in educational settings (see Nolen, 2007) and for investigating the role of culture in motivation (Zusho & Clayton, 2011). Moreover, these approaches may help motivational researchers work with educators to provide guidelines that are more realistic and useful for supporting motivation in classrooms by acknowledging the complexities of classrooms and better representing how multiple contextual components synergistically support motivation.

Fifth, we urge researchers to more carefully consider culture in the study of motivation. While this call is not new (Graham, 1994), it remains understudied. There are a number of recent theoretical reviews that thoughtfully discuss issues of culture, race, and ethnicity within the context of motivation research (e.g., Graham & Hudley, 2005; Kumar & Maehr, 2010; Zusho & Clayton, 2011). As these authors articulate, research on culture must move beyond simply identifying racial/ethnic or country-level differences to examine how meaningful conceptualizations of culture shape the nature of and variations in motivational phenomena.

Finally, while a variety of methods are used to study motivation, there is a heavy reliance on self-report instruments. Self-reports are useful for gaining access to social cognitive constructs like motivational self-beliefs; however, they have a number of drawbacks. Indeed, several studies suggest that students may not be interpreting items as intended (Karabenick et al., 2007; Koskey, Karabenick, Woolley, Bonney, & Dever, 2010; Urdan & Mestas, 2006). Thus, we urge researchers to continue to refine self-report measures while also employing other possible assessment techniques. Behavioral, observational, neuroimaging, facial recognition, and implicit techniques are among many methods that could be used to study motivation. For instance, Zhou and Winne (2012) employed goal traces (behavioral indicators operationalized as tags participants applied to selections of text and hyperlinks they clicked in an article) to collect in-the-moment goal orientations while students studied a passage. The goal traces and self-reported goals were correlated, but only goal traces significantly predicted test performance. Classroom observations are effectively employed to examine teachers' motivating practices and students' engagement (e.g., Jang et al., 2010; Turner et al., 1998), but are still relatively underutilized. Finally, recent efforts demonstrate that complex human motivational constructs can be understood through neuroscience methods (see Reeve & Lee, 2012, for a review).

## Conclusion

Research on motivation in educational settings continues to be a vibrant and productive area of study. As we have noted in this chapter, a great deal of progress in the study of motivation has occurred within the last decade. Researchers have continued to refine and advance our theoretical understanding of motivation, examined how motivation relates to engagement and learning, and explored how classroom contexts support it. One noteworthy advance we observed is the move beyond variable-centered analyses to consider how multiple forms of motivation function synergistically within individuals. We see this as quite fruitful, especially as researchers attempt to develop integrative approaches that move beyond the major theories outlined in this chapter. Relatedly, the use of situated or sociocultural perspectives may be particularly useful for understanding how motivation develops and is supported by educational contexts. Moreover, the increased use of diverse methods such as behavioral indicators of motivation and experience sampling designs may further clarify the processes by which motivation shapes academic outcomes. We are encouraged that the research on motivation continues to evolve and look forward to many more decades of productive motivational research.

## Notes

1. We refer to task value or value rather than individual components when various components of value were examined across similar studies or the primary research assessed the construct as a whole.
2. Also known as "catch" (Mitchell, 1993) and "emerging situational interest" (Krapp & Prenzel, 2011).
3. Also known as "hold" (Mitchell, 1993) or "stabilized situational interest" (Krapp & Prenzel, 2011).

## References

Aarts, H., & Custers, R. (2012). Unconscious goal pursuit: Nonconscious goal regulation and motivation. In R. Ryan (Ed.), *Oxford handbook of human motivation* (pp. 232–247). New York, NY: Oxford University Press.

Alexander, P. A., Murphy, P. K., Woods, B. S., Duhon, K. E., & Parker, D. (1997). College instruction and concomitant changes in students' knowledge, interest, and strategy use: A study of domain learning. *Contemporary Educational Psychology, 22*, 125–146.

Ames, C. (1992). Classrooms: Goals, structures, and student motivation. *Journal of Educational Psychology, 84*, 261–271.

Anderman, E. M., & Wolters, C. A. (2006). Goals, values, and affect: Influences on student motivation. In P. A. Alexander & P. H. Winne (Eds.), *Handbook of educational psychology* (pp. 369–389). Mahwah, NJ: Lawrence Erlbaum.

Archambault, I., Eccles, J. S., & Vida, M. N. (2010). Ability self-concepts and subjective value in literacy: Joint trajectories from grades 1 through 12. *Journal of Educational Psychology, 102*, 804–816.

Assor, A., Kaplan, H., Kanat-Maymon, Y., & Roth, G. (2005). Directly controlling teachers' behaviors as predictors of poor motivation and engagement in girls and boys: The role of anger and anxiety. *Learning and Instruction, 15*, 397–413.

Atkinson, J. W. (1964). *An introduction to motivation*. Princeton, NJ: Van Nostrand.

Bandura, A. (1986). *Social foundations of thought and action: A social cognitive theory*. Englewood Cliffs, NJ: Prentice Hall.

Bandura, A. (1997). *Self-efficacy: The exercise of control*. New York: Freeman.

Bandura, A. (2006). Toward a psychology of human agency. *Perspectives on Psychological Science, 1*, 164–180.

Bargh, J. A., Gollwitzer, P. M., Lee Chai, A., Barndollar, K., & Trotschel, R. (2001). The automated will: Nonconscious activation and pursuit of behavioral goals. *Journal of Personality and Social Psychology, 81*, 1014–1027.

Battle, A., & Wigfield, A. (2003). College women's value orientations toward family, career, and graduate school. *Journal of Vocational Behavior, 62*, 56–75.

Berlyne, D. E. (1960). *Conflict, arousal, and curiosity*. McGraw-Hill Series in Psychology. New York, NY: McGraw-Hill.

Blackwell, L. S., Trzesniewski, K. H., & Dweck, C. S. (2007). Implicit theories of intelligence predict achievement across an adolescent transition: A longitudinal study and an intervention. *Child Development, 78*, 246–263.

Bong, M. (2009). Age-related differences in achievement goal differentiation. *Journal of Educational Psychology, 101*, 879–896.

Bong, M., & Skaalvik, E. M. (2003). Academic self-concept and self-efficacy: How different are they really? *Educational Psychology Review, 15*, 1–40.

Braten, I., & Olaussen, B. S. (2005). Profiling individual differences in student motivation: A longitudinal cluster-analytic study in different academic contexts. *Contemporary Educational Psychology, 30*, 359–396.

Brophy, J. (2005). Goal theorists should move on from performance goals. *Educational Psychologist, 40*, 167–176.

Burton, K. D., Lydon, J. E., D'Alessandro, D. U., & Koestner, R. (2006). The differential effects of intrinsic and identified motivation on well-being and performance: Prospective, experimental, and implicit approaches to self-determination theory. *Journal of Personality and Social Psychology, 91*, 750–762.

Butler, R. (2012). Striving to connect: Extending an achievement goal approach to teacher motivation to include relational goals for teaching. *Journal of Educational Psychology, 104*, 726–742.

Chartrand, T. L., & Bargh, J. A. (2002). Nonconscious motivations: Their activation, operation, and consequences. In A. Tesser, D. A. Stapel, & J. V. Wood (Eds.), *Self and motivation: Emerging psychological perspectives* (pp. 13–41). Washington, DC: American Psychological Association.

Chen, J. A., & Usher, E. (2013). Profiles of the sources of science self-efficacy. *Learning and Individual Differences, 24*, 11–21.

Chen, P. P. (2003). Exploring the accuracy and predictability of the self-efficacy beliefs of seventh-grade mathematics students. *Learning and Individual Differences, 14*, 79–92.

Chow, A., Eccles, J. S., & Salmela-Aro, K. (2012). Task value profiles across subjects and aspirations to physical and IT-related sciences in the United States and Finland. *Developmental Psychology, 48*, 1612–1628.

Ciani, K. D., Sheldon, K. M., Hilpert, J. C., & Easter, M. A. (2011). Antecedents and trajectories of achievement goals: A self-determination theory perspective. *British Journal of Educational Psychology, 81*, 223–243.

Conley, A. M. (2012). Patterns of motivation beliefs: Combining achievement goal and expectancy-value perspectives. *Journal of Educational Psychology, 104*, 32–47.

Connell, J. P., & Wellborn, J. G. (1991). Competence, autonomy, and relatedness: A motivational analysis of self-system processes. In R. Gunnar & L. A. Sroufe (Eds.), *Minnesota symposia on child psychology* (Vol. 23, pp. 43–77). Hillsdale, NJ: Lawrence Erlbaum Associates.

Corpus, J. H., McClintic-Gilbert, M. S., & Hayenga, A. O. (2009). Within-year changes in children's intrinsic and extrinsic motivational orientations: Contextual predictors and academic outcomes. *Contemporary Educational Psychology, 34*, 154–166.

Covington, M. V. (1992). *Making the grade: A self-worth perspective on motivation and school reform*. New York, NY: Cambridge University Press.

Cury, F., Elliot, A. J., Da Fonseca, D., & Moller, A. C. (2006). The social-cognitive model of achievement motivation and the 2 x 2 achievement goal framework. *Journal of Personality and Social Psychology, 90*, 666–679.

Daniels, L. M., Haynes, T. L., Stupnisky, R. H., Perry, R. P., Newall, N. E., & Pekrun, R. (2008). Individual differences in achievement goals: A longitudinal study of cognitive, emotional, and achievement outcomes. *Contemporary Educational Psychology, 33*, 584–608.

Deci, E. L., & Ryan, R. M. (1985). *Intrinsic motivation and self-determination in human behavior*. New York: Plenum.

Denissen, J. J., Zarrett, N. R., & Eccles, J. S. (2007). I like to do it, I'm able, and I know I am: Longitudinal couplings between domain-specific achievement, self-concept, and interest. *Child Development, 78*, 430–447.

Dewey, J. (1913). *Interest and effort in education*. Boston, MA: Riverside.

Durik, A. M., & Harackiewicz, J. M. (2007). Different strokes for different folks: How individual interest moderates the effects of situational factors on task interest. *Journal of Educational Psychology, 99*, 597–610.

Durik, A. M., Vida, M., & Eccles, J. S. (2006). Task values and ability beliefs as predictors of high school literacy choices: A developmental analysis. *Journal of Educational Psychology, 98*, 382–393.

Dweck, C. S. (1999). *Self-theories: Their role in motivation, personality, and development*. Philadelphia: Taylor & Francis.

Dweck, C. S. (2006). *Mindset*. New York: Random House.

Dweck, C. S., & Grant, H. (2008). Self-theories, goals, and meanings. In J. Y. Shah & W. L. Gardner (Eds.), *Handbook of motivation science* (pp. 405–416). New York, NY: Guilford.

Dweck, C. S., & Leggett, E. (1988). A social-cognitive approach to motivation and personality. *Psychological Review, 95*, 256–273.

Eccles, J. (2005). Subjective task value and the Eccles et al. model of achievement-related choices. In A. J. Elliot & C. S. Dweck (Eds.), *Handbook of competence and motivation* (pp. 105–121). New York, NY: Guilford Publications.

Eccles, J. S., Adler, T. F., Futterman, R., Goff, S. B., Kaczala, C. M., Meece, J. L., et al. (1983). Expectancies, values, and academic behaviors. In J. T. Spence (Ed.), *Achievement and achievement motives* (pp. 75–146). San Francisco: Freeman.

Eccles, J. S., & Wigfield, A. (1995). In the mind of the actor: The structure of adolescents' achievement task values and expectancy-related beliefs. *Journal of Personality and Social Psychology, 21*, 215–225.

Elliot, A. J. (1999). Approach and avoidance motivation and achievement goals. *Educational Psychologist, 34*, 169–189.

Elliot, A. J., & McGregor, H. A. (2001). A 2 × 2 achievement goal framework. *Journal of Personality and Social Psychology, 80*, 501–519.

Elliot, A. J., Murayama, K., & Pekrun, R. (2011). A 3 × 2 achievement goal model. *Journal of Educational Psychology, 103*, 632–648.

Elliot, A. J., & Thrash, T. M. (2001). Achievement goals and the hierarchical model of achievement motivation. *Educational Psychology Review, 13*, 139–156.

Ferguson, Y. L., Kasser, T., & Jahng, S. (2010). Differences in life satisfaction and school satisfaction among adolescents from three nations: The role of perceived autonomy support. *Journal of Research on Adolescence, 21*, 649–661.

Ford, M. (1992). *Motivating humans: Goals, emotions, and personal agency beliefs*. Newbury Park, CA: Sage.

Frome, P. M., Alfeld, C. J., Eccles, J. S., & Barber, B. L. (2006). Why don't they want a male-dominated job? An investigation of young women who changed their occupational aspirations. *Educational Research and Evaluation, 12*, 359–372.

Fryer, J. W., & Elliot, A. J. (2007). Stability and change in achievement goals. *Journal of Educational Psychology, 99*, 700–714.

Fulmer, S. M., & Frijters, J. C. (2011). Motivation during an excessively challenging reading task: The buffering role of relative topic interest. *Journal of Experimental Education, 79*, 185–208.

Furrer, C., & Skinner, E. (2003). Sense of relatedness as a factor in children's academic engagement and performance. *Journal of Educational Psychology, 95*, 148–162.

Good, C., Aronson, J., & Inzlicht, M. (2003). Improving adolescents' standardized test performance: An intervention to reduce the effects of stereotype threat. *Journal of Applied Developmental Psychology, 24*, 645–662.

Graham, S. (1994). Motivation in African Americans. *Review of Educational Research, 64*, 55–117.

Graham, S., & Hudley, C. (2005). Race and ethnicity in the study of motivation and competence. In A. J. Elliot & C. S. Dweck (Eds.), *Handbook of competence and motivation* (pp. 392–413). New York, NY: Guilford Publications.

Graham, S., & Williams, C. (2009). An attributional approach to motivation in school. In K. R. Wentzel & A. Wigfield (Eds.), *Handbook of motivation at school* (pp. 11–33). New York, NY: Routledge.

Guthrie, J. T., Klauda, S. L., & Ho, A. N. (2013). Modeling the relationships among reading instruction, motivation, engagement, and achievement for adolescents. *Reading Research Quarterly, 48*, 9–26.

Harackiewicz, J. M., Durik, A. M., Barron, K. E., Linnenbrink-Garcia, L., & Tauer, J. M. (2008). The role of achievement goals in the development of interest: Reciprocal relations between achievement goals, interest, and performance. *Journal of Educational Psychology, 100*, 105–122.

Harter, S. (1998). The development of self-representations. In W. Damon (Series Ed.) & N. Eisenberg (Vol. Ed.), *Handbook of child psychology* (Vol. 3, 5th ed., pp. 553–617). New York: John Wiley.

Hayenga, A. O., & Corpus, J. H. (2010). Profiles of intrinsic and extrinsic motivations: A person-centered approach to motivation and achievement in middle school. *Motivation and Emotion, 34*, 371–383.

Haynes, T. L., Daniels, L. M., Stupnisky, R. H., Perry, R. P., & Hladkyj, S. (2008). The effect of attributional retraining on mastery and performance motivation among first-year college students. *Basic and Applied Social Psychology, 30*, 198–207.

Heider, F. (1958). *The psychology of interpersonal relations*. Hillsdale, NJ: Lawrence Erlbaum Associates.

Henderson, B. B., Marx, M. H., & Kim, Y. C. (1999). Academic interests and perceived competence in American, Japanese, and Korean children. *Journal of Cross-Cultural Psychology, 30*, 32–50.

Hidi, S. (2001). Interest, reading, and learning: Theoretical and practical considerations. *Educational Psychology Review, 13*, 191–209.

Hidi, S., & Renninger, K. A. (2006). The four-phase model of interest development. *Educational Psychologist, 41*, 111–127.

Hsieh, P. H. P., & Schallert, D. L. (2008). Implications from self-efficacy and attribution theories for an understanding of undergraduates' motivation in a foreign language course. *Contemporary Educational Psychology, 33*, 513–532.

Huang, C. (2011). Achievement goals and achievement emotions: A meta-analysis. *Educational Psychology Review, 23*, 359–388.

Huang, C. (2012). Discriminant and criterion-related validity of achievement goals in predicting academic achievement: A meta-analysis. *Journal of Educational Psychology, 104*, 48–73.

Hulleman, C. S., Durik, A. M., Schweigert, S. B., & Harackiewicz, J. M. (2008). Task values, achievement goals, and interest: An integrative analysis. *Journal of Educational Psychology, 100*, 398–416.

Hulleman, C. S., & Harackiewicz, J. M. (2009). Promoting interest and performance in high school science classes. *Science, 326*, 1410–1412.

Hulleman, C. S., Schrager, S. M., Bodmann, S. M., & Harackiewicz, J. M. (2010). A meta-analytic review of achievement goal measures: Different labels for the same constructs or different constructs with similar labels? *Psychological Bulletin, 136*, 422–449.

Husman, J., & Lens, W. (1999). The role of the future in the study of motivation. *Educational Psychologist, 34,* 113–125.

Jacobs, J. E., Lanza, S., Osgood, D. W., Eccles, J. S., & Wigfield, A. (2002). Changes in children's self-competence and values: Gender and domain differences across grades one through twelve. *Child Development, 73,* 509–527.

James, W. (1890). *The principles of psychology.* London: Macmillan.

Jang, H., Reeve, J. & Deci, E. L. (2010). Engaging students in learning activities: It is not autonomy support or structure but autonomy support and structure. *Journal of Educational Psychology, 102,* 588–600.

Jang, H., Reeve, J., Ryan, R. M., & Kim, A. (2009). Can self-determination theory explain what underlies the productive, satisfying learning experiences of collectivistically oriented Korean students? *Journal of Educational Psychology, 101,* 644–661.

Kaplan, A., & Maehr, M. L. (2007). The contributions and prospects of goal orientation theory. *Educational Psychology Review, 19,* 141–184.

Karabenick, S. A. (2004). Perceived achievement goal structure and college student help seeking. *Journal of Educational Psychology, 96,* 569–581.

Karabenick, S. A., Woolley, M. E., Friedel, J. M., Ammon, B. V., Blazevski, J., Bonney, C. R., De Groot, E., Gilbert, M., Musu, L., Kempler, T., & Kelly, K. L. (2007). Cognitive processing of self-report items in educational research: Do they think what we mean? *Educational Psychologist, 42,* 139–151.

Klassen, R. (2007). Using predictions to learn about the self-efficacy of early adolescents with and without learning disabilities. *Contemporary Educational Psychology, 32,* 173–187.

Klassen, R., & Krawchuk, L. (2009). Collective motivation beliefs of early adolescents working in small groups. *Journal of School Psychology, 47,* 101–120.

Klassen, R. M., Tze, V. M. C., Betts, S. M., & Gordon, K. A. (2011). Teacher efficacy research 1998-2009: Signs of progress or unfulfilled promise? *Educational Psychology Review, 23,* 21–43.

Klassen, R. M., & Usher, E. L. (2010). Self-efficacy in educational settings: Recent research and emerging directions. In T. C. Urdan & S. A. Karabenick (Eds.), *Advances in motivation and achievement: Vol. 16A. The decade ahead: Theoretical perspectives on motivation and achievement* (pp. 1–33). Bingley, UK: Emerald Publishing Group.

Koskey, K. L., Karabenick, S. A., Woolley, M. E., Bonney, C. R., & Dever, B. V. (2010). Cognitive validity of students' self-reports of classroom mastery goal structure: What students are thinking and why it matters. *Contemporary Educational Psychology, 35,* 254–263.

Krapp, A. (2002). Structural and dynamic aspects of interest development: Theoretical considerations from an ontogenetic perspective. *Learning and Instruction, 12,* 383–409.

Krapp, A., & Prenzel, M. (2011). Research on interest in science: Theories, methods, and findings. *International Journal of Science Education, 33,* 27–50.

Kumar, R., & Maehr, M. L. (2010). Schooling, cultural diversity, and student motivation. In J. Meece, & J. Eccles (Eds.) *Handbook of research on schools, schooling, and human development* (pp. 308–324). New York, NY: Routledge.

Lau, S., & Nie, Y. (2008). Interplay between personal goals and classroom goal structures in predicting student outcomes: A multilevel analysis of person–context interactions. *Journal of Educational Psychology, 100,* 15–29.

Lau, S., & Roeser, R. W. (2008). Cognitive abilities and motivational processes in science achievement and engagement: A person-centered analysis. *Learning and Individual Differences, 18,* 497–504.

Lepper, M. R., Corpus, J. H., & Iyengar, S. S. (2005). Intrinsic and extrinsic motivational orientations in the classroom: Age differences and academic correlates. *Journal of Educational Psychology, 97,* 184–196.

Liem, A. D., Lau, S., & Nie, Y. (2008). The role of self-efficacy, task value, and achievement goals in predicting learning strategies, task disengagement, peer relationship, and achievement outcome. *Contemporary Educational Psychology, 33,* 486–512.

Linnenbrink, E. A. (2005). The dilemma of performance-approach goals: The use of multiple goal contexts to promote students' motivation and learning. *Journal of Educational Psychology, 97,* 197–213.

Linnenbrink-Garcia, L., Middleton, M. J., Ciani, K. D., Easter, M. A., O'Keefe, P. A., & Zusho, A. (2012). The strength of the relation between performance-approach and performance-avoidance goal orientations: Theoretical, methodological, and instructional implications. *Educational Psychologist, 47,* 281–301.

Linnenbrink-Garcia, L., Patall, E. A., & Messersmith, E. E. (2013). Antecedents and consequences of situational interest. *British Journal of Educational Psychology, 83,* 591–614.

Linnenbrink-Garcia, L., Tyson, D. F., & Patall, E. A. (2008). When are achievement goal orientations beneficial for academic achievement? A closer look at moderating factors. *International Review of Social Psychology, 21,* 19–70.

Liu, K. S., Cheng, Y. Y., Chen, Y. L., & Wu, Y. Y. (2009). Longitudinal effects of educational expectations and achievement attributions on adolescents' academic achievements. *Adolescence, 44,* 911–924.

Lovejoy, C. M., & Durik, A. M. (2010). Self-handicapping: The interplay between self-set and assigned achievement goals. *Motivation and Emotion, 34,* 242–252.

Luo, W., Paris, S. G., Hogan, D., & Luo, Z. (2011). Do performance goals promote learning? A pattern analysis of Singapore students' achievement goals. *Contemporary Educational Psychology, 36,* 165–176.

Madjar, N., Kaplan, A., & Weinstock, M. (2011). Clarifying mastery-avoidance goals in high school: Distinguishing between intrapersonal and task-based standards of competence. *Contemporary Educational Psychology, 36,* 268–279.

Maehr, M. L., & Midgley, C. (1991). Enhancing student motivation: A schoolwide approach. *Educational Psychologist, 26,* 399–427.

Marsh, H. W., & O'Mara, A. J. (2008). Self-concept is as multidisciplinary as it is multidimensional: A review of theory, measurement, and practice in self-concept research. In H. W. Marsh, R. G. Craven, & D. M. McInerney (Eds.). *Self-processes, learning, and enabling human potential: Dynamic new approaches* (Vol. 3, pp. 87–118). Charlotte, NC: Information Age Publishing.

McClure, J., Meyer, L. H., Garisch, J., Fischer, R., Weir, K. F., & Walkey, F. H. (2011). Students' attributions for their best and worst marks: Do they relate to achievement? *Contemporary Educational Psychology, 36,* 71–81.

Miller, R. B., Greene, B. A., Montalvo, G. P., Ravindran, B., & Nichols, J. D. (1996). Engagement in academic work: The role of learning goals, future consequences, pleasing others, and perceived ability. *Contemporary Educational Psychology, 21,* 388–422.

Mitchell, M. (1993). Situational interest: Its multifaceted structure in the secondary school mathematics classroom. *Journal of Educational Psychology, 85,* 424–436.

Muis, K. R., & Edwards, O. (2009). Examining the stability of achievement goal orientation. *Contemporary Educational Psychology, 34,* 265–277.

Murayama, K., & Elliot, A. J. (2009). The joint influence of personal achievement goals and classroom goal structures on achievement-relevant outcomes. *Journal of Educational Psychology, 101,* 432–447.

Murphy, K., & Alexander, P. (2000) A motivated exploration of motivation terminology. *Contemporary Educational Psychology, 25,* 3–53.

Murphy, P. K., & Alexander, P. A. (2002). What counts? The predictive powers of subject-matter knowledge, strategic processing, and interest in domain-specific performance. *Journal of Experimental Education, 70,* 197–214.

Nagengast, B., Marsh, H. W., Scalas, L. F., Xu, M. K., Hau, K. T., & Trautwein, U. (2011). Who took the "×" out of expectancy-value theory? A psychological mystery, a substantive-methodological synergy, and a cross-national generalization. *Psychological Science, 22,* 1058–1066.

Natale, K., Viljaranta, J., Lerkkanen, M. K., Poikkeus, A. M., & Nurmi, J. E. (2009). Cross-lagged associations between kindergarten teachers' causal attributions and children's task motivation and performance in reading. *Educational Psychology, 29,* 603–619.

Nicholls, J. G. (1984). Achievement motivation: Conceptions of ability, subjective experience, task choice, and performance. *Psychological Review, 91,* 328–346.

Nolen, S. B. (2007). Young children's motivation to read and write: Development in social contexts. *Cognition & Instruction, 25,* 219–270.

Nolen, S. B., & Ward, C. J. (2008). Sociocultural and situative research on motivation. In M. Maehr, S. Karabenick, & T. Urdan (Eds.), *Social psychological perspective on motivation and achievement* (pp. 428–460). London, UK: Emerald Group.

O'Keefe, P., Ben-Eliyahu, A., & Linnenbrink-Garcia, L. (2013). Shaping achievement goal orientations in a mastery-structured environment and concomitant changes in related contingencies of self-worth. *Motivation and Emotion, 37*, 50–64.

Otis, N., Grouzet, F. M. E., & Pelletier, L. G. (2005). Latent motivational change in an academic setting: A 3-year longitudinal study. *Journal of Educational Psychology, 97*, 170–183.

Oyserman, D., Bybee, D., & Terry, K. (2006). Possible selves and academic outcomes: How and when possible selves impel action. *Journal of Personality and Social Psychology, 91, 188–204.*

Pajares, F. (1996). Self-efficacy beliefs in academic settings. *Review of Educational Research, 66*, 543–578.

Palmer, D. H. (2009). Student interest generated during an inquiry skills lesson. *Journal of Research in Science Teaching, 46*, 147–165.

Patall, E. A. (2012). The motivational complexity of choosing: A review of theory and research. In R. Ryan (Ed.), *Oxford handbook of human motivation* (pp. 249–279). New York, NY: Oxford University Press.

Patall, E. A. (2013). Constructing motivation through choice, interest, and interestingness. *Journal of Educational Psychology, 105*, 522–534.

Patall, E. A., Dacy, B. S., & Han, C. (2014). The role of competence in the effects of choice on motivation. *Journal of Experimental Social Psychology, 50*, 27–44.

Patrick, H., Kaplan, A., & Ryan, A. M. (2011). Positive classroom motivational environments: Convergence between mastery goal structure and classroom social climate. *Journal of Educational Psychology, 103*, 367–382.

Paulick, I., Watermann, R., & Nückles, M. (2013). Achievement goals and school achievement: The transition to different school tracks in secondary school. *Contemporary Educational Psychology, 38*, 75–86.

Pekrun, R. (2006). The control-value theory of achievement emotions: Assumptions, corollaries, and implications for educational research and practice. *Educational Psychology Review, 18*, 315–341.

Pekrun, R., & Perry, R. P. (2014). Control-value theory of achievement emotions. In R. Pekrun & L. Linnenbrink-Garcia (Eds.), *Handbook of emotions in education* (pp. 120–141). New York: Routledge.

Perez, T., Cromley, J. G., & Kaplan, A. (2014). The role of identity development, values, and costs in college STEM retention. *Journal of Educational Psychology, 106*, 315–329.

Perry, N. E., Turner, J. C., & Meyer, D. K. (2006). Classrooms as contexts for motivating learning. In P. A. Alexander & P. H. Winne (Eds.), *Handbook of educational psychology* (2nd ed., pp. 327–348). Mahwah, NJ: Lawrence Erlbaum.

Perry, R. P. (2003). Perceived (academic) control and causal thinking in achievement settings. *Canadian Psychology, 44*, 312–331.

Perry, R. P., Stupnisky, R. H., Daniels, L. M., & Haynes, T. L. (2008). Attributional (explanatory) thinking about failure in new achievement settings. *European Journal of Psychology of Education, 23*, 459–475.

Perry, R. P., Stupnisky, R. H., Hall, N. C., Chipperfield, J. G., & Weiner, B. (2010). Bad starts and better finishes: Attributional retraining and initial performance in competitive achievement settings. *Journal of Social and Clinical Psychology, 29*, 668–700.

Peterson, S. E., & Schreiber, J. B. (2006). An attributional analysis of personal and interpersonal motivation for collaborative projects. *Journal of Educational Psychology, 98*, 777–787.

Peterson, S. E., & Schreiber, J. B. (2012). Personal and interpersonal motivation for group projects: Replications of an attributional analysis. *Educational Psychology Review, 24*, 287–311.

Pintrich, P. R. (2000). Multiple goals, multiple pathways: The role of goal orientation in learning and achievement. *Journal of Educational Psychology, 92*, 544–555.

Ratelle, C. F., Guay, F., Vallerand, R. J., Larose, S., & Senecal, C. (2007). Autonomous, controlled, and amotivated types of academic motivation: A person-oriented analysis. *Journal of Educational Psychology, 99*, 734–746.

Reeve, J. (2009). Why teachers adopt a controlling motivating style toward students and how they can become more autonomy supportive. *Educational Psychologist, 44*, 159–175.

Reeve, J., & Jang, H. (2006). What teachers say and do to support students' autonomy during a learning activity. *Journal of Educational Psychology, 98*, 209–218.

Reeve, J. & Lee, W. (2012). Neuroscience and human motivation. In R. Ryan (Ed.), *Oxford handbook of human motivation* (pp. 365–380). New York, NY: Oxford University Press.

Renninger, K. A., & Hidi, S. (2002). Student interest and achievement: Developmental issues raised by a case study. In A. Wigfield & J. S. Eccles (Eds.), *Development of achievement motivation* (pp. 173–195). San Diego, CA: Academic Press.

Renninger, K. A., & Hidi, S. (2011). Revisiting the conceptualization, measurement, and generation of interest. *Educational Psychologist, 46*, 168–184.

Renninger, K., Hidi, S. E., & Krapp, A. E. (Eds.) (1992). *The role of interest in learning and development.* Hillsdale, NJ: Lawrence Erlbaum Associates.

Rodkin, P. C., Ryan, A. M., Jamison, R., & Wilson, T. (2013). Social goals, social behavior, and social status in middle childhood. *Developmental Psychology, 49*, 1139–1150.

Roorda, D. L., Koomen, H. M. Y., Spilt, J. L., & Ooart, F. J. (2011). The influence of affective teacher–student relationships on students' school engagement and achievement: A meta-analytic approach. *Review of Educational Research, 81*, 493–529.

Rotgans, J. I., & Schmidt, H. G. (2011). Situational interest and academic achievement in the active-learning classroom. *Learning and Instruction, 21*, 58–67.

Rotter, J. B. (1966). Generalized expectancies for internal versus external control of reinforcement. *Psychological Monographs: General and Applied, 80*, 1–28.

Ryan, A. M., & Patrick, H. (2001). The classroom social environment and changes in adolescents' motivation and engagement during middle school. *American Educational Research Journal, 38*, 437–460.

Ryan, A. M., & Shim, S. S. (2006). Social achievement goals: The nature and consequences of different orientations toward social competence. *Personality and Social Psychology Bulletin, 32*, 1246–1263.

Ryan, A. M., & Shim, S. S. (2008). An exploration of young adolescents' social achievement goals and social adjustment in middle school. *Journal of Educational Psychology, 100*, 672–687.

Ryan, R. M., & Connell, J. P. (1989). Perceived locus of causality and internalization: Examining reasons for acting in two domains. *Journal of Personality and Social Psychology, 57*, 749–761.

Ryan, R. M., & Deci, E. L. (2000). Self-determination theory and the facilitation of intrinsic motivation, social development, and well-being. *American Psychologist, 55*, 68–78.

Schiefele, U. (2009). Situational and individual interest. In K. R. Wentzel & A. Wigfield (Eds.), *Handbook of motivation at school* (pp. 197–222). New York: Routledge.

Schraw, G., & Lehman, S. (2001). Situational interest: A review of the literature and directions for future research. *Educational Psychology Review, 13*, 23–52.

Schunk, D. H., Meece, J. L., & Pintrich, P. R. (2014). *Motivation in education: Theory, research, and applications* (4th ed.). Upper Saddle River, NJ: Merrill Prentice Hall.

Schunk, D. H., & Pajares, F. (2005). Competence perceptions and academic functioning. In A. J. Elliot & C. S. Dweck (Eds.), *Handbook of competence and motivation* (pp. 85–104). New York: Guilford Press.

Senko, C., & Harackiewicz, J. M. (2005). Regulation of achievement goals: The role of competence feedback. *Journal of Educational Psychology, 97*, 320–336.

Senko, C., Hulleman, C. S., & Harackiewicz, J. M. (2011). Achievement goal theory at the crossroads: Old controversies, current challenges, and new directions. *Educational Psychologist, 46*, 26–47.

Shell, D. F., & Husman, J. (2008). Control, motivation, affect, and strategic self-regulation in the college classroom: A multidimensional phenomenon. *Journal of Educational Psychology, 100*, 443–459.

Shernoff, D. J., & Csikszentmihalyi, M. (2009). Flow in schools: Cultivating engaged learners and optimal learning environments. In R. Gilman, E. S. Huebner, & M. Furlong (Eds.), *Handbook of positive psychology in schools* (pp. 131–145). New York: Routledge.

Silvia, P. J. (2005). What is interesting? Exploring the appraisal structure of interest. *Emotion, 5*, 89–102.

Skinner, E. A. (1995). *Perceived control, motivation, and coping.* Thousand Oaks, CA: Sage Publications.

Soric, I., & Palekčic, M. (2009). The role of students' interests in self-regulated learning: The relationship between students' interests, learning strategies and causal attributions. *European Journal of Psychology of Education, 24,* 545–565.

Stroet, K., Opdenakker, M., & Minnaert, A. (2013). Effects of need supportive teaching on early adolescents' motivation and engagement: A review of the literature. *Educational Psychology Review, 9,* 65–87.

Trautwein, U., Marsh, H. W., Nagengast, B., Lüdtke, O., Nagy, G., & Jonkmann, K. (2012). Probing for the multiplicative term in modern expectancy–value theory: A latent interaction modeling study. *Journal of Educational Psychology, 104,* 763–777.

Tuominen-Soini, H., Salmela-Aro, K., & Niemivirta, M. (2012). Achievement goal orientations and academic well-being across the transition to upper secondary education. *Learning and Individual Differences, 22,* 290–305.

Turner, J. C., Gray, D. L., Anderman, L. H., Dawson, H. S., & Anderman, E. M. (2013). Getting to know my teacher: Does the relation between perceived mastery goal structures and perceived teacher support change across the school year? *Contemporary Educational Psychology, 38,* 316–317.

Turner, J. C., Meyer, D. K., Cox, K. E., Logan, C., DiCintio, M., & Thomas, C. (1998). Creating contexts for involvement in mathematics. *Journal of Educational Psychology, 90,* 730–745.

Turner, J. C., Warzon, K. B., & Christensen, A. (2011). Motivating mathematics learning: Changes in teachers' practices and beliefs during a nine-month collaboration. *American Educational Research Journal, 48,* 718–762.

Urdan, T. (2004). Using multiple methods to assess students' perceptions of classroom goal structures. *European Psychologist, 9,* 222–231.

Urdan, T. (2010). The challenges and promise of research on classroom goal structures. In J. L. Meece & J. S. Eccles (Eds.), *Handbook of research on schools, schooling, and human development* (pp. 92–108). New York: Routledge.

Urdan, T., & Mestas, M. (2006). The goals behind performance goals. *Journal of Educational Psychology, 98,* 354–365.

Usher, E. L., & Pajares, F. (2008). Sources of self-efficacy in school: Critical review of the literature and future directions. *Review of Educational Research, 78,* 751–796.

Vansteenkiste, M., Sierens, E., Goossens, L., Soenens, B., Dochy, F., Mouratidis, A., Aelterman, N., Haerens, L., & Beyers, M. (2012). Identifying configurations of perceived teacher autonomy support and structure: Associations with self-regulated learning, motivation and problem behavior. *Learning and Instruction, 22,* 431–439.

Vansteenkiste, M., Sierens, E., Soenens, B., Luyckx, K., & Lens, W. (2009). Motivational profiles from a self-determination perspective: The quality of motivation matters. *Journal of Educational Psychology, 101,* 671–688.

Vansteenkiste, M., Zhou, M., Lens, W., & Soenens, B. (2005). Experiences of autonomy and control among Chinese learners: Vitalizing or immobilizing? *Journal of Educational Psychology, 97,* 468–483.

Vispoel, W. P., & Austin, J. R. (1995). Success and failure in junior high school: A critical incident approach to understanding students' attributional beliefs. *American Educational Research Journal, 32,* 377–412.

Walker, C. O., Greene, B. A., & Mansell, R. A. (2006). Identification with academics, intrinsic/extrinsic motivation, and self-efficacy as predictors of cognitive engagement. *Learning and Individual Differences, 16,* 1–12.

Watt, H. M. (2004). Development of adolescents' self-perceptions, values, and task perceptions according to gender and domain in 7th through 11th grade Australian students. *Child Development, 75,* 1556–1574.

Weiner, B. (1985). An attributional theory of achievement motivation and emotion. *Psychological Review, 92,* 548–573.

Weiner, B. (2011). An attribution theory of motivation. In A. W. Kruglanski, P. A. M. Van Lange, & E. T. Higgins (Eds.) *Handbook of theories in social psychology* (Vol. 1, pp. 135–155). London, UK: Sage Publications.

White, R. W. (1959). Motivation reconsidered: The concept of competence. *Psychological Review, 66,* 297–333.

Wigfield, A., Battle, A., Keller, L. B., & Eccles, J. S. (2002). Sex differences in motivation, self-concept, career aspiration, and career choice: Implications for cognitive development. In A. McGillicuddy-De Lisi & R. De-Lisi (Eds.), *Biology, society, and behavior: The development of sex differences in cognition* (pp. 93–124). Westport, CT: Ablex Publishing.

Wigfield, A., Eccles, J. S., Schiefele, U., Roeser, R. W., & Davis-Kean, P. (2006). Development of achievement motivation. In N. Eisenberg, W. Damon, & R. M. Lerner (Eds.), *Handbook of child psychology: Vol. 3, Social, emotional, and personality development* (6th ed., pp. 933–1002). Hoboken, NJ: John Wiley.

Wigfield, A., Tonks, S., & Klauda, S. L. (2009). Expectancy-value theory. In K. R. Wentzel & A. Wigfield (Eds.), *Handbook of motivation at school* (pp. 55–75). New York: Routledge.

Wolters, C. A. (2004). Advancing achievement goal theory: Using goal structures and goal orientations to predict students' motivation, cognition, and achievement. *Journal of Educational Psychology, 96,* 236–250.

Wolters, C. A., Fan, W., & Daugherty, S. G. (2013). Examining achievement goals and causal attributions together as predictors of academic functioning. *Journal of Experimental Education, 81,* 295–321.

Wormington, S. V., Corpus, J. H., & Anderson, K. G. (2012). A person-centered investigation of academic motivation and its correlates in high school. *Learning and Individual Differences, 22,* 429–438.

Zhou, M., & Winne, P. H. (2012). Modeling academic achievement by self-reported versus traced goal orientation. *Learning and Instruction, 22,* 413–419.

Zusho, A., & Clayton, K. (2011). Culturalizing achievement goal theory and research. *Educational Psychologist, 46,* 239–260.

# 8

# Volition

*Gabriele Oettingen*
New York University

*Jana Schrage*
University of Hamburg, Germany

*Peter M. Gollwitzer*
New York University

Consider a teacher who is expressing concern about a student's academic performance. The teacher says the student lags behind the rest of the class, and needs to do well on an important, upcoming test. The student listens to the teacher's feedback: To prepare for the test, he decides to study an extra hour every day during the next few weeks. The incentive value of regularly studying an extra hour is high as the student wants to excel on the test. Also, he knows from past performance that he actually *can* study every day for an extra hour. Given a high incentive value and high expectations of successfully putting in extra work, the student is motivated and begins to add regular study time starting the next day. However, after a week has passed, the student has managed to add the extra hour just once. Even worse, he did not sleep well last night and is now overly tired. The student still intends to sit down and open his book that evening, but just then a friend calls and asks him over to watch an award-winning movie. In light of these difficulties and temptations, it is now volition that determines whether or not the student will give in and see the movie or go forward with his intention to stay home and study.

## Motivation and Volition

In this chapter, we explore how volitional processes affect behavior change. In contrast to motivational processes such as those affecting expectations and incentive values, volitional processes are needed when there is resistance to or conflict with attaining a desired future. In education, volitional processes support students, teachers, and administrators in mastering resistance or conflict (e.g., obstacles or temptations) on the way to reaching a desired future.

We conceptualize motivation as the energy to pursue a desired future and the direction that helps to channel this energy. Our definition builds upon that of Hull (1943), who proposed that variation in behavior is a function of intensity and direction. The intensity of a behavior is defined by the aroused energy (Duffy, 1934), whereas the direction of action is defined by whether the behavior is aimed at approaching or avoiding a certain stimulus (Atkinson, 1957; McClelland, 1985; see also Oettingen et al., 2009). The sources of intensity and direction are specified as motive disposition, expectation, and incentive value (Atkinson, 1957; Hull, 1943; Tolman, 1932).

Regarding the determinants of motivation, Gollwitzer (1990, 2012) coined the summary terms of desirability and feasibility. Desirability is defined as the expected value of a certain desired future (i.e., the perceived attractiveness of the expected short- and long-term consequences, within and outside the person, of having reached the desired future), while feasibility relates to expectations of attaining the desired future. Expectations are beliefs or judgments of perceived probabilities that are based on experiences in the past (e.g., Bandura, 1977; Mischel, 1973). Expectations come in different forms. There are: (a) expectations of whether or not one is capable of performing a certain behavior that is necessary to achieve a desired outcome (self-efficacy expectations: Bandura, 1977); (b) expectations of whether or not the performed behavior will lead to the desired outcome (outcome expectations: Bandura, 1977; Mischel, 1973); and (c) general expectations of whether or not one will reach the desired outcome (general expectations: Oettingen & Mayer, 2002).

Theory holds and research shows that beliefs pertaining to expectations and incentive values are the key determinants of motivation. Thus motivational strategies can be defined as those that are tailored to change perceived incentive values and expectations to attain a desired future. In educational contexts the aimed-for change of beliefs focuses on increasing the incentive value of a normative behavior (e.g., studying) and decreasing the incentive value of a non-normative behavior (e.g., attending class unprepared). At the same time, motivational procedures pertain to increasing expectations of performing the normative behavior. Chapter 7 (this volume) discusses the history of research on motivation, and Chapter 12 (this volume) discusses motivation interventions in education.

In contrast, the concept of *volition* comprises self-regulation strategies that target resistance and conflict (e.g., conflicts that may block or delay goal striving). Therefore, volitional strategies often help people to clarify goals when goals are ambiguous or equivocal; they prepare for potential obstacles standing in the way of attaining the desired future; and they enable individuals to stay on track and pursue their desired future even in the face of impediments, difficulties, and temptations. In line with this definition of volition, William James (1890) pointed out that volition is needed when a person faces resistance or conflict. James stated that:

> volition is a psychic or moral fact pure and simple, and is absolutely completed when the stable state of the idea is there. . . . The essential achievement of the will, in short, when it is most "voluntary", is to attend to a difficult object and hold it fast before the mind. (James, 1890, p. 446)

Accordingly, the use of volitional strategies supports individuals as they act upon the pre-existing incentive value of their desired futures and the expectations of attaining them. Put differently, using volitional strategies aims at translating high incentive value and expectations into respective behavior.

In the next sections, we provide an overview of the history and recent research on volitional processes and strategies that are relevant to educational settings. In particular, we discuss two volitional strategies and their combination to illustrate the role that volition plays in learning and performance. These strategies are mental contrasting and forming implementation intentions; combining mental contrasting with implementation intentions (MCII) forms a third kind of strategy.

## Volitional Processes and Interventions

As noted above, volition is required whenever people who have a desired future in mind face resistances or conflict (James, 1890; Oettingen, 2000, 2012; Oettingen, Wittchen, & Gollwitzer, 2013). In the context of education theory, volition plays a role in the translation of dispositions and processes of motivation into outcomes of learning and performance (e.g., Corno, 1993, 2004; Corno & Kanfer, 1993). Contemporary approaches to research on volition distinguish between top-down and bottom-up processes of volition (Boekaerts & Corno, 2005). In top-down processes the volition needed is determined by the goals that students pursue. In bottom-up processes the students react to stimuli in their environment (e.g., stressors) and adjust their volition to the situation. We will now briefly describe three prominent examples for the interplay of top-down and bottom-up volitional processes:

goal-shielding, the goal–subgoal hierarchy, and the regulation of conflicts between growth and well-being.

### Volitional Processes

*Goal shielding.* One serious challenge in goal pursuit is shielding the adopted goal from interfering goals and behaviors (Gollwitzer, Bayer, & McCulloch, 2005). Conducive for goal shielding are, for example, high goal commitment (Shah, Friedman, & Kruglanski, 2002) and an action orientation in contrast to a state orientation (Kuhl & Beckmann, 1994). Some assumed mechanisms that drive goal shielding are: environmental control, cognitive control, and emotion control (Kuhl & Beckmann, 1994). Furthermore, the interplay between a person's present emotions and the proximity of the goal seems to drive goal-shielding processes. If the goal is perceived as distal, positive emotions increase goal shielding because they signal high goal commitment. However, if the goal is perceived as proximal, positive emotions decrease goal shielding because they signal goal attainment; then negative emotions increase goal shielding (Louro, Pieters, & Zeelenberg, 2007).

*Goals and subgoals.* Recent research also takes into account that more than one goal is activated at any given time, and that every superordinate goal can be broken down into several subgoals (Fishbach, Shah, & Kruglanski, 2004). If the superordinate goal is activated, initial success regarding a subgoal signals high commitment to the superordinate goal; in contrast, initial failure on the subgoal indicates low commitment to the superordinate goal. If the superordinate goal is not activated, however, initial success on a subgoal signals goal attainment, whereas initial failure on a subgoal leaves the goal incomplete (Fishbach, Dhar, & Zhang, 2006). According to this approach, goal pursuit can only be understood in the context of the goal structure that characterizes the individual.

*Dual processing self-regulation model.* This model is specific to classroom learning and distinguishes between two pathways of self-regulation: the growth pathway and the well-being pathway (Boekaerts & Cascallar, 2006; Boekaerts & Corno, 2005). Assuming that on the growth pathway volition works top-down, students regulate their cognition, emotion, and behavior to pursue the respective goal (e.g., learning a new language). Assuming that on the well-being pathway volition works bottom-up, students regulate their cognition, emotion, and behavior to maintain their well-being in the face of hindrances (e.g., avoiding harm or protecting one's self-esteem). Students' self-regulation efforts in the well-being path are cue-driven as they react to hindrances and setbacks in their environment, trying to avoid further misery and instead stabilize well-being.

### Volitional Interventions

Various interventions attest to volitional processes in the field of education. Corno (1994) provides an overview of such interventions, differentiating them by three categories: (1) volitional interventions directed at particular students or content areas; (2) volitional interventions that focus on improving homework; and (3) interventions that aim at collaborative efforts with teachers to design classroom activities that promote volitional control.

### Volitional interventions directed at particular students and content areas.

Interventions in educational settings often focus only on subjects students learn in school or are directed at students who display particular problems (e.g., impulse control). However, domain specific instructions may provide insufficient context for retention and transfer (see e.g., Hattie, Biggs, & Purdie, 1996), and not all students need instruction in volitional control. One study by Perels, Dignath, and Schmitz (2009) used a pretest/post-test–control-group design to test a self-regulation intervention in sixth-grade mathematics students in Germany. They observed a teacher instructing one class using the regular math curriculum offering strategies for solving math problems (e.g., segmentation of complex problems into components; control group), and then observed the same teacher instructing another class in using self-regulation techniques when solving the math problems (e.g., dealing with distractions; intervention group). In the post-test, the intervention group reported more self-regulated behavior than the control group, while there was no difference in the pretest. In addition, only in the intervention group did scores of mathematical competences improve over time. Other interventions have targeted processes of volition and motivation in reading and writing for students who are particularly in need of help (Schunk & Zimmerman, 2007).

### Interventions for volitional enhancement during homework.

Homework can be considered a reference task for studying processes of volitional control. Specifically, it can be used to observe how volitional control is applied by students and how such control is taught by parents and teachers (Corno, 2011). In a recent example, Xu, Yuan, Xu, and Xu (2014) studied variables that predict time management in the context of mathematics homework in a large sample of Chinese secondary students. The more students reported to engage in volitional control (e.g., turn off the TV), the better they reported to manage their time (e.g., I set priorities and plan ahead), even though other important factors (e.g., prior math achievements) were statistically adjusted for. These results have implications for creating volition-enhancing interventions for parents and caregivers. Educators can teach students strategies to improve their homework routines, and students can share their effective strategies for doing homework with others in a class or via social media. Another reference task for studying volitional control is strategic reading (see Pressley et al., 1990, for interventions enhancing reading comprehension and fluency). This area of research is particularly important now that so much studying is done online or using a computer (for examples, see Corno, 2011).

### Collaborative interventions with teachers on curriculum development.

Randi (2005) collaborated with pre-service teachers to develop the teachers' volitional control skills, by teaching them the theoretical foundations of self-regulation as described in Boekaerts and Corno (2005), as well as knowledge about opportunities to use self-regulation strategies (e.g., emotion control strategies related to teaching effectively). The teachers were also encouraged to recall curricular experiences that allowed them to model specific volitional control strategies. They were taught to focus on negotiating opportunities to teach the curricula they had developed, on evaluating their own teaching practices, and on seeking feedback from mentors.

### Interventions deploying conscious and non-conscious processes.

Next to classifying interventions according to the needs in the classroom, as discussed above, volitional interventions may be grouped according to whether they deploy conscious processes versus processes that occur outside of awareness (non-conscious processes), or whether they use both conscious and non-conscious processes. Some approaches, including our own lines of investigation, focus on conscious volitional strategies that trigger volitional processes outside of awareness.

### Mental Contrasting

Fantasy realization theory (review by Oettingen, 2012) specifies a powerful volitional strategy of behavior change, referred to as mental contrasting. Mental contrasting involves engaging in fantasies about a desired future, and alongside reflecting realities that might impede attaining that future. Mental contrasting produces a wise use of energy: Heightened energy when people perceive their chances of success as being high, and reduced energy when people perceive their chances of success as being low (Oettingen, 2000; Oettingen, Pak, & Schnetter, 2001; Oettingen et al., 2009; summary by Oettingen, 2012).

In educational settings, when students mentally contrast, they first imagine a desired future (e.g., to get a good grade on an upcoming math test), and then imagine the reality that stands in the way of attaining this desired future (e.g., being distracted). Mental contrasting activates expectations of successfully overcoming the reality towards attaining the desired future: If these expectations are high, students will actively pursue (commit to and strive for) reaching the desired future of attaining a good grade. If expectations of success are low, students will refrain from realizing the desired future and will curb their efforts to reach this future, or let go of pursuing this future to save their resources for more promising endeavors (Oettingen et al., 2001). In this way, mental contrasting helps people differentiate between their pursuits, allowing them to invest their resources into futures that warrant success and to refrain from investing in futures they deem futile. Mental contrasting thus qualifies as a strategy that conserves energy and resources, both in the short and the long term.

Beyond mental contrasting, fantasy realization theory specifies three more modes of thought: (a) indulging, which means imagining the desired future without considering the reality; (b) dwelling, focusing on the reality without the desired future in mind; and (c) reverse contrasting, first focusing on the present reality and thereafter elaborating on the desired future. In contrast to mental contrasting, indulging does not juxtapose the resisting reality to the positive future, and dwelling does not incorporate the desired future into thoughts about the reality. Such one-sided thoughts and images do not signal that resistances need to be overcome to attain the desired future (indulging) and they do not suggest in which direction to act (dwelling). Finally, with respect to reverse contrasting, it is important to keep in mind that the effects of mental contrasting depend on people perceiving the present reality as impeding the desired future. In mental contrasting, individuals first imagine the desired future, and thus the future works as the reference point. Only then do they elaborate the present reality. Thus the reality can change its meaning and become an obstacle to attain the desired future (Kappes, Wendt, Reinelt, & Oettingen, 2013). Reversing this order (i.e., reverse contrasting), by first imagining the present reality, and then the desired future, does not present the reality as impeding or standing in the way of the desired future. Therefore, reverse contrasting does not promote goal pursuit and behavior change in line with expectations of success (e.g., Kappes et al., 2013; Oettingen et al., 2001, Study 3; Sevincer & Oettingen, 2013). In sum, indulging, dwelling, or reverse contrasting do not activate expectations of success and none of them leads to prudent pursuit of the future that is in line with one's chances to attain the desired future (Oettingen et al., 2001; Oettingen, 2012).

Think about the classroom context, and an elementary-school student who wants to improve her reading skills during the next term. The student's incentive value is high; she loves science fiction and is keen on learning how to read the books on her own. She has high expectations of successfully improving her reading skills; thus far, she has been a good student. Using mental contrasting, the student first vividly imagines how truly wonderful it would be to read her favorite science fiction book all by herself, independently and without any assistance from her parents (desired future). Then she identifies what it is in herself that holds her back from practicing her reading skills. What is her main obstacle? The student discovers that her main obstacle is that she is constantly distracted by social media, with all the tempting news of her friends (obstacle of the present reality). She now imagines these feelings of temptation, how she is tempted to look at her friends' cool pictures and getting the latest news. After this short imagery-based exercise of mental contrasting, the student recognizes that constantly looking at her social media outlets prevents her from becoming an independent and self-reliant reader. Now she will shut off her media applications, at least for a while, and practice reading.

***Effects of mental contrasting.*** Mental contrasting has been shown to effectively change behavior in many different educational settings and with diverse student samples (see summary by Oettingen, 2012). For example, one experimental study investigated first-year students in a vocational school for computer programming. For these students, mathematics was the most critical subject and they viewed improving their math skills as highly desirable. Oettingen et al. (2001, Study 4) instructed the participants to identify factors they associated with excelling in mathematics (participants named e.g., better chances to get a good job, to simply be happy), and to identify aspects of their present reality that may stand in their way of excelling (participants named e.g., not enough sleep and partying). Three modes of thought were then experimentally induced. Participants were directed to imagine and write about two aspects of their desired future and two aspects of their present reality, in an alternating order, beginning with the desired future (mental contrasting condition). Alternatively, they had to mentally elaborate four aspects of the desired future (indulging condition) or four aspects of the present reality (dwelling condition). Participants were then asked, directly following the experimental procedure, to rate (on five-point scales) how energized they felt with respect to excelling in mathematics (e.g., how active, eventful, energetic). Two weeks later, participants' teachers reported how much effort each student had invested in schoolwork during the past 2 weeks. In addition, the teachers provided course grades for each student during that time period.

For students in the mental contrasting condition, the link between expectations of success and being energized was significantly stronger than in the indulging and dwelling conditions. In addition, mental contrasting students were found to have exerted significantly more effort, and earned grades in line with their expectations of success: Those with high expectations of success felt most energized, exerted most effort, and were awarded with the highest grades. The reverse was true for those with low expectations of success. Students in the indulging and dwelling conditions ranged in between, regardless of their expectations of success.

A series of further experimental studies replicated these results. Those pertinent to education involved: studying abroad in university students (Oettingen et al., 2001, Study 2), acquiring English as a foreign language in middle-school students (Oettingen, Hönig, & Gollwitzer, 2000, Study 1), excelling in giving an ad hoc presentation in university students (Oettingen et al., 2009, Study 2), seeking help from academic experts in university students (Oettingen, Stephens, Mayer, & Brinkmann, 2010, Study 1), increasing tolerance towards members of minorities in high-school students (Oettingen, Mayer, Thorpe, Janetzke, & Lorenz, 2005, Study 2), and successfully combining work and family life while raising a child as a graduate student (Oettingen, 2000, Study 2). Further, strength of goal pursuit was assessed in these studies by cognitive (e.g., making plans), affective (e.g., feelings of responsibility to attain the desired future), motivational (e.g., feelings of disappointment), and behavioral indicators (e.g., exerted effort and spent resources). Indicators were measured subjectively (e.g., self-report) and objectively (e.g., content analysis, independent observations), directly after the experiment or weeks and months later. Across experiments, the described pattern of findings was observed: Participants with high expectations in the mental contrasting condition vigorously pursued their desired future, while participants with low expectations decreased their efforts or let go altogether. Participants in the indulging or dwelling conditions pursued their future with moderate effort and success regardless of whether their expectations of success were high or low. To summarize, only mental contrasting participants regulated their goal pursuit so that their resources were protected. They showed high investment when the attainment of the future was likely and low or no investment when attainment was unlikely.

It was hypothesized and found that mental contrasting does not change expectations of success, but activates pre-existing expectations of success, translating them into goal pursuit and behavior change (Oettingen, 2012). In two studies, Oettingen, Marquardt, and Gollwitzer (2012) investigated whether mental contrasting translates expectations into heightened effort and performance even if they are induced *in situ* via positive situational feedback. The authors used a creativity task to provide positive or moderate bogus feedback to college students. Thereafter participants engaged in mental contrasting, indulging, dwelling, or in contrasting irrelevant content. Mental contrasting increased creative performance after positive feedback compared with moderate feedback. Indulging, dwelling, and irrelevant contrasting did not change creative performance, regardless of feedback. Importantly, by manipulating expectations through bogus feedback, the Oettingen et al. (2012) studies showed that mental contrasting indeed translates expectations of success into behavior change, rather than affecting a third variable that may underlie both expectations of success and behavior. Further, these studies suggest that if the prerequisite of high expectations of success is not met, then such expectations can be induced on the spot through the provision of positive performance feedback. This is an important finding for teachers who wish to increase energy and study efforts in their students. By providing students with doable challenges (e.g., in math) and giving them respective positive feedback, teachers can take advantage of the students' heightened expectations: mental contrasting will then effectively increase students' efforts and successful performance, even in areas and tasks that they had not been strong in originally (e.g., to excel in math tests).

***Processes of mental contrasting.*** The effects of mental contrasting on behavior change are mediated by cognitive and motivational processes. As for cognitive changes, mental contrasting paired with high expectations strengthens the mental associations between future and the obstacle of reality as well as between the obstacle and the instrumental means to overcome it. It also changes the meaning of reality, in that the reality now becomes interpreted as an obstacle (Kappes & Oettingen, 2014; Kappes, Oettingen, & Pak, 2012; Kappes et al., 2013). Regarding motivational changes, mental contrasting catalyzes energy (measured by systolic blood pressure). That is, when prospects are good, it heightens energy,

when they are bad it relaxes, so that the saved energy can be used for alternative projects. Importantly, changes in energy mediate the relation between expectations and goal pursuit (Oettingen et al., 2009; Sevincer, Busatta, & Oettingen, 2014). Finally, regarding responses to negative feedback, mental contrasting changes the ways students deal with negative feedback. When the desired future seems reachable, negative feedback is processed as valuable information for reaching the desired future. It is processed without impairing a student's subjective competence, and it bolsters beneficial attributions (Kappes et al., 2012).

Taken together, mental contrasting will help students to attain success (e.g., excelling in a test, being friendly to the teacher) without consciously exerting effort. That is, the described processes mediating the effects of mental contrasting happen outside of awareness. Specifically, the building of mental associations between the desired future (e.g., good job opportunities) and obstacles of the present reality (e.g., poor language skills), and between the obstacles and instrumental means that deal with these obstacles (e.g., asking the teacher for help with language homework) will lead the student to actually go ahead and realize the desired future (e.g., ask the teacher for support; e.g., Oettingen et al., 2010c). Again, without awareness, mental contrasting will also provide the necessary energy and effort to reach the desired future (e.g., seek the teacher's help).

It comes as no surprise, then, that objective measures of effort and performance show the effects of mental contrasting more clearly than self-report measures. In other words, it may be hard for students to report on the exerted effort, as this effort is triggered outside of awareness. Finally, mental contrasting prepares them to effectively respond to critical feedback, by allowing them to non-consciously process immanently useful information entailed in the negative feedback. Mental contrasting is beneficial also because it shelters students from taking negative feedback from their teacher personally. Reducing students' defensiveness should aid student–teacher interactions when negative feedback is impending. In their entirety the reported processes instigated by mental contrasting support students to master some of the most difficult tasks in the educational context: initiating appropriate behavior change and carrying on in light of difficulties and setbacks.

***Mental contrasting as a metacognitive intervention.*** So far, mental contrasting has been shown to be a volitional self-regulation strategy that helps people initiate and sustain behavior change across time and in the face of difficulties. The question arises whether mental contrasting could be taught as a metacognitive strategy, that is, as a strategy that implies thinking about one's own thinking (Flavell, 1979). Can students learn mental contrasting as a skill that enables them to wisely select and prudently pursue their own idiosyncratic wishes? Can teachers and administrators learn and adopt the strategy in everyday life? Such use of mental contrasting may support individuals as they study, teach, or provide other services of schooling that call for effective time management and prioritizing goals.

*Effective time management and decision making.* Corno (2001) made the case that time and resource management as well as prioritizing goals is an important volitional skill for students in school and in everyday life. Mental contrasting, which promotes selective goal pursuit, should benefit students, teachers, and administrators by improving their time management and decision making. The effectiveness of mental contrasting for time management and decision making was shown in a study with middle-level health care administrators who had to work on many projects simultaneously and constantly adjust their time schedules (Oettingen, Mayer, & Brinkmann, 2010). The administrators were taught mental contrasting as a metacognitive strategy. That is, participants learned how to apply mental contrasting to a host of wishes or concerns in their everyday lives.

The administrators were randomly assigned to two conditions. In one condition, participants were taught to use mental contrasting regarding important everyday concerns, while participants in the other condition were taught to indulge in respective future fantasies. Participants generated concerns such as solving a conflict with an employee, writing a report, or organizing a dinner party, all of which they then either practiced using mental contrasting or indulging. The selected problems had to be controllable and participants needed to be able to act upon them. However, participants also had to feel somewhat uneasy about how to solve them. Each participant practiced the respective strategy (mental contrasting vs. indulging) using at least six such problems, and were then told to apply it to as many problems as possible during the upcoming weeks (Oettingen et al., 2010a). Two weeks later, compared to those in the indulging condition, participants in the mental contrasting condition reported to have managed their time more effectively and to have made better everyday life decisions.

As outlined above, mental contrasting with low expectations of success leads to relatively weak goal pursuit or even goal disengagement. However, sometimes goal disengagement from certain focal goals is unwanted for ethical or practical reasons. For example, it is not desirable for students to disengage from the goal of attending school or learning basic skills such as reading, writing, or math. In these cases, mental contrasting can still strengthen goal pursuit, if expectations of success are high. There are three ways to ensure that all participants who use mental contrasting hold high expectations of success. As described above, one way to instill positive expectations *in situ* is by giving positive performance feedback (Oettingen et al., 2012). Another way is to assign participants a new task, for which they have no pre-existing performance experiences and to assure them that it is feasible for them to succeed (A. Gollwitzer, Oettingen, Kirby, Duckworth, & Mayer, 2011). And finally, one can ask participants to generate an idiosyncratic (academic or well-being) wish or concern that is challenging yet feasible (Oettingen, 2012).

*Learning a foreign language.* Applying the second of the three options, A. Gollwitzer et al. (2011) showed in two studies that mental contrasting managed to heighten academic performance for elementary and middle-school children. The intervention was directed at second- and third-graders in Germany and fifth-graders in the United States. The children had to either learn vocabulary in a foreign language (English for the German participants) or they had to learn to say *thank you* in ten different languages (participants were fifth-graders in the United States). To guarantee high expectations of success, participants were not given the opportunity to gain prior experience with the task and it was ensured that it was possible for all students to succeed (A. Gollwitzer et al., 2011). Across studies, participants in the mental contrasting condition were more successful in learning the new vocabulary than students in the indulging (control) condition.

*Increasing well-being: Eating healthier and becoming more active.* Applying the third option mentioned above, college students who were interested in improving their well-being named respective idiosyncratic wishes for the next 2 weeks (e.g., eating healthier, losing weight). Thereafter, they were either instructed to mental contrast or indulge in fulfilling these wishes (Johannessen, Oettingen, & Mayer, 2012); a third group received no treatment. Two weeks later, compared to those in the indulging or no treatment condition, students in the mental contrasting condition reported an overall lower calorie intake, as they consumed less high-calorie foods and more low-calorie foods (Johannessen et al., 2012). Interestingly, the effects of mental contrasting transferred across domains. Students in the mental contrasting also reported more physical activity compared to participants in the other two conditions (Johannessen et al., 2012).

***Summary.*** Mental contrasting is a volitional strategy that allows for both engagement to, and disengagement from, desired futures—depending on the feasibility of realizing the envisioned future. Specifically, mental contrasting produces cognitive changes (e.g., mental associations, changes in the meaning of reality), energy (e.g., systolic blood pressure), and constructive mastery of negative feedback (e.g., careful processing of information) that in turn predicts behavior change in line with how feasible the desired future is perceived. Thus, mental contrasting is a conscious strategy that produces changes in cognition outside of awareness, which in turn predicts the observed behavior change. Engaging in promising and disengaging from futile futures guarantees that a person who uses mental contrasting saves resources for successfully managing everyday life and long-term development. Mental contrasting is easy to apply and can be taught as a metacognitive strategy, unfolding its effects in such diverse life domains as excelling in academic performance, promoting one's health and well-being, and managing time and other resources.

### Implementation Intentions

When pursuing academic goals, students are often confronted with the following challenges: they need to get started and take the first steps toward pursuing their goals; they must stay on track when goal striving has started; they should not overextend when striving for a given goal; and finally, they should disengage from an unattainable goal or futile means of attaining that goal (Gollwitzer & Sheeran, 2006). Planning in advance how one wants to deal with these challenges is an effective remedy. Gollwitzer (1993, 1999, 2014) highlighted the importance of forming implementation intentions that specify plans with the format of "If situation $X$ is encountered, then I will perform the goal-directed response $Y$!" Thus, implementation intentions define when, where, and how one wants to act. For instance, a student who wants to make more constructive contributions in class might form the following if-then plan: "And if another student is desperately trying to answer a difficult question, then I'll immediately jump to his rescue!" Empirical data support the assumption that implementation intentions help raise the rate of goal attainment. A meta-analysis based on close to a hundred studies shows a medium to large effect on increased rate of goal attainment ($d = 0.61$; Gollwitzer & Sheeran, 2006).

***Underlying processes of implementation intention effects.*** Research on the underlying processes of implementation intention effects has revealed that implementation intentions facilitate goal attainment on the basis of psychological mechanisms that relate to both the anticipated situation (specified in the if-part of the plan) and the association created between the if-part and the then-part of the plan (Gollwitzer, 1999). Because forming an implementation intention implies the selection of a critical future situation, the mental representation of this situation becomes highly activated and hence more accessible. For instance, Achtziger, Bayer, and Gollwitzer (2012) observed in a cued recall experiment that participants more effectively recalled the available situational opportunities to attain a set goal, given that these opportunities had been specified in if-then links (i.e., in implementation intentions); this effect showed up no matter whether the cued recall was requested 15 minutes or 24 hours later. Furthermore, a study by Parks-Stamm, Gollwitzer, and Oettingen (2007), using a lexical decision task paradigm, showed that implementation intentions not only increased the activation level of the specified critical cues, they also diminished the activation level of non-specified competing situational cues.

Forming implementation intentions creates strong associations between the specified critical situations and goal-directed responses. Thus, the execution of the goal-directed response, once the critical situational cue is encountered, can be expected to exhibit features of strong associations, such as automaticity in terms of immediacy, efficiency, and no need for conscious intent. Indeed, there is vast empirical evidence that if-then planners act more quickly (e.g., Gollwitzer & Brandstätter, 1997, Experiment 3), deal more effectively with cognitive demands (e.g., speed-up effects still emerge under high cognitive load and thus qualify as efficient; e.g., Brandstätter, Lengfelder, & Gollwitzer, 2001), and do not need to consciously intend to act in the critical moment (e.g., Bayer, Achtziger, Gollwitzer, & Moskowitz, 2009).

Further support for the hypothesis that action control by implementation intentions qualifies as automatic is also obtained in studies assessing brain data. In a functional magnetic resonance imaging study reported by Gilbert, Gollwitzer, Cohen, Oettingen, and Burgess (2009), acting on the basis of goal intentions was associated with brain activity in the lateral rostral prefrontal cortex, whereas acting on the basis of implementation intentions was associated with brain activity in the medial rostral prefrontal cortex. Brain activity in the latter area is known to be associated with bottom-up (stimulus) control of action, whereas brain activity in the former area is known to be related to top-down (goal) control of action (Burgess, Dumontheil, & Gilbert, 2007). Moreover, the automaticity of implementation intentions effects has also been supported by studies that collected brain data employing electroencephalography (e.g., Gallo, Keil, McCulloch, Rockstroh, & Gollwitzer, 2009, Study 3).

But do these postulated processes actually mediate implementation intention effects on goal attainment? There is supportive evidence for this assumption. In the Gilbert et al. (2009) study, the increased brain activity in the medial rostral prefrontal cortex matched the increase in prospective memory performance in participants who had formed implementation intentions. Moreover, studies by Webb and Sheeran (2007, 2008) found that the effects of if-then plans on goal attainment were mediated simultaneously by the accessibility of the specified situational cues and by the strength of the association between these cues and the intended response. The search for further mediating variables has shown that neither an increase in goal commitment nor an increase in self-efficacy qualifies as a potential alternative mediator of implementation intention effects.

***Implementation intentions as a means to overcome typical challenges of goal striving.*** The effects of implementation intentions have been demonstrated in the educational, interpersonal, health, and environmental domains, with respect to each of the four challenges to effective goal striving: getting started, staying on track, and disengaging from futile and inappropriate goals, as well as avoiding resource depletion. With respect to the first problem, implementation intentions were found to help individuals *get started* with goal striving in terms of remembering to act and overcoming an initial reluctance to act (e.g., see summary by Gollwitzer & Oettingen, 2011). Accordingly, it seems safe to assume that if-then plans can be used effectively to help students and teachers fight procrastination (e.g., getting started with homework or getting started with grading students' homework: Wieber & Gollwitzer, 2010).

However, many goals cannot be accomplished by a simple, discrete, one-shot action because they require people to keep striving over an extended period of time. *Staying on track* may then become very difficult when certain internal stimuli (e.g., being nervous) or external stimuli (e.g., distractions) interfere with the ongoing goal pursuit (e.g., going to bed that guarantees a satisfying sleep: Loft & Cameron, 2013). With respect to shielding an ongoing goal pursuit from inside stimuli, implementation intentions were demonstrated to be effective with respect to performance anxiety (Achtziger, Gollwitzer, & Sheeran, 2008), test anxiety (Parks-Stamm, Gollwitzer, & Oettingen, 2010), social anxiety (Webb, Onanaiye, Sheeran, Reidy, & Lavda, 2010), as well as general anxiety (Varley, Webb, & Sheeran, 2011). Implementation intentions have also been demonstrated to be effective in shielding goal pursuit from outside stimuli. For instance, they helped college students who were trying to solve math problems to shield themselves from distractive video clips ("If I see moving pictures or hear some noise, then I'll ignore them!": Gollwitzer & Schaal, 1998). Analogous findings were obtained with children of 6–8 years of age (Wieber, Suchodoletz, Heikamp, Trommsdorff, & Gollwitzer, 2011). Ignore-implementation intentions were highly effective in a classification task (categorizing vehicles vs. animals, presented on a computer screen), even when the distractions were highly attractive (i.e., cartoon movie sequences), and no matter whether these distractions appeared inside or outside the children's sight.

Implementation intentions may use different formats. For instance, if a student wants to keep studying even though the students next to her start a loud conversation, she can form suppression-oriented implementation intentions, such as "And if the students around me get noisy, then I will not get upset!" The then-component of such suppression-oriented implementation intentions negated the critical behavior (in the present example "then I will not get upset"). However, it may also specify a replacement behavior (". . . , then I will stay calm and ask them in a friendly manner to be more quiet!") or focus on ignoring the critical cue (". . . , then I will just ignore the noise!"). Recent research (Adriaanse, van Oosten, de Ridder, de Wit, & Evers, 2011) suggests that "negation" implementation intentions are less effective than the latter two types (i.e., replacement and ignore implementation intentions). Implementation intentions specifically geared towards stabilizing the ongoing goal striving are particularly effective (e.g., using if-then plans that explicate in detail what needs to be done to reach the goal; Bayer et al.,2009). In fact, it even blocked the disruptive effects created by inappropriate moods, ego depletion, or feelings of insecurity.

Goals or means that are no longer feasible and/or desirable in their current form may require individuals to adjust goal striving and to *disengage* from a goal or a chosen means to achieve that goal. Such disengagement from unattainable goals or dysfunctional means can free up resources and minimize negative affect resulting from repeated failure feedback (Carver & Scheier, 1998; Locke & Latham, 1990, 2006). Implementation intentions help to master this third challenge of effective goal pursuit (i.e., *functional disengagement*) by: (a) specifying negative feedback as a critical cue; and (b) linking this cue to switching to an alternative goal or means (e.g., a different way of studying for an academic test; Henderson, Gollwitzer, & Oettingen, 2007).

Finally, regarding the fourth challenge of effective goal pursuit, *not overextending oneself*, forming implementation intentions prevents resource depletion. Specifically, it enables individuals to engage in automated goal striving. As a consequence, the self should not become depleted (Muraven & Baumeister, 2000) when goal striving is regulated by implementation intentions. Indeed, in studies using different ego-depletion paradigms, research participants who used implementation intentions to self-regulate in one task did not show reduced self-regulatory capacity in a subsequent task (e.g., switching from one academic task to the next; Webb & Sheeran, 2003).

***When effective goal striving gets particularly hard.*** The following three situations ask for more powerful self-regulation: (a) situations in which a person's knowledge and skills constrain performance, such as having to solve difficult math problems; (b) situations in which a competitor limits one's performance, such as competitive sports; and (c) situations in which the wanted behavior (e.g., paying attention in class) conflicts with established habits favoring an antagonistic response (e.g., chatting with one's classmate). For all three of these situations, implementation intentions turned out to be beneficial.

Implementation intentions were found to enhance participants' performance on the Raven intelligence test, which consists of a series of problems to be solved (Bayer & Gollwitzer, 2007). The implementation intention "If I start a new problem, then I will tell myself: I can do it!" was more effective than the respective goal intention "I will tell myself: I can do it!" Tennis players participating in competitive tennis tournaments using implementation intentions effectively coped with critical situations during the game (e.g., "If I'm falling behind, then I'll tell myself: Stay concentrated!"; Achtziger et al., 2008).

Finally, assuming that action control by implementation intentions is immediate and efficient, a horserace model of action control suggests that implementation intentions can be used to deal with antagonistic habitual responses (Adriaanse, Gollwitzer, de Ridder, de Wit, & Kroese, 2011). Implementation intentions that specify responses contrary to the habitual responses (Cohen, Bayer, Jaudas, & Gollwitzer, 2008), have been shown to effectively reduce habitual responses, such as stereotyping (e.g., "When I see the face of someone who looks different from me, then I will think 'safe'!"; e.g., Gollwitzer & Schaal, 1998; Mendoza, Gollwitzer, & Amodio, 2010; Stewart & Payne, 2008).

Still, forming implementation intentions may not always succeed in blocking habitual responses. Whether the habitual response or the if-then guided response will "win the race" depends on the relative strength of the two behavioral orientations (Webb, Sheeran, & Luszczynska, 2009). This implies that controlling strong habits requires the formation of strong implementation intentions (e.g., trying to break the bad habit of watching TV when one gets home from school by an if-then plan to first do one's homework). Forming strong implementation intentions can be achieved by various measures. One pertains to creating particularly strong links between situational cues (if-component) and goal-directed responses (then-component) by asking participants to use mental imagery (e.g., Knäuper, Roseman, Johnson, & Krantz, 2009). Also, certain formats of implementation intentions (i.e., replacement and ignore implementation intentions) seem to be more effective in fighting habits than others (i.e., negation implementation intentions), and some formats seem to work better for some people than others (e.g., test-anxious individuals particularly benefit from ignore implementation intentions; Parks-Stamm et al., 2010). Finally, one has to keep in mind that behavior change cannot only be achieved by breaking old habits; one can also form new habits in new situational contexts (e.g., doing one's homework in the library before one goes home).

*Moderators of implementation intention effects.* Recent research has identified a number of moderators of implementation intention effects on goal attainment. First, implementation intentions only benefit goal attainment when commitment to both the goal is high (Sheeran, Webb, & Gollwitzer, 2005) and to executing the implementation intention is high (Achtziger et al., 2012, Study 2). Second, person attributes play a role. In undergraduate students (Webb, Christian, & Armitage, 2007), attendance in class was studied as a function of conscientiousness, openness to experience, goal intentions, and implementation intentions. Increased class attendance due to planning occurred only for low/moderately conscientious students as high conscientious students showed a perfect class attendance to begin with. This finding is in line with the repeated observation (Gollwitzer & Sheeran, 2006) that implementation intention effects are stronger when used for difficult rather than easy goals.

Moreover, implementation intention effects do not seem to depend on a person's lack of self-regulatory capacity (i.e., executive control resources; Hall, Zehr, Ng, & Zanna, 2012). It comes as no surprise then, that implementation intentions have been found to benefit children with attention deficit hyperactivity disorder (ADHD). According to the dual-pathway model (Sonuga-Barke, 2002), ADHD impairs behavioral control in two ways: (a) through an inhibitory dysfunction leading to poor task engagement and inattentiveness; and (b) through a deregulation of reward mechanisms leading to a higher preference for immediate rewards. Children with ADHD benefit from forming implementation intentions by improving both functions (e.g., Gawrilow & Gollwitzer, 2008; Gawrilow, Gollwitzer, & Oettingen, 2011a) as well as their ability to delay gratification (Gawrilow, Gollwitzer, & Oettingen, 2011b).

*Summary.* Forming implementation intentions is a volitional strategy that links cognitive, affective, or behavioral responses that are instrumental to reaching desired outcomes to critical situational cues. As a consequence, when the critical situation is encountered, the specified response is executed immediately, effortlessly, and without conscious intent. If-then planning can thus be understood as a self-regulation tool that allows for strategically delegating one's action control to critical situational cues.

There are two new lines of implementation intention research (see Gollwitzer, 2014) that are of relevance to improving the cooperation, communication, and interaction between students, teachers, and administrators. The first pertains to the use of implementation intentions in groups. This research asks whether individual group members can use implementation intentions to promote collaboration and thus improve group performance, and whether groups can also use we-implementation intentions ("If we encounter . . . , then we will . . . !") to promote group performance. The second new line of implementation intention research explores whether if-then plans can be used to benefit communication and social interaction. For instance, one question is whether implementation intentions can boost interest in sustained contact and close interpersonal distance in anxiety-provoking interactions (e.g., interracial interactions).

## Mental Contrasting with Implementation Intentions as a Metacognitive Intervention

The two volitional strategies of mental contrasting and implementation intentions have been combined to form a strategy called *mental contrasting with implementation intentions* (MCII). MCII is found to be more effective in changing behavior than each of the two alone, as the two strategies support each other. As mental contrasting of feasible wishes strengthens the non-conscious association between reality and instrumental means (Kappes et al., 2012; Oettingen, 2012), explicitly forming implementation intentions strengthens this association even further. Mental contrasting in turn benefits the effects of implementation intentions. Specifically, it prepares the application of implementation intentions in two ways: (a) Mental contrasting of feasible wishes fosters goal commitment and energization, and goal commitment is a necessary prerequisite for implementation intentions to be effective (Sheeran et al., 2005); and (b) in mental contrasting the idiosyncratic obstacles and means to pursue the desired future are specified, so that the obstacle can work as the if-component of a given implementation intention, and the instrumental means as the then-component. In sum, *if-then* plans as part of MCII may look like: "If . . . (obstacle), then I will . . . (respond to overcome or circumvent the obstacle)."

*MCII is more effective than MC and II alone.* MCII has been found to be more effective than mental contrasting and forming implementation intentions alone (Adriaanse et al., 2010; Kirk, Oettingen, & Gollwitzer, 2013; see summary by Oettingen, 2012). For example, MCII helped college students more in breaking snacking habits than mental contrasting only and forming implementation intention only. Importantly, mental contrasting did increase perceived clarity about personal obstacles towards reducing unhealthy snacking. These findings suggest that MCII may also be a valid strategy for fighting bad habits in educational settings (e.g., procrastination).

What underlying processes make MCII so effective for behavior change? Mental contrasting creates clarity about one's personal obstacles which can then be used as critical cues in the formation of implementation intentions (e.g., if my friends call, then I will tell them that I need to do my homework). Indeed, when Adriaanse, de Ridder, and de Wit

(2009) compared the effectiveness of if-then plans that were personalized vs. kept general (i.e., specifically referred to each participant's unique action control problem vs. a general action control problem), it was the personalized if-then plans that turned out to be more effective.

### MCII improves academic performance in school-children.

Duckworth, Grant, Loew, Oettingen, and Gollwitzer (2011) conducted an intervention study with university-bound high-school students preparing for the Preliminary SAT (PSAT) over the summer. Students first wrote down two positive outcomes they associated with completing all of the practice tests in the workbook (e.g. "I would feel good about myself"), and two obstacles of the present reality (e.g. "I'm distracted") that could interfere with this task. They then rewrote the previously stated first outcome, imagined it as vividly as possible, and then wrote their thoughts and images down. This procedure was repeated for the first obstacle, the second named positive outcome, and the second obstacle. Students then proposed a specific solution for each obstacle. Specifically, they completed two if–then plans in the following way: "If (obstacle), then I will (solution)." Finally, each student received a 12th edition of Barron's *How to prepare for the PSAT* workbook (Green & Wolf, 2004). These workbooks were collected in October, immediately after students had completed their PSAT. Students who applied MCII completed 60% more questions in their workbooks than control participants who had to write a short essay on an influential person or event in their life.

MCII also turned out to be helpful for the self-regulation of school-related concerns in middle-school schoolchildren at risk for ADHD (Gawrilow, Morgenroth, Schultz, Oettingen, & Gollwitzer, 2013). Students received a standard learning style or a learning style plus MCII intervention. The MCII pertained to students' most important school-related concern (e.g., be more attentive in French class). When parents rated their children's management of school-related activities (e.g., homework is done reliably, vocabulary is learned, desk is tidy) two weeks later, both children at risk and not at risk for ADHD benefited from MCII, more than from the learning style intervention. Importantly, the more ADHD symptoms the children showed before the intervention, the more they benefited from the MCII intervention.

Economically disadvantaged middle-school children participated in a further MCII study (Duckworth, Kirby, A. Gollwitzer, & Oettingen, 2013). Prior to the intervention, teachers were asked to rate children in their classroom behavior during the previous month. Baseline academic performance was assessed using three indicators from the official record: grade point average (GPA), attendance, and conduct. At the beginning of the third quarter, children were randomly assigned to complete either the MCII or a positive thinking control exercise. The children in both conditions targeted their most important personal wishes related to schoolwork. Trained interventionists met with the children in groups of four to five during three 1-hour sessions. After the third quarter, the three indicators of academic performance

(GPA, attendance, and conduct) were obtained again. Compared to children in the control condition, children that were taught how to apply MCII significantly improved their GPA, attendance, and conduct.

***Summary.*** MCII is a volitional strategy that combines two effective self-regulation strategies. By mentally contrasting the desired future with the present reality, students, teachers, and administrators identify what in themselves holds them back from attaining what they would like to achieve in the future. If they deem their wished-for future as reachable, they become energized and actively pursue the desired future; if they deem it as futile they let go and turn to alternative pursuits. Forming implementation intentions on top of mental contrasting enables them to master even highly challenging obstacles. MCII is easy to apply and particularly effective for people with special needs, such as children at risk for ADHD and children of low socioeconomic background. Therefore, MCII qualifies as an effective volitional strategy that children, teachers, and administrators can use to better their everyday life and long-term development (for instructions of how to learn and apply MCII in students and during one's everyday life, see woopmylife.org. WOOP stands for wish outcome obstacle plan).

### Individual Differences in Volition

The previous sections focused on understanding the processes underlying volition and respective behavior change interventions. But there are also individual difference perspectives on volition (see Corno, 2001, on habits). One line of research relates education outcomes to individual differences, such as the conscientiousness factor of the Big Five personality model, which encompasses dependability, punctuality, and orderliness (see Chapter 13, this volume; and McCrae & Costa, 1987). Another line (see Duckworth, 2009) distinguishes between two person-related attributes relevant to volition: grit and self-control.

Grit is defined as the tendency to sustain interest in and effort toward long-term goals; it is operationalized using the grit scale, a Likert-type self-report scale that includes items such as: "I am a hard worker" and "I finish whatever I begin." Self-control is defined as voluntary regulation of behavioral, emotional, and attentional impulses in the presence of momentarily gratifying temptations or diversions; it is operationalized using a scale with items such as: "My mind wandered when I should have been listening" and "I talked back to my teacher or parent when I was upset" (Duckworth & Carlson, 2013). Grit and self-control predict objectively measured performance over and above measures of talent. For instance, in longitudinal studies, grit predicts surviving the arduous first summer of training at West Point, reaching the final rounds of the National Spelling Bee, retention in the U.S. Special Forces, retention and performance among novice teachers, and graduation from Chicago public high schools. These predictions are observed after statistically adjusting for measures such as IQ, SAT, or standardized achievement test scores, as well as physical fitness scores.

In cross-sectional studies, grit correlates with lifetime educational attainment and, inversely, lifetime career changes and divorce.

Self-control predicts report card grades (and changes in report card grades over time) more strongly than measures of intelligence (Duckworth, Tsukayama, & May, 2010). Finally, recent research has looked at two distinct measures of academic performance—report card grades and standardized achievement test scores—and their different relations with self-control and intelligence. In three separate samples, self-control prospectively predicted changes in report card grades more accurately than intelligence scores, but intelligence was found to be a better predictor of changes in standardized achievement test scores (Duckworth, Quinn, & Tsukayama, 2012).

It is important to recognize that individual difference approaches to volition can easily be integrated into the process models described above. For instance, Webb et al. (2007) used an implementation intention intervention to help undergraduate college students to show up for class on time. They observed that only students low in conscientiousness benefited from the implementation intention intervention (as the students high in conscientiousness showed up on time to begin with). In other words, it was those students who had problems with showing up on time (i.e., the students who needed volition to overcome barriers to achieving the desired outcome of being punctual) who benefited from employing a self-regulation strategy.

While Webb et al. (2007) combine personality and process approaches to volition in terms of moderation of self-regulation processes by personality variables, there is also the possibility of combining the two approaches in terms of explicating distinct self-regulation processes for different types of people. This approach has been explored by Kuhl (1985) who differentiates individuals with an action orientation from those with a state orientation (i.e., individuals who show high vs. low cognition-behavior consistencies). His extensive empirical research (Kuhl, 2000; Kuhl, Kazén, & Koole, 2006) has by now delineated in detail what psychological processes (i.e., patterns of interactions among four cognitive systems: intention memory, extension memory, discrepancy-sensitive object recognition, and intuitive behavior control) ultimately lead to different levels of self-regulatory abilities.

Corno et al. (2002) suggest that studying individual differences in self-regulation across school settings might benefit from differentially looking at cognitive versus affective versus conative (motivational and volitional) individual differences (see also Corno, 2001). For example, with respect to affect, models may be developed for studying the influence of anxiety and mood on self-regulation; these influences may be moderated by temperament-related differences in reactivity and motivations, such as efficacy as well as problem- versus emotion-focused styles of coping with stress (Boekaerts, 1987; see also Folkman & Lazarus, 1985). Further, with respect to cognition, it might be worthwhile differentiating a deep approach to processing of information in learning situations versus a surface approach (Entwistle, 1989) and investigating how these different approaches relate to grit and self-regulation. Finally, with respect to conation, one might want to investigate how students' work styles, such as detached and disengaged versus committed, hopeful, and engaged (Ainley, 1993), may determine to what extent students benefit from using various volitional strategies.

## Conclusion and Future Research

One of the major challenges in education is to keep students striving for the attainment of future outcomes that are beneficial for them and for their context. A first step to master this challenge is to strengthen students' motivation by heightening both incentive value of academic achievement (desirability) and relevant expectations (feasibility). But in addition to the motivational processes that establish desirability and feasibility of academic goals, students need volition to ensure that they do not pull back from challenging tasks and long-term goals in the face of resistance and conflict (e.g., do not give up in math, or drop out of school). Volitional strategies like mental contrasting and forming implementation intentions, and especially the combination of the two, can help students reach attractive and attainable future outcomes by preparing themselves to master upcoming obstacles and setbacks. A big advantage of MCII is its simplicity. It can be taught as a metacognitive strategy in a very short time, and it can be applied during everyday life with relative ease. Importantly, students need no special skills or personal attributes to learn and apply MCII as it can be acquired by students of different walks of life and cultures, and used in diverse contexts to solve a wide array of different tasks.

Because MCII can be used for any wish and concern, it should benefit the mastery of the various challenges arising from the individual vulnerabilities described above. For example, referring to the example of a deep versus surface approach to information processing, it would be important to investigate whether MCII and other self-regulation strategies (e.g., goal shielding, distancing) can help students to flexibly adopt one mode of information processing versus another (Entwistle, 1989). Research might test whether teaching MCII to students would foster the surface approach when preparing for an upcoming test, especially when there is only a short time left to study. In contrast, for learning basic skills that a student needs in order to build a career in a particular field (e.g., basics in physics for a student aspiring to attend graduate school), MCII should promote adopting a deep approach. By allowing the student to fully understand which future she wishes for and which of her own obstacles are in the way, MCII will provide clarity whether surface or deep information processing is called for.

Similarly, future research may investigate MCII or other self-regulation procedures in the context of the dual processing self-regulation model (Boekaerts & Niemivirta, 2000). Specifically, MCII might readily support the growth pathway (top-down process of goal achievement) as the wished-for future in this case pertains to an improvement of the status quo. In the well-being pathway, students focus on preventing negative futures. Here the desired future pertains to keeping the status quo ("How nice would it be if I kept my GPA high?" or "How nice would it be if I continued to have a close relationship with my teacher?"). Alternatively, students could be asked to mentally contrast a potential negative future (e.g., "I might upset my teacher") with the positive reality that they might lose (e.g., the close relationship to the teacher right now), so that the students commit to preserving the valuable present reality. Such mental contrasting instills avoidance (rather than approach goals, e.g., Oettingen, Mayer, & Thorpe, 2010b), which may be particularly helpful in educational settings whenever the well-being path is concerned and when emotion regulation is called for.

Finally, Corno et al. (2002) have noted that the research in education has not focused enough on hypotheses of how affect and conation relate to cognition. Our own research investigating self-regulation strategies may be seen as a step in that direction. Research on MCII addresses the regulation of cognition (e.g., stereotypic or schematic thinking), emotion (e.g., anxiety, anger), and behavior (effort, performance). Indeed, applying MCII to a particular wish (e.g., being more friendly to a teacher) will have downstream consequences benefiting all three areas—cognition (e.g., interpreting the teacher's behavior in a more friendly light), emotion (e.g., feeling better after interacting with the teacher), and conation (e.g., using a more respectful tone of voice when talking to the teacher). Finally, engaging in MCII entails procedures that involve all three pathways. It instigates cognition (e.g., mental associations outside of awareness), emotions (e.g., feelings of energy; anticipated disappointment), and behavior (e.g., fighting back in light of setbacks) that mediate changes in observable performance and actual success. Future research should also focus on how these pathways interact when it comes to long-term consequences of MCII (e.g., to what extent do changes in emotion predict changes in performance, or the other way around).

In the present chapter, we defined volition and discussed respective processes that help to face resistance and resolve conflict in goal pursuit and behavior change. We also identified effective volitional strategies that students can learn and then apply on their own. These strategies support students, teachers, and administrators in identifying what they really want in the future and what kinds of obstacles stand in their way; they also help individuals to make plans and to ultimately overcome these obstacles. Importantly, for theory and research, these volitional strategies build on existing incentive values and expectations of success, thereby translating motivation into behavior change and goal attainment.

## References

Achtziger, A., Bayer, U. C., & Gollwitzer, P. M. (2012). Committing to implementation intentions: Attention and memory effects for selected situational cues. *Motivation and Emotion, 36*, 287–300.

Achtziger, A., Gollwitzer, P. M., & Sheeran, P. (2008). Implementation intentions and shielding goal striving from unwanted thoughts and feelings. *Personality and Social Psychology Bulletin, 34*, 381–393.

Adriaanse, M. A., de Ridder, D. T. D., & de Wit, J. B. F. (2009). Finding the critical cue: Implementation intentions to change one's diet work best when tailored to personally relevant reasons for unhealthy eating. *Personality and Social Psychology Bulletin, 35*, 60–71.

Adriaanse, M. A., Gollwitzer, P. M., de Ridder, D. T. D., de Wit, J. B. F., & Kroese, F. M. (2011). Breaking habits with implementation intentions: A test of underlying processes. *Personality and Social Psychology Bulletin, 37*, 502–512.

Adriaanse, M. A., Oettingen, G., Gollwitzer, P. M., Hennes, E. P., de Ridder, D. T. D., & de Wit, J. B. F. (2010). When planning is not enough: Fighting unhealthy snacking habits by mental contrasting with implementation intentions (MCII). *European Journal of Social Psychology, 40*, 1277–1293.

Adriaanse, M. A., van Oosten, J. M., de Ridder, D. T., de Wit, J. B., & Evers, C. (2011). Planning what not to eat: Ironic effects of implementation intentions negating unhealthy habits. *Personality and Social Psychology Bulletin, 37*, 69–81.

Ainley, M. (1993). Styles of engagement with learning: A multidimensional assessment of their relationship with strategy use and school achievement. *Journal of Educational Psychology, 85*, 395–405.

Atkinson, J. W. (1957). Motivational determinants of risk-taking behavior. *Psychological Review, 64*, 359–372.

Bandura, A. (1977). Self-efficacy: Toward a unifying theory of behavioral change. *Psychological Review, 84*, 191–215.

Bayer, U. C., Achtziger, A., Gollwitzer, P. M., & Moskowitz, G. B. (2009). Responding to subliminal cues: Do if-then plans facilitate action preparation and initiation without conscious intent? *Social Cognition, 27*, 183–201.

Bayer, U. C., & Gollwitzer, P. M. (2007). Boosting scholastic test scores by willpower: The role of implementation intentions. *Self and Identity, 6*, 1–19.

Boekaerts, M. (1987). Individual differences in the appraisal of learning tasks: An integrative view on emotion and cognition. *Communication and Cognition, 20*, 207–224.

Boekaerts, M., & Cascallar, E. (2006). How far have we moved toward the integration of theory and practice in self-regulation? *Educational Psychology Review, 18*, 199–210.

Boekaerts, M. & Corno, L. (2005). Self-regulation in the classroom: A perspective on assessment and intervention. *Applied Psychology: An International Review, 54*, 199–231.

Boekaerts, M., & Niemivirta, M. (2000). Self-regulated learning: Finding a balance between learning goals and ego-protective goals. In M. Boekaerts, P. R. Pintrich, & M. Zeidner (Eds.), *Handbook of self-regulation* (pp. 417–451). San Diego, CA: Academic Press.

Brandstätter, V., Lengfelder, A., & Gollwitzer, P. M. (2001). Implementation intentions and efficient action initiation. *Journal of Personality and Social Psychology, 81*, 946–960.

Burgess, P. W., Dumontheil, I., & Gilbert, S. J. (2007). The gateway hypothesis of rostral PFC (Area 10) function. *Trends in Cognitive Sciences, 11*, 290–298.

Carver, C. S., & Scheier, M. (1998). *On the self-regulation of behavior.* New York, NY: Cambridge University Press.

Cohen, A-L., Bayer, U. C., Jaudas, A., & Gollwitzer, P. M. (2008). Self-regulatory strategy and executive control: Implementation intentions modulate task switching and Simon task performance. *Psychological Research, 72*, 12–26.

Corno, L. (1993). The best-laid plans: Modern conceptions of volition and educational research. *Educational Researcher, 22*, 14–22.

Corno, L. (1994). Student volition and education: Outcomes, influences, and practices. In D. Schunk & B. Zimmerman (Eds.), *Self-regulation of learning and performance: Issues and applications* (pp. 229–254). Hillsdale, NJ: Erlbaum.

Corno, L. (2001). Volitional aspects of self-regulated learning. In B. J. Zimmerman & D. H. Schunk (Eds.), *Self-regulated learning and academic achievement: Theoretical perspectives* (2nd ed., pp. 191–226). Mahwah, NJ: Lawrence Erlbaum.

Corno, L. (2004). Introduction to the special issue work habits and work styles: Volition in education. *Teachers College Record, 106*, 1669–1694.

Corno, L. (2011). Studying self-regulation habits. In B. Zimmerman & D. Schunk (Eds.), *Handbook of self-regulation of learning and performance* (pp. 361–375). New York: Routledge.

Corno, L., Cronbach, L. J., Kupermintz, H., Lohman, D., Mandinach, E.B., Porteus, A. W., et al. (2002). *Remaking the concept of aptitude: Extending the legacy of R. E. Snow.* Mahwah, NJ: Lawrence Erlbaum Associates.

Corno, L., & Kanfer, R. (1993). The role of volition in learning and performance. *Review of Research in Education, 19,* 301–341.

Duckworth, A. L. (2009). (Over and) beyond high-stakes testing. *American Psychologist, 64,* 279–280.

Duckworth, A. L., & Carlson, S. M. (2013). Self-regulation and school success. In B. W. Sokol, F. M. E. Grouzet, & U. Müller (Eds.), *Self-regulation and autonomy: Social and developmental dimensions of human conduct* (pp. 208–230). New York: Cambridge University Press.

Duckworth, A. L., Grant, H., Loew, B., Oettingen, G., & Gollwitzer, P. M. (2011). Self-regulation strategies improve self-discipline in adolescents: Benefits of mental contrasting and implementation intentions. *Educational Psychology, 31,* 17–26.

Duckworth, A. L., Kirby, T. A., Gollwitzer, A., & Oettingen, G. (2013). From fantasy to action: Mental Contrasting with Implementation Intentions (MCII) improves academic performance in children. *Social Psychological and Personality Science, 4,* 745–753.

Duckworth, A. L., Quinn, P., & Tsukayama, E. (2012). What *No Child Left Behind* leaves behind: The roles of IQ and self-control in predicting standardized achievement test scores and report card grades. *Journal of Educational Psychology, 104,* 439–451.

Duckworth, A. L., Tsukayama, E., & May, H. (2010). Establishing causality using longitudinal hierarchical linear modeling: An illustration predicting achievement from self-control. *Social Psychology and Personality Science, 1,* 311–317.

Duffy, E. (1934). Emotion: An example of the need for reorientation in psychology. *Psychological Review, 41,* 184–198.

Entwistle, N. J. (1989). *Styles of learning and teaching: An integrated outline of educational psychology for students, teachers and lecturers.* London, UK: David Fulton Publishers.

Fishbach, A., Dhar, R., & Zhang, Y. (2006). Subgoals as substitutes or complements: The role of goal accessibility. *Journal of Personality and Social Psychology, 91,* 232–242.

Fishbach, A., Shah, J. Y., & Kruglanski, A. W. (2004). Emotional transfer in goal systems. *Journal of Experimental Social Psychology, 40,* 723–738.

Flavell, J. H. (1979). Metacognition and cognitive monitoring: A new area of cognitive-developmental inquiry. *American Psychologist, 34,* 906–911.

Folkman, S., & Lazarus, R. S. (1985). If it changes it must be a process: Study of emotion and coping during three stages of a college examination. *Journal of Personality and Social Psychology, 48,* 150–170.

Gallo, I. S., Keil, A., McCulloch, K. C., Rockstroh, B., & Gollwitzer, P. M. (2009). Strategic automation of emotion regulation. *Journal of Personality and Social Psychology, 96,* 11–31.

Gawrilow, C., & Gollwitzer, P. M. (2008). Implementation intentions facilitate response inhibition in children with ADHD. *Cognitive Therapy and Research, 32,* 261–280.

Gawrilow, C., Gollwitzer, P. M., & Oettingen, G. (2011a). If-then plans benefit executive functions in children with ADHD. *Journal of Social and Clinical Psychology, 30,* 616–646.

Gawrilow, C., Gollwitzer, P. M., & Oettingen, G. (2011b). If-then plans benefit delay of gratification performance in children with and without ADHD. *Cognitive Therapy and Research, 35,* 442–455.

Gawrilow, C., Morgenroth, K., Schultz, R., Oettingen, G., & Gollwitzer, P. M. (2013). Mental contrasting with implementation intentions enhances self-regulation of goal pursuit in schoolchildren at risk for ADHD. *Motivation and Emotion, 37,* 134–145.

Gilbert, S. J., Gollwitzer, P. M., Cohen, A. L., Oettingen, G., & Burgess, P. W. (2009). Separable brain systems supporting cued versus self-initiated realization of delayed intentions. *Journal of Experimental Psychology: Learning, Memory, and Cognition, 35,* 905–915.

Gollwitzer, A., Oettingen, G., Kirby, T. A., Duckworth, A. L., & Mayer, D. (2011). Mental contrasting facilitates academic performance in school children. *Motivation and Emotion, 35,* 403–412.

Gollwitzer, P. M. (1990). Action phases and mind-sets. In E. T. Higgins & R. M. Sorrentino (Eds.), *Handbook of motivation and cognition: Foundations of social behavior* (Vol. 2, pp. 53–92). New York, NY: Guilford Press.

Gollwitzer, P. M. (1993). Goal achievement: The role of intentions. *European Review of Social Psychology, 4,* 141–185.

Gollwitzer, P. M. (1999). Implementation intentions: Strong effects of simple plans. *American Psychologist, 54,* 493–503.

Gollwitzer, P. M. (2012). Mindset theory of action phases. In P. Van Lange, A. W. Kruglanski, & E. T. Higgins (Eds.), *Handbook of theories of social psychology* (Vol. 1, pp. 526–545). London: Sage Publications.

Gollwitzer, P. M. (2014). Weakness of the will: Is a quick fix possible? *Motivation and Emotion, 38,* 305–322.

Gollwitzer, P. M., Bayer, U. C., & McCulloch, K. C. (2005). The control of the unwanted. In R. Hassin, J. Uleman, & J. A. Bargh (Eds.), *The new unconscious* (pp. 485–515). Oxford: Oxford University Press.

Gollwitzer, P. M., & Brandstätter, V. (1997). Implementation intentions and effective goal pursuit. *Journal of Personality and Social Psychology, 73,* 186–199.

Gollwitzer, P. M., & Oettingen, G. (2011). Planning promotes goal striving. In K. D. Vohs & R. F. Baumeister (Eds.), *Handbook of self-regulation: Research, theory, and applications* (2nd ed., pp. 162–185). New York, NY: Guilford.

Gollwitzer, P. M., & Schaal, B. (1998). Metacognition in action: The importance of implementation intentions. *Personality and Social Psychology Review, 2,* 124–136.

Gollwitzer, P. M., & Sheeran, P. (2006). Implementation intentions and goal achievement: A meta-analysis of effects and processes. *Advances in Experimental Social Psychology, 38,* 69–119.

Green, S. W., & Wolf, I. K. (2004). *Barron's how to prepare for the PSAT/NMSQT: PSAT/national merit scholarship qualifying test* (12th ed.). Hauppauge, NY: Barron's Educational Series.

Hall, P. A., Zehr, C., Ng, M., & Zanna, M. P. (2012). Implementation intentions for physical activity in supportive and unsupportive environmental conditions: An examination of intention-behavior consistency. *Journal of Experimental Social Psychology, 48,* 432–436.

Hattie, J., Biggs, J., & Purdie, N. (1996). Effects of learning skills intervention on student learning: A meta-analysis. *Review of Educational Research, 66,* 99–136.

Henderson, M. D., Gollwitzer, P. M., & Oettingen, G. (2007). Implementation intentions and disengagement from a failing course of action. *Journal of Behavioral Decision Making, 20,* 81–102.

Hull, C. L. (1943). *Principles of behavior: An introduction to behavior theory. The Century Psychology Series.* New York, NY: Appleton-Century-Crofts.

James, W. (1890). *The principles of psychology.* New York, NY: Holt.

Johannessen, K. B., Oettingen, G., & Mayer, D. (2012). Mental contrasting of a dieting wish improves self-reported health behavior. *Psychology & Health, 27,* 43–58.

Kappes, A., & Oettingen, G. (2014). The emergence of goal pursuit: Mental contrasting connects future and reality. *Journal of Experimental Social Psychology, 54,* 25–39.

Kappes, A., Oettingen, G., & Pak, H. (2012). Mental contrasting and the self-regulation of responding to negative feedback. *Personality and Social Psychology Bulletin, 38,* 845–857.

Kappes, A., Wendt, M., Reinelt, T., & Oettingen, G. (2013). Mental contrasting changes the meaning of reality. *Journal of Experimental Social Psychology, 49,* 797–810.

Kirk, D., Oettingen, G., & Gollwitzer, P. M. (2013). Promoting integrative bargaining: Mental contrasting with implementation intentions. *International Journal of Conflict Management, 24,* 148–165.

Knäuper, B., Roseman, M., Johnson, P. J., & Krantz, L. H. (2009). Using mental imagery to enhance the effectiveness of implementation intentions. *Current Psychology, 28,* 181–186.

Kuhl, J. (1985). Volitional mediators of cognition-behavior consistency: Self-regulatory processes and action versus state orientation. In J. Kuhl & J. Beckmann (1985), *Action control. From cognition to behavior* (pp. 101–128). New York, NY: Springer

Kuhl, J. (2000). The volitional basis of Personality Systems Interaction Theory: Applications in learning and treatment contexts. *International Journal of Educational Research, 33,* 665–703.

Kuhl, J., & Beckmann, J. (1994). *Volition and personality: Action versus state orientation.* Goettingen: Hogrefe & Huber.

Kuhl, J., Kazén, M., & Koole, S. L. (2006). Putting self-regulation theory into practice: A user's manual. *Applied Psychology: An International Review, 55*, 408–418.

Locke, E. A., & Latham, G. P. (1990). *A theory of goal setting and task performance.* Englewood Cliffs, NJ: Prentice Hall.

Locke, E. A., & Latham, G. P. (2006). New directions in goal-setting theory. *Current Directions in Psychological Science, 15*, 265–268.

Loft, M. H., & Cameron, L. D. (2013). Using mental imagery to deliver self-regulation techniques to improve sleep behaviors. *Annals of Behavioral Medicine, 46*, 260–272.

Louro, M. J., Pieters, R., & Zeelenberg, M. (2007). Dynamics of multiple-goal pursuit. *Journal of Personality and Social Psychology, 93*, 174–193.

McClelland, D. C. (1985). How motives, skills, and values determine what people do. *American Psychologist, 40*, 812–825.

McCrae, R. R., & Costa, P. T. (1987). Validation of the five-factor model of personality across instruments and observers. *Journal of Personality and Social Psychology, 52*, 81–90.

Mendoza, S. A., Gollwitzer, P. M., & Amodio, D. M. (2010). Reducing the expression of implicit stereotypes: Reflexive control through implementation intentions. *Personality and Social Psychology Bulletin, 36*, 512–523.

Mischel, W. (1973). Toward a cognitive social learning reconceptualization of personality. *Psychological Review, 80*, 252–283.

Muraven, M., & Baumeister, R. F. (2000). Self-regulation and depletion of limited resources: Does self-control resemble a muscle? *Psychological Bulletin, 126*, 247–259.

Oettingen, G. (2000). Expectancy effects on behavior depend on self-regulatory thought. *Social Cognition, 18*, 101–129.

Oettingen, G. (2012). Future thought and behavior change. *European Review of Social Psychology, 23*, 1–63.

Oettingen, G., Hönig, G., & Gollwitzer, P. M. (2000). Effective self-regulation of goal attainment. *International Journal of Educational Research, 33*, 705–732.

Oettingen, G., Marquardt, M. K., & Gollwitzer, P. M. (2012). Mental contrasting turns positive feedback on creative potential into successful performance. *Journal of Experimental Social Psychology, 48*, 990–996.

Oettingen, G., & Mayer, D. (2002). The motivating function of thinking about the future: Expectations versus fantasies. *Journal of Personality and Social Psychology, 83*, 1198–1212.

Oettingen, G., Mayer, D., & Brinkmann, B. (2010a). Mental contrasting of future and reality: Managing the demands of everyday life in health care professionals. *Journal of Personnel Psychology, 9*, 138–144.

Oettingen, G., Mayer, D., Sevincer, A. T., Stephens, E. J., Pak, H.-J., & Hagenah, M. (2009). Mental contrasting and goal commitment: The mediating role of energization. *Personality and Social Psychology Bulletin, 35*, 608–622.

Oettingen, G., Mayer, D., & Thorpe, J. (2010b). Self-regulation of commitment to reduce cigarette consumption: Mental contrasting of future with reality. *Psychology and Health, 25*, 961–977.

Oettingen, G., Mayer, D., Thorpe, J. S., Janetzke, H., & Lorenz, S. (2005). Turning fantasies about positive and negative futures into self-improvement goals. *Motivation and Emotion, 29*, 237–267.

Oettingen, G., Pak, H.-J., & Schnetter, K. (2001). Self-regulation of goal-setting: Turning free fantasies about the future into binding goals. *Journal of Personality and Social Psychology, 80*, 736–753.

Oettingen, G., Stephens, E. J., Mayer, D., & Brinkmann, B. (2010c). Mental contrasting and the self-regulation of helping relations. *Social Cognition, 28*, 490–508.

Oettingen, G., Wittchen, M., & Gollwitzer, P. M. (2013). Regulating goal pursuit through mental contrasting with implementation intentions. In E. A. Locke & G. P. Latham (Eds.), *New developments in goal setting and task performance* (pp. 523–548). New York, NY: Brunner-Routledge.

Parks-Stamm, E. J., Gollwitzer, P. M., & Oettingen, G. (2007). Action control by implementation intentions: Effective cue detection and efficient response initiation. *Social Cognition, 25*, 248–266.

Parks-Stamm, E. J., Gollwitzer, P. M., & Oettingen, G. (2010). Implementation intentions and test anxiety: Shielding academic performance from distraction. *Learning and Individual Differences, 20*, 30–33.

Perels, F., Dignath, C., & Schmitz, B. (2009). Is it possible to improve mathematical achievement by means of self-regulation strategies? Evaluation of an intervention in regular math class. *European Journal of Psychology of Education, 24*, 17–31.

Pressley, M., Woloshyn, V., Lysynchuk, L. M., Martin, V., Wood, E., & Willoughby, T. (1990). A primer of research on cognitive strategy instruction: The important issues and how to address them. *Educational Psychology Review, 2*, 1–58.

Randi, J. (2005). Teachers as self-regulated learners. *Teachers College Record, 10*, 1825–1853.

Schunk, D. H. & Zimmerman, B. J. (2007). Influencing children's self-efficacy and self-regulation of reading and writing through modeling. *Reading & Writing Quarterly: Overcoming Learning Difficulties, 23*, 7–25.

Sevincer, A. T., Busatta, P. D., & Oettingen, G. (2014). Mental contrasting and transfer of energization. *Personality and Social Psychology Bulletin, 40*, 139–152.

Sevincer, A. T., & Oettingen, G. (2013). Spontaneous mental contrasting and selective goal pursuit. *Personality and Social Psychology Bulletin, 39*, 1240–1254.

Shah, J. Y., Friedman, R., & Kruglanski, A. W. (2002). Forgetting all else: On the antecedents and consequences of goal shielding. *Journal of Personality and Social Psychology, 83*, 1261–1280.

Sheeran, P., Webb, T. L., & Gollwitzer, P. M. (2005). The interplay between goal intentions and implementation intentions. *Personality and Social Psychology Bulletin, 31*, 87–98.

Sonuga-Barke, E. J. (2002). Psychological heterogeneity in AD/HD—A dual pathway model of behavior and cognition. *Behavioural Brain Research, 130*, 29–36.

Stewart, B. D., & Payne, B. K. (2008). Bringing automatic stereotyping under control: Implementation intentions as efficient means of thought control. *Personality and Social Psychology Bulletin, 34*, 1332–1345.

Tolman, E. (1932). *Purposive behavior in animals and men.* Berkeley, CA: University of California Press.

Varley, R., Webb, T. L., & Sheeran, P. (2011). Making self-help more helpful: A randomized controlled trial of the impact of augmenting self-help materials with implementation intentions in promoting the effective self-management of anxiety symptoms. *Journal of Consulting and Clinical Psychology, 79*, 123–128.

Webb, T. L., Christian J., & Armitage, C. J. (2007). Helping students turn up for class: Does personality moderate the effectiveness of an implementation intention intervention? *Learning and Individual Differences, 17*, 316–327.

Webb, T. L., Onanaiye, M., Sheeran, P., Reidy, J., & Lavda, S. (2010). Using implementation intentions to modify the effects of social anxiety on attention and responses to evaluative situations. *Personality and Social Psychology Bulletin, 36*, 612–627.

Webb, T. L., & Sheeran, P. (2003). Can implementation intentions help to overcome ego-depletion? *Journal of Experimental Social Psychology, 39*, 279–286.

Webb, T. L., & Sheeran, P. (2007). How do implementation intentions promote goal attainment? A test of component processes. *Journal of Experimental Social Psychology, 43*, 295–302.

Webb, T. L., & Sheeran, P. (2008). Mechanisms of implementation intention effects: The role of goal intentions, self-efficacy, and accessibility of plan components. *British Journal of Social Psychology, 47*, 373–395.

Webb, T. L., Sheeran, P., & Luszczynska, A. (2009). Planning to break unwanted habits: Habit strength moderates implementation intention effects on behaviour change. *British Journal of Social Psychology, 48*, 507–523.

Wieber, F., & Gollwitzer, P. M. (2010). Overcoming procrastination through Implementation Intentions. In C. Andreou and M. D. White (Eds.), *The thief of time: Philosophical essays on procrastination* (pp. 185–205). New York: Oxford University Press.

Wieber, F., von Suchodoletz, A., Heikamp, T., Trommsdorff, G., & Gollwitzer, P. M. (2011). If-then planning helps school-aged children to ignore attractive distractions. *Social Psychology, 42*, 39–47.

Xu, J., Yuan, R., Xu, B., & Xu, M. (2014). Modeling students' time management in math homework. *Learning and Individual Differences, 34*, 33–42.

# Part III

## Learner Readiness and Development

# 9

# Human Cognitive Abilities

## Their Organization, Development, and Use

*Patrick C. Kyllonen*
Educational Testing Service

Some students learn quickly; others take much longer. One explanation is that students come to school with widely varying learning experiences and are differentially prepared. Another is that students differ in their cognitive abilities. Even if students came to school with the same set of learning experiences, they would still differ in how quickly they learned due to ability differences. These explanations are not incompatible and most people—experts and non-experts—believe both to be true. Their relative importance has been the subject of heated debate for decades, if not centuries, and is unlikely to be resolved soon. This chapter summarizes what we know about human abilities, framed in the context of their measurement and organization. It also discusses cognitive ability development and the use of ability measures.

## The Organization of Human Abilities

### The General (g) Factor

The idea that people can be characterized by ability has been with us for centuries, but the scientific identification of human cognitive ability is typically attributed to Spearman (1904). Spearman studied performance on a wide variety of school (e.g., spelling, arithmetic) and psychology laboratory tasks (e.g., susceptibility to illusions) and found that performance on one task positively predicted performance on the others, a finding known as *positive manifold*. He further proposed a simple mathematical model, *vanishing tetrad differences,* to account for the correlations: For any subset of four tests, the product of the correlations of any two of them equals the product of the correlations of any other two, indicating unidimensionality. Spearman proposed general ability, or *g*, as an explanation for positive manifold, and the sufficiency of *g*, combined with test specificities, which he called *s*, as a way to characterize human abilities.

Spearman's finding of a general ability factor has held up remarkably well. To illustrate, the Program for International Student Assessment (PISA), which measures 15-year-old students' cognitive abilities in approximately 70 countries, found high correlations among three achievement domains: $r$ (mathematics, reading) = 0.84, $r$ (mathematics, science) = 0.89, and $r$ (reading, science) = 0.87 (OECD, 2012, Table 12.4), suggesting a strong, common factor. Similar results are found for all four PISA cycles, including problem solving for PISA 2003 ($r$ = 0.89, 0.82, 0.78, between problem solving and mathematics, reading, and science, respectively).

### Group Factors

Despite the power of the *g* factor in predicting performance on cognitive tests, since Spearman many studies have sought to identify additional factors. A key figure was Thurstone (1934), who proposed that in a battery of tests there might be *group factors* with several tests having something in common beyond the general factor, for example, "the ability to write fast, facility with geometrical figures, or a large vocabulary" (p. 4). Thurstone introduced exploratory factor analysis to test this hypothesis, in which factors are extracted successively from a correlation matrix, with communality estimates on the diagonal of that matrix, and rotation of axes to simple structure. This method led to the primary mental abilities proposal (Thurstone, 1938)—word fluency, verbal comprehension, spatial visualization, number facility, associative memory, reasoning, and perceptual speed. Later research programs, such as Guilford's (1956), attempted to identify an even larger number of cognitive ability factors.

Although historical accounts often cast "general" vs. "multiple intelligences" perspectives as opposing, they are reconcilable. Thurstone (1947) suggested that correlated group factors indicated a *g* factor, and Holzinger and Swineford (1937) introduced a bifactor method that identified both general and group factors (see Gustafsson & Balke, 1993). Schmid and Leiman (1957) developed a hierarchical method of extracting factors, and Vernon (1965) summarized research on a variety of tests best summarized by a hierarchical model. (Hierarchical and bifactor models themselves are compatible: Yung, Thissen, & McLeod, 1999.) The concept of a general factor and more specific group factors is not completely dependent on factor analysis: It is also captured with alternative methods of characterizing correlation matrices such as non-metric multidimensional scaling (Snow, Kyllonen, & Marshalek, 1984).

### The Fluid-Crystallized Distinction

A perspective not strictly compatible with the Spearman–Thurstone hierarchical framework is the Horn–Cattell (1966) model, which distinguishes two general abilities. Fluid intelligence (Gf) is the ability called upon during abstract reasoning and problem solving, particularly in novel situations; crystallized intelligence (Gc) reflects conceptual and verbal knowledge acquired through education and experience. Fluid ability is invested in learning to yield crystallized ability (Horn & Cattell, 1967). A source of evidence for the Gf–Gc distinction is differential growth patterns: Gf peaks as early as in one's twenties and declines slowly thereafter; in contrast, Gc grows, or at least does not decline until much later in life.

So, are there one or two gs? Gustafsson (1984) proposed that there is only one g, but it is identical to Gf. He based this on descriptions of g and Gf by various researchers, and showed that the two were factor analytically identical. Some studies have not corroborated this result, and so Valentin Kvist and Gustafsson (2008) suggested that this might be due to the effects of differential opportunities to learn. They found that within culturally homogeneous groups (Swedish non-immigrants, European immigrants, and non-European immigrants) g and Gf were identical (r = 1.0), and only when the data were pooled did the g–Gf correlation attenuate (to r = 0.83). That is, in a group with roughly the same opportunities to learn (e.g., Swedish non-immigrants) the expected r (g, Gf) = 1.0 relationship was observed, but when groups with differing opportunities to learn (e.g., Swedish native speakers vs. immigrants who spoke Swedish as a second language) were pooled, the correlation was reduced because a factor in addition to Gf, opportunity to learn, contributed to performance on other g measures.

### The Consensus Model: Carroll and CHC

Carroll (1993) summarized essentially all available research on human cognitive abilities by reanalyzing approximately 450 datasets (with several thousand test scores) using an exploratory hierarchical method. The results suggested a three-stratum model with g at the third stratum, eight factors at the second stratum—fluid intelligence (Gf), crystallized intelligence (Gc), general learning and memory (Gy), broad visual perception (Gv), broad auditory perception (Ga), broad retrieval ability (Glr), broad cognitive speediness (Gs), and reaction time/decision speed (Gt)—and numerous factors at the third stratum

(e.g., within Gf there is general sequential reasoning, induction, quantitative reasoning, and Piagetian reasoning; within Gc there is language development, verbal language comprehension, lexical knowledge, and 13 more abilities).

A combination of the Carroll (1993) framework, acknowledging the importance of the Gf–Gc distinction (Cattell, 1941) and the expansion of Gf–Gc into a broader abilities framework (e.g., Horn, 1989), is now commonly referred to as CHC (Cattell–Horn–Carroll) theory (McGrew, 2009). The CHC framework serves as the basis for several commercial intelligence test batteries (Kaufman & Kaufman, 2004; Woodcock, McGrew, & Mather, 2007) and is regarded as the foundation for psychoeducational assessment in school psychology (Flanagan & Harrison, 2012).

## Critiques: Achievements and Limitations of the Consensus Abilities Framework

The consensus cognitive abilities framework can be seen as representing a kind of "end of history" of human abilities. In 1994, Sternberg said of Carroll's (1993) tour de force that, "There is nothing like it, nor is there likely to be"; it represents "a culmination . . . of the psychometric approach to intelligence" (p. 65). This was written over 20 years ago, and there has not been a game-changing critique of the general framework during that time. Sternberg in that same article suggested that the Carroll framework was in danger of not appealing to as wide an array of "stakeholders" as newer alternatives, such as Gardner's (1983) multiple intelligences theory and his own practical intelligence framework, which takes context into account (Sternberg & Wagner, 1986). However, these alternatives have not fared well in the interim (e.g., Gottfredson, 2003; McDaniel & Whetzel, 2005; Visser, Ashton, & Vernon, 2006a, 2006b).

Still, the consensus abilities framework can be improved and elaborated upon as evidence accrues within the factor-analytic tradition (e.g., Carroll, 2003). McGrew (2009) provided justifications for new abilities such as tactile (Gh), kinesthetic (Gk), and olfactory (Go) abilities; domain-specific knowledge (Gkn); psychomotor ability (Gp); and psychomotor speed (Gps). Johnson and Bouchard (2005) proposed a related model, called the g-VPR (for verbal, perceptual, and image rotation), which does not seem qualitatively different from the CHC model, but has a different emphasis. This model may be more useful in studies emphasizing the neuroscientific underpinnings of cognitive ability. In particular, Hunt (2011) argues that, consistent with the g-VPR model, there is evidence for separate brain systems handling language and perceptual processing, and that there is a biological distinction that mirrors the distinction between mental rotation (where male–female differences are large) and the analysis of static figures (where the distinctions are small or favor women).

It is useful to consider a broader perspective on the status of the consensus abilities framework. Certainly the cognitive abilities measurement framework is sound and useful, but it is not universally accepted as a basis for understanding human abilities. Table 9.1 presents a list of some of the key criticisms, which are elaborated on in later sections of this chapter.

**Table 9.1    Common Criticisms of the Consensus Framework on Cognitive Ability**

1.  Tests are not authentic or relevant to real life. Tests are too brief a sample of behavior and there is a need for authentic assessment (Hakel, 1998).
    **Counter**: "*Authentic tasks*" duplicate traditional tests (e.g., Sonnleitner, Keller, Martin, & Brunner, 2013). Tests predict real-world outcomes.

2.  The consensus framework is limited to the tests analyzed. This is a theory about tests that happen to have been developed, particularly paper-and-pencil multiple-choice tests, not about human abilities per se.
    **Counter**: Alternative formats have been evaluated (e.g., motion picture tests during the 1950s). Still, technology opens the door to new kinds of measures, such as videos, simulations, eye movements, and physiological responses.

3.  The methodology of the analysis of test score covariances is limited. Additional methodologies should be used. Intelligence "is too important to be left to the psychometricians" (Gardner, 1999).
    **Counter**: Psychometricians are exploring alternative methodologies for measuring cognitive ability using games and simulations (e.g., Mislevy et al., 2014), data mining (He, 2013), and physiological neuroscience measurements (Kane & Engle, 2002), among others.

4.  Abilities are fixed, if not inherited, and there is not much that can be done about them in school.
    **Counter**: Abilities are not fixed—schooling reliably improves them (Brinch & Galloway, 2011), and a steady growth in test scores over the past half-century suggests that abilities, measured by tests, improve (Flynn, 2007).

5.  We do not know what human abilities are, or what tests actually measure: "intelligence as a measurable capacity must at the start be defined as the capacity to do well in an intelligence test. Intelligence is what the tests test" (Boring, 1923).
    **Counter**: There has been a concerted effort to understand the meaning of test scores from a basic psychological (Hunt, 2012) and neuroscientific perspective (e.g., see Chapter 5, this volume).

6.  There are factors that threaten the validity of test scores, such as fatigue, emotional strain, practice, room temperature, affect, test-wiseness, motivation (Cronbach, 1970).
    **Counter**: This is an active area of research with studies on the effects of score disclosure and financial incentives (Duckworth, Quinn, Lynam, Loeber, & Stouthamer-Loeber, 2011; Liu, Bridgeman, & Adler, 2013), stereotype threat (Ganley, Mingle, Ryan, Ryan, Vasilyeva, & Perry, 2013; Steele & Aronson, 1995), and beliefs about the nature of intelligence (Dweck and Master, 2009).

7.  Tests may be unfair to subgroups.
    **Counter**: The importance of establishing fairness is recognized in the Test Standards (American Educational Research Association, American Psychological Association, National Council on Measurement in Education, 2014).

8.  Aptitude (ability) and achievement are clearly separate concepts.
    **Counter**: Since Binet (1905) ability tests have been cognitive tasks drawn from school curricula that separate those who do well in school from those who do poorly (e.g., vocabulary, reading comprehension, sentence completion, arithmetic). There is not a distinction in the heritability of Gf and Gc (e.g., Mackintosh, 2011, Chapter 2). Secular growth (Flynn, 2007) affects Gf more than Gc, Although there are differences between Gf and Gc measures, the two factors are so highly correlated that the distinction can be ignored for many purposes (e.g., Hunt, 2012).

## Individual-Level Validity

Cognitive test scores are relatively rank-order stable over time. For example, Deary, Whalley, Lemmon, Crawford, and Starr (2000) readministered a general abilities test, the Moray House Test, consisting of verbal, spatial, numerical, and reasoning items, to a group of 77-year-olds who had taken the same test 66 years earlier as 11-year-olds, and found a correlation of $r = 0.63$ (adjusted to 0.73 when correcting for range restriction in the retested sample). Thirteen years later, with the 90-year-old cohort group (and a 77-year time difference) the correlation was $r = 0.54$ (adjusted to 0.67 when correcting for range restriction) (Deary, Pattie, & Starr, 2013).

### Predictions of Education and Workplace Success

But do cognitive test scores predict other life events? From its very beginnings, the rise in popularity and scientific acceptance of modern cognitive abilities measurement has been tied to its capability for predicting important and complex real-world outcomes relatively efficiently. The world's first intelligence test, the Binet-Simon scale, was promoted for its ability to differentiate normal from mentally challenged schoolchildren in France. The Army Alpha test was lauded for its success "(a) to aid in segregating the mentally

incompetent, (b) to classify men according to their mental capacity, (c) to assist in selecting competent men for responsible positions." (Yoachum & Yerkes, 1920, p. xi). Since then hundreds of studies have been conducted on the relationship between cognitive ability test scores and various life outcomes. Thorndike (1986) showed a correlation between an overall score on the Differential Aptitude Test Battery and grades (across many schools) of $r = 0.5$–0.6. In higher education admissions studies, cognitive ability measured by admissions tests of verbal comprehension, mathematics reasoning, and logical reasoning predict outcomes such as first-year grade point average ($r = 0.35$–0.60), degree completion ($r = 0.10$–0.40), qualifying and licensure exams ($r = 0.30$–0.65) and research productivity and publication citations ($r = 0.10$–0.25) (Kuncel & Hezlett, 2007).

Cognitive ability measures also predict success in the workplace. At the high end of ability, Lubinski, Benbow and colleagues have shown that students scoring relatively high on the SAT at age 13 are far more likely than others to attain a degree, get a doctorate, publish novels, have high incomes, secure patents, and be happy (Ferriman-Robertson, Smeets, Lubinski, & Benbow, 2010; Lubinski & Benbow, 2006; Park, Lubinski, & Benbow, 2013). In the normal-ability range, Schmidt and Hunter (1998) suggested high correlations between cognitive test scores and workplace outcomes ($r = 0.56$ with test scores in job training courses and $r = 0.51$ with supervisor ratings, after range restriction adjustments). Ree and Earles (1992) similarly found a high correlation ($r = 0.42$, no range restriction adjustment) between a first principal component score from the Armed Services Vocational Aptitude Battery (ASVAB, comprising ten diverse subtests—general science, arithmetic reasoning, word knowledge, paragraph comprehension, math knowledge, electronics information, auto information, shop information, mechanical comprehension, and assembling objects) and U.S. Air Force training grades (from multiple-choice knowledge tests from 82 job training courses, ranging from electronics troubleshooting to security police, with $n = 72,000$). Findings from the Army's *Project A* study (McHenry, Hough, Toquam, Hanson, & Ashworth, 1990) were similar. Ree, Earles, and Teachout (1994) also investigated prediction of other criteria—hands-on-performance tests, an interview work sample test, and a walk-through performance test—and found uncorrected correlations from $r = 0.10$–$0.34$ on jobs ranging from personnel specialist to radio operator, mechanic, and air traffic controller. Gottfredson (2002) summarizes data suggesting that the predictiveness of test scores increases as job complexity increases (e.g., from packer to attorney). She, along with Lubinski and Humphreys (1997), Jensen (1998), O'Toole and Stankov (1992), also identified other real-world variables correlated with cognitive test scores, such as health, crime, divorce rate, illegitimate births, accidents, and longevity.

### Differential Validity

From this summary of predictive validity studies it should be noted that Gf and Gc are often treated interchangeably as measures of general cognitive ability, the Gf–Gc compound (Corno et al., 2002). Tests such as the SAT and ASVAB largely measure Gc (Roberts et al., 2000), but are sometimes described as measures of intelligence; this is true of other measures reviewed here as well. An ASVAB review panel recommended including specific Gf measures in future versions (Drasgow, Embretson, Kyllonen, & Schmitt, 2006). But the finding also raises the broader question, what is the evidence that other cognitive ability measures besides Gf and Gc predict life outcomes? An issue of the 1986 volume of the *Journal of Vocational Behavior* was devoted to "the g factor in employment." Humphreys (1986) summarized his experiences in the Air Force on evaluating evidence for differential validity. He wrote that he and his coworkers were influenced by Thurstone's primary mental abilities scheme, and that they attempted to create factor-pure tests, but he was "quickly disillusioned"

> as we accumulated predictive validities and factor analyses of dozens of tests and thousands of examinees. We were able to define dependably many group factors, but found little differential validity for the multiple factors. (Differential validity is defined as stable differential regression weights for the prediction of multiple criteria.) (p. 421)

This characterizes much of the state of affairs with the consensus model: It is possible to find replicable structures of test intercorrelations through factor analysis. However, consensus model factors other than g, Gf, and Gc do not appear to have differential validity. The Brunswick symmetry hypothesis (Wittmann & Suess, 1999) explains this as a shortage of studies that have examined criterion outcomes matching factors other than g, Gf, and Gc. And there is still evidence for differential validity even for the ASVAB (Alley, 1994; Zeidner & Johnson, 1994).

However, there are at least two consensus model factors other than g, Gf, and Gc, for which there is particularly strong evidence for differential validity. One is *spatial ability* (broad visual perception, Gv, in Carroll's (1993) scheme). Lubinski and colleagues (Lubinski, 2010; Wai, Lubinski, and Benbow, 2009; Webb, Lubinski, & Benbow, 2007) summarized results from several studies suggesting that spatial ability had incremental validity over other measures (e.g., SAT scores) in identifying young students who went on to major in a science, technology, engineering, and mathematics (STEM) discipline, take a job in a STEM field, majored and ended up in occupations in visual arts, and had publications and patents in technical areas (Kell, Lubinski, Benbow, & Steiger, 2013). Snow (1999) lamented the fact that spatial ability has long been underappreciated as adding value to traditional assessments.[1]

Another construct showing differential validity is *creativity* (*idea production* or *broad retrieval ability*, Gr, in Carroll's scheme). Several studies (Bennett & Rock, 1995; Frederiksen & Ward, 1975) have found that *idea production* measures, such as ones obtained from tests of *formulating hypotheses*, and *measuring constructs*, predicted graduate school outcomes beyond the prediction by GRE verbal and mathematics scores. Similarly, another idea production task, *consequences,* has been shown to predict leadership abilities and Army officer career outcomes controlling for cognitive ability test scores (Mumford, Marks, Connelly, Zaccaro, & Johnson, 1998).

### Why do Cognitive Tests Predict Outcomes?

The evidence is fairly clear that abilities measured by cognitive tests predict important real-world outcomes, and that different abilities—g, Gf, Gc, Gv, Gr—differentially predict outcomes. This is, and has been for the past 100 years, of enormous practical significance, which explains why schools and employers continue to use ability tests for making admissions, placement, selection, and assignment decisions. However, the causes for why ability tests predict outcomes are not established. The fundamental problem is that predictive studies are based on correlations. Abilities cannot be randomly assigned to individuals at various dosage levels; we can explore their effects in a randomized trial. Instead we have to rely on correlation patterns and occasional natural experiments to investigate the causal relationships between abilities and outcomes.

Why does this make a difference? The issue of nature vs. nurture has been at the core of the abilities debate since its beginnings (e.g., Harris, 1998). Group differences (e.g., Herrnstein & Murray, 1994; Murray, 1998), the predictive power of personality and interests vs. abilities (Ackerman & Beier, 2003), personality and socioeconomic status vs. abilities (Lubinski, 2009; Roberts, Kuncel, Shiner, Caspi, & Goldberg, 2007; Sackett, Kuncel, Arneson, Cooper, & Waters, 2009), and the relative importance of abilities vs. educational attainment (e.g., Bowles, Gintis, & Osborne, 2001) have competed as explanations for student achievement, workplace, and life outcomes, and have sparked debates about the best societal investments.

For example, although it has long been thought that cognitive abilities are the most important determinants of educational attainment and labor market outcomes (e.g., Herrnstein & Murray, 1994; Jensen, 1998), there is good evidence that non-cognitive skills (such as persistence) may be as important and perhaps even more important in some cases. One source of evidence for this is that cognitive skills, as measured by test scores, only account for a small fraction of the effect of educational attainment on labor market outcomes (Bowles, Gintis, & Osborne, 2001). This leaves the possibility that something else, its effect on the development of non-cognitive skills, is what is responsible for schooling's effect on wages and employment and staying out of trouble (Heckman, Stixrud, & Urzua, 2006; Levin, 2012). A longitudinal study (Lindqvist & Vestman, 2011) evaluated over 14,000 Swedish enlistees aged 18 or 19 who were given two assessments during conscription: a comprehensive abilities battery (synonyms, induction, metal folding, and technical comprehension), and a 25-minute interview by a trained clinical psychologist intended to evaluate an applicant's responsibility, independence, outgoingness, persistence, emotional stability, initiative, and ability to adjust to life in the armed forces. Twenty years later, cognitive skill was found to be a stronger predictor of educational attainment than non-cognitive skill, suggesting the importance of education in transforming cognitive ability to labor market outcomes. However, non-cognitive skills compared to cognitive skills were found to be stronger predictors of employment and stronger predictors of earnings, particularly for those at the low end of the earnings distribution (see also Chapters 7, 8, and 11, this volume). Cognitive skills were found to be a more important predictor of wages for those earning above the fiftieth percentile. This is a finding consistent with Gottfredson's (1997) finding that cognitive tests were more predictive of success at higher occupational levels.

## Country-Level Validity

Cognitive ability tests can be evaluated at the national as well as individual level. Several researchers in psychology and economics have compared nations on their average cognitive ability test scores, based on either intelligence quotient (IQ) or achievement tests. Jones (2011) argues that cognitive skills have only moderate relations to earnings, but are strongly correlated with national outcomes, and suggests several reasons why that might be so. National cognitive ability predicts gross domestic product (GDP) (Jones & Schneider, 2006) and GDP growth over the past three to five decades; cognitive ability inequality within a country also predicts earnings inequality within that country (Hanushek

& Woessmann, 2010). Educational attainment predicts GDP growth, but adding cognitive ability substantially increases the prediction. Disentangling the effects of schooling compared to the effects of cognitive abilities is difficult because schooling increases cognitive ability, but cognitive ability also increases educational attainment (Heckman et al., 2006). There are some differences in whether cognitive ability is measured by achievement or IQ scores; achievement scores provide better predictions (Hunt & Wittmann, 2008).

National cognitive ability predicts outcomes besides earnings and economic growth. Rindermann (2007) showed high correlations (between $r = 0.30$ and $0.70$) between national cognitive ability and rule of law, quality of bureaucracy, economic freedom, and rate of solved homicides, and negative correlations ($r = -0.22$ to $-0.73$) with fertility rate, economic inequality, HIV infection rate, government spending (per GDP), homicide rate, and war. Whetzel and McDaniel (2006) showed a high correlation between national cognitive ability and national well-being (also replicated at the state level; Pesta, McDaniel, & Bertsch, 2010).

Hunt (2012) argues that national differences in cognitive ability exist, whether measured by achievement or IQ tests. Whether these national (as well as individual) differences are innate or due to the environment has been a long-standing controversy (e.g., Ceci & Williams, 2009). Hunt argues that national differences are largely due to environmental factors, such as the amount of schooling (early education and educational attainment), studying practices, the home environment, and attitudes towards learning and education. Clearly there is substantial evidence that environmental factors are important and therefore it is important for policy makers to acknowledge national cognitive ability differences and develop policies to address them.

Research on country-level validity has been conducted using both IQ and achievement tests. However, tests have been treated interchangeably, due to their high correlation, and other than the Hunt and Wittmann (2008) study, there has been little, if any, research on differential validity of human cognitive abilities at the national level.

## What is an Ability?

Spearman suggested that $g$ could be characterized as mental energy, but this was metaphorical, as there was no independent evidence for the claim. Another metaphorical attempt was Thomson's bonds theory (Bartholomew, Deary, & Lawn, 2009), which suggested that a general factor did not imply a single cognitive capability, but could just as easily arise from a situation in which any two tasks required a common set of independent bonds (e.g., stimulus–response associations), different tasks required different overlapping bonds, and that no subset of bonds was common to all tasks. But again, this was primarily metaphorical, as no independent evidence outside of the correlation matrix itself was brought forward as evidence.

### *The Cognitive Revolution*

In the 1970s, with the growth of cognitive psychology, the situation changed. Numerous researchers began to identify the underpinnings of cognitive ability test behavior. The "cognitive correlates" method involved identifying basic information-processing tasks that correlated with cognitive abilities. The idea was to use basic information-processing tasks to help shed light on the processing requirements of abilities tests (e.g., Hunt, Lunneborg, & Lewis, 1975). The "cognitive components" method used subtraction to identify the basic components of reasoning, spatial ability, or other cognitive abilities (e.g., Sternberg, 1977). Processing stages were isolated by comparing performance on a regular test item with simplified versions of that item. There were many variants on these methods and considerable enthusiasm about their potential for revealing something deep about the nature of abilities. For example, Ackerman (1987) integrated traditional abilities models with skill development models from the human factors literature.

## Working Memory and the Cognitive Abilities Measurement Framework

A successful example of the use of a cognitive correlates approach was a study by Kyllonen and Christal (1990), which administered the ASVAB and dozens of cognitive abilities tests to a couple thousand military enlistees along with dozens of measures of working-memory capacity prepared from Baddeley and Hitch's (1974) definition of tasks requiring simultaneous storage and processing of incoming information. The two constructs were highly correlated (the latent variable correlation was estimated at about 0.90). Since then a number of studies have attempted to determine which abilities and working-memory components are responsible for the relationship. A recent paper by Conway and Kovacs (2013) reviewed neuroimaging and behavioral research, suggesting that it is the executive/attentional component of working memory and the Gf component of ability that is responsible for the high correlation between g and working memory.

A larger framework for thinking about the information-processing underpinnings of cognitive abilities was the cognitive abilities measurement framework (Kyllonen, 1994, 1995), based on a consensus information-processing model. The framework posited that the major information-processing components for cognitive ability were working memory, long-term declarative and procedural knowledge stores, and a parameter governing the speed of information flow through the system. Each of these components could serve as a source of individual differences—the capacity of working memory, the speed of processing, the breadth of the declarative and procedural stores, and the efficiency of declarative and procedural learning. A test battery was developed from this framework (the Advanced Personnel Testing battery, APT), and validated against training grades (Sawin, Earles, Goff, & Chaiken, 2001). Although there were some suggestions for incremental validity of the APT over the ASVAB, the more important aspect of the effort was its heuristic value in showing the commonality between information-processing psychology and traditional psychometrics. The modern view (e.g., Underwood, 1975) is that the two fields are not really distinguishable, and that the psychometric methodology

serving as the basis for differential psychology, the discipline for identifying abilities, can be used also for identifying skills in information-processing psychology. For example, Miyake et al. (2000) used confirmatory factor analysis to explore the structure of executive functions (shifting attention, updating, and inhibition) in working memory.

### Neuroscience

In recent years, much of the energy in trying to define abilities seems to have shifted towards neuroscience (Gray & Thompson, 2004; see also Chapter 5, this volume). Several reviews summarize current understanding of the relationship between working memory, executive functioning, and neurological correlates (Conway, Moore, & Kane, 2009; Gray, Chabris, & Braver, 2003; Osaka, Logie, & D'Esposito, 2007). Although the field is plagued by small sample sizes due to high costs for data collection, as well as constraints on the nature of tasks due to the susceptibility to extraneous effects in brain imaging, data collection and analysis technology is improving rapidly and one can imagine a comprehensive brain-mapping study soon that identifies neurological correlates of all the abilities in the CHC consensus framework.

## Development of Abilities

Cognitive abilities increase with age at least through late adolescence and early adulthood, and even later adulthood in some cases. Thus, the concept of the IQ was invented to enable comparisons between people conditioned on age. A person with a high IQ is a person who outperforms others *his or her age* on cognitive ability tests. Test scores (e.g., SAT scores) required to qualify in talent searches (Webb et al., 2007) are not remarkable but for the fact that they are achieved at an early age (e.g., at age 12 rather than at age 17). All this demonstrates the obvious, that abilities develop with age. And, again, one of the arguments for the fluid vs. crystallized abilities distinction is that fluid abilities (including perceptual speed, inductive reasoning, spatial ability) peak relatively early (mid twenties) and decline in early adulthood, whereas crystallized abilities (including vocabulary, verbal ability, verbal memory) rise through one's thirties and perhaps even later, remain stable, and only decline much later in life (McArdle, Hamagami, Meredith, & Bradway, 2000). These results vary somewhat depending on whether studies are conducted using a dataset that is cross-sectional (peak tends to be earlier, perhaps due to general trends in growth of IQ scores over time) or longitudinal (peak tends to be later).

Desjardins and Warnke (2012) summarized the literature on cognitive skills growth, identifying a variety of effects (e.g., cohort, period, genetic, social, skills practice, physical and mental activity, education, and background effects), and distinguishing different types of cognitive skills. A key finding is that "education, training, and a number of physical, social and mental activities have all been implicated as possible factors which help to mitigate the age-related decline in cognitive skills [which] suggests that policy can make a difference" (p. 55). The authors point out the important role cross-national cognitive surveys, such as the Program for International Assessment of Adult Competencies, can play in disentangling the various influences on cognitive skill growth and decline.

The number of years a person spends studying in school is correlated with cognitive ability levels. Ceci and Williams (1997) identified seven types of evidence suggesting the relationship is not just correlational but that schooling raised cognitive ability. These were: (a) a negative correlation between IQ and age for children who attended school intermittently during their school-age years; (b) lower IQ and achievement scores for children who began school late; (c) high scores for those staying in school longer to avoid the draft in the United States during the Viet Nam war; (d) lower scores for those dropping out of school before graduation; (e) declines in scores due to summer vacation; (f) higher IQs for those with birthdays early in the year due to longer mandatory school attendance; and (g) children of the same age who receive different levels of schooling due to age entry requirements have scores that are most reflective of their years in school than of their chronological age. Most of these sources of evidence are essentially natural experiments that enable a causal interpretation of the effects of schooling on IQ.

Cliffordson and Gustafsson (2008) applied a method called the continuous age/continuous treatment (CC method, similar to regression discontinuity) to a dataset of 48,269 male military enlistees' test scores measuring Gf, Gc, and Gv abilities. They addressed whether schooling per se affected test scores beyond natural developmental growth and concluded that it did, and at the rate of 2.7 IQ points per year, consistent in size with other estimates. They also noted differential effects on growth due to educational tracks and even with curricular emphases within tracks; for example, the highest growth was associated with the technology track. They also found that for Gf ability specifically, schooling was associated with 4.2–4.8 IQ points per year.

A comparable estimate of 3.7 IQ points per year of school was suggested by a natural experiment in Norway, which changed compulsory schooling from seventh grade to ninth grade in the 1960s (Brinch & Galloway, 2011). Different communities in Norway adopted the change at different times (during a short window), making it possible to evaluate the effects of the additional mandatory schooling. All citizens were given a comprehensive abilities test at age 19 due to compulsory military service, which enabled the estimation of the effects of additional schooling on cognitive abilities.

In addition to the growth in cognitive abilities due to schooling, Flynn (1987) documented massive gains in American IQ scores from 1932 to 1978, followed by the observation of similar gains in 14 nations and later still more. The American Psychological Association commissioned a task force resulting in a book (Neisser, 1998) exploring the phenomenon (e.g., growth primarily in Gf, not in Gc; growth more at the lower than higher ends of the distribution), its possible causes (e.g., home factors, family size, nutrition, increased schooling, test familiarity) and its implications (e.g., narrowing of the achievement gap between subgroups). The Brinch and Galloway (2011) study suggested that increased schooling might have accounted for about one-third of the Flynn effect in Norway. It also appears to be the case that the Flynn effect may be slowing to a halt in developed nations (Teasdale & Owen, 2008), even though it may be continuing in developing nations (Flynn & Rossi-Casé, 2012), suggesting that national cognitive ability differences could be shrinking.

Finally, there is evidence that, like schooling, work experience contributes to cognitive skills development. The International Adult Literacy Survey (OECD & Statistics Canada, 2000) from 22 countries (16 languages) showed that cognitive skill levels (quantitative, verbal, and document literacy) were correlated with labor force participation, particularly with more high-status jobs (i.e., ones requiring greater education levels), how skills were used on the job, participation in education and workforce training, and the demand for cognitive skills at home.

## Trainability of Abilities

Studies of identical and fraternal twins reared apart (e.g., Plomin, Pedersen, Lichtenstein, & McClearn, 1994), as well as long-term test–retest studies (Deary et al., 2013), have led to a commonplace view that cognitive abilities are heritable, fixed, unaffected by schooling and the environment, and rank-order stable across time. While there is some evidence for those positions, the review above suggests that schooling, environmental effects, and a secular trend all have improved cognitive abilities, sometimes dramatically. In addition studies have specifically targeted cognitive abilities improvement. These range from nutritional interventions, early-childhood intervention programs, programs taught in schools designed to teach general cognitive skills, to recent programs designed to improve working-memory capacity.

### Early Childhood Studies

Protzko, Aronson, and Blair (2013) maintain the Database of Raising Intelligence, a continuously updated catalog of randomized trials designed to increase cognitive abilities. Meta-analyses from this database have shown that several interventions do appear to boost intelligence of young children: dietary supplements to pregnant mothers or infant formula supplements (0.24 effect size, about 3–4 IQ points), early-childhood intervention programs for low-socioeconomic status children (0.45 effect size; higher than the 0.23 given by Camilli, Vargas, Ryan, & Barnett, 2010), interactive reading with children (0.40 effect size), and sending children to preschool (0.51 effect size). Two programs have been studied in great detail: the Highscope Perry Preschool program (Schweinhart, Barnes, & Weikart, 1993) and the Abecederian program (Campbell et al., 2008), with the finding that the programs did boost IQ, although the effects faded somewhat over time (for the Abecedarian program, benefits were retained to age 40). Barnett (2011) concluded that these two small programs were among the most successful and their features ought to be compared to others to determine why. Regardless, it is important to note that there are additional benefits for these programs besides boosting IQ, such as higher educational attainment, decreased likelihood of being unemployed, on welfare, or having committed a crime, and greater earnings. These consequences have suggested that the rate of return on these programs is approximately 7–10% (Heckman, 2006; Heckman, Moon, Pinto, Savelyev, & Yavitz, 2010).

### Interventions with Schoolchildren and Adults

During the 1980s there were a number of programs developed and tried out in schools designed to improve general cognitive abilities, rather than specific curricular skills (Chipman, Segal, & Glaser, 1985; Nickerson, Perkins, & Smith, 1985; Segal, Chipman, & Glaser, 1985). Perhaps the expectations were too high, or the implementations were unsound, but these programs and this approach of teaching general cognitive abilities were not deemed wildly successful, and so attention moved to other topics. One program that was successful is Venezuela's Project Intelligence. This was a 3-year national intervention to improve the national cognitive ability level of the population. The first 2 years were essentially dress rehearsals, but in the final year, a randomized trial (matching classes) of six schools, 24 classes, and 30–40 seventh-graders per class were given non-curricular thinking skills lessons and practice for 4 days per week. Lessons covered classification, deductive and inductive reasoning, critical language use, hypothesis generation, problem solving, and decision making (Herrnstein, Nickerson, de Sanchez, & Swets, 1986). A battery of multiple-choice tests (e.g,. Otis-Lennon School Ability Test, Cattell Culture Fair Test, General Ability Tests; plus a 3.5-hour Target Ability Test designed to reflect the processes but not content taught) was administered by ministry officials as pretests, interim tests, and posttests. In addition, some far transfer tests, including a design task, oral and open-ended tasks, and an oral reasoning task, were administered. For all tasks there was a significant treatment effect, effect sizes ranging from 0.10 to 0.75, with suggestions that the benefits were in line with lesson emphasis. Unfortunately, no follow-up, short- or long-term, was attempted and so we know little about the long-term benefits of the program.

### Working-memory Training

It seems reasonable that an intense year-long cognitive training treatment such as was given in Project Intelligence would result in improvements in performance on cognitive tasks, even tasks that were not that similar to the ones that were the focus of training. But a rather surprising result came from a study showing that even a relatively short cognitive training program, this one training working-memory skills, resulted in improvements in one's ability to perform Gf reasoning tasks (Jaeggi, Buschkuehl, Jonides, & Perrig, 2008). The intervention, given to 70 young male and female adults for 8–19 days (with a control group) was a dual "n-back" task requiring participants to monitor auditory and visual targets presented sequentially, 3 seconds per target, and to indicate whether the target was in the same position or was the same consonant sound as the target from $n$ (= 3 or 4) trials previous.

Before the first training session, and after the last one, participants were administered Gf tasks, Raven's Progressive Matrices (RPM), and a more difficult variant of the RPM, and two working-memory span tests. The findings were that both treatment and control groups showed improvement in Gf from pretest to posttest (for the control group, a retest effect), but the treatment group showed significantly more (effect size of 0.65 vs. 0.25); the effect size was correlated with training dosage, and was not solely due to an improvement in working-memory span. The authors attributed the effect to practice in controlling attention. The study has received considerable attention (e.g., Morrison & Chein, 2011) but the dust has not yet settled on how reliable the phenomenon is and there is a concern that this might be a short-term, task-specific learning effect that does not generalize (Melby-Lervåg & Hulme, 2013; Shipstead, Redick, & Engle, 2012). Nevertheless the study—and others like it—is one more indicator that cognitive abilities might not be as immutable as once thought, and that they may be amenable to direct instruction.

### Expertise

Since the 1960s, studies have shown that specific cognitive abilities, ranging from playing chess, memorizing circuit diagrams, taxi driving, interpreting radiology images, to memory span itself, are highly amenable to training. And that expertise is not so much a matter of heritable, immutable abilities as it is a matter of sheer practice. For example, Ericsson, Chase, and Faloon (1980) were able to improve the memory span score of one student from a normal 7 to an unbelievable 79 (with digits read at one per second), as a result of 230 hours of practice (interestingly, after that training, the student's letter span remained at 6). This has led to the "10 years, 10,000 hours" mantra of expertise, popularized by Gladwell (2009) based on expertise research (Ericsson, Charness, Feltovich, & Hoffman, 2006). The expertise movement can be understood as a strongly environmental position on the nature of skills development. The field provides many demonstrations suggesting that any cognitive skill or ability is improvable through lots of practice, particularly deliberate practice—structured, mindful, and purposeful.

Ackerman (1987, 2007) has shown that expertise growth trajectories are moderated by cognitive abilities, particularly general cognitive ability in the early stages of skill development and knowledge acquisition. Macnamara, Hambrick, and Oswald (2014) conducted a meta-analysis showing that hours of deliberate practice accounted for only 12% of variance in performance overall (correlation of 0.35), but 26% of the variance in game performance, 21% for music, 18% for sports, and less than 5% for education and professions, suggesting that expertise is not accounted for by deliberate practice alone and might be explained by other factors, such as the age at which a person starts practice, and cognitive abilities.

### Other Influences on Test Scores

There are many influences on test scores besides abilities. These *construct-irrelevant* factors can affect inferences drawn from test score distributions, such as age and subgroup differences. For example, if a subgroup were less motivated on average than another subgroup, or a subgroup's first language were a language other than the test language, then it would be inappropriate to draw conclusions about group differences based on test scores. In general there are many possible other influences (e.g., disabilities, fatigue, stereotype threat, beliefs about the nature of intelligence, time of day, stressors, room temperature, drugs and alcohol, life events). Two of the most studied influences are motivation and the speed–accuracy tradeoff.

### Motivation

Several recent studies suggest that motivation can play a large role in test performance, particularly when the test is perceived by the test taker to be low stakes. Researchers often examine item response patterns for indications of random responding during data analysis but this is not systematically done, and there are likely many datasets contaminated with this kind of random responding. If aberrant response patterns are low frequency and distributed evenly, then there is not a large problem (other than attenuated validity coefficients); but if contaminated data are produced more by some groups than others, then this would create problems in inferences about group differences. Wise and Kong (2005) have suggested examining data for response time effort, indicated by short response times, which may indicate low motivation.

The magnitude of the motivation effect is potentially large. Duckworth, Quinn, Lynam, Loeber, and Stouthamer-Loeber (2011) conducted a meta-analysis of random-assignment studies that offered material incentives (e.g., typically small monetary payments) for test performance. They found a large effect size (0.64 SD) on test performance and found that motivation incentives were more effective for low scorers, implicating motivation as a possible cause for low scores in low-stakes testing. Segal (2012) compared performance on the coding speed test (a) given as part of a low-stakes survey study (the National Longitudinal Survey of Youth) versus (b) given as part of a high-stakes entrance exam for the armed forces (ASVAB) and found differences (e.g., prediction of future earnings, controlling for cognitive ability) suggesting a motivation component. Liu, Bridgeman, and Adler (2013) conducted a random-assignment incentive study examining motivation effects on a multiple-choice and essay test of critical thinking given to college students. Both the treatment and control groups were given standard written instructions (e.g., "your answers on the tests will only be used for research purposes") but the treatment group was given the additional instruction that "your test scores may be released to faculty in your college or to potential employers to evaluate your academic ability." They found an effect size of 0.41 for this simple manipulation (see their Table 4, $d_{cp}$).

### Speed–Accuracy Tradeoff

There has been a long-standing recognition in abilities measurement that response time is a dimension of test performance

separate from accuracy. Tests have been categorized as power (e.g., most of the sample completes the test) or speeded (e.g., most of the sample fails to complete), and the difference in performance has been called the speed-level distinction (Lohman, 1989). It is reflected in Carroll's (1993) and the CHC model as two separate second stratum factors, one called cognitive speediness (Gs) and the other called decision/reaction time/speed (Gt). Test takers can choose to go slowly and be more accurate or go more quickly and make more errors, a speed–accuracy tradeoff, and only the scoring procedure itself can determine the optimal tradeoff. Van der Linden (2007) developed a general framework for modeling accuracy and response time together in a hierarchical item–response theory model. It can be used to combine speediness with accuracy to make a better measure of ability. That is, response speed serves as collateral information to measure ability, which turns out to be particularly useful in measuring ability at the extremes of the ability distribution (Ranger, 2013).

### Outside the Realm of Cognitive Constructs

Sternberg (1985) and Gardner (1999) have argued that conventional discussions about human abilities overlook important ones, such as practical intelligence, creativity (Sternberg), and bodily-kinesthetic ability (Gardner). In fact, a human performance taxonomy based on the same principles as the cognitive ability taxonomies does include bodily-kinesthetic ability (Fleishman, 1972). Gottfredson (2003) points out that general cognitive ability relates to many aspects of practical intelligence. And creativity itself is part of the consensus model (the factor Gr, broad retrieval ability). Thus, the criticisms of Sternberg and Gardner are addressed in current abilities frameworks. However, there are cognitive abilities that are not included in the consensus framework because they are mostly uncorrelated with general cognitive ability, and thus truly might measure something different.

### Cognitive Biases and Heuristics

The field of cognitive biases and heuristics is based on studies that show that people tend to make systematic errors in thinking due to mental shortcuts (invoking "System 1 thinking") rather than thinking things through ("System 2 thinking") (Kahneman, 2011). Examples include confirmation bias (attending to evidence that confirms hypotheses and ignoring disconfirming evidence), fundamental attribution error (attributing others' mistakes to their character, but one's own to circumstance), base rate fallacy (calculating the likelihood of an event based on available information and ignoring the prior probability), projection fallacy (believing that others share one's own beliefs and attitudes), and the anchoring effect (using a local context to frame a current choice rather than taking a big-picture perspective). Stanovich and West (2008) investigated several biases and concluded that many were uncorrelated with cognitive ability (their Table 8 lists 14 biases that fail to correlate with cognitive ability and 14 that do correlate). Their explanation is that people will take the mental shortcuts that lead to errors unless characteristics of the task or reminders tell them not to. Some tasks do not invite the mental shortcuts, and others do. For example, "cognitive reflection tasks" (Frederick, 2005), which invite System 1 responding, have been found to be better at predicting susceptibility to cognitive biases than a composite measure of cognitive ability (Toplak, West, & Stanovich, 2011).

### Confidence and Metacognition

A particular kind of cognitive bias (cognitive optimism) is our inability to recognize our lack of intellectual and social skill in domains where we lack skill and failure to recognize others' skill, unless we are trained for that skill (Dunning, Johnson, Ehrlinger, & Kruger, 2003). Stankov and colleagues see this as a lack of calibration between confidence and performance. They have shown that confidence operates like an independent ability, correlated moderately with metacognition (Kleitman & Stankov, 2007), separate from general cognitive ability, but nevertheless incrementally predictive of intellectual tasks, such as tests of listening comprehension, speaking ability, and numeracy (Stankov & Lee, 2008). This may relate to self-regulation, as discussed in Chapter 8, this volume.

### Emotional Intelligence

Since Goleman's (1995) popular book, the concept of emotional intelligence (EI) has attracted considerable attention in scientific as well as pop culture circles. At its core EI represents cognitive skills that relate to processing and reasoning about emotional information (Mayer, Roberts, & Barsade, 2008), specifically, perceiving, using, understanding, and managing emotions (Mayer, Salovey, & Caruso, 2012). A growing consensus has emerged for two distinct ways to measure EI, through ratings ("trait EI") and performance measures ("ability EI" or "information-processing EI") (Petrides & Furnham, 2000). Trait EI ratings are similar to standard personality tests; EI performance measures include tests such as determining an emotion denoted by combining two adjectives, or perceiving the emotion expressed in a picture of a face, or abstract art. MacCann, Joseph, Newman, and Roberts (2014) have recently suggested that ability EI deserves standing as a second-stratum CHC factor, Gei, similar in status to Gc or Gv. They administered performance EI measures along with measures of fluid ability (Gf), crystallized intelligence (Gc), quantitative reasoning (Gq), visual processing (Gv), and broad retrieval ability (Gr) to 700 U.S. college students, and found support for a CHC-like hierarchical model, with EI at the second stratum, loading approximately 0.8 on a third-stratum g factor. This is one of the larger, more sophisticated studies of EI measures to date, placing them into a larger context of cognitive abilities measurement.

### Conclusions and New Directions

Cognitive abilities measurement, traced back to Galton's observations of normally distributed individual differences, Spearman's observations regarding the sufficiency of a general cognitive abilities factor, and Binet's construction of an intelligence test battery to identify the academic abilities of schoolchildren, is an applied and theoretical success story in educational psychology. In applications, ability measurement is perhaps more ubiquitous than ever, with more implications for policy, as indicated by the attention given large-scale domestic and international assessments of mathematical, verbal, and problem-solving literacy. Such assessments are used to compare states and nations and to draw lessons through comparative analysis to improve educational systems around the world. Despite the focus on curricular improvements in the United States resulting from No Child Left Behind legislation, there has nevertheless been a steady thread of attention given to the development of general, transferable cognitive abilities, for example through early-childhood education efforts. The general–specific pendulum swings back and forth, and a prediction is that efforts such as working-memory training, and general skills training will make a comeback.

In measurement, technology enables a much richer yet affordable means to present information (test questions) and collect responses from examinees, which can be seen already in identification of new abilities such as EI, scientific inquiry skills, or technology and engineering literacy skills that benefit from richer stimulus presentations and response possibilities (see also Chapter 3, this volume). In the future we are likely to see more applications using game-like tests, that present more realistic information in the form of video and computer-generated imagery graphics, and enabling the recording of eye movements and gestures through systems like Microsoft's Kinect. We also should expect concomitant increased synergies between neuroscience and abilities measurement (see Chapter 5, this volume).

On the construct side, we are likely to see increasing attempts to measure what have sometimes been called non-cognitive skills—teamwork, work ethic, communication skills, collaborative problem solving, tolerance for diversity— using performance measures. The EI work (MacCann et al., 2014) represents a step along these lines, but more is coming. PISA 2015 introduced a collaborative problem-solving measure, involving collaboration with an agent; future cycles of international assessments are likely to introduce human– human collaborative problem solving. Efforts like these will continue and undoubtedly expand our ideas on the organization, development, and use of human cognitive abilities.

### Acknowledgments

Support for this chapter comes from Educational Testing Service's Research Center for Academic and Workforce Readiness and Success (R&D). The author thanks Lyn Corno, David Lubinski, and Jan-Eric Gustafsson for their helpful comments and suggestions.

### Note

1. He wrote: "There is good evidence that [visual-spatial reasoning] relates to specialized achievements in fields such as architecture, dentistry,

engineering, and medicine . . . Given this plus the longstanding anecdotal evidence on the role of visualization in scientific discovery, . . . it is incredible that there has been so little programmatic research on admissions testing in this domain" (p. 136). (The author thanks David Lubinski for this find.)

# References

Ackerman, P. L. (1987). Individual differences in skill learning: An integration of psychometric and information processing perspectives. *Psychological Bulletin, 102,* 3–27.

Ackerman, P. L. (2007). New developments in understanding skilled performance. *Current Directions in Psychological Science, 16,* 235–239.

Ackerman, P. L., & Beier, M. E. (2003). Intelligence, personality, and interests in the career choice process. *Journal of Career Assessment, 11,* 205–218.

Alley, W. E. (1994). Recent advances in classification theory and practice. In M. G. Rumsey, C. B. Valker, and J. H. Harris (Eds.), *Personnel selection and classification* (pp. 431–442). Hillsdale, NJ: Lawrence Erlbaum Associates.

American Educational Research Association, American Psychological Association, National Council on Measurement in Education (2014). *The standards for educational and psychological testing.* Washington, DC: AERA Books and Publications.

Baddeley, A. D., & Hitch, G. (1974). Working memory. In G. H. Bower (Ed.), *The psychology of learning and motivation: Advances in research and theory* (Vol. 8, pp. 47–89). New York: Academic Press.

Barnett, W. S. (2011). Effectiveness of early educational intervention. *Science, 333,* 975–978.

Bartholomew, D. J., Deary, I. J., & Lawn, M. (2009). A new lease of life for Thomson's bonds model of intelligence. *Psychological Review, 116,* 567–579.

Bennett, R. E., & Rock, D. A. (1995). Generalizability, validity, and examinee perceptions of a computer-delivered formulating hypotheses test. *Journal of Educational Measurement, 32,* 19–36.

Binet, A. (1905/1916). New methods for the diagnosis of the intellectual level of subnormals. In E. S. Kite (Trans.), *The development of intelligence in children.* Vineland, NJ: Publications of the Training School at Vineland. (Originally published 1905 in *L'Année Psychologique, 12,* 191–244.)

Boring, E. G. (1923). Intelligence as the tests test it. *New Republic, 36,* 35–37.

Bowles, S., Gintis, H., & Osborne, M. (2001). The determinants of individual earnings: Skills, preferences, and schooling. *Journal of Economic Literature, 39,* 1137–1176.

Brinch, C. N. & Galloway, T. A. (2011). Schooling in adolescence raises IQ scores. *Proceedings of the National Academy of Sciences (PNAS),* 109, 425–430.

Camilli, G., Vargas, S., Ryan, S., & Barnett, W. S. (2010). Meta-analysis of the effects of early education interventions on cognitive and social development. *Teachers College Record, 112,* 579–620.

Campbell, F. A., Wasik, B. H., Pungello, E., Burchinal, M., Barbarin, O., Kainz, K., Sparling, J. J., & Ramey, C. T. (2008). Young adult outcomes of the Abecedarian and CARE early childhood educational interventions. *Early Childhood Research Quarterly, 23,* 452–466.

Carroll, J. B. (1993). *Human cognitive abilities: A survey of factor-analytic studies.* New York: Cambridge University Press.

Carroll, J. B. (2003). The higher-stratum structure of cognitive abilities: Current evidence supports g and about ten broad factors. In H. Nyborg (Ed.), *The scientific study of general intelligence: Tribute to Arthur R. Jensen* (pp. 5–21). Boston, MA: Pergamon Press.

Cattell, R. B. (1941). Some theoretical issues in adult intelligence testing. *Psychological Bulletin, 38,* 592.

Ceci, S. J., & Williams, W. M. (1997). Schooling, intelligence, and income. *American Psychologist, 52,* 1051–1058.

Ceci, S. J., & Williams, W. M. (2009). Should scientists study race and IQ? The scientific truth must be pursued. *Nature, 437,* 788–789.

Chipman, S. F., Segal, J. W., & Glaser, R. (Eds.) (1985). *Thinking and learning skills. Vol. 2: Research and open questions.* Hillsdale, NJ: Lawrence Erlbaum Associates.

Cliffordson, C., & Gustafsson, J.-E. (2008). Effects of age and schooling on intellectual performance: Estimates obtained from analysis of continuous variation in age and length of schooling. *Intelligence, 36,* 143–152.

Conway, A. R., & Kovacs, K. (2013). Individual differences in intelligence and working memory: A review of latent variable models. *Psychology of Learning and Motivation, 58,* 233–270.

Conway, A. R. A., Moore, A. B., & Kane, M. J. (2009). Recent trends in the cognitive neuroscience of working memory. *Cortex, 45,* 262–268.

Corno, L., Cronbach, L. J., Kupermintz, H., Lohman, D. F., Mandinach, E. B., Porteus, A. W., & Talbert, J. E. (2002). *Remaking the concept of aptitude: Extending the legacy of Richard E. Snow.* Mahwah, NJ: Lawrence Erlbaum Associates Publishers.

Cronbach, L. J. (1970). *Essentials of psychological testing.* New York: Harper & Row.

Deary, I. J., Pattie, A., & Starr, J. M. (2013). The stability of intelligence from age 11 to age 90 years: The Lothian birth cohort of 1921. *Psychological Science, 24*(12), 2361–2368.

Deary, I. J., Whalley, L. J., Lemmon, H., Crawford, J. R., & Starr, J. M. (2000). The stability of individual differences in mental ability from childhood to old age: Follow-up of the 1932 Scottish Mental Survey. *Intelligence, 28*(1), 49–55.

Desjardins, R., & Warnke, A. (2012). *Ageing and skills: A review and analysis of skill gain and skill loss over the lifespan and over time.* OECD Education Working Papers, No. 72. Paris: OECD Publishing.

Drasgow, F., Embretson, S., Kyllonen, P., & Schmitt, N. (2006). *Technical review of the Armed Forces Vocational Aptitude Battery.* Alexandria, VA: Human Resources Research Organization.

Duckworth, A. L., Quinn, P. D., Lynam, D. R., Loeber, R., & Stouthamer-Loeber, M. (2011). Role of test motivation in intelligence testing. *Proceedings of the National Academy of Sciences of the United States of America, 108,* 7716–7720.

Dunning, D., Johnson, K., Ehrlinger, J., & Kruger, J. (2003). Why people fail to recognize their own incompetence. *Current Directions in Psychological Science, 12*(3), 83–87.

Dweck, C. S., & Master, A. (2009). Self theories and motivation. In K. Wentzel, & A. Wigfield (Eds.), *Handbook of motivation at school* (pp. 123–140). New York: Routledge.

Ericsson, K. A., Charness, N., Feltovich, P., & Hoffman, R. R. (2006). *Cambridge handbook on expertise and expert performance.* New York: Cambridge University Press.

Ericsson, K. A., Chase, W. G., & Faloon, S. (1980). Acquisition of a memory skill. *Science, 208*(4448), 1181–1182.

Ferriman-Robertson, K., Smeets, S., Lubinski, D., & Benbow, C. P. (2010). Beyond the threshold hypothesis: Even among the gifted and top math/science graduate students, cognitive abilities, vocational interests, and lifestyle preferences matter for career choice, performance, and persistence. *Current Directions in Psychological Science, 19,* 346–351.

Flanagan, D. P., & Harrison, P. L. (2012). *Contemporary intellectual assessment: Theories, tests, and issues* (3rd ed.). New York: The Guilford Press.

Fleishman, E. A. (1972). On the relation between abilities, learning, and human performance. *American Psychologist, 27,* 1017–1032.

Flynn, J. R. (1987). Massive IQ gains in 14 nations: What IQ tests really measure. *Psychological Bulletin, 101*(2), 171–191.

Flynn, J. R. (2007). *What is intelligence? Beyond the Flynn effect.* Cambridge, MA: Cambridge University Press.

Flynn, J. R., & Rossi-Casé, L. (2012). IQ gains in Argentina between 1964 and 1998. *Intelligence, 40,* 145–150.

Frederick, S. (2005). Cognitive reflection and decision making. *Journal of Economic Perspectives, 19,* 25–42.

Frederiksen, N., & Ward, W. C. (1975). *Development of measures for the study of creativity.* GRE Board Professional Report GREB No. 72-2P; also ETS RB No. 75-18. Princeton, NJ: Educational Testing Service.

Ganley, C. M., Mingle, L. A., Ryan, A. M., Ryan, K., Vasilyeva, M., & Perry, M. (2013). An examination of stereotype threat effects on girls' mathematics performance. *Developmental Psychology, 49*(10), 1886–1897.

Gardner, H. (1983). *Frames of mind: The theory of multiple intelligences.* New York: Basic Books.

Gardner, H. (1999). Who owns intelligence? *The Atlantic Monthly, 283,* 67–76.

Gladwell, M. (2009). *Outliers: The story of success.* New York: Little, Brown.

Goleman, D. (1995). *Emotional intelligence: Why it can matter more than IQ.* London: Bloomsbury.

Gottfredson, L. S. (1997). Why g matters: The complexity of everyday life. *Intelligence, 24*(1), 79–132.

Gottfredson, L. S. (2002). Where and why g matters: Not a mystery. *Human Performance, 15*(1–2), 25–46.

Gottfredson, L. (2003). Dissecting practical intelligence theory: Its claims and its evidence. *Intelligence, 31,* 343–397.

Gray, J. R., Chabris, C. F., & Braver, T. S. (2003). Neural mechanisms of general fluid intelligence. *Nature Neuroscience, 6*(3), 316–322.

Gray, J. R., & Thompson, P. M. (2004). Neurobiology of intelligence: Science and ethics. *Nature Reviews, 5,* 471–482.

Guilford, J. P. (1956). The structure of intellect. *Psychological Bulletin, 53,* 267–293.

Gustafsson, J.-E. (1984). A unifying model for the structure of intellectual abilities. *Intelligence, 8,* 179–203.

Gustafsson, J. E., & Balke, G. (1993). General and specific abilities as predictors of school achievement. *Multivariate Behavioral Research, 28,* 407–434.

Hakel, M. D. (Ed.) (1998). *Beyond multiple choice.* Mahwah, NJ: Lawrence Erlbaum Associates.

Hanushek, E. A., & Woessmann, L. (2010). *The economics of international differences in educational achievement.* Working Paper 15949. Cambridge, MA: National Bureau of Economic Research.

Harris, J. R. (1998). *The nurture assumption: Why children turn out the way they do.* New York: Free Press.

He, J. (2013). *Text mining and IRT for psychiatric and psychological assessment.* PhD thesis, University of Twente, Enschede, the Netherlands.

Heckman, J. J. (2006). Skill formation and the economics of investing in disadvantaged children. *Science, 312,* 1900–1902.

Heckman, J. J., Moon, S. H., Pinto, R., Savelyev, P. A., & Yavitz, A. (2010). The rate of return to the HighScope Perry preschool program. *Journal of Public Economics, 94,* 114–128.

Heckman, J. J., Stixrud, J., & Urzua, S. (2006). The effects of cognitive and noncognitive abilities on labor market outcomes and social behavior. *Journal of Labor Economics, 24,* 411–482.

Herrnstein, R. J., & Murray, C. (1994). *The bell curve: Intelligence and class structure in American life.* New York: Free Press.

Herrnstein, R. J., Nickerson, R. S., de Sanchez, M., & Swets, J. A. (1986). Teaching thinking skills. *American Psychologist, 41,* 1279–1289.

Holzinger, K. J., & Swineford, F. (1937). The bi-factor method. *Psychometrika, 2,* 41–54.

Horn, J. L. (1989). Models for intelligence. In R. Linn (Ed.), *Intelligence: Measurement, theory, and public policy* (pp. 29–73). Urbana, IL: University of Illinois Press.

Horn, J. L., & Cattell, R. B. (1966). Refinement of the theory of fluid and crystallized intelligences. *Journal of Educational Psychology, 57,* 253–270.

Horn, J. L., & Cattell, R. B. (1967). Age differences in fluid and crystallized intelligence. *Acta Psychologica, 26,* 107–129.

Humphreys, L. G. (1986). An analysis and evaluation of test and item bias in the prediction context. *Journal of Applied Psychology, 71*(2), 327–333.

Hunt, E. (2011). *Human intelligence.* New York: Cambridge University Press.

Hunt, E. (2012). What makes nations intelligent? *Perspectives on Psychological Science, 7,* 284–306.

Hunt, E. B., Lunneborg, C., & Lewis, J. (1975). What does it mean to be high verbal? *Cognitive Psychology, 7,* 194–227.

Hunt, E., & Wittmann, W. (2008). National intelligence and national prosperity. *Intelligence, 36,* 1–9.

Jaeggi, S. M., Buschkuehl, M., Jonides, J., & Perrig, W. J. (2008). Improving fluid intelligence with training on working memory. *Proceedings of the National Academy of Sciences, 105*(19), 6829–6833.

Jensen, A. R. (1998). *The g factor: The science of mental ability (Human evolution, behavior, and intelligence).* Westport, CT: Praeger.

Johnson, W., & Bouchard, T. J., Jr. (2005). The structure of human intelligence: It is verbal, perceptual, and image rotation (VPR), not fluid and crystallized. *Intelligence, 33,* 393–416.

Jones, G. (2011). National IQ and national productivity: The hive mind across Asia. *Asian Developmental Review, 28,* 51–71.

Jones, G., & Schneider, W. J. (2006). Intelligence, human capital, and economic growth: A Bayesian averageing of classical estimates (BACE) approach. *Journal of Economic Growth, 11,* 71–93.

Kahneman, D. (2011). *Thinking fast and slow.* New York: Farrar, Straus, & Giroux.

Kane, M. J., & Engle, R. W. (2002). The role of prefrontal cortex in working memory capacity, executive attention, and general fluid intelligence: An individual differences perspective. *Psychonomic Bulletin & Review, 9,* 637–671.

Kaufman, A., & Kaufman, N. (2004). *Manual of the Kaufman Assessment Battery for Children,* 2nd ed. San Antonio, TX: Pearson Assessment.

Kell, H. J., Lubinski, D., Benbow, C. P., & Steiger, J. H. (2013). Creativity and technical innovation: Spatial ability's unique role. *Psychological Science, 24,* 1831–1836.

Kleitman, S., & Stankov, L. (2007). Self-confidence and metacognitive processes. *Learning and Individual Differences, 17,* 161–173.

Kuncel, N. R., & Hezlett, S. A. (2007). Standardized tests predict graduate students' success. *Science, 315,* 1080–1081.

Kyllonen, P. C. (1994). Cognitive abilities testing: An agenda for the 1990s. In M. G. Rumsey, C. B. Walker, & J. H. Harris (Eds.), *Personnel selection and classification* (pp. 103–129). Hillsdale, NJ: Lawrence Erlbaum Associates.

Kyllonen, P. C. (1995). CAM: A theoretical framework for cognitive abilities measurement. In D. K. Detterman (Ed.), *Current topics in human intelligence* (Vol. 4, pp. 307–359). New York: Springer-Verlag.

Kyllonen, P. C., & Christal, R. E. (1990). Reasoning ability is (little more than) working-memory capacity?! *Intelligence, 14*(4), 389–433.

Levin, H. M. (2012). The utility and need for incorporating noncognitive skills into large-scale educational assessments. In M. von Davier, E. Gonzalez, I. Kirsch, & K. Yamamoto (Eds.), *The role of international large-scale assessments: Perspectives from technology, economy, & educational research* (pp. 67–86). New York: Springer.

Lindqvist, E., & Vestman, R. (2011). The labor market returns to cognitive and noncognitive ability: Evidence from the Swedish enlistent. *American Economic Journal: Applied Economics, 3,* 101–128.

Liu, O. L., Bridgeman, B., & Adler, R. (2013). Learning outcomes assessment in higher education: Motivation matters. *Educational Researcher, 41,* 352–362.

Lohman, D. (1989). Estimating individual differences in information processing models using speed-accuracy models. In R. Kanfer, P. Ackerman, & R. Cudeck (Eds.), *Abilities, motivation, and methodology: The Minnesota symposium on learning and individual differences* (pp. 119–164). Hillsdale, NJ: Lawrence Erlbaum Associates.

Lubinski, D. (2009). Cognitive epidemiology: With emphasis on untangling cognitive ability and socioeconomic status. *Intelligence, 37,* 625–633.

Lubinski, D. (2010). Neglected aspects and truncated appraisals in vocational counseling: Interpreting the interest-efficacy association from a broader perspective. *Journal of Counseling Psychology, 57,* 226–238.

Lubinski, D., & Benbow, C. P. (2006). Study of mathematically precocious youth after 35 years: Uncovering antecedents for the development of math-science expertise. *Perspectives on Psychological Science, 1,* 316–345.

Lubinski, D., & Humphreys, L. G. (1997). Incorporating general intelligence into epidemiology and the social sciences. *Intelligence, 24,* 159–201

MacCann, C., Joseph, D. L., Newman, D. A., & Roberts, R. D. (2014). Emotional intelligence is a second-stratum factor of intelligence: Evidence from hierarchical and bifactor models. *Emotion, 14*(2), 358–374.

Mackintosh, N. (2011). *IQ and human intelligence* (2nd ed.). Oxford: Oxford University Press.

Macnamara, B. N., Hambrick, D. Z., & Oswald F. L. (2014). Deliberate practice and performance in music, games, sports, education, and professions: A meta-analysis. *Psychological Science, 25*(8), 1608–1618.

Mayer, J. D., Roberts, R. D., & Barsade, S. G. (2008). Human abilities: Emotional intelligence. *Annual Review of Psychology, 59*, 507–536.

Mayer, J. D., Salovey, P., & Caruso, D. R. (2012). The validity of the MSCEIT: Additional analyses and evidence. *Emotion Review, 4,* 403–408.

McArdle, J. J., Hamagami, F., Meredith, W., & Bradway, K. P. (2000). Modeling the dynamic hypotheses of Gf–Gc theory using longitudinal life-span data. *Learning and Individual Differences, 12*(1), 53–79.

McDaniel, M. A., & Whetzel, D. L. (2005). Situational judgment test research: Informing the debate on practical intelligence theory. *Intelligence, 33,* 515–525.

McGrew, K. S. (2009). CHC theory and the human cognitive abilities project: Standing on the shoulders of the giants of psychometric intelligence research. *Intelligence, 37,* 1–10.

McHenry, J. J., Hough, L. M., Toquam, J. L., Hanson, M. A., & Ashworth, S. (1990). Project A validity results: The relationship between predictor and criterion domains. *Personnel Psychology, 43,* 335–354.

Melby-Lervåg, M., & Hulme, C. (2013). Is working memory training effective? A meta-analytic review. *Developmental Psychology, 49*(2), 270–291.

Mislevy, R. J., Oranje, A., Bauer, M. I., von Davier, A., Hao, J., Corrigan, S., Hoffman, E., DiCerbo, K., & John, M. (2014). *Psychometric considerations in game-based assessment.* CreateSpace Independent Publishing Platform. Retrieved from http://www.instituteofplay.org/wp-content/uploads/2014/02/GlassLab_GBA1_WhitePaperFull.pdf (accessed 15 March 2014).

Miyake, A., Friedman, N. P., Emerson, M. J., Witzki, A. H., Howerter, A., & Wager, T. D. (2000). The unity and diversity of executive functions and their contributions to complex "frontal lobe" tasks: A latent variable analysis. *Cognitive Psychology, 41,* 49–100.

Morrison, A. B., & Chein, J. M. (2011). Does working memory training work? The promise and challenges of enhancing cognition by training working memory. *Psychonomic Bulletin & Review, 18*(1), 46–60.

Mumford, M. D., Marks, M. A., Connelly, M. S., Zaccaro, S. J., & Johnson, J. F. (1998). Domain-based scoring in divergent-thinking tests: Validation evidence in an occupational sample. *Creativity Research Journal, 11*(2), 151–163.

Murray, C. (1998). *Income, inequality, and IQ.* Washington, DC: American Enterprise Institute.

Neisser, U. E. (1998). *The rising curve: Long-term gains in IQ and related measures.* Washington, DC: American Psychological Association.

Nickerson, R. S., Perkins, D. N., & Smith, E. E. (1985). *The teaching of thinking.* Hillsdale, NJ: Erlbaum.

OECD (2012). *PISA 2009 Technical Report.* PISA, OECD Publishing. Retrieved from http://dx.doi.org/10.1787/9789264167872-en (accessed 13 March 2015).

OECD and Statistics Canada. (2000). *Literacy in the information age: Final report of the international adult literacy survey.* Paris: OECD Publications.

Osaka, N., Logie, R. H., & D'Esposito, M. (Eds.). (2007). *The cognitive neuroscience of working memory.* New York: Oxford University Press.

O'Toole, B. I., & Stankov, L. (1992). Ultimate validity of psychological tests. *Personality and individual differences, 13*(6), 699–716.

Park, G., Lubinski, D., & Benbow, C. P. (2013). When less is more: Effects of grade skipping on adult STEM accomplishments among mathematically precocious youth. *Journal of Educational Psychology, 105,* 176–198.

Pesta, B. J., McDaniel, M. A., & Bertsch, S. (2010). Toward an index of well-being for the fifty U.S. States. *Intelligence, 38,* 160–168.

Petrides, K. V., & Furnham, A. (2000). On the dimensional structure of emotional intelligence. *Personality and Individual Differences, 29*(2), 313–320.

Plomin, R., Pedersen, N. L., Lichtenstein, P., & McClearn, G. E. (1994). Variability and stability in cognitive abilities are largely genetic later in life. *Behavior Genetics, 24*(3), 207–215.

Protzko, J., Aronson, J., & Blair, C. (2013). How to make a young child smarter: Evidence from the Database of Raising Intelligence. *Perspectives on Psychological Science, 8*(1), 25–40.

Ranger, J. (2013). A note on the hierarchical model for responses and response times in tests of van der Linden (2007). *Psychometrika, 78*(3), 538–544.

Ree, M. J., & Earles, J. A. (1992). Intelligence is the best predictor of job performance. *Current Directions in Psychological Science, 1,* 86–89.

Ree, M. J., Earles, J. A., & Teachout, M. S. (1994). Predicting job performance: Not much more than g. *Journal of Applied Psychology, 79*(4), 518.

Rindermann, H. (2007). The g-factor of international cognitive ability comparisons: The homogeneity of results in PISA, TIMSS, PIRLS and IQ-tests across nations. *European Journal of Personality, 21,* 667–706.

Roberts, B. W., Kuncel, N. R., Shiner, R., Caspi, A., & Goldberg, L. R. (2007). The power of personality: The comparative validity of personality traits, socioeconomic status, and cognitive ability for predicting important life outcomes. *Perspectives on Psychological Science, 2*(4), 313–345.

Roberts, R. D., Goff, G. N., Anjoul, F., Kyllonen, P. C., Pallier, G., & Stankov, L. (2000). The Armed Services Vocational Batter (ASVAB) – Little more than acculturated learning (Gc)!?, *Learning and Individual Differences 12,* 81–103.

Sackett, P. R., Kuncel, N. R., Arneson, J. J., Cooper, S. R., & Waters, S. D. (2009). Does socioeconomic status explain the relationship between admissions tests and post-secondary academic performance? *Psychological Bulletin, 135,* 1–22.

Sawin, L., Earles, J., Goff, N., & Chaiken, S. R. (2001). *Advanced personnel testing project.* Final report. Technical report no. AFRL-HE-AZ-TP-2001-0004 ADA399062. Mesa, AZ: Air Force Research Laboratory Warfighter Training Research Division (AFRL/HEA).

Schmid, J., & Leiman, J. M. (1957). The development of hierarchical factor solutions. *Psychometrika, 22*(1), 53–61.

Schmidt, F. L., & Hunter, J. E. (1998). The validity and utility of selection methods in personnel psychology: Practical and theoretical implications of 85 years of research findings. *Psychological Bulletin, 124*(2), 262–274.

Schweinhart, L. J., Barnes, H. V., & Weikart, D. P. (1993). *Significant benefits: The High/Scope Perry preschool study through age 27.* Ypsilanti, MI: High/Scope Press.

Segal, C. (2012). Working when no one is watching: Motivation, test scores, and economic success. *Management Science, 58*(8), 1438–1457.

Segal, J. W., Chipman, S. F., & Glaser, R. (1985). *Thinking and learning skills: Relating instruction to research.* London: Routledge.

Shipstead, Z., Redick, T. S., & Engle, R. W. (2012). Is working memory training effective? *Psychological Bulletin, 138*(4), 628.

Snow, R. E. (1999). Commentary: Expanding the breadth and depth of admissions testing. In S. Messick (Ed.), *Assessment in higher education* (pp. 133–140). Hillsdale, NJ: Erlbaum.

Snow, R.E., Kyllonen, P.C., & Marshalek, B. (1984). The topography of ability and learning correlations. In R. J. Sternberg (Ed.), *Advances in the psychology of human intelligence* (Vol. 2., pp. 47–103). Hillsdale, NJ: Lawrence Erlbaum Associates.

Sonnleitner, P., Keller, U., Martin, R., & Brunner, M. (2013). Students' complex problem-solving abilities: Their structure and relations to reasoning ability and educational success. *Intelligence, 41,* 289–305.

Spearman, C. (1904). "General intelligence," objectively determined and measured. *American Journal of Psychology, 15*(2), 201–292.

Stankov, L. & Lee, J. (2008). Confidence and cognitive test performance. *Journal of Educational Psychology, 100,* 961–976.

Stanovich, K. E., & West, R. F. (2008). On the relative independence of thinking biases and cognitive ability. *Journal of Personality and Social Psychology, 94,* 672–695.

Steele, C. M., & Aronson, J. (1995). Stereotype threat and the intellectual test performance of African Americans. *Journal of Personality and Social Psychology, 69*(5), 797–811.

Sternberg, R. J. (1977). *Intelligence, information processing, and analogical reasoning: The componential analysis of human abilities.* Hillsdale, NJ: Lawrence Erlbaum Associates.

Sternberg, R. J. (1985). *Beyond IQ: A triarchic theory of intelligence.* Cambridge: Cambridge University Press.

Sternberg, R. J. (1994). 468 factor-analyzed data sets: What they tell us and don't tell us about human intelligence. [Review of John B. Carroll, *Human cognitive abilities.*] *Psychological Science, 5*(2), 63–65.

Sternberg, R. J., & Wagner, R. K. (Eds.). (1986). *Practical intelligence: Nature and origins of competence in the everyday world.* New York: Cambridge University Press.

Teasdale, T. W., & Owen, D. R. (2008). Secular declines in cognitive test scores: A reversal of the Flynn effect. *Intelligence, 36,* 121–126.

Thorndike, R. L. (1986). The role of general ability in prediction. *Journal of Vocational Behavior, 29*(3), 332–339.

Thurstone, L. L. (1934). The vectors of mind. *Psychological Review, 41*(1), 1.

Thurstone, L. L. (1938). Primary mental abilities. *Psychometric Monographs, 1,* ix–121.

Thurstone, L. L. (1947). *Multiple factor analysis.* Chicago, IL: University of Chicago Press.

Toplak, M. E., West, R. F., & Stanovich, K. E. (2011). The Cognitive Reflection Test as a predictor of performance on heuristics and biases tasks. *Memory & Cognition, 39,* 1275–1289.

Underwood, B. J. (1975). Individual differences as a crucible in theory construction. *American Psychologist, 30,* 128–134.

Valentin Kvist, A. V., & Gustafsson, J.-E. (2008). The relation between fluid intelligence and the general factor as a function of cultural background: A test of Cattell's investment theory. *Intelligence, 36*(5), 422–436.

van der Linden, W. (2007). A hierarchical framework for modeling speed and accuracy on test items. *Psychometrika, 72,* 287–308.

Vernon, P. E. (1965). Ability factors and environmental influences. *American Psychologist, 20*(9), 723–733.

Visser, B. A., Ashton, M. C., & Vernon, P. A. (2006a). Beyond g: Putting multiple intelligences theory to the test. *Intelligence, 34,* 487–502.

Visser, B. A., Ashton, M. C., & Vernon, P. A. (2006b). g and the measurement of multiple intelligences: A response to Gardner. *Intelligence, 34,* 507–510.

Wai, J., Lubinski, D., & Benbow, C. P. (2009). Spatial ability for STEM domains: Aligning over 50 years of cumulative psychological knowledge solidifies its importance. *Journal of Educational Psychology, 101*(4), 817–835.

Webb, R. M., Lubinski, D., & Benbow, C. P. (2007). Spatial ability: A neglected dimension in talent searches for intellectually precocious youth. *Journal of Educational Psychology, 99,* 397–420.

Whetzel, D. L., & McDaniel, M. A. (2006). Prediction of national wealth. *Intelligence, 34*(5), 449–458.

Wise, S. L., & Kong, X. (2005). Response time effort: A new measure of examinee motivation in computer-based tests. *Applied Measurement in Education, 18*(2), 163–183.

Wittmann, W. W., & Suess, H. M. (1999). Investigating the paths between working memory, intelligence, knowledge, and complex problem-solving performances via Brunswick symmetry. In P. Ackerman, P. C. Kyllonen, & R. D. Roberts (Eds.), *Learning and individual differences: Process, trait, and content determinants* (pp. 77–108). Washington, DC: American Psychological Association.

Woodcock, R. W., McGrew, K. S., & Mather, N. (2007). *Woodcock-Johnson® III Normative Update (NU) complete.* Rolling Meadows, IL: Riverside Publishing.

Yoachum, C. S., & Yerkes, R. M. (Eds.) (1920). *Army mental tests.* New York: Henry Holt.

Yung Y.-F., Thissen, D., & McLeod, L. D. (1999). On the relation between the higher-order factor model and the hierarchical factor model. *Psychometrika, 64,* 113–128.

Zeidner, J., & Johnson, C. D. (1994). Is personnel classification a concept whose time has passed? In M. G. Rumsey, C. B. Valker, & J. H. Harris (Eds.), *Personnel selection and classification* (pp. 377–410). Hillsdale, NJ: Lawrence Erlbaum Associates.

# 10

# Cognition and Cognitive Disabilities

*H. Lee Swanson*
University of California, Riverside

The study of cognition as applied to human behavior has been characterized as an attempt to understand the nature of human intelligence and how people think (Anderson, 1976). Thus, to understand disorders of cognition in children, as well as adults, requires a focus on various domains of intelligent behavior. These domains cover a host of areas such as language, reading, arithmetic, motor skills, attention, and social interactions, to mention a few. To limit our review, we will focus on children with specific cognitive difficulties. Specific cognitive disabilities can be contrasted with general cognitive disabilities. Children with general cognitive disabilities experience inefficiencies and deficits across a wide range of skills. Children with Down's syndrome, for example, frequently have problems mastering multiple academic skills, whereas children with specific learning disabilities have isolated deficits in cognition related to problems in areas such as reading or math. In practice, the distinction between specific and general learning difficulties is based on a standardized intelligence test (Cheung et al., 2012; Haworth et al., 2009; Hulme & Snowling, 2009; McGrath et al., 2011). Individuals with intelligence quotient (IQ) scores below a certain threshold, such as 75, may be viewed as having general to moderate disabilities, whereas those within the average range of intelligence (e.g., 85–120) may suffer more specialized deficits in specified areas of learning (e.g., math or reading). There are several excellent texts (e.g., Alloway & Gathercole, 2007; Hulme & Snowling, 2009; Yeates, Ris, Taylor, & Pennington, 2010) that provide an indepth review of developmental disorders of cognition related to language and learning. The reader is referred to those sources for a more comprehensive review of the literature than this chapter can provide.

## Cognitive Models

Without a doubt, there are a number of models that experts in the field have used to explain inefficiencies in cognition for children who have average intelligence (e.g., McGrath

et al., 2011). For example, one set of models tends to specify how the brain is related to behavior (brain–behavior relationships; e.g., Di Martino et al., 2009). Another seeks to account for the nature of specific cognitive deficits in specific domains of functioning, such as language, spatial cognition, social behavior, and executive capacity (e.g., Nittrouer & Pennington, 2010). Others draw in part from the cognitive sciences and in part from experimental psychology. There are some models that take cross-fertilization into consideration, such as research related to neuroscience, advances in technology (e.g., transcranial magnetic stimulation, functional magnetic resonance imaging, and diffuse tensor imaging), and genetics (e.g., Pennington et al., 2009, 2012). These data are brought into the context of the child's experience within her environment and the cognitive changes that occur within the child over the course of development.

Given the constraints of this chapter, however, we cannot cover the various degrees of complexity that may underlie cognitive disabilities in children. Instead, we narrow our focus on cognitive processes that may underlie some academic difficulties experienced by such children. Specifically, we elected to discuss problems related to working memory (WM) because it encapsulates several areas of cognition and academic achievement (e.g., Swanson & Alloway, 2012). To capture this literature, the outcomes of several meta-analyses are reviewed.

However, prior to summarizing the literature on this topic, it is important to indicate how memory performance was categorized and the advantages of meta-analyses.

## Memory

To understand the role of memory as an underlying factor of specific disabilities, we divide our review along the lines outlined by Baddeley (Baddeley, 2012; Baddeley & Logie, 1999) on WM. The majority of research linking memory to performance on academic measures follows the tripartite view of WM by Baddeley (e.g., Baddeley, 1986; Baddeley

& Logie, 1999). This relatively simple model has accommodated a number of experimental studies of normal adults, children, and neuropsychological patients (see Gathercole & Baddeley, 1993, for a review of earlier studies). Although Baddeley's multicomponent model was primarily developed from research on adult samples, the model also has an excellent fit to the WM performance of children (Alloway, Gathercole, Willis, & Adams, 2004; Gathercole, Pickering, Ambridge, & Wearing, 2004; Swanson, 2008).

This tripartite view characterizes WM as comprising a central executive controlling system that interacts with a set of two subsidiary storage systems: the speech-based phonological loop and the visual-spatial sketchpad. The central executive is involved in the control and regulation of the WM system. According to Baddeley (Baddeley, 2012; Baddeley & Logie, 1999), WM coordinates the two subordinate systems, focusing and switching attention, and activating representations within long-term memory (LTM). The central executive is thought to play an important role in "controlled attention," which coincides with Norman and Shallice's (1986) supervisory attentional system (SAS) model. The phonological loop, commonly referred to as verbal short-term memory (STM) storage, is responsible for the temporary storage of verbal information; items are held within a phonological store of limited duration, and the items are maintained within a store through the process of subvocal articulation. The visual-spatial sketchpad is responsible for the storage of visual-spatial information over brief periods and plays a key role in the generation and manipulation of mental images. This model has been revised to include an episodic buffer (Baddeley, 2000); however, support for the tripartite model has been found across various age groups of children (Gathercole et al., 2004; Swanson, Jerman, & Zheng, 2008). We will briefly review published syntheses that have divided the findings on children's disabilities along the dimensions of Baddeley's multicomponent model.

### Synthesis of the Memory Literature

Because of the extensive number of studies on children's cognitive disabilities and memory, this chapter relied on the published outcomes of meta-analyses, when possible, to summarize the findings on the relationship between the components of WM and children's cognitive disabilities. Meta-analysis, coined earlier by Gene Glass (Glass, McGraw, & Smith, 1981), refers to a statistical technique used to synthesize data from separate comparable studies in order to obtain a quantitative summary of research that addresses a common question. There are many different metrics to describe an effect size; one of the most popular is the d-index. The d-index, by Cohen (1988), is a scale-free measure of the separation between two group means that is used when one variable in the relation is dichotomous (e.g., children with cognitive disabilities vs. children without cognitive disabilities) and the other is continuous. Calculating the d-index for any study involves dividing the difference between the two group means by either their average standard deviation or the standard deviation of the control group. To make ds more

interpretable, statisticians have adopted Cohen's (1988) system for classifying ds in terms of their size (i.e., 0.00–0.19 is described as trivial; 0.20–0.49, small; 0.50–0.79, moderate; 0.80 or higher, large).

There are a number of advantages of meta-analysis over traditional narrative techniques for synthesizing research. First, the structured methodology of meta-analysis requires careful review and analysis of all contributing research. As such, meta-analysis overcomes biases associated with the reliance on single studies, or subsets of studies that inevitably occur in narrative reviews of a literature. Second, meta-analysis allows for even small and non-significant effects to contribute to the overall conclusions and avoids wasting data because a sample size was too small and significance was not achieved. Finally, meta-analysis can address questions about variables that moderate effects. Specifically, meta-analysis provides a formal means for testing whether different features of studies can explain variation in their outcomes.

Given this introduction, we summarize meta-analyses findings on WM performance of children with cognitive disabilities. The criteria for selecting articles reporting outcomes related to a meta-analysis were those: (a) that included children of public school age (age 5–18 years) with specific cognitive disabilities; (b) that reported comparisons between children with cognitive disabilities with average intelligence and children without cognitive disabilities on memory measures; and (c) for which the results were reported in a refereed journal. As previously mentioned, the findings from these syntheses were divided into the three components of the Baddeley model. Although this division is important to understand the process that may underlie various cognitive disability groups, it is important to note that problems related to these components of WM are not completely independent. For example, problems in the central executive system would no doubt be related to potential problems in the various storage systems (e.g., visual-spatial sketchpad). Unfortunately, not all syntheses on WM and cognitive disabilities reported effect sizes. However, when possible we report the component or components found in the synthesized literature that have yielded the largest effect sizes and/or differences between children with and without cognitive disabilities.

### Executive System

The central executive monitors the control processes in WM (e.g., Baddeley, 2012; Kane, Conway, Hambrick, & Engle, 2007). There have been a number of cognitive activities assigned to the central executive, including coordination of subsidiary memory systems, control of encoding and retrieval strategies, switching of attention in manipulation of material held related to the verbal and visual-spatial systems, and the retrieval of knowledge from LTM (e.g., Baddeley, 2012; Miyake, Friedman, Emerson, Witzki, & Howerter, 2000). Although there is an issue of whether the central executive is a unitary system (it is conceptualized as either being unitary (Baddeley, 1986) or composed of multiple domain-specific executives (Goldman-Rakic, 1995)), there is some agreement that the central executive has some capacity limitations that influence the efficiency of these operations (e.g., for allocating attention to, performing operations on). Executive functioning has separable operations (e.g., inhibition, updating, attention switching), but these operations may share some underlying commonalities (e.g., see Miyake et al., 2000, for a review).

Several studies suggest that individual differences in the executive component of WM are directly related to achievement (e.g., reading comprehension) in individuals with average or above-average intelligence (e.g., Booth, Boyle, & Kelly, 2010; Daneman & Carpenter, 1980; Swanson & Alloway, 2012). Thus, children scoring within the normal range on an IQ measure may have difficulties with executive processing that are not isolated to those with depressed intelligence (i.e., intellectually disabled individuals). As indicated below, deficits in the executive system of WM have been attributed to children with specific difficulties in math or reading comprehension. Not all children with executive processing deficits have problems in WM. For example, children with autism may have deficits in executive processing that do not entail the executive system of WM. We review some of the synthesis findings on these three groups of children.

### Specific Learning Disorder with Impairment in Math

The new American Psychiatric Association (2013) *Diagnostic and Statistical Manual of Mental Disorders* (DSM-5) views a specific learning disorder in math as reflecting a neurodevelopmental disorder of biological origin. This disability is manifested in math performance that is markedly below age level that is not attributed to intellectual, developmental, neurological, or motor disorders. This broad category of difficulties encapsulates children referred to as having math disability (MD) or suffering from dyscalculia. Several studies (Badian, 1983; Geary, 2013) estimate that approximately 6–7% of the school-age population has MD. Although this figure may be inflated due to variations in definition (e.g., Reigosa-Crespo et al., 2012, suggest the figure varies around 3%), a significant number of children in U.S. schools demonstrate poor achievement in mathematics. Although not a quantitative analysis, one of the most comprehensive syntheses of the cognitive literature of MD was provided by Geary (1993; also see Geary, 2013). His earlier review indicated that children with MD are a heterogeneous group and show one of three types of cognitive disorders: semantic memory (e.g., characterized as having weak fact retrieval and high error rates in recall), procedural (developmentally immature procedures in numerical calculations), and visual-spatial math disorders (e.g., have difficulties representing numerical information spatially).

The cognitive, as well as neural, mechanisms underlying these types of math disorders are still under investigation. There is some consensus, however, that arithmetic facts in children with MD are not retrieved accurately, and various deficits may reflect various forms of deficits related to neural structures, specifically the left basal ganglia, thalamus, and the left parieto-occipitotemporal areas (e.g., Dehaene

& Cohen, 1997). Regardless of the type of disorder and the theoretical account for MD, the majority of studies suggest that children with MD have some type of memory deficit. Theories of the representation of arithmetic facts in LTM indicate that performance on simple arithmetic depends on retrieval from LTM. The strength to which associations are stored, and hence, the probability of retrieving them correctly, depends in part on experience, with associations being formed each time an arithmetic problem is encountered, regardless of whether the association is correct. Thus, the ability to utilize WM resources to temporarily store numbers when attempting to reach an answer is of significant importance in learning arithmetic.

A comprehensive meta-analysis of the published literature focused on identifying the cognitive processes that underlie MD (Swanson & Jerman, 2006). The synthesis focused on the cognitive functioning of children with MD when compared to: (a) average-achieving children, (b) children with reading disabilities (RD); and (c) children with comorbid disabilities (RD + MD). A summary of the results on memory functioning related to children with MD and their comparison group is as follows. Average achievers outperformed children with MD on measures of verbal WM ($M = -0.70$), visual-spatial WM ($M = -0.63$), STM for words ($M = -0.45$), STM for numbers ($M = -0.26$), and LTM ($M = -0.72$). The results further indicated that children with MD outperformed children with comorbid disabilities (MD + RD) on measures of LTM ($M = 0.44$), STM for words ($M = 0.71$), verbal WM ($M = 0.30$), but not STM for numbers ($M = -0.08$). Interestingly, the effect sizes on the same measures for children with MD and those with RD were small (effect sizes range from $-0.30$ to $0.16$).

Hierarchical linear modeling showed that the magnitude of effect sizes in overall cognitive functioning between MD and average achievers was primarily related to WM deficits related to the executive system when the effects of all other variables (e.g., age, IQ, reading level, other cognitive domain categories) were partialed out. These findings are consistent with a more recent meta-analysis (David, 2012) that yielded larger effect sizes in favor of controls when compared to children with MD on the executive component of WM. However, no clear-cut differences emerged between children with MD and RD on several memory measures. Swanson, Jerman, and Zheng (2009) extended their meta-analysis to address this issue. They reasoned that the poor differentiation between children with MD and those with RD occurred because the studies included samples with poor arithmetic skills accompanied by relatively low reading skills.

The Swanson et al. (2009) results indicated moderate (0.50 to high) effect sizes in favor of age-matched average-achieving children on measures of verbal WM ($M = -0.53$), visual-spatial WM ($M = -0.63$), and LTM ($M = -0.87$). Children with MD were also differentiated from children with combined reading and math disabilities. Specifically, the effect sizes in favor of the MD group when compared to the comorbid group were found on measures of verbal WM ($M = 0.88$), LTM ($M = 0.58$) and visual-spatial WM ($M = 0.63$). Interestingly, an advantage was found for the comorbid group on measures of STM for digits ($M = -0.55$). In contrast to comparisons with the comorbid group, children with MD could not be clearly differentiated from children with RD on measures related to the phonological loop (STM) or executive system of WM (effect size ranges from $-0.01$ to $0.10$). Children with RD did yield small advantage on measures of visual WM when compared to children with MD ($M = 0.30$). Overall, the results from these two meta-analyses provide weak support for the assumption that distinct WM processes separate children with MD from children with RD.

In summary, syntheses of the literature have attributed to MD, when compared to average achievers, deficits in the executive components of WM (see Geary, 2013). However, comparisons between children with MD and children with RD on measures that tap the components of WM have yielded trivial or small effect sizes. Thus, it is possible that an important correlate of memory problems in children with MD is reading.

### Reading Comprehension Impairment

Children with reading comprehension impairments can recognize words accurately, but have problems understanding the meaning of what they have read in terms of accuracy and speed. Although there are no population-based studies of this disorder, individual studies (e.g. Nation, Adams, Bowyer-Crane, & Snowling, 1999) suggest that approximately 10% of samples of children with reading problems have reading comprehension difficulties (Snowling & Hulme, 2012). No doubt, understanding text involves some of the same processes as comprehending spoken language. Memory problems in children with dyslexia are understood in terms of decoding deficits, which are strongly associated with the phonological loop (to be discussed). Therefore, it is expected that the phonological memory would be normal in children with reading comprehension impairments.

Because phonological STM is just one component of a WM system, other components of a WM system have been investigated. A meta-analysis of this research (Carretti, Borella, Cornoldi, & De Beni, 2009) found problems in comprehension related to a general WM system as well as a specific system in children with poor comprehension. For example, Carretti et al.'s meta-analysis of the literature (18 published studies) on specific reading comprehension difficulties found that tasks that require attention control and the processing of verbal information were the best measures to distinguish between poor and good comprehenders. Poor comprehenders were more disadvantaged on complex span tasks (tasks that draw on the executive system of WM) that involved verbal material than good comprehenders. In contrast, poor comprehenders were comparable in performance to good comprehenders on measures of visual-spatial complex (effect size = 0.29) span tasks and simple span (STM or phonological loop) tasks (effect size = 0.36). They concluded that poor comprehension depends partially on the verbal WM modality (effect sizes in favor of good comprehenders varied from 0.75 to 1.07). This synthesis also suggested that a failure of the attention control component of WM underlies

poor comprehension. The synthesis found that poor comprehenders were more likely to express difficulties in updating information as well as inhibiting irrelevant information when compared to good comprehenders.

In summary, the literature suggests that WM is an important marker of reading comprehension difficulties (also see Locascio, Mahone, Eason, & Cutting, 2010; Pimperton & Nation, 2010; Ricketts, 2011). In addition, the literature suggests that children of average intelligence who have a specific deficit in comprehension suffer problems related to the executive system of WM.

### Autism Spectrum Disorder

According to the DSM-5 (American Psychiatric Association, 2013) autism spectrum disorder is defined as describing such children that reflect persistent communication and social interaction deficits in multiple situations. These deficits reflect restricted, repetitive behavior and interests and are manifested in the early developmental period. These deficits may be associated with or without intellectual impairment or with or without accompanying language impairment. In general, autism reflects a severe persistent social impairment that occurs in combination with problems in both verbal and non-verbal communication. There is some debate in the literature about the prevailing incidence of autism and this most likely relates to a widely accepted condition referred to autism spectrum disorder. Autism spectrum disorder includes classic autism, as well as Asperger syndrome, high-functioning autism, and atypical autism. Current estimates place the prevalence of autism spectrum disorder at approximately one in every hundred children (e.g., Davidovitch, Hemo, Manning-Courtney, & Fombonne, 2013; Russell, Rodgers, Ukoumunne, & Ford, 2014).

An executive processing hypothesis has gained some interest in describing autism because behaviors in such children reflect poor executive controls (e.g., rigidity, perseveration, and repetitive behaviors). However, there is little evidence of how WM is impaired in children with autism (see Belleville, Ménard, Mottron, & Ménard, 2006, for review). Although WM is not a single homogeneous system, the majority of studies indicate that the WM abilities of children with autism are in the normal range. For example, a study by Ozonoff and Strayer (2001) examined the WM in high-functioning autistic children, children diagnosed with Tourette's syndrome, and a typically developing control group. They found no group differences across various dependent measures of WM. Although performance was correlated with both age and IQ, they concluded that WM is not one of the executive functions seriously impaired in autism.

In summary, the results of the various syntheses suggest that autistic children do not show moderate or severe deficits in WM when compared to typically developing children.

### Phonological Loop

In Baddeley's model (2012; Baddeley & Logie, 1999), the phonological loop is specialized for the retention of verbal information over short periods of time. It is composed of both a phonological store, which holds information in phonological form, and a rehearsal process, which serves to maintain representations in the phonological store (see Baddeley, Gathercole, & Papagno, 1998, for an extensive review). The phonological loop has been considered a key area of impairment for children with RD and specific language impairment (e.g., Nithart et al., 2009).

### Specific Learning Disorder with Impairment in Reading

The new DSM-5 (American Psychiatric Association, 2013) views a specific learning disorder in reading as reflecting a neurodevelopmental disorder of biological origin. This disability is manifested in reading performance markedly below age level that is not attributed to intellectual, developmental, neurological, or motor disorders. This broad category includes more specific deficits referred to as dyslexia or RD. The incidence of dyslexia in public schools has been reported to vary between 5% and 17% in the United States (McCandliss & Noble, 2003), although more conservative estimated prevalence rates range from 5% to 7% of the general population. The National Institute of Neurological Disorders and Stroke (2010) gives the following definition for dyslexia:

> Dyslexia is a brain-based type of learning disability that specifically impairs a person's ability to read. These individuals typically read at levels significantly lower than expected despite having normal intelligence. Although the disorder varies from person to person, common characteristics among people with dyslexia are difficulty with spelling, phonological processing (the manipulation of sounds), and/or rapid visual-verbal responding.

Several studies indicate that children with RD (dyslexia) have specific localized low-order processing deficits. A cognitive process consistently implicated in RD is phonological awareness. Phonological awareness is "the ability to attend explicitly to the phonological structure of spoken words" (Scarborough, 1998, p. 95). Dyslexia is viewed as a specific developmental disorder for which a modular impairment in phoneme-grapheme system knowledge, or a phonological deficit, has been postulated. Thus, there is a strong application related to our understanding of the role of the phonological loop as it relates to dyslexia or also referred to as RD.

The manifestations of deficits in the phonological loop include poor acquisition of sight words, poor performance on phonological awareness tasks, slow naming speed, and impaired verbal STM. Several studies suggest that difficulties in the phonological loop may lie at the root of word-learning problems in children (e.g., see Melby-Lervåg, Lyster, & Hulme, 2012). For example, children with RD are less able to generate pronunciations for unfamiliar or nonsense words than skilled readers (e.g., Siegel, 1993), suggesting a deficit in utilization or operation of the phonological recoding function of the articulatory control process.

Swanson, Zheng, and Jerman (2009) synthesized research that compared children with and without RD on measures

of the phonological loop (STM) and the executive system of WM (tasks that included simultaneous processing and storage). In general, 578 effect sizes were computed across a broad range of age, reading, and IQ scores, yielding a mean effect size across studies of –0.89 (SD = 1.03) in favor of children without RD. In all, 257 effect sizes were in the moderate range for STM measures (M = –0.61, 95% confidence range of –0.65 to –0.58) and 320 effect sizes were in the moderate range for WM measures (M = –0.67, 95% confidence range of –0.68 to –0.64). The results indicated that children with RD were distinctively disadvantaged compared to average readers on (a) STM measures requiring the recall of phonemes and digit sequences and (b) WM measures requiring the simultaneous processing and storage of digits within sentence sequences and final words from unrelated sentences. No significant moderating effects emerged for age, IQ, or reading level on memory effect sizes. In addition these difficulties, related to STM and WM, have emerged when synthesizing the literature on adults with RD (e.g., Swanson & Hsieh, 2009).

In summary, syntheses of the published literature on RD indicated that domain-specific STM (measures of the phonological loop) and WM (measures reflective of the executive system) deficits persisted across age, suggesting that children with RD fail to efficiently draw or monitor resources from both a phonological and executive system. The outcomes of this earlier synthesis are consistent with more recent studies (Johnson, Humphrey, Mellard, Woods, & Swanson, 2010; Menghini, Finzi, Carlesimo, & Vicari, 2011), again showing that RD involves difficulties in both the phonological loop and the executive system. What is unclear from the literature, however, is whether deficits in phonological loop create a bottleneck in the processing of information in the executive system or whether problems in the phonological loop and executive system reflect independent difficulties.

*Specific language impairment.* The term communication disorder is used in the DSM-5 (American Psychiatric Association, 2013) to describe children with persistent deficits in comprehension or production of language (e.g., spoken, written) substantially below age level, beginning in the early developmental period. Specific language impairment is typically identified through the achievement of low scores on a standardized language measures and intelligence scores falling within the normal range. Hulme and Snowling's (2009) comprehensive review indicated that 3–6% of the child population suffers from various aspects related to specific language impairment. This figure varies related to the type of language impairment because heterogeneity exists within the sample related to vocabulary, grammar, and phonology (Archibald & Gathercole, 2006a, 2006b).

A comprehensive review of the literature by Montgomery, Magimairaj, and Finney (2010) showed a strong relationship between STM (phonological loop) and processing speed in children with specific language impairment which in turn led to widespread negative effects in language learning and functioning, including the partial processing of words, grammatical forms, and syntactic structures. Memory limitations were viewed as affecting the acquisition representations of language processes as well as children's efficacy and how they store, access, and retrieve coordinate-stored information related to input and output of language.

Although Montgomery and colleagues' (2010) review focused on the literature related to phonological loop (STM system), the researchers also reviewed studies showing that such children suffered problems in a general executive capacity or attentional capacity system. Three activities of the executive system of WM were reviewed: shifting, updating, and attentional control. Children with specific language impairment were found to be comparable in shifting, but were weak in updating related to WM, and poor attention control (also see Henry, Messer, & Nash, 2012). Their review also suggested that WM capacity and linguistic knowledge were not necessarily separable mental constructs. Rather, WM capacity reflected the activation of specific linguistic representations in LTM. In this view, WM capacity was viewed as a reflection of weak linguistic representations.

The above syntheses do not imply however, that children with specific language impairment do not suffer from problems in visual-spatial WM. A recent meta-analysis (Vugs, Cuperus, Hendriks, & Verhoeven, 2013) suggests that visual-spatial WM (visual-spatial sketchpad) is affected in these children. Their results indicated such children showed effect sizes for visual-spatial storage of $d = 0.49$ and of storage + processing of $d = 0.63$ when compared to their counterparts. However, their synthesis suggested that the deficit in verbal aspects of WM in children with specific language impairment could be "two to three times larger than the deficit in their visuospatial WM" (Vugs et al., 2013, p. 2593).

Taken together, the results suggest that clear deficits in verbal components of WM emerge for children with SLI. However, the findings related to problem in visual-spatial WM, suggesting that problems may extend to more domain-general deficits in WM.

**Visual-Spatial Sketchpad**

The visual-spatial sketchpad is specialized for the processing and storage of visual material, spatial material, or both, and for linguistic information that can be recoded into imaginal forms (see Baddeley, 2000, 2012 for a review). Measures of visual-spatial WM (visual-spatial sketchpad) have primarily focused on memory for visual patterns (e.g., Logie, 1986). Gathercole and Pickering (2000) found that visual-spatial WM abilities, as well as measures of central executive processing, were associated with attainment levels on a national curriculum (U.K.) for children aged 6–7 years. Children who showed marked difficulties in curriculum attainment also showed marked difficulties in visual-spatial WM.

There have been few quantitative syntheses, to the author's knowledge, that have covered the visual-spatial difficulties of children with cognitive disabilities. A meta-analysis (Swanson & Jerman, 2006) of children with math disabilities, for example, did not find strong support for the notion that math disabilities were related to visual-spatial disorders (however, see Mammarella, Lucangeli, & Cornoldi, 2010). Some links

to specific cognitive deficits in visual-spatial WM, however, have been found in children with attention deficit hyperactivity disorder (ADHD), coordination disorders, and Williams syndrome. These findings are briefly reviewed.

*Attention Deficit Hyperactivity Disorder*

ADHD is a chronic condition that impairs an individual's ability to control attention in an optimal manner. DSM-5 (American Psychiatric Association, 2013) views ADHD as reflecting a "persistent pattern of inattention and/or hyperactivity-impulsivity that interferes with functioning or development beginning in childhood, and present across more than one setting" (p. 61). The incidence of ADHD is between approximately 3 and 5% of children of primary school age (e.g., DSM-5). ADHD is somewhat dissimilar from some of the other cognitive disabilities we have reviewed thus far, since disabilities related to RD, specific language deficits, and math disabilities might be seen as modular disorders. In contrast, ADHD is much less clear in terms of specific cognitive explanations. However, behavioral inhibition or executive functioning as reflected in high-level supervisory systems has characterized this disability (e.g., Tillman, Eninger, Forssman, & Bohlin, 2011). As such, ADHD is a difficult disorder to characterize on the cognitive level, but there have been several studies that tie ADHD to problems in visual WM performance.

For example, Martinussen, Hayden, Hogg-Johnson, and Tannock's (2005) meta-analysis reviewed studies that compared ADHD and control children on WM tasks. Their synthesis showed that children with ADHD reflected greater deficits in spatial-memory storage tasks (average effect size of 0.85) and spatial central executive tasks (average effect size of 1.06) than verbal storage or verbal central executive tasks (mean effect sizes range from 0.40 to 0.47). Their synthesis of the literature also suggested that these WM problems could not be accounted for by general differences in language skill or general intelligence. In general, their synthesis suggested that spatial WM is a specific area of difficulty for children with ADHD.

Other meta-analyses have examined executive processing tasks as a means of differentiating ADHD from other disabilities (Willcutt, Doyl, Nigg, Faraone, & Pennington, 2005). These executive processing tasks have assessed response inhibition, updating (WM), and task shifting. The largest difference in favor of the control group emerged on measures of response inhibition and WM. However, the magnitude differences on some of these tasks (effect sizes ranged from 0.40 to 0.60) were somewhat smaller than would be expected if these executive processing tasks were a major cause of the disorder. Overall, the Willcutt et al. (2005) synthesis raised concerns as to whether deficits in executive functioning per se are a sufficient or necessary cause of ADHD.

In summary, the literature suggests that children with ADHD suffer problems in WM, primarily on tasks that draw upon the visual-spatial sketchpad. However, problems in WM are perhaps secondary when compared to cognitive activities related to other areas of executive processing, such as the monitoring of attention (e.g., Willcutt et al., 2005).

## Coordination Disorders

The DSM-5 (American Psychiatric Association, 2013) defines coordination disorders as motor skill development substantially below a child's age group that interferes with normal activities, and begins in the "early developmental period." These problems cannot be attributed to intellectual disabilities, visual problems, or a neurological condition such as cerebral palsy. The criteria for diagnosing children with developmental coordination disorders (DCD) focus on problems in motor coordination that are clearly out of line with the child's chronological age and intellectual functioning. These problems interfere with academic achievement in areas such as handwriting and/or activities related to everyday life such as sports games and perhaps learning to dress. The prevalence of this disability in the general population is estimated between 5% and 18%, depending on the level or point of the cutoff scores for determining risk (Alloway, 2011). The cognitive explanation for DCD has focused on perceptual deficits, visual perceptual deficits, problems in kinesthetic perception, and balance/postural control (Alloway, 2011).

Alloway's (2006) and Wilson, Ruddock, Smits-Engelsman, Polatajko, and Blank's (2013) syntheses of the literature suggested that visual-spatial deficits were related to children's impaired development of a "sensorimotor map" and "one's position in space." Their syntheses suggested that children with DCD perform poorly on all WM measures in terms of standardized scores; however, their performance levels on visual-spatial WM (visual-spatial sketchpad) measures were substantially lower than verbal WM, verbal STM, and visual-spatial STM tasks. An interesting finding from Alloway's synthesis (2006) was that the performance of children with DCD on visual-spatial STM tasks was no worse than their performance on verbal STM and verbal WM tasks. Although the visual STM tests involved some motor skills, her synthesis suggested that children with DCD struggled with dual task demands (process and storage component on a visual-spatial WM task) related to the processing of visual-spatial information and motor coordination.

In summary, the literature suggests that children with DCD experience a selective deficit in visual-spatial WM that is linked with movement planning and motor control.

*Williams syndrome.* Williams syndrome is a rare neural developmental disorder characterized by a distinctive facial appearance and a developmental delay in visual-spatial abilities coupled with strong language skills (Gonçalves et al., 2011). Williams syndrome is caused by a deletion of 26 genes from the long arm of chromosome 7. Williams syndrome is viewed as a disorder in which individuals have an extensive reliance on verbal WM and language acquisition, which is stronger than would be found for typically developing children. The study of Williams syndrome is of interest because it suggests some of the independence among verbal and visual-spatial systems. The cognitive profile for Williams syndrome is characterized by a relative strength in the phonological loop (verbal STM, as typically measured by a digit recall task), but a severe weakness in the visual-spatial sketchpad (visual-spatial memory).

Rowe and Mervis' (2007) review of the literature found that WM tasks that included verbal material for individuals with Williams syndrome when compared to typically developing children followed the normal effects of word length, phonological similarity, and concreteness. However, children with Williams syndrome experienced clear difficulties in tasks that required visual-spatial construction. A meta-analysis by Lifshitz et al. (Lifshitz, Shtein, Weiss, & Svisrisky, 2011a; Lifshitz, Shtein, Weiss, & Vakil, 2011b) that included five articles that compared children with Williams syndrome to typically developing children found that the mean effect size differences on verbal memory tasks was approximately 0.45. Although the effect size was moderate, the authors argue that children with Williams syndrome have a preserved explicit verbal memory system when compared to their visual-spatial WM system.

In summary, children with Williams syndrome are characterized as having a severe weakness in the visual-spatial WM system when compared to their verbal WM skills. However, weaknesses in verbal WM are also apparent when compared to their normal-achieving counterparts.

## The Paradox of Normal Intelligence

There is no doubt that a paradox exists in the findings related to specific cognitive disabilities and overall normal intellectual functioning. Given that children within the average range on intelligence measures perform with difficulties on tasks that tap specific components of WM (updating, suppression of competing traces), what is the role of WM on intelligence in children with specific cognitive disabilities? How is it that children with specific deficits in cognitive processes have average intelligence? We did not come across a single review that examined these issues. These are particularly complex issues because performance on WM tasks is strongly correlated with intelligence (e.g., Ackerman, Beier, & Boyle, 2002; Duncan, Schramm, Thompson, & Dumontheil, 2012; Chuderski, 2013; Kyllonen & Christal, 1990).

Three points can be considered when tackling this issue. First, the relationship between WM and intelligence may be indirect (e.g., Alloway, 2009). Crinella and Yu (2000) reviewed literature suggesting a weak relationship between IQ and executive processing with normal-achieving children. Similarly, the literature clearly shows that poor readers with high IQ levels, when compared to poor readers with low IQ levels, can yield statistically equivalent performance on cognitive measures (e.g., phonological processing; Hoskyn & Swanson, 2000; Siegel, 1993). Further, these commonalities in performance are not isolated to memory or phonological processing measures (see Hoskyn & Swanson, 2000 for a meta-analysis comparing RD and garden-variety poor achievers across an array of cognitive measures). For example, weak to moderate relations exists between WM and fluid intelligence (performance on the Raven Colored Progressive Matrices test) in children with RD. Swanson and Alexander (1997) found that the magnitude of the correlations between executive processing and fluid intelligence (Raven Colored Progressive Matrices test) varied between 0.04 and 0.34

in RD and between –0.05 and 0.46 in average readers (see Swanson & Alexander, 1997, Table 4).

Second, children with specific cognitive disabilities may use different routes or processes to problem solve, even though solution accuracy is comparable to chronologically matched peers. For example, Swanson (1988, 1993) found that children with RD successfully set up a series of sub-goals for task solution. Further, the children with RD's problem-solving performance was statistically comparable to their chronologically matched peers on a number of fluid measures of intelligence (Picture Arrangement subtest on the Wechsler Children's Intelligence Test, Swanson, 1988; Tower of Hanoi, Combinatorial, and Pendulum Task; Swanson, 1993). However, the studies also found that individuals with RD in some cases relied on different cognitive routes than skilled readers in problem solving. For example, on measures of fluid intelligence, problem solving was augmented by "emphasizing problem representation (defining the problem, identifying relevant information or facts given about the problem) rather than procedural knowledge or processes used to identify algorithms" (Swanson, 1993, p. 864). Thus, there is evidence to suggest that performance by individuals with RD on fluid measures of intelligence may involve some form of compensatory processing. However, little research has focused on the compensatory processes that underlie the links between intelligence and executive processing.

Finally, individuals may achieve scores within the range of normal intelligence because the information they experience in their environment does not always place high demands on their WM. A standardized test of WM (S-Cognitive Processing Test: Swanson, 1995) shows, for example, that the majority of children with serious academic difficulties (learning disabilities) scored in the 21st percentile on WM measures (scaled scores across 11 subtests hovered around 8, or a standard score of 88; see Swanson, 1995, p. 167), suggesting they have a very weak, but adequate WM ability to process information and then store information over the long term. Of course, they may use other experiences by pulling up from LTM things that they already know to help in the processing of information. With the accumulation of LTM links and connections, there is some control over the processing demands of new information. Thus, this control over processing demands may reduce any potential links between intelligence and WM. No doubt, the processes that link specific processing deficits with normal intelligence have not been elucidated.

## Discussion and Implications

This chapter reviewed studies that synthesized research on WM for children with specific cognitive deficits. WM was selected as a focus because of its significant relationship to behaviors such as learning to read, compute, acquire language, coordinate motor behaviors, and/or monitor attention. Performance on specific components of WM was further considered in the analysis since confirmatory factor analysis models have provided support of a multicomponent model (Baddeley, 2012; Baddeley & Logie, 1999) when applied to children (e.g., Alloway et al., 2004; Gathercole et al., 2004; Swanson, 2008).

The synthesized studies reviewed here have shown that children with average intelligence experience specific difficulties in reading, math, language, and writing (i.e., motor coordination) that are related to problems in WM. However, in our review we did not find clear support for the notion that a specific deficit in a particular component of WM underlies a specific cognitive disability. That is, when children with cognitive disabilities were compared to children matched on measures of intelligence without cognitive disabilities, the effect sizes in favor of children without cognitive difficulties may be larger in one component of WM when compared to another, but children with cognitive disabilities may also yield a weakness across other components of WM. For example, children with RD (dyslexia) when compared to their peers were found to experience deficits in the phonological loop, but were also found deficient in the executive component of WM (e.g., Swanson et al., 2009a). Likewise, children with serious difficulties related to the visual-spatial sketchpad (Williams syndrome) were found to have difficulties related to the phonological loop (Lifshitz et al., 2011a, 2011b). What these findings suggest is that, although a neurodevelopmental inefficiency of biological origin may underlie such children's disability, the manifestations of these inefficiencies may reflect problems across multiple components of WM.

So what are the educational implications of these findings? We suggest two applications. The first relates to assessment. Assuming that variables such as general intelligence, quality of instruction, and related environmental variables in the classroom are controlled or accounted for, the literature suggests that some of the specific learning difficulties experienced by children are related to the phonological loop (a component of WM that specializes in the retention of speech-based information), the visual-spatial sketchpad (a component that focuses on visual-spatial processing) and/ or the executive system (a component that focuses on controlled attention) of WM. A number of the syntheses suggested that some children with cognitive disabilities are more likely to experience more severe deficits in one component of WM than another. For example, children with RD (dyslexia) and specific language deficits are distinctly disadvantaged compared to their peers for remembering verbal information, specifically phonological items (phonemes). Children with DCD or ADHD do poorly on visual-spatial WM tasks. In contrast, children with math disabilities or reading comprehension deficits do poorly on tasks that reflect the monitoring of process and storage demands, a characteristic of the executive system.

However, it is also important to note in this assessment process that problems in one area of WM do not mean they will not experience difficulties in another. For example, it is important to note that the phonological loop is of service in complex cognition, such as reading comprehension and problem solving. Thus, this simple subsystem is not the only aspect of WM that is deeply rooted in more complex activities experienced by children who have serious academic problems. Situations that place high demands on processing, which in turn place demands on controlled attentional processing (such as monitoring limited resources, suppressing conflicting information, updating information), place children with problems in verbal and visual storage (phonological loop, visual-spatial sketchpad) at a clear disadvantage when compared with their chronological-aged average-achieving counterparts.

The second relates to intervention. Current research has provided some directions for remediation of WM difficulties. For example, there is evidence emerging that children's WM can be improved upon with training (e.g., Klingberg, 2012; Melby-Lervåg & Hulme, 2013) and dynamic testing (e.g., Swanson, 2011). However, these levels of improvement have as yet to be directly linked to improvements in children's academic performance (Melby-Lervåg & Hulme, 2013). Unfortunately, at this point the evidence that links WM to achievement is correlation and/or relies on quasi-experimental designs and therefore further experimentation is necessary.

Where should we go from here? Our synthesis of the "synthesized literature" suggests there are gaping holes in our knowledge about how WM and learning in children with cognitive disabilities are related, and therefore additional research is needed. Some areas of "residual ignorance" (to coin a phrase by Baddeley) are as follows:

***Why is WM related to cognitive disabilities and academic achievement?*** Additional research needs to be directed toward explaining why WM tasks are good predictors of academic performance. Although, for example, it makes sense that controlled attention ability (e.g., the ability to switch attention between processing and storage requirements) may be particularly good accounting for reading comprehension and/or problem-solving deficits, but not necessarily for simple sight word recognition (dyslexia), this has not yet been tested experimentally. No doubt, the complexity of the task determines whether general or domain-specific factors come into play. However, different capacity-limited factors may come into play in predicting achievement across elementary, junior high and high school. Further, one can only speculate on how children with reading and math disabilities are able to attain normal levels of functioning in everyday cognition.

***How processes are represented.*** We do not know how the basic mechanisms of WM are represented in children who experience serious deficits in reading and/or math. Basic mechanisms have been explored in some detail in the area of phonological loop (Baddeley et al., 1998); however, processes related to the integrated nature of storage and processing characteristic of WM tasks have not been adequately studied. In addition, research is unclear about primary mechanisms within the executive system that separate low- and high-WM groups as it applies to information maintenance. This is because monitoring activities are intertwined with maintaining information. That is, monitoring activities such as: (a) switching attention between multiple tasks; (b) active

inhibition or suppression of irrelevant information; (c) updating information; and (d) planning and sequencing intended actions are very much related to information maintenance. Further, it is difficult to know how all of these particular activities are related to one another, or if, in fact, they are independent.

***Instructional contributions.*** Classroom research has not identified all factors of WM amenable to particular manipulations, such as extended practice, specific instructions, and strategy use. For instructional purposes, specific research needs to be directed toward the ways in which LTM contribute to WM. Further research is necessary to determine how LTM representations can be activated or taught to support WM operations. If we can show that an enhancement of domain-specific WM factor is primarily related to a learned skill or knowledge, then clearly an environmental factor (e.g., instruction) plays an important role.

In summary, this review suggests that a WM system underlies some of the cognitive disabilities experienced by children. Although WM is obviously not the only skill that contributes to academic difficulties in children, WM does play a significance role in accounting for individual differences in children's academic performance. Depending on the academic task, age, and type of learning problem (reading and/or math), general and specific WM systems may be involved in learning and academic difficulties.

## References

Ackerman, P. L., Beier, M. E., & Boyle, M. O. (2002). Individual differences in working memory within a nomological network of cognitive and perceptual speed abilities. *Journal of Experimental Psychology: General, 131,* 567–589.

Alloway, T. P. (2006). Working memory skills in children with developmental coordination disorder. In T. P. Alloway & S. E. Gathercole (Eds.), *Working memory and neurodevelopmental disorders* (pp. 161–186). New York, NY: Psychology Press.

Alloway, T. P. (2009). Working memory, but not IQ, predicts subsequent learning in children with learning difficulties. *European Journal of Psychological Assessment, 25*(2), 92–98.

Alloway, T. P. (2011). A comparison of working memory profiles in children with ADHD and DCD. *Child Neuropsychology, 17*(5), 483–494.

Alloway, T. P., & Gathercole, S. E. (Eds.) (2007). *Working memory and neurodevelopmental disorders.* New York, NY: Psychology Press.

Alloway, T. P., Gathercole, S. E., Willis, C., & Adams, A. (2004). A structural analysis of working memory and related cognitive skills in young children. *Journal of Experimental Child Psychology, 87,* 85–106.

American Psychiatric Association. (2013). *Diagnostic and statistical manual of mental disorders, fifth edition.* Washington, DC: American Psychiatric Association.

Anderson, J. (1976). *Cognitive psychology.* New York: Freeman.

Archibald, L. M. D., & Gathercole, S. E. (2006a). Short-term and working memory in specific language impairment. *International Journal of Language & Communication Disorders, 41*(6), 675–693.

Archibald, L. M. D., & Gathercole, S. E. (2006b). Short-term memory and working memory in specific language impairment. In T. P. Alloway & S. E. Gathercole (Eds.), *Working memory and neurodevelopmental disorders* (pp. 139–160). New York, NY: Psychology Press.

Baddeley, A. D. (1986). *Working memory.* London: Oxford University Press.

Baddeley, A. (2000). The episodic buffer: A new component of working memory? *Trends in Cognitive Sciences, 4,* 417–423.

Baddeley, A. (2012). Working memory: Theories, models, and controversies. *Annual Review of Psychology, 63,* 1–29.

Baddeley, A. D., Gathercole, S. E., & Papagno, C. (1998). The phonological loop as a language learning device. *Psychological Review, 105*, 158–173.

Baddeley, A. D., & Logie, R. H. (1999). The multiple-component model. In A. Miyake & P. Shah (Eds.), *Models of working memory: Mechanisms of active maintenance and executive control* (pp. 28–61). Cambridge, UK: Cambridge University Press.

Badian, N. A. (1983). Arithmetic and nonverbal learning. In H. R. Myklebust (Ed.), *Progress in learning disabilities* (Vol. 5, pp. 235–264). New York: Grune and Stratton.

Belleville, S., Ménard, É., Mottron, L., & Ménard, M. (2006). Working memory in autism. In T. P. Alloway & S. E. Gathercole (Eds.), *Working memory and neurodevelopmental disorders* (pp. 213–238). New York, NY: Psychology Press.

Booth, J. N., Boyle, J. M. E., & Kelly, S. W. (2010). Do tasks make a difference? Accounting for heterogeneity of performance of children with reading difficulties on tasks of executive function: Findings from a meta-analysis. *British Journal of Developmental Psychology. Special Issue: Developmental Disorders of Language and Literacy, 28*(1), 133–176.

Carretti, B., Borella, E., Cornoldi, C., & De Beni, R. (2009). Role of working memory in explaining the performance of individuals with specific reading comprehension difficulties: A meta-analysis. *Learning and Individual Differences, 19*(2), 245–251.

Cheung, C. H. M., Wood, A. C., Paloyelis, Y., Arias-Vasquez, A., Buitelaar, J. K., Franke, B., . . . Kuntsi, J. (2012). Aetiology for the covariation between combined type ADHD and reading difficulties in a family study: The role of IQ. *Journal of Child Psychology and Psychiatry, 53*(8), 864–873.

Chuderski, A. (2013). When are fluid intelligence and working memory isomorphic and when are they not? *Intelligence, 41*(4), 244–262.

Cohen, J. (1988) *Statistical power analysis for the behavioral sciences.* NewYork: Academic Press.

Crinella, F., & Yu, J. (2000). Brain mechanisms and intelligence: Psychometric g and executive function. *Intelligence, 27*, 299–327.

Daneman, M., & Carpenter P. A. (1980). Individual differences in working memory and reading. *Journal of Verbal Learning and Verbal Behavior, 19*, 450–466.

David, C. V. (2012). Working memory deficits in math learning difficulties: A meta-analysis. *International Journal of Developmental Disabilities, 58*(2), 67–84.

Davidovitch, M., Hemo, B., Manning-Courtney, P., & Fombonne, E. (2013). Prevalence and incidence of autism spectrum disorder in an Israeli population. *Journal of Autism and Developmental Disorders, 43*(4), 785–793.

Dehaene, S., & Cohen, L. (1997). Cerebral pathways for calculation: Double disassociation between rote verbal and quantitative knowledge of arithmetic. *Cortex, 33*, 2219–2250.

Di Martino, A., Ross, K., Uddin, L. Q., Sklar, A. B., Castellanos, F. X., & Milham, M. P. (2009). Functional brain correlates of social and nonsocial processes in autism spectrum disorders: An activation likelihood estimation meta-analysis. *Biological Psychiatry, 65*(1), 63–74.

Duncan, J., Schramm, M., Thompson, R., & Dumontheil, I. (2012). Task rules, working memory, and fluid intelligence. *Psychonomic Bulletin & Review, 19*(5), 864–870.

Gathercole, S. E., & Baddeley, A. D. (1993). *Working memory and language.* Hove, UK: Erlbaum.

Gathercole, S. E., & Pickering, S. J. (2000). Working memory deficits in children with low achievements in the national curriculum at 7 years of age. *British Journal of Educational Psychology, 70*(2), 177–194.

Gathercole, S. E., Pickering, S. J., Ambridge, B., & Wearing, H. (2004). The structure of working memory from 4 to 15 years of age. *Developmental Psychology, 40*, 177–190.

Geary, D. C. (1993). Mathematical disabilities: Cognition, neuropsychological and genetic components. *Psychological Bulletin, 114*, 345–362.

Geary, D. C. (2013). Learning disabilities in mathematics: Recent advances. In H. L. Swanson, K. Harris, & S. Graham (Eds.), *Handbook of learning disabilities* (2nd ed., pp. 239–255). New York: Guilford.

Glass, G. V., McGraw, B., & Smith, M. L. (1981). *Meta-analysis in social research.* Beverly Hills, CA: Sage.

Goldman-Rakic, P. S. (1995). Architecture of the prefrontal cortex and the central executive. *Annals of the New York Academy of Sciences, 769*, 71–83.

Gonçalves, Ó. F., Pinheiro, A. P., Sampaio, A., Sousa, N., Férnandez, M., & Henriques, M. (2011). Autobiographical narratives in Williams syndrome: Structural, process and content dimensions. *Journal of Developmental and Physical Disabilities, 23*(4), 289–302.

Haworth, C. M. A., Kovas, Y., Harlaar, N., Hayiou-Thomas, M., Petrill, S. A., Dale, P. S., & Plomin, R. (2009). Generalist genes and learning disabilities: A multivariate genetic analysis of low performance in reading, mathematics, language and general cognitive ability in a sample of 8000 12-year-old twins. *Journal of Child Psychology and Psychiatry, 50*(10), 1318–1325.

Henry, L. A., Messer, D. J., & Nash, G. (2012). Executive functioning in children with specific language impairment. *Journal of Child Psychology and Psychiatry, 53*(1), 37–45.

Hoskyn, M., & Swanson, H. L. (2000). Cognitive processing of low achievers and children with reading disabilities: A selective meta-analytic review of the published literature. *School Psychology Review, 29*, 102–119.

Hulme, C. C., & Snowling, M. J. (2009). *Developmental disorders of language and cognition.* West Sussex, UK: Wiley.

Johnson, E. S., Humphrey, M., Mellard, D. F., Woods, K., & Swanson, H. L. (2010). Cognitive processing deficits and students with specific learning disabilities: A selective meta-analysis of the literature. *Learning Disability Quarterly, 33*(1), 3–18.

Kane, M. J., Conway, A. R., Hambrick, D. Z., & Engle, R. W. (2007). Variation in working memory capacity as variation in executive attention and control. In A. Conway, C. Jarrold, M. J. Kanem, A. Miyake, & J. Towse (Eds.), *Variation in working memory* (pp. 21–48). New York: Oxford University Press.

Klingberg, T. (2012). Is working memory capacity fixed? *Journal of Applied Research in Memory and Cognition, 1*(3), 194–196.

Kyllonen, P. C., & Christal, R. E. (1990). Reasoning ability is (little more than) working memory capacity?! *Intelligence, 14*, 389–433.

Lifshitz, H., Shtein, S., Weiss, I., & Svisrsky, N. (2011a). Explicit memory among individuals with mild and moderate intellectual disability: Educational implications. *European Journal of Special Needs Education, 26*(1), 113–124.

Lifshitz, H., Shtein, S., Weiss, I., & Vakil, E. (2011b). Meta-analysis of explicit memory studies in populations with intellectual disability. *European Journal of Special Needs Education, 26*(1), 93–111.

Locascio, G., Mahone, E. M., Eason, S. H., & Cutting, L. E. (2010). Executive dysfunction among children with reading comprehension deficits. *Journal of Learning Disabilities, 43*(5), 441–454.

Logie, R. H. (1986). Visuo-spatial processing in working memory. *Quarterly Journal of Experimental Psychology, 38A*, 229–247.

Mammarella, I. C., Lucangeli, D., & Cornoldi, C. (2010). Spatial working memory and arithmetic deficits in children with nonverbal learning difficulties. *Journal of Learning Disabilities, 43*(5), 455–468.

Martinussen, R., Hayden, J., Hogg-Johnson, S., & Tannock, R. (2005). A meta-analysis of working memory impairments in children with attention-deficit/hyperactivity disorder. *Journal of the American Academy of Child & Adolescent Psychiatry, 44*(4), 377–384.

McCandliss, B. D., & Noble, K. G. (2003). The development of reading impairment: A cognitive neuroscience model. *Mental Retardation and Developmental Disabilities Research Reviews, 9*(3), 196–204.

McGrath, L. M., Pennington, B. F., Shanahan, M. A., Santerre-Lemmon, L. E., Barnard, H. D., Willcutt, E. G., . . . Olson, R. K. (2011). A multiple deficit model of reading disability and attention-deficit/hyperactivity disorder: Searching for shared cognitive deficits. *Journal of Child Psychology and Psychiatry, 52*(5), 547–557.

Menghini, D., Finzi, A., Carlesimo, G. A., & Vicari, S. (2011). Working memory impairment in children with developmental dyslexia: Is it just a phonological deficit? *Developmental Neuropsychology, 36*(2), 199–213.

Melby-Lervåg, M., & Hulme, C. (2013). Is working memory training effective? A meta-analytic review. *Developmental Psychology, 49*(2), 270–291.

Melby-Lervåg, M., Lyster, S. H., & Hulme, C. (2012). Phonological skills and their role in learning to read: A meta-analytic review. *Psychological Bulletin, 138*(2), 322–352.

Miyake, A., Friedman, N. P., Emerson, M. J., Witzki, A. H., & Howerter, A. (2000). The unity and diversity of executive functions and their contributions to complex "frontal lobe" tasks: A latent variable analysis. *Cognitive Psychology, 41,* 49–100.

Montgomery, J. W., Magimairaj, B. M., & Finney, M. C. (2010). Working memory and specific language impairment: An update on the relation and perspectives on assessment and treatment. *American Journal of Speech-Language Pathology, 19*(1), 78–94.

Nation, K., Adams, J. W., Bowyer-Crane, C. A., & Snowling, M. J. (1999). Working memory deficits in poor comprehenders reflect underlying language impairments. *Journal of Experimental Child Psychology, 73,* 139–158.

National Institute of Neurological Disorders and Stroke. (12 May 2010). Retrieved from http://www.ninds.nih.gov/disorders/dyslexia/dyslexia. htm (accessed November 1, 2012).

Nithart, C., Demont, E., Majerus, S., Leybaert, J., Poncelet, M., & Metz-Lutz, M. (2009). Reading disabilities in SLI and dyslexia result from distinct phonological impairments. *Developmental Neuropsychology, 34*(3), 296–311.

Nittrouer, S., & Pennington, B. (2010). New approaches to the study of childhood language disorders. *Current Directions in Psychological Science, 19*(5), 308–313.

Norman, D., & Shallice, T. (1986). Attention to action: Willed and automatic control of behavior. In R. J. Davidson, G. E. Schwartz, & D. E. Shapiro (Eds.) *Consciousness and self-regulation: Advances in research and theory* (Vol. 4, pp. 1–18). New York: Plenum.

Ozonoff, S., & Strayer, D. L. (2001). Further evidence of intact working memory in autism. *Journal of Autism and Developmental Disorders, 31*(3), 257–263.

Pennington, B. F., McGrath, L. M., Rosenberg, J., Barnard, H., Smith, S. D., Willcutt, E. G., . . . Olson, R. K. (2009). Gene × environment interactions in reading disability and attention-deficit/hyperactivity disorder. *Developmental Psychology, 45*(1), 77–89.

Pennington, B. F., Santerre-Lemmon, L., Rosenberg, J., MacDonald, B., Boada, R., Friend, A., . . . Olson, R. K. (2012). Individual prediction of dyslexia by single versus multiple deficit models. *Journal of Abnormal Psychology, 121*(1), 212–224.

Pimperton, H., & Nation, K. (2010). Suppressing irrelevant information from working memory: Evidence for domain-specific deficits in poor comprehenders. *Journal of Memory and Language, 62*(4), 380–391.

Reigosa-Crespo, V., Valdés-Sosa, M., Butterworth, B., Estévez, N., Rodríguez, M., Santos, E., . . . Lage, A. (2012). Basic numerical capacities and prevalence of developmental dyscalculia: The Havana survey. *Developmental Psychology, 48*(1), 123–135.

Ricketts, J. (2011). Research review: Reading comprehension in developmental disorders of language and communication. *Journal of Child Psychology and Psychiatry, 52*(11), 1111–1123.

Rowe, M., & Mervis, C. B. (2007). Working memory in Williams syndrome. In T. P. Alloway & S. E. Gathercole (Eds.), *Working memory and neurodevelopmental disorders* (pp. 267–294). New York: Psychology Press.

Russell, G., Rodgers, L. R., Ukoumunne, O. C., & Ford, T. (2014). Prevalence of parent-reported ASD and ADHD in the UK: Findings from the millennium cohort study. *Journal of Autism and Developmental Disorders, 44*(1), 31–40.

Scarborough, H. S. (1998). Early identification of children at risk for reading disabilities: Phonological awareness and some other promising predictors. In B Shapiro, P. Accardo, & A. Capute (Eds.), *Specific reading disability: A view of the spectrum* (pp. 75–119). Timonium, MD: York Press.

Siegel, L. S. (1993). Phonological processing deficits as a basis for reading disabilities. *Developmental Review, 13,* 246–257.

Snowling, M. J., & Hulme, C. (2012). Annual research review: The nature and classification of reading disorders—a commentary on proposals for DSM-5. *Journal of Child Psychology and Psychiatry, 53*(5), 593–607.

Swanson, H. L. (1988). Learning disabled children's problem solving. *Intelligence, 12,* 261–278.

Swanson, H. L. (1993). An information processing analysis of learning disabled children's problem solving. *American Educational Research Journal, 30,* 861–893.

Swanson, H. L. (1995). *S-Cognitive Processing Test (S-CPT): A dynamic assessment measure* (p. 122). Austin, TX: PRO-ED.

Swanson, H. L. (2008). Working memory and intelligence in children: What develops? *Journal of Educational Psychology, 100,* 581–602.

Swanson, H. L. (2011). Dynamic testing, working memory, and reading comprehension growth in children with reading disabilities. *Journal of Learning Disabilities, 44*(4), 358–371.

Swanson, H. L., & Alexander, J. (1997). Cognitive processes as predictors of word recognition and reading comprehension in learning disabled and skilled readers: Revisiting the specificity hypothesis. *Journal of Educational Psychology, 89,* 128–158.

Swanson, H. L., & Alloway, T. P. (2012). *Working memory, learning, and academic achievement.* In K. Harris, S. Graham, & T. Urdan (Eds.), *APA educational psychology handbook* (Vol. 1, pp. 327–366). Washington, DC: American Psychological Association.

Swanson, H. L., & Hsieh, C. (2009). Reading disabilities in adults: A selective meta-analysis of the literature. *Review of Educational Research, 79*(4), 1362–1390.

Swanson, H. L., & Jerman, O. (2006). Math disabilities: A selective meta-analysis of the literature. *Review of Educational Research, 76,* 249–274.

Swanson, H. L., Jerman, O., & Zheng, X. (2008). Growth in working memory and mathematical problem solving in children at risk and not at risk for serious math difficulties. *Journal of Educational Psychology, 100*(2), 343–379.

Swanson, H. L., Jerman, O., & Zheng, X. (2009a). Math disabilities and reading disabilities: Can they be separated? *Journal of Psychoeducational Assessment, 27*(3), 175–196.

Swanson, H. L., Zheng, X., & Jerman, O. (2009b). Working memory, short-term memory and reading disabilities: A selective meta-analysis of the literature. *Journal of Learning Disabilities, 42,* 260–287.

Tillman, C., Eninger, L., Forssman, L., & Bohlin, G. (2011). The relation between working memory components and ADHD symptoms from a developmental perspective. *Developmental Neuropsychology, 36*(2), 181–198.

Vugs, B., Cuperus, J., Hendriks, M., & Verhoeven, L. (2013). Visuospatial working memory in specific language impairment: A meta-analysis. *Research in Developmental Disabilities, 34*(9), 2586–2597.

Willcutt, E. G., Doyle, A. E., Nigg, J. T., Faraone, S. V., & Pennington, B. F. (2005). Validity of the executive function theory of attention-deficit/hyperactivity disorder: A meta-analytic review. *Biological Psychiatry, 57*(11), 1336–1346.

Wilson, P. H., Ruddock, S., Smits-Engelsman, B., Polatajko, H., & Blank, R. (2013). Understanding performance deficits in developmental coordination disorder: A meta-analysis of recent research. *Developmental Medicine & Child Neurology, 55*(3), 217–228.

Yeates, K. O., Ris, M. D., Taylor, H. G., & Pennington, B. F. (2010). *Pediatric neuropsychology: Research, theory, and practice* (2nd ed.). New York: Guilford.

# 11

# Personal Capability Beliefs

*ELLEN L. USHER*
University of Kentucky

"Beliefs are rules for action." In 1885, William James, father of American psychology, echoed these five words from his friend and fellow philosopher, Charles Sanders Peirce, who considered them to be the ideological cornerstone of pragmatism. This chapter adopts the same premise, put forth by numerous others, that the beliefs individuals hold are excellent indicators of what people choose, what they perceive and experience, and ultimately what they do (Dewey, 1933; Rokeach, 1968). The chapter focuses on the development and functional value of *personal capability beliefs*—primarily learners' beliefs—in educational settings (see Chapter 30, this volume, for a thoughtful review of research and theory on teachers' beliefs).

Despite the emphasis that James (1892/2001) placed on the self as a key determinant of thought and action, the dominant psychological theories of the first half of the twentieth century relegated *self as agent* to the sidelines. To the psychoanalysts, human functioning was explained as the result of concealed inner impulses. To the behaviorists, internal influences were banished as causal agents altogether; the sole focus was on environmental contingencies as both causes and reinforcers of behavior. Not until the second half of the twentieth century was *self* reintroduced as an important determinant of individual functioning, growth, and health, this time by humanistic psychologists (e.g., Maslow, 1968; Rogers, 1947) and social cognitive theorists (e.g., Bandura, 1986).

Study of the self-system once again found favor in the science of psychology and, in turn, became of interest to educational researchers and practitioners. This work began to confirm what James and Peirce conjectured 100 years prior: learners' beliefs about their own capabilities are related to cognitive, affective, and behavioral outcomes (see Pajares & Schunk, 2002, for a historical review). In fact, in the first edition of this *Handbook of Educational Psychology*, Graham and Weiner (1996) asserted that the study of the self "reflects what is probably the main new direction in the field of motivation" and may soon dominate the field altogether (p. 77). Abundant research has been conducted on self-processes

over the past decade. This explains why two chapters were devoted to competence and self-beliefs in the 2006 edition of this handbook (i.e., Roeser, Peck, & Nasir, 2006; Schunk & Zimmerman, 2006) and one to self-concept in a recent related handbook (i.e., Marsh, Xu, & Martin, 2012).

The broad aim of this chapter is to bring readers up to date with the research on personal capability beliefs and to chart new pathways for future understanding. The chapter begins by addressing terminology and definitions useful in the study of personal capability beliefs in educational settings; it then offers a description and overview of several such beliefs, situating each in its theoretical home. Key research findings are discussed; these demonstrate how beliefs are related to behavioral and affective variables and how they develop and change. This section also reviews notable individual and group differences. The next section describes prominent methodological approaches used to investigate capability beliefs; this includes suggestions for ways in which capability beliefs can be operationalized, assessed, and modeled. The chapter concludes with suggestions for future research on personal capability beliefs.

## Personal Capability Beliefs: Terminology and Definitions

Of the studies focused on learner motivation that have filled education and psychology journals in recent decades, many have included some measure of learners' beliefs about their capabilities. A discerning reader will be quick to notice that the terminology researchers use to describe personal capability beliefs is diverse, if not downright confusing. Terms such as *self-concept of ability, self-efficacy, academic competence beliefs, self-esteem, ability conceptions, expectancy for success, outcome expectations*, and *implicit theory of intelligence* populate educational and developmental psychology journals. As the research on self-beliefs in academic settings has grown, new terms have emerged. With respect to personal capability beliefs as with other motivation constructs, "similar terminology is being used to mark varied constructs or . . . the same construct is being referenced by different language" (Murphy & Alexander, 2000, p. 5). These terms sometimes signify confusion on the part of researchers; however, they also likely point to the intricate system of beliefs that humans hold, each denoting a slightly different self-view. The combined influence of these self-beliefs, along with other factors both internal and external to the individual, makes learners more or less motivated to act.

To gain a better understanding of how learners' beliefs guide action and how those beliefs develop, one must look beyond the confusing semantic signposts to two critical questions. First, what is the theoretical home of the construct under investigation? This, of course, requires some background reading and knowledge of theory. Second, how are the beliefs in question measured and operationalized? For example, if the belief signpost in a study reads "self-efficacy," the reader should look to see that self-efficacy has been situated within social cognitive theory and assessed in a manner consistent with this theory. If it has not, the critical reader might ask, "What, then, *has* been measured?" These questions are addressed in more detail later; first, it is necessary to define terms to be used and review some conceptual distinctions in research on personal capability beliefs.

### Ability Versus Capability

The general term, *personal capability beliefs,* here refers to the beliefs learners hold about their potential to carry out the various learning tasks before them. Though small, a distinction exists between the meaning of "ability" and "capability." *Ability*, which comes from the Latin *habilis*, refers to a skill or competence in doing or performing that has already been acquired. *Capability* refers to the potential to develop a skill or competency in the future or to perform a given task under varying conditions. I judge myself as *able* to write; however, I may not judge myself as *capable* of writing a novel this summer. In other words, capability depends in part on one's ability but also on other cognitive and motivational variables, such as effort and persistence, and on one's assessment of contextual demands. A child might be *able* to add two-digit numbers but *incapable* of adding 50 such numbers within 30 minutes. A person's beliefs therefore reflect both actuality and potentiality (Maslow, 1968). Students' beliefs about what they can do presently, what they can do under varying circumstances, and what they can learn to do in the future might differ, and each can be important to investigate.

### Competence Versus Control Beliefs

With the paradigm shift from behaviorism, diverse frameworks accorded self-beliefs a prominent role in predicting and explaining human motivation and behavior. These frameworks, some of which are described below, emphasized two types of self-beliefs, which Schunk and Zimmerman (2006) classified as *competence* and *control* beliefs. As noted above, competence beliefs refer to individuals' perceptions of their ability or capability to meet task and situational demands. They answer the general question, "Can I perform task *X*?" and are based on individuals' evaluations of the skills they bring to a given situation or challenge. Competence beliefs are considered means- or process-related beliefs because they refer to the means by which individuals reach desired ends. Control beliefs, on the other hand, refer to individuals' perceptions of outcomes or ends that their actions will bring about. Control beliefs answer the general question, "If I perform *X*, will I achieve *Y*?" In this sense, control beliefs do not refer to one's perceived abilities or capabilities but to beliefs that one's actions will bring about desired outcomes.

Competence and control beliefs are independent predictors of human motivation and behavior (Bandura, 1997). A young student might believe herself competent as a reader but might not feel that she has much control over the grade she will earn on the comprehension test she must take when she finishes her book. Even learners who feel competent may not expect positive results if they do not believe they can control the outcomes of their efforts. Factors external to the learner, such as a teacher's inflexible assessment standards or the competitive nature of the class, may undermine a learner's sense of control. Conversely, a learner might feel that his grade in his mathematics class is within his control, but if he lacks a sense of competence, he may not achieve desired ends. Both a belief in one's own competence and a sense that outcomes are within one's control are critical motivating factors. Readers interested in a more detailed account of how competence and control beliefs have been theoretically situated and empirically examined are referred to Schunk and Zimmerman (2006).

### Relative Versus Absolute Criteria

Beliefs can be formed with relative and absolute criteria in mind. I may consider myself an accomplished pianist when, in the privacy of my own home, I master a page of music by learning to play it fluently (an absolute, self-set standard). If I were to invite a concert pianist to play the same piece of music and then judge my own abilities relative to his (a comparative standard), my self-perception would undoubtedly wane. A label of proficiency might be conferred by my piano teacher if I could meet her standard of 100% accuracy (an absolute, externally-set standard). In some situations, clear performance criteria exist by which learners can gauge their progress. In many situations, however, no absolute standards exist. In such circumstances people may judge their capabilities by social comparative means or by monitoring their progress toward self-set goals (regardless of the external criteria available). A thorough understanding of self-perceptions requires consideration of the relative versus absolute means by which individuals judge what they can do. The standards by which a given learner measures herself depend on numerous factors such as the academic domain, the nature of the task, personal characteristics, age of the learner, and the learning climate.

Much of the research described herein does not distinguish between ability versus capability, competence and control, or relative and absolute measures of perceived competence. But these distinctions are not simply semantic; the words researchers choose often reflect differences in the nature of the underlying beliefs to which they point.

## Personal Capability Beliefs: Diverse Theoretical Perspectives

Types of personal capability beliefs are defined in different theoretical frameworks. In educational settings, much research conducted within the past decade has targeted kindergarten through Grade 12 populations.

### Self-Concept Theory

*Self-concept* has historically referred to a global self-view that comprises the many self-perceptions one accumulates across life experiences (Hattie, 1992; James, 1892/2001; Wylie, 1989). One's self-concept is commonly conceptualized as both hierarchical and multidimensional in nature (Marsh & Craven, 2006). An individual's self-perceptions in specific domains of learning (e.g., mathematics, language) combine to form an *academic self-concept*, which, alongside self-concepts developed in other spheres of functioning (e.g., physical, social), form the individual's overall composite self-concept (Marsh, Trautwein, Lüdtke, & Köller, 2008). In school-based research, researchers tend to measure self-concept as students' cognitive self-assessment of their scholastic ability or competence (e.g., Harter, 2012). Researchers who have assessed students' domain-specific self-concept have reported that self-concept in one domain may be unrelated to self-concept in another (Marsh et al., 2012). For example, students' perceptions about their mathematics competence may be dissimilar to their views of their reading competence.

A wealth of research on self-concept over the past three decades has targeted school-aged populations (for a comprehensive review of self-concept research in education, see Marsh et al., 2012). Domain-general measures of self-concept appear only weakly related (and sometimes unrelated) to academic performance and motivation (Baumeister, Campbell, Krueger, & Vohs, 2003; Hattie, 1992). Likewise, self-esteem, which refers to an overall feeling of one's worth as a person, is similarly unrelated to performance. When assessed at a domain-specific level, however, one's self-concept of ability is a good predictor of these same outcomes (Marsh & Craven, 2006).

In the past decade, researchers have examined two explanatory views regarding the direction of influence between academic self-concept and academic achievement. The *self-enhancement view* posits that when their self-concept is robust, learners will experience increased academic achievement. In this view, enhancing self-concept in turn increases achievement. The *skill development view*

suggests that, by building requisite skills and performance, students will develop a positive self-concept. Evidence from reciprocal effects models has shown a bidirectional pattern of influence: academic self-concept and academic achievement are mutually reinforcing (Marsh & O'Mara, 2008). The implication of this finding is that teachers and parents should attend to the development of students' academic skills and academic self-views.

### Social Cognitive Theory

From a social cognitive theoretical perspective, personal, behavioral, and environmental factors influence each other in a dynamic process of triadic reciprocality (Bandura, 1986). Personal factors include the beliefs individuals hold about what they can do, or *self-efficacy*. Self-efficacy influences and is influenced by actual performances. Bandura (1997) contended that individuals with robust beliefs of personal efficacy are more motivated, tend to engage tasks in novel ways, take more risks, and persist when they encounter challenges.

Self-efficacy is distinct from other personal capability beliefs, such as self-concept. Academic self-efficacy refers to one's perceived capability to accomplish given academic tasks and can be thought of in terms of *can do* statements (e.g., "I can solve algebraic equations with one variable"). Self-concept of ability, on the other hand, refers to a broader self-evaluation of competence within an academic domain (e.g., "Work in mathematics classes is easy for me"). Although both types of self-judgments are related to competence, they are typically assessed at different levels of specificity (Bong & Skaalvik, 2003). Self-efficacy questions reveal how confident a learner feels that she can accomplish given tasks or succeed at academic activities. Self-concept questions reveal how learners evaluate their own competence in a particular academic domain.

Students' efficacy judgments are also related to, but distinct from, their expectations about the outcomes that their actions will bring about. Outcome expectations refer to a belief that a certain outcome (whether physical, social, or self-evaluative) will result from one's actions (Bandura, 1997). The academic outcomes that students expect are largely dependent on beliefs in their personal efficacy to perform and learn the skills required to bring about those outcomes. For example, a student must earn a particular grade point average (performance) to receive an award (outcome). Because the award is directly contingent on her performance, her efficacy beliefs relative to her performance will likely be consistent with her expectations of receiving the award. As this example illustrates, self-efficacy and outcome expectations are often correlated, particularly in activities where outcomes depend directly on the quality of one's performance. Some exceptions to this pattern can be noted, however. When outcomes are not directly dependent on one's performance, such as in environments rife with prejudice or bias, efficacy beliefs and outcome expectations may operate independently (Bandura, 1997). If a student faces a prejudiced or oppressive teacher, he may not expect a favorable outcome, even if he believes himself academically capable. A student with high self-efficacy for physics may nevertheless hold a reserved expectation about the outcome of her physics test because of her instructor's harsh grading practices. The less personal control a learner has over the outcomes of her actions, the less correlated her efficacy beliefs will be to her outcome expectations. Both self-efficacy and outcomes expectations can be important aspects of learners' motivation and performance.

The influence of personal efficacy beliefs on subsequent academic achievement has been consistently documented (for reviews, see Klassen & Usher, 2010; Pajares, 1997). Students with higher self-efficacy for particular tasks attain higher levels of success (e.g., higher scores). Self-efficacy has also been shown to influence self-regulatory processes such as goal setting and self-monitoring (Zimmerman & Cleary, 2006). Students with higher self-efficacy for self-regulation organize their work and manage their time more effectively (Klassen et al., 2009); they also report lower anxiety, higher mastery goals, and higher achievement (Usher & Pajares, 2008a). As was the case with self-concept, reciprocal effects models have shown a consistent bidirectional relationship between self-efficacy and achievement. Williams and Williams (2010) found support for a reciprocal relationship between high-school students' mathematics self-efficacy and achievement in 26 national contexts.

### Self-Determination Theory

From the perspective of self-determination theory, individuals are said to be *self-determining* (i.e., intrinsically motivated) in an activity to the extent that they are meeting three primary psychological needs: the need to feel competent, autonomous, and related to others (Deci & Ryan, 1985). The need for competence, or having the skills necessary to succeed in a given pursuit, is considered a partial source of intrinsic motivation. Students feel a sense of competence when they master their environment. They feel a sense of autonomy when they fully endorse or get behind their own actions. To become intrinsically motivated, "people must not only experience perceived competence (or self-efficacy), they must also experience their behavior to be self-determined" or "accompanied by a sense of autonomy" (Ryan & Deci, 2000, p. 58). In this respect, self-determination theory, like social cognitive theory, emphasizes the importance of students' need for a sense of competence and control in learning activities.

The bulk of the research conducted within the self-determination framework and applied to educational settings has focused on the degree to which students feel and are permitted to be autonomous in the learning process (see Reeve, 2004). However, some scholars have included some measure of perceived competence. For example, De Naeghel, Van Keer, Vansteenkiste, and Rosseel (2012) examined the influence of autonomous motivation, controlled motivation, and self-concept on elementary-school students' engagement, frequency, and comprehension in reading. Reading self-concept was related to all three reading outcomes; autonomous motivation was only related to reading frequency. Similarly, competence beliefs, relatedness, and perceived autonomy were all three related to changes in early adolescents' behavioral

and emotional engagement and disaffection (Skinner, Furrer, Marchand, & Kindermann, 2008).

### Expectancy-Value Theory

Expectancy-value theory posits that academic motivation is the result of learners' expectations of success and the degree to which they value academic activities. *Expectancy* refers to a learner's belief that he or she will do well on a given academic task in the future. *Value* offers information about why a learner engages in an activity (e.g., intrinsic value, attainment value, utility value, perceived cost; see Chapter 7, this volume, for a more detailed description of the value component of this theory). The theory holds that students' expectancy beliefs and the degree to which they value achievement-related tasks are related to school performance, academic choices, and persistence (Eccles & Wigfield, 2002). Unlike the expectancy-value theoretical frameworks put forth by earlier scholars, contemporary expectancy-value frameworks, based largely on research conducted in diverse school settings, offer a broader perspective and emphasize how the social and cultural environment influences the development of students' motivation (Wigfield, Tonks, & Klauda, 2009). Rather than focusing narrowly on whether a student expects to perform successfully, this broader view defines expectancy in terms of students' beliefs about how well they will perform on academic tasks. These beliefs are conceptually distinct from students' competence or ability beliefs, which refer to judgments of one's current ability (Wigfield & Eccles, 2002). Both expectancies and ability beliefs jointly contribute to student motivation and learning. Evidence from research across a variety of academic domains has shown that students who hold higher expectations for success and more positive ability beliefs experience more school success and show greater persistence for academic tasks (Wigfield et al., 2009).

A sizeable body of research within the expectancy-value framework has been devoted to understanding how students' subject-specific ability beliefs and values develop and change throughout childhood and adolescence (e.g., Fredricks & Eccles, 2002; Gniewosz, Eccles, & Noack, 2012; Jacobs, Lanza, Osgood, Eccles, & Wigfield, 2002). Findings generally show that students report lower self-concepts of ability as they progress through school, particularly during school transitions (e.g., elementary to middle school). Eccles and colleagues have suggested that systematic differences in school- and classroom-level structures, such as an increasing orientation toward performance and relative ability in secondary schools, are at odds with the developmental needs of learners. However, the relationship between ability beliefs and performance outcomes grows stronger as students move from the elementary- to middle-school years, indicating that greater attention should be paid to constructing learning environments that match the developmental needs of students whose beliefs are still nascent (see Eccles & Roeser, 2011).

### Implicit Theory of Intelligence

Researchers have contended that the view of intelligence that students hold—whether as a fixed trait or an incremental quantity that can change with effort—influences how they approach their academic work and respond to setbacks. This mindset has been referred to as a learner's *implicit theory of intelligence* (Dweck, 2006). Students are typically asked to respond to general statements about their intelligence (e.g., "You have a certain amount of intelligence, and you really can't do much to change it"; Dweck, 1999). Beliefs about the fixed or malleable nature of intelligence are then compared with students' motivation and academic outcomes. Blackwell, Trzesniewski, and Dweck (2007) found that students who held an incremental theory of intelligence (i.e., that one's intelligence can improve with effort) at the beginning of junior high school reported more positive motivation beliefs (e.g., a learning goal orientation, belief that effort was necessary for improvement) and achieved higher scores in mathematics two years later than did students who held a more fixed view.

Assessing one's implicit theory of intelligence in a domain-general manner may not evoke the same psychological response as assessing one's domain-specific views of ability. For example, a learner may view her overall intelligence as relatively fixed but believe herself capable of improving as a writer. Few researchers have investigated implicit theories of ability in different academic domains. For example, Chen and Usher (2013) found that adolescents who held a more malleable view of science ability were more likely to draw from multiple sources of information when forming their science self-efficacy than were students who viewed science ability as fixed. These and other studies suggest that one's implicit theories of ability and intelligence may be considered as framing belief systems that influence how learners attend to and select information, experience phenomena, and come to understand themselves (e.g., Mangels, Butterfield, Lamb, Good, & Dweck, 2006).

### Personal Capability Beliefs Related to Self-Regulation

Researchers have increasingly noted the importance of the underlying self-regulatory skillset that guides the learning process in different areas. To be successful, students must plan, organize, implement study strategies, manage their time, set goals, and monitor their progress. Just as students form beliefs about their capabilities to meet subject-area objectives (e.g., to understand the symbolism in a Hemingway novel), they also develop beliefs about their self-regulatory capabilities (e.g., to maintain focus while reading Hemingway). Knowledge alone does not ensure that a learner puts skills to effective use; learners must also possess a belief in their capability to use self-regulatory skills effectively (Zimmerman, 2011; Zimmerman & Cleary, 2006).

Just as they form beliefs about their academic competencies, learners hold beliefs about their capability to use appropriate self-regulatory strategies and to exercise self-control (Schunk & Usher, 2011). Students' self-efficacy for self-regulated learning has been shown to predict academic motivation, achievement, successful strategy use, and school completion (Caprara et al., 2008; Usher & Pajares, 2008a). For example,

junior high-school students who reported higher self-efficacy for self-regulated learning earned higher achievement scores, even when prior achievement, gender, socioeconomic status, personality, and intelligence—covariates that have been shown to be closely related to achievement—were controlled (Zuffiano et al., 2013). Students who believed themselves capable of regulating their academic work also achieved more academically. Researchers who have investigated students' actual self-disciplined behavior have similarly found that more disciplined students reap an achievement advantage at school, and that girls are more self-disciplined than boys (Duckworth & Seligman, 2006). Linking personal capability beliefs about self-regulation to actual self-regulatory behavior (e.g., third-person reports of self-regulation, -control, -discipline, grit; see Duckworth & Kern, 2011) could shed light on the benefit of such beliefs.

### Relationship Between Personal Capability Beliefs and Other Outcomes

In numerous studies involving tens of thousands of students of different ages, researchers have shown that the beliefs students hold about their own capabilities (i.e., academic self-concept, self-efficacy, perceived competence) predict student achievement on numerous measures of academic competence ranging from standardized tests, school-assigned grades, subject-area tests, and other school assignments (e.g., Klassen & Usher, 2010; Marsh & Craven, 2006). Personal capability beliefs often remain predictive of achievement even when past achievement is controlled, which attests to the powerful influence of beliefs on future performances. Students who doubt their academic capabilities perform less well at school and are at greater risk for academic difficulty.

Personal capability beliefs have also been shown to predict choice behavior such as course selection, field of study in high school or college, and career choice. Data from a large-scale longitudinal study that followed students from 805 high schools in England and Germany showed that high-school students' self-concept of ability in mathematics and English was related to their university entry and choice of university major (Parker et al., 2012). Students with higher mathematics self-concept were more likely to pursue mathematics study, whereas those with higher self-concept in English were more likely to enter more verbal majors such as humanities. Meta-analysis results from 45 studies conducted primarily with college students have similarly shown that the influence of environmental supports and barriers on students' career goals depend in part on students' level of self-efficacy (Sheu et al., 2010). Students with higher self-efficacy in a given domain also report higher outcome expectations and greater interest in their domain-related career goals.

Learners' cognitive and metacognitive experiences are also influenced by their beliefs about their own capabilities. Those with a high sense of personal efficacy foresee their own success. They rehearse successful scenarios and anticipate favorable outcomes (Bandura, 1997). These rehearsals make students more likely to implement successful strategies during their academic performances (Zimmerman, 2011).

Students who believe in their academic capabilities are more likely to handle setbacks and challenges effectively. They report pursuing their academic activities to improve their own skills and learning. Conversely, learners beset with self-doubt are more likely to engage in self-handicapping strategies such as procrastination (Klassen et al., 2009). They dwell on the possibility of their own failure and imagine worst-case scenarios. They employ preventive strategies to avoid appearing incompetent (Usher & Pajares, 2008a).

Capability beliefs, which are cognitive judgments, can affect and be affected by learners' emotion and motivation (see Chapters 6 and 7). For example, Wolters, Fan, and Daugherty (2013) found that learners who are sure of their own capabilities make attributions that uphold those beliefs. They attribute their success to their own ability rather than to their effort; they tend to attribute failure to internal, unstable causes such as insufficient effort. On the other hand, a self-doubting student attributes failure to stable causes such as poor ability (Dweck, 2006). Adolescents who tend to engage in work for learning and content mastery also report higher self-efficacy (Pajares, Britner, & Valiante, 2000). Those who try to avoid looking incompetent tend to doubt what they can do, and in turn undermine their own potential for success. Low self-efficacy is associated with a host of negative emotions, including stress and depression (Bandura, 1997). Emotions related to achieving are linked to learners' competence perceptions and their sense of control in determining their academic outcomes; a high sense of perceived efficacy and control brings about joy and hope; a low sense of efficacy and control is often accompanied by anxiety or hopelessness (Pekrun, 2006).

## Development of Personal Capability Beliefs

A lifetime of experience interacting with one's environment and one's own inner stirrings offer a wealth of information about one's present and future competencies (Bandura, 1997; Wigfield & Eccles, 2002). Experience is filtered through multiple frames of reference—both internal and external—that channel learners' interpretations of the events that happen to them (Marsh et al., 2012). The learning context provides an important and often influential backdrop for capability beliefs to be examined and modified.

### Enactive Experience

Direct, or *enactive*, experience of success or failure can have a profound influence on a young learner's self-view. Seeing oneself overcome extreme odds can fundamentally alter one's sense of efficacy; repeated failures can reinforce a sense of inadequacy and self-doubt (Bandura, 1997). Learners evaluate their performances in relation to others or to the internal or external expectations set for and by them. Completing 75% of a test correctly may be a roaring success for a certain student in a certain context and an utter devastation to another. One's own performances are typically a strong source of one's perceived capability. In general, perceived mastery experiences have been shown to outweigh other types of information when

predicting students' efficacy beliefs (Usher & Pajares, 2008b). However, this is not the case for all students and likely varies according to situational factors.

### Social Comparison and Modeling

Another means by which learners assess their own capabilities is social comparison. Students revise their academic self-concept in terms of how their own accomplishments compare to those of their peers (Schunk, 1987). Two students with the same record of academic accomplishment may develop different conceptions about their capability according to the social standards by which they evaluate their own performances (Marsh et al., 2008). Researchers have shown that a student's academic self-concept depends not only on personal accomplishment but also on the accomplishments of others in the student's nearby environment (e.g., classroom, program of study, or school). Being a "big fish in a little pond," that is, achieving higher than one's lower-ability classmates, raises one's academic self-concept (Marsh et al., 2008). On the other hand, being surrounded by "big fish"—high-achieving classmates—has been shown to lower students' academic self-concept. Even when students are themselves high achievers, if the average ability level of their class or school is high, their academic self-concept tends to suffer. Students also revise their beliefs about what they can do as they see others accomplish similar tasks. For example, female engineers reported that they became convinced of their own efficacy for engineering by watching close family members who were engineers (Zeldin, Britner, & Pajares, 2008).

### Social Messages

The messages students receive from others also influence how they will come to view their own capabilities. Bandura (1997) noted that "it is more difficult to instill enduringly high beliefs of personal efficacy by persuasory means alone than it is to undermine such beliefs" (p. 104). Harsh evaluations of one's capabilities are not easily forgotten (Pajares, 2006). Researchers have found that certain types of teacher feedback (e.g., positive, specific, effort, and ability feedback) can have beneficial effects on students' beliefs in their own capabilities, depending on an individual's stage of learning and level of success (see Hattie & Timperley, 2007, for a review). The differential effects of evaluative feedback from others can be attributed to the various ways the feedback is framed, the context in which it is provided, characteristics of the evaluator, the developmental stage of the learner, and how the messenger is perceived by the recipient (Bandura, 1997). Some researchers have investigated the relative influence of effort feedback versus ability feedback on student outcomes. Dweck and her colleagues have reported that effort feedback (e.g., "You worked hard on that problem") is more effective than ability feedback (e.g., "You're very good at this") for improving students' persistence, enjoyment, and performance, particularly when students experience failure or setback (see Dweck, 2006). However, Schunk (1984) found that providing students with ability feedback led to greater gains in efficacy beliefs and performance than did providing effort feedback. Even so, feedback that emphasizes ability may be detrimental to self-efficacy when learners encounter difficulty, even if it does boost self-efficacy when learning is relatively easy (Pajares, 2006).

### *Emotional and Physiological Arousal*

Individuals learn to read their own emotional and physiological states when they approach tasks as signs of what they can and cannot do. A student whose palms drip with sweat as he stands before his classmates to deliver a speech might interpret his physiological state as a sure sign that he cannot possibly perform well. Another student may step before the class and interpret his rush of excitement as an indicator that he can ace his delivery. Researchers have consistently found that students who experience high levels of anxiety in mathematics, science, writing, and general academics report lower self-efficacy in these same areas (Usher & Pajares, 2008b). The influence of learners' emotion is covered in greater depth in Chapter 6 of this volume.

### *Use of Capability-Related Information*

Assessing the influence of any source of capability-related information requires attention to a number of factors. First, experiences become influential only when cognitively processed. An external observer may view a student's creative essay as a written work of art, but unless the student interprets the work as a success, his beliefs in his writing capability might not improve. Second, students integrate information across multiple sources when forming their capability beliefs (Bandura, 1997). Some research evidence has suggested that the combined and individual influence of these sources of information varies as a function of developmental and contextual differences (see Usher & Pajares, 2008b, for a review). For instance, Spinath and Spinath (2005) found that, as students progressed through elementary school, their ability perceptions were better explained by their teachers' evaluations of them than by their parents'. Girls may be more attentive to information transmitted socially (e.g., messages from others, exposure to social models) than are boys (Usher & Pajares, 2006). Learners from different cultural backgrounds may also attend to ability-related information differently. For example, middle-school students who have been historically marginalized by the cultures in which they learn were more attuned to social messages than were those from privileged cultural backgrounds (Usher, 2009). High-school students whose outlook on ability was more malleable interpreted their experiences in unique ways from those who viewed ability as primarily unchangeable (Chen & Usher, 2013). Capability beliefs might even be partly explained by genetic factors. In an investigation of 3,785 pairs of twins, researchers found that considerable variation in self-perceived abilities could be explained by heritable factors (Greven, Harlaar, Kovas, Chamorro-Premuzic, & Plomin, 2009).

### *Developmental Trajectories*

A number of longitudinal investigations have shed light on how students' personal capability beliefs develop and change over the course of schooling. As noted previously, research shows that academic self-concept declines as students progress through school (e.g., Archambault, Eccles, & Vida, 2010; Wigfield, Eccles, & Rodriguez, 1998). Self-efficacy for self-regulated learning has also been shown to decline as students transition from junior to senior high school (Caprara et al., 2008). Conversely, students with more stable efficacy beliefs earn higher school grades and are more likely to remain in school.

Belief patterns over time vary according to context (e.g., age, domain, ability level, gender). Some researchers have reported a curvilinear pattern in self-efficacy change in the upper-elementary grades such that academic self-efficacy declines between Grades 3 and 4 and increases at the end of primary school in Grades 5 and 6 (Hornstra, Van der Veen, Peetsma, & Volman, 2013). Jacobs et al. (2002) found that patterns in students' competence beliefs across Grades 1 to 12 differed as a function of academic domain. Whereas students' language arts competence beliefs declined during elementary school, these beliefs stabilized as students completed high school. In mathematics and sports, however, students' competence beliefs declined steadily over time. Watt (2004) found that adolescent boys' perceptions of their talent in English remained stable from middle school to high school, but girls' talent perceptions declined. In the studies of both Jacobs et al. and Watt, boys and girls reported lower talent perceptions in mathematics over time.

Despite the fact that longitudinal investigations show considerable individual differences in self-belief trajectories (e.g., Hornstra et al., 2013), most trajectories still show a decline (Archambault et al., 2010). The general decline in students' capability perceptions over time has been attributed to a number of factors, including the increasing cognitive demand of advanced academic content, change in the composition of student peer groups, and changes in schooling practices (Eccles & Roeser, 2011). When learners move from the more communal and mastery-oriented environment of elementary school to the more formal, competitive-oriented environment of middle school, they begin to shift their frame of reference to external sources. As a result of school structures that do not match the developmental needs of the learner (i.e., a poor fit between the learner's developmental stage and learning environment), many begin to doubt their own capabilities (Wigfield & Eccles, 2002).

### Group Differences in Personal Capability Beliefs

Pajares (2007) wisely cautioned that "research findings and generalizations drawn from educational psychology broadly, and motivation theory and research in particular, cannot be taken as general rules that are independent of contextual variation" (p. 19). The general findings reported above should be viewed in concert with findings from more contextualized research that has aimed at examining patterns in students' beliefs as a function of context and of group identification, such as gender, ethnicity, nationality, and economic class.

Gender differences in students' capability perceptions have been documented in numerous studies. In a recent meta-analysis of 187 studies of academic self-efficacy, Huang (2012) found that male students report slightly higher self-efficacy than do female students overall, but that the direction and magnitude of gender differences depend on the academic domain under investigation. Female students report higher self-efficacy in language arts and music, whereas male students report higher self-efficacy in mathematics, computer science, and social sciences. In their analysis of large-scale data collected in 30 countries, Williams and Williams (2010) similarly found that, when mathematics achievement is held constant, high-school girls report lower mathematics skills self-efficacy than do boys. Gender differences in self-efficacy appear to increase as students age (Huang, 2012). However, not all studies have observed this trend (e.g., Jacobs et al., 2002). Some researchers have found no gender differences in students' self-efficacy, but have shown that boys and girls report different exposure to *sources* of self-efficacy. For example, sixth-grade girls reported receiving more positive persuasory messages from others and having been exposed more often to capable models than did boys (Usher & Pajares, 2006). For girls but not for boys, social persuasions were a significant predictor of academic self-efficacy. Several explanations are possible. Girls may indeed receive (or *perceive*) more messages about their capabilities than boys. Girls may also rely more on the messages they receive when judging their own capabilities.

Some researchers have examined differences in self-beliefs among students from various ethnic groups. Students in ethnic minorities have reported stronger beliefs in their personal capabilities than other students (Hornstra et al., 2013). And yet, African American students' capability beliefs are generally equal to or greater than those of their White counterparts, even in the face of lower achievement (Graham, 1994). African American students and Indo Canadian students have also been shown to differ from European-origin students in the import they place on social messages when forming their beliefs about what they can do academically (Klassen, 2004a; and see Usher, 2009; Usher & Pajares, 2008b). Some have posited that higher self-concept and self-efficacy reported by certain ethnic-minority students may reflect an ego-protective tendency among groups that have been historically oppressed (Steele, 2010). Investigations that take a wider sociocultural approach may provide a more accurate picture of students' self-beliefs. For example, Eccles, Wong, and Peck (2006) found that the degree to which African American middle-school students perceived racial discrimination from their teachers and peers was related to a decline in students' ability self-concepts across two school years. The influence of social class has been much less examined with regard to the development of capability beliefs.

Cross-cultural research on personal capability beliefs has grown in the past two decades. Large-scale datasets have permitted cross-national comparisons of students' beliefs and the sources and outcomes of those beliefs. Research based on data from the Program for International Student Assessment (PISA), which uses nationally representative samples of 15-year-olds from dozens of countries, has shown that students who attend academically selective schools with high average achievement suffer a negative effect on their academic self-concept (Nagengast & Marsh, 2012). Self-concept has also been shown to mediate the relationship of high-school students' prior achievement and career aspirations across 34 countries. In a review of cross-cultural studies of self-efficacy, Klassen (2004b) found that non-Western cultural groups tend to report lower efficacy beliefs than do Western groups. Although self-efficacy has been shown to be a consistent predictor of achievement across cultures, self-efficacy research has primarily been conducted in culturally Western settings and with students from middle- or upper-class families (Klassen & Usher, 2010), thus more work is needed in other cultural contexts.

## Methodological Considerations

This section addresses the prominent methodological approaches that have been used to investigate personal capability beliefs and suggests ways in which beliefs might be alternatively operationalized, assessed, and modeled. Most researchers have relied on quantitative methods to investigate capability beliefs. This section describes some of the limitations of using this approach exclusively.

### *Measurement*

Personal capability beliefs are typically assessed using self-report measures with Likert-type response scales. Students evaluate the strength of their beliefs by endorsing each statement at a certain level. The content of these statements reflects conceptual distinctions of various capability-related judgments. The discriminating reader will look to the items used to assess a construct for a clear notion of what set of beliefs the items actually assess, whether items are conceptually consistent, and whether they are true to the theoretical homes from which they are purportedly derived. This is no small task. Marsh et al. (2012) pointed to the jingle fallacy that plagues self-belief research: "two scales with similar names might measure different constructs, whereas two scales with apparently dissimilar labels might measure similar constructs" (p. 432). Adding to the complication, researchers have often included self-beliefs from different theoretical traditions in the same study or in complex models (Murphy & Alexander, 2000). A review of self-efficacy research conducted between 2000 and 2009 revealed that 51% of the self-efficacy measures used were incongruent with the measurement criteria outlined by Bandura (2006; Klassen & Usher, 2010). As Wigfield et al. (2009) aptly observed, "One of the measurement challenges for researchers is matching theoretical constructs to appropriate measurement tools" (p. 59).

Because personal capability beliefs vary in scope, the items used to assess them should be carefully worded. If one intends to measure self-concept, for instance, then items should be worded differently than if one's intent is to measure self-efficacy (Bong, 2006). Measures of self-concept typically include items related to perceived competence in reference to others (e.g., "Compared to others my age I am good at math") and past performances (e.g., "I have always done well in math classes"; Marsh, 1992). Such items would not be considered measures of self-efficacy, which refers to a can-do judgment of one's capability to successfully perform or learn to do a given task (e.g., "How confident are you that you can . . . successfully divide fractions?" or " . . . learn to do complex mathematics problems?"). Self-efficacy items should also reflect varying degrees of task difficulty (see Bandura, 2006).

As noted earlier, competence beliefs refer to one's capability beliefs in an area, and control beliefs refer to one's certainty that one's actions will bring about desired outcomes. Schunk and Zimmerman (2006) pointed out that many researchers have used measures that assess both types of beliefs simultaneously. The item "I believe I can score well enough on the test to make an A" contains both a judgment of competence (scoring well enough) and of control (making an A). Measures that combine items reflecting conceptually distinct constructs mask the relative contribution of each type of belief in prediction models.

Despite their theoretical perspective, researchers who have investigated personal capability beliefs generally agree that domain-specific measures offer the best predictive utility when explaining domain-specific academic functioning (Bandura, 1997; Marsh et al., 2012). For example, meta-analysis has revealed that the strength of the relationship between academic self-concept and achievement varies as a function of the specificity of the self-concept measure (Huang, 2011). Vague or global measures of self-concept or self-efficacy, although perhaps appropriate for predicting general educational outcomes, are not useful for predicting specific outcomes. On the other hand, "judgments of competence need not be so microscopically operationalized that their assessment loses all sense of practical utility" (Pajares, 1997, p. 13). Determining the appropriate level of generality/specificity requires careful consideration of the particular aims of the research (Schunk & Pajares, 2005).

If measures to assess students' perceived capability are to predict behavioral or performance outcomes, they must correspond in content and specificity with the outcomes they are intended to predict. Lack of correspondence between belief and outcome can weaken observed effects (Bandura, 2006). The greater the correspondence, the greater will be the belief's predictive power. A middle-school teacher who wants to know whether her students' beliefs about their writing capabilities are related to their writing quality must first determine how quality will be defined given the learning objectives (e.g., Is the writing expository, descriptive, or narrative?). The teacher can then assess beliefs germane to the writing task. Researchers who wish to investigate the predictive validity of perceived capability must first seek to assess beliefs that are most relevant to the course of action and skill set that will be required of the learner. The criterion task should be the point of departure for crafting appropriate belief measures.

reported perceptions about other aspects of school, such as their interest level or academic goals, and their achievement. For instance, of 210 articles published on academic self-efficacy between 2000 and 2009, 89% used quantitative analyses to examine data (Klassen & Usher, 2010). Although most of the studies were cross-sectional and correlational in design, about one-fourth included data from more than one time point.

Investigations that invoke a temporal lag in data collection are better suited for modeling hypothesized relationships between beliefs and outcomes (Valentine, DuBois, & Cooper, 2004). Longitudinal designs permit researchers to monitor changes in students' beliefs over time and therefore offer a promising avenue for examining inter- and intraindividual changes (Schunk & Pajares, 2005). Multilevel modeling techniques can help researchers parse out the variance in self-beliefs explained by contextual factors at multiple levels (i.e., teachers, classrooms, schools). For example, Joët, Usher, and Bressoux (2011) found that variation in children's academic self-efficacy was partly explained by the average self-efficacy level of students in a student's class.

Personal capability beliefs have historically been investigated from a variable-centered perspective, which investigates how specific variables predict the academic outcomes of most or all students. Some educational psychologists have advocated for a person-centered approach, which accounts for the unique and complex psychological processes that shape individual patterns of belief and action (Snyder & Linnenbrink-Garcia, 2013). For example, using latent profile analysis, Chen and Usher (2013) found that individual high-school students relied on different combinations of efficacy-relevant information when forming their beliefs about their science capabilities. Modeling the hypothesized sources of self-efficacy in this way enabled the researchers to examine not only the additive effects that traditional measures such as multiple linear regression can model, but combinatory effects as well. Similarly, a person-centered analysis revealed a more nuanced picture of the relationship among self-efficacy, interest, gender, and high-school students' conceptual change than would have been obtained from a variable-centered approach (Linnenbrink-Garcia, Pugh, Koskey, & Stewart, 2012).

Theoretical questions must guide method. Including a measure of perceived capability in a complex model of academic motivation without providing a rationale risks obscuring what is known about how those beliefs function. The utility of testing complex analytic models should be weighed against their potential benefit to theory and practice. Qualitative methods, such as interviews, open-ended response techniques, and thought-listing procedures, can permit researchers to gain an in-depth picture of how learners' beliefs develop and operate (Usher, 2009). Mobile technologies can also permit investigators to obtain moment-to-moment glimpses of how learners' beliefs function in everyday settings.

### Design and Analysis

Students' capability perceptions are typically collected via a survey or questionnaire and examined in relation to students'

### Directions for Future Research

Pursuing new avenues of research can help elucidate the role of personal capability beliefs in academic functioning and human development. As has been shown, the fact that capability beliefs serve as guides for behavior is well documented. Perhaps the field would be served by research that can clarify *how* and *under what conditions* learners come to form and alter their beliefs and how those beliefs *change in magnitude and influence* over time. Researchers have pointed to the need for additional investigations on the sources of capability beliefs such as self-efficacy (Usher & Pajares, 2008b). Most investigations have focused on experiences that build perceived competence (e.g., successful performances, positive evaluative messages, exposure to competent models). Investigating the experiences that undermine self-efficacy might provide a more complete picture of how some students become convinced of their inefficacy. Such investigations could include measures that reflect failure experiences (e.g., "I have performed poorly on mathematics tests") or could target learners who have been identified as at risk for academic failure.

Researchers should also consider influences beyond those typically examined. For example, how might the availability of assistance or the method of content delivery affect students' beliefs? How might autonomy-supportive or restrictive environments affect them? Investigating whether students tend to rely on the same or different sources of capability-related information (e.g., social messages, exposure to models) over time and across contexts would also prove informative. Some experiences or accomplishments might be considered transformative such that they affect perceived ability in other areas. For example, might athletic accomplishment transfer to the academic realm? Might an intense experience such as a study-abroad course or an outdoors education retreat offer transformative personal insights that change one's perspective and perceived capabilities? These questions point to how individuals construe their experiences. Formulas, heuristics, biases—the lens through which individuals interpret what happens to them—are central to how experiences shape beliefs. Following corrective feedback from the teacher, one student finds himself amidst a catastrophe, another shrugs it off without a second thought, and a third rallies to the challenge by changing his approach. Research should investigate the ways in which students frame their academic experiences (and perhaps their lives) and in turn alter their capability perceptions.

Intervention studies permit researchers to test the mechanisms by which capability beliefs change. Most intervention studies in education have been aimed at assessing the influence of instructional, programmatic, or curricular changes on specific learning objectives such as skill development and achievement. The effectiveness of innovative teaching approaches or novel curricula can be evaluated not only in terms of learning and behavioral outcomes but also in terms of changes in learners' perceived capabilities. The inclusion of perceived capability measures would enable researchers to view whether school-based changes have corresponding psychological effects (see Cleary, 2009).

Other interventions directly target students' motivation and capability beliefs (see Wentzel & Wigfield, 2007, and Chapter 12, this volume). Such interventions are becoming more common and hold promise for demonstrating how learners view themselves and their capabilities under varying conditions. Experimental designs are particularly useful. For example, Blackwell et al. (2007) randomly assigned some middle-school students to attend an 8-week workshop that emphasized brain growth as a result of persistence on challenging problems. Others in a control group attended a study skills workshop. Students who received the intervention not only reported more malleable views of intelligence but also earned higher mathematics grades than students in the control group.

Short-term interventions that require low-cost participatory involvement from students may be effective at bringing about lasting attitudinal and behavioral change (Yeager & Walton, 2011). An example comes from a burgeoning area of research on mindfulness, which suggests that individuals who engage in contemplative practices such as meditation or mindful movement show improvements in their emotion regulation, cognition, attention, motivation, and self-representation (Davidson et al., 2012). Engaging in contemplative practice might lead to changes in a learner's self-construal. Through the cultivation of awareness, learners practice volitional ways of thinking about, experiencing, and making sense of their experiences (Roeser & Peck, 2009). These practices differ from automatic ways of processing information and may offer "numerous opportunities for the development of new ways of understanding oneself and one's attempts to learn and be resilient during the process of learning" (Roeser & Peck, 2009, p. 129; see Chapter 8, this volume). Using an experimental intervention design, researchers can address whether brief classroom-based contemplative practices influence learners' beliefs about their academic and self-regulatory capabilities (Greenberg & Harris, 2012). Researchers who wish to implement such motivation interventions in schools still face many challenges, however, such as remaining true to an intervention's theoretical underpinnings, ensuring systematic delivery in school settings that are much "noisier" than laboratories, and maintaining sensitivity to diverse needs.

Novel methodological approaches might shed light on how contextual factors influence students' beliefs. Observational measures are useful for assessing classroom practices and can be examined in correlation with students' beliefs in different learning contexts. For example, capability beliefs might be formed in distinct ways in various classroom configurations: competitive or cooperative, teacher- or student-centered, or technology-heavy (e.g., one device per student) vs. technology-light (few or no digital devices). Similar methods can be used to show the relationship between teacher-level variables (e.g., teacher self-efficacy, teacher competence, pedagogical approach, teacher background) and student beliefs. What teacher practices lead to positive changes in personal capability beliefs? What practices undermine students' self-perceptions? Multilevel models can allow researchers to parse out variation in self-beliefs due to teachers, classrooms, or schools. Using results obtained from sophisticated quantitative analyses to select participants for targeted follow-up interviews could create a rich description of how beliefs develop in different contexts. Qualitative inquiry would enable researchers to explore the complex ways in which particular students make sense of their environment and experience.

Research designs should take into account not only the immediate but also the long-term consequences of the beliefs students hold about their own capabilities. Although the bulk of the longitudinal research on self-perceived capabilities has examined self-concept, additional work is needed to show how other beliefs evolve as students progress through school. What factors are associated with increasing or decreasing self-beliefs over time? Are growth trajectories similar for boys and girls or for students of different socioeconomic backgrounds, for instance? As noted earlier, most studies of students' self-efficacy have been correlational and cross-sectional in nature. More evidence of the causal relationship between self-efficacy and various outcomes is also needed and will require that data be temporally spaced.

The bulk of the research on personal capability beliefs has been conducted in the area of mathematics. Less is known about how learners' beliefs develop and are related to outcomes in other academic disciplines. For example, social studies, civics, music, art, engineering, history, science, and language learning have seen less research in this area and warrant further exploration. Researchers could also compare sources and effects of personal capability beliefs across disciplinary contexts. Such efforts might also address the extent to which personal capability beliefs generalize from one domain to another.

Advancing digital technologies have placed personalized content at one's fingertips and brought remote social environments into one's own home. People can now select their social environments in unprecedented ways. Some evidence has shown that personal capability beliefs (i.e., self-efficacy) influence learning outcomes in computer-based learning environments (Moos & Azevedo, 2009). More research is needed to examine how personal capability beliefs affect and are affected by different virtual environments. Because educational units have relied increasingly on technologies to deliver content, researchers should examine learners' technology-related competence beliefs and how they develop and function. How do beliefs influence technology adoption and implementation? How do they affect learning? One can only imagine how students who doubt their capabilities with technology might fare in high-tech learning environments. The ubiquity of technology also places a higher demand on learners to regulate their own activities. Those with high self-efficacy for self-regulated learning may benefit from technology-rich learning modalities; those who do not believe themselves capable of modulating electronic distraction may not fare as well (Schunk & Usher, 2011). Learners likely vary in their perceptions about how well they can regulate their use of and exposure to social and academic technologies; what might these variations predict?

Despite the assumption made at the start of this chapter that beliefs are rules for action, in some cases, beliefs and actions are misaligned. Consider the question, "What shall we do with overconfident students?" Albert Bandura said in an American Psychological Association address in 1998

that, "One cannot afford to be a realist." By this he meant that beliefs that slightly exceed one's ability may in fact provide the incentive for one to take a risk, and eventually, to grow. But this is a fair question, particularly at a time when comedy sketches poke fun at a society that tells kids, "You can do anything!" Although most students' perceived capabilities are linearly related to their achievement, there are those individuals for whom a large discrepancy between the two exists. These are so-called "poorly calibrated" students, whose beliefs do not correspond with their actions, and they may be at considerable academic risk. Overconfidence can lead to complacency when remedial action is needed (Zimmerman, 2011). Underconfidence might put students at even greater risk; otherwise able students who are beset by self-doubt shortchange themselves and squander their own potential. Although researchers have addressed this conceptually (e.g., Pajares, 2006), few have empirically examined poor calibration between self-perceived capability and actual skill (see Alexander, 2013). A first step is to determine how best to identify poorly calibrated students. A host of research questions can then be addressed. For instance, are certain students more likely to overestimate or underestimate what they can do? Do these students use unique approaches for making sense of capability-related information? Identifying those with poor calibration between beliefs and outcome might become a useful diagnostic tool for targeted interventions.

Last but not least, researchers should seek to expand the cultural contexts in which personal capability beliefs are examined (Pajares, 2007). An overwhelming number of studies in social and educational psychology have been conducted in so-called "WEIRD" (Western, educated, industrialized, rich, and democratic) societies (Henrich, Heine, & Norenzayan, 2010). Cross-national comparative research offers excellent information, but most has focused on high-school students. Less is known about how younger students, particularly those in elementary school, develop their self-beliefs. Research documenting the psychological landscape of students living in poverty or in rural settings is also scarce, as is research in urban areas and in schools predominantly attended by students from historically marginalized ethnic groups.

### Conclusion and Implications

In 2006, an internet search generated over half a million web pages for the term "self-efficacy" (Pajares, 2006). At the time of this chapter's writing, a Google search generated 9.6 million results; "self-concept of ability" generated 28.2 million. It would seem that interest in self-beliefs has grown by leaps and bounds. Several pertinent implications are worth emphasis in closing. First, beliefs related to one's academic capabilities must be developed and nurtured *in conjunction with* the development of academic skills. Attempts at ego or self-esteem boosting will have short-lived and perhaps even harmful results (see Baumeister et al., 2003). Inviting learners to experience failure as a normal part of growth can help ground their beliefs on their own perseverant accomplishments. Second, most students live in a culture where rewards and recognition programs, ability grouping, and other overt (and covert) means of publicizing ability-related information are readily available. Such information can shake students' beliefs in their own capabilities (Pajares, 2006). As noted above, researchers have shown that self-concept suffers when students perceive that they are surrounded by more capable peers. One way of addressing this is by changing school structures and systems. However, investigating dispositions within the individual that might mitigate the potentially harmful effects of social comparative information would be also useful. Teachers and parents can also help convey the message that the pond is big enough for all fish to thrive. Third, teachers should monitor and attend to students' changing self-beliefs and their association with changing learning structures. To do this will require the cultivation of compassionate awareness so that teachers can "be totally and nonselectively present to the student—to each student" (Noddings, 1984, p. 180). Teachers must also critically examine school structures that, though mainstream and longstanding, may be unsupportive of or detrimental to students' developing self-conceptions. Calming the busyness and stress that interfere with the capacity for openness and awareness will enable practitioners to attend to how students interpret their own experiences and feelings and alter their self-beliefs.

It seems fair to assume that most parents want their children to develop a healthy self-view. Nothing facilitates this more than unconditional love and positive regard. These support the child's natural development into a being unique to the world. As young people grow and ego develops, they naturally begin to look to external sources for validation. But this hardly marks the end of the road to so-called self-knowledge. The way of knowing oneself is not permanent but evolving. This evolution might be toward understanding that which James (1892/2001) called the *I*, a Knower whose vantage point transcends the external and habitual ways in which we come to know ourselves. What would happen to the Self if the individual suspended or dropped the ego involvement of the many *Me*s (i.e., social, material) that receive so much attention? What then would be the role of external sources in changing self-beliefs? Would a Self continue to exist? Japanese Zen Master Dogen once wrote, "To study the Way is to study the self. To study the self is to forget the self. To forget the self is to be enlightened by all things" (Kim, 2004, p. xxiv). Perhaps beyond self-concepts lies a Knower who understands that our fullest capabilities are yet to be found. This knowledge gives beliefs their motivating power. Perhaps, then, the best advice parents and teachers can give learners is what Christopher Robin shared with Pooh (Geurs, 1997): "Promise me you'll always remember: You're braver than you believe, and stronger than you seem, and smarter than you think."

# References

Alexander, P. A. (2013). Calibration: What is it and why it matters? An introduction to the special issue on calibrating calibration. *Learning and Instruction, 24*, 1–3.

Archambault, I., Eccles, J. S., & Vida, M. N. (2010). Ability self-concepts and subjective value in literacy: Joint trajectories from grades 1 through 12. *Journal of Educational Psychology, 102*, 804–816.

Bandura, A. (1986). *Social foundations of thought and action: A social cognitive theory*. Englewood Cliffs, NJ: Prentice Hall.

Bandura, A. (1997). *Self-efficacy: The exercise of control*. New York: Freeman.

Bandura, A. (1998). *Exercise of agency in accenting the positive*. Invited address delivered at the meeting of the American Psychological Association, San Francisco.

Bandura, A. (2006). Guide for constructing self-efficacy scales. In F. Pajares & T. Urdan (Eds.), *Adolescence and education, Vol. 5: Self-efficacy and adolescence* (pp. 307–337). Greenwich, CT: Information Age Publishing.

Baumeister, R. F., Campbell, J. D., Krueger, J. I., & Vohs, K. D. (2003). Does high self-esteem cause better performance, interpersonal success, happiness, or healthier lifestyles? *Psychological Science in the Public Interest, 4*, 1–44.

Blackwell, L. S., Trzesniewski, K. H., & Dweck, C. S. (2007). Implicit theories of intelligence predict achievement across an adolescent transition: A longitudinal study and an intervention. *Child Development, 78*, 246–263.

Bong, M. (2006). Asking the right question: How confident are you that you could successfully perform these tasks? In F. Pajares & T. C. Urdan (Eds.), *Adolescence and education: Vol. 5. Self-efficacy beliefs of adolescents* (pp. 287–305). Greenwich, CT: Information Age.

Bong, M., & Skaalvik, E. M. (2003). Academic self-concept and self-efficacy: How different are they really? *Educational Psychology Review, 15*, 1–40.

Caprara, G. V., Fida, R., Vecchione, M., Del Bove, G., Vecchio, G. M., Barbaranelli, C., & Bandura, A. (2008). Longitudinal analysis of the role of perceived self-efficacy for self-regulated learning in academic continuance and achievement. *Journal of Educational Psychology, 100*(3), 525–534.

Chen, J. A., & Usher, E. L. (2013). Profiles of the sources of science self-efficacy. *Learning and Individual Differences, 24*, 11–21.

Cleary, T. J. (2009). Monitoring trends and accuracy of self-efficacy beliefs during interventions: Advantages and potential applications to school-based settings. *Psychology in the Schools, 46*(2), 154–171.

Davidson, R. J., Dunne, J., Eccles, J. S., Engle, A., Greenberg, M., Jennings, P., . . . & Vago, D. (2012). Contemplative practices and mental training: Prospects for American education. *Child Development Perspectives, 6*, 146–153.

Deci, E. L., & Ryan, R. M. (1985). *Intrinsic motivation and self-determination in human behavior*. New York: Plenum.

De Naeghel, J., Van Keer, H., Vansteenkiste, M., & Rosseel, Y. (2012). The relation between elementary students' recreational and academic reading motivation, reading frequency, engagement, and comprehension: A self-determination theory perspective. *Journal of Educational Psychology, 104*(4), 1006–1021.

Dewey, J. (1933). *How we think*. Boston: D. C. Heath.

Duckworth, A. L., & Kern, M. L. (2011). A meta-analysis of the convergent validity of self-control measures. *Journal of Research in Personality, 35*, 259–268.

Duckworth, A. L., & Seligman, M. E. P. (2006). Self-discipline gives girls the edge: Gender in self-discipline, grades, and achievement test scores. *Journal of Educational Psychology, 98*, 198–208.

Dweck, C. S. (1999). *Self-theories: Their role in motivation, personality, and development*. Philadelphia, PA: Taylor and Francis.

Dweck, C. S. (2006). *Mindset*. New York: Random House.

Eccles, J. S., & Roeser, R. W. (2011). Schools as developmental contexts during adolescence. *Journal of Research on Adolescence, 21*, 225–241.

Eccles, J. S., & Wigfield, A. (2002). Motivational beliefs, values, and goals. *Annual Review of Psychology, 53*, 109–132.

Eccles, J. S., Wong, C. A., & Peck, S. C. (2006). Ethnicity as a social context for the development of African American adolescents. *Journal of School Psychology, 44*(5), 407–426.

Fredricks, J., & Eccles, J. S. (2002). Children's competence and value beliefs from childhood through adolescence: Growth trajectories in two male-sex-typed domains. *Developmental Psychology, 38*, 519–533.

Geurs, K. (Producer and Director). (1997). *Pooh's grand adventure: The search for Christopher Robin* [Motion picture]. USA: Walt Disney Television Animation.

Gniewosz, B., Eccles, J. S., & Noack, P. (2012). Secondary school transition and the use of different sources of information for the construction of the academic self-concept. *Social Development, 21*(3), 537–557.

Graham, S. (1994). Motivation in African Americans. *Review of Educational Research, 64*, 55–118.

Graham, S., & Weiner, B. (1996). Theories and principles of motivation. In D. C. Berliner & R. C. Calfee (Eds.), *Handbook of educational psychology* (pp. 63–84). New York: Simon & Schuster Macmillan.

Greenberg, M. T., & Harris, A. R. (2012). Nurturing mindfulness in children and youth: Current state of research. *Child Development Perspectives, 6*(2), 161–166.

Greven, C. U., Harlaar, N., Kovas, Y., Chamorro-Premuzic, T., & Plomin, R. (2009). More than just IQ: School achievement is predicted by self-perceived abilities—but for genetic rather than environmental reasons. *Psychological Science, 20*(6), 753–762.

Harter, S. (2012). *The construction of the self: Developmental and sociocultural foundations* (2nd ed.). New York: The Guilford Press.

Hattie, J. (1992). *Self-concept*. Hillsdale, NJ: Lawrence Erlbaum.

Hattie, J., & Timperley, H. (2007). The power of feedback. *Review of Educational Research, 77*, 81–112.

Henrich, J., Heine, S. J., & Norenzayan, A. (2010). The weirdest people in the world? *The Behavioral and Brain Sciences, 33*(2–3), 61–83.

Hornstra, L., Van der Veen, I., Peetsma, T., & Volman, M. (2013). Developments in motivation and achievement during primary school: A longitudinal study on group-specific differences. *Learning and Individual Differences, 23*, 195–204.

Huang, C. J. (2011). Self-concept and academic achievement: A meta-analysis of longitudinal relations. *Journal of School Psychology, 49*(5), 505–528.

Huang, C. (2012). Gender differences in academic self-efficacy: A meta-analysis. *European Journal of Psychology of Education, 28*(1), 1–35.

Jacobs, J. E., Lanza, S., Osgood, D. W., Eccles, J. S., & Wigfield, A. (2002). Changes in children's self-competence and values: Gender and domain differences across grades one through twelve. *Child Development, 73*, 509–527.

James, W. (1892/2001). *Psychology: The briefer course*. New York: Dover.

Joët, G., Usher, E. L., & Bressoux, P. (2011). Sources of self-efficacy: An investigation of elementary school students in France. *Journal of Educational Psychology, 103*(3), 649–663.

Kim, H.-J. (2004). *Eihei Dōgen: Mystical realist*. Somerville, MA: Wisdom Publications.

Klassen, R. (2004a). A cross-cultural investigation of the efficacy beliefs of South Asian immigrant and Anglo non-immigrant early adolescents. *Journal of Educational Psychology. 96*, 731–742.

Klassen, R. M. (2004b). Optimism and realism: A review of self-efficacy from a cross-cultural perspective. *International Journal of Psychology, 39*, 205–230.

Klassen, R. M., Ang, R., Chong, W. H., Krawchuk, L. L., Huan, V., Wong, I., & Yeo, L. S. (2009). A cross-cultural study of adolescent procrastination. *Journal of Research on Adolescence, 19*, 799–811.

Klassen, R. M., & Usher, E. L. (2010). Self-efficacy in educational settings: Recent research and emerging directions. In T. C. Urdan & S. A. Karabenick (Eds.), *Advances in motivation and achievement: Vol. 16A. The decade ahead: Theoretical perspectives on motivation and achievement* (pp. 1–33). Bingley, UK: Emerald Publishing Group.

Linnenbrink-Garcia, L., Pugh, K., Koskey, K. L. K., & Stewart, V. (2012). Developing conceptual understanding of natural selection: The role of interest, efficacy, and basic prior knowledge. *Journal of Experimental Education, 80*, 45–68.

Mangels, J. A., Butterfield, B., Lamb, J., Good, C., & Dweck, C. S. (2006). Why do beliefs about intelligence influence learning success? A social cognitive neuroscience model. *Social Cognitive and Affective Neuroscience, 1*(2), 75–86.

Marsh, H. W. (1992). *Self-description questionnaire III: Manual*. Sydney: University of Western Sydney, SELF Research Centre.

Marsh, H. W., & Craven, R. G. (2006). Reciprocal effects of self-concept and performance from a multidimensional perspective: Beyond seductive pleasure and unidimensional perspectives. *Perspectives on Psychological Science, 1*, 133–163.

Marsh, H. W., & O'Mara, A. (2008). Reciprocal effects between academic self-concept, self-esteem, achievement and attainment over seven adolescent years: Unidimensional and multidimensional perspectives of self-concept. *Personality and Social Psychology Bulletin, 34*, 542–552.

Marsh, H. W., Trautwein, U., Lüdtke, O., & Köller, O. (2008). Social comparison and big-fish-little-pond effects on self-concept and other self-belief constructs: Role of generalized and specific others. *Journal of Educational Psychology, 100*, 510–524.

Marsh, H. W., Xu, M., & Martin, A. J. (2012). Self-concept: A synergy of theory, method, and application. In K. R. Harris, S. Graham, & T. C. Urdan (Eds.) *APA educational psychology handbook, Vol. 1: Theories, constructs, and critical issues* (pp. 427–458). Washington, DC: American Psychological Association.

Maslow, A. H. (1968). *Toward a psychology of being*. New York: Van Nostrand Reinhold.

Moos, D. C., & Azevedo, R. (2009). Learning with computer-based learning environments: A literature review of computer self-efficacy. *Review of Educational Research, 79*(2), 576–600.

Murphy, P. K., & Alexander, P. A. (2000). A motivated exploration of motivation terminology. *Contemporary Educational Psychology, 25*, 3–53.

Nagengast, B., & Marsh, H. W. (2012). Big fish in little ponds aspire more: Mediation and cross-cultural generalizability of school-average ability effects on self-concept and career aspirations in science. *Journal of Educational Psychology, 104*(4), 1033–1053.

Noddings, N. (1984). *Caring: A feminine approach to ethics and moral education*. Berkeley, CA: University of California Press.

Pajares, F. (1997). Current directions in self-efficacy research. In M. Maehr & P. R. Pintrich (Eds.). *Advances in motivation and achievement.* (Vol. 10, pp. 1–49). Greenwich, CT: JAI Press.

Pajares, F. (2006). Self-efficacy during childhood and adolescence: Implications for teachers and parents. In F. Pajares & T. Urdan (Eds.), *Adolescence and education, Vol. 5: Self-efficacy beliefs of adolescents* (pp. 339–367). Greenwich, CT: Information Age Publishing.

Pajares, F. (2007). Culturalizing educational psychology. In F. Salili & R. Hoosain (Eds.), *Culture, motivation, and learning* (pp. 19–42). Charlotte, NC: Information Age.

Pajares, F., Britner, S. L., & Valiante, G. (2000). Relation between achievement goals and self-beliefs of middle school students in writing and science. *Contemporary Educational Psychology, 25*, 406–422.

Pajares, F., & Schunk, D. H. (2002). Self-efficacy and self-belief in psychology and education: A historical perspective. In J. Aronson & D. Cordova (Eds.), *Psychology of education: Personal and interpersonal forces* (pp. 5–25). New York: Academic Press.

Parker, P. D., Schoon, I., Tsai, Y.-M., Nagy, G., Trautwein, U., & Eccles, J. S. (2012). Achievement, agency, gender, and socioeconomic background as predictors of post-school choices: A multicontext study. *Developmental Psychology, 48*, 1629–1642.

Pekrun, R. (2006). The control-value theory of achievement emotions: Assumptions, corollaries, and implications for educational research and practice. *Educational Psychology Review, 18*, 315–341.

Reeve, J. (2004). Self-determination theory applied to educational settings. In E. L. Deci and R. M. Ryan (Eds.), *Handbook of self-determination research* (pp. 183–203). Rochester, NY: University of Rochester Press.

Roeser, R. W., & Peck, S. C. (2009). An education in awareness: Self, motivation, and self-regulated learning in contemplative perspective. *Educational Psychologist, 44*, 119–136.

Roeser, R. W., Peck, S. C., & Nasir, N. S. (2006). Self and identity processes in school motivation, learning, and achievement. In P. A. Alexander & P. H. Winne (Eds.), *Handbook of educational psychology* (pp. 391–424). Mahwah, NJ: Lawrence Erlbaum Associates.

Rogers, C. R. (1947). Some observations on the organization of personality. *American Psychologist, 2*, 358–368.

Rokeach, M. (1968). *Beliefs, attitudes, and values: A theory of organization and change*. San Francisco: Jossey-Bass.

Ryan, R. M., & Deci, E. L. (2000). Intrinsic and extrinsic motivations: Classic definitions and new directions. *Contemporary Educational Psychology, 25*, 54–67.

Schunk, D. H. (1984). Sequential attributional feedback and children's achievement behaviors. *Journal of Educational Psychology, 76,* 1159–1169.

Schunk, D. H. (1987). Peer models and children's behavioral change. *Review of Educational Research, 57,* 149–174.

Schunk, D. H., & Pajares, F. (2005). Competence perceptions and academic functioning. In A. J. Elliot & C. Dweck (Eds.), *Handbook of competence and motivation* (pp. 85–104). New York: Guilford Press.

Schunk, D. H., & Usher, E. L. (2011). Assessing self-efficacy for self-regulated learning. In B. J. Zimmerman, & D. H. Schunk (Eds.), *Handbook of self-regulation of learning and performance* (pp. 282–297). New York, NY: Routledge.

Schunk, D. H., & Zimmerman, B. J. (2006). Competence and control beliefs: Distinguishing the means and ends. In P. A. Alexander, & P. H. Winne (Eds.), *Handbook of educational psychology,* 2nd ed. (pp. 349–367). New York, NY: Lawrence Erlbaum Associates.

Sheu, H.-B., Lent, R. W., Brown, S. D., Miller, M. J., Hennessy, K. D., & Duffy, R. D. (2010). Testing the choice model of social cognitive career theory across Holland themes: A meta-analytic path analysis. *Journal of Vocational Behavior, 76,* 252–264.

Skinner, E., Furrer, C., Marchand, G., & Kindermann, T. (2008). Engagement and disaffection in the classroom: Part of a larger motivational dynamic? *Journal of Educational Psychology, 100,* 765–781.

Snyder, K. E., & Linnenbrink-Garcia, L. (2013). A developmental, person-centered approach to exploring multiple motivational pathways in gifted underachievement. *Educational Psychologist, 48*(4), 209–228.

Spinath, B., & Spinath, F. M. (2005). Longitudinal analysis of the link between learning motivation and competence beliefs among elementary school children. *Learning and Instruction, 15*(2), 87–102.

Steele, C. M. (2010). *Whistling Vivaldi and other clues to how stereotypes affect us.* New York, NY: W. H. Norton.

Watt, H. M. G. (2004). Development of adolescents' self-perceptions, values, and task perceptions according to gender and domain in 7th- through 11th-grade Australian students. *Child Development, 75,* 1556–1574.

Wentzel, K. R., & Wigfield, A. (2007). Motivational interventions that work: Themes and remaining issues. *Educational Psychologist, 42*(4), 261–271.

Wigfield, A., & Eccles, J. S. (2002). The development of competence beliefs, expectancies for success, and achievement values from childhood through adolescence. In A. Wigfield & J. S. Eccles (Eds.), *Development of achievement motivation* (pp. 91–120). San Diego, CA: Academic Press.

Wigfield, A., Eccles, J. S., & Rodriguez, D. (1998). The development of children's motivation in school contexts. *Review of Research in Education, 23,* 73–118.

Wigfield, A., Tonks, S., & Klauda, S. L. (2009). Expectancy-value theory. In K. R. Wentzel & A. Wigfield (Eds.), *Handbook of motivation at school* (pp. 55–76). Mahwah, NJ: Lawrence Erlbaum Associates.

Williams, T., & Williams, K. (2010). Self-efficacy and performance in mathematics: Reciprocal determinism in 33 nations. *Journal of Educational Psychology, 102*(2), 453–466.

Wolters, C. A., Fan, W., & Daugherty, S. G. (2013). Examining achievement goals and causal attributions together as predictors of academic functioning. *Journal of Experimental Education, 81,* 295–321.

Wylie, R. C. (1989). *Measures of self-concept.* Lincoln, NE: University of Nebraska Press.

Usher, E. L. (2009). Sources of middle school students' self-efficacy in mathematics: A qualitative investigation of student, teacher, and parent perspectives. *American Educational Research Journal, 46,* 275-314.

Usher, E. L., & Pajares, F. (2006). Sources of academic and self-regulatory efficacy beliefs of entering middle school students. *Contemporary Educational Psychology, 31,* 125–141.

Usher, E. L., & Pajares, F. (2008a). Self-efficacy for self-regulated learning: A validation study. *Educational and Psychological Measurement, 68,* 443–463.

Usher, E. L., & Pajares, F. (2008b). Sources of self-efficacy in school: Critical review of the literature and future directions. *Review of Educational Research, 78,* 751–796.

Valentine, J. C., DuBois, D. L., & Cooper, H. (2004). The relation between self-beliefs and academic achievement: A meta-analytic review. *Educational Psychologist, 39,* 111–133.

Yeager, D. S., & Walton, G. M. (2011). Social-psychological interventions in education: They're not magic. *Review of Educational Research, 81*(2), 267–301.

Zeldin, A. L., Britner, S. L., & Pajares, F. (2008). A comparative study of the self-efficacy beliefs of successful men and women in mathematics, science, and technology careers. *Journal of Research in Science Teaching, 45,* 1036–1058.

Zimmerman, B. J. (2011). Motivational sources and outcomes of self-regulated learning and performance. In B. J. Zimmerman & D. H. Schunk (Eds.), *Handbook of self-regulation of learning and performance* (pp. 49–64). New York, NY: Taylor & Francis.

Zimmerman, B. J., & Cleary, T. J. (2006). Adolescents' development of personal agency. In F. Pajares & T. Urdan (Eds.), *Adolescence and education, Vol. 5: Self-efficacy beliefs of adolescents* (pp. 45–69). Greenwich, CT: Information Age.

Zuffiano, A., Alessandri, G., Gerbino, M., Kanacri, B. P. L., Di Giunta, L., Milioni, M., & Caprara, G. V. (2013). Academic achievement: The unique contribution of self-efficacy beliefs in self-regulated learning beyond intelligence, personality traits, and self-esteem. *Learning and Individual Differences, 23,* 158–162.

# 12

# Motivation Interventions in Education

## Bridging Theory, Research, and Practice

*Chris S. Hulleman*
University of Virginia

*Kenn E. Barron*
James Madison University

[T]he job of the educational psychologist is to psychologize about authentic educational problems and issues, and not simply to bring psychology to education, as if we were missionaries carrying out the Lord's work. (Berliner, 2006, p. 23)

To the extent that psychologists [are] willing to walk down a two-way street with educators, there is increased hope for realizing the long-held goal of applying the science of learning to education. Striving to achieve this goal is a worthwhile adventure that offers advantages both to educational practice and psychological theory. (Mayer, 2012, p. 250)

The field of motivation research within educational psychology has been especially generative over the last several decades, in particular by producing theories, constructs, and tests thereof. However, this research productivity has not resulted in comparable benefits for educational practice (Berliner, 2006; Kaplan, Katz, & Flum, 2012). Our current methods have been unbalanced in favor of observational, correlational, and laboratory studies that often have implications for practice but do not end up changing practice. In other words, we have "brought psychology to education" by developing theories and constructs without regard for solving the practical problems of educators. Although helpful in advancing theory, this test-theory-first, solve-problems-second approach has served to exacerbate gaps between research and practice. Fortunately, there is an alternative.

In this chapter, we consider how intervention studies can help educational psychologists walk with practitioners and bridge the research–practice divide, particularly in the area of student motivation. In Part 1, we consider the case for intervention research as a bridge between motivation theory and research, on the one hand, and practice, on the other. In Part 2, we review two different intervention approaches

for conducting motivational interventions: targeted interventions and multicomponent interventions. In Part 3, we provide a detailed case study of each intervention approach. In Part 4, we offer conclusions and recommendations for next steps.

## Part 1: Motivation Research in Education: The Case for Interventions

As psychologists, we are trained in our earliest methodology classes that research is motivated by three major goals: to describe, predict, or explain human behavior. In addition, we are exposed to the major research methodologies that allow us to answer each of these goals, by using observational methods for description, correlational methods for prediction, and experimental methods for causation (or quasi-experimental methods for limited causation). Whereas each methodology has merit, many of our earliest undergraduate psychology courses in methodology are entitled experimental psychology, thus implying a preference or bias for one particular methodological approach over others (Perlman & McCann, 2005). But non-experimental methods hold an important place for initiating and advancing research. When little is known about a topic, one of the best starting points is to simply observe the phenomenon of interest to answer the question: "What is $X$?" For example, how many students feel self-efficacy and value for their math class? This in turn can quickly lead to explorations of how two or more observed phenomena are related to each other to answer a more sophisticated question: "Does $X$ predict $Y$?" For example, what short-term and long-term educational outcomes are predicted by students' feelings of self-efficacy and value?

As a field, we have learned a great deal about important motivational variables through observational and

160

correlational methods, and how those variables are linked to key adaptive student outcomes. Research on self-efficacy and value reveals that both generally decline as students progress through school (e.g., Jacobs, Lanza, Osgood, Eccles, & Wigfield, 2002), and that self-efficacy and value predict unique educational outcomes. Self-efficacy is generally a stronger predictor of performance outcome such as grades and standardized test scores, whereas value is a stronger predictor of continued course taking and interest in that subject (for reviews see Wigfield & Eccles, 2000; Wigfield & Cambria, 2010). Another benefit of adopting non-experimental methods, especially in real-world educational contexts, is when it is unethical or unrealistic to manipulate the behavior of interest (Harackiewicz & Barron, 2004).

However, the ability to establish causation and answer the question "Does $X$ cause $Y$?" requires an experimental or interventionist approach, where a researcher can formally manipulate and introduce an independent variable to see the effect it has on an observable outcome (cf. Shavelson, Phillips, Towne, & Feuer, 2003). Finding the underlying cause is often seen as the pinnacle of research and the culmination of a research continuum that may start out as non-experimental but end with a clear causal test (Shadish, Cook, & Campbell, 2002). This also allows us to best answer to teachers and school administrators who ask us what they can change to increase the self-efficacy and value of their students. We want to be able to say, if you do $X$, it will cause your students to have more of $Y$. Unfortunately, even though our earliest methodology courses emphasize experimental methods, as a motivational field, we have conducted far less work that would fall under either an experimental or interventionist approach.

In this chapter we address this shortcoming by reviewing the current state of intervention work that has been conducted in the field of motivation. We define an intervention as a manipulation implemented by an external agent (i.e., teacher, researcher) that was intended to change students' cognitions, emotions, and/or behaviors (Lazowski & Hulleman, 2013). As such, utilizing an intervention methodology does not require a randomized experiment. Instead, we consider intervention to be an umbrella term that includes a variety of methodological approaches, including randomized experiments and design-based research (Kaplan et al., 2012), both of which are reviewed by Penuel and Frank in Chapter 2 of this handbook.

In a randomized field experiment (i.e., randomized control trial), the effectiveness of an intervention is tested in the field on a particular population of interest by randomly assigning individuals to either a treatment group or a control group. It is held as a gold standard for validating the effectiveness of the treatment free from biases that occur when participation is self-selected or non-random (Schneider, Carnoy, Kilpatrick, Schmidt, & Shavelson, 2005; Shadish et al., 2002). Design-based research is a general label for an emerging body of approaches in which researchers and practitioners work in iterative cycles in naturalistic settings to test and refine interventions to improve learning and instruction (e.g., Brown,

1992; Design-based Research Collective, 2003). Penuel and Frank (Chapter 2, this volume) liken this methodology to engineering, where prototype testing is at the center of learning what does and does not work. Qualitative and/or quantitative evidence is collected to test the success or failure of an intervention, and then a team reflects on that data to inform changes to the intervention for the next round of testing.

Although formal tests of randomized interventions are a great way to establish causality, they're not the only reason to conduct intervention research (Shavelson et al., 2003). In fact, an arguably more important reason to conduct intervention research is to operationalize our theoretical constructs as potential educational practices that boost motivation and learning. It is one thing, for example, to observe that students with higher self-efficacy or perceived value for math at the beginning of a course perform better and learn more at the end of the course. It is another thing, entirely, to recommend changes in teaching practices based on this observation. What should teachers do differently to increase students' self-efficacy and help them find value in math? Should they change how they talk about student successes and failures? The grading structure? The content of what they teach? The types of learning activities they provide for students? The only way to make clear recommendations about what practitioners should actually do based on our theories and research is to develop recommendations for practice, and then systematically engage in intervention research to test their effects on student learning outcomes. It is in precisely these situations, when potential intervention ideas are being developed, that design-based studies and other types of quasi-experiments provide important information (see Chapter 2, this volume; Kaplan et al., 2012; Shavelson et al., 2003). For example, how well received are the suggested learning activities by students? How easy are they to implement by teachers? How different are the recommendations from current practice? All these questions may best be answered outside of a randomized experiment.

The research methods selected have clear implications for the conclusions that can be drawn from the work (Barron, Brown, Egan, Gesualdi, & Marchuk, 2008; Harackiewicz & Barron, 2004). Most notable is the tradeoff between cause and effect (i.e., internal validity) and generalizability (i.e., external validity; Shadish et al., 2002). One reason researchers choose to study phenomena in laboratory settings is to gain experimental control to isolate the variables of interest, while holding extraneous variables constant. Although helpful in establishing internal validity, a laboratory setting is subject to artificiality that threatens generalizability. Similar challenges exist even for randomized field experiments, which are often forced to sacrifice external validity in order to establish cause and effect (Schneider et al., 2005).

Researchers in the field of social psychology have referred to this tradeoff as the social psychologist's dilemma (Aronson, Wilson, & Brewer, 1998). Partially because we were both trained as experimental social psychologists, we have been inspired by Cialdini's (1980; Mortensen & Cialdini, 2010) challenge to the field. He argued that far too many social psychologists worked exclusively in laboratory research settings to test theoretical ideas. He noted this was especially problematic when the laboratory setting was artificial and overly controlled. Instead of trying to capture effects in the lab, he suggested that research efforts were better spent studying effects that already appear to be powerful in naturalistic settings. As an alternative approach, Cialdini proposed the concept of full-cycle social psychology. Hypotheses about phenomena should first be derived from observing those phenomena naturalistically in the real world. Then, research should be conducted in a controlled laboratory setting to determine the causes for why it might occur. Finally, verification should be continued back in a field setting, which often generates new hypotheses to start the cycle anew. By starting and ending in naturalistic field settings, Cialdini argued we would have a better model for theory building and theory testing, integrating both basic and applied research to solve real-world problems.

Our colleague, David Daniel, makes a similar plea when writing to learning scientists in his field of cognitive psychology (Daniel, 2012). In response to the call for widespread adoption of laboratory-based research findings (Roediger & Pyc, 2012), Daniel argued that a systematic "vetting" process is needed to verify if laboratory-based findings translate to actual, real-world classroom settings. Daniel proposed five steps to evaluate whether we can take a laboratory finding and apply it successfully to change practice in the classroom:

1. Begin with exploration in the lab to find *promising findings.*
2. Move to careful experimentation in select classrooms to yield a *promising principle.*
3. Develop and design classroom/teacher-friendly methods integrating the *promising principle* into an everyday *promising practice* and to help ensure the fidelity of the intervention.
4. Continue coordinated experimentation in more diverse and complex classroom settings to yield a teaching *best practice.*
5. Disseminate and continue refining the *best practice.*

Others have raised similar concerns about the broad application of laboratory findings to the field (Dunlosky & Rawson, 2012; Mayer, 2012; Pellegrino, 2012). In motivation research, Pintrich (2003) made a call for a motivational science approach that focused on use-inspired research; that is, research inspired by practical questions, grounded in theory, and guided by systematic inquiry. Writing over a decade ago, Pintrich identified motivation research that had established the first two steps of Daniel's (2012) process. Pintrich identified five motivational generalizations (step 1) that yielded 14 design principles for classroom instruction (step 2, see Pintrich, 2003, Table 2). However, motivation researchers have been less fruitful on the last three steps of Daniel's process, and have been unable to develop promising and best practices.

It is within this context that we highlight intervention research as a crucial methodological tool in bridging the research–practice gap. We do not propose that interventions should be the only focus of motivational researchers, nor do we argue that all interventions must be tested using randomized field experiments (Shavelson et al., 2003). Rather, as noted in the beginning of our chapter, research methods in motivation have been unbalanced, heavily favoring observational, correlational, and laboratory designs. Further, in order for interventions to provide effective direction for educational practice, interventions need to be use-inspired (Pintrich, 2003) and focused on solving practical problems of educators (Berliner, 2006; Kaplan et al., 2012). They also need to be guided by theory, of which the field of motivation has plenty. In the following sections, we review the current state of motivation interventions in education, and highlight two different intervention approaches that hold promise for impacting practice.

## Part 2: Motivation Interventions in Education: An Overview

Two main approaches to interventions grounded in motivation theory exist in the research literature. First, there are targeted interventions that leverage precise psychological mechanisms to enhance subsequent learning outcomes (for reviews, see Lazowski & Hulleman, 2013; Yeager & Walton, 2011). Targeted interventions tend to be briefer in duration and focus on one or two components of motivation. Second, there are more comprehensive interventions that integrate multiple motivation components and often leverage motivation alongside specific curricular content (e.g., literacy) or pedagogical practices (e.g., cooperative learning) to enhance specific academic knowledge and skills (e.g., Guthrie, Wigfield, & VonSecker, 2000; Martin, 2008).

### Targeted Motivation Interventions

We have organized targeted student motivation interventions into four main areas that synthesize the constructs that motivate students in classrooms. Three of the areas are adapted from Pintrich's (2003, Table 2) review of motivation research in education: expectancy and control beliefs, interest and value, and goals. To these we add the fourth area of research that has re-emerged in the decade since Pintrich's article was published: the psychological costs of engaging in academic tasks (Barron & Hulleman, in press; Eccles (Parsons) et al., 1983), such as the anxiety and stress that students face when they experience fear of failure or stereotype threat (e.g., Steele, 1997). Below, we offer some exemplar intervention studies within each of the four areas, with an emphasis on interventions implemented in the field as opposed to those tested within the laboratory.

***Expectancy and Control Beliefs Interventions.*** In general, this category of interventions helps students feel more confident to learn and achieve in a specific academic context and to be in control of producing their achievement outcomes. Within the research literature, there are a number of associated constructs that have been investigated under this umbrella, including the perceived competence to perform specific academic tasks (e.g., self-efficacy, competence beliefs), to obtain a specific performance level (e.g., expectancies, outcome expectations), perceptions of the reasons students succeed or fail on academic tasks (e.g., attributions), and how much control they have to create a positive outcome. Although numerous theoretical approaches exist (Bandura, 1997; Eccles (Parsons) et al., 1983; Pekrun, 2006; Skinner, 1996; Weiner, 2010), the general idea is that students who believe they have more expectancy and control over their behavior and learning are more successful. For example, Weiner (1972) proposed that students attribute success and failure on academic tasks to ability, effort, perceived task difficulty, or luck. Adaptive attributions involve ascribing success to more stable factors (e.g., ability) and failure to less stable factors (e.g., effort, task difficulty). If individuals attribute success to a less stable factor (e.g., good luck) or failure to a more stable factor (e.g., lack of ability), then they will be uncertain about future success.

For example, Dweck's (1999) theory about the malleability of intelligence posits that students who have a growth mindset (i.e., belief that intelligence increases over time by engaging in challenging learning activities) are more confident and learn more than students who have a fixed mindset (i.e., belief that intelligence does not change over time, regardless of effort or experiences). By helping students understand that being challenged can facilitate their learning, an intervention that targets growth mindsets enhances confidence in the ability to learn and achieve performance outcomes. Blackwell, Trzesniewski, and Dweck (2007) developed an eight-part intervention to enhance growth mindsets in classrooms. Six of the 1-hour sessions instructed students on the latest research on how the brain develops and grows. Two additional 1-hour sessions focused on helping students understand that their brains can grow through persistence through difficulty and using appropriate learning strategies. Students who were randomly assigned to the mindset intervention had higher academic performance compared to those in the control condition. Other versions of the intervention replicated this effect in high-school and college students (e.g., Aronson, Fried, & Good, 2002).

In addition to growth mindset, interventions that directly train students to think differently about the causes of their success and failure have been shown to be effective. For example, intervention work aimed at changing students' perceived control have focused primarily on changing cognitive attributions. Many of these interventions provide students with training about ascribing academic success to things that are within their control (e.g., effort) and that academic difficulties can be overcome. These control-enhancing interventions have been found to be successful in increasing perceived academic control, which in turn mediates effects on improved academic motivation and achievement outcomes (e.g., Hall, Hladkyj, Perry, & Ruthig, 2004; Perry, Stupnisky, Hall, Chipperfield, & Weiner, 2010). Furthermore, many of these intervention studies sought to alter the attributions that low-performing students made regarding their academic achievement from one of low ability to one underscoring the importance of effort. These shifts in attributions

have improved course grades (e.g., Boese, Stewart, Perry, & Hamm, 2013), exam performance (e.g., Struthers & Perry, 1996), and standardized test scores (e.g., Wilson & Linville, 1985).

The perception of choice can also enhance students' perceived control, motivation, and subsequent learning outcomes (Lepper & Henderlong, 2000). For example, Patall, Cooper, and Wynn (2010) randomly assigned high-school students to receive a choice of homework assignments or no choice. Students in the choice condition had higher self-reported intrinsic motivation and perceived competence, and also performed better on the unit exam, than students in the no-choice condition. Vansteenkiste and colleagues (Vansteenkiste, Simons, Lens, Sheldon, & Deci, 2004) randomly assigned college students to conditions that appeared to have more or less choice. The perceived-choice condition boosted students' depth of processing, persistence, and test performance compared to the no-choice condition.

Finally, Haney and Durlak (1998) reviewed the literature on self-efficacy interventions in both academic and clinical contexts, and found them to be effective at enhancing children's subsequent behavioral (e.g., teacher ratings of student classroom behavior), personality (e.g., self-report measures of depression), and academic outcomes (e.g. standardized test results).

***Value and Interest Interventions.*** This category of interventions targets students' perceptions of the reasons why they see value and meaning in an academic activity. Pintrich (2003) proposed separate categories for interest and value constructs, but we see the two as inextricably linked in that value is an important component of interest (cf. Hidi & Renninger, 2006). A number of theoretical frameworks outline the importance of value and interest, including the expectancy-value framework (e.g., Eccles (Parsons) et al., 1983), self-determination theory (Deci & Ryan, 1985), and interest theory (Hidi & Renninger, 2006). Students could perceive value for an activity because it is fun and enjoyable (e.g., intrinsic value, interest, intrinsic motivation), an important part of their sense of self (e.g., attainment value, integrated regulation), a means to attaining an important current or future goal (e.g., utility value, identified regulation), a way of pleasing others (e.g., introjected regulation), or a way to obtain a reward or avoid a punishment (e.g., extrinsic motivation) (Hulleman, Barron, Kosovich, & Lazowski, in press).

Interventions that focus on intrinsic value tend to identify tasks and activities that students find interesting and intrinsically motivating, which are then compared to those that are less interesting and enjoyable on various learning outcomes. This research generally finds support for using interesting tasks as beneficial for interest and value, as well as learning outcomes such as depth of processing, attention, and achievement (e.g., Ainley, Hidi, & Berndorff, 2002; Schaffner & Schiefele, 2007; for a review see Hidi, 1990). Field interventions that target utility value tend to emphasize the usefulness and relevance of learning material for the student's present and future life, and have found that these interventions enhance both intrinsic motivation and achievement (e.g., Hulleman & Harackiewicz, 2009; Oyserman, Terry, & Bybee, 2002; Yeager et al., 2014). Interventions focusing on extrinsic motivation demonstrate that tangible, extrinsic rewards can undermine students' motivation to engage in academic tasks, particularly if the rewards are unrelated to future task engagement (e.g., Marinak & Gambrell, 2008), if the task is already interesting to students (e.g., Deci, Koestner, & Ryan, 2001), and are perceived as controlling or are expected (e.g., Reeve et al., 2002). However, rewards that contain some informational value, such as providing feedback on performance quality, can be less undermining for future motivation and performance (Pintrich, 2003).

*Goal Interventions.* This category of interventions targets the goals that students set for themselves in the academic context. In the academic literature, goals have been approached from a variety of perspectives. Goal-setting researchers examine the specific, target goals students can set for performance, such as answering a specific number of math problems correctly (Harackiewicz & Sansone, 1991; Locke & Latham, 2002). Achievement goal researchers focus on the reason behind the goal pursuit, such as whether students are trying to learn and develop skills (mastery goals), perform better than others (performance goals), or achieve a set performance level (outcome goals) (for a review, see Senko, Hulleman, & Harackiewicz, 2011). Other researchers have focused on the process of goal pursuit, and how developing specific behavioral plans can facilitate goal achievement (e.g., Gollwitzer, 1999; see Chapter 8, this volume).

Although the observational and laboratory experimental research on goals in academic contexts has been prolific (for reviews, see Elliot, 2005; Harackiewicz, Barron, & Elliot, 1998; Pintrich, 2003; Senko et al., 2011), the field testing of achievement goal interventions in actual education contexts has lagged behind. Anderman, Maehr, and Midgley (1999) observed differences between two middle schools, one that was more mastery-focused and one that was more performance-focused. Maehr and Midgley (1996) report on the design of an intervention intended to reform an entire middle school to utilize more mastery-focused practices. However, no empirical results of the intervention are reported. Linnenbrink (2005) classified teachers as being more mastery-focused, performance-focused, or both goal-focused, and then structured small-group activities in each classroom to be consistent with the teacher's observed achievement goal profile. This quasi-experimental design revealed that students whose teachers and cooperative learning groups emphasized learning strategies consistent with both mastery and performance goals had the best outcomes. Muis, Ranellucci, Franco, and Crippen (2013) manipulated the feedback that undergraduate students received based on achievement goal theory. Undergraduate students were randomly assigned to receive quiz feedback that emphasized the importance of learning and improvement (mastery),

demonstrating individual competence and high scores compared to others (performance), both improvement and besting others (combined mastery and performance), or simply received their quiz score (control). The results indicated that performance feedback increased academic performance relative to control and mastery feedback.

In contrast to the paucity of interventions inspired by achievement goal research, there have been several interventions designed to test whether helping students develop specific behavioral plans facilitates goal attainment and learning outcomes. In a series of field studies, Gollwitzer and colleagues tested a series of interventions that helped students commit to specific goal-related behaviors at specific times and locations (i.e., implementation intentions; Gollwitzer, 1999). In one study, undergraduate students were asked to complete a report over winter break. Students who were randomly assigned to committing to a specific time and place to work on the report were more likely to complete the report than those who were simply asked to commit to turning the report in by a specific date (Gollwitzer & Brandstätter, 1997). This intervention approach has been adapted and found to boost effort and school performance with elementary-, middle-, and high-school students (e.g., Gollwitzer, Oettingen, Kirby, & Duckworth, 2011). Similarly, Morisano and colleagues (Morisano, Hirsh, Peterson, Pihl, & Shore, 2010) developed an online goal-setting program that guides students through steps for setting personal goals with detailed strategies for achievement. In comparison to a control condition that received questionnaires about positive psychology and wrote about past experiences, students randomly assigned to the goal-setting condition demonstrated higher academic performance and retention.

*Psychological Cost Interventions.* This category of interventions targets the negative aspects of engaging in academic tasks, often referred to as psychological cost (Barron & Hulleman, in press; Eccles (Parsons) et al., 1983). One psychological cost that can occur in academic settings is when students identify with a group that is stereotyped to underperform (e.g., girls aren't as good as boys in math). Known as stereotype threat, this cost can undermine academic performance and persistence, resulting in a sorting mechanism that reduces minority success and completion rates in high school and college (Steele, 1997). An intervention designed to ameliorate this perceived threat has been developed and tested by Cohen and colleagues (e.g., Cohen, Garcia, Apfel, & Master, 2006; Cohen, Garcia, Purdie-Vaughns, Apfel, & Brzustoski, 2009). Students randomly assigned to the affirmation condition wrote about their top most important values, whereas students assigned to the control condition wrote about their least important values. By writing about their most important values, students affirmed core aspects of themselves, which serves as a buffer against threats occurring in another domain. In a sample of seventh-grade students, the values affirmation intervention reduced the black–white achievement gap by 40% (Cohen et al., 2006). In a 2-year follow-up, the benefits of the intervention were particularly acute for low-achieving black students who increased their performance by 0.41 grade point average (GPA) points relative to the control group (Cohen et al., 2009). This intervention effect has been replicated with other minority groups, such as Latino American middle-school students (e.g., Sherman et al., 2013) and first-generation college students (Harackiewicz et al., 2014).

In addition to identity threat, students can also experience psychological cost if they feel anxious about not belonging or fitting in with other students. These feelings of belonging uncertainty can lead to students withdrawing from the academic experience and subsequently poorer academic outcomes. In a series of studies, Walton and Cohen developed an intervention targeting students' feelings of belonging (Walton & Cohen, 2007, 2011). In one study (Walton & Cohen, 2011), students randomly assigned to the intervention condition read results of a survey and quotes from other students that emphasized that everyone struggles with some aspects of college initially, but that these initial difficulties were temporary. In essence, students learned that there were other students like them who also felt like they did not fit in, and who eventually succeeded in college. Their results indicated that African American students, who were more likely to be uncertain about belonging, benefited with increased GPA and self-reported health and well-being.

Finally, students also experience psychological cost when they become highly anxious in testing situations. The cognitive component of anxiety, worrying, taxes working memory and undermines student performance on quizzes and exams. Several writing interventions have been developed that target the cognitive component of worry in testing situations. For example, Ramirez and Beilock (2011) randomly assigned high-school students to write about their exam-related worries (intervention condition) or to write about something not related to the exam (control condition). Highly anxious students in the intervention condition outperformed those in the control condition. Similarly, Jamieson, Mendes, Blackstock, and Schmader (2010) developed an intervention that helped students reappraise their pre-exam arousal and anxiety as a facilitator of performance. Undergraduates in the reappraisal condition outperformed their peers randomly assigned to the control group on the GRE math exam several months later.

***Summary.*** Our review of targeted interventions highlights there is a growing body of intervention studies now being conducted that operationalize motivation constructs in field settings and successfully enhance educational outcomes. A recent meta-analysis of over 60 motivation interventions in education contexts indicates that these interventions have an average effect size of over half a standard deviation (Lazowski & Hulleman, 2013). This research evidence, which demonstrates that targeted psychological interventions can have significant and meaningful impacts on students' educational outcomes, should energize the field to translate theoretical constructs into interventions that can lead to changes in educational practice.

## *Multicomponent Motivation Interventions*

Thus far, we have reviewed interventions that target a single motivational construct or component. However, to be maximally effective, an intervention may need to address multiple facets of the student experience. These interventions could target multiple motivational constructs, or these interventions could include pedagogical elements that target particular types of learning, such as reading or mathematics. As a group, such multicomponent interventions have received less experimental evaluation in the literature, so the associated empirical base is not as strong. Below, we review two promising examples of multicomponent interventions in the literature that address motivational processes to enhance student learning outcomes.

A multicomponent intervention developed by Andrew Martin provides an example of comprehensive motivation intervention. Designed using an integrative motivation and engagement framework known as The Wheel (Martin, 2008), this intervention targets students adaptive and maladaptive behaviors and cognitions. Delivered over the course of 13 modules, students are guided through instruction on the 11 aspects of the wheel: self-efficacy and mastery (expectancy and control beliefs); valuing (value and interest); anxiety, failure avoidance, uncertain control, self-handicapping, and disengagement (cost); and persistence, planning, and task management (learning skills). Initial quasi-experimental results indicate that the intervention boosted students' self-reported motivation, maladaptive cognitions, and persistence.

The Concept-Oriented Reading Instruction (CORI) intervention provides an example of a multicomponent intervention that combines motivational aspects with reading strategy instruction. Developed by John Guthrie and Allan Wigfield, CORI links reading fiction and non-fiction books to science activities (Guthrie et al., 2000). This reading program is organized into thematic units designed to target five motivational processes: self-efficacy and mastery goals, perceived autonomy and intrinsically motivating activities, and collaborative work that provides social support for learning (Guthrie, McCrae, & Klauda, 2007). A meta-analysis of 11 quasi-experimental studies demonstrates that the CORI intervention improves students' reading strategy use, self-reported reading motivation, and achievement (Guthrie et al., 2007).

Certainly, there are additional interventions in the literature that may indirectly impact motivation, but that were not designed to function primarily through motivation mechanisms. For example, in a special issue of the *Educational Psychologist* edited by Wigfield and Wentzel, the authors of different articles discuss school-wide reform efforts to create positive social and emotional climates for children (Juvonen, 2007), small learning community reforms (Felner, Seitsinger, Brand, Burns, & Bolton, 2007), and social skills training for aggressive children (Hudley, Graham, & Taylor, 2007). Such interventions connect to literature on social-emotional interventions (for a review, see Durlak, Weissberg, Dymnicki, Taylor, & Schellinger, 2011), and indirectly target motivation through instruction in social and emotional skills (e.g., Brackett, Rivers, Reyes, & Salovey, 2013), rather than by directly targeting motivation as the primary mechanism of change (Rimm-Kaufman & Hulleman, in press).

## Part 3: Motivation Interventions in Education: Two Case Studies

In this section, we present two case studies of how to develop and test interventions designed to address an important problem of practice. We present these as indepth exemplars of the important role of interventions in bridging the research–practice gap in the psychology of education. The first case study stems from our work to enhance the perceived utility value of learning specific academic content. The second case study stems from the Carnegie Foundation for the Advancement of Teaching's work to address student success rates in community college by altering the pathway through which students complete developmental mathematics courses. We conclude each case study by highlighting implications for theory, research, and practice.

### The Utility-Value Intervention

The utility-value intervention is grounded in the expectancy-value framework of student motivation (Eccles (Parsons) et al., 1983). The motivation intervention was inspired by a practical problem: How does a first-year, graduate teaching assistant increase the motivation of his undergraduate students to learn statistics? One intuitive method of engaging students in the learning process is to increase the value of educational topics—that is, the personal relevance and utility of school material—to students' lives. In the expectancy-value framework, student motivation to learn is a function of two components: how well we expect to do on the task (expectancy) and how valuable the outcomes of task engagement are perceived to be (value).

Faced with the challenge of students who lack value for statistics, an obvious way was to help students discover how the statistical techniques they were learning applied to their lives in some way (utility value). This seemed more plausible than convincing students that learning statistics was fun (intrinsic value) or an important part of their identity (attainment value). In addition, non-experimental work has revealed that utility value was predictive of both performance and interest in coursework (e.g., Hulleman, Durik, Schweigert, & Harackiewicz, 2008; Simons, Dewitte, & Lens, 2003). As a result, we designed a laboratory study to examine whether the theoretical construct of utility value could be enhanced through intervention and thereby increase motivation for learning. In this initial study (Hulleman, Godes, Hendricks, & Harackiewicz, 2010, Study 1), undergraduate psychology students were brought into the laboratory to learn a new method of computing arithmetic using mental math techniques rather than relying on paper and pencil or calculators. Before the learning session, participants were randomly assigned to one of two conditions. In the experimental condition, participants wrote about how a mental math technique applied to their lives in some way. In the control condition,

students wrote a summary of how to use the technique. The findings revealed that students who wrote about the personal relevance of the technique reported more utility value for math at the end of the session, and were more interested in learning more mental math techniques, than participants in the control condition. These findings were especially true for students who had lower math expectancies.

Buoyed by these initial results from the laboratory, we conducted three randomized field experiments in classrooms. First, we replicated these results in an introductory college psychology class and found that students who wrote about the relevance of what they were learning were more interested in psychology at the end of the semester than students in the control condition (Hulleman et al., 2010, Study 2). Students in the utility-value writing condition maintained their interest in psychology over time, whereas students in the control writing condition exhibited a decline in interest across five time points in the semester (Harackiewicz, Hulleman, & Pastor, 2009). These results were replicated in ten high-school science classrooms (Hulleman & Harackiewicz, 2009). In this case, we found that the intervention enhanced both academic performance and subsequent interest in science for low-performing students in the utility-value writing condition compared to the control writing condition. Third, we replicated these results in an unpublished study in an undergraduate statistics course (Hulleman, An, Hendricks, & Harackiewicz, 2013). This time, we found that low-expectancy students in the utility-value writing condition intended to take more statistics courses in the future than those in the control writing condition. Across all three studies, the findings were particularly evident for students who had low performance expectations at the beginning of the semester or who performed poorly on initial exams.

These four studies led us to consider whether we could enhance the perceived utility value for learning specific content outside the classroom. This time, the practical problem was the leaky academic pipeline in science, technology, engineering, and math (STEM). Specifically, students' lack of preparation in high school leads to a severe drop in interest in STEM majors and careers in college and beyond (Simpkins, Davis-Kean, & Eccles, 2006). Inspired by the potential role that parents play in students' educational trajectories (Jodl, Michael, Malanchuk, Eccles, & Sameroff, 2001), we developed an intervention that encouraged parents to talk to their children about the utility value of math and science (Harackiewicz, Rozek, Hulleman, & Hyde, 2012). Our thinking was that parents, as key socializers and influencers of their teenagers' course-taking decisions in high school (Eccles (Parsons) et al., 1983), could benefit from the knowledge of how taking math and science courses in high school was relevant to their children's lives. This intervention was delivered via two brochures mailed to parents, plus access to a website, while their children were in tenth and eleventh grade. The results revealed that students of parents who were randomly assigned to receive the intervention took nearly one additional math or science course in their last 2 years of high school than students of parents who did not receive the materials.

***Implications for Theory and Research.*** This research supports the expectancy-value framework proposed by Eccles (Parsons) et al. (1983) that postulates that motivation is partially determined by the extent to which individuals ascribe meaning and value to activities. First, the utility-value intervention, which encourages students to discover the connections between their lives and their topic of study, is effective because it encourages students to see greater purpose and utility in what they are studying. This affirms the basic tenets of the theoretical framework.

Second, our results reveal causal relationships between theorized constructs and outcomes across different contexts and age groups. Despite the extensive body of research within the expectancy-value tradition, little of that research has been experimental. We do not dismiss the importance of non-experimental work. In fact, non-experimental work has been important for the development of theory, and observing and assessing student motivation within real-world contexts. However, additional experimental tests of theory offer a more rigorous test of the theory, moving beyond the information that can be learned from interviews, observations, and correlational studies.

Third, when experimental studies are conducted, unexpected or counterintuitive findings can be revealed that diverge from non-experimental findings. For example, although not explicitly stated by Eccles (Parsons) et al.'s (1983) expectancy-value framework, the overwhelming majority of research within this framework in educational psychology has focused on the independent, main effects of expectancies and values on learning outcomes (cf. Nagengast et al., 2011). The findings from this non-experimental work imply that value interventions, if they work, should universally apply to all students. In contrast, our results challenge how expectancies and values contribute to motivation by revealing an interaction between value and expectancy. In our studies, we found that the utility-value intervention was most effective at increasing student interest and achievement for those with lower expectancies. Further, we find that low-expectancy students who are explicitly told why an academic activity is important to their lives demonstrate worse learning outcomes (e.g., Durik & Harackiewicz, 2007).

The take-away message is that care needs to be taken in terms of how value is influenced. Thus, it is through a combination of methodological approaches that we can best understand the phenomena that occur in schools, and the role that situational and personality factors play in sustaining and promoting optimally motivated behavior (Harackiewicz & Barron, 2004).

***Implications for Practice.*** The utility-value intervention work enables us to provide recommendations to practitioners about the effectiveness of interventions based on enhancing students' perceived value for the material. The effectiveness of this brief, low-cost intervention should be encouraging to practitioners wishing to enhance student motivation and learning. However, because the intervention was most effective for students with low perceived or actual competence, this may not be a one-size-fits-all strategy (Durik, Hulleman,

& Harackiewicz, in press). Thus, our recommendations are not so simple as to say that utility-value interventions are good for everyone. Instead, it is important to be mindful of individual differences when employing strategies intended to enhance motivation (cf. Berliner, 2002; Daniel, 2012). Further, the utility-value interventions presented here provide an exemplar case for teachers to consider including in their teaching practices. Variations of this intervention within different educational contexts can be made based on content area, teacher expertise, and student characteristics. Rather than providing the magic bullet for helping students discover value in course content, this intervention provides a blueprint for teachers to use within their own unique classroom contexts and students.

### The Carnegie Community College Intervention

Directly targeting perceptions of value proved to be an effective approach to address the problem of disengagement in introductory statistics for the graduate teaching assistant, and also for high school science. However, can targeting a single construct, such as utility value, create change in a more pervasive and complex problem, such as low persistence and graduation rates in community college? Perhaps an intervention with multiple components is needed to address this more systemic problem. In the United States, students are enrolling in community college in ever-increasing numbers, with nearly 13 million students enrolled in a community college in the fall of 2012, and nearly half of all undergraduate students having received a community college degree (American Association of Community Colleges, 2014). However, as many as 54% of students in community colleges fail to reach college-ready math proficiency, even with remediation through developmental curricula (Bailey, Jeong, & Cho, 2010; Le, Rogers, & Santos, 2011). Furthermore, students are taking and failing such "developmental" math courses (also known as remedial mathematics courses), aimed at preparing students for college-level math curriculum, as many as ten times (Bryk, Gomez, & Grunow, 2010). This has significant consequences for future employment opportunities, as many jobs today require a solid understanding of mathematical concepts (National Science Board, 2006).

This practical and significant problem inspired the Carnegie Foundation to develop a comprehensive intervention that included multiple components. The goal of the project is to raise developmental math completion rates from 5% to 50% within 5 years (Silva & White, 2012). Doing so requires addressing not only student motivation, but also the courses that students take, pedagogical practices, and assessment. As part of its ongoing efforts to address wide-ranging educational problems in a unique way, the Carnegie Foundation employed an improvement science approach (Bryk et al., 2010), which is another variation of design-based research. The approach starts with a problem of practice, develops hypotheses based on evidence from the research world and the practice world, tests change ideas based on these hypotheses in a rigorous way, and scales what works. Based on improvement models in health care and business, this approach requires researchers and practitioners to work closely together at each step, including hypothesis generation, data collection, intervention development and testing, and scaling up.

First, the course sequence for developmental math was revised through a partnership with Charles A. Dana Center at the University of Texas-Austin. The goal was to create a two-course sequence that students could complete within one academic year. The revised courses include developmental components that teach students learning skills and strategies, and encourage students to connect the material to the world around them (i.e., value). Next, students' motivation and strategies to persist through learning challenges, called productive persistence, was defined according to five general psychological constructs: study skills, expectancy beliefs, value, belonging, and faculty support of students' skills and mindsets. The conceptual model of productive persistence was developed iteratively through cooperation between psychological researchers and community college math faculty. The math instructors identified important gaps in student persistence and skills in the developmental math context, and the researchers connected these skill and mindset gaps to current psychological theory and research. Improvement science methods were then used to develop and test psychological interventions that could be embedded within the course (i.e., the Starting Strong package). Associated measures of productive persistence were also created to fit within the logistical constraints of the math courses. An initial pool of nearly 1,000 items was reduced to 26 that could be completed within 3 minutes during students' weekly lab sessions, thus providing important data on student progress and responsiveness to interventions during the semester.

The initial results of this effort have been striking. In just the first year, the community colleges that participated in the Carnegie program raised their developmental math completion rates to over 50% (Silva & White, 2012). The work, started in 2008, is ongoing. The ultimate goal is to continue to expand this work to other community colleges, and to increase the success rate far beyond 50%, utilizing iterative cycles of testing and revision.

***Implications for Theory and Research.*** Because this is a multicomponent intervention, it is difficult to isolate which factors are primarily responsible for the improvement. But that's not the focus of this effort. Instead, the most important goal is addressing the persistence problem. However, there are important lessons for theory and research. For example, Dweck's growth mindset intervention has now been scaled up in hundreds of community college classrooms, and is serving as a contributing factor to the success of the program. The work of the community college network demonstrates that psychological interventions, such as the growth mindset intervention, can be translated into practice when researchers and practitioners engage in collaborative work. This is an exciting development for other constructs and interventions grounded in motivation theory—rather than simply providing suggestive implications for teachers, there is real promise to directly influence educational practices. For example,

current research in the network is examining different ways in which instructors might reinforce student growth mindsets via daily interactions, email communications, and performance feedback (J. Myung, personal communication, October 1, 2014).

***Implications for Practice.*** The initial success of the community college partnership highlights the promise of researcher–practitioner partnerships in general to impact practice, and more specifically for instructors to employ lessons from motivation research to facilitate student learning outcomes. Future work needs to continue to translate the burgeoning literature on motivational interventions into educational practices. Knowledge of motivation theory and research is accessible to practitioners if they are willing to work with researchers to translate promising principles into promising practices, and eventually best practices that can be implemented at scale (Daniel, 2012).

## Part 4: Conclusion

Simply put, from a theoretical, research, and practical perspective, intervention studies facilitate our understanding about which interventions are most effective in improving educational outcomes in a way that observational and correlational research cannot. Whether the research design is experimental or not, this understanding can guide recommendations for educational practice based on appropriate scientific evidence. It is not enough to simply know that some motivation constructs are correlated with important student outcomes. What is needed are interventions, designed to target motivational constructs and processes, that in turn enhance educational outcomes. Importantly, when such interventions are guided by practical questions and developed in collaboration between researchers and practitioners, they have the potential to solve fundamental challenges of educational practice.

So, with such obvious benefits, why are such studies lacking in our body of motivation research? When reflecting on the differences between hard sciences and soft sciences, Berliner (2002) suggested this was a false dichotomy. Instead, he proposed that a better distinction might be easy-to-do science vs. hard-to-do science. Education research, as it turns out, may be the hardest science of all to do:

> We do our science under conditions that physical scientists find intolerable! We face particular problems and must deal with local conditions that limit generalizations and theory building—problems that are different from those faced by the easier-to-do sciences . . . In education, broad theories and ecological generalizations often fail because they cannot incorporate the enormous number or determine the power of the contexts within which human beings find themselves. (Berliner, 2002, pp. 18-19)

Within educational research in general, and motivational research in particular, non-experimental methods typically are the easier-to-do science and interventions and experimental methods are the harder-to-do science. Conducting high-quality intervention research requires time, money, and resources, especially when considering newer forms of intervention research that work in collaboration with educators. But with the right investments in how we train the next generation of educational psychologists and how we fund research, we can provide the necessary training and incentives to take up the call for this important work.

# References

Ainley, M., Hidi, S., & Berndorff, D. (2002). Interest, learning, and the psychological processes that mediate their relationship. *Journal of Educational Psychology, 94*(3), 545–561.

American Association of Community Colleges. (2014). *Community college fact sheet 2014.* Retrieved from http://www.aacc.nche.edu/AboutCC/Documents/Facts14_Data_R3.pdf (accessed May 31, 2014).

Anderman, E. M., Maehr, M. L., & Midgley, C. (1999). Declining motivation after the transition to middle school: Schools can make a difference. *Journal of Research and Development in Education, 32*(3), 131–147.

Aronson, J., Fried, C. B., & Good, C. (2002). Reducing the effects of stereotype threat on African-American college students by shaping theories of intelligence. *Journal of Experimental Social Psychology, 38*(2), 113–125.

Aronson, E., Wilson, T. D., & Brewer, M. B. (1998). Experimentation in social psychology. In D. Gilbert, S. Fiske, & G. Lindzey (Eds), *The handbook of social psychology, Vols. 1 and 2* (4th ed., pp. 99–142). New York, NY: McGraw-Hill.

Bailey, T., Jeong, D. W., & Cho, S. W. (2010). Referral, enrollment, and completion in developmental education sequences in community colleges. *Economics of Education Review, 29*, 255–270.

Bandura, A. (1997). *Self-efficacy: The exercise of control.* New York: Freeman.

Barron, K. E., Brown, A. R., Egan, T. E., Gesualdi, C. R., & Marchuk, K. A. (2008). Validity. In S. F. Davis & W. Buskist (Eds.), *21st century psychology: A reference handbook* (pp. 55–64). Thousand Oaks, CA: Sage.

Barron, K. E., & Hulleman, C. S. (in press). Expectancy-value-cost model of motivation. To appear in J. D. Wright (Ed.), *International Encyclopedia of Social & Behavioral Sciences* (2nd ed.). Oxford: Elsevier.

Berliner, D. C. (2002). Comment: Educational research: The hardest science of all. *Educational Researcher, 31*(8), 18–20.

Berliner, D. C. (2006). Educational psychology: Searching for essence throughout a century of influence. In P. A. Alexander & P. H. Winne (Eds.), *Handbook of educational psychology* (2nd ed., pp. 3–42). New York: Psychology Press.

Blackwell, L. S., Trzesniewski, K. H., & Dweck, C. S. (2007). Implicit theories of intelligence predict achievement across an adolescent transition: A longitudinal study and an intervention. *Child Development, 78*(1), 246–263.

Boese, G. D. B., Stewart, T. L., Perry, R. P., & Hamm, J. M. (2013). Assisting failure-prone individuals to navigate achievement transitions using a cognitive motivation treatment (attributional retraining). *Journal of Applied Social Psychology, 43*, 1946–1955.

Brackett, M. A., Rivers, S. E., Reyes, M. R., & Salovey, P. (2013). Enhancing academic performance and social and emotional competence with the RULER feeling words curriculum. *Learning and Individual Differences, 22*, 218–224.

Brown, A. L. (1992). Design experiments: Theoretical and methodological challenges in creating complex interventions in classroom settings. *Journal of the Learning Sciences, 2*(2), 141–178.

Bryk, A. S., Gomez, L. M., & Grunow, A. (2010). *Getting ideas into action: Building networked improvement communities in education.* Stanford, CA: Carnegie Foundation for the Advancement of Teaching.

Cialdini, R. B. (1980). Full-cycle social psychology. *Applied Social Psychology Annual, 1*, 21–47.

Cohen, G. L., Garcia, J., Apfel, N., & Master, A. (2006). Reducing the racial achievement gap: A social-psychological intervention. *Science, 313*, 1307–1310.

Cohen, G. L., Garcia, J., Purdie-Vaughns, V., Apfel, N., & Brzustoski, P. (2009). Recursive processes in self-affirmation: Intervening to close the minority achievement gap. *Science, 324*(5925), 400–403.

Daniel, D. B. (2012). Promising principles: Translating the science of learning to educational practice. *Journal of Applied Research in Memory and Cognition, 1*(4), 251–253.

Deci, E. L., Koestner, R., & Ryan, R. M. (2001). Extrinsic rewards and intrinsic motivation in education: Reconsidered once again. *Review of Educational Research, 71*(1), 1–27.

Deci, E. L., & Ryan, R. M. (1985). *Self-determination.* New York: Plenum Press.

Design-based Research Collective. (2003). Design-based research: An emerging paradigm for educational inquiry. *Educational Researcher, 32*(1), 5–8.

Dunlosky, J., & Rawson, K. A. (2012). Overconfidence produces underachievement: Inaccurate self evaluations undermine students' learning and retention. *Learning and Instruction, 22*(4), 271–280.

Durik, A. M., & Harackiewicz, J. M. (2007). Different strokes for different folks: How individual interest moderates the effects of situational factors on task interest. *Journal of Educational Psychology, 99*(3), 597–610.

Durik, A. M., Hulleman, C. S., & Harackiewicz, J. M. (in press). One size fits some: Instructional enhancements to promote interest. In K. A. Renninger & M. Nieswandt (Eds.), *Interest, the self, and K-16 mathematics and science learning.* Washington, DC: American Educational Research Association.

Durlak, J. A., Weissberg, R. P., Dymnicki, A. B., Taylor, R. D., & Schellinger, K. B. (2011). The impact of enhancing students' social and emotional learning: A meta-analysis of school-based universal interventions. *Child Development, 82*(1), 405–432.

Dweck, C. S. (1999). *Self-theories: Their role in motivation, personality, and development.* Philadelphia: Taylor and Francis/Psychology Press.

Eccles (Parsons), J. S., Adler, T. F., Futterman, R., Goff, S. B., Kaczala, C. M., Meece, J. L., & Midgley, C. (1983). *Expectancies, values, and academic behaviors.* In J. T. Spence (Ed.), *Achievement and achievement motivation* (pp. 75–146). San Francisco, CA: W. H. Freeman.

Elliot, A. J. (2005). A conceptual history of the achievement goal construct. In A. J. Elliot & C. S. Dweck (Eds.), *Handbook of competence and motivation* (pp. 52–72). New York: Guilford.

Felner, R. D., Seitsinger, A., Brand, S., Burns, A., & Bolton, N. (2007). Creating small learning communities: Lessons from the project on high performing learning communities about "what works" in creating productive, developmentally enhancing, learning contexts. *Educational Psychologist, 42*, 209–221.

Gollwitzer, P. M. (1999). Implementation intentions: Strong effects of simple plans. *American Psychologist, 54*(7), 493–503.

Gollwitzer, P. M., & Brandstätter, V. (1997). Implementation intentions and effective goal pursuit. *Journal of Personality and Social Psychology, 73*(1), 186–199.

Gollwitzer, A., Oettingen, G., Kirby, T., & Duckworth, A. L. (2011). Mental contrasting facilitates academic performance in school children. *Motivation and Emotion, 35*, 403–412.

Guthrie, J. T., McCrae, A., & Klauda, S. L. (2007). Contributions of concept-oriented reading instruction to knowledge about interventions for motivations in reading. *Educational Psychologist, 42*, 237–250.

Guthrie, J. T., Wigfield, A., & VonSecker, C. (2000). Effects of integrated instruction on motivation and strategy use in reading. *Journal of Educational Psychology, 92*(2), 331–341.

Hall, N. C., Hladkyj, S., Perry, R. P., & Ruthig, J. C. (2004). The role of attributional retraining and elaborative learning in college students' academic development. *Journal of Social Psychology, 144*(6), 591–612.

Haney, P., & Durlak, J. A. (1998). Changing self-esteem in children and adolescents: A meta-analytical review. *Journal of Clinical Child Psychology, 27*(4), 423–433.

Harackiewicz, J. M., & Barron, K. E. (2004). Conducting social psychological research in educational settings: "Lessons we learned in school". In C. Sansone, C. Morf, & A. Panter (Eds.), *Handbook of methods in social psychology* (pp. 471–484). Thousand Oaks, CA: Sage Publications.

Harackiewicz, J. M., Barron, K. E., & Elliot, A. J. (1998). Rethinking achievement goals: When are they adaptive for college students and why? *Educational Psychologist, 33*(1), 1–21.

Harackiewicz, J. M., Canning, E. A., Tibbetts, Y., Giffen, C. J., Blair, S. S., Rouse, D. I., & Hyde, J. S. (2014). Closing the social class achievement gap for first-generation students in undergraduate biology. *Journal of Educational Psychology, 106*(2), 375–389.

Harackiewicz, J. M., Hulleman, C. S., & Pastor, D. A. (2009). *Developmental trajectories of interest within semester-long courses in high school science and introductory psychology.* Paper presented at the European Association for Research on Learning and Instruction (EARLI) Biennial Conference. Munich, Germany.

Harackiewicz, J. M., Rozek, C. R., Hulleman, C. S., & Hyde, J. S. (2012). Helping parents motivate their teens in mathematics and science: An experimental test. *Psychological Science, 23*(8), 899–906.

Harackiewicz, J. M., & Sansone, C. (1991). Goals and intrinsic motivation: You *can* get there from here. In M. Maehr & P. Pintrich (Eds.), *Advances in motivation and achievement* (Vol. 7, pp. 21–49). Greenwich, CT: JAI Press.

Hidi, S. (1990). Interest and its contribution as a mental resource for learning. *Review of Educational Research, 60*(4), 549–571.

Hidi, S., & Renninger, K. A. (2006). The four-phase model of interest development. *Educational Psychologist, 41*(2), 111–127.

Hudley, C., Graham, S., & Taylor, A. (2007). Reducing aggressive behavior and increasing motivation in school: The evolution of an intervention to strengthen school adjustment. *Educational Psychologist, 42,* 251–260.

Hulleman, C. S., An, B., Hendricks, B., & Harackiewicz, J. M. (2013). *Expectancy-value effects on interest and performance in college statistics classes.* Manuscript in preparation.

Hulleman, C. S., Barron, K. E., Kosovich, J. J., & Lazowski, R. (in press). Expectancy-value models of achievement motivation in education. In A. A. Lipnevich, F. Preckel, & R. D. Robers (Eds.), *Psychosocial skills and school systems in the twenty-first century: Theory, research, and applications.* New York: Springer.

Hulleman, C. S., Durik, A. M., Schweigert, S. B., & Harackiewicz, J. M. (2008). Task values, achievement goals, and interest: An integrative analysis. *Journal of Educational Psychology, 100,* 398–416.

Hulleman, C. S., Godes, O., Hendricks, B., & Harackiewicz, J. M. (2010). Enhancing interest and performance with a utility value intervention. *Journal of Educational Psychology, 102*(4), 880–895.

Hulleman, C. S., & Harackiewicz, J. M. (2009). Promoting interest and performance in high school science classes. *Science, 326,* 1410–1412.

Jacobs, J. E., Lanza, S., Osgood, D. W., Eccles, J. S., & Wigfield, A. (2002). Changes in children's self-competence and values: Gender and domain differences across grades one through twelve. *Child Development, 73,* 509–527.

Jamieson, J. P., Mendes, W. B., Blackstock, E., & Schmader, T. (2010). Turning the knots in your stomach into bows: Reappraising arousal improves performance on the GRE. *Journal of Experimental Social Psychology, 46*(1), 208–212.

Jodl, K. M., Michael, A., Malanchuk, O., Eccles, J. S., & Sameroff, A. (2001). Parents' roles in shaping early adolescents' occupational aspirations. *Child Development, 72,* 1247–1265.

Juvonen, J. (2007). Reforming middle schools: Focus on continuity, social connectedness, and engagement. *Educational Psychologist, 42*(4), 197–208.

Kaplan, A., Katz, I., & Flum, H. (2012). Motivation theory in educational practice: Knowledge claims, challenges, and future directions. In K. R. Harris, S. Graham, & T. C. Urdan (Eds.), *Educational psychology handbook, Vol 2: Individual differences and cultural and contextual factors* (pp. 165–194). Washington, DC: American Psychological Association.

Lazowski, R. A., & Hulleman, C. S. (2013). *Motivation interventions in education: A meta-analytic review.* Paper presented at the American Educational Research Association annual meeting.

Le, C., Rogers, K. R., & Santos, J. (2011). Innovations in developmental math: Community colleges enhance support for nontraditional students. *Jobs for the Future.* Retrieved from http://www.jff.org/sites/default/files/MetLife-DevMath-040711.pdf (accessed 13 March 2015).

Lepper, M. R., & Henderlong, J. (2000). Turning "play" into "work" and "work" into "play": 25 years of research on intrinsic versus extrinsic motivation. In C. Sansone & J. M. Harackiewicz (Eds.), *Intrinsic and extrinsic motivation: The search for optimal motivation and performance* (pp. 257–307). New York: Academic Press.

Linnenbrink, E. A. (2005). The dilemma of performance-approach goals: The use of multiple goal contexts to promote students' motivation and learning. *Journal of Educational Psychology, 97,* 197–213.

Locke, E. A., & Latham, G. P. (2002). Building a practically useful theory of goal setting and task motivation: A 35-year odyssey. *American Psychologist, 57*(9), 705–717.

Maehr, M. L., & Midgley, C. (1996). *Transforming school cultures.* Boulder, CO: Westview Press.

Marinak, B. A., & Gambrell, L. B. (2008). Intrinsic motivation and rewards: What sustains young children's engagement with text? *Literacy Research and Instruction, 47,* 9–26.

Martin, A. J. (2008). Enhancing student motivation and engagement: The effects of a multidimensional intervention. *Contemporary Educational Psychology, 33,* 239–269.

Mayer, R. E. (2012). Advances in applying the science of learning to education: An historical perspective. *Journal of Applied Research in Memory and Cognition, 1*(4), 249–250.

Morisano, D., Hirsh, J. B., Peterson, J. B., Pihl, R. O., & Shore, B. M. (2010). Setting, elaborating, and reflecting on personal goals improves academic performance. *Journal of Applied Psychology, 416*(839), 4291.

Mortensen, C. R., & Cialdini, R. B. (2010). Full-cycle social psychology for theory and application. *Social and Personality Psychology Compass, 4*(1), 53–63.

Muis, K. R., Ranellucci, J., Franco, G. M., & Crippen, K. J. (2013). The interactive effects of personal achievement goals and performance feedback in an undergraduate science class. *Journal of Experimental Education, 81*(4), 556–578.

Nagengast, B., Marsh, H. W., Scalas, L. F., Xu, M. K., Hau, K. T., & Trautwein, U. (2011). Who took the "x" out of expectancy-value theory? A psychological mystery, a substantive-methodological synergy, and a cross-national generalization. *Psychological Science, 22*(8), 1058–1066.

National Science Board. (2006). *America's pressing challenge: Building a stronger foundation* (NSB06-02). Retrieved from http://www.nsf.gov/statistics/nsb0602/ (accessed February 19, 2015).

Oyserman, D., Terry, K., & Bybee, D. (2002). A possible selves intervention to enhance school involvement. *Journal of Adolescence, 25*(3), 313–326.

Patall, E. A., Cooper, H., & Wynn, S. R. (2010). The effectiveness and relative importance of choice in the classroom. *Journal of Educational Psychology, 102*(4), 896–915.

Pekrun, R. (2006). The control-value theory of achievement emotions: Assumptions, corollaries, and implications for educational research and practice. *Educational Psychology Review, 18,* 315–341.

Pellegrino, J. W. (2012). From cognitive principles to instructional practices: The devil is often in the details. *Journal of Applied Research in Memory and Cognition, 1*(4), 260–262.

Perlman, B., & McCann, L. I. (2005). Undergraduate research experiences in psychology: A national study of courses and curricula. *Teaching of Psychology, 32,* 5–14.

Perry, R. P., Stupnisky, R. H., Hall, N. C., Chipperfield, J. G., & Weiner, B. (2010). Bad starts and better finishes: Attributional retraining and initial performance in competitive achievement settings. *Journal of Social and Clinical Psychology, 29*(6), 668–700.

Pintrich, P. R. (2003). A motivational science perspective on the role of student motivation in learning and teaching contexts. *Journal of Educational Psychology, 95*(4), 667–686.

Ramirez, G., & Beilock, S. L. (2011). Writing about testing worries boosts exam performance in the classroom. *Science, 331*(6014), 211–213.

Rimm-Kaufman, S. E., & Hulleman, C. S. (in press). Social and emotional learning in elementary school settings. In J. Durlak & R. Weissberg (Eds.), *The handbook of social and emotional learning.* New York: Guilford.

Roediger III, H. L., & Pyc, M. A. (2012). Inexpensive techniques to improve education: Applying cognitive psychology to enhance educational practice. *Journal of Applied Research in Memory and Cognition, 1*(4), 242–248.

Schaffner, E., & Schiefele, U. (2007). The effect of experimental manipulation of student motivation on the situational representation of text. *Learning and Instruction, 17*(6), 755–772.

Schneider, B., Carnoy, M., Kilpatrick, J., Schmidt, W. H., & Shavelson, R. J. (2005). *Estimating causal effects using experimental and observational designs*. Washington, DC: American Educational Research Association.

Senko, C., Hulleman, C. S., & Harackiewicz, J. M. (2011). Achievement goal theory at the crossroads: Old controversies, current challenges, and new directions. *Educational Psychologist, 46*(1), 26–47.

Shadish, W. R., Cook, T. D., & Campbell, D. T. (2002). *Experimental and quasi-experimental designs for generalized causal inference.* Boston, MA: Houghton Mifflin.

Shavelson, R. J., Phillips, D. C., Towne, L., & Feuer, M. J. (2003). On the science of education design studies. *Educational Researcher, 32*(1), 25–28.

Sherman, D. K., Hartson, K. A., Binning, K. R., Purdie-Vaughns, V., Garcia, J., Taborsky-Barba, S., & Cohen, G. L. (2013). Deflecting the trajectory and changing the narrative: How self-affirmation affects academic performance and motivation under identity threat. *Journal of Personality and Social Psychology, 104*(4), 591–618.

Silva, E., & White, T. (2012). *Pathways to improvement: Using psychological strategies to help college students master developmental math.* Stanford, CA: Carnegie Foundation for the Advancement of Teaching.

Simons, J., Dewitte, S. & Lens, W. (2003). "Don't do it for me. Do it for yourself!" Stressing the personal relevance enhances motivation in physical education. *Journal of Sport and Exercise Psychology, 25*, 145–160.

Simpkins, S. D., Davis-Kean, P., & Eccles, J. S. (2006). Math and science motivation: A longitudinal examination of the links between choices and beliefs. *Developmental Psychology, 42*, 70–83.

Skinner, E. A. (1996). A guide to constructs of control. *Journal of Personality and Social Psychology, 71*, 549–570.

Steele, C. M. (1997). A threat in the air: How stereotypes shape intellectual identity and performance. *American Psychologist, 52*(6), 613–629.

Struthers, C. W., & Perry, R. P. (1996). Attributional style, attributional retraining, and inoculation against motivational deficits. *Social Psychology of Education, 1(2)*, 171–187.

Vansteenkiste, M., Simons, J., Lens, W., Sheldon, K. M., & Deci, E. L. (2004). Motivating learning, performance, and persistence: The synergistic effects of intrinsic goal contents and autonomy-supportive contexts. *Journal of Personality and Social Psychology, 87*(2), 246.

Walton, G. M., & Cohen, G. L. (2007). A question of belonging: Race, social fit, and achievement. *Journal of Personality and Social Psychology, 92*(1), 82.

Walton, G. M., & Cohen, G. L. (2011). A brief social-belonging intervention improves academic and health outcomes among minority students. *Science, 331*, 1447–1451.

Weiner, B. (1972). *Theories of motivation: From mechanism to cognition.* Oxford, England: Markham.

Weiner, B. (2010). The development of an attribution-based theory of motivation: A history of ideas. *Educational Psychologist, 45*(1), 28–36.

Wigfield, A., & Cambria, J. (2010). Students' achievement values, goal orientations, and interest: Definitions, development, and relations to achievement outcomes. *Developmental Review, 30*, 1–35.

Wigfield, A., & Eccles, J. S. (2000). Expectancy-value theory of achievement motivation. *Contemporary Educational Psychology, 25*, 68–81.

Wilson, T. D., & Linville, P. W. (1985). Improving the performance of college freshmen with attributional techniques. *Journal of Personality and Social Psychology, 49*(1), 287.

Yeager, D. S., Henderson, M., Paunesku, D., Walton, G. M., D'Mello, S., Spitzer, B. J., & Duckworth, A. L. (2014). Boring but important: A self-transcendent purpose for learning fosters academic self-regulation. *Journal of Personality and Social Psychology, 107*, 559–580.

Yeager, D. S., & Walton, G. M. (2011). Social-psychological interventions in education: They're not magic. *Review of Educational Research, 8*(2), 267–301.

# 13

# Beyond the Shadow

## The Role of Personality and Temperament in Learning[1]

*Arthur E. Poropat*
Griffith University, Australia

Educational concerns have provided much of the impetus for clarifying individual differences, especially with respect to identifying factors underlying academic performance. For example, Binet and Simon were contracted to develop techniques for identifying students who would succeed or struggle at school, ultimately leading to the Stanford-Binet Intelligence Scales (Wolf, 1973). Spearman instead used measures of academic performance (standardized test scores) as a central component of his research that resulted in the identification of the general cognitive ability or intelligence factor he termed *g* (Spearman, 1927). Around the same time, in one of the first self-consciously scientific studies of "character," Webb (1915) obtained ratings from older students on "qualities" that could be "conceived as having a general and fundamental bearing upon the total personality" (p. 12), such as "Tendency *not* to abandon tasks in face of obstacles" (p. 55). These ratings were used to identify what would now be called a personality factor, which was both independent of *g* and strongly associated with measures of academic performance. Webb labeled this *w*, the *will* factor. But whereas later research gave substantial support for the role of *g*-linked factors in learning, most twentieth-century reviewers concluded that correlations of personality with learning and associated outcomes were too inconsistent to be relied upon (De Raad & Schouwenburg, 1996; Harris, 1940; Margrain, 1978).

Recent meta-analyses have changed this picture, providing reliable evidence for the role of personality in learning and education. The five-factor model of personality (FFM) enabled these meta-analyses, so it is necessary to understand the FFM to properly appreciate their conclusions. Consequently, this chapter proceeds as follows. After a review of the FFM, a comparison and integration of the FFM with alternative, temperament-based models is provided. The FFM is then used to organize research on personality in relation to learning, with each dimension reviewed using the following framework: (a) a description of each FFM

dimension and its associated traits is provided; (b) links with learning and academic performance outcomes are summarized; (c) possible explanations and mechanisms underlying these links are considered. Alternative models of personality and their roles in learning and performance are then briefly considered, before examining measurement issues that complicate consideration of personality with respect to learning. Practical implications of the review are then discussed, before providing an integrating conclusion.

## The FFM and Temperament

The FFM currently dominates personality research, both generally and within educational psychology. For example, a recent empirical review of individual differences and their role within postsecondary education (Richardson, Abraham, & Bond, 2012) obtained twice as many reports using FFM-based measures than all non-FFM personality studies combined. The FFM was developed on the basis of the lexical hypothesis, which was originally conceived by Galton (1884) before later development by Allport and Odbert (1936) and Norman (1963). In brief, the lexical hypothesis is that languages will have more descriptors (especially adjectives) for the most important individual differences. For example, as cars grew in importance within modern societies, so did the number of words for makes and models of car. In similar manner, languages have more descriptors distinguishing between people on important dimensions, such as social dominance or predictability. Research based upon the lexical hypothesis led to an extended series of factor analyses using common English adjectives for describing personality, which ultimately converged on the FFM (Saucier & Goldberg, 2001). These factors are: agreeableness (warm and accommodating), conscientiousness (dutiful and diligent), emotional stability (ranging from calm to anxious), extraversion (talkative and sociable), and openness (curious, intellectual, and creative). Although currently the pre-eminent model of personality, the FFM is not universally accepted and does not consistently emerge from factor analyses in different languages (De Raad et al., 2010); more will be said on this later in the chapter.

Given its basis in linguistic descriptors, the FFM is inherently linked to an individual's reputation (i.e., the way in which she is perceived and described by herself and others) rather than underlying processes or influences (Saucier & Goldberg, 2001), such as neurological or endocrinological functioning. As such, personality as reflected in the FFM can be contrasted with these underlying influences that are presumed to appear early in development and without training or instruction, and that are often referred to as qualities of temperament (Rothbart, 2007). From this perspective, personality has been argued to reflect the interaction of temperament with later development and experience (Rothbart, 2007).

One of the earliest models of temperament was presented by Thomas, Chess, and Birch (1968), who analyzed children's behaviors into major components, such as: activity level, rhythmicity, adaptability, intensity of reaction, quality of mood, distractibility, and attention span and persistence. Although Buss and Plomin's (1975) model was partly based on similar observations, these authors also drew upon behavioral comparisons with non-human species to produce a simplified model comprised of emotionality, sociability, activity, and shyness. More recently, Rothbart (2007) and colleagues (Rothbart, Ahadi, Hershey, & Fisher, 2001) applied a theoretical framework of temperament in which an individual's reactivity to stimuli was argued to interact with processes for control of that reactivity, leading to a model of basic dimensions, namely effortful control, negative affectivity, and extraversion/surgency. The first assessment of these dimensions was the Children's Behavioral Questionnaire (Rothbart et al., 2001), which was designed for use with children aged from 3 through 7 years, but adaptations have been developed for adolescents (Capaldi & Rothbart, 1992) and adults (Evans & Rothbart, 2007).

Although Mervielde, De Clercq, De Fruyt, and Van Leeuwen (2005) argued that observed differences between models of temperament and the FFM are "more apparent than real" (p. 134), this is only partly supported by empirical evidence. De Pauw, Mervielde, and Van Leeuwen (2009) analyzed ratings of an FFM measure alongside several temperament assessments and found two factors almost entirely composed of temperament scales, while openness did not align with any temperament scales. So, despite similarities, FFM factors and temperament are not redundant (De Pauw et al., 2009). Consequently, the following review both integrates and contrasts research on personality and temperament with respect to learning and education.

## Personality/Temperament and Learning Processes/ Outcomes

If the lexical hypothesis is correct, lexical personality factors should be associated with socially important outcomes such as learning and educational performance. As outlined below, recent meta-analyses have confirmed this, showing correlations with academic performance that rival or exceed those with *g*-linked measures. This is particularly significant given that academic performance has been claimed to be the primary validating criterion for *g*-linked measures (Chamorro-Premuzic & Furnham, 2006). So, within the context of learning and education, personality has emerged from *g*'s shadow.

Outcomes of learning, especially academic performance as measured by grades and grade point average (GPA), have been the focus of most research on personality and learning. Several recent meta-analyses (Connelly & Ones, 2010; Poropat, 2009, 2014a, 2014b; Richardson et al., 2012) systematically reviewed this literature, so only headline meta-analytic correlations of FFM measures with academic performance are reported here.[2] These correlations assume linear relationships that may not always hold in educational situations (e.g., as exemplified by the complicated relationship between arousal, context, and performance known as the Yerkes-Dodson law: Hanoch & Vitouch, 2004). Further, these meta-analyses focus upon academic performance, which is an outcome and hence only an indicator of the learning process itself. So, in the following sections the major components of personality and temperament are explained and their relationships are clarified, prior to presenting evidence of their associations with prominent learning outcomes. Finally research on personality and temperament and their links with learning processes is considered in order to elucidate these relationships.

### Agreeableness/Prosociality

***Description and associated traits.*** Agreeableness is one of three personality factors that De Raad et al. (2010) found in each language they examined, and so may be a universal personality dimension. Shiner and Caspi (2003) argued that agreeableness reflects prosocial tendencies as opposed to antagonistic behavior, and agreeableness was related to temperament-based measures of adaptability and anger in De Pauw et al.'s (2009) research.

***Links with learning outcomes.*** Meta-analytic correlations of self-rated agreeableness with elementary-level academic performance (0.30) are relatively strong, but correlations at secondary and postsecondary levels are much lower (0.05 and 0.06). Correlations with academic performance are more consistent when agreeableness is other-rated (e.g., ratings are provided by parents or teachers)—elementary: 0.09; secondary 0.09; postsecondary: 0.12. Apart from the anomalous finding in elementary education (which is discussed in a later section), agreeableness is only modestly associated with learning outcomes.

***Explanations and mechanisms.*** Higher levels of agreeableness may help students establish positive relationships, potentially facilitating learning (Saklofske, Austin, Mastoras, Beaton, & Osborne, 2012). Agreeableness is linked with higher levels of extrinsic motivation, meaning that more agreeable students are able to see the value of something they have to comply with but do not like (Clark & Schroth, 2010), which may explain their additional efforts outside of formal schooling, such as doing more homework (Lubbers, Van der Werf, Kuyper, & Hendriks, 2010). Agreeableness is also linked with time management and effort regulation (Bidjerano & Dai, 2007), which in turn are linked to GPA (Bidjerano & Dai, 2007). This capacity for compliance makes students high in agreeableness more likely to work well in teams and to cooperate with guidance, such as that provided by teachers.

### Conscientiousness/Effortful Control

***Description and associated traits.*** Like agreeableness, De Raad et al. (2010) found that conscientiousness reliably emerges from emic lexical personality factor analyses across languages. Apart from being widely validated, conscientiousness is one of the longest-recognized personality dimensions, with much in common with Webb's (1915) *w* factor, and more attention has been paid to researching conscientiousness in education than any other personality variable (Richardson et al., 2012). Conscientiousness has been both theoretically (Mervielde et al., 2005) and empirically linked with effortful control (De Pauw et al., 2009), which in turn has been linked with both the human brain's executive attention network and human genetic markers (Rothbart, 2007), providing a possible basis for conscientiousness.

***Links with learning outcomes.*** Regardless of the culture in which a study was conducted, or whether a study is undertaken at elementary ($r = 0.28$), secondary ($r = 0.21$), or postsecondary ($r = 0.23$) levels of education (Poropat, 2009), conscientiousness is the most important personality predictor of academic performance. These correlations are much stronger when conscientiousness is rated by someone other than the self (Poropat, 2014a, 2014b), with correlations highest in elementary education (0.50), and still substantial in secondary and postsecondary education (0.38). The decline in these correlations at higher academic levels may be due to range restriction from lower levels of educational participation, but it is not as substantial as corresponding declines in correlations of intelligence with academic performance (0.58, 0.24, 0.23: Poropat, 2009). Notably, the link between other-rated conscientiousness and academic performance at secondary and postsecondary levels is one of few examples of academic performance having a stronger meta-analytic correlation with a non-cognitive individual difference variable than with intelligence.

***Explanations and mechanisms.*** In Rothbart's (2007) conception, effortful control encompasses self-regulation, persistence, and the ability to notice and take pleasure in low-intensity stimuli. These aspects support the capacity to choose and pursue actions while screening out distractions, and detecting and correcting errors. Consistent with earlier arguments, a range of behaviors linked with effortful control have been subsumed within the conscientiousness factor, including adhering to social norms, planfulness, and rule following (Roberts, Jackson, Fayard, Edmonds, & Meints, 2009).

One explanation for why conscientiousness appears to affect learning is it increases exposure of students to learning tasks and environments. The ability to stay involved in educational activities is crucial to learning (Credé, Roch, & Kieszczynka, 2010), as are goal setting and planning, and the monitoring and management of time (Hattie, 2009), each of which help to keep students involved with learning. At its most basic level, study involvement means staying enrolled, and Komarraju and Karau (2005) found that conscientiousness was strongly correlated with motivations to persist with study (0.60). Active management of time mediates the conscientiousness–academic performance relationship among part-time students, who tend to have greater demands upon their time (MacCann, Fogarty, & Roberts, 2012), while Bidjerano and Dai (2007) linked conscientiousness with allocation of study time and self-regulation of learning. Conscientiousness is correlated with motivation for learning-related activities (Steinmayr, Bipp, & Spinath, 2011) undertaken outside of teacher supervision (Lubbers et al., 2010) that contributes to learning outcomes (Zhang, Nurmi, Kiuru, Lerkkanen, & Aunola, 2011; see also Chapters 7 and 8 in this volume). The relationship of conscientiousness with academic performance is partly mediated by use of a strategic learning approach, in which students adapt their learning activities to the demands of assessment (Swanberg & Martinsen, 2010). Students higher on conscientiousness also have stronger intentions to transfer learning (Yamkovenko & Holton, 2010).

Conscientiousness is linked with managing stress by focusing on learning-associated tasks (Saklofske et al., 2012), or using problem-focused coping (MacCann, Lipnevich, Burrus, & Roberts, 2012). More conscientious students appear to manage their stress by changing focus from extrinsic performance goals, in which grades or other performance measures are targeted, to intrinsic learning goals, in which learning itself is attended to (see Chapter 7, this volume). Consistent with this, more conscientious students experience less tension when focused on learning rather than performance (Cianci, Klein, & Seijts, 2010) and have higher levels of positive feelings (MacCann, Lipnevich, et al., 2012), while effortful control is associated with fewer behavior problems (Rothbart, 2007). So, conscientiousness and associated factors both minimize stress and ameliorate the consequences of stress, which in turn contribute to learning.

Recent research has shown that conscientiousness and related constructs have a complicated relationship with intelligence. Since Binet and Simon, intelligence has typically been understood as maximal performance (Ackerman & Heggestad, 1997), yet actual scores on intelligence tests are commonly confounded by test-taking motivation, with meta-analytic estimates of the effects of incentive-based motivation on intelligence scores as high as 1.6 standard deviations (Duckworth, Quinn, Lynam, Loeber, & Stouthamer-Loeber, 2011). Consistent with this, student effort, as assessed by observing test-taking behavior, has been shown to account for as much as 30% of covariance between intelligence scores and subsequent academic performance (Duckworth et al., 2011). So, despite efforts by test administrators to prompt maximal effort and hence performance, individual differences in effortful behavior affect both intelligence scores and the observed relationships between intelligence and learning outcomes. Effort and ability have long been recognized to interact in their effect upon learning (Cronbach & Snow, 1977): being smart and making an effort are both good for learning, but *effort provides greater opportunity to demonstrate and profit from being smart.*

These interactive effects of effort and ability upon learning outcomes were well described by Richard Snow, especially as presented in the unique volume developing his work but compiled posthumously (Corno et al., 2002). A recent report demonstrating some of these effects was presented by Duckworth, Quinn, and Tsukayama (2012), who found that intelligence but not self-control predicted the degree of learning measured by standardized tests of achievement, although the reverse held for school-based tests. Duckworth et al. (2012) argued that intelligence helps students learn independently of school-related activities and self-control affects the degree to which students study and maintain focus on learning activities set within school. However, an alternative interpretation is that intelligence tests and standardized tests use similar formats ("common method variance"), being based on structured items developed independently of specific school curricula. The assessments of self-control used by Duckworth et al. (2012) relied on adult ratings based on observations within schools; likewise, the school-based performance measures were based on teacher assessments of children's behavioral demonstrations of learning achievements within schools. So, these results may be due to the type of behavior reflected in the various measures. This issue of measurement effects is revisited in a later section.

Despite the promise of conscientiousness, effortful control, and related constructs as explanatory factors for learning readiness and outcomes, many of the conclusions in this section remain tentative. The strength of associations between conscientiousness and learning is not under question, but the nature of those relationships will not be properly understood without active exploration of the underlying dynamics. The ability to consider these dynamics is limited by the fact that most studies cited here used correlational, cross-sectional designs. Researchers are encouraged to adopt alternative research methodologies, especially longitudinal, experimental and quasi-experimental, and rigorous case studies. For example, it would be valuable to examine over time the extent to which more conscientious students use techniques that have been demonstrated to affect learning. Optimally, such research would build upon and integrate extensive and ongoing research on self-regulated learning (see Winne, 2014, for a recent overview), potentially enhancing understanding of both educational and personality phenomena.

### Emotional Stability/Negative Affectivity

***Description and associated traits.*** Emotional stability (also commonly labeled by its opposite pole—neuroticism) is not reliably found across cultures (De Raad et al., 2010), but is reliably (negatively) related to temperament measures of negative affectivity, apparently based on intensity of reaction to stimuli and distractibility control (De Pauw et al., 2009). Given considerable evidence for a biological basis to negative affectivity (Rothbart, 2007), it seems that this aspect of temperament, and by implication emotional stability, represents a substantive individual difference.

***Links with learning outcomes.*** When self-rated, emotional stability has its highest correlation with academic performance in elementary education (0.20), falling to non-significant values in secondary (0.01) and postsecondary education. Yet other-rated emotional stability has a similar correlation with academic performance in elementary education (0.18), but this does not decline at higher levels of education (0.19). So, it appears that emotional stability still affects learning among older students, but self-ratings of older students become detached from academic performance, possibly as a result of older students adjusting their self-ratings in line with social desirability.

***Explanations and mechanisms.*** Negative affectivity (and hence, low emotional stability) is associated with heightened anticipation of, and sensitivity to: (a) distressing stimuli; (b) interruption of tasks and blocking of goals based on negative affect; and (c) slow recovery from feelings of distress (Rothbart, 2007). As such, emotional stability should be linked with aspects of learning that require integration of externally provided information that provokes emotional reactions. When confronted with anxiety-provoking stimuli, more anxious individuals ruminate more, enhancing memory for objects of rumination but actively interfering with other specific contents from within learning situations (Kircanski, Craske, & Bjork, 2008). Consistent with this, low emotional stability makes people less willing to focus on and consequently less able to learn from errors (Zhao, 2011), while high emotional stability results in greater focus on homework activities, leading to better academic performance (Lubbers et al., 2010).

Emotional stability is negatively associated with academic motivations of avoidance (Payne, Youngcourt, & Beaubien, 2007), debilitating anxiety, withdrawing, and being discouraged (Komarraju & Karau, 2005). Higher levels of emotional stability are associated with lower attention to extrinsic motivators (Clark & Schroth, 2010; Komarraju, Karau, & Schmeck, 2009). Yet, people who score low on emotional stability are actually more motivated to learn (Zhao, 2011), possibly because of error-prompted guilt or shame producing greater focus on learning to avoid future mistakes. This may partly explain the anomalous finding of Mellanby and Zimdars (2011), whose sample of female students with high trait anxiety did better in final-year assessments than less anxious women. However, these authors noted their sample was unusual, with exceptionally high academic performance and intelligence, making their results difficult to generalize.

Future research on emotional stability with respect to learning may profit from considering relevant factors that have been shown to contribute to learning. Such factors are likely to include attending to and integrating feedback, dealing with challenges, managing cognitive overload, and enhancing the capacity to persist in the face of "desirable difficulties" that foster learning despite their experienced inconvenience (Graesser, 2009).

## Extraversion/Surgency

**Description and associated traits.**  Extraversion is clearly linked to temperament measures of surgency, activity, and sociability (De Pauw et al., 2009), and is one of the personality factors reliably found across cultures (De Raad et al., 2010). Extraversion/surgency is linked with temperament aspects, including activity level, low behavioral inhibition, high approach towards novelty, positive affect, impulsivity, and affiliation, linking extraversion with interpersonal behavior (De Pauw et al., 2009).

**Links with learning outcomes.**  In one of the first and largest single school-based studies of personality, Eysenck and Cookson (1969) found extraversion had a modest association with academic performance ($r = 0.12$–0.13) in elementary education. On this basis, Eysenck and Cookson (1969) argued that extraverted students have more interaction, leading to more learning. Meta-analytic correlations of self-rated extraversion and academic performance are higher at elementary (0.18) than secondary (–0.03) and postsecondary (–0.01) levels of education, but the predicted negative correlations are small enough to be meaningless. Correlations of academic performance with other-rated extraversion are likewise of greatest magnitude at the elementary level (0.11), but become trivial at secondary and postsecondary levels (0.04).

**Explanations and mechanisms.**  Poropat (2009) suggested that behaviors associated with extraversion are likely to catch the attention of teachers, which may either result in more support or make it easier to grade an elementary-level student (Poropat, 2009). Consistent with this, elementary education teachers tend to think shy children are less intelligent and less academically able (Coplan, Hughes, Bosacki, & Rose-Krasnor, 2011). Further, Poropat (2009) argued that the reduced opportunity for consistent observation of students in secondary and postsecondary education, combined with more rigorous approaches to assessment, is likely to make teacher–student relationship-linked effects on academic performance less potent after elementary school.

Alternatively, extraversion may only affect learning in very specific circumstances, when higher levels of approach or impulsive behaviors arising from motivations such as curiosity, and the desire to play and explore social limits (Bernard, 2010), result in students having greater levels of experience. An example of this was reported by Orvis,

Brusso, Wasserman, and Fisher (2011), who found that extraversion only affected performance when learners were able to explore learning environments. Given that even students with attention deficit hyperactivity disorder have been found to learn more if they impulsively blurt out answers (Tymms & Merrell, 2011), possibly because generating responses to questions is an effective tool for enhancing learning (Graesser, 2009), it appears likely that extraverted students may also benefit from impulsive responding and exploration. So, extraversion may contribute to learning through enhancing experience but especially in learning environments with opportunities for learner control and exploration.

Extraversion has been linked with other learning motivations, apparently as a consequence of social responses to extraverted behaviors. According to Clark and Schroth (2010), extraversion is associated with introjected extrinsic motivation, in which students comply out of obligation or guilt, but it also is linked with external regulation, in which students comply to gain rewards or avoid punishments. The social interaction component to extraversion is further complicated by the tendency for more extraverted students to actively seek help from others (Bidjerano & Dai, 2007). This focus on external regulation and assistance may help to counteract some of the negative consequences of the impulsive aspects of surgency, such as associated difficulties with self-regulating learning, which are in turn likely to limit learning achievements (Graesser, 2009).

The range of different effects of extraversion upon learning and learning motivation and learning strategy make it unlikely that previously reported meta-analytic studies of extraversion and academic performance will reveal much about associated underlying processes. This is because meta-analyses average out variations of the type described in this section, a problem exacerbated by the reliance on aggregate measures of academic performance. Systematic research programs pursuing finer-grained questions are necessary to address the social complexity of extraversion in learning.

## Openness

**Description and associated traits.**  Openness is the most controversial of the FFM factors because of questions about its basic content (von Stumm, Hell, & Chamorro-Premuzic, 2011), the fact it is not consistently obtained in emic personality factor analyses across cultures (De Raad et al., 2010), and the observation that it does not have a clear parallel in childhood temperament (De Pauw et al., 2009; Shiner, 2000). Part of the confusion around the nature of openness arises from questions about the coherence of the factor, which has often been separated into two facets: an artistic and thoughtful component featuring interests in aesthetics and fantasy; and an intellectual engagement component focused upon thinking and curiosity, often referred to as *intellect* (von Stumm et al., 2011). A further complication is that, unlike other FFM traits, openness is commonly found to correlate with measures of intelligence (Goff & Ackerman, 1992), with the intellect component appearing to be the particular focus of this relationship (von Stumm et al., 2011).

However within this review, "openness" will be used as the generic term for measures of this FFM dimension.

***Links with learning outcomes.*** Despite these complications, openness is the personality dimension most closely associated with learning and academic performance, after conscientiousness. Self-rated openness is most highly correlated with academic performance in elementary education (0.24), falling in secondary (0.12) and postsecondary (0.07) education. Significantly stronger correlations are obtained when openness is other-rated at elementary (0.43) and secondary/postsecondary (0.28) levels, exceeding correlations of intelligence with academic performance (Poropat, 2014b).

***Explanations and mechanisms.*** A review of research by Goff and Ackerman (1992) highlighted theoretically meaningful links between openness and intelligence, and von Stumm and Ackerman (2013) argued that this association was based on common links with intellectual investment, the tendency to pursue and enjoy effortful intellectual activities. There is compelling independent evidence for von Stumm and Ackerman's thesis, based upon links between openness and various motivational constructs. To begin with, openness is significantly associated with motivations such as curiosity and desire to achieve greater ability (Bernard, 2010), and with intrinsic motivation to know, enjoyment of thinking, and self-improvement (Clark & Schroth, 2010; Komarraju & Karau, 2005). In a meta-analysis focused upon the motivational construct of goal orientation, Payne et al. (2007) found that the correlation of learning goal orientation (a focus on goals of learning and mastery rather than performance or outcomes) with openness (0.44) was the strongest between any FFM and goal orientation measure, while other research has shown that learning goal orientation mediates the relationship between openness and learning outcomes (Steinmayr et al., 2011). In a study of personality and learning that was rare both for being longitudinal and examining learning outside of educational settings, Hambrick, Pink, Meinz, Pettibone, and Oswald (2008) looked at the acquisition of knowledge of current events. The effect of g on acquisition of current events knowledge was non-significant, but openness affected interest in current events, which in turn led to greater current-events knowledge both directly and by increasing exposure to relevant news. This is consistent with the idea that learning is influenced by intellectual investment more than by maximal intellectual ability.

Openness-related motivations are expressed in specific sets of actions or learning strategies. Bidjerano and Dai (2007) found that the learning strategies of metacognition, elaboration, critical thinking, time management, and effort regulation were all associated with openness, but only time management and effort regulation were linked to academic performance. A deep learning strategy, in which students aim at understanding rather than reproducing knowledge, is particularly associated with openness rather than the other FFM dimensions (Chamorro-Premuzic & Furnham, 2009), and deep learning mediates the openness–academic performance relationship (Swanberg & Martinsen, 2010).

These relationships between openness, learning strategies, and learning outcomes can be complicated by the learning environment. Students who are higher in openness learn more when they can exercise their curiosity and desire to learn by controlling their learning process (Orvis et al., 2011). However, students who are lower on openness learn most when they have *fewer* opportunities to control their learning (Orvis et al., 2011), presenting a challenge to teachers dealing with students who vary substantially on this dimension.

Given the apparent value of openness and related constructs for learning, it is surprising that there has not been more research on its association with factors that have been demonstrated to improve learning and academic performance. For example, there are straightforward arguments for expecting openness to be associated with learning-related factors listed by Graesser (2009), such as: asking and answering "deep" questions; responding to apparent contradictions and paradoxes; cognitive flexibility; metacognition; and discovery learning. Yet the fact that openness is not related to performance goal orientation may mean that students who are high on openness learn more, but do not care to exchange performance for grades. Future researchers are encouraged to consider how openness is related to these other consequences for learning-related behaviors.

## Other Factors and Constructs

Apart from the models of temperament, few theoretically based personality models have been used in research on learning, the most notable exception being the Eysenckian personality model (Eysenck & Eysenck, 1975; Poropat, 2011a). Despite a substantial history of use in educational research, measures of the Eysenckian dimensions have demonstrated only minor associations with learning outcomes, all of which can be accounted for by the FFM. Moreover, the Eysenckian Psychoticism scale in particular is psychometrically unsound in educational settings (Poropat, 2011a). There appears to be little to be gained in continued use of this model in empirical studies in education.

A few other personality factors have been examined with respect to learning. Despite being negatively correlated with conscientiousness, playfulness, especially the aspects of spontaneous and creative playfulness, is positively correlated with university grades (Proyer, 2011). A recent meta-analysis showed that chronotype, which refers to whether an individual is more alert in the morning or evening, is reliably but modestly associated with academic performance (Preckel, Lipnevich, Schneider, & Roberts, 2011). There may be some potential in further exploring these constructs, possibly by integrating them with learning strategies.

One of the most widely researched current theories of personality is reinforcement sensitivity theory (RST), which, as its name suggests, was heavily influenced in its development by work on sensitivity to appetitive and aversive stimuli within the context of behavioral learning theory (Corr, 2004). A growing body of research has examined the implications of RST for learning in response to different reinforcement parameters (Leue & Beauducel, 2008), but the status of

RST as an account of individual differences in learning processes remains at best unproven (Matthews, 2007). Further, it is difficult to find a report that tests the implications of RST for learning outside of the laboratory, especially in academic or organizational settings. This represents an obvious and important oversight for RST, which future researchers are encouraged to address.

Also relatively underresearched in the context of learning are the temperament constructs of perceptual sensitivity, distractibility, and threshold. This is despite the fact that these constructs have clear implications for learning, associated with the centrality of attentional focus within learning processes. A rare example is Mullola et al. (2010), who in a large study ($n = 3,212$) found distractibility had substantial correlations with grades (–0.44 to –0.48). Unfortunately, the distractibility scale also had large correlations with other measures (e.g., persistence: –0.80 to –0.86), so it is unclear what was being measured. Validity studies to refine relevant measures will assist future explorations of the role of these underresearched aspects of temperament in learning and education.

## Measurement Moderators of Personality–Academic Performance Correlations

Within the foregoing review, one of the strongest effects was the substantial variation in validity between self- and other-rated measures of personality as statistical predictors of academic performance. Table 13.1 provides a summary of recent meta-analytic estimates of correlations between FFM-based personality measures and academic performance that were initially reported by Poropat (2014a, 2014b). Several of the moderating effects presented in Table 13.1 are substantial, such as the increase in validity of conscientiousness at elementary level ($\Delta r^2 = 0.17$), while the correlation with emotional stability at secondary and postsecondary levels shifts from negligible to modest but meaningful. The magnitude of this effect can best be appreciated by noting that the correlations of academic performance with other-rated conscientiousness are of similar magnitude to the strongest previously reported influences on learning outcomes, including feedback (Hattie & Timperley, 2007) and class attendance (Credé et al., 2010).

Research in other areas has demonstrated incremental validity for socially valued outcomes of other- over self-rated personality (Connelly & Ones, 2010), so the increases

in correlations summarized in Table 13.1 have precedents. However at the elementary level, correlations with agreeableness and extraversion decline when these are other-rated. To make sense of this pattern, it is necessary to consider how varying the source of a rating affects the rating process and hence the rating that is provided.

Some of the more important factors that have been found to contribute to the creation of personality ratings include: the access that a rater has to observations of a ratee (e.g., how long the ratee has been known; the range of situations within which the ratee has been observed; ability to access ratee's feelings, thoughts, and intentions); the rater's method of combining and interpreting observations; and the rater's intentions in providing a rating (e.g., to present the ratee positively, negatively, or accurately: Funder, 2001; Kenny & West, 2010). So, every rating incorporates effects that reflect the target or ratee, the rater, and their relationship. Consequently, other-ratings can be more or less favorable, reliable, or predictively valid than self-ratings, but neither can be accepted as true in any absolute sense (Poropat & Corr, 2015).

These insights are not new: a side note of Webb's (1915) research was a consideration of factors that were linked to observers, such as those that are due to idiosyncratic rater perspectives. Historically, there was a degree of suspicion about the use of self-raters, and much initial development work for several major personality models, including the Sixteen Personality Factor Questionnaire, Eysenck Personality Inventory, and the FFM (e.g., Cattell, 1943; Eysenck, 1947; Norman, 1963), was conducted using other-raters. The decline in use of other-raters appears to have been due to shifts away from methodological behaviorism with its emphasis on behaviors observed by others, combined with the relative ease of acquiring self-ratings (Hofstee, 1994), and denials that rating source substantially affected measurement validity (Cattell, 1984).

The consequences of using other-rated measures of personality were systematically reviewed by Connelly and Ones (2010). One of the tools they used was comparison of criterion-based validity of self- and other-rated personality. As can be seen in Table 13.1, all other-rated FFM dimensions had higher correlations with academic performance at secondary and postsecondary levels of education, which should indicate that other-rated measures were more accurate (cf., Funder, 2001). But applying the same reasoning implies that other-rated agreeableness and extraversion were *less* accurate at

**Table 13.1  Correlations of Academic Performance with Self- and Other-rated Personality**

| Academic Level | Rater | Agreeableness | Conscientiousness | Emotional Stability | Extraversion | Openness |
|---|---|---|---|---|---|---|
| Primary | Self | 0.30 | 0.28 | 0.20 | 0.18 | 0.24 |
| Primary | Other | 0.09*** | 0.50*** | 0.18 | 0.11* | 0.43*** |
| Secondary | Self | 0.05 | 0.21 | 0.01 | –0.03 | 0.12 |
| Tertiary | Self | 0.06 | 0.23 | –.001 | –.001 | 0.07 |
| Secondary/Tertiary | Other | 0.10** | 0.38*** | 0.18*** | 0.05*** | 0.28*** |

Significant differences between correlations with self- and other-rated personality measures at the same educational level are indicated by: * $p < 0.05$; ** $p < 0.01$; *** $p < 0.001$.

elementary level. Given the independently observed validity problems with children's self-ratings of personality (Allik, Laidra, Realo, & Pullman, 2004; Poropat, 2009; Soto, John, Gosling, & Potter, 2008), this is difficult to accept.

Apart from criterion-based validity, Connelly and Ones (2010) also used self–other agreement to test rating accuracy, and found that self–other correlations are highest between close family members. Yet, even when these are corrected using test–retest reliabilities, the amount of shared variance ranges between a quarter (agreeableness: $r = 0.50$; $r^2 = 0.25$) and a little more than a third (extraversion: $r = 0.61$; $r^2 = 0.37$) of total variance (Connelly & Ones, 2010). The corresponding levels of shared variance are even lower when other-raters are not family members. When compared with test–retest reliabilities for other-rated FFM measures (ranging from 0.81 to 0.85: Connelly & Ones, 2010), these various results indicate that there is much reliable variance in personality ratings that is not shared between self- and other-raters. The following sections consider what this reliable but unshared variance may be.

### Parsing Personality Ratings with Respect to Learning Outcomes

Classical test theory accounts assume measures are composed of only true score (trait variance) and error (random variation), but this cannot account for such findings. Part of the problem is that rater-linked reliable variance is systematic and not error; for example, self- and other-rater-linked variance can be strongly correlated (Lance, Dawson, Birkelbach, & Hoffman, 2010). A more complicated parsing of measures of personality is required in order to properly understand the relationships reported in Table 13.1.

One factor that appears to contribute to differences in validity between self- and other-rated personality is the set of observations upon which the ratings are based. Vazire (2010) argued for the existence of a persistent asymmetry in observational knowledge between self- and other-raters, with self-raters having privileged access to thoughts and feelings, while other-raters may have better access to behaviors. Other-raters will also be more focused upon aspects of the ratee's personality that are of value to the other-rater, and behaviors are more valuable to others than are thoughts and feelings (Gill & Swann, 2004). It is on this basis that Connelly and Hülsheger (2012) argued that other-raters will provide more useful assessments for predicting behavioral criteria such as performance. Poropat (2014b) extended this argument, claiming that this focus upon behavior will enhance the prediction of behavioral measures of learning outcomes, such as grades and GPA (Campbell, 1999), simply because behaviors provide the best prediction of behaviors (Ouellette & Wood, 1998). This analysis echoes the explanation of Duckworth et al.'s (2012) differential prediction of academic performance—assessments that adopt comparable formats and are based on similar types of behavioral observation produce higher correlations.

While these arguments help to explain much of the incremental validity of other-ratings, especially at secondary and postsecondary level, the relative decline in validity for other-ratings of agreeableness and extraversion in elementary education requires different explanations. One possible explanation is based on the fact that self- and other-raters have different motivations when providing ratings: specifically, self-raters have self-serving biases that result in more positive ratings (Vazire, 2010). Effective enhancement of self-ratings requires comprehension of what ratings would be self-enhancing and so more positive ratings should be correlated with comprehension, at least up until the age when most or all self-raters have the minimal ability required to comprehend a personality questionnaire. John and Robins (1993) found that agreeableness is one of the more strongly evaluative FFM dimensions, so this would help to explain the shift in correlations of academic performance with this personality dimension. However, extraversion was the least evaluative dimension in their study, precluding a similar explanation. However, extraversion is treated differently in elementary education, with teachers having significantly more positive evaluations of extraverted/outgoing children with respect to both intelligence and academic performance (Coplan et al., 2011). So, the higher correlations for self-rated personality in elementary education may be due to the combined effects of self-presentation, social desirability, and teacher–student interactions. Future researchers could explore this by using personality measures that are less subject to comprehension issues, such as that developed by Measelle, John, Ablow, Cowan, and Cowan (2005).

The larger implication of this discussion of moderating effects associated with self- and other-ratings and learning outcomes is that factors that are largely independent of learning may nevertheless have substantial effects on observed relationships between personality and learning. These measurement issues do not get to the heart of why personality is associated with learning; rather, they demonstrate that researchers need to be more careful with their choice of measurement strategy. Nonetheless, if it is true that other-ratings are more closely linked to learning outcomes because they are more closely linked with behaviors, this provides a clearer basis for identifying the strategies that successful learners find most useful.

### Range of Observations or Contexts

Personality ratings can also vary with respect to the range of observations. Specifically, most personality assessments are obtained using a general frame-of-reference, in which raters are asked to respond with respect to the ratee as they typically are (Schmit, Ryan, Stierwalt, & Powell, 1995). But, raters can use different frames-of-reference, for example, by assessing a target with respect to how they typically are at work or at school. With other-raters who only know the ratee within a specific context, such instructions would have little effect: such raters use the *de facto* frame-of-reference imposed by their situationally limited range of observations. But self-raters have a much broader range of observations to call upon, so using a constrained frame-of-reference may bring their range of observations into line with the *de facto* frame-of-reference used by other-raters.

Lievens, De Corte, and Schollaert (2008) reported two studies in which university students were asked to rate their own personality using an at-school frame-of-reference. When an at-school frame-of-reference was used, uncorrected correlations of conscientiousness with GPA rose in one study from 0.09 to 0.37, and to 0.38 in another. The at-school correlations were comparable with the correlation with other-rated conscientiousness at postsecondary level reported in Table 13.1. However, correlations of GPA with openness were not significantly different when an at-school frame-of-reference was used. So, the range of observations used within different frames-of-reference may explain some of the moderating effects of rating source, but it does not explain all of these.

## Personality and Intelligence

As discussed previously, recent findings have demonstrated that there are substantial motivational factors that contribute to intelligence test scores, and that these motivational components account for a significant proportion of the relationship between intelligence and learning. Such a finding can cut two ways—if motivation overlaps with scores on intelligence, it seems likely that mental ability overlaps with personality scores. With respect to self-rated personality, the correlations with intelligence are negligible, with only the correlation with openness (0.15) being notable (Poropat, 2009). Few studies have reported correlations between intelligence and other-rated personality, and these have been highly variable. For example, Asendorpf and van Aken (2003) reported correlations with conscientiousness ranging from 0.01 to 0.46, and correlations with openness ranging from 0.28 to 0.52. These correlations appear to be slightly lower in secondary education (i.e., conscientiousness: 0.13; openness: 0.29: Bratko, Chamorro-Premuzic, & Saks, 2006). Once again, the strongest correlations are those of intelligence with openness, which is consistent with the review of openness presented earlier in this chapter. Likewise, observed correlations of intelligence with other-rated conscientiousness are consistent with effortful control contributing to intelligence test scores. However, it also reasonable to argue that more intelligent students are more able to learn skills that contribute to openness and effortful control, making the causal direction ambiguous without further research.

These correlations raise questions regarding whether intelligence explains observed relationships of personality with learning outcomes, potentially due to measurement confounds. When self-rated personality–academic performance correlations are controlled for intelligence, effects on observed correlations are largest in elementary education, especially for correlations with emotional stability (0.20 to 0.11) and extraversion (0.18 to 0.06: Poropat, 2009). At higher educational levels, controlling for intelligence has little effect, even slightly increasing correlations (Poropat, 2009). For other-rated personality, controlling for intelligence had most effect on correlations with openness in postsecondary education (0.28 to 0.21), but this correlation

remained comparable with the correlation of intelligence itself with academic performance (Poropat, 2014a, 2014b). So, personality and intelligence have important independent and interacting contributions to learning outcomes, as previously argued by Snow and his colleagues (Talbert & Cronbach, 2002).

## Measurement Issues—General Conclusions

Measurement has long been central to understanding both personality and learning, as well as their interaction. The strength of the moderating effects due to rater source and frame-of-reference is consistent with the idea that personality and learning are associated because of shared behaviors, while overlaps between personality and measures of intelligence are likewise indicative of complex relationships with and implications for learning and learning outcomes. The preceding review of personality and learning processes/outcomes is also consistent with shared behaviors accounting for the relationships between these.

## Practical Applications of Personality in Educational Settings

The relationship between personality and learning is on a much sounder foundation than ever, and is beginning to indicate that early researchers' hopes may be realized. Yet much work remains before it is possible to provide sound practical applications of many of the findings. In this section, I speculate on some areas that seem likely to profit from these endeavors.

## Support for Learning

Personality scores have long been used in career counseling and student development, but there is further potential for guiding students, based upon the associations reviewed in this chapter. Personality assessments should be able to assist with identifying students who are likely to benefit from developmental programs, as well as guide decisions about appropriate assistance with learning strategies for those students.

Even simply providing students with well-structured feedback on their personality and its implications for learning may prove valuable. Research from clinical psychology demonstrates that providing clients with feedback on assessments is useful in itself, producing significant client change and facilitating subsequent clinical work (Poston & Hanson, 2010). Similar benefits may come from well-structured feedback programs based on knowledge of the various links between personality and learning, so researchers and practitioners should consider examining the use of personality assessment as a feedback tool for remedial and facilitative coaching and training in learning contexts.

## Selection

Poropat (2009) specifically referred to the potential of personality assessments as tools for selecting students into competitive educational programs. The relative size of the associations summarized in this chapter makes this an area that should be of great interest. However, before practical application of personality assessment to educational selection, a range of issues need to be addressed. To begin with, most studies of personality and learning have been cross-sectional, and longitudinal evidence is necessary to ensure genuine predictive validity. More concerning is the issue of motivated responding, in which applicants respond in a manner likely to enhance their prospects. Other-ratings eliminate self-motivated faking, but have their own problems: other-raters with good knowledge of applicants are also likely to have stronger relationships with them, and so may be motivated to adjust ratings as a measure of support. Avoiding this by using other-raters with limited relationships with applicants may produce less valid and potentially worthless assessments. Further, other-ratings may raise issues of adverse impact, especially when they come from a different group to applicants. Alternative assessment methods may prove valuable, such as use of implicit (Johnson & Saboe, 2011) or behavioral (Jackson et al., 2010) measures, but these require further validation. So, although interest in this area should be encouraged, personality should not be used for educational selection until these issues are resolved.

### *Personality and Learner Readiness: Learning a Personality to Enhance Learning?*

Many personality researchers implicitly or explicitly assume personality is a largely enduring feature, resistant to change (Roberts, Walton, & Viechtbauer, 2006). Against this position comes accumulating evidence that personality does indeed change, as a consequence of not only normal maturational processes but also specific life experiences (Edmonds, Jackson, Fayard, & Roberts, 2008; Sutin, Costa, Wethington, & Eaton, 2010). Although unusual within personality research, direct attempts at changing enduring aspects of learners has long been actively encouraged within education, such as Graesser's (2009) advocacy of training to enhance effort regulation (sa., Pashler et al., 2007).

Within educational contexts, various researchers have successfully improved learner performance by teaching them how to alter factors associated with personality, including openness (Jackson, Hill, Payne, Roberts, & Stine-Morrow, 2012) and socioemotional competence (Brackett, Rivers, Reyes, & Salovey, 2012). Greater focus has been given to conscientiousness-related factors, especially effortful control (Barnett et al., 2008; Diamond, Barnett, Thomas, & Munro, 2007), but also self-regulation (Eisenberg & Sulik, 2012) and self-regulated learning (Vandevelde, Van Keer, & De Wever, 2011; Winne, 2014). Berkman, Graham, and Fisher (2012) provide a thorough review of research on training for self-control, which makes it clear that these factors can be ameliorated by appropriate interventions (see Chapter 7 in this volume).

Such efforts are consistent with the substantial research tradition considering the interaction of individual differences with educational activities (Snow, 1996). From this perspective, the primary function of education is aptitude development (Snow, 1996), placing a premium on teachers' abilities to adapt learning activities to both accommodate and develop students' aptitudes (Corno, 2008). Care should be taken to distinguish this approach from attempts to match teaching with learning styles, which can be counterproductive (Bjork, Dunlosky, & Kornell, 2013). However, the apparent teachability of personality aptitudes adds weight to calls for adoption of adaptive teaching practices (Corno, 2008).

Further, it can be reasonably claimed that one of the major goals of formal education itself is to change personality. Bowles, Gintis, and Meyer (1999) argued that schooling is primarily undertaken to prepare students for employment by developing capacities for rule following, dependability, unsupervised performance, and internalization of norms, each of which has obvious associations with conscientiousness especially (e.g., see Roberts, Chernyshenko, Stark, & Goldberg, 2005; Roberts et al., 2009). This parallel has been used to explain why academic and work performance have similar relationships to personality (Lounsbury, Gibson, Sundstrom, Wilburn, & Loveland, 2004; Poropat, 2009, 2011b). So, training students to be more employable appears to be intended to change their personalities to better suit their future employers.

Despite this, rigorous assessments of efforts at guiding the development of learning-related aspects of personality have been relatively few, with most efforts restricted to early development (Jackson et al., 2012 provided a rare exception). Attempts to train personality-relevant skills provide an opportunity for both personality and educational researchers to engage in experimental studies of fundamental relationships between personality and learning, providing an alternative to cross-sectional correlational research designs, which are virtually ubiquitous in personality research. Such efforts should be strongly encouraged.

### Conclusion

It is more than a decade since Heckman and Rubinstein (2001) began their review of "non-cognitive skills" by mocking academic research that treated individual success as solely due to cognitive ability. Yet, these authors felt compelled to compare non-cognitive skills to the "dark matter" of astrophysics, because both are important within their field but ill described. Subsequent reviews have refined the identification of that "dark matter," refusing to define something meaningful in the negative, and confirming the substantial positive role for personality in learning and education. But, while personality has come out of the shadow of intelligence and much has been learned about links between personality and learning activities and processes, substantial lack of clarity remains.

The research reviewed in this chapter clearly identified at least one dominant contributor to learning. Whether it is labeled conscientiousness, effortful control, will-power, *w*, or self-regulation, there is a central component to personality that is reliably and strongly associated with learning and academic outcomes. This conclusion is strengthened by recognizing the importance of conative (motivational and volitional) processes, which are documented elsewhere in this volume. Correlations of learning variables with openness indicate that this and associated constructs are also important, apparently reflecting a role for intrinsic interest in learning. Likewise, emotional stability has now been shown to have a significant, meaningful role at all levels of formal education.

As important as these conclusions are, so is the argument that much, if not all, of the observed association of personality with learning is due to overlaps between the observable behaviors that inform personality ratings with the observable behaviors demonstrated in learning strategies, and the observable behaviors assessed in measures of learning outcomes such as academic achievement and other accomplishments. Such a conclusion does not imply that non-behavioral components of personality and learning are unimportant, but it does imply that historically dominant research methods limit the ability to properly assess these factors and their relationships. Rather than closing a door, this represents a substantial opportunity for researchers and practitioners who either choose to more effectively focus on the behavioral measurement of key constructs in this field (e.g., Jackson et al., 2010), or adopt new methodologies that enable effective access to thoughts and feelings in this area of research (see Chapter 6 in this volume).

Effective assessment of the causal structure of the relationship between personality and learning also requires different methodologies to those currently dominant. Cross-sectional, correlational studies have established a substantial basis and framework, but are probably reaching the point of diminishing returns. Instead, researchers must actively consider using experiments, quasi-experiments, and longitudinal studies, as well as qualitative exploratory analyses. Experimental research integrating training on personality-linked variables that are hypothesized to affect learning processes and outcomes appear to be particularly promising.

Alongside research considerations, there is much opportunity for educational practitioners to explore applications of personality in academic and other learning-focused settings. Using personality to select among applicants for competitive educational programs is still premature at best; using personality to guide educators and learners is clearly justified.

The questions for future theory development should no longer be about whether personality and temperament play important roles in learning, but about how these various factors interact. The emerging evidence that it is possible to actively intervene to affect these factors and their relationships gives cause for optimism for researchers and educators, and, most importantly, for learners.

## Notes

1. I happily acknowledge the contribution of Lyn Corno, Carolyn MacCann, and Philip Ackerman, along with my research students Melissa Wiemers and Dan Cummings, whose advice substantially improved this chapter.

2. All of the meta-analytic correlations of self-rated FFM with academic performance reported here were derived from Poropat (2009) for self-rated FFM, while those with other-rated FFM came from Poropat (2014a, 2014b). Richardson et al. (2012) also reported meta-analytic correlations for self-rated FFM and postsecondary academic performance, but these were based on slightly smaller aggregate samples and were not significantly different from those reported by Poropat (2009). Connelly and Ones (2010) also reported meta-analytic correlations between other-rated FFM and academic performance at secondary and post-secondary level, but their estimates were based on samples three to five times smaller than those of Poropat (2014b), and used scales that were not designed to assess the FFM. Poropat (2014b) found no systematic differences in correlations between secondary and postsecondary education, so reported just the one aggregate estimate for each FFM dimension. Unless otherwise stated, all cited meta-analytic correlations (including those with intelligence) have been corrected for measurement reliability, in line with the recommendations of Schmidt and Hunter (1996). However, it should be noted that these estimates will typically exceed correlations observed in practice.

## References

Ackerman, P. L., & Heggestad, E. D. (1997). Intelligence, personality, and interests: Evidence for overlapping traits. *Psychological Bulletin, 121*(2), 219–245.

Allik, J., Laidra, K., Realo, A., & Pullman, H. (2004). Personality development from 12 to 18 years of age: Changes in mean levels and structure of traits. *European Journal of Personality, 18*, 445–462.

Allport, G. W., & Odbert, H. S. (1936). Trait names: A psycho-lexical study. *Psychological Monographs, 47*(1, Whole No. 211).

Asendorpf, J. B., & van Aken, M. A. G. (2003). Validity of Big Five personality judgments in childhood: A 9 year longitudinal study. *European Journal of Personality, 17*(1), 1–17.

Barnett, W. S., Jung, K., Yarosz, D. J., Thomas, J., Hornbeck, A., Stechuk, R., & Burns, S. (2008). Educational effects of the Tools of the Mind curriculum: A randomized trial. *Early Childhood Research Quarterly, 23*(3), 299–313.

Berkman, E. T., Graham, A. M., & Fisher, P. A. (2012). Training self-control: A domain-general translational neuroscience approach. *Child Development Perspectives, 6*(4), 374–384.

Bernard, L. C. (2010). Motivation and personality: Relationships between putative motive dimensions and the five factor model of personality. *Psychological Reports, 106*(2), 613–631.

Bidjerano, T., & Dai, D.Y. (2007). The relationship between the big-five model of personality and self-regulated learning strategies. *Learning and Individual Differences, 17*(1), 69–81.

Bjork, R. A., Dunlosky, J., & Kornell, N. (2013). Self-regulated learning: Beliefs, techniques, and illusions. *Annual Review of Psychology, 64*, 417–444.

Bowles, S., Gintis, H., & Meyer, P. (1999). The long shadow of work: Education, the family, and the reproduction of the social division of labor. *Critical Sociology, 25*(2/3), 286–305.

Brackett, M. A., Rivers, S. E., Reyes, M. R., & Salovey, P. (2012). Enhancing academic performance and social and emotional competence with the RULER feeling words curriculum. *Learning and Individual Differences, 22*(2), 218–224.

Bratko, D., Chamorro-Premuzic, T., & Saks, Z. (2006). Personality and school performance: Incremental validity of self- and peer-ratings over intelligence. *Personality and Individual Differences, 41*, 131–142.

Buss, D. M., & Plomin, R. (1975). *A temperament theory of personality development.* New York: Wiley.

Campbell, J. P. (1999). The definition and measurement of performance in the new age. In D. R. Ilgen & E. D. Pulakos (Eds.), *The changing nature of performance: Implications for staffing, motivation, and development* (pp. 399–430). San Francisco, CA: Jossey-Bass.

Capaldi, D. M., & Rothbart, M. K. (1992). Development and validation of an early adolescent temperament measure. *Journal of Early Adolescence, 12*(2), 153–173.

Cattell, R. B. (1943). The description of personality: Basic traits resolved into clusters. *Journal of Abnormal and Social Psychology, 38*, 476–506.

Chamorro-Premuzic, T., & Furnham, A. (2006). Intellectual competence and the intelligent personality: A third way in differential psychology. *Review of General Psychology, 10*(3), 251–267.

Chamorro-Premuzic, T., & Furnham, A. (2009). Mainly openness: The relationship between the Big Five personality traits and learning approaches. *Learning and Individual Differences, 19*(4), 524–529.

Cianci, A. M., Klein, H. J., & Seijts, G. H. (2010). The effect of negative feedback on tension and subsequent performance: The main and interactive effects of goal content and conscientiousness. *Journal of Applied Psychology, 95*(4), 618–630.

Clark, M. H., & Schroth, C. A. (2010). Examining relationships between academic motivation and personality among college students. *Learning and Individual Differences, 20*, 19–24.

Connelly, B. S., & Hülsheger, U. R. (2012). A narrower scope or a clearer lens for personality? Examining sources of observers' advantages over self-reports for predicting performance. *Journal of Personality, 80*(3), 603–631.

Connelly, B. S., & Ones, D. S. (2010). An other perspective on personality: Meta-analytic integration of observers' accuracy & predictive validity. *Psychological Bulletin, 136*(6), 1092–1122.

Coplan, R. J., Hughes, K., Bosacki, S., & Rose-Krasnor, L. (2011). Is silence golden? Elementary school teachers' strategies and beliefs regarding hypothetical shy/quiet and exuberant/talkative children. *Journal of Educational Psychology, 103*(4), 939–951.

Cattell, R. B. (1984). The voyage of a laboratory. *Multivariate Behavioral Research, 19*, 121–174.

Corno, L. (2008). On teaching adaptively. *Educational Psychologist, 43*(3), 161–173.

Corno, L., Cronbach, L. J., Kupermintz, H. K., Lohman, D. H., Mandinach, E. B., Porteus, A., Talbert J. for the Stanford Aptitude Seminar (2002). *Remaking the concept of aptitude: Extending the legacy of Richard E. Snow.* Mahweh, NJ: Erlbaum.

Corr, P. J. (2004). Reinforcement sensitivity theory and personality. *Neuroscience and Biobehavioral Reviews, 28*(3), 317–332.

Credé, M., Roch, S. G., & Kieszczynka, U. M. (2010). Class attendance in college: A meta-analytic review of the relationship of class attendance with grades and student characteristics. *Review of Educational Research, 80*(2), 272–295.

Cronbach, L. J., & Snow, R. E. (1977). *Aptitudes and instructional methods: A handbook for research on interactions.* New York: Irvington.

De Pauw, S. S. W., Mervielde, I., & Van Leeuwen, K. G. (2009). How are traits related to problem behavior in preschoolers? Similarities and contrasts between temperament and personality. *Journal of Abnormal Child Psychology, 37*(3), 309–325.

De Raad, B., Barelds, D. P. H., Ostendorf, F., Mlačić, B., Di Blas, L., Hřebíčková, M., . . . Perugini, M. (2010). Only three factors of personality description are fully replicable across languages: A comparison of 14 trait taxonomies. *Journal of Personality & Social Psychology, 98*(1), 160–173.

De Raad, B., & Schouwenburg, H. C. (1996). Personality in learning and education: A review. *European Journal of Personality, 10*, 303–336.

Diamond, A., Barnett, W. S., Thomas, J., & Munro, S. (2007). The early years—Preschool program improves cognitive control. *Science, 318*(5855), 1387–1388.

Duckworth, A. L., Quinn, P. D., Lynam, D. R., Loeber, R., & Stouthamer-Loeber, M. (2011). Role of test motivation in intelligence testing. *Proceedings of the National Academy of Sciences, 108*(19), 7716–7720.

Duckworth, A. L., Quinn, P. D., & Tsukayama, E. (2012). What no child left behind leaves behind: The roles of IQ and self-control in predicting standardized achievement test scores and report card grades. *Journal of Educational Psychology, 104*(2), 439–451.

Edmonds, G. W., Jackson, J. J., Fayard, J. V., & Roberts, B. W. (2008). Is character fate, or is there hope to change my personality yet? *Social and Personality Psychology Compass, 2*(1), 399–413.

Eisenberg, N., & Sulik, M. J. (2012). Emotion-related self-regulation in children. *Teaching of Psychology, 39*(1), 77–83.

Evans, D. E., & Rothbart, M. K. (2007). Developing a model for adult temperament. *Journal of Research in Personality, 41*, 868–888.

Eysenck, H. J. (1947). *Dimensions of personality.* London: Routledge and Kegan Paul.

Eysenck, H. J., & Cookson, D. (1969). Personality in primary school children: 1. Ability and achievement. *British Journal of Educational Psychology, 39*, 109–122.

Eysenck, H. J., & Eysenck, S. B. G. (1975). *Manual of the Eysenck personality questionnaire.* London: Hodder and Stoughton.

Funder, D. C. (2001). Accuracy in personality judgement: Research and theory concerning an obvious question. In B. W. Roberts & R. T. Hogan (Eds.), *Personality psychology in the workplace.* (pp. 121–140). Washington, DC: American Psychological Association.

Galton, F. (1884). Measurement of character. *Fortnightly Review, 36*, 179–185.

Gill, M. J., & Swann Jr, W. B. (2004). On what it means to know someone: A matter of pragmatics. *Journal of Personality and Social Psychology, 86*(3), 405–418.

Goff, M., & Ackerman, P. L. (1992). Personality–intelligence relations: Assessment of typical intellectual engagement. *Journal of Educational Psychology, 84*(4), 537–552.

Graesser, A. C. (2009). Inaugural editorial for *Journal of Educational Psychology. Journal of Educational Psychology, 101*(2), 259–261.

Hambrick, D. Z., Pink, J. E., Meinz, E. J., Pettibone, J. C., & Oswald, F. L. (2008). The roles of ability, personality, and interests in acquiring current events knowledge: A longitudinal study. *Intelligence, 36*, 261–278.

Hanoch, Y., & Vitouch, O. (2004). When less is more: Information, emotional arousal and the ecological reframing of the Yerkes-Dodson law. *Theory & Psychology, 14*(4), 427–452.

Harris, D. (1940). Factors affecting college grades: A review of the literature, 1930–1937. *Psychological Bulletin, 37*(3), 125–166.

Hattie, J. A. (2009). *Visible learning: A synthesis of meta-analyses relating to achievement.* Abingdon, Oxon, UK: Routledge.

Hattie, J. A., & Timperley, H. (2007). The power of feedback. *Review of Educational Research, 77*(1), 81–112.

Heckman, J. J., & Rubinstein, Y. (2001). The importance of noncognitive skills: Lessons from the GED testing program. *American Economic Review, 91*(2), 145–149.

Hofstee, W. K. B. (1994). Who should own the definition of personality? *European Journal of Personality, 8*, 149–162.

Jackson, J. J., Hill, P. L., Payne, B. R., Roberts, B. W., & Stine-Morrow, E. A. L. (2012). Can an old dog learn (and want to experience) new tricks? Cognitive training increases openness to experience in older adults. *Psychology and Aging, 27*(2), 286–292.

Jackson, J. J., Wood, D., Bogg, T., Walton, K. E., Harms, P. D., & Roberts, B. W. (2010). What do conscientious people do? Development and validation of the Behavioral Indicators of Conscientiousness (BIC). *Journal of Research in Personality, 44*(4), 501–511.

John, O. P., & Robins, R. W. (1993). Determinants of interjudge agreement on personality traits: The Big Five domains, observability, evaluativeness, and the unique perspective of the self. *Journal of Personality, 61*(4), 521–551.

Johnson, R. E., & Saboe, K. N. (2011). Measuring implicit traits in organizational research: Development of an indirect measure of employee implicit self-concept. *Organizational Research Methods, 14*(3), 530–547.

Kenny, D. A., & West, T. V. (2010). Similarity and agreement in self- and other-perception: A meta-analysis. *Personality and Social Psychology Review, 14*(2), 196–213.

Kircanski, K., Craske, M. G., & Bjork, R. (2008). Thought suppression enhances memory bias for threat material. *Behaviour Research and Therapy, 46*, 462–476.

Komarraju, M., & Karau, S. J. (2005). The relationship between the big five personality traits and academic motivation. *Personality and Individual Differences, 39*, 557–567.

Komarraju, M., Karau, S. J., & Schmeck, R. R. (2009). Role of the Big Five personality traits in predicting college students' academic motivation and achievement. *Learning and Individual Differences, 19*, 47–52.

Lance, C. E., Dawson, B., Birkelbach, D., & Hoffman, B. J. (2010). Method effects, measurement error, and substantive conclusions. *Organizational Research Methods, 13*(3), 435–455.

Leue, A., & Beauducel, A. (2008). A meta-analysis of reinforcement sensitivity theory: On performance parameters in reinforcement tasks. *Personality and Social Psychology Review, 12*(4), 353–369.

Lievens, F., De Corte, W., & Schollaert, E. (2008). A closer look at the frame-of-reference effect in personality scale scores and validity. *Journal of Applied Psychology, 93*(2), 268–279.

Lounsbury, J. W., Gibson, L. W., Sundstrom, E., Wilburn, D., & Loveland, J. M. (2004). An empirical investigation of the proposition that 'School is Work': A comparison of personality-performance correlations in school and work settings. *Journal of Education and Work, 17*(1), 119–131.

Lubbers, M. J., Van der Werf, M. P. C., Kuyper, H., & Hendriks, A. A. J. (2010). Does homework behavior mediate the relation between personality and academic performance? *Learning and Individual Differences, 20*(3), 203–208.

MacCann, C., Fogarty, G. J., & Roberts, R. D. (2012). Strategies for success in education: Time management is more important for part-time than full-time community college students. *Learning and Individual Differences, 22*, 618–623.

MacCann, C., Lipnevich, A. A., Burrus, J., & Roberts, R. D. (2012). The best years of our lives? Coping with stress predicts school grades, life satisfaction, and feelings about high school. *Learning and Individual Differences, 22*(2), 235–241.

Margrain, S. A. (1978). Student characteristics and academic performance in higher education: A review. *Research in Higher Education, 8*(2), 111–123.

Matthews, G. (2007). Reinforcement Sensitivity Theory: A critique from cognitive science. In P. J. Corr (Ed.), *The Reinforcement Sensitivity Theory of personality.* Cambridge: Cambridge University Press.

Measelle, J. R., John, O. P., Ablow, J. C., Cowan, P. A., & Cowan, C. P. (2005). Can children provide coherent, stable, and valid self-reports on the Big Five dimensions? A longitudinal study from ages 5 to 7. *Journal of Personality & Social Psychology, 89*(1), 90–106.

Mellanby, J., & Zimdars, A. (2011). Trait anxiety and final degree performance at the University of Oxford. *Higher Education, 61*(4), 357–370.

Mervielde, I., De Clercq, B., De Fruyt, F., & Van Leeuwen, K. G. (2005). Temperament, personality, and developmental psychopathology as childhood antecedents of personality disorders. *Journal of Personality Disorders, 19*(2), 171–201.

Mullola, S., Ravaja, N., Lipsanen, J., Hirstio-Snellman, P., Alatupa, S., & Keltikangas-Jarvinen, L. (2010). Teacher-perceived temperament and educational competence as predictors of school grades. *Learning and Individual Differences, 20*(3), 209–214.

Norman, W. T. (1963). Toward an adequate taxonomy of personality attributes: Replicated factor structure in peer nomination personality ratings. *Journal of Abnormal and Social Psychology, 66*, 574–583.

Orvis, K. A., Brusso, R. C., Wasserman, M. E., & Fisher, S. L. (2011). E-nabled for e-learning? The moderating role of personality in determining the optimal degree of learner control in an e-learning environment. *Human Performance, 24*(1), 60–78.

Ouellette, J. A., & Wood, W. (1998). Habit and intention in everyday life: The multiple processes by which past behavior predicts future behavior. *Psychological Bulletin, 124*(1), 54–74.

Pashler, H., Bain, P., Bottge, B., Graesser, A. C., Koedinger, K., McDaniel, M., & Metcalf, J. (2007). *Organizing instruction and study to improve student learning.* Retrieved from http://ncer.ed.gov (accessed February 19, 2015).

Payne, S. C., Youngcourt, S. S., & Beaubien, J. M. (2007). A meta-analytic examination of the goal orientation nomological net. *Journal of Applied Psychology, 92*(1), 128–150.

Poropat, A. E. (2009). A meta-analysis of the five-factor model of personality and academic performance. *Psychological Bulletin, 135*(2), 322–338.

Poropat, A. E. (2011a). The Eysenckian personality factors and their correlations with academic performance. *British Journal of Educational Psychology, 81*(1), 41–58.

Poropat, A. E. (2011b). The role of citizenship performance in academic achievement and graduate employability. *Education + Training, 53*(6), 499–514.

Poropat, A. E. (2014a). A meta-analysis of adult-rated child personality and academic performance in primary education. *British Journal of Educational Psychology, 84*(2), 239–252.

Poropat, A. E. (2014b). A meta-analysis of other-rated personality and academic performance. *Learning and Individual Differences, 34*(1), 24–32.

Poropat, A. E., & Corr, P. J. (2015). Thinking bigger: The Cronbachian paradigm & personality theory integration. *Journal of Research in Personality, 56*(1), 59–69. doi: 10.1016/j.jrp.2014.10.006.

Poston, J. M., & Hanson, W. E. (2010). Meta-analysis of psychological assessment as a therapeutic intervention. *Psychological Assessment, 22*(2), 203–212.

Preckel, F., Lipnevich, A. A., Schneider, S., & Roberts, R. D. (2011). Chronotype, cognitive abilities, and academic achievement: A meta-analytic investigation. *Learning and Individual Differences, 21*(5), 483–492.

Proyer, R. T. (2011). Being playful and smart? The relations of adult playfulness with psychometric and self-estimated intelligence and academic performance. *Learning and Individual Differences, 21*, 463–467.

Richardson, M., Abraham, C., & Bond, R. (2012). Psychological correlates of university students' academic performance: A systematic review and meta-analysis. *Psychological Bulletin, 138*(2), 363–387.

Roberts, B. W., Chernyshenko, O. S., Stark, S., & Goldberg, L. R. (2005). The structure of conscientiousness: An empirical investigation based on seven major personality questionnaires. *Personnel Psychology, 58*(1), 103–139.

Roberts, B. W., Jackson, J. J., Fayard, J. V., Edmonds, G., & Meints, J. (2009). Conscientiousness. In M. R. Leary & R. H. Hoyle (Eds.), *Handbook of individual differences in social behavior* (pp. 369–381). New York, NY: Guilford.

Roberts, B. W., Walton, K. E., & Viechtbauer, W. (2006). Personality traits change in adulthood: Reply to Costa and McCrae (2006). *Psychological Bulletin, 132*(1), 29–32.

Rothbart, M. K. (2007). Temperament, development, and personality. *Current Directions in Psychological Science, 16*(4), 207–212.

Rothbart, M. K., Ahadi, S. A., Hershey, K. L., & Fisher, P. (2001). Investigations of temperament at three to seven years: The children's behavior questionnaire. *Child Development, 72*, 1394–1408.

Saklofske, D. H., Austin, E. J., Mastoras, S. M., Beaton, L., & Osborne, S. E. (2012). Relationships of personality, affect, emotional intelligence and coping with student stress and academic success: Different patterns of association for stress and success. *Learning and Individual Differences, 22*(2), 251–257.

Saucier, G., & Goldberg, L. R. (2001). Lexical studies of indigenous personality factors: Premises, products and prospects. *Journal of Personality, 69*(6), 847–879.

Schmidt, F. L., & Hunter, J. E. (1996). Measurement error in psychological research: Lessons from 26 research scenarios. *Psychological Methods, 1*, 199–223.

Schmit, M. J., Ryan, A. M., Stierwalt, S. L., & Powell, A. B. (1995). Frame-of-reference effects on personality scale scores and criterion-related validity. *Journal of Applied Psychology, 80*(5), 607–620.

Shiner, R. L. (2000). Linking childhood personality with adaptation: Evidence for continuity and change across time into late adolescence. *Journal of Personality and Social Psychology, 78*(2), 310–325.

Shiner, R. L., & Caspi, A. (2003). Personality differences in childhood and adolescence: Measurement, development, and consequences. *Journal of Child Psychology and Psychiatry, 44*(1), 2–32.

Snow, R. E. (1996). Aptitude development and education. *Psychology Public Policy and Law, 2*(3–4), 536–560.

Soto, C. J., John, O. P., Gosling, S. D., & Potter, J. (2008). The developmental psychometrics of Big Five self-reports: Acquiescence, factor structure, coherence, and differentiation from ages 10 to 20. *Journal of Personality and Social Psychology, 94*(4), 718–737.

Spearman, C. (1927). *The abilities of man.* London: Macmillan.

Steinmayr, R., Bipp, T., & Spinath, B. (2011). Goal orientations predict academic performance beyond intelligence and personality. *Learning and Individual Differences, 21*(2), 196–200.

Sutin, A. R., Costa, P. T., Wethington, E., & Eaton, W. (2010). Turning points and lessons learned: Stressful life events and personality trait development across middle adulthood. *Psychology and Aging, 25*(3), 524–533.

Swanberg, A. B., & Martinsen, O. L. (2010). Personality, approaches to learning and achievement. *Educational Psychology, 30*(1), 75–88.

Thomas, A., Chess, S., & Birch, H. G. (1968). *Temperament and behavior disorders in children.* New York: New York University Press.

Tymms, P., & Merrell, C. (2011). ADHD and academic attainment: Is there an advantage in impulsivity? *Learning and Individual Differences, 21*(6), 753–758.

Vandevelde, S., Van Keer, H., & De Wever, B. (2011). Exploring the impact of student tutoring on at-risk fifth and sixth graders' self-regulated learning. *Learning and Individual Differences, 21*, 419–425.

Vazire, S. (2010). Who knows what about a person? The self-other knowledge asymmetry (SOKA) model. *Journal of Personality & Social Psychology, 98*(2), 281–300.

von Stumm, S., & Ackerman, P. L. (2013). Investment and intellect: A review and meta-analysis. *Psychological Bulletin, 139*(4), 841–869.

von Stumm, S., Hell, B., & Chamorro-Premuzic, T. (2011). The hungry mind: Intellectual curiosity is the third pillar of academic performance. *Perspectives on Psychological Science, 6*(6), 574–588.

Webb, E. (1915). *Character and intelligence: An attempt at an exact study of character.* Cambridge, UK: Cambridge University Press.

Winne, P. H. (2014). Issues in researching self-regulated learning as patterns of events. *Metacognition and Learning, 9*(2), 229–237.

Wolf, T. H. (1973). *Alfred Binet.* Chicago, IL: University of Chicago Press.

Yamkovenko, B., & Holton, E. (2010). Toward a theoretical model of dispositional influences on transfer of learning: A test of a structural model. *Human Resource Development Quarterly, 21*(4), 381–410.

Zhang, X., Nurmi, J.-E., Kiuru, N., Lerkkanen, M.-K., & Aunola, K. (2011). A teacher-report measure of children's task-avoidant behavior: A validation study of the Behavioral Strategy Rating Scale. *Learning and Individual Differences, 21*(6), 690–698.

Zhao, B. (2011). Learning from errors: The role of context, emotion, and personality. *Journal of Organizational Behavior, 32*, 435–463.

# 14

# Cultural, Racial/Ethnic, and Linguistic Diversity and Identity

*Na'ilah Suad Nasir*
University of California, Berkeley

*Stephanie J. Rowley*
University of Michigan

*William Perez*
Claremont Graduate University

## Introduction

How do identity processes relate to schooling? This is an age-old question in the education literature. Accordingly, it has been the subject of numerous studies over several decades. A foremost concern in this body of research has been the ways that cultural, racial, and linguistic identities shape students' engagement and achievement. This research has been linked to efforts to understand, document, and ameliorate what has been viewed as educational underperformance of minority students in U.S. schools. Whereas much of the early research in this area focused on the psychological processes and academic achievements of individual or groups of students, more recent research attends to the nature of the sociopolitical school and community contexts that youths navigate.

Establishing robust racial/ethnic and linguistic identities is a key aspect of development that relates significantly to schooling experiences and outcomes (Davidson, 1996; Fuligni, Witkow, & Garcia, 2005; Roeser et al., 2008; Yip, Seaton, & Sellers, 2006). Positive identities are associated with better health and education outcomes and can buffer the negative effects of racial/ethnic discrimination (Rivas-Drake et al., 2014). In a highly racially and linguistically segregated society like the United States, constructing a healthy identity can be challenging for those individuals who often endure a host of negative perceptions about their group and experience limited access to high-quality social and educational services (Darling-Hammond, 2010; Spencer, 2006). Thus, understanding the connections between racial, cultural, and linguistic identities is critical to understand how to best support such students.

Rather than attempting a comprehensive review of this large literature, for this chapter, our discussion takes up three key tasks. First, we describe five foundational research issues on identity and schooling pertaining to non-dominant minority youth. We examine the topics of: (a) oppositional identities and "acting white"; (b) stereotype threat; (c) exclusion and the effects of discrimination; (d) the role of classroom structures on identities; and (e) the relations among ethnic identity, language proficiency, and academic achievement.

Second, we turn to three compelling trends in recent research on identity and schooling for minority youth: (a) scholarship on schools as sites of racial socialization; (b) research on language brokering and language practice in relation to identity; and (c) a growing body of research that identifies school success as a form of resistance among minority youth.

Finally, we conclude the chapter by suggesting potential gaps in the literature and delineating promising directions for future research. We opine that research must increasingly speak to the complex ways that multiple identities are experienced; these considerations of intersectionality are crucial for developing a next generation of identity studies. Therefore, we call for multilevel analyses, interdisciplinary research, and identity research based on increasingly prevalent demographic groups.

We primarily focus on research pertaining to African American and Latino youth,[1] yet where appropriate, we discuss research on Asian American and Pacific Islander students. This, in part, reflects the existing large body of research on identity and schooling (Umaña-Taylor et al., 2014). Although we consider the experiences of K-12 students, our review reflects the state of the research, which has been primarily concerned with adolescents because adolescence is when identity processes are most salient (Erikson, 1968).

### Key Term Definitions

Our definition of *culture* incorporates anthropological notions including traditions, customs, ways of knowing, and ways of being that provide the structure for daily life (Kroeber & Kluckholm, 1952; Weisner, 2002). In addition, we utilize concepts of culture that build on the tradition of Vygotsky (1978), which call attention to the ways that culture is created, maintained, and changed locally, as people, in concert with social others, enact daily routines within the context of their personal and cultural goals and available resources (Rogoff, 2003).

*Race* is also a complex and debated topic. Social scientists suggest that race is a socially constructed concept and that there is no scientific evidence to support biologically defined racial categories (Omi & Winant, 1994; Smedley & Smedley, 2005). Race serves the purpose of marginalizing some while maintaining social privilege for others (Fredrickson, 2002; Hany-Lopez, 1996) and racial categories often facilitate and justify the unequal distribution of social goods (Omi & Winant, 1994). Rivas-Drake and colleagues (2014) argue that it is vital to understand that "race indicates power and connotes the ongoing hierarchy in which one group considers other groups as different and inferior" (p. 41).

Numerous scholars advocate for the understanding and naming of the processes of racialization (e.g., Barot & Bird, 2001; Nasir, 2012), including social, interactional, and positional processes that make race salient in daily experiences. At the psychological level, studies have shown that disadvantaged group members can internalize a perception of their own inferiority in order to justify the social order (Jost, Banaji, & Nosek, 2004). Racialization processes occur through interpersonal interactions of daily life and through the ways in which access to resources is structured (Murji & Solomos, 2005).

*Ethnicity*, although a commonly used term, is sometimes utilized as a euphemism for race or culture (Gutiérrez & Rogoff, 2003). We understand ethnicity as referring to the social group with a national or cultural affiliation to which one belongs. Frequently conflated with culture, ethnic groups are seen as sharing a distinct identity that characterizes members of the group, though they may also be defined in terms of geographic area or shared history (Nagel, 1994).

Finally, it is important to be clear about what we mean by the term *identity*. Fundamental to our perspective is a cultural-developmental theoretical frame. The development of identity and its continual reconstruction is a normative developmental task (Erikson, 1968; Roeser, Peck, & Nasir, 2006; Spencer & Markstrom-Adams, 1990), particularly salient in pre-adolescence, adolescence, and early adulthood. Identities are fundamentally tied to the local social and cultural contexts within which they develop (Way, Hernández,

Rogers, & Hughes, 2013; Wortham, 2006). This perspective is consistent with sociocultural (Rogoff, 2003) and ecological theories of development (Bronfenbrenner, 1993; Spencer, 2006) that highlight the centrality of cultural activities and practices to individual development. Identities often develop as young people engage in school and everyday activities and practices.

It is through interactions, roles, and the positioning of self and others that identity develops. It is not a global construct; it is instead an accumulation of moments in cultural spaces that can be viewed both in terms of the individual and of positioning by the social world. This view is consistent with Erikson's (1968) theory that includes personal and social identity, and the classic symbolic interactionist school, which focuses on identity negotiated in local social interactions and informed by cultural expectations and norms (Mead, 1934). For our purposes then, identity is not achieved at one point in time but is continually negotiated and renegotiated in the social and cultural settings of which one is a part. *Racial/ ethnic identity* is thus defined as "how one views oneself relative to his or her own ethnic group, namely his or her sense of ethnic or racial group belonging or attachment" (Way et al., 2013, p. 408).

One of the ways racial/ethnic identities are conceptualized is as *scripts* (Oyserman & Destin, 2010), or *narratives* that attach a particular meaning to racial group membership (Nasir & Shah, 2011). Other research has highlighted the multidimensional nature of racial identities, and the ways in which they can vary by gender and neighborhood context (Fhagen-Smith, Vandiver, Worrell, & Cross, 2010).

## Foundational Issues and Theories

We begin by describing several foundational issues and theories in the research on the relation between cultural, racial/ ethnic, linguistic identities, and educational and psychological well-being. Specifically, we consider the bodies of research on oppositional identities, stereotype threat, exclusion, and the effects of discrimination, the relation between classroom structures and identities, and the relations between ethnic identity, language proficiency, and academic achievement. We are particularly concerned with research that has implications for thinking about the processes and outcomes of educational and psychological well-being.

### Oppositional Identities and "Acting White"

Many early studies of ethnic-minority student motivation and performance employed a cultural deficit approach, suggesting that students of color perform poorly in school because they fail to value achievement, associate academic excellence with whites, or have developed maladaptive attitudes toward achievement. Fordham and Ogbu (1986; Ogbu, 2008) suggested that youth of color adopt oppositional cultural frameworks in response to oppression and limited opportunities for upward social mobility. This may include the adoption of linguistic, behavioral, or religious styles that differ from mainstream cultural frames. Ogbu (2008) found that African American youth tend to sanction high-achieving peers by saying that they are "acting white." Moreover, high-achieving African American students may distance themselves from other African Americans as a way of reducing the "burden of acting white." Alternatively, these students may underperform to maintain ties to the black community.

Recent psychological research on "acting white" has moved beyond an examination of whether or not students view high achievement as "acting white" and has begun to account for a range of beliefs around the connection between white cultural norms and high achievement. One line of research has examined how students understand and respond to being labeled as "acting white," illustrating that the accusation of "acting white" by peers is a source of anxiety for adolescents and can trigger an examination of one's black identity, even calling one's authenticity into question (Murray, Neal-Barnett, Demmings, & Stadulis, 2012).

A number of empirical studies suggest that Ogbu's theory is limited and in some cases incorrect by demonstrating that African American youth adhere to mainstream achievement ideologies (e.g., Ainsworth-Darnell & Downey, 1998). In a large study of African American students in 11 high schools, Tyson, Darity, and Castellino (2005) found that, although some high-achieving African Americans were accused of "acting white," it was most prevalent in schools with the greatest racial stratification across academic tracks (see also Fryer & Levitt, 2006). Similarly, Fryer and Torelli (2010) note that "acting white" is more common in schools that are less than 20% black than it is in schools that were more than 80% black. This suggests that schools where African American students are in the minority are settings where there is a narrow stereotypical definition of what it means to be black. These findings are consonant with Carter's (2012) comparative study that found that in both the United States and in South Africa, in majority-minority schools, black children found access to a broader range of identity options (and were less held to stereotypical black identities).

Other researchers have noted that, although many students of color suffer the social costs of being in advanced courses, many find adaptive ways of coping with the associated tensions (e.g., Horvat & Lewis, 2003; Mickelson & Velasco, 2006). Carter's (2005) work demonstrates that youth of color use dominant and non-dominant cultural styles across settings to negotiate the social demands of multiple contexts. Thus, research shows that, although oppositional racial identities do exist, their presence is context-dependent (Carter, 2005; Mickelson & Velasco, 2006). Ford and Harris (2008) find that perceptions of race and schooling, and the connections between them, vary significantly with the achievement level of the students, with gifted students being more academically oriented and less affected by negative peer relationships.

Although Fordham and Ogbu (1986) suggest that "racelessness" is an adaptive response to the "burden of acting white," numerous studies have shown that a positive sense of connection to a racial or ethnic group is associated with healthy academic outcomes. Feelings of racial/ethnic belonging are positively associated with several motivational factors, including classroom engagement, academic self-efficacy, aspirations, and educational attainment (Chavous et al., 2003; Oyserman, Harrison, & Bybee, 2001; Thomas, Townsend, & Belgrave, 2003).

### Stereotype Threat

Stereotype threat describes the psychological risk that comes with the possibility of confirming a negative stereotype associated with a self-relevant social identity (Steele & Aronson, 1995). Steele and Aronson's original study demonstrated that subtle experimental manipulations designed to prime negative racial intellectual stereotypes led to underperformance in African American students. African American, but not European American, college students who reported their race before taking a test underperformed relative to their peers who did not. Similarly, African American students who were told that a test that they were to take was diagnostic of intelligence underperformed relative to those who were told that the test was just a set of word problems. Steele and Aronson suggested that these manipulations reminded African American students of negative race-related stereotypes, taxing their cognitive abilities and leading to depressed performance. What is compelling about this research is that the stereotype need not be invoked specifically; rather, simply triggering membership in the group and giving a task in a stereotyped domain is enough to lower performance. This research points to the ways race, gender, and academic performance can operate at an implicit level.

An interesting premise of the stereotype threat theory is that the effect can occur even in individuals from relatively high-status groups. For example, although white men typically are not susceptible to race-related stereotype threat, one study found that white men's performance on a math test was reduced when they were primed to think about the superior math performance of Asian Americans before taking a math test (Aronson et al., 1999). Still, African American and Latino students are more likely than white and Asian American students to be exposed to subtle contextual cues that may have the effect of priming negative stereotypes in their daily classroom activities. Past research on disidentification (see next paragraph), suggests that students of color who regularly experience stereotype threat may disengage from the negatively stereotyped domain (e.g., education) (Steele, 1992).

Disidentification is the process by which individuals realign their self-concept so that their performance in a domain no longer bears on their self-regard in that domain (Steele, 1992). Accordingly, Osborne (1995) found that, as African American students move from middle school through high school, the correlation between their academic achievement and their self-esteem declines. Schmader, Major, and Gramzow (2001) posit that, after repeated exposure to negative discrimination and stereotypes, students of color may discount feedback from teachers, devalue performance in the domain, and/or disengage. In addition to stereotype threat, where one is threatened by an outside group, Cohen and Garcia (2005) identified the phenomenon, collective threat, which describes the threat that a member of a shared social group might confirm a negative stereotype about the group. It tends to be strongest among select demographic groups, such as African Americans and Latinos. Similar to stereotype threat, collective threat undermines performance.

Although the implicit nature of stereotype threat and the ubiquitous nature of stereotype cues in American educational institutions make stereotype threat a particularly pernicious issue, a number of studies demonstrate that stereotype threat effects can be reduced. Good, Aronson, and Inzlicht (2003) found that teaching students to believe that intelligence is malleable lessened the effect of stereotype threat. Martens, Johns, Greenberg, and Schimel (2006) found that having participants write self-affirmations before taking a test eliminated the effect of the stereotype threat manipulation. Cohen, Steele, and Ross (1999) also noted that giving students of color critical and reassuring feedback improved their sense of trust and reduced stereotype threat.

### Exclusion and the Psychological Effects of Discrimination

The research literature on racial inclusion and exclusion, racial bias, and discrimination also informs our understanding of how racial/ethnic, cultural, and linguistic identities relate to schooling outcomes and experiences. More specifically, since self-appraisal processes are deeply connected to how one is perceived by others (Spencer, 1999), experiences of exclusion, discrimination, and racial bias have the potential to shape students' identities in multiple ways. In this section, we highlight some important scholarship in this area, paying particular attention to studies that focus on school-age populations and have implications for thinking about schooling outcomes and processes.

One of the ways in which discrimination manifests in schools is in peer relationships, where racial bias can be expressed as social exclusion. Scholars have argued that peer social exclusion is very powerful, and reflects both cognitive and moral developmental processes. Studies on race-based social exclusion have revealed several important findings. By and large, youth tend to view race-based peer exclusion as unfair and morally wrong (Killen & Stangor, 2001). Nevertheless, older children are more likely to find race-based exclusion acceptable, especially if they judge that inclusion would threaten group functioning. Children who are members of minority groups deemed instances of peer exclusion as based on race and believed that race-based exclusion occurred more often than did their non-minority peers (Killen, Henning, Kelly, Crystal, & Ruck, 2007).

Whereas much of this research has examined explicit social exclusion processes and reasoning, some have argued that racial biases are rooted in implicit cognitive processes. Implicit biases are unconscious beliefs about social groups that may be positive or negative and that are activated involuntarily (Greenwald & Krieger, 2006). Explicit biases can be consciously reported. Studies utilizing implicit measures illustrate that about twice as many people show bias on implicit measures as on explicit measures. Studies have

shown that as children get older they are more motivated to suppress explicit racial biases, but are still affected by explicit bias (Rutland, Cameron, Milne, & McGeorge, 2005). These findings highlight that the pervasiveness of racial stereotypes is not just related to the beliefs individuals are aware of but rather may be held at a subconscious level that may be even more challenging to change.

Other related research examines the ways that racial discrimination affects young people psychologically and academically. Scholars have argued that dealing with racial discrimination is simply a fact of life for minorities in contemporary American society (Feagin & Vera, 1995; Kluegel & Bobo, 1993). Although racial discrimination is common in the daily experiences of marginalized groups, it still deeply affects them in multiple ways, including decreased life satisfaction, increased stress (Utsey, Ponterotto, Reynolds, & Cancelli, 2000), and negative mental health outcomes (McCoy & Major, 2003). Studies that have examined youths' experiences find that discrimination regularly occurs within educational contexts (Fisher, Wallace, & Fenton, 2000). Ethnic-minority students perceive that they are routinely discouraged from taking advanced-level courses, have been given lower grades because of racial prejudice, and are disciplined more harshly than their white counterparts (Fisher et al., 2000). These experiences of discrimination in school were related to lowered self-esteem. The number of perceived incidents of discrimination also varies by racial identification, whereby more highly identified minority students recount more instances of discrimination (Sellers, Caldwell, Schmeelk-Cone, & Zimmerman, 2003). Moreover, students for whom racial identity was central report lower levels of psychological distress in relation to discrimination experiences (Romero, Edwards, Fryberg, & Orduña, 2014), indicating that strong racial identities can have a protective effect in the face of discrimination.

In addition to discrimination based on race, students, especially Hispanic and Southeast Asian students, have reported discrimination based on English-language proficiency (Fisher et al., 2000; Rumbaut & Ima, 1988). Studies have shown that having an accent can also be a source of negative stereotyping and discrimination (Dovidio, Gluszek, John, Ditlmann, & Lagunes, 2010). This is consistent with the sociolinguistic notion of "linguistic profiling" in which individuals are stereotyped and discriminated against on the basis of sounding Hispanic or African American (Baugh, 2007). Language associated with black and Hispanic communities (e.g., Ebonics and Spanish) tends to be undervalued and stigmatized, such that speakers of these dialects and languages are more likely to be denied an opportunity to view an apartment (Baugh, 2007), and are stigmatized and excluded in schools (Olsen, 1997).

### The Relation of Classroom Structures and Pedagogy to Identities

Schools and classrooms are key sites for the formation of racial, cultural, and linguistic identities. Social cues in schools can teach students about the school's valuing of diverse perspectives, positioning of various social groups, and racial-ethnic epistemologies. In addition, the structure of schools and the nature of the pedagogy can send clear messages to students that have implications for their developing racial/ethnic, linguistic, and academic identities.

Ability grouping is one aspect of school structure that may impact identities. Ability tracking leads African American and Latino students to experience a very different context than whites and Asian Americans, even within integrated schools. For this reason, Oakes (2005) calls tracking "second-generation segregation." African American and Latino students are vastly overrepresented in special education classes and underrepresented among those identified as gifted (National Education Association, 2011). Even in cases where students have some choice in class selection, African American and Latino students in integrated schools are overrepresented in lower tracks, and segregated schools tend to have disproportionate numbers of low-level courses.

Not only are there well-documented academic consequences of ability tracking on African American and Latino students, there is evidence of negative effects on racial/ethnic identity development. As noted, black and Latino students are more likely to be accused of "acting white" in schools where they are severely underrepresented in advanced courses (Mickelson & Velasco, 2006; Tyson, 2006). Mickelson and Velasco (2006) suggest that oppositional racial identities (e.g., those identities linking African Americans with academic failures) may develop in highly stratified contexts where it is easier to make the visual connection between race and ability grouping.

In addition, social processes *within* classrooms matter for students' identities. Research shows that classroom discourse and curricular content can impact social and racial/ethnic identities. Wortham (2006) found that elementary students took up ideas from the social studies lesson to position one another socially in the classroom. Langer-Osuna (2011) and Herrenkohl and Mertyl (2010) have similarly shown that students adopt and ascribe racial and social identities to themselves and one another as they engage the mathematics and science curriculum. Research on culturally relevant pedagogy has illustrated the power of curriculum that centers the cultural experience of the students to support access to positive racial identities and increased engagement and learning (Howard, 2010; Ladson-Billings, 1993). This point is further illustrated by C. Lee (2007), who studied what she called cultural modeling where teachers draw on cultural datasets or topics and material that are culturally relevant for students in order to teach core concepts in academic disciplines. C. Lee finds that students in classrooms where cultural modeling was used learned more and felt more connected to their learning than did students in comparison classrooms. Gutiérrez and Rogoff (2003) describe the importance of building on "cultural repertoires of practice" which encourage cycles of expansive learning.

Research has noted that cultural differences in ways of doing and knowing (e.g., different cultural repertoires of practice) may also play a role in how classroom processes relate to the learning and identities of students. Studies have demonstrated that African American students learn best in school contexts that align with cultural expressions in their homes, including movement (Boykin & Cunningham, 2001) and collaborative learning (Ellison, Boykin, Tyler, & Dillihunt, 2005). Highlighting the cultural underpinnings of these results are other studies showing that, although communalistic and cooperative learning contexts (see Serpell, Boykin, Madhere, & Nasim, 2006 for a description of the difference) benefit both African American and European American students, African American students benefit to a greater degree than whites (Boykin & Bailey, 2000; Serpell et al., 2006).

The differing cultural repertoires of practice of African American students have several implications for their developing racial identities. First, behavioral styles that may not initially be associated with racial or ethnic background become racialized as youth move into formal schooling (Boykin & Cunningham, 2001). African American students begin to learn that "black" cultural styles are viewed as oppositional in the classroom and may feel compelled to choose between their preferred behavioral repertoires and those of the mainstream, disrupting early feelings of group affinity. Second, this discontinuity may be especially problematic in integrated schools where cultural styles, academic performance, and racial identity may be more tightly coupled and may lay the foundation for later oppositional identities (Tyson, 2006). This research highlights the importance of the pedagogical setting to provide resources for positive racial/ethnic and academic identities in school.

### Ethnic Identity, Language Proficiency, and Academic Achievement

The research literature on youth from immigrant and linguistically diverse backgrounds highlights the variability in the relation between academic, racial/ethnic and linguistic identities. Bilingualism and ethnic identity have consistently been positively associated with academic self-concept and achievement among children of immigrants (Portes & Rumbaut, 2001). In addition, proficiency in the home language is an important component of ethnic identity for both recent immigrant adolescents and those living in immigrant households. For example, Kim and Chao (2009) find that heritage language proficiency and ethnic identity make independent and significant contributions to the school effort of second-generation Mexican adolescents. For first-, second-, and third-generation Mexican youth, being proficient in Spanish reading and writing is associated with higher effort in school. For these youth, the extra effort it takes to acquire heritage-language fluency and explore identity may help to clarify their sense of self, which in turn may enhance or increase their motivation in school (Fuligni et al., 2005).

As immigrant youth acculturate over time, they become more aware of racial and ethnic stereotypes, and ethnic identity begins to take on an important role as a protective factor for academic success (Suarez-Orozco & Suarez-Orozco, 2001). While perceived discrimination is a risk factor for educational success, a positive ethnic identity promotes success among immigrant youth (Garcia Coll & Marks, 2009). Specifically, Fuligni et al. (2005) found that adolescents who believed that their ethnicity was a central aspect of their self-concepts and held positive regard for their ethnic groups believed in a greater utility of education and school success, had more intrinsic interest in school, identified more with school, and believed they were respected by their school. In another recent study, Dominican immigrant children with a more central ethnic identity rated school as more important, and those who held positive regard for their ethnic group had more intrinsic motivation toward academics (Lawrence, Bachman, & Ruble, 2007). Latino immigrant youth may face ethnic discrimination that puts them at risk for academic disengagement but some may also hold strong ethnic identities that help them maintain positive attitudes about school. In addition to ethnic identity directly predicting academic outcomes, it is likely to play a second role as well as a moderator (Greene, Way, & Pahl, 2006; Umaña-Taylor & Updegraff, 2007; Wong, Eccles, & Sameroff, 2003). Having a strong, positive ethnic identity seems to buffer or mitigate negative effects associated with perceiving discrimination.

Although school contextual variables predict children's perceptions of discrimination and ethnic identity, such contexts also influence whether those perceptions of discrimination and ethnic identity are in turn related to academic outcomes. For example, Brown and Chu (2012) found that, for immigrant children who were in the minority in their school community, a positive and important ethnic identity was critical, both as a direct predictor of positive academic outcomes and as a buffer against teacher discrimination. Children in these school contexts are arguably the most vulnerable, belonging to a minority ethnic group at a school that does not highly value multiculturalism. At these schools, it seems that feeling positively about their ethnic group is particularly important for holding positive attitudes about school, performing well, and maintaining those positive attitudes in the face of teacher discrimination. In contrast, at predominantly Latino schools that valued diversity, ethnic identity and perceptions of discrimination were unrelated to academic attitudes (Brown & Chu, 2012). Although children at these schools perceived more discrimination overall, it was not linked to academic attitudes.

Ogbu (1991) argued that the social identifications of immigrant adolescents, whom he referred to as voluntary minorities, have important implications for academic motivation and achievement. Previous ethnographic research suggested that West Indian and Mexican youth from immigrant families who identify with their parents' cultural origins tend to be more attached to school and attain greater academic success than their peers who assume the more Americanized ethnic identity labels, such as *black* or *Chicano* (Rumbaut, 1994; Waters, 1999). However, current trends in social identity theory suggest that members of low-status groups attempt to improve their standing by challenging prevailing characteristics of their group, redefining the essential features of their group, and engaging in

social comparisons on other dimensions that are advantageous to them (Hogg, 2003). Thus, in terms of ethnic labels and educational orientation, adolescents who identify with Americanized ethnic labels such as *Latino* or *Chicano* may still show high levels of academic motivation and achievement because they define their ethnic labels differently than the larger society, where such labels are associated with negative stereotypes of academic failure. Identifying with such ethnic labels as a source of pride, these adolescents redefine the meaning of being Latino or Chicano as including a strong desire to achieve in school despite the many challenges they face (Zarate, Bhimji, & Reese, 2005).

What seems to be most important for academic success is that immigrant adolescents strongly identify with their ethnic background and specific ethnic labels, whatever they may be. For example, Fuligni and colleagues (2005) found that Mexican and Chinese adolescents who believed that their ethnicity was a central aspect of their selves and who held positive regard for their ethnic groups were more positive about education in general and their school specifically. Regardless of their chosen ethnic labels, these adolescents liked school, found it more interesting, and believed it was important and useful. Adolescents with stronger ethnic identity also believed that their schools valued and respected them.

The research on the ethnic identities of immigrant youth mirrors findings on students of color more generally, which indicate that a sense of pride in one's racial or ethnic group is also correlated with positive achievement outcomes for both children and adults (e.g., Bowman & Howard, 1985; Chavous et al., 2003; Wong et al., 2003). In addition, some studies have shown that more assimilationist beliefs (e.g., endorsement of mainstream views) are associated with less positive school outcomes for youth of color (Sellers, Chavous, & Cooke, 1998; Spencer, Noll, Stolzfus, & Harpalani, 2001).

Taken together, the scholarship on cultural, racial/ethnic, and linguistic identities, and the ways they are associated with schooling and academic outcomes, has enriched our understandings of the nature of racial/ethnic and linguistic identities, the cultural nature of these identities, and the range of ways they are brought to bear on schooling processes or on processes of well-being more generally. Next, we turn to a discussion of current trends in the research on these identities as they intersect with processes of schooling.

## Current Trends in Research on Cultural, Racial/ Ethnic, and Linguistic Identities

In this section, we highlight several compelling trends in the current scholarship on identity and educational and psychological well-being, and describe the research in relation to these trends. This section is not an exhaustive review; rather we focus on a small number of trends that move in new directions and add to a nuanced understanding of important processes and interactions. Often, these approaches are cross-cultural, multimethod, theoretically important, and interdisciplinary. Specifically, we discuss three key trends: (a) understanding schools as important sites of racialization processes; (b) the connection between identity and language-brokering processes; and (c) a focus on school success as a form of resistance.

## Schools as Sites of Racialization

One important trend in current research on racial, ethnic, and linguistic identities is the scholarly work that highlights racial socialization processes as key aspects of life in schools. In other words, schools are not simply places to which people bring racial identities or cultural identities, but rather, schools are sites of construction of those identities. This includes research that examines racialization processes and racial socialization at the whole-school level (Lewis, 2003; Pollock, 2004), but also processes of racialization and racial socialization inside classrooms, including mathematics and science classrooms (Nasir & Shah, 2011; Varelas, Martin, & Kane, 2012). At the whole-school level, scholars have pointed to the ways that schools convey strong and persistent messages about race. These messages position white and Asian students as high-achieving and "smart" and portray black and Latino students as not intellectually inclined and as students with behavior problems, or less parental support for achievement (Lewis, 2003; Nasir, Snyder, Shah, & Ross, 2012; Pollock, 2004). At times, these messages are overt, and are sometimes articulated by teachers or peers, and at other times by structures that privilege some students while marginalizing others (Conchas & Vigil, 2010; Noguera & Wing, 2006). Lewis's (2003) ethnographic study of three elementary schools with very different racial demographics illustrated that in majority-minority schools, as well as in predominantly white schools, African American and Latino students were stigmatized and that this process of positioning students and families of color as less capable was perpetrated by school personnel and by school-involved parents. Thus, the racial socialization that occurs in schools is jointly accomplished by multiple stakeholders acting in concert (Davidson, 1996).

Nasir (2012) conducted a qualitative study of racial identity processes and access in a poorly resourced urban high school, and showed that students made use of available social categories at their school site (which varied by academic track) to develop their own racial and academic identities. More specifically, students in the higher academic track had well-developed positive racial identities, associated with African American history and educational excellence, while students that were non-college-bound saw their racial identities as being connected to their street identities. These identities were supported by the ways students were positioned by teachers and peers in school, and by the social resources to which they had access.

Carter (2012) similarly showed that the identity processes of individual students are tied not only to the racial constitution of the student body, but also to the range of identity options made available for students in local school sites. She reported findings from a cross-national study of several hundred students in eight schools in South Africa and the United States. She found that racial group membership, and its relation to academic engagement, was more problematic for students from marginalized groups when there were fewer minority students at their schools. In majority-minority schools, students from marginalized groups were afforded greater opportunities to attain academic freedom, in part because they were not so beholden to negative racial stereotypes.

Davidson (1996) examined racialization processes in a California multiethnic high school. She conducted indepth case studies of 54 students and showed that not only were students racialized by virtue of race, but they were also racialized (and racialized themselves) by virtue of language. Davidson tells the story of a Latina student who spoke Spanish 2 days a week for the entire day (including in her predominantly white honors classes) as a means of resisting the oppressive ways she felt that she was seen and positioned by school personnel.

Other scholars have studied identity development and race in academic disciplines and K-12 classrooms (Ladson-Billings, 1993; C. Lee, 2007; Martin, 2006). For instance, Varelas et al. (2012) theorize the connections between racial, academic, and disciplinary (e.g., science and math) identities. They draw on multiple studies of math and science classrooms in elementary and middle school to argue that classrooms vary how they support marginalized students in successfully attaining both disciplinary and positive racial/ethnic identities. Further, important messages about these identities were conveyed in day-to-day interactions. C. Lee (2007) writes about the process of "cultural modeling," whereby teachers utilize students' cultural datasets to teach important literary analysis tools to urban African American students in urban schools. In both of these examples, scholars highlight how schooling environments racialize students through complex and subtle social positioning processes.

Research on racialization in schools is supported by recent race theory scholarship that outlines the ways that race and racism continue to operate even in spaces where people see themselves as color-blind. For instance, Bonilla-Silva (2006) has argued that schools often operate on principles of "color-blind racism," which include a nuanced set of beliefs and ideologies that allow one to deny the existence or power of race, while at the same time benefiting from racial privilege. Recent scholarship on whiteness theory (Leonardo, 2009) also calls out the subtle and pervasive ways that racialization persists in schools, and describes the very nuanced ways that white privilege operates in schools to perpetuate inequality (Leonardo, 2009).

## Language Brokering and Language Practice in Relation to Identity

Researchers have recently begun to expand our understanding of how linguistic practices and proficiency in multiple languages shape the racial/ethnic identities of children and young adults. The ability to speak two languages fosters close ties to the native and host culture (Phinney, Romero, Nava, & Huang, 2001). Scholars have identified "language brokering" as a practice of children of immigrants that involves translating and interpreting for parents and others. Research with adolescent language brokers has shown that the experience of language brokering positively contributes to feelings of social self-efficacy, biculturalism, acculturation, and academic performance (Acoach & Webb, 2004; Buriel, Perez, DeMent, Chavez, & Moran, 1998). Furthermore, heritage language proficiency is a strong contributor to ethnic identity (Phinney et al., 2001). For example, proficiency in Spanish is a strong indicator of both cultural affiliation and level of acculturation for many Latinos (Cuéllar & González, 2000). Children and adolescents who language broker have the opportunity to build stronger ties with the home culture and become bicultural. Consequently, language brokering may contribute to the formation of a strong ethnic identity. A strong ethnic identity has been associated with scholastic self-competence (Davey, Fish, Eaker, & Klock, 2003) and psychological well-being (R. M. Lee, 2003). At the same time, individuals who view language brokering as a positive experience develop a stronger sense of ethnic identity (LeFromboise, Coleman, & Gerton, 1993).

Language brokering places individuals into situations where they must navigate more than one culture, which may foster the sense of belonging, feelings, and attitudes toward the family's ethnic group, and create opportunities for understanding the family's ethnic-minority status. Language brokering tends to involve understanding the nuances of culture and the heritage language; therefore, language brokers may develop closer adherence to cultural values, which may be reflected in stronger ethnic identity development. During language-brokering activities, parents often discuss their heritage culture, practice traditions, and teach children about their ethnic culture—a process known as familial ethnic socialization (Umaña-Taylor, Alfaro, Bamaca, & Guimond, 2009; Umaña-Taylor & Fine, 2004). Familial ethnic socialization has been positively associated with ethnic identity and academic motivation (Huynh & Fuligni, 2008; Umaña-Taylor & Fine, 2004).

Weisskirch (2005) reported that language brokering was associated with greater ethnic identity exploration, even after accounting for level of acculturation. Moreover, positive feelings when engaging in language brokering were positively associated with greater ethnic identity, ethnic identity exploration, and ethnic identity affirmation. During the brokering process, adolescents may directly encounter institutional barriers or observe discriminatory treatment of their parents due to their limited English proficiency, and these experiences may make adolescents more hypervigilant both to their own language minority status and to more covert racial or ethnic microaggressions (e.g., Sue, Lin, Torino, Capodilupo, & Rivera, 2009). As a result, language brokering may influence the development of academic competencies (Chao, 2006; McQuillan & Tse, 1995).

Some studies have documented positive effects of language brokering that may result in higher academic success, including the development of strong metalinguistic and interpersonal skills (Valdés, 2003), increased confidence and maturity (McQuillan & Tse, 1995; Walinchowski, 2001), academic self-efficacy (Buriel et al., 1998), and pride at being able to help their families (DeMent & Buriel, 1999; Valdés, Chavez, & Angelelli, 2003). Furthermore, language brokering facilitates bilingualism by enhancing cognitive skills, and increasing comprehension of adult-level texts (Dorner, Orellana, & Li-Grining, 2007; Wu & Kim, 2009). Buriel et al. (1998) argued that the brokering process enhanced the cognitive skills of bilingual children who interpret for their parents. Language brokering may also increase metalinguistic skills (Duran, 2008; Garcia, 2006; J. S. Lee & Bowen, 2006) and social abilities (Chao, 2006; Han, 2006; Tabor & Collier, 2002). The complex translation strategies that are employed during language brokering by children may result in higher academic outcomes than those of non-brokering peers. For example, the process could result in increased school-related vocabulary and experience in certain language activities that require the same skills students need to achieve academic, cognitive, and linguistic competencies (Garcia, 2006; Han, 2006).

In their study of Mexican immigrants in Chicago, Dorner and colleagues (2007) found that higher levels of language brokering were significantly linked to better scores on fifth- and sixth-grade standardized reading tests. Similarly, Orellana, Renolds, Dorner, and Meza (2003) found a positive relation between language brokering and reading and math achievement test scores. In another study, Orellana (2009) noted that language brokers with transcultural skills and language-brokering experience had higher scores on standardized tests in reading and math. These arguments may explain why many Asian immigrant children who become language brokers have high achievement (J. S. Lee & Bowen, 2006). In sum, these studies suggest positive effects of language brokering on children's cognitive, academic, and behavioral development.

### School Success as a Form of Resistance

A growing number of studies suggest that some minority children respond to racism and discrimination in ways that promote educational attainment and academic excellence (Cammarota, 2004; Carter Andrews, 2008; Harris & Marsh, 2010; O'Connor, 1997; Sanders, 1997; Yosso, 2002a, 2002b). Though not discounting the oppositional identity work of Ogbu (1991), these recent studies suggest minority youth have more than one response to racism that can result in different educational outcomes. For example, studies focused on African Americans find that some youth possess a strong achievement orientation that is reflected in their multifaceted and continuous struggle for equal educational opportunity, attainment, and success (Carter Andrews, 2008; O'Connor, 1997; Sanders, 1997). One way in which students of color reconcile "the irreconcilable conflict" (Ogbu, 1991) is by using school success as a form of resistance. Scholars have defined this resistance in various ways in their work—"conformist resistance" (Fordham, 1999; Yosso, 2002a), "positive resistance" (Valenzuela, 1999) "academic resilience" (Gayles, 2005), and "transformational resistance" (Cammarota, 2004).

Some scholars define resistance as succeeding in school to reject racism as a structural barrier to students' upward mobility (Carter Andrews, 2008; Gayles, 2005; O'Connor, 1997; Sanders, 1997; Yosso, 2002a). For some students, school success as a resistance strategy represents a commitment to maintaining a historically rooted ideology of racial uplift and thriving against all odds. African American students who embody this characterization have been called race-conscious high achievers (Foster, 2005). These students have an achievement ideology that is collective and resistant in nature rather than collective and oppositional. By conceptualizing success in the context of being a proud member of the African American community, some participants develop an achievement ethos that reflects an understanding of success despite systemic forces that oppress them. These youth conceptualize achievement as integral, rather than separate from being African American, in order to sustain high levels of school success (Nasir, 2012; Oyserman, Gant, & Ager, 1995). Similarly, Carter Andrews (2008) describes "critical race achievement" as an ideology expressed by African American students that reflects resistance, resilience, and a redefinition of achievement. In her research, these students possessed a critical consciousness about racism and the challenges it presents to their present and future opportunities as well as those of other members of their racial group. Thus, students develop adaptive strategies for overcoming racism in the school context that allow them to maintain high academic achievement and a strong racial/ethnic self-concept (Carter Andrews, 2008).

Oyserman and colleagues' (1995) framework of identity development attempts to account for the experiences of youth who must conceptualize plausible paths toward academic success in a context unfavorable to members of their group. By conceptualizing achievement as embedded within one's sense of self as an African American, youths do not experience contradiction and tension between achievement and their African American identity (Oyserman et al., 1995). Thus, school success is thought to be dependent on three things: (a) seeing oneself as a member of the racial group (i.e., connectedness); (b) being aware of stereotypes and limitations to one's present and future social and economic outcomes (i.e., awareness of racism); and (c) developing a perspective of self as succeeding as a racial group member (i.e., achievement as an African American). Oyserman and colleagues (1995) also note that identity negotiation for African American youth should involve the dual task of assembling a positive sense of self, while discrediting negative identities attributed to African Americans. However, in contrast to becoming raceless, they posit that a sense of self as part of kin and community and interacting with the group are important components of African American identity that provide a sense of meaning and purpose. They tie the self to normative strategies for goal attainment, particularly school achievement. Therefore, in addition to discrediting negative stereotypes about the black community, it is important for African Americans who seek academic success, coupled with positive psychological health, to maintain attachment to the fictive kinship system and associate positive meaning to this membership. According to O'Connor (1997),

students aware of such injustices identify their "collective struggle" as the factor that leads them to continue to excel. For example, Sanders (1997) found that eighth-grade African American students with a high awareness of racial discrimination respond to discrimination in ways that are conducive, rather than detrimental, to academic success.

Education researchers have also described a type of student achievement among marginalized students of color that they call "conformist resistance" (Solórzano & Delgado Bernal, 2001; Valenzuela, 1999; Yosso, 2002a). "Conformist resistance" centers on using education, or at least persevering to obtain educational credentials, to counter societal inequalities without challenging the systemic oppressions of schooling. Valenzuela (1999) uses the term "positive resistance" to denote student achievement deployed as a strategy to counter social oppression. Solórzano and Delgado Bernal (2001) expand on this argument, contending that students may adopt a "transformational resistance," which they define as a deeper level of critical awareness and a social justice orientation to work for social change. Studying the influence of media on Chicana/o community college students, Yosso (2002b) identified a "prove them wrong" approach among students, described as the motivation for Latino youth to challenge negative media representations by succeeding in their own lives and serving as  positive examples for others. Similarly, Arellano and Padilla's (1996) investigation of Latino college students at a prestigious university found that, for resilient students, perceived disparities in opportunities afforded to others, as well as a sense of affiliation with other Latinos, constituted important motivational resources.

## Promising Directions for Future Research

In this final section, we consider potential gaps in research and identify promising directions for future research. We argue that there are several potentially promising directions for future research, building on critical issues in contemporary society around culture, race, language, identity, and schooling. One critical area for future research is the complex interplay of multiple gendered, linguistic, and racialized identities. Much of the research has examined race- or language-based identities but less frequently has research examined, from a psychological perspective, how people manage multiple marginalized identities, nor how these identities intersect in complex ways with the environment, or with schooling settings in particular. Whereas scholarship on intersectionality theory (Crenshaw, 1991) has articulated the important implications of being at the intersections of multiple identities, rarely have these experiences been examined in relation to schooling outcomes or processes. Perhaps one exception is the recent surge of scholarship on men and boys of color (Edley & Ruiz de Velasco, 2010).

A related area is the study of new and complex identity forms, and new configurations of the settings within which marginalized students construct racial, cultural, and linguistic identities. This includes the study of the growing population of black middle-class students, who too often face similar academic outcomes as their less well-resourced peers. Multiracial students are another growing demographic group (Lusk, Taylor, Nanney, & Austin, 2010). There is much research needed to understand the experience of multiracial students, including the linguistic identities of those students raised in multilingual households, and the racial identities of biracial students growing up in different kinds of social and school settings. In addition, research might address the experiences of language groups other than Spanish in U.S. schools and society.

In addition to considering new groups of students and students with complex configurations of identities, another promising area is developing alternate quantitative and qualitative research methods and utilizing multimethod designs to consider the interplay of social structures and sociopolitical trends, local teaching and learning environments, and developing racial, ethnic, cultural, and linguistic identities in relation to student achievement and educational experiences. For example, outmigration from inner cities in major metropolitan areas has caused the demographic reconstitution of suburban neighborhoods, whose schools are being asked to serve this new population of students. We know very little about the experience of students or about their identity processes that occur within high-minority, higher-poverty suburban schools (Morris, 2009). Multilevel models would be useful in such studies because they consider nested structure (i.e., multilevel models consider the individual in contexts such as schools or the communities). Another example would be a study of shifting student identities in relation to district-level reforms, particularly reforms that have to do with equity or the experiences of language-minority students. This line of research would also benefit from building on advances in multilevel and interdisciplinary research, as well as research in the tradition of translational science and human science (Penuel & Fishman, 2012).

Research on racial, ethnic, cultural, and linguistic identities of students should also address the important demographic and ideological shifts that have occurred over time. For instance, today's youth are coming of age in an era that has been referred to as "post-racial." Whereas the degree to which race is declining in significance is certainly debatable, the national discourse on race, culture, and language has shifted in important ways, which likely impacts the developing identities of young people.

In conclusion, there exists a burgeoning body of research relevant to understanding the relation between racial, cultural, and linguistic identities and schooling outcomes. The development of healthy identities is critical to young people's sense of selves and their academic outcomes. Additionally, healthy identities provide a layer of support in successfully navigating the inequality and racism they face in everyday life. The body of research provides significant information about the importance of healthy identities; yet, we do very little in schools or as a society to support the development of such identities. Moving forward, it is critical that we find ways to better support students as they work to craft consequential racial/ethnic, cultural, and linguistic identities in schools.

## Note

1. We use multiple terms throughout the chapter to denote racial and ethnic group membership, including African American, black, Latino, Hispanic, white, Caucasian, and Asian American. We use racial/ethnic terms for the same group interchangeably, in order to reflect the terms that the authors use in the original studies, as well as to communicate the range of terms used in the research literature.

## References

Acoach, C. L. & Webb, L. M. (2004). The influence of language brokering on Hispanic teenagers' acculturation, academic performance, and nonverbal decoding skills: A preliminary study. *The Howard Journal of Communications, 15,* 1–19.

Ainsworth-Darnell, J. W., & Downey, D. D. (1998). Assessing the oppositional culture explanation for racial/ethnic differences in school performance. *American Sociological Review, 63*(4), 536–553.

Arellano, A. R., & Padilla, A. M. (1996). Academic invulnerability among a select group of Latino university students. *Hispanic Journal of Behavioral Sciences, 18,* 485–507.

Aronson, J., Lustina, M. J., Good, C., Keough, K., Steele, C. M., & Brown, J. (1999). When white men can't do math: Necessary and sufficient factors in stereotype threat. *Journal of Experimental Social Psychology, 35*(1), 29–46.

Barot, R. & Bird, J. (2001). Racialization: The genealogy and critique of a concept. *Ethnic and Racial Studies, 24*(4), 601–618.

Baugh, J. (2007). Linguistic contributions to the advancement of racial justice within and beyond the African diaspora. *Language and Linguistics Compass, 1*(4), 331–349.

Bonilla-Silva, E. (2006). *Racism without racists: Color-blind racism and the persistence of racial inequality in the United States.* Lanham, MD: Rowman & Littlefield.

Bowman, P. J., & Howard, C. (1985). Race-related socialization, motivation, and academic achievement: A study of Black youths in three-generation families. *Journal of American Academy of Child Psychiatry, 24,* 134–141.

Boykin, A. W., & Bailey, C. (2000). *The role of cultural factors in school relevant cognitive functioning: Synthesis of findings on cultural contexts, cultural orientations, and individual differences.* Report No. 42. Washington, D.C.: Howard University, Center for Research on the Education of Students Placed At Risk (CRESPAR).

Boykin, A. W., & Cunningham, R. T. (2001). The effects of movement expressiveness in story content and learning context on the analogical reasoning performance of African American children. *Journal of Negro Education, 70,* 72–83.

Bronfenbrenner, U. (1993). The ecology of cognitive development. In R.H. Wozniak & K. W. Fischer (Eds.), *Development in context: Acting and thinking in specific environments* (pp. 3–44). Hillsdale, NJ: Erlbaum.

Brown, C., & Chu, H. (2012). Discrimination, ethnic identity, and academic outcomes of Mexican immigrant children: The importance of school context. *Child Development, 83*(5), 1477–1485.

Buriel, R., Perez, W., DeMent, T., Chavez, D. V., & Moran, V. R. (1998). The relationship of language brokering to academic performance, biculturalism and self-efficacy among Latino adolescents. *Hispanic Journal of Behavioral Sciences, 20,* 283–297.

Cammarota, J. (2004). The gendered and racialized pathways of Latina and Latino youth: Different struggles, different resistances in the urban context. *Anthropology and Education Quarterly, 35*(1), 53–74.

Carter, P. (2005). *Keeping it real.* New York, NY: Oxford University Press.

Carter, P. (2012). *Stubborn roots: Race, culture, and inequality in U.S. and South African schools.* New York, NY: Oxford University Press.

Carter Andrews, D. J. (2008). Achievement as resistance: The development of a critical race achievement ideology among Black achievers. *Harvard Educational Review, 78*(3), 466–497.

Chao, R. (2006). The prevalence and consequences of adolescents' language brokering for their immigrant parents. In M. Bornstein & L. Cote (Eds.), *Acculturation and parent child relationships: Measurement and development* (pp. 271–296). Mahwah, NJ: Erlbaum.

Chavous, T. M., Bernat, D. H., Schmeelk-Cone, K., Caldwell, C., Kohn-Wood, L., & Zimmerman, M. A. (2003). Racial identity and academic attainment among African American adolescents. *Child Development, 74,* 1076–1090.

Cohen, G. L., & Garcia, J. (2005). "I am us": Negative stereotypes as collective threats. *Journal of Personality and Social Psychology, 89*(4), 566.

Cohen, G. L., Steele, C. M., & Ross, L. D. (1999). The mentor's dilemma: Providing critical feedback across the racial divide. *Personality and Social Psychology Bulletin, 25*(10), 1302–1318.

Conchas, G., & Vigil, D. (2010). Multiple marginality and urban education: Community and school socialization among low-income Mexican-descent youth. *Journal of Education for Students Placed at Risk, 15*(1–2), 51–65.

Crenshaw, K. (1991). Mapping the margins: Intersectionality, identity politics, and violence against women of color. *Stanford Law Review, 43*(6), 1241–1299.

Cuéllar, I., & González, G. (2000). Cultural identity description and cultural formulation for Hispanics. In R. H. Dana (Ed.), *Handbook of cross-cultural and multicultural personality assessment* (pp. 605–621). Mahwah, NJ: Erlbaum.

Darling-Hammond, L. (2010). *The flat world and education: How America's commitment to equity will determine our future.* New York, NY: Teachers College Press.

Davey, M., Fish, D. G., Eaker, L. S., & Klock, K. (2003). Ethnic identity in an American White minority group. *Identity, 3,* 143–158.

Davidson, A. (1996). *Making and molding identities in schools: Student narratives on race, gender, and academic engagement.* Albany, NY: State University of New York.

DeMent, T., & Buriel, R. (1999). *Children as cultural brokers: Recollections of college students.* Paper presented at the SPSSI Conference on Immigrants and Immigration, Toronto, Canada.

Dorner, L. M., Orellana, M. F., & Li-Grining, C. P. (2007). "I helped my mom," and it helped me: Translating the skills of language brokers into improved standardized test scores. *American Journal of Education, 113,* 451–478.

Dovidio, J., Gluszek, A., John, M., Ditlmann, R., & Lagunes, P. (2010). Understanding bias toward Latinos: Discrimination, dimensions of difference, and experience of exclusion. *Journal of Social Issues, 66*(1), 59–78.

Duran, R. P. (2008). Assessing English-language learners' achievement. *Review of Research in Education, 32,* 292–327.

Edley, C. & Ruiz de Velasco, J. (2010). *Changing places: How communities will improve the health of boys of color.* Berkeley, CA: University of California.

Ellison, C. M., Boykin, A. W., Tyler, K. M., & Dillihunt, M. L. (2005). Examining classroom learning preferences among elementary school students. *Social Behavior and Personality, 33,* 699–708.

Erikson, E. (1968) *Identity: Youth and crisis.* New York, NY: Norton.

Feagin, J. R., & Vera, H. (1995). *White racism.* New York, NY: Routledge.

Fhagen-Smith, P., Vandiver, B., Worrell, F., & Cross, W. (2010). (Re) Examining racial identity attitude differences across gender, community type, and socioeconomic status among African American college students. *Identity: An International Journal of Theory and Research, 10*(3), 164–180.

Fisher, C. B., Wallace, S. A., & Fenton, R. E. (2000). Discrimination distress during adolescence. *Journal of Youth and Adolescence, 29*(6), 679–695.

Ford, D. & Harris, J. H. (2008). Perceptions and attitudes of Black students toward school, achievement, and other educational variables. *Child Development, 67*(3), 1141–1152.

Fordham, S. (1999). Dissin' "the standard": Ebonics as guerrilla warfare at Capital High. *Anthropology and Education Quarterly, 30*(3), 272–293.

Fordham, S., & Ogbu, J. U. (1986). Black students' school success: Coping with the burden of "acting White." *The Urban Review, 18*(3), 176–206.

Foster, K. M. (2005). Gods or vermin: Alternative readings of the African American experience among African and African American college students. *Transforming Anthropology, 13*(1), 34–46.

Fredrickson, G. M. (2002). *Racism: A short history.* Princeton, NJ: Princeton University Press.

Fryer, R. G., & Levitt, S. D. (2006). The black–white test score gap through third grade. *American Law and Economics Review, 8*(2), 249–281.

Fryer, R.G., & Torelli, P. (2010). An empirical analysis of 'acting white.' *Journal of Public Economics, 94,* 380–396.

Fuligni, A. J., Witkow, M., & Garcia, C. (2005). Ethnic identity and the academic adjustment of adolescents from Mexican, Chinese, and European backgrounds. *Developmental Psychology, 41,* 799–811.

Garcia, E. E. (2006). *Teaching and learning in two languages.* New York, NY: Teachers College Press.

Garcia Coll, C., & Marks, A. K. (2009). *Immigrant stories: Ethnicity and academics in middle childhood.* New York, NY: Oxford University Press.

Gayles, J. (2005). Playing the game and paying the price: Academic resilience among three high-achieving African American males. *Anthropology and Education Quarterly, 36*(3), 250–264.

Good, C., Aronson, J., & Inzlicht, M. (2003). Improving adolescents' standardized test performance: An intervention to reduce the effects of stereotype threat. *Journal of Applied Developmental Psychology, 24*(6), 645–662.

Greene, M., Way, N., & Pahl, K. (2006). Trajectories of perceived adult and peer discrimination among Black, Latino, and Asian American adolescents: Patterns and psychological correlates. *Developmental Psychology, 42,* 218–238.

Greenwald, A., & Krieger, L. H. (2006). Implicit bias: Scientific foundations. *California Law Review, 94*(4), 945–967.

Gutiérrez, K. D., & Rogoff, B. (2003). Cultural ways of learning: Individual traits or repertoires of practice. *Educational Researcher, 32*(5), 19–25.

Han, W. (2006). Academic achievements of children in immigrant families. *Educational Research and Review, 1*(8), 286–318.

Hany-Lopez, I. (1996). *White by law: The legal construction of race.* New York: New York University.

Harris, A. L., & Marsh, K. (2010). Is a raceless identity an effective strategy for academic success among Blacks? *Social Science Quarterly, 91*(5), 1242–1263.

Herrenkohl, L. & Mertyl, V. (2010). *How students come to be, know, and do: A case for a broad view of learning.* New York, NY: Cambridge University Press.

Hogg, M. (2003). Social identity. In M. R. Leary & J. P. Tangney (Eds.), *Handbook of self and identity* (pp. 462–479). New York, NY: Guilford.

Horvat, E. M., & Lewis, K. S. (2003). Reassessing the "burden of 'acting white'": The importance of peer groups in managing academic success. *Sociology of Education, 76*(4), 265–280.

Howard, T. S. (2010). *Why race and culture matter in schools: Closing the achievement gap in America's classrooms.* New York, NY: Teachers College Press.

Huynh, V. W., & Fuligni, A. J. (2008). Ethnic socialization and the academic adjustment of adolescents from Mexican, Chinese, and European backgrounds. *Developmental Psychology, 44,* 1202–1208.

Jost, J. T., Banaji, M. R., & Nosek, B. A. (2004). A decade of system justification theory: Accumulated evidence of conscious and unconscious bolstering of the status quo. *Political Psychology, 25*(6), 881–919.

Killen, M., Henning, A., Kelly, M., Crystal, D., & Ruck, M. (2007). Evaluations of interracial peer encounters by majority and minority US children and adolescents. *International Journal of Behavioral Development, 31*(5), 491–500.

Killen, M., & Stangor, C. (2001). Children's reasoning about inclusion and exclusion in gender and race peer group contexts. *Child Development, 72*(1), 174–186.

Kim, S. Y., & Chao, R. K. (2009). Heritage language fluency, ethnic identity, and school effort of immigrant Chinese and Mexican adolescents. *Cultural Diversity and Ethnic Minority Psychology, 15*(1), 27–37.

Kluegel, J. R. & Bobo, L. (1993). Opposition to race-targeting: Self-interest, stratification ideology, or racial attitudes. *American Sociological Review, 58*(4), 443–464.

Kroeber, A. L., & Kluckholm, C. (1952). *Culture: A critical review of concepts and definitions.* Cambridge, MA: Papers of the Peabody Museum of American Archeology and Ethnology.

Ladson-Billings, G. (1993). *The dreamkeepers: Successful teaching for African American students.* San Francisco, CA: Jossey Bass.

Langer-Osuna, J. (2011). How Brianna became bossy and Kofi came out smart: Understanding the differentially mediated identity and engagement of two group leaders in a project-based mathematics classroom. *The Canadian Journal for Science, Mathematics, and Technology Education, 11*(3), 207–225.

Lawrence, J. S., Bachman, M., & Ruble, D. N. (2007). Ethnicity, ethnic identity, and school valuing among children from immigrant and non-immigrant families. In A. J. Fuligni (Ed.), *Contesting stereotypes and creating identities* (pp. 136–159). New York, NY: Russell Sage Foundation.

Lee, C. (2007). *Cultural literacy and learning: Taking bloom in the midst of the whirlwind.* New York, NY: Teachers College Press.

Lee, J. S., & Bowen, N. K. (2006). Parent involvement, cultural capital, and the achievement gap among elementary school children. *American Educational Research Journal, 43*(2), 193–218.

Lee, R. M. (2003). Do ethnic identity and other-group orientation protect against discrimination for Asian Americans? *Journal of Counseling Psychology, 50*, 133–141.

LeFromboise, T., Coleman, H. L. K., & Gerton, J. (1993). Psychological impact of biculturalism: Evidence and theory. *Psychological Bulletin, 114*, 395–412.

Leonardo, Z. (2009). *Race, whiteness, and education.* New York, NY: Routledge.

Lewis, A. (2003). *Race in the schoolyard: Negotiating the color line in classrooms and communities.* New Brunswick, NJ: Rutgers University Press.

Lusk, E., Taylor, M., Nanney, J., & Austin, C. (2010). Biracial identity and its relation to self-esteem and depression in mixed Black/White biracial individuals. *Journal of Ethnic and Cultural Diversity in Social Work, 19*(2), 109–126.

Martens, M., Johns, J., Greenberg, J., & Schimel, J. (2006). Combating stereotype threat: The effect of self-affirmation on women's intellectual performance. *Journal of Experimental Social Psychology, 42*, 236–243.

Martin, D. B. (2006). Mathematics learning and participation as racialized forms of experience: African American parents speak on the struggle for mathematics literacy. *Mathematical Thinking and Learning, 8*(3), 197–229.

McCoy, S. & Major, B. (2003). Group identification moderates emotional responses to perceived prejudice. *Personality and Social Psychological Bulletin, 40*(8), 1005–1017.

McQuillan, J., & Tse, L. (1995). Child language brokering in linguistic minority communities: Effects on cultural interaction, cognition, and literacy. *Language and Education, 9*, 195–215.

Mead, G. H. (1934). *Mind, self, and society.* Chicago, IL: University of Chicago Press.

Mickelson, R. A., & Velasco, A. E. (2006). Bring it on! Diverse responses to "acting white" among academically able Black adolescents. In E. M. Horvat and C. O'Connor (Eds.), *Beyond acting white: Reframing the debate on Black student achievement* (pp. 27–56). New York, NY: Rowman & Littlefield.

Morris, J. (2009). *Troubling the waters: Fulfilling the promise of quality public schooling for Black children.* New York, NY: Teachers College Press.

Murji, K. & Solomos, J. (2005). *Racialization: Studies in theory and practice.* New York, NY: Oxford University Press.

Murray, M. S., Neal-Barnett, A., Demmings, J. L., & Stadulis, R. (2012). The acting White accusation, racial identity, and anxiety in African American adolescents. *Journal of Anxiety Disorders, 26*, 526–531.

Nagel, J. (1994). Constructing ethnicity: Creating and recreating ethnic identity and culture. *Social Problems, 41*(1), 152–176.

Nasir, N. (2012). *Racialized identities: Race and achievement for African-American youth.* Stanford, CA: Stanford University Press.

Nasir, N. S., & Shah, N. (2011). On defense: African American males making sense of racialized narratives in mathematics education. *Journal of African American Males in Education, 2*(1), 24–45.

Nasir, N. S., Snyder, C. R., Shah, N., & Ross, K. M. (2012). Stereotypes, storylines, and the learning process. *Human Development, 55*(5–6), 285–301.

National Education Association. (2011). *Race against time: Educating Black boys.* Washington, D.C.: National Education Association.

Noguera, P., & Wing, J. (2006). *Unfinished business: Closing the racial achievement gap in our schools.* San Francisco, CA: Jossey Bass.

Oakes, J. (2005). *Keeping track: How schools structure inequality* (2nd ed.). New Haven, CT: Yale University Press.

O'Connor, C. (1997). Dispositions toward (collective) struggle and educational resilience in the inner city. *American Educational Research Journal, 34*, 593–629.

Ogbu, J. U. (1991). Immigrant and involuntary minorities in comparative perspective. In M. A. Gibson & J. U. Ogbu (Eds.), *Minority status and schooling: A comparative study of immigrant and involuntary minorities* (pp. 3–36). New York, NY: Garland.

Ogbu, J. U. (2008). *Minority status, oppositional culture, & schooling.* New York, NY: Routledge.

Olsen, L. (1997). *Made in America: Immigrant students in our public schools.* New York, NY: New Press.

Omi, M., & Winant, H. (1994). *Racial formation in the United States: From the 1960s to the 1990s.* New York, NY: Routledge.

Orellana, M. F. (2009). *Translating childhoods: Immigrant youth, language, and culture.* New Brunswick, NJ: Rutgers University Press.

Orellana, M. F., Renolds, J., Dorner, L. & Meza, A. (2003). In other words: Translating or "para-phrasing" as a family literacy practice in immigrant households. *Reading Research Quarterly, 38*(1), 12–34.

Osborne, J. W. (1995). Academics, self-esteem, and race: A look at the underlying assumptions of the disidentification hypothesis. *Personality and Social Psychology Bulletin, 21*, 449–455.

Oyserman, D., & Destin, M. (2010). Identity-based motivation: Implications for intervention. *The Counseling Psychologist, 38*, 1001–1043.

Oyserman, D., Gant, L., & Ager, J. (1995). A socially contextualized model of African American identity: Possible selves and school persistence. *Journal of Personality and Social Psychology, 69*(6), 1216–1232.

Oyserman, D., Harrison, K., & Bybee, D. (2001). Can racial identity be promotive of academic efficacy? *International Journal of Behavioral Development, 25*, 379–385.

Penuel, W. R., & Fishman, B. J. (2012). Large-scale science education intervention research we can use. *Journal of Research in Science Teaching, 49*(3), 281–304.

Phinney, J. S., Romero, I., Nava, M., & Huang, D. (2001). The role of language, parents, and peers in ethnic identity among adolescents in immigrant families. *Journal of Youth and Adolescence, 30*, 135–153.

Pollock, M. (2004). *Colormute: Race talk dilemmas in an American school.* Princeton, NJ: Princeton University Press.

Portes, A., & Rumbaut, R. G. (2001). *Legacies: The story of the immigrant second generation.* Los Angeles, CA: University of California Press.

Rivas-Drake, D., Seaton, E. K., Markstrom, C., Quintana, S., Syed, M., Lee, R. M., . . . Ethnic and Racial Identity in the 21st Century Study Group. (2014). Ethnic and racial identity in adolescence: Implications for psychosocial, academic, and health outcomes. *Child Development, 85*(1), 40–57.

Roeser, R., Galloway, M., Casey-Cannon, S., Watson, C., Keller, L., & Tan, E. (2008). Identity representation in patterns of school achievement and well-being among early adolescent girls: Variable and person-centered approaches. *Journal of Early Adolescence, 28*(1), 115–152.

Roeser, R. W., Peck, S. C., & Nasir, N. S. (2006). Self and identity processes in school motivation, learning, and achievement. In P. A. Alexander & P. H. Winne (Eds.), *Handbook of educational psychology,* 2nd ed. (pp. 391–424). Mahwah, NJ: Erlbaum.

Rogoff, B. (2003). *The cultural nature of human development.* New York, NY: Oxford University Press.

Romero, A. J., Edwards, L. M., Fryberg, S. A., & Orduña, M. (2014). Resilience to discrimination stress across ethnic identity stages of development. *Journal of Applied Social Psychology, 44*, 1–11.

Rumbaut, R. G. (1994). The crucible within: Ethnic identity, self-esteem and segmented assimilation among children of immigrants. *International Migration Review, 28*, 748–794.

Rumbaut, R. G. & Ima, K. (1988). *The adaptation of Southeast Asian refugee youth: A comparative study.* Washington, D.C.: Office of Refugee Resettlement.

Rutland, A., Cameron, L., Milne, A., & McGeorge, P. (2005). Social norms and self-presentation: Children's implicit and explicit intergroup attitudes. *Child Development, 76*(2), 451–466.

Sanders, M. G. (1997). Overcoming obstacles: Academic achievement as a response to racism and discrimination. *Journal of Negro Education, 66,* 83–93.

Schmader, T., Major, B., & Gramzow, R. H. (2001). Coping with ethnic stereotypes in the academic domain: Perceived injustice and psychological disengagement. *Journal of Social Issues, 57,* 93–111.

Sellers, R. M., Caldwell, C. H., Schmeelk-Cone, K. H., & Zimmerman, M. A. (2003). Racial identity, racial discrimination, perceived stress, and psychological distress among African American young adults. *Journal of Health and Social Behavior, 44,* 302–317.

Sellers, R. M., Chavous, T. M., & Cooke, D. Y. (1998). Racial ideology and racial centrality as predictors of African American college students' academic performance. *Journal of Black Psychology, 24*(1), 8–27.

Serpell, Z., Boykin, A. W., Madhere, S., & Nasim, A. (2006). The significance of contextual factors on African American students' transfer of learning. *Journal of Black Psychology, 32,* 418–441.

Smedley, A., & Smedley, B. D. (2005). Race as biology is fiction, racism as a social problem is real. *American Psychologist, 60,* 16–26.

Solórzano, D. G., & Delgado Bernal, D. (2001). Examining transformational resistance through a critical race and LatCrit Theory framework: Chicana and Chicano students in an urban context. *Urban Education, 36*(3), 308–342.

Spencer, M. B. (1999). Social and cultural influences on school adjustment: The application of an identity-focused cultural ecological perspective. *Educational Psychologist, 34*(1), 43–57.

Spencer, M. B. (2006). Phenomenology and ecological systems theory: Development of diverse groups. In W. Damon & R. Lerner (Eds.), *Handbook of child psychology, Vol. 1: Theoretical models of human development,* 6th ed. (pp. 829–893). New York, NY: Wiley.

Spencer, M. B. & Markstrom-Adams, C. (1990). Identity processes among racial and ethnic minority children in America. *Child Development, 61*(2), 290–310.

Spencer, M. B., Noll, E., Stolzfus, J., & Harpalani, V. (2001). Identity and school adjustment: Revisiting the "acting White" assumption. *Educational Psychologist, 36,* 21–30.

Steele, C. M. (1992). Race and the schooling of African Americans. *The Atlantic Monthly, 269*(4), 68–78.

Steele, C. M., & Aronson, J. (1995). Stereotype threat and intellectual test performance of African Americans. *Journal of Personality and Social Psychology, 69,* 797–811.

Suarez-Orozco, C., & Suarez-Orozco, M. M. (2001). *Children of immigration.* Cambridge, MA: Harvard University Press.

Sue, D., Lin, A., Torino, G., Capodilupo, C., & Rivera, D. (2009). Racial microaggressions and difficult dialogues on race in the classroom. *Cultural Diversity and Ethnic Minority Psychology, 15,* 183–190.

Tabor, W., & Collier, V. (2002). *A national study of school effectiveness for language minority students' long term academic achievement.* Santa Cruz, CA: Center for the Research on Education.

Thomas, D. E., Townsend, T. G., & Belgrave, F. Z. (2003). The influence of cultural and racial identification on the psychosocial adjustment of inner-city African American children in school. *American Journal of Community Psychology, 32*(3–4), 217–228.

Tyson, K. (2006). The making of a "burden": Tracing the development of a "burden of acting white." In E. M. Horvat and C. O'Connor (Eds.), *Beyond acting White: Reframing the debate on Black student achievement* (pp. 57–90). New York, NY: Rowman & Littlefield.

Tyson, K., Darity, W., Jr., & Castellino, D. R. (2005). It's not "a Black thing": Understanding the burden of acting White and other dilemmas of high achievement. *American Sociological Review, 70,* 582–605.

Umaña-Taylor, A. J., Alfaro, E. C., Bamaca, M. Y., & Guimond, A. B. (2009). The central role of familial ethnic socialization in Latino adolescents' cultural orientation. *Journal of Marriage and Family, 71,* 46–60.

Umaña-Taylor, A. J., & Fine, M. A. (2004). Examining ethnic identity among Mexican-origin adolescents living in the United States. *Hispanic Journal of Behavioral Sciences, 26,* 36–59.

Umaña-Taylor, A. J., Lee, R., Rivas-Drake, D., Syed, M., Quintana, S., Cross, W., . . . Yip, T. (2014). Ethnic and racial identity during adolescence and into young adulthood: An integrated conceptualization. *Child Development, 85*(1), 21–39.

Umaña-Taylor, A. J., & Updegraff, K. A. (2007). Latino adolescents' mental health: Exploring the interrelations among discrimination, ethnic identity, cultural orientation, self-esteem, and depressive symptoms. *Journal of Adolescence, 30,* 549–567.

Utsey, S., Ponterotto, J., Reynolds, A., & Cancelli, A. (2000). Racial discrimination, coping, life satisfaction, and self-esteem among African Americans. *Journal of Counseling & Development, 78,* 72–80.

Valdés, G. (Ed.). (2003). *Expanding definitions of giftedness: The case of young interpreters from immigrant countries.* Mahwah, NJ: Erlbaum.

Valdés, G., Chavez, C., & Angelelli, C. (2003). A performance team: Young interpreters and their parents. In G. Valdés (Ed.), *Expanding definitions of giftedness: The case of young interpreters from immigrant countries* (pp. 42–81). Mahwah, NJ: Erlbaum.

Valenzuela, A. (1999). *Subtractive schooling: U.S.-Mexican youth and the politics of caring.* Albany, NY: State University of New York Press.

Varelas, M., Martin, D., & Kane, J. (2012). Content learning and identity construction: A framework to strengthen African American students' mathematics and science learning in urban elementary schools. *Human Development, 55,* 319–339.

Vygotsky, L. S. (1978). *Mind in society: The development of higher psychological processes.* Cambridge, MA: Harvard University Press.

Walinchowski, M. (2001). *Language brokering: Laying the foundation for success and bilingualism.* Paper presentation at the Annual Educational Research Exchange, College Station, TX.

Waters, M. C. (1999). *Black identities: West Indian immigrant dreams and American realities.* New York, NY: Russell Sage Foundation.

Way, N., Hernández, M. G., Rogers, L. O., & Hughes, D. L. (2013). "I'm not going to become no rapper": Stereotypes as a context of ethnic and racial identity development. *Journal of Adolescent Research, 28*(4), 407–430.

Weisner, T. (2002). Ecocultural understanding of children's developmental pathways. *Human Development, 45*(4), 275–281.

Weisskirch, R. S. (2005). The relationship of language brokering to ethnic identity for Latino early adolescents. *Hispanic Journal of Behavioral Sciences, 27,* 286–299.

Wong, C. A., Eccles, J. S., & Sameroff, A. (2003). The influence of ethnic discrimination and ethnic identification on African American adolescents' school and socioemotional adjustment. *Journal of Personality, 71,* 1197–1232.

Wortham, S. E. F. (2006). *Learning identity: The joint emergence of social identification and academic learning.* New York, NY: Cambridge University Press.

Wu, N., & Kim, S. Y. (2009). Chinese American adolescents' perceptions of the language brokering experience as a sense of burden and sense of efficacy. *Journal of Youth and Adolescence, 38,* 703–718.

Yip, T., Seaton, E. K., & Sellers, R. M. (2006). African American racial identity across the lifespan: A cluster analysis of identity status, identity content and depression among adolescents, emerging adults and adults. *Child Development, 77,* 1504–1517.

Yosso, T. J. (2002a). Toward a critical race curriculum. *Equity & Excellence in Education, 35*(2), 93-107.

Yosso, T. J. (2002b). Critical race media literacy: Challenging deficit discourse about Chicana/os. *Journal of Popular Film and Television, 30*(1), 52–63.

Zarate, M. E., Bhimji, F., & Reese, L. (2005). Ethnic identity and academic achievement among Latino/a adolescents. *Journal of Latinos and Education, 4,* 95–114.

# 15

# Language Development

*ALISON L. BAILEY*[1]
University of California, Los Angeles

*ANNA OSIPOVA*
California State University, Los Angeles

*KIMBERLY REYNOLDS KELLY*
California State University, Long Beach

What *develops* when we refer to language development? Before birth, children begin acquiring knowledge of the sounds of language, and by the end of the school years they have command of not only a fully fledged sound system but of complex sentence structures, conventions governing grammatical forms, expressive abilities with thousands of words, and receptive understanding of thousands more. Add to this language repertoires that include agile linguistic and discourse adaptations based on degrees of formality and changes in context that can create differences in talk at home, with friends, and in school. With new educational policies to enhance academic standards, children in U.S. schools will increasingly need to orally communicate English language arts, mathematics, and science content knowledge by effectively formulating arguments using evidence and by providing well-crafted explanations of processes and procedures (e.g., *Common Core State Standards*, National Governors Association Center for Best Practices, Council of Chief State School Officers (CCSSO), 2010; *Next Generation Science Standards,* NGSS Lead States, 2013).

Previous editions of the *Handbook of Educational Psychology* have been absent a chapter on language development. A language development chapter in this edition likely indicates more recent acknowledgment of the protracted development of language, as well as increased attention to oral language connections to literacy development and academic content learning. Furthermore, children may be exposed to two languages simultaneously from birth or sequentially before the age of 3 years, and therefore have opportunity to develop two languages as a first language (L1). Developing a second or additional language (L2) beyond this age is a process of second-language acquisition (SLA). In instances of neuro-atypical development, including hearing

impairment, developmental disorder such as autism spectrum disorder (ASD), or language-based disorders such as specific language impairment and learning disabilities (LD), the course and pace of development may differ and need to be additionally accounted for. We also include descriptions of assessment approaches and supplemental measures for tracing development in the different language domains (see Appendix 15.1).

## The Study of Child Language Development

Roger Brown (1973) and his students were among the first to conduct systematic studies of language development in the modern era, relying on spontaneous language samples collected in the homes of young children. Transcripts were subjected to linguistic analysis to reveal early word meanings, word combinations, and grammatical forms (e.g., verb agreement, prepositions). Other seminal researchers (e.g., Snow, 1981) continued in the tradition of nineteenth-century naturalists by adopting a participant-observer approach to study the speech of their own children in authentic contexts (Hoff, 2009).

Supplementing these approaches are psycholinguistic studies designed to elicit naturalistic interactions under controlled conditions (e.g., timed parent–child interactions around the same set of objects), as well as strategically administered tasks used primarily to generate data on less common features that would otherwise require hours of sampling to observe them occurring spontaneously (e.g., passive forms in English) (Dick, Wulfeck, Krupa-Kwiatkowski, & Bates, 2004). Such methods are valuable ways to elicit production or reveal tacit comprehension of specific linguistic features. Language development research also continues to rely on sociolinguistic studies of spontaneous language conducted with authentic conversations and personal narratives exchanged in the home and with teacher and student discussions in the classroom. Verbatim language data can be transcribed and described using qualitative analytic techniques, such as conversational, discourse, and narrative analyses, or quantified and analyzed using descriptive and inferential statistics in experimental and correlational research designs (see Genishi & Glupczynski, 2006, for review).

## Biological Foundations

Specialized vocal apparatus and a human brain are required for oral language. At birth, the vocal tract is immature, and the tongue, larynx, and glottis develop at different rates. Each reaches adult size anywhere from 7 to 18 years, allowing for articulation of a range of speech sounds (e.g., Vorperian et al., 2005). Historically, *Broca's area* and *Wernicke's area* in the left hemisphere of the cerebral cortex were believed to be primarily responsible for language production and comprehension, respectively. Exceptions to left-hemisphere lateralization (besides in many left-handed individuals) are pragmatic aspects of language, including prosody and understanding non-literal meanings (e.g., sarcasm). Advances in electromagnetic and neuroimaging methods show *middle* and *inferior temporal gyri* implicated in aspects of speech processing once attributed to Broca's area (Poeppel, Idsardi, & van Wassenhove, 2008), and the *inferior parietal lobule* functioning as a connective center for auditory, visual, and sensory processing linked to phonological processing and access to word meaning in print (Vigneau et al., 2006).

*Myelination* (production of an essential insulating layer around the axon of neurons) is implicated in overall language performance of children (Pujol et al., 2006). Sex differences in the rate of myelination may explain higher incidence of language disorders in boys compared to girls (Bishop, 1987), possibly due to deleterious effects of testosterone on myelination. Indeed, hormonal differences sensitive to both genetic and environmental factors are believed responsible for sex-specific differences in language development, favoring girls (Galsworthy, Dionne, Dale, & Plomin, 2000). To date, neurobiological explanations of sex differences in language development remain controversial (e.g., Wallentin, 2009) and are possibly confounded by gender biases in language socialization (see below), as well as in diagnosis (Tomblin, 1996). Nevertheless, large-scale twin studies show that genetic factors impact language development (see Stromswold, 2010, for review); specific genes can be identified as responsible for growth in language-related subcortical regions during embryonic development (Spiteri et al., 2007).

### Evolutionary Accounts of Language Development

Possession of the physiological structures of the vocal tract and brain does not explain why a complex system like language should have developed in humans. However, an evolutionary perspective does explain the selective advantage to oral language production of the unique positioning and shape of the human larynx, mouth, and teeth (Lieberman, 2007). Despite the possible .costs to sacrificing safety and efficiency (e.g., risk of choking from food crossing the airway to the lungs, malnutrition from few/small molars inefficiently extracting nutrients), the advantages of the resulting vocal tract capable of producing speech sounds must have greatly increased chances of human survival (Hoff, 2009) (see MacWhinney, 2005, for alternative accounts).

Locke's (2006) hypothesis of a biological selective advantage provides an ontological or individual account of the initial intent to communicate vocally. The *parent selection hypothesis,* similar to Bowlby's (1969) proposal of *ethological attachment theory* before it, states that infants who vocalize with more effective care-elicitation signals, as opposed to unpleasant and inconsolable stress crying, are more likely to receive care. This in turn results in the infant more effectively structuring her vocalizing behavior (Chisholm, 2003). Moreover, neurobiological research indicates that, upon hearing the human voice during stressful situations, oxytocin is released in the typically developing infant brain (Seltzer, Ziegler, & Pollak, 2010). Such pleasurable reinforcement from brain biochemical reactions may further strengthen the desire to initiate interactions by cooing and babbling. In contrast, neuroimaging studies of infants with ASD reveal disruptions of these biochemical reactions, which may explain disruptions in their language development trajectories (Abrams et al., 2013).

### A Shift from Critical to Sensitive Periods for Language Development

A critical period or biologically determined timeframe between early childhood and puberty has long been hypothesized for language development (e.g., Lenneberg, 1967). Evidence for the importance of early exposure has most recently been drawn from studies of congenitally deaf children that demonstrate the lack of intervention (e.g., cochlear implant) by 7–10 years results in deleterious effects to speech and communication (Connor, Craig, Raudenbush, Heavner, & Zwolan, 2006), and previously from cases of extreme environmental deprivation in early life (e.g., Curtiss, 1977). The benefits of language exposure in early childhood to native-like SLA acquisition in adulthood are also evident following years of relative disuse, particularly with regard to phonology and grammar (Au, Oh, Knightly, Jun, & Romo, 2008). However, age-of-arrival and linguistic competence continue to be correlated in L2 learners who immigrate well beyond puberty (e.g., Birdsong, 2005), supporting the existence of a sensitive period when input to the brain is optimal, rather than a strict critical period.

Brain plasticity helps to explain children's greater sensitivity to learning an L1 or L2 in the early years of life. Childhood and adolescence are periods of *synaptogenesis,* when the brain recognizes and makes sense of auditory and visual input by forging and strengthening connections between neurons. As connections are refined, strengthened, and eliminated through a process of synaptic pruning (see Casey, Tottenham, Liston,

& Durston, 2005, for review), the brain is primed for language acquisition. Thereafter, acquiring certain aspects of language to native-like competence appears difficult.

## Social Contexts of Language Development

The social contexts under which language develops reveal explanatory mechanisms for group and individual differences (see Hoff, 2006, for review). Studies have predominantly been confined to young children and their families and have documented differences primarily in terms of parental socioeconomic status and cultural expectations and supports for language development. Although there is documented individual variation in child and parent language within groups sharing similar characteristics such as lower socioeconomic status (e.g., Bailey & Moughamian, 2007), group-level social factors have nevertheless been used to predict the kinds of language children are exposed to and acquire, as well as rate of language development. For example, in a naturalistic study of *child-directed speech* (CDS), Rowe (2008) found that parent education and income were related to CDS, which in turn was a predictor of children's vocabulary abilities 1 year later. The effects of socioeconomic status on features of CDS were mediated by parental knowledge of child development: higher-socioeconomic status parents had greater knowledge of child development which in turn impacted their interactions with their children.

In terms of cultural differences, form, content, and structure of personal narratives vary depending on practices valued by a speech community (Heath, 1983). For example, topic-associating narratives, typical of some African American communities, link several generally related events that shift in time and setting (Michaels, 1981). Succinct narratives with few details are typical of Japanese children, whereas North American children of European descent typically tell elaborated narratives with temporal or causal sequences (Minami & McCabe, 1995). However, despite cultural differences between American mothers who label and Japanese mothers who focus on social routines (*say bye-bye*), both American and Japanese children acquire relatively more early nouns (object labels) than early verbs (action words) (Fernald & Morikawa, 1993). This finding is reported for other languages, suggesting aspects of acquisition are universal and the degree of *imageability* of nouns (i.e., ease of mentally picturing words) predicts development (McDonough, Song, Hirsh-Pasek, Golinkoff, & Lannon, 2011).

Individual variation in language development has been attributed to exposure to multiple languages, gender, birth order, characteristics of the caregiver, peer interactions, quality of child care setting, media exposure, and school environment (Hoff, 2006). For example, parent–child interactions can differ along gender lines, with daughters eliciting more words from their mothers and longer sentences from their fathers in contrast to sons (Lovas, 2011). A naturalistic study of children's use of discourse markers (words that signal changes in the flow of talk such as, *then, OK*) with peers by Escalera (2009), however, found girls and boys used comparable markers in comparable conversational contexts (e.g.,

bargaining, sound play, narrating). In such cases, gender differences in language usage may be attributable to the different social contexts in which boys and girls are typically situated rather than to inherently gendered language (see Kyratzis & Cook-Gumperz, 2008, for review). Elsewhere, language development is attributed to the interplay of socialization practices and biological sex differences (e.g., Galsworthy et al., 2000). In another example of socialization practices, academic registers are encountered in schooling contexts and tend to be formal, decontextualized styles of language with linguistic and discourse features that may differ across the content areas (see Bailey, 2012, for review). Capabilities in tailoring language forms (e.g., lexical precision, embedded clauses) to the demands of their functions (e.g., describing a literary character's motives, explaining the water cycle process) are hallmarks of development in school contexts (e.g., Schleppegrell, 2001).

## Inclusion of Bi/Multilingual and Neuro-atypical Development

With the U.S. Census Bureau (2010) reporting that more than 55 million U.S. residents over age 5 speak a language other than English at home (specifically, 21% of 5–17-year-olds), a focus on L2 development is imperative. Kindergarten-12th-grade students who are formally tested and determined to have insufficient proficiency in English to access the school curriculum without language support services are designated English-language learners (ELL students, also referred to as dual-language learners, limited English-proficient students, and most recently, emergent bilinguals; García, 2009). ELL students comprise an estimated 4.4 million students (9.1% of the U.S. student population) and approximately 80% are Spanish-speaking (National Center for Education Statistics (NCES), 2014); ELL students are the fastest-growing segment of the student population (Flores, Batalova, & Fix, 2012). These numbers do not include children whose parents increasingly foster SLA through enrollment in language immersion programs (Bailey & Osipova, 2015).

The chapter would also not be complete without accounts of neuro-atypical language development. Specifically, we elaborate on language development in children with hearing impairments, intellectual disabilities, specific language impairment, ASD, and LD. NCES (2013) reports the following prevalence of these disorders in children aged 3–21: hearing impairments 0.2%, intellectual disabilities 0.9%, speech or language impairment 2.8%, ASD 0.8%. We focus on children with LD throughout, not only due to a higher prevalence (4.8% of all students, 37% of those receiving special education services: NCES, 2013), but also to the unique nature of the disorder that manifests itself in multiple language domains.

## Key Theories of L1, L2, and Neuro-atypical Development

Theories of L1 development in neuro-typically developing children have coalesced around either innate mechanisms that organize information specific to language or general learning principles that serve in a variety of learning situations supported through interactions with the environment. Specifically, nativist theories of language development, also referred to as generative or linguistic theories, propose that there is a specialized innate language acquisition device used to organize speech input in particular ways. Language is argued to use specialized mechanisms or mental processes that constrain the acquisitional task (Chomsky, 1965). Such domain-specific processes operating on a set of linguistic-invariant parts (principles) and a finite set of options (parameters) are known as *universal grammar* (UG). Using verbal input, children select the parameter options of UG to generate the grammar of their specific L1 (e.g., marking grammatical gender if required in their language). The appeal of a theory combining a language acquisition device and UG is its ability to explain how children can sort through large amounts of generally rapid and fragmented speech to acquire a full-fledged language so quickly.

In contrast to nativist positions, psychological or constructivist theories (e.g., Piaget, 1952) propose domain-general cognitive processes. Such general learning mechanisms applied to language include symbolic thinking, cause–effect understanding, analogy, and pattern analysis abilities, and development involves children's increasing memory capacity and construction of new knowledge. Vygotsky's (1978) account of learning as inherently social explains how these general learning mechanisms might be effectively supported in the task of learning language. Specifically, a social constructivist or interactionist account posits that learning is embedded in an individual's social encounters (e.g., talk at meal times, collaborating with classmates). Learning is first external (social, interpersonal, and regulated by expert others) and becomes internalized (intrapersonal and self-regulated). Consequently, language can be viewed as a rule-governed cultural activity mediated by interaction with parents, caregivers, siblings, teachers, and more accomplished peers. Language development is aided by the modeling, scaffolding (i.e., graduated assistance), and routines offered by others shaping a child's environment (Bruner, 1985). This assistance is thought to operate most effectively if presented within a child's *zone of proximal development*— the distance between what children achieve independently and what they achieve with assistance from a more expert interactant (Vygotsky, 1978).

Sociocultural perspectives, also with origins in Vygotsky's work, offer contextualized theories of language development that include the historical and cultural contexts in which children develop (John-Steiner & Mahn, 1996). These perspectives take account of societal factors such as discontinuities in the communicative practices of schools and children's families. Specifically, inequalities in the status of languages and cultures in contact are thought to impact children's motivation and their identities as learners (Gee, 1991). Most recently, language as a *complex adaptive system* has been posited to unify the roles of experience, social interaction, and cognitive mechanisms. Under this view, structures of language emerge from these interrelated facets to explain both L1 and L2 acquisition (e.g., Ellis & Larsen-Freeman, 2009).

Among theories specific to SLA, a *common underlying language proficiency* is argued to account for interdependence between a child's languages and explain the transfer of knowledge between them (Cummins, 2000; Genesee, Lindholm-Leary, Saunders, & Christian, 2006). Sociocultural perspectives view SLA as a process of developing multicompetencies distributed across languages and consequently reframe more traditional views that position children as needing to overcome linguistic deficits to reach the goal of native-like proficiency in their L2 (Cook, 2008). In contrast, nativist theories typically explain acquisition of L2 as the resetting of UG parameters set initially to the L1 grammar (see Montrul & Yoon, 2009, for review).

Theories of atypical language development are often extensions of L1 theories and variably account for atypical development in terms of deviance, delay, or difference. Although behaviorist accounts that posit stimulus–response mechanisms have generally been discounted as failing to adequately explain development, they remain influential in language intervention (Spreckley & Boyd, 2009). Nativist theories have proposed that children may not recognize the obligatory setting of UG parameters. For example, children with specific language impairments are hypothesized to extend an optional infinitive phase in their grammars during which tense and subject–verb agreement (e.g., *she walk*[+*ed*, +*s*]) are not specified (Rice, 2013).

### Theories of Oral Language–Literacy Connections

While this chapter has oral language as the main focus, there are important ties to later literacy development that warrant a closer examination of theoretical approaches that take both into account. The *emergent literacy* view places the two modes of communication on a developmental continuum with antecedents to reading and writing behaviors occurring in oral language practices from birth (e.g., storytelling and storybook-reading routines with caregivers) (e.g., Teale & Sulzby, 1986). Children's metalinguistic awareness, by which they reflect on the forms and meanings of language, increases with such encounters so they come to understand that meaning can be made with both sound and print. Under the *comprehensive language approach to early literacy,* children's early literacy development is connected not only to phonological awareness—the oral language ability most commonly tied to early literacy and a target of direct instruction (e.g., rhyme as a prelude to phoneme–grapheme correspondences in decoding), but to additional components of oral language such as vocabulary knowledge (Dickinson, McCabe, Anastasopoulos, Peisner-Feinberg, & Poe, 2003).

*Decontextualized* language abilities acquired in extended oral discourse such as narration are also frequently tied to reading comprehension (Snow, 1991). The decontextualized nature of narrative resembles that of print language in that both require cohesive text without the contextual support of an immediate physical or social environment. Furthermore,

Snow, Burns, and Griffin (1998) suggest that narrative discourse shares basic cognitive processes with reading comprehension (lexical, syntactic, and inferential). Consequently, Bailey and Moughamain (2007) have conceptualized the oral language–literacy connection at the discourse level to be one of *rehearsal* of shared linguistic and cognitive skills, with the potential to hone these skills orally years in advance of formal literacy instruction. Oral language–literacy connections also apply to SLA and cross-linguistic situations (see August & Shanahan, 2006, for review)

## Phonological Development

### Phonological Development in Neuro-typical, Monolingual Contexts

Children's processing of speech sounds, or phonological processing, requires the combination of phonemes, the smallest units of sound, to form syllables, which together comprise words. By their first birthdays, children are typically turning their non-linguistic *vocalizations* (e.g., cries) into linguistic *verbalizations*, delighting their listeners with phonetically consistent forms used to label objects and actions in their environments (e.g., /baba/ always used for "bottle"). Some consonant sounds (e.g., bilabial /m/) are mastered by age 2, whereas other consonants (e.g., fricative /θ/, the onset sound in *think*) are still being acquired as late as age 6–7 (Dodd, Holm, Hua, & Crosbie, 2003). During preschool and the early elementary grades, children gain control of multisyllabic word productions, and acquire morpho-phonological rules (e.g., plural suffixes /s/, /z/, and /əz/ depend on prior voicing and sibilant sounds in the word, as in *cats, dogs,* and *horses*).

Children's phonological awareness also increases rapidly during these years (Lonigan, 2007) and is demonstrated by the ability to segment words into smaller sound units, as well as identify sound similarities across two or more words (i.e., onset phonemes and rimes, the ending phonemes). The predictive and reciprocal relationships between phonological awareness and later literacy are well documented (e.g., Dickinson et al., 2003; Lonigan, 2007). Furthermore, children's increasing cognitive capacities and literacy instruction itself can facilitate phonological awareness (Cunningham & Carroll, 2011). Finally, exposure to peers who may speak a different dialect from that of the home is especially influential to speech throughout adolescence (Gee, Allen, & Clinton, 2001).

### Phonological Development in Neuro-typical, Bi/Multilingual Contexts

For young children exposed to two or more languages, phonological development may involve the acquisition of a single undifferentiated system, or two separate phonological systems. A review by Hambly, Wren, Mcleod, and Roulstone (2013) suggests stronger evidence for two phonological systems that interact and/or transfer features from one language to the other. For example, interaction may lead Japanese–English bilingual children to produce sounds that differ from those of monolinguals of both languages (Harada, 2006), and transfer can be either negative (e.g., producing the French nasalized form /dɑ̃s/ for *dance* in both French and English) or positive (e.g., vowel sounds are perceived and produced identically in L1 and L2). If children are acquiring the L2 beyond the sensitive period, the likelihood of their speech production sounding native-like may diminish (Au et al., 2008).

As with L1 phonological development, phonological awareness plays a key role in L2 reading. Different languages may attune children to different features of the phonological system. For example, Spanish L1 children may initially be sensitive to the syllabic structure of the language and only later on, and possibly with the influence of reading, do they come to segment at the phonemic level needed for reading English. Nevertheless, their overall Spanish phonological awareness predicts reading abilities in both Spanish and English (see Denton, Hasbrouck, Weaver, & Riccio, 2000, for review). Even in instances where languages do not share an orthographic system, Gottardo, Chiappe, Yan, Siegel, and Gu (2006) report significant correlations between Chinese phonological processing (i.e., rhyme detection) of Chinese-speaking ELL students and their English phonological processing. The findings support Durgunoğlu's (2002) claim that phonological awareness is language-general metalinguistic knowledge that need only be acquired once to apply to different languages/orthographic systems.

### Phonological Development in Neuro-atypical Contexts: Hearing Impairment and Learning Disability

Hearing impairment includes a wide range of hearing loss from slight (15–25 dB) to profound (70+ dB) (Hunt & Marshall, 2005) and makes processing of spoken language a challenge. Children may have either congenital hearing loss present at birth or acquired hearing loss. For the latter, the age at which hearing loss is acquired is important because it determines the degree to which the phonological system has developed. Children with hearing loss typically demonstrate noticeable delays in their phonological development even if they receive hearing aids as early as 5 months of age (Houston et al., 2012). Certain tasks connected to training of phonological awareness (e.g., rhyme detection, pseudoword repetition, word discrimination) are particularly challenging for children with hearing loss and negatively impact growth of children's receptive vocabulary (James, Rajput, Brinton, & Goswami, 2009) as well as grammar comprehension and production (Caselli, Rinaldi, Varuzza, Giuliani, & Burdo, 2012). According to Ormel, Hermans, Knoors, Hendriks, and Verhoeven (2010), in contrast to hearing children and those with partial hearing loss, for whom phonology is critical for reading development, the majority of deaf children apply a more holistic approach to word recognition. Many of these children consider sign language their L1 and written language their L2. American Sign Language (ASL) is in fact acquired in a comparable sequence to the oral language of hearing children, but the onset of ASL is typically 4 months sooner (around 8 months) (Anderson & Reilly, 2002).

Children with reading disability (who comprise up to 80% of students with LD; Shaywitz, Morris, & Shaywitz, 2008) struggle with phonological tasks from early childhood through adolescence. Kindergarten students at risk acquire phonological skills more slowly than their neuro-typical peers (Smith, Scott, Roberts, & Locke, 2008), and these unresolved phonological difficulties affect spelling and reading skills into adolescence.

## Lexical and Semantic Development

### Lexical and Semantic Development in Neuro-typical, Monolingual Contexts

Although some children begin to reliably *recognize* words from a speech stream at 8 months (e.g., Johnson & Jusczyk, 2001), their first word *productions* typically occur between 10 and 14 months (Fenson et al., 1994). When children have approximately 50 words in their lexicons (repertoire of all words), lexical growth accelerates (Goldfield & Reznick, 1990). Whether all children experience a *word spurt* is questionable but the average rate of acquisition after this milestone is reached is between 10 and 20 new words per week (Ganger & Brent, 2004). By the time children reach first grade, estimates of their vocabularies range from 6,000 words (Chall, 1987) to 14,000 words (Carey, 1978). Hart and Risley (1995) attributed this variability largely to the amount and quality of language input a child receives, with children exposed to larger amounts of input developing larger, more diverse vocabularies than children with limited language exposure.

Through a process of *fast mapping*, children come to understand the meanings of words by connecting items in their conceptual domain to new words, typically, after a single exposure (Carey, 1978). To explain how they do so, Markman (1991) argues that children use a number of assumptions to constrain the number of possible word meanings, including that a new word: (a) likely refers to the whole object, rather than its parts (*whole-object assumption*); (b) includes other objects of the same or similar category (*taxonomic assumption*); and (c) maps to novel objects rather than being an additional label for familiar objects (*principle of mutual exclusivity*). Receptive fast-mapping skills tend to outpace expressive fast mapping (e.g., Kan & Kohnert, 2008). The order in which children learn words also reflects the relative complexity of the concepts to which the words refer (cf., McDonough et al., 2011). Children use semantic, syntactic, and pragmatic information to extract word meaning (Clark, 2004), and feedback from more experienced others helps refine their word mappings; for example, they benefit from lexically rich conversations with caregivers (Weizman & Snow, 2001).

Children's semantic networks become more complex as their vocabularies grow and become organized by similarities and differences in semantic relationships (Aitchison, 2012; cf. Beckage, Smith, & Hills, 2011). The vocabulary children are later exposed to in classroom discourse and texts enriches their semantic networks and places higher demands on them as vocabulary in an academic register may contain many abstract/technical concepts (e.g., Bailey, 2012), and is lexically diverse and comprised of many derived forms (e.g., Schleppegrell, 2001). Furthermore, research has established a strong reciprocal relationship between oral vocabulary and reading (Snow et al., 1998). Reading can become the main source of new vocabulary knowledge (Nagy & Anderson, 1984), and words that appear more frequently in text are more likely to be learned and less likely to be forgotten (Brown, Waring, & Donkaewbua, 2008).

### Lexical and Semantic Development in Neuro-typical, Bi/Multilingual Contexts

Most research findings in L2 lexical development are interpreted as evidence for children's initial awareness of two separate lexicons for their languages. As much as 30% of bilingual children's early words are translation equivalents across their two languages (e.g., *cat* in English and *el gato* in Spanish), which may be sufficient overlap to suggest children are aware of acquiring the vocabulary of two different language systems (Pearson, Fernández, & Oller, 1995). If children were organizing their lexicon as one system, the overlap would contravene the *principle of mutual exclusivity* and leave unexplained why they entertain more than one word per semantic concept. In fact, bilingual children may be more flexible and precocious word learners than monolingual children because they understand that this principle can in fact be contravened not just for acquiring two lexicons but in the acquisition of synonyms or words that share similar meaning within a language, such as adjectives (e.g., *big, large*) (Yoshida, 2008).

Bilingual children, however, do not acquire two words to encode each underlying concept. Consequently, they may not have the same number of words as their monolingual peers, although with two languages combined, they may have larger vocabularies. Bilingual children's vocabulary development reflects the dominance of the different contexts they experience; they have difficulty providing speech samples for analysis in a less supported language (20% or less of reported activities), suggesting a minimum input threshold by which lexical acquisition reliably occurs (see Oller, Pearson, & Cobo-Lewis, 2007, for review).

An important feature of SLA is transfer of word knowledge to L2 for concepts already lexicalized in L1. As with L1 acquisition, although highly correlated, receptive vocabulary develops in advance of expressive vocabulary (Kan & Kohnert, 2008). ELL students begin school knowing fewer English words than their monolingual peers (Mancilla-Martinez & Lesaux, 2011), although they may acquire new vocabulary more quickly than English monolinguals (Silverman, 2007). Often everyday terms in Spanish (e.g., *fácil/easy*) are cognates sharing a Latinate root with English low-frequency words (*facile and facilitate*) that are more typically used in formal or academic registers. As reported for L1, vocabulary knowledge also plays an important role in literacy development. However, unlike monolingual students, students whose L1 shares a common orthography with

English draw on their vocabulary knowledge of both languages as an oral language base for literacy development in English (August & Shanahan, 2006).

### *Lexical and Semantic Development in Neuro-atypical Contexts: Intellectual Disabilities and Learning Disabilities*

Children with intellectual disabilities demonstrate significantly delayed lexical development due to impacted speed of lexical access and working-memory weaknesses (Danielsson, Henry, Rönnberg, & Nilsson, 2010). Semantic development in this population occurs similarly to neuro-typical children, only much later, typically in adolescence (Roberts, Price, & Malkin, 2007). Receptive vocabulary is comparable to or slightly lower than neuro-typical development and less delayed than expressive vocabulary (Roberts et al., 2007).

Children with LD also have a more limited vocabulary than their peers (Koutsoftas & Gray, 2012). According to Scarborough (1990), while vocabularies of children with dyslexia at 30 months of age were comparable to peers, their vocabularies were comparatively less developed at 36 months. Throughout the school years, lexical and semantic development of students with LD is further affected by reading difficulties, resulting in slower than neuro-typical vocabulary growth (e.g., Ebbers & Denton, 2008).

### Morphological and Syntactic Development

### *Morphological and Syntactic Development in Neuro-typical, Monolingual Contexts*

After first combining two words or morphemes (i.e., the smallest unit of meaning), around the second birthday, children begin to produce longer and more complex syntactic constructions. A number of characteristics contribute to the increasing syntactic complexity of children's language (see Scott, 2004, for review). By the start of formal schooling, children have acquired most obligatory forms of inflectional morphology (i.e., grammatical markers for tense, person, number, gender) and syntactic rules (e.g., for formulating declarative statements, questions, and imperatives) (Diessel, 2004). However, children's mastery of certain syntactic structures (e.g., passive constructions) and metasyntactic knowledge of forms continue to develop throughout adolescence (Nippold, 2007).

Children's sentence comprehension mostly outpaces their sentence production. For example, Hirsh-Pasek and Golinkoff (1991) found young children know that word order conveys meaning before they even produce two-word utterances. However, comprehension of some grammatical forms particularly in complex sentences (e.g., rare word order) challenges children even into adolescence (Dick et al., 2004). Although children as young as age 3 can make metalinguistic judgments and productions involving language structures (Chaney, 1992), exposure to print and literacy education once children enter formal schooling provides more explicit information about sentence structure. Furthermore, switching from everyday, informal language to the academic

registers found in classrooms often requires a shift in sentence complexity (Christie, 2012). Children transition from conjoining simple sentences with repetitive "and," for example, to embedding clauses that create complex syntactic structures capturing advanced semantic relationships (e.g., "*I brush my teeth <u>because</u> my dentist told me to. I got cavities a lot <u>even though</u> I don't eat that much candy,*" Bailey & Heritage, 2014).

### *Morphological and Syntactic Development in Neuro-typical, Bi/Multilingual Contexts*

In young children acquiring two first languages simultaneously, the consensus is that the two grammars are differentiated from the earliest stages of one-word production (Genesee, 2001). Genesee argued that the two grammars develop largely autonomously with rates similar to those of monolinguals. Others have found slower rates, attributing delays to less exposure to each of the two languages (Gathercole, 2007). Two grammatical systems may also initially exert undue influences in terms of transfer of syntactic rules from one language to the other. For example, the adjective position may differ across the two languages (e.g., *las mesas verdes* in Spanish may result in \**the tables green* in English). Rather than being interpreted as evidence of a different course of syntactic development, such transfer is argued to be the result of superficial performance errors (Hoff, 2009). Gathercole (2007) argues that such transfer is most likely to occur in highly balanced bilingual children due to the greater degree of overlapping contexts for L1 and L2 usage.

The stages of grammatical development in SLA mirror those reported for L1, with the notable exception of using L1 as a SLA strategy (see *codeswitching* below). Children may also exhibit a silent period in which they actively gather data on their new languages, building receptive language skills before willingly expressing themselves in L2. Children subsequently transition to productive uses of their L2, first using simple sentences and then more complex forms until they are flexibly using a full repertoire of syntactic structures largely accurately (e.g., Tabors, 2008). Factors such as age of arrival in the L2 majority society, verbal aptitude, or a general underlying language proficiency, and motivation may all play a role in the SLA process and ultimate variability in attainment of L2 proficiency (see Dixon et al., 2012, for review). The interplay of amount of exposure and context of acquisition is particularly complex with degree of English grammatical proficiency less a function of amount of English exposure or use in the home context, and more a function of the instructional quality of English (Gutiérrez-Clellen & Kreiter, 2003).

### *Morphological and Syntactic Development in Neuro-atypical Contexts: Specific Language Impairment and Learning Disability*

Specific language impairment is a developmental language disorder characterized by "receptive and expressive language deficits, including . . . omission of morphological markers . . . shorter length of utterance [co-occurring] with age-appropriate non-verbal abilities" (Epstein & Phillips, 2009, p. 286). Contributing factors include deficits in sensory processing, the linguistic system, and impacted working memory (see Leonard, 2014, for review). Morphosyntactic challenges in children with specific language impairment can be traced to early childhood; 30–60% are considered late talkers by age 2 and continue to demonstrate lags in their language development at age 4 (LaParo, Justice, Skibbe, & Pianta, 2004). Smith-Lock, Leitao, Lambert, and Nickels (2003) demonstrated that morphological tasks prove difficult for preschool children, while school-aged children struggle with syntax. These difficulties persist into adolescence and adulthood, impacting decoding, comprehension, and production of both narrative and expository texts (Marinis, 2011). Research also points to frequent comorbidity of specific language impairment with LD (van der Lely & Marshall, 2010).

## Discourse and Pragmatic Development

### Discourse and Pragmatic Development in Neuro-typical, Monolingual Contexts

Language used in social interaction typically involves *discourse,* or the organization of language beyond the level of the sentence. Traditionally, the study of discourse has considered separately *conversation* and other genres of *extended discourse* (e.g., narration, argumentation). According to Grice (1957), conversation is governed by two basic principles: turn taking and cooperation. Most children take turns with an action or verbal reply by 12 months (Garvey & Berninger, 1981). Children competently produce contingent replies to questions, declarative statements, and commands by age 3 (e.g., Bloom, Rocissano, & Hood, 1976). However, children have been found to respond *less* readily to maternal questions and *increase* their non-contingent responses at age 5, asserting their autonomy as they become more competent conversationalists by ignoring their mothers' conversational supports and instead initiating their own topics (Kelly & Bailey, 2013a). Moreover, Kelly and Bailey (2013b) have demonstrated interdependence between the different discourse genres with development of narrative abilities (minimally two temporally or causally sequenced clauses about past events; Labov, 1972) occurring within the context of conversations with caretakers; children progress from dependence on assistance toward competent independent narration (Kelly & Bailey, 2013a).

McCabe and Peterson (1991) found narrative macrostructure becomes more complex with age; initially narratives contain multiple event clauses but are told out of temporal sequence. During the preschool years, children gradually map the sequence of events in their stories on to the order in which the events must have actually occurred, but the narrative is often cut short at an evaluative climax, or the high point. By age 6, neuro-typical children from mainstream English-speaking homes can produce well-sequenced narratives that build to a climax and bring the action to a resolution. During the school years, children's narratives become longer and contain more

details about the specifics of the events, and a large degree of individual variation in abilities exists amongst adults.

Communicative competence (Hymes, 1967) is the ability to employ language appropriately in social situations. Doing so successfully requires *pragmatic knowledge*, or the understanding of the communicative functions and governing conventions of language. The development of a number of *speech acts* to convey intents (e.g., requesting, commenting) starts as early as the first year of life (Snow, Pan, Imbens-Bailey, & Herman, 1996); however, control of more advanced linguistic devices during extended discourse continues to develop well into middle childhood, including use of non-literal language (Bernicot, Laval, & Chaminaud, 2007), cohesive ties between referents, and a widening repertoire of causal and temporal discourse markers (Bailey & Heritage, 2014). Metapragmatic knowledge, the ability to reflect on links between linguistic devices and communicative contexts, is also acquired later in childhood, and the rate at which children acquire metapragmatic knowledge about speech acts progresses differentially contributing to individual variation (Bernicot et al., 2007).

### Discourse and Pragmatic Development in Neuro-typical, Bi/Multilingual Contexts

As in L1, most studies of the discourse development of bilingual children have focused on development of narrative abilities, particularly with Spanish–English bilinguals. Narrative development need not be the same across a child's two languages, particularly if the discourse characteristics of the two speech/cultural communities are different. For example, Fiestas and Peña (2004) found that 4–6-year-old fluent bilingual children's Spanish-language stories contained greater adverbial clauses than their English-language stories. Given narrative discourse requires control over domains of language at the word, sentence, and discourse levels, it is unlikely for bilingual children to be equally skilled in narration across their languages if they show dominance in one language. This is particularly true in SLA situations where children may not have an opportunity to develop discourse-level abilities in their L1 before beginning the acquisition of L2, or where L2 becomes the dominant language through exposure to schooling. Bailey, Moughamian, and Dingle (2008), for example, found that elementary students who had been Spanish-dominant at kindergarten entry produced grammatically complex Spanish-language narratives but these were not as structurally sophisticated as their English-language narratives. As with other language domains, there is evidence of cross-linguistic transfer of skills with Spanish-story structure abilities in kindergarten, predicting children's first-grade English narrative quality (Uccelli & Páez, 2007). Moreover, as in L1 contexts, oral narrative abilities predict reading abilities. L1 story generation abilities of young ELL students not only predicted their reading scores in L1 but also their reading scores in English, their L2 (Miller et al., 2006).

Pragmatic development in bilingual children may be particularly precocious compared with that of their monolingual peers (Yoshida, 2008). The pragmatic abilities of bilingual students are perhaps most evident in their intentional linguistic practices. With at least two languages at their command, bilingual students can do "more" with language than their monolingual peers. *Translanguaging* is the pragmatic ability in which multiple languages "are negotiated for communication" and the speaker demonstrates multilingual situational competence (Canagarajah, 2011, p. 1). Included in this repertoire is *codeswitching*, in which children might borrow a single word from their other language, or switch between languages during or between utterances. Initially considered evidence of confusion between two languages, codeswitching is now largely viewed as rule-governed (e.g., MacSwan, 2000) and as having important social/interactional functions (e.g., Reyes, 2004). According to Vu, Bailey, and Howes (2010), even children as young as 5 have sociopragmatic uses for switching languages in order to follow their interlocutors' switching behaviors, and not simply because they have lexical gaps in one of their two languages. As children mature they become attuned to situational changes that require a switch in language, such as different interlocutors, settings, and topics.

Much as their monolingual peers, children learning an L2 encounter new registers to add to their pragmatic repertoires at school entry. For ELL students, the necessity for academic English language before fully participating in content learning has been debated. For example, the notion of decontextualized language has been questioned and it is argued that ELL students can access new academic content learning through contextualized language uses (see Bailey, 2012, for review). However, Duschl, Schweingruber, and Shouse (2007) note that at the word level, for instance, scientific argumentation often features "abstract nouns . . . derived from verbs" and "technical terms that have different meaning than in everyday use" (p.189). These and other complex or unfamiliar language features may place language demands on ELL students as they engage with academic content (Christie, 2012).

### *Discourse and Pragmatic Development in Neuro-atypical Contexts: Autism Spectrum Disorder and Learning Disability*

Individuals with ASD experience challenges in social interaction (American Psychiatric Association, 2013). Whereas 60–65% of individuals with ASD develop language to communicate, their trajectory of language development is uneven and is characterized by difficulties in initiating and maintaining conversations (Paul, Orlovski, Marcinko, & Volkmar, 2009). Pragmatic skills, such as joint attention abilities (Charman, Drew, Baird, & Baird, 2003) and early comprehension skills, such as responding to name and reacting to questions (Dawson, Meltzoff, Osterling, Rinaldi, & Brown, 1998), are impaired. Difficulty with deictic terms (words that index the position of the speaker, such as *here, that*) and personal pronouns continues into later childhood (Arnold, Bennetto, & Diehl, 2009). An underdeveloped theory of mind is a potential root of difficulties with turn taking, less frequent and narrow-ranging speech acts, trouble with

taking perspective, and providing relevant responses (Paul et al., 2009).

Children with LD also experience difficulties with discourse (Paul, 2001), including limited sensitivity to text organization and structure and difficulty producing factual statements even when topics are well known to them (Walker, Shippen, Alberto, Houchins, & Cihak, 2005). The demands presented by academic discourse result in limited spoken production: children with LD have been found to produce 40–60% of the language produced by their neuro-typical peers in classroom settings (Walker et al., 2005). Lapadat (1991) reported that students with LD also exhibit "consistent and pervasive deficits in conversation" (p. 147), resulting from language deficits rather than inadequate knowledge or understanding of social norms.

### Implications for Educators

Language development requires ongoing attention from educators, whether in the areas of L1 and L2, or in the context of disabilities. To date, educators working in general education in particular are neither provided deep knowledge of how language develops nor trained in oral language instruction and assessment (Understanding Language (UL) Initiative, 2012). Contexts that will need the support of teachers are children's uses of language to access academic content tasks and display the content learning that new college and career-ready standards require (CCSSO, 2010). However, language development is not only for the purpose of content learning; teachers must also foster the language children will inevitably need for self-expression and for effective interpersonal communication. In this context, a dialogue between educators and families is necessary to share research-based practices leading to successful language learning.

Research findings emphasize a balanced exposure to each language and quality of bilingual interactions as critical for success (Grosjean, 2009). Educators and families need to know that learning two first languages can be advantageous for children, including children with disabilities, despite the common misconceptions that they should be exposed to only one language. The loss of L1 in this population disrupts linguistic and socioemotional development (Espinosa, 2008), while dual-language exposure promotes overall language development and is a preferable culturally and linguistically responsive practice (Fredman, 2006).

Our review of neuro-typical, monolingual development suggests educators might best foster school-age children's oral language by focusing on the functions or purposes to which language is put (Schleppegrell, 2001), and by teaching discourse-level skills such as dialogue (conversation) and monologue (i.e., narration) that have embedded within them phonological, lexical, semantic, morphological, and syntactic demands, rather than teaching these domains of language as discrete, decontextualized skills (Christie, 2012). In particular, expanding and monitoring growth (see Appendix 15.1) in students' repertoires beyond the narrative genre to include expository language uses such as argumentation, and scaffolding collaborations between peers will be increasingly critical for academic success (CCSSO, 2010).

Due to immigration throughout the school years, students may be acquiring L2 at any grade level, with implications for both language and educational outcomes. Understanding SLA is important because multilingualism in the U.S. schooling context is often seen as deleterious to social and academic achievements. ELL students are vulnerable to underachievement, dropout, and restricted pathways to high-quality instruction (Gándara, 2005). The educational field has yet to coalesce around a specific set of instructional practices for SLA, in part because of the great variety in background experiences that L2 learners bring to the acquisitional task, and in part because the efficacy of language instructional programs and interventions has not been well established (Saunders, Goldenberg, & Marcelletti, 2013). Approaches to how language is best taught—through its use during meaningful real-world activities or during targeted instruction of language forms and functions—are still being debated, although general guidelines are available (e.g., UL Initiative, 2012), and facilitating the oral and written language of ELL students, especially academic registers, is the responsibility of all teachers (Shatz & Wilkinson, 2013).

With regard to neuro-atypical development, it is important for teachers who work in inclusive classrooms to trace their students' reading and writing difficulties to the oral language domains that are at the core of many literacy difficulties and to develop targeted interventions. Multicomponent interventions targeting deficits in oral language by providing students with explicit and direct instruction in phonological awareness and multisyllabic word decoding, especially within small-group contexts, have led to significant results (Vaughn et al., 2012).

## Closing Remarks

Normative studies of oral language development in school-age children and adolescents have largely been neglected, along with studies of effective instructional and assessment materials. Yet research on the progression of oral language relevant for acquiring new academic content knowledge has never been timelier for U.S. educators (Bailey & Heritage, 2014), particularly so for understanding language trajectories of academically vulnerable students with low socioeconomic status and ELL backgrounds (Hoff, 2013). Furthermore, recognition of the interdependence of oral language and literacy calls for a new generation of research studies of these modalities to better understand mutual influences.

Our review of L2 development reveals a growing trend for research recognizing linguistic and cognitive resources such as multicompetencies and translanguaging practices, and the need to study how best to capitalize on these developmental strengths while teaching. In the case of cultivating transfer between languages, students may need assistance to become aware of similarities in languages (Genesee et al., 2006). Research is required to determine what programming (e.g., L2 immersion or dual-language) and what approaches (e.g., form-focused instruction or authentic language use, or some combination) under what circumstances (e.g., L1 literacy) best support effective language learning. Finally, it is important to continue to extend research on language development in students with disabilities beyond early childhood; the few studies conducted with older children suggest their language takes different trajectories from those of their neuro-typical peers as they progress through adolescence.

**Appendix 15.1   Description of assessment approaches and supplemental measures of language development**

| | Neuro-typical, Monolingual Development | Neuro-typical, Bi/multilingual Development* | Neuro-atypical Development |
|---|---|---|---|
| Phonological domain | Commercial assessments of the ability to manipulate individual phonemes (e.g., delete, segment, elide) and phoneme combinations; identify sound onsets and rimes | Spanish adaptations of commercial assessments (normed on Spanish monolingual speakers)<br><br>Supplemental measures: phonological MLU | Commercial clinical assessments of phonological processing, also hearing and sound production/acquisition. Supplemental measures: rhyme judgment, pseudoword repetition/ discrimination, and sentence recall tasks |
| Lexical and semantic domains | Commercial assessments of receptive and expressive vocabulary (e.g., pointing to/ naming of picture plates) | Spanish adaptations of commercial assessments normed on Spanish-speaking populations or bilingual Spanish/English-speaking populations | Commercial clinical assessments of word meaning and usage |
| Morphological and syntactic domains | Measures of the repertoire of sentence structures and grammatical morphology Supplemental measures: mean length of utterance (MLU), MLU of five longest utterances; Brown's (1973) 14 first morphemes | Commercial assessments of English syntax and a partner language | Commercial clinical assessments of morphosyntactic acquisition.<br><br>Supplemental measures: language samples elicited with picture and narrative prompts to create obligatory contexts for inflectional morphology |
| Discourse and pragmatic domains | Inventories of children's communicative intents<br><br>Supplemental measures: Conversation (including during collaboration between peers), narration, and expository language uses such as argumentation elicited using naturalistic techniques or using questions and observations in authentic settings (i.e., formative assessment; see Chapter 29, this volume). | Formative assessment of translanguaging skills<br><br>See also supplemental measures: neuro-typical, monolingual development | Commercial clinical rating scales and profiles frequently based on observation. Diagnostic interview schedules<br><br>See also supplemental measures: neuro-typical, monolingual development |

* Commercial norm-referenced English-language proficiency assessments and state standards-based summative English language proficiency assessments are designed to measure English development of English-language learner students in both oral language and literacy and cover much of the content of the different language domains.

# Note

1.  We thank Eric Anderman, Terry Au, and Louise Wilkinson for their insightful and careful reviews of a previous draft of this Chapter.

# References

Abrams, D. A., Lynch, C. J., Cheng, K. M., Phillips, J., Supekar, K., Ryali, S., . . . & Meno, V. (2013). Underconnectivity between voice-selective cortex and reward circuitry in children with autism. *Proceedings of the National Academy of Sciences, 110*(29), 12060–12065.

Aitchison, J. (2012). *Words in the mind: An introduction to the mental lexicon* (4th ed.). Oxford, England: Wiley-Blackwell.

American Psychiatric Association. (2013). *Diagnostic and statistical manual of mental disorders* (5th ed.). Washington, DC: American Psychiatric Association.

Anderson, D., & Reilly, J. (2002). The MacArthur communicative development inventory: Normative data for American Sign Language. *Journal of Deaf Studies and Deaf Education, 7*(2), 83–106.

Arnold, J. E., Bennetto, L., & Diehl, J. J. (2009). Reference production in young speakers with and without autism: Effects of discourse status and processing constraints. *Cognition, 110*(2), 131–146.

Au, T. K. F., Oh, J. S., Knightly, L. M., Jun, S. A., & Romo, L. F. (2008). Salvaging a childhood language. *Journal of Memory and Language, 58*(4), 998–1011.

August, D., & Shanahan, T. (Eds.) (2006). *Developing literacy in second-language learners*. Mahwah, NJ: Erlbaum.

Bailey, A. L. (2012). Academic English. In J. Banks (Ed.), *Encyclopedia of diversity in education* (pp. 3–9). Thousand Oaks, CA: Sage.

Bailey, A. L. & Heritage, M. (2014). The role of language learning progressions in improved instruction and assessment of English language learners. *TESOL Quarterly, 48*(3), 480–506.

Bailey, A. L., & Moughamian, A. C. (2007). Telling stories their way: Narrative scaffolding with emergent readers and readers. *Narrative Inquiry, 17*(2), 203–229.

Bailey, A. L., Moughamian, A. C., & Dingle, M. (2008). The contribution of Spanish language narration to the assessment of early academic performance of Latino students. In A. McCabe, A. L. Bailey, & G. Melzi (Eds.), *Spanish-language narration and literacy: Culture, cognition, and emotion* (pp. 296–331). New York, NY: Cambridge University Press.

Bailey, A. L. & Osipova, A. (2015). *Multilingual development and education: Home and school contexts for creating and sustaining the linguistic resources of children*. Cambridge, UK: Cambridge University Press.

Beckage, N., Smith, L., & Hills, T. (2011). Small worlds and semantic network growth in typical and late talkers. *PloS One, 6*(5), e19348.

Bernicot, J., Laval, V., & Chaminaud, S. (2007). Nonliteral language forms in children: In what order are they acquired in pragmatics and metapragmatics? *Journal of Pragmatics, 39*(12), 2115–2132.

Birdsong, D. (2005). Interpreting age effects in second language acquisition. In J. F. Kroll & A. M. B. de Groot (Eds.), *Handbook of bilingualism: Psycholinguistic approaches* (pp. 109–127). New York, NY: Oxford University Press.

Bishop, D. V. M. (1987). The causes of specific developmental language disorder ("developmental dysphasia"). *Journal of Child Psychology and Psychiatry, 28*(1), 1–8.

Bloom, L., Rocissano, L., & Hood, L. (1976). Adult–child discourse: Developmental interaction between information processing and linguistic knowledge. *Cognitive Psychology, 8*(4), 521–552.

Bowlby, J. (1969). *Attachment and loss: Vol. 1. Attachment*. New York, NY: Basic Books.

Brown, R. (1973). *A first language: The early stages*. Cambridge, MA: Harvard University Press.

Brown, R., Waring, R., & Donkaewbua, S. (2008). Incidental vocabulary acquisition from reading, reading-while-listening, and listening to stories. *Reading in a Foreign Language, 20*(2), 136–163.

Bruner, J. (1985). *Child's talk: Learning to use language*. Oxford, England: Oxford University Press.

Canagarajah, S. (2011). Translanguaging in the classroom: Emerging issues for research and pedagogy. *Applied Linguistics Review, 2*, 1–27.

Carey, S. (1978). The child as word learner. In M. Halle, J. Bresnan, & G. A. Miller (Eds.), *Linguistic theory and psychological reality* (pp. 359–373). Cambridge, MA: MIT Press.

Caselli, M., Rinaldi, P., Varuzza, C., Giuliani, A., & Burdo, S. (2012). Cochlear implant in the second year of life: Lexical and grammatical outcomes. *Journal of Speech, Language, and Hearing Research, 55*(2), 382–394.

Casey, B. J., Tottenham, N., Liston, C., & Durston, S. (2005). Imaging the developing brain: What have we learned about cognitive development? *Trends in Cognitive Sciences, 9*(3), 104–110.

Chall, J. S. (1987). Two vocabularies for reading: Recognition and meaning. In M. G. McKeown & M. E. Curtis (Eds.), *The nature of vocabulary acquisition* (pp. 7–17). Hillsdale, NJ: Erlbaum.

Chaney, C. (1992). Language development, metalinguistic skills, and print awareness in 3-year-old children. *Applied Psycholinguistics, 13*(04), 485–514.

Charman, T., Drew, A., Baird, C., & Baird, G. (2003). Measuring early language development in preschool children with autism spectrum disorder using the MacArthur Communicative Development Inventory (Infant Form). *Journal of Child Language, 30*(01), 213–236.

Chisholm, J. S. (2003). Uncertainty, contingency, and attachment: A life history theory of theory of mind. In K. Sterelny & J. Fitness (Eds.), *From mating to mentality: Evaluating evolutionary psychology* (pp. 125–153). Hove, England: Psychology Press.

Chomsky, N. (1965). *Aspects of the theory of syntax* (No. 11). Cambridge, MA: MIT Press.

Christie, F. (2012). *Language education throughout the school years: A functional perspective*. Malden, MA: Wiley-Blackwell.

Clark, E. (2004). How language acquisition builds on cognitive development. *Trends in Cognitive Sciences, 8*(10), 472–478.

Connor, C. M., Craig, H. K., Raudenbush, S. W., Heavner, K., & Zwolan, T. A. (2006). The age at which young deaf children receive cochlear implants and their vocabulary and speech-production growth: Is there an added value for early implantation? *Ear and Hearing, 27*(6), 628–644.

Cook, V. (2008). Multi-competence: Black hole or wormhole for second language acquisition research. In Z. Han (Ed.), *Understanding second language process, 25* (pp. 16–26). Clevedon, England: Multilingual Matters.

Cummins, J. (2000). *Language, power, and pedagogy: Bilingual children in the crossfire*. Clevedon, England: Multilingual Matters.

Cunningham, A., & Carroll, J. (2011). Reading-related skills in earlier- and later-schooled children. *Scientific Studies of Reading, 15*(3), 244–266.

Curtiss, S. (1977). *Genie: A psycholinguistic study of a modern-day "wild child."* New York, NY: Academic Press.

Danielsson, H., Henry, L., Rönnberg, J., & Nilsson, L. (2010). Executive functions in individuals with intellectual disability. *Research in Developmental Disabilities, 31*(6), 1299–1304.

Dawson, G., Meltzoff, A. N., Osterling, J., Rinaldi, J. & Brown, E. (1998). Children with autism fail to orient to naturally occurring social stimuli. *Journal of Autism and Developmental Disorders, 28*(6), 479–485.

Denton, C. A., Hasbrouck, J. E., Weaver, L. R., & Riccio, C. A. (2000). What do we know about phonological awareness in Spanish? *Reading Psychology, 21*(4), 335–352.

Dick, F., Wulfeck, B., Krupa-Kwiatkowski, M., & Bates, E. (2004). The development of complex sentence interpretation in typically developing children compared with children with specific language impairments or early unilateral focal lesions. *Developmental Science, 7*(3), 360–377.

Dickinson, D. K., McCabe, A., Anastasopoulos, L., Peisner-Feinberg, E. S., & Poe, M. D. (2003). The comprehensive language approach to early literacy: The interrelationships among vocabulary, phonological sensitivity, and print knowledge among preschool-aged children. *Journal of Educational Psychology, 95*(3), 465–481.

Diessel, H. (2004). *The acquisition of complex sentences*. New York, NY: Cambridge University Press.

Dixon, L. Q., Zhao, J., Shin, J. Y., Wu, S., Su, J. H., Burgess-Brigham, R., . . . & Snow, C. (2012). What we know about second language acquisition: A synthesis from four perspectives. *Review of Educational Research, 82*(1), 5–60.

Dodd, B., Holm, A., Hua, Z., & Crosbie, S. (2003). Phonological development: A normative study of British English-speaking children. *Clinical Linguistics & Phonetics, 17*(8), 617–643.

Durgunoğlu, A. Y. (2002). Cross-linguistic transfer in literacy development and implications for language learners. *Annals of Dyslexia, 52*(1), 189–204.

Duschl, R. A., Schweingruber, H. A., & Shouse, A. W. (Eds.). (2007). *Taking science to school: Learning and teaching science in grades K-8.* Washington, DC: National Academies Press.

Ebbers, S. M., & Denton, C. A. (2008). A root awakening: Vocabulary instruction for older students with reading difficulties. *Learning Disabilities Research & Practice, 23*(2), 90–102.

Ellis, N. C., & Larsen-Freeman, D. (2009). *Language as a complex adaptive system.* Malden, MA: Wiley-Blackwell.

Epstein, S., & Phillips, J. (2009). Storytelling skills of children with specific language impairment. *Child Language Teaching & Therapy, 25*(3), 285–300.

Escalera, E. A. (2009). Gender differences in children's use of discourse markers: Separate worlds or different contexts? *Journal of Pragmatics, 41*(12), 2479–2495.

Espinosa, L. M. (2008). *Challenging common myths about young English language learners* (Policy Brief No. 8). Foundation for Child Development. Retrieved from http://fcd-us.org/sites/default/files/MythsOfTeachingELLsEspinosa.pdf (accessed February 19, 2015).

Fenson, L., Dale, P., Reznick, S., Bates, E., Thal, D., & Pethick, S. (1994). Variability in early communicative development. *Monographs of the Society for Research in Child Development, Serial No. 242, 59*(5), i–185.

Fernald, A., & Morikawa, H. (1993). Common themes and cultural variations in Japanese and American mothers' speech to infants. *Child Development, 64*(3), 637–656.

Fiestas, C. E., & Peña, E. D. (2004). Narrative discourse in bilingual children: Language and task effects. *Language, Speech, and Hearing Services in Schools, 35*(2), 155–168.

Flores, S. M., Batalova, J., & Fix, M. (2012). *The educational trajectories of English language learners in Texas.* Washington, DC: The Migration Policy Institute.

Fredman, M. (2006) Recommendations for working with bilingual children. *Folia Phoniatica et Logopaedica, 58*(6), 456–464.

Galsworthy, M. J., Dionne, G., Dale, P. S. & Plomin, R. (2000). Sex differences in early verbal and non-verbal cognitive development. *Developmental Science, 3*(2), 206–215.

Gándara, P. (2005). *Fragile futures: Risk and vulnerability among Latino high achievers* (Policy Information Report). Princeton, NJ: ETS.

Ganger, J., & Brent, M.R. (2004). Reexamining the vocabulary spurt. *Developmental Psychology, 40*(4), 621–632.

García, O. (2009). *Bilingual education in the 21st century: A global perspective.* Oxford, England: Wiley-Blackwell.

Garvey, C., & Berninger, G. (1981). Timing and turn taking in children's conversations. *Discourse Processes, 4*(1), 27–57.

Gathercole, V. C. M. (2007). Miami and North Wales, so far and yet so near: A constructivist account of morphosyntactic development in bilingual children. *International Journal of Bilingual Education and Bilingualism, 10*(3), 224–247.

Gee, J. (1991). Socio-cultural approaches to literacy (literacies). *Annual Review of Applied Linguistics, 12,* 31–48.

Gee, J. P., Allen, A-R., & Clinton, K. (2001). Language, class, and identity: Teenagers fashioning themselves through language. *Linguistics and Education, 12*(2), 175–194.

Genesee, F. (2001). Bilingual first language acquisition: Exploring the limits of the language faculty. *Annual Review of Applied Linguistics, 21,* 153–168.

Genesee, F., Lindholm-Leary, K.J., Saunders, W. & Christian, D. (2006). *Educating English language learners: A synthesis of empirical evidence.* New York, NY: Cambridge University Press.

Genishi, C., & Glupczynski, T. (2006). Language and literacy research: Multiple methods and perspectives. In J. L. Green, G. Camilli, P. B. Elmore, & E. Grace (Eds.), *Handbook of complementary methods in education research* (pp. 657–679). Mahwah, NJ: Erlbaum.

Goldfield, B. A., & Reznick, J. S. (1990). Early lexical acquisition: Rate, content, and the vocabulary spurt. *Journal of Child Language, 17*(1), 171–183.

Gottardo, A., Chiappe, P., Yan, B., Siegel, L., & Gu, Y. (2006). Relationships between first and second language phonological processing skills and reading in Chinese-English speakers living in English-speaking contexts. *Educational Psychology, 26*(3), 367–393.

Grice, H. P. (1957). Meaning. *Philosophical Review, 66,* 377–388.

Grosjean, F. (2009). What parents want to know about bilingualism. *The Bilingual Family Newsletter, 26*(4), 1–6.

Gutiérrez-Clellen, V. F., & Kreiter, J. (2003). Understanding child bilingual acquisition using parent and teacher reports. *Applied Psycholinguistics, 24*(2), 267–288.

Hambly, H., Wren, Y., Mcleod, S., & Roulstone, S. (2013). The influence of bilingualism on speech production: A systematic review. *International Journal of Language & Communication Disorders, 48*(1), 1–24.

Harada, T. (2006). The acquisition of single and geminate stops by English-speaking children in a Japanese immersion program. *Studies in Second Language Acquisition, 28*(04), 601–632.

Hart, B., & Risley, T. R. (1995). *Meaningful differences in the everyday experiences of young children.* Baltimore, MD: Brookes.

Heath, S. B. (1983). *Ways with words: Language, life and work in communities and classrooms.* Cambridge, England: Cambridge University Press.

Hirsh-Pasek, K., & Golinkoff, R. M. (1991). Language comprehension: A new look at some old themes. In N. Krasnegor, D. Rumbaugh, M. Studdert-Kennedy, & R. Schiefelbusch (Eds.), *Biological and behavior determinants of language development* (pp. 301–320). Hillsdale, NJ: Erlbaum.

Hoff, E. (2006). How social contexts support and shape language development. *Developmental Review, 26*(1), 55–88.

Hoff, E. (2009). *Language development* (4th ed.). Belmont, CA: Wadsworth Cengage Learning.

Hoff, E. (2013). Interpreting the early language trajectories of children from low-SES and language minority homes: Implications for closing achievement gaps. *Developmental Psychology, 49*(1), 4–14.

Houston, D. M., Beer, J., Bergeson, T. R., Chin, S. B., Pisoni, D. B., & Miyamoto, R. T. (2012). The ear is connected to the brain: Some new directions in the study of children with cochlear implants at Indiana University. *Journal of the American Academy of Audiology, 23*(6), 446–463.

Hunt, N., & Marshall, K. (2005). *Exceptional children and youth* (4th ed.). Boston, MA: Houghton Mifflin.

Hymes, D. H. (1967). Models of the interaction of language and social setting. *Journal of Social Issues, 23*(2), 8–38.

James, D., Rajput, K., Brinton, J., & Goswami, U. (2009). Orthographic influences, vocabulary development, and phonological awareness in deaf children who use cochlear implants. *Applied Psycholinguistics, 30*(4), 659–684.

John-Steiner, V., & Mahn, H. (1996). Sociocultural approaches to learning and development: A Vygotskian framework. *Educational Psychologist, 31*(3–4), 191–206.

Johnson, E. K., & Jusczyk, P. W. (2001). Word segmentation by 8-month-olds: When speech cues count more than statistics. *Journal of Memory and Language, 44*(4), 548–567.

Kan, P. F., & Kohnert, K. (2008). Fast mapping by bilingual children. *Journal of Child Language, 35*(03), 495–514.

Kelly, K. R., & Bailey, A. L. (2013a). Becoming independent storytellers: Modeling children's development of narrative macrostructure. *First Language, 33*(1), 68–88.

Kelly, K. R., & Bailey, A. L. (2013b). The dual development of conversational and narrative discourse: Mother and child interactions during narrative co-construction. *Merrill-Palmer Quarterly, 59*(4), 426–460.

Koutsoftas, A. D., & Gray, S. (2012). Comparison of narrative and expository writing in students with and without language-learning disabilities. *Language, Speech & Hearing Services In Schools, 43*(4), 395–409.

Kyratzis, A., & Cook-Gumperz, J. (2008). Language socialization and gendered practices in childhood. *Encyclopedia of Language and Education, 8,* 145–157.

Labov, W. (1972). *Language in the inner city.* Philadelphia, PA: University of Pennsylvania Press.

Lapadat, J. C. (1991). Pragmatic language skills of students with language and/or learning disabilities: A quantitative synthesis. *Journal of Learning Disabilities, 24*(3), 147–158.

LaParo, K. M., Justice, L., Skibbe, L. E., & Pianta, R. C. (2004). Relations among maternal, child, and demographic factors and the persistence of preschool language impairment. *American Journal of Speech-Language Pathology, 13*(4), 291–303.

Lenneberg, E. H. (1967). *Biological foundations of language.* New York, NY: Wiley.

Leonard, L. B. (2014). *Children with specific language impairment.* Cambridge, MA: MIT Press.

Lieberman, P. (2007). The evolution of human speech: Its anatomical and neural bases. *Current Anthropology, 48*(1), 39–53.

Locke, L. J. (2006). Parental selection of vocal behavior: Crying, cooing, babbling, and the evolution of language. *Human Nature, 17*(2), 155–168.

Lonigan, C. J. (2007). Vocabulary development and the development of phonological awareness skills in preschool children. In R. K. Wagner, A. E. Muse, & K. R. Tannenbaum (Eds.), *Vocabulary acquisition: Implications for reading comprehension* (pp. 15–31). New York, NY: Guilford.

Lovas, G. S. (2011). Gender and patterns of language development in mother-toddler and father-toddler dyads. *First Language, 31*(1), 83–108.

MacSwan, J. (2000). The architecture of the bilingual language faculty: Evidence from intrasentential code switching. *Bilingualism: Language and Cognition, 3*(01), 37–54.

MacWhinney, B. (2005). Language evolution and human development. In D. Bjorklund and A. Pellegrini (Eds.). *Constraints on word learning: Speculations about their nature, origins, and domain specificity* (pp. 383–410). New York, NY: Guilford.

Mancilla-Martinez, J., & Lesaux, N. K. (2011). Early home language use and later vocabulary development. *Journal of Educational Psychology, 103*(3), 535–546.

Marinis, T. (2011). On the nature and cause of Specific Language Impairment: A view from sentence processing and infant research. *Lingua, 121*(2), 463–475.

Markman, E. (1991). The whole-object, taxonomic, and mutual exclusivity assumptions as initial constraints on word meanings. In S. A. Gelman & J. P. Byrnes (Eds.), *Perspectives on language and thought: Interrelations in development* (pp. 72–106). Cambridge, England: Cambridge University Press.

McCabe, A., & Peterson, C. (1991). Getting the story: A longitudinal study of parental styles in eliciting narratives and developing narrative skill. In A. McCabe & C. Peterson (Eds.), *Developing narrative structure* (pp. 217–253). Hillsdale, NJ: Erlbaum.

McDonough, C., Song, L., Hirsh-Pasek, K., Golinkoff, R. M., & Lannon, R. (2011). An image is worth a thousand words: Why nouns tend to dominate verbs in early word learning. *Developmental Science, 14*(2), 181–189.

Michaels, S. (1981). "Sharing time": Children's narrative styles and differential access to literacy. *Language in Society, 10*(3), 423–442.

Miller, J. F., Heilmann, J., Nockerts, A., Iglesias, A., Fabiano, L., & Francis, D. J. (2006). Oral language and reading in bilingual children. *Learning Disabilities Research & Practice, 21*(1), 30–43.

Minami, M., & McCabe, A. (1995). Rice balls and bear hunts: Japanese and North American family narrative patterns. *Journal of Child Language, 22*(02), 423–423.

Montrul, S., & Yoon, J. (2009). Putting parameters in their proper place. *Second Language Research, 25*(2), 291–311.

Nagy, W. E., & Anderson, R. C. (1984). How many words are there in printed school English. *Reading Research Quarterly, 19*(3), 304–330.

National Center for Education Statistics. (2013). *Digest of Education Statistics, 2012. (NCES 2014-015). Table 48.* Washington, DC: U.S. Department of Education. Retrieved from http://nces.ed.gov/fastfacts/display.asp?id=64 (accessed February 19, 2015).

National Center for Education Statistics. (2014). *The Condition of Education 2014 (NCES 2014-083).* Washington, DC: U.S. Department of Education. Retrieved from http://nces.ed.gov/pubs2014/2014083.pdf (accessed February 19, 2015).

National Governors Association Center for Best Practices, Council of Chief State School Officers. (2010). *Common Core State Standards.* Washington, DC: Author.

NGSS Lead States. (2013). *Next generation science standards: For states, by state*s. Washington, DC: The National Academies Press.

Nippold, M. A. (2007). *Later language development: School-age children, adolescents, and young adults* (3rd ed.). Austin, TX: Pro-Ed.

Oller, D. K., Pearson, B. Z., & Cobo-Lewis, A. B. (2007). Profile effects in early bilingual language and literacy. *Applied Psycholinguistics, 28*(02), 191–230.

Ormel, E., Hermans, D., Knoors, H., Hendriks, A., & Verhoeven, L. (2010). Phonological activation during visual word recognition in deaf and hearing children. *Journal of Speech, Language, and Hearing Research, 53*(4), 801–820.

Paul, R. (2001). *Language disorders from infancy through adolescence.* St. Louis, MO: Mosby.

Paul, R., Orlovski, S. M., Marcinko, H. C., & Volkmar, F. (2009). Conversational behaviors in youth with high-functioning ASD and Asperger syndrome. *Journal of Autism and Developmental Disorders, 39*(1), 115–125.

Pearson, B. Z., Fernández, S. C, & Oller, D. K (1995). Cross-language synonyms in the lexicons of bilingual infants: One language or two? *Journal of Child Language, 22*(2), 345–368.

Piaget, J. (1952). *The origins of intelligence in children.* New York, NY: International University Press.

Poeppel, D., Idsardi, W. J., & van Wassenhove, V. (2008). Speech perception at the interface of neurobiology and linguistics. *Philosophical Transactions of the Royal Society, 363* (1493), 1071–1086.

Pujol, J., Soriano-Mas, C., Ortiz, H., Sebastián-Gallés, N. Losilla, J. M., & Deus, J. (2006). Myelination of language-related areas in the developing brain. *Neurology, 66*(3), 339–343.

Reyes, I. (2004). Functions of code switching in school children's conversations. *Bilingual Research Journal, 28*(1), 77–98.

Rice, M. L. (2013). Language growth and genetics of specific language impairment. *International Journal of Speech-Language Pathology, 15*(3), 223–233.

Roberts, J. E., Price, J., & Malkin, C. (2007). Language and communication development in Down syndrome. *Mental Retardation & Developmental Disabilities Research Reviews, 13*(1), 26–35.

Rowe, M. L. (2008). Child-directed speech: relation to socioeconomic status, knowledge of child development and child vocabulary skill. *Journal of Child Language, 35*(1), 185–205.

Saunders, W., Goldenberg, C., & Marcelletti, D. (2013). English language development. *American Educator, 37*(2), 13–25.

Scarborough, H. S. (1990). Very early language deficits in dyslexic children. *Child Development, 61*(6), 1728–1743.

Schleppegrell, M. (2001). Linguistic features of the language of schooling. *Linguistics and Education, 12*(4), 431–459.

Scott, C. M. (2004). Syntactic contributions to literacy learning. In C. A. Stone, E. R. Silliman, B. J. Ehren, & K. Apel (Eds.), *Handbook of language and literacy: Development and disorders* (pp. 340–362). New York, NY: Guilford.

Seltzer, L. J., Ziegler, T. E., & Pollak, S. D. (2010). Social vocalizations can release oxytocin in humans. *Proceedings of Biological Science*s, *277*(1694), 2661–2666.

Shatz, M., & Wilkinson, L. C. (2013). *Understanding language in diverse classrooms: A primer for all teachers.* New York, NY: Routledge.

Shaywitz, S. E., Morris, R., & Shaywitz, B. A. (2008). The education of dyslexic children from childhood to young adulthood. *Annual Review of Psychology, 59*(1), 451–475.

Silverman, R. D. (2007). Vocabulary development of English-language and English-only learners in kindergarten. *The Elementary School Journal, 107*(4), 365–383.

Smith, S., Scott, K. A., Roberts, J., & Locke, J. L. (2008). Disabled readers' performance on tasks of phonological processing, rapid naming, and letter knowledge before and after kindergarten. *Learning Disabilities Research & Practice, 23*(3), 113–124.

Smith-Lock, K. M., Leitao, S., Lambert, L., & Nickels, L. (2003). Effective intervention for expressive grammar in children with specific language impairment. *International Journal of Language & Communication Disorders, 48*(3), 265–282.

Snow, C. E. (1981). The uses of imitation. *Journal of Child Language, 8*(1), 205–212.

Snow, C. E. (1991). The theoretical basis for relationships between language and literacy in development. *Journal of Research in Childhood Education, 6*(1), 5–10.

Snow, C. E., Burns, M. S., & Griffin, P. (Eds.). (1998). *Preventing reading difficulties in young children.* Washington, DC: National Academies Press.

Snow, C. E., Pan, B. A., Imbens-Bailey, A., & Herman, J. (1996). Learning how to say what one means: A longitudinal study of children's speech act use. *Social Development, 5*(1), 56–84.

Spiteri, E., Konopka, G., Coppola, G., Bomar, J., Oldham, M., Ou, J., . . . & Geschwind, D. H. (2007). Identification of the transcriptional targets of FOXP2, a gene linked to speech and language, in developing human brain. *American Journal of Human Genetics, 81*(6), 1144–1157.

Spreckley, M., & Boyd, R. (2009). Efficacy of applied behavioral intervention in preschool children with autism for improving cognitive, language, and adaptive behavior: A systematic review and meta-analysis. *Journal of Pediatrics, 154*(3), 338–344.

Stromswold, K. (2010). Genetics and the evolution of language: What genetic studies reveal about the evolution of language. *Evolution of Language: Biolinguistic Perspectives,* 176–193.

Tabors, P. O. (2008). *One child, two languages: A guide for preschool educators of children learning English as a second language* (2nd ed.). Baltimore, MD: Brookes.

Teale, W. H., & Sulzby, E. (1986). *Emergent literacy: Writing and reading.* Norwood, NJ: Ablex.

Tomblin, J. B. (1996). Genetic and environmental contributions to the risk for specific language impairment. In M. L. Rice (Ed.), *Toward a genetics of language* (pp. 191–210). Mahwah, NJ: Erlbaum.

Uccelli, P., & Páez, M. M. (2007). Narrative and vocabulary development of bilingual children from kindergarten to first grade: Developmental changes and associations among English and Spanish skills. *Language, Speech, and Hearing Services in Schools, 38*(3), 225–236.

Understanding Language Initiative. (2012). Stanford University Graduate School of Education. Retrieved from http://ell.stanford.edu/ (accessed February 19, 2015).

U.S. Census Bureau. (2010). *United States Census 2010. American Community Survey Table B16001 "Language spoken at home by ability to speak English for the population 5 years and older".* Retrieved from http://www.census.gov/2010census/data/ (accessed February 19, 2015).

van der Lely, H. J., & Marshall, C. R. (2010). Assessing component language deficits in the early detection of reading difficulty risk. *Journal of Learning Disabilities, 43*(4), 357–368.

Vaughn, S., Wexler, J., Leroux, A., Roberts, G., Denton, C., Barth, A., & Fletcher, J. (2012). Effects of intensive reading intervention for eighth-grade students with persistently inadequate response to intervention. *Journal of Learning Disabilities, 45*(6), 515–525.

Vigneau, M., Beaucousin, V., Herve, P. Y., Duffau, H., Crivello, F., Houde, O., Mazoyer, B., & Tzourio-Mazoyer, N. (2006). Meta-analyzing left hemisphere language areas: Phonology, semantics, and sentence processing. *Neuroimage, 30*(4), 1414–1432.

Vorperian, H. K., Kent, R. D., Lindstrom, M. J., Kalina, C. M., Gentry, L. R., & Yandell, B. S. (2005). Development of vocal tract length during childhood: A magnetic resonance imaging study. *Journal of the Acoustical Society of America, 117*(1), 338–350.

Vu, J. A., Bailey, A. L. & Howes, C. (2010). Code-switching in narrative story-completion tasks in Mexican-heritage preschoolers. *Bilingual Research Journal, 33*(2), 200–219.

Vygotsky, L. S. (1978). *Mind and society: The development of higher mental processes.* Cambridge, MA: Harvard University Press.

Walker, B., Shippen, M. E., Alberto, P., Houchins, D. E., & Cihak, D. F. (2005). Using the expressive writing program to improve the writing skills of high school students with learning disabilities. *Learning Disabilities Research & Practice, 20*(3), 175–183.

Wallentin, M. (2009). Putative sex differences in verbal abilities and language cortex: A critical review. *Brain and Language, 108*(3), 175–183.

Weizman, Z. O., & Snow, C. E. (2001). Lexical output as related to children's vocabulary acquisition: Effects of sophisticated exposure and support for meaning. *Developmental Psychology, 37*(2), 265–279.

Yoshida, H. (2008). The cognitive consequence of early bilingualism. *Zero to Three, 29*(2), 26–30.

# 16

# Character Education, Moral Education, and Moral-Character Education

*Cary J. Roseth*[1]
Michigan State University

Few people would argue with the idea that children's moral and character formation is a foundational goal for parents and schools. In fact, many argue that there is no such thing as a values-free education because every decision that is made about what to teach (and what not to), how to enforce discipline, and how to balance one individual's needs with those of everyone else informs students about what is worth doing, what is right and wrong, and what constitutes social justice (Sizer & Sizer, 1999).

Yet such broad agreement about the importance of moral and character education does not extend to the particulars of what it is or how to do it. To the contrary, historically, moral and character education have been associated with opposing philosophical traditions, psychological theories, and pedagogical approaches (Lapsley & Yeager, 2013). Character educators have tended to reject the indirect methods favored by moral educators (e.g., moral discussions) as promoting moral relativism (e.g., Lickona, 1991; Ryan & Bohlin, 1999), while moral educators have rejected the direct instructional methods favored by character educators (e.g., the use of rewards, habit formation) as indoctrination (e.g., Kohlberg & Mayer, 1972). As noted by Lapsley and Yeager (2013), these divisions even extend to academia, where moral and character education have different professional societies (e.g., Association for Moral Education, the Character Education Partnership) and different professional journals (e.g., *Journal of Moral Education, Journal of Research in Character Education*).

Fortunately, these historical divisions have recently given way to a "new era in character education" (Damon, 2002) where there is "more consensus than controversy" (Lapsley & Yeager, 2013, p. 289), and scholars "ignore the inevitable semantic squabbles and get down to the business of fostering the development of character in youth" (Berkowitz, 2012, p. 248). The present chapter reflects this integrative view of moral-character education but situates it within the historical divisions between moral and character education. This approach is intended to be especially helpful to new readers, as reading the integrative moral-character literature without this background can be disorienting, much like joining an ongoing conversation without any idea what people are talking about. Situating the integrative approach within historic divisions makes explicit the way different conceptualizations of morality, character, and moral character inform different developmental models and different educational programs. It also clarifies the way different scholars think about "what counts" as moral-character education.

To be clear, situating the integrative approach to moral-character education within the field's historic divisions is *not* meant to rekindle "sterile old oppositions" (Damon, 2002, p. ix), nor to undermine integrative efforts. The integrative approach and the broad goal of supporting positive youth development are both commendable. For theory and research in educational psychology, however, one must consider whether the benefits of integration outweigh the potential loss of information about what distinguishes moral and character education.

The chapter is divided into four parts. The first part introduces terminology. The second part considers morality and character as developmental processes and what this implies for education. The third part reviews programmatic approaches to moral-character education. And finally, the fourth part summarizes major points and future challenges.

## Terminology

The terms morality, character, and moral character are often used interchangeably, especially within the contemporary literature on moral-character education (Berkowitz, 2012; Lapsley & Yeager, 2013). In part, this reflects the way the popularity of these terms has varied across time. In the United States, for example, the term "character education" was favored during the first half of the twentieth century, while "moral education" and "values clarification" were favored during the latter half. More recently (i.e., mid-1990s through present), the terms "character education" and "moral-character education" have both been used as umbrella terms for the field. Complicating things further, the contemporary literature also includes many programmatic approaches that do not refer explicitly to morality or character development (e.g., social-emotional learning, positive youth development, service learning), but still focus on outcomes of interest to moral-character education. Such a proliferation of terms makes it difficult to define the boundaries of the field and understand what counts as moral and character education (Lapsley & Yeager, 2013). The next section begins to address the issue by considering important distinctions among terms.

## Morality

*Morality* denotes the distinction between right and wrong and the way we ought to treat one another. The term "ought" is key to understanding the term because it connotes that moral concerns are universal, obligatory, and unalterable by consensus (Turiel, 2006).

Historically, one of the defining controversies in moral and character education has been whether philosophy or psychology should determine what constitutes right and wrong (Blasi, 1990; Kristjánsson, 2009). On one side of the debate, Kohlberg (e.g., Kohlberg, 1984; Colby & Kohlberg, 1987) and others (e.g., Carr, 1991) have argued that psychological explanations of morality must be grounded in philosophical explanations to avoid moral relativism. Other scholars have argued that defining moral psychology in terms of moral philosophy limits the field to particular moral dimensions (e.g., justice; Blasi, 1990; see also Gilligan, 1982) and narrow developmental models (Lapsley & Carlo, 2014).

Contemporary efforts to integrate moral-character education suggest that many psychologists have stopped trying to resolve moral philosophical questions and, instead, focus on psychological issues (Lapsley & Narvaez, 2005, 2008). Thus, Kohlberg's paradigmatic moral stage theory no longer delimits what counts as moral psychology and the field has expanded to include a much broader spectrum of psychological disciplines, theories, and methods (Lapsley & Carlo, 2014). Consequently, *psychological* definitions of morality are no longer limited to universal, obligatory, and unalterable standards of conduct. This is a significant change from the past and suggests that almost any conception of right and wrong, good and bad, and virtue and vice may be conceptualized as "moral." Time will tell whether this advances the field or results in more confusion and controversy about what counts as moral psychology.

## Character

*Character* derives from the Greek word meaning "to mark," and denotes an enduring quality (or qualities) of a person.

Within the moral and character education literatures, the term also typically connotes enduring *moral* qualities—e.g., Narvaez and Lapsley (2009) define character as the "moral dimension of personality" (p. 243). Definitions like this make qualifications (e.g., good) unnecessary because character already connotes a moral evaluation.

Yet not all scholars define character as moral. For example, Allport (1937) excluded character from his conceptualization of personality because, in his view, character was a normative concept while personality is morally neutral (Cawley, Martin, & Johnson, 2000). Likewise, Lickona and Davidson (2004) distinguish between performance and moral character, the former referring to the qualities needed to develop competence (diligence, perseverance, positive attitude, hard work) and the latter to ethical qualities (integrity, caring, justice, respect, cooperation). This represents an expansive definition of character because it adds a range of positive dispositions to the traditional emphasis on morality and virtue.

Historically, what it means to define character as an *enduring* quality has also been problematic, as theorists and researchers alike have struggled to explain how character can be both enduring and highly malleable (for a review, see Desteno & Valdesolo, 2011). After all, character is not the only factor that influences individual behavior, as different situations can make a person more or less fair and more or less honest.

## Moral Character

Defining *moral character* is not as straightforward as combining the terms moral and character to denote an enduring quality of a person whose qualities are considered to be universally good (i.e., moral). Consider, for example, a student who never cheats on tests but always breaks other school rules (e.g., refuses to address teachers by their last name). The moral character of this student may be described positively (e.g., good, virtuous) because he/she always follows the moral rule (Don't cheat) and, strictly speaking, arbitrary school rules do not bear on moral character. Yet this definition would strike many as inconsistent with moral-character education's broader goal of helping students to become responsible members of a democratic society (Althof & Berkowitz, 2006). Thus, the term moral character tends to be used broadly to refer to:

> the capacity to think about right and wrong, experience moral emotions (guilt, empathy, compassion), engage in moral behaviors (sharing, donating to charity, telling the truth), believe in moral goods, demonstrate an enduring tendency to act with honesty, altruism, responsibility, and other characteristics that support moral functioning. (Berkowitz, 2002, p. 48)

Here, it is important to note that moral character is used to describe everything related to living a good life well, which is consistent with the expansive definition of character noted above.

## Ethics

*Ethics* denote the standards by which actions are judged right or wrong. Thus, whereas values describe what is important, ethics *prescribe* what is and is not an acceptable manner to behave in relation to a given value. Ethics differ from morals because they are, by definition, socially determined within a particular time and context. Morality, at least as defined by philosophers, is universal, obligatory, and unalterable.

## Values

Although popular conceptions of *value* connote the importance of something, in the moral and character education literatures the term refers to a principled preference (Carr, 1991) or disposition (Carr, 2011). Thus, value differs from mere liking because it connotes reasoned justification and a motivated inclination while liking connotes an arbitrary preference that may or may not be justified and may or may not motivate action (Carr, 2011). In the strongest Aristotelian conception, values also differ from mere adherence to rules or principles because they connote qualities that a person cannot simply choose or ignore (Carr, 2011).

## Habits, Traits, and Virtues

The terms habits, traits, and virtues have all been used to describe moral and character formation. For example, Lapsley and Narvaez (2006) define moral character as "a manifestation of certain personality *traits* called *virtues* that dispose one to *habitual* courses of action" (original emphasis) (p. 2). *Habits* denote the tendency to respond to a particular situation in a particular way. *Traits* denote a person's dispositional tendencies that endure across time and situations. *Virtues* denote positive traits that are deemed morally good. When authors use virtue and character interchangeably, it suggests that character connotes a moral trait.

## Summary

In sum, the moral and character education literatures are notorious for non-consensual terminology (Berkowitz, 2012). In part, this is because some terms are used interchangeably (e.g., character trait = virtue; moral character = character) and scholars disagree on hierarchical relationships. Thus, it is not always clear whether character is being used interchangeably with moral character, or if moral character represents a subcomponent of character.

## Moral and Character Education as Developmental Processes

Having reviewed the "linguistic minefield" (Berkowitz, 2012, p. 248) surrounding terminology, the next question is where morality and character come from. This is a difficult question to answer because morality and character are multifaceted phenomena and developmental models vary as a function of how broadly or narrowly one conceptualizes the domain. Different components of morality and character also have their own developmental trajectories, and different developments likely build on prior and concurrent developments (Lapsley & Carlo, 2014). For example, empathy emerges in infancy (Hoffman, 2000), moral reasoning in preschool (Turiel, 2006), and moral identity emerges during late childhood and early adolescence (Hardy & Carlo, 2005), but the extent to which they are integrated or isolated competencies remains largely unknown.

It is beyond the scope of this chapter to provide a comprehensive review of all of the developmental models, milestones, and processes related to moral and character development. The next section therefore focuses on what developmental considerations imply for education.

### Character Development

This section considers three broad accounts of character development: habit formation, direct socialization, and personality development.

***Habit formation.*** Traditional conceptions of character development and the controversies surrounding them have their roots in classical philosophy (Arthur, 2008). For example, Aristotle's view that one becomes a good person by practicing and repeating a behavior informs character education's traditional emphasis on habit formation. From this perspective, people with good character behave well by way of habit (Ryan & Lickona, 1992) and without conscious deliberation (Steutel & Spiecker, 2004).

This view is typically contrasted with Plato's argument that being good depends on first knowing what is good. According to Arthur (2008), however, this overstates the difference between Aristotle and Plato's positions, as both argued that character involves *voluntarily* doing the right thing and for the right reason. What these scholars did not agree on was whether the behavioral components precede the cognitive components of character development and, by extension, whether character educators should emphasize habit formation or developing moral reasoning capabilities (Arthur, 2008).

During the twentieth century, a similar debate has surrounded psychological conceptions of character development (Blasi, 2005). Behaviorists (e.g., Skinner, 1971) argued that character development reflects a history of conditioning, with desired behaviors increasing (i.e., becoming habits) when parents and educators reinforce them, and undesired behaviors decreasing when they are punished (Burton & Kunce, 1995). In contrast, cognitive theorists focused on the mediating role of cognition, with stage theorists (e.g., Piaget, Kohlberg) emphasizing developmental-structural issues and social cognitive theory (Bandura, 1986) emphasizing the reinforcement of modeled behaviors and individuals' beliefs about their capabilities and the expected outcomes of their actions.

***Direct socialization.*** Direct socialization models assume that character develops from the "outside in" and emphasize the role of the environment in shaping children's character. Simply put, good environments socialize good children and bad environments do the opposite.

Religious perspectives argue that divine law dictates what counts as a good environment, which of course invites controversy about *'Whose values?'* should be taught in character education. In the United States, Christianity served as the religious basis for character education in public schools for much of the eighteenth and nineteenth centuries (Cunningham, 2005).

The shift toward secular bases for character education coincided with progressive educators' condemnation of direct socialization approaches such as exhortation, didactic instruction, and punishment. Dewey (1908) argued that these approaches not only fail to support character development, but also cultivate passivity and conformity, disconnecting character education from the social contexts in which it is most meaningful (Lapsley & Narvaez, 2005). According to Dewey (1908), students should instead become actively involved in constructing their own moral meaning through social interaction, moral discussion, and democratic practices.

Historically, the debate over *Whose values?* and the role of direct instruction has been intense. Just as some moral psychologists (e.g., Kohlberg) believed that philosophy must take the lead in determining what counts as moral psychology, many advocates of direct instruction also believe that what counts as "good" character is enduring and cannot be subjected to matters of consensus or individual discovery (e.g., Ryan & Bohlin, 1999). Instead, fundamental knowledge about right and wrong must be transmitted directly to successive generations.

***Personality development.*** Another way to conceptualize character development is in terms of personality traits, or the ways in which individuals differ from one other. Thinking about individual differences highlights the way different experiences (e.g., reinforcement histories, parenting styles) can influence different developmental trajectories. Unlike habit formation and direct socialization, however, personality psychology also suggests that character traits may be, to some extent, biologically inherited (see e.g., altruism; Hoffman, 2000; Chapter 13, this volume). This represents a major shift in psychological thinking and moves the question of where morality and character come from proximate levels of analysis to ultimate questions about how some traits may have contributed to survival and reproduction in the course of evolution (Peterson & Seligman, 2004). Rather than assume that children take on their parents' values because they are socialized to do so, thinking about character in terms of personality development reminds us that parent–child similarities may also be due to genetic similarity.

Taking an individual difference perspective also invites questions about which patterns of traits differentiate people of different character. For example, Walker and colleagues have examined which traits tend to be found together in individuals considered to be moral exemplars (e.g., Walker & Hennig, 2004). These findings provide a rich summary of the ways moral exemplars differ from other individuals but do not clarify whether particular traits are necessary and sufficient for someone to be considered an "exemplar," or if multiple traits are needed to characterize accurately the way one individual differs from another.

The individual difference perspective also invites questions about *moral identity,* or the "ways, and the extent to which, individuals integrate their morality in their subjective sense of personal identity" (Nucci, 2001, p. 128). Moral identity is an individual difference variable because some individuals consider moral concerns (e.g., being good, just) as a core feature of their sense of self, whereas others incorporate morality to the self to a lesser degree. Readers are referred to Narvaez and Lapsley (2009) for a more comprehensive treatment of moral identity.

***Summary.*** In sum, habit formation, direct socialization, and personality development offer three different perspectives on where character comes from. Habit formation emphasizes the role of practice and repeated behavior in the development of dispositional tendencies; direct socialization emphasizes the role of adult instruction; and personality development emphasizes the way individuals differ from each other. None of these accounts has much to say about the role of cognition in children's character development, though some scholars have argued that easily activated cognitive schemas and behavioral scripts may also inform individual differences (see e.g., Lapsley & Narvaez, 2006).

### Moral Development

Historically, cognitive-oriented psychologists focused on the development of morality rather than character and, in particular, on *moral reasoning,* or decision making about whether a given act is right and wrong. The field is most closely aligned with the cognitive-developmental perspective and, in particular, three moral stage theorists: namely, Piaget (1932/1965), Kohlberg (1984), and Turiel (1983, 1998). Given space restrictions, this chapter only reviews Kohlberg's theory of moral development and Turiel's social-cognitive domain theory.

***Kohlberg.*** Kohlberg (e.g., Kohlberg, 1984; Colby & Kohlberg, 1987) argued that morality develops through three moral levels in an invariant sequence, and that individuals do not regress to earlier stages of moral judgment once they have attained a higher stage of development. Instead, through development, cognitive structures evolve from and displace earlier structures by way of hierarchical integration. These assertions contrast with Piaget, who maintained that stages only represent "broad divisions of moral development" (Piaget, 1932/1965, p. 175) and, consequently, are likely to overlap at any given point in development.

Research tends to support Kohlberg's theory in broad terms (Lapsley, 2006), with studies conducted in many different countries showing a strong positive correlation between age and stage of moral reasoning (Colby & Kohlberg, 1987). However, research only partially supports Kohlberg's assertion that moral development progresses through an invariant and universal sequence of moral stages. For example, various longitudinal studies have shown that moral reasoning progresses in the order predicted by Kohlberg (i.e., Stage 1, then Stage 2, etc.) (Colby, Kohlberg, Gibbs, & Lieberman, 1983; Rest, Narvaez, Bebeau, & Thoma, 1999), and that most individuals do not progress beyond Stage 3 or 4 (Boom, Brugman, & van der Heijden, 2001). Research has also shown that the expression of moral stages varies across contexts (Carpendale, 2000) and between Western and non-Western cultures (Harkness, Edwards, & Super, 1981; Snarey & Keljo, 1991). Thus, research suggests that moral development progresses in a universal order but is also situated in culturally specific contexts.

Research also supports Kohlberg's (1984) assertion that moving from the preconventional to conventional level of moral reasoning is associated with perspective taking (e.g., Walker, 1980), and that moving from the conventional to postconventional level is associated with abstract reasoning (i.e., formal operations) (Tomlinson-Keasey & Keasey, 1974). However, advanced education is also associated with higher levels of moral reasoning (Rest et al., 1999), which suggests that perspective taking and formal operations are necessary but not sufficient prerequisites for moral growth. Social experiences that emphasize conflict and compromise may also be needed to move beyond the conventional level (Killen & de Waal, 2000; Tichy, Johnson, Johnson, & Roseth, 2010).

Critics of Kohlberg's theory of moral development have questioned whether the theory is biased towards individual rights and justice over social harmony (Helwig & Turiel, 2002) and moral authority (Turiel & Wainryb, 2000), because cross-cultural studies show that postconventional morality is only found in Western democracies (Harkness et al., 1981; Snarey & Keljo, 1991). Critics such as Carol Gilligan (1982) have also argued that Kohlberg's theory values a male-oriented morality of justice over a female-oriented morality of care. Research has largely failed to support this criticism, however, showing that men and women are equally likely to rely on justice-based principles when moral dilemmas involve individual rights and care-based principles when moral dilemmas involve relationships (Jaffee & Hyde, 2000).

Critics have also questioned whether Kohlberg's theory underestimates children's moral capacity, as research on distributive justice has shown that even 5- and 6-year-olds have developed sophisticated conceptions of what is fair when deciding how to allocate limited resources (e.g., toys, candies) (e.g., Damon, 1988; see also Fehr, Bernhard, & Rockenbach, 2008; Gummerum, Keller, Takezawa, & Mata, 2008). Research on prosocial moral reasoning has also shown that elementary-school children consider the needs of others when deciding whether to help, share with, or comfort others (Eisenberg, Fabes, & Spinrad, 2006).

Finally, critics have also questioned whether Kohlberg's theory is too narrow, focusing too heavily on moral reasoning and failing to account for other aspects of moral psychology such as moral affect, moral behavior, and moral identity.

As detailed below, contemporary scholars have addressed this issue by taking a more integrative and expansive approach to moral-character development (for a review, see Lapsley & Carlo, 2014).

Despite these criticisms, Kohlberg's theory has several implications for moral education. For example, research has shown that moral growth occurs when groups of peers are asked to come to consensus on controversial issues (e.g., Berkowitz & Gibbs, 1983; Tichy et al., 2010), or participate in small democracies within schools (e.g., the Just Community School; Power & Makogon, 1995). During these activities, the teacher's role is to minimize direct instruction and, instead, facilitate student discussion. This is not to say that adults have no role in Kohlbergian moral development, as research suggests that differences between peer and parent effects disappear when parents present their reasoning in a positive and supportive way (Walker, Hennig, & Krettenauer, 2000). What matters, it seems, is that children do not perceive adult's moral challenges to be threatening or coercive.

***Social-cognitive domain theory.*** Social-cognitive domain theory (Turiel, 2006) differentiates between moral, social-conventional, and the personal domains. Morality is a distinct developmental and conceptual domain and concerns obligatory and universally applicable principles of how we ought to treat one other (e.g., justice, welfare, rights). The social-conventional domain concerns rules, norms, and practices that are defined by consensus and agreement and therefore contextually relative and arbitrary. The personal domain refers to individual concerns such as privacy, body integrity and control, and individual preference.

In short, whereas Kohlberg (1984) described moral growth in terms of a single moral developmental trajectory, social-cognitive domain theory posits that the moral, social-conventional, and personal domains are differentiated in early experience and follow distinct developmental trajectories. Importantly, these three domains are also seen as operating on their own and in coordination with the other domains (for a full review of social-cognitive domain theory, see Turiel, 2006).

Considerable research supports social-cognitive domain theory and the differentiation of the moral, social-conventional, and personal domains. For example, research supports the idea of three different rule domains across cultures, though the content of specific domains may differ (Miller & Bersoff, 1995). Research has also shown that children begin making a distinction between the moral and social-conventional domains by 3–4-years-old (Smetana & Braeges, 1990), and even report they would disobey an authority figure's command (e.g., parent, teacher, God) to violate a moral rule (e.g., hitting, stealing) but not a social-conventional rule (e.g., working on Sunday) (Nucci & Turiel, 1993).

Broadly, research also supports the view that the three domains are associated with different social developmental contexts. For example, adults are more likely to highlight the consequences of moral violations (e.g., hitting harms victims, not sharing is unfair to others), but emphasize the importance of obeying rules when children violate social conventions (Nucci & Weber, 1995). Developmentally, these two different experiences may inform the distinctions children make between different categories of judgment (Turiel, 2006).

Domain theory's more complex account of moral development suggests that moral education involves more than helping students to move through progressively higher levels of moral reasoning. Moral educators may also help students to develop conceptions of the social-conventional and personal domains and, in turn, learn how to evaluate and coordinate these conceptions with the moral aspects of everyday life (Turiel, 2006). Domain theory also suggests that even children's resistance to conventions (e.g., norms for dress, ways of addressing adults, manners) all contribute to students' understanding of the purposes of social standards and their capacity for moral reflection (Smetana, 2006). This stands in sharp contrast to Kohlberg's dismissal of social conventions as an inferior basis for moral judgment.

*Summary.* In sum, cognitive-developmental perspectives on moral development suggest that moral reasoning cannot be understood solely in terms of environmental influences, nor can moral educators rely exclusively on direct instruction or reinforcement histories to support children's moral growth. Instead, moral education must account for the way children actively construct their own conceptions of right and wrong within the constraints of their current levels of cognitive development. This last point highlights the importance of developmentally appropriate forms of classroom management and conflict resolution, and the need to provide students with *relevant* social experiences; that is, social experiences that encourage them to re-evaluate and alter current moral perspectives but do not make them feel threatened.

### Moral-Character Development

In part, theory and research on moral-character has emerged in response to the historic divide between moral and character psychology. Taking an integrative and expansive approach, the term "moral character" now tends to be used broadly to refer to all characteristics that motivate and enable doing the right thing (Berkowitz, 2012).

Of course, expanding the moral-character domain has made it difficult to determine what counts as moral-character education. After all, supporting positive youth development may be conceptualized broadly, and it does not necessarily follow that programs designed to foster morality, virtue, and good character are psychologically equivalent to programs designed to prevent youth crime, illegal drug use, and other forms of antisocial behavior. On the contrary, taking such a broad view of moral-character education may reduce the construct to "a catalog of psychosocial interventions and risk prevention programs . . . that make no reference to morality, virtue or character" (Lapsley & Yeager, 2013, p. 299).

The debate surrounding the boundaries of moral-character education and whether it should be defined broadly or narrowly will not be resolved here. Instead, what readers must recognize is that taking an expansive view of moral-character

education has prompted a new debate about whether the domain should include any school-based program that fosters positive outcomes and/or reduces negative outcomes, or limit itself to only those programs that include ethical considerations in their treatment and/or outcomes.

The remainder of this section turns to the question of where moral character comes from and what this implies for moral-character education. A relational developmental systems perspective is considered first, followed by a model of the moral person.

***Relational developmental systems.*** Whereas traditional accounts of character development emphasize experience (e.g., habit formation, direct socialization) and cognitive-developmentalists emphasize the mediating role of cognition, a much more complex model is required to describe and explain the development of moral character. Relational development systems models provide one such perspective by emphasizing bidirectional relations between the developing individual and multiple levels of his/her changing context (Overton, 2010). Examples of such models include Bronfenbrenner's ecological systems perspective (e.g., Bronfenbrenner & Morris, 2006), Thelen and Smith's dynamic systems theory (Thelen & Smith, 2006), and Magnusson's holistic person–context interaction theory (e.g., Magnusson & Stattin, 2006).

Broadly, relational development systems theoretical models may be represented in terms of the plasticity and the multivariate nature of individual–context causal relations. *Plasticity,* or the idea that there is always some potential for systematic change across the life span (Lerner et al., 2011), emphasizes that individual–context relations are always in flux and therefore always able to adapt to new conditions. Thus, individual–context relations are best described in terms of dynamic stability because, even when they look stable, they have the potential to change (Thelen & Smith, 2006). For moral and character education, this suggests that any individual's developmental trajectory can change for better or worse at any given time. It also suggests that, rather than conceptualize children as having or not having some static ability (e.g., trait, habit), moral character should be thought of in dynamic terms, as constantly reflecting and interacting with the changing developmental and environmental context in which it is embedded (Lerner et al., 2011).

*Multicausality,* or the idea that multiple factors simultaneously contribute to a given individual–context relation, highlights the sheer complexity of relational developmental systems and the idea that no one factor (e.g., experience, cognitive structures) can be assumed to have causal primacy. Thus, the person and the environment represent a system rather than distinct sources of influence, and maturation and experience are inextricably fused in a way that causality exists between the two rather than within either one. Importantly, multicausality also suggests that different developmental timescales must be understood as unified and coherent, and that behavior reflects the interaction between current context and evolutionary and ontogenetic histories. For moral-character education, this suggests that the best way to understand moral character is within longitudinal studies. That is, the effects of any one intervention strategy (e.g., curriculum, the use of rewards and punishment, moral dialogue among peers) cannot be understood as distinct from the multidimensional context in which it is embedded.

The sheer complexity associated with relational developmental systems models can be overwhelming. Plasticity and multicausality prompt questions about whether main effects can even exist (e.g., Plomin, 1986), and whether empirical research can ever capture the number of variables informing outcomes (see Chapter 2, this volume). For moral-character education, however, this complexity also implies that there is *always* the potential that individual–context relations can change (see e.g., Kaplan, Crockett, & Tivnan, 2014). Thus, complexity also offers hope that educators can align youth strengths with ecological resources that promote positive individual–context relations (Lerner et al., 2011).

Kochanska's (e.g., Kochanska, 2002) work on the development of conscience provides an illustrative example of the way a relational development systems perspective can advance our understanding of moral-character development. Kochanska's research suggests that children who grow up in a *mutually responsive dyad*—in close, cooperative, and affectively positive relationships—are more likely than children who do not to embrace their parents' values and develop a strong conscience (Kochanska, 2002) and strong self-regulation skills (Kochanska, Aksan, Prisco, & Adams, 2008). This developmental trajectory is multicausal, however, as longitudinal studies have shown that children's proneness to anger (Kochanska, Aksan, & Carlson, 2005), guilt and effortful control (Kochanska, Barry, Stellern, & O'Blenesss, 2009a), and parental power assertion (a form of harsh parenting) (Kochanska, Barry, Jimenez, Hollatz, & Woodard, 2009b) interact with qualities of the parent–child dyad. The developmental trajectory of conscience is also plastic, as children's committed compliance has also been shown to vary across 'Do' (e.g., clean up toys) and 'Don't' (e.g., refrain from playing with an attractive toy) contexts (Kochanska, Coy, & Murray, 2001) and between mothers and fathers (Kochanska et al., 2005).

***The moral person.***   One of the benefits of an expansive (rather than narrow) view of moral character is understanding how different dimensions of morality and character coalesce into a moral person. Whether such unity even exists has long been debated, with theorists questioning whether virtues like justice and caring cohere within a person the same way that, say, intellectual curiosity, creativity, and preference for novelty cohere within a person with an open personality (Carr, 1991). Other possibilities exist, of course, as being fair and caring does not necessarily preclude from being lazy and gluttonous.

Taking an expansive view, Berkowitz's (2012) model of the moral person includes a moral self-system (moral identity and conscience) and both moral and non-moral aspects of cognition, affect, and behavior. The moral aspects of cognition include sociomoral reasoning and knowledge of moral facts, and the non-moral aspects include intrapsychic intelligence, critical thinking, social cognition, and general

knowledge. The moral aspects of affect include emotions such as empathy, sympathy, compassion, guilt, and shame, as well as moral motivations such as altruism and a concern for the common good. Non-moral aspects of motivation and affect include performance orientation (e.g., need for achievement and achievement motivations) and emotions such as curiosity. The moral aspects of behavior include behaviors that promote justice, enhance the welfare of others, protect human rights (e.g., charitable giving, telling the truth, protecting the weak), as well as social-emotional learning competencies such as conflict resolution skills. Non-moral behaviors include all manifestations of performance character such as persevering on a task and self-reflection, as well as social-emotional learning competencies such as anger management.

The value of such an elaborate model is descriptive, as it situates the moral self-system and moral cognition, emotion, and behavior within a person's non-moral yet foundational competencies. What is less clear is whether the model lends itself to specific hypotheses about specific features (mechanisms) of the moral person, the way they relate to each other, different antecedents, and specific short- and long-term outcomes. Taking a relational developmental systems perspective also highlights the need to understand whether specific features of the moral person operate similarly for different-age youth (or race, ethnicity, religion, sex, ability level, etc.) from different families and communities (Lerner et al., 2011). These factors are also likely to interact with different features of moral-character education programs, which means that a complete account of moral functioning must situate the moral person within an even more elaborate model of the environment in which he or she is embedded.

***Summary.***   In sum, there are advantages and disadvantages to an expansive definition of moral character and moral-character education. To the extent that the historical division between morality and character exaggerated their differences, the integrative approach maximizes construct validity (Cronbach, 1971) and suggests that there is nothing incompatible about the development of morality and character. The integrative approach also suggests that there is nothing incompatible about moral and character education because habit formation, direct socialization, character traits, and the development of moral reasoning may all contribute to moral-character formation (Berkowitz, 2012; Damon, 2002).

One of the obvious disadvantages of the expansive view is that it becomes difficult to determine what counts as moral character. This is especially true for moral-character education because different programs (e.g., social-emotional learning, positive youth development, service learning) share the common goal of helping young people to learn to live a good life well. However, linking programs solely by their common goal reveals very little about developmental trajectories or mechanisms of change and, at the extreme, one begins to wonder whether the term "moral character" will ultimately link theory, research, and practice in name only.

## Programmatic Approaches to Moral-Character Education

This section reviews prominent, contemporary approaches to moral-character education. Because of the diversity and number of programs related to moral-character education, only categories of programs and representative examples are considered. However, both expansive and non-expansive (i.e., ethically focused) approaches to character education are included, as this provides points of comparison when considering what counts as moral-character education. This section also includes an account of *what works* in moral-character education.

In this section the term "character" is used to refer to moral and non-moral aspects of character education, as it provides the broadest umbrella for programs of interest to moral and character educators. The term "moral-character" is therefore used deliberately to specify programmatic features that emphasize ethical considerations.

### Character Education Partnership

The Character Education Partnership (CEP) is an umbrella organization serving school- and community-based character education programs. The CEP does not represent one particular programmatic approach but, instead, identifies 11 principles to guide site-specific program planning and evaluation (Beland, 2003). Specifically, the CEP asserts that good character education programs are built on core ethical and performance values (Principle 1), and thus advocates an explicit focus on moral development rather than an expansive approach that includes both moral- and non-moral-character education programs. The CEP also asserts that effective character education involves a proactive (Principle 3) and holistic approach to teaching core values so that students can understand, care about, and act in accordance with those values (Principle 2). Thus, effective character education involves more than habit formation or moral reasoning, and must provide students with relevant opportunities to demonstrate good character and grapple with real-life ethical dilemmas (Principle 5).

Recognizing the importance of social context, the CEP also emphasizes creating a caring community (Principle 4). It asserts that every member of the school community must share responsibility for (Principle 8) and assume a leadership role in the support of character education (Principle 9), including engaging with families and community members (Principle 10).

Because students come to schools with diverse skills and needs, the CEP asserts that effective character education also involves both challenging and differentiated instruction (Principle 6), which fosters individual students' sense of autonomy and intrinsic motivation (Principle 7). Thus, students should not perceive that character education is personally irrelevant, threatening, or coercive. Finally, to make sure all of this is happening, the CEP asserts that effective character education must also regularly assess the ethical culture of the school, the development of the staff as character educators, and students' understanding of, commitment to, and action upon core values (Principle 11).

The CEP Principles provide a useful way to conceptualize what effective, programmatic approaches to character education involve. Recently, it has also developed a rubric (*Character Education Quality Standards*) that may be used to evaluate school programs, as the actual implementation of character education varies widely, even among programs that subscribe to CEP's 11 principles (Berkowitz, 2012).

### Educating for Character

*Educating for Character* is the title of Thomas Lickona's (1991) best-selling book outlining the role of school and family in children's character education. Here, I use the title more broadly to refer to his extensive writing on character education (e.g., Lickona, 1991, 2004; Lickona & Davidson, 2004). Like the CEP, Lickona and colleagues provide a conceptual framework for character education rather than a specific program. Specifically, Lickona and Davidson (2004) identify seven principles of effective character education, which are largely consistent with the CEP's principles and will not be detailed here. One difference, however, is that Lickona and Davidson (2004) argue that character development should be a cornerstone of a school's mission, rather than a co- or extracurricular focus.

### Positive Youth Development

Positive Youth Development (PYD) provides another conceptual framework for character education that emphasizes children's developmental strengths rather than risks and deficits. Specifically, PYD programs strive to help youth develop what Lerner et al. (2005) describe as the 5Cs (competence, confidence, character, connection, and caring) that they need to be successful members of society. The basic premise is that healthy development can be optimized when a youth's strengths are aligned with family, school and community resources that support positive growth (Lerner et al., 2011). By emphasizing alignment, PYD stresses the relation between youth and their social context rather than the particular attributes of either one. The PYD framework does not make any explicit reference to morality or ethics, but the outcomes associated with the approach are certainly of interest to character educators.

As a broad conceptual umbrella, there are literally thousands of programs that may be conceptualized as promoting PYD (Lerner et al., 2011). For example, in a survey of 71 youth-serving organizations, Roth and Brooks-Gunn (2003) found that the primary goal of 77% of programs was to promote youth competencies, while 54% also reported prevention goals (e.g., substance abuse, school dropout, violence, and gang activity). To date, there have also been two reviews of the effectiveness of PYD programs: Roth and colleagues (Roth, Brooks-Gunn, Murray, & Foster, 1998) identified 15 program evaluations and Catalano and colleagues (Catalano, Berglund, Ryan, Lonczak, & Hawkins, 2004) identified 25 program evaluations. In general, both reviews found evidence of effectiveness and identified several program features that moderated results. For example, Roth et al. (1998) found that better results were associated with more comprehensive and sustained programs, while Catalano et al. (2004) found increased effects with structured curriculums and youth contact lasting at least 9 months.

One of the most rigorously examined PYD programs is the 4-H Study of Positive Youth Development (for full review, see Lerner et al., 2011). Producing more than 40 empirical publications to date, this cohort sequential longitudinal study included almost 7,000 youth and about 3,500 of their parents from 41 states. Results support the view that alignment between youth strengths and ecological resources enhances positive youth development. Findings also indicate there are three youth strengths that are especially important for optimal outcomes (goal selection, strategy optimization, and compensating for obstacles) (Freund & Baltes, 2002), and that youth development programs are key ecological resources (Lerner et al., 2005; Theokas & Lerner, 2006). Findings also suggest that the most effective youth development programs include three assets: positive adult–youth relationships, life-skill building, and youth participation and leadership (Lerner et al., 2011). Finally, PYD (as measured by the 5Cs) has also been linked to adolescents' civic engagement (Lerner, 2004).

The 5Cs operationalize the developmental strengths that youth need to optimize healthy development and, like the 11 CEP Principles, provide an effective way to conceptualize PYD (Roth & Brooks-Gunn, 2003). As with the CEP principles, however, it remains unclear how to translate the 5C framework into specific youth development programs (though see Napolitano, Bowers, Gestsdóttir, & Chase, 2011).

### Child Development Project

The Child Development Project (CDP) is a comprehensive, elementary-school program designed to enhance children's prosocial development by strengthening the sense of community in school. The program's basic premise is that children have fundamental needs for autonomy, competence, and belonging, and the extent to which a school community satisfies these needs influences whether students identify with and internalize the school's goals, values, and norms. This premise, broadly referred to as the "Caring School Communities" approach to character education by Lapsley and Narvaez (2006), is well documented in psychology (e.g., Hamre & Pianta, 2001; Juvonen, 2006; Roseth, Johnson, & Johnson, 2008) and character education in particular (e.g., Battistich, 2008; Noddings, 2002). Readers interested in a more comprehensive review of the CDP's theoretical roots and program elements are directed to Battistich (2008).

To promote a sense of community, CDP students work collaboratively, giving and receiving help from cross-age buddies, and participating in school-wide projects. CDP teachers also hold class meetings to discuss and reflect upon prosocial values such as fairness and social responsibility. Three separate longitudinal trials support the efficacy

of this approach, with CDP students demonstrating more prosocial behavior in the classroom compared to controls (Solomon, Watson, Delucchi, Schaps, & Battistich, 1988), enhanced conflict resolution skills (Battistich, Solomon, Watson, Solomon, & Schaps, 1989), and more democratic values (Solomon, Watson, Schaps, Battistich, & Solomon, 1990). CDP students were also more likely than controls to view their classrooms as communities (Battistich, Solomon, Watson, & Schaps, 1996). In follow-up testing, intermediate-school teachers also rated former CDP students higher than former control students in conflict resolution skills, self-esteem, and popularity (Solomon, Watson, & Battistich, 2002).

While the CDP is "undoubtedly among the most thoroughly and rigorously evaluated programs in the character education literature" (Battistich, 2008, p. 337), it should be noted that What Works Clearinghouse (WWC), maintained by the U.S. Department of Education's Institute for Educational Sciences (IES), reports that the CDP has only "potentially positive effects on behaviors" and "no discernable effects" on knowledge, attitudes, values, and academic achievement (U.S. Department of Education, 2007). The WWC's conclusions are based on recalculating the statistical significance of the CDP's various outcomes after controlling for the clustered nature of the data (e.g., within classrooms or schools) and for multiple comparisons. Recognizing this limitation, Battistich (2008) notes that the direction and size of the observed differences between CDP and comparison schools remain unchanged and that follow-up studies suggest that the effects of the CDP on school-related, social, and moral outcomes in elementary school remained through the middle-school years. This is compelling evidence and one can only hope that funding will be made available for the CDP to be studied in a fully randomized experiment involving a large number of diverse schools.

### Social-Emotional Learning

Another conceptual framework for character education is social-emotional learning (Lapsley & Narvaez, 2006). Like the PYD framework, social-emotional learning focuses on the development of competencies that enhance positive outcomes and prevent problems (Durlak, Weissberg, Dymnicki, Taylor, & Schellinger, 2011).

The Collaborative to Advance Social and Emotional Learning has identified four key social-emotional learning competencies that overlap with character education: self–other awareness (e.g., perspective taking), self-regulation (e.g., goal setting, emotional regulation, perseverance), decision making (awareness of social norms, critical thinking, taking responsibility), and social skills (e.g., cooperation, conflict resolution). Social-emotional learning has been shown to be strongly associated with academic outcomes (e.g., Elias, Zins, Graczyk, & Weissberg, 2003) and programs that enhance social-emotional learning competencies have been shown to prevent various problem behaviors (e.g., Wilson, Gottfredson, & Najaka, 2001).

## Service Learning

Service learning is another programmatic approach to character education. Broadly defined as "doing good for others" (Tolman, 2003), service learning is different from community service because it includes specific learning objectives and links service activities to academic curricula (Pritchard, 2002). The basic premise is that service learning provides students with moral lessons about fairness and justice, moral action, and opportunities to develop a sense of community (Hart, 2005). Supporting this approach, student participation in service learning has been shown to increase civic engagement, promote moral-civic identity, and improve grades (e.g., Flanagan, 2004).

## What Works

There are two different accounts of "what works" in character education.

***What Works Clearinghouse.*** Representing a narrow view of the domain, the first is the WWC, established by the U.S. Department of Education and maintained by the IES. According to the IES, what counts as character education are school-based programs (i.e., practice, strategy, or policy) associated with core virtues (e.g., respect, responsibility, fairness, caring, citizenship) and designed to positively influence moral and ethical reasoning, emotions, and behaviors. Programs that focus on a single competency (e.g., conflict resolution) or single risk behaviors (e.g., drug abuse, unsafe sexual behavior) do not count as character education. To be included in the report, the IES also requires that research studies meet specific evidentiary criteria (e.g., conducted during last 20 years, randomized control trial or quasi-experimental study with strong control, measures with adequate reliability, minimal overall and differential attrition). The WWC report was last updated in 2007.

Amazingly, only 13 out of 41 programs met the IES evidentiary criteria to be included in the report and, of these, only two programs were found to have positive effects: The Too Good for Drugs and Violence program was found to have positive effects on high-school students' knowledge, attitudes, and values, and the Positive Action program was found to have positive effects on K-12 students' behavior and academic achievement. Two other programs—Building Decision Skills (combined with service learning) and Too Good for Violence—were found to have potentially positive effects on students' knowledge, attitudes, and values, and five programs (Caring School Community, Connect with Kids, Lions Quest—Skills for Adolescence, Too Good for Drugs, and Too Good for Violence) were found to have potentially positive effects on students' behavior.

***Berkowitz and colleagues.*** Unsatisfied with the IES definition of what counts as character education and their exacting evidentiary standards, Marvin Berkowitz and colleagues have reported their own version of *What Works in Character Education* (Berkowitz, Battistich, & Bier, 2008; Berkowitz & Bier, 2004). Whereas IES only considered programs explicitly involving moral and ethical components, the Berkowitz report defined character education more expansively and also included studies that reported on outcomes of interest to character education. The Berkowitz report also used much less restrictive evidentiary criteria than the IES.

Using this expansive approach, Berkowitz and colleagues identified many more programs demonstrating empirical evidence of effective character education. In fact, only seven of the 33 programs in the Berkowitz report were included in the IES report. Of these 33 programs, 18 were explicitly identified as character education programs, and 27 included some form of social-emotional curricula (e.g., social skills instruction, self-management, decision making). Four broad categories of outcomes were reported: risk behavior, prosocial competencies, school-based outcomes (e.g., academic achievement), and social-emotional functioning. And strong and moderate support for the effectiveness of different programs was found for all of these outcomes, though the pattern of results varied by program and specific outcome. Some of the programs deemed effective by Berkowitz et al. that were not included in IES' WWC included (but were not limited to) the CDP, Just Communities, Moral Dilemma Discussion, PYD, and the Seattle Social Development Project.

Resolving the differences between the IES and Berkowitz et al. reports is a matter for another day. For now, what both reports suggest is that the evidence for effective character education is quite thin.

## Summary

In sum, this section reviewed six programmatic approaches to moral-character education. Three of these approaches represented conceptual frameworks rather than specific programs (Character Education Partnership, Educating for Character, and PYD), and only two programs have been extensively studied (4-H study of PYD, CDP). Social-emotional learning and service learning reflect an expansive approach to character education, as neither explicitly involves ethical considerations but have been shown to influence outcomes of interest to character educators. Finally, what works in character education clearly depends on how one defines the domain and what standards one uses for evidence.

## Conclusions

Despite broad agreement about the importance of moral and character education, many theoretical and practical questions remain about what it is, how it occurs, and the efficacy of educational programs. These questions have deep philosophical and religious roots that have influenced developmental psychologists' questions about where morality and character come from, and educational psychologists' questions about whether morality and character can be taught.

This chapter makes clear that educational and developmental processes are equally important when considering how morality and character are learned and taught. Historically, character and moral education represented distinct paradigms. Traditional conceptions of character development and education emphasized habit formation and direct socialization, while more recent efforts have focused on personality development. Historically, moral development and associated educational approaches focused narrowly on cognition and the way youth judge right and wrong (e.g., Piaget, Kohlberg) and differentiate between moral, social, and personal conventions (e.g., Turiel). Kohlberg especially defined moral development exclusively in terms of universal (Kantian) ethics.

More recently, a new era of scholarship has tried to move beyond historic divisions by taking an integrative approach to conceptions of morality and character. This integrative approach requires a meta-theoretical conception of where moral character comes from, as exemplified by the relational developmental systems perspective. The integrative approach has also led to more complete models of the moral person in which both moral and non-moral components are thought to influence moral character. As illustrated by Kochanska's work on conscience development, the integrative approach has shown that moral character is neither taught by socialization (e.g., caregivers, parents, teachers) nor passively caught by youth through experience. Instead, developmental relational systems theory and a growing body of evidence suggest that moral character is more accurately conceptualized as *brought, taught, and caught*. Even infants are predisposed to grasp matters of right and wrong, and children's temperament interacts with adult socialization and other relevant experiences in a reciprocal and dynamic process. This realization highlights the plasticity of moral character and the extent to which it is dynamically stable within specific ecologies. For moral-character education, it also suggests that morality and character involve an alignment between youth strengths and ecological resources.

The integrative approach to moral-character education represents an important first step in overcoming the conceptual and professional obstacles that, historically, have prevented theory development and determining best practice (cf. Lerner et al., 2011). But much work remains to be done, as disagreements remain about what counts as moral-character education and what works when comparing different programmatic approaches. There also remains little explicit linkage between models of developmental change and specific program components and, as a result, theory, research, and practice remain largely disconnected. Lerner et al. (2011) describe this lack of integration as the "fundamental problematic" (p. 57) within the field of PYD, and the same can be said of the moral-character education field. After all, it is only through integrating theory, research, and practice that educational psychologists can know what specific developmental and educative features relate to specific outcomes for specific youth in specific ecological contexts.

## Note

1.  I want to thank Lyn Corno, Darcia Narvaez, and Richard Lerner for their thoughtful reviews of previous drafts of this chapter. I also want to thank Timothy Knox, who first helped me to appreciate what "ought" and "is" imply for education.

## References

Allport, G. W. (1937). *Personality: A psychological interpretation.* New York: Holt.

Althof, W., & Berkowitz, M. W. (2006). Moral education and character education: Their relationship and roles in citizenship education. *Journal of Moral Education, 35,* 495–518.

Arthur, J. (2008). Traditional approaches to character education in Britain and America. In L. Nucci & D. Narvaez (Eds.), *Handbook of moral and character education* (pp. 80–98). New York, NY: Routledge.

Bandura, A. (1986). *Social foundations of thoughts and action.* Englewood Cliffs, NJ: Prentice-Hall.

Battistich, V. (2008). The child development project: Creating caring school communities. In L. Nucci & D. Narvaez (Eds.), *Handbook of moral and character education* (pp. 328–351). New York, NY: Routledge.

Battistich, V., Solomon, D., Watson, M., & Schaps, E. (1996). *Enhancing students' engagement, participation and democratic values and attitudes.* Ann Arbor, MI: Society for the Psychological Study of Social Issues.

Battistich, V., Solomon, D., Watson, M., Solomon, J., & Schaps, E. (1989). Effects of an elementary school program to enhance prosocial behavior on children's social problem-solving skills and strategies. *Journal of Applied Developmental Psychology, 10,* 147–169.

Beland, K. (2003, Series Ed.) *Eleven principles sourcebook: How to achieve quality character education in K-12 schools.* Washington, DC: Character Education Partnership.

Berkowitz, M. W. (2002). The science of character education. In W. Damon (Ed.), *Bringing in a new era in character education* (pp. 43–63). Stanford, CA: Hoover Institution Press.

Berkowitz, M. W. (2012). Moral and character education. In K. R. Harris, S. Graham, & T. Urdan (Eds.), *Educational psychology handbook, Vol. 2. Individual differences and cultural and contextual factors* (pp. 247–264). Washington, D.C.: American Psychological Association.

Berkowitz, M. W., Battistich, V. A., & Bier, M. C. (2008). What works in character education: What is known and what needs to be known. In L. Nucci & D. Narvaez (Eds.), *Handbook of moral and character education* (pp. 414–431). New York, NY: Routledge.

Berkowitz, M. W., & Bier, M. (2004). *What works in character education: A research-driven guide for educators.* Washington, DC: Character Education Partnership.

Berkowitz, M. W., & Gibbs, J. (1983). Measuring the developmental features of moral discussion. *Merrill-Palmer Quarterly, 29,* 399–410.

Blasi, A. (1990). How should psychologists define morality? Or, The negative side effects of philosophy's influence on psychology. In T. Wren (Ed.), *The moral domain: Essays on the ongoing discussion between philosophy and the social sciences* (pp. 38–70). Cambridge, MA: MIT Press.

Blasi, A. (2005). Moral character: A psychological approach. In D. K. Lapsley & F. C. Power (Eds.), *Character psychology and character education* (pp. 18–35). Notre Dame, IN: University of Notre Dame Press.

Boom, J., Brugman, D., & van der Heijden, P. G. (2001). Hierarchical structure of moral stages assessed by a sorting task. *Child Development, 72,* 535–548.

Bronfenbrenner, U., & Morris, P. A. (2006). The bioecological model of human development. In W. Damon (Series Ed.) & R. M. Lerner (Vol. Ed.), *Handbook of child psychology: Vol. 1. Theoretical models of human development* (6th ed., pp. 793–828). Hoboken, NJ: Wiley.

Burton, R., & Kunce, L. (1995). Behavioral models of moral development: A brief history and integration. In W. Kurtines & J. Gewirtz (Eds.), *Moral development: An introduction* (pp. 141–171). Needham Heights, MA: Allyn & Bacon.

Carpendale, J. I. M. (2000). Kohlberg and Piaget on stages of moral reasoning. *Developmental Review, 20,* 181–205.

Carr, D. (1991). *Educating the virtues: An essay on the philosophical psychology of moral and education.* London, UK: Routledge.

Carr, D. (2011). Values, virtues, and professional development in education and teaching. *International Journal of Educational Research, 50,* 171–176.

Catalano, R. F., Berglund, M. L., Ryan, J. A., Lonczak, H. S., & Hawkins, J. D. (2004). Positive youth development in the United States: Research findings on evaluations of youth development programs. *Annals of the American Academy of Political and Social Science.* [*Special issue*] *Positive Development: Realizing the Potential of Youth, 591,* 98–124.

Cawley, M. J., Martin, J. E., & Johnson, J. A. (2000). A virtues approach to personality. *Personality and Individual Differences, 28,* 997–1013.

Colby, A., & Kohlberg, L. (1987). *The measurement of moral judgment: Vol. 1. Theoretical foundations and research validation.* New York, NY: Cambridge University Press.

Colby, A., Kohlberg, L., Gibbs, J., & Lieberman, N. (1983). A longitudinal study of moral judgment. *Monographs of the Society for Research in Child Development, 48*(1–2, Serial No. 200).

Cronbach, L. J. (1971). Validity. In R. L. Thorndike (Ed.), *Educational measurement* (pp. 443–507). Washington, DC: American Council on Education.

Cunningham, C. A. (2005). A certain and reasoned art: The rise and fall of character education in America. In D. K. Lapsley & F. C. Power (Eds.), *Character psychology and character education* (pp. 166–200). Notre Dame, IN: University of Notre Dame Press.

Damon, W. (1988). *The moral child: Nurturing children's natural moral growth.* New York: The Free Press.

Damon, W. (Ed.). (2002). *Bringing in a new era in character education.* Stanford, CA: Hoover Institute Press.

Desteno, D., & Valdesolo, P. (2011). *Out of character: Surprising truths about the liar, cheat, sinner (and saint) lurking in all of us.* New York: Three Rivers Press.

Dewey, J. (1908). *Moral principles in education.* Boston: Houghton Mifflin.

Durlak, J. A., Weissberg, R. P., Dymnicki, A. B., Taylor, R. D., & Schellinger, K. B. (2011). The impact of enhancing students' social and emotional learning: A meta-analysis of school based universal interventions. *Child Development, 82,* 405–432.

Eisenberg, N., Fabes, R. A., & Spinrad, T. L. (2006). Prosocial development. In W. Damon & R. M. Lerner (Series Eds.) & N. Eisenberg (Vol. Ed.), *Handbook of child psychology: Vol. 3. Social, emotional, and personality development* (6th ed., pp. 646–718). New York, NY: Wiley.

Elias, M. J., Zins, J. E., Graczyk, P. A., & Weissberg, R. P. (2003). Implementation, sustainability, and scaling up of social-emotional and academic innovations in public schools. *School Psychology Review, 32,* 303–319.

Fehr, E., Bernhard, H., & Rockenbach, B. (2008). Egalitarianism in young children. *Nature, 454,* 1079–1083.

Flanagan, C. (2004). Volunteerism, leadership, political socialization and civic engagement. In R. Lerner & L. Steinberg (Eds.), *Handbook of adolescent psychology* (2nd ed., pp. 721–746). New York: Wiley.

Freund, A. M., & Baltes, P. B. (2002). Life-management strategies of selection, optimization and compensation: Measurement by self-report and construct validity. *Journal of Personality and Social Psychology, 82,* 642–662.

Gilligan, C. (1982). *In a different voice: Psychological theory and women's development.* Cambridge, MA: Harvard University Press.

Gummerum, M., Keller, M., Takezawa, M., & Mata, J. (2008). To give or not to give: Children and adolescents' sharing and moral negotiations in economic decision situations. *Child Development, 79,* 562–576.

Hamre, B. K., & Pianta, R. C. (2001). Early teacher–child relationships and the trajectory of children's school outcomes through eighth grade. *Child Development, 72,* 625–638.

Hardy, S. & Carlo, G. (2005). Identity as a source of moral motivation. *Human Development, 48,* 222–256.

Harkness, S., Edwards, C. P., & Super, C. M. (1981). Social roles and moral reasoning. A case study in a rural African community. *Developmental Psychology, 34,* 1220–1232.

Hart, D. (2005). The development of moral identity. *Nebraska Symposium on Motivation, 51,* 165–196.

Helwig, C. C., & Turiel, E. (2002). Children's social and moral reasoning. In P. K. Smith & C. H. Hart (Eds.), *Blackwell handbook of childhood social development.* Oxford: Blackwell.

Hoffman, M. (2000). *Empathy and moral development: Implications for caring and justice.* Cambridge, UK: Cambridge University Press.

Jaffee, S., & Hyde, J. S. (2000). Gender differences in moral orientation: A meta-analysis. *Psychological Bulletin, 126,* 703–726.

Juvonen, J. J. (2006). Sense of belonging, social bonds, and school functioning. In P. A. Alexander & P. H. Winne (Eds.), *Handbook of educational psychology* (pp. 655–674). Mahwah, NJ: Erlbaum.

Kaplan, U., Crockett, C. E., & Tivnan, T. (2014). Moral motivation of college students through multiple developmental structures: Evidence of intrapersonal variability in a complex dynamic system. *Motivation & Emotion, 38,* 336–352.

Killen, M., & de Waal, F. (2000). The evolution and development of morality. In F. Aureli and F. de Waal (Eds.), *Natural conflict resolution.* Berkeley, CA: University of California Press.

Kochanska, G. (2002). Committed compliance, moral self and internalization: A mediated model. *Developmental Psychology, 38,* 339–351.

Kochanska, G., Aksan, N. & Carlson, J. J. (2005). Temperament, relationships, and young children's receptive cooperation with their parents. *Developmental Psychology, 41,* 648–660.

Kochanska, G., Aksan, N., Prisco, T. R., & Adams, E. E. (2008). Mother–child and father–child mutually responsive orientation in the first two years and children's outcomes at preschool age: Mechanisms of influence. *Child Development, 79,* 30–44.

Kochanska, G., Barry, R. A., Jimenez, N. B., Hollatz, A. L., & Woodard, J. (2009). Guilt and effortful control: Two mechanisms that prevent disruptive developmental trajectories. *Journal of Personality and Social Psychology, 97,* 322–333.

Kochanska, G., Barry, R. A., Stellern, S. A., & O'Bleness, J. J. (2009). Early attachment organization moderates the parent–child mutually coercive pathway to children's antisocial conduct. *Child Development, 80,* 1288–1300.

Kochanska, G., Coy, K. C., & Murray, K. T. (2001). The development of self-regulation in the first four years of life. *Child Development, 72,* 1091–1111.

Kohlberg, L. (1984). Moral stages and moralization: The cognitive developmental approach. In L. Kohlberg (Ed.), *The psychology of moral development: The nature and validity of moral stages* (pp. 170–205). San Francisco, CA: Harper & Row.

Kohlberg, L., & Mayer, R. (1972). Development as the aim of education. *Harvard Educational Review, 42,* 449–496.

Kristjánsson, K. (2009). Does moral psychology need moral theory? The case of self-research. *Theory & Psychology, 19,* 816–836.

Lapsley, D. K. (2006). Moral stage theory. In M. Killen & J. Smetana (Eds.), *Handbook of moral development* (pp. 37–66). Mahwah, NJ: Erlbaum.

Lapsley, D. K., & Carlo, G. (2014). Moral development at the crossroads: New trends and possible futures. *Developmental Psychology, 50,* 1–7.

Lapsley, D. K., & Narvaez, D. (2005). Moral psychology at the crossroads. In D. K. Lapsley & F. C. Power (Eds.), *Character psychology and character education* (pp. 18–35). Notre Dame, IN: University of Notre Dame Press.

Lapsley, D. K., & Narvaez, D. (2006). Character education. In W. Damon & R. Lerner (Series Eds.), A. Renninger & I. Siegel (Vol. Eds.), *Handbook of child psychology: Vol. 4. Child psychology in practice* (6th ed., pp. 248–296). New York, NY: Wiley.

Lapsley, D. K., & Narvaez, D. (2008). "Psychologized morality" and its discontents, or, do good fences make good neighbors? In F. Oser & W. Veugelers (Eds.), *Getting involved: Global citizenship development and sources of moral value* (pp. 279–292). Rotterdam, The Netherlands: Sense Publishers.

Lapsley, D. K., & Yeager, D. (2013). Moral character education. In I. Weiner (Series Ed.), W. Reynolds (Ed.), & G. Miller (Ed.), *Handbook of psychology: Vol. 7: Educational psychology* (pp. 147–177). New York, NY: Wiley.

Lerner, R. M. (2004). *Liberty: Thriving and civic engagement among American youth.* Thousand Oaks, CA: Sage Publications.

Lerner, R. M., Lerner, J. V., Almerigi, J., Theokas, C., Phelps, E., Gestsdottir, S., et al. (2005). Positive youth development, participation in community youth development programs, and community contributions of fifth grade adolescents: Findings from the first wave of the 4-H Study of Positive Youth Development. *Journal of Early Adolescence, 25,* 17–71.

Lerner, R. M., Lerner, J. V., Lewin-Bizan, S., Bowers, E. P., Boyd, M. J., et al. (2011). Positive youth development: Processes, program, and problematics. *Journal of Early Adolescence, 6,* 41–64.

Lickona, T. (1991). *Educating for character: How our schools can teach respect and responsibility.* New York, NY: Bantam.

Lickona, T. (2004). *Character matters.* New York: Touchstone.

Lickona, T., & Davidson, M. (2004). *Smart and good high schools: Developing excellence and ethics for success in school, work and beyond.* Cortland, NY: Center for the 4th and 5th Rs (Respect and Responsibility).

Magnusson, D., & Stattin, H. (2006). The person in context: A holistic-interactionistic approach. In W. Damon (Series Ed.) & R. M. Lerner (Vol. Ed.), *Handbook of child psychology* (6th ed., pp. 400–464). Hoboken, NJ: John Wiley.

Miller, J. G., & Bersoff, D. M. (1995). Development in the context of everyday family relationships: Culture, interpersonal morality, and adaptation. In M. Killen & D. Hart (Eds.), *Morality in everyday life: Developmental perspectives* (pp. 259–282). New York: Cambridge University Press.

Napolitano, C. M., Bowers, E. P., Gestsdóttir, S., & Chase, P. (2011). The development of intentional self-regulation in adolescence: Describing, explaining, and optimizing its link to positive youth development. In R. M. Lerner, J. V. Lerner, & J. B. Benson (Eds.), *Advances in child development and behavior* (pp. 17–36). London, England: Elsevier.

Narvaez, D., & Lapsley, D. K. (2009). Moral identity, moral functioning and the development of moral identity. In D. M. Bartels, C. W. Bauman, L. J. Skitka, & D. L. Medin (Eds.), *Moral judgment and decision-making: The psychology of learning and motivation: Advances in research and theory* (pp. 237–274). San Diego, CA: Elsevier Academic Press.

Noddings, N. (2002). *Educating moral people.* New York: Teachers College Press.

Nucci, L. (2001). *Education in the moral domain.* Cambridge, UK: Cambridge University Press.

Nucci, L. P., & Turiel, E. (1993). God's word, religious rules, and their relation to Christian and Jewish children's concepts of morality. *Child Development, 64,* 1475–1491.

Nucci, L. P., & Weber, E. K. (1995). Social interactions in the home and the development of young children's conceptions of the personal. *Child Development, 66,* 1438–1452.

Overton, W. F. (2010). Life-span development: Concepts and issues. In R. M. Lerner (Ed-in-chief) & W. F. Overton (Vol. Ed.), *The handbook of life-span development: Vol. 1. Cognition, biology, and methods* (pp. 1–29). Hoboken, NJ: Wiley.

Peterson, C., & Seligman, M. (2004). *Character strengths and virtues: A classification and handbook.* Washington, DC: American Psychological Association.

Piaget, J. (1932/1965). *The moral judgment of the child.* New York, NY: Free Press.

Plomin, R. (1986). *Development, genetics, and psychology.* Hillsdale, NJ: Erlbaum, Power & Makogon.

Power, F. C., & Makogon, T. (1995). The just community approach to care. *Journal for a Just and Caring Education, 2,* 9–24.

Pritchard, I. (2002). Community service and service-learning in America: The state of the art. In A. Furco & S. H. Billig (Eds.), *Service learning: The essence of the pedagogy* (pp. 3–20). Greenwich, CT: Information Age Press.

Rest, J., Narvaez, D., Bebeau, M. J., & Thoma, S. J. (1999). *Postconventional moral thinking: A neo-Kohlbergian approach.* Mahwah, NJ: Lawrence Erlbaum Associates.

Roseth, C. J., Johnson, D. W., & Johnson, R. T. (2008). Promoting early adolescents' achievement and peer relationships: The effects of cooperative, competitive, and individualistic goal structures. *Psychological Bulletin, 134,* 223–246.

Roth, J. L., & Brooks-Gunn, J. (2003). What exactly is a youth development program? Answers from research and practice. *Applied Developmental Science, 7,* 94–111.

Roth, J., Brooks-Gunn, J., Murray, L., & Foster, W. (1998). Promoting healthy adolescents: Synthesis of youth development program evaluations. *Journal of Research on Adolescence, 8,* 423–459.

Ryan, K., & Bohlin, K. E. (1999). *Building character in schools: Practical ways to bring moral instruction to life.* San Francisco, CA: Jossey-Bass.

Ryan, K., & Lickona, T. (Eds.). (1992). *Character development in schools and beyond.* Washington, DC: Council for Research in Values and Philosophy.

Sizer, T. R., & Sizer, N. F. (1999). *The students are watching: Schools and the moral contract.* Boston, MA: Beacon Press.

Skinner, B. F. (1971). *Beyond freedom and dignity.* New York: Knopf.

Smetana, J. G. (2006). Social domain theory: Consistencies and variations in children's moral and social judgments. In M. Killen & J. G. Smetana (Eds.), *Handbook of moral development* (pp. 119–153). Mahwah, NJ: Erlbaum.

Smetana, J., & Braeges, J. L. (1990). The development of toddlers' moral and conventional judgments. *Merrill–Palmer Quarterly, 36,* 329–346.

Snarey, J., & Keljo, K. (1991). The cross-cultural expansion of moral development theory. *Handbook of moral behavior and development* (Vol. 1, pp. 395-424). Hillsdale, NJ: Erlbaum.

Solomon, D., Watson, M., & Battistich, V. (2002). Teaching and school effects on moral/prosocial development. In V. Richardson (Ed.), *Handbook of research on teaching* (pp. 566–603). Washington, DC: American Educational Research Association.

Solomon, D., Watson, M., Delucchi, I., Schaps, E., & Battistich, V. (1988). Enhancing children's prosocial behavior in the classroom. *American Educational Research Journal, 25,* 527–554.

Solomon, D., Watson, M., Schaps, E., Battistich, V, & Solomon, J. (1990). Cooperative learning as part of a comprehensive classroom program designed to promote prosocial development. In S. Sharan (Ed.), *Cooperative learning: Theory and research* (pp. 231–260). New York: Praeger.

Steutel, J., & Spiecker, B. (2004). Cultivating sentimental dispositions through Aristotelian habituation. *Journal of the Philosophy of Education, 38,* 531–549.

Thelen, E., & Smith, L. B. (2006). Dynamic systems theories. In W. Damon (Series Ed.) & R.M. Lerner (Vol. Ed.), *Handbook of child psychology: Vol. 1. Theoretical models of human development* (6th ed., pp. 258–312). Hoboken, NJ: Wiley.

Theokas, C., & Lerner, R. M. (2006). Observed ecological assets in families, schools, and neighborhoods: Conceptualization, measurement and relations with positive and negative developmental outcomes. *Applied Developmental Science, 10,* 61–74.

Tichy, M. L., Johnson, D. W., Johnson, R. T., & Roseth, C. J. (2010). The impact of constructive controversy on moral development. *Journal of Applied Social Psychology, 40,* 765–787.

Tolman, J. (2003). *Providing opportunities for moral action: A guide to Principle 5 of the eleven principles of effective character education.* Washington, DC: Character Education Partnership.

Tomlinson-Keasey, C., & Keasey, C. B. (1974). The mediating role of cognitive development in moral judgment. *Child Development, 45,* 291–298.

Turiel, E. (1983). *The development of social knowledge: Morality and convention.* Cambridge, UK: Cambridge University Press.

Turiel, E. (1998). The development of morality. In W. Damon (Ed.), *Handbook of child psychology* (5th ed.). Volume 3. N. Eisenberg (Ed.), *Social, emotional, and personality development* (pp. 863–932). New York: Wiley.

Turiel, E. (2006). The development of morality. In W. Damon & R. M. Lerner (Eds.), *Handbook of child psychology* (6th ed.). Volume 3. N. Eisenberg (Ed.), *Social, emotional, and personality development.* New York: Wiley.

Turiel, E., & Wainryb, C. (2000). Social life in culture: Judgments, conflict, and subversion. *Child Development, 71,* 250–256.

U.S. Department of Education, Institute of Education Sciences, What Works Clearinghouse. (April, 2007). *Caring school community (formerly, the child development project).* Retrieved from http://whatworks.ed.gov (accessed 13 March 2015).

Walker, L. (1980). Cognitive and perspective-taking prerequisites for moral development. *Child Development, 51,* 131–139.

Walker, L. J., & Hennig, K. H. (2004). Differing conceptions of moral exemplarity: Just, brave and caring. *Journal of Personality and Social Psychology, 86,* 629–647.

Walker, L. J., Hennig, K. H., & Krettenauer, T. (2000). Parent and peer contexts for children's moral reasoning development. *Child Development, 71,* 1033–1048.

Wilson, D. B., Gottfredson, D. C., & Najaka, S. S. (2001). School-based prevention of problem behaviors: A meta-analysis. *Journal of Quantitative Psychology, 17,* 171–247.

# Part IV

**Building Knowledge and
Subject Matter Expertise**

# 17

# Literacy for Schooling

## Two-Tiered Scaffolding for Learning and Teaching

**IAN A. G. WILKINSON**
The Ohio State University

**JANET S. GAFFNEY**
University of Auckland, New Zealand

Teaching then can be likened to a conversation in which you listen to the speaker carefully before you reply. (Clay, 1985, p. 6)

Like our predecessors, presumably, we saw the invitation to author a chapter in the *Handbook of Educational Psychology* as an opportunity to assay the field and reflect the zeitgeist in literacy research and instruction. In the first volume of the *Handbook,* Hiebert and Raphael (1996) examined the relationship between theories of learning in educational psychology and literacy research and practice. In the second volume, Alvermann, Fitzgerald, and Simpson (2006) took stock of classroom-based, instructional studies of reading, and Graham (2006) reviewed research on writing. In this third volume, our goal is no less noble—to review instructional research in literacy published since the previous edition that has made, or is likely to make, a significant impact on the field. Our hope was to identify practices that have meaningful, sustainable influences on students' literacy learning.

Looking back over the past 30 years of literacy research, we as a community of literacy scholars can take pride in our progress. We have amassed a considerable body of research and theory about literacy learning and teaching and we know, with reasonable surety, what constitutes quality literacy instruction. As is evident in research syntheses such as *Becoming a Nation of Readers* (Anderson, Hiebert, Scott, & Wilkinson, 1985), *Preventing Reading Difficulties in Young Children* (Snow, Burns, & Griffin, 1998), the *Report of the National Reading Panel* (National Institute of Child Health and Human Development, 2000), and the *Report of the National Early Literacy Panel* (National Institute for Literacy, 2008), there is considerable consensus as to what should be the foci of instruction (i.e., oral language skills,

alphabetics, fluency, vocabulary, comprehension, writing) and the teaching practices to be used to improve students' literacy.

The defining challenge of the past decade has been to help teachers implement these practices and adapt them to students' needs. The observation that traditional one-shot professional development workshops are unlikely to lead to substantial or sustained shifts in teachers' practices is common knowledge (Cochran-Smith & Lytle, 1999; Englert & Tarrant, 1995). Consensus is emerging that effective professional development and support for teachers need to include several elements: a focus on subject-matter content and students' learning, opportunities for active learning, coherence with existing standards and curricula, prolonged duration, and collective participation and collaboration (Desimone, 2009). These essential elements have been echoed in numerous other publications on professional development (e.g., Ball & Cohen, 1999; Darling-Hammond, Wei, Andree, Richardson, & Orphanos, 2009; Garet, Porter, Desimone, Birman, & Yoon, 2001). The challenge for literacy scholars over the past decade has been to apply these elements to help teachers implement productive instructional practices, and to evaluate the consequences for students' literacy learning.

To accomplish our goal of identifying the most influential work in our field, and to reflect the zeitgeist, we used *two-tiered scaffolding* (Gaffney & Anderson, 1991) as a theoretical frame to guide our search, analysis, and interpretation of literacy intervention research published over the last decade. This framework proposes two tiers of support for literacy learning and teaching: the support provided to students by a teacher or more capable other, and the support provided to the teacher or more capable other by teacher education, professional development, or some other system of support.

We argue that both tiers of support need to be in place to provide a robust framework for instruction. We further argue that the key to success of two-tiered scaffolding is an interactive relationship between the tiers and movement towards independence at both tiers. Within this framework, we chose to organize our review in terms of four contexts for literacy learning and teaching: one-to-one (i.e., tutoring), small-group, whole-class, and school-wide.

We employed a multipronged approach to identify studies of literacy instruction that embodied two-tiered scaffolding. First, using Gaffney and Anderson's (1991) description of the framework, we identified prototypical studies of two-tiered scaffolding for each instructional context. Second, using these prototypical studies as exemplars, we conducted a manual search for relevant articles published from 2004 (the last year covered by the previous *Handbook*) through June 2014 in ten premier journals that publish research in literacy by educational psychologists: *American Educational Research Journal, British Journal of Educational Psychology, Early Childhood Research Quarterly, The Elementary School Journal, Cognition and Instruction, Journal of Educational Psychology, Journal of Research in Reading, Reading Research Quarterly, Reading and Writing*, and *Scientific Studies of Reading*. Our percent agreement in identifying relevant articles from the manual search, based on two of the journals, was 97%. Third, we conducted searches of the ERIC and PsycINFO databases using the following combination of terms, limiting our search to empirical studies published from 2004 through June 2014: *(intervention OR tutoring) AND (professional development OR coach\*) AND (reading OR writing OR literacy OR oral language OR vocabulary OR comprehension)*. Our percent agreement in identifying relevant studies from titles and abstracts, based on a 10% random sample of records, was 88%. Fourth, we combed the references in reports of relevant studies to identify additional sources.

To be eligible for inclusion in this review, a study had to meet certain criteria. First, it had to be an empirical investigation of an instructional intervention in literacy with students in grades K-12. For our purposes, literacy encompassed reading, writing, and use of oral language, including verbal reasoning, communication and narrative skills, and academic discourse. Second, the study had to be relevant to English-language arts or to social studies or science instruction if the focus was on literacy. Third, the study must have been reported in a government report or peer-reviewed journal published in 2004 or more recently. Fourth, at least two tiers of support for literacy learning had to be in evidence. Most instructional research provides the opportunity to examine tier 1, the interactions between students and a teacher or more capable other. To examine tier 2, we restricted our review to studies in which support was provided to teachers, teacher candidates, parents, volunteers, or peers to develop targeted expertise that was intended to endure beyond the scope of the study. Thus, studies in which researchers carried out the teaching or where the purpose was solely to evaluate a program rather than to enhance the professional learning of teachers or other instructors were excluded from our review.

The purpose of this chapter, then, is to provide a comprehensive coverage of research on literacy for schooling conducted in the United States and abroad that encompasses teacher professional development or support, teaching practices, and student learning within a framework that is consistent with two-tiered scaffolding. In the next section, we describe in more detail the framework proposed by Gaffney and Anderson (1991). We then review studies that embody the framework, organized in terms of four contexts for literacy learning and teaching: tutorial interventions, small-group instruction, whole-class instruction, and school-wide improvement. For each context, we summarize the studies in a table and indicate our judgment of the strength of evidence for effects on student learning. The latter uses a rating system inspired by Slavin (2008) that considers study design, evidence of teacher growth, and magnitude of student outcomes (see Appendix 17.1). For each context, we provide a brief narrative describing exemplary or illustrative studies and our summation of the state of research in the area. We then provide a critique of the research from the perspective of two-tiered scaffolding. We conclude by considering implications for research, policy, and practice.

## Two-Tiered Scaffolding for Learning and Teaching

Scaffolding is a construct proffered by Wood, Bruner, and Ross (1976) and implicit in Vygotsky's (1981) sociocultural theory of development and the notion of the *zone of proximal development*. Social collaboration, which could be verbal, non-verbal, or a combination, between a novice and a more knowledgeable other to promote the learner's increasing independence in challenging tasks is the quintessence of scaffolding. The scaffolding metaphor has been advanced by developmental and cognitive psychologists and featured in many instructional interventions (e.g., Brown, 1985; Clay & Cazden, 1990; Jadallah et al., 2011; Rogoff & Wertsch, 1984; Tharp & Gallimore, 1988; Van Lier, 2007).

Gaffney and Anderson (1991) extended the metaphor by proposing two tiers of support for literacy learning and teaching. The first tier of scaffolding is a teacher or more capable other (e.g., parent, volunteer, peer) providing support for a student. The second tier of scaffolding is the support necessary to assist the teacher or more capable other in supporting a student in a manner consistent with the method located in the first tier. The second tier may encompass teacher education, professional development, or some other system of support (including technology) that facilitates the capacity of the expert.[1]

The two-tiered scaffolding framework has two entailments. The first is that a coherent articulation between the two tiers makes for a robust framework for instruction. Given that the individual in the role of the teacher is the common element across tiers, designing interventions with this assumption in the forefront is not only theoretically, but also practically, sound. We argue that the key to success of two-tiered scaffolding is an interactive relationship between the two tiers—that is, that the methods used to teach students and the processes used to support teachers, or more capable others, in teaching students need to be congruent with and responsive to each other. According to Gaffney and Anderson (1991), in robust interventions the student is the *driver* of both tiers, which enhances the connection between tiers and, hypothetically, the effectiveness of the intervention outcomes for students and teachers. The second entailment is gradual release of responsibility (Pearson & Gallagher, 1983) or handover (Van Lier, 2007). Scaffolding is intended to provide temporary support for learning that gives way to increased independence, enabling individuals to access more advanced learning. Although commonly applied to teaching children, contingent scaffolding is also essential for teaching teachers, teacher candidates, parents, volunteers, and peers to develop understanding and instructional expertise with a new approach, method, or intervention (hence, the demise of the one-shot workshop). Implementers need contingent scaffolding to develop prowess in using novel interventions within teaching contexts. Analogous to teaching interactions with students, the design of tier 2 must account for the gradual and differential uptake of responsibility and facility with innovative interventions on the part of the teacher or more knowledgeable other.

A prototype of two-tiered scaffolding is Reading Recovery (Clay, 2005a, 2005b). This is a school-based literacy intervention in which a cohort of teachers engage in professional learning, meeting weekly over a school year, in sessions facilitated by a teacher leader while simultaneously providing individual tutoring to first-graders with the highest need of support.[2] In each session, discussions are fueled by the teachers' observations and interpretations of real-time interactions of a colleague tutoring a child, with the explicit goal of increasing the momentum of the child's learning by contributing to the colleague's effectiveness. In this way, the two tiers (teacher–child, teacher leader–teacher) are interdependent, with the first tier, school-based, driving the content and learning of the second tier (professional development)—which is not the typical direction of influence in this relationship. At both tiers, responsibility for independent action gradually shifts from expert to novice, that is, from teacher leader to teacher, and from teacher to student. The goal is for both the teacher and the student to function independently at increasingly higher levels of expertise.

## Contexts for Literacy Learning and Teaching

### Tutorial Interventions

In terms of school-based literacy, one-to-one tutoring was the keystone of early-intervention research and practice for students who did not sufficiently benefit from classroom teaching. Juel's (1988) study of the cycle of literacy failure experienced by young learners without the opportunity for assistance across the primary grades catalyzed the tutoring movement. In the first decade, volunteers engaged in after-school and community-based tutoring and teaching assistants (e.g., Title I) provided in-school support. With the expansion of Reading Recovery in North America and the federal requirement that certified teachers provide Title I services, the emphasis shifted from volunteers to preparing teachers and teacher candidates in effective tutoring. Funding in the United States from No Child Left Behind (2001) and its legislative predecessors (i.e., Elementary and Secondary Education Act of 1965; Improving America's Schools Act of 1994) provided the impetus to target funding on the early elementary grades with the goal of prevention rather than remediation. The 18 studies in this section reflect the range of one-to-one tutorial interventions offered by Reading Recovery teachers, classroom teachers, pre-service candidates, and parents and paraprofessionals. We summarize these studies in Table 17.1.

Overall, studies of Reading Recovery addressed the efficiency, effectiveness, and durability of this seasoned intervention. The key features of Reading Recovery that exemplified the origin of two-tiered scaffolding model (Gaffney & Anderson, 1991) endure in the seven U.S. and U.K. studies. Schwartz's (2005) study offers an innovative and robust design for evaluating the intervention and ensuring participation by eligible children. Thirty-seven pairs of at-risk first-graders from the same classrooms were identified by their teachers at the beginning of the school year, and students in each pair were randomly assigned to participate in Reading Recovery either during the first or second half of the year; their performance was also compared with that of high- and low-average students at three points in time across the year. The evidence for "closing the gap" between the students who participated in Reading Recovery and their average peers was clear for the Reading Recovery participants on text reading and writing vocabulary and less apparent on measures of constrained skills (e.g., letter identification). It is noteworthy that 86% of the students in the second intake made little progress in text reading during the first half of the year.

Findings from Burroughs-Lange and Douetil's (2007) study suggest a promising avenue of research on the impact of tutorial interventions on system-level improvement. They compared the literacy outcomes over 1 year in schools in poor urban settings implementing Reading Recovery ($n = 21$) with those implementing an alternative intervention ($n = 21$). Their results suggest that the impact of professional development for tutoring may permeate literacy practices in classrooms and schools.

Although small in scale, an extension of the Interactive Strategies Approach (Gelzheiser, Scanlon, Vellutino, Hallgren-Flynn, & Schatschneider (2011) is exemplary of two-tiered scaffolding. In the Gelzheiser et al. (2011) study, five teachers individually tutored five fourth-graders with individual education plans for 40 minutes daily for a half-year each. The students had not responded to classroom or small-group instruction. An extended interactive strategies approach (ISA-X) that comprised reading, discussion, and writing of social-studies texts was the target intervention. In addition to 5 days of concentrated professional development prior to the tutoring, the content of the subsequent workshop days and on-site coaching derived from the researchers' interactions with the teachers and analysis of audio- and video-taped lessons. Fidelity of implementation was monitored

**Table 17.1   Two-tiered Scaffolding Studies of Individual Tutorial Interventions**

| Reading Recovery | Intervention (Tier 1) | Professional Development (PD)/Support (Tier 2) | Quality of Articulation | Release of Responsibility | Strength of Evidence |
|---|---|---|---|---|---|
| Bufalino et al. (2010) | Reading Recovery / Gr1 | Yearlong, weekly PD sessions / in-school support | Strong | P → T<br>T → S | Moderate |
| Burroughs-Lange & Douetil (2007) | Reading Recovery / alternative / Yr1 | Yearlong, weekly PD sessions / in-school support | Strong | No indication | Moderate |
| Fitzgerald & Ramsbotham (2004) | Reading Recovery / Gr1 | Yearlong, weekly PD sessions / in-school support | Strong | No indication | Limited |
| Hurry & Sylva (2007) | Reading Recovery phonological / Yr2 | Yearlong, bimonthly sessions / in-school support | Strong | P → T<br>T → S | Moderate |
| Kelly et al. (2008) | Reading Recovery / Gr1 | Yearlong, weekly PD sessions / in-school support | Strong | P → T<br>T → S | Limited |
| Schwartz (2005) | Reading Recovery / Gr1 | Yearlong, weekly PD sessions / in-school support | Strong | P → T<br>T → S | Moderate |

| Teacher Interventions | Intervention (Tier 1) | Professional Development/Support (Tier 2) | Quality of Articulation | Release of Responsibility | Strength of Evidence |
|---|---|---|---|---|---|
| Atkinson & Colby (2006) | Reading clinic / elementary | Grad course  feedback on tutoring / emails | Strong | P → T<br>T → S | Insufficient |
| Ehri et al. (2007) | Reading rescue / Gr1 | 30 hours PD (initial, distributed) / in-school support / peer coaching | Weak | No indication | Moderate |
| Gelzheiser et al. (2011) | Interactive strategies approach-ext. / Gr4 | 48 hours PD (initial, midyear) / on-site coaching / discussion of videos / emails | Strong | T → S | Strong |
| Vernon-Feagans et al. (2013) | Targeted reading intervention / GrK&1 | 18 hours PD (initial) / biweekly webcam coaching | Strong | No indication | Moderate |

| Pre-service Teachers | Intervention (Tier 1) | Professional Development/Support (Tier 2) | Quality of Articulation | Release of Responsibility | Strength of Evidence |
|---|---|---|---|---|---|
| Al Otaiba & Lake (2007) | TAILS / Gr2 | 6 hours PD on TAILS and DIBELS / in-school support—America Reads' coordinators | Weak | No indication | Insufficient |
| Al Otaiba et al. (2012) | TAILS and Book Buddies / GrK&1 | Early literacy course and fieldwork | Weak | No indication | Limited |
| Spear-Swerling & Brucker (2004) | Tutoring in reading and spelling / Gr2 | 6 hours language arts course on word structure / on-site supervision | Weak | No indication | Limited |
| Spear-Swerling (2009) | Tutoring program / Gr2 | Eight weekly sessions / in-class support-teacher leader | Strong | No indication | Limited |

| Parents & Paraprofessionals | Intervention (Tier 1) | Professional Development/Support (Tier 2) | Quality of Articulation | Release of Responsibility | Strength of Evidence |
|---|---|---|---|---|---|
| Brown et al. (2005) | Next Steps / Gr2&3 | 20 hours PD (distributed), in-class coaching by lead trainer, on-site support | Strong | P → Para/T<br>Para/T → S | Moderate |
| Chow et al. (2010) | Parent–child / dialogic reading / GrK | 1 hour (initial), biweekly phone contacts | None | Parent → Child | Limited |
| Levin & Aram (2012) | Mother–child dyadic activities / 5–6-year-olds | Group-specific workshop (initial) / weekly home visits | Strong | P → Mother<br>Mother → Child | Limited |
| Sylva et al. (2008) | SPOKES Incredible Years + literacy / 5–6-yr-olds | 30 hours Incredible Years (distrib.) + home visit / 25 hours literacy (distrib.) / 15 hours top up (distrib.) | Weak | No indication | Limited |

P = provider; T = teacher; S = student; TAILS = Tutor-Assisted Intensive Learning Strategies; DIBELS = Dynamic Indicators of Basic Early Literacy Skills; SPOKES = Supporting Parents on Kids Education in Schools.

on key intervention components. The teachers' focus on students' independence was a major theme of the professional development. In fact, a stated goal of the professional development was "how to scaffold students and to gradually release responsibility for strategy use to students" (p. 291). Results showed a large, statistically significant effect ($d = 1.68$)

on measures of basic reading skills, text-reading accuracy, and comprehension, though not on standardized measures ($d = 0.06$).

***Summation.***   Given the historical role that individual tutoring has played in literacy learning, especially for young children who experience difficulty in getting their learning underway in school, we expected a more sophisticated paradigm of research to have evolved. Exemplary studies of tutorial interventions are rare, however, with Gelzheiser et al.'s (2011) study being the sole standout in this category. The studies of Reading Recovery and other teacher interventions represent a kaleidoscope array, each with a different focus. Nonetheless, a significant pattern in this body of research is the extensive nature of the professional development provided prior to intervention and distributed throughout implementation, combined with ongoing teaching support. Clearly, the days of one-shot workshops have waned, at least in terms of published research. The status of research on pre-service teachers is of greatest concern, given the importance of preparing teachers with literacy expertise and the ongoing challenges of accountability for teacher education. Perhaps reflecting the dominant influence of coursework and separation from teaching that all too often typifies pre-service education, the design of field experiences begs for greater coherence with coursework and a clear route for the teaching of children to feed into the course sessions to facilitate the development of teachers' flexibility in responding, especially in one-to-one tutoring. In the case of the studies of pre-service teachers, one might ask the question, who is the tutoring serving?

### Small-Group Instruction

We located only 11 studies of small-group instruction in literacy that fit the two-tiered scaffolding framework. These are summarized in Table 17.2. We grouped these into four categories: comprehensive programs involving small-group instruction, small-group instruction as a supplement to classroom reading instruction, tutoring in small groups, and instructional activities to enhance the quality of oral group discourse. Most studies targeted students in the early grades and students who, for reasons of poverty, language, and the like, were at risk of literacy failure.

**Table 17.2  Two-tiered Scaffolding Studies of Small-group Instruction**

| Comprehensive Instruction | Intervention (Tier 1) | Professional Development/Support (Tier 2) | Quality of Articulation | Release of Responsibility | Strength of Evidence |
|---|---|---|---|---|---|
| Estrada (2005) | Five standards / Gr1 | Seminars / collaboration / coaching | Strong | P → T  T → S | Limited* |
| Frost & Sorenson (2007) | EMMA / Gr3 | Training / weekly and monthly meetings / personal web-based guidance | Strong | P → T  T → S | Insufficient |
| Klingner et al. (2004) | CSR / Gr4 | 6 hours (initial) / in-class support / materials | Weak | T → S | Insufficient |
| Menzies et al. (2008) | Early reading / Gr1 | Weekly grade-level meetings / bimonthly staff meetings / ongoing assessment | Weak | No indication | Insufficient |

| Supplemental Instruction | Intervention (Tier 1) | Professional Development/Support (Tier 2) | Quality of Articulation | Release of Responsibility | Strength of Evidence |
|---|---|---|---|---|---|
| Denton et al. (2010) | Responsive reading / Gr1 | 18 hours (initial) year 1 / 6 hours (initial) year 2 / 12 hours follow-up each year / some coaching (various) | Weak | T → S | Strong |
| Harris et al. (2015) | Self-regulated strategy dev. writing / Gr2 | 12–14 hours (2 days in teacher teams) / in-class support / materials | Weak | P → T  T → S | Limited |
| Mathes et al. (2005) | Responsive reading or proactive reading / Gr1 | 42 hours (initial) year 1 / 12 hours (initial) year 2 / monthly meetings each year / coaching | Strong | T → S (responsive reading) | Strong |
| Vaughn et al. (2006) | English early reading / Gr1 | 18 hours (initial, distributed) / meetings / coaching | Weak | No indication | Strong |

| Tutoring in Groups | Intervention (Tier 1) | Professional Development/Support (Tier 2) | Quality of Articulation | Release of Responsibility | Strength of Evidence |
|---|---|---|---|---|---|
| Iversen et al. (2005) | Modified reading recovery / Gr1 | Weekly 2 hours in-service | Strong | T → S | Limited |
| Nesselrodt & Alger (2005) | Academic tutoring / Gr7–8 | 3–4.5+ hours (initial, sometimes distributed) / supervision / materials | Weak | No indication | Insufficient |

| Group Discourse | Intervention (Tier 1) | Professional Development/Support (Tier 2) | Quality of Articulation | Release of Responsibility | Strength of Evidence |
|---|---|---|---|---|---|
| Sutherland (2006) | Exploratory talk / 11–12-year-olds | Some form of instruction / coaching | Strong | P → T  T → S | Limited* |

P = provider; T = teacher; S = student; *=effect sizes cannot be calculated; EMMA = Epi-Meta-Mastery-Approach; CSR = Collaborative Strategic Reading.

From the inception of our review, Estrada's (2005) case study of professional development in the Five Standards of Effective Pedagogy[3] (Tharp, Estrada, Dalton, & Yamauchi, 2000) served as a prototypical example of two-tiered scaffolding and small-group instruction. Over 3 years, Estrada worked with a teacher in a two-way Spanish–English bilingual immersion first-grade classroom with many high-poverty English-language learners. She assisted the teacher to incorporate the Five Standards into her teacher-led, small-group reading instruction through a combination of collaborative professional development seminars, follow-up observations and video taping, and individual after-school consultations. Estrada noted: "To contextualize the learning process, real problems and real products came directly from teachers' small-group reading instruction" (p. 330). Hence, there was a high degree of interactivity between tiers. Moreover, because scaffolding is inherent in the Five Standards framework, we assume that gradual release of responsibility was a feature of both tiers. Although the design of the qualitative study limits the ability to make causal inferences, Estrada made a compelling argument that the professional development was associated with improvements in the quality of instruction and she reported "dramatic increases" (p. 357) in students' reading performance over the 3 years.

Mathes et al.'s (2005) and Denton et al.'s (2010) studies present something of an anomaly from a two-tiered scaffolding perspective. Mathes et al. (2005) conducted a study of the efficacy of two programs, Responsive Reading and Proactive Reading, as supplements to classroom-reading instruction. Responsive Reading derived from a cognitive apprenticeship model (Brown, Collins, & Duguid, 1989) and comprised modeling, guided, and independent practice; Proactive Reading derived from Direct Instruction (Carnine, Silbert, Kame'enui, & Tarver, 2004). Extensive support for teachers and a high degree of articulation between tiers characterized both programs. Results showed that the two interventions produced robust growth on multiple measures of reading compared to a program of enhanced classroom instruction. Denton et al. (2010; see also Denton, Swanson, & Mathes, 2007) conducted a subsequent scale-up study of responsive reading. Despite providing more modest support for teachers and fewer opportunities for articulation between tiers, they reported even stronger effects. Presumably the scaffolding built into the responsive reading program was sufficient to address students' needs.

*Summation.* Although we identified only 11 studies of small-group instruction that qualified for inclusion, those that provided extensive and distributed support, good articulation between tiers, and release of responsibility showed sizeable benefits in student achievement (with our rating of the strength of evidence being limited only by the design of the studies). We caution, however, that many of the studies narrowly qualified for inclusion because the teacher training seemed more for the purpose of evaluating the interventions than for supporting teacher learning. We note also that, with the exception of Estrada (2005) and Iversen, Tunmer, and Chapman (2005), rarely was the support for teachers

tailored to the particular demands of small-group instruction (e.g., consideration of group dynamics and norms).

### Whole-Class Instruction

Within the period covered by our review, we found 31 studies (three from one article) of whole-class instruction in literacy that met our criteria. These are summarized in Table 17.3. We grouped these studies into seven categories: writing instruction, class-wide peer tutoring, English-language learning, content-area literacy instruction, individualized student instruction (ISI), direct comparisons of professional development (professional development manifold), and comprehensive programs. In our view, Connor and colleagues' (e.g., Connor et al., 2011b) studies of ISI, Greenleaf et al.'s (2011) study of literacy instruction in science, and Sailors and Price's (2010) study of coaching provide the best, most illustrative examples of two-tiered scaffolding involving whole-class instruction. In this section, we also discuss Garet et al.'s (2008) large-scale study of coaching as their findings provide an interesting contrast to those of Sailors and Price for the purpose of our review.

Connor et al.'s (2011b) study of ISI served as a prototypical example of two-tiered scaffolding at the class level. Connor and colleagues (Al Otaiba et al., 2011; Connor et al., 2009, 2011a, 2011b, 2013) conducted a series of cluster randomized control field trials comparing ISI supported by A2i (assessment to instruction) software with more conventional instruction in kindergarten, first, second, and third grades. Students were assessed on a battery of measures in fall, winter, and spring, and scores on these measures were used in the A2i software to compute recommended amounts and types of instruction (meaning- or code-focused; whole-class, small-group, or individual; teacher- or student-managed). The authors refer to A2i "as an instructional decision support system" (Connor et al., 2011b, p. 195). Tier 1 comprised differentiated instruction on the part of the teachers; tier 2 comprised the periodic support given to teachers via the software in combination with prior and ongoing professional development. In a real sense, then, tier 1 and tier 2 informed each other. Teacher fidelity to the recommended instruction varied but in most studies individualized instruction produced substantial effects on standardized measures relative to controls. Connor et al.'s (2013) study showed a large cumulative effect for students who received ISI from first through third grade (we inferred evidence of teacher change from other studies). In Connor et al.'s (2011b) third-grade study, the effects were weaker than in the other studies, probably because the authors used a robust form of vocabulary instruction for the control condition.

Greenleaf et al. (2011) examined the effects of professional development in Reading Apprenticeship on ninth- and tenth-grade teachers' abilities to integrate disciplinary literacy practices in science teaching in biology. Reading Apprenticeship is an instructional framework in which teachers make explicit the comprehension strategies and processes involved in understanding texts in academic disciplines. The professional development included a sequence of daylong

**Table 17.3   Two-tiered Scaffolding Studies of Whole-class Instruction**

| Writing | Intervention (Tier 1) | Professional Development/Support (Tier 2) | Quality of Articulation | Release of Responsibility | Strength of Evidence |
|---|---|---|---|---|---|
| Coe et al. (2011) | 6+1 trait writing model / Gr5 | 36 hours (initial, distributed) / monthly letter / online assistance / manual | Weak | No indication | Insufficient |
| Festas et al. (2015) | Self-regulated strategy dev. writing / Gr8 | 14 hours (2 days) / after-school support / materials | Weak | P → T<br>T → S | Limited |
| Harris et al. (2012) | Self-regulated strategy dev. writing / Gr2-3 | 12 hours (2 days in teacher teams, 1 week apart) / in-class support / materials | Weak | P → T<br>T → S | Limited |
| Kim et al. (2011) | Cognitive strategies for writing / Gr6–12 ELL | 46 hours (distributed) / monthly meetings / coaching / assessment / materials | Weak | T → S | Limited |

| Class-wide Peer Tutoring | Intervention (Tier 1) | Professional Development/Support (Tier 2) | Quality of Articulation | Release of Responsibility | Strength of Evidence |
|---|---|---|---|---|---|
| McMaster et al. (2013) | K-PALS / K | University vs. district support (4 hours initial / 2 booster sessions / in-class support / e-mail) | Weak | No indication | Moderate |
| Stein et al. (2008) | K-PALS / K | 6 hours (initial) / 2 booster sessions / in-class support / materials vs. other levels of support | Weak | No indication | Moderate |
| Van Keer & Verhaeghe (2005a) | Peer tutoring in comp. strategies / Gr2 and 5 | Extensive (initial, distributed) / coaching / materials | Strong | T → S | Limited |
| Van Keer & Verhaeghe (2005b) | Peer tutoring in comp. strategies / Gr2 and 5 | 35 hours (initial, distributed, coaching) / manual vs. 13 hours (initial, in-class support) / manual | Strong | T → S | Insufficient |

| English-language Learning | Intervention (Tier 1) | Professional Development/Support (Tier 2) | Quality of Articulation | Release of Responsibility | Strength of Evidence |
|---|---|---|---|---|---|
| Echevarria et al. (2006) | SIOP writing / Gr6–8 | 18+ hours (initial, distributed) / email | Strong | No indication | Moderate |
| Echevarria et al. (2011) | SIOP / Gr7 | 15 hours (initial) / coaching / material | Strong | No indication | Insufficient |
| Short et al. (2012) | SIOP / Gr6–12 | 42 hours (initial, distributed) / coaching / email | Strong | No indication | Limited |
| Tong et al. (2010) | English language & literacy / K-2 | 54 hours per year (distributed) | Strong | No indication | Strong* |

| Content-area Literacy | Intervention (Tier 1) | Professional Development/Support (Tier 2) | Quality of Articulation | Release of Responsibility | Strength of Evidence |
|---|---|---|---|---|---|
| Greenleaf et al. (2011) | Reading apprenticeship / Gr9–10 | 60 hours (initial, distributed) / online assistance | Strong | P → T<br>T → S | Moderate |
| McKeown & Beck (2004) | Questioning the author / Gr3–6 | 18 hours (initial), in-class support, instructional resources | Weak | No indication | Insufficient |
| Simmons et al. (2010) | Comp. or vocab. instr. / Gr4 | 18 hours (distributed) | Strong | T → S | Moderate |

| Individualized Student Instruction | Intervention (Tier 1) | Professional Development/Support (Tier 2) | Quality of Articulation | Release of Responsibility | Strength of Evidence |
|---|---|---|---|---|---|
| Al-Otaiba et al. (2011) | ISI / K | 6 hours (initial) / A2i / coaching / in-class support / materials | Strong | No indication | Strong |
| Connor et al. (2009) | ISI / Gr1 | 18 hours (initial, distributed) / A2i / coaching | Strong | No indication | Strong* |
| Connor et al. (2011a) | ISI / Gr1 | 9 hours (distributed) / A2i / coaching | Strong | No indication | Strong |
| Connor et al. (2011b) | ISI / Gr3 | 12 hours (initial, distributed) / A2i / coaching | Strong | No indication | Limited |
| Connor et al. (2013) | ISI / Gr1–3 | 3 hours (initial) / A2i / monthly teacher meetings / coaching / in-class support | Strong | No indication | Strong |

| Professional Development Manifold | Intervention (Tier 1) | Professional Development/Support (Tier 2) | Quality of Articulation | Release of Responsibility | Strength of Evidence |
|---|---|---|---|---|---|
| Garet et al. (2008) | NRP components / Gr2 | 45 hours (initial, distributed) / 62 hours coaching vs. 45 hours (initial, distributed) vs. business-as-usual | Weak | T → S | Insufficient |

*(continued)*

**Table 17.3**    *(continued)*

| Professional Development Manifold | Intervention (Tier 1) | Professional Development/Support (Tier 2) | Quality of Articulation | Release of Responsibility | Strength of Evidence |
|---|---|---|---|---|---|
| Gersten et al. (2010) | Vocabulary & comprehension instr. / Gr1 | Summer institute / 16 study groups vs. summer institute / contracted hours of professional development | Strong | No indication | Limited |
| Lovett et al. (2008) | Phast Paces / Gr9–10 | 48–60 hours (initial, distributed) / in-class support / coaching vs. control | Strong | No indication | Limited |
| Sailors & Price (2010) | Comprehension strategy instr. / Gr2–8 | 12 hours (initial) / coaching vs. 12 hours (initial) | Strong | P → T T → S | Moderate |
| Scanlon et al. (2008) | Interactive strategies approach / K | 18 hours (initial, distributed) / coaching / materials vs. baseline (no professional development) | Strong | P → T | Moderate |

| Comprehensive Programs | Intervention (Tier 1) | Professional Development/Support (Tier 2) | Quality of Articulation | Release of Responsibility | Strength of Evidence |
|---|---|---|---|---|---|
| Borman et al. (2008) | Open court reading / Gr1–5 | 12–18 hours (initial) / in-class support / materials | Weak | No indication | Insufficient |
| Doherty & Hilberg (2008) Study 1 | 5 standards of effective pedagogy / Gr3 and 4 | Workshops in initial 2 years | None | No indication | Insufficient |
| Study 2 | 5 standards of effective pedagogy / Gr1–3 | 6 hours (distributed) on instructional conversations / coaching in instructional conversations | Weak | No indication | Limited |
| Study 3 | 5 standards of effective pedagogy / Gr3–5 | 3 workshops (distributed) / coaching | Weak | No indication | Insufficient |
| Ferguson et al. (2011) | Think about it / 5–6-year-olds | 18 hours (initial, distributed) / weekly meetings / in-class support / materials | Strong | T → S | Moderate |
| McCutchen et al. (2009) | Literacy instruction / Gr3–5 | 78 hours (initial, distributed) / in-class support | Weak | No indication | Limited |

P = provider; T = teacher; S = student; *=effect sizes cannot be calculated; ELL = English-language learners; K-PALS = Kindergarten PALS; SIOP = Sheltered Instruction Observation Protocol; ISI = Individualized Student Instruction; NRP = National Reading Panel.

sessions, involving summer institutes and follow-up sessions during the school year, with multiple opportunities to try new methods and examine students' responses. Both the instructional framework and the professional development had a generative capacity intended to foster students' and teachers' independent problem solving. After 2 years, teachers showed an increased ability to integrate literacy instruction in their science teaching and students showed statistically significant and meaningful gains on standardized tests in reading and biology relative to control students. Although effect sizes were slightly less than 0.30, results were tempered by the fact that the treatment group comprised a higher percentage of low-performing students. We judged the strength of evidence from this study to be moderate.

In a large-scale cluster randomized control study commissioned by the U.S. Department of Education, Garet et al. (2008) examined the benefits of coaching in early reading instruction on teacher practices and student reading achievement. In a yearlong study in 90 high-poverty schools in six districts with 270 grade 2 teachers and 5,500 students, they compared the effects of: (a) prior and distributed professional development implemented via 8 days of teacher institute; (b) the same institute plus over 60 hours of coaching; and (c) business-as-usual professional development provided by school districts. Although the coaching had positive (but not statistically significant) effects on teacher practices at the end of 1 year, no significant differences were found between

conditions in students' scores on standardized tests. At the end of a second, follow-up year, there were no significant differences in teacher practices or student achievement.

These results stand in sharp contrast to those of Sailors and Price (2010), who reported significant and meaningful benefits of coaching for teachers and students in a cluster randomized study of comprehension strategy instruction intervention in Grades 2 through 8. From a two-tiered scaffolding perspective, what differentiates the two studies is the articulation between tiers and release of responsibility. Whereas the ongoing coaching in Sailors and Price's study allowed for a high degree of interactivity between tiers, and there was evidence of progression towards independence for both teachers and students, this does not appear to have been the case in Garet et al. (2008). In Garet et al., the structured nature of the coaching and the core reading programs used by schools may have rendered the instruction relatively impervious to change.

***Summation.***    The last decade has seen no shortage of studies of whole-class instruction that involved extensive and distributed professional development and support for teachers. In many of the studies, researchers employed large-scale, cluster randomized field trials and the focus of the research was tilted towards evaluating the interventions rather more than furthering teachers' expertise to improve students' literacy. Moreover, although extensive professional development and support were integral to implementing the interventions, the descriptions often lacked details as to what actually transpired. Another problem with many of the studies concerned the fidelity of implementation of the classroom instruction or the professional development. Many of the studies showed wide variation in implementation or lacked convincing evidence of fidelity.

### School-wide Improvement

The passage of the No Child Left Behind Act in 2001 was an impetus to scale up literacy interventions within and across schools in the United States and to establish a link between professional development, literacy teaching, and students'

literacy achievement. We categorized studies as school-wide (also termed school-reform efforts) if the intent of the intervention extended beyond individual classrooms to a school, multiple schools, or a region. An unanticipated caveat arose during our categorization process as studies of school-wide interventions most often reported data from limited grade levels, such as K-2, K and 4, or a single grade. We pondered whether these studies should be designated as class- or school-wide. Our resolution was to accept the authors' appellation of school-wide reform as reflective of their intended scope. The 26 studies that met the criteria for two-tiered scaffolding clustered into five categories: coaching, Reading First, Success for All, professional development manifold, and English-language learning. Summaries of these studies appear in Table 17.4.

**Table 17.4    Two-tiered Scaffolding Studies of School-wide Improvement Interventions**

| Coaching and Teams | Intervention (Tier 1) | Professional Development (PD)/Support (Tier 2) | Quality of Articulation | Release of Responsibility | Strength of Evidence |
|---|---|---|---|---|---|
| Biancarosa et al. (2010) | Literacy collaborative / GrK–2 | 40 hours initial / 12 hours annual PD / in-classroom coaching | Strong | C → T T → S | Moderate |
| Matsumura et al. (2010) | Classroom discussions / Gr4–5 | Weekly grade-level meetings PD / in-classroom coaching | Strong | No indication | Strong |
| Porche et al. (2012) | Collaborative lang. & literacy instr. / GrK and 4 | 36 hours initial PD with modules / in-classroom coaching | Strong | No indication | Limited |
| Zakierski & Siegel (2010) | ELA time / read aloud / take-home rdg. / Gr4 | Weekly grade-level meetings PD / using data / collaborative teams | Weak | No indication | Insufficient |
| **Reading First** | **Intervention (Tier 1)** | **Professional Development/Support (Tier 2)** | **Quality of Articulation** | **Release of Responsibility** | **Strength of Evidence** |
| Carlisle & Berebitsky (2011) | Phonics and small-group instruction / Gr1 | Year 1: 27 hours PD / Year 2: current study / weekly meetings / coaching | Strong | No indication | Limited |
| Elish-Piper & L'Allier (2011) | Five key components / GrK-3 | PD in-classroom coaching on five key components | Strong | No indication | Limited |
| Walpole et al. (2010) | Reading, small group, differentiated instr., read aloud / GrK–3 | Coaching outside (PD) and inside classrooms | Strong | No indication | Insufficient |
| **Success for All** | **Intervention (Tier 1)** | **Professional Development/Support (Tier 2)** | **Quality of Articulation** | **Release of Responsibility** | **Strength of Evidence** |
| Borman et al. (2007) | SFA / GrK-2 | 18 hours PD (initial) / ongoing, on-site support | Strong | No indication | Moderate |
| Chambers et al. (2006) | SFA + multimedia / Gr1 | 18 hours PD (initial) / ongoing, on-site support | Strong | No indication | Limited |
| Hanselman & Borman (2013) | SFA *Reading Wings* w/o *Reading Roots* / Gr3–5 | 18 hours PD (initial) / ongoing, on-site support, school-solutions team | Strong | No indication | Insufficient |
| Munoz & Dossett (2004) | SFA / Gr3 | 18 hours PD (initial) / ongoing, on-site support, family support team | Strong | No indication | Limited |
| Skindrud & Gersten (2006) | SFA vs. open court / Gr2–3 | SFA: 18 hours PD (initial) / on-site support, implementation visits / open court: 24 hours PD new teachers / 24 hours for advanced training/ reading coach / monthly meetings | Strong | No indication | Moderate |
| **Professional Development Manifold** | **Intervention (Tier 1)** | **Professional Development/Support (Tier 2)** | **Quality of Articulation** | **Release of Responsibility** | **Strength of Evidence** |
| Dowell (2012) | Guided reading / GrK–5 | Weekly literacy course PD / alternative online option Scholastic Red / coaching | Strong | P → T | Insufficient |
| Epstein (2005) | Action team summaries / GrK– 5 | PD / development, monitoring, and evaluation by on-site facilitator / site visits / family-community | Weak | No indication | Limited |

*(continued)*

**Table 17.4**    *(continued)*

| Professional Development Manifold | Intervention (Tier 1) | Professional Development/Support (Tier 2) | Quality of Articulation | Release of Responsibility | Strength of Evidence |
|---|---|---|---|---|---|
| Herlihy & Kemple (2004) | Small-communities / cooperative lng. / Gr6–8 | 38 hours PD over 2 years / in-class coaching / school-based lead teachers | Weak | No indication | Limited |
| Kennedy & Shiel (2010) | Balanced differentiated instruction / Gr1–2 | Biweekly meetings over 2 years in collaborative PD/in-class support | Strong | P → T<br>T → S | Moderate |
| Lai et al. (2009) | Reading comprehension / Yrs 4–6 | Collaborative data analysis / PD sessions / guided learning circles, action research | Strong | No indication | Moderate |
| O'Connor et al. (2005) | Classroom, small-group teaching / GrK–3 | 26 hours PD (distributed) / 5 key components / 4 meetings / class visits | Strong | No indication | Strong |
| Phillips et al. (2004) | Core instructional settings / Yr1 | 30 hours PD (distributed) in school teams | Strong | T → S | Moderate |
| Taylor et al. (2004) | Effective reading instruction / Gr2–5 | School-level reform, 10 components / large and small-group / CIERA website / feedback | Strong | P → T<br>T → S | Strong |
| Whitehead (2010) | Literacy initiative / Yrs 8–11 | Externally funded PD by regional coordinators, in-school literacy leaders and learning coordinators / support at staff, department, and individual levels | Strong | No indication | Limited |

| ELL/ESOL | Intervention (Tier 1) | Professional Development/Support (Tier 2) | Quality of Articulation | Release of Responsibility | Strength of Evidence |
|---|---|---|---|---|---|
| Arens et al. (2012) | On Our Way to English (OWE) / Gr1–4 | 3 hours PD (initial) OWE; varied delivery of RISE modules by site coordinators | Weak | No indication | Insufficient |
| August et al. (2009) | Project QuEST science / Gr6 | 3 PD sessions (initial, distributed) / weekly mentoring | Strong | No indication | Moderate/ limited |
| Lee et al. (2007) | Science curriculum units / Gr3 | 30 hours PD / science units, inquiry activities, linguistic scaffolding | Weak | T → S | Insufficient |
| Lee et al. (2008) | Science curriculum units / Gr3 | 30 hours PD / science units, inquiry approach, linguistic and cultural practices | Weak | T → S | Limited |
| Lee et al. (2011) | Science curriculum units / Gr 3 | 30 hours PD / science units, inquiry approach, linguistic practices | Weak | T → S | Insufficient |

C = coach; P = provider; T = teacher; S = student; ELA = English Language Arts; SFA = Success for All; ESOL = English for Speakers of Other Languages; CIERA = Center for the Improvement of Early Reading Achievement; RISE = Responsive Instruction for Success in English.

Taylor, Pearson, Peterson, and Rodriguez' (2004) school-change study served as a prototypical example of two-tiered scaffolding at the school level. The 13 schools (eight in second year, five in first year) were a mix of high-poverty sites in urban, suburban, and rural areas, which varied in terms of proportion of English-language learners and persons of color. Researchers attended to school-level variables (e.g., leadership, collaboration, home–school links) simultaneously with effective classroom instruction (e.g., high-level questioning, comprehension strategies, vocabulary) in Grades 2–5. Professional development combined large-group sessions on school-reform activities and small, study-group sessions on effective reading practices with classroom feedback distributed across the year. The intervention addressed classroom and school-wide change of both students and teachers. Students' growth in reading comprehension from the first to second year of implementation was explained by the school- and classroom-level variables. The strong articulation and reciprocal influence between tiers was verified by the high-effort reform schools outperforming the low-effort reform schools in the second year of implementation. Transfer of knowledge and skills from coaches to teachers and teachers to students was in evidence in teacher interviews and observations. Multiple measures of fidelity of implementation of

teaching and professional development that included interviews, observations, and artifacts were used.

O'Connor, Fulmer, Harty, and Bell's (2005) longitudinal lag-design study of a layered approach to reading intervention allowed comparison of participating teachers with control teachers, not yet participating, as a grade cohort was added to the professional development scheme each year. The authors noted dramatic improvements in teaching as the professional development rolled to the next grade cohort and second- and third-graders significantly outperformed the control students on all reading measures except word identification.

***Summation.***    All of the school-wide studies were conducted in high-need, elementary schools with only three studies venturing into middle (August, Branum-Martin, Cardenas-Hagan, & Francis, 2009; Herlihy & Kemple, 2004) or secondary schools (Whitehead, 2010). Schools were designated as high need in terms of students' achievement, socioeconomic status, cultural and linguistic diversity, mobility, and urban settings. The interventions were multicomponent, with writing included in only four studies (Biancarosa, Bryk, & Dexter, 2010; Kennedy & Shiel, 2010; Phillips, McNaughton, & MacDonald, 2004; Porche, Pallante, & Snow, 2012). Release of responsibility at both tiers was evident in only three studies (Biancarosa et al., 2010; Kennedy & Shiel, 2010; Taylor et al., 2004). In the majority of studies, we judged the quality of articulation between tiers as strong. For example, strong articulation and bidirectional influence between tiers are built into the structure of the comprehensive reform model of Success for All (Slavin, Madden, Dolan, & Wasik, 1996). Descriptions of organic, collaborative, professional development approaches to non-prescriptive, responsive interventions are more challenging to convey. Two research teams, Lai, McNaughton, Amituanai-Toloa, Turner, and Hsiao (2009) and Phillips et al. (2004), were especially adroit at explaining complex processes at both tiers.

Although all of the researchers designated their studies as school-wide interventions, we note that none reported school-wide data. Rather, researchers identified specific grade levels (e.g., Grades 2, 4, and 5) as targets for administering their measures and analyzing outcomes. Most of the studies were conducted over a single school year, with a few exceptions (Biancarosa et al., 2010; Herlihy & Kemple, 2004; Kennedy & Shiel, 2010; O'Connor et al., 2005; Taylor et al., 2004). Multiyear implementations of school-wide reforms showed cumulative benefits in terms of teachers' take-up of interventions and students' literacy growth.

## Research in Literacy From the Perspective of Two-Tiered Scaffolding

Our purpose in writing this chapter was to provide a thorough review of recent research in literacy that encompassed teacher professional development or support, teaching practices, and student learning within a framework consistent with two-tiered scaffolding. We used this framework to help identify practices that are likely to have meaningful, sustainable influences on literacy learning. Our assumption was that a coherent articulation between the professional development and support provided to teachers or more capable others (tier 2) and the interactions with students (tier 1), combined with a push towards independence at both tiers, would make for a robust framework for instruction and help establish a logical, even causal, relationship between professional development/support and student learning. In this section, we provide a critique of the research from a two-tiered scaffolding perspective. We also reflect on the support studies provide for the framework.

Our quest for robust instructional interventions bore fruit in some contexts. There is an abundance of research on tutorial interventions, class-level interventions, and whole-school improvement where researchers have provided extensive and distributed professional development and support that fit the two-tiered framework. The same cannot be said of research on small-group instruction in literacy. As noted earlier, we found few studies of small-group instruction consistent with two-tiered scaffolding and most that qualified did so only narrowly because the focus was more on evaluation of programs than on support for teacher learning. Professional development and support that address the particular demands and affordances of the small-group setting is an area ripe for research.

We found the quality of articulation between professional development/support and student learning was strongest among studies of school-wide improvement, and less so among studies of class-level and tutorial interventions. Under the umbrella of school-wide literacy interventions, we saw a shift in focus from *organizational* features emanating from the precedents of effective-schools research and comprehensive school reform to a focus on *literacy* writ large (e.g., Reading First). In school-wide studies, professional development seems to be the bridge that links the context for teachers' learning with the context of teachers design for students' learning. Among class-level interventions, research on ISI by Connor and colleagues (Al Otaiba et al., 2011; Connor et al., 2009, 2011a, 2011b, 2013) showed strong articulation between tiers. Greenleaf et al.'s (2011) work in Reading Apprenticeship and Sailors and Price's (2010) work in comprehension strategy instruction were also exemplary of an interactive relationship between tiers. Among tutorial interventions, studies of Reading Recovery and Gelzheiser et al.'s (2011) study of ISA-X were exemplary in this regard.

By contrast, we found relatively few studies that attended to the need for teachers and students to function independently at increasingly higher levels of expertise. By definition, we rated most studies of Reading Recovery as strong in this area. Attending to the transfer of responsibility from teacher leader to teacher and from teacher to child is a distinctive feature of Reading Recovery. It may be that gradual release of responsibility was a feature of other interventions, but the authors failed to report it in their descriptions. Be that as it may, we urge researchers to give more attention to scaffolding for independence in professional development and instructional contexts.

We are compelled to mention two important programs of research in school-wide change that were excluded from our analysis: School-Based Inquiry—Getting Results (Gallimore, Ermeling, Saunders, & Goldenberg, 2009; Saunders, Goldenberg, & Gallimore, 2009) and the South Carolina Reading Intervention (Stephens et al., 2007, 2011). These two programs were wittingly skewed towards teacher professional development. Close reading of the publications and supplemental references provided little access to information about tier 1, which led to their exclusion. These change models present a challenge to researchers to increase the transparency of teaching practices implemented at tier 1 when the professional-development emphasis is promoting an organic, inquiry-based, build-your-own model.

We turn now to the support the studies provide for two-tiered scaffolding. We caution that establishing relationships between teacher professional development/support, teaching practices, and student achievement is not easy. It is difficult to know whether a "lack of evidence of efficacy was caused by inherent flaws in the instructional model or in the focus, sequence, and timing of the professional development model" (Doherty & Hilberg, 2008, p. 205). In other words, the content of instruction matters. Poor research design can also mitigate effects. We also presume that the critical elements of two-tiered scaffolding, and their benefits, are hard to detect when instructional programs are so highly structured that instruction is impermeable to change or so broad that they fail to gain traction in the classroom. Highly structured programs make it difficult for teachers to be responsive to student learning; broad approaches may lack practical strategies for implementation.

That said, more often than not we found that extensive and distributed professional development/support for teaching was associated with moderate to strong evidence of effects when there was strong articulation between tiers and efforts to achieve gradual release of responsibility. Moreover, we found the two-tiered framework afforded considerable insight when we were trying to make sense of seemingly anomalous outcomes (e.g., Garet et al.'s, 2008, and Sailors & Price's, 2010, studies of coaching). Two-tiered scaffolding offers considerable explanatory power and may be a necessary—though not sufficient—condition for positive student outcomes.

## Conclusion

We conclude by looking across instructional contexts to discern the currents beneath the surface that have implications for research, policy, and practice. Through our analysis of professional development intervention studies, which were predominantly conducted at the early elementary levels in high-need schools, we were able to identify areas where we determined that the field is headed in the right direction, elements that might be missing, and current challenges. Substantial initial and distributed professional development opportunities with in-class support, use of multiple student outcome measures, and use of multiple and varied teacher-fidelity measures characterize areas where the field is moving in the *right* direction. Missing elements are writing interventions, attention to social validity (i.e., participants' perceptions of ease, effectiveness, and sustainability of procedures), and sufficient attention to scaffolding for independence of children and teachers. Current challenges are: (a) providing sufficiently rich descriptions of organically designed and complex professional development; (b) ensuring the coherence and connection between the learning of teachers and

the learning of their students; (c) promoting the influence of teaching–learning interactions on professional development and teacher education; (d) monitoring fidelity of implementation; and (e) interventions for students in the intermediate grades, middle school, and junior and senior high schools.

Importantly, we note our selection and analysis of literacy intervention studies were theoretically driven. The field, however, has been driven by features of professional development proposed by Desimone (2009) and others that are lacking in theoretical coherence (viz., content focus, active learning, coherence, duration, and collective participation) and do not seem to yield consistent success (Hill, Beisiegel, & Jacob, 2013). The lens of two-tiered scaffolding allowed us to go beneath the criteria to understand why these features might be important and why literacy interventions might or might not have worked. Two-tiered scaffolding is not only evaluative but also formative. Attending to the quality of the articulation between tiers, the direction of the influence, and the intentional transfer of responsibility in both the professional development and teaching tiers has the power to substantially lift the plane of design of literacy interventions.

We are not suggesting that two-tiered scaffolding is the only theoretical frame to bring to bear on professional development for literacy interventions. Educational psychologists who do work in literacy have a rich array of theories of learning to apply in their research and practice (Hiebert & Raphael, 1996). We recommend that the next era of professional development-intervention research address the complexity of the reciprocal learning processes of teachers and students and that researchers prioritize the theoretical rationales for their approaches to professional development. We argue that researchers must not only use robust literacy interventions and quality professional development or support, they must also make the hinge between tiers transparent.

## Appendix 17.1    Criteria for Judgment of Strength of Evidence

**Strong evidence**

Randomized or cluster randomized design

Evidence of teacher change/difference in practices in expected direction

Evidence of student growth (effect size greater than or equal to +0.30 on most standardized measures; there must be at least one standardized measure)

**Moderate evidence**

Any design

Evidence of teacher change/difference in practices in expected direction

Evidence of student growth (effect size greater than or equal to +0.30 on most standardized measures in experimental design study, or *much* greater than expected growth on most standardized measures in single-group or case study design; there must be at least one standardized measure)

or

Same criteria as for strong evidence, but study is compromised in some way (e.g., uncertain fidelity, only self-report measure(s) of teacher change, limited measurement of student outcomes)

**Limited evidence**

Any design

At least some evidence of teacher change/difference in practices in expected direction

Some evidence of student growth (effect size of +0.20 to <+0.30 on most standardized measures or effect size greater than +0.50 on most researcher-developed measures in experimental design study, or greater than expected growth on most measures in single-group or case study design)

**Insufficient evidence**

No evidence of teacher change/difference in practices in expected direction

or

No evidence of student growth (effect size < +0.20 on most standardized measures or non-significant effect on most researcher-developed measures in experimental design study, or no greater than expected growth on most measures in single-group or case study design)

Note: Evidence of teacher change/difference in practices could come from fidelity data or separate (e.g., observational) data on teachers.

## Acknowledgment

We gratefully acknowledge the assistance of Robert Drewry and Lauren Donnan in identifying, selecting, and coding studies. Their contributions were invaluable in assisting us to complete this chapter.

## Notes

1. The term *tiers* as used by Gaffney and Anderson (1991) as descriptors of teaching children (tier 1) and preparation of teachers (tier 2) is distinct from the more recent use of tiers as levels of intervention in the response-to-intervention scheme.
2. In some countries, Reading Recovery professional-development sessions for teachers in the initial year are held every 2 weeks and the term "tutors" is used synonymously with "teacher leaders." The U.S. terminology will be used to correspond with the context of most of the studies in this review.
3. The Five Standards comprise a set of pedagogical principles for effective instruction, especially with learners of diverse backgrounds: joint productive activity, developing language and literacy across the curriculum, contextualizing learning, challenging students towards complex thinking, and instructional conversations.
4. * Studies that meet the criteria for two-tiered scaffolding and that are summarized in tables.

## References[4]

*Al Otaiba, S., Connor, C. M., Folsom, J. S., Greulich, L., Meadows, J., & Li, Z. (2011). Assessment data-informed guidance to individualize kindergarten reading instruction: Findings from a cluster-randomized control field trial. *The Elementary School Journal, 111*(4), 535–560.

*Al Otaiba, S., & Lake, V. E. (2007). Preparing special educators to teach reading and use curriculum-based assessments. *Reading and Writing, 20*, 591–617.

*Al Otaiba, S., Lake, V. E., Greulich, L., Folsom, J. S., & Guidry, L. (2012). Preparing beginning reading teachers: An experimental comparison of initial early literacy field experiences. *Reading and Writing, 25*, 109–129.

Alvermann, D. E., Fitzgerald, J., & Simpson, M. (2006). Teaching and learning in reading. In P. A. Alexander and P. H. Winne (Eds.), *Handbook of educational psychology* (2nd ed., pp. 427–455). Mahwah, NJ: Erlbaum.

Anderson, R. C., Hiebert, E. H., Scott, J. A., & Wilkinson, I. A. G. (1985). *Becoming a nation of readers: The report of the Commission on Reading.* Champaign, IL: Center for the Study of Reading; Washington, DC: National Institute of Education.

*Arens, S. A., Stoker, G., Barker, J., Shebby, S., Wang, X., Cicchinelli, L. F., & Williams, J. M. (2012). Effects of curriculum and teacher professional development on the language proficiency of elementary English language learner students in the Central Region. Research Report No. 2012-4013. Retrieved from Institute of Education Sciences website: http://ncee.ed.gov (accessed February 18, 2015).

*Atkinson, T. S., & Colby, S. A. (2006). Who's teaching, who's learning? Analyzing the professional growth of graduate student tutors. *Mentoring & Tutoring, 14*, 227–245.

*August, D., Branum-Martin, L., Cardenas-Hagan, E., & Francis, D. J. (2009). The impact of an instructional intervention on the science and language learning of middle grade English language learners. *Journal of Research on Educational Effectiveness, 2*, 345–376.

Ball, D., & Cohen, D. (1999). Developing practice, developing practitioners: Toward a practice-based theory of professional education. In L. Darling-Hammond & D. Sykes (Eds.), *Teaching as the learning profession: Handbook of policy and practice.* San Francisco, CA: Jossey-Bass.

*Biancarosa, G., Bryk, A. S., & Dexter, E. R. (2010). Assessing the value-added effects of literacy collaborative professional development on student learning. *The Elementary School Journal, 111*(1), 7–34.

*Borman, G. D., Dowling, N. M., & Schneck, C. (2008). A multisite cluster randomized trial of Open Court Reading. *Educational Evaluation and Policy Analysis, 30*(4), 389–407.

*Borman, G. D., Slavin, R. E., Cheung, A. C., Chamberlain, A. M., Madden, N. A., & Chambers, B. (2007). Final reading outcomes of the national randomized field trial of Success for All. *American Educational Research Journal, 44*, 701–731.

Brown, A. L. (1985). *Teaching students to think as they read: Implications for curriculum reform.* Technical Report No. 58. Champaign, IL: Center for the Study of Reading.

Brown, J. S., Collins, A., & Duguid, P. (1989). Situated cognition and the culture of learning. *Educational Researcher, 18*, 32–42.

*Brown, K. J., Morris, D., & Fields, M. (2005). Intervention after grade 1: Serving increased numbers of struggling readers effectively. *Journal of Literacy Research, 37*(1), 61–94.

*Bufalino, J., Wang, C., Gómez-Bellengé, F. X., & Zalud, G. (2010). What's possible for first-grade at-risk literacy learners receiving early intervention services. *Literacy Teaching and Learning, 15*(1), 1–15.

*Burroughs-Lange, S., & Douetil, J. (2007). Literacy progress of young children from poor urban settings: A Reading Recovery comparison study. *Literacy Teaching and Learning, 12*(1), 19–46.

*Carlisle, J. F., & Berebitsky, D. (2011). Literacy coaching as a component of professional development. *Reading and Writing, 24*, 773–800.

Carnine, D.W., Silbert, J., Kame'enui, E. J., & Tarver, S. G. (2004). Direct instruction reading (4th ed.). Upper Saddle River, NJ: Merrill-Prentice Hall.

*Chambers, B., Cheung, A. C., Madden, N. A., Slavin, R. E., & Gifford, R. (2006). Achievement effects of embedded multimedia in a success for all reading program. *Journal of Educational Psychology, 98*, 232–237.

*Chow, B. W. Y., McBride-Chang, C., & Cheung, H. (2010). Parent–child reading in English as a second language: Effects on language and literacy development of Chinese kindergarteners. *Journal of Research in Reading, 33*, 284–301.

Clay, M. M. (1985). The early detection of reading difficulties (3rd ed.). Auckland, New Zealand: Heinemann.

Clay, M. M. (2005a). *Literacy lessons designed for individuals: Part one why? when? and how?* Portsmouth, NH: Heinemann.

Clay, M. M. (2005b). *Literacy lessons designed for individuals: Part two teaching procedures.* Portsmouth, NH: Heinemann.

Clay, M. M. & Cazden, C. B. (1990). A Vygotskian interpretation of Reading Recovery. In L. C. Moll (Ed.), *Vygotsky and education: Instructional implications and applications of sociohistorical psychology* (pp. 206–222). New York: Cambridge University Press.

Cochran-Smith, M., & Lytle, S. (1999). Relationship of knowledge and practice: Teacher learning in communities. In A. Iran-Nejad & C. D. Pearson (Eds.), *Review of research in education* (Vol. 24, pp. 249–306). Washington, DC: American Educational Research Association.

*Coe, M., Hanita, M., Nishioka, V., & Smiley, R. (2011). *An investigation of the impact of the 6+1 trait writing model on grade 5 student writing achievement.* NCEE 2012-4100. Washington, D.C.: National Center for Education Evaluation and Regional Assistance, Institute of Education Sciences, U.S. Department of Education.

*Connor, C. M., Morrison, F. J., Schatschneider, C., Toste, J. R., Lundblom, E., & Fishman, B. (2011a). Effective classroom instruction: Implications of child characteristics by reading instruction interactions on first graders' word reading achievement. *Journal of Research on Educational Effectiveness, 4*, 173–207.

*Connor, C. M., Morrison, F. J., Fishman, B., Giuliani, S., Luck, M., Underwood, P. S., . . . Schatschneider, C. (2011b). Testing the impact of child characteristics × instruction interactions on third graders' reading comprehension by differentiating literacy instruction. *Reading Research Quarterly, 46*(3), 189–221.

*Connor, C. M., Morrison, F. J, Fishman, B., Crowe, E. C., Al Otaiba, S., & Schatschneider, C. (2013). A longitudinal cluster-randomized controlled study on the accumulating effects of individualized literacy instruction on students' reading from first through third grade. *Psychological Science, 24*(8), 1409–1419.

*Connor, C. M., Piasta, S. B., Fishman, B., Glasney, S., Schatschneider, C., Crow, E., . . . Morrison, F. J. (2009). Individualizing student instruction precisely: Effects of child x instruction interactions on first graders' literacy development. *Child Development, 80*(1), 77–100.

Darling-Hammond, L., Wei, R. C., Andree, A., Richardson, N., & Orphanos, S. (2009). *Professional learning in the learning profession: A status report on teacher development in the United States and abroad.* Dallas, TX: National Staff Development Council.

*Denton, C. A., Mimon, K., Mathes, P. G., Swanson, E. A., Kethley, C., Kurz, T. B., & Shih, M. (2010). Effectiveness of a supplemental early reading intervention scaled up in multiple schools. *Exceptional Children, 76*(4), 394–416.

Denton, C. A., Swanson, E. A., & Mathes, P. G. (2007). Assessment-based instructional coaching provided to reading intervention teachers. *Reading and Writing, 20*(6), 569–590.

Desimone, L. M. (2009). Improving impact studies of teachers' professional development: Toward better conceptualizations and measures. *Educational Researcher, 38*, 181–199.

*Doherty, R. W., & Hilberg, S. R. (2008). Efficacy of Five Standards in raising student achievement: Findings from three studies. *Journal of Educational Research, 101*(4), 195–206.

*Dowell, M. M. S. (2012). Addressing the complexities of literacy and urban teaching in the USA: Strategic professional development as intervention. *Teaching Education, 23*(1), 25–50.

*Echevarria, J., Richards-Tutor, C., Canges, R., & Francis, D. (2011). Using the SIOP model to promote the acquisition of language and science concepts with English learners. *Bilingual Research Journal, 34*(3), 334–351.

*Echevarria, J., Short, D., & Powers, K. (2006). School reform and standards-based education: An instructional model for English language learners. *Journal of Educational Research*, 99, 195–211.

*Ehri, L. C., Dreyer, L. G., Flugman, B., & Gross, A. (2007). Reading rescue: An effective tutoring intervention model for language-minority students who are struggling readers in first grade. *American Educational Research Journal, 44*, 414–448.

*Elish-Piper, L., & L'Allier, S. K. (2011). Examining the relationship between literacy coaching and student reading gains in grades K–3. *The Elementary School Journal, 112*(1), 83–106.

Englert, C. S., & Tarrant, K. L. (1995). Creating collaborative cultures for educational change. *Remedial and Special Education, 16*(6), 325–336, 353.

*Epstein, J. L. (2005). A case study of the partnership schools comprehensive school reform (CSR) model. *The Elementary School Journal, 106*(2), 151–170.

*Estrada, P. (2005). The courage to grow: A researcher and a teacher linking professional development with small-group reading instruction and student achievement. *Research in the Teaching of English, 39*(4), 320–364.

*Ferguson, N., Currie, L. A., Paul, M., & Topping, K. (2011). The longitudinal impact of a comprehensive literacy intervention. *Educational Research, 53*, 237–256.

*Festas, I., Oliveira, A. L., Rebelo, J. A., Damião, M. H., Harris, K., & Graham, S. (2015). Professional development in self-regulated strategy development: Effects on the writing performance of eighth grade Portuguese students. *Contemporary Educational Psychology, 40*, 17–27.

*Fitzgerald, J., & Ramsbotham, A. (2004). First-graders' cognitive and strategic development in Reading Recovery reading and writing. *Reading Research and Instruction, 44*(1), 1–31.

*Frost, J., & Sorenson, P. M. (2007). The effects of a comprehensive reading intervention programme for grade 3 children. *Journal of Research in Reading, 30*(3), 270–286.

Gaffney, J. S., & Anderson, R. C. (1991). Two-tiered scaffolding: Congruent processes of teaching and learning. In E. H. Hiebert (Ed.), *Literacy for a diverse society: Perspectives, programs, and policies* (pp. 184–198). NY: Teachers College.

Gallimore, R., Ermeling, B. A., Saunders, W. M., & Goldenberg, C. (2009). Moving the learning of teaching closer to practice: Teacher education implications of school-based inquiry teams. *The Elementary School Journal, 109*, 537–553.

*Garet, M. S., Cronen, S., Eaton, M., Kurki, A., Ludwig, M., Jones, W., . . . & Sztejnberg, L. (2008). The impact of two professional development interventions on early reading instruction and achievement. Research Report No. 2008-4030. Retrieved from Institute of Education Sciences website: http://ies.ed.gov/ncee (accessed February 18, 2015).

Garet, M. S., Porter, A. C., Desimone, L., Birman, B. F., & Yoon, K. S. (2001). What makes professional development effective? Results from a national sample of teachers. *American Educational Research Journal, 38*, 915–945.

*Gelzheiser, L. M., Scanlon, D., Vellutino, F., Hallgren-Flynn, L., & Schatschneider, C. (2011). Effects of the interactive strategies approach—extended: A responsive and comprehensive intervention for intermediate-grade struggling readers. *The Elementary School Journal, 112*, 280–306.

*Gersten, R., Dimino, J., Jayanthi, M., Kim, J. S., & Santoro, L. E. (2010). Teacher study group: Impact of the professional development model on reading instruction and student outcomes in first grade classrooms. *American Educational Research Journal, 47*(3), 694–739.

Graham, S. (2006). Writing. In P. A. Alexander and P. H. Winne (Eds.), *Handbook of educational psychology* (2nd ed., pp. 457–478). Mahwah, NJ: Erlbaum.

*Greenleaf, C. L., Litman, C., Hanson, T. L., Rosen, R., Boscardin, C. K., Herman, J., . . . Jones, B. (2011). Integrating literacy and science in biology: Teaching and learning impacts of reading apprenticeship professional development. *American Educational Research Journal, 48*(3), 647–717.

*Hanselman, P., & Borman, G. D. (2013). The impacts of success for all on reading achievement in grades 3–5: Does intervening during the later elementary grades produce the same benefits as intervening early? *Educational Evaluation and Policy Analysis, 35*, 237–251.

*Harris, K. R., Graham, S., & Adkins, M. (2015). Practice-based professional development and self-regulated strategy development for Tier 2, at-risk writers in second grade. *Contemporary Educational Psychology, 40*, 5–16.

*Harris, K. R., Lane, K. L., Graham, S., Driscoll, S. A., Sandmel, K., Brindle, M., & Schatschneider, C. (2012). Practice-based professional development for self-regulated strategies development in writing: A randomized controlled study. *Journal of Teacher Education, 63*(2), 103–119.

*Herlihy, C. M., & Kemple, J. J. (2004). *The Talent Development Middle School model: Context, components, and initial impacts on students' performance and attendance.* New York: MDRC.

Hiebert, E. H., & Raphael, T. E. (1996). Psychological perspectives on literacy and extensions to educational practice. In D. C. Berliner and R. C. Calfee (Eds.), *Handbook of educational psychology* (pp. 550–602). New York: Macmillan.

Hill, H. C, Beisiegel, M., & Jacob, R. (2013). Professional development research: Consensus, crossroads, and challenges. *Educational Researcher, 42*, 476–487.

*Hurry, J., & Sylva, K. (2007). Long-term outcomes of early reading intervention. *Journal of Research in Reading, 30*, 227–248.

*Iversen, S., Tunmer, W. E., & Chapman, J. W. (2005). The effects of varying group size on the Reading Recovery approach to preventive early intervention. *Journal of Learning Disabilities, 38*(5), 456–472.

Jadallah, M., Anderson, R. C., Nguyen-Jahiel, K., Miller, M., Kim, I.-H., Kuo, L.-J., . . . Dong, T. (2011). Influence of a teacher's scaffolding moves during child-led small-group discussions. *American Educational Research Journal, 48*, 194–230.

Juel, C. (1988). Learning to read and write: A longitudinal study of fifty-four children from first through fourth grade. *Journal of Educational Psychology, 80*, 437–447.

*Kelly, P. R., Gómez-Bellengé, F.-X., Chen, J., & Schulz, M. M. (2008). Learner outcomes for English language learner low readers in an early intervention. *TESOL Quarterly, 42*, 235–260.

*Kennedy, E., & Shiel, G. (2010). Raising literacy levels with collaborative on-site professional development in a disadvantaged school. *The Reading Teacher, 63*, 372–383.

*Kim, J. S., Olson, C. B., Scarcella, R., Kramer, J., Pearson, M., van Dyk, D., Collins, P., & Land, R. E. (2011). A randomized experiment of a cognitive strategies approach to text-based analytical writing for mainstreamed Latino English language learners in grades 6 to 12. *Journal of Research on Educational Effectiveness, 4*, 231–263.

*Klingner, J. K., Vaughn, S., Arguelle, M. E., Hughes, M. T., & Leftwich, S. A. (2004). Collaborative strategic reading: "Real-world" lessons from classroom teachers. *Remedial and Special Education, 25*(5), 291–302.

*Lai, M. K., McNaughton, S., Amituanai-Toloa, M., Turner, R., & Hsiao, S. (2009). Sustained acceleration of achievement in reading comprehension: The New Zealand experience. *Reading Research Quarterly, 44*(1), 30–56.

*Lee, O., Lewis, S., Adamson, K., Maerten-Rivera, J., & Secada, W. G. (2007). Urban elementary school teachers' knowledge and practices in teaching science to English language learners. *Science Education, 92*, 733–758.

*Lee, O., Maerten-Rivera, J., Penfield, R. D., LeRoy, K., & Secada, W. G. (2008). Science achievement of English language learners in urban elementary schools: Results of a first-year professional development intervention. *Journal of Research in Science Teaching, 45*(1), 31–52.

*Lee, O., Penfield, R. D., & Buxton, C. A. (2011). Relationship between "form" and "content" in science writing among English language learners. *Teachers College Record, 113*, 1401–1434.

*Levin, I., & Aram, D. (2012). Mother–child joint writing and storybook reading and their effects on kindergartners' literacy: an intervention study. *Reading and Writing, 25*, 217–249.

*Lovett, M. W., Lacerenza, L., De Palma, M., Benson, N. J., Steinbach, K. A., & Frijters, J. C. (2008). Preparing teachers to remediate reading disabilities in high school: What is needed for effective professional development? *Teaching and Teacher Education, 24*, 1083–1097.

*Mathes, P. G., Denton, C. A., Fletcher, J. M., Anthony, J. L., Francis, D. J., & Schatschneider, C. (2005). The effects of theoretically different instruction and student characteristics on the skills of struggling readers. *Reading Research Quarterly, 40*(2), 148–182.

*Matsumura, L. C., Garnier, H. E., Correnti, R., Junker, B., & Bickel, D. D. (2010). Investigating the effectiveness of a comprehensive literacy coaching program in schools with high teacher mobility. *The Elementary School Journal, 111*(1), 35–62.

*McCutchen, D., Green, L., Abbott, R. D., & Sanders, E. A. (2009). Further evidence for teacher knowledge: Supporting struggling readers in grades three through five. *Reading and Writing, 22*, 401–423.

*McKeown, M. G., & Beck, I. L. (2004). Transforming knowledge into professional development resources: Six teachers implement a model of teaching for understanding text. *The Elementary School Journal, 104*(5), 391–408.

*McMaster, K. L., Han, I., Coolong-Chaffin, M., & Fuchs, D. (2013). Promoting teachers' use of scientifically based instruction: A comparison of university versus district support. *The Elementary School Journal, 113*(3), 303–330.

*Menzies, H. M., Mahdavi, J. N., & Lewis, J. L. (2008). Early intervention in reading: From research to practice. *Remedial and Special Education, 29*(2), 67–77.

*Munoz, M. A., & Dossett, D. H. (2004). Educating students placed at risk: Evaluating the impact of Success for All in urban settings. *Journal of Education for Students Placed at Risk, 9*, 261–277.

National Institute for Literacy. (2008). *Developing early literacy: Report of the National Early Literacy Panel*. Washington, DC: National Institute for Literacy.

National Institute of Child Health and Human Development. (2000). *Report of the National Reading Panel. Teaching children to read: An evidence-based assessment of the scientific research literature on reading and its implications for reading instruction.* NIH Publication No. 00-4769. Washington, D.C.: U.S. Government Printing Office.

*Nesselrodt, P. S., & Alger, C. L. (2005). Extending opportunity to learn for students placed at risk. *Journal of Education for Students Placed at Risk, 10*(2), 207–224.

No Child Left Behind Act of 2001, P.L. 107-110 (2001). Retrieved from http://www2.ed.gov/policy/elsec/leg/esea02/index.html (accessed 13 March 2015).

*O'Connor, R. E., Fulmer, D., Harty, K. R., & Bell, K. M. (2005). Layers of reading intervention in kindergarten through third grade changes in teaching and student outcomes. *Journal of Learning Disabilities, 38*, 440–455.

Pearson, P. D., & Gallagher, M. C. (1983). The instruction of reading comprehension. *Contemporary Educational Psychology, 8*, 317–344.

*Phillips, G., McNaughton, S., & MacDonald, S. (2004). Managing the mismatch: Enhancing early literacy progress for children with diverse language and cultural identities in mainstream urban schools in New Zealand. *Journal of Educational Psychology, 96*, 309–323.

*Porche, M. V., Pallante, D. H., & Snow, C. E. (2012). Professional development for reading achievement: Results from the collaborative language and literacy instruction project (CLLIP). *The Elementary School Journal, 112*(4), 649–671.

Rogoff, B., & Wertsch, J. V. (Eds.). (1984). *New directions for child development: No. 23: Children's learning in the "zone of proximal development."* San Francisco, CA: Jossey Bass.

*Sailors, M., & Price, L. R. (2010). Professional development that supports the teaching of cognitive reading strategy instruction. *The Elementary School Journal, 110*(3), 301–322.

Saunders, W. M., Goldenberg, C. N., & Gallimore, R. (2009). Increasing achievement by focusing grade-level teams on improving classroom learning: A prospective, quasi-experimental study of title I schools. *American Educational Research Journal, 46*, 1006–1033.

*Scanlon, D. M., Gelzheiser, L. M., Vellutino, F. R., Schatschneider, C., & Sweeney, J. M. (2008). Reducing the incidence of early reading difficulties: Professional development for classroom teachers vs. direct interventions for children. *Learning and Individual Differences, 18*(3), 346–359.

*Schwartz, R. M. (2005). Literacy learning of at-risk first-grade students in the Reading Recovery early intervention. *Journal of Educational Psychology, 97*, 257–267.

*Short, D. J., Fidelman, C. G., & Louguit, M. (2012). Developing academic language in English language learners through sheltered instruction. *TESOL Quarterly, 46*(2), 334–361.

*Simmons, D., Hairrell, A., Edmonds, M., Vaughn, S., Larsen, R., Wilson, V., . . . Byrns, G. (2010). A comparison of multiple-strategy models: Effects on fourth-grade students' general and content-specific reading comprehension and vocabulary development. *Journal of Research on Educational Effectiveness, 3*, 121–156.

*Skindrud, K., & Gersten, R. (2006). An evaluation of two contrasting approaches for improving reading achievement in a large urban district. *The Elementary School Journal, 106*, 389–408.

Slavin, R.E. (2008). What works? Issues in synthesizing education program evaluations. *Educational Researcher, 37*(1), 5–14.

Slavin, R. E., Madden, N. A., Dolan, L. J., & Wasik, B. A. (1996). *Every child, every school: Success for all*. Thousand Oaks, CA: Corwin.

Snow, C. E., Burns, M. S., & Griffin, P. (Eds.). (1998). *Preventing reading difficulties in young children*. Washington, DC: National Academy Press.

*Spear-Swerling, L. (2009). A literacy tutoring experience for prospective special educators and struggling second graders. *Journal of Learning Disabilities, 42*, 431–443.

*Spear-Swerling, L., & Brucker, P. O. (2004). Preparing novice teachers to develop basic reading and spelling skills in children. *Annals of Dyslexia, 54*, 332–359.

*Stein, M. L., Berends, M., Fuchs, D., McMaster, K., Saenz, L., Yen, L., Fuchs, L. S., & Compton, D. (2008). Scaling up an early reading program: Relationships among teacher support, fidelity of implementation, and student performance across different sites and years. *Educational Evaluation and Policy Analysis, 30*(4), 368–388.

Stephens, D., Morgan, D. N., DeFord, D., Donnelly, A., Hamil, E., Crowder, K., . . . Leigh, S. R. (2011). The impact of literacy coaches on teachers' beliefs and practices. *Journal of Literacy Research, 43*(3), 215–249.

Stephens, D., Morgan, D., Donnelly, A., DeFord, D., Young, J., Seaman, M., . . . Meyer, P. (2007). *The South Carolina Reading Initiative: NCTE's reading initiative as a statewide staff development project*. Urbana, IL: National Council of Teachers of English.

*Sutherland, J. (2006). Promoting group talk and higher-order thinking n pupils by 'coaching' secondary English trainee teachers. *Literacy, 40*(2), 106–114.

*Sylva, K., Scott, S., Totsika, V., Ereky-Stevens, K., & Crook, C. (2008). Training parents to help their children read: A randomized control trial. *British Journal of Educational Psychology, 78*, 435–455.

*Taylor, B. M., Pearson, P. D., Peterson, D. S., & Rodriguez, M. C. (2004). The CIERA school change framework: An evidence-based approach to professional development and school reading improvement. *Reading Research Quarterly, 40*(1), 40–69.

Tharp, R. G., Estrada, P., Dalton, S., & Yamauchi, L. (2000). *Teaching transformed: Achieving excellence, fairness, inclusion, and harmony*. Boulder, CO: Westview Press.

Tharp, R. G., & Gallimore, R. (1988). *Rousing minds to life: Teaching, learning, and schooling in social context*. New York: Cambridge University Press.

*Tong, F., Irby, B. J., Lara-Alecio, R., Yoon, M., & Mathes, P. (2010). Hispanic English learners' responses to longitudinal English instructional intervention and the effect of gender: A multilevel analysis. *The Elementary School Journal, 110*(4), 542–566.

*Van Keer, H., & Verhaeghe, J. P. (2005a). Effects of explicit reading strategies instruction and peer tutoring on second and fifth graders' reading comprehension and self-efficacy perceptions. *Journal of Experimental Education, 73*(4), 291–329.

*Van Keer, H., & Verhaeghe, J. P. (2005b). Comparing two teacher development programs for innovating reading comprehension instruction with regard to teachers' experiences and student outcomes. *Teaching and Teacher Education, 21*, 543–562.

Van Lier, L. (2007). Action-based teaching, autonomy and identity. *Innovation in Language Learning and Teaching, 1*(1), 46–65.

*Vaughn, S., Mathes, P., Linan-Thompson, S., Cirino, P., Carlson, C., Pollard-Durodola, S., . . . Francis, D. (2006). Effectiveness of an English intervention for first-grade English language learners at risk for reading problems. *The Elementary School Journal, 107*(2), 153–180.

*Vernon-Feagans, L., Kainz, K., Hedrick, A., Ginsberg, M., & Amendum, S. (2013). Live webcam coaching to help early elementary classroom teachers provide effective literacy instruction for struggling readers: The targeted reading intervention. *Journal of Educational Psychology, 105*(4), 1175–1187.

Vygotsky, L. S. (1981). The genesis of higher mental functions. In J. W. Wertsch (Ed.), *The concept of activity in Soviet psychology* (pp. 144–188). Armonk, NY: Sharpe.

*Walpole, S., McKenna, M. C., Uribe-Zarain, X., & Lamitina, D. (2010). The relationships between coaching and instruction in the primary grades: Evidence from high-poverty schools. *The Elementary School Journal, 111*(1), 115–140.

*Whitehead, D. (2010). The year after: Sustaining the effects of literacy professional development in New Zealand secondary schools. *Language and Education, 24*, 133–149.

Wood, D., Bruner, J. S., & Ross, G. (1976). The role of tutoring in problem solving. *Journal of Child Psychology and Psychiatry and Allied Disciplines, 17*, 89–100.

*Zakierski, M., & Siegel, A. (2010). Creating collaborative literacy teams to increase reading achievement in urban settings. *Journal of College Teaching & Learning, 7*(4), 25–28.

# 18

# Warm Change about Hot Topics

## The Role of Motivation and Emotion in Attitude and Conceptual Change about Controversial Science Topics

*Gale M. Sinatra*
University of Southern California

*Viviane Seyranian*
California State Polytechnic University, Pomona

Students and the general public often consider current scientific topics such as biological evolution, climate change, stem cell research, vaccinations, and genetically modified food *controversial*. However, the degree of controversy is in the eye of the beholder. Science is conducted at the edge of the known, thus cutting-edge science can be controversial even among those engaged in the research directly. However, many issues within a field of study are largely resolved from a scientific standpoint, but are still considered controversial from the public's perception. As an example, 98% of climate scientists concur that we are in a period of warming and humans are contributing significantly to this trend (Intergovernmental Panel on Climate Change, 2007). Thus, this point is not controversial within the climate science community. However, the *projections* for future average temperatures still have a degree of uncertainty—somewhere between 2 and 6° is the best estimate (Intergovernmental Panel on Climate Change, 2007). The degree of uncertainty in projections may contribute to the public's perception that climate change is more controversial than scientists perceive it to be. Similarly, there is a high level of certainty within the scientific community that vaccines are not linked to autism, and yet the causes of autism are still uncertain, leading some members of the public to resist vaccinating their children (Sinatra, Kienhues, & Hofer, 2014).

Topics perceived as controversial present unique challenges for teachers, students, and members of the public who must weigh these issues in learning, reasoning, and decision making. These challenges include many factors, such as understanding uncertainty (Lindley, 2006) and appreciating

complexity (Hmelo-Silver & Azevedo, 2006), both inherent to understanding controversial topics (Sinatra et al., 2014a).

A trend in media and popular outlets, school boards, and more recently in textbooks is to present "both sides" of every science topic in the interest of "fair and balanced" presentation. This is misleading, as it gives the impression of a greater degree of controversy than actually exists among members of the scientific community. Students in classrooms, learners in out-of-school environments, and members of the general public hold both attitudes and conceptual knowledge about controversial science topics that impact their learning, engagement, and acceptance of scientific ideas (Sinatra et al., 2014a). Further, recent research on the *warming trend* (Sinatra, 2005), and on motivated reasoning (Jost, Glaser, Kruglanski, & Sulloway, 2003), shows that the processes of attitude change and conceptual change are significantly impacted by motivation and emotion, and are not likely to be overcome by simply filling in gaps in knowledge (Sinatra et al., 2014a).

Our purpose for this chapter is to present a view of the challenges of fostering attitude and conceptual change on controversial topics in science that will inform research and teaching. We begin by drawing distinctions between attitudes, beliefs, and conceptual knowledge. We argue that these distinctions are necessary for a more complete understanding of the change process. Then, we provide an overview of two literatures that until recently were considered in isolation: attitude change and conceptual change. In these literature reviews, we pay particular attention to the role motivation and emotion play in understanding and acceptance of controversial science topics. Next, we consider the intersection of conceptual change and attitude change by proposing a framework for exploring change. Next, we discuss the methodological challenges facing this field of study. Finally, we conclude with directions for future research.

### Attitude Change and Conceptual Change: Important Distinctions

What do you know about stem cell research? What is your attitude towards stem cell research? As researchers, when we pose these two questions, are we asking about two fundamentally different constructs? Can we empirically and theoretically distinguish between these constructs? If these differences exist, are they relevant and important to educators and researchers? Over ten years ago, Southerland, Sinatra, and Matthews argued that such questions "are at the very heart of science teaching and research" (2001, p. 327). Yet, in the last decade, rather than more conceptual clarity, we perceive that there has been a greater blurring of the constructs of attitude change and conceptual change in academic and public discourse. Attitudes are related to beliefs, and here is where the lines begin to blur. Murphy and Mason note that,

> most educational psychology researchers seem to avoid differentiating between knowledge and beliefs by either using the terms interchangeably or by only referring to knowledge or beliefs. In this way, researchers avoid the issue of the relations among these constructs. (2006, p. 306)

Southerland et al. (2001) argued that there are important differences between knowledge, beliefs, attitudes, and acceptance that matter for how we conceptualize research in science education. For controversial topics, we argue that the distinctions are not only important, but are critical for research and teaching. Therefore, we propose a framework for conceptualizing attitude and knowledge change that we feel may contribute to productive research on the intersection of these important constructs.

### Attitude Change and Conceptual Change about Controversial Topics

Before we can consider attitudes and conceptual change, we must first consider the conceptual distinctions between attitudes and concepts as well as the distinction between knowledge and belief. Then, we discuss relevant models of attitude change and conceptual change.

### Attitudes and Attitude Change

The study of attitudes has been fundamental to the field of social psychology since its inception (Allport, 1935; McGuire, 1985; Prislin & Crano, 2008). Despite the centrality of the attitude concept in social psychology, surprisingly, the definition of attitudes still remains elusive (Banaji & Heiphetz, 2010), with hundreds of definitions prevalent in the literature (Albarracín, Johnson, Zanna, & Kumale, 2005). Various attitude scholars (e.g., Eagly & Chaiken, 1993) have noted that the common thread running through the majority of these definitions is that an *attitude consists of an evaluation of a person, object, or entity*. That is, an attitude describes the *valence* (e.g., like–dislike, favor or disfavor) evoked by an attitude object. This idea is also echoed in the most widely cited definition of attitudes by Eagly and Chaiken (1993), who defined an attitude as "a psychological tendency that is expressed by evaluating a particular entity with some degree of favor or disfavor" (p. 1).

*Attitudinal components.* When conceptualized as evaluative judgments, attitudes are described as consisting of three components related to the attitude object: (a) behaviors; (b) affect; and (c) cognition. The behavioral intention or response is interpreted to relay a positive or negative evaluation of the attitude object. For example, attitude theorists would argue that the act of wishing a friend "happy birthday" on Facebook might express a positive evaluation of the friend.

The *affective* component of attitudes consists of the feelings, emotions, or moods evoked by, and associated with, the attitude object. Affective reactions are usually positive (e.g., joy) or negative (e.g., sadness) and contribute to evaluative responding. In recent years, there has been an increased emphasis on the affective component of attitudes as these are more readily accessible and may contribute more to behavioral outcomes than the cognitive component (Banaji & Heiphetz, 2010; Forgas, 2010).

Attitude theorists often describe the cognitive component of attitudes as an evaluative reaction to beliefs about an attitude object. In this context, *beliefs* are defined as associations formed between an attitude object and some related attribute (Eagly & Chaiken, 1998). We propose that a more fine-grained definition of beliefs is called for, particularly when considering attitudes from the vantage point of controversial science topics and attitude or conceptual change. The cognitive component of attitudes entails an evaluative reaction to one of the following types of beliefs: (a) *unjustified beliefs*, which are associations between an attitude object and a related attribute that has emerged from experience (by "unjustified," we mean to suggest that the belief is held with insufficient justification or warrant to be called knowledge), or (b) *justified true beliefs (knowledge)*, which are associations between an attitude object and a related attribute that has sufficient justifications and warrants to be called knowledge. For example, a scientist's hypothesis may be construed as a belief until substantial scientific evidence supporting the hypothesis is gathered to justify calling the belief *knowledge*.

As such, attitudes can consist of valenced evaluative reactions to unjustified beliefs (e.g., the Holocaust never happened) or justified true beliefs (e.g., the earth rotates around the sun). Note that this is consistent with a definition of conceptual knowledge as *justified true belief*. Even though conceptual knowledge is by definition not valenced in and of itself, it can conjure up evaluative reactions in people in a similar manner as unjustified beliefs. For example, a person may have conceptual knowledge about stem cells. That is, he may understand what a stem cell is and hold justified knowledge about stem cell research. At an evaluative level, however, he may react negatively to this knowledge. In other words, this reaction may contribute evaluative information that may inform his attitudes about stem cell research. Therefore, one can hold attitudes about both types of beliefs, the unjustified and the justified (or knowledge). In the same vein, attitudes can also be changed about both types of beliefs (see Attitude Change and Persuasion section, below). This idea suggests a novel way of considering the link between conceptual knowledge and attitudes. We will return to this point later and elaborate more on the relationship between attitudes and conceptual knowledge when considering the attitude–conceptual change framework. For now, it is important to highlight the idea that attitudes can be informed by one or two types of beliefs, unjustified and justified true beliefs, which can operate alone or simultaneously to inform evaluations.

Attitudes may be primarily based on behavioral, affective, or cognitive components or they may consist of evaluative responses that integrate these aspects. For instance, a student's positive evaluation of physical education class may stem from her belief that exercise leads to good health (cognitive), that she feels happy during exercise (affective), engages in it often (behavior), or a combination of one or more of these components. Attitude scholars also consider the relative consistency of the evaluative information *across* the behavioral, affective, or cognitive components. For example, a person might believe that bungee jumping is safe (positive cognitive evaluation) but experience fear and panic when considering the prospect of taking the plunge (negative affective evaluation). In this example, there is an inconsistency across components, which contributes disparate evaluative information to the overall attitude.

It is also possible to have inconsistencies *within* evaluative components—for instance, *within* the cognitive component. Consider attitudes about controversial topics. For controversial science topics, there are usually different camps (pro or con). Each camp presents its own set of information, statistics, beliefs, and rationales to substantiate its position. As such, individuals may be exposed to disparate and potentially conflicting information from each side and their attitudes will contain evaluative judgments regarding beliefs from both camps. Along these lines, Pratkanis (1989) noted that attitudes about controversial issues are more likely to contain bipolar structures, that is, information from both sides of an issue is represented in memory. Non-controversial issues are more likely to be represented with a unipolar structure that predominantly contains information that is in line with the attitude. Eagly and Chaiken (1998) argue that "it may be mainly in the face of clear-cut social conflict on an issue that people's attitudes become bipolar in the sense that they divide their knowledge into clusters of congenial and uncongenial ideas" (p. 274).

Expanding on this idea, we propose that an attitude about a controversial issue may become bipolar particularly when it is associated with one's collective self or social identity (Tajfel & Turner, 1986) and there is some type of tension that characterizes relations between the ingroup and outgroup. In this circumstance, attitudes may become bipolar because different attitudinal poles help to distinguish the ingroup from the outgroup. For example, negative attitudes towards whaling may be associated with a social identity such as an anti-whaling Greenpeace activist, yet the activist will also possess considerable information about the beliefs of the outgroup (whalers).

An attitude may have either a bipolar or unipolar structure, and at the same time, it may be related to another attitude or sets of attitudes, which may be embedded within more global structures (Eagly & Chaiken, 1998). Related attitudes tend to cluster together in a constellation, not unlike related conceptual knowledge. For instance, attitudes about gun control and gays in the military are associated (Alvaro & Crano, 1997; Crano, 2012). Attitudes that are highly integrated with values are termed *ideologies* (Banaji & Heiphetz, 2010). Similar to individual attitudes, ideologies may also have bipolar structures, as a person may possess information about both sides of the ideological spectrum. Take, for example, the liberal–conservative ideology. Conservatives and liberals may hold considerable information about the other side's position on social and political issues. That is not to say the beliefs and information concerning the positions of the "other side" are always accurate. For instance, a conservative from the United States may have some understanding about communism or socialism, but also hold a variety of misconceptions, and a liberal may have some understanding of nuclear power but may also hold some misconceptions. When attitudes are based on misconceptions, they may be particularly resistant to change unless the misconception is corrected. In this case, *attitudinal change may be dependent on conceptual change.* Prior to developing this idea, let us first consider attitude change and persuasion.

### Attitude Change and Persuasion

Attitude change occurs when an evaluation about a justified or unjustified belief is moved in a different direction. An attitude can move in a direction that is in line with the original evaluation (polarize) or it can move in the opposite direction or towards neutrality compared to the original evaluation (depolarize). Until the 1950s, there was little understanding of attitude change and the processes that encourage it (persuasion). The pioneering efforts of the Yale group, a team of 30 scholars led by Carl Hovland, spurred the field of attitude change and persuasion (Johnson, Miao, & Smith-McLallen, 2005). More contemporary research and theories of persuasion stand on the shoulders of this earlier work and extend it by proposing a dual process of persuasion (Chaiken, 1980; Petty & Cacioppo, 1986a).

***The Elaboration Likelihood Model (ELM).*** The ELM (Petty & Cacioppo, 1986b) is a model of how persuasion may occur through one of two processes. When one encounters a persuasive message, the extent to which the message is processed depends on one's motivation and ability to process the message. The motivation and ability to process a message depend on a confluence of situational and individual difference variables; however, people tend to be most motivated to elaborate on information when it is personally relevant (Petty & Cacioppo, 1979). When one is sufficiently motivated and able to process a message, ELM would predict that central route processing is employed to carefully scrutinize and comb through all of the available information concerning the attitude object. As such, individuals will compare the message with their previous knowledge and beliefs and evaluate its merit. If the quality of the message is strong, this type of intense and effortful message consideration will likely elicit attitude change. If message quality is weak, effortful message consideration will reduce the likelihood of attitude change as there is little merit to the message. Attitudes changed as a result of effortful consideration (or high elaboration) and strong message quality tend to be strong, resistant to subsequent persuasion efforts, and more predictive of behavior (Petty, Haugtvedt, & Smith, 1995).

When one is insufficiently motivated or unable to process a message, ELM predicts that peripheral route processing is more likely to be employed, whereby individuals are less likely to carefully process a message. Since message content is not closely attended to during peripheral route processing, message quality is not a factor that influences attitude change. Instead, peripheral cues play a pivotal role. Peripheral cues are factors that are peripheral to the logic of the argument, which may comprise of variables such as source credibility or attractiveness. Peripheral cues could also comprise of heuristics (Chaiken, 1980) or simple decision rules such as "experts tend to be correct" in making judgments. When people use the peripheral route processing, they are more likely to form weaker attitudes that may be fleeting (Petty & Wegener, 1998).

The ELM assumes that elaboration is objective when a particular judgment is not preferred prior to message exposure. However, biased message processing is also possible when individuals hold a favored attitudinal position or have relatively one-sided knowledge prior to message exposure. In particular, Petty and Wegener (1998) argue that individuals with a biased store of knowledge have more information to draw on to bolster their own side and they can better see the flaws of opposing arguments. As a result, their attitudes can become even more polarized due to counterattitudinal message exposure (Lord, Ross, & Lepper, 1979).

***Source credibility.*** Source credibility usually refers to the level of *expertise* (i.e., knowledge and ability to provide accurate information) and *trustworthiness* (i.e., honesty) associated with a source (Petty & Wegener, 1998). Research has widely corroborated the power of highly credible sources to influence attitude change, particularly when messages are of low personal relevance (for a review, see Pornpitakpan, 2004). Research shows that source credibility can have differential impacts. It can act as a peripheral cue when individuals are not processing the message deeply (Petty & Wegener, 1998). When individuals do engage deeply with the message, the quality of message arguments is more important than source credibility in influencing attitudes (Petty, Cacioppo, & Goldman, 1981). However, when a message is personally relevant, source credibility may take on alternative roles. It can spur message-relevant thoughts (Heesacker, Petty, & Cacioppo, 1983), bias processing (Chaiken & Maheswaran, 1994), or could act as an argument that bolsters message quality (Kaufman, Stasson, & Hart, 1999).

***Group membership: ingroup and outgroup.*** Another important source variable that may influence consideration of controversial issues is ingroup and outgroup status. An *ingroup* is a group of people with whom a person shares common group membership (e.g., ethnicity, religion). Not all group memberships are important to individuals. For the ingroup to become psychologically meaningful, individuals must attach emotional significance or identify with the group such that the group becomes a part of their social identity (Tajfel & Turner, 1986). In this case, the individual is said to highly identify with the group. An *outgroup* is a group of people with whom an individual does not share common group membership, and does not identify.

Research suggests that a message associated with an ingroup member holds more persuasive power than the same message from an outgroup member (see Turner, 1991). These findings may be explained by social categorization theory, which suggests that individuals tend to conform to the attitudes, norms, and behaviors (prototypes) of ingroups, particularly those with which they highly identify (Turner, 1991). For example, a faculty member may be more persuaded by a message to change tenure review guidelines if the source of the message is from another faculty member (ingroup) than a student (outgroup). If the individual does not have the motivation or ability to process the message, ingroup or outgroup status may serve as a peripheral cue in influencing attitude change (Wood, 2000).

Recent research suggests that ingroup sources may be more persuasive in altering attitudes about justified beliefs than in changing justified beliefs themselves. Seyranian, Lombardi, and Sinatra (in submission) recently provided experimental evidence showing that attitudes about scientific views on climate change (justified by evidence) were more amenable to persuasion by an ingroup source than an outgroup source. On the other hand, the plausibility of climate change (more subjective and thus could be considered to have weaker justification) was more likely to be influenced by an outgroup source than an ingroup source. The rationale for this discrepancy is that individuals tend to consult with similar others (i.e., ingroups) on attitudinal judgments because they are more likely to share their own worldviews, beliefs, and values. Ingroup members are also likely to share similar biases, which may interfere with objective judgments (e.g., groupthink). Dissimilar sources (i.e., outgroups) are more likely to be consulted for knowledge-based judgments that are verifiably right or wrong because outgroups are less likely to share the same biases and will likely possess different strengths and weaknesses than the ingroup. As such, they may have worthwhile perspective to share for knowledge judgments (Crano & Seyranian, 2009).

## Conceptual Knowledge and Conceptual Change

Conceptual change describes a special case of learning when the to-be-learned information conflicts with the learner's background knowledge and is often referred to as a process of *knowledge restructuring* (see, for example, Dole & Sinatra, 1998; Murphy & Mason, 2006). Much of the information we learn is new, or only vaguely familiar. While we may hold some fragmented pieces of knowledge about the topic (Smith, diSessa, & Roschelle, 1993), we may not have a rich, developed, interconnected representation of the concept in memory. From our point of view, conceptual change describes the scenario when the learner holds a conception that is connected to other concepts in background knowledge, can be used in reasoning or problem-solving tasks (likely ineffectually, since it is misconceived), and it is in conflict with the new information.

In the parlance of attitudes and attitude change discussed above, one would say that knowledge that is misconceived is not well justified and therefore is technically a *belief*. It is important to note that, in the conceptual change literature, this terminology is not typically used. If the term "belief" is used, it is used in a variety of ways, as there is no common definition of belief or belief change. Conceptual change researchers typically describe concepts as consistent or inconsistent with scientific understanding. In our review below, we use the terms used in the conceptual change literature to avoid confusion, and we note where differences lie.

Many perspectives exist on the nature of conceptual change learning (for a review of several perspectives, see Vosniadou, 2008). Major perspectives that have significantly influenced our understanding of the change process when confronted with controversial topics include those from developmental psychology (Carey, 2009; Vosniadou, 2008), cognitive science (Chi, 1992; Ohlsson, 2009), science education (Posner, Strike, Hewson, & Gertzog, 1982; Strike & Posner, 1992), and educational psychology (Dole & Sinatra, 1998; Murphy & Mason, 2006; Sinatra, 2005). Next, we briefly review each of these perspectives with an eye towards how they inform our current view.

***Developmental perspectives.*** The origin and development of conceptual knowledge are of deep and central concern to all of psychology, but are foundational to any understanding of conceptual change. Most researchers describe conceptual knowledge as categorical in nature. That is, "a concept can be viewed as belonging to some category" (Chi, 2008, p. 62). We view concepts as rich, interconnected representations of categorical knowledge in memory. A key aspect of the type of conceptual knowledge relative to learning is that it is generative. It allows the knower to draw inferences, make predictions, and think and reason with that conceptual knowledge, which can be small units of thought, mental models, or schemata.

The developmental perspective describes how, through the process of conceptual change, young children acquire new conceptual representations that are qualitatively different than their prior conceptions. These new representations afford new ways of thinking and reasoning about not only the new concept, but about other concepts. Developmentalists trace the origins and restructuring of core concepts such as the concept of "number," "agency," and "living thing," that are fundamental to thinking and reasoning in a variety of domains (Carey, 2009). Carey described these changes as so fundamental that the new representations are incommensurate with prior ones, meaning that the prior representation is forever lost to the individual. (For an alternative perspective on the persistence of prior conceptions post conceptual change, see Shtulman & Valcarcel, 2012.)

Developmental conceptual change of this sort is viewed as driven primarily by maturational processes as the child interacts with her environment. It should be contrasted with the restructuring of concepts that is triggered by instruction. A quintessential example of *instructionally induced conceptual change* (Inagaki & Hatano, 2008) is the well-documented shift in young children's knowledge of the shape of the earth (Vosniadou & Brewer, 1992).

A major difference in maturationally versus instructionally induced conceptual change is that the first may occur without deliberate instruction to bring about change, but the second is unlikely to do so. That is, young children are unlikely to adopt a spherical view of the earth on their own, since the notion is counterintuitive and belies their everyday experience. Even direct instruction on the shape of the earth often results in *synthetic conceptions* (Vosniadou, 1999), or the blending of the original flat-earth concept with the round concept to form the conception that the earth is shaped like a pancake. Once a child has shifted her conception of the shape of the earth, the new spherical earth conception affords (but by no means assures) the acquisition of scientifically correct conceptions of the day/night cycle and seasonal change. And yet, these conceptions are themselves often resistant to instruction designed to overcome misconceptions (Posner et al., 1982).

Thus, we learn several key points from developmental perspectives on conceptual change that pertain to our interest in controversial topics: (a) conceptual knowledge is categorical in nature; (b) conceptual knowledge is constructed in part from everyday experiences that often conflict with scientific understandings (thus, it could be characterized as unjustified beliefs); (c) conceptual knowledge relevant to learning in academic domains, whether scientifically accurate or inaccurate, is highly interconnected with other knowledge and is generative in that it impacts thinking and reasoning about other concepts and domains; and (d) change in one concept affords, but does not necessarily bring about, change in a related concept.

***Cognitive Science Perspective.*** Two perspectives from cognitive science have influenced our thinking on conceptual change regarding controversial topics. The first is that of Chi and her work on conceptual change as a process of *ontological shifts* (Chi, 1992). According to Chi, since conceptual knowledge is categorical in nature, the learner can mistakenly miscategorize concepts, leading to reasoning and problem-solving difficulties. According to Chi, the process of conceptual change is one of restructuring miscategorized knowledge to a new or different *ontological* category (Chi, 1992). Ontological categories are distinguished by different properties. According to this view, the category *process* can be described as taking place over time, but cannot have the property of color, whereas an *entity* can have the property of color, but cannot be described as taking place over time. So, a baseball game or baking a cake could be described as a process, but not an *entity* (Chi, 2008). According to this view, conceptual change is described as a shift from thinking about a concept such as heat as belonging to one ontological category (entity) to thinking about heat as belonging to a different ontological category (process) (Chi, 1992).

An alternative cognitive science perspective that informs our thinking is that of Ohlsson (2009, 2011). Ohlsson rejects the notion that conceptual change is about transforming or restructuring knowledge. Rather, he views the change process as one of seeing a phenomenon from a new theoretical lens, a process he calls resubsumption (Ohlsson, 2009). So, according to this perspective, conceptual change occurs when a learner discovers that there are two ways of thinking about a phenomenon. Ohlsson (2009) calls the process by which experiences with the phenomenon activate both theories *bisociation*. Bisociation is an insight but does not necessarily cause the cognitive conflict, disequilibrium, or restructuring of categorical knowledge theorized by other conceptual change researchers. Ultimately, the choice to think about the phenomenon through the lens of the alternative theory is driven by *cognitive utility* according to this view.

A key difference among these perspectives is the degree to which prior knowledge undergoes radical restructuring (Chi, 1992), is lost to the individual (Carey, 2009), or if the individual merely thinks about the concept from a new perspective, thereby leaving the original knowledge intact (Ohlsson, 2009). A recent study by Shtulman and Valcarcel (2012) was designed to explore precisely this issue. They asked: when conceptual change occurs, "what happens to the earlier theories? Are they overwritten or merely suppressed?" (Shtulman & Valcarcel, 2012, p. 209). In this study, college students were asked to verify information under speeded conditions. Some statements were consistent with both scientific and naïve theories (such as the "moon revolves around the sun") and some statements were consistent with scientific but not naïve theories (such as the "Earth revolves around the sun"; Shtulman & Valcarcel, 2012, p. 209). Participants were slower and less accurate to verify information from ten different domains when the statement was inconsistent with *prior* naïve beliefs. In addition, it was domains that individuals learn earlier in childhood (astronomy), rather than later in adolescence (genetics) that showed the greatest degree of cognitive conflict. Shtulman and Valcarcel concluded that their "findings suggest that naïve theories are suppressed by scientific theories but not supplanted by them" (Shtulman & Valcarcel, 2012, p. 213).

What we take away from these scholars' contributions is that: (a) consistent with the developmental perspective, conceptual knowledge is categorical and concepts are embedded within a hierarchy of rich, interconnected conceptual knowledge; (b) individuals confer characteristics to their conceptual knowledge based on characteristics of the superordinate conceptual knowledge; and (c) non-scientific knowledge may persist even after conceptual change and may be evoked in reasoning under certain conditions.

***Science education perspectives.*** Science education researchers have been influential to our thinking about conceptual change and productive for the conceptual change field more broadly. This work began as an attempt to explain the apparent resistance to instruction that science educators encountered in classrooms (White & Gunstone, 2008). Science instruction designed to promote scientific understanding often failed to surmount students' naïve conceptions, even when those concepts were targeted. In what some refer to as the "classic approach" to conceptual change (Vosniadou, 2008), science educators likened conceptual change to paradigmatic shifts in science because students exhibited ideas that were consistent with earlier scientific theories (e.g., the flat earth) (Posner et al., 1982). Also, science education researchers initially viewed individual and paradigmatic change processes as analogous.

Posner and his colleagues (Posner et al., 1982; Strike & Posner, 1992) described the conditions they viewed as necessary for instruction to overcome students' misconceptions. First, students must be put in a situation that promotes dissatisfaction with existing conceptions. For example, dissatisfaction may occur when individuals are confronted with anomalous data (Chinn & Brewer, 1993). Then, students must find the new conception *intelligible*, *plausible*, and *fruitful* (Posner et al., 1982). In other words, instruction must be designed to assure that the students find the new information comprehensible, and judge it as having higher plausibility than their original conception (Lombardi, Sinatra, & Nussbaum, 2013). Finally, the new idea must be generative, in that it must explain other phenomena.

We have learned from science educators that: (a) alternative conceptions can be resistant to instruction, even with instruction designed to promote change; (b) comprehensibility is a key factor for the design of conceptual change pedagogy; and (c) plausibility reappraisal is important for promoting conceptual change on controversial topics (Lombardi, Nussbaum, & Sinatra, in submission; Lombardi et al., 2013).

***Educational psychology perspectives.*** Educational psychology perspectives on conceptual change research are fairly recent compared to the long and rich history of developmental, cognitive science, and science education perspectives. Significant contributions from educational psychologists begin with Chinn and Brewer's account of students' difficulty accommodating anomalous data (Chinn & Brewer, 1993) and extend to recent efforts to integrate motivation into conceptual change (Sinatra, 2005).

From our perspective, educational psychologists' recent contributions have been the integration of cognition, affect, and motivation (often referred to as "hot" constructs) to advance our understanding of *motivated change*. Understanding how beliefs, emotions, and motivation contribute to the change process has been the focus of research on what Sinatra (2005) called the "warming trend" inspired by the influential article, "Beyond cold conceptual change" (Pintrich, Marx, & Boyle, 1993). There have been several recent reviews of Pintrich et al.'s contributions, and the bourgeoning body of empirical work that has come out of their call for a view of conceptual change that begins to take into account hot constructs. Therefore, we do not overview the "next generation" of conceptual change models here (for reviews, see Murphy & Alexander, 2008; Murphy & Mason, 2006; Sinatra, 2005; Sinatra & Mason, 2008).

The influence of attitude change and persuasion research on this conceptualization of conceptual change is evident. Each model blends attitude change and conceptual change research (e.g., Dole & Sinatra, 1998; Gregoire, 2003; Murphy, 2007; Murphy & Mason, 2006), drawing on the ELM (Petty & Cacioppo, 1986b). As we have described, the ELM is a dual-process model of attitude change and persuasion in that it proposes there are two routes to change, a central and a peripheral route. It is the central route (the systematic or deep processing route) that is more likely to produce change than the superficial, low-engagement, or peripheral route.

These accounts of conceptual change also draw directly or indirectly on the notion of levels of processing from cognitive psychology (Craik & Lockhart, 1972) or what has more recently come to be understood as System 1 versus System 2 processing (Kahneman, 2011; Stanovich, 2010). Cognitive psychologists have described the architecture of cognition as differentiated in two distinct forms of processing to provide a "work around" for the limited capacity constraints imposed by working memory:

> System 1 operates automatically and quickly, with little or no effort and no sense of voluntary control. System 2 allocates attention to the effortful mental activities that demand it, including complex computations. The operations of System 2 are often associated with the subjective experience of agency, choice, and concentration. (Kahneman, 2011, pp. 20–21)

Educational psychologists have also drawn on multiple domains (most notably, cognitive psychology, social psychology, and philosophy) to provide an account of *epistemic conceptual change* (Sinatra & Chinn, 2011). Sinatra and Chinn describe epistemic conceptual change as a change in thinking about the nature of knowledge itself, not just in conceptual understanding. For example, if a student views scientific knowledge as certain, she might need to change her views about scientific uncertainty before she could accept that the level of uncertainty in climate models does not undermine the warranted conclusion that the climate is warming. This type of change requires deep processing, motivated engagement, or effortful thinking and reasoning.

In sum, our perspective on conceptual change draws on research from developmental psychology, cognitive science, science education, and educational psychology. In the next section, we describe a new framework for attitude and conceptual change we hope will inform research on controversial science topics that calls for attitude change and conceptual change to be distinguished.

### Attitude Change/Conceptual Change Framework

As described in our review, for over 15 years, conceptual change researchers have integrated persuasion into conceptual change research. This has brought significant progress to our field. However, our work on controversial science topics has led us to posit that the field would be well served by recognizing that a degree of distinction between attitude change and conceptual change should be maintained. In this section, we posit that it is both theoretically and empirically possible to describe a 2 × 2 framework of attitudes and conceptual knowledge about a particular topic (Figure 18.1) which distinguishes these two constructs. According to this framework, an individual can be either in favor of an idea or against it while at the same time either holding misconceptions about the topic or having an accurate conception of the topic. This creates four profiles, which we label, only for the purposes of discussion, Profile A, B, C, and D. Next, we describe each in turn.

Profile A describes an individual who has accurate (justified) knowledge about a topic and holds a favorable attitude towards that topic. Thus we call this first profile, *Pro-Justified*. A stem cell researcher might fit Profile A in that she may favor stem cell research for the treatment of Alzheimer's disease and hold an accurate conception of stem cells' role in the treatment of that disease. Another example could be a college astronomy student who understands the International Astronomical Union's (IAU) redefinition of the concept "planet" that caused them to reclassify Pluto to dwarf planetary status (International Astronomical Union Press Release, 2006, August 24). At the same time, he accepts the IAU's decision to demote Pluto, and favors Pluto's new classification. Thus, he holds both a positive attitude about the new definition of planet and Pluto's reclassification as well as an accurate conception of the concept of planet.

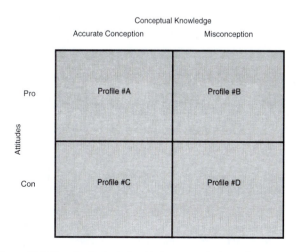

**Figure 18.1** Hypothesized relationship between attitudes and conceptual knowledge.

Profile B describes an individual with favorable attitudes about a topic but who holds misconceptions about that topic; thus this knowledge is not well justified and should be considered a belief (Pro-Unjustified). To return to the stem cell topic, consider a parent who holds out hope for a stem cell treatment for her child's autism. Here, the parent would hold a positive attitude towards the use of stem cells in the treatment of disorders, but likely holds a number of misconceptions about the nature of stem cells and their potential in treatment. She may also hold related misconceptions about the nature of autism and the utility of stem cells for the treatment of autism. Thus, her beliefs about the relation between autism and stem cell treatments are not well justified. Consider a second example of a middle-school student learning about climate change. The student may hold a positive attitude about human-induced climate change. This student accepts that climate change is occurring, accepts that humans have a role, and is favorably disposed towards taking mitigative actions to curb climate change effects through both his own actions and through policy change. However, his conceptual knowledge is flawed in that he thinks that pollution is causing the greenhouse effect and thus pollution is ultimately responsible for climate change. In this case, correcting the misconception may also influence the attitude and perhaps even attitudinal valence. In a science classroom, correcting these types of student misconceptions via a conceptual change pedagogical approach may or may not impact students' attitudes.

An individual with accurate conceptual knowledge who holds unfavorable attitudes (Con-Justified) would characterize Profile C. An example here could be a policy analyst who understands that humans are impacting the climate, but who is not favorably disposed towards taking either personal steps to mitigate climate change or recommending policy changes. A variety of reasons could contribute to the negative attitude toward mitigation strategies. Perhaps this individual feels that one person's behaviors are not that important in the grand scheme of things; thus, she does not believe her actions alone would make a difference. Perhaps she is opposed to climate change policy initiatives because she feels they will be too costly and create too much of a negative impact on national debt. A second example could be an investment banker who holds an accurate conception of the role repackaged junk mortgages had in the financial crisis, but is opposed to regulatory actions that would limit this practice. We could speculate that his motives here could be related to personal interest, but other motives or beliefs could impact this perspective. It is a matter of debate whether it is in the domain of education to attempt to influence students who hold justified beliefs but motivated attitudes (Crano & Prislin, 2006; Sinatra & Kardash, 2004).

Finally, the last profile, Profile D, is the one likely to be very familiar to change researchers (Con-Unjustified). These are individuals who have a negative attitude towards a topic and simultaneously hold misconceptions about that topic. An example could be a person who is opposed to emergency contraception and believes that "morning-after pills" cause an abortion. Another example could be a parent who opposes evolution education and believes that students would be taught that humans evolved from modern-day apes. This situation is likely very common in science education. Perhaps due to the misconception, the student has formed a negative attitude that may bias processing of subsequent information regarding scientific perspectives on climate change or evolution. In this way, the attitude itself becomes an obstacle to knowledge change as well as to the development of accurate scientific understanding. In this particular case, correcting the scientific misconception through conceptual change efforts may also influence subsequent attitudes (see for example, Heddy, Sinatra, & Danielson, 2014).

In terms of prominence, Profile D (Con-Unjustified) might in fact be the most common of our four profiles if we consider only controversial topics. That is, since controversial science topics are at once complex and difficult to understand, and at the same time have significant impact for policy and practice, the profile of negative attitudes and misconceptions co-occurring might be the most prevalent. We would predict that Profile B might be next in prevalence—those with positive attitudes and misconceptions (Pro-Unjustified). Again, this would be due to the prevalence of misconceptions about controversial science topics. Perhaps Profile A would be next in prevalence (Pro-Justified), followed by Profile C (Con-Justified) as least common, although these last two conjectures are highly speculative and all of these predications warrant empirical investigation. It is safer to predict that the likely distribution of individuals across the four profiles would differ substantially if non-controversial topics were considered. Profile A (Pro-Justified) or Profile B (Pro-Unjustified) may be the more prevalent for non-controversial topics. Again, these predictions warrant empirical investigation.

### Attitude and Conceptual Change on Controversial Topics

Whereas a large body of literature exists in both attitude change and conceptual change, few studies have explored both constructs in the same study. Even fewer have explored both attitude and conceptual change on controversial topics.

A recent study conducted by Heddy et al. (2014) examined the attitude change and conceptual change framework by asking undergraduate students enrolled in psychology courses to read a text designed to refute misconceptions about genetically modified organisms (GMOs). The topic of GMOs is interesting because, unlike evolution and climate change (which are rejected more often by conservatives), both liberals and conservatives vary widely in their knowledge and attitudes about GMOs. The results showed that, for individuals who held negative attitudes and misconceptions (con-unjustified) about GMOs, reading a refutation text promoted conceptual change and a shift in attitudes towards more positive evaluations. Similarly, participants who held a positive attitude and misconceptions (pro-unjustified) prior to reading the refutation text also changed their conceptions, but their attitudes remained positive.

These findings were interpreted as providing some support for the hypotheses of the attitudes and knowledge profiles and suggest that overcoming misconceptions can shift attitudes in some instances. Further, the results highlight the importance of drawing distinctions among knowledge, attitudes, and beliefs. That is, when participants experienced change in the knowledge of GMOs, it affected their belief systems, and shifted their attitudes in a positive direction (if they were originally leaning negative). We posit that these more positive attitudes would likely influence subsequent learning about GMOs.

From the research in both areas, we do know that a number of motivational and affective variables influence, if not determine, the likelihood of change. Several motivational and affective constructs have been explored in conceptual change, including epistemic beliefs (Sinatra, Southerland, McConaughy, & Demastes, 2003), interest (Andre & Windschitl, 2003), achievement goals (Linnenbrink & Pintrich, 2003), emotions (Pugh, Linnenbrink-Garcia, Koskey, Stewart, & Manzey, 2010), and task values (Johnson & Sinatra, 2012). Much of this work has been extensively reviewed elsewhere (Sinatra & Chinn, 2011; Sinatra & Mason, 2008). Therefore, we focus primarily on two constructs that are particularly relevant to controversial science topics here—emotions and plausibility.

One area that has been of increasing interest is the role of emotions in science learning in general and in conceptual change in particular (for a review, see Sinatra, Broughton, & Lombardi, 2014b). Emotions are related to individuals' acceptance or rejection of scientific perspectives as well as their willingness to engage with specific controversial topics. Specifically, positive emotions are related to greater acceptance, engagement, and conceptual change whereas negative emotions are associated with lack of engagement and resistance to change (see Sinatra et al., 2014a). Engagement is critical to both attitude change (Petty & Cacioppo, 1986b) and conceptual change (Dole & Sinatra, 1998). Therefore, promoting positive emotions is seen as one means of bolstering engagement and promoting attitude and conceptual change (Broughton, Sinatra, & Nussbaum, 2011; Heddy & Sinatra, 2013).

The relation among these variables was demonstrated in a recent study by Broughton et al. (2011), who explored students' topic emotions as they learned that Pluto had been reclassified to a dwarf planet. Negative emotions were related to negative attitudes about the reclassification. After reading and discussing the scientific rationale behind the reclassification, fifth- and sixth-grade students changed both their attitudes towards the reclassification and their conceptual understanding about the definition of planet toward the scientifically accepted view. In addition, after instruction, students showed a dampening of the negative emotions they had reported when they first learned of the demotion. This study suggests that attitude change and conceptual change are related and may be associated with strong emotions when the topic is controversial. This study also supports our contention that, in some cases, conceptual change may foster attitude change. In this study, the intervention was designed to promote a change in students' conceptual understanding of the redefinition of planet, yet it ultimately shifted attitudes

in favor of the IAU decision to reclassify Pluto. This may be because the conception formed the basis of the attitude. Therefore, shifting the conception simultaneously shifted the attitude.

Heddy and Sinatra (2013) also found that students' emotions about a controversial topic can shift with instruction. They employed the Teaching for Transformative Experience in Science (TTES) pedagogical approach to teach university students enrolled in education classes about biological evolution. TTES promotes engagement with course content in out-of-school settings (Pugh et al., 2010). Results showed that students who learned through the TTES method showed greater enjoyment for learning about biological evolution compared to students who experienced a more traditional lecture, reading, and discussion-based pedagogical approach. They also increased their understanding of the topic and evidenced a reduction of topic-related misconceptions. Thus, in both studies, the interventions designed to promote attitude and/or conceptual change also fostered change in emotions, suggesting that the relationship between emotions and attitude or conceptual change may be reciprocal.

The types of emotion, as well as emotional valence and intensity, are important to consider when exploring controversial topics. Broughton, Pekrun, and Sinatra (2012) demonstrated that both positive (interest) and negative (anxiety) emotions were associated with misconceptions. However, emotions such as curiosity, interest, and anxiety were more intense for topics when individuals held more misconceptions (about climate change and genetically modified foods) compared to topics where they exhibited fewer misconceptions (airport body scanners). This again suggests that, in situations that call for attitude and/or conceptual change, a key aspect of the change process may entail overcoming strong emotions.

Another construct that may be particularly important in attitude and conceptual change about controversial topics is plausibility. Plausibility figures prominently in several perspectives on conceptual change (Chinn & Brewer, 1993; Dole & Sinatra, 1998; Posner et al., 1982). It may be even more critical when there is a *plausibility gap* (Lombardi et al., in submission) between individual and scientific conceptions of a phenomenon, as there often is with controversial topics. Recently, Lombardi, Sinatra, and Nussbaum (2013) showed that when students considered two competing models, the model they considered more plausible was more likely to be considered correct. They also demonstrated that, through critical evaluation, middle-school students could reconsider their plausibility judgments.

Previously, Lombardi and Sinatra (2012) found that shifts in plausibility perceptions about climate change accounted for a change in college students' conceptions about weather and climate distinctions, but they did not attempt to shift those perceptions directly. Rather, students were enrolled in a geoscience course on climate change, and their perceptions shifted with content instruction over the course of the semester. In the study with middle-school students, plausibility perceptions of human-induced climate change were increased through the use of critical evaluation of model-link-evidence diagrams (Chinn & Buckland, 2012). Students viewed the scientific concept of human impacts on climate as more plausible than the skeptic model of increased solar activity after this instruction. They also experienced sustained conceptual change regarding their understanding of climate change measured at a 6-month delay.

Finally, a study with teachers shows that plausibility is related to emotions. Lombardi and Sinatra (2013) showed that pre-service elementary and in-service secondary science teachers' emotions about climate change (including anger and hopelessness) significantly predicted plausibility perceptions, with more anger associated with lesser plausibility and greater hopelessness associated with higher plausibility. Those who do not currently teach about climate change exhibited greater anger than those who do. Teachers with negative emotions and views of climate change as implausible may impart a negative stance towards controversial science topics to their students.

Like emotions, we view plausibility as contributing to a profile of attitude and conceptual change. That is, we believe this research suggests that plausibility and emotions, along with the previously reviewed motivational constructs (self-efficacy, task value, interest, epistemic motives) serve as leverage points for shifting negative attitudes and misconceptions about complex and controversial science topics. Specifically, if plausibility judgments can be increased and negative emotions tempered, then motivational interventions may be able to promote a value for the content, or interest in the topic, and help to shift attitudes and conceptual knowledge.

## A Research Agenda on Warm Change on Hot Topics: Next Steps

Controversial topics present unique challenges for educators, scientists, researchers, writers, and even politicians interested in promoting attitude and/or conceptual change. Arguably, there is much commonality in the change process whether one hopes to impact attitudes or conceptual knowledge. Motivations and emotions are implicated in the change process for both attitudes and knowledge. Both are embedded in a rich psychological, social, and cultural context that steers the change process in new directions at every turn. However, we believe much can be learned from looking at attitude change and conceptual change as unique, but related, processes. We have tried to provide a "primer" on two rich and complex bodies of literature for those who wish to explore these interconnections. Finally, we have provided a framework for examining the combined influences of both types of change, which we hope inspires researchers to test, confirm, or challenge our hypotheses.

Much work has yet to be done and many challenges must be confronted as we move forward along this conceptual landscape. There are theoretical, methodological, and measurement challenges that must be confronted. Definitions of attitudes, beliefs, and concepts are often murky, if not absent from much of the published work on these constructs. Defining terms, as Alexander and her colleagues have often called for (see, for example, Alexander, Shallert, & Hare,

1991), is much needed as we move forward. There are unique methodological challenges for researchers exploring controversial topics. Researchers might be met with resistance by students, teachers, family members, or members of the community when a controversial topic is the basis of the research. Both of us have been confronted with those who wish to shut down our research efforts when exploring a controversial science topic. We advise those who endeavor to explore such topics to take extra steps beyond those required by Institutional Review Boards, or others in oversight of research, by reaching out carefully and cautiously to community members to engage with them as collaborators in the research effort to the extent possible.

Measurement challenges abound in research examining both conceptual change and attitude change. Of paramount importance is distinguishing among attitudes, beliefs, and knowledge in order to operationalize these concepts for research. Then, considerable attention must be paid to developing appropriate measures of knowledge and attitudes. We suggest using self-report measures such as Likert-type scale or semantic differential scales to measure attitudes. Conceptual knowledge can be measured in any number of ways, including tradition test item types (such as multiple-choice, short-answer, essays), concept maps, or even self-reported knowledge (for an array of techniques, see Vosniadou, 2013). Beliefs are often measured using self-reported Likert scales (see, for example, Buehl, Alexander, & Murphy, 2002).

The challenges of studying motivation and affect in educational settings are also well documented and include construct definition, the accuracy of self-report measures, and the challenges of triangulating data (see, for example, Buehl et al., 2002). Particularly challenging is conducting classroom-based research on controversial science topics, which can meet with resistance from students, parents, teachers, and administrators. There is naturally a desire to resist controversial topics in science instruction, yet the outcome of such resistance is to risk portraying science as a cold and rational endeavor consisting of a set of reified facts. The science that is interesting and engaging for scientists, science enthusiasts, students, and teachers is at the cutting edge of the known, where controversies abound. However, we would argue, it is also at this edge where interest in science can be most successfully fostered.

Much work is needed to capitalize on such intriguing controversial topics, while optimizing affective and motivational reactions towards promoting learning, not resistance. Additional controversial topics must be explored. Topics are unique in the emotions that they invoke (Pekrun & Linnenbrink-Garcia, 2014), so as we explore more topics, we can promote understanding of the complex interplay of emotions and motivation in attitude and conceptual change. Much more research is also needed on teachers' emotions, motives, and attitudes towards controversial topics, and how these reactions impact their teaching. Finding ways to temper teachers' negative emotions and even possible bias in teaching controversial science topics is a topic little explored.

We need to put what we have learned to work in creating powerful learning environments that capitalize on adaptive emotions and motives, and take into account attitudes and conceptual knowledge in the service of learning both science content and epistemic practices of science. In sum, we argue for the importance of understanding the roles of both attitudes and conceptual knowledge, in order to promote change in both when learning about complex, controversial science topics.

Finally, the work on attitude and conceptual change about hot topics needs to extend to other domains. Despite the recent surge of conceptual change work in domains outside of science (see, for example, Limón, 2002), little work has been done to explore attitudes and conceptual understandings of controversies in domains such as history. We have begun to extend our work into the domain of history, and we call for others to do the same. As the research on warm change about hot topics progresses, we hope to see researchers consider both attitudes and conceptual knowledge about controversial topics.

# References

Albarracín, D., Johnson, B. T., Zanna, M. P., & Kumale, G. T. (2005). Attitudes: Introduction and scope. In D. Albarracín, B. T. Johnson, & M. P. Zanna (Eds.), *The handbook of attitudes* (pp. 3–20). Mahwah, NJ: Lawrence Erlbaum.

Alexander, P. A., Shallert, D. L., & Hare, V. C. (1991). Coming to terms: How researchers in learning and literacy talk about knowledge. *Review of Educational Research, 61*, 315–343.

Allport, G. W. (1935). Attitudes. In C. Murchison (Ed.), *Handbook of social psychology* (pp. 798–884). Worcester, MA: Clark University Press.

Alvaro, E., & Crano, W. D. (1997). Indirect minority influence: Evidence for leniency in source evaluation and counterargumentation. *Journal of Personality and Social Psychology, 7*, 949–964.

Andre, T., & Windschitl, M. (2003). Interest, epistemological belief, and intentional conceptual change. In G. M. Sinatra & P. R. Pintrich (Eds.), *Intentional conceptual change* (pp. 173–197). Mahwah, NJ: Lawrence Erlbaum Associates.

Banaji, M. R., & Heiphetz, L. (2010). Attitudes. In S. T. Fiske, D. Gilbert, & G. Lindsey (Eds.), *The handbook of social psychology*. Hoboken, NJ: John Wiley.

Broughton, S. H., Pekrun, R., & Sinatra, G. M. (2012). *Climate change, genetically modified foods, airport body scanners: Investigating students' emotions related to science topics*. Paper presented at the American Educational Research Association, Vancouver, CA.

Broughton, S. H., Sinatra, G. M., & Nussbaum, E. M. (2011). "Pluto has been a planet my whole life!" Emotions, attitudes, and conceptual change in elementary students' learning about Pluto's reclassification. *Research in Science Education, 1–22*.

Buehl, M. M., Alexander, P. A., & Murphy, P. K. (2002). Beliefs about schooled knowledge: Domain specific or domain general? *Contemporary Educational Psychology, 27*, 415–449.

Carey, S. (2009). *The origin of concepts*. New York, NY: Oxford University Press.

Chaiken, S. (1980). Heuristic versus systematic information processing and the use of sources versus message cues in persuasion. *Journal of Personality and Social Psychology, 39*, 752–766.

Chaiken, S., & Maheswaran, D. (1994). Heuristic processing can bias systemic processing: Effects of source credibility, argument ambiguity, and task importance on attitude judgment. *Journal of Personality and Social Psychology, 66*, 460–473.

Chi, M. T. H. (1992). Conceptual change within and across ontological categories: Examples from learning and discovery in science. In R. N. Giere (Ed.), *Minnesota studies in the philosophy of science: Vol. XV. Cognitive models of science* (Vol. XV, pp. 129–186). Minneapolis, MN: University of Minnesota Press.

Chi, M. T. H. (2008). Three types of conceptual change: Belief revision, mental model transformation, and categorical shift. In S. Vosniadou (Ed.), *International handbook of research on conceptual change* (pp. 61–82). New York, NY: Routledge.

Chinn, C. A., & Brewer, W. F. (1993). The role of anomalous data in knowledge acquisition: A theoretical framework and implications for science instruction. *Review of Educational Research, 63*, 1–49.

Chinn, C. A., & Buckland, L. A. (2012). Model-based instruction: Fostering change in evolutionary conceptions and in epistemic practices. In K. Rosengren, E. M. Evans, S. K. Brem, & G. M. Sinatra (Eds.), *Model-based instruction: Fostering change in evolutionary conceptions and in epistemic practices*. New York, NY: Oxford University Press.

Craik, F. I. M., & Lockhart, R. S. (1972). Levels of processing: A framework for memory research. *Journal of Verbal Learning and Verbal Behavior, 11*, 671–684.

Crano, W. D. (2012). *The rules of influence: Winning when you're in the minority*. New York, NY: St. Martin's Press.

Crano, W. D., & Prislin, R. (2006). Attitudes and persuasion. *Annual Review of Psychology, 57*, 345–374.

Crano, W. D., & Seyranian, V. (2009). How minorities prevail: The context/comparison-leniency contract model. *Journal of Social Issues, 65*, 335–363.

Dole, J. A., & Sinatra, G. M. (1998). Reconceptualizing change in the cognitive construction of knowledge. *Educational Psychologist, 33*(2/3), 109–128.

Eagly, A. H., & Chaiken, S. (1993). *The psychology of attitudes*. Fort Worth, TX: Harcourt Brace.

Eagly, A. H., & Chaiken, S. (1998). Attitude structure and function. In D. Gilbert, S. T. Fiske, & G. Lindsey (Eds.), *The handbook of social psychology* (4th ed., Vol. 2, pp. 269–322). New York, NY: Oxford University Press.

Forgas, J. P. (2010). Affective influence on the formation, expression, and change of attitudes. In J. P. Forgas, J. Cooper, & W. D. Crano (Eds.), *The psychology of attitudes and attitude change* (pp. 141–162). New York, NY: Oxford University Press.

Gregoire, M. (2003). Is it a challenge or a threat? A dual-process model of teachers' cognition and appraisal process during conceptual change. *Educational Psychology Review, 15*, 117–155.

Heddy, B. C., & Sinatra, G. M. (2013). Transforming misconceptions: Using transformative experience to promote positive affect and conceptual change in students learning about biological evolution. *Science Education, 97*, 725–744.

Heddy, B. C., Sinatra, G. M., & Danielson, R. W. (2014). *Modifying attitudes, emotions, and conceptual knowledge about genetically modified foods*. Paper presented at the American Educational Research Association, Philadelphia, PA.

Heesacker, M., Petty, R. E., & Cacioppo, J. T. (1983). Field dependence and attitude change: Source credibility can alter persuasion by affecting message relevant thinking. *Journal of Personality, 51*, 653–666.

Hmelo-Silver, C. E., & Azevedo, R. (2006). Understanding complex systems: Some core challenges. *Journal of Learning Sciences, 15*(1), 53–61.

Inagaki, K., & Hatano, G. (2008). Conceptual change in naive biology. In S. Vosniadou (Ed.), *International handbook of research on conceptual change* (pp. 240–262). New York, NY: Routledge.

Intergovernmental Panel on Climate Change. (2007). *Climate change 2007: Synthesis report—summary for policymakers*. Geneva, Switzerland: World Meteorological Organization.

International Astronomical Union Press Release. (2006). Retrieved from http://www.iau.org/news/pressreleases/detail/iau0603/ (accessed April 19, 2007).

Johnson, B. T., Miao, G. R., & Smith-McLallen, A. (2005). Communication and attitude change: Causes, processes, and effects. In D. Albarracín, B. T. Johnson, & M. P. Zanna (Eds.), *The handbook of attitudes* (pp. 617–669). Mahway, NJ: Lawrence Erlbaum Associates.

Johnson, M., & Sinatra, G. M. (2012). Use of task-value instructional inductions for facilitating engagement and conceptual change. *Contemporary Educational Psychology, 30*, 51–63.

Jost, J. T., Glaser, J., Kruglanski, A. W., & Sulloway, F. J. (2003). Political conservatism as motivated social cognition. *Psychological Bulletin, 129*, 339–375.

Kahneman, D. (2011). *Thinking fast and slow*. New York, NY: Farrar, Straus, & Giroux.

Kaufman, D. Q., Stasson, M. F., & Hart, J. W. (1999). Are the tabloids always wrong or is that just what we think? Need for cognition and perceptions of articles in print media. *Journal of Applied Social Psychology, 29*, 1984–2000.

Limón, M. (2002). Conceptual change in history. In M. Limón (Ed.), *Reconsidering conceptual change: Issues in theory and practice*. Hingham, MA: Kluwer Academic Publishers.

Lindley, D. V. (2006). *Understanding uncertainty*. Hoboken, NJ: John Wiley.

Linnenbrink, E. A., & Pintrich, P. R. (2003). Achievement goals and intentional conceptual change. In G. M. Sinatra & P. R. Pintrich (Eds.), *Intentional conceptual change* (pp. 347–374). Mahwah, NJ: Lawrence Erlbaum Associates.

Lombardi, D., Nussbaum, E. M., & Sinatra, G. M. (in submission). Plausibility judgments in conceptual change and epistemic cognition. *Educational Psychologist*.

Lombardi, D., & Sinatra, G. M. (2012). College students' perceptions about the plausibility of human-induced climate change. *Research in Science Education, 42*(2), 201–217.

Lombardi, D., & Sinatra, G. M. (2013). Emotions when teaching about human-induced climate change. *International Journal of Science Education, 35*, 167–191.

Lombardi, D., Sinatra, G. M., & Nussbaum, E. M. (2013). Plausibility reappraisals and shifts in middle school students' climate change conceptions. *Learning and Instruction, 27*, 50–62.

Lord, C. G., Ross, L., & Lepper, M. R. (1979). Biased assimilation and attitude polarization: The effects of prior theories on subsequently considered evidence. *Journal of Personality and Social Psychology, 37*, 2098–2109.

McGuire, W. J. (1985). Attitudes and attitude change. In F. Lindzey & E. Aronson (Eds.), *Handbook of social psychology* (3rd ed., Vol. 2, pp. 233–346). New York, NY: Random House.

Murphy, P. K. (2007). The eye of the beholder: The interplay of social and cognitive components in change. *Educational Psychologist, 42*(1), 41–53.

Murphy, P. K., & Alexander, P. A. (2008). The role of knowledge, beliefs, and interest in the conceptual change process: A synthesis and meta-analysis of the research. In S. Vosniadou (Ed.), *International handbook of research on conceptual change* (pp. 582–616). New York, NY: Routledge.

Murphy, P. K., & Mason, L. (2006). Changing knowledge and beliefs. In P. Alexander & P. Winne (Eds.), *Handbook of educational psychology* (pp. 305–324). Mahwah, NJ: Lawrence Erlbaum Associates.

Ohlsson, S. (2009). Resubsumption: A possible mechanism for conceptual change and belief revision. *Educational Psychologist, 44*(1), 20–40.

Ohlsson, S. (2011). *Deep learning: How the mind overrides experience*. New York, NY: Cambridge University Press.

Pekrun, R., & Linnenbrink-Garcia, L. (2014). *International handbook of emotions in education*. New York, NY: Routledge.

Petty, R. E., & Cacioppo, J. T. (1979). Issue involvement can increase or decrease persuasion by enhancing message-relevant cognitive responses. *Journal of Personality and Social Psychology, 37*, 1915–1926.

Petty, R. E., & Cacioppo, J. T. (1986a). *Communication and persuasion: Central and peripheral routes to attitude change*. New York: Springer-Verlag.

Petty, R. E., & Cacioppo, J. T. (1986b). The elaboration likelihood model of persuasion. In L. Berkowitz (Ed.), *Advances in experimental social psychology* (Vol. 19, pp. 123–205). New York, NY: Academic Press.

Petty, R. E., Cacioppo, J. T., & Goldman, R. (1981). Personal involvement as a determinant of argument-based persuasion. *Journal of Personality and Social Psychology, 4*, 847–855.

Petty, R. E., Haugtvedt, C. P., & Smith, S. M. (1995). Message elaboration as a determinant of attitude strength. In R. E. Petty & J. A. Krosnick (Eds.), *Attitude strength: Antecedents and consequences*. Hillsdale, NJ: Lawrence Erlbaum Associates.

Petty, R. E., & Wegener, D. T. (1998). Attitude change: Multiple roles for persuasion variables. In D. Gilbert, S. T. Fiske, & G. Lindsey (Eds.), *The handbook of social psychology* (4th ed., Vol. 2, pp. 332–390). New York, NY: Oxford University Press.

Pintrich, P. R., Marx, R., & Boyle, R. (1993). Beyond cold conceptual change: The role of motivational beliefs and classroom contextual factors in the process of conceptual change. *Review of Educational Research, 63*, 167–199.

Pornpitakpan, C. (2004). The persuasiveness of source credibility: A critical review of five decades' evidence. *Journal of Applied Social Psychology, 34*, 243–281.

Posner, G. J., Strike, K. A., Hewson, P. W., & Gertzog, W. A. (1982). Accommodation of a scientific conception: Towards a theory of conceptual change. *Science Education, 67*(4), 489–508.

Pratkanis, A. R. (1989). The cognitive representation of attitudes. In A. R. Pratkanis, S. J. Breckler, & A. G. Greenwald (Eds.), *Attitude structure and function* (pp. 71–98). Hillsdale, NJ: Lawrence Erlbaum Associates.

Prislin, R., & Crano, W. D. (2008). Attitudes and attitude change: The fourth peak. In W. D. Crano & R. Prislin (Eds.), *Attitudes and attitude change: Frontiers of social psychology* (pp. 3–15). New York, NY: Psychology Press.

Pugh, K. J., Linnenbrink-Garcia, L., Koskey, K. L. K., Stewart, V. C., & Manzey, C. (2010). Motivation, learning, and transformative experience: A study of deep engagement in science. *Science Education, 94*(1), 1–28.

Seyranian, V., Lombardi, D., & Sinatra, G. M. (in preparation). The context comparison model: Examining attitude change and plausibility judgments concerning climate change.

Shtulman, A., & Valcarcel, J. (2012). Scientific knowledge suppresses but does not supplant earlier intuitions. *Cognition, 124*, 209–215.

Sinatra, G. M. (2005). The "warming trend" in conceptual change research: The legacy of Paul R. Pintrich. *Educational Psychologist, 40*(2), 107–115.

Sinatra, G. M., Broughton, S. H., & Lombardi, D. (2014b). Emotions in science education. In R. Pekrun & L. Linnenbrink-Garcia (Eds.), *International handbook of emotions in education* (pp. 415–436). New York, NY: Routledge.

Sinatra, G. M., & Chinn, C. A. (2011). Thinking and reasoning in science: Promoting epistemic conceptual change. In K. Harris, C. B. McCormick, G. M. Sinatra, & J. Sweller (Eds.), *Critical theories and models of learning and development relevant to learning and teaching* (Vol. 1, pp. 257–282). Washington, DC: APA Publisher.

Sinatra, G. M., & Kardash, C. M. (2004). Teacher candidates' epistemological beliefs, dispositions, and views on teaching as persuasion. *Contemporary Educational Psychology, 29*, 483–498.

Sinatra, G. M., Kienhues, D., & Hofer, B. K. (2014a). Addressing challenges to public understanding of science: Epistemic cognition, motivated reasoning, and concpetual change. *Educational Psychologist, 49*(2), 123–138.

Sinatra, G. M., & Mason, L. (2008). Beyond knowledge: Learner characteristics influencing conceptual change. In S. Vosniadou (Ed.), *International handbook of research on conceptual change* (pp. 560–582). Netherlands: Springer.

Sinatra, G. M., Southerland, S. A., McConaughy, F., & Demastes, J. (2003). Intentions and beliefs in students' understanding and acceptance of biological evolution. *Journal of Research in Science Teaching, 40*(5), 510–528.

Smith, J. P., diSessa, A. A., & Roschelle, J. (1993). Misconceptions reconceived: A constructivist analysis of knowledge in transition. *Journal of Learning Sciences, 3*, 115–163.

Southerland, S. A., Sinatra, G. M., & Matthews, M. (2001). Belief, knowledge, and science education. *Educational Psychology Review, 13*, 325–351.

Stanovich, K. E. (2010). *Decision making and rationality in the modern world*. New York, NY: Oxford University Press.

Strike, K. A., & Posner, G. J. (1992). A revisionist theory of conceptual change. In R. Duschl & R. Hamilton (Eds.), *Philosophy of science, cognitive psychology, and educational theory and practice* (pp. 147–176). New York: State University of New York Press.

Tajfel, H., & Turner, J. C. (1986). Dimensions of majority and minority groups. In S. Worchel & W. G. Austin (Eds.), *Psychology of intergroup relations* (2nd ed., pp. 7–24). Chicago, IL: Nelson-Hall.

Turner, J. C. (1991). *Social influence*. Buckingham, UK: Open University Press.

Vosniadou, S. (1999). Preface. In W. Schnotz, S. Vosniadou, & M. Carretero (Eds.), *New perspectives on conceptual change* (pp. xiii–xxiv). Amsterdam: Pergamon.

Vosniadou, S. (Ed.). (2008). *International handbook of conceptual change*. New York: Routledge.

Vosniadou, S. (2013). *International handbook of conceptual change* (2nd ed.). New York, NY: Routledge.

Vosniadou, S., & Brewer, W. F. (1992). Mental models of the earth: A study of conceptual change in childhood. *Cognitive Psychology, 24*, 535–585.

White, R. T., & Gunstone, R. F. (2008). The conceptual change approach and the teaching of science. In S. Vosniadou (Ed.), *International handbook of research on conceptual change* (pp. 619–628). New York, NY: Routledge.

Wood, W. (2000). Attitude change: Persuasion and social influence. *Annual Review of Psychology, 51*, 539–570.

# 19

# Toward an Educational Psychology
# of Mathematics Education

*Jon R. Star*
Harvard University

*Bethany Rittle-Johnson*
Vanderbilt University

In this chapter we review a selection of current research as a way to explore relations between the disciplines of mathematics education and educational psychology. We believe that we are entering a new and exciting phase in the relation between these two disciplines, where researchers are bringing the discipline of psychology to bear on problems in mathematics education in interesting ways that take seriously the realities of classroom teaching and learning. Stated somewhat differently, we believe that the field is beginning to conceptualize what an educational psychology of mathematics education might look like.

It seems useful to begin this effort by looking back briefly at the last two chapters in prior handbooks from 1996 and 2006, as they portray a very different picture of the relations between educational psychology and mathematics education as we do here. Starting with the 1996 chapter (De Corte, Greer, & Verschaffel, 1996), we find that De Corte and colleagues present a very broad and historical look at the fields of mathematics education and educational psychology, exploring the ways that these two fields have influenced each other and have explored similar kinds of learning and teaching challenges. From this 1996 chapter, one can identify strong theoretical and empirical connections between educational psychology and mathematics education, particularly in the 1980s and early 1990s.

In contrast, the 2006 chapter (Schoenfeld, 2006) is primarily a chapter about the field of mathematics education, chronicling recent advances and themes of interest in mathematics education; arguably, Schoenfeld's (2006) chapter as written would have been quite appropriate in a volume devoted exclusively to research in mathematics education and is only peripherally related to educational psychology. At the time when the 2006 chapter was written, there were articles published in educational psychology journals that included

mathematics as a context. Yet (judging from Schoenfeld's decision to not review this research in his chapter) one can perhaps infer that many of the 2000-era educational psychology articles that related to mathematics were not viewed as centrally about mathematics teaching and learning per se but rather as using mathematics as a convenient discipline to study broader psychological phenomena. Schoenfeld's (2006) chapter was written during the so-called "math wars," a particularly turbulent time in mathematics education when tensions between mathematics education researchers and psychologists reached a peak (see Schoenfeld, 2004).

Thus, based on the most recent 2006 handbook chapter, one might conclude that, in the very recent past, there has been some disconnect between educational psychology and mathematics education. In other disciplines, in the past 20 or 30 years, psychology and psychologists have played an increasingly important role in research about teaching and learning. The prime example is perhaps the field of reading. At least since Jeanne Chall's work in the 1960s, psychologists (as well as experts from other fields such as linguistics) have exerted a large influence on the ways that we teach children how to read—an influence on research and teaching practice that continues to be quite strong to the present. Yet in mathematics education, the connection between psychology and education appears to have peaked in the early 1990s. Many mathematics education researchers do not view psychology as an especially important discipline for their field and instead look to other fields such as sociology and anthropology for guidance on theoretical frameworks and research methods. Yet, perhaps as a result of the research that we discuss below, this situation may be changing, with psychology again offering more meaningful and useful contributions to our search for solutions to pressing problems of mathematics teaching and learning.

In selecting what research to highlight in this chapter, we have chosen to focus on researchers and research themes that we find helpful in understanding what an educational psychology of mathematics education is or might be. Our purposeful sample is by no means exhaustive but rather selected in support of our larger aims for the chapter. We highlight research that is of interest to the community of educational psychologists but also thoughtfully connects with mathematics education. We discuss research grounded in mathematics not merely as a matter of convenience or interest but in recognition of the unique features of mathematics that make it distinct. Consistent with similar perspectives from within educational research (e.g., Burkhardt & Schoenfeld, 2003; Brown, 1997), we review research that is firmly grounded in basic psychological research but which also seeks to directly impact the classroom. We seek to showcase work done by teams of researchers, including mathematics educators and psychologists, in an attempt to make the work more genuine and germane to problems of mathematics teaching and learning.

Our explicit hope is that this chapter might lead to continued development of an educational psychology of mathematics education, prompting traditionally trained educational psychologists to seek out mathematics educators as research partners, and vice versa. The challenges that we face in improving the teaching and learning of mathematics are complex and require an interdisciplinary approach—this interdisciplinarity is crucial to our vision of an educational psychology of mathematics education. To summarize, this chapter has two goals. First, we seek to provide a brief review of a few of the major advances in research within the field of educational psychology that have occurred since the publication of the last handbook chapter and that relate to mathematics teaching and learning. And second, in reflecting on the research that we review, we seek to advance a more general conversation on the nature of an educational psychology of mathematics education.

Before beginning, it is important to note that we do not make fine-grained distinctions here between various subfields of psychology in order to determine what is, and what is not, *educational* psychology, strictly speaking. For example, researchers who might consider themselves developmental psychologists, cognitive psychologists, and/or applied developmental psychologists have conducted much of the research that we include. From the perspective of mathematics teaching and learning, these distinctions among types of psychologists do not appear to be especially relevant. As a result, we generally use the more generic term *psychologists* to refer to scholars who conduct psychological research on education (e.g., who focus on learners' mental processes in their work).

## Recent and Prominent Psychological Research on Mathematics Education

In the sections that follow, we review a collection of recent research that meets most or all of the criteria mentioned above: research that incorporates a psychological perspective on learners' mental processes, often from teams that include psychologists, that reflects a sincere interest and a deep appreciation of the complexities of teaching and learning in classrooms, and that is grounded in the discipline of mathematics in recognition of the unique features of this discipline and its importance in today's society. To arrive at the collection of research described below, we searched recent issues of prominent journals that publish psychological work, with the intent of identifying recent research on mathematics learning that focused on school-aged student populations (from pre-kindergarten through middle school). We sought to identify areas where there were clumps of recent and significant research—multiple publications, often by multiple author teams. We organize our review by the approximate age of students, beginning with early mathematics learning in preschool and then moving into the elementary and middle grades.

### *Preschool Mathematics Learning*

In the past 30+ years, developmental research has highlighted the depth of young children's informal mathematical competencies (e.g., Gelman & Gallistel, 1978; Wynn, 1992). Simultaneously, educational policy research has demonstrated the critical importance of early education to children's subsequent school success (Duncan & Murnane, 2011); knowledge gaps that exist at the beginning of formal schooling can persist throughout the lifespan. In consideration of both of these research trends, the past decade has seen an increase in the attention paid by researchers and educators to children's early mathematics learning. The development and evaluation of preschool mathematics curricula is one example of a body of research that emerges from psychology but that also is firmly grounded within the discipline of mathematics. In particular, two teams of researchers have developed, implemented, and evaluated two innovative preschool mathematics curricula. One team (Starkey and Klein) are both psychologists, while the other team (Clements and Sarama) are both mathematics educators (who attend carefully to learners' mental processes, with publications in psychology journals). While efforts to develop and evaluate preschool mathematics curricula predate their work, these scholars' efforts have significantly advanced our thinking about the types/level of mathematics that children can and should learn in preschool.

Clements and Sarama developed and evaluated the *Building Blocks* curriculum, a pre-K to Grade 2 software-based mathematics curriculum that is intended to help children find and extend mathematics in everyday activities (Clements & Sarama, 2007, 2011; Clements, Sarama, Spitter, Lange, & Wolfe, 2011; Clements, Sarama, & Liu, 2008). A critical feature is that the curriculum is based upon *learning trajectories*, which they define as:

descriptions of children's thinking and learning in a specific mathematical domain and a related, conjectured route through a set of instructional tasks designed to engender those mental processes or actions hypothesized to move children through a developmental progression of levels of thinking, created with the intent of supporting children's achievement of specific goals in that mathematical domain. (Clements & Sarama, 2004, p. 83)

These learning trajectories are empirically derived and provide useful frameworks for the development of mathematical thinking about particular topics over time, such as shape or measurement (Clements, Wilson, & Sarama, 2004; Szilagyi, Clements, & Sarama, 2013). For example, from pre-kindergarten to second grade, children typically progress through seven phases of understanding of length measurement, beginning with recognizing that length is an attribute of objects to comparing lengths of two objects using a third object to measuring via repeated use of a unit (Szilagyi et al., 2013). Further, *Building Blocks* has been found to be effective in promoting students' learning of mathematics, in both small studies and large randomized controlled trials (Klein, Starkey, Clements, Sarama, & Iyer, 2008; Sarama, Clements, Starkey, Klein, & Wakeley, 2008).

Similarly, Starkey and Klein developed the *Pre-K Mathematics* curriculum, which consists of small-group math activities with concrete manipulatives that can be used both in classrooms and at home (Klein, Starkey, & Ramirez, 2002). The activities in *Pre-K Mathematics* drew upon developmental research on students' early mathematics knowledge (e.g., Ginsburg, Klein, & Starkey, 1998). Studies have shown that *Pre-K Mathematics* is effective at improving preschool students' mathematical knowledge (e.g., Starkey, Klein, & Wakeley, 2004).

Considering both of these interventions, it is interesting to note that the development of mathematics content in these curricula represented a significant improvement over the status quo. Explicit mathematics instruction in preschool (where it even exists) typically consists of an assortment of mathematics topics, often without careful thought about what young children are mathematically capable of and what might be important for their subsequent success in kindergarten and beyond; as Clements and Sarama note, "Early childhood teachers often believe that they are 'doing mathematics' when they provide puzzles, blocks and songs. Even when they teach mathematics, that content is usually not the main focus, but is embedded in a fine-motor or reading activity" (Clements & Sarama, 2011, p. 968). These two lines of intervention research, along with each program's associated teacher professional development and efficacy research, are an important example of research that is psychological in nature (e.g., carefully attends to children's mental processes) and which tackles important problems in mathematics teaching and learning.

### Development of Symbolic Number Sense

In recent years, psychologists have been tackling how children learn to give meaning or sense to symbolic numbers, where number sense is defined as accurately representing the magnitude of symbolic numbers. One prominent line of recent research by Siegler and colleagues has focused on developing number sense for Arabic numerals (Booth & Siegler, 2006, 2008; Laski & Siegler, 2007; Opfer & Siegler, 2007; Ramani, Hitti, & Siegler, 2012; Ramani & Siegler, 2008, 2011; Siegler & Booth, 2004; Siegler & Opfer, 2003; Siegler & Ramani, 2008, 2009). They focus on number line estimation tasks, where (for example) children were presented with a number line with no marks on it other than 0 on one end and 100 on the other end. Children were given various Arabic numerals between 0 and 100 and asked to estimate the position of these given numbers. One might perhaps expect children to respond to this task by indicating awareness of the linearity that (to adults) is inherent in the number line—that the distance between 0 and 10, for example, is the same as the distance between 90 and 100. Yet Siegler and colleagues' results suggest that younger children's estimates more closely fit a logarithmic function, where estimates exaggerate differences in number magnitude for smaller numbers and compress differences for larger numbers—so that the distance between 0 and 10 would be viewed as more than the distance between 90 and 100. Such a logarithmic function suggests reliance on an approximate number sense that does not yet attach specific magnitudes to particular numbers. Furthermore, Siegler and colleagues' work has suggested an interesting developmental progression: A shift from logarithmic to linear patterns of number line estimates has been found to occur during preschool for 0–10 number lines, between kindergarten and second grade for 0–100 number lines, and between second and fourth grade for 0–1,000 ones among children from middle-income families (Booth & Siegler, 2006; Siegler & Booth, 2004; Siegler & Ramani, 2008). In addition, more linear representation of magnitude is associated with higher performance on standardized mathematics assessments (Booth & Siegler, 2006).

What might underlie increasingly precise representation of the magnitude of Arabic numerals? Siegler and colleagues propose that experience playing certain kinds of board games that have linear arrangements of numbers (e.g., where squares are numbered linearly such as from 1 to 10, such as in the first row of the game *Chutes and Ladders*) might support this development. They have tested this hypothesis with low-income preschoolers, who are much less likely to have a linear representation of the magnitude of the Arabic numerals from 0 to 10 than their middle-income peers. Playing a linear board game, even for relatively short periods of time (e.g., four 15-minute sessions), led preschoolers to make reliable and lasting gains in their estimation, counting, and numeral identification abilities. These gains were not found when children played games that were otherwise identical except that the squares had different colors rather than different numbers or when the game board was circular rather than linear (Ramani & Siegler, 2008, 2011; Siegler & Ramani, 2008, 2009). In addition, similar findings were obtained when the study was repeated in a small-group learning activity in classrooms, both under the supervision of a researcher as well as by a classroom teacher (Ramani et al., 2012).

Although this line of research is relatively new, with results that warrant further exploration and refinement (Ebersbach, Luwel, & Verschaffel, 2013), Siegler and colleagues' work is noteworthy for its use of ecological valid representations and settings. Both number lines and linear board games are omnipresent in preschool and elementary-school classrooms and are routinely used to support mathematics learning and teaching. The research of Siegler and colleagues highlighted the ways students naturally reason with these representations, as well as how the representations can be used as a means towards improving students' mathematical thinking in classroom settings.

## Use of Concrete Manipulatives in Elementary Mathematics Learning

We move now to research on mathematics teaching and learning with slightly older children. Particularly with elementary-school students, the use of concrete manipulatives in mathematics teaching has been on the rise for many years; a recent meta-analysis confirms that manipulatives generally improve mathematics achievement (Carbonneau, Marley, & Selig, 2013). However, over the past several years, scholars have attempted to more carefully tackle the issue of how, when, and why concrete manipulatives might or might not be useful in children's mathematics learning (Brown, McNeil, & Glenberg, 2009; Kaminski, Sloutsky, & Heckler, 2008, 2009; Martin, 2009; McNeil & Jarvin, 2007; McNeil & Uttal, 2009; McNeil, Uttal, Jarvin, & Sternberg, 2009; Sarama & Clements, 2009; Uttal, O'Doherty, Newland, Hand, & DeLoache, 2009).

Historically, both mathematics educators and educational psychologists may have assumed that manipulatives that resemble objects that children are familiar with (e.g., pizza, apples, baseballs) will aid in mathematics learning, given that these familiar objects ground abstract mathematical concepts in the real world. However, evidence is mounting that using these familiar objects as manipulatives can convey superficial and potentially distracting information to learners. Familiar objects have properties that may not be relevant to how they are used as mathematical manipulatives (e.g., shape, common uses, taste); these features may draw learners' attention to the object itself rather than to the abstract concepts that the object represents. For example, 6–8-year-olds who learned to read simple bar graphs that included pictures of discrete countable objects learned less than children who learned with monochromatic bar graphs without pictures because they learned an inappropriate strategy, which was to count the number of objects, rather than to learn to read the y-axis (Kaminski & Sloutsky, 2013). Current research suggests that teachers should consider using simple, bland materials such as solid-colored fraction tiles, which may avoid some of the potential difficulties noted above. Bland materials may make it easier for students to focus on the mathematics that the objects are intended to represent, rather than the objects themselves.

Concreteness fading, in which instruction begins with concrete manipulatives and systematically fades to abstract contexts without manipulatives, has emerged as an instructional method to harness the benefits of familiar manipulatives and abstract contexts (see Fyfe, McNeil, Son, & Goldstone, 2014, for a review). Importantly, concreteness fading allows learners to benefit from the familiar, concrete context, while still encouraging them to generalize their informal knowledge to more conventional, symbolic formats. Resulting knowledge is not only grounded and meaningful, but abstract

and portable (e.g., Goldstone & Son, 2005; McNeil & Fyfe, 2012). The results from this psychological research are consistent with comparable work from within the education literature (Bruner, 1966; Gravemeijer, 2002; Lesh, 1979).

One noteworthy feature of this research literature on the use of manipulatives was the use of both empirical work and theory from psychology to bear on a current and core issue in mathematics teaching and learning. The central and productive role of physical manipulatives, as well as concrete, real-world experiences in mathematics classrooms more generally, was for many years largely unquestioned in mathematics education. As psychologists such as Kaminski, McNeil, Uttal, and colleagues began to more carefully consider the affordances and constraints of manipulatives, some of these unexamined assumptions within mathematics education came under scrutiny. This psychological research on manipulatives also led to interesting and important conversations in the research literature, as witnessed by the various reaction papers that were subsequently published by mathematics educators (De Bock, Deprez, Van Dooren, Roelens, & Verschaffel, 2011; M. G. Jones, 2009).

## Word Problem Solving in Arithmetic

Another long-standing concern in mathematics education that has received recent research attention is word problem solving. Children's challenges with word problem solving in mathematics, including in arithmetic and in algebra, have been the focus of research in mathematics education for many years (e.g., Cawley, Fitzmaurice, Shaw, Kahn, & Bates, 1979; Kilpatrick, 1968; Polya, 1945). Psychological research into the 1980s and 1990s proved to be very influential in advancing thinking about how to ameliorate students' difficulties with word problem solving (Cummins, 1991; Cummins, Kintsch, Reusser, & Weimer, 1988; De Corte & Verschaffel, 1985, 1987; De Corte, Verschaffel, & De Win, 1985; Reed, 1987, 1989, 1999; Reed, Dempster, & Ettinger, 1985; Reed & Evans, 1987; Riley & Greeno, 1988), although this research was largely descriptive and not conducted in classrooms. However, recent years have seen a great deal of renewed interest in word problem solving, led by special education and psychology researchers investigating challenges faced by struggling learners.

In particular, in separate but related programs of research, Fuchs, Jitendra, and colleagues have developed and evaluated curricular interventions aimed at helping students solve word problems in mathematics (Fuchs et al., 2006, 2008a, 2008b, 2010; Griffin & Jitendra, 2009; Jitendra et al., 2007, 2009; Jitendra, Sczesniak, Griffin, & Deatline-Buchman, 2007; Jitendra & Star, 2011, 2012; Jitendra, Star, Dupuis, & Rodriguez, 2013; Jitendra, Star, Rodriguez, Lindell, & Someki, 2011; Powell, 2011; Yan Ping, Jitendra, & Deatline-Buchman, 2005). The interventions are centrally focused on helping students categorize word problems into problem types—an approach with a long history both in psychology (e.g., Riley, Greeno, & Heller, 1983) and with some support in mathematics education (e.g., Carpenter & Moser, 1984, but see also Verschaffel, Greer, & De Corte, 2007).

Once students learn to sort problems into types, they can more easily apply a useful diagram, equation, or plan that can help in the solution of problems of that type, even when unfamiliar problem features, such as irrelevant information, are introduced.

Of note with this recent work on word problem solving is the researchers' interest in evaluating curricular interventions in authentic classroom environments, often at scale. After developing and evaluating short interventions in small-scale settings, including the lab or researcher-led classrooms, the research programs of Fuchs, Jitendra, and colleagues progressively scaled up to experimentally evaluate longer word problem-solving units (e.g., in Fuchs et al. (2008a), the intervention lasted 16 weeks), with larger numbers of students and classrooms (e.g., Jitendra et al., 2013 worked with 1,163 students in 42 classrooms). The challenges and costs associated with conducting large-scale intervention studies are formidable and include recruiting large numbers of teachers, schools, and districts; providing teacher professional development; developing measures of implementation fidelity; and using increasingly sophisticated techniques for quantitative analysis of multilevel data. Yet, by moving to scale, these researchers have demonstrated the power of their interventions for improving students' word problem solving under actual classroom conditions, perhaps increasingly the likelihood of adoption of this work in schools.

### Meaning of the Equals Sign

In the past decade, a large number of studies have explored students' knowledge of the concept of mathematical equivalence. Symbolically, the equals sign is used to indicate the mathematical equivalence of two expressions, and it is a critically important idea that is first introduced in the elementary grades. Teachers and researchers have long known that too many students view the equals sign as a "do-something" symbol that means to simply add up all of the numbers in equations with operations on both sides of the equal sign (Kieran, 1981). As students are exposed to equals signs in a greater variety of mathematics problems (e.g., arithmetic equations in non-traditional formats such as $8 + ? = 9 - ?$ or $? = 5 + 6$ or algebraic equations such as $2x + 1 = 5$), this limited conception of the equals sign becomes increasingly problematic.

Recent research has significantly advanced our understanding of this phenomenon (Alibali, Knuth, Hattikudur, McNeil, & Stephens, 2007; I. Jones & Pratt, 2012; I. Jones, Inglis, Gilmore, & Dowens, 2012; Knuth, Alibali, Hattikudur, McNeil, & Stephens, 2008; Knuth, Stephens, McNeil, & Alibali, 2006; Matthews, Rittle-Johnson, McEldoon, & Taylor, 2012; McNeil, 2007, 2008; McNeil & Alibali, 2004, 2005; McNeil et al., 2012; McNeil, Fyfe, Petersen, Dunwiddie, & Brletic-Shipley, 2011; McNeil et al., 2006; Powell & Fuchs, 2010; Sherman & Bisanz, 2009; Stephens et al., 2013). For example, various researchers have conducted experiments in elementary and middle-school classrooms to document the prevalence of this limited conception of the equals sign, to more precisely identify the factors influencing the development of equals sign knowledge, and to evaluate interventions that can improve students' understanding of this important concept. For example, instruction on the meaning of the equal sign in the context of the traditional equation format $a + b = c$ is less effective than when the instruction is presented in the context of equations such as $a = a$ (McNeil, 2008), and practicing arithmetic facts presented in the format $c = a + b$ rather than $a + b = c$ leads to greater understanding of mathematical equivalence (McNeil et al., 2011). In addition, research has provided confirmation of the link between students' knowledge of equivalence in elementary school and their subsequent performance on algebra tasks several years later (Alibali et al., 2007; Knuth et al., 2006; McNeil et al., 2006)—equivalence may serve as a key conceptual level that helps students move from arithmetic to algebra.

This line of research stands to have a substantial impact on mathematics curricula and teaching. In the United States, the Common Core State Standards now include understanding of the meaning of the equals sign as a first-grade standard (National Governors Association Center for Best Practices & Council of Chief State School Officers, 2010). Previously, the vast majority of instructional examples were presented by teachers and texts in a traditional "operations on the left side" format, $3 + 7 =$ ___ (Powell, 2012); evidence suggests that the exclusive use of this format may be contributing to students' misconceptions (McNeil et al., 2006). However, recently published elementary math textbooks appear to contain some diversity in problem formats (e.g., $3 + 7 = 2 + $ ___; ___ $= 3 + 7$), although a recent analysis of a commonly used mathematics textbook, *enVisionMath* (Scott Foresman Addison Wesley, 2011), indicates that the second- to fourth-grade textbooks still only included the equals sign in the context of operations on both sides of the equals sign on less than 5% of instances of the equals sign (Rittle-Johnson, 2013).

One interesting and noteworthy feature of recent research on equivalence can be seen in the composition of research teams that are responsible for the work described above. Much of this research has been generated by teams of researchers that include developmental psychologists, cognitive scientists, and mathematics education researchers, as well as scholars for whom it is difficult to determine what might be the most appropriate label. As a consequence, the resulting research has been published in an extraordinary range of outlets, ranging from *Cognitive Science, Child Development*, and *Journal of Educational Psychology*, to top-tier mathematics education journals such as *Journal for Research in Mathematics Education* and *Mathematical Thinking and Learning*. The high quality of this work, its broad reach in terms of publications, and its impact on mathematics teaching practice all appear to be a consequence of the interdisciplinarity of the researchers.

### Cross-cultural Studies of Elementary Mathematics Teaching

Another area of recent research that aligns with the goals of this chapter is the work of Perry and colleagues on cross-cultural studies of mathematics teaching, particularly with regard to similarities and differences in elementary math instruction in China and the United States. International comparative studies of mathematics learning and teaching have played an important role in mathematics education and policy for at least the past 30 years. Seminal psychological research in the 1980s comparing U.S., Japanese, and Taiwanese students (e.g., Stevenson, Lee, & Stigler, 1986) was instrumental in the establishment of both the influential Trends in International Mathematics and Science Study (TIMSS) and Programme for International Student Assessment (PISA), which have collected international data on student achievement regularly since the mid-1990s.

Perry and colleagues have been engaged in numerous psychological studies on mathematics pedagogy. Building on initial studies that focused on U.S. teachers' instructional practices such as questioning, instructional explanations, and gestures (Hamm & Perry, 2002; Flevares & Perry, 2001; Perry, 2000), Perry and colleagues have more recently conducted a series of studies comparing U.S. and Chinese elementary-school teachers' mathematical instructional practices, including how teachers created opportunities for students to engage in extended discourse (Schleppenbach, Perry, Miller, Sims, & Fang, 2007), how teachers respond to students' errors (Schleppenbach, Flevares, Sims, & Perry, 2007), differences in teachers' beliefs about how students learn math (Correa, Perry, Sims, Miller, & Fang, 2008), and differences in teacher pedagogies related to student engagement and behavior management (Lan et al., 2009). For example, Schleppenbach and colleagues (Schleppenbach et al., 2007b) analyzed lesson videos from fourth- and fifth-grade teachers in the United States and China to identify instances in which teachers and students engaged in indepth mathematical discussions. Their findings indicated that Chinese teachers engaged in more of these types of discussions than U.S. teachers, and also that the length of each discussion episode was longer in Chinese classrooms as compared to U.S. classrooms. Furthermore, Chinese teachers' discussions tended to push students to draw connections between specific problems and more general mathematical principles, whereas U.S. teachers' discussions tended to focus mostly on computation.

This research is noteworthy for several reasons. First, within the realm of psychology, the work of Perry and colleagues is somewhat unusual in that it explores content-specific (e.g., mathematics) pedagogical practices. Psychological research tends to explore learning and/or motivational processes at the student or individual level, with less of an emphasis on teaching, particularly content-specific instruction. Second, this work represents a timely response from psychologists to an issue of great importance to mathematics education, where interest in supporting teachers in their implementation of high-quality, student-led discussions is very high. Third, the methodology used here—fine-grained analyses of instructional videos—is well aligned with methodologies typically used in mathematics education research, enhancing the ability of this work to connect to and be used by researchers and teachers in mathematics education. Finally, it is also worth noting that this research team

has published its work in a variety of psychology and education journals, including those read by mathematics practitioners (Sims, 2008).

## Algebra Equation Solving in Middle and High School

Finally, there is increasing awareness among math education researchers and policy makers of the importance of algebra, both for students' success in later math courses but also for providing students with the knowledge and skills for harnessing new technologies and taking advantage of job opportunities resulting from them (Adelman, 2006; National Mathematics Advisory Panel, 2008). Psychologists have long been interested in problem solving in algebra (e.g., Carroll, 1994; Cooper & Sweller, 1987; Mayer, 1982), but there is renewed interest in psychological research on understanding students' challenges in algebra as well as designing and evaluating educational interventions that improve performance in algebra.

In particular, collaborative teams of mathematics education and psychology researchers have recently conducted research on algebra learning and teaching in authentic classroom environments. Here we highlight our own work on the comparison of worked examples in algebra (Rittle-Johnson & Star, 2007, 2009; Rittle-Johnson, Star, & Durkin, 2009, 2012). Other research teams are following a similar path, focusing on the effectiveness of incorporating incorrect examples and diagrams (e.g., Booth & Davenport, 2013; Booth, Lange, Koedinger, & Newton, 2013; Booth & Koedinger, 2012).

The promise of learning from worked examples is well established in the psychological literature (e.g., see Atkinson, Derry, Renkl, & Wortham, 2000, for a review). Similarly, a rich literature points to the importance of comparison for learning and transfer (e.g., Gentner, 1983; Gick & Holyoak, 1980). However, very few studies have explored whether and how these findings from cognitive science on worked examples and comparison could be implemented in math classrooms. Rather, studies typically examined instructional interventions that were quite brief, were conducted in laboratory settings, and often utilized undergraduate students as subjects. Our work, a collaboration between a developmental psychologist (Rittle-Johnson) and a mathematics education researcher (Star), sought to evaluate how comparison of worked examples could support learning within mathematics classrooms (Rittle-Johnson & Star, 2011).

We first conducted a series of small experimental studies in classrooms, where we redesigned two to three lessons on algebra equation solving and implemented these lessons during students' mathematics classes. We began by showing that comparison of worked examples of different solution methods improved students' mathematical knowledge more than sequential study of the same worked examples (Rittle-Johnson & Star, 2007). Further studies yielded a more complex picture of the potential effectiveness of comparison of worked examples, suggesting the importance of what is being compared (e.g., the same problem solved in two different ways, two different problems solved the same way; Rittle-Johnson & Star, 2009), the impact of prior knowledge on students' ability to learn from comparison (Rittle-Johnson et al., 2009), and when during instruction comparison of examples is implemented (Rittle-Johnson et al., 2012).

These results prompted us to develop and then evaluate a year-long intervention using comparison of worked examples in algebra classrooms. After the development of and piloting of a set of supplemental curriculum materials, we worked with 141 Algebra I teachers and their students over a period of 2 years to determine whether a curriculum that included regular comparison of worked examples led to learning gains, as compared to a business-as-usual control. The results of this large and complex study were somewhat messy, but we did find a marginally significant dosage effect—in that increased exposure to the supplemental curriculum materials led to marginally significant gains in procedural knowledge (Star et al., 2015).

The challenges and costs associated with conducting this type of large-scale intervention studies are formidable and include recruiting large numbers of teachers, schools, and districts; providing teacher professional development; developing measures of implementation fidelity; and using increasingly sophisticated techniques for quantitative analysis of multilevel data. Yet by moving to scale, our work demonstrates the potential power of comparison of worked examples for improving students' algebra learning under actual classroom conditions, perhaps increasingly the likelihood of adoption of this work in schools. Finally, the larger study afforded us the opportunity to qualitatively explore issues of great interest to the mathematics education community, including instructional practices related to the implementation of comparison (Lynch & Star, 2014a), what kinds of professional development experiences help teachers implement this approach (Newton & Star, 2013), and which kinds of students might optimally benefit (Lynch & Star, 2014b; Newton, Star, & Lynch, 2010).

## Toward an Educational Psychology of Mathematics Education

With this selective review of recent research in mind, we move now to considering the nature of and contributions of psychological research to mathematics education more generally. As noted above, we believe we are in the midst of a new phase in the relationship between the disciplines of psychology and mathematics education, such that psychological research is viewed as more central to practice and policy in mathematics education. The recent research described above, though firmly grounded in psychology, has successfully entered an international conversation about the teaching and learning of mathematics—a conversation that in recent years has seemed somewhat resistant to considering the views of psychologists. What features of this research have increased its relevance to mathematics education? What can be learned from this research about the important role educational psychology can continue to play in research, policy, and practice related to mathematics education?

Our answers to these questions have been foreshadowed by the features identified as noteworthy in the paragraphs above. For the research on preschool mathematics curricula, we commented on the seriousness with which these researchers considered issues of mathematical thinking and content. In the work on number sense, we pointed to the use of ecologically valid representations and settings. We noted that recent work on concrete manipulatives and on cross-cultural instructional practices has brought psychological research to bear on a core issue from the practice of mathematics teaching and learning. Similarly, both the word problem research and our research on comparison of worked examples in algebra have made a deliberate effort to move from laboratory research to at-scale work in authentic classroom environments. And we commented that the work on mathematical equivalence and algebra has been influential on theory and practice in part due to the efforts of an interdisciplinary group of researchers who have made broad efforts to disseminate their work in a variety of outlets.

Of course this is not a new issue for the field—the desire to connect and the difficulties of connecting psychological research with educational practice have been a persistent theme in the field for some time. Yet in the past, the central concern appeared to be how to make psychological research *relevant* to practice; researchers did work that they perceived might be important to education, and they subsequently endeavored to communicate and apply this research to those in education. Connecting research with practice typically meant taking studies that had been conceptualized and implemented by psychological researchers and (after the fact) attempting to make these results available and useful to educational researchers and practitioners. Traditionally researchers have been viewed as the producers of knowledge and educators as the consumers of such knowledge.

In contrast, we would argue that an increasing number of psychological researchers have begun to conceptualize the relationship between research and mathematics education practice (and even their professional identities) as lying at the intersection of research and practice. At present, ideas for research often begin in the world of educational practice—scholars think about the challenges faced by students and teachers in educational settings and then design research programs to try to address these challenges. Rather than endeavoring to apply research *to* practice after the fact, researchers now see and try to take advantage of the reciprocal relationships between research and educational practice: Research can inform practice, but practice also can inform research (Burkhardt & Schoenfeld, 2003). Instead of trying to *apply* our research to practice, we now seek to do research that *is* inherently relevant to and driven by the needs of practice, consistent with the call made by Ann Brown to psychologists more than 15 years ago (Brown, 1997). When research is initiated with awareness of and interest in problems of educational practice, the application of research to practice is less forced, as the research is already tightly tied to practice. In our conceptualization of an educational psychology of mathematics education, doing research that is relevant to practice is central. Note that the claim here is not that the model of applying research to practice is necessarily problematic, but rather that more and more contemporary scholars view the relationship between research and practice as reciprocal (for a similar argument in science education, see Klahr & Li, 2005.)

Doing research that is consistent with this reciprocal vision of the relationship between research and practice is a complex endeavor (Burkhardt & Schoenfeld, 2003). Abstracting from the research exemplars discussed above, we offer the following suggestions that can help lead to research within educational psychology that is maximally relevant to mathematics education practice—what we refer to as an educational psychology of mathematics education. Note that each of these suggestions points to ways that researchers ground their research in problems of mathematics educational practice.

A first and central suggestion is that research should be firmly situated within the domain of mathematics. Research that is intended to be relevant to mathematics teaching and learning must be grounded in mathematics and should include mathematical content that is coherent, deep, and consistent with the current best thinking of mathematicians and mathematics educators about what content should be taught in schools. We have learned and will continue to learn a great deal from content-generic basic research, but impacting educational practice likely requires research to be more strongly connected to a school discipline such as mathematics. It is probably no longer sufficient for psychological researchers who are interested in impacting mathematics education to select target mathematical content based on convenience. Rather, target math concepts and procedures should be present and emphasized in the current curriculum, in order to increase the likelihood that educators can and will attend to the research results. Consider the content domains of the research described above, which included mathematical equivalence and word problem solving. Interest in these topics comes directly from mathematics education practice, which enabled the researchers to conduct careful investigations that were likely to be impactful.

This kind of careful consideration of mathematical content poses numerous challenges for researchers who are interested in impacting educational practice. First, mathematical topics that are currently taught in schools may be different than those learned when researchers themselves were in schools. Second and related, psychological researchers may not bring sufficient expertise in mathematics to adequately investigate the mathematics that is currently taught in middle and high school, and the difficulties students face when learning it. On this point, it is perhaps not surprising to observe that the selection of exemplary research described above is heavily weighted toward preschool and elementary school mathematics. Responding to these challenges may require rethinking the composition of research teams engaging in this work, as we return to below.

A second suggestion that can lead to useful and impactful mathematics education research within educational psychology is to incorporate the current "messy" state of school instructional environments into study designs. Having an impact on mathematics education practice requires research that shows an appreciation of the complexities of classrooms, including the challenges of working with students in large groups under strict time constraints, with diverse populations of learners, and with teachers who may have limited training and/or available time to try something new. In the past, many educational psychology researchers may have been reluctant to situate studies of mathematics learning and teaching in authentic classroom environments, perhaps because of the seemingly unavoidable methodological and logistical challenges inherent in doing so. Psychologists also have a strong preference for experimental research that involves random assignment of learners to conditions in order to support causal claims. Classroom-based research requires creative solutions to random assignment. With the increasing sophistication of both analytical methods and research designs, educational psychological researchers can and should pursue studies in classrooms—as some of the exemplar research described above has done. As noted above, in our work (e.g., Rittle-Johnson & Star, 2007, 2009) we have created intervention materials to use during classroom partner work, randomly assigning pairs of students to a condition within a classroom. This allowed us to conduct experimental research in classrooms without necessitating the large number of classrooms required when randomly assigning classroom to condition. Others have created alternative versions of student booklets that are randomly assigned to students within a classroom and used in conjunction with the same whole-class instruction (McNeil, 2008). Psychological research also needs to incorporate contemporary teaching practices, such as students working in groups and teachers as facilitators (see Chapter 26, this volume). Otherwise, the research may appear less applicable to policy makers and leaders in mathematics education, regardless of the importance of the results.

Third, impactful educational psychological research in mathematics education must incorporate research topics and methods that take into consideration actual and current problems of practice. Selecting topics for research should be guided not only by researchers' interest and knowledge of the field but also by what mathematics educators identify as their most pressing concerns and areas where psychological research might be especially informative. For example, researchers might consider exploring unquestioned educational assumptions (e.g., as in the research on manipulatives, above) or persistent areas of great difficulty for students (e.g., as in the research on word problems, above) or teachers (e.g., as in the cross-cultural work on math instruction, above). As another example, research can attempt to unpack complex instructional practices to determine what works, when, why, and for whom—as we have tried to do in our work on the benefits of comparison for mathematics learning (Rittle-Johnson & Star, 2007, 2009; Rittle-Johnson et al., 2009; Star & Rittle-Johnson, 2009). Relevant research does not necessarily seek to identify or pursue a problem that is unknown by mathematics educators, but rather to highlight or forefront a known problem in innovative ways.

With respect to research methods, it is important for educational psychologists to incorporate research methods that help reveal why things work, in addition to what works. In the recent past, mathematics education researchers tended to specialize in fine-grained qualitative explorations of classroom learning, with a focus on the "why," while psychologists focused on quantitative studies in the lab that explored "what works." For maximal relevance to educational practice, educational psychologists should consider blurring these boundaries, such as incorporating opportunities for qualitative data collection within quantitative studies. For example, as part of our experimental work in classrooms we have examined audiotapes of partner dialogues from high- and low-learning pairs to gather potential reasons for why students learned different amounts from our intervention materials (Rittle-Johnson & Star, 2007). Similarly, Brown (1992) conducted case studies on a few children based on clinical interviews while completing a larger, quantitative evaluation of a classroom science intervention.

Finally, all three of the suggestions above clearly point to the need for interdisciplinary research teams that include educational psychologists, mathematics education researchers, mathematicians, and mathematics teachers. Psychologists bring knowledge of diverse research methods and analytic techniques as well as knowledge of basic mental processes that are vital in conducting high-quality educational research. However, traditionally trained psychologists may not be qualified to do the research that needs to be done—perhaps as a result of insufficient content knowledge of mathematics and/or lack of familiarity with and access to authentic educational settings. Research with the potential for maximal relevance incorporates mathematics education experts in the design and implementation of the research, consults with teachers and students in schools, and also seeks out opportunities for dissemination that might reach mathematics education researchers and/or practitioners, including articles in practitioner and mathematics education research journals and presentations at math education conferences. Research teams that are composed of an array of scholars from psychology, education, and mathematics are more likely to be able to tackle the formidable challenges associated with producing high-quality, maximally relevant research on the teaching and learning of mathematics.

# References

Adelman, C. (2006). *The toolbox revisited: Paths to degree completion from high school though college*. Washington, DC: United States Department of Education.

Alibali, M. W., Knuth, E. J., Hattikudur, S., McNeil, N. M., & Stephens, A. C. (2007). A longitudinal examination of middle school students' understanding of the equal sign and equivalent equations. *Mathematical Thinking and Learning, 9*(3), 221–246.

Atkinson, R. K., Derry, S., Renkl, A., & Wortham, D. (2000). Learning from examples: Instructional principles from the worked examples research. *Review of Educational Research, 70*(2), 181–214.

Booth, J. L., & Davenport, J. (2013). The role of problem representation and feature knowledge in algebraic equation solving. *Journal of Mathematical Behavior, 32*, 415–423.

Booth, J. L., & Koedinger, K. R. (2012). Are diagrams always helpful tools? Developmental and individual differences in the effect of presentation format on student problem solving. *British Journal of Educational Psychology, 82*, 492–511.

Booth, J., Lange, K., Koedinger, K., & Newton, K. (2013). Using example problems to improve student learning in algebra: Differentiating between correct and incorrect examples. *Learning and Instruction, 25*, 24–34.

Booth, J. L., & Siegler, R. S. (2006). Developmental and individual differences in pure numerical estimation. *Developmental Psychology, 42*(1), 189–201.

Booth, J. L., & Siegler, R. S. (2008). Numerical magnitude representations influence arithmetic learning. *Child Development, 79*(4), 1016–1031.

Brown, A. L. (1992). Design experiments: Theoretical and methodological challenges in creating complex interventions in classroom settings. *Journal of the Learning Sciences, 2*(2), 141.

Brown, A. L. (1997). Transforming schools into communities of thinking and learning about serious matters. *American Psychologist, 52*(4), 399–413.

Brown, M. C., McNeil, N. M., & Glenberg, A. M. (2009). Using concreteness in education: Real problems, potential solutions. *Child Development Perspectives, 3*(3), 160–164.

Bruner, J. S. (1966). *Toward a theory of instruction*. Cambridge, MA: Harvard University Press.

Burkhardt, H., & Schoenfeld, A. (2003). Improving educational research: Toward a more useful, more influential, and better funded enterprise. *Educational Researcher, 32*(9), 3–14.

Carbonneau, K. J., Marley, S. C., & Selig, J. P. (2013). A meta-analysis of the efficacy of teaching mathematics with concrete manipulatives. *Journal of Educational Psychology, 105*(2), 380–400.

Carpenter, T. P., & Moser, J. M. (1984). The acquisition of addition and subtraction concepts in grades one through three. *Journal for Research in Mathematics Education, 15*, 179–202.

Carroll, W. (1994). Using worked examples as an instructional support in the algebra classroom. *Journal of Educational Psychology, 86*(3), 360–367.

Cawley, J. F., Fitzmaurice, A. M., Shaw, R. A., Kahn, H., & Bates, H. (1979). Math word problems: Suggestions for LD students. *Learning Disability Quarterly, 2*, 25–41.

Clements, D. H., & Sarama, J. (2004). Learning trajectories in mathematics education. *Mathematical Thinking & Learning, 6*(2), 81–89.

Clements, D. H., & Sarama, J. (2007). Effects of a preschool mathematics curriculum: Summative research on the Building Blocks project. *Journal for Research in Mathematics Education, 38*(2), 136–163.

Clements, D. H., & Sarama, J. (2011). Early childhood mathematics intervention. *Science, 333*(6045), 968–970.

Clements, D. H., Sarama, J. H., & Liu, X. H. (2008). Development of a measure of early mathematics achievement using the Rasch model: the Research-Based Early Maths Assessment. *Educational Psychology, 28*(4), 457–482.

Clements, D. H., Sarama, J., Spitter, M. E., Lange, A. A., & Wolfe, C. B. (2011). Mathematics learned by young children in an intervention based on learning trajectories: A large-scale cluster randomized trial. *Journal for Research in Mathematics Education, 42*(2), 127–166.

Clements, D. H., Wilson, D. C., & Sarama, J. (2004). Young children's composition of geometric figures: A learning trajectory. *Mathematical Thinking & Learning, 6*(2), 163–184.

Cooper, G., & Sweller, J. (1987). Effects of schema acquisition and rule automation on mathematical problem-solving transfer. *Journal of Educational Psychology, 79*(4), 347–362.

Correa, C., Perry, M., Sims, L., Miller, K., & Fang, G. (2008). Connected and culturally embedded beliefs: Chinese and U.S. teachers talk about how their students best learn mathematics. *Teaching and Teacher Education, 24*, 140–153.

Cummins, D. D. (1991). Children's interpretations of arithmetic word problems. *Cognition & Instruction, 8*(3), 261.

Cummins, D. D., Kintsch, W., Reusser, K., & Weimer, R. (1988). The role of understanding in solving word problems. *Cognitive Psychology, 20*(4), 405–438.

De Corte, E., Greer, B., & Verschaffel, L. (1996). Mathematics teaching and learning. In D. Berliner & R. Calfee (Eds.), *Handbook of educational psychology* (pp. 491–549). New York: Simon & Schuster Macmillan.

De Corte, E., & Verschaffel, L. (1985). Beginning first graders' initial representation of arithmetic word problems. *Journal of Mathematical Behavior, 4*(1), 3–21.

De Corte, E., & Verschaffel, L. (1987). The effect of semantic structure on first graders' strategies for solving addition and subtraction word problems. *Journal for Research inMathematics Education, 18*(5), 363–381.

De Corte, E., Verschaffel, L., & De Win, L. (1985). Influence of rewording verbal problems on children's problem representations and solutions. *Journal of Educational Psychology, 77*(4), 460–470.

De Bock, D., Deprez, J., Van Dooren, W., Roelens, M., & Verschaffel, L. (2011). Abstract or concrete examples in learning mathematics? A replication and elaboration of Kaminski, Sloutsky, and Heckler's study. *Journal for Research in Mathematics Education, 42*(2), 109–126.

Duncan, G. J., & Murnane, R. J. (Eds.). (2011). *Whither opportunity: Rising inequality, schools, and children's life chances.* New York: Russell Sage Foundation.

Ebersbach, M., Luwel, K., & Verschaffel, L. (2013). Apples and pears in studies on magnitude estimations. *Frontiers in Cognitive Science, 4*(332), 1–6.

Flevares, L. M., & Perry, M. (2001). How many do you see? Teachers' use of multiple representations in place-value instruction. *Journal of Educational Psychology, 93*, 330–345.

Fuchs, L. S., Fuchs, D., Craddock, C., Hollenbeck, K. N., Hamlett, C. L., & Schatschneider, C. (2008a). Effects of small-group tutoring with and without validated classroom instruction on at-risk students' math problem solving: Are two tiers of prevention better than one? *Journal of Educational Psychology, 100*(3), 491–509.

Fuchs, L. S., Fuchs, D., Finelli, R., Courey, S. J., Hamlett, C. L., Sones, E. M., & Hope, S. K. (2006). Teaching third graders about real-life mathematical problem solving: A randomized controlled study. *Elementary School Journal, 106*(4), 293–311.

Fuchs, L. S., Seethaler, P. M., Powell, S. R., Fuchs, D., Hamlett, C. L., & Fletcher, J. M. (2008b). Effects of preventative tutoring on the mathematical problem solving of third-grade students with math and reading difficulties. *Exceptional Children, 74*(2), 155–173.

Fuchs, L. S., Zumeta, R. O., Schumacher, R. F., Powell, S. R., Seethaler, P. M., Hamlett, C. L., & Fuchs, D. (2010). The effects of schema-broadening instruction on second graders' word-problem performance and their ability to represent word problems with algebraic equations: A randomized control study. *Elementary School Journal, 110*(4), 440–463.

Fyfe, E. R., McNeil, N. M., Son, J. Y., & Goldstone, R. L. (2014). Concreteness fading in mathematics and science instruction: A systematic review. *Educational Psychology Review, 26*, 9–25.

Gelman, R., & Gallistel, C. R. (1978). *The child's understanding of number.* Cambridge, MA: Harvard University Press.

Gentner, D. (1983). Structure-mapping: A theoretical framework for analogy. *Cognitive Science, 7*, 155–170.

Gick, M. L., & Holyoak, K. J. (1980). Analogical problem solving. *Cognitive Psychology, 12*, 306–355.

Ginsburg, H. P., Klein, A., & Starkey, P. (1998). The development of children's mathematical thinking: Connecting research with practice. In W. Damon, I. E. Sigel & K. A. Renninger (Eds.), *Handbook of child psychology: Child psychology in practice* (5th ed., Vol. 4, pp. 401–476). New York: Wiley.

Goldstone, R. L., & Son, J. Y. (2005). The transfer of scientific principles using concrete and idealized simulations. *Journal of the Learning Sciences, 14*, 69–110.

Gravemeijer, K. (2002). Preamble: From models to modeling. In K. Gravemeijer, R. Lehrer, B. Oers, & L. Verschaffel (Eds.), *Symbolizing, modeling and tool use in mathematics education* (pp. 7–22). Dordrecht, the Netherlands: Kluwer.

Griffin, C. C., & Jitendra, A. K. (2009). Word problem-solving instruction in inclusive third-grade mathematics classrooms. *Journal of Educational Research, 102*(3), 187–202.

Hamm, J. V. & Perry, M. P. (2002). Learning mathematics in first grade: On whose authority? *Journal of Educational Psychology, 94*, 126–137.

Jitendra, A. K., Griffin, C. C., Haria, P., Leh, J., Adams, A., & Kaduvettoor, A. (2007). A comparison of single and multiple strategy instruction on third-grade students' mathematical problem solving. *Journal of Educational Psychology, 99*(1), 115–127.

Jitendra, A. K., Sczesniak, E., Griffin, C. C., & Deatline-Buchman, A. (2007). Mathematical word problem solving in third-grade classrooms. *Journal of Educational Research, 100*(5), 283–302.

Jitendra, A. K., & Star, J. R. (2011). Meeting the needs of students with learning disabilities in inclusive mathematics classrooms: The role of schema-based instruction on mathematical problem-solving. *Theory Into Practice, 50*(1), 12–19.

Jitendra, A. K., & Star, J. R. (2012). An exploratory study contrasting high- and low-achieving students' percent word problem solving. *Learning & Individual Differences, 22*(1), 151–158.

Jitendra, A. K., Star, J. R., Dupuis, D. N., & Rodriguez, M. C. (2013). Effectiveness of schema-based instruction for improving seventh-grade students' proportional reasoning: A randomized experiment. *Journal of Research on Educational Effectiveness, 6*(2), 114–136.

Jitendra, A. K., Star, J. R., Rodriguez, M., Lindell, M., & Someki, F. (2011). Improving students' proportional thinking using schema-based instruction. *Learning and Instruction, 21*(6), 731–745.

Jitendra, A. K., Star, J. R., Starosta, K., Leh, J. M., Sood, S., Caskie, G., Hughes, C., & Mack, T. R. (2009). Improving seventh grade students' learning of ratio and proportion: The role of schema-based instruction. *Contemporary Educational Psychology, 34*(3), 250–264.

Jones, I., Inglis, M., Gilmore, C., & Dowens, M. (2012). Substitution and sameness: Two components of a relational conception of the equals sign. *Journal of Experimental Child Psychology, 13*(1), 166–176.

Jones, I., & Pratt, D. (2012). A substituting meaning for the equals sign in arithmetic notating tasks. *Journal for Research in Mathematics Education, 43*(1), 2–33.

Jones, M. G. (2009). Transfer, abstraction, and context. *Journal for Research in Mathematics Education, 40*(2), 80–89.

Kaminski, J. A., & Sloutsky, V. M. (2013). Extraneous perceptual information interferes with children's acquisition of mathematical knowledge. *Journal of Educational Psychology, 105*(2), 351–363.

Kaminski, J. A., Sloutsky, V. M., & Heckler, A. F. (2008). The advantage of abstract examples in learning math. *Science, 320*(5875), 454–455.

Kaminski, J. A., Sloutsky, V. M., & Heckler, A. (2009). Transfer of mathematical knowledge: The portability of generic instantiations. *Child Development Perspectives, 3*(3), 151–155.

Kieran, C. (1981). Concepts associated with the equality symbol. *Educational Studies in Mathematics, 12*, 317–326.

Kilpatrick, J. (1968). *Analyzing the solution of word problems in mathematics: An exploratory study.* Palo Alto, CA: Stanford University.

Klahr, D., & Li, J. (2005). Cognitive research and elementary science instruction: From the laboratory, to the classroom, and back. *Journal of Science Education and Technology, 14*, 217–238.

Klein, A., Starkey, P., Clements, D., Sarama, J., & Iyer, R. (2008). Effects of a pre-kindergarten mathematics intervention: A randomized experiment. *Journal of Research on Educational Effectiveness, 1*(3), 155–178.

Klein, A., Starkey, P., & Ramirez, A. (2002). *Pre-K mathematics curriculum.* Glendale, IL: Scott Foresman.

Knuth, E. J., Alibali, M. W., Hattikudur, S., McNeil, N. M., & Stephens, A. C. (2008). The importance of equal sign understanding in the middle grades. *Mathematics Teaching in the Middle School, 13*(9), 514–519.

Knuth, E. J., Stephens, A. C., McNeil, N. M., & Alibali, M. W. (2006). Does understanding the equal sign matter? Evidence from solving equations. *Journal for Research in Mathematics Education, 36*(4), 297–312.

Lan, X., Ponitz, C., Miller, K., Li, S., Cortina, K., Perry, M., & Fang, G. (2009). Keeping their attention: Classroom practices associated with behavioral engagement in first grade mathematics classes in China and the United States. *Early Childhood Research Quarterly, 24*(2), 198–211.

Laski, E. V., & Siegler, R. S. (2007). Is 27 a big number? Correlational and causal connections among numerical categorization, number line estimation, and numerical magnitude comparison. *Child Development, 78*(6), 1723–1743.

Lesh, R. (1979). Mathematical learning disabilities: Considerations for identification, diagnosis, and remediation. In R. Lesh, D. Mierkiewicz, & M. Kantowski (Eds.), *Applied mathematical problem solving* (pp. 111–180). Columbus, OH: ERIC.

Lynch, K., & Star, J. R. (2014a). Teachers' views about multiple strategies in middle and high school mathematics. *Mathematical Thinking and Learning, 16*(2), 85–108.

Lynch, K., & Star, J. R. (2014b). Views of struggling students on instruction incorporating multiple strategies in Algebra I: An exploratory study. *Journal for Research in Mathematics Education, 45*(1), 6–18.

Martin, T. (2009). A theory of physically distributed learning: How external environments and internal states interact in mathematics learning. *Child Development Perspectives, 3*(3), 140–144.

Matthews, P., Rittle-Johnson, B., McEldoon, K., & Taylor, R. (2012). Measure for measure: What combining diverse measures reveals about children's understanding of the equal sign as an indicator of mathematical equality. *Journal for Research in Mathematics Education, 43*(3), 316–350.

Mayer, R. (1982). Memory for algebra story problems. *Journal of Educational Psychology, 74*(2), 199–216.

McNeil, N. M. (2007). U-shaped development in math: 7-year-olds outperform 9-year-olds on equivalence problems. *Developmental Psychology, 43*(3), 687–695.

McNeil, N. M. (2008). Limitations to teaching children 2 + 2 = 4: Typical arithmetic problems can hinder learning of mathematical equivalence. *Child Development, 79*(5), 1524–1537.

McNeil, N. M., & Alibali, M. W. (2004). You'll see what you mean: Students encode equations based on their knowledge of arithmetic. *Cognitive Science, 28*(3), 451–466.

McNeil, N. M., & Alibali, M. W. (2005). Why won't you change your mind? Knowledge of operational patterns hinders learning and performance on equations. *Child Development, 76*(4), 883–899.

McNeil, N. M., & Fyfe, E. R. (2012). "Concreteness fading" promotes transfer of mathematical knowledge. *Learning and Instruction, 22*, 440–448.

McNeil, N. M., & Jarvin, L. (2007). When theories don't add up: Disentangling the manipulatives debate. *Theory Into Practice, 46*(4), 309–316.

McNeil, N. M., & Uttal, D. H. (2009). Rethinking the use of concrete materials in learning: Perspectives from development and education. *Child Development Perspectives, 3*(3), 137–139.

McNeil, N. M., Chesney, D. L., Matthews, P. G., Fyfe, E. R., Petersen, L. A., Dunwiddie, A. E., & Wheeler, M. C. (2012). It pays to be organized: Organizing arithmetic practice around equivalent values facilitates understanding of math equivalence. *Journal of Educational Psychology, 104*(4), 1109–1121.

McNeil, N. M., Fyfe, E. R., Petersen, L. A., Dunwiddie, A. E., & Brletic-Shipley, H. (2011). Benefits of practicing 4 = 2 + 2: Nontraditional problem formats facilitate children's understanding of mathematical equivalence. *Child Development, 82*(5), 1620–1633.

McNeil, N. M., Grandau, L., Knuth, E. J., Alibali, M. W., Stephens, A. C., Hattikudur, S., & Krill, D. E. (2006). Middle-school students' understanding of the equal sign: The books they read can't help. *Cognition and Instruction, 24*(3), 367–385.

McNeil, N. M., Uttal, D. H., Jarvin, L., & Sternberg, R. J. (2009). Should you show me the money? Concrete objects both hurt and help performance on mathematics problems. *Learning and Instruction, 19*(2), 171–184.

National Governors Association Center for Best Practices, & Council of Chief State School Officers. (2010). *Common core state standards (mathematics)*. Washington, D.C.: National Governors Association Center for Best Practices, Council of Chief State School Officers.

National Mathematics Advisory Panel. (2008). *Foundations for success: The final report of the National Mathematics Advisory Panel*. Washington, DC: U.S. Department of Education. Retrieved from http://www2.ed.gov/about/bdscomm/list/mathpanel/report/final-report.pdf (accessed May 13, 2014).

Newton, K. J., & Star, J. R. (2013). Exploring the nature and impact of model teaching with worked example pairs. *Mathematics Teacher Educator, 2*(1), 86–102.

Newton, K., Star, J. R., & Lynch, K. (2010). Exploring the development of flexibility in struggling algebra students. *Mathematical Thinking and Learning, 12*(4), 282–305.

Opfer, J. E., & Siegler, R. S. (2007). Representational change and children's numerical estimation. *Cognitive Psychology, 55*(3), 169–195.

Perry, M. (2000). Explanations of mathematical concepts in Japanese, Chinese, and US first- and fifth-grade classrooms. *Cognition and Instruction, 18*(2), 181–207.

Polya, G. (1945). *How to solve it* (2nd ed.). Princeton, NJ: Princeton University Press.

Powell, S. R. (2011). Solving word problems using schemas: A review of the literature. *Learning Disabilities Research & Practice, 26*(2), 94–108.

Powell, S. R. (2012). Equations and the equal sign in elementary mathematics textbooks. *Elementary School Journal, 112*(4), 627–648.

Powell, S. R., & Fuchs, L. S. (2010). Contribution of equal-sign instruction beyond word-problem tutoring for third-grade students with mathematics difficulty. *Journal of Educational Psychology, 102*(2), 381–394.

Ramani, G. B., Hitti, A., & Siegler, R. S. (2012). Taking it to the classroom: Number board games as a small group learning activity. *Journal of Educational Psychology, 104*(3), 661–672.

Ramani, G. B., & Siegler, R. S. (2008). Promoting broad and stable improvements in low-income children's numerical knowledge through playing number board games. *Child Development, 79*(2), 375–394.

Ramani, G. B., & Siegler, R. S. (2011). Reducing the gap in numerical knowledge between low- and middle-income preschoolers. *Journal of Applied Developmental Psychology, 32*(3), 146–159.

Reed, S. K. (1987). A structure-mapping model for word problems. *Journal of Experimental Psychology: Learning, Memory, and Cognition, 13*, 124–139.

Reed, S. K. (1989). Constraints on the abstraction of solutions. *Journal of Educational Psychology, 81*(4), 532–540.

Reed, S. K. (1999). *Word problems: Research and curriculum reform*. Mahwah, NJ: Lawrence Erlbaum.

Reed, S. K., Dempster, A., & Ettinger, M. (1985). Usefulness of analogous solutions for solving algebra word problems. *Journal of Experimental Psychology: Learning, Memory, and Cognition, 11*(1), 106–125.

Reed, S. K., & Evans, A. C. (1987). Learning functional relations: A theoretical and instructional analysis. *Journal of Experimental Psychology: General, 116*(2), 106–118.

Riley, M. S., & Greeno, J. G. (1988). Developmental analysis of understanding language about quantities and of solving problems. *Cognition and Instruction, 5*(1), 49–101.

Riley, M. S., Greeno, J. G., & Heller, J. I. (1983). Development of children's problem-solving ability in arithmetic. In H. P. Ginsburg (Ed.), *The development of mathematical thinking* (pp. 153–196). New York: Academic Press.

Rittle-Johnson, B. (2013). *Context of the equal sign: A textbook analysis of enVisionMath*. Unpublished manuscript. Nashville, TN: Department of Psychology and Human Development, Vanderbilt University.

Rittle-Johnson, B., & Star, J. R. (2007). Does comparing solution methods facilitate conceptual and procedural knowledge? An experimental study on learning to solve equations. *Journal of Educational Psychology, 99*(3), 561–574.

Rittle-Johnson, B., & Star, J. R. (2009). Compared with what? The effects of different comparisons on conceptual knowledge and procedural flexibility for equation solving. *Journal of Educational Psychology, 101*(3), 529–544.

Rittle-Johnson, B., & Star, J. R. (2011). The power of comparison in learning and instruction: Learning outcomes supported by different types of comparisons. In B. Ross & J. Mestre (Eds.), *Psychology of learning and motivation: Cognition in education* (Vol. 55, pp. 199–226). San Diego, CA: Elsevier.

Rittle-Johnson, B., Star, J. R., & Durkin, K. (2009). The importance of prior knowledge when comparing examples: Influences on conceptual and procedural knowledge of equation solving. *Journal of Educational Psychology, 101*(4), 836–852.

Rittle-Johnson, B., Star, J. R., & Durkin, K. (2012). Developing procedural flexibility: When should multiple procedures be introduced? *British Journal of Educational Psychology, 82*, 436–455.

Sarama, J., & Clements, D. H. (2009). 'Concrete' computer manipulatives in mathematics education. *Child Development Perspectives, 3*(3), 145–150.

Sarama, J., Clements, D. H., Starkey, P., Klein, A., & Wakeley, A. (2008). Scaling up the implementation of a pre-kindergarten mathematics curriculum: Teaching for understanding with trajectories and technologies. *Journal of Research on Educational Effectiveness, 1*(2), 89–119.

Schleppenbach, M., Flevares, L. M., Sims, L. M., & Perry, M. (2007a). Teacher responses to student mistakes in Chinese and U.S. classrooms. *Elementary School Journal, 108*(2), 131–147.

Schleppenbach, M., Perry, M., Miller, K. F., Sims, L., & Fang, G. (2007b). The answer is only the beginning: Extended discourse in Chinese and U.S. mathematics classrooms. *Journal of Educational Psychology, 99*, 380–396.

Schoenfeld, A. (2004). The math wars. *Educational Policy, 18*, 253–286.

Schoenfeld, A. H. (2006). Mathematics teaching and learning. In P. A. Alexander & P. H. Winne (Eds.), *Handbook of educational psychology* (2nd ed., pp. 479–510). Mahwah, NJ: Erlbaum.

Scott Foresman Addison Wesley. (2011). *enVisionMATH*. Upper Saddle River, NJ: Pearson Education.

Sherman, J., & Bisanz, J. (2009). Equivalence in symbolic and nonsymbolic contexts: Benefits of solving problems with manipulatives. *Journal of Educational Psychology, 101*(1), 88–100.

Siegler, R. S., & Booth, J. L. (2004). Development of numerical estimation in young children. *Child Development, 75*(2), 428–444.

Siegler, R. S., & Opfer, J. E. (2003). The development of numerical estimation: Evidence for multiple representations of numerical quantity. *Psychological Science, 14*(3), 237–243.

Siegler, R. S., & Ramani, G. B. (2008). Playing linear numerical board games promotes low-income children's numerical development. *Developmental Science, 11*(5), 655–661.

Siegler, R. S., & Ramani, G. B. (2009). Playing linear number board games, but not circular ones, improves low-income preschoolers' numerical understanding. *Journal of Educational Psychology, 101*(3), 545–560.

Sims, L. (2008). Look who's talking: Differences in math talk in U.S. and Chinese classrooms. *Teaching Children Mathematics, 15*(2), 120–124.

Star, J. R., Pollack, C., Durkin, K., Rittle-Johnson, B., Lynch, K., Newton, K., & Gogolen, C. (2015). Learning from comparison in algebra. *Contemporary Educational Psychology, 40,* 41–54.

Star, J. R., & Rittle-Johnson, B. (2009). It pays to compare: An experimental study on computational estimation. *Journal of Experimental Child Psychology, 102,* 408–426.

Starkey, P., Klein, A., & Wakeley, A. (2004). Enhancing young children's mathematical knowledge through a pre-kindergarten mathematics intervention. *Early Childhood Research Quarterly, 19*(1), 99.

Stephens, A. C., Knuth, E. J., Blanton, M. L., Isler, I., Gardiner, A. M., & Marum, T. (2013). Equation structure and the meaning of the equal sign: The impact of task selection in eliciting elementary students' understandings. *Journal of Mathematical Behavior, 32*(2), 173–182.

Stevenson, H. W., Lee, S. Y., & Stigler, J. W. (1986). Mathematics achievement of Chinese, Japanese, and American Children. *Science, 231,* 693–699.

Szilagyi, J., Clements, D., & Sarama, J. (2013). Young children's understandings of length measurement: Evaluating a learning trajectory. *Journal for Research in Mathematics Education, 44*(3), 581–620.

Uttal, D. H., O'Doherty, K., Newland, R., Hand, L. L., & DeLoache, J. (2009). Dual representation and the linking of concrete and symbolic representations. *Child Development Perspectives, 3*(3), 156–159.

Verschaffel, L., Greer, B., & De Corte, E. (2007). Whole number concepts and operations. In F. K. Lester (Ed.), *Second handbook of research on mathematics teaching and learning* (pp. 557–628). Charlotte, NC: Information Age Publishing.

Wynn, K. (1992). Children's acquisition of the number words and the counting system. *Cognitive Psychology, 24*(2), 220.

Yan Ping, X., Jitendra, A. K., & Deatline-Buchman, A. (2005). Effects of mathematical word problem-solving instruction on middle school students with learning problems. *Journal of Special Education, 39*(3), 181–192.

# 20

# Functional Scientific Literacy

## Seeing the Science within the Words and Across the Web

*Iris Tabak*[1]
Ben-Gurion University of the Negev, Israel

Engaging in science is no longer the stronghold of professional scientists. Increasingly, laypeople are considering scientific findings in their everyday lives. The types of knowledge and skills that laypeople use to take civic action, assess risks, or make personal choices may correspond with those of practicing scientists, but have a distinct character (Feinstein, 2011; Ryder, 2001). These skills comprise a *functional* scientific literacy (Ryder, 2001). The advent of the world wide web creates a context where public engagement in science is associated with online information seeking (Brossard, 2013), and with multiple-document comprehension (MDC: Bromme & Goldman, 2014; Goldman & Scardamalia, 2013b; Stadtler & Bromme, 2013).

People seek scientific information for two main types of goal: leisure goals, such as satisfying curiosity; and instrumental goals, such as making a decision or solving a problem (Brossard, 2013; Segev & Baram-Tsabari, 2012). For example, of over 3,000 questions presented by the public to science editors, the top questions were distributed between curiosity questions, such as "why do tea leaves rotate in the middle of the cup when stirred?" and instrumental questions, such as "shall I turn off even energy-saving lamps when I leave a room?" (Artz & Wormer, 2011). The stakes for achieving accuracy and understanding are higher for instrumental goals. In this chapter, I focus on instrumental goals, and on research on adults and secondary-school students.

The ability to integrate information sources is germane to functional scientific literacy, because when people seek information on the world wide web they obtain multiple results for each of their queries. Therefore, understanding the public's capacity to engage with science relates to questions of how well people interpret and comprehend scientific information within information sources, how well they integrate information across information sources, and what factors enhance or impede these processes. Investigating these questions (not just in science) has mainly appeared under the topics of MDC (e.g., Goldman & Scardamalia, 2013b) and information problem solving (e.g., Brand-Gruwel & Stadtler, 2011).

Understanding how people learn from text is a tradition in educational psychology (see a content analysis of educational psychology journals: Nolen, 2009). Until recently, this has been associated with a focus on content acquisition versus understanding (Pearson, Moje, & Greenleaf, 2010). However, increased recognition of the role of literacy in the practice of scientists (Bazerman, 2004), in learning science (Norris & Phillips, 2003), and in how experience with scientific practices can develop literacy skills (Krajcik & Sutherland, 2010) has reframed these perspectives. Literacy goals are now part of the Next Generation Science Standards (National Research Council, 2012).

This chapter engages these trends in the study of the role of text in science learning. It examines questions concerning the intersection of MDC and everyday science problem solving. What skills facilitate problem solving? What characterizes the texts available for problem solving? How can we cultivate these skills? What are the implications for curriculum and instruction?

## The Knowledge Demands of Media Use in Everyday Science Problem Solving

What knowledge and skills facilitate everyday problem solving? Consider a patient trying to choose among alternative smoking cessation aids (adapted from Asher, Nasser, & Tabak, 2010). She reads a news brief stating that Drug A is more effective. The brief states that Study 1 found that 80% of patients stopped smoking with Drug A, while Study 2 found that only 70% stopped smoking with Drug B. Robust problem solving would draw on many facets of knowledge.

Initially, the problem solver might be wary of the definitive language used in this brief, wondering if it represents the level of confidence in the scientific community, and seek more information. She would compare the studies' relative merit, reconcile information between them, and ask how each study operationalized what it means to "stop smoking." This is an important step. Variable operationalization affects interpretation. If Study 1 operationalized "stopped smoking" as no smoking for 6 months, while Study 2 measured no smoking for 12 months, then this could challenge what on the surface appears to be a clinical advantage of Drug A.

The processes that this hypothetical problem solver went through were complex and drew on multiple forms of knowledge. The problem solver realized that the writing genre of media reports differs from academic reports, and that she needed other information in order to obtain the details she was interested in exploring. Next, she used knowledge of scientific experimentation, such as knowing that different scientists, even when working with the same variables, can operationalize these variables in different ways. She considered how these different choices influence experimental outcomes. Surface processing could result in choosing a drug that is only effective in the short term, when the goal is to find a long-term solution. Functional scientific literacy relies on applying an amalgam of rhetorical, epistemic, and science-specific knowledge in integrating information from multiple sources.

## A Snapshot of Current Use of Media in Everyday Science Problem Solving

The empirical evidence on the efficacy of using, primarily online, science information in naturalistic contexts is sparse and mixed (see Chapter 25, this volume). Some studies show that seeking information and attending to multiple sources predicts greater knowledge of the investigated topic (Kahlor & Rosenthal, 2009). Similarly, meta-analyses on the use of patient decision aids[2] show that patients who utilize decision aids end up with more knowledge than those who do not (Stacey et al., 2011).

Unfortunately, these studies leave open questions concerning how well the information is used. We cannot assess whether this new knowledge is integrated or robust (Ladwig, Dalrymple, Brossard, Scheufele, & Corley, 2012), nor gauge how deeply people examine details in information sources in order to weigh their relative merits (Elwyn & Miron-Shatz, 2010). In fact, people have difficulty with interpretation tasks such as assessing risk (Stacey et al., 2011).

People report feeling overwhelmed and frustrated by the amount of information and its inconsistencies (Ward, Henderson, Coveney, & Meyer, 2012). Rather than discriminate between sources, reconcile discrepancies, and integrate knowledge across sources, some people opt to turn to a single source on which to base their choice. The selection criteria tend to be driven by surface features, or institutional authority (e.g., cancer council site) (Ward et al., 2012), which may reduce complexity, but may not be optimal for informed decisions.

These studies of the public's use of scientific information do not reflect the deep processing depicted in the hypothetical scenario above. They do not reflect an effort to evaluate and integrate information across sources. Laboratory studies further suggest that most people are not prepared to engage in these processes.

## Multiple-Document Comprehension and Everyday Science Problem Solving

A current line of research, *MDC*, involves creating experimental contexts similar to everyday science problem solving. In these contexts, researchers ask participants to utilize a set of information sources in order to reason about a problem, such as assessing the health risks of cell phones, or advising a fictitious friend on the use of a medication. From this perspective, proficiency in evaluating, comprehending, and integrating multiple information sources is a component of functional scientific literacy (Bromme & Goldman, 2014; Stadtler & Bromme, 2013).

The *documents model* (Perfetti, Rouet, & Britt, 1999) underlies much of this research (Bråten, Britt, Strømsø, & Rouet, 2011; Goldman, Braasch, Wiley, Graesser, & Brodowinska, 2012; Goldman & Scardamalia, 2013b; Stadtler & Bromme, 2013). This framework posits that comprehending multiple documents includes constructing two complementary cognitive models: an *intertext model* and a *situation model*. This builds on research on single-text processing (e.g., Kintsch, 1988) that depicts text comprehension as consisting of constructing a representation of the information in the text (*text base*) and of inferences and interpretations that draw on prior knowledge in relation to the text (*situation model*). The intertext model extends the text base as it applies to representing the characteristics of individual documents and of the relationships between multiple (concurrently read) documents. It is, figuratively, a depiction of a set of interconnected nodes, where each node contains information about a document. Information about the document can include details about the author, information about its claims or evidence, as well as impressions of its quality. Assertions about relationships between these nodes (documents), such as whether their content is complementary or conflicting, can annotate the links between the nodes.

The studies share a similar setup. Typically, university undergraduates are presented with four to eight documents of 250–800 words that present information on an extant, often controversial topic, such as climate change, or health concerns and treatment options. Participants read the documents in order to provide a summary, an argumentative position, or to make a justified recommendation. Sometimes, participants write an essay in response to these tasks. Most of the documents that participants read are original or modified information sources from the internet. The documents contain information that conflicts with, is orthogonal to, or complements information in the other documents.

These studies employ a set of instruments that enable fine-grained distinctions between components of MDC. Instruments that measure memory for source-content links are an index of the strength of the intertext model. For example, participants can be asked to fill in which source from a list of sources is associated with a statement that is a restatement or paraphrase of a unique statement from one of the information sources that the participants read (e.g., Braasch, Rouet, Vibert, & Britt, 2012).

In addition to tests that measure recall of information, measures also include tests that require inferences beyond the explicit text. These deeper measures distinguish between comprehension within single documents by asking questions that can be answered based on information from a single document, and comprehension across texts (cross-text comprehension) by asking questions that can only be answered by making inferences based on information from two or more documents (e.g., Strømsø, Bråten, & Samuelstuen, 2008). Such cross-text comprehension is also measured through postreading essays that are assessed for presenting explanations that draw on information from multiple documents (e.g., Wiley et al., 2009) or that reflect competing positions from multiple documents (e.g., Stadtler, Scharrer, Skodzik, & Bromme, 2014).

### Attending to Source Information and Determining the Trustworthiness of Information Sources

Sourcing, using knowledge of the authors' expertise, affiliation, or interests to judge the trustworthiness or qualifications of the information (Wineburg, 1991), is a focus of research on MDC. In principle, sourcing can facilitate both intertext and situation model construction (Bråten, Strømsø, & Britt, 2009; Wiley et al., 2009). Sourcing can help readers construct an intertext model, because source information can mark a document's representational node and the link to its content. It can contribute to constructing a situation model, by helping readers direct their attention selectively to more relevant and trustworthy content (Goldman et al., 2012).

Despite its importance, participants do not engage much in spontaneous sourcing (Mason, Boldrin, & Ariasi, 2010; Wiley et al., 2009). Most participants discriminate between information sources based on surface relevance of the content to the topic of the experimental task (Bråten, Strømsø, & Salmerón, 2011; Wiley et al., 2009). Some sourcing might be tacit, because participants spend more time on trustworthy than less trustworthy sites (Goldman et al., 2012). Attending to author credibility is rare (Bråten et al., 2009; Bråten, Strømsø, et al., 2011; Wiley et al., 2009), but more likely when author expertise is salient (Stadtler, Scharrer, Brummernhenrich, & Bromme, 2013).

Sourcing can be a bidirectional process. People may first scan all of the sources to make an initial evaluation, but information they encounter later in the reading process may send them back to examine source information more critically (Goldman et al., 2012). Relationships between accurate evaluation of trustworthy sources and strategic processing that includes returning to previously read documents support this idea (Anmarkrud, Bråten, & Strømsø, 2014). Encountering conflicting information might trigger this process (Stadtler et al., 2014).

Interventions that present normative evaluation criteria can foster productive sourcing. The SEEK instructional model (Graesser et al., 2007; Wiley et al., 2009) encourages readers to evaluate four aspects of the documents: (a) the credibility of the *source*; (b) the presence and strength of supporting *evidence*; (c) the fit of the evidence to an *explanation* of the phenomenon; and (d) the fit of the new information to readers' existing *knowledge*.

Following SEEK instruction, participants, who worked with a worksheet prompting the SEEK criteria (e.g., "is the author knowledgeable?"), applied these criteria, and more accurately ranked site reliability in a subsequent unguided task than participants who did not receive such instruction (Mason, Junyent, & Tornatora, 2014; Wiley et al., 2009). Although these effects appear even with very short (e.g., 1-hour) interventions, a single guided experience may not be sufficient, because when participants experienced prompting while working on a single task, their sourcing did not outperform participants who did not receive such prompts (Graesser et al., 2007). Providing participants with an introduction to the sourcing criteria prior to the prompted task might also be an essential feature that distinguished the successful from the less successful interventions.

However, even the single prompted experience had an effect. The participants who received evaluation prompts were more likely to raise these critical perspectives in posttask essays. Similar online evaluation prompts, compared to no evaluation prompts, fostered stronger memory for source characteristics such as the authors' affiliation, as well as more connections between arguments and the sources on which they were based in a postreading essay (Stadtler & Bromme, 2007). Interestingly, these online evaluation prompts did not support better comprehension (Stadtler & Bromme, 2007).

Considering source information, such as author expertise, does not guarantee better comprehension, and can even bias reasoning. Participants who read documents presented as authored by medical doctors were more likely to reconcile differences between the documents based on unwarranted inferences than participants who read the same documents presented as authored by high-school students (Stadtler et al., 2013). Possibly, the expectation that all medical doctors were correct led participants to focus on reconciliation at the expense of evaluating their own inferences.

### Cross-text Comprehension

The need to coordinate and piece together information from multiple documents into a coherent understanding adds complexity to the challenges that characterize *single* scientific document comprehension (Graesser, León, & Otero, 2002), such as gleaning causality and contending with specialized terminology. As expected, strategies that contribute to single-document comprehension also contribute to MDC, such as relating the text to one's prior knowledge and trying to understand claims by using self-explanation. Purposeful back-and-forth movement among documents, rather than an exhaustive forward traversal, seems to support integration across texts (Anmarkrud et al., 2014; Bråten & Strømsø, 2011; Goldman et al., 2012).

Evaluating the relative scientific merit of the content of different documents, and using this assessment to regulate the effort, attention, and strategies used while reading different documents distinguishes those who learn more from the reading than those who learn less (Goldman et al., 2012). Two hundred and seventeen undergraduates completed an inventory on comprehension strategies immediately after reading a set of documents on climate change. Self-reports of trying to elaborate, compare, and integrate information between texts predicted cross-text comprehension (Bråten & Strømsø, 2011).

Considering the content of a currently read document in relation to content previously read in other documents is essential to cross-text comprehension. This process is especially productive when it includes moving between the documents in order to pursue conjectures, and make judgments about whether the information between documents is cumulative, subject to reconciliation, or requires selection between incompatible accounts. Think-aloud studies bring these processes to light. In think-alouds participants carry out the task while continually voicing their thoughts.

In a think-aloud examining how undergraduates read six documents conveying different perspectives on health hazards of cell phones, a third of participants' actions concerned identifying and learning new information, and most of these involved elaborating the text in order to connect information between documents (Anmarkrud et al., 2014). Navigation consisted mainly of backward linking to previously read documents. These linking strategies positively correlated with presenting more than one perspective in postreading essays. Think-aloud analysis by Goldman et al. (2012) included coding of intertext comments (e.g., "this goes directly back to what I read about the oceanic plate going below the continental plate"). Their findings also suggest that this type of processing is key to cross-text comprehension, but their sample was not large enough to discern significant patterns.

Considering documents in relation to each other, and intending to reconcile differences, may not be sufficient. Resolution strategies may prove difficult to apply. As a result, some individuals might have the goal of resolution, but revert to focusing on a single source after reaching an impasse in their attempt to evaluate, compare, and integrate information sources (Ferguson, Bråten, & Strømsø, 2012).

Ironically, aspects that make these tasks more challenging—conflicting information distributed across documents—are also aspects that contribute to comprehension. Participants who read conflicting accounts concerning diagnosis and treatment of high cholesterol in four separate documents remembered more conflicting information and mentioned more conflicts in postreading essays than participants who read the same information within a single continuous document (Stadtler et al., 2013). Perhaps the physical separation between documents makes it easier to create an intertext model relating claims to sources. The physical separation might disrupt reading, alerting readers to distinguish one document and its associated claims from another.

Similar processing might occur when readers encounter conflicting information. Participants reading two-sentence stories in which the second sentence was either consistent with or contradictory to the first sentence had a stronger memory for conflicting rather than consistent stories. Eye-tracking data revealed that participants reprocessed the text more for inconsistent than consistent stories (Braasch et al., 2012). Thus, encountering conflicting information might trigger reprocessing, and this rereading of the text can influence memory for the text, and perhaps enhance comprehension.

The relationship between conflicting information and comprehension hinges on how people respond to these conflicts. Do they reconcile the information based on causal coherence and evidence, or aggregate even incompatible information? People might react in this way because they believe that empiricism is key to scientific knowledge, or that there can only be one explanation, so all accounts must be reconciled in some way.

### Epistemic Cognition and Multiple-Document Comprehension

Epistemic cognition in MDC refers to the ways in which people use their beliefs about knowledge and knowing in order to judge the trustworthiness of sources and the merit of information, and to respond to conflicting information (Sinatra, Kienhues, & Hofer, 2014). Epistemic beliefs are increasingly regarded as domain- (e.g., Hofer, 2006), context-, and topic-specific (Bromme, Kienhues, & Stahl, 2008). Individual studies conceptualize epistemic beliefs in nuanced ways, but overall this corpus of research draws on the personal epistemology framework (Hofer & Pintrich, 1997). Epistemic cognition may drive the purposeful navigation between documents that facilitates comprehension. A number of studies point to relationships between beliefs and cross-text comprehension.

Think-aloud studies demonstrate that participants evoke epistemic beliefs spontaneously as they evaluate source information and encounter surprising, corroborating, or conflicting information (Barzilai & Zohar, 2012; Bråten, Ferguson, Strømsø, & Anmarkrud, 2014; Ferguson et al., 2012; Mason, Ariasi, & Boldrin, 2011; Mason et al., 2010). Consider the following quote from one of these studies (undergraduates examining potential hazards of cell phones):

> Also here they are pretty convinced that the mobile phone is harmful and that it would be better not to use it . . . if I want to maintain that the majority claim the harmfulness of mobile phones, I would like to see if this site, the site of the newspaper *La Repubblica,* is in line with the ministry of health and not with the others. Knowledge is made of claims that must be compared to understand better. (Mason et al., 2010, p. 623)

This quote alludes to a number of epistemic considerations that motivate the participant's plan to examine additional documents. For example, it suggests that the participant considers preponderance of evidence (i.e., "if I want to maintain that the majority claim") and alignment with authority (i.e., "with the ministry of health and not with the others") as standards of justification. The quote is striking in that it ends with an explicit mention of views of knowledge.

### Expecting Scientific Knowledge to be Complex and Evolving

Expecting knowledge about a topic to be complex can be conducive to MDC. Participants who considered knowledge about the topic to consist of detailed interrelated concepts performed better on postreading assessments than participants who considered knowledge about the topic to consist of an accumulation of facts (Bråten & Strømsø, 2009; Strømsø et al., 2008). This was true for test questions that required drawing inferences from single as well as multiple documents. Although not as strong, similar outcomes were found for believing that knowledge about the topic is tentative and evolving rather than certain (Bråten & Strømsø, 2009).

Porsch and Bromme (2011), working with a construct that overlaps with both simplicity and certainty, which they refer to as texture, sensitized participants to either a view of the texture of knowledge as vague and subject to debate or as exact and precise. Participants read different versions of an introduction to the investigation topic (tides): one that emphasized scientific controversies, or another that emphasized the accuracy of models of tides. Participants sensitized to an imprecise view of the topic reported that they would seek more sources in order to complete the task. Expecting knowledge to be complex may lead readers to seek connections among different sources.

### Justification Beliefs and Strategies

The impetus to examine different information sources and to evaluate one document with respect to another document's content can also be a function of the criteria people employ to sanction and adopt knowledge claims. Two sets of studies point to a relationship between such justification beliefs and MDC. Each study conceptualizes justification beliefs differently.

Mason and colleagues conducted think-aloud studies of high-school students (Mason et al., 2011) and undergraduates (Mason et al., 2010) reading about possible hazards of cell phones. They coded the participants' statements for epistemic considerations of source of knowledge, justification, simplicity, and certainty. They identified three types of justification: knowledge cannot be evaluated; knowledge needs to be evaluated in light of the participant's prior knowledge; and knowledge needs to be evaluated based on scientific evidence. Justification statements were the second most prevalent type of statement after source of knowledge, and the most prevalent of the statements referring to the content of the information sources. Participants' statements clustered into two patterns. One pattern focused almost entirely on source information, and the other included consideration of the information content, as exhibited, in part, by justification statements. This second pattern was associated with more learning, as reflected in a postreading essay (Mason et al., 2010, 2011).

The tenor of these findings, that an evaluative focus on document content is efficacious, is consistent with findings by Bråten, Strømsø and colleagues (e.g., Bråten, Ferguson, Strømsø, & Anmarkrud, 2013). However, rather than justification through scientific evidence, they point to justification through multiple sources as the most productive belief. Justification by multiple sources is a belief that checking multiple sources can reveal incorrect claims, and that in order to decide what is correct in natural science it is necessary to check multiple sources. They contrast this position with two other positions: personal justification that posits that knowledge about natural science is a personal opinion, and that any opinion is as good as another; and justification by authority that states that knowledge presented by a teacher, textbook, scientist, or scientific investigation is correct. Believing in justification by multiple sources, as measured through pretask questionnaires (Bråten et al., 2013) or through coding of think-aloud statements (Bråten et al., 2014), predicted mentioning and explaining multiple perspectives in postreading essays.

Both sets of studies reveal that people spontaneously consider criteria for sanctioning knowledge claims, and that a stance that triggers comparison, evaluation, and critique is productive. What remains unclear is whether the two groups' conceptualizations of justification reflect the same theoretical meaning. For example, Bråten et al.'s (2013) justification by multiple sources does not explicitly note evaluation of scientific evidence, and Mason et al.'s (2010) criteria of evaluating scientific evidence does not explicitly refer to cross-source corroboration.

### Task Goal and Qualities of Document Texts

Task goals and text features also modulate multiple-document processing. If participants are given the task of writing an argumentative or a descriptive essay they vary in the extent to which they integrate information and present multiple perspectives in their essays (Gil, Bråten, Vidàl-Abarca, & Strømsø, 2010; Stadtler et al., 2014; Wiley et al., 2009). High-school students presented with an MDC task as a precursor to a real-world event, such as planning a trip, were more likely to want to consult more sources than originally provided compared to students who received the same task as a typical school assignment (Porsch & Bromme, 2011).

Scharrer and colleagues (Scharrer, Britt, Stadtler, & Bromme, 2013; Scharrer, Stadtler, & Bromme, 2014) examined whether reading comprehensible texts in MDC skews people's judgment about the scientific merit of the information and about their ability to effectively reason about the topic. A comprehensible text includes features such as using simple language, avoiding specialized terminology, and repeating important information. People reading comprehensible texts were more likely to agree with the claims made in the text, and less likely to seek additional information or expert advice than people who read less comprehensible texts.

Textual features can focus readers on conflicting claims. Participants who read documents where conflicting information was signaled by statements like "in contrast . . ." or "contrary to . . . ." were more likely to remember conflicting information and to report more conflicts in a two-sided fashion in postreading essays than participants who read the same text without these textual signals (Stadtler et al., 2014).

Textual features may be just as important as reading strategies and epistemic cognition. Media communications, which are the public's central source for scientific information (Kahlor & Rosenthal, 2009; Segev & Baram-Tsabari, 2012), present information differently than textbooks and academic communications. In what follows, I first describe the goals and constraints that shape the form and content of science news.[3] Next, I present studies that examine how laypeople interpret science news.

## Media Genre and Everyday Scientific Problem Solving

### Characteristics of Science News Reports

Science news needs to provide information quickly and concisely, and must draw the readers' attention away from competing media posts (Boykoff & Rajan, 2007). A scientific news report often takes on the "inverted pyramid" structure (Jarman & McClune, 2010), placing the conclusions at the start of the article. In contrast, an academic publication usually presents conclusions after an account of related studies, of how the study was conducted, and of what was found (Bazerman, 2004; Goldman & Bisanz, 2002). Scientific news reports are shorter and less detailed than academic reports. Media reports include headlines and sound bites that highlight attention-grabbing aspects that are not necessarily the most salient points for scientists, and may not be composed by the journalist (Goldman & Bisanz, 2002; Jarman & McClune, 2010).

One of the transformations that take place in moving from academic to media reports is simplification (Goldman & Bisanz, 2002). Many methodological details, such as how subjects were assigned to treatment groups, or other qualifications are unreported. Interestingly, even though consumers, scientists, and journalists can agree on the type of details that should be included (Mountcastle-Shah et al., 2003), many of these details do not appear in the published reports (Zimmerman, Bisanz, Bisanz, Klein, & Klein, 2001). The degree of omission is high. Using a content completeness instrument that included items such as number of subjects included in the study and the type of control or comparison used, 228 reports covering 24 discoveries had a completeness score of less than 20%, with individual report scores ranging from 6% to 81% (Holtzman et al., 2005).

Science media reports are criticized for being inaccurate (Secko, Amend, & Friday, 2012). Rather than the reporting of misinformation, this may reflect simplification and omission. Analyses comparing media reports with comparable academic reports suggest that the information that *is* reported is accurate (Holtzman et al., 2005). However, this information is presented using linguistic devices to enhance

emotionality that are not common in academic reports (Ransohoff & Ransohoff, 2000). Even if not sensationalized, other qualities of the report may draw readers' attention from details that are pertinent to distinguishing speculation from assertion. Media texts accompanied by visuals (DiFrancesco & Young, 2011) can evoke emotional responses that affect interpretation (Ainley, Corrigan, & Richardson, 2005).

Selection and framing can skew the portrayal of scientific research. Journalists and editors decide which studies are newsworthy, what aspects of the findings to emphasize, and whether to convey the findings as positive, negative, a breakthrough, or a concern (Jarman & McClune, 2010). The values of journalism rather than the values of science drive these decisions (Anderson, 2012). For example, science news reports might exaggerate the benefits of particular discoveries or report on only a subset of the risks or benefits (Mountcastle-Shah et al., 2003; Moynihan et al., 2000), which can differ from scientists' evaluation of the discovery (cf., Logan, Zengjun, & Wilson, 2000).

The ethics of unbiased reporting can drive journalists to present competing accounts of an issue, even when no controversy exists in the scientific community. As a result, the media can create an illusion of controversy by presenting a balanced report of majority and minority scientific positions. Central examples of this phenomenon are the media coverage of climate change and of relationships between the measles, mumps, rubella (MMR) vaccine and the onset of autism (Boykoff & Rajan, 2007; Nisbet, 2009). In an attempt to draw readers' attention, reporters may take an ancillary finding that relates to current public interest, or has other public appeal, and present it as a central discovery (Jarman & McClune, 2010; Ransohoff & Ransohoff, 2000).

Conferences, interviews with scientists, press releases, and academic publications all serve as sources for media coverage of science. The media may treat all of these sources equally, even though the scientific community has implicit assumptions about which of these are more dependable. In addition, the language of science news tends to be more certain than tentative, hedging, academic writing (Fahnestock, 1986). Therefore, there are few, if any, structural, textual or visual cues to distinguish the report of frontier science from more established findings (Dunwoody, 1999; Rowan, 1999).

### Laypeople's Awareness of and Responses to Science News Genre

Laypeople may regard science media reports as a veridical account of scientific findings, rather than a construction that is the product of selection, interpretation, and framing. They may not realize that pertinent information is absent. As a result, they may approach these texts with a simple reception rather than an interpretive and critical stance. A number of studies reveal that high-school and university undergraduates have difficulty critiquing science news reports, and negotiating the scientific details in order to determine appropriate generalizations of the reported conclusions (Goldman & Bisanz, 2002; Yeaton, Smith, & Rogers, 1990). Moreover, they may not be aware of limitations in their reading, because in some studies participants rate their performance with confidence (Norris, Phillips, & Korpan, 2003; Scharrer, Bromme, Britt, & Stadtler, 2012)

Norris et al. (2003) examined how well university undergraduates across disciplinary majors could interpret scientific media reports. Undergraduates were given genuine media reports on current scientific topics. The reports were about 400–900 words in length and at a tenth-grade reading level. The students reported that these media reports were easy to read. They were successful in answering information lookup questions, so decoding and locating information in the text were not an obstacle. However, participants were only able to answer half of the interpretive questions correctly.

In reading science media reports, both high-school and university undergraduates seem to struggle with distinguishing an explanation from a description, and causality from explanation (Manuel, 2002; Norris & Phillips, 1994; Norris et al., 2003). Students had a hard time recognizing when one statement served as evidence in support of another statement (Manuel, 2002; Norris & Phillips, 1994), and tended to view all statements as equally true and justified. This might be a result of the educational system's strong socialization to textbooks as a source of knowledge. People might expect all texts to reflect the canonical, truth statement, form that textbooks use. In fact, when presented with a variety of sources that include science news reports, undergraduates rated textbooks as more trustworthy (Bråten, Strømsø, et al., 2011). This socialization may desensitize learners to the subtleties of language use. For example, despite taking a course on media and information literacy, some students did not realize that the author had a point of view and persuasion goals (Manuel, 2002). These students had expected persuasion to be associated with strong one-sided language; they expected the author's phrasing to be "really forcing it."

There also seems to be a disparity between the evaluation criteria for science news that laypeople generate and the criteria that they apply in practice. Undergraduates noted that information about a scientific study's methodology is helpful to include in evaluating science media reports (Korpan, Bisanz, Bisanz, & Henderson, 1997). Yet, undergraduates who were given science news reports and were asked to rate their credibility tended to base their judgment on whether they believed the conclusion (Bisanz, Zimmerman, & Bisanz, 1998). Participants were better able to distinguish high- from low-quality methodology, and were more likely to include methodological quality in their justification, when the topic of the news reports was a topic that was prevalent in educational curricula or the popular press (Bisanz et al., 1998).

Baram-Tsabari and Yarden (2005) found more promising results concerning how science learners contend with science news. They presented tenth-, eleventh-, and twelfth-grade students with a text that contained the same information as an authentic academic publication, but written to resemble the language and structure of a science news report. Unlike the students in the research reviewed above, these learners were able to respond to interpretation questions. Two differences might explain these discrepant outcomes. First, although written in the science news genre, the adapted report was based on and designed to include all of the information in the original academic report. Therefore, it may have included details not typically found in published news articles, and these details may have facilitated comprehension. In addition, the participants studied in a biology-major track, which means that they had educational experience with advanced topics that delve into the processes and products of professional biological research.

Methodological details as well as other textual features can mark texts as more scientific, but this may not be the central influence on laypeople's reasoning. Undergraduates identified the use of specialized terminology, of in-text citations and the report of methodology as signifying a more scientific, and consequently more credible, report (Thomm & Bromme, 2012). Yet, in reading in order to make a decision, such "scientificness" did not prove persuasive for these students. Instead, undergraduates were swayed by more approachable texts (Scharrer et al., 2012). People may conflate friendly prose with substantiated claims.

Science news and networked resources include different forms of textual, visual, and graphical representations that offer affordances and constraints for problem solving. The chapter reveals that current formal education does not prepare learners for MDC and for negotiating diverse genres. Learners need experience processing multiple documents in the science news genre, and in other genres that populate the world wide web.[4]

## Cultivating Functional Scientific Literacy

Recent research explores how to enact these types of experience in the classroom. It is not possible to include a review of the range of research on the use of texts or everyday problem solving in science learning. I present two illustrative examples.

### Reading, Evidence, and Argumentation in Disciplinary Instruction (READI)

Project READI (Goldman & Scardamalia, 2013a) builds on prior research, reviewed in this chapter, especially on the efficacy of the SEEK instructional model (e.g., Wiley et al., 2009). Similar to SEEK, the READI curriculum encourages learners to evaluate the credibility of sources, the scientific merit of source content, to build causal models that draw on information across sources, and to consider new information in light of prior knowledge. The curriculum also aims to help learners develop proficiency in the critical reading of multiple genres. In this project, learners use information sources to construct evidence-based recommendations for extant problems.

In one unit (Greenleaf, Brown, Goldman, & Ko, 2013), learners investigate the public health threat of an antibiotic-resistant bacteria, and formulate a recommendation on how to manage this threat. They use a variety of multimodal texts drawn from authentic professional and popular science information sources. The learners construct and critique causal explanations of the mechanisms of infection, resistance, and control of infection. The teacher models these processes, and guides learners throughout the unit. Initial learning outcomes show much promise (Greenleaf et al., 2013).

## SciJourn

The SciJourn project cultivates functional scientific literacy and emphasizes immersion in the science news genre by positioning learners as science news journalists (Polman & Hope, 2014). The learner-journalists propose a question, such as whether youth should get tattoos. They then use primary and secondary information sources to investigate different facets of this question, and to compose a news article on the topic. Participating classrooms publish an open-access online newspaper, and some classrooms publish a print newspaper edited by a professional science news editor. Curricular activities include both guided reading and writing. For example, a class will read a science news story together, stopping to discuss and critique the article, in order to uncover some of its strengths and weaknesses as a source of information (Kohnen, 2013).

The editorial review and revision process helps learners develop a repertoire of strategies for seeking information to evaluate claims, and to distinguish established from frontier science. For example, an editor might question a claim in an article draft, and encourage learners to examine primary literature. The subsequent encounter with primary sources can provide a purview into the relative position of the finding within the scientific literature. Assessments show that learners are better able to evaluate the factual accuracy of reports, as well as to identify when further information is needed and how it can be obtained. This was especially true for classrooms where teachers encouraged multiple revision focused on scientific content issues (Farrar, 2012).

## Implications for Research and Practice

The research reviewed in this chapter—the public surveys, experimental studies of MDC, reviews of the science news genre and laypeople's awareness of this genre—highlights that the public has increasing *material access* to scientific information, but that they do not have adequate *intellectual command* over these resources. A challenge for educational psychologists and science educators is to minimize this gap between access and command. We need to advance our understanding of MDC in science, and use it to inform curricular innovations. We need to consider whether prevailing curricula focused on scientific practices are relevant to cultivating functional scientific literacy.

### Advancing Understanding of Multiple-Document Comprehension in Science

#### Elaborating Science-specific Aspects of Multiple-Document Comprehension. Effective MDC strategies for scientific information may be different from effective strategies in other disciplines. Corroboration, identifying the same information in multiple primary sources as a way to identify trustworthy information and to construct a reliable account of the past, is a key strategy for historians (Wineburg, 1991).

Historical inquiry involves juxtaposing and interpreting period texts. Unlike historical inquiry, scientific inquiry often involves quantified measurements and experimentation (e.g., Chalmers, 1976). Consequently, corroboration may function differently in science. Current research does not explain much about how the practices and values of science figure in MDC of scientific information sources. Differences in the reading practices of experts in different disciplines suggest that research on MDC could benefit from research that would extend this knowledge.

Shanahan, Shanahan, and Misischia (2011) identified differences in the reading processes of a chemist, mathematician, and historian, each reading texts within his or her discipline. For example, the historian used information about the author for interpretation as well as for text selection. In contrast, the chemist used this information only to select texts, and the mathematician tried not to consider author information in interpretation. Comparing how scientists and historians examined the *same* set of historical documents (Gottlieb & Wineburg, 2012) reveals how disciplinary knowledge drives interpretation. Scientists viewed segments such as "beneficial Author of all the good" as evidence of the widespread belief in God. Historians contextualized this segment within the emergence of deism, and arrived at a different interpretation, viewing it as reflecting precursors to the separation of church and state (Gottlieb & Wineburg, 2012).

Future research on MDC can examine how scientists solve tasks used in prior research with laypeople. This research has the potential to uncover new MDC processes, because most research to date focused on novices with little scientific background. When participants do have knowledge of scientific practices they focus on considerations of the reported methodology more than lay participants (Yang, Chen, & Tsai, 2013).

#### Converging on Shared Conceptualizations of Epistemic Cognition. The literature review pointed to relationships between patterns of epistemic cognition and successful MDC. It also revealed that different studies employed different conceptualizations of epistemic beliefs, even when using the same labels, such as justification beliefs. This makes it difficult to generalize conclusions across MDC studies. There is a need to converge on shared conceptualizations of epistemic cognition.

Debates about conceptualizing epistemic cognition extend beyond the study of MDC. These debates explore how to articulate different frameworks (Chinn, Buckland, & Samarapungavan, 2011; Greene, Azevedo, & Torney-Purta, 2008). Some critiques question the appropriateness of studying epistemic cognition as a predefined set of positions rather than the orchestration of resources within the enactment of a reasoning activity (Elby & Hammer, 2001; Sandoval, 2005). A similar concern is whether different positions can be considered more or less efficacious in an absolute rather than context-specific sense (Bromme et al., 2008; Elby & Hammer, 2001).

Considering these debates in the context of science education adds even greater multivocality. In science education, alongside studies employing the personal epistemology framework (e.g., Hofer & Pintrich, 1997), are studies of nature of science (NOS) (e.g., Lederman, 2007), which focus specifically on beliefs about the production of knowledge in science. Studies of NOS rarely examine the role of NOS beliefs in MDC, but some studies examined NOS beliefs in reasoning about socioscientific issues (Zeidler, Walker, Ackett, & Simmons, 2002). There are some similarities between ideas in NOS and in personal epistemology, but some of the social and cultural aspects of the production of scientific knowledge addressed in NOS are not found in most personal epistemology studies (Wu & Tsai, 2010). There is mixed evidence concerning relationships between learners' views as measured by common personal epistemology and NOS instruments (Tabak & Weinstock, 2005; Wu & Tsai, 2010), and the variability of conceptualizations within NOS research makes such mapping even more difficult (for a critical review, see Deng, Chen, Tsai, & Chai, 2011).

The *aims, ideals and reliable processes* (AIR) model (Chinn et al., 2011; Chinn, Rinehart, & Buckland, 2014) offers a new conceptualization that responds to many past critiques and is compatible with NOS and personal epistemology. The model articulates three components of epistemic cognition: *Epistemic aims* and values are what people aim to achieve and how important achieving this goal is to them. Understanding or explaining may be epistemic aims. *Ideals* are the criteria used to evaluate how well the epistemic aims have been met. For example, a scientist might consider whether her account explains patterns of data not explained by prior accounts. Finally, *reliable processes* are schemas that specify the means to achieve epistemic aims reliably. Some examples of reliable processes in professional science include systematic comparisons and replication. The AIR model integrates different aspects of MDC highlighted in this chapter, and provides a way to focus on science-specific aspects. It combines attention to a particular task goal (aim), to different context-specific evaluation criteria (ideals), and to the particular methods that scientists might use to meet these criteria (reliable means).

### Are Learning Environments that Emulate Professional Scientific Practice Relevant to Cultivating Functional Scientific Literacy?

Research on curricular innovation in science focuses on activities that emulate scientific practices (Duschl & Hamilton, 2011; Linn & Eylon, 2006). Consider the actions and reasoning processes of science learners constructing a model of water pollution in a local pond. These actions include learning about contaminants and water characteristics, conducting observations of the pond in order to identify possible contaminants, and raising conjectures about the relationships between the sources of the contaminants, the ways in which they reach the pond, and their effect on water quality. The learners can articulate their conjectures in a scientific model, which they can then test against samples collected from the pond. This process is similar in its aims, reasoning, and practices to those that ecologists might employ, but different

from the process depicted earlier in the two example functional scientific literacy curricula. Are these types of activities relevant to learners who will not pursue science-oriented careers?

Learners who engage in such first-hand investigations can develop an understanding of the role of interpretive frameworks in science, as well as of the strengths and limitations of experimentation (Lehrer, Schauble, & Lucas, 2008). The learners in the example above need to decide which factors to specify in their model. In doing this, they realize that scientific models are selectively constructed representations of phenomena rather than replicas. Comparing models, they can see how different learners can make different, but accurate and justifiable, selection decisions.

Decisions about what factors to include or exclude result in different models and different explanations. These experiences may be the only way to become aware of these decisions. Primary scientific literature presents scientific models, but the idea that constructing the model involved a process of selection is implicit. Secondary sources will report the conclusions, and may not even present the model on which they are based.

These selection decisions are invisible to people who only see science through secondary sources. Yet, an appreciation for these types of decisions is precisely the understanding that enabled the hypothetical problem solver, in the opening section of the chapter, to recognize the nuanced differences in the clinical trials, and to realize that what appeared on the surface as a preferable drug was only effective in the short term. In coining the term functional scientific literacy, Ryder (2001) found that knowing what methods scientists use to make claims, and what standards are used to justify these claims, helps laypeople contend with scientific issues. Therefore, educational experiences that emulate professional scientific practices enhance MDC, and are just as important to learners who will not pursue careers in science as they are to those who will.

### Co-evolution of Scientific Media Reports and Media Awareness

Scientific media reports offer easy access to information that might otherwise be invisible to the public (Logan et al., 2000). However, they usually do not provide the information that is needed to evaluate findings (Zimmerman et al., 2001), or to compare findings across studies in order to make decisions. Such details may be a form of reporting that goes beyond the media's current goals, and may not be consonant with perspectives that see "science in the news" as its own expression of scientific ideas rather than a veridical summary of scientific reports (Anderson, 2012). Nonetheless, the journalism and science communication communities grapple with whether and how science media can play an educative role (Lewenstein, 2011; Rowan, 1999).

With time, we might witness concomitant changes in science news reports and in the public as discerning readers. Research reviewed in this chapter, such as on how signaled language (Stadtler et al., 2014) can help people to focus on conflicting claims, or on what details reports can include to facilitate problem solving (Jarman & McClune, 2010; Mountcastle-Shah et al., 2003), can guide such changes. Greater public awareness of information needs, alongside their increasing consumer power in networked spaces, might be a catalyst in this process (Maier, Rothmund, Retzbach, Otto, & Besley, 2014).

## Conclusion

Scientific understanding takes on a specialized meaning when considering laypeople in the information age. The public has unprecedented access to scientific information. Yet, the potential to use these resources is unmet. Research on MDC in science and on science news genre-awareness offers important guidance concerning the knowledge and skills that can enable laypeople to become discerning consumers of scientific information. Future research needs to extend our understanding of science-specific processes in MDC, and to converge on shared conceptualizations of epistemic cognition. Instruction needs to build on such research, and incorporate more experiences with everyday scientific problem solving. However, we should not abandon curricula focused on professional scientific practices. If learners have the opportunity to play the role of scientists, as well as gain a purview into the ways in which they might use the products of science in daily life, then they may be ready to take intellectual command over the information to which they have access.

## Notes

1. I thank Michael Weinstock, and members of the Learning in a Networked Society (LINKS) Israeli Center for Research Excellence, especially Sarit Barzilai and Shira Soffer-Vital, for helpful discussions. I thank Eric Anderman, Josh Radinsky, and two anonymous reviewers for productive feedback on an earlier draft.
2. Patient decision aids present information on treatment options and risks, as well as processing aids (e.g., checklists). They are similar to layperson use of media in everyday science problem solving.
3. The review draws on research on both print and digital media, but the characterizations and concerns that are described seem to hold for both print and online media reports (Gerhards & Schäfer, 2010).
4. Learning to contend with primary literature may also be necessary for functional scientific literacy. Research on adapting primary literature (Yarden, 2009) may inform these efforts.

## References

Ainley, M., Corrigan, M., & Richardson, N. (2005). Students, tasks and emotions: Identifying the contribution of emotions to students' reading of popular culture and popular science texts. *Learning and Instruction*, *15*(5), 433–447.

Anderson, M. M. (2012). *A functional conceptualization of understanding science in the news* (unpublished doctoral dissertation). Madison, WI: The University of Wisconsin—Madison.

Anmarkrud, Ø., Bråten, I., & Strømsø, H. I. (2014). Multiple-documents literacy: Strategic processing, source awareness, and argumentation when reading multiple conflicting documents. *Learning and Individual Differences*, *30*(0), 64–76.

Artz, K., & Wormer, H. (2011). What recipients ask for: An analysis of 'user question generated' science coverage. *Journalism*, *12*(7), 871–888.

Asher, I., Nasser, S., & Tabak, I. (2010). Putting the pieces together: The challenge and value of synthesizing disparate graphs in inquiry-based science learning. In K. Gomez, L. Lyons, & J. Radinsky (Eds.), *Learning in the disciplines: Proceedings of the 9th international conference of the learning sciences (ICLS 2010)* (Vol. 2, pp. 340–341). Chicago, IL: International Society of the Learning Sciences.

Baram-Tsabari, A., & Yarden, A. (2005). Text genre as a factor in the formation of scientific literacy. *Journal of Research in Science Teaching*, *42*(4), 403–428.

Barzilai, S., & Zohar, A. (2012). Epistemic thinking in action: Evaluating and integrating online sources. *Cognition and Instruction*, *30*(1), 39–85.

Bazerman, C. (2004). Speech acts, genres, and activity systems: How texts organize activity and people. In C. Bazerman & P. A. Prior (Eds.), *What writing does and how it does it: An introduction to analyzing texts and textual practices* (pp. 309–339). Mahwah, NJ: Erlbaum.

Bisanz, J., Zimmerman, C., & Bisanz, G.L. (1998). Everyday scientific literacy: Do students use information about the social context and methods of research to evaluate news briefs about science? *Alberta Journal of Educational Research*, *44*(2), 188.

Boykoff, M. T., & Rajan, S. R. (2007). Signals and noise. *EMBO Rep*, *8*(3), 207–211.

Braasch, J. G., Rouet, J.-F., Vibert, N., & Britt, M. A. (2012). Readers' use of source information in text comprehension. *Memory & Cognition*, *40*(3), 450–465.

Brand-Gruwel, S., & Stadtler, M. (2011). Solving information-based problems: Evaluating sources and information (special issue). *Learning and Instruction*, *21*(2).

Bråten, I., Britt, M. A., Strømsø, H. I., & Rouet, J.-F. (2011). The role of epistemic beliefs in the comprehension of multiple expository texts: Toward an integrated model. *Educational Psychologist*, *46*(1), 48–70.

Bråten, I., Ferguson, L., Strømsø, H., & Anmarkrud, Ø. (2013). Justification beliefs and multiple-documents comprehension. *European Journal of Psychology of Education*, *28*(3), 879–902.

Bråten, I., Ferguson, L. E., Strømsø, H. I., & Anmarkrud, Ø. (2014). Students working with multiple conflicting documents on a scientific issue: Relations between epistemic cognition while reading and sourcing and argumentation in essays. *British Journal of Educational Psychology*, *84*(1), 58–85.

Bråten, I., & Strømsø, H. I. (2009). Effects of task instruction and personal epistemology on the understanding of multiple texts about climate change. *Discourse Processes*, *47*(1), 1–31.

Bråten, I., & Strømsø, H. (2011). Measuring strategic processing when students read multiple texts. *Metacognition and Learning*, *6*(2), 111–130.

Bråten, I., Strømsø, H. I., & Britt, M. A. (2009). Trust matters: Examining the role of source evaluation in students' construction of meaning within and across multiple texts. *Reading Research Quarterly*, *44*(1), 6–28.

Bråten, I., Strømsø, H. I., & Salmerón, L. (2011). Trust and mistrust when students read multiple information sources about climate change. *Learning and Instruction*, *21*(2), 180–192.

Bromme, R., & Goldman, S. R. (2014). The public's bounded understanding of science. *Educational Psychologist*, *49*(2), 59–69.

Bromme, R., Kienhues, D., & Stahl, E. (2008). Knowledge and epistemological beliefs: An intimate but complicate relationship. In M. Khine (Ed.), *Knowing, knowledge and beliefs* (pp. 423–441). Amsterdam, Netherlands: Springer.

Brossard, D. (2013). New media landscapes and the science information consumer. *Proceedings of the National Academy of Sciences*, *110*(Supplement 3), 14096–14101.

Chalmers, A. F. (1976). *What is this thing called science?* Queensland, Australia: University of Queensland Press.

Chinn, C. A., Buckland, L. A., & Samarapungavan, A. L. A. (2011). Expanding the dimensions of epistemic cognition: Arguments from philosophy and psychology. *Educational Psychologist*, *46*(3), 141–167.

Chinn, C. A., Rinehart, R. W., & Buckland, L. A. (2014). Epistemic cognition and evaluating information: Applying the air model of epistemic cognition. In D. Rapp & J. Braasch (Eds.), *Processing inaccurate information* (pp. 425–454). Cambridge, MA: MIT Press.

Deng, F., Chen, D.-T., Tsai, C.-C., & Chai, C. S. (2011). Students' views of the nature of science: A critical review of research. *Science Education*, *95*(6), 961–999.

DiFrancesco, D. A., & Young, N. (2011). Seeing climate change: The visual construction of global warming in Canadian national print media. *Cultural Geographies, 18*(4), 517–536.

Dunwoody, S. (1999). Scientists, journalists, and the meaning of uncertainty. In S. M. Friedman, S. Dunwoody, & C. L. Rogers (Eds.), *Communicating uncertainty: Media coverage of new and controversial science* (pp. 59–79). Mahwah, NJ: Erlbaum.

Duschl, R. A., & Hamilton, R. (2011). Learning science. In R. E. Mayer & P. A. Alexander (Eds.), *Handbook of research on learning and instruction* (pp. 78–107). New York, NY: Routledge.

Elby, A., & Hammer, D. (2001). On the substance of a sophisticated epistemology. *Science Education, 85*(5), 554–567.

Elwyn, G., & Miron-Shatz, T. (2010). Deliberation before determination: The definition and evaluation of good decision making. *Health Expectations, 13*(2), 139–147.

Fahnestock, J. (1986). Accommodating science: The rhetorical life of scientific facts. *Written Communication, 3*(3), 275–296.

Farrar, C. (2012). *Assessing the impact participation in science journalism activities has on scientific literacy among high school students* (doctoral dissertation). ProQuest, UMI Dissertations Publishing (1015637958). St. Louis, MO: University of Missouri-St. Louis.

Feinstein, N. W. (2011). Salvaging science literacy. *Science Education, 95*(1), 168–185.

Ferguson, L. E., Bråten, I., & Strømsø, H. I. (2012). Epistemic cognition when students read multiple documents containing conflicting scientific evidence: A think-aloud study. *Learning and Instruction, 22*(2), 103–120.

Gerhards, J., & Schäfer, M. S. (2010). Is the internet a better public sphere? Comparing old and new media in the USA and Germany. *New Media & Society, 12*(1), 143–160.

Gil, L., Bråten, I., Vidal-Abarca, E., & Strømsø, H.I. (2010). Summary versus argument tasks when working with multiple documents: Which is better for whom? *Contemporary Educational Psychology, 35*(3), 157–173.

Goldman, S. R., & Bisanz, G. L. (2002). Toward a functional analysis of scientific genres: Implications for understanding and learning processes. In J. Otero, J. A. León, & A. C. Graesser (Eds.), *The psychology of science text comprehension* (pp. 19–50). Mahwah, NJ: Erlbaum.

Goldman, S. R., Braasch, J. L. G., Wiley, J., Graesser, A. C., & Brodowinska, K. (2012). Comprehending and learning from internet sources: Processing patterns of better and poorer learners. *Reading Research Quarterly, 47*(4), 356–381.

Goldman, S. R., & Scardamalia, M. (2013a). Managing, understanding, applying, and creating knowledge in the information age: Next-generation challenges and opportunities. *Cognition and Instruction, 31*(2), 255–269.

Goldman, S. R., & Scardamalia, M. (2013b). Multiple document comprehension (special issue). *Cognition and Instruction, 31*(2).

Gottlieb, E., & Wineburg, S. (2012). Between veritas and communitas: Epistemic switching in the reading of academic and sacred history. *Journal of the Learning Sciences, 21*(1), 84–129.

Graesser, A. C., León, J. A., & Otero, J. (2002). Introduction to the psychology of science text comprehension. In J. Otero, J. A. León, & A. C. Graesser (Eds.), *The psychology of science text comprehension* (pp. 1–15). Mahwah, NJ: Erlbaum.

Graesser, A. C., Wiley, J., Goldman, S. R., O'Reilly, T., Jeon, M., & McDaniel, B. (2007). SEEK web tutor: Fostering a critical stance while exploring the causes of volcanic eruption. *Metacognition and Learning, 2*(2–3), 89–105.

Greene, J. A., Azevedo, R., & Torney-Purta, J. (2008). Modeling epistemic and ontological cognition: Philosophical perspectives and methodological directions. *Educational Psychologist, 43*(3), 142–160.

Greenleaf, C., Brown, W., Goldman, S. R., & Ko, M.-L. (2013). *READI for science: Promoting scientific literacy practices through text-based investigations for middle and high school science teachers and students.* Washington, D.C.: NRC Workshop on Literacy for Science.

Hofer, B. K. (2006). Domain specificity of personal epistemology: Resolved questions, persistent issues, new models. *International Journal of Educational Research, 45*(1–2), 85–95.

Hofer, B. K., & Pintrich, P.R. (1997). The development of epistemological theories: Beliefs about knowledge and knowing and their relation to learning. *Review of Educational Research, 67*(1), 88–140.

Holtzman, N. A., Bernhardt, B. A., Mountcastle-Shah, E., Rodgers, J. E., Tambor, E., & Geller, G. (2005). The quality of media reports on discoveries related to human genetic diseases. *Public Health Genomics, 8*(3), 133–144.

Jarman, R., & McClune, B. (2010). Developing students' ability to engage critically with science in the news: Identifying elements of the 'media awareness' dimension. *The Curriculum Journal, 21*(1), 47–64.

Kahlor, L., & Rosenthal, S. (2009). If we seek, do we learn?: Predicting knowledge of global warming. *Science Communication, 30*(3), 380–414.

Kintsch, W. (1988). The role of knowledge in discourse comprehension: A construction-integration model. *Psychological Review, 95*(2), 163.

Kohnen, A. M. (2013). The authenticity spectrum: The case of a science journalism writing project. *English Journal, 102*(5), 28–34.

Korpan, C. A., Bisanz, G. L., Bisanz, J., & Henderson, J. M. (1997). Assessing literacy in science: Evaluation of scientific news briefs. *Science Education, 81*(5), 515–532.

Krajcik, J. S., & Sutherland, L. M. (2010). Supporting students in developing literacy in science. *Science, 328*(5977), 456–459.

Ladwig, P., Dalrymple, K. E., Brossard, D., Scheufele, D. A., & Corley, E. A. (2012). Perceived familiarity or factual knowledge? Comparing operationalizations of scientific understanding. *Science and Public Policy, 39*(6), 761–774.

Lederman, N. G. (2007). Nature of science: Past, present, and future. In S. K. Abell & N. G. Lederman (Eds.), *Handbook of research on science education* (Vol. I, pp. 831–880). Mahwah, NJ: Erlbaum.

Lehrer, R., Schauble, L., & Lucas, D. (2008). Supporting development of the epistemology of inquiry. *Cognitive Development, 23*(4), 512–529.

Lewenstein, B. V. (2011). Changing our ideas. *International Journal of Science Education, Part B, 1*(1), 17–21.

Linn, M. C., & Eylon, B.-S. (2006). Science education: Integrating views of learning and instruction. In P. A. Alexander & P. H. Winne (Eds.), *Handbook of educational psychology* (2nd ed., pp. 511–544). Mahwah, NJ: Erlbaum.

Logan, R. A., Zengjun, P., & Wilson, N. F. (2000). Science and medical coverage in the Los Angeles Times and the Washington Post: A six-year perspective. *Science Communication, 22*(1), 5–26.

Maier, M., Rothmund, T., Retzbach, A., Otto, L., & Besley, J. C. (2014). Informal learning through science media usage. *Educational Psychologist,* 1–18.

Manuel, K. (2002). How first-year college students read popular science: An experiment in teaching media literacy skills. *SIMILE: Studies In Media & Information Literacy Education, 2*(2), 1–12.

Mason, L., Ariasi, N., & Boldrin, A. (2011). Epistemic beliefs in action: Spontaneous reflections about knowledge and knowing during online information searching and their influence on learning. *Learning and Instruction, 21*(1), 137–151.

Mason, L., Boldrin, A., & Ariasi, N. (2010). Searching the web to learn about a controversial topic: Are students epistemically active? *Instructional Science, 38*(6), 607–633.

Mason, L., Junyent, A. A., & Tornatora, M. C. (2014). Epistemic evaluation and comprehension of web-source information on controversial science-related topics: Effects of a short-term instructional intervention. *Computers & Education, 76*(0), 143–157.

Mountcastle-Shah, E., Tambor, E., Bernhardt, B. A., Geller, G., Karaliukas, R., Rodgers, J. E., & Holtzman, N. A. (2003). Assessing mass media reporting of disease-related genetic discoveries: Development of an instrument and initial findings. *Science Communication, 24*(4), 458–478.

Moynihan, R., Bero, L., Ross-Degnan, D., Henry, D., Lee, K., Watkins, J., . . . Soumerai, S. B. (2000). Coverage by the news media of the benefits and risks of medications. *New England Journal of Medicine, 342*(22), 1645–1650.

National Research Council. (2012). *A framework for K-12 science education: Practices, crosscutting concepts, and core ideas.* Washington, DC: National Academies Press.

Nisbet, M. C. (2009). Communicating climate change: Why frames matter for public engagement. *Environment: Science and Policy for Sustainable Development, 51*(2), 12–23.

Nolen, A. L. (2009). The content of educational psychology: An analysis of top ranked journals from 2003 through 2007. *Educational Psychology Review, 21*(3), 279–289.

Norris, S. P., & Phillips, L. M. (1994). Interpreting pragmatic meaning when reading popular reports of science. *Journal of Research in Science Teaching, 31*(9), 947–967.

Norris, S. P., & Phillips, L. M. (2003). How literacy in its fundamental sense is central to scientific literacy. *Science Education, 87*(2), 224–240.

Norris, S. P., Phillips, L. M., & Korpan, C. A. (2003). University students' interpretation of media reports of science and its relationship to background knowledge, interest, and reading difficulty. *Public Understanding of Science, 12*(2), 123–145.

Pearson, P. D., Moje, E., & Greenleaf, C. (2010). Literacy and science: Each in the service of the other. *Science, 328*(5977), 459–463.

Perfetti, C. A., Rouet, J.–F., & Britt, M. A. (1999). Toward a theory of documents representation. In H. V. Oostendorp & S. R. Goldman (Eds.), *The construction of mental representations during reading* (pp. 88–108). Mahwah, NJ: Erlbaum.

Polman, J. L., & Hope, J. M. G. (2014). Science news stories as boundary objects affecting engagement with science. *Journal of Research in Science Teaching, 51*(3), 315–341.

Porsch, T., & Bromme, R. (2011). Effects of epistemological sensitization on source choices. *Instructional Science, 39*(6), 805–819.

Ransohoff, D. F., & Ransohoff, R. M. (2000). Sensationalism in the media: When scientists and journalists may be complicit collaborators. *Effective Clinical Practice, 4*(4), 185–188.

Rowan, K. E. (1999). Effective explanation of uncertain and complex science. In S. M. Friedman, S. Dunwoody, & C. L. Rogers (Eds.), *Communicating uncertainty: Media coverage of new and controversial science* (pp. 201–224). Mahwah, NJ: Erlbaum.

Ryder, J. (2001). Identifying science understanding for functional scientific literacy. *Studies in Science Education, 36*(1), 1–44.

Sandoval, W. A. (2005). Understanding students' practical epistemologies and their influence on learning through inquiry. *Science Education, 89*(4), 634–656.

Scharrer, L., Britt, M. A., Stadtler, M., & Bromme, R. (2013). Easy to understand but difficult to decide: Information comprehensibility and controversiality affect laypeople's science-based decisions. *Discourse Processes, 50*(6), 361–387.

Scharrer, L., Bromme, R., Britt, M. A., & Stadtler, M. (2012). The seduction of easiness: How science depictions influence laypeople's reliance on their own evaluation of scientific information. *Learning and Instruction, 22*(3), 231–243.

Scharrer, L., Stadtler, M., & Bromme, R. (2014). You'd better ask an expert: Mitigating the comprehensibility effect on laypeople's decisions about science-based knowledge claims. *Applied Cognitive Psychology, 28*(4), 465–471.

Secko, D. M., Amend, E., & Friday, T. (2012). Four models of science journalism. *Journalism Practice, 7*(1), 62–80.

Segev, E., & Baram-Tsabari, A. (2012). Seeking science information online: Data mining Google to better understand the roles of the media and the education system. *Public Understanding of Science, 21*(7), 813–829.

Shanahan, C., Shanahan, T., & Misischia, C. (2011). Analysis of expert readers in three disciplines: History, mathematics, and chemistry. *Journal of Literacy Research, 43*(4), 393–429.

Sinatra, G. M., Kienhues, D., & Hofer, B. K. (2014). Addressing challenges to public understanding of science: Epistemic cognition, motivated reasoning, and conceptual change. *Educational Psychologist*, 1–16.

Stacey, D., Bennett, C. L., Barry, M. J., Col, N. F., Eden, K. B., Holmes-Rovner, M., . . . Thomson, R. (2011). Decision aids for people facing health treatment or screening decisions. *Cochrane Database Syst Rev, 10*(10).

Stadtler, M., & Bromme, R. (2007). Dealing with multiple documents on the www: The role of metacognition in the formation of documents models. *International Journal of Computer-Supported Collaborative Learning, 2*(2–3), 191–210.

Stadtler, M., & Bromme, R. (2013). Multiple document comprehension: An approach to public understanding of science. *Cognition and Instruction, 31*(2), 122–129.

Stadtler, M., Scharrer, L., Brummernhenrich, B., & Bromme, R. (2013). Dealing with uncertainty: Readers' memory for and use of conflicting information from science texts as function of presentation format and source expertise. *Cognition and Instruction, 31*(2), 130–150.

Stadtler, M., Scharrer, L., Skodzik, T., & Bromme, R. (2014). Comprehending multiple documents on scientific controversies: Effects of reading goals and signaling rhetorical relationships. *Discourse Processes, 51*(1–2), 93–116.

Strømsø, H. I., Bråten, I., & Samuelstuen, M. S. (2008). Dimensions of topic-specific epistemological beliefs as predictors of multiple text understanding. *Learning and Instruction, 18*(6), 513–527.

Tabak, I., & Weinstock, M. P. (2005). Knowledge is knowledge is knowledge? The relationship between personal and scientific epistemologies. *Canadian Journal for Science, Mathematics and Technology Education, 5*(3), 307–328.

Thomm, E., & Bromme, R. (2012). "It should at least seem scientific!" Textual features of "scientificness" and their impact on lay assessments of online information. *Science Education, 96*(2), 187–211.

Ward, P. R., Henderson, J., Coveney, J., & Meyer, S. (2012). How do south Australian consumers negotiate and respond to information in the media about food and nutrition?: The importance of risk, trust and uncertainty. *Journal of Sociology, 48*(1), 23–41.

Wiley, J., Goldman, S. R., Graesser, A. C., Sanchez, C. A., Ash, I. K., & Hemmerich, J. A. (2009). Source evaluation, comprehension, and learning in internet science inquiry tasks. *American Educational Research Journal, 46*(4), 1060–1106.

Wineburg, S. S. (1991). Historical problem solving: A study of the cognitive processes used in the evaluation of documentary and pictorial evidence. *Journal of Educational Psychology, 83*(1), 73–87.

Wu, Y. T., & Tsai, C. C. (2010). High school students' informal reasoning regarding a socio-scientific issue, with relation to scientific epistemological beliefs and cognitive structures. *International Journal of Science Education, 33*(3), 371–400.

Yang, F.-Y., Chen, Y.-H., & Tsai, M.-J. (2013). How university students evaluate online information about a socio-scientific issue and the relationship with their epistemic beliefs. *Journal of Educational Technology & Society, 16*(3), 385–399.

Yarden, A. (2009). Reading scientific texts: Adapting primary literature for promoting scientific literacy. *Research in Science Education, 39*(3), 307–311.

Yeaton, W. H., Smith, D., & Rogers, K. (1990). Evaluating understanding of popular press reports of health research. *Health Education & Behavior, 17*(2), 223–234.

Zeidler, D. L., Walker, K. A., Ackett, W. A., & Simmons, M. L. (2002). Tangled up in views: Beliefs in the nature of science and responses to socioscientific dilemmas. *Science Education, 86*(3), 343–367.

Zimmerman, C., Bisanz, G. L., Bisanz, J., Klein, J. S., & Klein, P. (2001). Science at the supermarket: A comparison of what appears in the popular press, experts' advice to readers, and what students want to know. *Public Understanding of Science, 10*(1), 37–58.

# 21

# Studying Historical Understanding

*Chauncey Monte-Sano*
University of Michigan

*Abby Reisman*
University of Pennsylvania

In recent decades, the history classroom has been the site of much political wrangling (e.g., Nash, Crabtree, & Dunn, 2000). Yet, the studies reviewed here ask *how* to engage students in meaningful learning about the past, rather than *which* history to teach. For the past three decades, scholars in the anglophone world have looked to the professional discipline to build a model of what historical reasoning and understanding might look like in the classroom (e.g., VanSledright & Limón, 2006; Wineburg, 1996). Together, these scholars define historical understanding as a familiarity and facility with disciplinary ways of interpreting and reasoning with historical texts, an appreciation of the slippery nature of historical knowledge, and the application of conceptual, narrative, and discrete factual knowledge. The consensus has been that such processes come neither easily nor intuitively to students.

Early empirical research in the United Kingdom consisted of an effort to chart students' understanding of the nature of historical knowledge. British researchers studied students enrolled in the School's Council History 13–16 Project, a curriculum reform initiative founded in 1973 that sought to teach history as a "form of knowledge," with distinct concepts, ideas, and ways of conducting inquiry and establishing truth claims (Hirst, 1973). Researchers proposed developmental trajectories for adolescents' understanding of historical accounts (Shemilt, 1983), causation (Lee & Shemilt, 2009), and evidence (Lee & Shemilt, 2003). They found that early in their development students conceive history as a fixed story whereas later they recognize the interpretive, contextualized nature of history. British researchers also identified more and less sophisticated ways that students employ concepts in history, such as cause, change, time, and empathy (Lee & Ashby, 2000). In Canada, researchers have studied students' understanding of historical significance (Lévesque, 2008; Seixas, 1994) and the construct has been identified as

one of six foundational historical thinking concepts (http://www.historicalthinking.ca).

In the United States, early research on historical thinking focused on how adolescents process and interpret historical texts. Wineburg (1991) identified three heuristics that historians use in their evaluation of historical sources—sourcing, contextualization, and corroboration—that reflect disciplinary attention to authorship, audience, perspective, and temporal and geographic context. Wineburg determined that adolescents do not apply the same strategies when faced with conflicting accounts of the past. Others have confirmed both the limits of adolescent historical reasoning when compared with expert historians, as well as instructional supports that can prompt novices to reason historically (e.g., Rouet, Britt, Mason, & Perfetti, 1996; Stahl, Hynd, Britton, McNish, & Bosquet, 1996).

More recently, research in the United States on historical thinking has dovetailed with a national focus on adolescent literacy. In 2002, the Rand Corporation, an American nonprofit policy think tank, published a report on reading comprehension that highlighted the dearth of research on reading comprehension in secondary schools, despite increasing demands for advanced literacy (Snow, 2002). Soon after, the Carnegie Corporation published *Reading Next,* which targeted adolescent literacy (Biancarosa & Snow, 2006). The report was followed by the formation of the Carnegie Council on Advancing Adolescent Literacy (2010) and several additional reports (Graham & Perin, 2007; McCombs, Kirby, Barney, Darilek, & Magee, 2005), culminating with *Time to Act: An Agenda for Advancing Adolescent Literacy for College and Career Success* in 2010. Many North American researchers of historical thinking have responded by focusing on disciplinary literacy, exploring the effects of various instructional techniques and curricular interventions on adolescents' ability to read, think, and write about historical texts in a disciplinary fashion. As will be described below, this development of research on historical reading and writing has had direct and positive implications for classroom instruction. At the same time, by effectively equating historical thinking with particular ways of reading and writing, the body of literature runs the risk of closing itself off from important questions that concern how the past is used in the present: What motivates one's interest in the past? How does identity or collective memory shape how one understands the past? How do informal encounters with the past that occur outside the classroom influence students' historical understanding? And how do particular interpretations of the past, in turn, shape identity? Even if historical knowledge seeking were to occur, hypothetically, in some pure, universal space, it is quite clear that any such pursuit would be motivated by, and have direct implications for, lived experience.

German theorist Jörn Rüsen's "disciplinary matrix" (1993, p. 162) captures these different facets of historical understanding, depicting the relationship between the disciplinary work of inquiry and what he terms "life-practice" (Figure 21.1). In this cycle, historical investigations begin with and are motivated by particular interests; these interests are filtered through dominant theories or preconceptions about the past or human behavior; historical questions are then investigated using the disciplinary rules of empirical research, and ultimately represented in writing or other media. Yet, the process ultimately serves to orient the individual or society in time. That is, we study the past to better understand ourselves and our world.

Rüsen's work sits in a rich theoretical literature that has emerged in Europe and has wrestled with the nature of historical consciousness (e.g., von Borries, 1988). By contrast, research on historical thinking and history education in the anglophone world has been more empirical, though less focused on how the past is *used* in the present and what the implications of such uses are for classroom history instruction. For research on history education to truly address the nature and purposes of historical knowledge, it must ask questions not only about how students read and write about historical

texts, but also about how students respond to various uses of the past that they encounter. The ultimate goal of such a research program would be to help students become aware of how the past is used by themselves and those around them.

Drawing heavily from Rüsen's matrix, we have divided the review into two sections. The first half of the review discusses the research on the skills or practices that comprise the historical discipline, which in the past decade has largely attended to the demands of historical reading and writing. As a whole, this body of research contributes to our understanding of effective instructional resources and techniques that engage students in historical thinking in classrooms. In the second half of the review, we examine the relationship between historical study and lived experience (or, "life-practice"), in an effort to tease out the relationship between the school curriculum, informal encounters with the past, and individual identity. We believe that these studies contribute to a more robust conception of historical understanding that speaks to deep, underlying reasons for why we bother to study history at all.

Ultimately, we argue that the field stands to benefit from greater interaction between these two strands of research—that an emphasis on disciplinary literacy in the absence of the latter risks decoupling procedural knowledge and related strategies from underlying conceptual knowledge and historical understanding. At the same time, as Peter Lee argues in his discussion of Rüsen's matrix, classroom instruction matters: "history education must go above the line if students' historical consciousness is to be adequately developed" (Lee, 2004, p. 140). Only through formal education will students develop the tools and analytic frameworks with which to examine and understand their historical selves.

The proliferation of interest in the teaching and learning of history necessitated that we establish certain criteria for review. All the studies reviewed here: (a) appeared in blind and peer-reviewed journals with an acceptance rate of 50% or below; (b) were published since the last *Handbook of Educational Psychology* came out in 2006 *unless* we deemed them significant and they were not included in the 2006 review; (c) are empirical studies focused on *student* learning; (d) are empirical studies focused on reasoning or understanding, rather than factual recall (unless factual recall is one part of a larger conception of history learning); (e) are full, original reports of empirical studies rather than abbreviated summaries of research; and (f) are written in English. *If* books or book chapters reported on empirical research and focused on student learning we included them. We used the PsycInfo, ERIC, and JSTOR databases and conducted searches with terms such as "teaching history," "learning history," "historical thinking," "historical consciousness," or "primary sources" and reviewed the resulting lists of articles to check that they met our criteria. After careful consideration, we eliminated articles that either did not meet our criteria or did not use rigorous research methods.

## Historical Study and Disciplinary Practices

Building on foundational work in the field, researchers have engaged in small-scale classroom interventions that focus

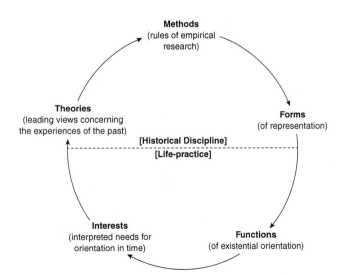

**Figure 21.1** Rüsen's disciplinary matrix.

on improving students' historical thinking. These studies use similar instructional modules, including central historical questions or problems, authentic historical sources, structures for analyzing and critiquing sources, and use of discussion and writing to facilitate and record students' interpretation of the sources and central question. These studies suggest that students in fifth grade (Swan, Hofer, & Locascio, 2008; VanSledright, 2002), ninth grade (Bain, 2006), and college (Hynd, Holschuh, & Hubbard, 2004) can learn to work with historical sources, develop interpretations based on those sources, think historically, and articulate the process of historical interpretation. Moreover, Bain (2006) and VanSledright (2002) argue that the challenge is as much about shifting students' epistemic stances toward history and textbook narratives as it is about teaching students particular disciplinary reading practices. Other researchers have also explored the nature and development of historical empathy (Brooks, 2011; Endacott, 2010; Kohlmeier, 2006), a term associated with a deep appreciation for the strangeness of the past. These studies examine emergent forms of historical empathy and suggest certain instructional techniques, such as discussion around texts, which help foster an empathetic orientation towards the strangeness of the past.

Other small-scale interventions in history classrooms have highlighted the learning of students with learning disabilities, yet these studies largely equate historical understanding with factual recall. In the one exception, Ferretti, MacArthur, and Okolo (2007) found that students in one eighth-grade class grew in their knowledge of American westward expansion *and* in their understanding of historical inquiry; however, students with learning disabilities learned less than their peers. The researchers speculate that, since students with disabilities knew less content at the outset of the study, they may have needed more support to make sense of the intervention.

Several scholars have explored student historical thinking with digital materials (e.g., Damico & Baildon, 2007) and e-platforms to support student historical inquiry. In a series of design experiments with an open learning environment that contains over 1,000 multimedia artifacts about the 1950s–1960s civil rights movement, Saye and Brush (2007) found that use of technology to create a problem-based historical investigation engaged learners, encouraged empathy, and challenged epistemological assumptions. However, the relationship between the technological learning environment and the development of deep knowledge and critical reasoning was less clear. Several studies of students engaged in computer-mediated historical inquiry projects (e.g., Yang & Huang, 2007) or games (Akkerman, Admiraal, & Huizenga, 2009) found positive effects for engagement and critical thinking, though many of these findings were largely based on student self-report in interviews and surveys. Hernandez-Ramos and De La Paz (2009) found that eighth-graders who constructed multimedia mini-documentaries showed significant growth in factual recall and some evidence of historical thinking when compared to control students who studied under more traditional instruction.

Together, these studies provide vivid examples of what successful instruction in historical thinking might entail, and the ways in which students respond to them. Their strength lies in their articulation of key features of instruction that can potentially be tested on a larger scale. Although the authors carefully consider students' thinking and illustrate their claims with student work, the generalizability of these studies is often limited by the small sample, the lack of a control condition, and the absence of baseline measures of historical thinking.

## Historical Reading

One of the consistent findings in the research on adolescent literacy is that domain-specific texts make unique demands on students' literacy and reasoning. These demands transcend general reading comprehension and include, in the case of history, an appreciation of the constructed nature of historical texts, and a skepticism of authoritative narratives. Unlike earlier studies on historical reading that tested whether or not the presence of multiple documents would prompt adolescents to read historically, recent studies have experimented with instructional manipulations that might prompt disciplinary historical reading.

***Text effects in cognitive studies.*** Several controlled experimental studies have examined whether certain text-based instructional manipulations can effectively promote student historical reasoning. For example, three studies shed light on the effect of texts on student disciplinary reading. Wolfe and Goldman (2005) conducted think-alouds with 44 sixth-graders as they read two contrasting accounts of the fall of Rome, and found that students were capable of reasoning across texts. It is important to note that the highly scaffolded texts were "structurally isomorphic" (p. 475); the only variation was the author's particular claim about the fall of Rome. In another study that manipulated texts, Paxton (2002) found effects for the insertion of an author's voice in an otherwise passive textbook. High-school students were assigned to one of two conditions: one read a text by an anonymous author who wrote in the third person and included little emotion or personal feeling; the other group read a text by a visible author who had a greater authorial presence. Students in the "visible" author condition tended to evaluate the texts and authors, think more about the history, write longer essays, and consider their audience in writing. Both studies shed light on the type of scaffolding that might foster historical reasoning in a classroom setting, though they do not reveal how students might respond to actual historical texts.

Logtenberg, van Boxtel, and van Hout-Wolters (2010) examined the effect of the type of texts students read on their interest and on the questions they asked. Students generated questions after reading narrative, expository, and problematizing (or, controversial) texts about the Industrial Revolution. The researchers found that narrative and problematizing texts provoked more situational interest and emotive questions than expository texts. However, one can argue that question-type and situational interest are distal proxies for historical thinking. van Boxtel and van Drie (2012) asked a different question related to historical texts—what allows students to successfully contextualize historical images and documents: historical knowledge or strategy use? The authors found that providing students with knowledge of key historical concepts, and helping them construct an associative network around those concepts, was most predictive of student success on contextualization tasks. This study underscores the importance of historical knowledge in leveraging student reasoning with and about historical texts.

In a study that manipulated instruction and text, Britt and Aglinskas (2002) designed a computer-based environment (Sourcer's Apprentice) that explicitly encouraged students to source and corroborate historical texts. In three distinct evaluation studies, researchers found that students improved at sourcing, contextualization, and corroboration, on a transfer task when compared to students in regular classroom or textbook-centered comparison conditions. The Sourcer's Apprentice environment featured a cognitive apprenticeship model of instruction (Brown, Collins, & Duguid, 1989), emphasizing a gradual transition to student independent work through modeling, coaching, and fading, as well as explicit instruction, and task decomposition. The researchers also suggest that presenting students with separate, distinct excerpts, rather than a single integrated text, may prompt students to attend to sourcing information. Whether these techniques transfer from the computer environment to actual classrooms lay beyond the scope of the study.

Another group of studies examined specific technological innovations and instructional scaffolds that could support students' historical reading and learning in online, hypertext, or multimedia learning environments. These include writing prompts and argumentation templates (Li & Lim, 2008), embedded annotations (Lee & Calandra, 2004), and different forms of textual representations (Mendez & Montanero, 2008; van Drie, van Boxtel, Erkens, & Kanselaar, 2005). As a whole, this branch of research remains largely exploratory, with primary emphasis on the development of instructional e-tools to support student learning. To the extent that the literature reports effects of specific technological innovations on student learning and historical reading, these have been modest and tentative.

### Large-scale studies of historical reading and thinking.
Two experimental and quasi-experimental studies have tested the effects of targeted classroom instruction on students' historical thinking. Nokes, Dole, and Hacker (2007) tested the effects of two crossed interventions on student learning: instruction that used a single history textbook versus multiple documents; and instruction that explicitly taught historical thinking heuristics versus instruction that focused on teaching content. When they placed 200 upper secondary students in one of four treatment conditions, they found that students in the condition that used multiple documents to learn content learned the most content, followed by the group that used multiple documents to learn about historical thinking heuristics. This finding serves as a response to critics who worry that incorporating multiple documents might detract from factual recall. Students in the groups that used multiple documents sourced and corroborated more often

than their counterparts. As for student growth in historical thinking, however, the study's findings were less robust. While researchers counted how many times students used certain strategies (i.e., sourcing and corroboration) in their final essays, they did not report whether such strategies helped students write plausible and compelling historical arguments, or led to deeper understanding of the nature of historical reasoning.

More recently, Reisman (2012a, 2012b) designed a curriculum intervention for upper secondary students and examined its effect on several measures, including student reading. In a quasi-experiment in five urban high schools, students in a "Reading Like a Historian" condition outperformed their counterparts on four measures: historical reading, general reasoning, factual recall, and generic reading comprehension. The intervention curriculum took the form of stand-alone "document-based lessons" that followed a predictable activity sequence: (a) presentation of relevant background knowledge; (b) independent or small-group analysis of historical documents; and (c) whole-class discussion. However, as in studies of historical writing instruction, the intervention centered on certain instructional techniques, including cognitive apprenticeship and explicit strategy instruction. By explicitly teaching students the strategies of disciplinary reading, the intervention sought to shift the students' orientation toward historical knowledge. Rather than extract fixed historical knowledge from the text, students learned to construct historical knowledge through the process of evaluating and reconciling competing claims about the past.

### Language demands in historical reading.    Functional linguists offer a different perspective on teaching historical reading. Motivated in part by the needs of English learners, these researchers have identified certain language demands of history classrooms. A major tenet of this field is that the texts of a given discipline can be distinguished by certain linguistic features and have a particular structure, grammar, and lexis. By developing students' awareness of the linguistic features of a discipline's texts, these scholars hope to improve students' reading, writing, and content understanding. For example, Schleppegrell, Achugar, and Oteiza (2004) analyzed middle-school history textbooks and found that textbooks described events without elaboration and without causal relationships, relied on nominalizations that hid human actors, and used conjunctions whose meaning varied and differed from everyday use. The authors proposed a series of instructional suggestions for revealing and making explicit the particular language demands of historical texts. In later work, Schleppegrell, Greer, and Taylor (2008) detail one teacher's implementation of a language-centered approach to teaching history, and its effect on students' reading and writing skills and understanding of the historical content.

Several researchers have examined the use of considerate texts among students with learning disabilities in both inclusive and disability-only history classrooms. For example, Espin, Cevasco, van den Broek, Baker, and Gersten (2007) focused on narrative texts and found that creating causal networks of events supported learning disabilities students' reading comprehension. Likewise, Harniss, Caros, and Gersten (2007) found that an experimental text designed to teach about the relationships between events was more effective than a conventional textbook in helping students with learning disabilities learn content. Williams and her colleagues (2007) found modest effects of explicit cause–effect text structure strategy instruction on "at-risk" second-graders' comprehension of informational social studies texts; they conclude that text comprehension strategies can be integrated into content teaching. Although neither these studies nor the functional linguistic research examines the effects on student disciplinary reading practices, the research highlights the importance of supporting basic reading comprehension in any instructional engagement with text.

***Expanding notions of text: historical thinking about films, physical spaces, and online texts.*** Several researchers have broadened the literature on historical thinking to include studies that examine how students and adults reason about unconventional texts, such as movies, physical spaces, and online materials. Marcus, Paxton, and Meyerson (2006) note that students fail to discern the perspective and constructed nature of film. Although students in their study claim that feature films are unreliable historical sources, they nonetheless incorporate information gleaned directly from films into their accounts of the past. Stoddard (2009) found a similar orientation in students towards documentary films, which they viewed as objective and impartial. Both studies emphasize the importance of the teacher's role in making explicit the constructed nature of film. More research is needed to better understand how films shape students' understanding of history.

Researchers have also stepped out of the classroom to examine how students and adults interact and reason about physical spaces. Baron (2012) examined how expert historians "read" a historical space, namely, the Old North Church in Boston, Massachusetts. Arguing that Wineburg's heuristics for reading documentary texts did not account for how experts reason about space, Baron identified five new heuristics from the historians' think-aloud protocols: origination (considering the building's origin), intertectonality (drawing comparisons with similar historical buildings), stratification (identifying the multiple strata of time evident in the building), supposition (offering hypotheses that explore reasons behind particular aspects of the building), and empathetic insight (considering the affective response of people who occupied the space at particular historical moments). Baron argues that awareness of these heuristics might allow novices to begin to ask "What are the multiple time periods evident in this building, and what do they tell me about its history?" (p. 844).

Finally, several researchers have examined students' historical reading of online texts. Manfra and Lee (2012) found that students were able to engage in some historical analysis when blogging about a single source with a scaffold, especially when topics involved relevant cultural experiences. Larson (2005) discusses the benefits of "threaded discussions" over face-to-face discussions for fostering student participation and supporting students' reading and writing;

however, Journell (2008) found that student comments in threaded discussion were often "unsubstantiated opinions that rarely challenged preexisting or canonical notions of history" and that active teacher facilitation is essential to successful online learning (p. 317). Damico, Baildon, Exter, and Guo (2009) found that some students use cultural resources and background knowledge to discern the perspective of particular websites, and are able to consider the various factors that affect how they read. By contrast, Calkins and Kelley (2009) found that undergraduates are not necessarily critical consumers of online information. The authors found that half of the 38 undergraduates who participated in an evaluation of Wikipedia demonstrated a dualistic (right–wrong) understanding of historical knowledge and were therefore troubled by the lack of authority in a Wikipedia entry. Only two students fell into Perry's (1970) commitment stage, whereby they "recognize that knowledge of the past is not complete or absolute" and that even Wikipedia could be a "useful, even scholarly, tool" (p. 131).

The research on historical reading in many ways confirms earlier findings that disciplinary practices do not come easily or naturally to students. However, the past decade has produced a robust body of research on the instructional interventions that might serve to promote historical reading.

## Historical Writing

Just as we have seen an increased emphasis on historical reading, we also note growth in researchers' attention to writing, although the writing research is narrower in scope. Researchers have conceptualized historical writing both as a representation of student thinking and understanding about the past, as well as evidence of student facility with historical argumentation. In a trend that echoes earlier work (e.g., Wiley & Voss, 1999; Young & Leinhardt, 1998) historical writing tasks continue to be composed of a prompt and a set of primary sources. However, in contrast to earlier work that focused on more elite students (e.g., students in college or advanced placement classes), recent research has examined student writing and its development with a broader population of students (e.g., De La Paz, 2005).

***Qualitative studies of historical writing.*** A cluster of studies have used qualitative methods to explore the particular disciplinary demands of historical writing. Beaufort's (2004) case study examined one college student's history writing over 3 years and found that, although the student's factual and thematic knowledge improved over time, his interpretive thinking and critical analysis lagged, making it difficult for him to construct evidence-based arguments. Beck and Jeffrey (2009) interviewed 11 students enrolled in tenth- and eleventh-grade humanities classes to explore their understanding of the demands of writing assignments in history and English. They found that students struggled to characterize their history writing assignments as interpretive. Although limited in their generalizability, these studies call for better understanding of the process by which students become immersed in the discourse of historical writing.

Monte-Sano's work suggests that teachers who present history as evidence-based interpretation, and who support students' reading comprehension and thinking, may improve students' disciplinary writing. Monte-Sano's comparative case study (2008, 2011) examined the writing instruction of three high-school teachers. Monte-Sano administered pre- and post essay assessments and identified teaching practices that coincided with students' growth in historical thinking and argument writing. Certain instructional techniques characterized those classrooms with marked growth in student writing, including: teaching students to annotate sources, providing feedback on students' interpretations, assigning informal writing prompts that focused students' attention on the author and that called for synthesis and argument, creating repeated opportunities for students to read multiple historical texts, and engaging in explicit instruction through a cognitive apprenticeship approach. Monte-Sano concluded that writing practice, without explicit instruction or attention to the nature of the reading and writing opportunities, was not sufficient to foster historical writing.

Analyzing student writing from the above study (*n* = 56), Monte-Sano (2010) identified five aspects that characterize the use of historical evidence in argumentative writing, including factual and interpretive accuracy, persuasiveness of evidence, sourcing of evidence, corroboration of evidence, and contextualization of evidence. Like conventional arguments, historical arguments include claims, evidence, and warrants; however, the nature of the warrants and evidence reflects historical ways of thinking. Monte-Sano found that students who lacked a conceptual understanding of history and historical interpretation wrote weaker essays because they misused or misinterpreted evidence, or because they integrated evidence without attending to key details such as where the evidence originated. In addition to providing a conceptual framework for historical argumentation, this study found that the majority of high-school students in this sample were able to integrate historical and conventional aspects of argumentation given supportive instructional settings.

Henriquez and Ruiz (2014) also highlight the relationship between reading, analysis, and writing and find students need help transitioning between each of these aspects of the writing process. Using discourse analysis to examine Chilean students' (ages 12–17) written explanations, the authors identify three ways that students constructed an explanation: *chronicle without a historical sense* (these are largely focused on individual will), *narrative without a historical sense* (these tend to focus on singular causes and do not evaluate evidence), and *narrative with a historical sense* (actors are social and political groups, causes and effects are linked, multiple causes are identified, evidence is evaluated).

Researchers have only begun to consider the particular language demands faced by English learners in history classrooms. In one such study, Fránquiz and Salinas (2011) found that the writing of newcomer students demonstrated growing mastery of both English-language literacy skills and historical thinking in the context of three document-based lessons. Explicit teaching of vocabulary and background knowledge,

built-in support for working with primary sources, and encouraging meaningful interactions about text supported student writing.

### Large-scale studies of writing and historical thinking.
De La Paz (2005) and De La Paz and Felton (2010) tested self-regulated strategy instruction, a form of cognitive apprenticeship, which maintains that cognitive acts like writing strategies remain invisible unless they are brought to the surface and named (Brown et al., 1989). Just as apprentices observe experts as they learn their craft, students must repeatedly see teachers practice the strategies of disciplinary writing. The approach emphasizes a gradual shift of responsibility over time, as students begin to practice disciplinary writing with teacher guidance, in small groups, and ultimately, individually.

De La Paz's initial study (2005) of 70 12- and 13-year-olds tested the effect of cognitive apprenticeship in argument writing and historical reasoning. Across a 12-lesson unit of instruction, she found growth in the persuasive writing and historical accuracy of students with and without disabilities in inclusive settings. However, effects on students' historical understanding were mixed and not evident in their writing. In a follow-up study of 160 upper secondary students (De La Paz & Felton, 2010), four units of instruction in historical reasoning and writing were implemented over the course of several months. Again, the study focused on the effect of cognitive apprenticeship, this time providing control classrooms with the same materials and prompts that they provided the treatment group, except for the instructional methods used to teach historical reading and writing. In examining the students' final essays, the researchers found that they were not only longer and more persuasive, but the treatment students developed more elaborate claims and rebuttals and used more documents than students in the control group.

De La Paz and Felton (2010) criticized prior research on argument writing instruction for overlooking the "intimate relationship between reading and writing processes," suggesting that "support for reading historical documents may help students to develop more sophisticated claims, evidence and counter-arguments in their writing, because they have built a sophisticated representation of the arguments found in the texts they have read" (p. 175). However, like Nokes et al. (2007), they continued to search for evidence of student disciplinary reading and textual comprehension in student essays. Whereas Nokes and colleagues tallied the strategies students used, De La Paz and Felton added up claims and references to documents. Once again, while promising, these tallies are indirect measures of students' depth of analysis or the sophistication of their understanding.

More recent work has looked substantively at 13- and 14-year-olds' writing by examining aspects of historical thinking (e.g., substantiation, perspective recognition, contextualization, and rebuttal) as well as overall argument-writing quality in students' essays (De La Paz et al., 2014; Monte-Sano, De La Paz, & Felton 2014). Building on prior studies, this project developed an 18-lesson curriculum (implemented across the school year) and professional development intervention using a cognitive apprenticeship approach to teach historical reading, thinking, and writing. The study found significant effects for the intervention on students' historical argument writing. Moreover, the study tests the scalability of such an intervention: compared to prior studies, the intervention occurred across a greater number of school sites, with a larger number of students, representing greater ethnic and academic diversity, and with teachers representing a range of expertise in teaching history and literacy with primary sources.

***Language demands in historical writing.*** Two projects (Coffin 2006a, 2006b; de Oliveira, 2011) have identified key linguistic features in students' historical writing. de Oliveira (2011) analyzed eighth- and eleventh-grade students' expository essays and found that successful students used themes to organize their essays, made logical connections using conjunctions, and elaborated on their ideas through repetition, grammatical metaphors, specific examples, and restatements of major points. By eleventh grade, the more effective essays also incorporated evaluative assessments, as well as the words or ideas of others, using concessions such as "although" to recognize different perspectives. Coffin (2006a, 2006b) also analyzed writing samples produced by students aged 11–17 years and cross-referenced these with curricular resources in an effort to define genres and subgenres of history writing in Australian secondary schools. She found that students are asked to write three particular genres over the course of their secondary schooling—recording, explaining, and arguing—each of which has its own purpose, structure, grammar, and lexis. Coffin (2006a) found that students' writing shifted over time, in accordance with the changing expectations for writing at different grade levels. For example, as older students began to write increasingly abstract interpretations, they also employed nominalization, integrated events into an argument rather than list events chronologically, and used a more evaluative lexis to argue the significance of events. The study does not make clear whether the collected writing samples simply reflect current practices, on the one hand, or students' developmental capacities for producing different kinds of texts at different ages, on the other.

Coffin (2006b) built on this work by developing an intervention that made explicit the structure, purpose, and linguistic features of historical texts. She found that student organization and text structure in the target genre improved. Coffin's study constitutes one of the few direct applications of functional linguistic research to classroom learning; in addition, this work represents a promising direction for future research on historical literacy.

### Historical Study and Lived Experience

The recent research on historical reading and writing has moved the field forward by identifying and exploring effective instructional interventions that engage students in disciplinary practices and potentially change students' epistemological understanding of historical knowledge.

However, collectively, these studies do not shed light on how classroom history intersects with student identity, with collective memory, and with the popular history that students encounter outside of the classroom. These questions matter because students bring their lived experiences to classroom encounters with the past, which have implications, in turn, for real life. A primary goal for all work on history education is for students to develop a degree of historical consciousness that allows them to locate themselves in the context of temporal change and to understand how their own experiences shape their view of the past.

***Cultural resources and historical understanding.*** Several studies suggest that students draw on diverse cultural resources to construct historical narratives. Two cross-generational studies examine the influence of the "cultural curriculum" on national memory and historical consciousness. Wineburg, Mosborg, Porat, and Duncan (2007) interviewed adolescents and their parents about the Vietnam War, using a photo elicitation method. Parents reacted differently to the events portrayed in photographs depending on their personal experiences, memories, and perspective of the war. Students, despite their differing schools, backgrounds, and religions, shared fairly uniform narratives of the war, derived from common cultural experiences, such as visiting the Vietnam Memorial Wall, or watching popular films.

In the second study, Wineburg and Monte-Sano (2008) also found cultural consensus among youth. In a survey administered to 4,000 individuals in the United States, the authors asked adolescents and adults over age 50 to list the "most famous Americans," not including presidents or their wives. Martin Luther King, Rosa Parks, and Harriet Tubman were some of the most commonly named individuals. Although black students included more African American figures than whites, white students included a majority of African American figures on their list. Black history and civil rights appeared front and center in respondents' consciousness. While this narrative may, in part, reflect changes to the school curriculum, it is also prominent in the cultural curriculum, in the ways we learn about the past outside of formal institutions (e.g., through reading, television or movies, and advertisements). Together, these studies highlight the myriad influences on historical consciousness and expand the notion of education beyond schooling (Wineburg et al., 2007, p. 70).

***Individual identity, group membership, and historical understanding.*** Several studies examined the roles that identity and group membership play in how people engage with and understand the past. Polman (2006) explored the individual identity trajectories and historical learning of students who designed an online virtual museum about abolitionism in an after-school History Web club. Where one student became a more committed student and history learner through his involvement in the club, another had a more limiting experience. Polman argues that the first student was more successful in part because his learning environment was more highly scaffolded, but also because he had a teacher who accepted and built on his identity as a computer gamer.

Several studies consider the role of religious and cultural affiliations in shaping students' thinking about the past. Barton and McCully (2010) interviewed adolescents in Northern Ireland from different religious affiliations, geographic regions, and schooling experiences using a set of images about people and events in the history of Ireland and Britain. As students sorted pictures into groups and chose the group with which they identified, the researchers found that students' views of history were not limited to the sectarian accounts from their families or communities. Instead, students learned about history from multiple sources—including school, which appeared to present a more balanced view. Students navigated among the competing narratives in an effort to formulate a coherent view on contemporary issues.

Porat (2006) and Mosborg (2002) underscore the relationship between religious and cultural affiliation and text processing. Porat found that students' narratives of a contentious event in Israeli history were shaped more by the interpretation of their social and political milieu than by the actual textbook account. Porat (2006) identified three key "mechanisms" that explained how students—hailing from opposing sides of the political and social spectrum in Israeli society—drew historical meaning from the textbook: first, students had expectations given the nature of a text or the topic; then, when students found that the text missed key elements, their prior knowledge or beliefs guided their insertion of meaning; finally, students integrated the textbook account with other memories or knowledge that they had of the event. Together, these mechanisms worked to privilege students' incoming beliefs—rooted in their political and social identities—over the literal text. Relatedly, Mosborg (2002) found that students from a Christian school and a college preparatory high school drew on different historical events when making sense of newspaper articles about school prayer and Starbucks' treatment of coffee workers from Guatemala. They also represented these news stories differently depending on their background.

A number of studies have highlighted the role that race and ethnicity play in how students interpret and understand the past. Epstein's (2009) work highlights the extent to which racial identity shapes historical narrative, regardless of instructional influence. She examined the ways in which white and black students understood historical actors and events in U.S. history, and found that, regardless of teachers' instruction, black students were more likely to emphasize persistent inequalities, violence, and conflict, whereas white students pointed to progress more often. By contrast, Hughes, Bigler, and Levy (2007) found some attitudinal shifts when they examined European American and African American students' reactions to learning about historical racism. They found that European American children became less biased towards African Americans when compared to students in the control condition, whereas African American students' racial attitudes did not vary by condition.

Peck (2010) lends insight into how adolescents with different ethnic identities might interpret national history. She asked multiethnic students who were born in Canada, recent immigrants, and Aboriginal students to select photos and create a timeline of Canadian history. Peck identified three narratives that students used to explain Canadian history and to locate themselves in this history: the "founding of the nation," the "diverse and harmonious Canada," and the "diverse but conflicted Canada" narrative (pp. 594–595). Peck suggests that ethnic identity is central to the process of narrative development and modification.

Hawkey and Prior (2011) used photo elicitation to determine how urban ethnic-minority students living in Britain view that country's history. The authors found that what the history students learned at home differs from what students learned in school, and that multiple identities influence students' thinking about history (e.g., that of their country, their parents or grandparents' country of origin, religious community, youth culture). Finally, An (2009) asked students to name the three most important people or events in U.S. history and justify their selections. She found that Korean adolescents in U.S. schools have a different sense of U.S. history depending on their migration status (e.g., study-abroad Korean youth, and Korean immigrants with and without a sense of national belonging to the United States).

In reality, people's identity and affiliation are not confined to any one trait. How, then, do people navigate more than one set of influences on their lived experience as they make sense of the past? In a study that turned the notion of epistemological purity on its head, Gottlieb and Wineburg (2012) studied adults who belong to multiple communities: religious believers who were also historians and religious skeptics who were historians or scientists. They found that, when faced with historical sources about the (sacred) biblical Exodus and the (secular) first American Thanksgiving, participants varied "their criteria for truth, reliability, and warrant according to the associations and allegiances that a given text triggered" (p. 111). The authors define this phenomenon of navigating among competing commitments as "epistemic switching." They conclude that historical consciousness is not a capacity that people have or don't have; rather it is "a form of thinking exercised in different ways and to different extents in different contexts" (p. 115). Clearly, individual identity and group membership influence students' historical consciousness and must be engaged directly and deliberately to support history learning.

***The school curriculum and historical understanding.*** Recent research has also highlighted the school curriculum's powerful role in shaping students' understanding of the past. In some ways, school curricula obstruct or limit historical consciousness. For example, Wills (2011) interviewed three fifth-graders about the origins of American history and discovered that their narratives contained significant misconceptions, including a belief that the Gold Rush was undertaken by early explorers in 1749. Rejecting a deficit model, he traced this misunderstanding to Wertsch's (2004) concept of "schematic narrative templates" in the curriculum that highlighted and reinforced certain themes, such as the European/majority American quest for gold and the abuse and mistreatment of Native Americans. Students integrated these themes into coherent, albeit historically inaccurate, narratives. In a survey of Argentine college students, Carretero and Kriger (2011) found that national history dominated their understanding of their country's origin, and that they had little awareness of competing narratives. Schweber (2008a) found that girls in a Lubavitch Yeshivah were not encouraged, and were therefore unable, to grasp or wrestle with the historical underpinnings of the Holocaust. Rather, their explanations of the atrocity were constrained by notions of Jewish "chosenness" and God's will, ideas that flourished in the girls' school setting. Lastly, Bekerman and Zembylas (2011) examine how teachers in an integrated bilingual school in Israel delegitimized certain emotional responses by students when discussing a controversial historical event, thereby privileging units of peoplehood/nation over individual, personal experience.

At the same time, the classroom can potentially be a site for developing students' historical consciousness. Levstik and Groth (2005) asked adolescents from Ghana to select pictures that would explain Ghana's history to someone from another country. The authors found trends that reflected the school curriculum: struggle, sacrifice, and unity were key themes in the narratives students constructed, and the history that emerged valued diversity and included multiethnic history. In the context of a long-term school project, Trofanenko (2008) found that U.S. eighth-graders were able to achieve a degree of historical consciousness and discern the constructed nature of the celebrated story of the Lewis and Clark expedition. In comparing how the story of Lewis and Clark was presented in the 1904 World's Fair and a 2004 bicentennial exhibit, students became aware that each representation reflected national concerns that were paramount at the time.

In another study where researchers tried to assess student awareness of how the past is used in the present, Seixas and Clark (2004) analyzed essays written by 53 twelfth-graders who responded to a contemporary debate about a historical monument: what should be done about a series of murals depicting the origin of British Columbia that include images of Aboriginal people that many found offensive? A majority of students suggested the murals be destroyed, a sizeable minority recommended that the murals be preserved to honor the past, while only a small minority (eight students) suggested that the murals be preserved but problematized. Moreover, over half the essays failed to distinguish between the colonial past and the representation of that past in the murals. In other words, these students equated the morality depicted in the representations (created in the 1930s) with the moral order of the colonial past. The authors suggest that historical instruction should prepare young people to "engage knowledgeably in debates about continuities and critical breaks in moral sensibilities over time" (p. 168). Both Trofanenko and Seixas and Clark point to ways that the development of historical consciousness might be explicitly brought into history instruction.

***Integrating school and lived experiences in support of historical understanding.*** A handful of studies effectively bridge the divide that we have erected in this review. Goldberg, Schwarz, and Porat (2008, 2011) explore whether the relationship between student identity, group membership, and historical understanding can change in the face of an opportunity to learn about the topic through engagement with multiple perspectives and class discussion. In the first study (Goldberg et al., 2008), Ashkenazi and Mizrahi Israeli students wrote their opinions about controversial historical topics that were more ("living") and less ("dormant") present in the nation's collective memory. Researchers found that students' narratives about the dormant topic became more certain once they had a chance to learn more about it, while their narratives about the living topic were initially quite certain and became less so once they were confronted with multiple perspectives. In the second study (Goldberg et al., 2011), the authors examined the interaction between students' ethnic background and their learning of a controversial historical topic. Sixty-four Israeli twelfth-graders of Ashkenazi and Mizrahi backgrounds were assigned to one of two conditions—a textbook or argumentative-disciplinary condition—to read about Israel's 1950s Melting Pot policy, which promoted cultural assimilation of Mizrahi immigrants to the dominant Ashkenazi/European culture. Although most students (both Ashkenazi and Mizrahi) initially held negative views of the policy, students who read and collectively discussed various positions on the issue were more likely to change their stance to a more favorable one, especially if they were Ashkenazi. The authors argue that the peer discussion in the argumentative-disciplinary condition promoted deeper historical understanding and an appreciation of evidence, and mitigated against anachronistic thinking (e.g., decrying 1950s policy makers for their lack of pluralistic thinking).

Kolikant and Pollack (2009) conducted another study designed to shift students' incoming notions about history. Researchers examined how Israeli Jews and Israeli Arabs worked within groups to analyze and write about multiple historical sources with different perspectives about the Balfour Declaration. Initially grouped by ethnicity, students arrived at ethnocentric interpretations of the event, highlighting the impact on their own group and portraying the other as passive. However, after critiquing each other's essays and discussion, students co-wrote essays that demonstrated change in their perceptions and recognition of different perspectives about the historical event. These studies suggest that, while lived experience certainly influences one's historical consciousness and thinking, this influence is not fixed; through careful instruction with texts that portray multiple perspectives, students' thinking about the past can shift.

## Assessing Historical Understanding

The limited research on assessment in history education critiques standard assessments of factual recall, and promotes measures that capture deeper learning. Reich (2009) conducted think-alouds with tenth-graders as they answered multiple-choice questions from the New York Regents exam and discovered a significant misalignment between the standard the test claimed to measure (historical analysis) and the reasoning of students who achieved correct answers primarily on the basis of "history content, literacy, and test-wiseness"

(p. 325). Reich concludes that selected response items do not capture more complex learning goals such as historical thinking and analysis.

Ercikan and Seixas (2011) explain the challenges involved in assessing historical thinking, including the inextricability of factual knowledge and higher-order thinking in history, the complexity of discipline-specific tasks, and the different components of historical thinking (e.g., continuity and change, historical significance). A handful of studies have taken on these challenges, in attempts to assess sourcing, contextualization, perspective taking, and evidence-based argument. One recent effort by Wineburg and his colleagues assesses historical reading strategies such as sourcing and contextualization using "Historical Assessments of Thinking" (HATs). HATs serve as quick, formative assessments that measure students' ability to *transfer* specific historical thinking practices to new documents and unfamiliar historical topics (Breakstone, Smith, & Wineburg, 2013).

Hartmann and Hasselhorn (2008) demonstrate how complicated it can be to measure historical perspective taking. The researchers created a scenario focused on whom to vote for in the 1930 election in the Weimar Republic. Respondents rated certain responses according to the likelihood that a given imaginary historical actor would have found them plausible. The possible actions ranged from presentist (least plausible) to historically contextualized (most plausible). The researchers translated students' selection of the contextualized responses as high scores on historical perspective taking. However, because students' history grades correlated strongly with their selection of contextualized responses to the scenario, it remains unclear whether their high scores on the measure indicated mastery of historical perspective taking or some other factor related to academic success.

Monte-Sano and De La Paz (2012) assessed high-school students' evidence-based argument writing, perspective recognition, and contextualization in response to four different kinds of essay prompts to see which tasks would best elicit historical thinking in students' writing. Using multiple regression, they found that the writing task explained 31% of the variance in students' overall historical reasoning. Those tasks that directed students to source, corroborate, or engage in causal analysis were the most effective, especially in prompting students to recognize and reconcile historical perspectives. Students' historical reasoning was weaker in response to writing tasks that prompted students to imagine themselves in a time/place and write from that point of view. Frost, de Pont, and Brailsford (2012) simply added weekly short writing tasks to a college history course and found that students' grades, attendance, course evaluations, and quality of discussion were quite strong. Without a comparison or control group, the findings were limited; however, together, the studies suggest that writing tasks may support students' historical learning.

Like the research literature discussed above, the extant assessment models of historical understanding largely focus on disciplinary practices. One exception comes out of Germany, and represents an effort to translate the largely theoretical work on historical consciousness into performance

standards, or measurable competencies. Körber (2011) shares a model of historical understanding that includes three procedural competencies and a basic competence: (a) an *inquiring competence*, which captures the ability to turn uncertainty into a question and investigation; (b) a *methodical competence*, which pertains to the process of investigation, the analysis of evidence, and the construction of a narrative; (c) a *competence of historical orientation*, which refers to the ability to *use* historical information "for personal or collective orientation in the present and the future" (p.150); and finally (d) a declarative or subject matter competence, which refers to the "case knowledge" required to reason historically. Körber suggests levels that reflect increasingly sophisticated mastery of each competence. Although, as Körber readily admits, much work remains to be done to test the empirical validity of this model, it is nonetheless promising in its effort to integrate the two halves of Rüsen's (1993) model—historical discipline and life experience.

The urgency for robust, valid assessments of historical thinking and understanding should be self-evident. First, in their absence, multiple-choice assessments focused only on factual recall will remain the norm. But, more importantly in the context of this review, until the field has precise and valid measures that capture agreed-upon student outcomes, the research on student historical learning will lag.

### Where Have We Been, Where Are We Going?

We are heartened by the amount and quality of research that has emerged in the past decade, and we believe both strands of research highlighted in this review—research on students' engagement with disciplinary practices and research on how students' lived experiences interact with historical study—make important contributions to our understanding of history education. Below, we suggest directions for future research before offering a final comment.

***Methodological balance.*** The research reviewed here primarily consists of small-scale qualitative studies, with a few exceptions representing larger-scale, experimental, or quasi-experimental work. While we advocate for more large-scale experimental studies, we also caution researchers to ground such work in discipline-based conceptions of history. Ultimately, a mix of qualitative and quantitative approaches will allow the field to both identify trends and make valid inferences about what students' performances indicate about their learning. The ultimate goal should be to understand better the conditions and environments that foster meaningful history learning.

***Learning progressions.*** We continue to lack a comprehensive and coherent view of student learning from elementary school through college. We have not moved far beyond the findings of the foundational and ambitious History 13–16 Project in the United Kingdom or the expert-novice studies of the 1990s to further define learning progressions, even on discrete components of historical thinking, literacy, or epistemology. In particular, we have little research on elementary students' history learning (see Filpot, 2009, for an exception), although some promising work has started on civics and economics topics (e.g., Halvorsen et al., 2012).

Only a handful of studies explore the relationship between students' development and their capacity to understand certain historical topics, and these pieces constitute some of the only research that has emerged on how younger children understand the past (e.g., Corriveau, Kim, Schwalen, & Harris, 2009; Hoodless, 2002; Schweber, 2008b). For example, Harris (2012) suggests that learning world history may be significantly different than learning the history of any one country. Such studies highlight how much more we need to know about students' historical understanding at varying developmental stages.

With regard to reading and writing history, we have only a rudimentary and incomplete sense of how students' historical literacy practices develop over time. What levels of text complexity are manageable for fifth-graders as opposed to eleventh-graders, for example? And how would a written argument constructed by a fifth-grader compare to that written by a tenth-grader? Clearly, any investigation of student development must continue in tandem with ongoing empirical work that seeks to identify and assess discrete components of historical understanding.

***The role of factual knowledge.*** While we applaud the emergent consensus that historical understanding transcends mere familiarity with historical information, we see factual knowledge and familiarity with narratives as the elephant in the review, evident in studies where students learned to source, but failed to contextualize (e.g., Nokes et al., 2007; Reisman, 2012a), or where persistent schematic narrative templates nonetheless incorporate historical inaccuracies (e.g., Wertsch, 2004). We would like to see more research that takes a close look at the role of factual knowledge as an independent variable. Whereas most scholars recognize the crucial role that factual knowledge plays in historical inquiry and analysis, few have closely examined the relationship between factual knowledge and historical thinking (see van Boxtel & van Drie, 2012 as an exception). We believe that further study of this relationship would yield a more robust model of historical understanding.

***Classroom discourse and discussion.*** A number of the studies cited here (e.g., Goldberg et al., 2011; Manfra & Lee, 2012) suggest the promise of discussion and interaction for supporting students' learning. Work in civic education has long lauded the benefits of discussion (e.g., Hess, 2009) and sociocultural learning theory underscores the value of interactive discourse. Curiously, there has been little empirical attention to discussion as a key classroom activity through which students encounter the past and develop understanding (see Reisman, 2015, for exception regarding whole-class discussion). Nor has there been much attention to the nature and role of classroom discourse in students' learning (see Bunch, 2009, for an exception). Greater attention to discussion and discourse more broadly has the potential to support students' historical learning and clarify how students navigate the complexity of the past.

***Teacher learning.*** Since we confined this chapter to student learning, we did not report on teacher education and professional development. With few exceptions (e.g., Conklin, 2014), research in teacher education and professional development does not link pre-service or in-service experiences and students' history learning in classrooms. Some research focuses on teacher learning over time (e.g., Conklin, 2008; Hicks, 2005; Monte-Sano & Budano, 2013), or approaches to measuring teacher learning (Maggioni, VanSledright, & Alexander, 2009). Together these studies do not paint a coherent picture of how we might best support teachers as they learn to teach for historical understanding. To support history learning, we call for a more systematic effort to identify the experiences, tasks, and environments that support new and veteran teachers' learning and to examine the effects of such factors on student learning.

***A closing comment.*** We have found that the research on historical understanding has largely pursued two sets of questions. One set asks whether and how students might be prompted to engage in the procedural practices of disciplinary historical thinking. The other set asks how students' lived experiences shape their understanding and interpretation of the past. We argue in this review that the field stands to benefit from greater interaction between these two strands of research, and we highlight a few studies that shed light on what this interaction might look like (e.g., Goldberg et al., 2008, 2011; Kolikant & Pollack, 2009).

In short, we encourage future researchers to be mindful of the ultimate goal of history education—historical understanding—and to consider how their particular research focus relates to other questions raised in the field. Moving forward, we encourage the field to develop a clearer understanding of how disciplinary practices, conceptual knowledge, epistemic orientation, lived experience, and factual knowledge intersect and interact to support historical understanding. In the course of a mere quarter century, history education has become a burgeoning field of scholarly interest. We are encouraged by the fact that the bulk of this research has focused on developing stimulating, intellectual experiences for students in real classrooms. We eagerly await future developments in the field.

## References

Akkerman, S., Admiraal, W., & Huizenga, J. (2009). Storification in history education: A mobile game in and about medieval Amsterdam. *Computers and Education, 52*(2), 449–459.

An, S. (2009). Learning US history in an age of globalization and transnational migration. *Journal of Curriculum Studies, 41*(6), 763–787.

Bain, R. (2006). Rounding up unusual suspects: Facing the authority hidden in the history classroom. *Teachers College Record, 108*(10), 2080–2114.

Baron, C. (2012). Understanding historical thinking at historic sites. *Journal of Educational Psychology, 104*(3), 833–847.

Barton, K., & McCully, A. (2010). "You can form your own point of view": Internally persuasive discourse in Northern Ireland students' encounters with history. *Teachers College Record, 112*(1), 142–181.

Beck, S., & Jeffery, J. (2009). Genre and thinking in academic writing tasks. *Journal of Literacy Research, 41*, 228–272.

Beaufort, A. (2004). Developmental gains of a history major: A case for building a theory of disciplinary writing expertise. *Research in the Teaching of English, 39*(2), 136–185.

Bekerman, Z., & Zembylas, M. (2011). The emotional complexities of teaching conflictual historical narratives: the case of integrated Palestinian–Jewish schools in Israel. *Teachers College Record, 113(5)*, 1004–1030.

Biancarosa, C., & Snow, C.E. (2006). *Reading next—A vision for action and research in middle and high school literacy: A report to Carnegie Corporation of New York* (2nd ed.). Washington, D.C.: Alliance for Excellent Education.

Breakstone, J., Smith, M., & Wineburg, S. (2013). Beyond the bubble in history/social studies assessments. *Phi Delta Kappan, 94(5)*, 53–57.

Britt, M., & Aglinskas, C. (2002). Improving students' ability to identify and use source information. *Cognition and Instruction, 20(4)*, 485–522.

Brooks, S. (2011). Historical empathy as perspective recognition and care in one secondary social studies classroom. *Theory and Research in Social Education, 39(2)*, 166–202.

Brown, J.S., Collins, A., & Duguid, P. (1989). Situated cognition and the culture of learning. *Educational Researcher, 18 (1)*, 32–42.

Bunch, G. (2009). "Going up there": Challenges and opportunities for language minority students during a mainstream classroom speech event. *Linguistics and Education, 20(2)*, 81–108.

Calkins, S., & Kelley, M. (2009). Who writes the past? Student perceptions of Wikipedia knowledge and credibility in a world history classroom. *Journal on Excellence in College Teaching, 20(3)*, 123–143.

Carnegie Council on Advancing Adolescent Literacy. (2010). *Time to act: An agenda for advancing adolescent literacy for college and career success.* New York, NY: Carnegie Corporation of New York.

Carretero, M., & Kriger, M. (2011). Historical representations and conflicts about indigenous people as national identities. *Culture and Psychology, 17(2)*, 177–195.

Coffin, C. (2006a). *Historical discourse: The language of time, cause, and evaluation.* London, England: Continuum.

Coffin, C. (2006b). Learning the language of school history: The role of linguistics in mapping the writing demands of the secondary school curriculum. *Journal of Curriculum Studies, 38(4)*, 413–429.

Conklin, H. (2008). Promise and problems in two divergent pathways: Preparing social studies teachers for the middle school level. *Theory and Research in Social Education, 36(1)*, 36–65.

Conklin, H. (2014). Student learning in the middle school social studies classroom: The role of differing teacher preparation. *The Elementary School Journal, 114(4)*, 455–478.

Corriveau, K., Kim, A., Schwalen, C., & Harris, P. (2009). Abraham Lincoln and Harry Potter: Children's differentiation between historical and fantasy characters. *Cognition, 113(2)*, 213–225.

Damico, J., & Baildon, M. (2007). Examining ways readers engage with websites during think-aloud sessions. *Journal of Adolescent and Adult Literacy, 51(3)*, 254–263.

Damico, J., Baildon, M., Exter, M., & Guo, S. (2009). Where we read from matters: Disciplinary literacy in a ninth-grade social studies classroom. *Journal of Adolescent and Adult Literacy, 53(4)*, 325–335.

De La Paz, S. (2005). Effects of historical reasoning instruction and writing strategy mastery in culturally and academically diverse middle school classrooms. *Journal of Educational Psychology, 97(2)*, 139–156.

De La Paz, S., & Felton, M. (2010). Reading and writing from multiple source documents in history: Effects of strategy instruction with low to average high school writers. *Contemporary Educational Psychology, 35(3)*, 174–192.

De La Paz, S., Felton, M., Monte-Sano, C., Croninger, R., Jackson, C., Deogracias, J. S., & Hoffman, B. P. (2014). Developing historical reading and writing with adolescent readers: Effects on student learning. *Theory and Research in Social Education, 42*, 228–274.

de Oliveira, L. C. (2011). *Knowing and writing school history: The language of students' expository writing and teachers' expectations.* Charlotte, NC: Information Age Publishing.

Endacott, J. (2010). Reconsidering affective engagement in historical empathy. *Theory and Research in Social Education, 38(1)*, 6–49.

Epstein, T. (2009). *Interpreting national history: Race, identity, and pedagogy in classrooms and communities.* New York: Routledge.

Ercikan, K., & Seixas, P. (2011). Assessment of higher order thinking: the case of historical thinking. In G. Schraw (Ed.), *Assessment of higher order thinking skills* (pp. 245–261). Scottsdale, AZ: Information Age Publishing.

Espin, C., Cevasco, J., van den Broek, P., Baker, S., & Gersten, R. (2007). History as narrative: The nature and quality of historical understanding for students with LD. *Journal of Learning Disabilities, 40(2)*, 174–182.

Ferretti, R., MacArthur, C., & Okolo, M. (2007). Students' misconceptions about U.S. westward migration. *Journal of Learning Disabilities, 40(2)*, 145–153.

Filpot, E. (2009). Bringing history home: A K-5 curriculum design. *The History Teacher, 42(3)*, 281–295.

Fránquiz, M., & Salinas, C. (2011). Newcomers developing English literacy through historical thinking and digitized primary sources. *Journal of Second Language Writing, 20(3)*, 196–210.

Frost, J., de Pont, G., & Brailsford, I. (2012). Expanding assessment methods and moments in history. *Assessment and Evaluation in Higher Education, 37(3)*, 293–304.

Goldberg, T., Schwarz, B., & Porat, D. (2008). Living and dormant collective memories as contexts of history learning. *Learning and Instruction, 18(3)*, 223–237.

Goldberg, T., Schwarz, B., & Porat, D. (2011). "Could they do it differently?" Narrative and argumentative changes in students' writing following discussion of "hot" historical issues. *Cognition and Instruction, 29(2)*, 185–217.

Gottlieb, E., & Wineburg, S. (2012). Between veritas and communitas: Epistemic switching in the reading of academic and sacred history. *Journal of the Learning Sciences, 21(1)*, 84–129.

Graham, S., & Perin, D. (2007). *Writing next: Effective strategies to improve writing of adolescents in middle and high schools.* Washington, D.C.: Alliance for Excellent Education.

Halvorsen, A-L., Duke, N., Brugar, K., Block, M., Strachan, S., Berka, M., & Brown, J. (2012). Narrowing the achievement gap in second-grade social studies and content area literacy: The promise of a project-based approach. *Theory and Research in Social Education, 40(3)*, 198–229.

Harniss, M., Caros, J., & Gersten, R. (2007). Impact of the design of U.S. history textbooks on content acquisition and academic engagement of special education students: An experimental investigation. *Journal of Learning Disabilities, 40(2)*, 100–110.

Harris, L. (2012). Conceptual devices in the work of world historians. *Cognition and Instruction, 30(4)*, 312–358.

Hartmann, U., & Hasselhorn, M. (2008). Historical perspective taking: A standardized measure for an aspect of students' historical thinking. *Learning and Individual Differences, 18(2)*, 264–270.

Hawkey, K., & Prior, J. (2011). History, memory cultures and meaning in the classroom. *Journal of Curriculum Studies, 43(2)*, 231–247.

Henriquez, R., & Ruiz, M. (2014). Chilean students learn to think historically: Construction of historical causation through the use of evidence in writing. *Linguistics and Education, 25*, 145–157.

Hernandez-Ramos, P., & De La Paz, S. (2009). Learning history in middle school by designing multimedia in a project-based learning experience. *Journal of Research on Technology in Education, 42(2)*, 151–173.

Hess, D. (2009). *Controversy in the classroom: The democratic power of discussion.* New York, NY: Routledge.

Hicks, D. (2005). Continuity and constraint: Case studies of becoming a teacher of history in England and the United States. *International Journal of Social Education, 20(1)*, 18–51.

Hirst, R. H. (1973). Liberal education and the nature of knowledge. In R. S. Peters (Ed.), *Philosophy of education* (pp. 87–101). Oxford: Oxford University Press.

Hughes, J., Bigler, R., & Levy, S. (2007). Consequences of learning about historical racism among European-American and African-American children. *Child Development, 78(6)*, 1689–1705.

Hoodless, P. (2002). An investigation into children's developing awareness of time and chronology in story. *Journal of Curriculum Studies, 34(2)*, 173–200.

Hynd, C., Holschuh, J., & Hubbard, B. (2004). Thinking like a historian: College students' reading of multiple historical documents. *Journal of Literacy Research, 36(2)*, 141–176.

Journell, W. (2008). Facilitating historical discussions using asynchronous communication: The role of the teacher. *Theory and Research in Social Education, 36(4)*, 317–355.

Kohlmeier, J. (2006). "Couldn't she just leave?": The relationship between consistently using class discussions and the development of historical empathy in a 9th grade world history course. *Theory and Research in Social Education, 34*(1), 34–57.

Kolikant, Y., & Pollack, S. (2009). The asymmetrical influence of identity: A triadic interaction among Israeli Jews, Israeli Arabs, and historical texts. *Journal of Curriculum Studies, 41*(5), 651–677.

Körber, A. (2011). German history didactics: From historical consciousness to historical competencies—and beyond? In H. Bjerg, C. Lenz, & E. Thorstensen (Eds.), *Historicizing the uses of the past: Scandinavian perspectives on history culture, historical consciousness and didactics of history related to World War II* (pp. 145–164). New Brunswick, NJ: Transaction Publishers.

Larson, B. (2005). Considering the move to electronic discussions. *Social Education, 69*(3), 162.

Lee, P. (2004). Understanding history. In P. Seixas (Ed.) *Theorizing historical consciousness* (pp. 129–164). Toronto: University of Toronto Press.

Lee, P., & Ashby, R. (2000). Progression in historical understanding among students ages 7–14. In P. Stearns, P. Seixas, & S. Wineburg (Eds.), *Knowing, teaching and learning history: National and international perspectives* (pp. 199–222). New York, NY: NYU Press.

Lee, J., & Calandra, B. (2004). Can embedded annotations help high school students perform problem solving tasks using a web-based historical document? *Journal of Research on Technology in Education, 37*(1), 65–84.

Lee, P., & Shemilt, D. (2003). A scaffold not a cage: Progression and progression models in history. *Teaching History, 113*, 13–23.

Lee, P., & Shemilt, D. (2009). Is any explanation better than none? *Teaching History, 137*, 42–49.

Lévesque, S. (2008). *Thinking historically: Educating students for the twenty-first century.* Toronto: University of Toronto Press.

Levstik, L., & Groth, J. (2005). "Ruled by our own people": Ghanaian adolescents' conceptions of citizenship. *Teachers College Record, 117*(4), 563–586.

Li, D., & Lim, C. (2008). Scaffolding online historical inquiry tasks: A case study of two secondary classrooms. *Computers and Education, 50*(4), 1394–1410.

Logtenberg, A., van Boxtel, C., & van Hout-Wolters, B. (2010). Stimulating situational interest and student questioning through three types of historical introductory texts. *European Journal of Psychology of Education, 26*(2), 179–198.

Maggioni, L., VanSledright, B., & Alexander, P. (2009). Walking on the borders: A measure of epistemic cognition in history. *Journal of Experimental Education, 77*(3), 187–213.

Manfra, M., & Lee, J. (2012). "You have to know the past to (blog) the present": Using an educational blog to engage students in U.S. history. *Computers in Schools, 29*, 118–134.

Marcus, A., Paxton, R., & Meyerson, P. (2006). "The reality of it all": History students read the movies. *Theory and Research in Social Education, 34*(3), 515–552.

McCombs, J. S., Kirby, S. N., Barney, H., Darilek, H., & Magee, S. (2005). *Achieving state and national literacy goals, a long uphill road: A report to Carnegie Corporation of New York.* Santa Monica, CA: RAND.

Mendez, J. M., & Montanero, M. (2008). Hypergraphics for history teaching—barriers for causal reasoning about history accounts. *Educational Technology and Society, 11*(4), 128–138.

Monte-Sano, C. (2008). Qualities of historical writing instruction: A comparative case study of two teachers' practice. *American Educational Research Journal, 45*(4), 1045–1079.

Monte-Sano, C. (2010). Disciplinary literacy in history: An exploration of the historical nature of adolescents' writing. *Journal of the Learning Sciences, 19*, 539–568.

Monte-Sano, C. (2011). Beyond reading comprehension and summary: Learning to read and write in history by focusing on evidence, perspective, and interpretation. *Curriculum Inquiry, 41*(2), 212–249.

Monte-Sano, C., & Budano, C. (2013). Developing and enacting pedagogical content knowledge for teaching history: An exploration of two novice teachers' growth over three years. *Journal of the Learning Sciences, 22*(2), 171–211.

Monte-Sano, C., & De La Paz, S. (2012). Using writing tasks to elicit adolescents' historical reasoning. *Journal of Literacy Research, 44*(30), 273–299.

Monte-Sano, C., De La Paz, S., & Felton, M. (2014). Implementing a disciplinary literacy curriculum for US history: Learning from expert middle

school teachers in diverse classrooms. *Journal of Curriculum Studies, 46*(4), 540–575.

Mosborg, S. (2002). Speaking of history: How adolescents use their knowledge of history in reading the daily news. *Cognition and Instruction, 20*(3), 323–358.

Nash, G., Crabtree, C., & Dunn, R. (2000). *History on trial: Culture wars and the teaching of the past.* New York, NY: Vintage.

Nokes, J., Dole, J., & Hacker, J. (2007). Teaching high school students to use heuristics while reading historical texts. *Journal of Educational Psychology, 99*(3), 492–504.

Paxton, R. (2002). The influence of author visibility on high school students solving a historical problem. *Cognition and Instruction, 20*(2), 197–248.

Peck, C. (2010). "It's not like [I'm] Chinese and Canadian. I am in between": Ethnicity and students' conceptions of historical significance. *Theory and Research in Social Education, 38*(4). 574–617.

Perry, W. (1970). *Forms of intellectual and ethical development in the college years: A scheme.* New York, NY: Holt, Rinehart and Winston.

Polman, J. (2006). Mastery and appropriation as means to understand the interplay of history learning and identity trajectories. *Journal of the Learning Sciences, 15*(2), 221–259.

Porat, D. (2006). Who fired first? Students' construction of meaning from one textbook account of the Israeli–Arab conflict. *Curriculum Inquiry, 36*(3), 251–271.

Reich, G. (2009). Testing historical knowledge: Standards, multiple-choice questions and student reasoning. *Theory and Research in Social Education, 37*(3), 325–360.

Reisman, A. (2012a). Reading like a historian: A document-based history curriculum intervention in urban high schools. *Cognition and Instruction, 31*(1), 86–112.

Reisman, A. (2012b). The "document-based lesson": Bringing disciplinary inquiry into high school history classrooms with adolescent struggling readers. *Journal of Curriculum Studies, 44*(2), 233–264.

Reisman, A. (2015). Entering the historical problem space: Whole-class text-based discussion in history class. *Teachers College Record, 117*(2), 1–44.

Rouet, J-F., Britt, M. A., Mason, R., & Perfetti, C. (1996). Using multiple sources of evidence to reason about history. *Journal of Educational Psychology, 88*(3), 478–493.

Rüsen, J. (1993). *Studies in metahistory.* Pretoria, South Africa: Human Sciences Research Council.

Saye, J., & Brush, T. (2007). Using technology-enhanced learning environments to support problem-based historical inquiry in secondary school classrooms. *Theory and Research in Social Education, 35*(2), 196–230.

Schleppegrell, M., Achugar, M., & Oteiza, T. (2004). The grammar of history: Enhancing content based instruction through a functional focus. *TESOL Quarterly, 38*(1), 67– 93.

Schleppegrell, M., Greer, S., & Taylor, S. (2008). Literacy in history: Language and meaning. *Australian Journal of Language and Literacy, 31*(2), 174–187.

Schweber, S. (2008a). "Here this is no why": Holocaust education at a Lubavitch girls' Yeshivah. *Jewish Social Studies, 14*(2), 156–185.

Schweber, S. (2008b). "What happened to their pets?": Third graders encounter the Holocaust. *Teachers College Record, 110*(10), 2073–2115.

Seixas, P. (1994). Students' understanding of historical significance. *Theory and Research in Social Education, 22*(3), 281–304.

Seixas, P., & Clark, P. (2004). Murals as monuments: Students' ideas about depictions of civilization in British Columbia. *American Journal of Education, 110*(2), 146– 171.

Shemilt, D. (1983). The devil's locomotive. *History and Theory, 22*(4), 1–18.

Snow, C. B. (2002). *Reading for understanding: Toward a research and development program in reading comprehension.* Santa Monica, CA: RAND.

Stahl, S. A., Hynd, C. R., Britton, B. K., McNish, M. M., & Bosquet, D. (1996). What happens when students read multiple source documents in history? *Reading Research Quarterly, 31*(4), 430–456.

Stoddard, J. (2009). The ideological implications of using "educational" film to teach controversial events. *Curriculum Inquiry, 39*(3), 407–433.

Swan, K., Hofer, M., & Locascio, D. (2008). The historical scene investigation (HIS) project: Instruction in the fifth grade social studies classroom. *International Journal of Social Education, 22*(2), 70–100.

Trofanenko, B. (2008) More than a single best narrative: Collective history and the transformation of historical consciousness. *Curriculum Inquiry, 38*(5), 579–603.

van Boxtel, C., & van Drie, J. (2012). "That's in the time of the Romans!" Knowledge and strategies students use to contextualize historical images and documents. *Cognition and Instruction, 30*(2), 113–145.

van Drie, J., van Boxtel, C., Erkens, G., & Kanselaar, G. (2005). Using representational tools to support historical reasoning in computer-supported collaborative learning. *Technology, Pedagogy and Education, 14*(1), 25–41.

VanSledright, B. (2002). Fifth graders investigating history in the classroom: Results from a researcher-practitioner design experiment. *The Elementary School Journal, 103*(2), 131–160.

VanSledright, B., & Limón, M. (2006). Learning and teaching social studies: A review of cognitive research in history and geography. In P. Alexander & P. Winne (Eds.), *Handbook of educational psychology* (pp. 545–570). Mahwah, NJ: Lawrence Erlbaum.

von Borries, B. (1988). *Learning history and historical consciousness: Empirical explorations to the acquisition and use of history.* Stuttgart, Germany: Ernst Klett.

Wertsch, J. (2004). Specific narratives and schematic narrative templates. In P. Seixas (Ed.), *Theorizing historical consciousness* (pp. 49–62). Toronto, Canada: University of Toronto Press.

Wiley, J., & Voss, J. (1999). Constructing arguments from multiple sources: Tasks that promote understanding and not just memory for text. *Journal of Educational Psychology, 91*(2), 301–311.

Williams, J., Nubla-Kung, A., Pollini, S., Stafford, K., Garcia, A., & Snyder, A. (2007). Teaching cause effect text structure through social studies content to at-risk second graders. *Journal of Learning Disabilities, 40*(2), 111–120.

Wills, J. (2011). Misremembering as mediated action: Schematic narrative templates and elementary students' narration of the past. *Theory and Research in Social Education, 39*(1), 115–144.

Wineburg, S. (1991). Historical problem solving: A study of the cognitive processes used in the evaluation of documentary and pictorial evidence. *Journal of Educational Psychology, 83*(1), 73–87.

Wineburg, S. S. (1996). The psychology of learning and teaching history. In R. C. Calfee & D. C. Berliner (Eds.), *Handbook of educational psychology* (pp. 423–437). New York, NY: Macmillan.

Wineburg, S., & Monte-Sano, C. (2008). "Famous Americans": The changing pantheon of American heroes. *Journal of American History, 95*(1), 1186–1202.

Wineburg, S., Mosborg, S., Porat, D., & Duncan, A. (2007). Common belief and the cultural curriculum: An intergenerational study of historical consciousness. *American Educational Research Journal, 44*(40), 40–76.

Wolfe, M., & Goldman, S. (2005). Relations between adolescents' text processing and reasoning. *Cognition and Instruction, 23*(4), 467–502.

Yang, S., & Huang, L. (2007). Computer-mediated critical doing history project. *Computers in Human Behavior, 23*(5), 2144–2162.

Young, E., & Leinhardt, G. (1998). Writing from primary documents: A way of knowing in history. *Written Communication, 15*(1), 25–68.

# 22

# Civic Education

*MARIO CARRETERO*
Autonoma University of Madrid, Spain

*HELEN HASTE*
Harvard University

*ANGELA BERMUDEZ*
Deusto University, Bilbao, Spain

Civic education is currently a field of vibrant research and practice that is producing significant pedagogical innovation. However, it is a contested field with intense discussions about its goals and what teaching and learning processes should be privileged. These discussions reflect a transition from "traditional" models of civic education to "new civics" that considerably extends the definitions of civic participation and the purposes of civic education. Underlying this transition is a basic tension between pedagogy that emphasizes the acquisition of knowledge through teacher instruction and pedagogy that emphasizes praxis, interaction with tools, objects, experiences, and people as the means to gain understanding. The former implies a "top-down" model, the latter, a more "bottom-up" model. In civic education they parallel a tension between seeing the purpose of civic education as increasing knowledge primarily about the nation's political institutions and history, and the purpose being to develop understanding, skills, agency, and motivation through hands-on experiences with civic issues and actions.

In this chapter we discuss the contributions of educational and developmental psychology to this renewed understanding of civic education, in particular, to redefining key learning processes, curriculum orientations in formal and informal learning environments, and different pathways to development. To conclude, we consider three examples of emerging research and practice that relate to "new civics": Civic education through new media, student engagement in critical deliberation of controversial issues, and how historical narratives and concepts are used in the construction of civic identity.

## Developmental Theory and Civic Education

Models of human development are the infrastructures that inform civic education. Advances in developmental psychology are affecting how civic education is conceived. For example, the term "political socialization," widely used in several social sciences, assumes a social learning theory model, in which the passive individual is molded by environmental factors such as conditioning and reinforcement; civic education is one agent of that molding process. However, for several decades, the emergent cognitive model within developmental psychology has cast the individual instead as an active agent in learning, selecting, organizing, and making meaning of experience and information. Further, this active model of the person has been extended by a neo-Vygotskian perspective which takes account of the individual's cultural context and experience.

Cultural models of development focus on the growing individual's social and cultural context, the narratives, values, knowledge, and norms of action to which the growing individual is exposed in different sociocultural settings, interactions, and experiences that promote or inhibit effective and relevant learning. Learning results not only from formal teaching of information, but also from individuals' interaction, dialogue, and performance of action within their social context. Meaning and understanding, therefore, are co-constructed and negotiated in social and cultural interactions, not merely processed in individual cognition. In cognitive developmental approaches, the individual actively is successively restructuring and reflecting, producing increasingly complex and abstract understanding. Within culturally oriented approaches, the active process also involves negotiating meaning through dialogue with others and with cultural resources.

These theoretical developments transform a view of civic education that was focused on the teaching and learning of factual knowledge and conventional values, primarily aiming to socialize the students as newcomers into an existing sociopolitical order. More cognitive developmental perspectives orient research and practice to new sets of questions: What elements of civic education are necessary to scaffold active learning and deep understanding? What happens in civic learning with increasing age? What happens in civic learning with increasing opportunity to engage with civic issues? The pedagogic implications are that education should focus on fostering in students an increasingly sophisticated and mature understanding of civic matters, and provide the right kinds of experiences and contexts for learning to facilitate active, effective, and meaningful processing. This takes civic learning beyond factual knowledge, to include conceptual understanding, cognitive and socioemotional skills, and moral judgment.

First, educators need to recognize and take account of the cultural messages and resources available to the growing individual (for example, linguistic, non-linguistic, and institutional messages about ethnicity, power, dominant values, and norms of behavior). Second, effective civic learning needs to use the resources of the cultural context, to facilitate interaction, critical reflection, and negotiation, for example with media and through experience and engagement with actual civic life. This includes paying attention to classroom and school climate (Campbell, 2008; Thapa, Cohen, Guffey, & Higgins D'Alessandro, 2013), community experience, service learning, family interactions, cultural narratives, norms and expectations, socioeconomic factors, and increasingly social media.

## The Building Blocks of Civic Learning

We can think of the dimensions of civic learning as building blocks that contribute in different ways to achieving the goals of civic education, reflecting different models of development. These are: civic knowledge and understanding; civic skills; civic values, motivation, and identity; and civic action. We will consider these also in the context of emergent developmental theories.

### Civic Knowledge and Understanding

Civic education typically has concentrated on conveying factual knowledge about democratic institutions, processes, and elements of national history. However, there is a growing consensus that citizens also require more diverse civic knowledge and understanding such as controversial issues, intergroup relations, local processes, or community affairs (Alexander, Pinson, & Yonah, 2011; Amadeo, Torney-Purta, Lehmann, Husfeldt, & Nikolova, 2002; Hess, 2009; Levinson, 2012). There is also growing consensus that civic knowledge alone is not enough to foster active and responsible civic engagement. There is a relation between civic knowledge and voting: those who intend to vote tend to have better knowledge (Carnegie Corporation of New York and CIRCLE Center for Information and Research on Civic Learning and Engagement, 2003) and knowledge is needed for routes to political participation, monitoring of government actions, and exercising rights and responsibilities (Cox, Jaramillo, & Reimers, 2005). However, an active civil society requires also understanding of concepts

and principles, the skills for reflective and responsible action, willingness to engage, and commitment to democratic values (Sherrod, Torney-Purta, & Flanagan, 2010; Torney-Purta, Lehmann, Oswald, & Schulz, 2001). Discrete knowledge becomes more meaningful as it is integrated with conceptual understanding. For example, students may "know" the list of core human rights, but they may not understand what the concept of "rights" actually entails, why they were codified in a particular historical time, or how they relate to specific conceptions of state.

The ability to understand civic and social concepts progresses in parallel with the development of conceptual thinking (Barrett, 2007). Students initially understand concepts in terms of more concrete characteristics and gradually progress to understand more abstract dimensions (Carretero, Castorina, & Levinas, 2013). From representing civic and social concepts as static and isolated there are gradually established increasingly complex conceptual networks in which different elements are interconnected, and in which every social and civic element is dynamically defined by its relation with other aspects of reality (Barrett, 2007; Berti & Andriolo, 2001). The pedagogical strategies employed and educational environment in which students learn significantly influence the level of sophistication of their conceptual understanding (Barrett & Davies, 2005; Berti, 2002).

This development is reflected in the conception of social institutions, as illustrated by several examples:

1. For younger students, civic institutions and social realities are embodied by those who represent them. Later they come to understand the societal functions of institutions within a wide range of systems and structures.
2. Younger students tend to believe that the various levels of social order are diverse and disconnected realities. For instance, cultural changes have no connection with political or economic factors, revolutions are simple confrontations between groups rather than structural changes affecting all aspects of society.
3. Social change is difficult to understand because things are as they are, social situations are immutable, and little change is possible.
4. Younger students tend to think that civil rights depend on the willingness of individuals. With further conceptual development they understand that their existence rests on political, economic, social, and cultural factors forming a multicausal structure.
5. Younger students understand a country's presidency only in terms of an individual and they also may have difficulty in understanding that a modern nation-state is not simply a territory or a group of inhabitants but an abstract concept that only emerged in modern societies.

### Civic Skills

A variety of skills are necessary for effective participation in civic life. For example, youth are expected to make sound political choices, to take part in processes of collective decision making, conflict resolution, and negotiation, in the discussion of controversial social and political issues, or the monitoring of government action on behalf of public interests. Whereas knowledge and conceptual understanding make up the declarative dimension of civic learning (know what), civic skills make up the procedural dimension that refers to what students should be able to do (know how). Civic skills are often divided into intellectual skills, participatory skills, and socioemotional skills (Fine, Bermudez, & Barr, 2007).

Cognitive skills refer to the capacities that enable citizens to analyze and synthesize information and arguments, as well as evaluate, reach conclusions, take and defend positions on matters of public concern (Kirlin, 2003). Examples include considering different perspectives (Hess, 2009), interrogating and interpreting political communication (Amadeo et al., 2002), and supporting positions with evidence and good argumentation (Youniss, 2011).

Participatory skills refer to a variety of social capacities for working with others that enable citizens to influence public and civic life by building coalitions, seeking consensus, negotiating differences, and managing conflict. Kirlin (2003) proposes a typology that includes skills for communication (public speaking, petitioning, lobbying, protesting), organization (mobilizing, securing funding, leading meetings), and collective decision making (coordinating perspectives, evaluating alternative solutions, etc.). Chi, Jastrzab, and Melchior (2006) add skills for group membership and for conflict resolution. The Latin American module of the International Civic and Citizenship Study measures skills for: (a) living together in peace (peaceful resolution of conflict, assertiveness, communication); (b) democratic participation (collective decision-making processes, advocacy, persuasive communication); and (c) plurality and diversity (multiperspectivity, confronting discrimination, and exclusion).

Socioemotional skills refer to the interpersonal capacities for handling oneself in healthy relationships with family, peers, and community members. Examples include dealing positively with peer pressure, developing non-abusive relationships, avoiding risky behavior, and coordinating one's needs with the needs of others (Diazgranados & Selman, 2014; Selman, 2003). For many, these interpersonal skills feed into wider societal dynamics and a culture that sustains "democracy as a way of life" (Sinclair, 2004; Sinclair, Davies, Obura, & Tibbits, 2008).

### Civic Values, Motivation, and Identity

A third dimension of civic learning comprises the development of values, motives, and identities that dispose citizens towards engaging effectively in democratic practices (Youniss & Levine, 2009). Traditional civic education approaches sought to instill in students civic values and attitudes regarded as essential for a virtuous citizen, such as taking responsibility for civic actions like voting and helping others, upholding the law, and monitoring current affairs in the media (Lickona, 1997). The preferred pedagogical strategies employ exemplar role models, illustrative story telling, negative and positive reinforcement of behavior. Indeed, it is important to transmit to younger generations a host of democratic values that societies have struggled to construct, such as tolerance and respect for diversity, concern with the rights and welfare of others, freedom, or justice.

However, in the more active model of the learner found in cognitive developmental and cultural psychology the appropriation of values is rooted in active meaning making and negotiation within social contexts. For this reason, these approaches privilege active pedagogical strategies such as the discussion of hypothetical or real moral dilemmas implicit in interpersonal and civic situations (Kohlberg, 1984; Power, Higgins, & Kohlberg, 1989; Selman & Kwok, 2010), the reflective analysis of moral contents in literature, or the creative production of personal moral narratives (Selman, 2003). These approaches foster a reflective appropriation of social values and the development of moral judgment.

Moral values play an important role in motivating civic action because they make civic issues personally relevant and provide a sense of purpose for civic action. It is evident that this profile of engagement is only partially accountable in terms of knowledge. Whereas young people express very little interest in conventional "politics" or in joining a political party, they are concerned about and active in many community and environmental issues (Haste & Hogan, 2006; Seider, 2012; Westheimer, 2008). Because community-based and single issues are frequently seen as morally charged they may contribute to a sense of personal responsibility. Motivations may come from a variety of interests, such as the common good, group solidarity, contesting oppressive practices, or gaining power (Flanagan, 2013; Haste, 2010; Haste & Hogan, 2006; Tausch et al., 2011; Yates & Youniss, 1999).

Affect and civic identity play significant roles. These are often absent when conventional civic education is defined in relation to macro political processes such as voting, rather than on what actually motivates behavior. For effective education it is essential to start from where young people's concerns and interests are, and to understand what are the different factors that motivate them to engage (Youniss, 2011). Individual and collective identities are increasingly recognized as key elements in the definition of civic motivation and commitments. For this reason, identity is crucial to why, when, and how people become engaged, and the meaning they make of such engagement in their particular sociocultural contexts (Haste, 2010).

Civic identity is not a fixed individual trait of the person's psychology, but rather an active and fluid psychosocial process though which citizens make sense of themselves in relation to their social reality, and negotiate their place and role within their civic communities. Thus, civic identity reflects the interplay between individual traits and preferences, and the different contexts in which the citizen is formed (Haste, 2014; Haste & Abrahams, 2008; Jensen, 2010; Kassimir & Flanagan, 2010; Seif, 2010).

Civic identity includes the person's sense of agency and efficacy. Agency refers to the sense of being a meaningful actor, responsible to one's community welfare. Efficacy refers to the confidence in one's ability to take action, effect change, and achieve the desired results. In the civic realm, efficacy also involves the belief that it is possible and worth trying to make a difference through public action and may determine whether a felt concern gets translated into engagement. Through civic practice students develop a positive sense of agency and efficacy (Beaumont, 2010; Haste, 2004, 2010; Kahne & Westheimer, 2006; Levinson, 2010, 2012).

### Civic Action

Opportunities for experiencing civic action constitute a fourth building block of learning (Beaumont, 2010; Levinson, 2010; Torney-Purta & Barber, 2011). Students interact in a variety of civic environments long before they become formal political citizens, providing opportunities for age-appropriate, relevant, and meaningful learning. For example, in schools and local communities, students are constantly confronted with situations that call them to stand up against prejudice, discrimination, and harassment (Selman & Kwok, 2010). School government affords opportunities for demonstrating civic voice (Oser, Althof, & Higgins-D'Alessandro, 2008). Families, peer groups, and social media often become sites for discussing controversial issues (Lievrouw, 2011). Young people bring to the classroom a wide variety of experiences with civic life; effective civic education needs to recognize their complexity, and rich teaching opportunities for a meaningful learning process (Rubin & Hayes, 2010; Rubin, Hayes, & Benson, 2009).

Experience with real-life civic action is important to cultivate civic identities that provide authentic and effective sources of motivation, purpose, responsibility, agency, and efficacy. "Hands-on" pedagogy helps students to grasp the deeper meaning of knowledge and concepts and to develop an increasing mastery of skills. Civic action can provide the means for reflective practice necessary to connect abstract ideas with real-life situations (Bennett, Freelon, & Wells, 2010; Hart & Gullan, 2010; Levinson, 2012; Kahne & Westheimer, 2006).

Studies of service learning found that adult civic participation was linked to community engagement in adolescence (Yates & Youniss, 1999; Youniss & Yates, 1997). Recent work on youth organizing in action has explored the evolution of a program and the ways that both individual and community development unfolds within it (Cammarota & Fine, 2008; Ginwright, 2008). An example is Ginwright's (2010) study of a black youth community initiative in Oakland, California. Community-based civic action is particularly salient among communities marginalized from the conventional political system, for example, among Native Americans (Martin & Chiodo, 2008).

This form of civic engagement focuses on cooperation around targeted problem solving regarding issues of common concern. Participation requires and fosters many democratic qualities: coming together, working with others, mediating differences, managing conflict, and establishing shared goals in order to regulate, direct, and develop common affairs with

a marked sense of "public good" (Bloch-Schulman, 2010; Kassimir & Flanagan, 2010; McIntosh & Youniss, 2010; Zukin, Keeter, Andolina, Jenins, & Della Carpini, 2006). The data suggest that a distinct sense of social responsibility underlies community activism, characterized by a commitment to partner with others in understanding problems, and responsiveness in developing and implementing solutions. Furthermore, community activism builds a strong sense of belonging to local environments and interdependence within them (Kassimir & Flanagan, 2010).

Youth participatory action research (YPAR) is an emergent version of community action, based in part on Freirian principles. The goal of YPAR is to generate positive identity, agency, and efficacy in the community through the ownership of local knowledge and expertise and integrating it with relevant scholarship. YPAR projects are student-led, but with advisory guidance from researchers; they draw upon unique local knowledge. The local actors are trained in skills, including exploring scholarly work, but the collaborative project is faithful to the authentic experience and interpretation of the community (Brown & Rodriguez, 2009; Cammarota & Fine, 2008; Flanagan & Christens, 2011). YPAR presents a challenge to conventional research models because of its strong ethnographic stance, but it also challenges the implicit deficit and pathological models that inform much work on minority and underprivileged groups.

## Conceptions of Democracy and "Good Citizenship"

In the last three decades, definitions of civic processes have expanded to include many more forms of participation, such as community involvement, and to recognize the importance of unconventional civic action such as protest. Plural and multifaceted characterization of civic engagement has redefined how we understand, investigate, and practice "civic education" (Sherrod et al., 2010). A fundamental discussion concerns the goals of civic education. What purpose is served by having an educated citizenry? What are the perceived threats posed by civic ignorance and apathy? What is a "good citizen"?

### The "Good Citizen"

Westheimer and Kahne (2004) found three distinct conceptions of a "good citizen" underlying both young people's concepts and the agendas of civic education programs: the personally responsible citizen, the participatory citizen, and the justice-oriented citizen. Personally responsible citizenship emphasizes being kind to other people, helping others in need, telling the truth, following the rules, maintaining harmony, and keeping the community clean and safe. Participatory citizenship prioritizes engagement with national, state, or local issues, working with community organizations and local government on relevant issues, and getting involved in improving and strengthening one's own community. Justice-oriented citizenship focuses on thinking critically about systemic problems in society and the possibilities of social transformation, and supporting social protest that challenges inequalities, even if this involves questioning law or authority.

These are not mutually exclusive. Individuals as well as educational programs may support, engage with, or promote more than one and they often intersect. For example, helping the underprivileged out of compassion leads at least some students to recognize that their plight reflects injustice (Yates & Youniss, 1999). *Facing History and Ourselves*, a curriculum for the study of racism and societal violence within a social justice agenda, builds purposeful connections with issues of discrimination and violence in interpersonal relationships, fostering students' understanding that they have various widening "circles of moral obligation" (Fine, 2004).

### Conceptions of Democracy and Agendas for Civic Education

Not all civic education takes place within systems of representative democracy. However, most current literature on civic education assumes democracy as the model and/or context for civic education (Gutmann & Thompson, 2004; Nussbaum, 2006). There is no single definition of "democracy." At the very least we can distinguish four conceptions, each of which informs different emphases of civic education programs: *procedural democracy*, *deliberative democracy*, *democracy as social justice*, and *democracy as a mode of living*. Each of these models of democracy privileges particular kinds of civic engagement, which in turn implies that civic education pursues different goals and engages different learning processes.

Procedural democracy, which underlies many civic education efforts, defines democracy as a system of political organization and decision making based on representative and participatory procedures that are grounded on principles of freedom, equality, and the rule of law. Civic education programs informed by this conception aim to provide students with the knowledge necessary to engage with formal institutions and mechanisms for political participation such as voting in elections or campaigning for parties.

Deliberative approaches to democracy share the underlying principles of procedural democracy, but they emphasize two core ideas that push the idea of "democracy" further. First, theorists stress the pervasiveness and importance of conflict, moral controversy, and dissent in social and political life (Gutmann & Thompson, 2004; Rawls, 1993). In practice procedural democracy privileges majority views, achieving consensus, compliance with convention, and keeping order. This emphasis on system stability may marginalize alternative views on public issues that are in the minority, controversial, novel, or particularly complex. Gutmann and Thompson also argue that the conventional mechanisms of procedural democracy, such as participation in elections or interest group bargaining, are not the most adequate to handle essential moral disagreements. Therefore, it is important that citizens have wide and active engagement in the deliberation of public issues. Civic education grounded on this perspective of democracy focuses on developing the capacities

for critical inquiry and moral and political argumentation, and strengthening students' voice to participate effectively in controversial dialogue (Hess, 2009; Hess & Gatti, 2010; Ruitenberg, 2009; Stitzlein, 2012).

Proponents of democracy as social justice argue that focusing on political procedures does not adequately represent the complex, unequal, and conflictive nature of citizenship in contemporary societies. An "authentic" or "deep" democracy must be committed to assert moral equality and to protect dignity in equal terms for all (West, 2004). Unless socioeconomic (distributive) justice is guaranteed, the essential values of democracy are at stake. Civic education programs informed by democracy as social justice stress the importance of developing students' capacity to critically understand the multiple forms of systemic violence, oppression, and exclusion (Blades & Richardson, 2006). They also emphasize helping youth to become agents of social change, capable of confronting these barriers (Arnot & Swartz, 2012; Cammarota & Fine, 2008; Levinson, 2012; Swartz, 2006). As Llewellyn, Cook, and Molina's (2010) work illustrates, putting social justice at the heart of student learning means preparing students to analyze power relationships, investigate the ambiguities of political issues, and embrace opportunities for social change.

A fourth conception defines democracy as a mode of living founded on values of inclusiveness, pluralism, fairness, cooperation, dialogue, and non-violent resolution of conflict (Biesta & Lawy, 2006; Nussbaum, 2006). Civic education programs informed by this perspective aim to develop students' sensitivity, habits, and capacities necessary to build and preserve relationships and connection across lines of difference (Noddings, 2005; Sinclair, 2004; Sinclair et al., 2008).

These different conceptions of democracy have implications for the definition of the knowledge, skills, and attributes privileged in civic education programs. For example, all models require civic knowledge. Yet, the contents emphasized are more or less comprehensive, with procedural views emphasizing knowledge of political institutions and constitutional procedures, deliberative models adding knowledge of current public issues, and social justice models adding knowledge of socioeconomic dynamics. Likewise, procedural models emphasize the development of cognitive skills for effective analysis of information, whereas deliberative and social justice models emphasize skills for critical inquiry and controversial dialogue. In turn, models based on the idea of a democracy as a way of life emphasize the development of cognitive and socioemotional skills necessary for fair and caring resolution of conflict.

### Changing Patterns and Definitions of Civic Engagement: Educational Implications

Worldwide, major changes in the extent and style of youth participation, the targets of concern, and particularly the means of expressing political action have broadened the definition of civic participation (both action and targets of engagement) beyond voting or conventional partisan support;

this is an essential component of "new civics." These changes support the psychological and pedagogical claim that civic motivation should be harnessed through young people's own concerns and that education should take account of routine experiences of the young, for instance, their use of technologies and media (Haste, 2004; Haste & Hogan, 2012). Bermudez (2012) synthesizes four key transformations that are particularly salient in the literature: Beyond electoral politics; voice as agency; local focus; and affirmative and transformative action.

### Beyond Electoral Politics

The political process has been redefined beyond electoral activity in representative democracies, to include the variety of efforts to affect government and the formation of public policy, whether through formal institutions, or through alternative channels such as social movements, protest activity, and grassroots organizing (Hart & Gullan, 2010; Haste, 2010; Seif, 2010). This transformation supports a more comprehensive definition of the knowledge content of civic education, as well as the attention given to participatory skills and to the development of a civic identity.

### Voice as Agency

It is increasingly recognized that citizens participate in the public sphere by expressing their views about contested issues, mobilizing and organizing to make their voices heard. In particular, new communication technologies afford a variety of effective means to mobilize others and express alternative ideas (Banaji & Buckingham, 2013; Earl & Kimport, 2011; Facer, 2011; McLeod, Shan, Hess, & Lee, 2010). This attention to voice as an important quality of good citizenship coincides with the increasing educational emphasis on the development of skills for the deliberation of controversial issues, participatory skills for working with others, and the attention to civic issues that are relevant to students' sense of civic identity (Apple, 2010; Haste, 2010).

### Local Focus

A shift in youth focus towards local matters reflects the increasing relevance of personal civic purpose. Civic engagement is increasingly associated with community practices rather than only conventional politics such as voting in elections (Fox et al., 2010; Kassimir & Flanagan, 2010). Pedagogically, this relates to the rise of civic education strategies such as action projects, youth-led and community-based research, and service learning (Cammarota & Fine, 2008; Flanagan & Christens, 2011).

### Affirmative and Transformative Action

Civic engagement has typically been conceived as system-affirmative activities that build on and sustain the prevailing sociopolitical order. However, grassroots organizations, social movements, and political activists highlight structural inequalities that must be recognized and transformed in truly democratic societies. For pedagogy, this implies critical inquiry and social justice agendas (Cammarota, 2007; Fox et al., 2010; Jensen, 2010; Levinson, 2012; Russell, Toomey, Crockett, & Laub, 2010; Seif, 2010).

### The Importance of Context in Civic Education

Context matters. How civic institutions develop and operate depends on sociohistorical context. Likewise, policies and practices in civic education vary across social and cultural contexts. For example, in violence-ridden societies, prioritizing learning how to manage interpersonal conflicts may be seen as a precursor of managing group conflicts. In the innovative K-12 curriculum established in Colombia a decade ago conflict management and human rights education were two core-organizing criteria of civic education (Jaramillo, 2005). In many Asian societies it is explicitly the obligation of a good citizen to take care of the community and to be proactive in maintaining social harmony, even prioritizing this above individual needs (Kennedy, Fairbrother, & Zhao, 2014).

Civic learning is therefore mediated by the individual's experience of membership in multiple cultural groups within larger communities, such as gender, ethnic, religious, or political groups. The meaning that people make of these experiences depends on how they construct and negotiate their identities in each of the groups to which they belong. Engaging civically is not the same for members of minority and discriminated groups that perceive themselves as "outsiders" as it is for members of majority and dominant groups that take their citizenship for granted. For example, students from communities that the system has not served well often fail to connect to civics education that privileges obedience and conformity to middle-class white values (Banks, 2001; Janmaat, 2008; Jensen, 2010; Russell et al., 2010).

We need to understand what are relevant experiences, whether within a formal or informal educational setting, and how to promote these for effective education. Biesta and Lawy (2006) argue that educational research, policy, and practice should not focus on teaching one predetermined canon of citizenship, but focus on understanding how young people's learning of democracy is situated in wider social orders in which the lives of young people unfold. Research across diverse populations demonstrates the plurality of civic practices and developmental paths (Kahne & Sporte, 2008; Kassimir & Flanagan, 2010; Seif, 2010; Zaff, Malanchuk, & Eccles, 2008). For instance, Martin and Chiodo (2008) studied the perceptions of eighth- and eleventh-grade American Indian students regarding citizenship. American Indian students saw citizenship as grounded in community service, and volunteering in tribal activities or participating in their local tribal organization as more relevant alternatives to conventional political activity such as voting and running for political office.

Civic learning is determined by the number, variety, and quality of the opportunities provided to students. Opportunities for civic engagement available to youth are not evenly distributed by social class, race, or ethnicity. Also, some young people's lived experiences result in decisions to civically disengage. Two sets of factors contribute to a lower rate of civic engagement among low-income and minority young adults: cumulative disadvantage—especially parental education—and different institutional opportunities for civic engagement, especially between college and non-college youth (Biesta & Lawy, 2006; Flanagan & Levine, 2010; Kahne & Sporte, 2008; Zaff, Kawashima-Ginsberg, & Lin, 2011).

Recognizing the contextual nature of civic education will contribute to aligning teaching practices and programs more effectively with the democratic ideals of pluralism and equality. Llewellyn et al. (2010) examined the perspectives on civic learning of teachers and students in four secondary schools in Ottawa, Canada. They found that, while students in their study had a breadth of knowledge about current civic issues that were relevant to them, civic education paid little attention to that. Both teachers and students claimed that this made it very difficult to encourage youth participation in democratic processes.

Mason, Cremin, and Warwick (2011) use an ecological systems approach to explore the civic learning experiences of three different groups of young people living in areas of socioeconomic disadvantage in Britain. They analyzed young people's experiences of expressing their voice, civic participation, volunteering, and altruism; their motivations for civic participation; and the challenges they face that may prevent civic participation and action. While there is variation in levels of civic engagement, their findings suggest that the lived experiences of some students lead them to decisions to civically disengage. Young people who were minimally engaged had more direct experience of crime, prejudice, poor education, and intrusive policing. Students commented on how several interactions with teachers, police officers, neighbors, and employers had taught them to disengage and keep their heads down. For example, some students explained that they were unhappy that the system for providing meals at their school had been modified in response to healthy-eating drives. The students were not opposed to healthy eating per se, but they were upset that they had not been involved in making a decision that affected them. They objected that the change was done to them rather than with them and their response was to deliberately boycott the school's meal service. The lack of consultation was described as a demotivating lesson that taught that they could not make a difference.

Finkel and Ernst (2005) conducted a study that examined the effects of a postapartheid civic education program (*Democracy for All*) on South African high-school students in the late 1990s. The results show that exposure to civic instruction (i.e., passive or lecture-based instruction) has relatively strong effects on political knowledge, while having no impact on political attitudes, values, and participatory dispositions such as civic duty, tolerance, institutional trust, or the acquisition of civic skills. These dimensions of civic learning require high degrees of active, participatory methods that give students the opportunity to practice democratic participation, exercise democratic skills, and adopt democratic values (e.g., role playing, dramatizations, group decision making, mock elections, mock trials, classroom discussions of political and social issues). Importantly, the effect of such methods is also seen for political knowledge.

Similarly, an evaluation of *Project Citizen* civic education program in Bosnia found that active involvement by students in developing and implementing actual public policy recommendations had a positive effect on several democratic orientations (Soule, 2000).

## The Process and Outcomes of Change: Three Examples

To exemplify this period of expansion and redefinition of civic education, we explore three examples. The first is the role of new media, the second is the importance of critical enquiry, and the third concerns how history teaching reflects goals of civic education.

### *The Increasing Role of New Media in Education*

New media present highly innovative opportunities for civic education. They challenge many traditional ways of teaching, as well as contribute to extensive democratization in society at large. These tools make possible radically new practices of civic engagement and civic education; their potential has yet to be fully realized. While in many non-Western countries, and in lower-socioeconomic groups everywhere, there is less access to computers, cell phones increasingly with internet access are now nearly universally available and in developing countries are used for many activities performed on PCs in industrialized countries. Such access will increase rapidly, as will the form and scope of media interaction.

The democratization facilitated by new media has been widely evident in rapid mobilization of social movements, in mainstream political activity such as electioneering, and in the huge volume of information and opinion conveyed through Twitter and blogging. These put the power of communication in the hands of ordinary citizens rather than only corporate media. How this power is used and how effective it is may be problematic; there are educational implications of preparing young people for selection, critical judgment, and online discussion (Apple, 2010; Banaji & Buckingham, 2013; Earl & Kimport, 2011; Facer, 2011; Haste, 2010; McLeod et al., 2010).

Facer (2011) summarizes the democratization benefits as "emerging networked publics and the related tools to support accountability, social movement-building and democracy" (p. 89). New media provide public spaces, schools can be sites for "doing" democracy, and inside and out of school new media provide places for social and civic learning. Citizen journalism leads to new forms of accountability, individual action can easily be aggregated, and traditional institutions can be bypassed. These are all tools for decision making and deliberation.

The "bottom-up" potentials of new media challenge non-collaborative learning models where the teacher's role is as conduit of the canon (Bers, 2008). When knowledge can be accessed by the individual learner via the internet, the teacher's role may shift from authority to choreographer. Collaborative learning, the creation of learning spaces, and the production of understanding require praxis, not just assimilation. New media hugely enlarge the scope of these learning contexts in all fields. This also reflects the shift to recognizing that learning must start from where the learners are, what their activities are, and what engages them (Rheingold, 2008). This is especially important in the civic domain. There is often a gap between the highly skilled and intensive out-of-school technology use and how technology is used in a traditional teaching framework.

The MacArthur Foundation's Youth and Participatory Politics research program, with nearly 3,000 U.S. respondents, has been a major source of data on youth and media in the civic context. For example, friendship-based, interest-based, and politics-based digital participation are different and also different media are used for different purposes (Cohen, Kahne, Bowyer, Middaugh, & Rogowski, 2012; Kahne, Middaugh, Lee, & Feezell, 2012). In one study, 41% engaged in participatory politics, which include starting an online discussion around politics, blogging on a political issue, or sharing politics-related material. Weinstein (2014) found that civically engaged young people vary in how they wish to present their civic identity and activities; some are happy to write about their civic interests in all their social media, others separate the topics they address in different media. Yet others avoid any overlap between social topics and their civic identity.

The patterns of media use in civic engagement suggest several education strategies. For example, Kahne, Lee, and Feezell (2012) found that greater digital media literacy experience in high school and college, in a California sample, was related to greater civic awareness, politically driven online participation, and greater exposure to diverse points of view, countering the view that young people select only those with whom they agree.

Interactive media provide spaces for "communities of practice" where learning and production of ideas and solutions are collaborative, and where civic identities are constituted through social practices. Ito (2010) argues that "engagement with media (itself a form of mediated sociability) is a constitutive part of how we learn to participate as culturally competent, social and knowledgeable beings" (p. 18). Games are increasingly being developed to expose young people to civic practices and to different community experiences (Bennett et al., 2010; Salen, 2007). Kahne, Middaugh, and Evans (2008) explored participation in games in which players helped others, organized groups or guilds, explored social or ethical issues, learned about a problem in society, or had to make decisions about how a community, city, or nation should be run. They found that game characteristics and the context of play rather than the quantity of game playing correlated with civic participation.

## Critical Inquiry and the Discussion of Controversial Issues

A significant body of theory and research stresses the importance of engaging students in rigorous critical inquiry and in open classroom discussion about relevant civic issues (Hess, 2009; Nussbaum, 2006). This is particularly salient in civic education informed by conceptions of democracy as deliberation and social justice that recognize the pervasiveness and importance of conflict, controversy, and dissent in social and political life, as well as the power relations and different forms of systemic violence, oppression, and exclusion that require change. In this spirit, Stitzlein (2012) argues that the legitimacy of democratic governance depends on the state obtaining the consent of the governed. But he points out that this requirement also entails the reverse: the possibility of dissent, or of raising disagreement and advocating for change when the needs and rights of people are not adequately taken care of. Critical inquiry and classroom discussion are also relevant strategies for civic education programs that seek to cultivate democracy as a way of living committed to values such as inclusiveness, pluralism, cooperation, dialogue, and non-violent resolution of conflict.

Generally speaking, deliberation processes engage people in discussion with others about public issues that are controversial but require collective decision making and action. Unlike debates where participants trade claims and counterclaims in an antagonistic process, deliberation requires dialogue and collaboration in constructing solutions that are infused with a perspective of "the public," and acceptable for the multiple sides (Hess, 2009). Studies conducted in different contexts demonstrate that engaging students in the deliberation of civic issues has persistent positive effects on different dimensions of civic learning. In a large-scale study of civic education of 14-year-olds in 28 countries, Torney-Purta et al. (2001) found that school-based experience of open discussion is a significant predictor of civic knowledge, tolerance, and support for democratic values. Kahne and Sporte (2008) obtained similar results in an indepth study of ten Chicago city high schools. Beaumont's (2010) study of undergraduate students across the United States also shows that it helps students to see politics as relevant to their own lives and concerns and to gain an increased sense of political efficacy.

Productive deliberation requires that participants have basic knowledge, skills, and dispositions to participate in the process of discussion, develop a sophisticated understanding of the issues at stake, and arrive at fair decisions that represent diverse interests. In fact, political theories of deliberation presuppose that people have the cognitive capacity to argue with reasons, evaluate claims and evidence, reflect on their own assumptions, offer justifications, and consider other perspectives (Reykowski, 2006; Rosenberg, 2007). Developmental theory and research have established the varied and complicated paths through which individuals in different contexts develop these capacities. This raises important challenges because in many situations students seem not to be ready to engage in deliberation. For instance, research on moral judgment shows that most people don't develop a postconventional reasoning, yet this is what enables an individual to consider the perspectives of others outside of their own groups of membership or to consider claims that go against the grain of societal conventions (Kohlberg, 1984). As several teachers report, students tend to vent their opinions with passion but with little thorough analysis, and quickly dismiss unfamiliar perspectives (Hess, 2009).

However, proponents of this kind of pedagogy argue that it is in the actual practice of dissent and dialogue that participants have the opportunity to develop these skills and dispositions (Nussbaum, 2006; Rosenberg, 2007; Stitzlein, 2012). When students engage in guided process of discussion with the aim of constructing a sophisticated understanding of complex issues and agreeing on reasonable courses of action, they practice how to listen, take different perspectives, ask questions of others, explain and justify their claims, attempt to persuade others, and challenge other viewpoints (Davies, 2008; Hess, 2009; Ruitenberg, 2009). Therefore, even if students have not fully developed these capacities and dispositions, the process of deliberation creates a context and a process that is favorable for their development. Likewise, it is an effective strategy acquiring knowledge, building informed opinions, and strengthening students' voice (Fishkin & Farrar, 2005).

### Critical Enquiry

It is important to stress the role of critical inquiry in deliberation. Critical inquiry engages with the complexities of civic life and its conflicts, rather than oversimplifying the problems that emerge in it and dismissing or silencing those who confront us (Nussbaum, 2006; Youniss, 2011). Pedagogy of critical inquiry can purposefully teach students to use a variety of cognitive tools for such purpose. Based on an analysis of different theoretical approaches and pedagogical models of critical inquiry, Bermudez (2015) proposes that teachers help students gain mastery of four cognitive tools for critical inquiry that are particularly relevant in in the social domain: Problem posing, reflective skepticism, multiperspectivity, and systemic thinking (Bermudez, 2015). Each of these tools serves to engage with a different dimension of the complexity of civic issues.

Problem posing is the tool for raising questions about issues that are potentially problematic, on which there is no consensus, or on which existing consensus needs to be disturbed. This resonates with Nussbaum's (2006) call for education to increase the freedom of the mind from tradition, dominant views, and established order. But once a controversy is raised, students must know how to analyze the ambiguities of political issues. Reflective skepticism is the tool that serves students through the careful examination of the reasonableness and validity of the different claims made, drawing upon both epistemological and moral criteria.

Multiperspectivity helps students to recognize different and often contending viewpoints and to coordinate them in

multivocal accounts and integrative solutions. These are fundamental aspects of a civil capacity to hear the other side and engage with conflict constructively in order to work towards shared goals (Beaumont, 2010; Davies, 2008; Hess, 2009; Mutz, 2006). Critical inquiry also requires that students learn to reconstruct the wider societal systems and historical process in which particular civic issues, institutions, practices, and principles are situated. This is the task of systemic thinking. Several authors point out that traditional civics and history education often teach concepts in a vacuum and present one-dimensional and triumphalist views of democracy. Their research shows that this does little to engage students' interest or to help them understand the complexities of civic struggles for freedom, inclusiveness, pluralism, or justice. Furthermore, systemic thinking is also indispensable if students are to understand that decisions taken today may have long-term effects, or that current practices and situations are the result of long-term and systemic dynamics. Similarly, in order to understand the notion of "public interest," students must learn to establish the interdependence that exists between various elements in a society.

Pedagogical approaches that emphasize student engagement in critical inquiry and deliberation resonate with three other important features of "new civics." First, they focus on issues of public concern that are highly significant to students and strive to connect what students learn with their own experience as emerging citizens (Beaumont, 2010; Cammarota & Fine, 2008; Hess, 2009; Rubin & Hayes, 2010; Youniss, 2011).

Second, critical inquiry and deliberation provide a constructive pedagogical approach to teach about the obstacles, flaws, and failures of democracy. Among others, Torney-Purta (2002) stresses that students need to learn about practices such as corruption or the monopoly of power that pose grave "threats to democracy." Others insist that they must learn to confront structural inequalities, the various forms of oppression and alienation that citizens endure in both emerging and established democracies (Fox et al., 2010; Levinson, 2010, Seif, 2010; Swartz, 2006). This relates to what Rubin and Hayes (2010) characterize as teaching in *contexts of disjuncture* in which many youths learn about democracy. Left unexamined, the contradiction between the principles of democracy and the lived experiences of students are likely to generate frustration, despair, and disenchantment. However, if addressed through critical inquiry and deliberation, there are better chances of fostering in students a more sophisticated understanding of the challenges and fragility of democracy and of the need and possibilities of transformative civic action (Alexander et al., 2011; Biesta and Lawy, 2006; Hart & Gullan, 2010; Llewellyn et al., 2010).

Third, the practice of critical inquiry and deliberation continuously draws upon students' identities as they try to make sense and negotiate the issues at stake. Bermudez (2012) analyzed an extensive online discussion among high-school students regarding issues such as slavery, current discrimination, and police brutality in the United States. Her study describes how students engaged in discursive processes of negotiation, affirmation, recognition, and contestation around competing identities, social narratives, value conflicts, and power differences. This process of negotiation sets in motion a social dynamic that intertwines with the intellectual dynamics of critical inquiry that affects how students come to understand social and historical events.

## Historical Narratives and Civic Education

The acquisition of historical concepts and narratives also has clear implications for civic education. First, most social concepts have a historical dimension that must be correctly represented. Second, history education has always been closely related to civic education through the development of both nationalism and patriotism (Van Sledright, 2008). Researchers identify two competing objectives of school history (Barton, 2008; Wineburg, 2001). We argue that history taught in any national school system attends to two different goals: to make students "love their country" and to make them "understand their past" (Seixas, 2004). In practice, more than half of school history content in most countries is related to national history and not to world history. There is an important contemporary debate about the presence of this national canon in school history (Grever & Stuurman, 2007).

In recent decades, scholarship on history education has recognized that this school subject may have an important function in the formation of critical and autonomous citizens (Barton, 2012). Because of this emerging conception, history teaching is no longer structured merely around superficial knowledge of political characters, dates, and significant events of the past. Instead, the objective is for students to understand both the processes of historical changes and the influence of these processes in the present. In other words, students can learn to think historically (Seixas, 2004; Wineburg, 2001) through a constructive use of both declarative and procedural historical knowledge (Monte-Sano, de la Paz, & Felton, 2014; Seixas & Morton, 2013).

Numerous historians and educational researchers have criticized school history curricula because of their nationalistic and patriotic educational practices both in and out of school (Berger, 2012; Carretero, 2011). This is particularly the case for patriotic rituals such as the Pledge of Allegiance, contents of national historical museums, and other informal educational devices such as TV series and media in general. Such formal and informal educational practices relating history education to civic education purvey an essentialist understanding of the concept and narrative of the nation (Lopez, Carretero, & Rodriguez-Moneo, 2015). That is to say, students tend to think that nations, particularly their own nation, have always existed and that things could not be otherwise.

Carretero and Bermudez (2012) have described four dimensions of historical narratives:

1. The historical subject is established in terms of inclusion and exclusion, radically opposing it to others as a coherent and homogeneous group. The national group is internally unified, and at the same time, it is set apart as absolutely different from another, often simplified, historical group.

2. Identification processes work in the narrative, attaching personal affect and value judgments to the unification and opposition mentioned above. The historical subject is referred to in the first-person plural "us," often logically opposed to "them," and valued more positively. A shared identity—a timeless national identity—between the present storyteller and the past historical subject is established.

3. The historical events are simplified around one common narrative theme, such as the search for freedom or territory. As indicated in other studies (e.g., Wertsch, 2002), this search only considers the freedom of a specific group: the freedom of the historical subject. The narrative tends to minimize, and avoids mentioning, the right to freedom of additional subjects, such as natives, slaves, or women. Also, this particular freedom is considered in a teleological way, as the pre-established outcome of the historical processes.

4. National identity is perceived as a natural property and a condition pre-existing the nation, instead of being considered as a consequence of social and historical processes.

The relation between identity and civic and historical understanding is important and a challenge for pedagogy. In one study, even though older students (eleventh-grade compared to seventh-grade students) showed a better historical understanding, half still held an essentialist concept of the nation (Carretero & Van Alphen, 2014). As Hammack (2010) argues, identity can be at the same time both a burden and a benefit in the process of historical comprehension. National identification could both hinder and promote historical and civic understanding. Lopez, Carretero, and Rodriguez-Moneo (2014) have shown that university students understand much better the historical concept of nation when it is not their own. These data highlight important questions for the pedagogical relationship between civic and historical understanding.

## Conclusion

Our goal with this chapter was to show the vibrancy of the field of civic education both in research and in pedagogical innovation. This vibrancy manifests in the emergence of "new civics," an approach to civic education that is grounded in recognizing the actual civic experience of youth in diverse sociocultural contexts, and seeks to engage students in hands-on reflexive practice as a means to help them make and negotiate meaning of civic issues, processes, and opportunities.

First we discuss how current developmental psychology contributes to transforming traditional civic education and giving rise to "new civics." We emphasize how these perspectives recast the student as an active learner, and expand the dimensions of civic learning to include a comprehensive base of civic and historical knowledge and conceptual understanding and a variety of cognitive, participatory, and motivational skills. A sociocultural perspective on development predicates that effective pedagogy needs to attend to cultural and context resources and engage students in critical reflection, dialogue, and negotiation around them.

Second, we explore issues that underlie the evolving definition of civic engagement. These include different meanings of democracy, as well as changes in the extent and style of youth participation, their targets of concern and particularly their means of expressing political action, for example, through new social media. A major consequence has been to broaden the definition of a "good citizen," beyond participating in conventional practices such as voting and party politics. These discussions expand the building blocks of civic learning, and the attention needed to hands-on learning through reflective engagement with relevant civic experiences, civic education through new media, and student engagement in critical inquiry and the deliberation of controversial issues.

A pressing challenge for future work is to continue expanding civic education grounded in students making and negotiating meaning around age-appropriate and culturally relevant civic experiences. This contrasts strongly with a civic education agenda that is designed to socialize students into a predefined political order, instead of considering what actually motivates citizens' behavior and harnessing that to foster a critical and transformative approach to civic life. This brings also the challenge of recognizing and strengthening cultural diversity in the experience and meaning of civic engagement, while equalizing the variety and quality of civic learning opportunities across social groups.

From a pedagogical perspective, an important challenge is to integrate the renewed building blocks of civic learning into a cohesive civic competence that sustains a democratic culture. An active civil society requires citizens who have relevant knowledge and deep understanding, but also the skills for reflective and responsible action, willingness to engage, and deep commitment to democratic values. In the absence of integration, factual knowledge, values, and skills are reduced to discrete elements that may not be applied or used consistently when needed. In contrast, when they interact with each other around projects of actual civic engagement, they transform into "usable knowledge" that is relevant, transferable, and applicable in a variety of real-life situations. This approach has a better potential of harnessing the developmental potential of individuals, taking stock of cultural resources made available to them. Particular attention must be given to research and practice that contribute to developing in students a critical understanding of social conflict and our means of resolution.

## Acknowledgments

This paper was written with the support of projects EDU-2013-42531 (DGICYT, Spain) and PICT 2012-1594 (ANPCYT, Argentina), both coordinated by the first author.

## References

Alexander, H., Pinson, H., & Yonah, Y. (2011). *Citizenship, education and social conflict*. New York: Routledge.

Amadeo, J., Torney-Purta, J., Lehmann, R., Husfeldt, V., & Nikolova, R. (2002). *Civic knowledge and engagement: An IEA study of upper secondary students in sixteen countries*. Amsterdam: International Association for the Evaluation of Educational Achievement. (IEA).

Apple, M. W. (2010). *Global crisis, social justice and education*. New York: Routledge.

Arnot, M., & Swartz, S. (2012). Youth citizenship and the politics of belonging. *Comparative Education, 48*(1) 1–10.

Banaji, S., & Buckingham, D. (2013). *The civic web: Young people, the internet and civic participation*. Cambridge, MA: MIT Press.

Banks, J. A. (2001). *Cultural diversity and education: Foundations, curriculum and teaching*. Boston: Pearson, Allyn & Bacon.

Barrett, M. (2007). *Children's knowledge, beliefs and feelings about nations and national groups*. NY: Psychology Press.

Barrett, M., & Davies, E. (Eds.). (2005). *Children's understanding of society*. NY: Psychology Press.

Barton, K. C. (2008). Research on students´ ideas about history. In L. Levstik & C. A. Tyson (Eds.), *Handbook of research in social studies education* (pp. 239–258). New York: Routledge.

Barton, K. C. (2012). Agency, choice and historical action: How history teaching can help students think about democratic decision making. *Citizenship Teaching and Learning, 7*, 131–142.

Beaumont, E. (2010). Political agency and empowerment: Pathways for developing a sense of political efficacy in young adults. In L.R. Sherrod, J. Torney-Purta, & C. Flanagan (Eds.), *Handbook of research on civic engagement and youth* (pp. 225–258). New York: Wiley.

Bennett, W. L., Freelon, D., & Wells, C. (2010). Changing citizen identity and the rise of participatory media culture. In L.R. Sherrod, J. Torney-Purta, & C. Flanagan (Eds.), *Handbook of research on civic engagement in youth* (pp. 393–423). New York: Wiley.

Berger, S. (2012). De-nationalizing history teaching and nationalizing it differently. In M. Carretero, M. Asensio & M. Rodríguez-Moneo (Eds.), *History education and the construction of national identities* (pp. 33–47). Charlotte, CT: Information Age Publishing.

Bermudez, A. (2012). Youth civic engagement: decline or transformation? A critical review. *Journal of Moral Education, 41*(4), 529–542.

Bermudez, A. (2015). Four tools for critical inquiry in history, social studies and civic education. *Revista de Estudios Sociales, 52*.

Bers, M. U. (2008). Civic identities, online technologies: From designing civic curriculum to supporting civic experiences. In L. Bennett (Ed.), *Civic life online: Learning how digital media can engage youth* (pp. 139–159). Cambridge, MA: MIT Press.

Berti, A. E. (2002). Children's understanding of society: Psychological studies and their educational implications. In *Children's understanding in the new Europe* (pp. 89–107). Stoke on Trent: Trentham Books.

Berti, A. E., & Andriolo, A. (2001). Third graders' understanding of core political concepts (law, nation-state, government) before and after teaching. *Genetic, Social, and General Psychology Monographs, 127*(4), 346–377.

Biesta, G., & Lawy, R. (2006). From teaching citizenship to learning democracy: Overcoming individualism in research, policy and practice. *Cambridge Journal of Education, 36*(1), 63–79.

Blades, D., & Richardson, G. (2006). Introduction: Troubling the canon of citizenship education. In G. Richardson & D. Blades (Eds.), *Troubling the canon of citizenship education* (pp. 1–9). New York: Peter Lang.

Bloch-Schulman, S. (2010). When the "best hope" is not so hopeful, what then? Democratic thinking, democratic pedagogies, and higher education. *Journal of Speculative Philosophy, 24*(4), 399–415.

Brown, T. M. & Rodriguez, L. F. (Eds.). (2009). Youth in participatory action research. *New directions for youth development*. San Francisco, CA: Jossey Bass.

Cammarota, J. (2007) A social justice approach to achievement: Guiding Latino/a students toward educational attainment with a challenging, socially relevant curriculum. *Equity and Excellence in Education, 40*(1), 87–96.

Cammarota, J., & Fine, M. (2008). *Revolutionizing education: Youth participatory action research in motion*. New York: Routledge.

Campbell, D. E. (2008). Voice in the classroom: How an open classroom climate fosters political engagement among adolescents. *Political Behavior, 30*, 437–454.

Carnegie Corporation of New York and CIRCLE Center for Information and Research on Civic Learning and Engagement (2003). *The civic mission of schools*. New York: Carnegie Corporation of New York and CIRCLE Center for Information and Research on Civic Learning and Engagement.

Carretero, M. (2011). Constructing patriotism. *Teaching history and memories in global worlds*. Charlotte, NC: Information Age Publishing.

Carretero, M., & Bermudez, A. (2012). Constructing histories. In J. Valsiner (Ed.), *Oxford handbook of culture and psychology* (pp. 625–646). Oxford: Oxford University Press.

Carretero, M., Castorina, J. A., & Levinas, M. L. (2013). Conceptual change and historical narratives about the nation: A theoretical and empirical approach. In S. Vosniadou (Ed.), *International handbook of research in conceptual change* (pp. 269–287). New York: Routledge.

Carretero, M., & Van Alphen, F. (2014). Do master narratives change among high school students? Analyzing national historical representations characteristics. *Cognition and Instruction*, *32*(3), 1–23.

Chi, B., Jastrzab, J., & Melchior, A. (2006). Developing indicators and measures of civic outcomes for elementary school students. *CIRCLE - Working paper 47: CIRCLE*. Medford, MA: The Center for Information and Research on Civic Learning and Engagement.

Cohen, C., Kahne, J., Bowyer, B., Middaugh, E., & Rogowski, J. (2012). *Participatory politics: New media and youth political action*. Retrieved from http://www.civicsurvey.org/publications/107 (accessed February 20, 2015).

Cox, C. B., Jaramillo, R., & Reimers, F. (2005). *Education for citizenship and democracy in the Americas: An agenda for action*. Washington, D.C.: Inter-American Development Bank.

Davies, L. (2008). *Educating against extremism*. Sterling, VA: Trentham Books.

Diazgranados, S., & Selman, R. (2014). How students' perceptions of the school climate affect their choice to upstand, bystand or join perpetrators of bullying. *Harvard Educational Review*, *84*(1).

Earl, J., & Kimport, K. (2011). *Digitally enabled social change*. Cambridge, MA: MIT Press.

Facer, K. (2011). *Learning futures: Education, technology and social change*. New York: Routledge.

Fine, M. (2004). *Making our children more humane: Facing history and ourselves as civic education*. Brookline: FHAO.

Fine, M., Bermudez, A., & Barr, D. (2007). *Civic learning survey—Developed for the National Professional Development and Evaluation Project (NPDEP), a longitudinal outcome study of the Facing History and Ourselves program from 2005–2010*. Brookline, MA: Facing History and Ourselves.

Finkel, S. E. & Ernst, H. R. (2005). Civic education in post-apartheid South Africa: Alternative paths to the development of political knowledge and democratic values. *Political Psychology*, *26*(3), 333–366.

Fishkin, J., and Farrar, C. (2005). Deliberative polling. In J. Gastil & P. Levine (Eds.), *The deliberative democracy handbook*. San Francisco: Jossey-Bass.

Flanagan, C. (2013). *Teenage citizens: The political theories of the young*. Cambridge, MA: Harvard University Press.

Flanagan, C. & Christens, B. D. (Eds.). (2011). Youth civic development: Work at the cutting edge. In *New directions for child and adolescent development* (p. 134). San Francisco, CA: Jossey Bass.

Flanagan, C., & Levine, P. (2010). Civic engagement and the transition to adulthood. *Future of Children*, *20*(1), 159–179.

Fox, M., Mediratta, K., Ruglis, J., Stoudt, B., Seema, S., & Fine, M. (2010). Critical youth engagement: Participatory action research and organizing. In L. R. Sherrod, J. Torney-Purta, & C. Flanagan (Eds.), *Handbook of research on civic engagement in youth* (pp. 621–649). Hoboken, NJ: John Wiley.

Ginwright, S. (2008). Collective radical imagination: Youth participatory action research and the art of emancipatory knowledge. In J. Cammarota & M. Fine (Eds.), *Revolutionizing education: Youth participatory action research in motion* (pp. 13–22). New York: Routledge.

Ginwright, S. (2010). *Black youth rising: Activism and radical healing in urban America*. New York: Teachers College Press.

Grever, M., & Stuurman, S. (Eds.) (2007). *Beyond the canon: History for the 21st century*. Basingstoke: Macmillan.

Gutmann, A., & Thompson, D. (2004). *Why deliberative democracy?* Princeton, NJ: Princeton University Press.

Hammack, P. L. (2010). Identity as burden or benefit? Youth, historical narrative, and the legacy of political conflict. *Human Development*, 53, 173–201.

Hart, D., & Gullan, R. (2010). The sources of adolescent activism: Historical and contemporary findings. In L. R. Sherrod, J. Torney-Purta, & C. Flanagan (Eds.), *Handbook of research on civic engagement in youth* (pp. 67–90). Hoboken, NJ: John Wiley.

Haste, H. (2004). Constructing the citizen. *Political Psychology*, *25*(3), 413–439.

Haste, H. (2010). Citizenship education: A critical look at a contested field. In L. R. Sherrod, J. Torney-Purta, & C. Flanagan (Eds.), *Handbook of research on civic engagement in youth* (pp. 161–188). Hoboken, NJ: John Wiley.

Haste, H. (2014). Culture, tools and subjectivity: The (re) construction of self. In T. Magioglou (Ed.), *Culture and political psychology* (pp. 27–48). Charlotte, NC: Information Age Publishers.

Haste, H., & Abrahams, S. (2008). Morality, culture and the dialogic self: Taking cultural pluralism seriously. *Journal of Moral Education*, *37*(3), 357–374.

Haste, H., & Hogan, A. (2006). Beyond conventional civic participation, beyond the moral–political divide: Young people and contemporary debates about citizenship. *Journal of Moral Education*, *35*(4), 473–493.

Haste, H., & Hogan, A. (2012). The future shapes the present: Scenarios, metaphors and civic action. In M. Carretero, M. Asensio, & M. Rodríguez-Moneo (Eds.), *History education and the construction of national identities* (pp. 311–326). Charlotte, CT: Information Age Publishing.

Hess, D. (2009). *Controversy in the classroom: The democratic power of discussion*. New York: Routledge.

Hess, D., & Gatti, L. (2010). Putting politics where it belongs: In the classroom. *New Directions for Higher Education*, *152*, 10–26.

Ito, M. (2010). *Hanging out, messing around and geeking out*. Cambridge, MA: MIT Press.

Janmaat, J. G. (2008). The civic attitudes of ethnic minority youth and the impact of citizenship education. *Journal of Ethnic and Migration Studies*, *34*(1), 27–54.

Jaramillo, R. (2005). The experience of Colombia. In V. Espinola (Ed.), *Education for citizenship and democracy in a globalized world: A comparative perspective* (pp. 87–90). Washington, DC: Inter-American Development Bank.

Jensen, L. A. (2010). Immigrant youth in the United States: Coming of age among diverse civic cultures. In, L. R. Sherrod, J. Torney-Purta, & C. Flanagan (Eds.), *Handbook of research on civic engagement in youth* (pp. 425–444). Hoboken, NJ: John Wiley.

Kahne, J., Lee, N., & Feezell, J. (2012). *Digital media literacy education and online civic and political participation*. Retrieved from http://www.civicsurvey.org/publications/46 (accessed February 20, 2015).

Kahne, J., Middaugh, E., & Evans, C. (2008). *The civic potential of video games. MacArthur Foundation*. Retrieved from http://www.digitallearning.macfound.org.

Kahne, J., Middaugh, E., Lee, N., & Feezell J. (2012). *Youth online activity and exposure to diverse perspectives*. Retrieved from http://www.civicsurvey.org/publications/203 (accessed February 20, 2014).

Kahne, J., & Sporte, S. (2008). Developing citizens: The impact of civic learning opportunities on students' commitment to civic participation. *American Educational Research Journal*, *45*(3), 738–766.

Kahne, J., & Westheimer, J. (2006) The limits of political efficacy: Educating citizens for a democratic society. *PSOnline*, April, 289–296.

Kassimir, R., & Flanagan, C. (2010). Youth civic engagement in the developing world: Challenges and opportunities. In L. R. Sherrod, J. Torney-Purta, & C. Flanagan (Eds.), *Handbook of research on civic engagement in youth* (pp. 91–113). Hoboken, NJ: John Wiley.

Kennedy, K. J., Fairbrother, G. P., & Zhao, Z. (2014). *Citizenship education in China: Preparing citizens for the "Chinese century"*. New York: Routledge.

Kirlin, M. (2003). The role of civic skills in fostering civic engagement. *CIRCLE -Working paper 06: CIRCLE*. Medford, MA: The Center for Information and Research on Civic Learning and Engagement.

Kohlberg, L. (1984). *The psychology of moral development: The nature and validity of moral stages*. San Francisco, CA: Harper & Row.

Levinson, M. (2010). The civic empowerment gap: Defining the problem and locating solutions. In L. R. Sherrod, J. Torney-Purta, & C. Flanagan (Eds.), *Handbook of research on civic engagement in youth* (pp. 331–361). Hoboken, NJ: John Wiley.

Levinson, M. (2012). *No citizen left behind*. Cambridge, MA: Harvard University Press.

Lickona, T. (1997). Educating for character: A comprehensive approach. In A. Molnar (Ed.), *The construction of children's character* (pp. 45–62). Chicago, IL: The University of Chicago Press.

Lievrouw, L. A. (2011). *Alternative and activist new media*. Cambridge, UK: Polity Press.

Llewellyn, K. R., Cook, S. A., & Molina, A. (2010). Civic learning: Moving from the apolitical to the socially just. *Journal of Curriculum Studies, 42*(6), 791–812.

Lopez, C., Carretero, M., & Rodriguez-Moneo, M. (2014). Telling a national narrative not of your own. Does it enable disciplinary historical understanding? *Culture & Psychology, 20*(4), 547–571.

Lopez, C., Carretero, M., & Rodriguez-Moneo, M. (2015). Conquest or reconquest? Students' conceptions of nation embedded in a historical narrative. *Journal of the Learning Sciences, 2*, 252–285.

Martin, L. A., & Chiodo, J.J. (2008). American Indian students speak out: What's good citizenship. *International Journal of Social Education, 23*(1), 1–26.

Mason, C., Cremin, H., & Warwick, P. (2011) Learning to (dis)engage? The socializing experiences of young people living in areas of socio-economic disadvantage. *British Journal of Educational Studies, 59*(4), 403–419.

McIntosh, H., & Youniss, J. (2010). Toward a political theory of political socialization of Youth. In L. R. Sherrod, J. Torney-Purta, & C. Flanagan (Eds.), *Handbook of research on civic engagement in youth* (pp. 23–41). Hoboken, NJ: John Wiley.

McLeod, J., Shan, D., Hess, D., & Lee, N. (2010). Communication and education: Creating competence for socialization into public life. In L. R. Sherrod, J. Torney-Purta, & C. Flanagan (Eds.), *Handbook of research on civic engagement in youth* (pp. 363–391). Hoboken, NJ: John Wiley.

Monte-Sano, C. S., de la Paz, S., & Felton, M. (2014). *Reading, thinking, and writing about history*. New York: Teachers College Press.

Mutz, D. C. (2006). *Hearing the other side: Deliberative versus participatory democracy*. New York: Cambridge University Press.

Noddings, N. (Ed.). (2005). *Educating citizens for global awareness*. New York: Teachers College Press.

Nussbaum, M. (2006). Education and democratic citizenship: Capabilities and quality education. *Journal of Human Development, 7*(3) 285–295.

Oser, F., Althof, W., & Higgins-D'Alessandro, A. (2008). The just community approach to moral education: System change or individual change? *Journal of Moral Education, 37*(3), 395–415.

Power, F. C., Higgins, A. & Kohlberg, L. (1989) *Lawrence Kohlberg's approach to moral education*. New York: Columbia Press.

Rawls, J. (1993). *Political liberalism*. New York: Columbia University Pres.

Reykowski, J. (2006). Deliberative democracy and "human nature": An empirical approach. *Political Psychology, 27*(3), 323–346.

Rheingold, H. (2008). Using participatory media and public voice to encourage civic engagement. In L. Bennett (Ed.), *Civic life online: Learning how digital media can engage youth* (pp. 97–118). Cambridge, MA: MIT Press.

Rosenberg, S. W. (2007). Rethinking democratic deliberation: The limits and potential of citizen participation. *Polity, 39*, 335–360.

Rubin, B., & Hayes, B. (2010). "No backpacks" versus "drugs and murder": The promise and complexity of youth civic action research. *Harvard Educational Review, 80*(3), 352–379.

Rubin, B., Hayes, B., & Benson, K. (2009). "It's the worst place to live": Urban youth and the challenge of school-based civic learning. *Theory Into Practice, 48*, 213–221.

Ruitenberg, C. W. (2009). Educating political adversaries: Chantal Mouffe and radical democratic citizenship education. *Studies on Philosophy of Education, 28*, 269–281.

Russell, S. T., Toomey, R. B., Crockett, J., & Laub, C. (2010). LGBT politics, youth activism, and civic engagement. In L. R. Sherrod, J. Torney-Purta, & C. Flanagan (Eds.), *Handbook of research on civic engagement in youth* (pp. 471–494). Hoboken, NJ: John Wiley.

Salen, K. (2007). *The ecology of games: Connecting youth, games, and learning*. Cambridge, MA: MIT Press.

Seider, S. (2012). *Character compass: How powerful school culture can point students towards success*. Cambridge, MA: Harvard University Press.

Seif, H. (2010). The civic life of Latina/o immigrant youth: Challenging boundaries and creating safe spaces. In L. R. Sherrod, J. Torney-Purta, & C. Flanagan (Eds.), *Handbook of research on civic engagement in youth* (pp. 445–470). Hoboken, NJ: John Wiley.

Seixas, P. (Ed.). (2004). *Theorizing historical consciousness*. Toronto: University of Toronto Press.

Seixas, P., & Morton, T. (2013). *The big six historical thinking concepts*. Independence, KY: Cingage Learning.

Selman, R. (2003). *The promotion of social awareness: Powerful lessons from the partnership of developmental theory and classroom practice*. New York: Russell Sage Foundation.

Selman, R., & Kwok, J. (2010). Informed social reflection: Its development and importance for adolescents' civic engagement. In L. R. Sherrod, J. Torney-Purta, & C. Flanagan (Eds.), *Handbook of research on civic engagement in youth* (pp. 651–685). Hoboken, NJ: John Wiley.

Sherrod, L. R., Torney-Purta, J., & Flanagan, C. (Eds.). (2010). *Handbook of research on civic engagement in youth*. Hoboken, NJ: John Wiley.

Sinclair, M. (2004). *Learning to live together: Building skills, values and attitudes for the twenty-first century*. Geneva: UNESCO-International Bureau of Education.

Sinclair, M., Davies, L., Obura, A., & Tibbits, F. (2008). Learning to live together. *Design, monitoring and evaluation of education for life skills, citizenship, peace and human rights*. Eschborn, Germany: UNESCO, IBE, GTZ.

Soule, S. (2000). *Beyond communism and war: The effect of civic education on the democratic attitudes and behavior of Bosnian and Herzegovinian youth*. Calabasas, CA: Center for Civic Education.

Stitzlein, S. M. (2012). *Teaching for dissent: Citizenship education and political activism*. Boulder, CO: Paradigm Publishers.

Swartz, S. (2006). A long walk to citizenship: Morality, justice and faith in the aftermath of apartheid. *Journal of Moral Education, 35*(4), 551–570.

Tausch, N., Becker, J. C., Spears, R., Christ, O., Saab, R., Singh, P., & Siddiqi, R. N. (2011). Explaining radical group behavior: Developing emotion and efficacy routes to normative and non-normative collective action. *Journal of Personality and Social Psychology, 101*(1), 129–148.

Thapa, A., Cohen, J., Guffey, S., & Higgins D'Alessandro, A. (2013). A review of school climate research. *Review of Educational Research, 83*(3), 357–387.

Torney-Purta, J. (2002) Patterns in the civic knowledge, engagement and attitudes of European adolescents: The IEA Civic Education Study. *European Journal of Education, 37*(2), 129–141.

Torney-Purta, J., & Barber, C. (2011). Fostering young people's support for participatory human rights through their developmental niches. *American Journal of Orthopsychiatry, 81*(4), 473–481.

Torney-Purta, J., Lehmann, R., Oswald, H., & Schulz, W. (2001). *Citizenship and education in twenty-eight countries: Civic knowledge and engagement at age fourteen*. Amsterdam: IEA.

Van Sledright, B. A. (2008). Narratives of nation-state, historical knowledge, and school history. *Review of Research in Education, 32*, 109–146.

Weinstein, E. (2014). The personal is political on social media: Online civic expression patterns and pathways among civically engaged youth. *International Journal of Communication, 8*, 210–233.

Wertsch, J. (2002). *Voices of collective remembering*. Cambridge, UK: Cambridge University Press.

West, C. (2004). *Democracy matters: Winning the fight against imperialism*. New York: Penguin.

Westheimer, J. (2008). On the relationship between political and moral engagement. In F. Oser & W. Veugelers (Eds.), *Getting involved: Global citizenship development and sources of moral values* (pp. 17–30). Rotterdam: Sense Publishers.

Westheimer, J., & Kahne, J. (2004). What kind of citizen? The politics of educating for democracy. *American Educational Research Journal, 41*(2), 237–269.

Wineburg, S. (2001). *Historical thinking and other unnatural acts: Charting the future of teaching the past*. Philadelphia, PA: Temple University Press.

Yates, M., & Youniss, J. (Eds.). (1999). *Roots of civic identity: International perspectives on community service and activism in youth*. New York: Cambridge University Press.

Youniss, J. (2011). Civic education: What schools can do to encourage civic identity and action. *Applied Developmental Science, 15*(2), 98–103.

Youniss, J., & Levine, P. (2009*). Engaging young people in civic life*. Nashville, TN: Vanderbilt University Press.

Youniss, J., & Yates, M. (1997). *Community service and social responsibility in youth*. Chicago, IL: University of Chicago Press.

Zaff, J. F., Kawashima-Ginsberg, K., & Lin, E. S. (2011). Advances in civic engagement research: Issues of civic measures and civic context. *Advances in Child Development and Behavior, 41*, 273–308.

Zaff, J. F., Malanchuk, O., & Eccles, J. (2008). Predicting positive citizenship from adolescence to young adulthood: The effects of a civic context. *Applied Developmental Sciences, 12*(8), 38–53.

Zukin, C., Keeter, S., Andolina, M., Jenins, K., & Della Carpini, M. X. (2006). *A new engagement? Political participation, civic life and the changing American citizen*. New York: Oxford University Press.

# Part V

## The Learning and Task Environment

# 23

# Sociocultural Perspectives on Literacy and Learning

*DAVID O'BRIEN*
University of Minnesota Twin Cities

*THERESA ROGERS*
University of British Columbia, Canada

Sociocultural frameworks have been popular for at least four decades in literacy research and pedagogy (e.g. Au, 1980; Dyson, 1993; Gee, 2000; Gutiérrez, 2008; Heath, 1983; Purcell-Gates, 1997, Street, 1984). They have also become increasingly prevalent in framing research questions and explanations for literacy learning and instruction (e.g., Green & Bloome, 1997; Heath, 1991; Lewis, Enciso, & Moje, 2007; Rueda, 2011). These frameworks are influenced largely by the writing of Lev Vygotsky (e.g., *Thought and Language*, 1986; *Mind in Society*, 1978), as well as work in sociolinguistics, anthropology, and critical theory. They stand in contrast to more traditional frameworks for explaining reading processes, assessment, and instruction, within the broader field of literacy, which derive from psychology and are aligned with experimental research. Specifically, the more traditional frameworks draw from cognitive, linguistic, and psycholinguistic views of reading processes with the end goal of developing better models of assessment and teaching.

In this chapter, we attempt to capture the bigger picture of evolving views on literacy under the auspices of sociocultural theory. We begin by connecting the more traditional psychological with sociocultural perspectives, by observing that literacy, like cognition, is most productively viewed as situated. Learners engaged in literacy activities are always simultaneously cognitive and sociocultural participants in situated practices. In this view of mind, learning is mediated by how learners engage with language, literacy, and other tools made available in social contexts (Roth & Lee, 2007; Vygotsky, 1986; see Chapter 1, this volume).

In the situated view of literacy, "text" is neither synonymous with "print" nor subject to linguistic and psycholinguistic rules such as those historically applied in defining connected written discourse, particularly in the context of the recent proliferation of digital and multimodal texts. Nor are literacy practices conflated with schooling and pedagogy in this view. Hence, many theoretical frameworks used to explain reading and writing processes from a traditional print-centric perspective will be inadequate from the standpoint of sociocultural theory, and may eventually be obsolete. This chapter, then, provides an overview of the influences of sociocultural perspectives on literacy research, and it does so in the context of broadened notions of texts, the subjects of reading and writing, and the implications for literacy learning and learners themselves as they participate in situated literacy practices across formal and informal contexts.

We take the position that psychological and sociocultural views can be complementary in research on literacy process and practices and can potentially yield richer theories of learning and teaching. Although we do not address problems related to instruction and assessment here, we do offer implications for research on teaching and learning with some examples from research in instructional contexts. Later in the chapter, we also attempt to explain how studies of digitization and its consequences can be framed as a subfield or focal area within recent literacy research. To do so we define and disambiguate often-confounded terms like "New Literacy Studies" (e.g., Street, 2003), "multimodal literacies" (e.g., Jewitt & Kress, 2003), "multiliteracies" (e.g., New London Group, 1996); and "new literacies" (e.g., Coiro, Knobel, Lankshear, & Leu, 2008)—categories or subfields that are evolving within the context of sociocultural perspectives on literacy.

## Broad Traditions of Psychological and Sociocultural Perspectives on Literacy

In the previous *Handbook of Educational Psychology,* the topics of literacy (Alvermann, Simpson, & Fitzgerald, 2006) and cultural perspectives (Martin, 2006) appeared as separate chapters. In this volume, Wilkinson and Gaffney review literacy intervention studies conducted in schools and classrooms to improve student knowledge in reading, writing, and use of oral language across grades K-12 (Chapter 17). Our chapter integrates sociocultural frameworks with literacy studies to conceptualize problems in educational psychology from a larger, more inclusive literacy perspective. We argue that teaching, learning, motivation, and engagement cannot be understood thoroughly without considering sociocultural dynamics, including how particular learners position themselves, and are positioned socially and discursively as they engage in situated literacy practices.

Also, in the previous handbook, Martin (2006) noted that educational psychology has been traditionally wedded to assumptions about persons, knowledge, and progress (see Chapter 1, this volume). Within these assumptions, learners who stand outside the sociocultural milieu are seen as rational; they are reflective, monitoring their situations, constructing knowledge, self-regulating, using fix-up strategies, and responding to individual tasks. "External" factors, originating in, for example, broader sociocultural contexts, are viewed as factors or variables that might, through interaction, impact the learner's internal state, selection and use of strategies, and performance outcomes.

Psychologists have historically tended to view these contextual factors as confoundings or possible threats to validity, quantified them, and then incorporated them into research designs to measure or control their effects. In contrast, socioculturalists view contextual factors as crucial, complex, often unquantifiable facets of a milieu central to interpreting how practices unfold and what they mean to participants and those studying participants (e.g., Cole & Wertsch, 1996; Purcell-Gates, 2012; Rogoff, 2003). Not only is this sociocultural milieu not to be controlled or factored out, it is considered inseparable from understanding human intentionality, engagement, cultural mediation, and participation based on the nature of each individual's identity, positionality, and agency in relation to others and to particular events and contexts.

Indeed, socioculturally grounded literacy scholars (e.g., Heath, 1983; Moll, Amanti, Neff, & González, 1992; Street, 1984, 1995) take the position that learning is situated and mediated by social practices: that is, mind and its psychological processes are unquestionably social, though individual actors make intellectual decisions and experience contexts uniquely. In fact, intellectual interdependency, mediated by social contexts and discourses, defines what is actually personal. For several decades, sociocultural theorists in literacy have contended that psychologists have downplayed or dismissed the sociocultural dimensions in their research questions and designs, as well as in instruction and assessment (Carey & Harste, 1988; Lewis et al., 2007).

For example, in the fourth edition of *Social Linguistics and Literacies* (2012), Gee noted: "When this book was first written [reference to the first edition in 1990] the traditional view of literacy was 'cognitive' or 'mental'. Literacy was seen as something residing primarily inside people's heads, not society." (p. 1) Lankshear and Knobel (2011) stated in a recent text on new literacies, "The point is, however, that whereas reading has traditionally been conceived in psychological terms, 'literacy' has always been much more of a 'sociological' concept" (p. 12). They continued, "In addition, the sociocultural approach to literacy overtly rejects the idea that textual practices are even largely, let alone solely, a matter of processes that 'go on in the head' or that essentially involve heads communicating with each other by means of graphic signs" (p. 12).

The critiques of psychology by socioculturalists arise for several related reasons. First, socioculturally positioned scholars who draw on anthropology, linguistics, or language study are often less familiar with psychology or its subfields and see this discipline as less important than their own. Consequently, they may tend to oversimplify or essentialize notions of psychology. Second, they believe that meaning making is exclusively or largely a collective, outside-of-the-head process, rather than primarily an inside-the-head process (as focused on by most psychologically oriented researchers). Third, researchers from these other disciplinary traditions may hold negative views of psychology because they believe that its dominance in education, in institutionalized ideologies, practices, and research, has led to devaluing or excluding sociocultural perspectives. The view is that psychologists have simultaneously ignored literacy itself as cultural and ideological sets of practices.

## Sociocultural and Psychological Perspectives as Complements in Literacy Theory and Research

As stated earlier, we believe that psychological and sociocultural views can be theoretical complements in studying literacy teaching and learning. Literacy and literacy practices involve interweaving of the cognitive and the sociocultural. Meaning is always situated, although the experiences and perspectives that make it possible must be represented, stored, and retrievable—part of cognition and mind. The ability to decode words, syntax, and semiotic systems is a transaction between the linguistic and psychological (e.g., Carey & Harste, 1988); that is, it is a psycholinguistic as well as a socially and culturally constituted process. Literacy scholars such as Kathy Au, Anne Dyson, and Annemarie Palinscar began to discuss sociocognitive and sociolinguistic perspectives on reading in the 1980s and 1990s, some in conjunction with the Center for the Study of Reading (CSR). In the early 1990s, under a research agenda conceptualized by Alvermann and Guthrie (1993), scholars affiliated with the National Reading Research Center (NRRC) studied reading as engagement in classrooms, "recognizing the social nature of cognition" (p. 2). Drawing from work such as socially and developmentally oriented research on intrinsic motivation (e.g., Deci & Ryan, 1992), these literacy studies marked another turning point in bridging more traditional cognitive and sociocultural perspectives (Guthrie & Coddington, 2009; Guthrie & Wigfield, 2000).

Therefore, just as "decoding" and making sense of texts entail social and psychological or psycholinguistic processes, approaches focusing on motivation and engagement with texts and literacy practices have come to be recognized for their social, cultural, and cognitive aspects. One's perceptions about ability, self-efficacy, and agency when presented with specific tasks, goals, and various assignments define the literacy event and practices. So, according to this perspective, situatedness can be seen as both a social *and* a psychological construct.

Of course, social and cultural psychologists (e.g., Cole, 1996; Scribner & Cole, 1981) have long studied the relationship between psychology and literacy. Scribner and Cole (1981) gathered evidence on the ways that literacy may or may not be related to specific kinds of abstract thinking, reasoning, and processing of information; and ultimately they were unable to link literacy to general cognitive consequences. And while Cole's (1996) writing illustrates how psychologists have historically marginalized the concept of culture, he also notes that "culture-inclusive" psychologists have not only figured out how to include culture, but have engaged in inquiry on culture-inclusive psychology in ways that are "scientifically acceptable" (p. 2). These inquiries and the theoretical frameworks that support them rely on theoretical constructs of literacy, linguistics, psycholinguistics, and cognition as complements in the human condition, and as necessary in understanding experiences in the world.

Throughout this chapter we maintain the perspective that neither a purely cognitive nor a purely sociocultural perspective—that is, a perspective that does not take into account a situated theory of mind—will help us to fully account for the potential of various kinds of literacy practices, policies, and instructional approaches to benefit a range of learners in particular contexts and over time.

## Contributions of Multiple Disciplines to a Sociocultural View of Literacy: The "Social Turn"

In this section we outline how various lines of scholarship, which fall under the increasingly unwieldy rubric of "sociocultural" theory, have informed contemporary perspectives on literacy learning in and out of schools. We begin with the many influences on the "social turn" in literacy. While Vygotsky's (1978) theory of language and thought—particularly his notion that reasoning is mediated by cultural signs and symbols—is often central to such discussions, the social turn in literacy is also influenced by work originating in the interrelated disciplines of cognitive psychology, sociolinguistics, sociology, anthropology, literary theory, and critical and poststructural theories.

### *Toward Literacy as a Social Practice: Anthropological and Sociolinguistic Perspectives*

In the late 1970s and early 1980s in the United States, literacy studies reflected the "cognitive revolution" emanating from the work of cognitive theorists and reading researchers. This scholarship displayed rich cross-fertilizations of cognitive theory, psycholinguistic theory, and educational practice, and included work drawing on schema theory and reading as information processing (Anderson, 1977; Anderson & Pearson, 1984); the development of teaching strategies for reading comprehension and interpretation (e.g., Tierney & Cunningham, 1984); and connections between reading and writing processes (Tierney & Pearson, 1983). While this research took into account some social and cultural issues related to reading and writing processes, these issues, as we noted above, were often seen as variables in studies that ultimately focused on individual learning outcomes. This line of inquiry continues to be the basis of much ongoing literacy research while also influencing practice in schools in the form of instructional reading strategies, writing process curricula, and approaches to assessment (see Chapter 17, this volume).

However, due largely to a revival of interest in the work of Vygotsky in the late 1970s, many scholars of literacy and language were shifting their interest to the role of social situatedness in shaping understanding. This perspective influenced cognitive theorists, many of whom view cognition as mediated by the role of social contexts during learning tasks. As Mills (2010) noted, offshoots from this interest in social contexts and social construction include the community of scholars studying situated cognition (Brown, Collins, & Duguid, 1989; Greeno, 1997; Lave, 1988), communities of practice, and situated learning (e.g., Lave & Wenger, 1991).

While this sociocognitive work was just beginning to take hold in the field, a rich parallel tradition in anthropology and sociolinguistics began to inform the way educators were thinking about literacy practices beyond schools. Most notably, in the early 1980s, Shirley Brice Heath's work (1983) began to influence new conceptualizations of literacy as a social practice. Her key argument was that the uses of language and ways of communicating are socially and culturally produced, as evidenced by her study of two very different working-class communities in the southern United States. The communities had contrasting patterns of orality and literacy practices, which in turn contrasted with "mainstream" or more dominant literacy practices and with school literacy practices. She illustrated these differences through rich ethnographic descriptions of the varying uses of storytelling and written literacy practices. As Heath (1982) stated, "Literacy events must . . . be interpreted in relation to the larger sociocultural patterns which they exemplify or reflect" (p. 74).

Much of what we now call "family and community literacy research" (Barton & Hamilton, 1998; Moll et al., 1992; Purcell-Gates, 1997) is concerned with literacy in everyday lives, echoing Heath's work in various ways. For instance, Taylor and Dorsey-Gaines (1988) argued that even when homes are filled with a range of rich literacy practices, children can experience a disjuncture between home and school language and literacy practices. Researchers working from a critical perspective argued against locating risk primarily within families, rather than focusing on the ways schools might be more sensitive and responsive to variations across home, community, and school literacy practices (see Delpit, 1986; Swadener & Lubeck, 1995).

Around the same time that Heath's book, *Ways with Words,* was published, Brian Street argued in *Literacy in Theory and Practice* (1984) that any analysis of literacy practices is by definition a study of ideology, and related to the particular social, historical, and political contexts in which it is situated. He contrasted this view with perspectives that view literacy to be a set of neutral, decontextualized, transferable skills, or what he termed an "autonomous" theory of literacy. In this book, Street draws on, among other theorists, the work of Scribner and Cole (1981) and Labov (1973) to debunk the "great divide" theory of literacy, i.e., that preliterate societies lack the capability for rational or logical thinking (Goody & Watt, 1963; Ong, 1967). Street also draws on Graff's (1979) argument related to the "literacy myth"—that increased literacy skills necessarily result in economic, social, and cultural success; in fact, the meanings and functions of literacy in people's lives are much more contextually laden. Although aspects of Street's argument have been critiqued (see, for example, Brandt & Clinton, 2002), his work continues to be a key influence on social practice views of literacy in particular and on sociocultural literacy perspectives more broadly.

Other sociolinguists in the field of language and literacy in the 1980s and 1990s provided additional rich analyses of the social contexts of literacy and literacy instruction in schools. Exemplars include David Bloome and Judith Green's sociolinguistic perspectives on reading (Bloome & Green, 1984), Bloome's (1985) discussion of classroom reading as a social process, and McDermott's (1977) and Cazden's (1988) sociolinguistic work on classroom language. This research used ethnographic and linguistic tools to perform close analyses of the moment-by-moment interactions among teachers and students that create classroom literacy events. For example, Courtney Cazden (1988) argued that patterns of language use affect what counts as knowledge in a classroom. For instance, she analyzed the tensions arising from the interaction of children's stories in classrooms and teacher questions during sharing time. Teachers' questions often communicate the valued forms of narrative and meaning making. She also argues for the limiting discourse pattern of interaction–response–evaluation common in classrooms, a pattern which does not allow for elaboration, explanation, and other ways to expand thinking. These researchers illustrate how such interactions affect the ways students are able to participate in the collective meaning-making and knowledge-producing process.

Research drawing on anthropological and sociological perspectives provided new lenses for analyzing and understanding how literacy learning and instruction take place both in and beyond schools. Key concepts emerged from this work, including the concepts of literacy events, family and community literacy, literacy as ideological, and literacy as situated social practices. As Barton and Hamilton (2000) put it, social relationships are a crucial element of literacy practices, since practices "are more usefully understood as existing in the relationships between people, within groups and communities, rather than as a set of properties residing in individuals" (p. 8).

### The New Literacy Studies

One body of research resulting from the traditions just described has come to be known as the New Literacy Studies (NLS). NLS scholars focus on the recognition of literacy practices as local—i.e., as situated in place and time, and in relation to power, i.e., in terms of what people are able to do with literacy. NLS scholars also observe that some literacy practices seem to "count" more than others—that is, to have more credibility or legitimacy (Street, 2003). School literacy practices, for instance, count more than community literacy practices. As noted above, there is also an emphasis in NLS on written and spoken language as a continuum rather than a divide—this is a particularly important perspective as we begin to address and analyze the range of texts and modalities in any given literacy event. More specifically, this area of research ushers in a shift away from what is observable in literacy events to include the less visible social, historical, cultural, and political aspects of literacy practices—including beliefs and values, power relationships and struggles, connections to larger domains of social practice, and historical contexts.

The NLS perspective emerged starting in the early 1980s as a multidisciplinary, socioculturally situated alternative formulation of literacy. Rather than viewing this perspective as complementary to a cognitive view, NLS scholars intended to provide a *replacement* for an autonomous view of literacy (Street, 1984). The emphasis was on the importance of looking at reading, writing, speaking, and other literate acts as embedded in, and developing out of, social practices *rather* than as sets of cognitive skills. Street (1993) similarly characterized NLS as the replacement for a "psychologistic and culturally narrow" view of literacy that had dominated literacy research until the 1980s. The "new" field of study, he noted, was informed by anthropological, sociolinguistic, and cross-cultural perspectives. In 1984, Street lamented that NLS, although emerging in importance overall in the broad field of literacy, had still not replaced the older, autonomous view of literacy which he claimed was popular among both psychologists and "educationalists."

NLS scholars claim that the autonomous view of literacy, the antithesis of NLS, has been and will continue to be sustained based on the misconceptions of psychologists, psychometricians, and educationists that certain types of literacy practices, defined through the acquisition of clearly defined and assessed skills, lead to higher-order cognitive skills and, hence, better performance on a range of abstract reasoning tasks (Gee, 1990). In contrast, and in alignment with Scribner and Cole, NLS scholars contend that specific literacy practices, apprenticed from within specific sociocultural contexts with varying demands, account for success on contextualized tasks, rather than a generic cognitive ability tied to decontextualized literacy skills. In fact, this notion of decontextualized literacy skills is epitomized in standardized assessments of reading and writing used to define student competence and drive school curricula.

NLS researchers have more recently focused on social semiotic notions of multimodality, particularly on the features of various modes and genres, to expand definitions of reading and literacy and consider how we might change policy and practices associated with literacy teaching in schools (e.g., Rowsell, Kress, Pahl, & Street, 2013). These scholars argue that, while NLS emphasizes the understanding of social environments, the addition of a social semiotic multimodal perspective emphasizes the resources of meaning making. These resources include print, image, gestural, digital, and speech modes and the genres or forms of social interaction in relation to the modal resources being used. This perspective applied to reading, for instance, would more fully consider the rich repertoire of literacy practices children experience in their everyday lives, from bedtime reading, to exposure to public signage, to engagement with communicative technologies. Rowsell et al. (2013) argue that approach broadens our theoretical models of reading and acknowledges the increasing importance of semiotic skills among learners.

The new emphasis described above can be at least partly a result of a critique of the NLS perspective put forth by Brandt and Clinton (2002). Brandt and Clinton (2002) argued that an overly local perspective on literacy events represented by the work in NLS does not take into account the influence of more global literacy technologies and concomitant tools/objects (Latour, 2005). For instance, computers and the internet are global technologies that carry reading and writing practices in and out of local contexts (e.g., filling out a census to join an abstract constituency, or creating a website and receiving "hits"). These authors show how such tools and practices can travel across contexts and be accompanied by ideological struggles that also need to be part of a sociocultural view of literacy. That is, conceptualizations of literacy as bounded events fail to acknowledge that most literacy practices are shaped both by the activity of local actors and influences distant to that setting.

In fact, as Brandt and Clinton (2002) point out, it is not uncommon for particular kinds of literacy practices and objects to travel from more distant contexts, outlining what they call transcontextual features of literacy events and therefore calling for a "literacy-in-action" model. As they ask: "Can we not see the ways that literacy arises out of local, particular, situated human interactions while seeing how it also regularly arrives from other places—infiltrating, disjointing, and displacing local life?" (p. 333). We would argue that, in fact, a more complementary view of literacy would take into account learners' understandings of the literacy demands in a particular social context in which it resides, as well as the various literacy experiences that the learner brings from other contexts and experiences.

In summary, sociocultural researchers are investigating new forms of literacy practice that include a range of modalities, text forms, and digital tools. And they are grappling with issues of the local and more global contexts of literacy events and practices, the material tools and objects that are mediated in and also mediate literacy events and practices, and how agency and power are manifested among participants of literacy events and practices. Those relatively few sociocultural literacy researchers who attempt to bridge the gap between the cognitive and the social perspectives of literacy by arguing for the interwoven role of individual cognition call for a "situated cognition" view. In this view, cognitive processes are considered as situated in particular literacy learning contexts, and influenced by the histories and practices of participants as well as the larger institutional

discourses of schooling and educational policy (e.g., Purcell-Gates, 2012). Others ask interesting questions such as how we might understand local problems and potentials of literacy in ways that can be recontextualized for new situations and contexts (Stephens, 2000). We return to this tension, the relationship of sociocognitive aspects of learning in new textual environments to the larger sociocultural contexts of literacy practice, later in the chapter.

### The Influence of the New London Group and "Multiliteracies" Theory

Drawing on both sociocultural concepts, including the work of NLS and the emerging digital and multilingual landscape of schooling, a group of literacy scholars came together in the mid-1990s to develop the concept of multiliteracies and to advocate for a corresponding curricular framework. Multiliteracies includes two components: first, there is the notion that global communication requires multiple channels and media; and second is the idea that multiple literacies are constituted by, and constitutive of, the multiplicity of cultures and linguistic contexts in which literacy practices occur (Cope & Kalantzis, 2000). Hence multiliteracies represents a way to conceptualize how literacy(ies) intersect with NLS. The New London Group (NLG) that embraced these ideas included sociolinguists, critical and feminist literacy researchers, and functional linguists, including many theorists and researchers discussed above (such as Courtney Cazden, Norman Fairclough, James Gee, Alan Luke, Carmen Luke, and Gunther Kress). Two key concepts guided the NLG: (a) that in increasingly diverse and globalized societies (both culturally and linguistically), students need to develop sophisticated abilities to negotiate a range of registers, dialects, and languages and texts; and (b) in light of the proliferation of new, multimodal technologies, literacy pedagogy needs to account for the burgeoning variety of text forms associated with information and multimedia technologies. This group brought together many new perspectives guiding sociocultural research in literacy and attempted to create an overarching model of pedagogical practice.

The NLG argued that the human mind is "embodied, situated and social" and that "human knowledge is embedded in social, cultural and material contexts" (New London Group, 1996, p. 82). However, in what they called the "International Multiliteracies Project," they defined the limits of immersive, situated practices of learning on their own, and argued for the place of overt instruction, critical framing, and transformative practices to develop cultural and critical understanding associated with sophisticated multiliteracy practices. As the NLG stated: "Multiliteracies also creates a different kind of pedagogy, one in which language and other modes of meaning are dynamic, representational resources, constantly being remade by their users as they work to achieve their various cultural purposes" (New London Group, 1996, p. 6). The components of their pedagogical model were based on the notion of design. They argued that learners use available designs, such as linguistic grammars and semiotic systems, to redesign and create meaningful texts and representations of their learning. One example offered from an English class invited students to analyze the conventions of song lyrics, music, and video from a contemporary singer. They then immerse themselves in contemporary music and are taught the grammars and semiotic systems, and the cross-cultural meanings, and then write, perform, and create their own music video (Cope and Kalantzis, 2001).

Contemporary critics point to the prescriptive nature of the NLG documents and the model of pedagogy they put forth which was and still is largely untested (e.g., Leander & Boldt, 2013). However, the multiliteracies framework attempted to move the field toward a closer look at issues such as the role of multiple modes as representational resources while reasserting critical perspectives—particularly in relation to the capacity of young people to critically redesign texts, to represent themselves and their identities, and to participate in social life. The NLG project continues to play a role in drawing attention to, advancing, and complementing contemporary views of sociocultural literacy and literacy research, and more recently, "new literacies" and "new literacies research" (Coiro et al., 2008).

### Critical, Linguistic, and Poststructural Perspectives and Influences on Sociocultural Theories of Literacy

While it is beyond the scope of this chapter to discuss in detail the many and various philosophical, linguistic, and political theories that have influenced approaches to literacy research, it is important to provide a sense of the range of these influences on the work of scholars in the various traditions of sociocultural literacy theory. What is of particular importance is how theories of power, discourse, identity, and agency are integral to many of the conceptual frameworks found in this body of work.

As in other fields and disciplines, literacy researchers use the word "critical" in a number of ways, ranging from describing a more analytic or evaluative stance toward text to referring to a more overtly political or Marxist stance toward texts, reading, and the world. The latter is illustrated by the traditions of critical literacy that emanate from Brazilian educator Paulo Freire, as well as the Birmingham School of Cultural Studies; these traditions influenced literacy research and practice in North America, Australia, England, South Africa, and beyond.

In his seminal work with peasants in Brazil, Paulo Freire developed a dialogical model of literacy teaching that focused on reading the word *and* the world (Freire & Macedo, 1987) with a goal of transforming the world through social action and reflection, which he called "praxis" (Freire, 1970, 1993). Scholars who have contributed to this rich tradition in critical literacy include Michael Apple, Henry Giroux, Peter McLaren, Jean Anyon, Vivian Vasquez, and others. Parallel traditions in Australia, Canada, the United Kingdom, and South Africa are slightly more focused on critical text and discourse analysis, and include scholars such as Alan Luke, Peter Freebody, Colin Lankshear, Hilary Janks, and Barbara Comber.

The key influence of critical perspectives on sociocultural approaches to literacy is the idea that all knowledge building is, in effect, an active political as well as cognitive process. What is learned emanates from the lives, interests, and desires of the learners. In this view, knowledge is jointly or dialogically produced between learners and teachers; and it is produced in and from particular social, cultural, and historical contexts. In short, the position holds that education, literacy, and texts are never politically neutral sites of learning, and both learners and teachers are developed or redeveloped through critical literacy instruction. Even very young and early literacy learners engage in activities that question texts, authors, and discourses in relation to who and what societal values and structures are represented, emphasized, and privileged. A useful example of what this means for literacy instruction when incorporated into a comprehensive teaching framework is the Four Resources Model developed by Allan Luke and Peter Freebody (1999). This model includes attention to a repertoire of capabilities deemed necessary for students to acquire to become literate: breaking the code, meaning making through texts, understanding how texts function socially and culturally, and critically analyzing and transforming texts.

While cultural studies, also influenced by Marxist theory (e.g. Gramsci's cultural Marxism), have had influence on media studies (e.g., Kellner, 1995), they have also informed sociocultural perspectives on literacy. Cultural studies critique aspects of power, capitalism, and nationalism, as well as the race, gender, and sexual discrimination seen as inherent in dominant discourses. This work is also influential in relation to multimodal and digital literacies with its critical approach to examining the production, interpretation, and reception of cultural artifacts within particular contexts and the concomitant political and ideological uses and outcomes. The parameters of analysis extend beyond institutions, focusing on popular culture, media, and in literacy education, the texts and processes involved in "out-of-school" literacies (Hull & Schultz, 2002).

Various critical language awareness, functional, and poststructural perspectives on language have also deeply influenced how researchers think about literacy practices as sociocultural in the larger sense. Emanating from various linguistic and philosophical roots, theorists such as Halliday, Fairclough, Foucault, and Bakhtin broadly focus on the relationship of everyday language in use to larger social, cultural, and historical functions and meanings. Feminist, cultural, and poststructural perspectives have deepened these analyses, particularly the work of Davies on discursive positioning (Davies & Harré, 1990) and Holland and her colleagues (Holland, Lachicotte, Skinner, & Cain, 1998) on figured worlds in cultural settings, both of which draw attention to the role of individual positioning and agency within discourses that take place in social and cultural contexts. Contemporary sociocultural studies of situated literacy practices in classrooms, for instance, might analyze the linguistic genres and larger discourse structures of an event and look for ways that students might enter, position themselves, improvise, or get excluded from participating. These observations would then be related as a result to various forms of engagement and resistance.

Once language-in-use became a focus of much research in education, approaches to analyzing discourse *in situ* were developed. Discourse analysis tools analyze meaning as it is constructed in particular contexts or social activities, and in relation to identity positioning of the participants. As Moje and Luke (2009) noted, "It is common, of late, to frame literacy practices as either precursors to and producers of identities or as the outgrowth of particular identifications with the world" (p. 415). Yet, they argue, few researchers up to this point are clear about what particular conceptualizations of identity they are indexing; Moje and Luke (2009) therefore attempt to outline what they see as five key ways that literacy researchers conceptualize identity as socially situated, mediated, or produced: (a) difference; (b) sense of self/subjectivity; (c) mind or consciousness; (d) narrative; and (e) position. Each of these conceptualizations, though overlapping in various ways, will result in slightly different understandings of how identity and literacy influence one another in sociocultural approaches to studying particular literacy events and processes.

Perhaps one of the most important outcomes of such efforts—indeed, of social science more generally—is to understand the relationship between the discourses of everyday language and the larger cultural and political aspects of language—such as status, ethical judgments, negotiations of social goods, and the connections between moment-to-moment interactions and larger institutional discourses. Gee (1990), for instance, points to the discourses associated with everyday language use and those associated with institutional and cultural power—a theoretical position reminiscent of the work of Foucault, and especially the work of Bakhtin on primary and secondary discourses (Bakhtin, 1986).

These theoretical frameworks, and others, such as Bourdieu's (1991) theory of social, symbolic, and cultural capital, are foundational to some current research that is situated in the larger rubric of sociocultural literacy research. Often, in educational contexts, researchers will rely on various approaches to sociolinguistic or discourse analysis and to investigations of the role of identity, agency, and power inherent in socially situated literacy events and practices (see e.g., Chapter 28, this volume).

### *New Literacies and the Digital "Turn"*

Throughout the 1990s and 2000s scholars began to discuss multiple literacies, including "multiliteracies" (Cope & Kalantzis, 2000; New London Group, 1996), multimodal literacies (cf. Jewitt & Kress, 2003; O'Halloran & Smith, 2011; Street, Pahl, & Rowsell, 2009), visual literacy (e.g., Kress & van Leeuwen, 2006), digital literacy (e.g., Lankshear & Knobel, 2008), technology and literacy, and informational literacy. Literacy researchers from the subfields of reading, writing, and English education/language arts began studying the advent of, and experimenting with, new forms of

technology in their research projects (e.g., Flood, Heath, & Lapp, 2004; Leu, 2000; O'Brien, 2003; Reinking, 1994; Rubin & Bruce, 1984; Tierney & Damarin, 1998). With this said, new literacies can be seen as a messy or ill-structured domain (Spiro, Feltovich, Jacobson, & Coulson, 1993).

The term "new literacies" first appeared in 1993 when David Buckingham, in collaboration with media colleagues Chris Abbott and Julian Sefton-Green, acknowledged the emerging literature of "new literacies" as a possible construct for organizing future scholarly and pedagogical work (Lankshear & Knobel, 2013). These authors argued for "a new definition of literacy" more adaptable to a range of cultures and communication options. They noted a blurring of boundaries between traditional print text and media that was also accompanied by a blurring of the conventional boundaries between reading and writing, readers and writers, and consumers and producers ("prosumers") of various forms of text.

Indeed, by the end of the 1990s, the term *new literacies* was more likely to be used to refer to a range of "posttypographic" texts (Lankshear & Knobel, 2003), reading and writing, and a newly emerging amalgamation of sociocultural perspectives, digital literacy, popular culture, multimodality, and media studies. The "turn" tag, associated with the social shift in literacy discussed previously, has also been attached to the shift toward digital literacies and new media—i.e., the digital turn (Mills, 2010). As is the case with multiple literacies, multiliteracies, and new literacies, digital literacies are defined differently by different scholars. For example, Mills (2010) defines digital literacy simply as "sign-making practices using digital tools." Dobson and Willinsky (2009) argue that digital literacies are "remarkably continuous" with print literacies, pointing out that the effects of digital on print literacy are not unlike the effects of print literacy on oral language.

Other scholars defined new literacies as "the rapid and continuous changes in the ways in which we read, write, view, listen, compose and communicate information" (Coiro et al., 2008, p. 8). These authors argue that new literacies reflect increased demands for reading, writing, viewing, and communicating as new texts mutate into complex, hybrid semiotic systems (C. Luke, 2003). Among the hallmarks of the new literacies associated with the digital turn are that they are perceived to be more democratic (Dobson & Willinsky, 2009) and to foster more participatory, collaborative, and distributed engagements (Jenkins, Purushotma, Clinton, Weigel, & Robison, 2009; Knobel & Lankshear, 2007).

The terms "new literacies" and "new literacies research," then, have become an umbrella for an increasingly broad and somewhat unwieldy range of research. The *Handbook of Research in New Literacies* (Coiro et al., 2008) includes multimodal research on, for instance, the role of text and image relations in meaning making (Stein, 2008; Unsworth, 2008), the influence of popular cultural texts on youth literacy (Beach & O'Brien, 2008; Black, 2008; Hagood, 2008) and reading, writing, and interacting in online environments (Lam, 2008; Leu, Everett Cacopardo, Zawilinski, Mcverry,

& O'Byrne, 2012; Lewis & Fabos, 2005). As a collection, it spans analyses that draw on more cognitive and psycholinguistic approaches to online literacies and those in the area of sociocultural literacy with a focus on the social practices of literacies. As Coiro et al. (2008) point out in their introduction, literacy acquisition is likely ultimately to be redefined as the ability to continuously adapt to new literacies required by new technologies in specific ways to suit particular purposes and goals.

Lankshear and Knobel (2003) contend that new literacies research is more than a move away from traditional or more technical literacy research. It is, in fact, an acknowledgment of new *kinds* of literacies, largely influenced by "digital literacies" but also by other new and continuously developing forms of cultural productions (e.g. zines—small self-published magazines for fans or specialized groups often found online, and culture jamming—the practice of disrupting media culture through, for example, recreating logos and posting on mass media sites). They also note that many of the key influences on what is understood as new literacies research come from other disciplines. The problem, of course, with these expanding notions of literacy is that the term "literacy" begins to lose any coherent reference. It can now mean anything from decoding print text to producing a range of multimedia and multigenre texts on the web. Therefore, literacy researchers, and particularly researchers whose work falls under the rubric of new literacies, find it increasingly important to locate their work in this complex and changing landscape and to specify what kinds of literacy practices they are examining.

One active area of new literacies research that interfaces with media literacy focuses on youth as producers of cultural media as they experiment with the semiotic power of multimodality (Hull & Nelson, 2005; Stein, 2008). Studies show how youth appropriate and transform modes and resources of popular culture to subvert and rewrite media representations (Hull & Greeno, 2006), and comment on and critique their social worlds (Hill & Vasudevan, 2008; Morrell, 2007; Sefton-Green, 1998, 2006; Soep, 2006). In work with marginalized youth and video production in and out of schools, for example, Rogers and colleagues (Rogers, Winters, LaMonde & Perry, 2010; Rogers, Winters, Perry, & LaMonde, 2014) analyzed the ways in which youth draw upon the affordances of a range of text genres and the multimodal resources of arts and film making to critically engage with and reflect on their identity positions and engage in larger cultural discourses. This new form of authoring illustrates the ways in which youth are becoming flexible creators and designers of multimodal genres using a range of cultural resources. The research underscores the need for creating opportunities in schools that can support discursive and textual sophistication and reflective critical analysis. Analyses that have been historically associated with print text are thus being extended to a wider range of text and media forms.

Indeed, this growing complexity of literacy research not only changes the way scholars study literacy, it illuminates the continuities and discontinuities between school-based literacy

policies and practices and the myriad literacy engagements that take place in both formal and informal learning contexts (Hull and Schultz, 2002; see Chapter 24, this volume). An important illustration of this growing mismatch between in- and out-of-school literacy practices is the arena of assessment practices (see Chapter 29, this volume). The digital environment brings into clearer focus the role of not only a range of text types but also genres that are widely accessed by young readers in and out of schools, and across more and less formal educational contexts. Against the backdrop of literacy "reinventing" itself in "New Times" (Luke & Elkins, 1998), and with the impact of the internet and accessible digital media emerging as more formidable than educators might have thought, changes will be needed for teachers and classrooms to more adequately assess media-related literacy abilities and skills of youth (Alvermann & Hagood, 2000). Fifteen years after Alvermann and Hagood made these observations and worked to define media-related literacies from a multidisciplinary perspective, literacy practices in schools have become increasingly multimodal and digital; nevertheless, assessments are mostly unaltered, unable to accommodate students' abilities to critique, produce, mix, and transpose across modalities and platforms (e.g., Rowsell et al., 2013).

Accordingly, our analysis suggests that scholarship in educational psychology with reference to sociocultural theories of literacy, and more recently, the new literacies foci within sociocultural theories, is, and will increasingly be, the study of how literacy practices and texts are mediated by digital technologies and spaces. These technologies and spaces are situated in a variety of social contexts, including schools and other formal and informal learning settings, workplaces, and recreational settings. Digital literacy practices have also prompted a range of research questions related to how notions of text, reading, writing, discussing, and using other literacy practices have changed through their mediation by digital tools and collaborative work in collective digital spaces. Other questions need to address how digital texts, in turn, reposition young readers and writers (Wohlwend & Lewis, 2010; see Chapter 3, this volume).

## New Considerations for Research on Learning and Instruction Across Formal and Informal Learning Contexts

To discuss new considerations for research drawing on this overview of sociocultural perspectives on literacy, we turn to Cole and Wertsch (1996) to help summarize some of our key points about bridging psychological and sociocultural perspectives with significance for rich theorizing about the learning and teaching of literacy. In their classic piece on the importance of social mediation in mind, cognition, and learning, Cole and Wertsch present a reasoned critique of Piaget and Vygotsky. In the end, they argue for the importance of both the cognitive and social. After paraphrasing their themes, we discuss implications for research in which sociocultural and cognitive literacy can be studied concurrently and to the advantage of each.

## The Role of Cultural Mediation

Cole and Wertsch's key theme, which we have discussed in this chapter, is that cultural mediation, as articulated by cultural-historical psychologists, is key to knowledge construction and learning. Humans learn in "environments" where the ways in which they learn are mediated by tools, including language, and their acquired disciplinary knowledge as well as the personal qualities they bring to situations. The meanings of tools, language, and other symbol systems that mediate learning are historically situated and culturally defined. Hence, although it seems logical to study selected psychological aspects of teaching and learning as cognitive, affective, or conative processes, these processes are always socially, culturally, and historically situated. And, although one can take the position that learning, including how it is impacted by internal psychological states, is affected by contexts (which we discuss below), context itself is ambiguous and simplistically rendered in research unless it is carefully defined as situated practice.

To give an example of the complexity of cultural mediation, Hull and Stornaiuolo (2014) situate their research in the world. Using frameworks from theories of cosmopolitanism (Appadurai, 1996) and situated broadly in NLS, these authors explore how youth, via dialogue across a private global social network, construct identities as cosmopolitan citizens. A challenge of this work was to foster and study dialogue across differences in culture, language, ideology, and geography. A key question was how young people might be positioned by their social networks to develop effective and ethical responses to local and global concerns in our digital age (see Chapter 25, this volume). In order to study cosmopolitan literacy, Hull and Stornaiuolo used mixed-methods, design-based research (see Chapter 2, this volume) in which they collected an array of ethnographic data and used analyses such as multimodal analysis; in addition, they collected a variety of quantitative data via an analytic program built into the network tool called Space2Cre8 (http://www.space2cre8.com).

## The Location of Mind

If knowledge construction and learning are socially mediated, then, contrary to the biological position taken by many psychologists, the location of mind and cognition is not solely in the head. Again, as others in this volume have argued cogently, "higher psychological" processes can be considered as "transactions" between the biological individual and sociocultural—which includes engaging in activities, and using various resources, tools, and artifacts. Hence, inquiries into teaching and learning that account for mind may be better targeted within *activities* rather than on individuals, working on tasks. Likewise, the "unit of analysis" is better seen as the activity rather than the individual (Engeström, 1987). The activity is an embodiment of action (Burnett, Merchant, Pahl, & Rowsell, 2014).

To take one example, consider the research by Beach and O'Brien (2015), who sought to explore how "app affordances" (with "app" referring to simple programs that can be loaded on to digital devices for various applications) were tied to literacy practices that students can use to support learning and enact activities. These authors demonstrate how the activity in which each digital app is used shapes learning—initially, as a mediational tool (or multiple tools). They further posit that this mediated learning—the "app in use" takes precedence over the app in and of itself based on its predesigned learning affordances that presuppose certain kinds of engagement and learning. The socially mediated learning position is situated in the *activity*, and this sits in contrast to the notion that affordances are predesigned into learning tools like digital applications or apps. Work such as this provides a robust view of literacy and literacy learning with reference to location of mind in the activity.

## Context and Action

Context is never a static, given element—it is never a set of fixed features of a learning environment, as it has been traditionally characterized in psychological research. A context supports and enables certain actions; but it does not exist statically, as an environment entered by actors that affects them. Rather, context is also *constructed* by the actors and their actions—actors and context are in flux and dynamically intertwined. Hence, the most accurate unit in understanding learning may be "mediated action in context." When learners learn, biological processes co-occur and are co-defined by sociocultural actions as learners use mediation tools in specific activities.

Lewis and Tierney (2013) attempted to understand, among other constructions, the "geography of emotion"—that is, how emotion is mobilized by students in curriculum tasks. These authors viewed emotion as an action "that involves social agents and mediating signs or tools such as language, texts, bodies (gestures), objects, and space" (p. 293). They attempted to understand how emotion is mobilized through action by studying mediated discursive practices in a high-school English/history class where students engaged with media and documentary film making. Lewis and Tierney's study requires looking at emotion, not as a pre-existing affective state that influences action (a more typical psychological position), but as constructed through a given context in social action. It also draws from work on embodied critical engagement (illustrated through action such as gesture, movement, or volume, for example), which may reveal the tension students feel between their own histories and the underpinning ideologies in classroom discourse.

Now that we have explored the assumptions of socially and culturally mediated understanding with some research exemplars, we can consider some questions that might continue to guide research based on these assumptions. In the introduction to the first major compilation of research in new literacies mostly within the digital turn, Coiro et al. (2008) noted that a difficult challenge in studying new literacies was that it was so new that we lacked theoretical frameworks—there were few well-defined constructs and research methods to match the complexity of the emerging subfield. Now, several years after the publication of that volume, while scholars have enjoyed some progress, most of the big questions remain, and these questions drive current research. Although we have pointed out in this chapter that NLS and its attendant views of the centrality of the sociocultural context itself is not so new, what is new are studies in the digital turn era of the broader "new literacies" field.

The most urgent broad question Coiro et al. (2008) posed was this: How do the internet and other information and communication technologies alter the nature of literacy? The most intriguing aspect of this inquiry is the extent to which researchers should continue to study literacy skills, strategies, and practices, based on existing frameworks that are developed from print-centric theories and models of connected written discourse. The fields of educational psychology and literacy both draw upon tomes of this print-centric work in multiple handbooks and other volumes. Another key issue is to what extent we want to continue to study engagement with texts and literacy as isolated encounters of an individual learner drawing from her or his repertoire of skills and strategies when these new literacies practices are increasingly collaborative and social, as well as supported by technologies that will only make them more so. For the broad field of educational psychology to which this volume speaks, these questions, among many others, arise:

1. What new models of text, written discourse processing, context, and the relationship between texts and learning are needed as education moves increasingly into digital, multimodal representation? This question will demand both an immediate response and new forms of research dissemination. The notion that texts can be defined as linearly presented print organized around identifiable structures is rapidly changing; linguistic and psycholinguistic processing elements of texts are collaborative, multimodal, and intermedial products, created by multiple authors in shared virtual and social spaces.

2. How do these new texts, multimodal spaces, and new social and literacy practices, and the collaborative production of ideas, engender new forms of motivation and engagement that will sustain attention and learning beyond what was traditionally possible? For instance, researchers have begun to ask how notions of identity, emotion, and embodiment are entwined with various kinds of literacy activities, contexts, and practices in and across mediated spaces.

3. How will we define, teach, and assess these new digital competencies—the skills, strategies, and collaborative and participatory stances that distinguish the most skilled literate competence from less competence or measured proficiency? What skills or practices travel from print-centered to digitally mediated contexts and what constitutes new forms of competence and proficiency? Researchers, for instance, will need to study how learners take up and learn to navigate particular kinds of digital affordances in the service of their goals or required outcomes.

4. What new methodologies, or adaptations of more traditional methodologies, will best serve us as we research new literacy practices? Current methodologies include ethnographic studies, discourse analyses, semiotic analyses, and activity theory, with gaining popularity of mixed methods. Some new technologies permit the digital collection of data in virtual spaces, enabling new ways to collect and annotate video, as well as to analyze

and triangulate multimodal data with new analysis software like VideoAnt annotation of videos (http://ant.umn.edu) or using FlipGrid (http://flipgrid.com/info/) videos as a multimodal data source to study, for example, teacher reflection.

The convergence of sociocultural perspectives on literacy and new forms of literacy will continue to shape and reshape the research agenda for teaching and learning across formal and informal educational contexts. Indeed, we are far from the first to note this sea change in literacy research. Notions of literacy as mediated cognitive and social practices that include the almost endless possibilities of multimodal and digital affordances, which we have attempted to at least briefly explore in this chapter, point to a compelling paradigm shift in how we think about literacy, how we research literacy practices, and the implications for teaching and learning.

## References

Alvermann, D. E., & Guthrie, J. T. (1993). *Themes and directions of the National Reading Research Center.* Athens, GA: National Reading Research Center, Universities of Georgia and Maryland.

Alvermann, D. E., & Hagood, M. C. (2000). Critical media literacy: Research, theory, and practice in "new times". *Journal of Educational Research, 93*(3), 193.

Alvermann, D., Simpson, M., & Fitzgerald, J. (2006). Teaching and learning in reading. In P. Alexander & P. Winne (Eds.), *Handbook of educational psychology* (2nd ed., pp. 427–456). New York: Routledge.

Anderson, R. C. (1977). The notion of schemata and the educational enterprise. In R. C. Anderson, R. J. Spiro, & W. E. Montague (Eds.), *Schooling and the acquisition of knowledge.* Hillside, NJ: Erlbaum.

Anderson, R. C., & Pearson, P. D. (1984). A schema-theoretic view of basic processes in reading comprehension. In P. D. Pearson, R. Barr, M. L. Kamil, & P. Mosenthal (Eds.), *Handbook of reading research* (pp. 255–291). New York: Longman.

Appadurai, A. (1996). *Modernity at large: Cultural dimensions of globalization.* Minneapolis, MN: University of Minnesota Press.

Au, K. (1980). Participation structures in a reading lesson with Hawaiian children. *Anthropology and Education Quarterly, 11*, 91–115.

Bakhtin, M. M. (1986). *Speech genres and other late essays.* Austin, TX: University of Texas Press.

Barton, D., & Hamilton, M. (1998). *Local literacies: Reading and writing in one community.* London: Routledge.

Barton, D., & Hamilton, M. (2000). Introduction: Exploring situated literacies. In D. Barton, M. Hamilton, & R. Ivanic (Eds.), *Situated literacies: Reading and writing in context* (pp. 1–15). New York: Routledge.

Beach, R., & O'Brien, D. (2008). Teaching popular-culture texts in the classroom. In J. Coiro, M. Knobel, C. Lankshear, & D. J. Leu (Eds.), *Handbook of research on new literacies* (pp. 775–804). New York: Lawrence Erlbaum Associates.

Beach, R., & O'Brien, D. (2015). *Using apps for learning across the curriculum: A literacy-based framework and guide.* New York: Routledge.

Black, R. W. (2008). *Adolescents and online fan fiction* (Vol. 23). New York: Peter Lang.

Bloome, D. (1985). Reading as a social process. *Language Arts, 62*, 134–142.

Bloome, D., & Green, J. (1984). Directions in the sociolinguistic study of reading. In P. D. Pearson, R. Barr, M. L. Kamil, & P. Mosenthal (Eds.), *Handbook of reading research* (pp. 395–421). New York: Longman.

Bourdieu, P. (1991). *Language and symbolic power.* Cambridge, MA: Harvard University Press.

Brandt, D., & Clinton, K. (2002). Limits of the local: Expanding perspectives on literacy as a social practice. *Journal of Literacy Research, 34*(3), 337–356.

Brown, J. S., Collins, A., & Duguid, P. (1989). Situated cognition and the culture of learning. *Educational Researcher, 18*(1), 32–41.

Burnett, C., Merchant, G., Pahl, K., & Rowsell, J. (2014). The (im) materiality of literacy: The significance of subjectivity to new literacies research. *Discourse: Studies in the Cultural Politics of Education, 35*(1), 90–103.

Carey, R.F., & Harste, J.C. (1988). Comprehension as context: Toward reconsideration of a transactional theory of reading. In R. J. Tierney, P. Anders, & J. Mitchell (Eds.), *Understanding readers' understanding.* Hillsdale, NJ: Erlbaum.

Cazden, C. B. (1988). *Classroom discourse: The language of teaching and learning* (pp. 159–181). Portsmouth, NH: Heinemann.

Coiro, J., Knobel, M., Lankshear, C., & Leu, D. J. (Eds.). (2008). *The handbook of research in new literacies.* New York: Lawrence Erlbaum.

Cole, M. (1996). *Cultural psychology: A once and future discipline.* Cambridge, MA: Belknap of Harvard University Press.

Cole, M., & Wertsch, J. V. (1996). Beyond the individual-social antinomy in discussions of Piaget and Vygotsky. *Human Development, 39*(5), 250–256.

Cope, B., & Kalantzis, M. (Eds.). (2000). *Multiliteracies: Literacy learning and the design of social futures.* London: Routledge.

Cope, B., & Kalantzis, M. (2001). *Putting multiliteracies to the test.* Adelaide, South Australia: Australian Literacy Educators' Association.

Davies, B., & Harré, R. (1990). Positioning: The discursive production of selves. *Journal for the Theory of Social Behaviour, 20,* 43–63.

Deci, E. L., & Ryan, R. M. (1992). The initiation and regulation of intrinsically motivated learning and achievement. In A. K. Boggiano & T. S. Pittman (Eds.), *Achievement and motivation: A social-developmental perspective* (pp. 9–36). New York: Cambridge University Press.

Delpit, L. D. (1986). Skills and other dilemmas of a progressive Black educator. *Harvard Educational Review, 56*(4), 379–385.

Dobson, T., & Willinsky, J. (2009). Digital literacies. In D. Olsen & N. Torrance (Eds.), *The Cambridge handbook of literacy* (pp. 286–312). New York: Cambridge University Press.

Dyson, A. H. (1993). A sociocultural perspective on symbolic development in primary grade classrooms. *New Directions for Child and Adolescent Development, 61,* 25–39.

Engeström, Y. (1987). *Learning by expanding: An activity-theoretical approach to developmental research.* Helsinki: Orienta-Konsultit.

Flood, J., Heath, S. B., & Lapp, D. (2004). (Eds.). *Handbook of teaching literacy through the communicative and visual arts.* New York: Prentice Hall.

Freire, P. (1970). *Pedagogy of the oppressed* (M. Bergman Ramos, trans.). New York: Continuum.

Freire, P. (1993). *Pedagogy of the oppressed* (rev. ed.). New York: Continuum, 1970.

Freire, P., & Macedo, D. (1987). *Reading the word and the world.* South Hadley, MA: Bergin & Garvey.

Gee, J. P. (1990). *Social linguistics and literacies: Ideology in discourses.* Bristol, PA: Falmer.

Gee, J. P. (2000). The new literacy studies. In D. Barton, M. Hamilton, & R. Ivanic (Eds.), *Situated literacies: Reading and writing in context* (pp. 180–196). London: Routledge.

Gee, J. P. (2012). *Social linguistics and literacies: Ideology and discourses* (4th ed.). New York: Routledge.

Goody, J., & Watt, I. (1963). The consequences of literacy. *Comparative Studies in Society and History, 5*(03), 304–345.

Graff, H. J. (1979). *The literacy myth: Literacy and social structure in the nineteenth-century city.* New York: Academic Press.

Green, J., & Bloome, D. (1997). Ethnography and ethnographers of and in education: A situated perspective. In J. Flood, S. B. Heath, & D. Lapp (Eds.), *Research on teaching literacy through the communicative and visual arts* (pp. 181–202). New York: Macmillan.

Greeno, J. G. (1997). On claims that answer the wrong questions. *Educational Researcher, 26*(1), 5–17.

Guthrie, J. T., & Coddington, C. S. (2009). Reading motivation. In K. R. Wentzel & A. Wigfield (Eds.), *Handbook of motivation at school* (pp. 503–525). New York: Routledge.

Guthrie, J. T., & Wigfield, A. (2000). Engagement and motivation in reading. In M. L. Kamil, P. Mosenthal, P. D. Pearson, & R. Barr (Eds.), *Handbook of reading research, volume III* (pp. 403–422). Mahwah, NJ: Lawrence Erlbaum.

Gutiérrez, K. D. (2008). Developing a sociocritical literacy in the third space. *Reading Research Quarterly, 43*(2), 148–164.

Hagood, M. C. (2008). Intersection of popular culture, identities, and new literacies research. In J. Coiro, M. Knobel, C. Lankshear, & D. J. Leu (Eds.), *Handbook of research on new literacies* (pp. 531–551). New York: Lawrence Erlbaum.

Heath, S. B. (1982). What no bedtime story means: Narrative skills at home and school. *Language in society, 11*(01), 49–76.

Heath, S. B. (1983). *Ways with words.* Cambridge: Cambridge University Press.

Heath, S. B. (1991). The sense of being literate: Historical and cross-cultural features. In R. Barr, M. L. Kamil, P. Mosenthal, & P. D. Pearson (Eds.), *Handbook of reading research, volume II* (pp. 3–23). Mahwah, NJ: Lawrence Erlbaum.

Hill, M. L., & Vasudevan, L. (2008). *Media, learning, and sites of possibility.* New York: Peter Lang.

Holland, D., Lachicotte, W., Skinner, C., & Cain, C. (1998). *Identity and agency in cultural worlds.* Cambridge, MA: Harvard University Press.

Hull, G., & Greeno, J. (2006). Identity and agency in non-school and school worlds. In Z. Bekerman, N. Burbules, & D. Silberman-Keller (Eds.), *Learning in places: The informal education reader* (pp. 77–98). New York: Peter Lang.

Hull, G., & Nelson, M. E. (2005). Locating the semiotic power of multimodality. *Written Communication, 22,* 224–261.

Hull, G., & Schultz, K. (Eds.). (2002). *Schools out! Bridging out-of-school literacies with classroom practice.* New York: Teachers College Press.

Hull, G., & Stornaiuolo, A. (2014). Cosmopolitan literacies, social networks, and "proper distance": striving to understand in a global world. *Curriculum Inquiry, 44*(1), 15–44.

Jenkins, H., Purushotma, R., Clinton, K., Weigel, M., & Robinson, A. J. (2009). *Confronting the challenges of participatory culture.* Cambridge, MA: MIT Press.

Jewitt, C., & Kress, G. (Eds.). (2003). *Multimodal literacy.* New York: Peter Lang.

Kellner, D. (1995). *Media culture: Cultural studies, identity and politics between the modern and the postmodern.* London: Routledge.

Knobel, M., & Lankshear, C. (Eds.). (2007). *A new literacies sampler.* New York: Peter Lang.

Kress, G., & Van Leeuwen, T. (2006). *Reading images: The grammar of visual design* (2nd ed.). New York: Routledge.

Labov, W. (1973). The logic of non-standard English. In R. W. Bailey & J. L. Robinson (Eds.), *Varieties of present-day English* (pp. 319–354). New York: Macmillan.

Lam, W. S. E. (2008). Language socialization in online communities. In P. A. Duff and N. H. Hornberger (Eds.), *Encyclopedia of language and education* (2nd ed., pp. 2859–2869). New York: Springer.

Lankshear, C., & Knobel, M. (2003). *New literacies: Changing knowledge and classroom learning.* Buckingham, UK: Open University Press.

Lankshear, C., & Knobel, M. (Eds.). (2008). *Digital literacies: Concepts, policies, and practices.* New York: Peter Lang.

Lankshear, C., & Knobel, M. (2011). *New literacies: Everyday practices and social learning.* Berkshire, England: Open University Press.

Lankshear, C., & Knobel, M. (2013). Introduction: Social and cultural studies of new literacies from an educational perspective. In C. Lankshear & M. Knobel (Eds.), *A new literacies reader* (pp. 1–19). New York: Peter Lang.

Latour, B. (2005). *Reassembling the social: An introduction to actor-network-theory.* New York: Oxford University Press.

Lave, J. (1988). *The culture of acquisition and the practice of understanding* (pp. 259–286). Palo Alto, CA: Institute for Research on Learning.

Lave, J., & Wenger, E. (1991). *Situated learning: Legitimate peripheral participation.* Cambridge, MA: Cambridge University Press.

Leander, K., & Boldt, G. (2013). Rereading "A pedagogy of multiliteracies": bodies, texts, and emergence. *Journal of Literacy Research, 45*(1), 22–46.

Leu, D. J. (2000). Literacy and technology: Deictic consequences for literacy education in an information age. In M. L. Kamil, P. Mosenthal, P. D. Pearson, & R. Barr (Eds.), *Handbook of reading research, volume III* (pp. 743–770). Mahwah, NJ: Lawrence Erlbaum.

Leu, D. J., Everett Cacopardo, H., Zawilinski, J., Mcverry, G., & O'Byrne, W. I. (2012). New literacies of online reading comprehension. In C. A. Chapelle (Ed.), *The encyclopedia of applied linguistics.* Oxford, UK: John Wiley.

Lewis, C., & Fabos, B. (2005). Instant messaging, literacies, and social identities. *Reading Research Quarterly*, *40*(4), 470–501.

Lewis, C., Enciso, P., & Moje, E. B. (Eds.). (2007). *Reframing sociocultural research on literacy: Identity, agency, and power*. New York: Routledge.

Lewis, C., & Tierney, J. D. (2013). Mobilizing emotion in an urban classroom: Producing identities and transforming signs in a race-related discussion. *Linguistics and Education, 24*, 289–304

Luke, A., & Elkins, J. (1998). Reinventing literacy in "new times". *Journal of Adolescent and Adult Literacy, 42*, 4–7.

Luke, A., & Freebody, P. (1999). Further notes on the four resources model. *Reading Online, 3*.

Luke, C. (2003). Pedagogy, connectivity, multimodality, and interdisciplinarity. *Reading Research Quarterly*, *38*(3), 397–403.

Martin, J. (2006). Social cultural perspectives in educational psychology. In P. Alexander & P. H. Winne (Eds.), *Handbook of educational psychology* (2nd ed., pp. 595–614). New York: Routledge.

McDermott, R. P. (1977). Social relations as contexts for learning in school. *Harvard Educational Review*, *47*(2), 198–213.

Mills, K. A. (2010). A review of the "digital turn" in the new literacy studies. *Review of Educational Research*, *80*(2), 246–271.

Moje, E. B., & Luke, A. (2009). Literacy and identity: Examining the metaphors in history and contemporary research. *Reading Research Quarterly*, *44*(4), 415–437.

Moll, L., Amanti, C., Neff, D., & Gonzalez, N. (1992). Funds of knowledge for teaching: Using a qualitative approach to connect homes and classrooms. *Theory into Practice, 31*, 132–141.

Morrell, E. (2007). Critical literacy and popular culture in urban education: Toward a pedagogy of access and dissent. In C. Clark & M. Blackburn (Eds.), *Working with/in the local: New directions in literacy research for political action* (pp. 235–254). New York: Peter Lang.

New London Group. (1996). A pedagogy of multiliteracies: Designing social futures. *Harvard Educational Review, 66*(1), 60–92.

O'Brien, D. G. (2003). Juxtaposing traditional and intermedial literacies to redefine the competence of struggling adolescents. *Reading Online, 6*(7).

O'Halloran, K. L., & Smith, B. A. (Eds.). (2011). *Multimodal studies: Exploring issues and domains*. New York: Routledge.

Ong, W. J. (1967). *The presence of the word: Some prolegomena for cultural and religious history*. New Haven, CT: Yale University Press.

Purcell-Gates, V. (1997). *Other people's words: The cycle of low literacy*. Cambridge, MA: Harvard University Press.

Purcell-Gates, V. (2012). Epistemological tensions in reading research and a vision for the future. *Reading Research Quarterly, 47*(4), 465–471.

Reinking, D. (1994). *Electronic literacy*. Athens, GA and College Park, MD: National Reading Research Center, Universities of Georgia and Maryland.

Rogers, T., Winters, K., LaMonde, A., & Perry, M. (2010). From image to ideology: Analyzing shifting identity positions of marginalized youth across the cultural sites of video production. *Pedagogies: An International Journal, 5*(4), 298–312.

Rogers, T., Winters, K., Perry, M., & LaMonde, A. (2014). *Youth, critical literacies and civic engagement: Arts, media and literacy in the lives of adolescents*. New York: Routledge.

Rogoff, B. (2003). *The cultural nature of human development*. New York: Oxford University Press.

Roth, W. M., & Lee, Y.J. (2007). "Vygotsky's neglected legacy": Cultural-historical activity theory. *Review of Educational Research, 77*(2), 186–232.

Rowsell, J., Kress, G., Pahl, K., & Street, B. (2013). Multimodal approaches to the reading theoretical models of the reading process. In D. E. Alvermann, N. J. Unrau & R. B. Ruddell (Eds.), *Theoretical models and reading processes* (6th ed.). Newark, DE: International Reading Association.

Rueda, R. (2011). Cultural perspectives in reading research and instruction. In M. Kamil, P. D. Pearson, E. B. Moje, & P. P. Afflerbach (Eds.), *Handbook of reading research, volume IV* (pp. 84–103). New York: Routledge.

Rubin, A., & Bruce, B. C. (1984). *Quill: Reading and writing with a microcomputer*. Report no. 48. Champaign, IL: Center for the Study of Reading, University of Illinois.

Scribner, S., & Cole, M. (1981). *The psychology of literacy*. Cambridge, MA: Harvard University Press.

Sefton-Green, J. (Ed.). (1998). *Digital diversions*. London: UCL Press.

Sefton-Green, J. (2006). Youth, technology and media cultures. In J. Green, & A. Luke (Eds.), *Review of research in education* (pp. 279–306). Washington, DC: American Educational Research Association.

Soep, E. (2006). Beyond literacy and voice in youth media production. *McGill Journal of Education*, *41*(3), 197–213.

Spiro, R. J., Feltovich, P. J., Jacobson, M. J., & Coulson, R. L. (1993). Cognitive flexibility, constructivism, and hypertext: Random access instruction for advanced knowledge acquisition in ill-structured domains. In T. M Duffy & D. H. Jonassen (Eds.), *Constructivism and the technology of instruction: A conversation* (pp. 57–75). Hillsdale, NJ: Lawrence Erlbaum Associates.

Stein, P. (2008). Multimodal instructional practices. In J. Coiro, M. Knobel, C. Lankshear, & D. J. Leu (Eds.), *The handbook of research in new literacies*. New York: Lawrence Erlbaum.

Stephens, K. (2000). A critical discussion of the 'new literacy studies'. *British Journal of Educational Studies*, *48*(1), 10–23.

Street, B. (1984). *Literacy in theory and practice*. Cambridge, UK: Cambridge University Press.

Street, B. (1993). Introduction: The new literacy studies. In B. V. Street (Ed.), *Cross-cultural approaches to literacy* (pp. 1–21). New York: Cambridge University Press.

Street, B. V. (1995). *Social literacies: Critical approaches to literacy in development, ethnography, and education*. New York: Longman.

Street, B. (2003). What's new in new literacy studies: Critical approaches to literacy in theory and practice. *Current Issues in Comparative Education*, *5*(2), 77–91.

Street, B., Pahl, K., & Rowsell, J. (2009). *Multimodality and new literacy studies*. In C. Jewitt (Ed.), *The Routledge handbook of multimodal analysis* (pp. 191–200). London: Routledge.

Swadener, B. B., & Lubeck, S. (Eds.). (1995). *Children and families "at promise": Deconstructing the discourse of risk*. Albany, NY: SUNY Press.

Taylor, D., & Dorsey-Gaines, C. (1988). *Growing up literate: Learning from inner-city parents*. Portsmouth, NH: Heinemann.

Tierney, R. J., & Cunningham, J. W. (1984). Research on teaching reading comprehension. In P. D. Pearson, R. Barr, M. L. Kamil & P. Mosenthal (Eds.), *Handbook of reading research* (pp. 609–655). Mahwah, NJ: Lawrence Erlbaum Associates.

Tierney, R. J., & Damarin, S. (1998). Technology as enfranchisement and cultural development: Crisscrossing symbol systems, paradigm shifts, and social-cultural considerations. In D. Reinking, M. McKenna, L.D. Labbo, & R. D. Kieffer (Eds.), *Handbook of literacy and technology* (pp. 278–295). Mahwah, NJ: Lawrence Erlbaum.

Tierney, R. J., & Pearson, P. D. (1983). *Toward a composing model of reading*. Champaign, IL: University of Illinois at Urbana-Champaign. Center for the Study of Reading, Bolt Beranek and Newman Inc., & National Institute of Education.

Unsworth, L. (2008). Multiliteracies, e-literature and English teaching. *Language and Education*, *22*(1), 62–75.

Vygotsky, L. S. (1978). *Mind in society*. Cambridge, MA: Harvard University Press.

Vygotsky, L. S. (1986). *Thought and language* (A. Kozulin, trans.). Cambridge, MA: MIT Press.

Wohlwend, K. E., & Lewis, C. (2010). Critical literacy, critical engagement, and digital technology: Convergence and embodiment in global spheres. In D. Lapp, & D. Fisher (Eds.), *Handbook of research on teaching English language arts* (pp. 188–194). New York: Routledge.

# 24

# Learning Environments In and Out of School

*BRIGID BARRON*
Stanford University

*PHILIP BELL*[1]
University of Washington

This is an exciting time to be studying learning and learning environments, both in and out of school. Since the publication of the last *Handbook of Educational Psychology* in 2006, there has been growing interest in research that goes beyond schools to focus on the variety of settings that provide opportunities to learn (Banks, Au, Ball, Bell, & Gordon, 2007; Barron, 2006; Bell, Lewenstein, Shouse, & Feder, 2009; Bevan, Bell, Stevens, & Razfar, 2013). Persistent concerns about achievement gaps linked to income inequality raise questions about how we can increase access to inspiring out-of-school activities. Rapid changes in the availability of mobile devices, communication platforms, and networked resources have in turn raised additional questions about how virtual spaces and resources catalyze new learning experiences and how they can be used to expand creative agency equitably and enrich personal learning ecologies (Barron, 2006; Greenhow, Robelia, & Hughes, 2009; Warschauer & Matuchniak, 2010). There is a clear need to develop ideas, prototypes, and design knowledge that will advance our capacity to create hybrid environments that build connections across homes, schools, and communities to strengthen learning opportunities. This work is particularly important to address the needs of those learners who have been marginalized or underresourced.

This chapter synthesizes foundational and recent research studies related to these issues and articulates directions for the future. We build on the previous edition of the *Handbook* that began to make the case for a cross-setting research agenda (e.g., Bransford et al., 2006; Perry, Turner, & Meyer, 2006). The discussion is organized in four sections. In the first section we frame our review with a theoretical perspective that foregrounds *learning in relation to cultural practices*. In the second section, we review research that informs our understanding of *varieties of learning environments*, with an emphasis on out-of-school settings. We make

connections and highlight contrasts to what is known about successful school-based learning environments, particularly project-based approaches designed for engaging learners in ambitious work. In the third section, we turn to research that helps us understand how *learning takes place across settings and time*. We identify conditions associated with catalysts and barriers to cross-setting learning, including the roles of learner interests, practice-linked identities, and learning partners who help coordinate opportunities, often over extended timeframes. In the final section, we outline several *directions for research* with a special emphasis on design-based research and the need for work that can continue to advance a social justice agenda of equal opportunities to learn for all (Moss, Pullin, Gee, Haertel, & Young, 2008).

## Learning in Relation to Cultural Practices

There is a growing interdisciplinary consensus that interest in understanding learning across time and contexts must be understood in relation to cultural practices (Cole, 1996; Nasir, Rosebery, Warren, & Lee, 2006; Rogoff, 2003). This social and historical view of learning has led to two important breakthroughs that open up new avenues for inquiry. First, there has been an important conceptual and methodological move away from privileging individual learners as the focal unit of analysis. This shift includes recognition that pedagogical approaches are cultural achievements that reflect historically grounded practices and are themselves continually revised and adapted to changing local conditions (Tomasello, 2009; Vygotsky, 1978). There is new emphasis on understanding social processes underlying developmental change (Meltzoff, Kuhl, Movellan, & Sejnowski, 2009), and this is made possible in part by neuroscience advances that reveal developmental changes before they can be seen in human behavior. Second, there has been a move away from conceptualizing learning as tied only to specific places, to learning as distributed and assembled across a variety of environments. In these environs, learners and their partners play important roles as designers who choose and craft configurations of social and material resources. This view leads to an analytic focus on pathways of learning, the role of learning networks in shaping these patterns, and suggests that any space might be conceived of as permeable and open to multiple influences rather than as closed, container-like settings (Barron, 2006; Leander, Phillips, & Taylor, 2010).

Both of these shifts are important for how we think about developing more equitable opportunities for learning. An asset-based cultural perspective demonstrates how non-dominant communities engage in creative practices to generate powerful learning arrangements that map to local interests, values, contexts, practices, and histories (Bang, Warren, Rosebery & Medin, 2012; Barron, Gomez, Pinkard, & Martin, 2014c; Bell, Tzou, Bricker, & Baines, 2012; Schwartz & Gutiérrez, in press). New lines of scholarship are beginning to document community learning processes and expertise development systematically and in relation to diverse social and ecological niches. The goal is to understand these cultural niches as important sites of learning (Kral & Heath, 2013) and to learn how such educational capital can be recognized and leveraged for broader social purposes (Bell et al., 2009).

By recognizing the intersecting roles of families, communities, organizations, and institutions in nurturing young learners, we are better positioned to recognize and leverage local forms of expertise and to attend to how histories of structural inequalities, economic circumstances, discrimination, and associated stresses can constrain access to learning opportunities. For example, studies that investigate extracurricular expenditures highlight the ways that dispensable income allows parents to supplement school learning with enrichment-oriented activities, materials, and a wide range of academically focused supports in out-of-school time during the school year and over the summer (Bennett, Lutz, & Jayaram, 2012; Chin & Phillips, 2004; Duncan & Murnane, 2014; Lareau, 2011). The many thousands of dollars that wealthy families spend on children each year pay for books, computing tools, travel opportunities, summer camps, organizational memberships, gear and clothing for specialized hobbies, transportation and enrollment fees, tutors, test preparation classes, access to academically oriented online communities, and entry fees to cultural institutions like museums. Differences in access to these out-of-school learning resources are likely contributors to differences in academic achievement, but there is increasing evidence that lack of access is also linked to missed opportunities for the development of domain-related interests (Archer et al., 2012; Ben-Eliyahu, Rhodes, & Scales, 2014; Bennett et al., 2012; Scales, Benson, & Roehlkepartain, 2011).

The good news is that intentionally designed, community-based programs that build on youth assets can help bridge experience gaps to which differences in family affluence contribute. Quantitative studies have shown that participation in diverse sets of activities, social networks, and domains is linked to social and school-related outcomes, including ideas about a learner's future, mental health, prosocial behavior, civic engagement, and academic skills in the near term and over years (e.g., Eccles & Gootman, 2002; Lerner, Almerigi, Theokas, Lerner, 2005). These findings about youth development mostly focus on early adolescence and general measures of well-being. However, they make clear the importance of developing innovative, theory-driven models that can engage young people in inspiring learning opportunities beyond the school day.

The term *organized activities* is used by youth development researchers to refer to settings that are primarily led by adults, invite voluntary participation, have a regular schedule, and are designed to support specific skills (Mahoney, Larson, & Eccles, 2005). Activities within these programs range widely in their structure, goals, institutional grounding, stability, funding, and the time commitment expected from learners (Bevan et al., 2010). Some are housed within stable cultural institutions such as libraries, churches, museums, zoos, or aquaria where visitors come on their own schedule and staff may be offered some professional training. Sports teams, theatre groups, musical ensembles, art organizations, and national organizations like FIRST Robotics provide intensive collaborative design or performance challenges often under the guidance of adults with domain expertise (Yim, Chow, & Dunbar, 2000). Large national organizations such as 4H, the YMCA, Girl Scouts and Boy Scouts, though largely led by volunteers at the local level, have institutional infrastructure and histories that support the development of a common set of activities and professional development experiences to help staff complete them (Rogoff, Topping, Baker-Sennett, & Lacasa, 2002).

The heterogeneity of out-of-school learning settings, and the relative novelty of some of their pedagogical approaches, present an immediate challenge for learning researchers but provide an incredibly rich, longer-term opportunity to expand the ways that we conceptualize and envision learning. To complement theoretical motivational principles such as those described in Chapter 7 (this volume), we need grounded images of practice that can inform the design of powerful learning experiences. To develop better theories of contexts of learning we need detailed accounts of the social and relational practices in these spaces, the nature and content of activities, and the opportunities for participation and experience they provide (Bohnert, Fredricks, & Randall, 2010; Eccles & Gootman, 2002; Rose-Krasnor, 2009; Vadeboncoeur, 2006). Research that takes a learning sciences and sociocultural perspective can provide such accounts (see Chapter 2, this volume).

## Varieties of Learning Environments

In the history of cognitive and sociocultural research on learning in and out of school, schools have been associated with the term *formal*; non-school settings have been referred to as *informal* (see Bransford et al., 2006; Scribner & Cole, 1973, for reviews). This contrast served to highlight different types of learning arrangements, processes, and outcomes (e.g., Bransford, Brown, & Cocking, 2000; Resnick, 1987), as well as to focus attention on how learning takes place without the bundle of practices that constitute what Tyack and Tobin (1994) aptly described as the "grammar of schooling" (p. 454). Though the forms of assessment and norms for participation in informal environments might look very different from those in schools, they are neither haphazard nor unstructured (Heath, 2001). Informal environments lend themselves to expert-supported engagement in authentic project work, with formalized roles, routine practices, and professional review that are consequential for expertise development, similar to what can take place in reform-oriented classrooms organized around problem- and project-based learning (Barron et al., 1998). Practices such as observation, imitation, collaboration, and apprenticeship take place in schools (Goodwin & Kryatzis, 2007; Rogoff, Paradise, Arauz, Correa-Chavez, & Angelillo, 2003), while processes that we typically associate with Western schooling such as quizzing or memorizing can be observed in homes and among peers engaging in non-school learning (Henze, 1992; Sénéchal & LeFevre, 2002).

Although the field has moved beyond simple dichotomies such as formal and informal, or school and non-school experiences, contrasting environments remains an important analytical heuristic for making visible similarities and differences in how they are organized and what they offer for learning (Bransford et al., 2006; Hull & Greeno, 2006; Resnick, 1987; Rogoff et al., 2003; Sefton-Green, 2013). Situated perspectives of learning and cognition have provided frameworks that help surface these. Constructs such as "intent participation" (p. 176) draw attention to learning processes such as close observation and listening-in on ongoing activities (Rogoff, 2003), and the "community-of-practice" perspective introduces the idea of inbound and outbound trajectories to describe changes in involvement of newcomers with understanding of norms and expectations (Lave & Wenger, 1991). The theory of guided participation (Rogoff, 1990) attends to roles of more- and less- expert partners, and the concept of participation structures (Au, 1980) helps identify routines that organize interactions. The construct of positioning (Harré & van Langenhove, 1999) attends to the dynamic, relational dimensions of learning interactions, regardless of where they take place.

The nature of adult–youth and peer-based relationships in non-school environments varies widely (Sullivan & Larson, 2009). Forms of learning partnerships are diverse and differentially suited for providing learners with views of more expert performance and supports for trajectories to competence (Nasir et al., 2006). Informal teaching approaches are often emergent and related to particular histories of participants and institutions. Conceptualizing dimensions of variability in learning partnerships is important for theorizing features associated with the generativity of non-traditional learning environments. Below we consider research focused on forms of guided participation. We begin with studies that focus on guided participation in co-located face-to-face settings and then review studies of interactions in online affinity spaces (Gee, 2005).

## Co-located Learning Settings

Making visible forms of guidance requires detailed observations of events, activities, and interactions between participants over time. Studies of workplace learning (Bailey & Barley, 2011), sports teams (Heath, 1991; Nasir & Hand, 2008), and intergenerational apprenticeships (Greenfield, 2004) reveal the variety of types of teaching/learning interactions that are powerful for expertise development. For example, Kirshner (2008) used ethnographic methods to study three civic engagement programs focused on multiracial activism. The research categorized prototypical forms of guidance in terms of a relative focus on following youth vs. adult interests and the degree of collaborative work. In one program, led by a university-based research center, adults took on *a neutral facilitator role that promoted student interests* and explicitly refrained from taking over decision making and project management, and from interjecting their own political views into the process. In a second program, housed in a community-based youth advocacy program, guidance followed an *apprenticeship model* with adults coaching, pitching in to complete tasks, and openly sharing their own political views. In the third program, hosted in an environmental justice organization, the model began with facilitation but moved to what Kirshner (2008) described as "joint work" (p. 73) organized around conference planning for youth and adult political officials. In this collaborative arrangement, the boundaries between youth and adults were blurred, with an intense focus on planning the best conference possible. These forms of guidance offered different opportunities to learn. For example, although the facilitation model allowed young people to learn to take initiative and manage group meetings, the apprenticeship model offered explicit modeling around persuasive speech, helping to make the domain of work visible (Nasir et al., 2006). The joint work model allowed youth to observe and participate in mature practices alongside adult professionals, providing even more explicit modeling.

Soep and Chávez (2010) described an approach to apprenticeship they call "collegial pedagogy" (p. 49), designed to support young journalists in Youth Radio, an award-winning media company. To prepare for original reporting work, novices are guided through a series of increasingly intensive experiences, including organized classes and peer mentoring focused on genres of reporting. Later they work directly with adult reporters or editors and are paid as interns to produce material. Consistent with established practices of documentary newsrooms, youth and adults engage in the collaborative framing of original work, but the young journalists ultimately have editorial power. The negotiation of stories is a key learning opportunity in this setting and critically important given the extended digital afterlife of published work.

By working so closely with established journalists, the more novice authors were given access to how seasoned writers anticipated reactions of diverse audiences to the stories they helped create, making invisible aspects of expertise transparent and available for reflection.

Guided participation in meaningful social practices relies upon productive social positioning of learners. The concept of positioning, drawn from studies of everyday discourse (Harré & van Langenhove, 1999; Holland & Leander, 2004; see Bricker & Bell, 2012b for a summary), focuses on how interactions are enacted such that people have shifting opportunities to take on, adapt, or reject particular roles, stances, or personas (Holland, Lachicotte, Skinner, & Cain, 1998; Nasir & Saxe, 2003). Social positions dynamically regulate the rights and responsibilities of actors in a given context of shared action. Relevant to our understanding of learning are occasions where a learner is offered different types of relationships to content by adults or peers, for example as a person capable of understanding content, contributing to a knowledge base or archive, having the authority to critique, or being able to teach others. This kind of moment-to-moment positioning can support or discourage participation and powerfully illustrates ways that young people can be cast in marginalized roles (e.g., Tzou, Scalone, & Bell, 2010; Wortham, 2004). It has also been used to show how students are positioned in positive ways. In a study of mathematics classrooms, Esmonde (2009) found that students were positioned in a variety of powerful roles, including those of expert or facilitator, when working on problems in groups.

In less hierarchical and more youth-controlled settings the importance of self-positioning becomes central as learners actively take on or reject tutoring or tutee roles and modify settings to support learning. Ma and Munter (2014) studied the dialectical relationship between activity and setting in skateboard parks. Learning opportunities were crafted when skaters chose to perform novel tricks in order to get feedback from peers, request tips, and observe more experienced peers. The park space was strategically "edited" (p. 39) to allow for more focused learning episodes. This work highlights how physical sites are not passive backgrounds or prefabricated containers for activity. The material arrangement of the built environment can be recruited to support the learning of the youth working to refine their practice within the site.

Whereas moment-to-moment social positioning is highly dynamic, project-based roles offer more stable ways of contributing to a learning experience. A growing body of work that focuses on project-based environments where learners are given roles as guides, teachers, or producers of teaching artifacts shows how these opportunities are powerful ways to both recognize and build expertise (see Barron & Darling-Hammond, 2010, for a review). Longer-term projects afford authentic roles as creators and contributors, and allow interdisciplinary pursuits that match work in professional endeavors. Research on learning in subjects such as the visual arts (Heath, 2004), musical apprenticeships (Mertl, 2009), sports (Heath, 1991), out-of-school science (Calabrese Barton & Tan, 2010; Heath, 2012; Polman & Miller, 2010), various digital hobbies (Barron, 2010; Ching & Kafai, 2008; Sheridan, 2011), and urban planning for biking safety (Taylor & Hall, 2013) has shown that the choosing of active roles on authentic projects can lead to growth in technical skills and content knowledge. Active role taking can also support students' identities as authors and creators. As a result of such activities, advances in language and problem-solving skills have been documented, marked by increases in hypothetical and counterfactual talk about possibility, conditional thinking, reasoning about contingency, strategies for getting clarification, and deeper perspective taking (Heath, 1999, 2001).

Learning environments also differ in the extent to which the core activities are framed as relevant to future activities. Engle (2006) hypothesized that if students come to understand that what they are doing is relevant to an ongoing intellectual conversation that extends across time, they will be more likely to choose to use what they learn in novel situations. She contrasts this future-oriented, more expansive frame with the more typical classwork framing, where topics are considered individually and are bound to the present. Being an author or researcher helps socialize students into roles as idea generators and sharers, preparing them for future opportunities to use what they have learned and signaling the social expectation that learners would be able to comment upon and challenge related ideas. Jurow, Hall, and Ma (2008) offer another example of expansive framing, a form of exchange they called "re-contextualizing" conversations (p. 1). These were initiated by working professional biologists invited to attend a middle-school math class where students had been developing population models of biological systems. They used a discursive strategy that invited students to consider how their models fit different contexts. It was an intentional design strategy to hybridize the environment in a way that served to position learners as developing experts with the support of disciplinary experts. The technique allowed students to try on new ways of thinking to act more like disciplinary experts in the school environment.

Understanding how learners are positioned in interactions by others, how they position themselves, and how activities are framed as more or less bounded in time, place, and community is relevant to both in school and out-of-school learning environments. These are also central for thinking about equity. Increasingly we are coming to understand the power of cultural stereotypes of both people and academic domains (Cheryan & Plaut, 2010). Racial and gender-based stereotypes appear to develop early (Cvencek, Meltzoff, & Greenwald, 2011; Cvencek, Nasir, O'Connor, Wischnia, & Meltzoff, 2014). Stereotype threat (Steele & Aronson, 1995) and the unintentional positioning of students as less capable can work together to diminish participation. The need for intentional repositioning is made clear in design experiments that start out with a social justice goal, only to find that patterns reassert themselves despite the best of intentions (see Barron et al., 2014c; Sims, 2014, for examples). Youth from non-dominant communities are frequently positioned as less capable; as a result, these youth can have a difficult time viewing themselves as being prepared for challenging academic pursuits (see Chapter 27, this volume). Socially positioning youth as developing experts and providing them with opportunities and supports associated with sophisticated intellectual work can help them overcome negative stereotypes and self-perceptions; however, attention to these dynamics has to be ongoing.

An important line of work reframes and extends the local sense-making practices developed and maintained by indigenous communities (González, Moll, & Amanti, 2013). Ethnographic and design-based studies led by Bang and Medin (2010) focus on the land-based practices of indigenous communities in the United States, which are often multigenerational arrangements focused on socializing youth into important epistemic practices and conceptual knowledge. A culturally expansive approach makes local practices a leading focus of instruction, and thereby leverages and extends the epistemologies, knowledge, and practices of the community in relation to new learning goals (Bang & Medin, 2010; Barton & Tan, 2010; Bell et al., 2012). These authors argue that it is important to teach from a relational epistemology, in contrast to a Western, Eurocentric perspective, because it is better aligned with how indigenous communities have historically made, and currently continue to make, sense of the natural world. A relational epistemology highlights the interconnections between components of a system (e.g., an ecosystem), including humans, whereas the dominant, Eurocentric view focuses on categorizing elements and typically excludes humans and built environments as integrated into the natural world.

The relational epistemology is often marginalized in traditional science instruction—when it can actually be viewed as having a deep correspondence with professional scientific knowledge (see Chapter 20, this volume). By recognizing a broader variety of sense-making practices and arenas for everyday competence, these environments frequently expand the forms of relevant work related to a given domain in comparison to how the domain is framed in traditional academic terms (Calabrese Barton, 2003; Stevens, 2013). This explicit epistemological framing (Berland & Hammer, 2012; Greeno, 2009) attends to participants' understanding of kinds of knowledge that are relevant for use in their activity and the kinds of information they need to construct to succeed in their activity (e.g., what kind of information would count as a solution to a problem). This explicit framing is crucial for native youth, who are often left having to navigate these multiple, conflicting epistemologies on their own. Moreover, the cultural and cognitive specifics of particular communities are documented as central forms of expertise and provide us with a more inclusive understanding of cognition and learning (Henrich, Heine, & Norenzayan, 2010)—as well as crucial educational design insights to inform education.

### Online Affinity Groups

In contrast to the mostly adult organized settings reviewed above, interest-driven online learning environments are more self-organizing and led by learners. Scholarship focused on these affinity groups is in its infancy, although studies that have been completed are provocative. Digitally based youth cultures are organized around interest-driven online communities where participants contribute to blogs and discussion boards, and share original video, animation, stories, and learning resources. For instance, using discourse analysis, studies of multiplayer online games documented scientific and mathematical hypothetical reasoning in the context of discussion and game play of MMOGs, known as massively multiplayer online games (Steinkuehler & Williams, 2009). An ethnographic study of an MMOG highlighted how a large, distributed collective appropriated new tools and learned to coordinate and refine joint action over the course of months (Chen, 2009).

Online, fan-based affinity groups organized around popular fiction, games, or television shows offer a range of ways for readers to engage in reading, contribute to discussion about texts, author fan fiction, and get feedback on original writing or analysis (Black, 2009). Ethnographic studies of these sites and their participants show the ways that community members socialize one another to use conventions and establish the credibility of an analysis, for example, by adding quotes and page numbers in reference to episodes or character depictions (Curwood, 2013). Even in communities that are organized around televised entertainment, academic disciplinary practices may be recruited. For instance, in a study of an online Wiki site that attracted fans of the televised historical drama *The Tudors*, an analysis of posts collected over a 5-month period revealed that, in this online space, debates about the historical accuracy of character portrayals and events took place. Disciplinary heuristics were observed, including contextualization and corroboration (Matthews, in press). Members used a range of types of sources to support their arguments. Questions about sources led to members searching for more information, which then led to the learning of new topics participants had not previously considered.

Several forms of self-directed, voluntary learning were also described in a study of contributors to an online film discussion site, with learning distributed among on- and offline activities (Sheridan, 2008). These included reading and writing about films, watching films alone or in larger groups organized for special screenings, subscribing to film magazines, and writing fiction based on films. These highly personalized routines functioned to build background knowledge, helped viewers find films to watch, inspired imaginative work, and supported the capacity to interpret and critique films.

Online creative communities have also grown around introductory programming tools that allow for the development of digital media for storytelling, game design, and animation. Many of these projects begin by taking an existing project and modifying images or code. In studies of the online "Scratch community," researchers have documented emergent practices of providing learning resources to one another (Kafai & Peppler, 2014), as well as generating norms around ethical practices like crediting ownership by referencing the origins of code or images used in media products. A culture of remixing in the Scratch community is particularly common (Monroy-Hernández, 2007), suggesting that this ethical practice was an important innovation for the community.

Other, rapidly growing online communities have emerged around the DIY or "Maker" movement reviewed in several recent publications (Kafai & Peppler, 2014; Peppler & Bender, 2013). Digital and physical production projects form the basis for highly active online communities where sharing learning and inspiration resources is a central form of exchange. Again, participation in the online communities is frequently combined with participation in co-located physical spaces, made possible by initiatives being sponsored by libraries, museums, neighborhood organizations, and households. A culture of generous sharing of tips for newcomers was also found in a study of Whyville.Net—an online virtual world (Fields & Kafai, 2010). The studies reviewed above focus on specific settings and the learning dynamics within them. We now turn to studies that attempt to go beyond a single space and conceptualize when learning moves and flows across settings and time.

## Learning Across Settings and Time

The review above focused on studies carried out in particular settings. However, learning is increasingly conceptualized as distributed across settings and extended time periods, with learners and their partners in learning playing an important role in assembling resources, establishing connections, and making choices about what, when, where, and how to learn (see Chapter 23, this volume). This broader conceptualization of learning is grounded in ecological and sociocultural perspectives that emerged from a desire to better articulate the interdependencies between child and environmental variables in development and acknowledge the tight intertwining of person and context in producing developmental change (Bronfenbrenner, 1979; Cole, 1996; Lee, 2008; Lerner, 1991; Lewin, 1951; Rogoff, 2003). In the early formulations of these perspectives, development was conceptualized as occurring as a result of microinteractional processes across short time frames within contexts and across settings. This broadly ecological view of learning foregrounds the permeability of settings and suggests we look for possible connections between learning at home, school, or in community settings as well as document missed opportunities associated with institutional borders (Phelan, Davidson, & Cao, 1991). Below we review research that speaks to some of the conditions associated with cross-setting learning.

### Interests as a Resource for Cross-setting Learning

A significant body of work has accumulated that shows a positive relationship between interest and motivation, attention, and vocational choices (see Hidi & Renninger, 2006, for review). Interest-driven learning is thought to be particularly important for development because it requires self-regulation, the defining and pursuit of goals, and reflection on how well one is doing. Interests can also support forms of academic resiliency, for example, in overcoming challenges in processing text (Fink, 2000). Personally meaningful interest-driven pursuits are also correlated with a connection to school, and well-being more generally (Ben-Eliyahu et al., 2014). There is some evidence that identification with disciplinary domains during the adolescent years is predictive of the completion of a related college major for about 20% of college graduates (Tai, Qi Liu, Maltese, & Fan, 2006).

What do we know about how interests emerge? Large-scale quantitative longitudinal studies point to the importance of understanding the role of families (Croll, 2009; Dabney, Chakraverty, & Tai, 2013). Smaller-scale naturalistic studies also document how from an early age interests are shared between parents and children, between siblings, and in relation to broader networks of relatives and friends who spend time together at home. Parents indirectly influence interests by providing particular toys or media, by arranging social activities or excursions, and by arranging interest-related internships or volunteer experiences (Zimmerman, 2012). Provision of materials that match a child's interest can encourage sustained exploration of a topic that can in turn develop both content knowledge and interest (Fender & Crowley, 2007; Leibham, Alexander, Johnson, Neitzel & Reis-Henrie, 2005).

More directly, parents contribute to interests by engaging in co-activity such as playing board games, reading aloud to children, engaging in building projects, or using digital media together. In these shared contexts, parents can express their enthusiasm, explanations can be provided spontaneously or in response to questions, and children have an opportunity to demonstrate their interest or lack of it in particular activities and content. For example, in an ethnographic study of musical parenting, intergenerational practices of singing and music making were documented as well as reciprocal child–parent interest in listening and producing traditional, popular, and spiritual songs (Gibson, 2009). Relatedly, Goodwin (2007) described one family's "occasioned knowledge exploration" (p. 97) that routinely emerged during daily walks, dinners, car rides, or bedtime stories. Within these interactions, playful imaginative conversations were connected to prior knowledge when a child asked questions and parents provided detailed explanations. Not surprisingly, the internet is being used as a resource to explore children's and parents' interests, through curated collections of media and information seeking about emergent topics (Barron, Levinson, & Matthews, 2013; Takeuchi & Stevens, 2011).

Though studies of cross-setting influences in very young children's interests are rare, there is some work that has shown links between interests expressed at home and at school. In a prospective study, 4-year-olds' interests were tracked for a year through parent report and then researchers observed the children in their kindergarten classrooms. Consistent with the idea that interests can transfer across settings, observational data revealed interest-linked differences in the type of information that children contributed to discussions and the information they pursued through questions or requests for help (Neitzel, Alexander, & Johnson, 2008; Rowe & Neitzel, 2010). In an ethnographic study of learning across preschool and home settings, Mehus, Stevens, and Grigholm (2013) traced examples of home-based activities related to measurement observed as children traveled to the classroom setting. Interests originating in school and traveling home have also been reported. In an experiment that used the television show *Sid the Science Kid* as an anchor for inquiry and discussion, Penuel et al. (2010) found that preschool children initiated more science talk at home than they did in control conditions.

Some researchers suggest that only middle-class parents support their children's interest-driven learning as part of a broader process of concerted cultivation (e.g., Lareau, 2011). Other ethnographic studies counter this broad generalization, while confirming the role of resources in a family's ability to fully develop expertise in areas of interest (Barron, 2010; Bell et al., 2012; Chin & Phillips; 2004). For example, recent studies of family media practices show how interest-driven, boundary-crossing learning was supported by repertoires of new media practices. In a study of recent immigrants from Mexico and Central America, Levinson (2014) found that parents used free translator tools to better understand their child's homework and used search engines to find content related to the interests of their children, including biographies of historical figures, transportation, and dinosaurs. Often these were topics introduced at school. In an ethnographic study of how low-income Hispanic families leverage cell phones for play, learning, and safety, Schwartz and Gutiérrez (in press) found that in the Ramirez family, both mother's and father's interests were shared with their children and that these interests were further developed in an out-of-school community setting. The mother's interests in cooking and cooking shows were shared by her daughters and led to collaborative practices of looking up information, developing play scripts around cooking competitions, and the collaborative production of a home video.

### Stabilization of Practice-linked Identities Through Social Recognition Work

The incorporation of *identity* has been increasingly important for conceptualizing these cross-setting learning dynamics as it helps make visible relationships between persons, domains, and pursuits over time (Holland & Leander, 2004; Hull & Greeno, 2006; Lave & Wenger, 1991). For example Nasir and Hand (2008) develop the idea of practice-linked identities (see Chapter 14, this volume). This construct expands notions of identity development from more individually focused, psychological perspectives, to a more social and situated view that considers how people form understandings of themselves through deepening engagement in culturally and historically situated and socially enacted practices, as well as how interactions with peers and adults can shift individual perspectives. These authors illustrate this view with a study of young athletes on a track team, analyzing the interrelationships between resources, including physical practice

space, interactions with a coach and teammates, and the goals and credos of the sport. Becoming a hurdler, for example, requires mastering material resources, including the track, uniforms, spikes, and hurdles. Explicit communication that positions particular team members as future athletes (e.g., "you are going to be a hurdler") bolsters the connection between a novice athlete and the track practice, particularly when he or she encounters challenges in mastering a specific skill. It also means more focused coaching, which then deepens athletes' expertise and identification with the sport, or practice-linked identities.

Studies that follow interests over time suggest that engagement is often fluctuating, idiosyncratic, and supported by varied social and material resources. This variability can be seen in studies of hobbies and how they develop (e.g., Liu & Falk, 2013), in studies of talented teens (Csikszentmihalyi, Rathunde, & Whalen, 1997), and in retrospective case studies of professionals who demonstrated excellence in their areas of expertise by age 40 (Bloom, 1985). What kinds of resources support stable engagement? In a case study of amateur astronomers, Azevedo (2013) found significant variability among practitioners that associated with unique personal preferences in the form of values, beliefs, and long-term goals related to the same hobby. Some participants were motivated to seek out constellations for their aesthetic qualities but were also motivated by the opportunity to teach. For other participants, being recognized as an expert through certificates or awards was an important driver of particular lines of activity. Reading, observing, drawing, and building were also common lines of practice tied to particular preferences and these were practices that often showed up in other aspects of a hobbyist's life. Separate lines of activity were made possible and constrained by specific conditions of practice that included things like time, money, access to material infrastructure, community norms, and the availability of social partners.

As we noted earlier, recent research shows how social reputations influence the practice-linked identities of individuals through the mechanism of social positioning—the shaping of evolving rights and responsibilities of individuals within specific social contexts (Bricker & Bell, 2012b). It is thought that these recurrent moments of being positioned as a developing expert promote the social affiliation and sense of belonging needed to more fully identify with specific communities of practice (Luehmann, 2009). The social recognition work that takes place within communities associated with expertise development is a central feature of the learning process and the associated stabilization of identities. When being recognized as an expert leads to invitations to teach or work for pay, there is the added benefit of a new setting for learning. Examples of this kind of recognition offered by schools or other organized learning settings were found in studies of teens with programming expertise who were invited to take on work for pay or become teaching assistants (Barron, Martin, Takeuchi, & Fithian, 2009), teens who have created social networks designed for political discussion and invited to lead workshops for teachers (Barron et al., 2014c), and longitudinal studies of girls involved in community-oriented science clubs asked to create educational artifacts (Calabrese Barton et al., 2013). Similar results occurred in research inside of a Citizen Science project where specialized expertise in local insects was recruited to create field guides for the broader community (Barron, Martin, & Mertl, 2014b), and in ethnographies of voluntary expertise development where social reputations were found to be both a marker and a maker of expertise (Bricker & Bell, 2012a).

Several extended ethnographic cases detail how the stabilization of practice-linked identities is supported through parents' social recognition of a child's interest and developing expertise. These cases also address how parents further resource that learning pathway at more ambitious levels of participation (Barron, 2006; Bricker & Bell, 2012a, 2014). For example, in a study of Silicon Valley teens with practice-linked identities related to computing (Barron et al., 2009), parents brokered opportunities for their children by connecting them with new people or places that provided chances for them to deepen their expertise. More directly, they collaborated with their sons and daughters to build robots, engage in playful programming activities, or learn HTML. These forms of guidance provided views into workplace learning practices when parents made connections between their child's activity and what they themselves experienced as professionals, or when parents arranged for their children to develop paid work experience using their technical expertise. Although parents were important, activities contributing to teens' learning ecologies were distributed across home, online, school, and neighborhood sites. Teens pursued tutorials online, read books, joined online communities, chose to take technology-focused electives, and developed relationships with mentors.

Mentors and extended family members can also be critical brokers and sponsors of new opportunities (Brandt, 2001; DuBois, Portillo, Rhodes, Silverthorn, & Valentine, 2011). Zimmerman (2012) documented how a family's participation in their faith community practices led their daughter to be connected with multiple, supportive godparents—some of whom provided the girl with different domain-related mentoring and learning resources (e.g., to learn mathematics, to use technology). In a 4-year study of engineering students, Stevens, O'Connor, Garrison, Jocuns, and Amos (2008) showed how the parent of a friend, who was an engineering professor, nurtured a childhood interest in engineering through the establishment of an airplane club. Many years later this interest translated into the pursuit of an engineering major at a public university. Academic challenges threatened to block completion but the mentorship of his professor friend, and perhaps most importantly, the brokering of an internship in a company, led to significant shifts in the friend's expertise that enabled him to excel in the end.

Disconnects between home- and school-centered interests are also important to understand. Learners define and pursue broad, multifaceted disciplines like science or history in divergent ways, in the context of available activities and resources. In a multisited ethnography, researchers documented unfolding cultural learning pathways (Bell, Bricker, Reeve, Zimmerman & Tzou, 2013), especially those related to science and technology, which youth from a culturally and linguistically diverse immigrant community navigated over a 4-year period across hundreds of social settings. In addition to the ethnographic accounts, the research team also developed an ecologically validated interview that allowed them to understand the disparate ways in which the youth perceived "science" in relation to the practices in their lives (Zimmerman & Bell, 2014). The analysis highlighted the multifaceted and divergent personal meanings that learners associate with such broad disciplinary labels—some viewed science as activities they only conducted in school; others had their science-related interests focused on personal hobbies; and others interpreted science as being centrally about specific subdisciplines (e.g., chemistry, paleontology, technology development). Still others saw most of life's activities as meaningfully connecting to science.

Through the linked set of child ethnographies, the Bell team highlighted a range of sophisticated and often highly innovative social and material arrangements used to support the cultural learning pathways of youth's voluntary expertise development (Bell et al., 2012). Many of the families were living under constrained financial conditions, and yet were still resourceful and able to dedicate much of their discretionary funds to support their children's interest-driven expertise development when it was seen as prosocial or potentially advantageous in the long term. One family engaged in a complex set of elective technological and gaming practices not connected to their children's school pursuits (Bricker & Bell, 2012a). The family had a well-developed arrangement for passing down technologies to the younger members of the family over time, allowing for apprenticeship learning arrangements. Coordinated sets of social, material, and technological resources allowed one youth to cultivate his gaming practice, identify with it, and develop precocious expertise in multiple genres and platforms by the end of elementary school (e.g., chess, MMOG). Other youth also decided to pursue their science-related expertise development in out-of-school time, but not bring that knowledge to school (although that would have been appropriate). In one case, a deep interest in and growing knowledge of chemistry by a fifth-grade girl could be traced back to the rather culturally unique preschool play experiences of "mixing" with her cousin, and the recognition of this interest and ongoing resourcing by her mother and an extended family member. However, the girl also sometimes elected not to leverage this expertise in relevant moments of schooling (Bricker & Bell, 2014).

Peer perceptions of the expertise youth develop can also strongly influence how they highlight or hide their interests and identities across different settings. In yet another of the cases, a young girl had a multiyear learning pathway developing which focused on understanding and taking care of animals through a systematic proto-scientific practice.

She chose to keep this secret from her peers at school so as to not be viewed as a "geek" or "nerd" who loves science (Zimmerman, 2012). Informal education programs also helped initiate multiyear learning pathways of youth, including that of one young man who developed design expertise (Bricker & Bell, in review). A 1-week summer program in the third grade led to the multiyear pursuit where he cultivated his practice, developed deep resiliency in technical trouble shooting, and learned to create innovative designs. Again, much of this expertise was not viewed as relevant to his schooling.

Practice-linked identity development is a slow and non-linear process. Personal and program goals do not always mesh automatically. Dawes and Larson (2011) interviewed teens and young adults who were participating in one of ten art or leadership programs. Only a subset of youth were identified as having a positive shift in the intensity of their connection to the programs, accounted for by the integration of personal goals with program activities—a specific form of hybridity more easily accomplished in out-of-school time than in the classroom, where mandated learning goals strongly constrain what can be learned. These goals included learning for the future, developing specific skills and competencies, and conceptualizing a sense of purpose beyond the self.

The match between pre-existing interests and mentor interests is also important. In a 3-year, longitudinal study following learners participating in afterschool clubs, variation in practice-linked identities, predictions for future learning, and technical expertise were associated with the match between mentor and learner interests and whether contests and other project-based opportunities allowed for the exploration of specific interests. Despite this variability, self-sustained learning in the form of creating novel projects or teaching others did emerge over time (Barron, Martin, & Mertl, 2014a). Specific forms of intentional positioning were important, including recognizing expertise through invitations to take on roles—for instance, (a) asking members to speak at forums, participate in committees, or lead workshops; and (b) recruiting bystanders by offering personal invitations to students who were less engaged.

Contrasting learning biographies within and across communities make visible the extensive differences in resources that learners have access to, as well as the significant differences in the amount of experience with particular domains that can emerge long before middle school. These are differences sometimes due to stark contrasts in personal learning networks at home or school, but they can also be traced to variation in adults' noticing of potential interests, or a child's skills in recruiting the attention of mentors, teachers, or parents (Barron et al., 2014a; Crowley, Barron, Knutson, & Martin, in press). The ethnographic case studies reviewed here highlight the importance of being socially positioned as a developing expert in a domain, the social and material resourcing of deepening engagement in practices over years, and the support in knowing how to navigate personal interests in relation to the competing expectations and value systems of multiple institutions and organizations.

## Directions for Research

We began this chapter with an emphasis on the importance of designing for equity and we close with some ideas for future research that might advance a social justice agenda. Differential access to inspiring out-of-school learning resources no doubt contributes to differences in academic achievement. There is, however, increasing evidence that such access is also linked to missed opportunities for the development of committed interests related to particular domains. These findings lend urgency to the tasks of theory development and to the study of novel varieties of learning environments. Our review of research suggests several important directions for future work; namely, further conceptualizing and supporting roles for mentors; design-based research that spans organizations and sites for learning; and new metrics for assessing outcomes linked to opportunities to learn across the life spaces of youth.

### Conceptualizing and Supporting Hybrid Roles for Mentors

Our review suggests that defining new forms of pedagogy, hybrid roles, and interactional practices for educators is both a major challenge and an opportunity for the field of non-school learning (also see Chan et al., 2013; Erickson, McDonald, & Elder, 2009). We need to know more about how face-to-face and online interpersonal interactions between educators, youth, and peers best recruit joint attention, engagement, and trust. We also need to understand more about how adults in community spaces and in homes can position learners in ways that help connect them to additional opportunities to learn and develop practice-linked identities. We now have several empirical examples of ways that adults broker new opportunities, frame experiences, and make suggestions about future pathways. More of this kind of work would be useful, particularly if we want to find ways to help adults imagine new ways of connecting young people to social and material resources that can help them continue to learn, and deepen their connection to practices and possible selves. Equally important are studies that will help us understand interactional or cultural barriers. Adults serve intentionally or unintentionally as gatekeepers who can block access to resources or may not value youth practices that are interest-driven.

It is likely that new forms of professional development for mentors and educators will be needed. Earlier studies of urban, community-based organizations identified a number of characteristics of "wizards" (p. 37)—adults who lead youth-oriented organizations and are able to earn the loyalty and respect of the youth they serve (McLaughlin, Irby, & Langman, 1994). These characteristics included positive perception of and emphasis on youth assets rather than problems, personal connections to neighborhoods, a willingness to work for little pay, a sensibility of giving back to their own communities, and a belief that they can make a difference in young people's futures. One conclusion that might be drawn is that these adults are so unique and their vocations so highly personal that it is impossible to support newcomers in this role. However, some research suggests that, contrary to the notion that high-quality mentorship is found rather than developed, collective work to co-develop one's practice can be a powerful way for adults to generate new ideas about varied ways to position mentees for leadership, teaching, and the imaginative work of envisioning their possible futures (Barron et al., 2014c). Basic research on mentor development and design experiments is needed to advance our capacity to support guides, coaches, and artist-mentors in their essential work.

## Design-Based Research and New Methods for Coordinating Learning Across Settings

The ecological metaphor is being taken up not only as an analytical tool, but also as a design resource. There is great interest in developing new forms of collaboration among schools and other learning organizations. Systemic approaches to design are emerging that are organized to build synergies across school and out-of-school time (Bevan et al., 2010; Itō et al., 2013). Questions about how we can intentionally catalyze cross-setting learning have gained currency with rapidly changing technologies that provide novel opportunities for the design of hybrid forms of curriculum-based learning that span virtual and co-located settings. The promise in this approach is that participation in activities in multiple learning environments over time and across spaces can serve to build cultural learning pathways, which will link experiences in discrete learning settings into developmental trajectories of participation.

Innovations in cross-setting learning need to be documented, both to support the continuous improvement process that Bryk and Gomez call "networked improvement communities" (Bryk, Gomez, & Grunow, 2011), but also to help ensure that generative models can spread, scale, and can be sustained (Coburn, Catterson, Higgs, & Morel, 2013; Lawson & Lawson, 2013). We especially need to know how they come to support youth from underresourced communities and the qualities of the competencies they cultivate.

## New Methods to Track Sustained Engagement

If the field begins to take seriously the potential benefit of hybrid, systemic designs to connect learning across settings, then we will need to develop methods that can measure sustained engagement and document practices and conditions associated with successful synergies. Some of the research we reviewed suggests that when learners begin to develop their own projects, set their own goals for learning, find resources that support their expertise development, build relationships that advance their agendas, and come to be recognized by others for their expertise, we can be confident that their learning is becoming more committed and will spawn the persistence needed for expertise development. These outcomes are in fact the ones that most educators would be delighted to see, but they are difficult to document without longitudinal research methods that can track the evolution of activities, artifacts, and relationships over time (Vossoughi & Gutiérrez, 2013; see Chapter 2, this volume). There is a significant need to develop metrics for outcomes that go beyond academic skills to include growth in interests and identities, self-efficacy for generating new ideas, repertoires of collaborative practices, depth and types of learning partnerships, future plans in relation to possible selves, and in meta-awareness of learning pathways and choices (see Chapter 12, this volume). These are not typically assessed, but map on to the kinds of inter- and intrapersonal competencies being highlighted in recent publications focused on the future of work and learning (Pellegrino & Hilton, 2012). They connect with positive outcomes called out in the youth development literature, such as initiative—the capacity to direct attention and effort toward challenging goals (Bohnert et al., 2010; Larson, 2000)—and the expertise literature, that highlights the importance of deliberate practice (Ericsson, 2004).

Future research will need to create novel methodologies to better understand learners as contributing designers of their own learning environments as they increasingly can make choices that allow them to craft configurations of experiences and locate resources made possible by digital platforms. New data collection tools, protocols, and data representations are needed to help us to see and document how learners coordinate resources (see Chapter 5, this volume) as they make choices to learn (Schwartz & Arena, 2013; see Chapter 29, this volume). Biographical methods are important for this kind of work but they are also costly. Learning analytic approaches that track the performance and artifact portfolios for learners across multiple sites of participation is a promising avenue to pursue. Self-documentation, the collection of digital traces of participation, and mobile platforms for multisited ethnography are all pioneering attempts to characterize new forms of learning.

This chapter adds to a set of recent research syntheses suggesting we design for a future where learning opportunities are distributed and connected across the settings of home, school, and community (e.g., Itō et al., 2013). New methods for research are required that can serve to document and inspire approaches that create synergies across the spaces where learners spend time. At the same time, although researchers and policymakers recognize the unique benefits that out-of-school learning opportunities may bring (Hirsch, Deutsch, and DuBois 2011), there is a danger that non-school time will be co-opted by school agendas, or that more informal spaces will become subject to school-like accountability structures and lose their distinctive features (Nocon & Cole, 2006). Better theories and studies of the forms and functions of out-of-school spaces may help prevent these possible outcomes. There is much to be done and much at stake.

## Note

1. The writing of this chapter was supported by the LIFE Science of Learning Center (Learning in Informal and Formal Environments), a National Science Foundation (NSF)-funded (REC-354453) effort and an NSF cyberlearning grant (REC-1124568). We thank Rogers Hall and Bronwyn Bevan for their insightful comments on the first version of the manuscript.

# References

Archer, L., DeWitt, J., Osborne, J., Dillon, J., Willis, B., & Wong, B. (2012). Science aspirations, capital, and family habitus: How families shape children's engagement and identification with science. *American Educational Research Journal, 49*(5), 881–908.

Au, K. H. P. (1980). Participation structures in a reading lesson with Hawaiian children: Analysis of a culturally appropriate instructional event. *Anthropology & Education Quarterly, 11*(2), 91–115.

Azevedo, F. S. (2013). The tailored practice of hobbies and its implication for the design of interest-driven learning environments. *Journal of the Learning Sciences, 22*(3), 462–510.

Bailey, D. E., & Barley, S. R. (2011). Teaching-learning ecologies: Mapping the environment to structure through action. *Organization Science, 22*(1), 262–285.

Bang, M., & Medin, D. (2010). Cultural processes in science education: Supporting the navigation of multiple epistemologies. *Science Education, 94*(6), 1008–1026.

Bang, M., Warren, B., Rosebery, A., & Medin, D. L. (2012). Relationality: Teaching and learning in the intersections of epistemology, the disciplines, and culture. *Human Development, 55*, 302–318.

Banks, J., Au, K., Ball, A., Bell, P., & Gordon, E. (2007). *Learning in and out of school in diverse environments: Life-long, life-wide, life-deep*. Seattle, WA: University of Washington.

Barron, B. (2006). Interest and self-sustained learning as catalysts of development: A learning ecology perspective. *Human Development, 49*(4), 193–224.

Barron, B. (2010). Conceptualizing and tracing learning pathways over time and setting. *National Society for the Study of Education Yearbook, 109*(1), 113–127.

Barron, B., & Darling-Hammond, L. (2010). Prospects and challenges for inquiry-based approaches to learning. In H. Dumont, D. Istance, & F. Benavides (Eds.), *The nature of learning: Using research to inspire practice*. Paris: OECD.

Barron, B., Gomez, K., Pinkard, N., & Martin, C. K. (2014c). *The Digital Youth Network: Cultivating digital media citizenship in urban communities*. Cambridge, MA: MIT Press.

Barron, B., Levinson, A., & Matthews, J. (2013). Parent and child interests as drivers of joint media engagement. In A. Levinson (Chair), *Joint media engagement: Diverse perspectives on how young children, families and teachers learn and interact with media together*. Symposium conducted at the Annual Meeting of the AERA, San Francisco, CA.

Barron, B., Martin, C. K., & Mertl, V. (2014a). Appropriating the process: Creative production within informal interactions and across settings. In B. Barron, K. Gomez, N. Pinkard, & C. K. Martin (Eds.), *The Digital Youth Network: Cultivating digital media citizenship in urban communities*. Cambridge, MA: MIT Press.

Barron, B., Martin, C. K., & Mertl, V. (2014b). Connecting to science through art: Examples from a Citizen Science project. Paper presented at the *NARST Annual International Conference*.

Barron, B., Martin, C. K., Takeuchi, L., & Fithian, R. (2009). Parents as learning partners in the development of technological fluency. *International Journal of Learning and Media, 1*(2), 55–77.

Barron, B., Schwartz, D. L., Vye, N. J., Moore, A., Petrosino, A., Zech, L., & Bransford, J. D. (1998). Doing with understanding: Lessons from research on problem- and project-based learning. *Journal of the Learning Sciences, 7*(3–4), 271–311.

Barton, A. C., & Tan, E. (2010) We be burnin'! Agency, identity, and science learning. *Journal of the Learning Sciences, 19*(2), 187–229.

Bell, P., Bricker, L. A., Reeve, S., Zimmerman, H. T., & Tzou, C. (2013). Discovering and supporting successful learning pathways of youth in and out of school: Accounting for the development of everyday expertise across settings. In B. Bevan, P. Bell, R. Stevens, & A. Razfar (Eds.), *LOST opportunities: Learning in out-of-school time* (pp. 119–140). Dordrecht, the Netherlands: Springer.

Bell, P., Lewenstein, B., Shouse, A. W., & Feder, M. A. (Eds.), Committee on Learning Science in Informal Environments, National Research Council. (2009). *Learning science in informal environments: People, places, and pursuits*. Washington, DC: The National Academies Press.

Bell, P., Tzou, C., Bricker, L. A., & Baines, A. D. (2012). Learning in diversities of structures of social practice: Accounting for how, why and where people learn science. *Human Development, 55*, 269–284.

Ben-Eliyahu, A., Rhodes, J. E., & Scales, P. (2014). The interest-driven pursuits of 15 year-olds: "Sparks" and their association with caring relationships and developmental outcomes. *Applied Developmental Science, 18*(2), 76–89.

Bennett, P. R., Lutz, A. C., & Jayaram, L. (2012). Beyond the schoolyard: The role of parenting logics, financial resources, and social institutions in the social class gap in structured activity participation. *Sociology of Education, 85*(2), 131–157.

Berland, L. K., & Hammer, D. (2012). Students' framings and their participation in scientific argumentation. In M. S. Khine (Ed.), *Perspectives on scientific argumentation* (pp. 73–93). New York, NY: Springer.

Bevan, B., Bell, P., Stevens, R., & Razfar, A. (Eds.) (2013). LOST opportunities: Learning in out-of-school time. In S. R. Steinberg & K. Tobin (Ser. Eds.), *Explorations of educational purpose* (Vol. 23). Dordrecht, the Netherlands: Springer.

Bevan, B., Dillon, J., Hein, G. E., Macdonald, M., Michalchik, V., Miller, D., Root, D., Rudder, L., Xanthoudaki, M., & Yoon, S. (2010). *Making science matter: Collaborations between informal science education organizations and schools. A CAISE Inquiry Group Report*. Washington, D.C.: Center for Advancement of Informal Science Education (CAISE).

Black, R. W. (2009). Online fan fiction, global identities, and imagination. *Research in the Teaching of English, 43*(4), 397–425.

Bloom, B. (1985). *Developing talent in young people*. New York: Ballantine.

Bohnert, A., Fredricks, J., & Randall, E. (2010). Capturing unique dimensions of youth organized activity involvement: Theoretical and methodological considerations. *Review of Educational Research, 80*(4), 576–610.

Brandt, D. (2001). *Literacy in American lives*. Cambridge, UK: Cambridge University Press.

Bransford, J. D., Brown, A., & Cocking, R. (2000). *How people learn: Mind, brain, experience and school* (expanded ed.). Washington DC: National Academy Press.

Bransford, J. D., Vye, N., Stevens, R., Kuhl, P., Schwartz, D., Bell, P., Meltzoff, A., Barron, B., Pea, R. D., Reeves, B., Roschelle, J., & Sabelli, N. (2006). Learning theories and education: Toward a decade of synergy. In P. Alexander & P. Winne (Eds.), *Handbook of educational psychology* (2nd ed., pp. 209–244). Mahwah, NJ: Erlbaum.

Bricker, L. A., & Bell, P. (2012a). "GodMode is his video game name": Situating learning and identity in structures of social practice. *Cultural Studies of Science Education, 7*(4), 883–902.

Bricker, L. A., & Bell, P. (2012b). Positioning, situated learning, and identity formation. In J. A. Banks (Ed.), *Encyclopedia of diversity in education* (Vol. 4, pp. 1677–1678). New York, NY: Sage.

Bricker, L. A., & Bell, P. (2014). "What comes to mind when you think of science? The perfumery!" Documenting science-related cultural learning pathways across contexts and timescales. *Journal of Research in Science Teaching, 51*(3), 260–285.

Bricker, L. A., & Bell, P. (in review). "I want to be an engineer": Network, framing, and positioning dynamics associated with youth STEM learning and expertise development.

Bronfenbrenner, U. (1979). Contexts of child rearing: Problems and prospects. *American Psychologist, 34*(10), 844–850.

Bryk, A. S., Gomez, L. M., & Grunow, A. (2011). Getting ideas into action: Building networked improvement communities in education. In M. T. Hallinan (Ed.), *Frontiers in sociology and social research: Vol. 1. Frontiers in sociology of education* (pp. 127–162). Dordrecht, the Netherlands: Springer.

Calabrese Barton, A. (2003). *Teaching science for social justice*. New York, NY: Teachers College Press.

Calabrese Barton, A., Kang, H., Tan, E., O'Neill, T. B., Bautista-Guerra, J., & Brecklin, C. (2013). Crafting a future in science: Tracing middle school girls' identity work over time and space. *American Educational Research Journal, 50*(1), 37–75.

Calabrese Barton, A., & Tan, E. (2010). We be burnin'! Agency, identity, and science learning. *Journal of the Learning Sciences, 19*(2), 187–229.

Chan, C. S., Rhodes, J. E., Howard, W. J., Lowe, S. R., Schwartz, S. E. O., & Herrera, C. (2013). Pathways of influence in school-based mentoring: The mediating role of parent and teacher relationships. *Journal of School Psychology*, *51*(1), 129–142.

Chen, M. G. (2009). Communication, coordination, and camaraderie in World of Warcraft. *Games and Culture*, *4*(1), 47–73.

Cheryan, S., & Plaut, V. C. (2010). Explaining underrepresentation: A theory of precluded interest. *Sex Roles*, *63*(7–8), 475–488.

Chin, T., & Phillips, M. (2004). Social reproduction and child-rearing practices: Social class, children's agency, and the summer activity gap. *Sociology of Education*, *77*(3), 185–210.

Ching, C., & Kafai, Y. B. (2008). Peer pedagogy: Student collaboration and reflection in a learning-through-design project. *The Teachers College Record*, *110*(12), 2601–2632.

Coburn, C. E., Catterson, A. K., Higgs, J., & Morel, R. (2013). *Spread and scale in the digital age: A report to the MacArthur Foundation*. Evanston, IL: Northwestern University.

Cole, M. (1996). *Cultural psychology: A once and future discipline*. Cambridge, MA: Harvard University Press.

Croll, P. (2009). Educational participation post-16: A longitudinal analysis of intentions and outcomes. *British Journal of Educational Studies*, *57*(4), 400–416.

Crowley, K., Barron, B. J., Knutson, K., & Martin, C. K. (in press). Interest and the development of pathways to science. To appear in K. A. Renninger, M. Nieswandt, & S. Hidi (Eds.), *Interest in mathematics and science learning and related activity*. Washington, DC: AERA.

Csikszentmihalyi, M., Rathunde, K., & Whalen, S. (1997). *Talented teenagers: The roots of success and failure*. Cambridge University Press.

Curwood, J. S. (2013). The hunger games: Literature, literacy, and online affinity spaces. *Language Arts*, *90*(6), 417–427.

Cvencek, D., Meltzoff, A. N., & Greenwald, A. G. (2011). Math–gender stereotypes in elementary school children. *Child Development*, *82*(3), 766–779.

Cvencek, D., Nasir, N. S., O'Connor, K., Wischnia, S., & Meltzoff, A. N. (2014). The development of math–race stereotypes: "They say Chinese people are the best at math." *Journal of Research on Adolescence*. http://dx.doi.org/10.1111/jora.12151.

Dabney, K. P., Chakraverty, D., & Tai, R. H. (2013). The association of family influence and initial interest in science. *Science Education*, *97*(3), 395–409.

Dawes, N. P., & Larson, R. (2011). How youth get engaged: Grounded-theory research on motivational development in organized youth programs. *Developmental Psychology*, *47*(1), 259–269.

DuBois, D. L., Portillo, N., Rhodes, J. E., Silverthorn, N., & Valentine, J. C. (2011). How effective are mentoring programs for youth? A systematic assessment of the evidence. *Psychological Science in the Public Interest*, *12*(2), 57–91.

Duncan, G. J., & Murnane, R. J. (2014). Growing income inequality threatens American education. *Phi Delta Kappan*, *95*(6), 8–14.

Eccles, J. S., & Gootman, J. A. (Eds.) (2002). *Community programs to promote youth development*. Washington, DC: National Academies Press.

Engle, R. A. (2006). Framing interactions to foster generative learning: A situative explanation of transfer in a community of learners classroom. *Journal of the Learning Sciences, 15*(4), 451–498.

Erickson, L. D., McDonald, S., & Elder, G. H. (2009). Informal mentors and education: Complementary or compensatory resources? *Sociology of Education*, *82*(4), 344–367.

Ericsson, K. A. (2004). Deliberate practice and the acquisition and maintenance of expert performance in medicine and related domains. *Academic Medicine*, *79*(10), S70–S81.

Esmonde, I. (2009). Ideas and identities: Supporting equity in cooperative mathematics learning. *Review of Educational Research*, *79*(2), 1008–1043.

Fender, J. G., & Crowley, K. (2007). How parent explanation changes what children learn from everyday scientific thinking. *Journal of Applied Developmental Psychology*, *28*(3), 189–210.

Fields, D. A., & Kafai, Y. B. (2010). "Stealing from Grandma" or generating cultural knowledge? Contestations and effects of cheating in a tween virtual world. *Games and Culture*, *5*(1), 64–87.

Fink, R. P. (2000). Gender, self-concept, and reading disabilities. *Thalamus: Journal of the International Academy for Research in Learning Disabilities*, *18*(1), 15–33.

Gibson, R. E. (2009). *Musical parenting: An ethnographic account of musical interactions of parents and young children*. Unpublished dissertation. University of Washington.

Gee, J. P. (2005). Semiotic social spaces and affinity spaces: From the Age of Mythology to today's schools. In D. Barton & K. Tusting (Eds.), *Beyond communities of practice: Language, power and social context* (pp. 214–232). Cambridge: Cambridge University Press.

González, N., Moll, L. C., & Amanti, C. (Eds.). (2013). *Funds of knowledge: Theorizing practices in households, communities, and classrooms*. New York, NY: Routledge.

Goodwin, M. H. (2007). Occasioned knowledge exploration in family interaction. *Discourse & Society*, *18*(1), 93–110.

Goodwin, M. H., & Kyratzis, A. (2007). Children socializing children: Practices for negotiating the social order among peers. *Research on Language and Social Interaction*, *40*(4), 279–289.

Greenfield, P. M. (2004). *Weaving generations together: Evolving creativity in the Zinacantec Maya*. Santa Fe, NM: SAR Press.

Greenhow, C., Robelia, B., & Hughes, J. E. (2009). Learning, teaching, and scholarship in a digital age: Web 2.0 and classroom research: What path should we take now? *Educational Researcher*, *38*(4), 246–259.

Greeno, J. G. (2009). A theory bite on contextualizing, framing, and positioning: A companion to Son and Goldstone. *Cognition and Instruction*, *27*(3), 269–275.

Harré, R., & van Langenhove, L. (Eds.) (1999). *Positioning theory: Moral contexts of intentional action*. Cambridge, UK: Blackwell.

Heath, S. B. (1991). "It's about winning!" The language of knowledge in baseball. In L. B. Resnick, J. M. Levine, & S. D. Teasley (Eds.), *Perspectives on socially shared cognition* (pp. 101–124). Washington, DC: American Psychological Association.

Heath, S. B. (1999). Dimensions of language development: Lessons from older children. In A. S. Masten (Ed.), *Cultural processes in child development: The Minnesota symposia on child psychology* (Vol. 29, pp. 59–75). Mahwah, NJ: Erlbaum.

Heath, S. B. (2001). Three's not a crowd: Plans, roles, and focus in the arts. *Educational Researcher*, *30*(7), 10–17.

Heath, S. B. (2004). Risks, rules, and roles: Youth perspectives on the work of learning for community development. In A. N. Perret-Clermont, C. Pontecorvo, L. B. Resnick, T. Zittoun, & B. Burge (Eds.), *Joining society: Social interaction and learning in adolescence and youth* (pp. 41–70). Cambridge, UK: Cambridge University Press.

Heath, S. B. (2012). Seeing our way into learning science in informal environments. In W. F. Tate IV (Ed.), *Research on schools, neighborhoods, and communities: Toward civic responsibility* (pp. 249–268). Lanham, MD: Rowan & Littlefield.

Henrich, J., Heine, S. J., & Norenzayan, A. (2010). The weirdest people in the world? *Behavioral and Brain Sciences*, *33*(2–3), 61–83.

Henze, R. C. (1992). *Informal teaching and learning: A study of everyday cognition in a Greek community*. New York, NY: Routledge.

Hidi, S., & Renninger, K. A. (2006). The four-phase model of interest development. *Educational Psychologist*, *41*(2), 111–127.

Hirsch, B. J., Deutsch, N. L., & DuBois, D. L. (2011). *After-school centers and youth development: Case studies of success and failure*. New York, NY: Cambridge University Press.

Holland, D., Lachicotte, W. Jr., Skinner, D., & Cain, C. (1998). *Identity and agency in cultural worlds*. Cambridge, MA: Harvard University Press.

Holland, D., & Leander, K. (2004). Ethnographic studies of positioning and subjectivity: An introduction. *Ethos*, *32*(2), 127–139.

Hull, G. A., & Greeno, J. G. (2006). Identity and agency in nonschool and school worlds. In Z. Bekerman, N. C. Burbules, & D. Silberman-Keller (Eds.), *Learning in places: The informal education reader* (pp. 77–98). New York, NY: Peter Lang.

Itō, M., Gutiérrez, K., Livingstone, S., Penuel, B., Rhodes, J., Salen, K., Schor, J., Sefton-Green, J., & Watkins, S. C. (2013). *Connected learning: An agenda for research and design*. Irvine, CA: Digital Media and Learning Research Hub.

Jurow, A. S., Hall, R., & Ma, J. Y. (2008). Expanding the disciplinary expertise of a middle school mathematics classroom: Re-contextualizing student models in conversations with visiting specialists. *Journal of the Learning Sciences, 17*(3), 338–380.

Kafai, Y. B. & Peppler, K. A. (2014). Transparency reconsidered: Creative, critical, and connected making with e-textiles. In M. Ratto & M. Boler (Eds.), *DIY citizenship: Critical making and social media* (pp. 179–188). Cambridge, MA: MIT Press.

Kirshner, B. (2008). Guided participation in three youth activism organizations: Facilitation, apprenticeship, and joint work. *Journal of the Learning Sciences, 17*(1), 60–101.

Kral, I., & Heath, S. B. (2013). The world with us: Sight and sound in the "cultural flows" of informal learning. An Indigenous Australian case. *Learning, Culture and Social Interaction, 2*(4), 227–237.

Lareau, A. (2011). *Unequal childhoods: Class, race, and family life* (2nd ed.). Oakland, CA: University of California Press.

Larson, R. W. (2000). Toward a psychology of positive youth development. *American Psychologist, 55*(1), 170.

Lave, J., & Wenger, E. (1991). *Situated learning: Legitimate peripheral participation*. New York, NY: Cambridge University Press.

Lawson, M. A., & Lawson, H. A. (2013). New conceptual frameworks for student engagement research, policy, and practice. *Review of Educational Research, 83*(3), 432–479.

Leander, K. M., Phillips, N. C., & Taylor, K. H. (2010). The changing social spaces of learning: Mapping new mobilities. *Review of Research in Education, 34*(1), 329–394.

Lee, C. D. (2008). The centrality of culture to the scientific study of learning and development: How an ecological framework in education research facilitates civic responsibility. *Educational Researcher, 37*(5), 267–279.

Leibham, M. E., Alexander, J. M., Johnson, K. E., Neitzel, C. L., & Reis-Henrie, F. P. (2005). Parenting behaviors associated with the maintenance of preschoolers' interests: A prospective longitudinal study. *Journal of Applied Developmental Psychology, 26*(4), 397–414.

Lerner, R. M. (1991). Changing organism–context relations as the basic process of development: A developmental contextual perspective. *Developmental Psychology, 27*(1), 27–32.

Lerner, R. M., Almerigi, J. B., Theokas, C., & Lerner, J. V. (2005). Positive youth development. *Journal of Early Adolescence, 25*(1), 10–16.

Levinson, A. (2014). *Tapping in: Latino family's home media practice*. Unpublished doctoral dissertation. Palo Alto, CA: Stanford University.

Lewin, K. (1951). *Field theory in social science: Selected theoretical papers*. (D. Cartwright, Ed.). New York: Harper.

Liu, C. C., & Falk, J. H. (2013). Serious fun: Viewing hobbyist activities through a learning lens. *International Journal of Science Education, Part B: Communication and Public Engagement, 4*(4), 343–355.

Luehmann, A. (2009). Accessing resources for identity development by urban students and teachers: Foregrounding context. *Cultural Studies of Science Education, 4*(1), 51–66.

Ma, J. Y., & Munter, C. (2014). The spatial production of learning opportunities in skateboard parks. *Mind, Culture, and Activity, 21*(3), 1–21.

Mahoney, J. L., Larson, R. W., & Eccles, J. S. (Eds.) (2005). *Organized activities as contexts of development: Extracurricular activities, after school and community programs*. Mahwah, NJ: Erlbaum.

Matthews, J. (in press). Historical inquiry in an informal online community: Source usage among TV fans. *Journal of the Learning Sciences*.

McLaughlin, M. W., Irby, M. A., & Langman, J. (1994). *Urban sanctuaries: Neighborhood organizations in the lives and futures of inner-city youth*. San Francisco, CA: Jossey-Bass.

Mehus, S., Stevens, R., & Grigholm, L. (2013). Doing science with others at preschool and at home: A comparison of contextually situated interactional configurations and their implications for learning. In B. Bevan, P. Bell, R. Stevens, & A. Razfar (Eds.), *LOST opportunities: Learning in out-of-school time* (pp. 141–165). Dordrecht, the Netherlands: Springer.

Meltzoff, A. N., Kuhl, P. K., Movellan, J., & Sejnowski, T. J. (2009). Foundations for a new science of learning. *Science, 325*(5938), 284–288.

Mertl, V. (2009). "Don't touch anything, it might break!" Adolescent musicians' accounts of collaboration and access to technologies seminal to their musical practice. In C. O'Malley, D. Suthers, P. Reimann, and A. Dimitracopoulou (Eds.), *Computer supported collaborative learning practices: CSCL2009 conference proceedings* (pp. 25–27). New Brunswick, NJ: International Society of the Learning Sciences.

Monroy-Hernández, A. (2007). ScratchR: Sharing user-generated programmable media. In (Ed.), *Proceedings of the 6th international conference on interaction design and children,* IDC 2007 (pp. 167–168). New York, NY: ACM.

Moss, P., Pullin, D. C., Gee, J. P., Haertel, E. H., & Young, L. J. (2008). *Assessment, equity, and opportunity to learn*. Cambridge, UK: Cambridge University Press.

Nasir, N. S., & Hand, V. (2008). From the court to the classroom: Opportunities for engagement, learning, and identity in basketball and classroom mathematics. *Journal of the Learning Sciences, 17*(2), 143–179.

Nasir, N. S., Rosebery, A., Warren, B., & Lee. C. (2006). Learning as a cultural process: Achieving equity through diversity. In R. K. Sawyer (Ed.), *The Cambridge handbook of the learning sciences* (pp. 489–504). Cambridge, UK: Cambridge University Press.

Nasir, N. S., & Saxe, G. B. (2003). Ethnic and academic identities: A cultural practice perspective on emerging tensions and their management in the lives of minority students. *Educational Researcher, 32*(5), 14–18.

Neitzel, C., Alexander, J. M., & Johnson, K. E. (2008). Children's early interest-based activities in the home and subsequent information contributions and pursuits in kindergarten. *Journal of Educational Psychology, 100*(4), 782.

Nocon, H., & Cole, M. (2006). Schools invasion of "after-school": Colonization, rationalization or expansion of access? In Z. Bekerman, N. C. Burbules & D. Silberman-Keller (Eds.), *Learning in places: The informal education reader* (pp. 99–122). New York, NY: Peter Lang.

Pellegrino, J. W., & Hilton, M. L. (Eds.), & National Research Council. (2012). *Education for life and work: Developing transferable knowledge and skills in the 21st century*. Washington, DC: The National Academies Press.

Penuel, W. R., Bates, L., Pasnik, S., Townsend, E., Gallagher, L. P., Llorente, C., & Hupert, N. (2010). The impact of a media-rich science curriculum on low-income preschoolers' science talk at home. In K. Gomez, J. Radinsky, & L. Lyons (Eds.), *Proceedings of the 9th International Conference of the Learning Sciences* (Vol. 1, pp. 238–245). New Brunswick, NJ: ISLS.

Peppler, K. A., & Bender, S. (2013). Maker movement spreads innovation one project at a time. *Phi Delta Kappan, 95*(3), 22–27.

Perry, N., Turner, J. C., & Meyer, D. K. (2006). Student engagement in the classroom. In P. Alexander & P. Winne (Eds.), *Handbook of educational psychology* (pp. 327–348). Mahwah, NJ: Erlbaum.

Phelan, P., Davidson, A. L., & Cao, H. T. (1991). Students' multiple worlds: Negotiating the boundaries of family, peer, and school cultures. *Anthropology & Education Quarterly, 22*(3), 224–250.

Polman, J. L., & Miller, D. (2010). Changing stories: Trajectories of identification among African American youth in a science outreach apprenticeship. *American Educational Research Journal, 47*(4), 879–918.

Resnick, L. B. (1987). The 1987 presidential address: Learning in school and out. *Educational Researcher, 16*(9), 13–20.

Rogoff, B. (1990). *Apprenticeship in thinking: Cognitive development in social context*. New York: Oxford University Press.

Rogoff, B. (2003). *The cultural nature of human development*. New York, NY: Oxford University Press.

Rogoff, B., Paradise, R., Arauz, R. M., Correa-Chavez, M., & Angelillo, C. (2003). Firsthand learning through intent participation. *Annual Review of Psychology, 54*(1), 175–203.

Rogoff, B., Topping, K., Baker-Sennett, J., & Lacasa, P. (2002). Mutual contributions of individuals, partners, and institutions: Planning to remember in Girl Scout cookie sales. *Social Development, 11*(2), 266–289.

Rose-Krasnor, L. (2009). Future directions in youth involvement research. *Social Development, 18*(2), 497–509.

Rowe, D. W., & Neitzel, C. (2010). Interest and agency in 2- and 3-year-olds' participation in emergent writing. *Reading Research Quarterly, 45*(2), 169–195.

Scales, P. C., Benson, P. L., & Roehlkepartain, E. C. (2011). Adolescent thriving: The role of sparks, relationships, and empowerment. *Journal of Youth and Adolescence, 40*(3), 263–277.

Schwartz, D. L., & Arena, D. (2013). *Measuring what matters most: Choice-based assessments for the digital age*. Cambridge, MA: MIT Press.

Schwartz, L., & Gutiérrez, K. (in press). Literacy studies and situated methods: Exploring the social organization of household activity and family media use. In J. Rowsell, & K. Pahl (Eds.), *The Routledge handbook of literacy studies*. New York, NY: Routledge.

Scribner, S., & Cole, M. (1973). Cognitive consequences of formal and informal education. *Science, 182*(4112), 553–559.

Sefton-Green, J. (2013). *Learning at not-school: A review of study, theory, and advocacy for education in non-formal settings*. Cambridge, MA: MIT Press.

Sénéchal, M., & LeFevre, J. A. (2002). Parental involvement in the development of children's reading skill: A five-year longitudinal study. *Child Development, 73*(2), 445–460.

Sheridan, K. M. (2008). Reading, writing and watching: The informal education of film fans. In J. Flood, D. Lapp, and S. B. Heath (Eds.), *Handbook on teaching literacy through the communicative, visual and performing arts* (2nd ed.). Mahwah, NJ: Erlbaum.

Sheridan, K. M. (2011). Envision and observe: Using the studio thinking framework for learning and teaching in digital arts. *Mind, Brain, and Education, 5*(1), 19–26.

Sims, C. (2014). From differentiated use to differentiating practices: Negotiating legitimate participation and the production of privileged identities. *Information, Communication & Society, 17*(6), 670–682.

Soep, E., & Chávez, V. (2010). *Drop that knowledge: Youth radio stories*. Oakland, CA: University of California Press.

Steele, C. M., & Aronson, J. (1995). Stereotype threat and the intellectual test performance of African Americans. *Journal of Personality and Social Psychology, 69*(5), 797.

Steinkuehler, C., & Williams, C. (2009). Math as narrative in WoW forum discussions. *The International Journal of Learning and Media, 1*(3).

Stevens, R. (2013). Introduction: What counts as math and science? In B. Bevan, P. Bell, R. Stevens, & A. Razfar (Eds.), *LOST opportunities: Learning in out-of-school time* (pp. 201–217). Dordrecht, the Netherlands: Springer.

Stevens, R., O'Connor, K., Garrison, L., Jocuns, A., & Amos, D. M. (2008). Becoming an engineer: Toward a three dimensional view of engineering learning. *Journal of Engineering Education, 97*(3), 355–368.

Sullivan, P. J., & Larson, R. W. (2009). Connecting youth to high-resource adults: Lessons from effective youth programs. *Journal of Adolescent Research, 25*(1), 99–123.

Tai, R. H., Qi Liu, C., Maltese, A. V., & Fan, X. (2006). Planning early for careers in science. *Science, 312*(5777), 1143–1144.

Takeuchi, L., & Stevens, R. (2011). *The new coviewing: Designing for learning through joint media engagement*. New York, NY: The Joan Ganz Cooney Center at Sesame Workshop.

Taylor, K. H., & Hall, R. (2013). Counter-mapping the neighborhood on bicycles: Mobilizing youth to reimagine the city. *Technology, Knowledge and Learning, 18*(1–2), 65–93.

Tomasello, M. (2009). *The cultural origins of human cognition*. Cambridge, MA: Harvard University Press.

Tyack, D., & Tobin, W. (1994). The "grammar" of schooling: Why has it been so hard to change? *American Educational Research Journal, 31*(3), 453–479.

Tzou, C. T., Scalone, G., & Bell, P. (2010). The role of environmental narratives and social positioning in how place gets constructed for and by youth: Implications for environmental science education for social justice. *Equity and Excellence in Education, 43*(5), 105–119.

Vadeboncoeur, J. A. (2006). Engaging young people: Learning in informal contexts. *Review of Research in Education, 30*(1), 239–278.

Vossoughi, S., & Gutiérrez, K. (2013). Toward a multi-sited ethnographic sensibility. In J. Vadeboncoeur (Ed.), *NSSE Yearbook*. New York, NY: Teachers College Press.

Vygotsky, L. S. (1978). *Mind in society: The development of higher psychological processes*. Cambridge, MA: Harvard University Press.

Warschauer, M., & Matuchniak, T. (2010). New technology and digital worlds: Analyzing evidence of equity in access, use, and outcomes. *Review of Research in Education, 34*(1), 179–225.

Wortham, S. (2004). The interdependence of social identification and learning. *American Educational Research Journal, 41*(3), 715–750.

Yim, M., Chow, M., & Dunbar, W. (2000). Eat, sleep, robotics. In A. Druin & J. Hendler (Eds.), *Robots for kids: Exploring new technologies for learning* (pp. 246–295). San Francisco, CA: Morgan Kaufman.

Zimmerman, H. T. (2012). Participating in science at home: Recognition work and learning in biology. *Journal of Research in Science Teaching, 49*(5), 597–630.

Zimmerman, H. T., & Bell, P. (2014). Where young people see science: Everyday activities connected to science. *International Journal of Science Education, 4*(1), 25–53.

# 25

# Networked Learning

*GARY NATRIELLO*
Teachers College, Columbia University

The examination of learning by educational psychologists has moved from a primary focus on the internal or intrapsychic dimensions to include the social and environmental factors that constitute conditions for learning (Bransford et al., 2006). This chapter contemplates a further extension of this trajectory and takes us where no handbook chapter has gone before, beyond the individual and beyond the immediate social environment to the network connections, some proximate and some distal, that increasingly and more obviously contribute to the learning opportunities of individuals in postindustrial societies. These networks that individuals may draw on for learning include both those with no intentional learning dimensions as well as those composed of resources deliberately created to foster learning. Advertising networks are an example of the former while online learning venues and applications are an example of the latter.

The chapter is organized in five sections. After an initial section on the recent interest in networks and learning, subsequent sections focus on social networks, local networks, and interest networks. A concluding section considers the implications and next steps for learning research on networks.

## Networks and Learning

Interest in networks and learning extends at least as far back as Illich's (1971) *Deschooling Society*, the book in which he developed the idea of learning webs to support self-directed learning as a replacement for institutionally based education. More recent discussions of networks and learning have emanated from diverse sources influenced both by new theoretical work on social networks and by the development of information and computing technologies with the capacity to connect individuals and information resources both near and far.

Marin and Wellman (2011) highlight the essential features of social networks and the accompanying analytic perspective. They begin by explaining that a social network is a set of members (also called "nodes") "connected by one or

more relations" (p. 11). The network perspective, therefore, focuses on relations among members, not their individual attributes. Moreover, it highlights "networks" where members each have a unique set of relations rather than groups where individuals share common attributes. Finally, network analyses consider relations not just between pairs of members but rather the patterns of relationships of all members of the network.

Citing these new technological connections along with the pace of the development of knowledge and the volume of knowledge, Siemens (2005) proposes what he terms "connectivism" as a learning theory for the digital age. The principles of connectivism highlight the benefits of a network perspective, chief among them the principle that "learning is a process of connecting specialized nodes or information sources" and that "nurturing and maintaining connections is needed to facilitate continual learning" (Siemens, 2005, pp. 5–6).

Whereas Siemens is motivated by the changing technology landscape to seek a new theoretical perspective on learning, commentators such as Tapscott (1998), Prensky (2001a, 2001b), and Howe and Strauss (2000) point to what they see as a generational change and the emergence of "digital natives" or "millennials" who have new levels of experience and skills in interaction with technologies and who consequently need a new kind of educational experience. However, Bennett, Maton, and Kervin (2008) point to the lack of an evidentiary base for most such claims and appeal to the widely shared sense of concern about the challenges of adjusting to technological change to explain how this issue has been raised to a level of prominence in public thinking that has outpaced the evidence. Nonetheless, the digital natives discussion has had an impact. Selwyn (2009) calls attention to the impact of the digital natives hypothesis, or what he recasts as the digital natives myth, in thinking about learning through network connections. The idea of youth as "digital natives" or the "net generation" who interact with rapidly developing technologies with confidence and expertise beyond that of adults echoes Mead's (1977) idea of a prefigurative culture in which adults learn from children due to the rapid pace of change. Selwyn's (2009, p. 372) conclusion that many youth engage technology in ways that are often "passive, solitary, sporadic, and unspectacular" provides a necessary empirical corrective, but the digital native narrative continues to drive interest in networks of students engaged in interactions that facilitate learning.

Jones (2004) points to the increasing engagement of learners with learning technologies on networked computers as a reason to pay greater attention to the network metaphor in thinking about learning. He argues that research on learning technologies must consider networks and theoretical and practical advances made in the study of networks. Moreover, he maintains that the network metaphor can bring together some of the central issues in learning theory and research, notably virtual communities and communities of practice, with the latter serving as a contrast to the idea of networked individualism highlighted by Castells (1996) in his discussions of networked society. For example, Jones points out that the emphasis on community within the theoretical approaches tied to virtual communities and communities of practice may underestimate the potential contribution to learning of the weaker and more distant ties highlighted in network analyses.

The various perspectives on networked learning together call attention to the growing potential of such connections in an era when computing and communications technologies are reshaping the costs and benefits of far-flung social connections. That these new conditions will have an impact on learning opportunities is inescapable.

## Social Networks

Studies of the social dimensions of learning opportunities and learning have begun to examine how the connections among individuals can impact learning and development. This section briefly considers four major themes in this area. First, the literature on peer relations, a fundamental element in social learning, is considered. Second, research on learning opportunities for individuals in social networks is discussed. Third, the properties of social networks that are associated with societal learning are reviewed. Finally, studies of educational contributions of contemporary online social networking sites are noted.

### Peer Relationships

The research literature on peer relationships and learning highlights the potential contributions to learning of positive peer interaction as well as the problems and barriers to learning connected with the lack of peer interaction or negative interactions. Wentzel and Watkins (2010) call attention to the contributions of peer interactions for learning in both formal and informal settings. They note that dyadic friendships and interaction with the broader peer group lead to gains in a number of cognitive competencies as well as greater learning task engagement. These effects operate through various means, including assistance, advice, modeling, or shared experiences, notably collaborative academic tasks. In addition to direct learning gains, positive peer relationships are associated with a sense of safety and positive affective outcomes.

Ladd (1999) examines the connections between peer relationships and social competence during childhood. For students in grade school, friendships are associated with socioemotional adjustment and academic competence. Conversely, rejection by peers, a case of what Portes (1998) labels "exclusion," leads to absenteeism, being retained in a grade level, and to problems making the transition to middle school.

Ryan (2001) found that peer relationships were related to both behavior and achievement. Students moving into middle school suffered less of an academic decline when the members of their peer group were high achievers. The potential for positive peer relations among schoolchildren to contribute to learning is clear. These peer relations are typically among a small number of children with close ties and typically within the same school or classroom.

### Learning Opportunities for Individuals in Social Networks

The distribution of information to support learning in networks poses certain challenges to individual learning. Because information is not distributed uniformly across individuals in networks, those in certain network positions have greater access than those in other network positions. Kang and Lerman (2013) consider these patterns as structural bottlenecks to information access. They find that social media users have access to different information from their friends depending on their position in the network. Individuals in positions where they are embedded in a group of others who are tightly connected share information on topics of most interest to those in the group.

Individuals in positions that bridge groups or in brokerage positions between different communities tend to have access to more diverse information. Individuals can act to enhance their access to information. For example, they can add more friends to their network. Increasing the number of friend connections results in access to more information within certain limitations. Specifically, the addition of friends leads to more information, but a saturation point seems to be reached at about 100 friends, and there are limitations on individual capacity to process the information. Schnettler (2009) provides a broader look at the patterns of clustering and reachability in networks in his discussion of small-world research.

Janicik and Larrick (2005) consider a slightly different challenge for individuals seeking to make use of networks for learning. Pointing to earlier work (Cook and Emerson, 1978) showing that missing relations in incomplete networks (i.e., those with missing relations among some members) affect the pattern of information flow, they consider how individuals learn to make sense of incomplete social networks. They note that individuals differ in their abilities to learn about incomplete networks and in their abilities to take advantage of such networks to, for example, secure unique knowledge. Their work demonstrates the interplay between network structures and social psychological dimensions that results in uneven learning opportunities.

Dobrow, Chandler, Murphy, and Kram (2012) examine networks for their contribution to human development with an emphasis on the employment setting. They consider both the density and the range of networks. Density or the interconnectedness of individuals seems to be associated with fewer opportunities for exploration in terms of role models due to a lack of breadth. Range or the number of different social arenas (e.g., workplace, school, community) represented among network contacts appears to be related to better performance on the job and greater satisfaction with careers and life in general. They also note the need for research to shed light on whether the characteristics of an individual's network change in response to learning needs as conditioned by age, career stage, and developmental stage.

### Network Social Learning

A line of research largely from economics and sociology offers additional insight into the properties of networks that contribute to learning. This literature focuses on the relation between networks and social learning, with social learning defined as the ability of a population to aggregate information (Gonzalez-Avella, Eguiluz, Marsili, Vega-Redondo, & Miguel, 2011). The basic setting for learning in these investigations involves multiple agents who are linked by information flows so that the actions and consequences of others provide information about the state of the environment. In this setting, if the set of choices is diverse, the choices of one agent can be expected to inform another (Sobel, 2000).

The literature on network social learning suggests a number of implications for learning from the structure and design of networks. First, if the social network makes accessing quality information easier (less costly), it could improve learning (i.e., enable agents to make better decisions). Conversely, if the network prevents access to quality information or makes it more difficult to access (more costly), then learning could be constrained. As Sobel (2000) notes, understanding the conditions where optimal learning does not occur could allow us to identify those actors who create environments to exploit learning deficiencies. For example, this type of framework might allow us to understand how some network structures favor full sharing of information to optimize decisions while others favor less than full sharing and so advantage some actors (e.g., advertisers) over others.

Some network structures may be more favorable to innovation and experimentation than others. Goyal (2003) examines the prospects for complete learning in societies with an infinite number of agents. He concludes that the structure of the network makes a difference. Goyal finds that a network supportive of experimentation and innovation: (a) should allow for what he terms "local independence" or the opportunity for a group of agents to have distinct sources of information to facilitate the assembly of new information, and (b) should also have connections across local groups so that knowledge of local success can spread across the network (Goyal, 2003, p. 56). The studies of Gonzalez-Avella et al. (2011) reinforce this point and conclude that social learning is enhanced by local interaction that supports "spatial nucleation and consolidation around the correct action" (p. 7), correct action that can then be spread more widely.

Marin and Wellman (2011) illustrate this point in offering a network analytic approach to understanding network social learning in Silicon Valley. They note that mobility among educational institutions and various employers increases the connections among organizations as people "moving from one organization to another bring their ideas, expertise, and tacit knowledge with them" (p. 13). This pattern of connections allows organizations to draw on diverse sources of knowledge and leads to an accelerated rate of innovation.

There are, of course, complications that can interfere with the genesis of learning in local groups and the spread of new knowledge more broadly. J. Lin (2005) studies simple communications networks as they impact the evolution of heterogeneous beliefs. He concludes that social learning includes many interactions that together create social conformism or herding behavior. Golub and Jackson (2010) consider the conditions under which the opinions in the larger society converge to what they term the "truth" or, more fully specified, what network conditions will lead a society of naïve agents to aggregate decentralized information appropriately. They conclude that the prospects for social learning or wisdom are determined by the geometry of the network. The disproportionate influence of some agent is the main obstacle to wisdom. Naïve agents can be misled and learning can be compromised by a small group of opinion leaders who receive substantial attention from others in the society. Social learning and wisdom are possible if the attention of agents is dispersed broadly enough.

Two studies illustrate the application of the network social learning perspective. Barrera and van de Bunt (2009) provide an example of applying the perspective within an organization. They examine the network effects on the development of trust among the staff of a dialysis department in a medium-size Dutch hospital. They found that interpersonal trust among these colleagues developed through a learning mechanism based on network connections; both prior connections between two individuals and those involving third parties in the network impact trust. Prior information relating to distrust had a stronger effect than prior information relating to trust.

Forkosh-Baruch and Hershkovitz (2012) examine the use of social networking sites by higher-education institutes in Israel for sharing scholarly research. Although they find that social networking sites such as Facebook and Twitter can be used to share research and support informal learning, they noted several limitations. First, they found an exponential distribution of activity, with most activity concentrated in only a few accounts. Second, they found that in many cases the social networking accounts of the research institutes are being managed by public relations offices and function much like commercial sites aimed at enlarging profit instead of being managed as social networking sites to facilitate social interaction and knowledge building.

## Studies of Educational Use of Social Networking Sites

Research on the use of social networking sites for learning has focused both on patterns of student use of available online resources and, on occasion, on more deliberate educational efforts by educators. Both self- or student-directed activities and more planned activities developed by educators reveal the potential for networked learning. Liccardi et al. (2007) examine the literature on social networks in computer science education. They identify several mechanisms by which social networks facilitate communication among students (e.g., introducing two individuals, inferring associations from mutual friends, word-of-mouth communications for information and advice) and several types of communities (e.g., informal knowledge communities, communities of practice, communities of interest, communities of commitment, and intentional networks to accomplish a specific task). They note that students with higher self-efficacy appear to be more likely to make use of social networks and that students need to adapt quickly to use such networks to their full potential. They cite student preferences for richer face-to-face communication over online networking for complex tasks requiring the involvement of multiple decision makers. They conclude that social networking sites offer advantages for finding people with shared interests but that they carry the negative consequences of sharing personal data.

Luckin et al. (2009) examine the use of Web 2.0 tools by students aged 11–16 in U.K. schools. They categorized student use patterns into four groups: researchers who confined their activities to reading, collaborators who engaged in file sharing, gaming, and communicating, and both producers and publishers who used social networking sites to share their experiences. Overall they characterize the use patterns as relatively unsophisticated with little analytical awareness, few instances of knowledge building, and limited production and publishing.

Ellison, Steinfield, and Lampe (2007) focus on the relation between the use of the social networking site Facebook by college students and the three types of social capital: bonding capital, characterized by N. Lin (1999) as involving strong ties and social integration helpful for defending and protecting existing resources; bridging capital, described by N. Lin (1999) as involving weaker ties or bridges helpful in reaching resources lacking in one's social circle for expanding chances of gaining resources; and what they call "maintained capital" or prior ties from high school. Facebook use seemed to be associated with the formation of all three types of social capital. Of particular note is the potential contribution of maintained social capital in supporting students through the transition into college. Students use the communications afforded by Facebook to maintain their high-school networks even as they acquire new networks associated with college.

The impact of bridging social capital is apparent in a study of high-school students. Greenhow and Robelia (2009) examine the role of another social networking site, MySpace, in the lives of 11 high-school-age students. They find that participation in MySpace supported students' social learning in several ways, including through what Greenhow and Robelia label "peer alumni support" or advice, information, and encouragement from former high-school friends who have transitioned to college. In addition, the high-school students in their study received validation and appreciation of their creative work and support for school tasks in the form of information about deadlines, planning for study groups, sharing educational resources, assembling project materials, brainstorming, and sharing written work and feedback.

Studies of German college students using StudiVZ, a German equivalent of Facebook, by Wodzicki, Schwammlein, and Moskaliuk (2012) also highlight the importance of social networking for students at the transition point into college. They found that students used StudiVZ to exchange knowledge related to their studies, that they joined study-related groups to share course materials, discuss course topics, and prepare for exams, and that about half of the groups formed were study-related. Moreover, they found that students used the social networking site for study-related matters, particularly during their first year of college.

Several studies provide more detailed insights into the ways that social networking sites are used to enhance learning opportunities. Fewkes and McCabe (2012) studied the use of Facebook by secondary-school students in Ontario. Although they found that use of Facebook for educational purposes and applications is ranked lowest of all the uses, 73% of the students in the study did make use of Facebook for educational purposes. Such uses included: supporting the work of lab groups in biology and chemistry and sharing links to science resources, asking teachers or friends about homework, participating in a teacher-led Facebook group that included all of the students from all of the same-level classes to discuss homework and share quiz and test reminders, discussing readings for an English exam, and sending oneself assignments to complete at home to bypass email blocks.

Kabilan, Ahmad, and Abidin (2010) surveyed undergraduate university students to determine if they consider Facebook a useful tool to support the learning of the English language. Students reported generally positive attitudes toward the use of Facebook for language learning. Among the advantages noted were the ability to practice the use of English, the free use of the language on Facebook in casual discussions and engaging social chats, and interactions in English between experts and novices. Students were motivated to use English on Facebook because the site relies on English. The necessary focus on meaning making for communication as opposed to mechanics was viewed as a strength and a confidence-building aspect.

Facebook provided an audience or a community for their work in developing English-language competence.

The use of Facebook to support learning among medical students was the focus of a study by Gray, Annabell, and Kennedy (2010). They found that one-fourth of the students in the study reported using Facebook for learning purposes. They followed four groups using Facebook for research, information sharing, and exam preparation. Although all of these tasks could be accomplished in the university's learning management system, students found them easier to handle through Facebook. The groups varied in the extent of educational use of Facebook, and these differences were largely related to group processes, not to the technologies employed. Overall, the medical students made modest use of the capabilities of Facebook and did not go beyond their university to create learning networks.

Learning from peers and others in networks appears to be a promising component of the evolving landscape for learning. This makes increasing our understanding of network organization and structure as they relate to the distribution of knowledge an important avenue for enhancing learning opportunities. The benefits of such greater understanding of network effects appear to accrue to both organizational and individual learning.

Early studies of learning in existing social networks suggest that we are at the initial stages of making full use of their potential to support learning. However, as Portes (1998) reminds us, in our enthusiasm about the potential of networks for enhancing learning we should not overlook the potential negative effects. Portes singles out four kinds of negative consequences: exclusion of outsiders, excessive claims made by less diligent members on the more diligent, restrictions on individual freedom associated with dense network ties, and downward-leveling norms in networks where members adopt an oppositional stance toward the mainstream. Emerging research on cyberbullying (Slonje, Smith, & Frisen, 2013) and gangs (Pyrooz, Decker, & Moule, 2013) online illustrates some of the negative dimensions.

### Local Networks

Among the networks that can provide resources for learning are those that are locally based, typically within some reasonable geographical proximity, and that permit frequent face-to-face interaction. Such local networks come with both opportunities and constraints as a function of their inherent limitations due to the physical distances they span. Communities, workplaces, families, schools, and local adolescent peer networks may each be examined to understand how local networks operate to impact learning. This section will focus on research that examines the learning resources provided through these types of local networks.

### *Communities*

Carroll and Rosson (2003), in their study of online community networks, note that such networks are created to help members of the proximate community manage information and activity. But such networks are undergirded by sets of morals and behavioral norms that arise to help individuals living in small, relatively isolated and stable groups avoid conflicts. This is one aspect that differentiates local networks from others; individuals in close proximity must both compete for local resources and depend upon one another in times of crisis. As Carroll and Rosson point out, in such communities the children may even marry into other families in the community. In such communities, members may share common meanings as well as a common purpose and ethical system, all of which makes it more likely that participants in the network will enact appropriate roles and attendant responsibilities. This, in turn, makes it more likely that the learning in such a network is purposeful or project-based, peer-oriented, and collaborative in the context of local facilitation.

Drawing on their work on the Milan Community Network, de Cindio and Ripamonti (2010) noted several additional unique features of local networks. They found that having a specific local interest allows individuals participating in the network to shift easily from the virtual to the real world and so connect online networking with concrete action such as organizing an event or a political protest. In addition, the possibilities of online interaction and information sharing, by relaxing constraints of time and space, allow local networks to overcome the limitations of traditional meeting places. This is particularly useful for larger local communities and in the case of individual citizens whose work and other obligations prevented participation. Such enhanced participation carries important implications for social learning. de Cindio and Ripamonti (2010) observed that online local community networks were able to gather very substantial amounts of knowledge of the community from exchanges among citizens and to collect such knowledge to develop civic intelligence. This, in turn, supported democratic development.

Chang's (2010) case study of the Zhabei Learning Community in Shanghai, China provides an example of a local network designed to promote individual development as well as community development. A key element in this particular community is the tight connection of the learning activities to the social and cultural context (i.e., the culture, history, social practices, and life of the community) and to the plans for community development. Another defining feature is the organization of local residential patterns according to learning goals. For example, apartment complexes are organized along learning themes, with a reading apartment complex for those who enjoy reading, a science and technology complex, and a gourmet complex.

A more content-specific learning theme addressed through various local networks was investigated by Nichols, Rowsell, Nixon, and Rainbird (2012) in their study of networks to support the early-childhood education and care learning needs of parents. Their international study examined the learning networks available in a church-sponsored refugee center, a community library, a shopping mall, and a clinic. They found evidence of learning opportunities in each of these settings that were accessed by different parts of the population for different purposes.

In studies of two separate communities, Leonard (2005) examined the network relations among children as opposed to those between children and adults. As she noted, children, like the elderly, are particularly dependent on the local environment, so local networks play prominently in their lives. The children interviewed in both communities cited the importance of physical facilities for gathering and noted the lack of things like playgrounds and play areas that could facilitate information exchange. Nonetheless, the children did develop networks for specific purposes. For example, Leonard found that children developed their own networks as potential sources of babysitting to generate income. Peers served as important sources of information about jobs, and children who recommended other children to jobs brought their personal ties to the recruitment process based on mutual trust. She also found that local networks for children differed, with some providing ties that connected families to the local community, and others including ties that extended to opportunities provided by wider networks outside the local community. These configurations of network ties led to horizons for learning in these two kinds of local networks that were quite different, with only those extending beyond the local community affording value beyond meeting immediate needs.

Somewhat like the playgrounds found lacking by the children studied by Leonard (2005), artifacts are viewed by Fischer (2006) as important elements of the local infrastructure to support distributed intelligence or distributed cognition. For example, artifacts such as historical records and archives of a local community support the long-term development of ideas. Documentation of local community events and actions provides a foundation upon which subsequent thinking and decisions can be advanced.

Communities provide useful focal settings for considering local networks. However, it is important to recall that, from a social network perspective, it is the network of relationships and not the common geographical setting that influences the behaviors, learning-related and otherwise, of the individuals involved (Marin & Wellman, 2011).

### Postsecondary Institutions

Colleges and universities have also been examined as the sites of local networks. An early study of the University of Wisconsin Student History Network (Huehner & Kallgren, 1999), based on the model of the literary society, revealed interest in participating on the part of both faculty and students. Discussions among network members surfaced issues related to editorial control and the necessary level of moderation, issues that would later be raised across a range of online learning networks. Because this network involved multiple campuses in the University of Wisconsin system, it came to encompass both local network ties and ties across campuses, for instance, ties that linked individuals at 2-year campuses to those at 4-year institutions in the system.

Fischer, Rohde, and Wulf (2007) developed a perspective on residential, research-based universities as sites of community-based learning networks that allow students to become members of the community of scholars while forging life-long bonds between students and the university. Drawing on case studies at the University of Colorado and the University of Siegen, Germany, they examined efforts to integrate community-based learning techniques into the computer science curriculum. These efforts were less successful when there was a mismatch between student expectations and program goals (for example, when passive learners with consumptive expectations confronted programs intending to provide opportunities for self-directed learning in the context of learning communities). When efforts were made to support enculturation into specific communities of practice, then learning operated through processes of collaboration, interaction, and diffusion.

Hommes et al. (2012) investigated the impact of student networks among undergraduate medical students. They considered three types of local social network relationships: friendship, giving information, and receiving information. Their findings revealed that these local network relationships were positively related to both student social integration and student learning.

In a study of medical school students, Woolf, Potts, Patel, and McManus (2012) examined the formation and impact of local social networks. They found that student gender, ethnicity, tutor assignments, and small-group assignments influenced their closeness in the local social network. Furthermore, students with closer network ties had more similar Year 2 exam scores. They interpreted these patterns to suggest that local social networks had an impact on academic performance beyond the impact of lectures and tutorials.

Langan, Cullen, and Shuker (2008) studied the learning network interactions among students and tutors during the completion of investigative bioscience projects in a residential field course with a particular focus on the impact of the size of the network experienced by students. They found that students participating in more network interactions did not lead to higher grades; higher-achieving students worked in smaller networks. Overall students interacted with about 40% of their peers and over 50% of the tutors, with the most critical interactions provided by tutors. Interaction patterns varied over the various stages of the project, with the start of the project involving the most interaction.

A study of the local student network connected to a physics learning center on campus was conducted by Brewe, Kramer, and Sawtelle (2012). They found that students who physically visited the learning center more often were more central participants in the network. Although there were no differences in network participation related to either gender or ethnicity, which they interpreted as evidence of an equitable learning environment, they did find that students majoring in physics were more involved in the network.

Schools provide the physical locations for students to assemble and create local networks. These networks facilitate interactions that can lead to enhanced engagement.

Some, but not all, of the interactions among motivated members lead to enhanced learning and opportunities, as all of the negative aspects identified earlier can arise in the local school context.

### Workplace

With organizations of all types confronting the need to respond to changing circumstances, it has never been more important to provide opportunities for employees to learn and develop new capacities. Investigations into local networks connected to the workplace have focused at both the level of individuals within work organizations and at the level of organizations within sets of organizations.

Pahor, Skerlavaj, and Dimovski (2008) considered learning networks in two companies that varied in terms of size, industry, and culture. They found that the learning networks exhibited clusters (or communities of practice) in which learning was more intense, that individuals were drawn to those higher on the corporate ladder as people to learn from, and that project settings provided for learning that involved the tacit transfer of knowledge through participation in the project activities.

Using an agent-based modeling approach, Rodan (2008) created a simulated learning organization of 85 agents (or rule-governed individual entities) to examine the impact of network structures on learning. Results indicated that learning seems to benefit from cross-cutting ties that reduce constraints in the network, from drawing on one's more knowledgeable contacts, and even more from relying on a consensus among contacts.

Chia and Foo (2006) conducted a study in which they examined both the content of the local network interaction as well as the type of network ties. For content they considered interactions around issues of procedural justice and around issues of interactional justice. For ties, they considered both expressive ties and instrumental ties in the local network (N. Lin, 1999). They found that for procedural justice issues, both expressive and instrumental ties were positively related, but in the case of interactional justice issues only expressive ties had a significant role. Overall, they concluded that the content of the issues, along with the type of network ties, shapes the ways that information is exchanged in the local network in the workplace.

A number of investigations have focused on local networks to foster learning at the organizational level in one or more organizations. Bottrup (2005) examined 11 Danish enterprises collaborating in a network to improve occupational health and safety conditions. Participating in the multi-workplace network allowed individuals to form bridging ties beyond their own organizations, but the process entailed a number of difficulties for learning. First, the process of self-reflection set in motion was very difficult for participants. Second, participants found it difficult to extract general patterns from the various institutional cases. Third, it was difficult to adapt general insights to the particulars of one's own workplace. Even when those in

the network learned something as individuals, the learning failed to become organizational due to lack of support and follow-up.

In a study of the prosthetics service in England, Knight and Pye (2004) considered learning networks in the workplace by examining how a group of organizations change as a group as a result of network participation. They examined the impact of network learning on improvements in collective capability, not by focusing on individual cognitive development but by focusing on the social, political, contextual, and practice-based nature of learning. In particular, they looked at professionalization within the organizations in the study as reflected in changes to network structures, practices, and interpretation.

Similarly, Kerosuo and Toiviainen (2011) examined patterns of learning across workplace boundaries in a regional learning network in Finland. They noted that learning at and across organizational boundaries involves a process of constructing and reconstructing boundaries. The episodes they studied in this learning network led the in-house developers to an expansion of the notion of workplace development through a lengthy learning process that transformed the object of learning from one limited to a particular organization into one that was regional. This organizational-level look at local learning networks in the workplace thus reinforces the importance of bridging ties for network learning.

Networks play a role in setting the conditions for learning in the workplace. Both those network connections internal to a single organization and those that extend to a relevant sector and even beyond can contribute to learning opportunities at individual and organizational levels.

### Families

Families represent another site for local networks. Bohanek et al. (2009) provide a graphic example of the local family network in action to support learning with their study of family dinnertime conversations. These conversations are shown to support children's developing autobiographical memory skills, self-concept, and emotional regulation. They note that through these dinnertime exchanges children learn not only how to become storytellers but also theory builders as they participate in the co-construction of family narratives. In conversations where the focus is on the social activities of both parents and children, the children can learn to negotiate smooth social interactions and to take the perspectives of others.

Ho (2010) examined intergenerational learning exchanges in Hong Kong families between Generation X parents and their Generation Y children. She found that learning in the local family networks was bi-directional between these generations, with some incidents where the parents played the leading role, some in which the children took the lead, and some where they were learning together. These patterns differed by content area. Parents led in areas involving life views and experiences, morals and values, manners and relationships. Chinese History, Chinese calligraphy, and hobbies were areas of joint learning. The younger generation took the lead in learning events centered in information technologies.

Delgado-Gaitan (2005) reports on studies of women from two California communities whose use of computers allowed access to resources for their families and their children. This enhanced information flow among the women carried over into their families as they taught one another to secure educational resources for their children and negotiate relations with school authorities.

Families provide important contexts for the development of local networks. They offer strong ties supported by long-term relationships in close proximity, and they can include weaker ties, both those where the nodes are parents and sometimes those where the nodes are children who have connections beyond the home.

### Adolescent Peer Networks

Some studies have considered the role of local peer networks as experienced by adolescent students. Phelan, Davidson, and Cao (1991) and Phelan, Yu, and Davidson (1994) developed a model of the multiple worlds negotiated by students as they move among family, school, and peer cultures. Students have connections to all of these worlds, and the degree to which these settings and the relevant actors in each are aligned makes it either easy or difficult for students to move among them. In different circumstances students adopt different networking strategies. When such worlds are congruent students move easily among them and foster connections among the actors across these different groups. When such worlds are not well aligned, students may avoid making bridging connections, and suffer the negative learning consequences.

Stanton-Salazar and colleagues (Stanton-Salazar & Dornbusch, 1995; Stanton-Salazar & Spina, 2005; Stanton-Salazar, 2010) have developed a line of work that examines the local information networks available to high-school students, particularly low-income high-school students. Stanton-Salazar and Dornbusch (1995) assessed the information networks of Mexican-origin high-school students. They highlighted the importance of ties to institutional agents, those individuals who controlled or influenced institutional resources that might be helpful for college admission or job placement. They found that all students enhanced their networks by incorporating non-family weak ties, but for higher-socioeconomic status students there was an added advantage because they also incorporated their high-status parents.

Stanton-Salazar and Spina (2005) focused on the role of supportive adolescent peer relationships and the potential of such relationships for helping adolescents develop behaviors vital to adult relationships and facilitating integration into adult institutional life. The peer networks of the adolescents in their study averaged between five and six people. Such peers provided emotional support, intimate counsel, or practice for the norm of reciprocity. Some of these relationships entailed multiple dimensions. Through the other adolescents in their peer networks, students were exposed to a panoramic view of the problems of others as well as strategies for responding. This vicarious learning allowed students to draw important lessons. Stanton-Salazar and Spina (2005) also found that the formation of supportive peer relationships is more likely in a facilitating institutional context.

The potential of institutional agents to have a positive impact on the networks of adolescents is highlighted by Stanton-Salazar (2010), who noted the importance of such agents to adolescent social development, academic performance, and preparation for adulthood. When students have access to such institutional agents, they extend their networks through bridging relationships. The impact of such network ties is dependent on the personal resources of these individuals, on their positional resources, and on the resources of others whom they are able to mobilize on behalf of the adolescents. Thus the nature of the network ties of the institutional agent comes to have a bearing on the learning and development opportunities of the adolescents connecting to them.

As children grow their networks shift in form and shape. They move from networks dominated by family members connected by close ties to networks that include non-family peers connected by a combination of close and weak ties. Just as important is the alignment of the various networks in which students find themselves, with more aligned networks allowing easier movement and better access to learning opportunities.

Various kinds of local networks provide resources that support learning. Whether these networks are rooted in common locales such as schools, workplaces, or families or even in more specialized settings such as prisons and fraternal organizations, such networks also offer important norms to structure online network relationships. Online networks aligned with local networks appear to make it easier for individuals, relationships, and actions to move from offline to online and back again. Such alignment supports the use of networks to serve as the basis for taking action.

### Interest Networks

Networks based on shared interests tend to be both specialized or one-dimensional and physically dispersed as individuals with common interests extend their connections. Such networks can be organized around professions, hobbies, or other shared interests or pursuits. Such interests can be cultivated through interactions with others with similar interests as well as through specialized media information resources. This section will review research that considers the learning resources available in such interest networks. In contrast to the local networks considered above, interest networks typically are not built on face-to-face interactions that are enhanced or extended by online technologies. In part as a result, they face certain dilemmas that are not encountered by local networks.

Selwyn (2000) reported on the formation and operation of a network for teachers and other professionals supporting students with special educational needs in the UK.

In the course of his investigation, use of the online forum grew in popularity, with postings increasing over a period of 2 years. He identified four use patterns apparent in the network interactions: (a) information exchanges; (b) empathetic exchanges; (c) a virtual respite; and (d) a sense of community for special-needs educators who are often the only member of school staffs with their designated responsibilities.

Closer inspection revealed some of the limitations of this forum as a learning network in the fullest sense. For instance, although the forum had over 900 members, more than one-third of the total messages posted came from 26 members who were frequent contributors. Selwyn observed that the sense of community or collaborative culture was transitory at best, with most members contributing only sporadically. He concluded that the online forum was a site for information or empathetic exchange for educators whose sense of community was elsewhere.

In another study of an electronic forum for science and math teachers in Indiana, Kling and Courtright (2003) attempted to provide a set of resources and online forums to support teachers in reflecting on their own practices and create a community of practice to engage in knowledge building. Like Selwyn, they found that participation in the forum was concentrated among a small percentage of the participating teachers, with only 6% of teachers posting ten or more times. Kling and Courtright concluded that, although the forum did function as an online resource for teachers, it did not develop sufficient trust and group identity to evolve into a community of practice.

In summarizing their experience with the online forum, Kling and Courtright (2003) made a distinction between strategies where the formation of a group is intended to be led by information technology and those where an existing group is supported and extended by information technology. They concluded that supporting and extending existing groups through online networks will be more fruitful because such an approach does not require complex processes of group formation and group development to occur via the online network. This highlights an important distinction between local networks based on existing relationships and online-only interest networks that lack such a face-to-face foundation.

A study of nine Usenet news groups by Fisher, Smith, and Welser (2006) reinforces and extends the patterns reported by Kling and Courtright (2003). The nine Usenet groups included several different genres of online network groups: question-and-answer groups, social support groups, discussion groups, and flame groups, i.e., those characterized by hostile or insulting interactions. Overall the patterns of participation can be described as very few active participants with a great number of inactive participants, e.g., across all of Usenet, 66% of posters have only one message (Fisher, Smith, and Welser, 2006, p. 6). However, there were differences in the distribution of participation associated with the group genre. For example, in the technical question-and-answer groups there is a pattern of responding to people who raised a question without otherwise participating (along with a pattern of maintaining ties to more senior group members), while in the politics group the preference was to engage those who were more active participants. Similarly, question-and-answer groups have many short threads while discussion-oriented groups have longer threads with greater involvement of certain individuals. Fisher, Smith, and Welser (2006) highlight the variations in roles and interaction patterns that exist across different network genres, but the general pattern of a small number of active participants prevails. This pattern suggests certain limitations of such networked interactions for the distribution of learning opportunities.

Despite the recognized difficulties in developing and sustaining meaningful online interest networks to support learning, there are studies that examine some examples that highlight dimensions that might be associated with success in creating broad participation in such learning networks. Lee and Trace (2009) reported on the online network among collectors of rubber ducks who tend to be geographically very dispersed. Individuals in this collector network exchanged various kinds of information, including: the availability of new ducks, tools and techniques for bidding or searching on eBay, the provenance of ducks, repair techniques, and the sources of rare ducks. Lee and Trace (2009) reported a significant amount of mentoring in the rubber duck collector community, with much of it through an online bulletin board. They noted that the object needs of these collectors were the motivation for the networking activity as collectors sought information to support their hobby. Although the online networking activities were driven by the collecting activities of members, there were no local networks driving online activities for these widely dispersed members. However, the online networking activities did sometimes result in offline networking, as when members of the online bulletin board site participated in an annual face-to-face gathering.

The online behavior of collectors is also the subject of a study by Case (2010), who spent 4 years studying coin collectors on eBay. The online interactions were focused on resolving ambiguities in eBay listings and deciding whether or not to bid on a particular coin. The members of the eBay coin-collecting group served as a source of advice, sometimes about coins in general and sometimes about the value of a specific coin. Case concludes that the internet is providing online reference material, visual resources about particular coins, and human information resources from other hobbyists.

In a study of online groups organized around health issues, Akrich (2010) found that these groups engage in collective learning activities that result in the development of experiential knowledge, the use of outside sources of medical knowledge, and the articulation of knowledge in the form of lay expertise. These groups develop as communities of practice that produce knowledge products. For example, one group developed an extensive bibliographic database of 2,200 references that was made available on a public website. Akrich went on to explain how such groups can develop further into what she termed epistemic communities, whose activities move from producing knowledge to influencing policies.

Influencing policy is also considered by Newig, Gunther, and Pahl-Wostl (2010) in their study of governance networks. They consider the key functions of networks that make them valuable at the level between markets and hierarchies, identifying information transmission among actors, and providing opportunities for the genuine exchange of ideas and arguments. To these they add network resilience as a third important function of networks to support learning. Their examination of the evidence leads them to conclude that "modular networks consisting of several subgroups with strong ties and several weak tie relations within the broader network can be expected to provide the strongest environment to foster learning" (Newig et al., 2010, p. 9), a pattern quite consistent with that identified by Kling and Courtright (2003).

A similar pattern of network connections is contemplated by Rajagopal, Brinke, Van Bruggen, and Sloep (2012) in their development of a model of personal learning networks. They cite Grabher and Ibert's (2006) three-layered approach of a communality layer of strong ties, a sociality layer of weak ties, and a connectivity layer of very weak ties. Drawing on a literature review, semi-structured interviews with individuals working in the social development sector, and a survey of participants of two networking events, they concluded that networking for networked learning entails recognizing and identifying the qualities of others and making associations of such qualities with one's own.

Interest networks demonstrate some of the challenges of establishing and growing robust networks of well-distributed connections. Such networks appear to be more readily developed from an interest base than from a technology base, and the most likely growth pattern may be as a result of an accumulation of distinct interests that generate high levels of commitment. Interest networks that combine subgroups with strong ties together with weak ties to other subgroups and the broader network appear to offer the most promise for facilitating learning.

## Conclusion

The resources to support and extend learning available through networks have never been greater. Yet we may still be near the beginning of the period of growth for networking capacities, with much more to come. Even now we can see the development of more complex resources and relationships in the form of things such as augmented reality displays, mobile devices, ubiquitous networks, and networked physical objects. As networks and networking capacities multiply and become more extended, more densely configured, and more diverse, there arise new challenges for learners and for those who conduct research with the aim of expanding learning opportunities, enhancing the appeal of connectivism as an approach to understanding learning (Siemens, 2005). Moreover, as networked opportunities grow to constitute a more prominent component of the learning landscape, they will be certain to capture the attention of policy makers concerned with promoting overall social welfare through education. Areas of concern for learners,

researchers, and policy makers include issues of quality, distribution, and engagement.

The quality of the resources and relationships available through networks will have a substantial impact on possibilities for learning for all concerned. We have seen how learners make use of all manner of network affordances as tools for learning. Although resources and relationships in networks exist in abundance, the learning potential of these elements differs widely. Although there are well-developed methods of determining quality from a learning perspective for traditionally produced and distributed learning resources, we have only begun to understand how learners make use of resources and relationships in networks to support their learning. Such understanding will be essential to develop criteria for assessing quality.

As we have seen, networks differ in their architectures and in the corresponding distributions of resources and relationships. These differences carry consequences for the opportunities of learners in different network locations to access resources and leverage relationships to support their learning. Understanding the variation in network configurations and the impact on learners will be a necessary step in developing an appreciation for the network architectures that support equitable distributions of learning opportunities. This knowledge might in turn lead to the development of policies to promote network structures that support the most learning for the most learners.

The abundance of resources and relationships to support learning available through networks will have little impact unless learners engage with them. As we have seen, the engagement of individuals is impacted by network characteristics, local contexts, and individual self-regulation. Understanding how these factors combine to determine engagement confronts us with important research questions such as the response to multiple networks representing diverse values and interests and the consequent impact on learning and development.

We stand at the beginning of a very exciting period for research on networked learning. Thanks to developments in computing and communications technologies, the opportunities for learning in networks have never been greater. Thanks to the developments in theory and research in educational psychology and learning, the capacity to study these opportunities has never been more robust.

## References

Akrich, M. (2010). From communities of practice to epistemic communities: Health mobilizations on the Internet. *Sociological Research Online, 15*(2). Retrieved from http://www.socresonline.org.uk/15/2/10.html (accessed February 20, 2015).

Barrera, D., & van de Bunt, G. (2009). Learning to trust: Networks effects through time. *European Sociological Review, 25*(6), 709–721.

Bennett, S., Maton, K., & Kervin, L. (2008). The 'digital natives' debate: A critical review of the evidence. *British Journal of Educational Technology, 39*, 775–786.

Bohanek, J., Fivush, R., Zaman, W., Lepore, C., Merchant, S., & Duke, M. (2009). Narrative interaction in family dinnertime conversations. *Merrill-Palmer Quarterly, 55*(4), 488–515.

Bottrup, P. (2005). Learning in a network: A "third way" between school learning and workplace learning? *Journal of Workplace Learning, 17*(8), 508–520.

Bransford, J., Stevens, R., Schwartz, D., Meltzoff, A., Pea, R., Roschelle, J., Vye, N., Kuhl, P., Bell, P., Barron, B., Reeves, B., & Sabelli, N. (2006). Learning theories and education: Toward a decade of progress. In P. Alexander, & P. Winne (Eds.), *Handbook of educational psychology* (2nd ed., pp. 209–244). New York, NY: Routledge.

Brewe, E., Kramer, L, & Sawtelle, V. (2012). Investigating student communities with network analysis of interactions in a physics learning center. *Physical Review, 8*(1), 010101, 1–9.

Carroll, J., & Rosson, M. (2003). A trajectory of community networks. *The Information Society, 19,* 381–393.

Case, D. (2010). A model of the information seeking and decision making of online coin buyers. *Information Research, 15*(4). Retrieved from http://InformationR.net/ir/15-4/paper448.html (accessed February 20, 2015).

Castells, M. (1996). *The information age: Economy, society, and culture. Volume 1: The rise of networked society.* Oxford, UK: Blackwell.

Chang, B. (2010). Local administrative districts serving as lifelong learning communities: A case study on the Zhabei Learning Community. *Adult Learning, 21*(3–4), 27–33.

Chia, H., & Foo, M. (2006). Workplaces as communities: The role of social networks in who seeks, gives, and accepts information on justice issues. *Journal of Community Psychology, 34*(3), 363–377.

Cook, K., & Emerson, R. (1978). Power, equity, and commitment in exchange networks. *American Sociological Review, 43,* 721–739.

de Cindio, F., & Ripamonti, L. (2010). Nature and roles for community networks in the information society. *AI and Society, 25,* 265–278.

Delgado-Gaitan, C. (2005). Family narratives in multiple literacies. *Anthropology and Education Quarterly, 36*(3), 265–272.

Dobrow, S., Chandler, D., Murphy, W., & Kram, K. (2012). A review of developmental networks: Incorporating a mutuality perspective. *Journal of Management, 38*(1), 210–242.

Ellison, N., Steinfield, C., & Lampe, C. (2007). The benefits of Facebook "friends": Social capital and college students' use of online social network sites. *Journal of Computer-Mediated Communication, 12*(4), article 1.

Fewkes, A., & McCabe, M. (2012). Facebook: Learning tool or distraction? *Journal of Digital Learning in Teacher Education, 28*(3), 92–98.

Fischer, G. (2006). Learning in communities: A distributed intelligence perspective. *Journal of Community Informatics, 2*(2). Retrieved from http://ci-journal.net/index.php/ciej/article/view/339/245 (accessed February 20, 2015).

Fischer, G., Rohde, M., & Wulf, V. (2007). Community-based learning: The core competency of residential, research-based universities. *International Journal of Computer Supported Collaborative Learning, 2*(1), 9–40.

Fisher, D., Smith, M., & Welser, H. (2006). You are who you talk to: Detecting roles in Usenet newsgroups. *Proceedings of the 39th Hawaii International Conference on System Sciences, vol. 3,* 59–68.

Forkosh-Baruch, A., & Hershkovitz, A. (2012). A case study of Israeli higher-education institutes sharing scholarly information with the community via social networks. *Internet and Higher Education, 15,* 58–68.

Golub, B., & Jackson, M. (2010). Naïve learning in social networks and the wisdom of crowds. *American Economic Journal, 2*(1), 112–149.

Gonzalez-Avella, J., Eguiluz, V., Marsili, M., Vega-Redondo, F., & Miguel, M. (2011). Threshold learning dynamics in social networks. *PLOS One, 6*(5), 1–9.

Goyal, S. (2003). Learning in networks: A survey. In G. Demange and M. Wooders (Eds.), *Group formation in economics: Networks, clubs, and coalitions* (pp. 122–169). Cambridge, UK: Cambridge University Press.

Grabher, G., & Ibert, O. (2006). Bad company? The ambiguity of personal knowledge networks. *Journal of Economic Geography, 6*(3), 251–271.

Gray, K., Annabell, L., & Kennedy, G. (2010). Medical students' use of Facebook to support learning: Insights from four case studies. *Medical Teacher, 32,* 971–976.

Greenhow, C., & Robelia, B. (2009). Old communication, new literacies: Social network sites as social learning resources. *Journal of Computer Mediated Communication, 14*(4), 1130–1161.

Ho, C. (2010). Intergenerational learning (between Generation X and Y) in learning families: A narrative inquiry. *International Education Studies, 3*(4), 59–72.

Hommes, J., Rienties, B., de Grave, W., Bos, G., Schuwirth, L., & Scherpbier, A. (2012). Visualizing the invisible: A network approach to reveal the informal social side of learning. *Advances in Health Science Education, 17,* 743–757.

Howe, N., & Strauss, W. (2000). *Millennials rising: The next great generation.* New York, NY: Vintage.

Huehner, D., & Kallgren, D. (1999). Technology and student-centered learning: The University of Wisconsin Student History Network Project. *The History Teacher, 33*(1), 41–54.

Illich, I. (1971). *Deschooling society.* New York, NY: Harper and Row.

Janicik, G., & Larrick, R. (2005). Social network schemas and the learning of incomplete networks. *Journal of Personality and Social Psychology, 88*(2), 348–364.

Jones, C. (2004). Networks and learning: Communities, practices and the metaphor of networks. *ALT-F, Research in Learning Technology, 12*(1), 82–93.

Kabilan, M., Ahmad, N., & Abidin, M. (2010). Facebook: An online environment for learning of English in institutions of higher education? *Internet and Higher Education, 13,* 179–187.

Kang, J., & Lerman, K. (2013). Structural and cognitive bottlenecks to information access in social networks. *Proceedings of the 24th ACM Conference on Hypertext and Social Media,* 51–59.

Kerosuo, H., & Toiviainen, H. (2011). Expansive learning across workplace boundaries. *International Journal of Educational Research, 50,* 48–54.

Kling, R., & Courtright, C. (2003). Group behavior and learning in electronic forums: A sociotechnical approach. *The Information Society, 19,* 221–223.

Knight, L., & Pye, A. (2004). Exploring the relationships between network change and network learning. *Management Learning, 35,* 473–490.

Ladd, G. (1999). Peer relationships and social competence during early and middle childhood. *Annual Review of Psychology, 50,* 339–359.

Langan, A., Cullen, W., & Shuker, D. (2008). Student learning networks on residential field courses: Does size matter? *Bioscience Education, 11.* Retrieved from www.bioscience.heacademy.ac.uk/journal/vol11/beej-11-1.pdf (accessed February 20, 2015).

Lee, C., & Trace, C. (2009). The role of information in a community of hobbyist collectors. *Journal of the American Society for Information Science and Technology, 60*(3), 621–637.

Leonard, M. (2005). Children, childhood, and social capital: Exploring the links. *Sociology, 39*(4), 605–622.

Liccardi, I., Ounas, A., Pau, R., Massey, E., Kinnunen, P., Lewthwaite, S., Midy, M., & Sakar, C. (2007). The role of social networks in student's learning experiences. *ACM SIGCSE Bulletin, 39*(4), 224–237.

Lin, J. (2005). Learning in a network economy. *Computational Economics, 25*(1), 59–74.

Lin, N. (1999). Building a network theory of social capital. *Connections, 22*(1), 28–51.

Luckin, R., Clark, W., Graber, R., Logan, K., Mee, A., & Oliver, M. (2009). Do Web 2.0 tools really open the door to learning? Practices, perceptions and profiles of 11–16-year-old students. *Learning, Media, and Technology, 34*(2), 87–104.

Marin, A., & Wellman, B. (2011). Social network analysis: An introduction. In J. Scott, & P. Carrington (Eds.), *The Sage handbook of social network analysis* (pp. 11–25). London, England: Sage.

Mead, M. (1977). *Culture and commitment: A study of the generation gap.* New York, NY: Panther.

Newig, J., Gunther, D., & Pahl-Wostl, C. (2010). Synapses in the network: Learning in governance networks in the context of environmental management. *Ecology and Society, 15*(4), article 24. Retrieved from http://www.ecologyandsociety.org/vol15/iss4/art24/ (accessed February 20, 2015).

Nichols, S., Rowsell, J., Nixon, H., & Rainbird, S. (2012). *Resourcing early learners: New networks, new actors.* New York, NY: Routledge.

Pahor, M., Skerlavaj, M., & Dimovski, V. (2008). Evidence for the network perspective on organizational learning. *Journal of the American Society for Information Science and Technology, 59*(12), 1985–1994.

Phelan, P., Davidson, A., & Cao, H. (1991). Students' multiple worlds: Negotiating the boundaries of family, peer, and school cultures. *Anthropology and Education Quarterly, 22*(3), 224–250.

Phelan, P., Yu, H., & Davidson, A. (1994). Navigating the psychosocial pressures of adolescence: The voices and experiences of high school youth. *American Educational Research Journal, 31*, 415–446.

Portes, A. (1998). Social capital: Its origins and applications in modern sociology. *Annual Review of Sociology, 24*, 1–24.

Prensky, M. (2001a). Digital natives, digital immigrants. *On the Horizon, 9*(5), 1–6.

Prensky, M. (2001b). Digital natives, digital immigrants, part II: Do they really think differently? *On the Horizon, 9*(6), 1–6.

Pyrooz, D., Decker, S., & Moule, R. (2013). Criminal and routine activities in online settings: Gangs, offenders, and the Internet. *Justice Quarterly, 30*(1), 1–29.

Rajagopal, K., Brinke, D., Van Bruggen, J., & Sloep, P. (2012). Understanding personal learning networks: Their structure, content, and the networking skills needed to optimally use them. *First Monday, 17*(1). Retrieved from http://firstmonday.org/ojs/index.php/fm/article/view/3559/3131 (accessed February 20, 2015).

Rodan, S. (2008). Organizational learning effects of (network) structure and (individual) strategy. *Computational and Mathematical Organizational Theory, 14*(3), 222–247.

Ryan, A. (2001). The peer group as a context for development of young adolescent motivation and achievement. *Child Development, 72*(4), 1135–1150.

Schnettler, S. (2009). A structured overview of 50 years of small-world research, *Social Networks, 31*(3), 165–178.

Selwyn, N. (2000). Creating a "connected" community? Teachers' use of an electronic discussion group. *Teachers College Record, 102*(4), 750–778.

Selwyn, N. (2009). The digital native—myth and reality. *Aslib Proceedings: New Information Perspectives, 61*(4), 364–379.

Siemens, G. (2005). Connectivism: A learning theory for the digital age. *International Journal of Instructional Technology and Distance Learning, 2*. Retrieved from http://www.itdl.org/Journal/Jan_05/article01.htm (accessed February 20, 2015).

Slonje, R., Smith, P., & Frisen A. (2013). The nature of cyberbullying and strategies for prevention. *Computers and Human Behavior, 29*(1), 26–32.

Sobel, J. (2000). "Economists' models of learning." *Journal of Economic Theory, 94*(2), 241–261.

Stanton-Salazar, R. (2010). A social capital framework for the study of institutional agents and their role in the empowerment of low-status students and youth. *Youth and Society, 43*, 1066–1109.

Stanton-Salazar, R., & Dornbusch, S. (1995). Social capital and the reproduction of inequality: Information networks among Mexican-origin high school students. *Sociology of Education, 68*, 116–135.

Stanton-Salazar, R., & Spina, S. (2005). Adolescent peer networks as a context for social and emotional support. *Youth and Society, 36*, 379–416.

Tapscott, D. (1998). *Growing up digital: The rise of the net generation.* New York, NY: McGraw-Hill.

Wentzel, K., & Watkins, D. (2010). Instruction based on peer interaction. In R. Mayer and P. Alexander (Eds.), *Handbook of learning and instruction* (pp. 322–343). New York, NY: Routledge.

Wodzicki, K., Schwammlein E., & Moskaliuk, J. (2012). "Actually, I wanted to learn": Study-related knowledge exchange on social networking sites. *Internet and Higher Education, 15*, 9–14.

Woolf, K., Potts, H., Patel, S., & McManus, C. (2012). The hidden medical school: A longitudinal study of how social networks form, and how they relate to academic performance. *Medical Teacher, 34*, 577–586.

# 26

# Collaborative Learning

*CINDY E. HMELO-SILVER*
Indiana University

*CLARK A. CHINN*
Rutgers University

Collaborative learning has become an increasingly important part of contemporary learning environments. Dillenbourg (1999) noted that it is surprisingly difficult to get researchers to agree on a definition of collaborative learning. He concluded that collaborative learning "describe[s] a situation in which particular forms of interaction among people are expected to occur, which would trigger learning mechanisms, but there is no guarantee that the expected interactions will actually occur" (p. 5). Roschelle and Teasley (1995) made the distinction that collaboration involves a coordinated attempt to construct and maintain a shared understanding of goals, whereas cooperation refers to a division of labor. Others disagree: Webb and Palincsar (1996) assert, "In collaboration, the thinking is distributed among members of the group. Although cooperative learning can occur without collaboration, collaborative learning is generally assumed to subsume cooperative learning" (p. 848). Thus, distinction between these two terms is blurry, and any attempt to resolve the question is likely to be idiosyncratic. In this chapter, we focus on small groups of learners working together towards a common goal, whether it is one that they have set themselves or one that has been externally set (e.g., by a teacher); the tasks are intended to promote learning through the interactions.

This chapter will briefly review the theoretical approaches to collaborative learning that draw from information-processing theory, sociocultural theory, regulatory theories, and the theory of knowledge building. We will briefly consider a range of methodologies that are used for research in collaborative learning starting with quantitative methodologies, and a general overview of qualitative methodologies. Following this, we will review productive collaborative processes and examine how these are implemented in a number of instructional approaches and issues in collaborative learning, such as argumentation, group investigations, communities of learners, and problem-based learning. In the final section, we will sample issues related to computer-supported collaborative learning (CSCL).

## Theoretical Frameworks for Collaborative Learning

Diverse theoretical frameworks have guided the research and design of collaborative learning methods. In this section, we discuss four theoretical frameworks that have been highly influential in contemporary research on collaborative learning: Information-processing theory; sociocultural theory; regulatory theories; and knowledge building or knowledge creation.

### Information-Processing Theory

Much research on collaborative learning has been guided explicitly or implicitly by information-processing theory. By treating student statements during collaborative interactions as products of and inputs to cognitive processing, researchers can explore processes that promote more effective learning. One central premise of information-processing theory is that elaborative processing of information improves understanding of and memory for that information (see Webb, 2013). Examples of effective elaborative processing in collaborative groups include explaining ideas, giving reasons, articulating goals and plans, articulating solution procedures, and so on (e.g., Chi & Wylie, 2014). A second premise is that learning can be enhanced by receiving appropriate information from others. By applying elaborative processing to new information, learners incorporate this information into long-term memory structures. Through appropriate design, peer groups can be encouraged to engage in overt, verbal elaborative processing as they discuss ideas and solve problems with peers. Similarly, by encountering alternative perspectives presented by peers, students receive new ideas that can help them develop better ideas themselves (Chi & Wylie, 2014). Webb (2013) has provided an excellent overview of research on collaborative learning grounded in information-processing theory.

Information-processing theory has established that working memory—where cognitive processing occurs—is very limited in capacity. Some theorists have argued that this makes learning from inquiry and problem solving inefficient, because engaging in inquiry overloads working memory (Kirschner, Sweller, & Clark, 2006). If it were true that inquiry impedes learning by overloading working memory, then it would follow that collaborative learning tasks should avoid inquiry. However, others have shown that working-memory limitations in inquiry can be effectively circumvented in group work via appropriate problem design and scaffolding (Chinn, Duncan, Dianovsky, & Rinehart, 2013; Hmelo-Silver, Duncan, & Chinn, 2007); these methods will be discussed later in the chapter.

### Sociocultural Theory

Vygotsky's sociocultural theory is another prevalent theory framing work on collaborative learning (Hakkarainen, Paavola, Kangas, & Seitamaa-Hakkarainen, 2013). Whereas information-processing theory is compatible with the view that students should learn component skills before learning the larger skills of which they are a part, sociocultural theorists observe that, outside of school, people typically learn through apprenticeships in which they participate in the whole activities from the outset. At the beginning, apprentices may undertake only minor tasks, but they observe and participate in the overall process and gain an overall sense of the process, and then they gradually undertake more and more of the tasks over time. Accordingly, sociocultural theorists advocate having collaborative groups engage in complex inquiry and problem solving of the sort that people carry out in real-world tasks. Rather than teaching component knowledge and skills (e.g., learning anatomy) before allowing students to engage in larger processes (developing diagnoses of patients based on presenting symptoms), students are helped to engage in the larger processes with scaffolds that provide help through the parts that they cannot initially do (e.g., learning anatomy in the context of developing diagnoses; Rogoff, Paradise, Arauz, Correa-Chávez, & Angelillo, 2003). Sociocultural theorists also posit that learning occurs in the *zone of proximal development*, which means that students learn best when they are engaged with tasks on which they need some help, but which they can accomplish with this help; thus, collaborative groups should be provided with authentic tasks and the scaffolds (i.e., instructional supports) needed to help them succeed at these tasks (Hogan & Tudge, 1999). Novices will receive many scaffolds that can be gradually faded, until they can succeed at the tasks on their own. In addition, learning includes learning to use the tools that experts use, such as data visualization software to generate graphs and charts in a science project.

For sociocultural theorists, the units of analysis lie in the interactive processes by which people come to share the norms and practices of their community. Although many studies using a sociocultural frame do report individual learning, there is at least an equally intense focus on groups, communities, and societies in examining processes of collaborative learning (Hogan & Tudge, 1999). Rather than viewing collaborative learning through an individual lens, sociocultural theorists point to processes such as group co-construction of norms, processes by which these norms spread through communities, and processes by which these practices are appropriated by individuals, who in turn help stimulate new changes in the practices themselves.

### Regulatory Theories

Recently researchers have brought contemporary self-regulatory theories to bear on understanding collaborative processes. Self-regulatory theories were developed to explain individual cognitive functioning (see Hadwin & Oshige, 2011); these theories identify core regulatory processes that individuals use, such as setting goals, making plans, executing strategies to accomplish goals, evaluating how one is doing, and adjusting plans if the goal has not been achieved (Winne, Hadwin, & Perry, 2013). Recently, researchers have expanded this theory to encompass collaborative processes in groups. In a burgeoning area of research, self-regulated learning theorists have developed new models of self-regulated learning at levels of analysis higher than the individual. These models have stressed that, in collaborative groups, there are processes of collaborative regulation by which groups must coordinate shared activities. These include assumptions that collaborative learning occurs within social systems engaged in a meaningful activity using social processes to regulate goal-directed interactions. These systems are composed of interdependent agents who demonstrate metacognitive processes that support interacting (Järvelä, Volet, & Järvenoja, 2010).

According to Winne et al. (2013), collaborative groups involve: (a) individual group members' self-regulation; (b) co-regulation in which group members are mutually aware of each other's goals, strategies, and evaluations; and (c) shared regulation in which there are shared, common goals, standards, focus of attention, and so on. As an example, consider a task in which students are working with a body of evidence to judge whether the global climate is becoming warmer because of activities. Individual regulation might occur when a student monitors her current, individual beliefs about the quality of a piece of evidence. Co-regulation involves the student's awareness of her co-collaborators' judgments of the evidence. Shared regulation could involve agreeing, as a group, that they will adopt the norm of ignoring anecdotal evidence and focusing instead on evidence with broad samples. Researchers have found that co-regulation and shared regulation (such as joint attention and shared understanding of a task) are important for successful group performance as well as individual growth in collaborative learning settings (Barron, 2003; Järvelä & Hadwin, 2013).

### Knowledge Building or Knowledge Creation

Although many collaborative learning methods have focused on individual learning as the goal, another approach to collaborative learning, called *knowledge building,* treats group knowledge creation itself as the goal (Hakkarainen et al., 2013; Scardamalia & Bereiter, 2006). The focus is less on individual knowledge acquisition than on the collective knowledge developed by the group. In professional settings, one mark of successful collaborative interaction is that the group produces new knowledge, as when scientists produce new empirical findings or a new theory or a human personnel group work out causes of absenteeism in their workplace (cf. Scardamalia & Bereiter, 2006). These researchers argue, analogously, that the focus in collaborative learning should be on increasing knowledge created by a classroom community; collaborative learning is successful if the joint work performed by the group or class improves the collective knowledge of the community. In this approach to collaborative learning, the units of analysis are primarily at group levels rather than individual levels. What students need to learn is precisely how to participate in these knowledge-building communities, as these abilities are just what their future adult communities will need to thrive. The perspective here is that adult achievements are generally collective achievements accomplished by teams; accordingly, the focus of education should be to foster the capabilities of students to build knowledge in groups.

## Methods for Studying Collaborative Learning

In studying collaborative learning, there is often a tension between studying processes and studying outcomes, as well as a tension between whether research questions can be better answered with quantitative, qualitative, or mixed methods. These methods are informed by theoretical perspectives (Jeong, Hmelo-Silver & Yu, 2014). Moreover, collaborative learning provides special challenges for quantitative researchers (Cress, 2008; Cress & Hesse, 2013). In this section, we briefly address some of these issues.

### Quantitative Methods for Studying Collaborative Learning

Quantitative methods may involve experimental or quasi-experimental designs. But they may also involve descriptive designs in which collaborative processes may be counted (e.g., Chi, 1997; Hmelo-Silver, Liu, & Jordan, 2009) and described, as well as more complex inferential approaches such as using regression to show relations among variables or sequential data analysis to suggest how different kinds of events vary temporally (A. Jeong, 2003). Methods and research designs need to be appropriate for research questions and units of analysis being studied.

One of the challenges of studying collaborative learning is identifying the appropriate unit of analysis. Collaborative learning research may deal with units at the level of: (a) individual events within interactions; (b) sequences of interactions; (c) individual learners; and (d) groups (Cress & Hesse, 2013). The units of analysis selected will constrain the analytic techniques and methods used to study them and may lend themselves to different analytic techniques (Lund & Suthers, 2013; Strijbos, Martens, Prins, & Jochems, 2006). For example, sequences of interactions might be studied through sequential data analysis (Erkens, Prangsma, & Jaspers, 2006) or statistical discourse analysis (Chiu, 2008). Studying learning outcomes may still require that the group be considered as the unit of analysis, as we discuss next (e.g., Derry, Hmelo-Silver, Nagarajan, Chernobilsky, & Beitzel, 2006). Researchers using quantitative techniques must plan for their data collection and analysis with this in mind, even when they use individual measures.

In experimental and quasi-experimental designs, inferential statistics are used to determine whether a manipulation had an effect. Experimental designs assume random sampling and assignment to conditions, something that is often violated in classroom settings and other educational contexts. Moreover, many commonly used inferential statistics make assumptions about the independence of units. This is particularly problematic in studies of collaborative learning as individual students are nested within groups. Dependent variables tend to be non-independent because group members talk with each other, between as well as within groups.

Another challenge is that some variables are measured at the individual level (e.g., gender, prior knowledge) and others are measured at the group level (e.g., whether students have assigned roles or not; Strijbos, Martens, Jochems, & Broers, 2004). Newer statistical methods such as multilevel analysis can be used to deal with the individual and group levels common to collaborative learning (Cress, 2008). A challenge in using multilevel analysis in collaborative learning is having a sufficiently large sample. There is a consensus that at least 50 groups are required to use multilevel analysis to study collaborative learning (Cress, 2008; Janssen, Cress, Erkens, & Kirschner, 2013). However, Cress (2008) suggests looking at whether the intraclass correlation is significant. This represents the degree to which members of a group are similar to each. If it is significant, then researchers are advised to use a more stringent alpha level.

Another quantitative analysis approach, sequential data analysis, has been used to analyze the probabilities of how likely one event is followed by another. In collaborative learning, this can refer to different kinds of discourse moves, such as argumentation (A. Jeong, 2003; Jeong, Clark, Sampson, & Menekse, 2011). To model dynamic collaboration processes (e.g., create new ideas, modify other ideas), *statistical discourse analysis* (Chiu, 2008; Chiu & Khoo, 2005) estimates the likelihood of each process during each utterance or online message and the influences of explanatory factors at multiple levels (e.g., turns of talk, individual, group, class).

Statistical discourse analysis also identifies pivotal moments that radically change a collaboration and models factors that influence the likelihood of these moments (Chiu, Molenaar, Chen, Wise, & Fujita, 2013).

## Blurring the Boundaries

Other methods for analyzing collaborative learning are more descriptive and begin to blur the boundaries between qualitative and quantitative methods. A common method for looking at collaborative learning data is through quantitative content analysis (Strijbos et al., 2006). In content analysis, coding categories are identified and quantified. Once quantified, these can be counted and can then be subject to other kinds of analyses. For example, Jeong et al. (2011) used a content analysis scheme of argumentation moves, such as warranting claims for their sequential data analysis to determine how particular argumentative discourse moves were followed (or not) by other discourse moves in online data. Note that the quantitative content analysis is used to provide the events or predictors in sequential data analysis and statistical discourse analysis.

Content analysis can also take a more qualitative turn, being used in an inductive analysis to identify patterns in collaborative learning data. In studying a collaborative problem-based learning tutorial, Hmelo-Silver first examined the collaborative problem-based learning tutorial process using a multidimensional content analysis and later created a visual representation of the different codes along a timeline. This allowed looking for temporal patterns and discovering that causal reasoning about a patient case was associated with group construction of a representation (Hmelo-Silver, 2003; Hmelo-Silver & Barrows, 2008). Note that the initial content analysis was driven by a deductive coding scheme, but identifying patterns of codes from the visual representation was accomplished inductively.

## Qualitative Methods for Analyzing Collaborative Learning

Unlike content analysis, which tends to be deductive, some qualitative methods rely on inductive analytic schemes. One of the challenges of using qualitative analysis is dealing with the emergent and distributed nature of collaborative learning (Sawyer, 2013). Qualitative methodologies are generally appropriate for studying collaborative learning processes because discursive processes are important mediators of collaborative learning. For example, in interaction analysis, researchers work in a team to analyze video data to understand naturally occurring social interactions (Jordan & Henderson, 1995). This allows analysts to see how a collaboration emerges and is distributed among group members. Hmelo-Silver, Katiç, Nagarajan, and Chernobilsky (2007) used interaction analysis to see how leadership was distributed in a problem-based learning group and how it was mediated by the artifacts that the group constructed. The researchers used this approach because there appeared to be a

phenomenon related to emergent leadership and group success (broadly defined).

For other qualitative methods, the researcher may use either inductive and/or deductive approaches based on the research question, availability of prior theory, or research to guide analysis. For example, in verbal data analysis, researchers tend to begin with a predefined coding scheme that might be modified to fit the data. Verbal data draw from the cognitive science tradition of think-aloud protocols that assume that verbalizations are a form of objective data that can be used to reveal cognitive processes and knowledge organization (Chi, 1997). Although it is similar to content analysis in quantifying data based on predefined coding schemes, it has a focus on cognitive processes, whereas content analysis has a broader purview, though H. Jeong (2013) notes that these differences have narrowed in recent years.

In conversation analysis, inductive methods are used in order to understand how the participants in a conversation produce their interpretations. Roschelle (1996) used conversation analysis to study how learners collaboratively achieved convergent conceptual change while using a simulation. In conversation analysis, an important unit of analysis is the adjacency pair and conversational sequences. Qualitative approaches tend to need extended time for analysis and a great deal of manuscript space to adequately report results, which makes it challenging to publish research in journals with strict page limits.

## Mixing Methods

Using mixed methods to study collaborative learning can help researchers in understanding the complex nature of collaborative learning (Hmelo-Silver, 2003). They allow the researcher to understand the four variables that are important for understanding collaborative learning: *individual outcomes*, *group processes*, *temporality*, and the *context* in which collaborative learning is situated (Puntambekar, 2013). This allows researchers to triangulate their data to better support their claims as well as being complementary—using one method to help explain findings from other methods. For example, Derry et al. (2006) studied how students learned in a hybrid problem-based learning intervention for pre-service teachers. Inferential statistics were used to examine pre- to posttest gains and demonstrated large effects for the individual learning outcomes. A content analysis of group discussion posts was used as part of a contrasting case analysis to try to understand how collaborative groups interacted with each other and the technological resources (electronic whiteboard, video, hypertext) of the learning environment. This contrasting case analysis used chronological visual representations of the codes and technology used to demonstrate that the more effective group used the technological resources more extensively to answer questions and build from each other's ideas in an iterative fashion. Thus, the mixed methods triangulated data on individual outcomes and group processes over time in the context of the course to determine the more and less effective groups and were complementary in providing insight into the collaborative learning processes.

### Frontiers in Analyzing Collaborative Learning

Although many familiar methods will continue to be used to analyze collaborative learning, newer methods such as hierarchical linear modeling, statistical discourse analysis, and learning analytics add new tools to the repertoire of collaborative learning researchers. Learning analytics is the collection, measurement, and analysis of data from learning in context (Siemens, 2013). Learning analytics offers great potential in using automated techniques that can identify patterns in collaborative learning contexts through capturing data from students' interactions with computers and each other. Some techniques use social network analysis and other analyses of computer logs. There are learning analytic techniques that take into account the semantic content of those interactions using techniques from computational linguistics (Rosé et al., 2008). In addition, newer software tools provide support for qualitative researchers to assist with coding and pattern identification. Together these offer opportunities for researchers to better understand productive collaborative processes.

### Productive Collaborative Processes

One outcome of research into collaborative learning has been the identification of processes that occur within collaborative learning that facilitate student learning, as well as processes that facilitate successful group products. Processes that have been identified include: (a) engagement; (b) positive interdependence; (c) mutual respect; (d) high-quality social and cognitive strategy use; (e) uptake of peers' ideas; (f) communication of alternative perspectives; (g) balanced participation; and (h) co-regulation and shared regulation. Effective methods that promote learning will succeed in promoting most or all of these productive processes, which we discuss further below. In the following section, we discuss a range of instructional methods that do indeed succeed in promoting these processes and, through them, greater learning.

### Engagement

Effective groups are deeply engaged in their task (Blumenfeld, Kempler, & Krajcik, 2006). They find the task interesting and are motivated to discuss issues around the task. Effective groups avoid the problem of social loafing, in which some students do little work with the expectation that others will do the work instead of them. Linnenbrink-Garcia, Rogat, and Koskey (2011) found that engagement when working in small groups was positively correlated with positive affect and negatively associated with negative affect. Engle and Conant (2002) emphasized that productive interactions are characterized by *disciplinary engagement*, in which students are not only engaged, but are engaged in authentic tasks of a discipline (such as scientific inquiry) using the norms of

that discipline (e.g., scientific norms for evaluating evidence and scientific claims). This means, for example, that science students appreciate that theory building is not a matter of simply finding "right" answers but using evidence to support theories, and that science progresses by argumentation over rival theories.

### Positive Interdependence

Positive interdependence occurs when students can achieve their goals only by helping each other, not by acting independently (Johnson & Johnson, 1991; Slavin, 1996). A task with positive interdependence requires that individual students cannot successfully do it alone; input from all group members is needed for success. Many group work tasks assigned by teachers do not require positive interdependence. For example, students working on routine end-of-chapter problems in a mathematics textbook may be well able to work on the problems individually without needing to talk with each other. In contrast, complex inquiry tasks, such as middle-school students developing a scientific model of how natural selection occurs based on complex evidence (Chinn & Buckland, 2012), cannot be accomplished without students pooling their ideas, as the task is too complex for most students to negotiate successfully alone. Thus, positive interdependence is established in such a task.

### Mutual Respect

Students are more likely to interact well if they respect each other (Cohen, 1994b; Johnson & Johnson, 1990). Mutual respect precludes a common problem in collaborative groups—interactions in which one member puts down others. Adams-Wiggins and Rogat (2013) found that effective inquiry in middle-school science classes is undermined when students focus on right answers and disparage group members who they think have gotten the wrong answer; what is missing from such interactions is a focus on disciplinary norms that emphasize that effective scientific inquiry means that very good ideas will turn out not to fit the evidence, and that science depends on these ideas being advanced and considered. Thus, all participants merit respect. Moreover, when students develop a genuine respect for each other, perceived status differences diminish (Cohen, 1994b).

### High-quality Social and Cognitive Strategy Use

Effective groups engage in high-quality strategy use, including both social strategies (Krol, Veenman, & Voeten, 2002) and cognitive strategies (Webb, 2013). Effective social strategies include turn taking in an orderly manner, refraining from hogging the floor, offering encouragement to peers, and asking for input from students who have not been contributing. Students may not know how to be helpful group members, and may need to learn these skills. In effective groups, students also develop and exhibit emergent leadership skills (Miller, Sun, Wu, & Anderson, 2013).

Students in effective groups also use high-level cognitive strategies. In a series of seminal studies, Webb investigated middle-school students working collaboratively in math classes (see Webb, 2013, for a review). She found that learning was strongly associated with giving certain types of help—particularly *explanations*. In contrast, *terminal help* (just telling the answer) impedes learning, particularly for the recipient. Also unproductive is *procedural description*, where students tell (for example) the steps in solving a mathematics problem without actually explaining why the steps should be followed. Research on more complex tasks has identified other kinds of productive strategies, such as elaboration, monitoring understanding, summarizing, representing problems, planning, revising, weighing evidence fairly, and constructing arguments (Chi & Wylie, 2014; Chinn, O'Donnell, & Jinks, 2000).

### Uptake of Peers' Ideas

Research by Webb and Farivar (1994) has pointed to the importance of uptake of peers' ideas. To take up a peer's idea, students must listen to the idea and then respond to it in some way. Webb and Farivar found that peers benefited from receiving a mathematical explanation from a peer only when they used that explanation, such as by trying out the explained principles right away on a new problem. Barron (2003) similarly found that uptake of ideas was critical in groups working on a challenging mathematics problem. Students who simply agreed with and/or repeated a peer's idea showed little growth, as did students who rejected ideas without any rationale. In contrast, students who offered explanation for a peer's ideas or initiated a discussion by asking a question about the ideas showed more progress.

### Communication of Alternative Perspectives

On tasks where students' ideas differ from the ideas to be learned, learning is facilitated when group members share their contrasting perspectives (Chi & Wylie, 2014; Perret-Clermont, 1980). Students can learn from alternative perspectives even when no student's initial perspective is correct (Ames & Murray, 1982). Higher levels of discourse are also stimulated by disagreement, as the divergence in viewpoints spurs students to discuss issues more fully (Chi & Wylie, 2014).

### Balanced Participation

Participation by students in a group need not be exactly equal to promote learning. Indeed, sociocultural theorists have observed that, in many learning settings, people initially participate peripherally, gradually contributing more as they gain more experience with the group and its tasks. But researchers studying collaborative learning in schools have generally found that it is desirable to promote substantial participation by each student because the opportunity to explain one's ideas to one's peers promotes learning (Webb, 2013), and it can be valuable to hear others' perspectives on challenging topics. A common problem in collaborative groups is the exclusion of some students by others.

### Co-regulation and Shared Regulation

As we noted earlier, successful work in groups requires students to be aware of their fellow group members' goals, strategies, standards, and products (Winne et al., 2013). It also requires that members develop a shared common goal, shared standards that they can use to accomplish their work, and joint attention on the same components of the task so that coordination of work is possible. This requires very complex cognitive effort to integrate information at different levels (individual and group); recently researchers have become very interested in these topics, but the work to identify critical processes is just beginning (Järvelä & Hadwin, 2013; Winne et al., 2013).

## Instructional Methods

During the past five decades, educational researchers have investigated a broad range of instructional methods designed to enhance collaborative learning by promoting the productive processes discussed previously. We discuss key instructional methods and issues in this section.

### Rewards

One important issue in collaborative learning is how to use grades and other rewards. Some researchers have argued that extrinsic rewards are essential for motivating productive group behavior (Slavin, 1996). Slavin and his colleagues have presented extensive empirical evidence supporting the use of group rewards for individual learning. With this system, all students in a group receive the same grade or reward, but the grade or reward is based on an average of group performance. For instance, a group of four students study spelling words together and then take a test. Their grade or reward is determined by taking the group members' average score on the spelling test. Because each group member's reward depends in part on the performance of their group mates, positive interdependence is established.

However, many researchers who investigate collaborative learning have objected to the use of extrinsic rewards to motivate student performance in groups because of concerns about undermining intrinsic motivation. There are limitations to the empirical research on which the pro-reward conclusion is based (Cohen, 1994b). First, the studies that find support for group rewards for individual products have usually not measured intrinsic motivation as a possible outcome of the method. Thus, it is possible that academic gains occur at a partial cost to intrinsic motivation (see Deci, Koestner, & Ryan, 2001). Second, for many educators, one goal of cooperative collaborative learning is to promote genuinely prosocial, caring, altruistic behavior by students. However, students are not—by definition—learning to help others altruistically when they are always rewarded for any help that they give (Noddings, 2002). Finally, the tasks used in the studies cited in Slavin's review tend to employ fairly low-level cognitive tasks, such as reviewing material on work sheets provided by the teacher. It is questionable whether a reward structure that is successful with lower-level cognitive tasks is appropriate for more complex tasks with greater situational interest (Cohen, 1994b), which we turn to next.

### Complex Tasks

The current trend in collaborative learning research is to develop instruction with complex tasks at higher cognitive levels. Positive interdependence is established in these tasks without rewards because the tasks are complex enough that students need each other's insights and perspective to be successful, and high-level strategy use is needed to successfully negotiate the tasks. External rewards are de-emphasized. For instance, inquiry environments may ask students to use evidence to develop scientific models or to choose between alternative scientific models. Students may be working with four or five studies bearing on whether there are people resistant to HIV; these studies vary in methodological quality and link to alternative models in complex ways (Chinn et al., 2013; Chinn & Buckland, 2012; Rinehart, Duncan, & Chinn, in press). Developing and evaluating models against data is a challenging task that can best be solved by students pooling their knowledge and engaging in reasoned argumentation to try to work out which model is best supported by the evidence.

Such tasks differ markedly from tasks such as working on the problems at the end of a chapter or answering worksheet questions. These tasks require more complex strategy use, and they have the potential to be highly motivating. Effective tasks are also relatively challenging and open-ended. When tasks are simple and have a single right answer, it is likely that a single student will produce the answer, circumventing productive group processes (Cohen, 1994a). Effective complex tasks invite students to consider multiple sources of information and to conduct various types of investigation (Krajcik, Blumenfeld, Marx, Bass, & Fredricks, 1998). Many researchers recommend that groups produce public artifacts. Artifacts encourage accountability to create intellectual products through their group work that others can see, and the artifacts themselves can stimulate further inquiry. For example, groups can develop models to explain a body of evidence bearing on how dissolving occurs and then, once the models are publicly displayed, students can discuss which of these models is best (Chinn & Buckland, 2012).

### Scaffolds

A major focus of research on collaborative learning has been to develop and investigate scaffolds that can improve collaborative learning processes. Scaffolds are aids that help students accomplish tasks that they could not accomplish on their own. For example, students might be overwhelmed if simply given the task of trying to work out which of two scientific models fits a large body of conflicting evidence better; these students might be enabled to succeed if they are coached to use a matrix to tabulate the evidence and show systematically which evidence supports each model (Rinehart et al., in press).

One prominent scaffold in recent research is the *collaboration script* (Fischer, Kollar, Stegmann, & Wecker, 2013). Under the label *collaboration scripts*, we are including a wide variety of methods that provide students with specific guidance about what they should say during collaborative interactions; this guidance is analogous to the scripts that provide guidance to actors in a play, except that, whereas a theatrical script specifies everything that actors say, an instructional script might direct students to state their position on a historical question and a reason for their position, but leave it to students to formulate their own position and reason. Scripted methods originated in research that had students work in pairs to take turns recalling material and checking each other's recall. Research on this method found strong learning benefits for it, ranging from elementary students (e.g., Fuchs, Fuchs, Mathes, & Simmons, 1997) to university students (e.g., O'Donnell, 1999).

Scripts can provide guidance at several different levels (Fischer et al., 2013). They can provide guidance in the grammatical expressions that can be used (e.g., giving examples of phrases like "I disagree because. . . ." They can also provide guidance in the order of actions to follow (e.g., first, plan your project; second, identify what needs to be addressed to implement the steps in the plan, and so on). They may provide information about the roles that learners are to take in the interactions.

King (1999) has developed a method called guided peer questioning, in which students read a text and then question each other about that text using question stems such as "Describe ___ in your own words" or "Explain why ____." King (1994) found that students using these stems learned more than control students when the question set included connection stems that encouraged explanations as well as connections across different passages, such as, "How does ___ tie in with ____ that we learned before?"

Research with scripts and analogous methods has yielded complex findings. For example, in a task involving learning about attribution theory, Weinberger, Ertl, Fischer, and Mandl (2005) found that epistemic scripts (e.g., directions to ask questions such as whether the cause of an attribution is internal or external) were not helpful, whereas social scripts (e.g., directions to discuss differences in opinion) were beneficial. But in other research, scripts analogous to Weinberger's epistemic scripts have been helpful (Linn, Clark, & Slotta, 2003). Davis (2003) found that seventh-graders learned more with more general inquiry prompts (e.g., What we're thinking about now is . . . ) than with more specific prompts (e.g., When we critique evidence, we need to . . . ). It may be that more expert learners benefit from more general prompts, whereas novice learners benefit from more specific prompts (Kalyuga, Ayres, Chandler, & Sweller, 2003). Scripts may also be effective when students are reluctant to exert the effort to use productive strategies without being prompted by the scripts (Fischer et al., 2013).

Scripts promote several of the productive collaborative processes discussed earlier. For example, a script that directs students to formulate an argument or a summary directly encourages students to use high-level cognitive strategies that foster learning. Scripts that direct learners to ask each other questions can function to promote more balanced participation and more uptake of ideas. By directing students explicitly to interact with each other, such as by directing students to respond to a partner's argument, scripts foster uptake of ideas, as well as positive interdependence; the task simply cannot be completed without working together.

Another type of scaffold that has been extensively explored in recent work is the use of roles. *Social roles* focus on social and procedural processes that the groups perform. For instance, one possible social role is discussion leader. The discussion leader is responsible for making sure that the discussion runs smoothly and that everyone is contributing. *Cognitive roles* focus on the use of particular cognitive strategies the group must use to solve a problem (Herrenkohl & Guerra, 1998). For example, a possible cognitive role is theory checker. The theory checker would be responsible for ensuring that the group was carefully checking their theories against the evidence, and would have learned questions that could be asked to aid in this task. Herrenkohl and Guerra (1998) found that students who used cognitive roles during peer presentations of inquiry investigations had more productive discussions than students who did not.

A class of scaffolds used particularly in CSCL research encompasses *group awareness tools*. These tools provide help to inform participants about their peers' participation. For example, the number of contributions by each participant can be kept on the screen, which provides information about whom they might direct questions to in order to bring more participants into the discussion. Another example is a tool that periodically polls and posts discussants' stances on issues under discussion to see what participants' current stances are; participants may discover that the apparent consensus was not really a consensus because two quieter participants were in disagreement, which can foster more indepth exploration of an issue. Janssen et al. (2013) discussed the effects of a range of group awareness tools.

In an analysis of scaffolds supporting students' motivation in inquiry practices, Belland, Kim, and Hannafin (2013) observed that, although the original conceptualization of scaffolds included motivational supports, subsequent research on scaffolds had neglected specific scaffolds designed to support motivation, such as scaffolds to encourage students to set mastery goals, to heighten self-efficacy, and to enhance student autonomy—all desirable components of student motivation (see Chapter 7, this volume). Belland et al. (2013) provided a taxonomy of scaffolds for collaborative inquiry to enhance these forms of motivation.

Finally, an important and potent scaffold is teachers' modeling of desired forms of discourse, together with them pressing students to use these forms of discourse (Jadallah et al.,

2011; Rogat, Witham, & Chinn, 2014; Webb, Nemer, & Ing, 2006). For example, teachers who both model the practice of giving good explanations and urge students to do the same can promote better explanations; however, teachers frequently fall short of these desired forms of discourse (Webb et al., 2006). Similarly, students who model how to give good reasons can promote better argumentative discourse (cf. Jadallah et al., 2011).

### Shared Norms

Different disciplines adopt different norms to guide their practices—norms such as principles for evaluating sources in history and journalism, norms for evaluating methodology in science, and norms for evaluating arguments in mathematics. With increasing awareness that many of these norms are largely discipline-specific, there has been increased research interest in fostering the development of appropriate disciplinary norms in collaborative group work. One way of doing this has been the explicit discussion and/or encouragement of these norms by teachers, such as teachers constantly emphasizing the importance of giving reasons for ideas in science and mathematics and insisting that students follow these norms during group work. Chinn and colleagues (2013) have employed explicit public epistemic criteria with model-based inquiry in middle schools. For example, students collaboratively develop the criteria that they use to evaluate each other's models—criteria such as "good models fit the evidence" and "good models are easy to understand." Dianovsky, Chinn, Duncan, and Rinehart (2013) presented evidence for the efficacy of using epistemic criteria in science classes.

### Status Treatments

Research by Cohen and her colleagues has documented the effectiveness of status treatments to help preclude status problems discussed earlier. Status treatments are interventions designed to reduce students' perceptions that some students are higher-status (e.g., more academically capable) than others. Because high-status students can dominate collaborative interactions (Adams-Wiggins & Rogat, 2013), it is imperative for teachers to take actions to reduce status effects. Two options have been validated by research. With the *multiple-abilities treatment* (Cohen, 1994b), teachers act persistently to inform and persuade students that there are many cognitive abilities that are needed to complete the complex tasks they are undertaking, such as hypothesizing, considering different points of view, creativity, problem solving, planning, writing, public speaking, and so on. Research has shown that the multiple-ability treatment reduces status differences within groups, although it does not eliminate them (Cohen, Lotan, & Catanzarite, 1988). With the treatment of *assigning competence to low-status students*, teachers observe groups, and when they notice a lower-status student making a good contribution, they publicly acknowledge the contribution, describing specifically what the student has done well. Another approach to assigning competence is to thoroughly train lower-status students to be experts in a task so that they can teach higher-status students how to do the task (Cohen, Lockheed, & Lohman, 1976). These status treatment methods are all designed to promote the productive processes of balanced interaction and mutual respect.

### Collaborative Learning Programs

In this final section, we discuss several well-researched instructional programs that prominently feature collaborative learning. Generally, these programs all incorporate many or most of the instructional methods discussed above, with the exception of rewards, and they are designed to promote the beneficial group processes discussed in the previous section.

***Problem-based learning and inquiry-based learning.*** Problem-based learning has its origins in medical education. Students in groups are presented with problems (such as the presenting symptoms of a patient and the results of selected medical tests) and are required to search out and study resources (typically written) to solve the problem. Students work with a facilitator, set their own learning goals, and work together to gather information and bring it to bear to solve the problem (Hmelo-Silver & Barrows, 2008). Researchers have found that problem-based learning in medical schools is effective at promoting students' reasoning and problem-solving abilities in contrast to traditional forms of learning (e.g., Schmidt, Van Der Molen, Te Windel, & Wijnen, 2009; Hmelo, 1998). Positive results have also been obtained with other student populations in other settings (Hmelo-Silver & DeSimone, 2013).

Inquiry-based learning is similar to problem-based learning (Hmelo-Silver et al., 2007a, noted that there are no clearcut factors that distinguish them in the literature), and has been extensively studied in science, mathematics, and history classes. Groups of students typically are engaged in using reasons and evidence appropriate to the discipline to develop claims. They are often encouraged to engage in argumentation to consider each other's perspectives, interpretations of evidence, and so on. Different instructional programs have used a wide array of the instructional supports discussed earlier (e.g., prompts, scripts, diagrammatic representations). Overall evidence strongly supports the instructional efficacy of these methods in promoting growth in students' reasoning and content understanding (Chinn et al., 2013).

One prominent model for inquiry learning is *Fostering a Community of Learners (FCL)* (Brown & Campione, 1994). Students in FCL engage in projects that employ the *jigsaw* procedure. In jigsaw, different groups of students specialize in different subtopics relevant to the overall problem. Then they come together in new groups to share what they have learned with fellow students who have specialized in all the different subtopics. The students combine their expertise to solve the problem. In FCL, the culminating activity is a public event in which they must integrate their individual expertise into a final product such as a presentation. This method employs positive interdependence in that it critically involves students in a need to share information with each other in order to succeed.

***Group investigation.*** In group investigation (Sharan & Sharan, 1992), teachers provide the class with a broad topic, and student groups select their own subtopics for investigation and decide how to investigate these subtopics. They carry out investigations, prepare and make presentations, which are evaluated by peer audiences, and the students then evaluate their investigations and receive feedback on them from teachers. Group investigation is thus a method that affords great autonomy for students to co-regulate their own learning. Researchers have found that students learning in classrooms with group investigation outperform control students learning in classrooms that did not use any collaborative learning (Sharan, Sharan, & Tan, 2013). The studies conducted span a variety of ages and subject matters. The positive results include not only cognitive outcomes but also affective outcomes, such as greater liking for members of ethnic groups other than one's own.

***Complex instruction.*** Complex instruction is a collaborative learning format that emphasizes complex tasks, roles, and reducing status differences (Cohen & Lotan, 1997). Students tackle complex problems that require multiple perspectives and diverse insights to solve. Teachers assign cognitive roles to students, and they regularly use the two methods for reducing status differences that we discussed earlier. Researchers have evaluated complex instruction with elementary- and middle-school students (Cohen et al., 1997). They found that students who learn using complex instruction outperformed students in control classes on a variety of measures, including some measures of standardized tests of reading and mathematics. Both elementary- and middle-school students benefited from participating in complex instruction.

***Preparation for future learning and productive failure.*** Recent work by Schwartz and colleagues (e.g., Schwartz, Chase, Oppezzo, & Chin, 2011) and by Kapur and colleagues (e.g., Kapur & Bielaczyc, 2012) has advanced a novel way to employ collaborative groups. Both teams of researchers have presented groups with challenging problems which they may not be able to solve, such as solving a problem that requires use of standard deviation without being given the standard deviation formula. Both research teams have found that groups that tackle these problems, even when unsuccessful, learn more from a subsequent lecture on the relevant constructs than students who have spent the same amount of time being taught the ideas and then practicing them, as in traditional instruction. Schwartz et al. view this inventive period as preparing students for future learning, and Kapur refers to this inventive period as productive failure. Both teams of researchers posit that, even when unsuccessful, students are learning relevant features of problems that make them better prepared to learn from explanations.

## Technology Support for Collaborative Learning.

Many collaborative learning programs now take advantage of technology, which has provided possibilities for collaborative learning that would not otherwise be possible (see Chapter 25, this volume). Indeed, technology has become part and parcel of many approaches to collaborative learning, in particular, in the growing field of CSCL. A central tenet of CSCL focuses on learning as participatory and the social process of creating joint meaning, with computers serving as the medium for interaction (Suthers, 2006). As Roschelle (2013) noted, CSCL exploits a range of technology affordances:

- Interactivity: Social affordances for productivity;
- Representational: Promoting attention to particular aspects of working with disciplinary knowledge and tasks;
- Guidance: Scaffolding collaborative learning practices.

Both synchronous (chat, video) and asynchronous approaches to collaborative learning are being used, but, as in face-to-face collaborative learning, scaffolding and support are needed. Technology can serve as a medium of communication, but it can also serve as a focus for collaboration, as when a group discusses how to interpret a simulation (Jeong & Hmelo-Silver, 2012; Roschelle, 1996). Technology can also be used to provide guidance and constraints on the collaborative learning process, such as with collaboration scripts (Fischer et al., 2013).

The technologies used in CSCL can be classified along a number of dimensions. They may allow learners to work at the same time, as in synchronous chat or video conferencing, or asynchronously, as in threaded discussions or wikis (Jeong & Hmelo-Silver, 2012). Moreover, in CSCL, learners may be working in the same place or they may be in distributed locations. In a content meta-analysis of CSCL literature, Jeong and Hmelo-Silver (2012) identified a broad range of technologies that are used for collaborative learning, with communications tools being the most common. At the same time, these different technologies supported a broad range of collaborative pedagogies.

### Guidance in CSCL

Guidance can be provided in a number of ways that help reduce the overall cognitive load that might be imposed by both collaboration and the use of technology (Goldman, 1991; Hmelo-Silver et al., 2007a; Peters & Slotta, 2010). Collaboration scripts, which we discussed earlier, are one approach to providing supports and have been heavily researched in CSCL (Fischer et al., 2013). Collaboration scripts can function at the macro level or the micro level. Macro scripts specify a sequence of activities in a pedagogical model (Dillenbourg & Hong, 2008). For example, in ConceptGrid, there is a sequence of six activities that implement a jigsaw approach to collaboration and mix individual, whole-class, and small-group tasks. STELLAR used a sequence of eight individual, small-group, and whole-class activities to support problem-based learning (Derry et al.,

2006). In contrast, micro scripts focus on dialogue elements at the level of turn taking, discourse moves, and collaborative roles. For example, Schellens, Van Keer, DeWever, and Valcke (2007) found that assigning student roles in asynchronous discussions led to superior learning outcomes compared with students who were not assigned roles. Micro scripts have also been used productively to support argumentation in CSCL (Stegmann, Wecker, Weinberger, & Fischer, 2011). Fischer et al. (2013) have recently proposed a theory of how these external collaboration scripts dynamically interact with a learner's internal collaboration scripts. These internal scripts are acquired through repeated participation in collaborative learning and are activated as cognitive resources in new collaborative learning situations. Fischer et al. argue that, as learners internalize external scripts, they become empowered as self-regulated learners.

### Knowledge Building in Knowledge Forum

The knowledge-building theoretical perspective, which we discussed at the beginning of the chapter, has been implemented with the Knowledge Forum platform. Knowledge Forum is a software tool that establishes a networked communal knowledge base in which students can contribute ideas in the form of text or multimedia notes (Scardamalia & Bereiter, 1993/1994; van Aalst, 2009; Zhang, Scardamalia, Reeve, & Messina, 2009). Knowledge building and the associated Knowledge Forum technology have been the subject of a great deal of research. For example, in a program of design-based research, Zhang et al. (2009) examined the effects of different grouping arrangements on collective cognitive responsibility and knowledge advancement, finding that opportunistic groups (i.e., groups that self-organized) led to the most advancement compared with teacher-organized or other fixed groups.

Bringing together students from Hong Kong and Canada, Lai and Law (2006) demonstrated that students experienced in a knowledge-building culture from Canada could provide peer scaffolding for students in Hong Kong, who were newer to this approach to instruction. However, van Aalst and Chan (2007) demonstrated that groups also have difficulty in reaching these ideals of knowledge building and are often focused on lower levels of collaboration. A challenge for knowledge building is professional development and creating a culture that supports knowledge-building practices (Bielaczyc, 2013; Hakkarainen, 2009).

### Creating Contexts for Collaborative Learning

One important aspect of collaboration is that learners need something to talk about—a problem or task context (Hmelo, Guzdial, & Turns, 1998). In an early attempt at CSCL, Hmelo et al. found that it was extraordinarily difficult to get sustained online discussion; however through trial and refinement, they found that anchoring discussions around student questions and projects promoted sustained engagement. Video and simulations can provide contexts for learners to engage with complex phenomena and provide a shared reference. They can provide learners with opportunities to display and repair their understanding (Hmelo, Nagarajan, & Day, 2000; Roschelle, 1996). Roschelle provided a detailed analysis of how two students constructed a convergent understanding of a physics concept through the shared use of a simulation. Hmelo et al. (2000) built on the idea of using simulations to support development of a joint problem space in a study of medical students learning to design clinical trials. Similarly, video can provide contexts for collaborative inquiry. The *Adventures of Jasper Woodbury* series provided video anchors for middle-school students to collaboratively engage in mathematical problem solving (Cognition and Technology Group at Vanderbilt, 1997). Barron (2000, 2003) studied how these video problems provided contexts for coordinating shared attention.

Video cases have also been used to provide CSCL contexts in teacher education (Derry et al., 2006; Zottmann et al., 2013), science inquiry (Sinha, Rogat, Adams-Wiggins, & Hmelo-Silver, under revision; Goldman et al., 1994), and medical education (Balslev, De Grave, Muijtjens, & Scherpbier, 2005; Chan, Lu, Ip, & Yip, 2012). Research on the use of these contexts, as in simulations, often emphasizes collaborative processes and disciplinary practices (e.g., modeling, argumentation).

Mobile CSCL now provides opportunities to blend real-life contexts with computer tools to support collaboration. As Looi, Wong, and Song (2013) observed, "learners are mobile, mobile technologies are ubiquitous and ready-at-hand and learners can learn and collaborate in context" (p. 420). These mobile devices may include cell phones, tablets, and other devices that are small and portable. Mobile CSCL devices provide instant access to both information and to distributed networks of communication and expertise (Squire, 2010). In-class, mobile CSCL can set a context for participatory simulations (e.g., Klopfer, Yoon, & Perry, 2005). In Environmental Detectives, participants worked in small teams in the role of environmental engineers in a watershed near the implementation site or local nature centers (Squire & Klopfer, 2007). With handheld computers equipped with GPS, students could engage in scientific inquiry practices to investigate environmental disasters. Using maps and computers, students could work across the spatially distributed inquiry contexts and negotiate complex problem spaces. This is a relatively new and potentially rich area for future research on collaborative learning.

### Collaboration in Informal Learning Environments

Increasing attention is being devoted to the role of technology in informal environments. Youth communities, such as the Computer Clubhouse, are important sites for informal CSCL (Peppler & Kafai, 2007). The Computer Clubhouses form networks of youth communities where young people can engage in creative media production and share their projects with peers. These networks become increasingly large, and, like the internet in general, increasingly integrated into the lives of young people outside of school walls (Kafai & Fields, 2013).

One focus for these sometime massive informal communities revolves around online games (Steinkuehler, 2006). Games have attracted much attention in providing motivation and opportunities to learn outside of school. Some multiplayer online games, such as Whyville, are specifically geared towards younger learners. Using an ethnographic approach, Fields and Kafai (2009) described how students in an after-school gaming club used resources, people, and different virtual spaces to learn particular gaming practices through peer helping.

A last focus for informal collaboration is through Web 2.0 tools, in which users are collaborative producers of information and not just consumers. Wikipedia is perhaps one of the best-known examples of a collaborative knowledge community (Bryant, Forte, & Bruckman, 2005). Participants' concern for the shared knowledge artifact (i.e., Wikipedia) reflects an orientation consistent with knowledge building. Greenhow, Robelia, and Hughes (2009) argue that we need to understand and take advantage of learning in the Web 2.0 world of social networks. Web 2.0 technologies such as wikis, social network sites, and the like can blur the boundaries between formal collaboration and more permeable communities.

### Conclusions

Collaborative learning continues to hold an important position in educational psychology and the learning sciences. Research in collaborative learning is driven by both theoretical and practical purposes. It is an exciting time for collaborative learning researchers. New methodological tools are being developed to help in understanding the processes and products of collaborations. Advanced statistical techniques such as hierarchical linear modeling and statistical discourse analysis offer opportunities for better understanding collaborative processes and products, and learning analytics may allow the study of collaborative learning on a larger scale than has been possible before now. Automated techniques might help provide formative feedback for students and information for teachers that can be used to improve learning.

A range of instructional approaches have been well researched, but a great deal more work from the collaborative learning research community is needed. Research is just beginning to examine the potential of software agents that can help to facilitate collaborative groups (Howley, Kumar, Mayfield, Dyke, & Rosé, 2013). Many of the collaborative learning techniques and CSCL have been studied in a limited range of populations and subject matters; there is a need to broaden the study of collaborative learning to understand what is common across techniques and what adaptations are need for particular disciplines and populations. The explosion of massive open online education may be a fad or may be here to stay—either way, it may also be a laboratory for understanding collaborative learning (and for students, feeling a social affiliation is important for completing these courses; Yang, Wen, & Rosé, 2014). The promise of technology offers new opportunities for research and development, especially in understanding collaborative informal learning and communities. Finally, many inquiry approaches to collaborative learning work well on small scales, but the question remains about how these can be implemented more broadly, as well as how we can support teachers in guiding productive collaboration processes during broader implementation.

# References

Adams-Wiggins, K., & Rogat, T. K. (2013). Variation in other-regulation and the implications for competence negotiation. In N. Rummel, M. Kapur, M. Nathan, & S. Puntambekar (Eds.), *To see the world and a grain of sand: Learning across levels of space, time and scale* (pp. 18–25). Madison, WI: International Society of the Learning Sciences.

Ames, G. J., & Murray, F. B. (1982). When two wrongs make a right: Promoting cognitive change by social conflict. *Developmental Psychology, 18*, 894–897.

Balslev, T., De Grave, W. S., Muijtjens, A. M., & Scherpbier, A. (2005). Comparison of text and video cases in a postgraduate problem-based learning format. *Medical Education, 39*(11), 1086–1092.

Barron, B. J. S. (2000). Achieving coordination in collaborative problem-solving groups. *Journal of the Learning Sciences, 8*, 403–436.

Barron, B. J. S. (2003). When smart groups fail. *Journal of the Learning Sciences, 12*, 307–359.

Belland, B. R., Kim, C., & Hannafin, M. J. (2013). A framework for designing scaffolds that improve motivation and cognition. *Educational Psychologist, 48*, 243–270.

Bielaczyc, K. (2013). Informing design research: Learning from teacher's designs of social infrastructures. *Journal of the Learning Sciences*, 258–311.

Blumenfeld, P. C., Kempler, T. M., & Krajcik, J. C. (2006). Motivation and cognitive engagement in learning environments. In R. K. Sawyer (Ed.), *The Cambridge handbook of the learning sciences* (pp. 475–488). Cambridge: Cambridge University Press.

Brown, A. L., & Campione, J. C. (1994). Guided discovery in a community of learners. In K. McGilly (Ed.), *Classroom lessons: Integrating cognitive theory and classroom practice* (pp. 229–270). Cambridge, MA: MIT Press.

Bryant, S. L., Forte, A., & Bruckman, A. (2005). *Becoming Wikipedian: Transformation of participation in a collaborative online encyclopedia.* Paper presented at the Proceedings of the 2005 international ACM SIGGROUP conference on supporting group work.

Chan, L. K., Lu, J., Ip, M. S., & Yip, A. L. (2012). Effects of video triggers on the PBL process. In S. Bridges, C. McGrah, & T. L. Whitehill (Eds.), *Problem-based learning in clinical education* (pp. 139–150). Dordrecht, Netherlands: Springer.

Chi, M. T. H. (1997). Quantifying qualitative analyses of verbal data: A practical guide. *Journal of the Learning Sciences, 6*, 271–315.

Chi, M. T. H., & Wylie, R. (2014). The ICAP framework: Linking cognitive engagement to active learning outcomes. *Educational Psychologist, 49*, 219–243.

Chinn, C. A., Duncan, R. G., Dianovsky, M., & Rinehart, R. (2013). Promoting conceptual change through inquiry. In S. Vosniadou (Ed.), *International handbook of conceptual change* (2nd ed., pp. 539–559). New York: Taylor & Francis.

Chinn, C. A., & Buckland, L. A. (2012). Model-based instruction: Fostering change in evolutionary conceptions and in epistemic practices. In K. S. Rosengren, S. K. Brem, E. M. Evans & G. M. Sinatra (Eds.), *Evolution challenges: Integrating research and practice in teaching and learning about evolution* (pp. 211–232). Oxford: Oxford University Press.

Chinn, C. A., O'Donnell, A. M., & Jinks, T. S. (2000). The structure of discourse in collaborative learning. *Journal of Experimental Education, 69*, 77–97.

Chiu, M. M. (2008). Flowing toward correct contributions during groups' mathematics problem solving: A statistical discourse analysis. *Journal of the Learning Sciences, 17*, 415–463.

Chiu, M. M., & Khoo, L. (2005). A new method for analyzing sequential processes. *Small Group Research, 36*, 600–631.

Chiu, M. M., Molenaar, I., Chen, G., Wise, A. F., & Fujita, N. (2013). Micro-analysis of collaborative processes that facilitate productive online discussions: Statistical discourse analyses of three cases. In M. Clara & E. B. Gregori (Eds.), *Assessment and evaluation of time factors in online teaching and learning* (pp. 232–263). Hershey, PA: IGI Global.

Cognition and Technology Group at Vanderbilt. (1997). *The Jasper project: Lessons in curriculum, instruction, assessment, and professional development.* Mahwah, NJ: Erlbaum.

Cohen, E. G. (1994a). *Designing groupwork: Strategies for the heterogeneous classroom* (2nd ed.). New York: Teachers College Press.

Cohen, E. G. (1994b). Restructuring the classroom: Conditions for productive small groups. *Review of Educational Research, 64*, 1–35.

Cohen, E. G., Bianchini, J. A., Cossey, R., Holthuis, N. C., Morphew, C. C., & Whitcomb, J. A. (1997). What did students learn? 1982–1994. In E. G. Cohen & R. A. Lotan (Eds.), *Working for equity in heterogeneous classrooms: Sociological theory in practice* (pp. 137–165). New York: Teachers College Press.

Cohen, E. G., Lockheed, M., & Lohman, M. (1976). The Center for Interracial Cooperation: A field experiment. *Sociology of Education, 49*, 47–58.

Cohen, E. G., & Lotan, R. A. (Eds.). (1997). *Working for equity in heterogeneous classrooms: Sociological theory in practice.* New York: Teachers College Press.

Cohen, E. G., Lotan, R., & Catanzarite, L. (1988). Can expectations for competence be treated in the classroom? In M. Webster, Jr. & M. Foschi (Eds.), *Status generalizations: New theory and research* (pp. 27–54). Stanford, CA: Stanford University Press.

Cress, U. (2008). The need for considering multilevel analysis in CSCL research—An appeal for the use of more advanced statistical methods. *International Journal of Computer Supported Collaborative Learning, 3*, 69–84.

Cress, U., & Hesse, F. (2013). Quantitative methods for studying small groups. In C. E. Hmelo-Silver, C. A. Chinn, C. K. K. Chan, & A. M. O'Donnell (Eds.), *International handbook of collaborative learning* (pp. 93–111). New York: Routledge.

Davis, E. A. (2003). Prompting middle school science students for productive reflection: Generic and directed prompts. *Journal of the Learning Sciences, 12*, 91–142.

Deci, E. L., Koestner, R., & Ryan, R. M. (2001). Extrinsic rewards and intrinsic motivation in education: Reconsidered once again. *Review of Educational Research, 71*, 1–27.

Derry, S. J., Hmelo-Silver, C. E., Nagarajan, A., Chernobilsky, E., & Beitzel, B. (2006). Cognitive transfer revisited: Can we exploit new media to solve old problems on a large scale? *Journal of Educational Computing Research, 35*, 145–162.

Dianovsky, M., Chinn, C. A., Duncan, R. G., & Rinehart, R. (2013). *Middle school students' reasoning about the relations between models and evidence.* Paper presented at the annual meeting of the American Educational Research Association, San Francisco.

Dillenbourg, P. (1999). What do you mean by 'collaborative learning'? In P. Dillenbourg (Ed.), *Collaborative learning: Cognitive and computational approaches* (pp. 1–19). Oxford: Elsevier.

Dillenbourg, P., & Hong, F. (2008). The mechanics of CSCL macro scripts. *International Journal of Computer Supported Collaborative Learning, 3*, 5–23.

Engle, R. A., & Conant, F. R. (2002). Guiding principles for fostering productive disciplinary engagement: Explaining an emergent argument in a community of learners classroom. *Cognition and Instruction, 20*, 399–483.

Erkens, G., Prangsma, M., & Jaspers, J. (2006). Planning and coordinating activities in collaborative learning. In A. M. O'Donnell, C. E. Hmelo-Silver & G. Erkens (Eds.), *Collaborative learning, reasoning, and technology* (pp. 233–263). Mahwah, NJ: Erlbaum.

Fields, D., & Kafai, Y. B. (2009). A connective ethnography of peer knowledge sharing and diffusion in a tween virtual world. *ijCSCL, 4*, 47–68.

Fischer, F., Kollar, I., Stegmann, K., & Wecker, C. (2013). Toward a script theory of guidance in computer-supported collaborative learning. *Educational Psychologist, 48*, 56–66.

Fuchs, D., Fuchs, L. S., Mathes, P. G., & Simmons, D. C. (1997). Peer-assisted learning strategies: Making classrooms more responsive to diversity. *American Educational Research Journal, 34*, 174–206.

Goldman, S. R. (1991). On derivation of instructional applications from cognitive theories: Commentary on Chandler and Sweller. *Cognition and Instruction, 8*, 333–342.

Goldman, S. R., Petrosino, A., Sherwood, R. D., Garrison, S., Hickey, D. T., Bransford, J. D., & Pellegrino, J. W. (1994). Multimedia environments for enhancing science instruction. In S. Vosniadou, E. DeCorte, & H. Mandl (Eds.), *Technology-based learning environments* (pp. 89–96). Berlin: Springer.

Greenhow, C., Robelia, B., & Hughes, J. E. (2009). Web 2.0 and classroom research: What path should we take now? *Educational Researcher, 38*, 246–259.

Hadwin, A., & Oshige, M. (2011). Self-regulation, coregulation, and socially shared regulation: Exploring perspectives of social in self-regulated learning theory. *Teachers College Record, 113*, 240–264.

Hakkarainen, K. (2009). A knowledge practice perspective on technology-mediated learning. *International Journal of Computer Supported Collaborative Learning, 4*, 213–231.

Hakkarainen, K., Paavola, S., Kangas, K., & Seitamaa-Hakkarainen, P. (2013). Sociocultural perspectives on collaborative learning. In C. E. Hmelo-Silver, C. A. Chinn, C. K. K. Chan, & A. M. O'Donnell (Eds.), *International handbook of collaborative learning* (pp. 57–73). New York: Routledge.

Herrenkohl, L. R., & Guerra, M. R. (1998). Participant structures, scientific discourse, and student engagement in fourth grade. *Cognition and Instruction, 16*, 431–473.

Hmelo, C. E. (1998). Problem-based learning: Effects on the early acquisition of cognitive skill in medicine. *Journal of the Learning Sciences, 7*, 173–208.

Hmelo, C. E., Guzdial, M., & Turns, J. (1998). Computer support for collaborative learning: Learning to support student engagement. *Journal of Interactive Learning Research, 9*, 107–130.

Hmelo, C. E., Nagarajan, A., & Day, R. S. (2000). Effects of high and low prior knowledge on construction of a joint problem space. *Journal of Experimental Education, 69*, 36–56.

Hmelo-Silver, C. E. (2003). Analyzing collaborative knowledge construction: Multiple methods for integrated understanding. *Computers and Education, 41*, 397–420.

Hmelo-Silver, C. E., & Barrows, H. S. (2008). Facilitating collaborative knowledge building. *Cognition and Instruction, 26*, 48–94.

Hmelo-Silver, C. E., & DeSimone, C. (2013). Problem-based learning: An instructional model of collaborative learning. In C. E. Hmelo-Silver, C. A. Chinn, C. K. K. Chan, & A. M. O'Donnell (Eds.), *International handbook of collaborative learning* (pp. 370–385). New York: Routledge.

Hmelo-Silver, C. E., Duncan, R. G., & Chinn, C. A. (2007a). Scaffolding and achievement in problem-based and inquiry learning: A response to Kirschner, Sweller, and Clark (2006). *Educational Psychologist, 42*, 99–107.

Hmelo-Silver, C. E., Katic, E., Nagarajan, A., & Chernobilsky, E. (2007b). Soft leaders, hard artifacts, and the groups we rarely see: Using video to understand peer-learning processes. In R. Goldman, R. D. Pea, B. J. S. Barron, & S. J. Derry (Eds.), *Video research in the learning sciences* (pp. 255–270). Mahwah, NJ: Erlbaum.

Hmelo-Silver, C. E., Liu, L., & Jordan, R. (2009). Visual representation of a multidimensional coding scheme for understanding technology-mediated learning about complex natural systems. *Research and Practice in Technology-Enhanced Learning Environments, 4*, 253–280.

Hogan, D. M., & Tudge, J. R. H. (1999). Implications of Vygotsky's theory for peer learning. In A. M. O'Donnell & A. King (Eds.), *Cognitive perspectives on peer learning* (pp. 39–65). Mahwah, NJ: Erlbaum.

Howley, I., Kumar, R., Mayfield, E., Dyke, G., & Rosé, C. P. (2013). Gaining insights from sociolinguistic style analysis for redesign of conversational agent based support for collaborative learning. In D. D. Suthers, K. Lund, C. P. Rosé, C. Teplovs, & N. Law (Eds.), *Productive multivocality in the analysis of group interactions* (pp. 477–494). New York: Springer.

Jadallah, M., Anderson, R. C., Nguyen-Jahiel, K., Miller, B. W., Kim, I.-H., Kuo, L.-J., . . . Wu, X. (2011). Influence of a teacher's scaffolding moves during child-led small-group discussions. *American Educational Research Journal, 48*, 194–230.

Janssen, J., Cress, U., Erkens, G., & Kirschner, P. A. (2013). Multilevel analysis for the analysis of collaborative learning. In C. E. Hmelo-Silver, C. Chinn, C. K. K. Chan, & A. M. O'Donnell (Eds.), *International handbook of collaborative learning* (pp. 112–125). New York: Routledge.

Järvelä, S., & Hadwin, A. F. (2013). New frontiers: Regulating learning in CSCL. *Educational Psychologist, 48*, 25–39.

Järvelä, S., Volet, S., & Järvenoja, H. (2010). Research on motivation in collaborative learning: Moving beyond the cognitive–situative divide and combining individual and social processes. *Educational Psychologist, 45*, 15–27.

Jeong, A. (2003). The sequential analysis of group interaction and critical thinking in online discussion threads. *American Journal of Distance Education, 17*, 25–43.

Jeong, A., Clark, D. B., Sampson, V. D., & Menekse, M. (2011). Sequential analysis of scientific argumentation in asynchronous online discussion. In S. Puntambekar, G. Erkens, & C. E. Hmelo-Silver (Eds.), *Analyzing interactions in CSCL* (pp. 207–232). New York: Springer.

Jeong, H. (2013). Verbal data analysis for understanding interactions. In C. E. Hmelo-Silver, C. A. Chinn, C. K. K. Chan, & A. M. O'Donnell (Eds.), *International handbook of collaborative learning* (pp. 168–181). New York: Routledge.

Jeong, H., & Hmelo-Silver, C. (2012). Technology supports in CSCL. In J. van Aalst, K. Thompson, M. J. Jacobson, & P. Reimann (Eds.), *The future of learning: Proceedings of the 10th international conference of the learning sciences (ICLS 2012)—Volume 1, Full Papers* (pp. 339–346). Sydney, Australia: ISLS.

Jeong, H., Hmelo-Silver, C. E., & Yu, Y. (2014). An examination of CSCL methodological practices and the influence of theoretical frameworks 2005–2009. *iJCSCL, 9*, 305–344.

Johnson, D., & Johnson, R. (1990). Cooperative learning and achievement. In S. Sharan (Ed.), *Cooperative learning: Theory and research* (pp. 23–37). New York: Praeger.

Johnson, D. W., & Johnson, R. T. (1991). *Learning together and along: Cooperative, competitive, and individualistic learning.* Englewood Cliffs, NJ: Prentice Hall.

Jordan, B., & Henderson, A. (1995). Interaction analysis: Foundations and practice. *Journal of the Learning Sciences, 4*, 39–103.

Kafai, Y. B., & Fields, D. (2013). Collaboration in informal learning environments: Access and participation in youth virtual communities. In C. E. Hmelo-Silver, C. A. Chinn, C. K. K. Chan, M. O'Connor, & A. M. O'Donnell (Eds.), *International handbook of collaborative learning* (pp. 480–494). New York: Routledge.

Kalyuga, S., Ayres, P., Chandler, P., & Sweller, J. (2003). The expertise reversal effect. *Educational Psychologist, 38*, 23–31.

Kapur, M., & Bielaczyc, K. (2012). Designing for productive failure. *Journal of the Learning Sciences, 21*(1), 45–83.

King, A. (1994). Guiding knowledge construction in the classroom: Effects of teaching children how to question and how to explain. *American Educational Research Journal, 31*, 338–368.

King, A. (1999). Discourse patterns for mediating peer learning. In A. M. O'Donnell & A. King (Eds.), *Cognitive perspectives on peer learning* (pp. 87–115). Mahwah, NJ: Erlbaum.

Kirschner, P. A., Sweller, J., & Clark, R. E. (2006). Why minimal guidance during instruction does not work: An analysis of the failure of constructivist, discovery, problem-based, experiential, and inquiry-based teaching. *Educational Psychologist, 41*, 75–86.

Klopfer, E., Yoon, S., & Perry, J. (2005). Using palm technology in participatory simulations of complex systems: A new take on ubiquitous and accessible mobile computing. *Journal of Science Education and Technology, 14*, 285–297.

Krajcik, J., Blumenfeld, P. C., Marx, R. W., Bass, K. M., & Fredricks, J. (1998). Inquiry in project-based science classrooms: Initial attempts by middle school students. *Journal of the Learning Sciences, 7*, 313–350.

Krol, K., Veenman, S., & Voeten, M. (2002). Toward a more cooperative classroom: Observations of teachers' instructional behaviors. *Journal of Classroom Interaction, 37*, 37–46.

Lai, M., & Law, N. (2006). Peer scaffolding of knowledge building through collaborative groups with differential learning experiences. *Journal of Educational Computing Research, 35,* 123–144.

Linn, M. C., Clark, D., & Slotta, J. D. (2003). WISE design for knowledge integration. *Science Education, 87,* 517–538.

Linnenbrink-Garcia, L., Rogat, T. K., & Koskey, K. L. K. (2011). Affect and engagement during small group instruction. *Contemporary Educational Psychology, 36,* 13–24.

Looi, C.-K., Wong, L.-H., & Song, Y. (2013). Mobile computer-supported collaborative learning. In C. E. Hmelo-Silver, C. K. K. Chan, C. Chinn, & A. M. O'Donnell (Eds.), *International handbook of collaborative learning* (pp. 420–436). New York: Routledge.

Lund, K., & Suthers, D. D. (2013). Methodological dimensions. In D. D. Suthers, K. Lund, C. P. Rosé, C. Teplovs, & N. Law (Eds.), *Productive multivocality in the analysis of group interactions* (pp. 21–33). New York: Springer.

Miller, B., Sun, J., Wu, X., & Anderson, R. C. (2013). Child leaders in collaborative groups. In C. E. Hmelo-Silver, C. A. Chinn, C. K. K. Chan, & A. M. O'Donnell (Eds.), *International handbook of collaborative learning* (pp. 268–279). New York: Routledge.

Noddings, N. (2002). *Educating moral people: A caring alternative to character education.* New York: Teachers College Press.

O'Donnell, A. M. (1999). Structuring dyadic interaction through scripted cooperation. In A. M. O'Donnell & A. King (Eds.), *Cognitive perspectives on peer learning* (pp. 179–196). Mahwah, NJ: Erlbaum.

Peppler, K., & Kafai, Y. B. (2007). From SuperGoo to Scratch: Exploring creative digital media production in informal learning. *Learning, Media and Technology, 32,* 149–166.

Perret-Clermont, A.-N. (1980). *Social interaction and cognitive development in children.* London: Academic Press.

Peters, V., & Slotta, J. D. (2010). Scaffolding knowledge communities in the classroom: New opportunities in the web 2.0 era. In M. J. Jacobson & P. Reimann (Eds.), *Designs for learning environments of the future: International perspectives from the learning sciences* (pp. 205–232). New York: Springer.

Puntambekar, S. (2013). Mixed methods for analyzing collaborative learning. In C. E. Hmelo-Silver, C. Chinn, C. K. K. Chan, & A. M. O'Donnell (Eds.), *International handbook of collaborative learning* (pp. 220–230). New York: Routledge.

Rinehart, R. W., Duncan, R. G., & Chinn, C. A. (in press). A scaffolding suite to support evidence-based modeling and argumentation. *Science Scope.*

Rogat, T. K., Witham, S. A., & Chinn, C. A. (2014). Teachers' autonomy relevant practices within an inquiry-based science curricular context: Extending the range of academically significant autonomy suppotive practices. *Teachers College Record, 116*(7), 1–46.

Rogoff, B., Paradise, R., Arauz, R. M., Correa-Chávez, M., & Angelillo, C. (2003). Firsthand learning through intent participation. *Annual Review of Psychology, 54,* 175–203.

Roschelle, J. (1996). Learning by collaborating: Convergent conceptual change. In T. D. Koschmann (Ed.), *CSCL: Theory and practice of an emerging paradigm* (pp. 209–248). Mahwah, NJ: Erlbaum.

Roschelle, J. (2013). Special issue on CSCL: Discussion. *Educational Psychologist, 48,* 67–70.

Roschelle, J., & Teasley, S. D. (1995). The construction of shared knowledge in collaborative problem solving. In *Computer supported collaborative learning* (pp. 69–97). New York: Springer.

Rosé, C. P., Wang, Y.-C., Yue, C., Arguello, J., Stegmann, K., Weinberger, A., & Fischer, F. (2008). Analyzing collaborative learning processes automatically: Exploiting the advances of computational linguistics in computer-supported collaborative learning. *International Journal of Computer Supported Collaborative Learning, 3,* 227–231.

Sawyer, R. K. (2013). Qualitative methodologies for studying small groups. In C. E. Hmelo-Silver, A. M. O'Donnell, C. K. K. Chan, & C. Chinn (Eds.), *International handbook of collaborative learning* (pp. 126–148). New York: Routledge.

Scardamalia, M., & Bereiter, C. (1993/1994). Computer support for knowledge-building communities. *Journal of the Learning Sciences, 3,* 265–284.

Scardamalia, M., & Bereiter, C. (2006). Knowledge building. In R. K. Sawyer (Ed.), *The Cambridge handbook of the learning sciences* (pp. 97–115). Cambridge: Cambridge University Press.

Schellens, T., Van Keer, H., De Wever, B., & Valcke, M. (2007). Scripting by assigning roles: Does it improve knowledge construction in asynchronous discussion groups? *International Journal of Computer Supported Collaborative Learning, 2,* 224–246.

Schmidt, H. G., Van Der Molen, H. T., Te Windel, W. W. R., & Wijnen, W. H. F. W. (2009). Constructivist, problem-based learning does work: A meta-analysis of curricular comparisons involving a single medical school. *Educational Psychologist, 44,* 227–249.

Schwartz, D. L., Chase, C. C., Oppezzo, M. A., & Chin, D. B. (2011). Practicing versus inventing with contrasting cases: The effects of telling first on learning and transfer. *Journal of Educational Psychology, 103,* 759–775.

Sharan, Y., & Sharan, S. (1992). *Expanding cooperative learning through group investigation.* New York: Teachers College Press.

Sharan, S., Sharan, Y., & Tan, I. G.-C. (2013). The group investigation approach to cooperative learning. In C. E. Hmelo-Silver, C. A. Chinn, C. K. K. Chan, & A. M. O'Donnell (Eds.), *International handbook of collaborative learning* (pp. 351–369). New York: Routledge.

Siemens, G. (2013). Learning analytics: The emergence of a discipline. *American Behavioral Scientist, 57,* 1380–1400.

Sinha, S., Rogat, T. K., Adams-Wiggins, K., & Hmelo-Silver, C. E. (in press). Collaborative group engagement in a computer-supported inquiry learning environment, *International Journal of Computer-Supported Collaborative Learning.*

Slavin, R. E. (1996). Research on cooperative learning and achievement: What we know, what we need to know. *Contemporary Educational Psychology, 21,* 43–69.

Squire, K. (2010). From information to experience: Place-based augmented reality games as a model for learning in a globally networked society. *Teachers College Record, 112,* 2565–2602.

Squire, K., & Klopfer, E. (2007). Augmented reality simulations on handheld computers. *Journal of the Learning Sciences, 16*(3), 71–413.

Stegmann, K., Wecker, C., Weinberger, A., & Fischer, F. (2011). Collaborative argumentation and cognitive elaboration in a computer-supported collaborative learning environment. *Instructional Science, 40,* 297–323.

Steinkuehler, C. A. (2006). Why game (culture) studies now? *Games and Culture, 1,* 97–102.

Strijbos, J. W., Martens, R. L., Jochems, W. M. G., & Broers, N. J. (2004). The effect of functional roles on group efficiency using multilevel modeling and content analysis to investigate computer-supported collaboration in small groups. *Small Group Research, 35,* 195–229.

Strijbos, J. W., Martens, R. L., Prins, F. J., & Jochems, W. M. G. (2006). Content analysis: What are they talking about? *Computers & Education, 46,* 29–48.

Suthers, D. D. (2006). Technology affordances for intersubjective meaning making. *International Journal of Computer Supported Collaborative Learning, 1,* 315–337.

van Aalst, J. (2009). Distinguishing between knowledge sharing, knowledge creating, and knowledge construction discourses. *International Journal of Computer Supported Collaborative Learning, 4,* 259–288.

van Aalst, J., & Chan, C. K. K. (2007). Student-directed assessment of knowledge building using electronic portfolios. *Journal of the Learning Sciences, 16,* 175–220.

Webb, N. M. (2013). Information processing approaches to collaborative learning. In C. E. Hmelo-Silver, C. A. Chinn, C. K. K. Chan, & A. M. O'Donnell (Eds.), *International handbook of collaborative learning* (pp. 19–40). New York: Routledge.

Webb, N. M., & Farivar, S. (1994). Promoting helping behavior in cooperative small groups in middle school mathematics. *American Educational Research Journal, 31,* 369–395.

Webb, N. M., Nemer, K. M., & Ing, M. (2006). Small-group reflections: Parallels between teacher discourse and student behavior in peer-directed groups. *Journal of the Learning Sciences, 15,* 63–119.

Webb, N. M., & Palincsar, A. S. (1996). Group processes in the classroom. In D. Berliner & R. Calfee (Eds.), *Handbook of educational psychology* (pp. 841–876). New York, NY: Macmillan.

Weinberger, A., Ertl, B., Fischer, F., & Mandl, H. (2005). Epistemic and social scripts in computer-supported collaborative learning. *Instructional Science, 33*, 1–30.

Winne, P. H., Hadwin, A. F., & Perry, N. E. (2013). Metacognition and computer-supported collaborative learning. In C. E. Hmelo-Silver, C. A. Chinn, C. K. K. Chan, & A. M. O'Donnell (Eds.), *International handbook of collaborative learning* (pp. 462–479). New York: Routledge.

Yang, D., Wen, M., & Rosé, C. P. (2014). Peer influence on student attrition in massively open online courses. In J. Stemper, Z. Pardos, M. Mavrikis, & B. M. McLaren (Eds.), *Proceedings of the 7th International Conference on Educational Data Mining* (pp. 405–406). Retrieved from http://educationaldatamining.org/EDM2014/uploads/procs2014/posters/81_EDM-2014-Poster.pdf (accessed March 13, 2015).

Zhang, J., Scardamalia, M., Reeve, R., & Messina, R. (2009). Designs for collective cognitive responsiiblity in knowledge building communities. *Journal of the Learning Sciences, 18*, 7–44.

Zottmann, J. M., Stegmann, K., Strijbos, J. W., Vogel, F., Wecker, C., & Fischer, F. (2013). Computer-supported collaborative learning with digital video cases in teacher education: The impact of teaching experience on knowledge convergence. *Computers in Human Behavior, 29*, 2100–2108.

# 27

# Black and Hispanic Students

## Cultural Differences within the Context of Education

*Donna Y. Ford*
Vanderbilt University

We are living in a nation of unparalleled cultural diversity and differences relative to factors such as race, language, income, socioeconomic status (SES), and more. Current and projective demographic data indicate that racially and culturally different (RCD) students—African American, Asian American, Hispanic American, and Native American—represent an increasingly large proportion of the national and school population. In many U.S. cities, school districts, and school buildings, these "minority" groups are actually the numerical majority.[1] Given ever-changing demographics, issues of culture, difference, and conflict must be addressed in discussions, theories, research, and prevention and intervention efforts among educators.

According to the *Condition of Education* (Aud et al., 2013; Kena et al., 2014), the racial distribution of public-school students enrolled in grades P-12 is consistently changing. To illustrate, from 1988 to 2011, the percentage of White students in U.S. public schools decreased from 68% to 52%; in contrast, Hispanic enrollment doubled, from 11% to 22%. Black students' enrollment decreased slightly, from 17% to 16%. Projections for 2020 are that non-White students will comprise over half of all public-school students.

Note that changes in student demographics are not matched by changes in teacher or school personnel demographics relative to race (and gender). According to the *Condition of Education* (Aud et al., 2013; Kena et al., 2014), the majority (85%) of teachers are White; 75% of teachers are women. Undeniably, the demographic gap between school professionals and students contributes to the achievement gap, with some explanations grounded in cultural clashes (Banks, 2010; Ford, 2013a, 2013b; Gay, 2010; Ladson-Billings, 2006, 2009). Clashes exist when the values, beliefs, customs, and traditions of racial and cultural groups are dissimilar and/or in opposition. In the sections below, I present an overview of key theories, models, and paradigms that center on how cultures are out of sync in schools for the aforementioned

two student groups. This discussion begins with theories and conceptions of culture, cultural differences, and cultural conflict based on the works of John Ogbu (regarding voluntary and involuntary minorities) and A. Wade Boykin (regarding characteristics of African American culture). Later sections focus on racial identity using the scholarship of William Cross, Jr.

## African American/Black Students

In education discourse, laws, reforms, and policies on "minority" students, African Americans have received the greatest attention compared to other non-White students and groups for at least two reasons: (a) because they have been the largest "minority" in U.S. history until the last decade; and (b) because they are experiencing the least amount of school success—high dropout rates, low graduation rates, low test scores, high suspension rates, high enrollment in special education, and low enrollment in gifted and advanced classes. The outcomes are especially negative for African Americans, as witnessed by their experiencing the least amount of success in many school settings (Losen & Gillespie, 2012; Losen & Martinez, 2013; see also various Schott Foundation reports, such as *The Urgency of Now*, 2012). Given this specific educational crisis, two federal initiatives have been created in the United States: (a) the White House Initiative on Educational Excellence for African Americans (http://www.ed.gov/edblogs/whieeaa/); and (b) My Brother's Keeper, which seeks to recruit some 80,000 African American male teachers (http://www.white house.gov/my-brothers-keeper). Evident in these works is that race and culture matter, and that far too many African American students are not faring well in our nation's schools, but can do better when prevention and intervention are targeted to their specific issues and needs.

Ogbu (1988, 1994; Ogbu & Davis, 2003) accurately noted that African Americans are the only RCD group to come to the United States in chains and shackles; they are the only group denied the legal right to an education for centuries. Many other RCD groups have come by choice; that is, in search of the proverbial American dream and/or to escape from horrific and oppressive conditions in their nation. They are immigrants and "voluntary minorities." This is not the case for African Americans—descendants of slaves who are the largest "involuntary" minority group in the United States.

Given academic and social data, the American dream has been elusive for far too many. The ways in which African Americans experience education is not similar to the way of other culturally different groups in our schools and nation. The vestiges of slavery, Jim Crow, and segregation continue to influence such students socially and educationally, contributing in meaningful ways to the achievement gap, overrepresentation in special education, overreferrals for suspensions, and underrepresentation in gifted education and classes for advanced learners. To be effective with such students, educational psychologists have come to grasp the importance of studying the historical and contemporary lives of their students. They seek to understand who African Americans are as individuals and as a group.

Culture matters in teaching, learning, and assessment. As will be discussed later, the beliefs, attitudes, values, customs, and traditions of a people affect their school experiences and how educational psychologists work with them. As the United States continues being a nation of immigrants, it behooves educators from all disciplines to avoid disregarding or negating their culture and cultural differences, which can result in cultural clashes and contribute to students' underachievement and professional burnout. For instance, numerous reports and studies indicate that, in urban schools, educator turnover is high, with educators (especially classroom teachers) leaving the profession within 2–5 years (e.g., Barton & Coley, 2009). If culture were insignificant, there would be fewer misunderstandings and better outcomes for such students and educators.

Worth noting is that when educators learn that their students are Hispanic or Asian, they appear to recognize that culture will be at work; not so, it seems with African Americans (Ford, 2011). As an illustration, when Americans travel to Mexico or another Hispanic country, they cannot deny that their experiences and encounters will involve cultural differences. In this case, educators in another culture are vulnerable and may experience cultural shock, as noted by Hofstede, Hofstede, and Minkov (2010), Oberg (1960), and Storti (2007). Likewise, when Hispanic students are enrolled in classes in the United States, cultural differences and clashes will exist. The impact of culture is significant, regardless of whether educators are traveling abroad or when students are under their charge in U.S. schools. To repeat, when the students are immigrants or the focus is on international students, educators seem to understand and are more willing to accommodate cultural differences. However, when the students are neither immigrants nor international, such accommodations appear to be tempered and cultural differences are discounted or trivialized, which has been found with Black

students (e.g., Ogbu, 1988). Blacks are not immigrants; they are not recent immigrants or new to the United States, which can and does result in the misguided mindset that they do not have a culture that is unique and/or influences what happens in schools. This may be one reason—and a significant one—for their generally poor educational outcomes compared to other RCD groups.

Like all racial groups, African Americans have a culture with subcultures based on such variables as gender, region, age, income, SES, and education. As Boykin and colleagues (Boykin, Tyler, & Miller, 2005; Boykin, Tyler, Watkins-Lewis, & Kizzie, 2006) explained and as summarized by Ford (2011) and Ford and Kea (2009), spirituality, affect, harmony, movement, verve, orality, expressive individualism/creativity, polychronicity, and communalism are a few noteworthy characteristics of Black culture (Table 27.1). As with any RCD group, we need to rely on generalizations rather than stereotypes for understanding, and to guide prevention and intervention designed to improve their educational outcomes. The characteristics listed in Table 27.1 by no means suggest that all African Americans have these qualities or characteristics. Instead, the point is that there are some fundamental features of Black culture that educators, including educational psychologists, should understand and consider when working to be culturally responsive in their practice and when building relationships with such students, families, communities, and groups.

Black students are often communal or socially oriented; this is defined as a collective and interdependent identity more than an individualistic and independent one. Communalism is also reflected in fictive kinship networks and extended families (e.g., Boykin et al., 2005; Ford, 2011; Hale, 1983, 2001; McAdoo, 2006; Shade, Kelly, & Oberg, 2001). The desire for social acceptance, belonging, affiliation, and bonding with others who share similar concerns, needs, and interests is strong. Communal support is a mechanism for individual and group preservation, as well as social identity. However, group identity can be an important source of vulnerability for Black students. For instance, for a number of historical and contemporary reasons related to racism and associated discrimination, African American students may develop an oppositional social identity (Ogbu, 1988, 1994; Ogbu & Davis, 2003) in which they consciously underperform in school to avoid being identified or affiliated with Whites—the group deemed to be their oppressors (Ford, 2010; Ford, Grantham, & Whiting, 2008), rebel against school and social authority figures who are perceived as racist and oppressive, and rail against any behavior associated with mainstream society—known as "acting White." All students confront negative peer pressures, and educational psychologists are frequently called upon to design prevention and intervention programs. Increasingly, it is being recognized that such efforts must be culturally responsive rather than color-blind and they should be tailored to each student group (Gay, 2010; Irvine, 1991, 2003; Ladson-Billings, 2009).

To protect their image (i.e., self-esteem, self-concept, and/or racial identity), some African American students

**Table 27.1  Afro-centric cultural qualities: An overview**

| | |
|---|---|
| Spirituality | • Belief that a non-material, religious force/spirit influences people's everyday lives; acceptance of a non-material higher force that pervades all of life's affairs<br>• External locus of control: "God willing . . . "<br>• Faithful; optimistic; resilient<br>• Intuitive |
| Harmony | • Environment, nature, and context are important; the notion that one's fate is interrelated with other elements in the scheme of things so that humankind and nature are harmonically conjoined; harmony—one's functioning is tightly linked to nature's order<br>• Relationships matter<br>• External locus of control—nature/supernatural rules<br>• Observant/perceptive: Reads the environment well; reads non-verbal behaviors well, including inconsistencies between verbal and non-verbal<br>• Keen sense of justice |
| Movement | • An emphasis on movement, rhythm, music, and dance<br>• Tactile and kinesthetic; a need to move, to be involved, to be active<br>• Expresses self well non-verbally |
| Verve | • A propensity for relatively high levels of stimulation; physical overexcitability<br>• Energetic and lively; has vitality<br>• Demonstrative and animated<br>• Tactile; kinesthetic; physical |
| Affect | • An emphasis on emotions and feelings; strong emotions<br>• Sensitivity to emotional cues and a tendency to be emotionally responsive<br>• Keen sense of justice, right and wrong<br>• Realness—faces life without pretense<br>• Transparent—shows and tells emotions, feelings, thoughts |
| Expressive individualism | • Creative, innovative<br>• Seeks and cultivates a distinctive personality and style; unique personal expression, personal style<br>• A proclivity for spontaneity<br>• Risk taker, independent, impulsive<br>• Musicality and rhythm<br>• Uncanny sense of humor; clever |
| Orality/oral tradition | • A preference for oral modes of communication—speaking and listening are treated as performances<br>• Call and response<br>• Digression ("off topic," circular, non-linear)<br>• Oral virtuosity—uses metaphorically colorful, graphic forms of spoken language (e.g., slang; storytelling, embellishments, jokes, metaphors); idiomatic expression<br>• Direct, forthright, blunt, "tells it like it is" |
| Communalism | • Social orientation:<br>  – A commitment to social connectedness—social bonds and responsibilities transcend individual privileges and obligations<br>  – A commitment to the fundamental interdependence/co-dependence of people and to the importance of social bonds and relationships<br>  – A strong need for affiliation and social acceptance/approval; social; extraverted<br>• Interdependent; collective worldview<br>• Group identity; group duty and sharing often more important than individual wants and needs |
| Social time perspective/ polychronic | • Quality view of time<br>• Time is circular, social<br>• Time is not a commodity; time is not the master<br>• The event is more important than the time; flexibility is valued<br>• Present-oriented; the here and now is what exists (the future is not guaranteed)<br>• Multitasking is being efficient and making the most of time |

Adapted from Ford (2011), based on the works of A. Wade Boykin and colleagues (e.g., 2006). Although some of these qualities may appear to be consistent with stereotyped views of this cultural group, Boykin has evidence to support this list.

develop ineffective and unproductive coping styles that further alienate them from school and, thus, can hinder their academic success. Far too many Black students play down and hide their academic abilities by becoming class clowns and not enrolling in or taking advantage of gifted and advanced placement classes (Ford, 2010; Ford et al., 2008; Weiss, Kreider, Lopez, & Chatman-Nelson, 2010). One hypothesis is that these African American students may have a *diffused identity,* depicted by negative racial identity and low racial salience. This can result in educational, social, and psychological adjustment problems. This identity most likely develops when the values, attitudes, and behaviors promoted in the home and school are incongruent or incompatible, resulting in barriers to African

American students' academic success. This said, there is also ample and growing evidence that healthy or positive Black identity correlates favorably with motivation and academic achievement in African American students (Rowley, Sellers, Chavous, & Smith, 1998; Sellers, Linder, Martin, & Lewis, 2006). These works support the need for educational psychologists to be familiar with racial identity models and theories for their RCD students.

## Hispanic American/Latino Students

Hispanic Americans or Latinos are the fastest-growing RCD group in the United States. They are the largest linguistically different group, representing about one-fourth of the nation's school-age population (Aud et al., 2013; Kena et al., 2014). The largest Hispanic subgroup in U.S. schools is Mexican (over 60%), and those who are undocumented are experiencing poor school outcomes at high rates.

Hispanic American students, in particular Mexicans, are confronted by high poverty and unemployment rates, and negative educational outcomes. Dropout rates are alarming—almost half leave school without a degree (Batalova & Fix, 2011; Kena et al., 2014; see http://www.nytimes.com/2011/11/25/nyregion/mexicans-in-new-york-city-lag-in-education.html?pagewanted=all&_r=0). Language is a major barrier, as many do not speak English as their first or primary language; this is compounded by educators' beliefs and controversy regarding foreign languages, bilingual education, and English-only policies in some states and schools. When language supports are not valued and provided, these students are unlikely to be successful (Shade et al., 2001; Trumbull & Rothstein-Fisch, 2008).

Educational prevention and interventions for Hispanic American students mainly pertain to language acquisition programs—bilingual education, Spanish immersion, English as a second language, or limited English proficiency. (For an overview of bilingual education, see National Association for Bilingual Education at http://www.nabe.org/BilingualEducation). The focus is understandably on students adopting English; however, students also would benefit if programs targeted educational professionals who are bilingual and/or culturally responsive to support such students. Educational psychologists can be more effective with Hispanic students when they recognize verbal strengths in such students and are responsive to their cultural and linguistics issues and needs.

Generally speaking, when it comes to culture, Hispanic Americans value non-material possessions, family bonds, concrete and real-world learning experiences, social and cooperative learning, student-centered classrooms, and active learning experiences (Shade et al., 2001; Trumbull & Rothstein-Fisch, 2008). Overall and with an acknowledgment of within-group differences, many Hispanics are united by customs, language, religion, and values; yet, they are also heterogeneous (e.g., Hofstede et al., 2010). Similarities and differences exist among Mexicans, Cubans, Puerto Ricans, and all other subgroups. Educational psychologists who are culturally competent have the potential to support such students through targeted programs and interventions. This does not mean speaking the language; rather, it means understanding, respecting, valuing, and being responsive to this racial and cultural group and subgroups.

One characteristic that is of paramount importance in many Hispanic cultures (and subcultures) is family commitment, which involves loyalty, a strong support system, a belief that a child's behavior reflects on the honor of the family, and a duty to care for family members. This strong sense of other-directedness conflicts with the U.S. mainstream emphasis and value on individualism (Hofstede, 1984, 1991; Hofstede et al., 2010; Shade et al., 2001; Trumbull & Rothstein-Fisch, 2008). In general, Hispanic cultures promote and value interdependence and cooperation in the attainment of goals.

This focus on collective identity can result in students' discomfort when there is individualistic competition in classes. The individual rather than group-oriented philosophy and ways of being contribute to negative school performance and outcomes, depicted by the White–Hispanic achievement gap (see Trumbull & Rothstein-Fisch, 2008 and http://www.education.com/reference/article/Ref_Hispanic_American/, The White House Initiative on Educational Excellence for Hispanics (retrieved from http://www.ed.gov/edblogs/hispanic-initiative/)).

As was noted with Black students, it is important that educational psychologists become familiar with the culture and subcultures of their Hispanic American students, and plan prevention and intervention activities and strategies in culturally responsive ways. Being a color-blind professional seems counterproductive and may result in programs and strategies that are ineffective.

## Achievement Gaps: African American and Hispanic American Students

Several terms have been adopted to describe or articulate the comparative and differential performance of African American and Hispanic American students compared to White students in school settings. The term "achievement gap" covers a broad range of terms on this issue—rigor gap, expectation gap, opportunity gap, resource gap, funding gap, teacher quality gap, performance gap, cultural gap, and more—but they share the reality that both African American and Hispanic American students seldom fare as well as White students in P-12 and higher education settings.

At least 16 correlates clustered into three contexts contribute significantly to the different outcomes of students (Barton & Coley, 2009), as indicated in Table 27.2. Explanations for and contributing factors to the achievement gap are multifaceted and complex; the gap starts at home and then increases during the formal school years. At the kindergarten level, there is a 1-year gap between Black and White students and between Hispanic Americans and Whites; however, by the 12th grade, there is a 4-year gap (e.g., Barton & Coley, 2009; Chatterji, 2006; Ladson-Billings, 2006; Reardon & Galindo, 2009). Given that the gap *widens* while CRD students are in school, we cannot place the blame solely on families and educators cannot be held blameless and unaccountable.

A focus on achievement, including the achievement gap, is incomplete without also discussing the overrepresentation of African American and Hispanic students in special education and among suspensions and expulsions (e.g., Losen & Gillespie, 2012; Losen & Martinez, 2013). It is also incomplete without attention to their underrepresentation in gifted education and advanced placement classes (College Board, 2014; Ford, 2013b; U.S. Department of Education, 2009, 2013). Black students, mostly males, are two to three times more likely than White students to be represented in high-incidence areas of special education—emotional and behavioral disorders, learning disability, intellectual disabilities, and developmental delay. The suspension rates are equally dismal. A report released in March 2014 by the U.S.

**Table 27.2  Achievement gap correlates: School, home, and health**

| | | |
|---|---|---|
| School correlates | 1. | Rigor (e.g., low expectations, lack of access to rigorous courses and programs) |
| | 2. | Teacher preparation (e.g., low/poor-quality teachers) |
| | 3. | Teacher experience (e.g., novice teachers, those with fewer than 5 years of teaching experience) |
| | 4. | Teacher absence/turnover (e.g., many substitute teachers) |
| | 5. | Class size (e.g., larger class sizes) |
| | 6. | Instructional technology (e.g., little or inadequate use of technology to augment instruction) |
| | 7. | Fear and safety (e.g., negative peer pressure, gangs, violence in school) |
| Home correlates | 1. | Parent involvement (e.g., little involvement in school settings) |
| | 2. | Parent–student ratio (e.g., single-parent homes; larger families) |
| | 3. | Reading and talking to children (e.g., little talking and reading with children) |
| | 4. | Excessive TV watching (e.g., too much time spent with media) |
| | 5. | Changing schools (e.g., results in playing catch-up and keep-up; transition issues) |
| | 6. | Summer loss (e.g., little or no focus on academics) |
| Health correlates | 1. | Hunger and nutrition (e.g., more prone to food insecurity due to higher rates of poverty) |
| | 2. | Low birth weight (e.g., inadequate health care, poor prenatal care; contributes to developmental delays and health issues) |
| | 3. | Environmental damage (e.g., lead poisoning, mercury poisoning as a function of living in older homes) |

Source: adapted from Barton and Coley (2009).

Department of Education indicated that the national average for suspensions among Black males was 20%—compared to 6% for Whites and 9% for Hispanics. Nationally, 12% of Black girls were suspended, compared to 2% of White girls and 4% of Hispanic girls (retrieved from http://www.washingtontimes.com/news/2014/mar/21/school-suspension-rates-higher-for-black-boys/). This is not new data. In 2012, although Black students made up only 18% of those enrolled in the schools sampled, they accounted for 35% of those suspended once, 46% of those suspended more than once, and 39% of all expulsions, according to the Civil Rights Data Collection's 2009–2010 statistics from 72,000 schools in 7,000 districts, serving about 85% of the nation's students. The data covered students from kindergarten age through high school (retrieved from http://www.nytimes.com/2012/03/06/education/black-students-face-more-harsh-discipline-data-shows.html).

Conversely, and just as troubling, African American and Hispanic students are poorly represented in gifted and advanced placement classes, with about 50% underrepresentation for African American students and almost 40% for Hispanic American students (U.S. Dept. of Education, Office for Civil Rights, 2013). Specifically, Black students represent 19% of public schools but 10% of gifted programs. Hispanic American students comprise 25% of gifted education but 16% of gifted programs.

Overrepresentation and underrepresentation in the two aforementioned programs share the problem of deficit thinking (e.g., stereotypes, biases, prejudices) by educators. Deficit

thinking (Valencia, 2010) results in unnecessary referrals to special education and for suspensions and expulsions, and contributes to underreferral for gifted education screening (Ford, 2013a, 2013b; Ford et al., 2008). Deficit thinking contributes to gifted education underrepresentation and special education overrepresentation; both representation issues are a clarion call for educational psychologists to be culturally competent.

### Racial Identity Considerations

To further understand the educational performance of Black and Hispanic American students, a discussion of psychological development is in order. This section focuses on racial identity, using a research-based model by William Cross Jr. (See Ponterotto and Pedersen (2003), Ponterotto, Casas, Suzuki, and Alexander (2001), and Marks, Settles, Cooke, Morgan, and Sellers (2004) for several other racial identity models that are useful in guiding educational psychologists in their work to effect changes that improve the achievement and educational outcomes of Black and Hispanic American students).

No one is born with a racial identity. Instead, racial identity is learned. Self-perception, self-image, and identity play significant roles in school achievement and behavior. However, traditional theories of self-related constructs seldom include racial identity as a component, despite the reality that race is central to the sense of self of many RCD groups (Cross, 1991, 1995; Cross & Vandiver, 2001). Unfortunately, and undeniably, RCD students confront issues of race, such as stereotypes, discrimination, and racial microaggressions, on a consistent basis (Sue, 2010), which affects their identity. Self-perception and pride are lifelong developmental processes that begin with a healthy sense of one's own racial identity.

Racial identity concerns one's self-perceptions and values regarding race, especially salience and valence, as described in the many studies by Robert Sellers and colleagues. For example, when racial salience and valence are high, students tend to have racial pride. Racial identity theories exist for Whites and three major RCD groups—Asian, African American, and Hispanic, as well as biracial students. Space limitations prohibit a detailed discussion of each theory. Several racial identity models and theories appear in Ponterotto and Pedersen (2003; Ponterotto et al., 2001) for White students and RCD groups (and subgroups). To repeat, research supporting these models appears in Ponterotto et al.'s handbook (2001), and a chapter by Marks et al. (2004).

**Black racial identity.**  In Cross' revised model of Black racial identity, Cross and Vandiver (2001) and Vandiver, Fhagen-Smith, Cokley, Cross, and Worrell (2001) describe how African Americans progress and regress in the process of becoming Afro-centric where racial identity and pride are positive and have high salience. This model has been modified several times due to extensive studies by Cross and colleagues, along with other scholars who have conducted studies using the Cross Racial Identity Scale (see Cross &

Vandiver, 2001; Cross, Vandiver, Worrell, & Fhagen-Smith, 2002; Vandiver et al., 2001). The original theory contained four stages or identity types (Cross, 1971), while the 2001 model contains three (i.e., encounter is no longer one of the stages or identity types).

The model is described in stages or by identity types. My focus herein is on P-12 students, thus, I address and support a developmental or stage model. A discussion of considerations and potential pros and cons of stage or developmental models of racial identity appear in Quintana (2007). Whether a racial identity model is developmental or not, it cannot be denied that, like self-esteem and self-concept, racial identity is an important component of one's self. Per Cross and Vandiver (2001),

> when Nigrescence Theory is applied to the study of Black identity change, the categories Pre-Encounter, Encounter, Immersion-Emersion, and Internalization-Commitment are viewed as *stages*. However, when the focus is on the socialization experiences, covering infancy through early adulthood, that result in the production of exemplars . . . then the exemplars are viewed as bounded and fairly stable identity or distinctive reference group orientations. (p. 375)

According to the model, African American students in stage 1 (pre-encounter) hold one of at least three attitudes toward race: (a) low racial salience attitudes; (b) social stigma attitudes; and (c) anti-Black attitudes. Those holding a low-salience attitude do not deny being physically Black, but they consider their Blackness as having an insignificant role in their daily lives, their well-being, or how they define themselves (Figure 27.1). Students with an assimilation identity have low racial salience. Their primary identity is as an American rather than African American. Blacks who have a stereotype or miseducation identity disidentify as Black, perhaps due to shame associated with stereotypes of other Blacks. Those who express self-hatred personify an even more extreme disregard for their racial status. Being White is preferred and desired.

These Black students seldom give much thought to race issues, and appear unaware of problems associated with prejudice and discrimination. Overall, pre-encounter students view themselves as "human beings who just happen to be Black" (Cross & Vandiver, 2001, p. 98). By default, in this stage 1, race is attributed some significance, in a neutral or negative sense. Anti-Black attitudes represent the most extreme type of pre-encounter identity, as such students see their racial status as negative, feel alienated from other Blacks and family, and do not value the Black community as a resource.

All three pre-encounter types (assimilation, stereotypes/miseducation, and self-hatred) favor European cultural perspectives of beauty, literature, the arts, communication styles, work ethic (e.g., American dream), and so on. In all cases, being supportive of other Blacks is not likely.

Based on encounters (e.g., racial prejudice and discrimination, microaggressions), Blacks experience an "identity metamorphosis" (Cross & Vandiver, 2001, p. 104); this significant event (or series of events) induces cognitive dissonance. These events, either positive or negative and either direct or indirect, strip away at pre-encounter attitudes and push African American students toward increased awareness of their status as racial beings. The encounter or encounters (e.g., microaggressions: see Sue, 2010; Sue, Capodilupo, & Holder, 2008) result in significant emotional changes—guilt, anger, rage, stress, and/or anxiety—for having trivialized, discounted, or denied the significance of race and associated inequities.

Stage 2 (immersion-emersion) is the "vortex of psychological Nigrescence" in which African American students discard their raceless, low racial salience, or pre-encounter identity and begin to construct a different and more salient frame of reference. Immersion-emersion is characterized by anxiety, particularly relative to becoming the proper or "right kind of Black person" (Cross, 1995, p. 106). The two identity subtypes are intense Black involvement and anti-White attitudes (Cross & Vandiver, 2001). Whites are now perceived as oppressive, racist, and inhumane. African Americans immerse themselves in a world of Blackness. For instance, they attend political or cultural meetings that focus on Black issues grounded in justice and equity.

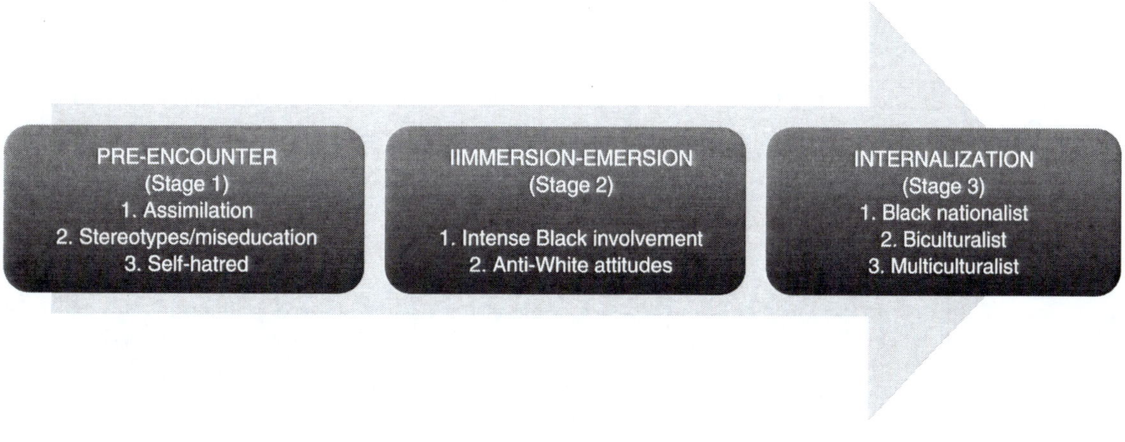

**PRE-ENCOUNTER**
(Stage 1)
1. Assimilation
2. Stereotypes/miseducation
3. Self-hatred

**IIMMERSION-EMERSION**
(Stage 2)
1. Intense Black involvement
2. Anti-White attitudes

**INTERNALIZATION**
(Stage 3)
1. Black nationalist
2. Biculturalist
3. Multiculturalist

**Figure 27.1** African American racial identity: Cross' stages and identity types.

African American students now accept themselves as racial beings. Common themes include dedication and commitment to the Black community and causes grounded in social and racial justice. When extreme, immersed African American students have difficulty controlling the impulse or desire to confront racism, even when their life is at stake. In the emersion phase, there is a marked decline in racist and emotional attitudes by African American students. This leveling off occurs when African American students encounter a mentor or role model, for instance, who emulates racial pride and salience, along with resilience in the face of oppression.

The last stage (internalization) represents the integration of a new identity characterized by healthy racial pride and high racial salience. There are three possible identity subtypes—nationalism, biculturalism, or multiculturalism. An internalized identity serves several functions: (a) to defend and protect African American students from psychological and racial problems; (b) to provide a sense of belonging and social affiliation; and (c) to provide a basis for interacting and communicating with people, cultures, and situations beyond being Black (Cross, 1995). It is important to note that internalization is change- or action-oriented, with a focus on change, equity, and being proactive at addressing social ills. Internalization represents self-advocacy and advocacy for those who are oppressed by income, gender, and perhaps other variables. Internalized African American students devote time and energy to discovering strategies and resources to translate their personal sense of Blackness into a plan of action—a commitment to Black affairs and improving the circumstances of African Americans and other disenfranchised groups (e.g., other RCD groups, groups who live in poverty).

Cross (1995) and Cross and Vandiver (2001) acknowledged that African Americans may regress or be stagnant in a stage or an identity type. This depends on their personality, support base, resources, and experiences at home, in school, in their communities and other contexts. For example, one can face encounters as an adolescent in school settings, have an immersion-emersion identity, and then get solid mentoring and become internalized. Years later as a college student or adult, this same individual can face encounters that increase anger and rage, which may result in regressing to immersion-emersion.

It is essential that African American and Latino students are not homogenized as racial beings. That is, racial identity is similar and different for all RCD students. Latinos or Hispanic Americans

generally hold a fundamentally different view of race. Many state that they are too racially mixed to settle on one of the government-sanctioned racial categories — white, black, American Indian, Alaska native, native Hawaiian, and a collection of Asian and Pacific Island backgrounds.
(Retrieved from http://www.nytimes.com/2012/01/14/us/for-many-latinos-race-is-more-culture-than-color.html?_r=0).

Hence, over 18 million Hispanic Americans checked the "other" box in the 2010 census—an indicator of the sharp disconnect between how Hispanics/Latinos view themselves and how the government and others want to count and categorize them. Many Hispanic Americans/Latinos argue that the country's race categories—indeed, the government's very conception of identity—"do not fit them" (retrieved from http://www.pewhispanic.org/2012/04/04/when-labels-dont-fit-hispanics-and-their-views-of-identity/).

Due to space limitations, all models of racial identity cannot be described here. Arce (1981) focused specifically on Chicano racial identity, with the stipulation that having a healthy racial identity for this RCD group involves: (a) cultural awareness; and (b) political awareness. Cultural awareness represents increased pride in Hispanic Americans' language, heritage, and cultural values. Political awareness represents the knowledge of their history in the United States, along with an awareness of the impact of discrimination or prejudice on this RCD population.

Unlike Cross (1995) and Cross and Vandiver (2001), Arce (1981) does not name stages in his racial identity development model for Chicanos. Nonetheless, the transitional descriptions are consistent with and somewhat aligned with other theories of racial identity. Ponterotto and Pedersen (2003) noted that the generic racial identity stages could be classified as: (a) forced identification; (b) internal quest; (c) acceptance; and (d) internalized racial/ethnic identity. During forced identification, Hispanic American students are identified by the general terms "Latino" or "Mexican American" by others. Those Latinos who adopt this imposed identity learn that it promotes a search for their cultural heritage—a quest for self-understanding relative to racial or ethnic identity (stage 2). This search leads to an acceptance of their group, and contributes to increased pride and commitment (stage 3). In the final stage, Hispanics (Latinos) develop a deeper, more substantive sense of affiliation and belonging to their group, and a desire to contribute to the group's overall well-being.

As all of these theories attest, becoming proud of one's culture as an RCD student does not happen in a vacuum, by accident, or without intent. Deliberate efforts by the students themselves and their peers, family, community, and schools provide opportunities for pride to develop. This is where a culturally responsive education comes into play.

## Culturally Responsive Education for Racially and Culturally Different Students

Decades ago, the American Association for Colleges of Teacher Education (1973) recognized that effective implementation of multicultural education has four foundational goals:

a. teaching values that support cultural diversity and differences, as well as individual uniqueness and differences;
b. promoting the qualitative expansion of existing cultures and their incorporation into the mainstream of American socioeconomic, cultural, and political life;
c. examining alternative and emerging lifestyles; and
d. fostering a philosophy of cultural responsiveness and equity.

However, there is too little consideration given to the cultural heritage that culturally different students—Black and Hispanic students—bring to classrooms and learning environments. Educational psychologists cannot conduct their work effectively absent of a clear definition of multicultural or culturally responsive education. Banks and Banks (1993) defined multicultural education as:

an educational reform movement designed to change the total educational environment so that students from racial and ethnic groups, both gender groups, exceptional students, and students from each social-class group will experience equal educational opportunities in schools, colleges and universities. (p. 359)

Culturally responsive education contributes to the psychological, social, affective/emotional, intellectual, and educational well-being of not only RCD students, but White students as well. Every student can benefit from an education that is culturally responsive (Banks, 1993, 2010; Ford, 2011; Gay, 2010; Shade et al., 2001; Trumbull & Rothstein-Fisch, 2008). Education is polemic and culturally assaultive when it caters to and capitalizes on the culture of White students more than other students (Ford, 2011). Too often, all students are given a homogenized curriculum and interventions that best meet the cultural, academic, intellectual, and affective/social-emotional interests and needs of White students, especially those in upper-income and SES groups. In this type of curriculum, African American and Hispanic American students can be marginalized, ignored, trivialized, or negated. This treatment of cultural diversity and difference(s) frequently affirms White students while undervaluing others. Likewise, homogenization espouses a color-blind or "culture-blind" philosophy, which is also offensive to RCD students. The result is that RCD students are denied opportunities to be valued and respected as RCD beings in schools (and the larger society). When educators seek to be color-blind, often as an ideal, equity is likened to equality and sameness; however, students are different in so many important ways that matter in educational settings. Therefore, in the process of seeking to achieve color-blindness/culture-blindness, educational psychologists risk negating, minimizing, or trivializing the richness and reality of diversity and differences (e.g., Steele, 2010; Sue, 2010; Sue et al., 2008).

Self-reflection among educational psychologists seems essential for change and progress. Why do *all* students need an education that is responsive in general and culturally responsive in particular? Why is this education essential for White and Hispanic and Black students? What is a culturally responsive education and what components are most vital? When is a culturally responsive education necessary? How can educators implement multicultural (culturally responsive) education so that it is an integral and integrated aspect of the educational process? Ford and Whiting (2008) share standards addressing students on the need for and their journey to becoming culturally competent students:

a. Engage responsibly in the cultural heritage and traditions of their community. Culturally competent students assume responsibility for their role in sustaining the well-being of the cultural

community and they demonstrate a lifelong commitment as community members and benefactors.
b. Build on the knowledge and skills of their cultural community as a foundation from which to achieve personal and academic success on a long-term basis. Culturally competent students demonstrate a capacity for and interest in learning about other cultures without diminishing personal integrity within their own and other cultures. They make effective use of their own cultural knowledge and skills to learn about the global world.
c. Participate actively and consistently in cultural environments. They feel confident and comfortable in other cultural settings and with people whose cultural backgrounds differ from their own. Such students adapt to different environments and see the myriad of advantages in being actively engaged in different cultural environments.
d. Engage effectively in learning activities that are based on traditional ways of knowing and learning. Culturally competent students identify and use appropriate sources of cultural knowledge to find solutions to everyday problems; they engage in realistic self-assessment to identify strengths and needs to maximize learning.
e. Demonstrate an awareness and appreciation of the relationships and processes of interaction of all elements in the community and world around them. Culturally competent students view their community and the world holistically, recognizing interdependence; they recognize how and why cultures change over time, and anticipate the challenges and changes that occur when different cultures come into contact. Culturally competent students discern the influence of cultural values and beliefs on interactions among people from different cultural backgrounds and contexts (Ford & Whiting, 2008).

As described next, educational psychologists benefit from becoming culturally aware, knowledgeable, skilled, and responsive. Cultural competence is a personal and professional survival skill.

### Instructional Models

Integrating culturally responsive education in schools and practice is a personal and professional commitment that becomes a reality with time, effort, persistence, and efficacy. Increased racial diversity among school personnel, modifications in curriculum and instruction, and philosophical changes can be implemented more effectively (that is, equitably) when educational psychologists are trained to be culturally competent. This will help them to enhance their work on individual differences relative to intelligence, cognitive development, affect, motivation, and self-concept and racial identity, as well as their role in learning, achievement, as assessment. Accordingly, such professionals will be more culturally inclusive in instructional design, educational technology, curriculum development, organizational learning, gifted education, special education, and classroom management.

Culturally competent educators are better equipped to identify and support strengths rather than weaknesses in RCD students. They have the following core characteristics: self-awareness and self-understanding; cultural awareness and understanding; social responsiveness and responsibility; and culturally sensitive techniques and strategies (Gay, 2010; Ladson-Billings, 2009).

*Self-awareness and self-understanding.* Culturally competent educators seek out and have greater self-awareness and understanding of their own biases, assumptions, and stereotypes. This comes from self-reflection—understanding our own cultural values and norms, and understanding how we all are a product of our experiences—specifically, culture. Such introspection helps educators to recognize how assumptions and biases influence their teaching and relationships with RCD individuals and groups (e.g., Ford, 2013a; Gay, 2010; Ladson-Billings, 2009; Storti, 2007).

*Cultural awareness and understanding.* Culturally competent educators understand, respect, and value the worldviews (e.g., values and norms) of RCD students. They do not harbor negative judgments, stereotypical judgments, and/or pre-judgments. Educators do not have to adopt the culture of their RCD students; instead, they respect that cultures are different and legitimate rather than substandard and trivial to the educational process. Through such reflection or looking inward, educational psychologists are better equipped to become more informed about how attitudes and beliefs influence teaching, learning, and assessment—all three influence their work and the way they relate to students and their families.

Culturally competent educators increase cultural awareness, understanding, and pride among *all* students. They adopt culturally responsive education, even in racially homogeneous settings (e.g., predominantly or all-White classrooms, schools, and communities). The absence of RCD students in such contexts is not used as an excuse to continue business as usual. Such educators are activists who seek positive changes on behalf of RCD students. As advocates, these school professionals seek equity in all areas of the educational process; they address inequities in instruction, materials, instruments, assessment, policies, and so forth by challenging barriers in school settings that hinder the educational outcomes of Black and Hispanic students.

*Cooperative learning.* Cooperative learning (Johnson & Johnson, 1994) is essential for Hispanic and African American students relative to building a sense of community and addressing culturally based ways of learning (Schul, 2012; Shade et al., 2001; Trumbull & Rothstein-Fisch, 2008). Educators must utilize a variety of cooperative learning techniques, relying less on competitive strategies. This strategy capitalizes on the cultural styles and preferences of RCD students to increase their achievement, engagement, and sense of belonging. Cooperative learning is a connection to how both groups tend to be reared at home—interdependence, social, family, and community are valued—with a decreased focus on individual competition. It is also important to recall components of Table 27.1 regarding the individual-collective continuum.

Cooperative learning holds promise for helping RCD students to feel more comfortable as they relate to and work with White classmates and educators. There is comfort when group identity is nurtured, as Hispanic and African American students can express themselves as a group or family (i.e., communal, collective, and interdependent) rather than individually (competitive). Cooperative learning makes Hispanic American and African American students interdependent, yet individually accountable. The two need not be mutually exclusive.

*Perspectives about time.* Notions of time are studied often in works on culture (e.g., Hoftstede et al., 2010). In most countries and cultures outside of the United States, time is polychronic rather than monochronic (e.g., Cohen, 2004; Luximon & Goonetilleke, 2010; and various works by Hofstede, 1984, 1991). A monochronic time system means that things and tasks are done one at a time and time is segmented into precise, small units. Under this system, time is scheduled, arranged, and managed by the clock in a literal way. However, when polychronic is the orientation, the event takes precedence over the hour; time is circular; time is unlimited. Educators would benefit from becoming familiar with different views about the concept of time, how they use time, and then transition African American and Hispanic American students into deadlines and class activities that require different timeframes and deadlines, and that have a different view of how time should be spent.

Students who are polychronic may not fare well in schools that are unforgiving and uncompromising by being wedded to a monochronic conception of time (Cohen, 2004; Hofstede, 1984, 1991; Luximon & Goonetilleke, 2010). Direct teaching/instruction regarding time management and organization is important. Concrete and real-world examples (such as being on time for a flight and work) for why being monochronic in U.S. school is a win–win is essential. This is not to say that deadlines are foreign to African American and Latino students; rather, the point is that time is perceived and spent differently across cultures and this can affect learning and teaching, even in U.S. classrooms.

*Communication style.* Whereas African American students tend to be direct about their views and can come across as blunt or rude, Hispanic students tend to be less direct and can come across as shy or lacking in self-confidence. Hispanic students tend to view the educational process as hierarchical, with teachers as the authority figure. Thus, some will not voluntarily talk in class, ask questions, admit to confusion, or ask for help (Ford, 2011). Speaking one to one with students can facilitate conversation, honesty, and a sense of agency, particularly among males who may hold macho views.

However, African American students are likely to be rather direct or blunt in their comments and views (see Boykin et al., 2005a, 2005b, 2006, and Table 27.1). Yet, African American males may be reserved when it comes to asking for help and support from teachers (e.g., Whiting, 2006). Hence, asking for help may be viewed as a sign of weakness and vulnerability, even more so among Black males. Many will prefer directives, specifics, and structure—leaving little room for confusion about teacher expectations on assignments. This is not to say that student choice must be eliminated; rather, that structure, clarity, and consistency are culturally responsive strategies that support these two groups of students, especially African American males.

## Multicultural Curriculum

Several studies and reports with African American and Hispanic students indicate that too many find the traditional curriculum irrelevant, thus contributing to disengagement and lower achievement, including the achievement gap. Although multicultural education is a commonly used concept, and is widely espoused in schools, the degree and quality of its implementation vary widely, and this variation has been attributed to inadequate training to ensure quality and integrity. Banks (1993, 1994, 1997, 2006, 2010) and Banks and Banks (1993, 2010) described four levels of integration of multicultural content into the curriculum (Figure 27.2).

In Level 1, the *contributions approach*, educators focus extensively, if not exclusively, on heroes, holidays, and discrete cultural elements and artifacts. According to Banks (1993, 2010) and Ford (2011), this is the most frequently adopted approach to multiculturalism in schools. A central feature of this approach is that the traditional, ethnocentric curriculum remains unchanged in its basic structure, goals, and salient characteristics. Cultural traditions—folklore, food, fashion, fun (e.g., music and dance)—may be

discussed, but insufficient attention is given to their meaning and significance to RCD groups and the larger U.S. context. Why do RCD groups celebrate alternative holidays and celebrations, or celebrate them in different ways (e.g., birthdays, childbirth, rites of passage, New Year's Eve, weddings, funerals/home goings)? These questions would not be raised or addressed at this level. As a result, students arguably learn little to nothing about the occasion, group, or individuals being celebrated. The contributions approach is cosmetic, superficial, and ancillary to the curriculum; it provides teachers with a quick, non-threatening way to "integrate" the curriculum, and teachers themselves can adopt this approach without knowing much about RCD groups. It also reinforces stereotypes about RCD students and groups by using safe, non-threatening heroes found acceptable to the mainstream (Ford, 2011).

In the *additive approach* (Level 2), the content, concepts, themes, and perspectives of RCD groups are added to the curriculum without changing its fundamental structure. That is, teachers may add a book, unit, or course that focuses on RCD groups, issues, or topics. While the content changes slightly, there is little restructuring of the curriculum relative to purposes and characteristics. RCD students learn little of their own history, and White students learn little of the history and contributions of other racial and cultural groups

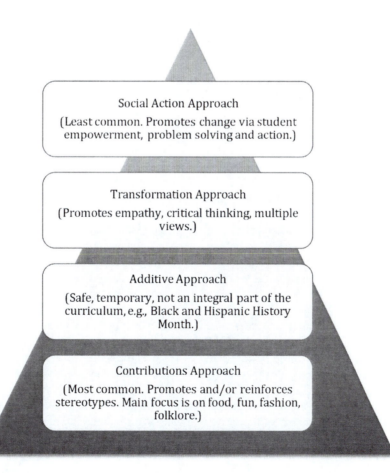

Social Action Approach
(Least common. Promotes change via student empowerment, problem solving and action.)

Transformation Approach
(Promotes empathy, critical thinking, multiple views.)

Additive Approach
(Safe, temporary, not an integral part of the curriculum, e.g., Black and Hispanic History Month.)

Contributions Approach
(Most common. Promotes and/or reinforces stereotypes. Main focus is on food, fun, fashion, folklore.)

**Figure 27.2** Overview of Banks' four levels of integrating multicultural content in the curriculum.

Adapted from Banks (2010) and Ford (2011).

in and to American society. The additive approach fails to help students view society from different perspectives and to understand how the histories of racial, cultural, economic, and religious groups are interconnected (Banks & Banks, 1993, 2010). This superficial approach requires little time, preparation, effort, training, and rethinking of curriculum and instruction. Students are actually miseducated if they are led to believe that the U.S. is postracial (i.e., that racism and related injustices do not exist in contemporary America).

In the third level, the *transformational approach*, at least two changes occur. First, the structure of the curriculum changes to empower students to view concepts, issues, events, and themes from the perspectives of RCD groups and/or from more than one view. This is a fundamental change from the previous two levels due to changes in the basic assumptions, goals, nature, and structure of the curriculum. The second fundamental change is that students are provided with the knowledge, dispositions, and skills to better understand the perspectives of RCD groups (e.g., empathy and compassion). Essentially, students are informed, enlightened, and empowered. This approach requires extensive curriculum revision, along with changes in teacher preparation, teacher attitudes and philosophies, student thinking, and much time, effort, and commitment.

At the *social action approach* (Level 4), students make decisions about important social issues and take action to solve and resolve them. Students are not socialized to accept mainstream ideologies, values, practices, and institutions. Instead, students are educated to feel empowered and proactive; they are provided with the knowledge, dispositions, and skills necessary to participate in social change. Student self-examination becomes central in this approach through value analysis, as well as decision making, problem solving, and social action skills training. For example, students examine, discuss, and interrogate past and contemporary issues surrounding prejudice and discrimination, and they develop solutions to improve race relations. According to Banks (1993, 2006, 2010), this approach/level is the least likely to be adopted by educators, primarily because they lack formal training, experience, understanding, and personal knowledge of other racial and cultural groups (e.g., histories, values, beliefs, customs). Some may also lack interest and the desire to be culturally responsive. Reason aside, knowledge without action does not improve social and cultural relations and behavior.

It should be evident that, at the highest levels, authentic and rigorous multicultural education requires extensive attitudinal, philosophical, and curricular changes, undergirded by a personal and professional commitment to be culturally responsive. Rigorous multicultural education helps students to accept their culture as an integral component of their overall development without relegating the culture of others to second-class status. Professional development/training is essential to ensure the integrity of Banks' model/level and implementation at the highest two levels of transformation and social action.

By increasing their knowledge about cultural and racial diversity and differences, every teacher and student can acquire an ethic of equity and social justice—a sense of

personal independence, social interdependence, personal responsibility, moral obligation, and social responsibility that can increase interest, motivation, and learning (Banks, 2006, 2010; Gay, 1993, 1997, 2002, 2010; Hale, 2001; Irvine, 2003).

## Summary and Conclusion

Culturally competent educators seek to deliver a more effective education to African American and Hispanic students, an education that is relevant and appropriate to students' interests and needs. This means adopting principles of learning that meet the academic, social-emotional, and psychological needs of RCD students, which is necessary to help close the documented achievement gaps.

Educators and educational psychologists who champion being culturally responsive create an education to achieve cultural pride, equity, and cultural congruency. This necessitates going beyond the subject matter to empower RCD students to value achievement (see Graham, 1994, for a seminal discussion) and to access social and cultural capital that benefits Whites, but is often elusive to so many Black and Hispanic students. Culturally competent educators who integrate the realities of students' lives, experiences, and cultures into their classrooms and curricula, while affirming and validating students' racial and cultural identities (Ladson-Billings, 2009), have the potential to close the various achievement gaps and inequities in school settings.

Several models of cultural competence exist to guide this process. To illustrate, consider the model from Mason (1993). Mason described six levels of cultural competence for individuals and organizations. The lowest level is cultural destructiveness, in which attitudes, policies, and practices hinder RCD individuals and groups. Also low is incapacity, whereby the educator and/or agency does not intentionally seek to be culturally assaultive; rather, the educator or agency lacks the skills or resources to work responsively with culturally different students. Blindness is also low. At this level, the educator and/or organization provide services with the objective of being unbiased. They function as if culture is insignificant. At a higher level is pre-competence, in which educators and organizations acknowledge cultural differences and make efforts to improve. The highest level, competence, is characterized by acceptance and respect of cultural differences, continued self-assessment, attention to the dynamics of cultural differences, and adoption of culturally relevant service models.

Storti (2007) shared a 2 × 2 typology based on competence and consciousness. Level 1 is called blissful ignorance (unconscious-incompetent). Here, individuals are not aware that cultural differences exist between themselves and another person or group. It does not occur to such individuals that they may be making cultural mistakes or perhaps misinterpreting much of the behavior going on around them. Level 2 is termed troubling ignorance (conscious-incompetent). Individuals realize that there are cultural differences between themselves and another person or group, but have little understanding about these differences. Individuals know there is a problem, but do not know the magnitude of the conflicts. At this level, individuals are worried about whether they will ever figure out differences in others.

Storti labels the third level as spontaneous sensitivity (unconscious-competent). Here, individuals know there are cultural differences between people, they know some of the differences and attempt to modify their own behavior to be sensitive to these differences. This does not come naturally, but individuals make a conscious effort to behave in culturally sensitive ways. They are in the process of replacing old intuitions with new ones. The highest level is spontaneous sensitivity (conscious-competent). Individuals no longer have to think about what they are doing in order to be culturally sensitive in a *familiar* culture. Culturally appropriate behavior comes naturally at this point, and individuals trust their intuition because it has been reconditioned by what has been learned and experienced about cross-cultural interactions.

Colleges and universities hold the primary responsibility of preparing future educators to work in P-12 settings. In terms of knowledge and understanding, preparation programs seek to develop future educators who are culturally competent, as described below.

1. *Knowledge and understanding* of: (a) principles of human development and the nature of individual and group differences; (b) the social, cognitive, emotional, and environmental factors that affect development; (c) a variety of methods for identifying and assessing students; (d) current and seminal research related to learning theory, giftedness, and creativity; and (e) theoretical models, program prototypes, and educational principles that offer appropriate foundations for developing differentiated curriculum for RCD students.

2. The *ability and training* to: (a) interpret and apply knowledge related to the needs of Black and Hispanic students; (b) identify and assess the unique or specific needs of RCD students; (c) act as a change agent in social, cultural, political, and economic environments inhibiting services to students; (d) vary teaching styles and instructional strategies to help RCD students meet their academic interests, goals, and needs; and (e) develop in RCD students the attitudes and skills needed to become independent, lifelong learners, to self-evaluate, and to set and pursue appropriate personal and academic goals for future success (Whiting, 2006).

Based on the analysis presented in this chapter, the following recommendations are provided for improving educators' competence to work with RCD students.

1. *Personal exposure and experience*: (a) increased self-understanding and views about working with non-White students by educations. This requires involvement in experiences that allow them to examine their own cultures, and to better understand the concept and significance of culture; and (b) close examination of their beliefs and assumptions regarding RCD students—including biases, stereotypes, and prejudices.

2. *Cultural exposure and experience*: (a) educators need opportunities and experiences that expose them to ways to become more culturally competent. These experiences cannot take place solely by reading books and articles; there must be ongoing opportunities to interact with RCD students, families, and communities—to become somewhat immersed in their lives; and (b) educators can benefit from early, consistent, and ongoing experiences that expose them to RCD students, families, and communities;

3. *Linguistic exposure and experience*: Again, with early and consistent experiences with linguistically different students, educators can come to understand the importance of language, and the implications of bilingualism and limited English proficiency in learning and achievement;

4. *Social exposure and experience*: Substantive preparation for educators can effectively address prejudice and discrimination in school settings, such as reducing racism, sexism, and classism in attitudes, assessment, and curriculum; the theories of Robert Merton, Gordon Allport, and Derald Sue are essential. As described by Ford, Trotman Scott, Moore, and Amos (2013), microaggressions, degrees of prejudice and discrimination, and attention to intentional and unintentional racism are all important.

5. *Culturally responsive curriculum and instruction*: To learn how to design, implement, and evaluate culturally responsive curriculum and instruction for all students. James Banks' model of how to infuse multicultural content in the curriculum is useful and rigorous. Ford (2011) adapted Banks's model, adding critical thinking by Bloom (Anderson et al., 2001); the resultant Bloom–Banks matrix offers educators ways to develop lesson plans that are rigorous *and* relevant. More information is presented in Ford (2011).

6. *Learning environment and classroom management*: Educators can learn how to develop supportive, affirming, and nurturing environments for RCD students; this competence will help to improve classroom management, which increases teaching and learning time and, thus, achievement.

## A Final Word

It cannot be denied that Black and Hispanic students individually and as groups are not faring well in our schools. The key indicator is the achievement gap; other indicators, such as the overrepresentation of such students in special education and among suspensions, as well as their underrepresentation in gifted education, are different manifestations of this same problem. The need for educational psychology to devote attention to these two groups is a non-trivial matter, especially given current and projected demographics showing that numbers of Hispanic and Black children are increasing quickly in schools and the nation at large. The racial demographics of teachers remains rather low and stagnant; accordingly, once again, the analysis I have presented in this chapter suggests that educators and educational psychologists who champion being culturally responsive have the potential to create an education that can help Black and Hispanic students to achieve cultural pride, equity, and cultural congruency.

## Note

1. The term "racially and culturally *different*" is preferred to "racially and culturally *diverse*," based on my belief that everyone has a culture. The problem is *how* educators view and respond to differences in race and culture. "Racially and culturally different" students are those who are different from the mainstream; they are non-White—Black, Hispanic American, American Indian, and Asian American.

## References

American Association of Colleges for Teacher Education, Commission on Multicultural Education. (1973). No one model American. *Journal of Teacher Education, 24,* 264–265.

Anderson, L. W. (Ed.), Krathwohl, D. R. (Ed.), Airasian, P. W., Cruikshank, K. A., Mayer, R. E., Pintrich, P. R., Raths, J., & Wittrock, M. C. (2001). *A taxonomy for learning, teaching, and assessing: A revision of Bloom's taxonomy of educational objectives.* New York: Longman.

Arce, C. A. (1981). A reconsideration of Chicano culture and identity. *Daedalus, 110,* 177–192.

Aud, S., Rathbun, A., Flicker-Wilkinson, S., Kristapovich, P., Wang, X., Shang, J., & Notter, L. (2013). *Condition of education 2013.* Washington, DC: National Center for Education Statistics.

Banks, J. A. (1993). Approaches to multicultural curricular reform. In J. A. Banks & C. A. M. Banks (Eds.), *Multicultural education: Issues and perspectives* (2nd ed.). Boston, MA: Allyn & Bacon.

Banks, J. A. (1994). Multicultural education: Historical development, dimensions, and practice. In L. D. Darling-Hammond (Ed.), *Review of research in education* (pp. 3–49). Washington, DC: American Educational Research Association.

Banks, J. A. (1997). *Teaching strategies for ethnic studies* (6th ed.). New York, NY: Allyn and Bacon.

Banks, J. A. (2006). *Cultural diversity in American education.* Boston, MA: Allyn & Bacon.

Banks, J. A. (2010). Approaches to multicultural curriculum reform. In J. A. Banks & C. A. M. Banks (Eds.), *Multicultural education: Issues and perspectives* (7th ed., pp. 233–258). Hoboken, NJ: John Wiley.

Banks, J. A., & Banks, C. A. M. (Eds.). (1993). *Multicultural education: Issues and perspectives* (2nd ed.). Boston, MA: Allyn & Bacon.

Banks, J. A., & Banks, C. A. M. (Eds.). (2010). *Multicultural education: Issues and perspectives* (7th ed.). Hoboken, NJ: John Wiley.

Barton, P. E., & Coley, R. J. (2009). *Parsing the achievement gap II.* Princeton, NJ: Educational Testing Services.

Batalova, J. & Fix, M. (2011). *Up for grabs: The gains and prospects of first- and second-generation youth adults.* Washington, DC: Migration Policy Institute.

Boykin, A. W., Albury, A., Tyler, K., Hurley, E., Bailey, C., & Miller, O. (2005a). Culture-based perceptions of academic achievement among low-income elementary students. *Cultural Diversity and Ethnic Minority Psychology, 11,* 339–350.

Boykin, A. W., Tyler, K. M., & Miller, O. A. (2005b). In search of cultural themes and their expressions in the dynamics of classroom life. *Urban Education, 40,* 521–549.

Boykin, A. W., Tyler, K. M., Watkins-Lewis, K. M., & Kizzie, K. (2006). Culture in the sanctioned classroom practices of elementary school teachers serving low-income African American students. *Journal of Education of Students Placed At-Risk, 11,* 161–173.

Chatterji, M. (2006). Reading achievement gaps, correlates, and moderators of early reading achievement: Evidence from the early childhood longitudinal study (ECLS) kindergarten to first grade sample. *Journal of Educational Psychology, 98*(3), 489–507.

Cohen, R. (2004). *Negotiating across cultures: International communication in an interdependent world* (rev. ed.). Washington, DC: United States Institute of Peace.

College Board. (2014). *10th Annual AP report to the nation.* New York: College Board.

Cross, W. E. (1971). The Negro-to-Black conversion experience. *Black World, 20*(9), 13–27.

Cross, W. E. (1991). *Shades of black: Diversity in African-American identity.* Philadelphia: Temple University Press.

Cross, W. E., Jr. (1995). The psychology of Nigrescence: Revising the Cross model. In J. G. Ponterotto, J. M. Casas, L. A. Suzuki, & C. M. Alexander (Eds.), *Handbook of culturally responsive counseling* (pp. 93–122). Thousand Oaks, CA: Sage.

Cross, W. E., Jr., & Vandiver, B. J. (2001). Nigrescence theory and measurement: Introducing the Cross Racial Identity Scale (CRIS). In J. G. Ponterotto, J. M. Casas, L. A. Suzuki, & C. M. Alexander (Eds.), *Handbook of multicultural counseling* (pp. 30–44). Thousand Oaks, CA: Sage.

Cross, W. E., Jr., Vandiver, B., Worrell, F., & Fhagen-Smith, P. (2002). Validating the Cross Racial Identity Scale. *Journal of Counseling Psychology, 49*(1), 71–85.

Ford, D. Y. (2010). *Reversing underachievement among gifted Black students* (2nd ed.). Waco, TX: Prufrock Press.

Ford, D. Y. (2011). *Multicultural gifted education* (2nd ed.). Waco, TX: Prufrock Press.

Ford, D. Y. (2013a). Gifted under-representation and prejudice: Learning from Allport and Merton. *Gifted Child Today, 36,* 62–68.

Ford, D. Y. (2013b). *Recruiting and retaining culturally different students in gifted education.* Waco, TX: Prufrock Press.

Ford, D. Y., Grantham, T. C., & Whiting, G. W. (2008). Culturally and linguistically diverse students in gifted education: Recruitment and retention issues. *Exceptional Children, 74*(3), 289–308.

Ford, D. Y., & Kea, C. D. (2009). Creating culturally responsive instruction: For students' sake and teachers' sake. *Focus on Exceptional Children, 41*(9), 1–18.

Ford, D. Y., Trotman Scott, M., Moore III, J. L., & Amos, S. O. (2013). Gifted education and culturally different students: Examining prejudice and discrimination via microaggressions. *Gifted Child Today, 36*(3), 205–208.

Ford, D. Y., & Whiting, G. W. (2008). Cultural competence: Preparing gifted students for a diverse society. *Roeper Review, 30*(2), 104–110.

Gay, G. (1993). Ethnic minorities and educational equality. In J. A. Banks & C. A. M. Banks (Eds.), *Culturally responsive education: Issues and perspectives* (2nd ed.) (pp. 171–194). Boston, MA: Allyn & Bacon.

Gay, G. (1997). Educational equity for students of color. In J. A. Banks & C. A. M. Banks (Eds.), *Culturally responsive education: Issues and perspectives* (3rd ed.) (pp. 195–228). Needham Heights, MA: Allyn & Bacon.

Gay, G. (2002). Preparing for culturally responsive teaching. *Journal of Teacher Education, 53,* 106–116.

Gay, G. (2010). *Culturally responsive teaching: Theory, research, and practice* (2nd ed.). New York, NY: Teachers College Press.

Graham, S. (1994). Motivation in African Americans. *Review of Educational Research, 64,* 55–118.

Hale, J. E. (1983). Black children: Their roots, culture, and learning styles. In O. N. Saracho & B. Spodek (Eds.), *Understanding the multicultural experience in early childhood education* (pp. 17–34). Washington, DC: National Association for the Education of Young Children.

Hale, J. E. (2001). *Learning while Black.* Baltimore, MD: The Johns Hopkins University Press.

Hofstede, G. (1984). *Culture's consequences: International differences in work-related values* (2nd ed.). Beverly Hills, CA: Sage.

Hofstede, G. (1991). *Cultures and organizations: Software of the mind.* New York, NY: McGraw-Hill.

Hofstede, G., Hofstede, G. J., & Minkov, M. (2010). *Cultures and organizations: Software of the mind* (3rd ed.). New York: McGraw-Hill.

Irvine, J. J. (1991). *Black students and school failure: Policies, practices, and prescriptions.* New York, NY: Praeger.

Irvine, J. J. (2003). *Educating teachers for diversity: Seeing through a cultural lens.* New York, NY: Teachers College Press.

Johnson, D., & Johnson, R. (1994). *Learning together and alone, cooperative, competitive, and individualistic learning.* Needham Heights, MA: Prentice-Hall.

Kena, G., Aud, S., Johnson, F., Wang, X., Zhang, J., Rathbun, A., Wilkinson-Flicker, S., and Kristapovich, P. (2014). *The condition of education 2014* (NCES 2014-083). Washington, DC: U.S. Department of Education, National Center for Education Statistics.

Ladson-Billings, G. (2006). From the achievement gap to the education debt: Understanding achievement in US schools. *Educational Researcher, 35*(7), 3–12.

Ladson-Billings, G. (2009). *The dreamkeepers: Successful teachers for African-American children* (2nd ed.). San Francisco: Jossey-Bass.

Losen, D. J., & Gillespie, J. (2012). *Opportunities suspended: The disparate impact of disciplinary exclusion from school.* Los Angeles, CA: UCLA Civil Rights Project.

Losen, D. J., & Martinez, T. E. (2013). Out of school suspension and expulsion. *Pediatrics 131*(3), e1000–e1007.

Luximon, Y., & Goonetilleke, R. S. (2010). The relationship between monochronicity, polychronicity and individual characteristics. *Behaviour & Information Technology, 29*(2), 187–198.

Marks, B., Settles, I. H., Cooke, D. Y., Morgan, L., & Sellers, R. M. (2004). African American racial identity: A review of contemporary models and measures. In R. L. Jones (Ed.), *Black psychology* (4th ed., pp. 383–404). Hampton, VA: Cobb & Henry.

Mason, J. (1993). *Cultural competence self-assessment questionnaire.* Portland, OR: Portland State University, Multicultural Initiative Project.

McAdoo, H. P. (2006). *Black families.* Newbury Park, CA: Sage.

Oberg, K. (1960). Culture shock & the problem of adjustment to new cultural environments. *Practical Anthropologist, 7,* 177–182.

Ogbu, J. U. (1988). Human intelligence testing: A cultural-ecological perspective. *Phi Kappa Phi Journal, 68,* 23–29.

Ogbu, J. U. (1994). From cultural differences to differences in cultural frame of reference. In P. M. Greenfield & R. Cocking (Eds.), *Cross-cultural roots of multicultural child development* (pp. 365–391). Hillsdale, NJ: Lawrence Erlbaum.

Ogbu, J. U., & Davis, A. (2003). *Black American students in an affluent suburb: A study of academic disengagement.* Mahwah, NJ: Lawrence Erlbaum.

Ponterotto, J. G., Casas, J. M., Suzuki, L. A., & Alexander, C. M. (Eds.). (2001). *Handbook of multicultural counseling* (2nd ed.). Thousand Oaks, CA: Sage.

Ponterotto, J. G., & Pedersen, P. B. (2003). *Preventing prejudice: A guide for counselors and educators* (2nd ed.). Newbury Park, CA: Sage.

Quintana, S. M. (2007). Racial and ethnic identity: Developmental perspectives and research. *Journal of Counseling Psychology, 54*(3), 259–270.

Reardon, S. F., & Galindo, C. (2009). The Hispanic–White achievement gap in math and reading in the elementary grades. *American Educational Research Journal, 46*(3), 853–891.

Rowley, S. A., Sellers, R. M., Chavous, T. M., & Smith, M. (1998). The relationship between racial identity and self-esteem in African American college and high school students. *Journal of Personality and Social Psychology, 74*(3), 715–724.

Schott Foundation. (2012). *The urgency of now: The Schott 50 state report on public education of Black males.* Cambridge, MA: Schott Foundation.

Schul, J. E. (2012). Revisiting an old friend: The practice and promise of cooperative learning for the twenty-first century. *The Social Studies, 102,* 88–93.

Sellers, R. M., Linder, N. C., Martin, P. P., & Lewis, R. L. (2006). Racial identity matters: The relationship between racial discrimination and psychological functioning in African American adolescents. *Journal of Research on Adolescence, 16*(2), 187–216.

Shade, B. J., Kelly, C., & Oberg, M. (2001). *Creating culturally responsive classrooms.* Washington, DC: American Psychological Association.

Steele, C. M. (2010). *Whistling Vivaldi and other clues to how stereotypes affect us.* New York: W. W. Norton.

Storti, C. (2007). *The art of crossing cultures* (2nd ed.). Boston, MA: Intercultural Press.

Sue, D. W. (2010). *Microaggressions in everyday life: Race, gender, and sexual orientation.* Hoboken, NJ: John Wiley.

Sue, D., Capodilupo, C. M., & Holder, A. M. B. (2008). Racial microaggressions in the life experience of Black Americans. *Professional Psychology: Research and Practice, 39,* 329–336.

Trumbull, E., & Rothstein-Fisch, C. (2008). Cultures in harmony. *Educational Leadership, 66*(1), 63–66.

U.S. Department of Education. (2009, 2013). *The Office for Civil Rights' civil rights data collection.* Retrieved from http://ocrdata.ed.gov/ (accessed March 13, 2015).

Valencia, R. R. (2010). *Dismantling contemporary deficit thinking: Educational thought and practice.* New York: Taylor and Francis.

Vandiver, B. J., Fhagen-Smith, P. E., Cokley, K. O., Cross, W. E., Jr., & Worrell, F. C. (2001). Cross Nigrescence model: From theory to scale to theory. *Journal of Multicultural Counseling and Development, 29,* 174–200.

Weiss, H. B., Kreider, H., Lopez, M. E., & Chatman-Nelson, C. (2010). *Preparing educators to engage families: Case studies using an ecological systems framework* (2nd edn). Thousand Oaks, CA: Sage.

Whiting, G. W. (2006). From at risk to at promise: Developing scholar identities among Black males. *Journal of Secondary Gifted Education, 17*(4), 222–229.

# 28

# Dialogic Instruction

## A New Frontier

**Sherice N. Clarke**
**Lauren B. Resnick**
University of Pittsburgh

**Carolyn Penstein Rosé**
Carnegie Mellon University

This chapter examines the role of dialogue in classroom learning. Classroom language has long been a focus of educational inquiry. The earliest investigations sought to understand the underlying logic of teacher–student interactions in the classroom (Bellack, Kliebard, Hyman, & Smith, 1966). They showed that verbal exchanges between teachers and students constitute much of classroom activity, and that most of these exchanges take the form of teacher questions or comments followed by student answers (Gall, 1970).

Interest in improving instruction led to a growth in studying of the quality of teacher questions in terms of the cognitive processes they elicited from students, and their effects on student achievement (Bloom & Krathwohl, 1956; Gall, 1970; Winne, 1979). Bloom's taxonomy (and similar frameworks) provided a way to rank the kinds of questions teachers ask in terms of the cognitive demands required to answer them. At the same time, work on the use of technology to support instruction drew upon these frameworks to build the first approaches to automating instruction through dialogue (Carbonell, 1969, 1970; Stevens & Collins, 1977).

The hypothesis at this time was that questions that elicited higher-order thinking processes would be associated with greater student achievement. However, empirical studies found little evidence to support the hypothesized correlation between higher-order questions and student achievement (Winne, 1979).

Around the same time, the ideas of Vygotsky and colleagues were being translated and making their way West. Blending these ideas with the ideas of Dewey, Mead, Bakhtin and (to some extent) Piaget, some psychological theorists began to offer a theory of mind and development that posited that individual cognition is shaped through social interaction, and verbal dialogue plays a special role in this process (Dewey, 1916; Mead, 1967; Vygotsky, 1962, 1978; Wertsch, 1979). These ideas advanced the notion that dialogue is a form of human learning.

As these ideas began to penetrate adjacent disciplines like sociology and linguistics, and their newly formed subfields of ethnomethodology (Garfinkel, 1967) and sociolinguistics (Hymes, 1977), theories of language were evolving. Sociologists and linguists were seeking theory that could account for the "social" and "cultural" nature of language and its production (Bourdieu, 1977; Hymes, 1977). New areas of scholarship in these fields, together with new technologies of the time (i.e., video recording), enabled indepth ethnographic studies of classroom activity and language not previously possible. These studies yielded insights about classroom life similar to those that educational psychologists had been documenting—classroom activity consisted primarily of dialogue in the form of questions and answers. Taken together, these investigations also revealed how most verbal interactions in classrooms were highly constrained, consisting primarily of recitation (a teacher's question followed by a solicitation of a student's response, followed by the teacher's evaluation of the student's response) (Mehan, 1979; Sinclair, Coulthard, & Council, 1975). Recitation would be classified as eliciting lower-order cognitive processes, according to Bloom's taxonomy, and was considered as limiting opportunities for student ownership over reasoning (Veel & Christie, 1999).

Over the last few decades a new form of instructional pedagogy has emerged (Alexander, 2008; Littleton & Howe, 2010; Resnick, Asterhan, & Clarke, in press; Resnick, Michaels, & O'Connor, 2010). We have come to refer to instructional dialogue that engages discussants in *inter*-mental reasoning processes to support the development of *intra*-mental reasoning processes as *dialogic instruction*. Dialogic instruction is grounded in a set of domain-specific ideas and concepts, e.g., science, mathematics, history, literature, that schools teach. Within these domains, students explain, reflect upon, and elaborate on their own and their peers' understandings of domain concepts. They engage in reasoned argumentation about subject matter: supporting claims with evidence, drawing logically grounded and justified conclusions, and negotiating disputes through argumentation. This form of dialogue has an implicit social contract; discussants endeavor to collaboratively engage in the sense-making process. This requires discussants to participate in verbal activities that externalize their emergent thinking, reason aloud about solutions offered, challenge one another's views, and clarify misunderstandings. It requires discussants to listen to, hear, and respond to their peers' contributions.

Dialogic instruction can be human-mediated (e.g., by a teacher or facilitator) or computer-mediated (e.g., facilitated by a computer agent serving as surrogate teacher) (Dyke, Adamson, Howley, & Rosé, 2013), in face-to-face settings or computer-mediated settings (Stahl, Koschmann, & Suthers, 2006). Unlike recitation, the primary role of the teacher (or computer-mediated surrogate) is to scaffold and elicit students' verbal reasoning. A wide range of participation structures found in classroom learning are qualitatively dialogic (e.g., cooperative learning, collaborative learning, argumentation, reciprocal teaching, group problem solving, peer tutoring, computer-supported collaborative learning).

Until quite recently it has appeared that direct instruction by an instructor (or computer-based tutor) was the only reliable way to ensure high levels of learning in core school subject matters (Klahr & Nigam, 2004). But in the past couple of decades there has been growing evidence that dialogue-rich instruction is worth the extra time and effort and may be able to produce large, measurable learning gains, including retention and transfer.

The next sections of the chapter bring together the body of evidence on human- and computer-supported dialogic instruction. We consider the best evidence on learning through dialogue in terms of traditional measures of school learning, which we refer to here as *academic outcomes*. We then review evidence that helps to explicate some of the mechanisms though which dialogic instruction supports growth in academic outcomes. We conclude by considering future directions for research and inquiry for the field.

## "Big Effects" of Dialogue

While dialogic instruction is a growing area of inquiry, a surprisingly small number of studies examine the relationship between participation in dialogue and learning outcomes. This small set of studies collectively provide robust evidence of the effects of dialogic instruction on valued academic outcomes. When considered as a whole, the evidence suggests that, when teachers (or computer-mediated surrogates) lead discussions of this kind, they can produce steep increases in student learning. We refer to these findings as the "big effects" of dialogic instruction. In assembling this data, we count the following as evidence of learning:

a. improved *initial learning*, in comparison with a control or reference group, on assessments of academic skills and knowledge that are developed and administered by an authority external to the school or classroom whose effectiveness is under study (these could be state or national examinations, or commercial standardized tests);

b. evidence of *retention* of academic skills and knowledge, again in comparison with a control or reference group, across several months or years;

c. evidence of *transfer* to domains of academic skill and knowledge other than the one taught in the study;

d. evidence of improvement in widely accepted forms of *reasoning* or *general intelligence*.

### *Initial Learning*

Several studies conducted in the 1980s experimented with discussion-rich approaches to mathematics instruction. These studies show that if teachers lead students in problem-solving discussions that elicit collaborative reasoning, students greatly outperform non-treated comparison groups on standardized tests.

The first case, *Math³*, is an intervention developed by a master teacher and a group of scholars to teach math in an elementary school serving ethnic-minority children from low-income families (Bill, Leer, Reams, & Resnick, 1992; Resnick, Bill, Lesgold, & Leer, 1991). Bill and colleagues developed an approach to instruction that would foster fluency in complex mathematical thinking. Math³ program consisted of math "story problems" that engaged students in a process of shared mathematical reasoning. Lessons entailed whole-class discussions, followed by teamwork and more discussion as each team reported out. The discussions were designed to prompt students to listen to each other's ideas and reflect on their own and others' reasoning, and encourage students to explicate their thinking. Discussions exposed students to core mathematical concepts and tasked them with reasoning about them.

Bill and colleagues conducted a 2-year study of the Math³ program. Bill taught two cohorts of students Math³ in almost every math class during the 2-year period. Cohort A started Math³ in the first grade; Cohort B, in second grade; and a Control Cohort consisted of Bill's students prior to the intervention as a comparison group (Resnick et al., 1991). Growth in academic outcomes was measured using existing assessments of student competence in math and reading, in addition to measures of the dialogic processes in the lessons. The school-administered California Achievement Test was used to measure student growth in academic outcomes from the Math³ intervention.

Dramatic changes in students' computational ability were documented. On the California Achievement Test, Cohorts A and B performed near the top of the scale in mathematics after Bill's dialogic-style teaching. However, the Control Cohort who did not receive the story-based lessons had relatively low achievement scores across the 3-year period of measurement.

The second case of the learning effects of dialogic instruction is *Project Challenge*, a similar mathematics program to Math[3]. Project Challenge was developed by a master teacher and scholars at Boston University for one of the lowest-performing school districts in Massachusetts. The team developed an intervention that would provide students with complex problems, projects, and arithmetic learning through games (Chapin & O'Connor, 2004).

Project Challenge lessons were taught 5 days a week and entailed discussions of the kind in Math[3], focusing on students' explanation of mathematical thinking. The intervention was given to four cohorts of 25 students each, beginning in the fourth grade and lasting 4 years.[1] The Massachusetts Comprehensive Assessment System (MCAS) state assessment was administered to measure learning outcomes of the intervention.

After 1 year, 57% of Project Challenge students scored "Advanced" or "Proficient" on the MCAS, compared with 38% in Massachusetts overall. After 3 years in Project Challenge, 82% of students scored in the "Advanced" or "Proficient" ranges, compared to only 40% for Massachusetts sixth-graders overall. Project Challenge results indicate that students' competencies did not simply grow during their years in the program, but grew exponentially over the 3-year period.

The evidence from Math[3] and Project Challenge suggests that, when teachers use dialogic approaches in mathematics instruction that engages students in a process of shared mathematical reasoning, students' general competencies in math increase dramatically. The effects of discussion seem to transcend the idiosyncrasies of particular discussions and discussion topics.

### Long-term Retention

A "tough" standard of effectiveness for any form of instruction would call for evidence that what students learned had more "staying power"—that it lasted longer than an academic year. Perhaps the most extensive demonstration of long-term learning effects comes from the *Cognitive Acceleration through Science Education* (CASE) program (Adey & Shayer, 1990, 1993). CASE had three core principles: (a) inducing *cognitive conflict*; (b) facilitating *social construction*; and (c) supporting the development of *metacognition*.

The CASE intervention was based on Piaget's schemata of formal operations e.g., control and exclusion of variables, equilibrium, ratio, and proportionality. Students (aged 11–14 years) were taught 30 lessons on practical problems in science class every other week for 2 years. Lessons were designed to induce cognitive conflict so as to disrupt existing knowledge structures to make them more receptive to conceptual change. Through discussing the problems and working to solve them, it was believed that students would be able to construct the schemata themselves. Teachers guide

students through the restructuring process, helping them to reason scientifically about problems. In these interventions, dialogue is the pedagogical tool used to support students' problem solving and scientific reasoning.

The study was conducted in schools serving a range of populations, with two to three classes assigned to the CASE intervention, and two to three matched classes assigned to serve as non-treated controls. Piagetian reasoning tasks were administered as pretests and posttests to examine cognitive development. School science assessments were used as delayed posttests of science achievement, 1 and 2 years after the intervention. In addition, results of students' performance on the science, math, and English portions of the national General Certificate of Secondary Education (GCSE) were examined as a delayed posttest of achievement 2 and 3 years after CASE.

Immediate posttests showed that CASE cohorts had no significant gains in science understanding over control students. However, delayed posttests and GCSE scores showed considerable gains in science achievement of CASE students. The most significant results were concentrated amongst two CASE cohorts. The first cohort showed modest gains on the school-based science assessment taken 1 year after the CASE intervention. However, they made considerable gains over and above the delayed posttest on the science portion of the GCSEs taken 2 years later, scoring on average one grade higher than control students. The second cohort had a similar pattern. They made significant gains on the delayed posttest in science taken 2 years after CASE, and retained these gains in science on the GCSEs 3 years later. The evidence from the CASE program indicates that one could not only *teach* the core "Piagetian schemata" (which constitute basic schemata for scientific and mathematical reasoning), but doing so can have long-term results, including better performance on state-administered exams several years later.

Our fourth case, a body of instruction gathered under the name of *Philosophy for Children* (P4C), also documents long-term retention effects (Lipman, 1981). The goal of the P4C program is to develop students' critical reasoning skills through collaborative philosophical inquiry (Topping & Trickey, 2007a, 2007b). Using a text or another stimulus, a teacher guides students through dialogue and questioning in which multiple answers are possible. Like CASE, P4C encourages cognitive conflict, involves learning processes that promote metacognitive development, and relies on the social construction of knowledge.

Topping and Trickey studied a variant of this program that was implemented in a school district in Scotland. They investigated whether the program of philosophical inquiry in the classroom had a measurable effect on children's cognitive reasoning ability, and whether learning would be retained. In weekly 1-hour lessons, the teachers' aim was for the class to construct deeper knowledge or a better solution than any one child could develop alone. Six classrooms participated in the P4C study, four as part of the intervention and two as controls. The control classes were presented with the same initial story, followed by a discussion, but did not experience weekly inquiry lessons. The Cognitive Abilities Test was administered before the intervention, and again after 16 months and 43 months.

The experimental group showed significant gains between the pretest and the first posttest, in verbal, non-verbal, and quantitative reasoning abilities, while the control group showed none. And despite no further intervention, the experimental group maintained these gains for 2 more years, while the control group's scores decreased over the same period.

Together these studies document long-term retention effects for up to 3 years from engaging in joint sense-making discussions in science and literature-cum-philosophy. These are sizable effects of the "staying power" of learning that occurs through discussions. The findings suggest that the process of engaging in these kinds of discussions promotes robust conceptual transformation.

## Transfer

Another "tough" standard of effectiveness of any instruction would call for evidence that what students learned spread to competencies and subject matter not directly taught. Three of our cases document evidence of domain transfer effects: namely, Math[3], Project Challenge, and CASE interventions.

In the Math[3] program, Bill and colleagues found that, in addition to gains that intervention cohorts had in math achievement on the Cognitive Abilities Test exam, their scores on the reading portion of the exam not only rose, but continued to rise when they were assessed after the first and second year of the intervention (Bill et al., 1992; Resnick et al., 1991). What is notable is that Bill did not teach reading, and the intervention involved little written work.

Project Challenge produced similar results. When scores on the English portion of the MCAS were examined, they found that Project Challenge students had steep increases in literacy in addition to math, over and above the performance of the students in Massachusetts receiving regular, non-dialogic instruction (Chapin & O'Connor, 2004). Both these interventions show evidence of transfer from math instruction to reading. Adey and Shayer found transfer results from dialogic-style science instruction in CASE when they compared intervention students' results with non-treated control classes (Adey & Shayer, 1993). GCSEs were administered 2–3 years after the CASE intervention (depending on the cohort). The results showed that students who participated in the CASE intervention in science showed considerable gains on the English and math portion of the GCSEs 2–3 years later. Thus, they document not only a sizable long-term retention effect of the program, but also domain transfer as a consequence of collaborative scientific inquiry discussions.

Together, these studies provide initial evidence that transfer is achievable through dialogic instruction. No theory of the day could account for these findings.[2] One-time gains could be chance, but these data show the same transfer effects from three different programs, with several cohorts of students over multiple years. Greeno and others suggest that the phenomena of domain transfer might be explained in terms of the cognitive processes engaged when students participate in discussions and the cognitive processes elicited on assessments in other domains (Greeno, Moore, & Smith, 1993; Koedinger, Corbett, & Perfetti, 2012). In other words, their conceptualization of transfer would suggest that students develop general capacities through dialogic instruction in one domain, and the capacities transfers when students are assessed in another domain. Nevertheless, what is particularly notable is that these studies are amongst the few studies that provide evidence that educational practices can actually promote domain transfer.

## Reasoning Development

Our final criterion for big effects of dialogic instruction is the development of reasoning ability. To date, there have been just a couple of studies of dialogic instruction that have documented these effects: P4C and Talk, Reasoning and Computers (TRAC).

As an outcome measure of the P4C program, Topping and Trickey administered the Cognitive Abilities Test, which measures the development of *non-verbal* and *quantitative* reasoning ability. Their findings show that students in treated conditions who were engaging in philosophical discussion of questions such as "what is truth?" increased both their non-verbal and quantitative reasoning (Topping & Trickey, 2007a). Students in the control classes decreased in their non-verbal and quantitative reasoning ability.

The fifth case is *TRAC*. Through TRAC, Mercer and colleagues sought to examine whether reasoning could be directly taught through collaborative computer-based activities (Mercer, Wegerif, & Dawes, 1999; Wegerif, Mercer, & Dawes, 1999). The aforementioned cases have been primarily been concerned with teaching domain concepts through dialogue, and studying the development of domain-specific outcomes. TRAC, however, sought to examine the language of collaborative reasoning itself. In doing so, Mercer and colleagues posited that if students were taught the language norms of effective collaborative reasoning, what the researchers referred to as "exploratory talk," then reasoning itself could be developed.

In the TRAC program teachers led students through lessons designed to raise students' awareness of the norms of "exploratory talk." The study involved four target classes of primary Grade 5 children, and four matched classes as control groups. The target classes received nine lessons of TRAC, and the control classes received business-as-usual instruction. To examine the impact of TRAC on target groups, the researchers collected two measures of reasoning development using the *Ravens Progressive Matrices* (RPM), a test of non-verbal reasoning ability. The first was an individual RPM test to measure individual growth in non-verbal reasoning, and the second a collaborative version, to test the development of group reasoning discussions. They posited that if there was a greater incidence of "exploratory talk" in group discussions that resulted in successful solutions to RPM items, then they would have evidence of relationship between language and reasoning development.

At the individual level, the authors found that children in both the treatment and control classes increased their performance on the RPM from the pretest to posttest, suggesting an increase in individual non-verbal reasoning ability for both groups as an outcome of instruction. At the group level, they examined the difference between group dialogues of successful and unsuccessful solutions to RPM items. They confirmed that group dialogues that resulted in successful solutions to RPM items included far greater exploratory talk than unsuccessful solutions, suggesting a relationship between language form and accurate reasoning. They also found that groups increased in their amount of exploratory talk from pretreatment group problem solving to posttreatment problem solving, suggesting that the intervention supported the development of exploratory talk. Groups in control classes decreased in the number of essential features of exploratory talk from pretest to posttest.

What Mercer and colleagues were setting out to examine was whether cognitive processes could be activated if instruction focused solely on teaching the language associated with those processes. What is striking about their findings is that the RPM is a measure of non-verbal reasoning ability. Increases in performance on the RPM provide direct evidence of increases in reasoning, and indirect evidence that collaborative dialogues that include argumentative talk support increases in reasoning ability. Like Topping and Trickey, they provide evidence of a kind that is impossible to ignore: the tethered nature of language and thought. Direct instruction of the linguistic forms of reasoning supports the development of reasoning itself.

### What Produces the Big Effects of Dialogic Instruction?

These five studies suggest that, when teachers lead students in structured collaborative sense-making discussions about subject matter, students not only learn the targeted content, but the learning can be retained for up to 3 years, transferred to other domains, and verbal and non-verbal reasoning can develop. These are powerful effects for the educational enterprise. But what is it about dialogic instruction that produces these big effects?

There are a few common features of the aforementioned studies. First, dialogue-intensive activities are facilitated by teachers who lead students in reasoned discussion within an academic domain about domain concepts (with the exception of Mercer et al., 1999). Second, the dialogue is purposeful. In other words, the discussions are oriented around tasks that create authentic reasons to engage in discussion. Third, teachers (or computer-mediated surrogates) elicit students' verbalizations of their emergent thinking to scaffold the social and linguistic norms of collaborative reasoning. Adey and Shayer's studies suggest a fourth criterion not described in the other big-effects studies; i.e., that the discussion task is one that induces cognitive conflict. These features describe the general conditions of dialogic instruction, but what is it that occurs through verbal interaction about academic subject matter that lends itself to the robust outcomes found in the big-effects studies? To address this question, we take an indepth look at dialogic instruction and learning, examining targeted studies of discussion-rich teaching that help to shed light on some of the mechanisms that support learning.

### Unpacking the Big Effects of Dialogue: Cognitive and Social

What are the processes engaged when an individual articulates her thinking in discussion? Are these the same processes that are engaged when an individual listens to peers during discussion? These are some of the questions that researchers have been asking in order to identify the mechanisms through which talk and dialogue support learning. The *big-effects* studies put a compelling set of evidence on the table of the academic outcomes that dialogic instruction can foster. But precisely how dialogic instruction fosters these steep increases in outcomes is not fully explicated. For this reason, in this section we consider targeted interventions of dialogic instruction and learning (and its close cousins) in order to identify the processes engaged when learners participate in dialogue.

### Talk "Moves" That Support Cognitive Processes

To examine the mechanisms through which dialogic instruction supports academic outcomes, researchers have looked towards the discourse itself—the "processes" of dialogic participation. Collaborative sense making in discussions provides insight into the underlying cognitive work of discussants. In particular, *talk moves*, a class of speech act, signify cognitive processes (Resnick et al., 2010; Searle, 1969), and social positioning in talk (Veel & Christie, 1999). For example, *elaboration* requires that a speaker has heard the previous utterance, understood it, and made sense of the ideas expressed in relation to his own current understanding. The elaboration, therefore, is an expression of the difference between a student and his peers' understanding. Talk moves have both a social function (e.g., listening and responding to one another) and an intellectual function (e.g., explanation, elaboration, reasoning) (Greeno, in press).

The use of certain talk moves (e.g., *explanation, reasoning, disagreement*) has been shown to support growth in academic outcomes. We consider the evidence on each of these moves, including the evidence they provide on both sides of dialogue: production (speaking) and reception (listening). While production and reception are dynamic and interchanging in natural dialogue, some studies have teased apart the effects in terms of these distinct roles.

***Explanation.*** Explanations are the externalization of knowledge or understanding (emergent or fully formed) in the form of a verbal utterance. Chi and colleagues' investigations of self-explanation provide some insight into the production side of explanation (Chi, Bassok, Lewis, Reimann, & Glaser, 1989; Chi, Slotta, & De Leeuw, 1994). Self-explanation is the process whereby individuals explain to themselves their understanding, e.g., verbally through think-aloud, in text, or *inner speech* (Vygotsky, 1962). Chi et al. have found that verbal self-explanations support success in problem solving. When the differences between students who were more or less successful at problem solving were examined, they found that one of the characteristics of successful problem solving was the greater incidence of self-explanations, and more robust explanations. Further, they have found that there is a positive effect of good explanations on learning. Accurate explanations yield higher learning gains on measures of knowledge and understanding.

Chi and colleagues (1989, 1994) claim that there are several cognitive processes at work when individuals articulate their understanding in the form of self-explanations. First, explanation drives the explainer to "fill in" missing, or not yet understood, parts of phenomena in order to provide a complete explanation. In other words, through explanation, the individual attempts to construct a coherent picture by making inferences, and in doing so, drives the second process: integration. Through explanation, the explainer integrates new knowledge with existing knowledge. Integration may lend itself to the third process, cognitive conflict, which is when an individual becomes aware of misconceptions and has an opportunity to correct them.

Self-explanations as typically conceptualized, however, are inherently monologic. In what ways are explanations to peers different from self-explanations? Researchers have found that the effects that have been documented on self-explanation persist when students explain to peers (Fuchs et al., 1997; Howe et al., 2007; King, 1992; King & Rosenshine, 1993; Slavin, 1987; Veenman, Denessen, van den Akker, & van der Rijt, 2005; Webb, 1991; Webb et al., 2009). When students explain domain concepts to their peers in dyads or small groups, they themselves perform better on outcome measures of knowledge and understanding. Peer explanation accuracy and sophistication have also been found to yield higher learning gains for explainers (King & Rosenshine, 1993; Veenman et al., 2005). However, Webb and colleagues have found that, while both "explainers" and receivers of explanations benefit from explanations in terms of increasing outcomes, the benefits for receivers are dependent upon their active cognitive engagement with the explanations (Webb & Mastergeorge, 2003; Webb, Troper, & Fall, 1995). They found that it is necessary for receivers to make immediate use of explanations to solve new problems (in the context of mathematics instruction) in order to achieve gains on posttest measures.

As mentioned, the explanatory process lends itself to situations of cognitive conflict, whereby an individual becomes aware of a disjuncture between her existing and new knowledge and provides an opportunity for integration of new knowledge. The transformation process is known as *conceptual change*. A growing number of studies have been investigating the ways in which dyadic or collaborative activities involving explanation support this transformation process (see Chapter 18, this volume).

Several studies have shown a positive relationship between explanations and conceptual change. However,

conceptual change in the form of a "radical transformation of knowledge structures" is not immediate (Asterhan & Schwarz, 2007, 2009; Howe, McWilliam, & Cross, 2005). When learning is measured immediately following collaborative problem-solving activities involving explanation, gains have been moderate. However, if a delayed posttest is given a week or two following collaborative activities involving explanation, learning gains for individuals in conditions involving explanation exceed their immediate posttests. This suggests that the radical transformation process that explanation lends itself to may take time to be synthesized and integrated. This is what Howe has referred to as an "incubation period" (Howe et al., 2005).

Examining the question of *who* benefits from explanations in terms of conceptual change, Asterhan and Schwarz (2009) found that this kind of deep conceptual shift is limited to individuals giving explanations, rather than those receiving explanations. Receivers benefit from explanation in terms of knowledge acquisition; however, they need to actively externalize their understanding for a radical transformation of understanding to occur.

***Transactive reasoning.*** *Transacts*, following Berkowitz and Gibbs (1983), are talk moves in which the reasoning of discussants is "interpenetrated." These are moves in which a speaker's utterance(s) builds on her own or another's thinking. To a certain extent, transactivity is the natural order of truly collaborative dialogue: (a) attentive to one another's ideas; and (b) progressive, the reasoning of discussants develops. While there has been a lot of interest in transacts as an indicator of productive learning dialogues, just a few studies have examined the effect of transactive moves in dialogue on learning.

Generally, researchers have found that the incidence of transactive moves during problem-solving discussions positively predicts problem-solving accuracy and learning of problem-solving skills (Azmitia & Montgomery, 1993; Berkowitz & Gibbs, 1983; Chinn, O'Donnell, & Jinks, 2000; Kruger, 1992, 1993; Teasley, 1997). There are two types of transactive exchanges that can occur: elaborating on one's own reasoning (*self-transacts*) and elaborating on another's reasoning (*other-oriented transacts*). Both self- and other-oriented transacts have been shown to support dyadic problem solving and the development of reasoning (Azmitia & Montgomery, 1993; Kruger, 1992; Teasley, 1997). If there is a complete absence of engagement with another's reasoning, however (in other words, excessive use of self-transacts in the context of problem-solving discussions), then the dyad's or group's performance can suffer (Barron, 2003; Kruger, 1992).

This research suggests that, while elaboration of one's own thinking is good for individual performance, overuse to the extent that the transactivity is akin to a monologue can be harmful for group problem solving. The "sweet spot" for collaborative discussions appears to be a combination of self-oriented and other-oriented transacts as it supports individual cognitive work, with the added benefit of the plurality of ideas from peers with which to reason (Chi, 2009). Analysis of the social properties of audio data from collaborative sessions suggests that the balance of self and other transacts reflects the extent to which students are listening to one another and valuing one another's respective perspectives (Gweon, Jain, Mc Donough, Raj, & Rosé, 2013). Thus, an overrepresentation of self-oriented transacts might be symptomatic of missed opportunities to reflect on the partner student's expressed reasoning.

A related area of inquiry has been the study of question asking during collaborative learning. Studies have examined the degree to which students asked each other questions during collaborative learning and the quality of those questions in relation to outcomes (King, 1992, 1999; King & Rosenshine, 1993; Rosenshine, Meister, & Chapman, 1996). Research has found that, when students ask each other questions during collaborative learning discussions, groups are more effective at problem solving and individual learning outcomes increase (King, 1999; Rosenshine et al., 1996).

The kinds of questions that carry the most weight in terms of supporting learning are those that elicit talk moves, e.g., eliciting explanations, elaborations, inferences. These are questions that in effect facilitate transactivity, by coordinating collaborative dialogue through the negotiation for meaning. Computer facilitators of collaborative learning that elicit these moves have also been found to produce more learning than found in otherwise equivalent groups that do not have that support (Adamson, Dyke, Jang, Rosé, 2014; Dyke et al., 2013).

In addition to facilitating group-level processes, question asking has been shown to be supportive of self-regulated learning. In particular, King (1999) found that when students were trained to use self-regulation questions to monitor their own understanding and coordinate collaborative dialogue, they were more effective at problem solving than students who were not trained.

### Challenges, disagreements, contradictions.

One of the advantages of collaborative learning in dyads, small groups or whole-class situations is that by virtue of the number of participants, discussion is a multiplier of ideas and perspectives. Engaging in dialogue versus working alone increases the probability that individuals will be exposed to a range of ideas beyond their own. The inherent multivocality of dialogue creates the conditions for challenges, disagreements, and contradictions of opinions and ideas to arise.

Challenges to ideas, disagreements, and contradictions have been shown to be productive for learning for a number of reasons. First, they have been shown to induce *sociocognitive conflict* (Kruger, 1993; Mugny & Doise, 1978). Sociocognitive conflict is induced when an individual is confronted with alternative or competing perspectives that challenge the person's current understanding. This state of conflict prompts the individual (whose understanding is challenged) to undergo a process of cognitive restructuring in order to integrate the new perspective into understanding—to re-achieve a state of equilibrium.

Second, the very nature of opposition and disequilibrium gives rise to elaborations, justifications, and resolutions, which are supportive of learning outcomes (Howe & McWilliam, 2006). Howe and colleagues, in particular, have shown that it is not the sheer number of disagreements in dialogues that is associated with posttest performance on problem-solving activities. Rather, it is the incidence of explanations, elaborations, and justifications that disagreement gives rise to (however frequent) that is associated with posttest gains (Howe et al., 2007). Similar to the effects of explanation on conceptual change, Howe and colleagues have found that disagreement is not only predictive of learning gains immediately following group collaboration, but also predictive of gains sustained well beyond the intervention, as much as 18 months later (Howe, 2010).

Kruger argues that learning gains from disagreements are not simply predicated on the social structure of activities, e.g., group or dyadic problem solving. Rather, the benefit for learning is located in the act of collaboratively wrestling with inferior solutions (Kruger, 1993). In this sense, dialogue that involves challenges, disagreements, and contradictions prompts peers to collaboratively participate in the process of cognitive restructuring.

### Social Processes

Thus far, our discussion has been limited to talk moves that support cognitive processes in dialogue. In what ways does the inherently social nature of dialogue shape what is said, and as a consequence, opportunities for learning through dialogue? Classroom dialogue is *socially contingent*. Utterances are a collaborative artifact, and contingent upon the interrelationship between discussants, time, and space (Goffman, 1959). There is a vast body of scholarship that explores the contingent nature of classroom dialogue (e.g., Chen & Chiu, 2008; Clarke, in press). However, we limit our review to the subset of studies that relate the social processes of dialogue to learning outcomes, as they help provide insight into the *big effects* of dialogue.

### Interpersonal effects.

There are several separate lines of inquiry into the interpersonal dynamics of dialogue and their impact on learning outcomes. This includes research that examines stable categories, e.g., relationship status, as well as research that examines more fluid categories, e.g., etiquette in dialogue. Together this body of work shows the connections between linguistic features of communication, underlying social processes, and cognitive processes that impact learning.

Research that has examined benefits of collaborating with friends versus acquaintances has shown consistent support for collaborating with friends (Azmitia & Montgomery, 1993; Barron, 2003; Ogan, Finkelstein, Walker, Carlson, & Cassell, 2012). Azmitia and Montgomery have found that friends not only use more transactive moves during problem solving in general, but there is a greater incidence of engagement with each other's reasoning during problem solving (other-oriented transacts). Engagement with a friend's reasoning has been found to be a strong predictor of problem-solving accuracy (Azmitia & Montgomery, 1993).

While the purely social aspects of language may connect more indirectly with learning processes than cognitive constructs like transactivity, there is evidence that they play an important facilitative role. As mentioned previously, acoustic style features that signal trust and respect between students are associated with increased prevalence of transactivity in conversation (Gweon et al., 2013). Similarly, Howley and colleagues have demonstrated that groups that show openness in their rhetorical strategies elicit more displays of reasoning from group members (Howley, Kumar, Mayfield, Dyke, & Rosé, 2013a).

Some research has examined the effect that rudeness can have on collaborative problem solving dialogue, and whether the incidence of rudeness has a global impact, e.g., ultimately impacting achievement. Not surprisingly, several studies found that rudeness can have immediate negative effects on the dialogue itself and ultimately a negative impact on achievement (Asterhan, 2013; Chiu & Khoo, 2003). There are qualitative differences in how polite disagreements versus adversarial disagreements are taken up by discussants, in terms of the ideas expressed by the disagreement. For example, Chiu and Khoo (2003) found that rude disagreements tend to spawn further rude disagreements by discussants. In addition, rude or adversarial disagreements lend themselves to collaboration breakdowns, where participants are no longer co-constructing, but rather talking past one another (Asterhan, 2013). Like the research on friendship and collaboration, there seems to be a positive relationship between rapport in dialogue and outcomes.

Similarly, Howley and colleagues have reported on the effects of confrontational remarks on collaboration in 2-day activity. They found that confrontational remarks from the first day of collaboration were associated with shifts in social positioning of students between Days 1 and 2. Recipients of confrontational comments on Day 1 became reluctant to try again on Day 2 when they reached a problem-solving impasse. This in turn reduced the needed practice they were able to get, which was associated with a corresponding reduction in learning (Howley, Mayfield, & Rosé, 2013b).

The dialogue produced between friends seems to be experienced in a qualitatively different manner from dialogue that appears similar in form but is experienced between acquaintances. In particular, Ogan and colleagues have shown that, while the surface features of dialogue might be the same when comparing friends and acquaintances, their communicative function is entirely dependent upon the relationship between discussants (Ogan et al., 2012). For example, they found that cues such as "confrontations" between friends in peer tutoring dyads were followed by productive responses that served to keep both participants coordinated on the problem-solving activity. However, with acquaintances, the same cue (confrontations) was threatening, and as a result, these cues had a negative impact on learning outcomes of these dyads.

Howley and colleagues also document that "confrontational behavior in collaboration has differential effects depending on the relational status of the students" (Howley et al., 2013a). These findings seem to suggest that the rapport that exists between friends versus acquaintances allows for more critical interaction, and these are the kinds of verbal interactions that are supportive of learning.

Other socially relevant group composition variables, such as ability-level groupings, have also been examined. The evidence on the relative benefits of collaborating with peers of the same ability level are somewhat mixed (Kruger, 1992; Mugny & Doise, 1978). Mixed-ability groups have been found to be both productive and counterproductive for collaborative problem solving. Mugny and Doise (1978) found that, when children were paired with children of the same ability level to solve spatial reasoning problems through dialogue, their collective performance did not improve. However, when children of intermediate ability level were paired with low-ability-level partners, the collaboration yielded improvements for both children. This gestalt effect however, was only found between the low and intermediate dyads, and not with the high–low dyads. Mugny and Doise argued that this could be explained by relative stability of problem-solving strategies used by high- and intermediate-level children. Intermediate children's strategies may be still emergent, therefore more malleable, allowing for more negotiation in collaboration with low-ability-level children. By contrast, in high–low dyads, low-ability-level children's problem solving improves to the level of their high-ability-level partner at posttest. Mugny and Doise suggest that this may be because high-ability-level children are disseminating their strategies to their low-ability-level partners, rather than collaboratively constructing them.

However, when Kruger examined the differences between peer (same ability level) vs. adult–child dyads (high–low ability level), she found that peers outperformed adult–child dyads on reasoning posttests (Kruger, 1992). In addition, peer dyads contained a greater number of transactive reasoning moves during the collaborative activity than did adult–child dyads.

***Temporal effects.*** How does time impact what occurs in dialogue? If we conceptualize class discussions as a kind of living organism, then Richard Anderson and colleagues have been examining the ways in which changes in the organism result in changes in the classroom ecology over time. Anderson and colleagues have been investigating what they refer to as the "snowball phenomenon," which is the way in which social and thinking practices, argument stratagems, emerge in discussions over time (Anderson et al., 2001).

Argument stratagems are a class of *talk moves* like those reviewed in the previous section. Anderson and colleagues suggest that acquiring argument stratagems means both understanding the form and function of these moves, as well as putting them to use in appropriate and meaningful ways. Discussions in which children are tasked with reasoning together provide authentic opportunities for discussants to observe their peers using argument stratagems effectively, and consequently internalize their appropriate form and use in argumentation. They argue that children's observations of effective use of a stratagem is what can account for the snowballing phenomenon that they have observed across a series of studies (Anderson et al., 2001; Li et al., 2007; Lin et al., 2012; Sun, Anderson, Lin, & Morris, in press). They have found that when children participate in successive discussions with peers, the use of stratagems spreads across the discussants over time, gradually increasing in the frequency of their use. This phenomenon has been documented in terms of social stratagems, e.g., leadership moves (Anderson et al., 2001; Li et al., 2007), as well as the use of cognitive stratagems such as the use of analogical reasoning (Lin et al., 2012; Sun et al., in press).

In short, Anderson and colleagues have documented how the norms of collaborative reasoning and reasoning itself become socially distributed over time. As individuals appropriate moves, they provide a model for peers. This modeling and appropriation work grows exponentially. Thus, this body of research shows the social and intellectual developmental process that unfolds as students participate in dialogue of this kind over time. This work highlights the key role that the students themselves play in bringing change to classroom discussion practices. Clarke and colleagues have found that initiating small groups of students into dialogic discussion practices using computer support is associated with corresponding positive effects on teacher uptake of dialogic facilitation practices in classroom discussions (Clarke et al., 2013).

Other temporal effects that operate at the micro level, at the level of utterances or a sequence of utterances, are those reported above on the effects of rudeness on collaboration and outcomes (Asterhan, 2013; Chiu & Khoo, 2003; Howley et al., 2013b).

***Identity effects.*** Identity has primarily been examined in terms of how relational identities impact participation in dialogue. A few studies have shown that gender and socioeconomic status (SES) are correlated with participation patterns in dialogue (Howe & McWilliam, 2001; Kelly, 2008). Howe and McWilliam and others have found that the frequency and complexity of children's talk moves were associated with SES, with children from high-SES backgrounds engaging in argumentation with greater frequency and complexity than children from low-SES backgrounds (Christie, 1999; Howe & McWilliam, 2001). These differences have been interpreted as a function of differences in language exposure in the home, rather than that of the relative capabilities of the children. Student dispositions, such as high self-efficacy beliefs in their ability to contribute meaningfully to a collaborative discussion, have been shown to be associated with the ways in which students are socially and epistemically positioned in discussions (Clarke, in press; Howley, Mayfield, & Rosé, 2011; Howley et al., 2012; see Chapter 11, this volume).

While these studies show demographic and dispositional effects on participation in dialogue, Clarke and colleagues

suggest that classroom micro cultures are co-constructed by teachers and students alike (Clarke, in press; Clarke et al., 2013). Verbal and non-verbal signals, such as who has the right to speak, to try out ideas, to get things wrong, or be correct, are in the ether, so to speak. Micro cultures can shape participation patterns, and may account for the differences in participation patterns associated with gender and SES that studies have reported. These results suggest that support for productive co-construction of micro cultures could help to overcome obstacles that students bring into the learning environment based on demographic and dispositional factors (see Chapter 27, this volume).

### Cognitive and Social Dimensions of Dialogic Instruction

The above body of evidence suggests that there are several processes at work when individuals engage in structured collaborative sense-making discussions about academic subject matter that support the development of the kind of learning described in the big-effects studies.

Explanation, transactive reasoning, and challenge/disagreement talk moves have been shown to support learning and long-term retention, as well as conceptual change and reasoning development when used in collaborative problem-solving discussions. However, the extent of the benefits for learning seems to be associated with the role that one inhabits with respect to the ideas produced (e.g., speaker or listener), and the extent to which one operates on those ideas. In other words, just *being there* in collaborative discussions seems to be an insufficient condition in order to benefit in terms of learning. Cognitive engagement with ideas and active use of ideas generated to solve problems seem to be necessary conditions for learning.

Dialogue in which the reasoning of discussants is interpenetrated supports problem solving and reasoning development. The evidence related to effects of transactivity suggests that it is not enough for individuals to externalize their thinking. Rather, the thinking made public must become an ideational artifact that is manipulated and developed by discussants over time. It is engagement in the manipulation of ideas that lends itself to development in reasoning ability. Challenges, disagreements, and contradictions are moves that are beneficial for learning because they induce productive cognitive processes (e.g., explanation and reasoning, sociocognitive conflict) that help to push individual thinking forward. These are moves that are transactive by their very definition.

Engaging in successive discussions serves as a practice space for individuals to learn and eventually appropriate productive talk moves (Anderson et al., 2001). However, discussants' willingness, actual participation, and quality of contributions in discussions can be mediated by social factors, e.g., identity, rapport, and etiquette.

While our review provides insight into some of the mechanisms through which dialogic instruction supports robust learning, our discussion is limited to the current state of the art. We have discussed the evidence of mechanisms that support learning, retention, and reasoning development;

however, we have not identified targeted dialogic instruction interventions that help to explain the mechanisms that support domain transfer. Much more scholarship is needed to understand the cognitive and social dimensions that support robust learning through dialogue.

## Into the Future

The findings on dialogic processes and outcomes make it possible to conclude that certain forms of instructional dialogue support steep increases in student learning. However, surveys of classroom language show that academically productive dialogue is rarely observed in low-performing schools (Pauli & Reusser, in press). Yet these are precisely the instructional settings that could benefit most from introducing rigorous forms of instruction to raise the achievement of students they serve in the short term, and enable greater life chances in the long term.

While we may want to make this form of instruction widespread practice, there is evidence that suggests scaling this kind of practice is not trivial. Longitudinal teacher-training efforts highlight how challenging it is to train teachers in low-performing schools, serving children of the greatest need, how to use dialogic instruction effectively (Clarke et al., 2013). There is a need to develop approaches that can leverage these insights on dialogic instruction, to improve instruction at scale.

In meeting this goal, the research in computer-supported collaborative learning shows promise for helping in this process (see Chapter 26, this volume). This is because we know that instructional technologies can play multiple roles in teaching and learning. In recent years, instructional technologies have developed intelligent computer agents that can play the role of a collaborative learning partner (Ogan et al., 2012), or as a facilitator of group discussion, leveraging insights on talk moves to dynamically support learning (Adamson et al., 2014; Dyke et al., 2013; Kumar, Rosé, Wang, Joshi, & Robinson, 2007).

Technological capacities are growing rapidly and there is already a substantial body of research that provides a foundation for more ambitious human–computer learning-oriented interaction in the future, especially as more attention is given towards learning at scale. We discuss here just a few lines of work that provide a glimpse of possibilities and challenges for the future.

The first is the use of technology as a research tool for the study of dialogic instruction. Technology can enable the experimental isolation of specific characteristics of discussion, to study the social and cognitive processes of dialogic instruction systematically (e.g., Adamson et al., 2014; Dyke et al., 2013; Kumar, Ai, Beuth, & Rosé, 2010; Kumar, Beuth, & Rosé, 2011). In order to uncover the mechanisms through which discussion impacts learning, we must isolate specific characteristics of discussion, possibly even at the level of presence or absence of specific talk moves. This level of experimental control is extremely difficult in the context of whole-class, teacher-led discussion; however, it is possible to achieve when the facilitator is a computer agent.

Technology can also play an important role in creating the rich learning environments in which to use dialogic instruction to support learning. Existing research in this area shows how computer agents can enhance the learning experiences of students. A limitation of the research to date, however, is that study of the uses of this kind of technology is short-term, e.g., one or two class periods. New questions are raised when such interventions take place over a more extended period of time, e.g., successive instruction over an academic year. This will raise questions such as how these technologies can adapt support to account for student growth in knowledge, reasoning, and collaborative skill (Adamson et al., 2014).

Finally, and perhaps of greatest interest to educational psychologists who support pre-service teacher instruction, technology could be used to dynamically support teachers (e.g., Chen, Clarke, & Resnick, 2014). The same kind of technologies that support students in collaborative learning can be repurposed to support teachers in facilitating the kind of discussions that support learning in real time (e.g., McLaren, Scheuer, & Miksáko, 2010).

## Notes

1. Cohort 1 received the Project Challenge intervention for 4 years, from Grade 4 through Grade 7. Cohorts 2–4 began the intervention in Year 2, receiving the program for 3 years, in Grades 4 through 6.
2. The search for transfer was associated with the development of educational psychology in the early part of the twentieth century. By and large, researchers did not find it, and by the 1980s, the question had changed to whether or not thinking skills could be taught in the abstract (Resnick, 1987).

## References

Adamson, D., Dyke, G., Jang, H. J., & Rosé, C. P. (2014). Towards an agile approach to adapting dynamic collaboration support to student needs. *International Journal of AI in Education 24*(1), 91–121.

Adey, P., & Shayer, M. (1990). Accelerating the development of formal thinking in middle and high school students. *Journal of Research in Science Teaching, 27*(3), 267–285.

Adey, P., & Shayer, M. (1993). An exploration of long-term far-transfer effects following an extended intervention program in the high school science curriculum. *Cognition and Instruction, 11*(1), 1–29.

Alexander, R. J. (2008). *Towards dialogic teaching: Rethinking classroom talk*. Cambridge: Dialogos.

Anderson, R. C., Nguyen-Jahiel, K., McNurlen, B., Archodidou, A., Kim, S.-Y., Reznitskaya, A., . . . Gilbert, L. (2001). The snowball phenomenon: Spread of ways of talking and ways of thinking across groups of children. *Cognition and Instruction, 19*(1), 1–46.

Asterhan, C. S. C. (2013). Epistemic and interpersonal dimensions of peer argumentation. In M. Baker, J. Andriessen, & S. Järvelä (Eds.), *Affective learning together: Social and emotional dimensions of collaborative learning* (pp. 251–271). London: Routledge.

Asterhan, C. S. C., & Schwarz, B. B. (2007). The effects of monological and dialogical argumentation on concept learning in evolutionary theory. *Journal of Educational Psychology, 99*(3), 626.

Asterhan, C. S. C., & Schwarz, B. B. (2009). The role of argumentation and explanation in conceptual change: Indications from protocol analyses of peer-to-peer dialogue. *Cognitive Science, 33*(3), 374–400.

Azmitia, M., & Montgomery, R. (1993). Friendship, transactive dialogues, and the development of scientific reasoning. *Social Development, 2*(3), 202–221.

Barron, B. (2003). When smart groups fail. *Journal of the Learning Sciences, 12*(3), 307–359.

Bellack, A. A., Kliebard, H. M., Hyman, R. T., & Smith, F. L. (1966). *The language of the classroom*. New York: Teachers College Press.

Berkowitz, M. W., & Gibbs, J. C. (1983). Measuring the developmental features of moral discussion. *Merrill-Palmer Quarterly, 29*(4), 399–410.

Bill, V., Leer, M., Reams, L., & Resnick, L. (1992). From cupcakes to equations: The structure of discourse in a primary mathematics classroom. *Verbum, 1, 2,* 63–85.

Bloom, B. S., & Krathwohl, D. R. (1956). *Taxonomy of educational objectives: The classification of educational goals. Handbook I: Cognitive domain.* New York: David McKay.

Bourdieu, P. (1977). The economics of linguistic exchanges. *Social Science Information, 16,* 645–668.

Carbonell, J. (1969). On man–computer interaction: A model and some related issues. *IEEE Transactions on Systems Science and Cybernetics, 5*(1), 16–26.

Carbonell, J. (1970). AI in CAI: An artificial intelligence approach to computer-assisted instruction. *IEEE Transactions on Man-Machine Systems, 11*(4), 190–202.

Chapin, S., & O'Connor, C. (2004). Project challenge: Identifying and developing talent in mathematics within low-income urban schools. *Boston University School of Education Research Report 1,* 1–6.

Chen, G., & Chiu, M. M. (2008). Online discussion processes: Effects of earlier messages' evaluations, knowledge content, social cues and personal information on later messages. *Computers & Education, 50*(3), 678–692.

Chen, G., Clarke, S. N., & Resnick, L. B. (2014). An analytic tool for supporting teachers' reflection on classroom talk. In J. L. Polman, E. A. Kyza, D. K. O'Neill, I. Tabak, W. R. Penuel, A. S. Jurow, K. O'Connor, T. Lee, & L. D'Amico (Eds.), *Learning and becoming in practice: The International Conference of the Learning Sciences (ICLS) 2014* (Vol. 1, pp. 583–590). Boulder, CO: International Society of the Learning Sciences.

Chi, M. T. (2009). Active-constructive-interactive: A conceptual framework for differentiating learning activities. *Topics in Cognitive Science, 1*(1), 73–105.

Chi, M. T., Bassok, M., Lewis, M. W., Reimann, P., & Glaser, R. (1989). Self-explanations: How students study and use examples in learning to solve problems. *Cognitive Science, 13*(2), 145–182.

Chi, M. T., Slotta, J. D., & De Leeuw, N. (1994). From things to processes: A theory of conceptual change for learning science concepts. *Learning and Instruction, 4*(1), 27–43.

Chinn, C. A., O'Donnell, A. M., & Jinks, T. S. (2000). The structure of discourse in collaborative learning. *Journal of Experimental Education, 69*(1), 77–97.

Chiu, M. M., & Khoo, L. (2003). Rudeness and status effects during group problem solving: Do they bias evaluations and reduce the likelihood of correct solutions? *Journal of Educational Psychology, 95*(3), 506.

Christie, F. (Ed.) (1999). *Pedagogy and the shaping of consciousness: Linguistic and social processes.* London: Cassell Academic.

Clarke, S. N. (in press). The right to speak. In L. B. Resnick, C. S. C. Asterhan, & S. N. Clarke (Eds.), *Socializing intelligence through academic talk and dialogue.* Washington, DC: American Educational Research Association.

Clarke, S. N., Chen, G., Stainton, C., Katz, S., Greeno, J. G., Resnick, L. B., . . . Rosé, C. P. (2013). The impact of CSCL beyond the online environment. In N. Rummel, M. Kapur, M. Nathan, & S. Puntambekar (Eds.), *To see the world and a grain of sand: Learning across levels of space, time, and scale: CSCL 2013* (Vol. 1, pp. 105–112). Madison, WI: International Society of the Learning Sciences.

Dewey, J. (1916). *Democracy and education.* New York: The Free Press.

Dyke, G., Adamson, A., Howley, I., & Rosé, C. P. (2013). Enhancing scientific reasoning and discussion with conversational agents. *IEEE Transactions on Learning Technologies* 6(3), special issue on Science Teaching, 240–247.

Fuchs, L. S., Fuchs, D., Hamlett, C. L., Phillips, N. B., Karns, K., & Dutka, S. (1997). Enhancing students' helping behavior during peer-mediated instruction with conceptual mathematical explanations. *The Elementary School Journal,* 223–249.

Gall, M. D. (1970). The use of questions in teaching. *Review of Educational Research,* 707–721.

Garfinkel, H. (1967). *Studies in ethnomethodology.* Englewood Cliffs, NJ: Prentice-Hall.

Goffman, E. (1959). *The presentation of self in everyday life.* New York: Anchor Books.

Greeno, J. G. (in press). Classroom talk sequences and learning. In L. B. Resnick, C. S. C. Asterhan, & S. N. Clarke (Eds.), *Socializing intelligence through academic talk and dialogue.* Washington, DC: American Educational Research Association.

Greeno, J. G., Moore, J. L., & Smith, D. R. (1993). Transfer of situated learning. In D. K. Detterman & R. Sternberg (Eds.), *Transfer on trial: Intelligence, cognition, and instruction* (pp. 99–197). Westport, CT: Ablex Publishing.

Gweon, G., Jain, M., Mc Donough, J., Raj, B., & Rosé, C. P. (2013). Measuring prevalence of other-oriented transactive contributions using an automated measure of speech style accommodation. *International Journal of Computer Supported Collaborative Learning 8*(2), 245–265.

Howe, C. (2010). Peer dialogue and cognitive development: A two-way relationship? In K. Littleton & C. Howe (Eds.), *Educational dialogues: Understanding and promoting productive interaction.* London: Routledge.

Howe, C., & McWilliam, D. (2001). Peer argument in educational settings variations due to socioeconomic status, gender, and activity context. *Journal of Language and Social Psychology, 20*(1–2), 61–80.

Howe, C., & McWilliam, D. (2006). Opposition in social interaction amongst children: Why intellectual benefits do not mean social costs. *Social Development, 15*(2), 205–231.

Howe, C., McWilliam, D., & Cross, G. (2005). Chance favours only the prepared mind: Incubation and the delayed effects of peer collaboration. *British Journal of Psychology, 96*(1), 67–93.

Howe, C., Tolmie, A., Thurston, A., Topping, K., Christie, D., Livingston, K., . . . Donaldson, C. (2007). Group work in elementary science: Towards organisational principles for supporting pupil learning. *Learning and Instruction, 17*(5), 549–563.

Howley, I., Adamson, D., Dyke, G., Mayfield, E., Beuth, J., & Rosé, C. P. (2012). Group composition and intelligent dialogue tutors for impacting students' self-efficacy. In S. A. Cerri, W. J. Clancey, G. Papadourakis, & K. K., Panourgia (Eds.), *ITS 2012 Proceedings of the 11th International conference on Intelligent Tutoring Systems,* Lecture notes in computer science (Vol. 7315; pp. 551–556). Chania, Crete, Greece: Springer-Verlag.

Howley, I., Kumar, R., Mayfield, E., Dyke, G., & Rosé, C. P. (2013a). Gaining insights from sociolinguistic style analysis for redesign of conversational agent based support for collaborative learning. In D. Suthers, K. Lund, C. P. Rosé, C. Teplovs, & N. Law (Eds.). *Productive multivocality in the analysis of group interactions,* edited volume. New York: Springer.

Howley, I., Mayfield, E., & Rosé, C. P. (2011). Missing something? Authority in collaborative learning. In *Proceedings of the 9th International Computer Supported Collaborative Learning Conference, Volume 1: Long Papers,* pp. 336–373. Rhodes: International Society of the Learning Sciences.

Howley, I., Mayfield, E., & Rosé, C. P. (2013b). Linguistic analysis methods for studying small groups. In C. Hmelo-Silver, A. O'Donnell, C. Chan, & C. Chinn (Eds.), *International handbook of collaborative learning.* New York: Routledge.

Hymes, D. (1977). *Foundations in sociolinguistics: An ethnographic approach.* London: Tavistock Publications.

Kelly, S. (2008). Race, social class, and student engagement in middle school English classrooms. *Social Science Research, 37,* 434–448.

King, A. (1992). Facilitating elaborative learning through guided student-generated questioning. *Educational Psychologist, 27*(1), 111–126.

King, A. (1999). Discourse patterns for mediating peer learning. In A. M. O'Donnell & A. King (Eds.), *Cognitive perspectives on peer learning.* Mahwah, NJ: Lawrence Erlbaum.

King, A., & Rosenshine, B. (1993). Effects of guided cooperative questioning on children's knowledge construction. *Journal of Experimental Education, 61*(2), 127–148.

Klahr, D., & Nigam, M. (2004). The equivalence of learning paths in early science instruction: Effects of direct instruction and discovery learning. *Psychological Science, 15,* 661–667.

Koedinger, K. R., Corbett, A. T., & Perfetti, C. (2012). The knowledge-learning-instruction framework: Bridging the science-practice chasm to enhance robust student learning. *Cognitive Science, 36*(5), 757–798.

Kruger, A. C. (1992). The effect of peer and adult–child transactive discussions on moral reasoning. *Merrill-Palmer Quarterly (1982–)*, 191–211.

Kruger, A. C. (1993). Peer collaboration: Conflict, cooperation, or both? *Social Development, 2*(3), 165–182.

Kumar, R., Ai, H., Beuth, J., & Rosé, C. P. (2010). Socially-capable conversational tutors can be effective in collaborative learning situations. In *Proceedings of Intelligent Tutoring Systems, lecture notes in computer science, Volume 6095*, pp. 156–164. Pittsburgh, PA: International Society of the Learning Sciences.

Kumar, R., Beuth, J., & Rosé, C. P. (2011). Conversational strategies that support idea generation productivity in groups. In *Proceedings of the 9th International Computer Supported Collaborative Learning Conference, Volume 1: Long papers*, pp. 398–405. Hong Kong: International Society of the Learning Sciences.

Kumar, R., Rosé, C. P., Wang, Y. C., Joshi, M., & Robinson, A. (2007). Tutorial dialogue as adaptive collaborative learning support. In *Proceedings of the 2007 conference on Artificial Intelligence in Education: building technology rich learning contexts that work*, pp. 383–390. Amsterdam, The Netherlands: IOS Press.

Li, Y., Anderson, R. C., Nguyen-Jahiel, K., Dong, T., Archodidou, A., Kim, I.-H., . . . Jadallah, M. (2007). Emergent leadership in children's discussion groups. *Cognition and Instruction, 25*(1), 1–2.

Lin, T.-J., Anderson, R. C., Hummel, J. E., Jadallah, M., Miller, B. W., Nguyen-Jahiel, K., . . . Wu, X. (2012). Children's use of analogy during collaborative reasoning. *Child Development, 83*(4), 1429–1443.

Lipman, M. (1981). Philosophy for children. In A. I. Costa (Ed.), *Developing minds: Programs for teaching thinking* (Vol. 2, pp. 35–38). Alexandria, VA: Association for Supervision and Curricular Development.

Littleton, K., & Howe, C. (2010). *Educational dialogues: Understanding and promoting productive interaction*. London: Routledge.

McLaren, B. M., Scheuer, O., & Miksáko, J. (2010). Supporting collaborative learning and e-discussions using artificial intelligence techniques. *International Journal of Artificial Intelligence in Education, 20*(1), 1–46.

Mead, G. H. (1967). *Mind, self, and society: From the standpoint of a social behaviorist* (Vol. 1): Chicago, IL: The University of Chicago Press.

Mehan, H. (1979). *Learning lessons: Social organization in the classroom*. Cambridge, MA: Harvard University Press.

Mercer, N., Wegerif, R., & Dawes, L. (1999). Children's talk and the development of reasoning in the classroom. *British Educational Research Journal, 25*(1), 95–111.

Mugny, G., & Doise, W. (1978). Socio-cognitive conflict and structure of individual and collective performances. *European Journal of Social Psychology, 8*(2), 181–192.

Ogan, A., Finkelstein, S., Walker, E., Carlson, R., & Cassell, J. (2012). Rudeness and rapport: Insults and learning gains in peer tutoring. *Intelligent Tutoring Systems* (pp. 11–21). Berlin: Springer.

Pauli, C., & Reusser, K. (in press). Discursive cultures of learning in (everyday) mathematics teaching: A video-based study on mathematics teaching in German and Swiss classrooms. In L. B. Resnick, C. S. C. Asterhan, & S. N. Clarke (Eds.), *Socializing intelligence through academic talk and dialogue*. Washington, DC: American Educational Research Association.

Resnick, L. B. (1987) *Education and learning to think*. Washington, DC: National Academy of Education Press.

Resnick, L. B., Asterhan, C. S. C., & Clarke, S. N. (Eds.). (in press). *Socializing intelligence through academic talk and dialogue*. Washington, DC: American Educational Research Association.

Resnick, L. B., Bill, V., Lesgold, S., & Leer, M. (1991). Thinking in arithmetic class. In B. Means, C. Chelemer, & M. S. Knapp (Eds.), *Teaching advanced skills to at-risk students: Views from research and practice*. San Francisco, CA: Jossey-Bass.

Resnick, L. B., Michaels, S., & O'Connor, C. (2010). How (well-structured) talk builds the mind. In D. Preiss & R. Sternberg (Eds.), *Innovations in educational psychology: Perspectives on learning, teaching and human development* (pp. 163–194). New York: Springer.

Rosenshine, B., Meister, C., & Chapman, S. (1996). Teaching students to generate questions: A review of the intervention studies. *Review of Educational Research, 66*(2), 181–221.

Searle, J. R. (1969). *Speech acts: An essay in the philosophy of language* (Vol. 626). Cambridge, UK: Cambridge University Press.

Sinclair, J. M. H., Coulthard, M., & Council, S. S. R. (1975). *Towards an analysis of discourse: The English used by teachers and pupils*. London: Oxford University Press.

Slavin, R. (1987). Ability grouping and student achievement in elementary schools: A best-evidence synthesis. *Review of Educational Research, 57*(3), 293–336.

Stahl, G., Koschmann, T., & Suthers, D. (2006). Computer-supported collaborative learning: An historical perspective. In R. K. Sawyer (Ed.), *Cambridge handbook of the learning sciences* (pp. 409–426). Cambridge, UK: Cambridge University Press.

Stevens, A., & Collins, A. (1977). The goal structure of a Socratic tutor. In *Proceedings of the National ACM Conference*. New York: Association for Computing Machinery.

Sun, J., Anderson, R. C., Lin, T., & Morris, J. (in press). Social and cognitive development during collaborative reasoning. In L. B. Resnick, C. S. C. Asterhan, & S. N. Clarke (Eds.), *Socializing intelligence through academic talk and dialogue*. Washington, DC: American Educational Research Association.

Teasley, S. D. (1997). Talking about reasoning: How important is the peer in peer collaboration? In L. B. Resnick, R. Säljö, C. Pontecorvo, & B. Burge (Eds.), *Discourse, tools and reasoning: Essays on situated cognition* (pp. 361–384). Berlin: Springer.

Topping, K. J., & Trickey, S. (2007a). Collaborative philosophical enquiry for school children: Cognitive effects at 10–12 years. *British Journal of Educational Psychology, 77*(2), 271–288.

Topping, K. J., & Trickey, S. (2007b). Collaborative philosophical inquiry for schoolchildren: Cognitive gains at 2 year follow up. *British Journal of Educational Psychology, 77*(4), 787–796.

Veel, R., & Christie, F. (1999). Language, knowledge and authority in school mathematics. In J. R. Martin, & F. Christie (Eds.), *Pedagogy and the shaping of consciousness: Linguistic and social processes* (pp. 185–216). London: Continuum.

Veenman, S., Denessen, E., van den Akker, A., & van der Rijt, J. (2005). Effects of a cooperative learning program on the elaborations of students during help seeking and help giving. *American Educational Research Journal, 42*, 115–151.

Vygotsky, L. S. (1962). *Thought and language*. Cambridge, MA: MIT Press.

Vygotsky, L. S. (1978). *Mind in society: The development of higher psychological processes*. Cambridge, MA: Harvard University Press.

Webb, N. M. (1991). Task-related verbal interaction and mathematics learning in small groups. *Journal for Research in Mathematics Education*, 366–389.

Webb, N. M., Franke, M. L., De, T., Chan, A. G., Freund, D., Shein, P., & Melkonian, D. K. (2009). 'Explain to your partner': teachers' instructional practices and students' dialogue in small groups. *Cambridge Journal of Education, 39*(1), 49–70.

Webb, N. M., & Mastergeorge, A. M. (2003). The development of students' helping behavior and learning in peer-directed small groups. *Cognition and Instruction, 21*(4), 361–428.

Webb, N. M., Troper, J. D., & Fall, R. (1995). Constructive activity and learning in collaborative small groups. *Journal of Educational Psychology, 87*, 406–423.

Wegerif, R., Mercer, N., & Dawes, L. (1999). From social interaction to individual reasoning: an empirical investigation of a possible socio-cultural model of cognitive development. *Learning and Instruction, 9*(6), 493–516.

Wertsch, J. V. (1979). From social interaction to higher psychological processes: A clarification and application of Vygotsky's theory. *Human Development, 22*(1), 1–22.

Winne, P. H. (1979). Experiments relating teachers' use of higher cognitive questions to student achievement. *Review of Educational Research*, 13–49.

# 29

# Assessment Illuminating Pathways to Learning

*Ellen B. Mandinach*
*Andrea A. Lash*[1]
WestEd

This chapter tackles new themes that are redefining educational assessment. It takes the position that educators can use evidence from assessments for learning and other data on learners in ways that inform their work and illuminate new pathways to learning.

Black and Wiliam (1998) and Stiggins (2002, 2005) characterized assessments *of* learning as distinct from assessments *for* learning. The former are assessments that measure the accumulation of learning or performance in a summative manner; for example, to hold schools accountable for student achievement. The latter constitute a process of moment-to-moment, day-to-day, or interim assessment that provides results to inform instruction in a more formative manner, by helping to guide teacher decisions. Assessments that inform learning emphasize the dynamic processes of assessment, rather than static models. Assessments that serve formative purposes are being adopted by school districts and even entire states as they recognize that annual summative tests are insufficiently linked to instruction (e.g., Arkansas Department of Education, 2007; Rodosky, 2009). Measures other than traditional summative assessments are increasingly being accepted and used even as understandings of these new forms of assessments are still developing (Pellegrino, 2010).

This chapter addresses the effects of assessments *for* learning, the process of formative assessment, and how research and development on some new topics are informing formative assessment. These topics include learning progressions, learning analytics, new technologies, and data use. Brought together, literature on these topics share similar theories of action; they all use evidence or data to support improved curriculum, teaching, and learning at different levels of feedback, decisions, and user groups, as well as different units of and strategies for analysis. Requirements for validity of different measures also share some similarities, such as alignment with learning goals, instructional sensitivity, accessibility and fairness, and utility for a given purpose. The use or interpretation of assessment information places different demands on reliability and other aspects of technical quality, and all require expert judgment to bring improvement to fruition. Data do not provide solutions; educators do, and the quality of those solutions depends on the skills, abilities, and knowledge that teachers bring to assessment situations.

Underlying these trends are principles derived from related measurement theory and research, many examples of which have been described elsewhere, in chapters published in previous volumes of this handbook and other handbooks of educational psychology (see e.g., Ercikan, 2006; Hambleton, 1996; Hosp, 2011). Today's work in assessment builds upon such theory and research at the same time that it differentiates the emergence of assessments to inform the teaching–learning process.

There is value in bringing the literatures on these related topics together to understand assessment and learning. They form a complex system with components that inform each other. Learning progressions provide a roadmap for data collection, learning analytics, and assessment. Technology provides a rich medium. Data serve to inform the entire process, comprising a continuum from in-the-moment to interim formative assessment, to longer-cycle, summary indicators for learning. A model of this system is displayed in Figure 29.1; this figure will be discussed further in the section titled "A Model for the Formative Assessment–Learning Progression Dynamic."

The model highlights how the data are fused in a feedback loop comprising the instruction and assessment process. The tighter the feedback loop or timing between assessment and decisions about next steps for instruction, the more informative the data. Assessment becomes part of the instructional process (Snow & Mandinach, 1999).

In the three major sections to follow we discuss how formative assessments can shed light on multiple aspects of students in education settings, how new technologies are transforming and enhancing the assessment and

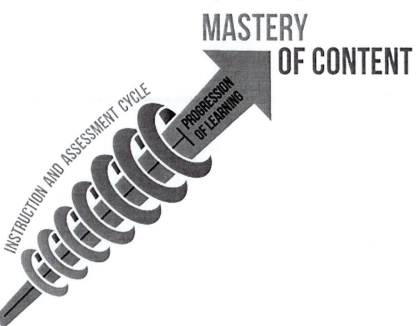

**Figure 29.1** The relationship of instruction and assessment with learning progressions.

decision-making processes surrounding them, and validity considerations necessary for proper interpretation and use of these assessments.

## Assessments and Learning

### The Formative-Summative Assessment Continuum

Assessments are used to gather evidence of student learning for a variety of types of decisions. Since implementation of the No Child Left Behind Act of 2001, students in public schools have been assessed annually with tests that survey a broad range of content. These summative assessments, which are used to form final judgments about student progress in meeting grade-level standards in mathematics and English-language arts, are administered to individual students at the end of a course of study. However, their purpose is not to identify an individual's learning needs. Instead, the results are aggregated over students within a class, grade, and school for accountability purposes, to monitor or evaluate schools and, increasingly, teachers. While these tests may identify students who lack knowledge and skills expected for their grade level, they do not identify the *reasons* students are not proficient. They do not identify misconceptions or misunderstandings students may hold that could help them and assist their teachers in designing instruction that promotes learning.

Over the past decade, the field has seen increasing interest in formative assessment, the purpose of which is to gather evidence of student learning that can guide instructional decisions. As noted, Black and Wiliam (1998) and Stiggins (2002, 2005) distinguished between assessments used for summative judgments and assessments to inform instruction

and learning. Formative assessment is a process rather than a test per se (Bennett, 2011; Frohbeiter, Greenwald, Stecher, & Schwartz, 2011; Heritage, 2013). In the process of formative assessment, student knowledge and understanding are monitored so that feedback can be given in a timely manner that is both informative and useful as a way to facilitate student growth. Therefore, the *process* of formative assessment, which includes instruction and the conversion of assessments into data, is intimately entwined with learning. It includes the establishment of goals and expected progressions of learning.

Pellegrino (2010) warned that distinctions across the formative–summative assessment continuum are not clear cut. In some situations, summative assessments might be used for more formative purposes and formative assessments used for more summative decisions. Herman (2013) notes that the key interacting elements of the formative assessment process include learning goals, assessment tasks, interpretations, and feedback. Although these components may be applicable for summative purposes, in formative situations there are different forms of assessment, closer ties to curriculum, and a learner-centered feedback cycle and interpretation.

### Central Characteristics of Formative Assessments

The formative assessment process can focus on individuals or groups of students. The process may be oral or written, open-ended, or closed-response. It may be initiated by teachers or by students and evaluated by students, their peers, or teachers. In theory, information from any assessment could be used formatively, to guide instruction; but in practice, the most useful assessments for this purpose would be closely linked to the curriculum and instructional content, and are often moment-to-moment, short cycle. Shavelson et al. (2008) identified degrees of formality in formative assessments. They may occur "on-the-fly"; that is, during the course of instruction in response to an opportunity, student action, or requested response. A teacher might, for example, ask a follow-up question in response to a student comment that suggests a possible misunderstanding. "Planned-for interactions" are questions or activities teachers design for the lesson in order to evaluate student understanding, while "curriculum-embedded" activities might be problems or questions included in a pre-packaged curriculum that students could use to evaluate their own understanding. The formative assessment process is diagnostic to inform subsequent instruction; that is, to help to identify where students are, but also to determine the challenges to their success—the roadblocks that might be overcome with pointed instruction.

Regardless of their form or timing, formative assessments monitor student progress toward learning goals. Underlying any formative assessment is a theory or model of how students develop the understanding or skills they are trying to learn. A useful tool for developing the student model of understanding is a so-called learning progression.

### Learning Progressions

Learning progressions have become a logical extension to assessment because they lay out the landscape of a domain in terms of chunking and sequencing requisite skills and knowledge embedded within a content area. For each learning progression there is a curricular aim or specific end goal. Along the progression are subskills and knowledge that build toward the targeted objective. Popham (2011) considers learning progressions as the "blueprints" for the formative assessment process. He defines them as: "a sequenced set of subskills or bodies of enabling knowledge that, it is thought, students must master en route to mastering a more remote target curricular aim" (Popham, 2008, p. 24).

Learning progressions are a foundation of the instruction and formative assessment process (Herman, 2013, 2014). They inform and guide the process. They provide indications of when assessments need to be given, data collected, or additional instruction prescribed. They are cues that help teachers to adjust instruction based on evidence of learning or gaps in learning. This student response-instructional process is consistent with the microadaptations of adaptive teaching (Corno, 2008) and instruction (Mosher, 2011). As learning progresses, it builds to an increasingly sophisticated understanding of content material over time; in turn, teaching needs to modify and adapt to facilitate the learning progression even further. Mosher (2011; Corcoran, Mosher, & Rogat, 2009) distinguishes traditional teaching or instruction from that based on learning progressions. The latter are designed using empirically tested knowledge of student learning and cognition within a domain.

Heritage (2008) notes that learning progressions must be aligned to and implemented with indepth domain knowledge. Heritage provides examples of several progressions that have been developed for diverse content areas. The work of Confrey and Maloney in mathematics (https://www.turnonccmath.net/) reflects how complex and dynamic progressions can become when the knowledge domain is specified comprehensively (Confrey & Maloney, 2012; Confrey, Maloney, & Corley, 2014; Maloney & Confrey, 2013; Sztajn, Confrey, Holt Wilson, & Edington, 2012).

### A Model for the Formative Assessment–Learning Progression Dynamic

Consider now the image presented in Figure 29.1. In the model, the learning progression is represented as an arrow showing the direction in which learning develops over time. It outlines the specific skills and knowledge that students need to acquire within a discipline. It identifies the order of skills students are expected to learn, and assumes that each skill builds upon previous ones. A learning progression, though it shows order, may also be non-linear (Confrey et al., 2014). Confrey, Nguyen, and Maloney (2011) used hexagons to represent the complexity of mathematics. Following Figure 29.1, as learning progresses, there may be some backward or sideways movement. In Figure 29.1, around the arrow, is the iterative cycle of instruction and assessment in the form of a kind of Slinky that expands and contracts according to the cycle's periodicity. Instruction is given. Students are assessed. Data are collected and analyzed, based on common misconceptions and evidence students need to learn in order to leave those misconceptions behind and move forward in the next steps along the learning progression.

Learning progressions may evolve into an essential component of the instruction and assessment cycle, but obstacles still remain. First, not all learning progressions embedded within content areas have been specified to the detail of Confrey's work; nor do all content areas lend themselves as readily as mathematics to learning progression analyses. Second, to work effectively, teachers must have sufficient pedagogical content knowledge, specialized knowledge about the progressions, and knowhow to integrate them into the instruction and assessment cycle (Gunckel, 2013). Furtak (2012) found that teachers have difficulty placing student work along the progression, which leads to problems interpreting from them in ways that translate into instructional action.

In sum, learning progressions have emerged from research as viable constructs that foster the process of formative assessment in critical ways. They may not, however, yet be readily transformed into the kinds of supports teachers need to implement formative assessment cycles (Gunckel, 2013). Finally, the National Research Council (2012) has raised questions about the empirical evidence that supports learning progressions; and indeed, according to this careful analysis, research results are mixed.

### Formative Assessment and Classroom Instruction

In classrooms where formative assessments are used routinely, the roles of students and teachers shift. As Herman (2010) notes:

Formative assessment itself involves a change in instructional practice. Rather than imparting knowledge in a transmission-oriented process, in formative assessment teachers guide students toward significant learning goals and actively engage students as assessors of themselves and their peers. Formative assessment occurs when teachers make their learning goals and success criteria explicit for students, gather evidence of how student learning is progressing, partner with students in a process of reciprocal feedback, and engage the classroom as a community to improve students' learning. (p. 511)

The classroom environment necessary for formative assessment is collaborative and supportive; students must be comfortable with questioning and constructive feedback. Students not only engage in assessment activities with their teachers, they also may be involved in self- and sometimes peer assessments. With formative assessment, students are in positions to evaluate their own understanding and to provide feedback to peers. They must know what they are expected to learn, and be able to evaluate progress toward those goals. Perhaps most importantly, when students understand that assessment information can help promote learning, and that is not being used for summative purposes alone, they can begin to regulate their own learning (Corno, 2008; OECD, 2005).

Teachers who use assessments formatively must not only determine whether students have learned target material but also probe students' thinking to understand why they may not have learned (Trumbull & Lash, 2013). This characteristic explains why teaching with formative assessment requires an underlying model of how students learn (such as a learning progression), knowledge about the actions that may be taken to move a student forward, and the ways that feedback may be provided to support learning.

Research on the effects of formative assessment shows its promise for promoting advanced learning in students; yet, as with the studies of learning progressions, reviews are mixed. One issue is the variety of techniques that researchers consider as formative. Most claims about the benefits of formative assessment reference the conclusions of a review by Black and Wiliam (1998), who summarized studies that evaluated some components of formative assessment. These authors found modest effect sizes (e.g., 0.20–0.30) when studies used rigorous research methods (Kingston & Nash, 2012) and particular strategies of formative assessment (Rich, Harrington, Him, & West, 2008; Wiliam, Lee, Harrison, & Black, 2004). A possible explanation for the small effects might be that, while teachers may learn about their students through the use of formative assessment, they may be unsure of what to do with the information they acquire through this process. The next step, for the teacher to determine whether and how to modify instruction, is not often addressed. Although teachers may gather and correctly interpret evidence of student learning, they may not be able to provide the feedback or identify the instruction students need to progress further, to more advanced levels (Heritage, Kim, Vendlinski, & Herman, 2009; Herman, Osmundson,

Ayala, Schneider, & Timms. 2006). We discuss this further later in the chapter.

### The Key Role of Feedback in Formative Assessment

Feedback is an essential element of formative assessment that distinguishes it from other forms of assessment and that should result in immediate action to improve instruction (Wiliam & Leahy, 2007). The provision for timely, targeted, and actionable feedback is a component for all assessments, but particularly in the formative assessment process (Hattie & Timperley, 2007; Ruiz-Primo & Li, 2013). The objective of feedback is to reduce the gap between a learner's current state and the desired goal. Decades of research on feedback (e.g., Dweck, 1975; Weiner, 1986) indicate that feedback should be given in a manner that does not communicate to students that poor performance or failure is due to unchangeable traits such as intelligence. Instead, feedback should be given about something malleable, such as effort or information that is constructive.

In research on data use, feedback also is noted as a central tenet. The Institute of Education Sciences practice guide on data use (Hamilton et al., 2009) recommends that students should become their own data-driven decision makers by learning how to examine their performance data and how to set goals. A component of this recommendation is the provision of "timely, specific, well-formatted, and constructive" feedback (p. 20). Such feedback should be given in a way that communicates students' strengths and weaknesses; it should be sufficiently concrete to help them understand the steps needed to improve their performance. The practice guide also suggests that teachers provide students with tools that can help them benefit from feedback and explain how these tools work, e.g., templates, lists of questions, worksheets, and rubrics.

As a component of formative assessment, feedback must also be descriptive, evidence-based, non-evaluative, and aligned with instructional objectives and outcomes within a given context (Heritage, 2010; McManus, 2008). It must lead to new learning (Heritage, 2010). Feedback should help students to understand what is needed to improve their performance. It addresses three questions: (a) where am I going? (b) where am I now? and (c) where to next? Ruiz-Primo and Li (2013) emphasize that formative feedback must be a component of the instruction and assessment cycle, rather than a discrete process. They outline several elements of formative feedback: (a) feedback linked to learning goals; (b) feedback based on a comparison of achieved and expected performance; (c) student involvement in feedback; (d) feedback as an instructional scaffold; (e) the intent to improve specific learning outcomes; (f) feedback that is accessible and practical; (g) feedback based on multiple sources of information; and (h) demonstrable alignment over time with a learning trajectory.

Hattie and Timperley's review of feedback (2007) provides a framework that is informed by three questions: Where am I going, how am I doing, and where to next? The major tenet is that feedback must be timely and constructive to be informative for teachers and students. The best timing for feedback seems to vary with the type of task. Immediate feedback for new or difficult tasks (Clariana, 1990) and those dealing with procedural knowledge (Dihoff, Brosvic, & Epstein, 2003) may be beneficial. However, feedback may be less productive if it is given while the student is actively engaged in a particular learning event (due to interference), and might best be delayed somewhat on simple tasks (Corno & Snow, 1986). Shute (2008) finds research results on feedback to be mixed and inconsistent, with some variables and characteristics related to positive outcomes, depending on setting, context, prior knowledge, learner characteristics, and task. Shute's review recommends that feedback should: (a) focus on the task, not the learner; (b) be elaborated; (c) be provided in manageable units; (d) be specific and clear; (e) be simple; (f) reduce uncertainty; (g) be objective; and (h) promote a learning goal orientation (a goal to master material rather than produce a high grade).

### How to Use Data for Decision Making

The process of using educational assessment data in a formative manner may be considered a form of data-driven decision making (hereafter referred to as DDDM). In recent years, DDDM has been promoted in policy and administrative literatures as a key method for improving educational systems. While they were developed within different disciplines, it is helpful to examine how formative assessment and DDDM relate. DDDM allows for use of different types of data—data that are not only formative assessments of students learning. DDDM is used with summative data as well as other kinds of information (e.g., data on student attendance and non-cognitive assessments) in so-called "data dashboards."

DDDM has been defined as an iterative inquiry cycle applied to: (a) examine a research question (Easton, 2009); (b) address readiness and improvement (Abbott, 2008); (c) assist in instructional decision making (Hamilton et al., 2009); and (d) form general theories of the skills and knowledge educators need to use to inform their practice (Gummer & Mandinach, 2015; Mandinach, Honey, Light, & Brunner, 2008; Means, Padilla, & Gallagher, 2010). A fundamental factor in DDDM is the notion of iterative, non-linear progressions and a cycle of inquiry. Data serve to provide insights that inform decisions (Mandinach & Jackson, 2012).

The Data Use for Improving Learning (2014) website contains a cycle specifically for formative assessment (http://datause.cse.ucla.edu/). The cycle begins with a learning progression to determine learning objectives and success criteria. It then moves to the collection and interpretation of the evidence that can be used to identify gaps in learning. The gap analysis provides feedback that facilitates the modification of instruction, the scaffolding for new learning, and ultimately closure of the learning gap.

Heritage (2010) also approaches the cyclical process of decision making from the perspective of formative assessment. The cycle includes curriculum, instruction, and feedback and data or evidence. It begins with learning goals that elicit evidence of the status of the learners' knowledge. The second stage is interpretation in which the data and evidence are examined for meaning in terms of student learning. The third stage is the decision about what to do that will improve student learning. Finally, there is an action taken to move toward the student learning goals.

A model of DDDM presented by Hamilton and colleagues (2009) directly relates to the topic of this chapter by focusing on the use of assessment data to inform instruction. The steps in the inquiry cycle include: (a) collecting and preparing student learning data from multiple sources; (b) interpreting the data and developing hypotheses about the instructional steps needed to improve student learning; and (c) modifying instruction in ways that will test out the hypotheses. Based on the results from this feedback cycle, teachers may need to collect more data, develop new hypotheses, and cycle through the iterative process once again. The notion of a cycle means that a teacher can actually begin anywhere in the process.

The models discussed above use slightly different terminology but all have identified a number of skills that are important to the inquiry process. Mandinach and colleagues (2008) likewise describe DDDM as a continuum of transforming data to information and ultimately to actionable knowledge, with skills that include the collection and organization of data; the analysis and summarization of information; and the synthesis and prioritization of knowledge that stimulates a decision, implementation, and assessment of the impact. The impact of outcomes determines if further data are needed, more analyses, or different prioritization.

It is essential in both formative assessment and DDDM for the targeted hypotheses to be testable and measurable and the results actionable (Mandinach et al., 2008). In the case of formative assessments, targeted hypotheses would include, for example, expectations teachers might have that changing their instruction would correct some student misconceptions. If the inquiry process yields knowledge on which action cannot be taken, then the implementation of the decision will be stifled. Mandinach, Friedman, and Gummer (2015) identified 59 skills teachers need to use data from formative learning assessments and other assessments effectively. These skills then became the basis for a conceptual framework for data literacy for teaching (Gummer & Mandinach, 2015). Two components of the inquiry cycle are the knowledge of how to transform data into information and knowledge of how to transform information into an instructional decision.

Extrapolating from these conceptual frameworks to assessments and learning, the following logic model pertains: The formative assessment process identifies questions, concerns, or learning issues that data are intended to inform. It yields data that require analysis and interpretation. The interpretation of data, in conjunction with teachers' content knowledge and pedagogical content knowledge (Shulman, 1986), enables teachers to determine a course of instructional actions (Gummer & Mandinach, 2015). Analyses of the impact of the instructional next steps will determine what new kinds of educational assessment data need to be collected, thereby restarting the inquiry process once again.

A key component of the process is the tightness of the feedback loop between when data are collected and when the instructional next steps are taken. Data and decisions differ if the feedback loop is moment-to-moment, versus daily, weekly, or even annually (Herman & Gribbons, 2001; Pellegrino, 2010). The National Council of Teachers of Mathematics (1995) distinguishes moment-to-moment, short-term, and long-term decisions. Moment-to-moment data might include a teacher's observation of a student or the determination of understanding based on the response to a question. Data collection is instantaneous and the decision-making process rapid. The feedback cycle expands all the way to what has been called autopsy data for teachers' instructional decision making. These are data that have been collected so far in the past (back by at least several months) that the link to current performance levels and instruction makes them virtually unusable. In general, the tighter the timing among assessments, data, and instruction, the more actionable the data become for instructional decisions made by teachers. This assumes that the data are sufficiently sensitive to relevant questions and aligned with learning goals.

Another tenet of DDDM is the coordination of multiple measures from which to inform a decision (Hamilton et al., 2009). This refers not just to multiple measures for the process of evaluating students' educational learning and achievement, but also that multiple and diverse sources of data provide more complete understanding of students' performance. These might be sources other than formative learning assessments, and may even include such disparate forms of data as attendance, health, behavior, demographics, or even time spent commuting to school. Such an array of sources can provide good context for describing a student and his/her learning needs. In the DDDM process, relevant data often also include student attitudes, engagement, or indicators of attention, in addition to the more cognitively oriented data sources that teachers glean from observations of student behavior during class discourse, small-group work, and discussions.

## Trends Made Possible by New Technologies
### The New Field of Learning Analytics

Among the technology and learning science community, a new field called learning analytics has emerged. Those who study learning analytics integrate assessment, data, and technology, with the objective of providing precise measurement of the processes of student learning (see http://www.solaresearch.org and Chapter 2, this volume). The field of learning analytics is also linked to work in the areas of personalized and blended learning (environments that mix online learning with classroom teaching) (Dieterle, 2014). The underlying theory for these paradigms is that learning activities delivered on technology platforms provide affordances for collecting data, measuring student learning and patterns of performance, and analyzing results that would not be possible in more traditional learning environments. The technology platforms such as gaming and simulation programs, adaptive instruction, and assessment provide for diverse and rich instruction and assessment, with the ability to record change in real time. The technologies also facilitate the collection of diverse and indepth sources of data (e.g., logfiles), in natural feedback loops to extract learner performance patterns through micro-measurements (DiCerbo & Behrens, 2014). These data are fine-grained, moment-to-moment, generated in real time, and actionable through analyses and immediate feedback (Baker, 2014). They also provide for analytics that inform decision making (Bienkowski, 2014).

The learning analytics that underlie blended or personalized learning environments contain creative technologies that are made available to both teachers and students. In the blended environment developed by Baker (2014), the environment functions to facilitate the customization of instruction as it provides the assessments of learning and diagnostic feedback in ways that can enhance student learning and educational practices. These new technologies are steeped in many of the principles that underlie effective data use. The technologies use assessment procedures that provide diagnostic feedback to students and teachers, putting the student at the center of the learning process (Bienkowski, 2014). They can facilitate triangulation among multiple data sources, making possible creative assessment strategies. These data enable teachers to differentiate instruction in ways that capitalize on students' strengths while remediating weaknesses; that is, to teach adaptively (Corno, 2008). The technologies enable teachers and students to access data not readily available without real-time data captures and analysis (Baker, 2014; Behrens, 2014).

The sorts of data produced in technology platforms include response times, time on task, response pattern traces, error patterns, and help-seeking behavior. Real-time data close the essential feedback loop among instruction, assessment, and the examination of data in ways that can facilitate the learning process. And, because this process of gathering the information is unobtrusive, it tends not to interfere with students as they work. Shute refers to unobtrusive measures as stealth assessment. In research still in an early phase, Shute and her colleagues show its promise for gathering information about qualities such as persistence and novelty in problem solving (Shute & Kim, 2013; Shute & Ventura, 2013).

### Technology Supports for Formative Assessment

While learning analytics use technology as a powerful medium for the analysis of learning, other technologies provide venues for creative assessments. Applications of new computer and web-based technologies to education offer the potential for improving the main task of assessments: to gather high-quality evidence of students' knowledge and skills that will be useful for the purpose for which it is intended. New technologies offer greater flexibility in how assessment tasks can be presented to students and in the ways students may respond to them, thus making it possible for a greater number of students to demonstrate their knowledge and skills. The technologies allow for greater diversity of data and may provide more rapid feedback because of their greater speed in processing information and their capacity to organize, manage, and retrieve assessment information. With new technologies come dynamic ways of representing information that, in combination with advances in theories of learning and psychometrics, may provide the means to gather useful evidence about a greater variety of student knowledge and skills. The technologies also allow the collection of data for dynamic and complex cognitive processes and performance patterns that would not be possible with more static media (Quellmalz & Pellegrino, 2009).

The flexibility offered by technologies in the methods of assessment delivery and response may improve the quality of the evidence obtained. Ideally, evidence gathered through assessments reflects only the target knowledge for which information is needed. In reality, assessment evidence will be influenced by other, alternative knowledge and skills that the assessment tasks tap inadvertently. Students' decoding skills may affect how well they understand instructions; their visual acuity may determine if they can respond on the correct line of an answer sheet; their working-memory capacity may affect their ability to complete the computations required for a mathematics problem. Validity improves with reduction of the impact of alternative knowledge and skills.

New technologies offer alternative methods to present information and responses that may reduce the impact of alternative knowledge and skills. Text-to-speech software allows instructions to be read to students. Manipulations in text size, fonts, colors, and contrast with background can improve clarity of text. Special support can be provided on demand. For example, calculators can be made available on screen for problems that are not intended to assess computation facts and dictionaries can be accessed on screen for tasks that are not intended to assess vocabulary. Speech-to-text translators, touch screens, and other input devices can reduce the impact of alternative knowledge and skills such as knowledge of the keyboard or manual dexterity.

With their capacities to manipulate large quantities of information rapidly, new technologies can improve the precision and efficiency of assessments. There are more choices to when and where assessments can be made. It is no longer necessary to stop instruction and administer assessments to groups of students when computers can present assessment tasks to individuals at any point in time. Computerized assessments can score responses rapidly to provide immediate feedback to teachers and students. When coupled with psychometric methods that model responses of students to items, computerized assessments may be designed to adapt to individual students, selecting tasks that best match the level of the students' performance. And, when linked closely to instruction, feedback might offer formative information to direct the next instructional steps (Pellegrino & Quellmalz, 2010). Because of the large capacity to organize and manipulate data, it may be possible with technology to link information gathered from individual students during the course of instruction to class or school-level information, making the data useful for a greater variety of decision making, not just

for instruction and learning (Pellegrino, 2010; Pellegrino, Chudowsky, & Glazer, 2001).

As researchers explore how features of new technologies can be adapted in education, the potential for alternative assessments grows. One promising feature is the dynamic representation of information. With the new technologies it is possible to display models of systems, for example, ecosystems or social systems, and to show how those systems change over time or with changes in model parameters. With dynamic representations, it may be possible to better assess complex knowledge and skills, such as scientific inquiry or complex problem solving, that have been difficult to assess with static representations (Pellegrino & Quellmalz, 2010; Quellmalz et al., 2011). The technology provides affordances that allow students to demonstrate learning. A second promising feature is the capacity to capture indicators performance during the course of learning. Examples include the stealth assessments previously mentioned—e.g., the time a student spends examining a particular feature of a task, the number of times the student returns to a particular portion of a lesson, or the number of times a student changes responses to an assessment.

A flourishing line of work has been the development and work around the intersection of formative assessment and technology. Quellmalz (2013) provides an examination of how technologies can be used to support formative assessment and notes:

> A new generation of assessments is moving beyond the use of technology only for resource collections or for test assembly, delivery, and scoring of conventional item formats. A goal of these new assessments is for technology to enable assessment of those aspects of cognition and performance that are complex and dynamic and that were previously impossible to assess directly. (p. 6)

The technologies provide affordances that enhance the learning and assessment process. For example, they can provide a wide range of assessment strategies that are linked to instructional goals, learning progressions, and criteria of success. They can elicit and record data and evidence of performance so teachers can analyze and interpret the results so additional instruction can be planned.

Research is examining the integration of technology-based formative assessments into domains such as science (Gobert, Sao Pedro, Baker, Toto, & Montalvo, 2012; Quellmalz, Timms, Silberglitt, & Buckley, 2012). Game-based assessment also is seen as a promising venue in which technologies and assessment are merging. These environments provide for personalized learning and assessment, but in the context of video games (Bagley & Shaffer, 2009; Bauer, 2014; Shute & Ventura, 2013). Some games require collaboration and are a venue to examine collaborative learning and assessment (Zapata-Rivera & Bauer, 2011). This work is still nascent and much more research is needed to understand the potentials and impact of such technologies.

## Validity Considerations and Conclusions

We conclude our chapter with two considerations that impact assessment and learning. We first briefly examine the validity literature as it pertains to assessment for learning. Our second consideration is the human capacity to use assessments and implement results; that is, the extent to which educators can be helped to become sufficiently knowledgeable about how to use data and assessments to inform the teaching–learning process.

### Reasoning About Evidence From Assessments

Validation questions for measurement can also relate to the teaching and learning process. Do the measurement activities elicit data that can inform the instructional–assessment cycle? Do the assessment questions or observations yield data that can identify learning strengths and weaknesses? Are the assessment events aligned with the curriculum and instruction?

An examination of the validity of assessment data requires an examination of the plausibility of the claims made based on the assessment information (Cronbach, 1988; Kane, 2006, 2013). Validity then is a feature of the claim being made about an assessment outcome—whether or not the process of assessment produces valid information. As such, validity may vary from one interpretation about a score from a test to another. As an example, a school might administer the middle-school test of arithmetic knowledge and skills at the end of a remedial summer program to students who were assigned randomly to either a new or traditional arithmetic course. In one use of the test, the school administrators planned to evaluate the quality of the new course by comparing the posttest scores of students who had studied arithmetic in the new and traditional courses. In this use, the school administrators interpret that the scores on the test are indicators of students' levels of arithmetic knowledge. In a second use, the school administrators planned to identify students eligible for enrollment in algebra the next school year. They interpreted the score on the test as an indicator of students' likelihood of successfully completing algebra in the future. These are two different interpretations of the test score; empirical evidence required to support the first would not necessarily support the second; and the claims being made about the scores may differ in their degree of validity.

In addition to examining validity of interpretations made about an assessment outcome, it is important to examine validity of the decisions based on the outcomes. Messick (1989) defined validity not only as the "adequacy and appropriateness" of inferences but also of "*actions*" based on the test scores or other modes of assessment (p. 13). Kane (2013) argued the importance not only of evaluating claims to support assessment interpretations but also the claims that support the *uses* of assessment information. Decisions based on assessment information will "involve a chain of inferences leading to claims about attributes of test takers and then to decisions made on the estimated values of the attribute" (p. 46). A decision rule to allow students to enroll in algebra only if they score above a criterion level on an arithmetic test is a decision rule that is based not only on the interpretation of the score as a measure of prerequisite knowledge for algebra, but also that the criterion score identifies the required

level of prerequisite skill. In evaluating validity when scores are the basis of decisions, the consequences of the rule are important outcomes to study (Kane, 2013; Messick, 1989).

When considering validity of score interpretations and uses, it is typical to think about developing validity arguments after assessments are designed and administered. Evidence-centered design (ECD; Mislevy & Haertel, 2006; Mislevy & Riconscente, 2005) provides a means for constructing assessments to support claims about score interpretation and use. ECD begins with the understanding that the interpretation of assessment results is reasoning from evidence. It begins by addressing the question of what behavior one would accept as evidence of the knowledge and skills that an assessment is being designed to measure. Next is the question of what tasks or activities would elicit the behavior. And, finally, what mathematical model best describes the relationship of the observed behavior to underlying knowledge and skills? Detailed analyses of the knowledge and skills and detailed task analyses take place, typically in multidisciplinary groups of experts from diverse fields, including psychometrics, learning, and disciplinary subject matter. The process results in templates that may guide development of assessment activities by identifying in detail key features of the tasks. Along with the templates for task design are specifications of scoring and the mathematical model for analysis of scores and a detailed specification of the validity argument to support a particular interpretation of the assessment results. ECD requires deep analysis of an assessment situation and the time and resources it requires may mean that it is most likely to be applied in developing large-scale, high-stakes assessments. However, the principles of ECD are so powerful that they hold promise even when applied informally by teachers seeking information about their classroom instruction.

### Validity and Formative Assessment

Like it is for other types of assessment, the primary activity for people using information from formative assessment is to reason from evidence, to make inferences about what a student knows, and to do so from a sample of information that may be incomplete or imprecise (Pellegrino et al., 2001). The quality of the inference for a particular purpose defines its validity: Are the instructional decisions made as a consequence of the assessment process accurate, suitable, and fair? Multiple claims must be substantiated to justify score inferences for a specific purpose.

In large-scale testing, statistical methods and traditional psychometric indicators may be used to evaluate the qualities of the inferences. These techniques would not be helpful to evaluate inferences from formative assessments. They require information gathered for a large number of students, on a large number of activities and days. Formative assessment might be used to evaluate a few students during the course of one lesson, and so the appropriate models are diagnostic and looking at levels/patterns of reasoning and thinking in addition to content knowledge. Traditional statistics use models of test interpretation that summarize the quantity rather than the qualities of student knowledge. These models focus on whether a student had acquired sufficient knowledge rather than the type of information useful to teachers in understanding student thinking, such as their reasoning or patterns in their thinking (Trumbull & Lash, 2013).

It may be that any problems with validity in a single formative assessment can be corrected over time because of the way they are used in classrooms. Teachers are able to evaluate student learning frequently with a variety of strategies that can be tailored to particular students (Durán, 2011). On repeated assessment, over time, teachers can correct any decisions that may have been in error and adjust instruction accordingly (Shavelson, Black, Wiliam, & Coffey, 2007). While a traditional statistical approach may not be useful to examine validity in classroom use, certain principles of assessment design still are helpful to teachers as they select and develop assessment methods. An understanding of the principles of ECD (Mislevy & Haertel, 2006) can help teachers identify tasks that will provide information on the knowledge and skills they want to target and avoid tapping other, unwanted, knowledge and skills. The following series of questions, based in part on Harris, Bauer, and Redman (2008) and Trumbull and Lash (2013), can help teachers develop valid assessment processes:

- What knowledge and skills do I wish to assess (e.g., knowledge, skills, processes, understanding toward competency in a particular part of a domain)?
- What is the cognitive/developmental path I would expect to see with regard to these knowledge and skills?
- What forms of evidence (i.e., observable features of students' performances and responses) would I need in order to determine the students' level of knowledge and skills?
- What are the characteristics of tasks that will elicit this evidence?
- What knowledge and skills that are not wanted (e.g., unnecessarily complex language, need for speed of response) might this type of formative assessment process introduce?
- How can I modify my formative assessment process to make it inclusive for all students, to minimize the impact of non-target knowledge and skills?

## Users of Assessment and Consumers of Data

As the National Research Council (2012) has noted, new conceptualizations of assessment will require professional development to prepare teachers to use the techniques effectively. Reports have laid out the skills and knowledge teachers need to acquire, e.g., the National Council for Accreditation of Teacher Education's Blue Ribbon Panel (2010) clinical recommendations for teacher preparation; the Council of Chief State School Officers' (CCSSO) Task Force (2012) on teacher preparation; the CCSSO Interstate Teacher Assessment and Support Consortium (InTASC, 2013) teaching standards, and the Council for the Accreditation of Educator Preparation Commission on Standards and Performance Reporting (2013) draft recommendations and standards. In all instances, the documents stress the importance of educators' capacity to use assessment data to inform instructional practice. The InTASC document consists of ten standards, only one of which is devoted to the six critical

dispositions, seven essential knowledge, and nine performances teachers need to demonstrate with respect to assessment. The assessment standard states:

> The teacher understands and uses multiple methods of assessment to engage learners in their own growth, to monitor learner progress, and to guide the teacher's and learner's decision making. (p. 30)

An examination of states' licensure codes and statutes indicated that 43 of 51 include knowledge of assessments as part of their requirements (Mandinach et al., 2015).

## Assessment Literacy and Data Literacy for Educators

There is a need to distinguish between assessment and data literacy (Mandinach & Gummer, 2013a). Assessment literacy is educators' ability to use assessments, to understand key concepts around measurement, and to understand what assessments are appropriate for particular purposes. Assessment literacy is a major component of the larger umbrella of data literacy. Data literacy includes the ability to use many different sources of data, not just formative assessments, but other information about students as well, such as student attendance, behavioral, demographic, and health data. A data-literate educator can "continuously and effectively access, interpret, act on, and communicate multiple types of data from state, local, classroom, and other sources in order to improve outcomes for students in a manner appropriate to their professional roles and responsibilities" (Data Quality Campaign, 2014, p. 1). Formative assessments that convey information about student progress in learning, of course, are a major source of data for teachers.

There has been confusion about these two constructs. The CCSSO Task Force (2012), for example, comprising several chief state school officers, tout the importance of assessment literacy in their discussion of the need for educators to draw upon more than just assessment results in their decision making. The report states that teacher candidates must be able to "use data from a variety of assessments as well as information on student attendance, student engagement, demographics, attendance, and school climate in order to develop or adjust instruction" (p. 2). Although assessments are central, including the other sources of data makes clear that what the report is actually discussing is the importance of *data* literacy. This is more than a semantic difference. Student performance is the most important data source to inform instructional decisions and promote learning. However, the other sources of data can provide a comprehensive picture by capturing essential contextual information that facilitates the interpretation of assessment results. Teachers will need to be not only assessment-literate, but also *data*-literate.

## Future Directions in Assessment

Assessments provide an essential repository of data about students' learning, their strengths and weaknesses, and the instructional remediation necessary for them to attain competence in a particular subject. As we have discussed, there are a variety of assessments, some more or less aligned to inform instruction and students' learning trajectories. The tighter the feedback loop among instruction, assessment, and the resulting data, the greater the potential to inform the learning and instructional process.

New models of assessment are being designed, and existing models are being retrofitted to maximize their information value. There are new national assessment programs being introduced (Center for K-12 Assessment & Performance Management at ETS, 2012; Herman & Linn, 2013; Partnership for Assessment of Readiness for College and Careers, 2013; Smarter Balanced Assessment Consortium, 2013). In many of these programs, distinctions between formative and summative assessments are not so clear. In the past, annual summative assessments were widely used for accountability and more local purposes. Today formative assessments are becoming a focus. This momentum reflects a philosophical shift to assessments that can inform instructional practice.

These changes and trends have implications for practice. Current and future educators need to be prepared to understand and use the new forms of educational assessment and be able to competently interpret the results in ways that transform data into actionable knowledge. Professional development (Heritage, 2010; Trumbull & Gerzon, 2013) and educator preparation programs (Mandinach et al., 2015) must flexibly adapt to the emerging trends. Courses on formative assessment and DDDM may need to be added to schools of education. Professional development should address the finding that, while teachers are able to understand and use assessment results, they may have difficulty determining instructional action (Heritage et al., 2009). Mandinach and Gummer (2013b) found that professional development providers who focus on data use need to help educators to attain data literacy skills *and* to take the next step toward connecting data to instructional actions. As teachers learn to combine their assessment and data literacy with pedagogical content knowledge to transform results into actionable instruction, they begin to show evidence of pedagogical data literacy (Mandinach, 2012).

The transition to assessments that can inform learning requires a culture shift, particularly from an accountability culture to a culture of improvement (Shepard, 2000; Wise, 2014). The Data Quality Campaign (Guidera, 2013) provided a catchy metaphor for thinking about this needed change in how we use data: Using data for accountability purposes is a hammer; using it for continuous improvement is a flashlight. Teachers who have access to and know how to use the right data from the right assessments can transform those data into actionable knowledge that can be used to guide instruction and enhance the learning process. But these data must be aligned to intended purposes and interpretations; that is, they must be instructionally valid, as previously described. The metaphorical and actual transformation is about providing information to students and teachers about where students are located along their learning progressions so that appropriate instructional actions can be determined and implemented. If the field is serious about continuous improvement at the student level, then it seems essential that policy makers, educators, and stakeholders recognize formative assessments and other sources of data as beacons of information illuminating the path toward learning and competence for all students.

## Note

1. The authors would like to acknowledge the insightful guidance of Lyn Corno. We also thank Joan Herman and Geneva Haertel for their thoughtful reviews of a previous draft of the chapter.

## References

Abbott, D. V. (2008). A functionality framework for educational organizations: Achieving accountability at scale. In E. B. Mandinach & M. Honey (Eds.), *Data-driven school improvement: Linking data and learning* (pp. 257–276). New York, NY: Teachers College Press.

Arkansas Department of Education. (2007). Arkansas educators learn what "formative assessment" really is. *Education Matters for Administrators, 1*(4), 3.

Bagley, E., & Shaffer, D. W. (2009). When people get in the way: Promoting civic thinking through epistemic gameplay. *International Journal of Gaming and Computer-Mediated Simulations (IJGCMS), 1*(1), 36–52.

Baker, R. (2014). *Toward demonstrating the value of learning analytics in education.* Paper presented at a presidential symposium at the annual meeting of the American Educational Research Association, Philadelphia, PA.

Bauer, M. (2014). *GlassLab: Creating game-based formative assessments using learning progressions.* Paper presented at the annual meeting of the American Educational Research Association, Philadelphia, PA.

Behrens, J. T. (2014). *Inferential foundations for learning analytics in the digital ocean.* Paper presented at a presidential symposium at the annual meeting of the American Educational Research Association, Philadelphia, PA.

Bennett, R. E. (2011). Formative assessment: A critical review. *Assessment in Education: Principles, Policy & Practice, 18*(1), 5–25.

Bienkowski, M. (2014). *Putting the learner at the center: Exposing analytics to learning.* Paper presented at a presidential symposium at the annual meeting of the American Educational Research Association, Philadelphia, PA.

Black, P., & Wiliam, D. (1998). Assessment and classroom learning. *Assessment in Education: Principles, Policy, and Practice, 5*(1), 7–74.

Blue Ribbon Panel on Clinical Preparation and Partnerships for Improved Student Learning. (2010). *Transforming teacher education through clinical practice: A national strategy to prepare effective teachers.* Washington, DC: National Council for Accreditation of Teachers Education.

Center for K-12 Assessment & Performance Management at ETS. (2012). *Coming together to raise achievement: New assessments for the Common Core State Standards.* Austin, TX: Center for K-12 Assessment & Performance Management at ETS.

Clariana, R. B. (1990). A comparison of answer until correct feedback and knowledge of correct response feedback under two conditions of contextualization. *Journal of Computer-Based Instruction, 17*(4), 125–129.

Confrey, J., & Maloney, A. (2012). *A learning trajectory framework in the CCSS-M.* Presentation at the North Carolina Council of Teachers of Mathematics Conference, Greensboro, NC.

Confrey, J., Maloney, A. P., & Corley, A. K. (2014). Learning trajectories: A framework for connecting standards with curriculum. *ZDM Mathematics Education,* 1–15.

Confrey, J., Nguyen, K. H., & Maloney, A. P. (2011). *Hexagon map of learning trajectories for K-8 Common Core mathematics standards.* Retrieved from https:/www.turnonccmath.net/p=map.

Corcoran, T., Mosher, F. A., & Rogat, A. (2009). *Learning progressions in science: An evidence based approach to reform.* Research Report No 63. Madison, WI: Consortium for Policy and Research in Education.

Corno, L. (2008). On teaching adaptively. *Educational Psychologist, 43*(3), 161–173.

Corno, L., & Snow, R. E. (1986). Adapting teaching to individual differences among learners. In M. C. Wittrock (Ed.), *Handbook of research on teaching* (3rd ed., pp. 605–629). New York, NY: Macmillan.

Council for the Accreditation of Educator Preparation Commission on Standards and Performance Reporting. (2013). *Draft recommendations for the CAEP board*. Washington, DC: CAEP.

Cronbach, L. J. (1988). Five perspectives on validity argument. In H. Wainer & H. Braun (Eds.), *Test validity* (pp. 3–17). Hillsdale, NJ: Lawrence Erlbaum.

Council of Chief State School Officers (CCSSO) Interstate Teacher Assessment and Support Consortium. (2013). *InTASC Model Core Teaching Standards and Learning Progressions for Teachers 1.0*. Washington, DC: CCSSO Interstate Teacher Assessment and Support Consortium.

Council of Chief State School Officers (CCSSO) Task Force on Teacher Preparation and Entry into the Profession. (2012). *Our responsibility, our promise: Transforming teacher preparation and entry into the profession*. Washington, DC: Council of Chief State School Officers.

Data Quality Campaign. (2014). *Teacher data literacy: It's about time*. Washington, DC: Data Quality Campaign.

Data Use for Improving Learning. (2014). *Formative assessment cycle*. Retrieved from http://datause.cse.ucla.edu/ (accessed February 20, 2015).

DiCerbo, K. E., & Behrens, J. T. (2014). *Impacts of the digital ocean*. London: Person.

Dieterle, E. (2014). *Discussion on learning analytics*. Presidential symposium at the annual meeting of the American Educational Research Association, Philadelphia, PA.

Dihoff, R. E., Brosvic, G. M., & Epstein, M. L. (2003). The role of feedback during academic testing: The delay retention revisited. *The Psychological Record, 53*, 533–548.

Durán, R. P. (2011). Ensuring valid educational assessments for ELL students. Scores, score interpretation, and assessment uses. In M. Basterra, E. Trumbull, & G. Solano-Flores (Eds.), *Cultural validity in assessment: Addressing linguistic and cultural diversity* (pp. 115–142). New York, NY: Routledge.

Dweck, C. (1975). The role of expectations and attributions in the alleviation of learned helplessness. *Journal of Personality and Social Psychology, 31*, 674–685.

Easton, J. Q. (2009). *Using data systems to drive school improvement*. Keynote address at the STATS-DC 2009 Conference, Bethesda, MD.

Ercikan, K. (2006). Developments in assessment of student learning. In P. A. Alexander & P. H. Winne (Eds.), *Handbook of educational psychology* (2nd ed., pp. 929–952). Mahwah, NJ: Lawrence Erlbaum Associates.

Frohbeiter, G., Greenwald, E., Stecher, B., & Schwartz, H. (2011). *Knowing and doing: What teachers learn from formative assessment and how they use information* (CRESST Report 802). Los Angeles, CA: UCLA National Center for Research on Evaluation, Standards, and Student Testing.

Furtak, E. M. (2012). Linking a learning progression for natural selection to teachers' enactment of formative assessment. *Journal of Research in Science Teaching, 49*, 1181–1210.

Gobert, J., Sao Padro, M., Baker, R. S., Toto, E., & Montalvo, O. (2012). Leveraging educational data mining for real time performance assessment of science inquiry skills within microworlds. *Journal of Educational Data Mining, 4*, 153–185.

Guidera, A. (2013). *Hammer to flashlight: Past, present, and future of education data use*. Presentation at Changing the Ground Game: Focus on People to Improve Data Use at the Local Level, Arlington, VA.

Gummer, E. S., & Mandinach, E. B. (2015). Building a conceptual framework for data literacy. *Teachers College Record, 117*(5). Retrieved from http://www.tcrecord.org/PrintContent.asp?ContentID=17856 (accessed March 13, 2015).

Gunckel, K. L. (2013). *Teacher knowledge for using learning progressions in classroom instruction and assessment*. Paper presented at the annual meeting of the American Educational Research Association, San Francisco, CA.

Hambleton, R. K. (1996). Advances in assessment models, methods, and practices. In D. C. Berliner & R. C. Calfee (Eds.), *Handbook of educational psychology* (1st ed., pp. 899–925). New York, NY: Simon & Schuster Macmillan.

Hamilton, L., Halverson, R., Jackson, S., Mandinach, E., Supovitz, J., & Wayman, J. (2009). *Using student achievement data to support instructional decision making* (NCEE 2009-4067). Washington, DC: National Center for Education Evaluation and Regional Assistance, Institute of Education Sciences, U.S. Department of Education.

Harris, K., Bauer, M., & Redman, M. (2008). *Cognitive based developmental models uses as a link between formative and summative assessment*. Princeton, NJ: Educational Testing Service.

Hattie, J., & Timperley, H. (2007). The power of feedback. *Review of Educational Research, 77*(1), 81–112.

Heritage, M. (2008). *Learning progressions: Supporting instruction and formative assessment*. Paper prepared for the Formative Assessment for Teachers and Students (FAST) State Collaborative on Assessment and Student Standards (SCASS) of the Council of Chief State School Officers (CCSSO). Washington, DC: CCSSO.

Heritage, M. (2010). *Formative assessment: Making it happen in the classroom*. Thousand Oaks, CA: Corwin Press.

Heritage, M. (2013). *Formative assessment in practice: A process of inquiry and action*. Cambridge, MA: Harvard Education Press.

Heritage, M., Kim, J., Vendlinski, T., & Herman, J. (2009). From evidence to action: A seamless process in formative assessment? *Educational Measurement: Issues and Practice, 28*(3), 24–31.

Herman, J. L. (2010). Impact of assessment on classroom practice. In E. L. Baker, B. McGaw, & P. Peterson (Eds.), *International encyclopedia of education* (pp. 506–511). Oxford: Elsevier.

Herman, J. L. (2013). *Formative assessment for next generation science standard: A proposed model*. Paper presented at the Invitational Research Symposium on Science Assessment, Washington, DC.

Herman, J. L. (2014). *Learning progressions for multi-dimensional formative assessment*. Paper presented at the annual conference of the American Educational Research Association, Philadelphia, PA.

Herman, J., & Gribbons, B. (2001). *Lessons learned in using data to support school inquiry and continuous improvement: Final report to the Stuart Foundation* (CSE Technical Report 535). Los Angeles, CA: UCLA National Center for Research on Evaluation, Standards, and Student Testing.

Herman, J., & Linn, R. (2013). *On the road to assessing deeper learning: The status of Smarter Balanced and PARCC assessment consortia* (CRESST Report 823). Los Angeles, CA: UCLA National Center for Research on Evaluation, Standards, and Student Testing.

Herman, J. L., Osmundson, E., Ayala, C., Schneider, S., & Timms, M. (2006). *The nature and impact of teachers' formative assessment practices* (CRESST Report 703). Los Angeles, CA: UCLA National Center for Research on Evaluation, Standards, and Student Testing.

Hosp, J. (2011). Using assessment data to make decisions about teaching and learning. In K. Harris, S. Graham, & T. Urdan (Eds.), *APA educational psychology handbook* (pp. 87–110). Washington, DC: American Psychological Association.

Kane, M. (2006). Validation. In R. L. Brennan (Ed.), *Educational measurement* (4th ed., pp. 18–64). Westport, CT: Praeger.

Kane, M. T. (2013) Validating the interpretations and uses of test scores. *Journal of Educational Measurement, 50*(1), 1–73.

Kingston, N., & Nash, B. (2012). Formative assessment: A meta-analysis and a call for research. *Educational Measurement: Issues and Practice, 30*(4), 28–37.

Maloney, A., & Confrey, J. (2013). *A learning trajectory framework for the common core: Turnonccmath for interpretation, instructional planning, and collaboration*. Presentation at the Association of Mathematics Teacher Educators Conference, Orlando, FL.

Mandinach, E. B. (2012). A perfect time for data use: Using data-driven decision making to inform practice. *Educational Psychologist, 47*(2), 71–85.

Mandinach, E. B., Friedman, J. M., & Gummer, E. S. (2015). How can schools of education help to build educators' capacity to use data: A systemic view of the issue. *Teachers College Record, 117*(5). Retrieved from http://www.tcrecord.org/PrintContent.asp?ContentID=17850 (accessed March 13, 2015).

Mandinach, E. B., & Gummer, E. S. (2013a). Defining data literacy: A report on a convening of experts. *Journal of Educational Research and Policy Studies, 13*(2), 6–28.

Mandinach, E. B., & Gummer, E. S. (2013b). A systemic view of implementing data literacy into educator preparation. *Educational Researcher, 42*(1), 30–37.

Mandinach, E. B., Honey, M., Light, D., & Brunner, C. (2008). A conceptual framework for data-driven decision making. In E. B. Mandinach & M. Honey (Eds.), *Data-driven school improvement: Linking data and learning* (pp. 13–31). New York, NY: Teachers College Press.

Mandinach, E. B., & Jackson, S. S. (2012). *Transforming teaching and learning through data-driven decision making.* Thousand Oaks, CA: Corwin.

McManus, S. (2008). *Attributes of effective formative assessment.* Washington, DC: CCSSO.

Means, B., Padilla, C., & Gallagher, L. (2010). *Use of education data at the local level: From accountability to instructional improvement.* Washington, DC: U.S. Department of Education, Office of Planning, Evaluation, and Policy Development.

Messick, S. (1989). Validity. In R. L. Linn (Ed.), *Educational measurement* (3rd ed., pp. 13–103). New York, NY: American Council on Education and Macmillan.

Mislevy, R. J., & Haertel, G. D. (2006). Implications of evidence-centered design for educational testing. *Educational Measurement: Issues and Practice, 25*(4), 6–20.

Mislevy, R. J., & Riconscente, M. M. (2005). *Evidence-centered assessment design: Layers, structure, and terminology* (PADI Technical Report 9). Menlo Park, CA: SRI, International.

Mosher, F. A. (2011). *The role of learning progressions in standards-based education reform.* CPRE Policy Briefs, RB-52. Philadelphia, PA: University of Pennsylvania, Graduate School of Education.

National Council of Teachers of Mathematics. (1995). *Assessment standards for school mathematics.* Reston, VA: National Council of Teachers of Mathematics.

National Research Council. (2012). *A framework for K-12 science education.* Washington, DC: National Academies Press.

OECD. (2005). *Formative assessment: Improving learning in secondary classrooms.* Center for Educational Research and Innovation. Retrieved from http://oecd.org (accessed February 20, 2015).

Partnership for Assessment of Readiness for College and Careers. (2013). *The PARCC assessment.* Retrieved from http://parcconline.org/parcc-assessment (accessed February 20, 2015).

Pellegrino, J. W. (2010). Technology and formative assessment. In P. Peterson, E. Baker, & B. McGaw (Eds.), *International encyclopedia of education* (Vol. 8; pp. 42–47). Oxford: Elsevier.

Pellegrino, J. W., Chudowsky, N., & Glaser, R. (2001). *Knowing what students know: The science and design of educational assessment.* Washington, DC: National Academy Press.

Pellegrino, J. W., & Quellmalz, E. S. (2010). Perspectives on the integration of technology and assessment. *Journal of Research on Technology in Education, 43*(2), 119–134.

Popham, W. J. (2008). *Transformative assessment in action.* Alexandria, VA: ASCD.

Popham, W. J. (2011). *Transformative assessment in action: An inside look at applying the process.* Alexandria, VA: ASCD.

Quellmalz, E. S. (2013). *Technology to support next-generation classroom formative assessment for learning.* San Francisco, CA: WestEd.

Quellmalz, E. S., & Pellegrino, J. W. (2009). Technology and testing. *Science, 323,* 75–79.

Quellmalz, E. S., Timms, M. J., Buckley, B. C., Davenport, J., Loveland, M., & Silberglitt, M. D. (2011). 21st century dynamic assessment. In M. Mayrath, J. Clarke-Midura, D. H. Robinson, & G. Schraw (Eds.), *Technology-based assessments for 21st century skills: Theoretical and practical implications from modern research* (pp. 55–89). Charlotte, NC: Information Age Publishing.

Quellmalz, E. S., Timms, M. J., Silberglitt, M. D., & Buckley, B. C. (2012). Science assessments for all: Integrating science simulations into balanced state science assessment systems. *Journal of Research in Science Teaching, 49*(3), 363–393.

Rich, C. C., Harrington, H., Him, J., & West, B. (2008). *Automated essay scoring in state formative and summative writing assessment.* Paper presented at the annual meeting of the American Educational Research Association, New York, NY.

Rodosky, R. (2009). Introduction. *Research & Evaluation Brief, 1*(3). Louisville, KY: Jefferson County Public Schools: Department of Accountability, Research & Planning.

Ruiz-Primo, M. A., & Li, M. (2013). Examining formative feedback in the classroom context: New research perspectives. In J. M. McMillan (Ed.), *Handbook of research on classroom assessment* (pp. 215–232). Thousand Oaks, CA: Sage.

Shavelson, R. J., Black, P. J., Wiliam, D., & Coffey, J. (2007). *On linking formative and summative functions in the design of large-scale assessment systems.* Stanford, CA: Stanford University School of Education, Stanford Education Assessment Lab.

Shavelson, R. J., Yin, Y., Furtak, E. M., Ruiz-Primo, M. A., Ayala, C. C., Young, D. B., et al. (2008). On the role and impact of formative assessment on science inquiry teaching and learning. In J. Coffey, R. Douglas, & C. Stearns (Eds.), *Assessing science learning* (pp. 21–36). Arlington, VA: NSTA Press.

Shepard, L. A. (2000). The role of assessment in a learning culture. *Educational Researcher, 29*(7), 4–14.

Shulman, L. S. (1986). Those who understand: Knowledge growth in teaching. *Educational Researcher, 15*(2). 4–14.

Shute, V. J. (2008). Focus on formative feedback. *Review of Educational Research, 78*(1), 153–189.

Shute, V. J., & Kim, Y. J. (2013). Formative and stealth assessment. In J. M. Spector, M. D. Merrill, J. Elen, & M. J. Bishop (Eds.), *Handbook of research on educational communications and technology* (4th ed.). New York, NY: Lawrence Erlbaum Associates.

Shute, V. J., & Ventura, M. (2013). *Measuring and supporting learning in games: Stealth assessment.* Cambridge, MA: The MIT Press.

Smarter Balanced Assessment Consortium. (2013). *Smarter balanced assessments.* Retrieved from http://www.smarterbalanced.org/smarter-balanced-assessments/ (accessed February 20, 2015).

Snow, R. E., & Mandinach, E. B. (1999). *Integrating instruction and assessment for classrooms and courses: Programs and prospects for research* (Special Monograph). Princeton, NJ: Educational Testing Service.

Stiggins, R. J. (2002). Assessment crisis: The absence of assessment for learning. *Phi Delta Kappan, 83*(10), 758–765.

Stiggins, R. (2005). From formative assessment to assessment FOR learning: A path to success on standards-based skills. *Phi Delta Kappan, 85*(4), 324–238.

Sztajn, P., Confrey, J., Holt Wilson, P., & Edgington, C. (2012). Learning trajectory based instruction: Toward a theory of teaching. *Educational Researcher, 41*(5), 147–156.

Trumbull, E., & Gerzon, N. (2013). *Professional development on formative assessment.* San Francisco, CA: WestEd.

Trumbull, E., & Lash. A. (2013). *Understanding formative assessment: Insights from learning theory and measurement theory.* San Francisco, CA: WestEd.

Weiner, B. (1986). *An attributional theory of motivation and emotion.* New York, NY: Springer-Verlag.

Wiliam, D., & Leahy, S. (2007). A theoretical foundation for formative assessment. In J. H. McMillan (Ed.), *Formative classroom assessment: Research, theory, and practice* (pp. 29–42). New York, NY: Teachers College Press.

Wiliam, D., Lee, C., Harrison, C., & Black, P. J. (2004). Teachers' developing assessment for learning: Impact on student involvement. *Assessment in Education: Principles, Policy, and Practice, 11*(1), 49–65.

Wise, B. (2014). *Policies and capacity enablers and barriers for learning analytics.* Paper presented at the annual meeting of the American Educational Research Association, Philadelphia, PA.

Zapata-Rivera, D., & Bauer, M. (2011). Exploring the role of games in educational assessment. In M. C. Mayrath, J. Clarke-Midura, D. Robinson, & G. Shraw (Eds.) *Technology-based assessments for 21st century skills: Theoretical and practical implications from modern research* (pp. 147–169). Charlotte, NC: Information Age Publishing.

# 30

# Being a Teacher

## Efficacy, Emotions, and Interpersonal
## Relationships in the Classroom

*Lynley H. Anderman*
The Ohio State University

*Robert M. Klassen*
University of York, United Kingdom

Teachers' professional lives are complex and demanding. In addition to enacting mandated curricula and being held accountable for students' progress in learning and performance, teachers also are answerable to parents and taxpayers who may have differing expectations. Finally, teachers are responsible for creating an orderly classroom environment that promotes the development of students with often widely varying backgrounds, talents, and needs. In this chapter, we discuss aspects of teachers' work as it takes place in the classroom, during the act of instruction. In particular, we focus on research in K-12 contexts rather than in higher-education classes (e.g., Menges & Austin, 2001) or informal learning contexts (e.g., Bell, Lewenstein, Shouse, & Feder, 2009). Even setting aside other dimensions of their professional lives, including activities that occur outside the classroom and responsibilities in enacting policy requirements, teachers' work is multifaceted and fluid. As teachers work to provide instruction, maintain student engagement, and monitor student progress, a range of cognitive, affective, and social processes interacts. In the first *Handbook of Educational Psychology,* Schuell (1996) noted:

> teacher effects are multidimensional. Although cognitive processes typically receive the most attention, cognition neither occurs in isolation nor is it the only psychological system that influences both the content and noncognitive outcomes that students acquire from an educational experience. Emotional, motivational, attitudinal, cultural, and other affective and social factors operate simultaneously with cognitive factors and play a critical role in determining what is learned. (p. 727)

We agree that teaching is multidimensional and complex. In particular, we conceptualize teachers' work as a dynamic system in which teachers' subject and pedagogical knowledge along with their *inner lives*—their emotions, engagement, and sense of efficacy—influence their interactions with students. These interactions, in turn, contribute to the ongoing development of teachers' knowledge and inner lives in a reciprocal manner. Teachers' working lives are not static, but are subject to change through the influence of external factors such as school and social contexts, the passage of time, and by the nature of teacher–student interactions. Thus, this system represents a constantly changing set of interacting influences that reflects the reciprocal relationship between the teacher, the teaching and social environment, and the student. This conceptualization is represented graphically in Figure 30.1.

The ways that teachers carry out the day-to-day tasks of teaching are influenced by the knowledge they possess, and the beliefs they hold about the nature of what constitutes successful teaching. Bransford, Darling-Hammond, and LePage (2005) suggest a framework of teacher knowledge that includes three intersecting areas, viz., knowledge of: (a) learners and their development; (b) subject matter and curriculum; and (c) teaching, pedagogy, assessment, and classroom management. The category of teacher beliefs encompasses a range of beliefs (e.g., see Woolfolk Hoy, Davis, & Pape, 2006), such as beliefs about students, including their learning and development, expectations for success, and epistemological beliefs (Buehl & Fives, 2009). Teacher efficacy, that is, judgments about individual and collective capabilities to influence student outcomes (e.g., Bandura, 1997), represents teachers' beliefs about the self or group rather than beliefs about students or the nature of teaching itself. Teacher emotions in the classroom include stress, anger, and burnout as well as their engagement, enjoyment, and enthusiasm (Schutz & Pekrun,

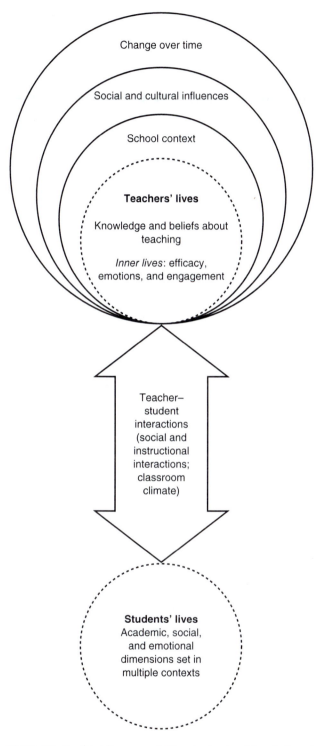

Change over time

Social and cultural influences

School context

**Teachers' lives**

Knowledge and beliefs about teaching

*Inner lives*: efficacy, emotions, and engagement

Teacher–student interactions (social and instructional interactions; classroom climate)

**Students' lives**
Academic, social, and emotional dimensions set in multiple contexts

**Figure 30.1** Teachers' lives are nested in school and social contexts, and change over time through interactions with students.

2007). Finally, teachers' social relationships and interactions with students include dyadic, interpersonal relationships, instructional interactions, and the social and managerial climate the teacher helps to create in the classroom (Anderman, Freeman & Mueller, 2007; Hamre et al., 2013).

To date, some of these areas of study have received considerably more attention than others. In particular, research on teachers' knowledge and beliefs has been conducted

for more than 30 years (Munby, Russell, & Martin, 2001), whereas the study of teachers' emotion has emerged relatively recently (e.g., Schutz & Pekrun, 2007). This pattern is illustrated by the coverage of related topics in the previous two editions of this *Handbook of Educational Psychology*. In the first edition, edited by Berliner and Calfee (1996), chapters were included on teachers' knowledge and beliefs (Calderhead, 1996) and the role of knowledge and beliefs in teacher education (Borko & Putnam, 1996). The second *Handbook* edition, edited by Alexander and Winne (2006), included a chapter specifically dedicated to teacher knowledge and beliefs (Woolfolk Hoy et al., 2006), which included discussion of beliefs at multiple levels, including teacher efficacy. In addition, Brophy (2006) provided an overview of observational studies of classroom teaching that included studies of teacher cognition, classroom climate, and teacher expectations. Finally, the study of teachers' knowledge and cognition has been a particular focus in teacher education. Teachers' knowledge and the role of teacher education in promoting and developing that knowledge have been featured in the *Handbook of Research on Teaching* (e.g., Munby et al., 2001) and the *Handbook of Research in Teacher Education* (e.g., Carter, 1990). Furthermore, the text *Preparing Teachers for a Changing World: What Teachers Should Learn and be Able to do* (Darling-Hammond & Bransford, 2005), sponsored by the National Academy of Education, echoes the emphasis on teacher knowledge and cognition, with less consideration of topics such as teacher efficacy, emotion, and relationships.

Since the publication of the second edition of this volume (Alexander & Winne, 2006), however, these latter topics have been the focus of considerable activity in terms of both empirical research and theoretical development. In this chapter, therefore, we discuss the areas of teacher efficacy and collective efficacy, teacher emotions in the classroom, including their motivation and engagement or experience of burnout (i.e., emotional exhaustion, depersonalization, and reduced personal efficacy), and finally their interpersonal relationships and interactions with students. Although we consider these topics separately, it is important to reiterate that all of these processes occur as part of a complex dynamic system, reciprocally influencing one another, during instruction.

### Teacher Efficacy Research

Teacher efficacy continues to be a fertile area of research. The previous *Handbook* considered how teaching experience influenced efficacy beliefs, how efficacy operates for specific tasks, like science teaching, and how collective efficacy develops in a school setting. Teacher efficacy is associated with positive outcomes: a recent meta-analysis (Klassen & Tze, 2014) shows teacher efficacy to be robustly associated with externally measured teaching effectiveness (defined as student achievement or observation ratings of teaching). The relationship between teacher efficacy and observed teaching performance ($d = 0.58$, $p < 0.01$) was considerably stronger than the relationship between teacher personality and observed teaching performance ($d = 0.16$, $p < 0.05$). As evidence has continued to build about how teacher efficacy is associated with teaching and learning, some new areas of focus are emerging.

One area of interest is how teacher efficacy develops from the period of pre-service teacher education through to later career stages. In the early years of research on teachers' motivation, investigators treated teachers' motivation beliefs as static, reflecting the tendency of early educational psychology research to overlook the effects of contextual factors on motivation, such as the passage of time. However, not all disciplines have taken an *atemporal* look at motivation: research outside the field of education suggests that the motivation beliefs of workers are influenced by career stage (e.g., Kooij, de Lange, Jansen, & Dikkers, 2008), and fluctuate according to the interaction of changes in both the worker and the work environment over time. Bandura (1997) hypothesized that self-efficacy remains relatively stable once established, but it is likely that teacher motivation develops with the passage of time, much as the motivation of workers in other fields changes over the career span.

Efficacy beliefs are conditional, dynamic, and reflective of environmental changes and challenges (Bandura, 2012; see Chapter 11, this volume). Examining the relationship between teaching experience and teachers' self-efficacy suggests that teacher efficacy develops over time, although the change may not follow a linear pattern. A number of studies have shown that teacher efficacy increases during the teaching practicum (e.g., Fives, Hamman, & Olivarez, 2007; Knoblauch & Woolfolk Hoy, 2008), although the pattern of increasing self-efficacy may not be linear once professional practice begins. For example, Woolfolk Hoy and Burke Spero (2005) saw self-efficacy increase during teacher education and the practicum, followed by a *reality shock*-inspired decrease in the first year of professional practice. Wolters and Daugherty (2007) examined changes in self-efficacy during professional practice, and found modest positive effects of teaching experience on self-efficacy for instructional strategies and self-efficacy for classroom management, but no effect of experience on self-efficacy for student engagement. Klassen and Chiu (2010) examined teachers' self-efficacy across career stages and found that years of experience were linked to forms of self-efficacy in a non-linear, inverted-U, curvilinear pattern, with efficacy increasing to a peak at about 23 years of experience, and then receding in late career. Changes in teacher efficacy may be influenced not only by teaching experience, but also by the psychosocial context of the work environment (e.g., amount of autonomy and quality of social and emotional interactions).

The myriad influences of efficacy beliefs also vary by cultural context. A recent study by Malinen et al. (2013) examined teachers' efficacy for teaching in inclusive classrooms using a large sample of practicing teachers from China, Finland, and South Africa. Results showed a strong effect of past experience on teacher efficacy across all settings, but particular contexts influenced how efficacy beliefs were experienced. For Chinese teachers, teacher type (mainstream or special education) was a strong influence on efficacy beliefs; for Finnish teachers the content of teacher training was influential; and for South African teachers, past interactions with persons with disabilities strongly influenced self-efficacy beliefs. Teacher efficacy is influenced by differences in cultural beliefs, expectations of what comprises effective teaching practice, and the background and diversity of student populations.

*Teachers' collective efficacy.* Theorists and policy makers increasingly conceptualize teaching as a collaborative endeavor (Hargreaves & Fullan, 2012), although, in practice, much of a teacher's work is performed in isolation. Teachers often plan their teaching or face student problems individually, with little time and opportunity to consult about immediate problems and issues. Collaboration is considered to be essential for success in almost all professions—with teaching no exception; however, observations of teachers in schools show that collaboration is neither embraced by all teachers nor, by itself, a guarantee of effective practice. The benefits of teacher collaboration can be multiplied by building *collective efficacy*; i.e., teachers' beliefs in their shared capabilities to accomplish valued goals through working collectively (Bandura, 1997). The degree to which teachers develop and nurture their collective efficacy is a critical factor influencing educational outcomes.

Research investigating teachers' collective efficacy has grown at a slower rate than research exploring teachers' self-efficacy, perhaps slowed by measurement inconsistencies (see Klassen, Tze, Betts, & Gordon, 2011, for a discussion of problems with collective efficacy measurement). Two recent studies have investigated aspects of student problem behavior and teachers' collective efficacy. In Norway, Sørlie and Torsheim (2011) used a two-wave longitudinal study to examine how collective efficacy predicted teacher perceptions of problem behavior over time. They found that Time 1 school-level collective efficacy predicted severe and less severe problem behavior at Time 2 (6 months later), and that the relationship was reciprocal; that is, that problem behavior at Time 1 also predicted Time 2 collective efficacy. The authors concluded that promoting perceptions of collective capability in school staff is one important way to positively influence school culture and lessen the negative influence of student problem behavior. To understand how best to achieve this result, Sørlie and Torsheim recommend further longitudinal studies on interventions aimed at raising teachers' collective efficacy beliefs.

In the United Kingdom, Gibbs and Powell (2011) investigated the relationship between teachers' self-efficacy, collective efficacy, and the rate of student expulsion from school. None of the self-efficacy variables was related to expulsion rate, but collective efficacy to address external influences was significantly related to the number of students excluded during the school year. The authors suggested that, in schools where teachers are confident that they can address adverse influences of home and community, fewer children are excluded due to problem behavior. These two studies together point out that teachers' collective efficacy is associated with school-wide student behavior patterns. Professional development programs that target building school-level efficacy beliefs, possibly through the pathway of explicitly and collectively targeting the four sources of efficacy (e.g., Ross & Bruce, 2007), may provide a productive way to address whole-school student behavior issues.

## Teacher Emotion in the Classroom

Research on teacher emotions has generated a great deal of attention in the last decade, continuing the emphasis in educational psychology on teacher well-being reflected by the research on teacher burnout conducted in the 1980s (e.g., Kyriacou, 1987). Chang (2009) provided an updated review that proposed a renewed emphasis on antecedents of burnout, and a greater focus on emotion regulation. Whereas early work on teachers' emotion focused on relatively straightforward models of burnout—e.g., that burnout was the direct result of emotional, physical, and attitudinal exhaustion developed from poor coping responses to stress (Kyriacou, 2001)—the recent surge in teachers' emotion research represents a more nuanced, multifaceted, and contextualized view of emotions built on stronger explanatory frameworks. An important recent development has been to conceptualize the transmission of emotions from teacher to student, thereby providing the hypothesis that teachers' emotional states and behavior influence student outcomes through their effects on student emotional states and behavior.

The range of teacher emotion research includes the study of factors such as enjoyment, anger, anxiety, and enthusiasm in the classroom. Frenzel, Goetz, Stephens, and Jacob (2009) conceptualized teachers' emotions as "achievement emotions," i.e., emotions that result from judgments of perceived success or failure in the attainment of instructional goals. In particular, Frenzel and colleagues focused on three emotions—enjoyment, anger, and anxiety—most experienced in daily life and prominent in research on teacher emotion, and traced the link between these emotions on teacher cognition and behavior. Of these three emotions, enjoyment was found to be experienced significantly more often by teachers than either anger or anxiety, with primary-school teachers experiencing higher mean levels of enjoyment than teachers in secondary schools. In particular, emotions experienced during teaching may influence the effectiveness of instruction, especially when these emotions are repeatedly experienced by teachers during social interactions with students inside and outside the classroom.

The importance of research on teacher emotions is underscored by the finding that the emotions teachers experience can be passed on to students. Frenzel, Goetz, Lüdtke, Pekrun, and Sutton (2009) tested the transmission of enjoyment teachers experience while teaching mathematics to the enjoyment students experience in math class. Using a social cognitive framework, the authors proposed a social perception model in which teachers communicate value and enjoyment of tasks through overt enthusiasm, but also through implicit hints about motivational orientation. In their sample of early-adolescent mathematics students and their teachers, teacher

enthusiasm mediated the relationship between teacher and student enjoyment, suggesting that observable teacher emotion-related behavior makes a difference in student emotional experiences. The result that emotions can be contagious is important because it suggests a pathway through which teachers can influence the emotional lives of students.

Teacher enthusiasm is an emotion easily noted by students, but it may not operate as a one-dimensional construct. Kunter, Frenzel, Nagy, Baumert, and Pekrun (2011) tested the dimensionality and context specificity of teacher enthusiasm, finding two dimensions—enthusiasm for teaching and enthusiasm for the subject—that varied according to contextual classroom variables. The two dimensions of teaching enthusiasm may hold implications for educating new teachers, some of whom may hold great enthusiasm for a subject, but not for teaching, and with others who are enthusiastic about the act of teaching, but less enthusiastic about specific subjects. Importantly, teaching enthusiasm may be a better predictor of teaching success than subject-matter enthusiasm (Kunter et al., 2011).

***Emotion regulation.*** Teachers often find themselves in challenging classroom situations where regulating the emotions they experience may be desirable. Sutton and Harper (2009) noted that emotion regulation consists of modifying cognitive processes (e.g., trying to displace blame targets), action tendencies (e.g., choosing not to express visible facial expressions when angry or when disappointed in a student's response), and even physiological tendencies (e.g., regulating heart rate and breathing patterns when upset). Three sets of beliefs have been proposed to explain teachers' emotion regulation: goal setting for emotion regulation, which consists of choosing to emphasize abstract or longer-term goals in place of short-term satisfaction (i.e., giving in to feelings of frustration); perceived effectiveness, referring to teachers' choice to override negative emotional experiences in place of behaviors that result in positive outcomes that reflect teaching effectiveness; and efficacy of emotion regulation, referring to the level of confidence a teacher has that negative emotions can be reduced and positive emotions can be communicated to students. Teachers reported emotion regulation strategies including antecedent-focused strategies, whereby trigger points are noted and managed, and response-focused strategies that included suppression of emotions (e.g., counting to ten), or reappraising emotion-laden experiences in search for more effective strategies and responses.

For many teachers, classroom management issues provoke high levels of negative emotions, necessitating the need to regulate these unpleasant emotions during teaching. Tsouloupas and colleagues (2010) found that, although teachers' perceptions of student misbehavior were directly associated with burnout, the emotion regulation strategies of cognitive reappraisal and expression suppression did not mediate the relationship as expected. Self-efficacy to manage student misbehavior did lessen the impact of perceptions of student misbehavior on feelings of burnout, with the authors proposing the need for professional development focused on developing management strategies. More recently,

Chang (2013) proposed and tested models of emotion regulation, appraisals of disruptive behavior, and burnout. She found that the intensity of unpleasant teacher emotions, such as anger or frustration, from even a single negative classroom incident was significantly related to feelings of burnout. Low problem-solving efficacy by teachers led to higher levels of frustration but problem-focused coping strategies reduced the effects of negative classroom incidents on feelings of burnout.

### Positive psychology's response to teacher burnout: Teacher engagement.

Positive psychology's influence on educational psychology can be seen in recent studies of work engagement, the flip side of burnout. Defined as a "positive, fulfilling, work-related state of mind that is characterized by vigor, dedication, and absorption" (Schaufeli, Bakker, & Salanova, 2006, p. 702), work engagement has received considerable research attention in general workplace settings over the last decade. Workers who are engaged devote energy, time, and effort to work tasks (the *vigor* component), view their work as significant and meaningful (the *dedication* component), and fully concentrate on tasks when at work (the *absorption* component). Schaufeli et al.'s *Utrecht Work Engagement Scale* (UWES) is perhaps the most frequently used measure of work engagement (Bakker, Albrecht, & Leiter, 2011), including with teachers. A recent cross-cultural validation study of this self-report instrument (Klassen et al., 2012a) found scores on it were related to teachers' job satisfaction across five countries—Australia, Canada, China, Indonesia, and Oman. The factor structure of the measure was not invariant across settings, however, with either one-factor or three-factor models fitting the data depending on country context. In addition, the authors noted that the kind of engagement conceptualized in the UWES did not map well on to the kind of work done by teachers in schools, and may not adequately capture how teachers experience engagement in school settings.

In response, a new teaching-responsive engagement measure—the Engaged Teachers Scale (ETS)—has been designed and validated (Klassen, Yerdelen, & Durksen, 2013) with four engagement factors—cognitive, emotional, social (students), and social (colleagues). The advantages of the ETS are that its items are contextualized in classroom examples, and its theoretical foundation is based on recent advances in engagement research (e.g., Rich, Lepine, & Crawford, 2010). The conceptualization of engagement in the ETS acknowledges social relationships with students as an important source of engagement, as well as the more typical relationships with colleagues seen in business-based models of engagement. However, the measure has not yet been tested in many contexts.

### Engagement over time.

Cross-sectional studies of teacher engagement do not provide information on fluctuations over time. All teachers have periods during their careers—a few minutes during a lesson, certain hours during a difficult day, or even longer periods of time during difficult career phases—where engagement fluctuates, but static measures do not capture these fluctuations. A few researchers have begun to study changes in engagement using multiple time points. Bakker and Bal (2010) measured weekly work engagement among a sample of novice teachers in the Netherlands, and found a relationship between variations in job resources (i.e., social support, performance feedback, supervision, and learning opportunities) and weekly reports of work engagement. Malmberg, Hagger, and Webster (2013) used electronic personal digital assistants to collect questionnaire data on 43 teachers' class-specific engagement during 1,055 individual lessons over a 2-week period. Situation-specific engagement varied between teachers and across classes, and was predicted by teachers' experience, level of domain-specific self-efficacy, and levels of student engagement.

Although teachers' engagement may fluctuate over time, most of the research to date has captured the constructs with self-report measures, and usually with a limited number of time points. Existing approaches such as experience sampling methods and new technologies such as mobile eye trackers (e.g., Jarodzka, van Gog, Dorr, Scheiter, & Gerjets, 2013) provide multiple data points of teachers' behavior and psychological states (engagement, emotions, motivation), which in turn can be linked with subjective measures of engagement. Specialist intraindividual analytic approaches not yet common in educational psychology are capable of describing real-life fluctuations in classrooms that can be measured with experience sampling or diary approaches. Analyzing the patterns of teacher–student interactions or emotional states during the course of the day provides an understanding of the shape of change that might fall outside the usual pre-specified change patterns (i.e., linear, quadratic, cubic) that are generated from conventional analysis approaches. Time-varying effect modeling (Tan, Shiyko, Li, Li, & Dierker, 2012) allows researchers to describe and predict irregular patterns of change that often characterize teachers' lives, and provides a better understanding of how teachers' psychological states change, often rapidly, over even short periods of time.

## Changes in the Inner Lives of Teachers across Career Stages

Teachers' self-efficacy, emotions, and engagement change over time (e.g., Bakker & Bal, 2010; Klassen & Chiu, 2010), but a consistent and coherent theoretical explanation of these temporal changes is yet to be developed. In addition, more empirical work is needed to test how the inner lives of teachers develop and change across career stages, and in particular, in late-career stages. Teachers' cognitive and emotional responses to student behavior, policy changes, and the daily demands inherent in the act of teaching evolve as careers progress (Huberman, 1989). According to Huberman, the characteristic reaction of novice teachers to early classroom experiences is that of survival ("Can I actually do this job?") and discovery ("I really love/hate this job"). Not surprisingly, cognitive and emotional states experienced by teachers are influenced by career stage. Much of the research on teachers' emotional and motivational states, however, has tended to ignore the age and career stage of respondents, or to focus primarily on teachers at the beginning stages of their careers (e.g., Richardson, Watt, & Devos, 2013).

Building on Huberman's work, Day and Gu (2009) found that a majority of teachers in mid-career (i.e., 8–23 years of teaching) experience increases in motivation and commitment (i.e., psychological attachment to their profession). In contrast, increased proportions of teachers in later career stages (24+ years of experience) report declining levels of motivation (i.e., feeling disenchanted, fatigued, trapped). But teachers in the late-career stage do not invariably experience decreasing engagement and motivation. For example, Veldman, van Tartwijk, Brekelmans, and Wubbels (2013) found that, for veteran teachers with high engagement and satisfaction, the perceived quality of teacher–student relationships played a central role in the positive views of their work; interestingly, the perception of quality of the relationship did not have to be shared by their students.

Evidence from research conducted outside educational psychology suggests that age interacts with emotional and motivational states over the course of a career (Kooij et al., 2008), although it is not clear how and why these changes occur. Kooij et al. propose that age-related factors—chronological age, physical health, self-perception, social perception, and skills obsolescence—had a negative impact on the motivation beliefs of older workers, and that motivation and emotions were influenced by an interaction of age-related factors. For instance, physical and mental health-related declines may be related to a deterioration of self-concept or changes in weighting of work- and leisure-related values, but stereotyped perceptions of peers also influence workers' motivation, and result in lowered affect, reduced skills, motivation, and opportunities for promotion. For late-career teachers, lower levels of motivation beliefs may be influenced not only by biological and psychological changes related to chronological age, but by student and peer perceptions of declining competence influenced by stereotyped beliefs about aging. Thus, age-related changes in efficacy, emotions, and interpersonal relationships are influenced not only by chronological age, but also by the psychosocial interactions and expectations of colleagues and students. As noted by Veldman et al. (2013), however, the quality of teacher–student relationships may hold the key for the successful passage through teachers' career stages.

### Teacher–Student Relationships

Teachers' relationships with their students have been the focus of a considerable body of research during the past two decades. At this time, it is well established that the nature of those relationships and of teachers' interactions with students plays an important role in shaping a range of student outcomes, including motivation and engagement, emotional well-being, school readiness, and academic learning and performance (e.g., Cornelius-White, 2007; Davis, 2003; Juvonen, 2006; Roorda, Koomen, Spilt, & Oort, 2011; Wentzel, 2010; Williford, Maier, Downer, Pianta, & Howes, 2013). Furthermore, there is emerging evidence that positive relationships and a sense of connectedness with students

may also be important for teachers' level of engagement and sense of well-being (Klassen, Perry, & Frenzel, 2012b). Teacher–student relationships are multifaceted, serve multiple roles, and have been studied from a range of theoretical perspectives. As noted by Davis (2003), the definition of a "high-quality" teacher–student relationship differs depending on those theoretical frames and the particular focus under study. In addition to interactions that focus on the delivery and explanation of curriculum content, teachers' interactions with students can be conceptualized as serving at least three important functions: (a) forming and maintaining an interpersonal, dyadic relationship with individual students; (b) fostering and managing a positive climate in the social context of the classroom; and (c) acting as a socializing agent, communicating and reinforcing societal norms, values, and expectations to students. Each of these functions creates and sustains a different aspect of the teacher–student relationship; and, although separate, these functions also inevitably overlap and intersect. Given this chapter's primary focus on teachers' beliefs and emotions in the context of instruction, we limit our discussion to the first two of these dimensions. Comprehensive reviews of teachers' role as socialization agents are available elsewhere (e.g., Evertson & Weinstein, 2006; Wentzel & Looney, 2007).

***Teachers' interpersonal relationships with students.*** Research that focuses on the nature of interpersonal relationships teachers have with individual students includes topics such as social support from teachers (e.g., Turner, Gray, Anderman, Dawson, & Anderman, 2013; Wentzel, 1998), closeness or conflict in the relationship (e.g., Hamre & Pianta, 2007; Ladd, Birch & Buhs, 1999), teachers' expectations for behavior and achievement (Wentzel, 2010), teacher control (e.g., Brekelmans, Mainhard, den Brok, & Wubbels, 2011) and, for young children, the degree of dependence or independence students exhibit in their relationships with teachers (e.g., Burchinal, Peisner-Feinberg, Pianta, & Howes, 2002; Pianta, Steinberg, & Rollins, 1995).

Much of the research on the affective quality of teacher–student relationships is grounded in attachment theory (e.g., Ainsworth, 1989; Bowlby, 1979, 1998) and, thus, has a developmental emphasis. Based in research on young children's relationships with their parents, the attachment perspective assumes that those early attachment relationships form the basis for future relationships with other adults, including teachers. This perspective on teacher–student relationships places considerable emphasis on the characteristics and developmental history the individual child brings into the classroom. Those who have enjoyed securely attached relationships with parents and caregivers are set up to have high-quality relationships with their teachers. In this conceptualization, teachers' perceptions of their relationships with individual students seem to reflect their interpretations of and responses to student characteristics and, perhaps, similarities between the teacher and student. Longitudinal studies that examine young children's adjustment to school, conceptualized in terms of their cognitive and social-emotional development, have established the importance of closeness, dependency, and conflict in their relationships with teachers. For example, Pianta et al. (1995) found that students with warm, close, communicative relationships with their kindergarten teachers were better adjusted in second grade than were those who had angry, dependent relationships. Furthermore, conflictual relationships with teachers appear to negatively influence students' academic gains over time (Crosnoe et al., 2010).

Perhaps because of an emphasis on attachment models, much of the research on teacher–student relationships has focused on preschool and elementary-aged students and reflects an assumption that younger students are more strongly influenced by their relationships with teachers than are older students. Roorda et al. (2011) examined this assumption in a meta-analysis of 99 studies of the associations between teacher–student relationships and students' engagement and achievement. Roorda et al. distinguished between positive (close, supportive, trusting) and negative (conflictual, neglectful, rejecting) relationships. Their results suggest that the effects of positive relationships on both engagement and achievement were stronger in secondary-school students than those in elementary grades, whereas the reverse was true for the effects of negative relationships. This finding has important implications for supporting students' academic success. For secondary students, the importance of positive relationships with teachers must be considered in light of other studies that suggest such positive relationships become less common as students move through school (e.g., Furrer & Skinner, 2003; Midgley, Feldlaufer, & Eccles, 1989). Because secondary students interact with multiple different teachers each day, and spend less time with each, the opportunities to develop close positive relationships are reduced. In addition, differences in the design and requirements of teacher preparation programs for secondary compared to elementary levels may include less emphasis on student development and affective aspects of teaching practice (Patrick, Anderman, Shalter, & Duffin, 2011).

For elementary-aged students, the stronger effects of negative teacher–student relationships on both engagement and academic achievement emphasize the importance of prompt intervention into conflictual or unsupportive teacher–student relationships. Roorda et al. (2011) discuss the possibility that negative teacher–student relationships may have a cumulative effect over time, influencing and being influenced by students' low achievement and externalizing behaviors. Helping teachers of young children avoid the cascading effects of negative relationships, behavior, and achievement may have the potential to prevent students' later disengagement from school (Finn, 1989).

### Differences in teachers' relationships with students.
Given the significance of high-quality teacher–student relationships, emerging evidence that the characteristics of those relationships tend to be somewhat stable for individual students, across different teachers and years, is particularly important. Jerome, Hamre, and Pianta (2008) examined teacher reports of closeness and conflict with individual students from kindergarten through sixth grade. Greater stability

in scores was found for conflict than for closeness, with average levels of conflict peaking in Grades 3 and 4, then declining somewhat. Initial levels in kindergarten were partially predicted by student-level variables (e.g., externalizing behavior, entering academic skills) and by family and demographic variables. For example, teachers reported greater conflict in their relationships with: (a) African American children, as compared to all other ethnicities; (b) those who spent more time in childcare; and (c) children whose mothers' parenting was rated as less sensitive, based on the average of standardized observations conducted by researchers when the children were 6, 15, 24, 36, and 54 months of age. Maternal sensitivity in this research represented a multidimensional construct including affective expressiveness and support, cognitive stimulation, and provision of autonomy. Similarly, teachers reported feeling less of a close connection with boys, compared to girls, and with those from home environments that were rated lower on a home observation measure (including physical, experiential, and relational components) and with lower academic scores. It should be noted that the measures of maternal sensitivity and quality of home environment were significantly correlated with maternal education (r = 0.49 and 0.47, respectively), the only measure of socioeconomic risk included in the study. Undoubtedly, some of the items in these observed composites, such as provision of learning materials and stimulation of cognitive development, may reflect the stressors of families living in poverty. These early-childhood experiences generally predicted teachers' ratings at kindergarten but did not predict change in their ratings over time; in other words, teachers reported less closeness and more conflict with boys, African American students, and those with lower academic skills at entry to kindergarten and those patterns tended to persist over time and across teachers.

These findings highlight important differences in students' experiences of their relationships with their teachers. In addition to potential differences in relationships based on students' age, teachers' relationships with students may vary based on cultural, ethnic, or socioeconomic backgrounds that differ from their own. The sample of teachers in the longitudinal study described above (Jerome et al., 2008) was predominantly white. One potential explanation for teachers' reports of greater conflict with African American students is offered by Tyler, Boykin, and Walton (2006). They found that white elementary teachers' perceptions of hypothetical students' motivation and academic achievement differed based on cultural learning orientations that reflected either mainstream cultural or Afro-cultural themes. That is, white teachers' preferences for classroom behavior that reflects mainstream cultural orientations may play out in their relationships with students from other backgrounds. In keeping with this suggestion, Saft and Pianta (2001) examined Caucasian, African American, and Hispanic teachers' reports of their relationships with preschool and kindergarten students. Teachers were more likely to rate their relationships with children of their same ethnic background more positively than those with students from other backgrounds; this was particularly true for Hispanic students (see Chapter 27, this volume). Teachers reported greater closeness and especially less conflict and dependency in their relationships with students who shared their ethnic background.

The studies discussed above report differences in teachers' perceptions of their relationships with students from different cultural backgrounds. Less is known, however, about differences in students' perceptions of those same relationships. This is important because teachers' and students' perceptions even within the same classroom may not agree (Brekelmans et al., 2011). In a study conducted in the Netherlands, den Brok, van Tartwijk, Wubbels, and Veldman (2010) examined differences in students' perceptions of their relationships with teachers in terms of two dimensions: *teacher influence* (the degree of control teachers have over classroom behavior) and *proximity* (closeness or agreement between teacher and students) for four ethnic groups: Dutch, Turkish, Moroccan, and Surinamese. They also compared non-Dutch students in terms of level of acculturation, distinguishing between first- and second-generation immigrants. Their results showed mean level differences in perceived influence and proximity across ethnic groups; Moroccan and Turkish students perceived more teacher influence than did Dutch students, and Turkish students also perceived more teacher proximity than did Dutch students. In addition to mean level differences in students' perceptions, however, these researchers also examined differences in the strength of associations between perceived relationships and student outcomes. The total (direct and indirect) effect of perceptions of teacher influence on students' subject-specific attitudes and grades was negative for students from Dutch and Moroccan backgrounds but positive for those with a Turkish or Surinamese background. In contrast, perceived proximity had a positive total effect on both attitudes and grades for students from all groups. Finally, students' perceptions explained more variance in the attitudes of non-Dutch (minority) students than those from the majority culture. Thus, although students' perceptions of closeness in their relationships with teachers were similarly positive across groups, the perception of teachers' controlling behavior had differential effects. The authors note, "it is important for teachers to realize that they are not only perceived differently by different ethnic groups of students, but also that the strength and direction of effect of their behavior might be different for students from various ethnic groups" (p. 218).

As noted earlier, the research on differences in teacher–student relationships based on students' age and grade level has implications for teacher education in terms of the importance of preparing teachers to foster and maintain close, positive relationships with students at different developmental stages. Similarly, the research on differences based on students' ethnic and cultural backgrounds highlights the importance of preparing teachers to work with diverse student populations and promoting teachers' awareness of their own culturally based preferences and interpretations of student behavior (Gay, 2000). These concerns are discussed in greater depth elsewhere in this volume (see Chapters 14 and 27).

***Teacher caring.*** An alternative framework for considering dyadic relationships between teachers and students is provided by Noddings' (1988, 1992, 2012) work on caring relations in teaching. Teacher caring often is treated by other researchers as a more global construct that characterizes a given classroom's social-emotional climate, or from the perspective of student perceptions only (e.g., Wentzel, 1997); this work is discussed below. Noddings, however, emphasizes the individualized and reciprocal nature of a caring relation between teacher and student. She states: "although these potentially caring relations are not equal, both parties contribute to the establishment and maintenance of caring" (Noddings, 2012, p. 772). In other words, although the term *teacher caring* seems to focus on the characteristics and actions of the teacher, Noddings argues that a relationship between teacher and student can only be considered "caring" if the student *feels cared for* and responds in a way that maintains communication and relationship. The student's perception of caring is critical; no good intention or behavior on the teacher's part creates a caring relationship without it. The teacher's role, then, is to listen closely and attend to individual students' expressed needs and interests, rather than to assume she knows what students need or that all students have the same needs. Importantly, conceptualizing caring as meeting students' needs implies that caring is more than affective (feeling and communicating empathy) but also requires thinking and knowledge. That is, "caring also implies competence" (Noddings, 2012, p. 776) in that teachers' ability to respond to multiple students' intellectual needs and interests will make significant demands on the teachers' depth and breadth of knowledge. In addition to promoting students' engagement and learning, such caring relations between teachers and students should promote the moral education and growth of both participants: "the teacher models not only admirable patterns of intellectual activity but also desirable ways of interacting with people. Such teachers treat students with respect and consideration and encourage them to treat each other in a similar fashion" (Noddings, 1988, p. 223).

Recent discussions of care theory are addressing the interface of caring and equity, or justice, in educational settings, including whether care and justice are incompatible in the process of setting educational policy and pedagogy, or can be integrated in a meaningful way (e.g., Katz, Noddings, & Strike, 1999; Noddings, 2007). These theoretical debates address very real, practical dilemmas faced by teachers in the course of their practice. For example, zero-tolerance policies related to specific student behaviors may be viewed as equitable, in that every instance of a particular transgression results in the same consequences. Periodically, however, the popular media exposes cases where such policies have resulted in clearly unreasonable outcomes (e.g., Nash-Wood, 2011; Rubinkam, 2013) that might have been avoided if behavior were instead addressed from a caring perspective that considered the developmental and individual needs of students. The challenge of balancing equity concerns and caring also has direct implications for school reform policies. Noddings (2007) argues that curriculum reforms that require common standards and that narrow students' focus to traditional academic courses, although superficially appearing to promote equity in achievement, do not respect the individual needs and interests of students—that is, do not reflect a caring perspective.

***Teacher–student relationships as a dimension of classroom climate.*** As noted earlier, a somewhat different approach to studying teacher–student relationships focuses less on the dynamics of specific dyadic relationships and considers teacher characteristics and behavior that foster an overall climate of positive regard, respect, and caring. This body of work draws on several theoretical perspectives, including seminal research on classroom climate (e.g., Fraser & Fisher, 1982; Moos & Moos, 1978), as well as social-psychological theories of affiliation and belonging (e.g., Baumeister & Leary, 1995; Goodenow, 1992; Ryan & Deci, 2000). Much of this research is based on student self-reports, often obtained through surveys, that permit examining associations between different dimensions of students' perceptions and a range of student outcomes, including aspects of students' academic and social motivation, self-regulation and effort, cheating, school adjustment, and achievement (e.g., Goodenow, 1993; Murdock, Anderman, & Hodge, 2000; Murdock, Miller, & Kohlhardt, 2004; Ryan & Patrick, 2001; Wentzel, 1997).

Overall, the findings of this body of research are remarkably consistent in terms of the importance of students' positive perceptions of the interpersonal climate of their classes and their teachers' classroom practices. The sense that one is accepted, respected, and cared for, and that one's teacher promotes a climate of mutual respect and prosocial values is consistently linked with desirable motivational, academic, and developmental outcomes (see Anderman & Freeman, 2004; Juvonen, 2006; Wentzel, 2010, for reviews). Less is known, however, about the particular teacher behaviors, practices, or characteristics that promote these perceptions in students (Anderman & Freeman, 2004).

Some researchers have attempted to address this question by having students report on their teacher's characteristics. For example, Ryan and Patrick (2001) asked middle-school students about the extent to which their math teachers provided interpersonal support and promoted both interaction and mutual respect among classmates. These variables were then entered into regression analyses as predictors of measures of students' self-reported motivation and engagement. Although such approaches contribute to understandings of how different dimensions of students' perceptions are associated with one another, they do not provide strong evidence of what teachers actually do to encourage those perceptions. Such questions require moving beyond traditional constructed response survey methods to include more open-ended explorations of classroom interactions. In examining the notion of teachers' pedagogical caring, Wentzel (1997) asked middle-school students to list three things "that teachers do to show that they care about you" (p. 414) and three things that show they do not care about you. Students' responses were then coded into categories such as democratic interactions, nurturance, and rule setting. Once again, however, the specific behaviors or interactions that teachers were engaged in were unclear.

The substantial body of research conducted by Pianta and his colleagues represents an important development in the study of teacher–student interactions in the classroom (e.g., Hamre & Pianta, 2007; Hamre et al., 2013; Pianta & Hamre, 2009; Williford et al., 2013). These researchers propose a model of effective teaching conceptualized in terms of three major categories of interactions, including emotional support, classroom organization, and instructional support. The three categories are measured using an observational instrument, the Classroom Assessment Scoring System (Pianta, Hamre, & Mintz, 2012). Developed initially in early-childhood settings, this instrument has now been adapted for teachers of older students (Pianta et al., 2012). The focus on observable behaviors in the classroom has both strengths and limitations. If the goal is to evaluate teacher effectiveness in promoting student performance, the ability to "attend to aspects of teachers' jobs that can be reliably observed and assessed" (Hamre et al., 2013, p. 463) is crucial. Nevertheless, reliance on teachers' observable behavior, even when broadly assessed, inevitably limits the perspective on teachers' work in the classroom, omitting information on teachers' real-time decision making that drives the behavior and the perceptions of students who make up the other half of classroom interactions.

One way to address this limitation is through the use of multiple data sources collected from both teachers and students. For example, Anderman, Andrzejewski, and Allen (2011) used students' survey reports to identify high-school teachers who were perceived as creating a classroom environment that supported positive motivational and learning-related beliefs, and then conducted direct observations to provide a rich description of those teachers' practice. They documented examples of teacher–student interactions that fostered positive interpersonal relationships with students while simultaneously maintaining students' behavioral and cognitive engagement, such as the use of self-disclosure and varying participation structures within lessons.

An even more complex methodology was developed by Strati and Schmidt (2013) to examine teachers' provision of challenge and support in high-school science classrooms. The researchers used a combination of the experience sampling method to generate student reports of their own engagement and time-coded video observations of the classroom. Students' responses could then be directly linked to the record of their interactions with the teacher that immediately preceded those responses. What emerges from these and similar studies (e.g., Fulmer & Turner, 2013) is the complexity of teachers' relationships and interactions with students, where seemingly straightforward actions (such as circling the classroom to monitor small-group activity or responding to students' requests for assistance) can either support or undermine multiple purposes simultaneously.

Despite the large and growing body of research on teacher–student relationships, a number of important areas remain for future study. First, much of the published research currently available has been conducted within the United States. In the meta-analysis conducted by Roorda et al. (2011), 77 of the 99 empirical studies were conducted within the United

States. Although there are notable exceptions, such as the work of Wubbels, den Brok, and their colleagues (e.g., Brekelmans et al., 2011; den Brok et al., 2010; Wubbels, den Brok, Veldman, & van Tartwijk, 2006), the literature base is still unbalanced. More international research will help clarify which patterns are specific to particular societies and which are more universal.

Secondly, there is a need for much more research on effective prevention and intervention into negative teacher–student relationships. Empirically supported approaches that help teachers develop more appropriate support for students at all developmental levels, particularly those who are at risk of failure or who demonstrate oppositional behavior, are needed. More integration of the literature on student–teacher relationships and on culturally responsive pedagogy also is needed. As noted earlier, the ability to make recommendations for practice requires methodological approaches that move beyond reliance on survey measures alone and cross-sectional designs. Direct observations of classroom interactions are helpful, but the combination of multiple methods and inclusion of multiple informants (e.g., teachers, students, and observers) are most likely to provide robust recommendations for teacher education and intervention efforts.

## Conclusions and Future Directions

This overview of research on teachers' efficacy, emotions, and interpersonal relationships in the classroom highlights the continuing contributions being made by educational psychologists to our understanding of teachers' work. At the time of writing, there is considerable research activity in all of the areas we have discussed. An important development is the emerging focus on teachers' experiences and emotion in the classroom and changes in those experiences across their careers. Similarly, the ongoing development in theorizing about the social relationships in a classroom, and teachers' sense of personal and collective efficacy, all represent significant areas of progress. Nevertheless, in many ways, the current picture of teachers' lives in the classroom is incomplete. Specifically, in relation to the topics discussed here, we suggest some key areas for further development in the field.

First, there is a need for greater conceptual integration that crosses over areas of study, such as teacher efficacy, emotional experiences in the classroom, and relationships between teachers and students that, too often, are examined in isolation. There is a strong tendency for researchers to narrow their focus to examine topics separately when these processes co-occur in practice, and there is good evidence that they are interactive. For example, researchers could explore those constellations of teacher beliefs, relationships with students, and interaction patterns during instruction that lead to positive learning and motivational outcomes for students, as well as positive emotional experiences and engagement for teachers. As noted earlier, the potential role of teachers' emotions and perceptions of relationships with students in triggering cascading effects that lead to differing patterns of student development, engagement, and learning

merits greater examination. Such complex research questions clearly have implications for the design and methodology used in studies. Researchers now operate in a time of rapid development of statistical analytic approaches (see Chapter 4, this volume). There has been an increase in the thoughtful combination of multiple methodologies that have the potential to capture the complexity of teachers' lives in the classroom. We envision this trend continuing and revealing new, more valid understandings of teachers' work.

In addition to more complex descriptions of teachers' work in the classroom and longitudinal studies examining causal effects, the field would benefit from more intervention-based studies, moving into "Pasteur's quadrant" (Pintrich, 2000). That is, the need is pressing to apply emerging classroom research findings to teacher education and professional development practices and, perhaps, teacher selection. This requires greater understanding of how to promote change in teachers' beliefs, perceptions, and emotional functioning in the classroom. Coupled with this is the need for a greater emphasis on understanding collective beliefs, collaboration, and the ways teachers' beliefs and emotions are influenced by interactions with colleagues, students, and the larger community. Finally, we see a continuing need for a global perspective, examining similarities and differences in teacher characteristics and experiences across international boundaries.

## References

Ainsworth, M. D. S. (1989). Attachments beyond infancy. *American Psychologist, 44,* 709–716.

Alexander, P. A., & Winne, P. H. (2006). *Handbook of educational psychology* (2nd ed.). Mahwah, NJ: Lawrence Erlbaum.

Anderman, L. H., Andrezejewski, C. E., & Allen, J. (2011). How do teachers support students' motivation and learning in their classrooms? *Teachers College Record, 113,* 969–1003.

Anderman, L. H., & Freeman, T. M. (2004). Students' sense of belonging in school. In P. R. Pintrich & M. L. Maehr (Eds.), *Advances in motivation and achievement: Vol. 13: Motivating students, improving schools: The legacy of Carol Midgley* (pp. 27–63). Boston, MA: Elsevier.

Anderman, L. H., Freeman, T. M., & Mueller, C. (2007). The "social" side of social context: Interpersonal and affiliative dimensions of students' experiences and academic dishonesty. In E. M. Anderman & T. B. Murdock (Eds.), *Psychological perspectives on academic cheating* (pp. 203–228). New York: Academic Press.

Bakker, A. B., & Bal, P. M. (2010). Weekly work engagement and performance: A study among starting teachers. *British Journal of Educational Psychology, 83,* 189–206.

Bakker, A. B., Albrecht, S. L., & Leiter, M. P. (2011). Key questions regarding work engagement. *European Journal of Work and Organizational Psychology, 20,* 4–28.

Bandura, A. (1997). *Self-efficacy: The exercise of control.* New York: Freeman.

Bandura, A. (2012). On the functional properties of perceived self-efficacy revisited. *Journal of Management, 38,* 9–44.

Baumeister, R. F., & Leary, M. R. (1995). The need to belong: Desire for interpersonal attachments as a fundamental human motivation. *Psychological Bulletin, 117,* 497–529.

Bell, P., Lewenstein, B., Shouse, A. W., & Feder, M. A. (Eds.) (2009). *Learning science in informal environments: People, places and pursuits.* Washington, D. C.: National Academies Press.

Berliner, D. C., & Calfee, R. C. (Eds.). (1996). *Handbook of educational psychology.* New York: Macmillan.

Borko, H., & Putnam, R. (1996). Learning to teach. In D. C. Berliner & R. C. Calfee (Eds.), *Handbook of educational psychology* (pp. 673–708). New York: Macmillan.

Bowlby, J. (1979). *The making and breaking of affectional bonds.* London, UK: Tavistock.

Bowlby, J. (1998). *A secure base: Parent–child attachment and healthy development.* London: Basic Books.

Bransford, J., Darling-Hammond, L., & LePage, P. (2005). Introduction. In L. Darling-Hammond & J. Bransford (Eds.), *Preparing teachers for a changing world: What teachers should learn and be able to do* (pp. 1–39). San Francisco, CA: John Wiley.

Brekelmans, M., Mainhard, T., den Brok, P., & Wubbels, T. (2011). Teacher control and affiliation: Do students and teachers agree? *Journal of Classroom Interaction, 46*(1), 17–26.

Brophy, J. (2006). Observational research on generic aspects of classroom teaching. In P. A. Alexander & P. H. Winne (Eds.), *Handbook of educational psychology* (2nd ed., pp. 755–780). Mahwah, NJ: Lawrence Erlbaum.

Buehl, M. M., & Fives, H. (2009). Exploring teachers' beliefs about teaching knowledge: Where does it come from? Does it change? *Journal of Experimental Education, 77,* 367–407.

Burchinal, M. R., Peisner-Feinberg, E., Pianta, R., & Howes, C. (2002). Development of academic skills from preschool through second grade: Family and classroom predictors of developmental trajectories. *Journal of School Psychology, 40,* 415–436.

Calderhead, J. (1996). Teachers: Beliefs and knowledge. In D. C. Berliner & R. C. Calfee (Eds.), *Handbook of educational psychology* (pp. 709–725). New York: Macmillan.

Carter, K. (1990). Teachers' knowledge and learning to teach. In W. R. Houston (Ed.), *Handbook of research in teacher education* (pp. 291–310). New York: Macmillan.

Chang, M.-L. (2009). An appraisal perspective of teacher burnout: Examining the emotional work of teachers. *Educational Psychology Review, 21,* 193–218.

Chang, M.-L. (2013). Toward a theoretical model to understand teacher emotions and teacher burnout in the context of student misbehavior: Appraisal, regulation and coping. *Motivation and Emotions, 37,* 799–817.

Cornelius-White, J. (2007). Learner-centered teacher-student relationships are effective: A meta-analysis. *Review of Educational Research, 77,* 113–143.

Crosnoe, R., Morrison, F., Burchinal, M., Pianta, R., Keating, D., Friedman, S. L., Clarke-Stewart, K. A., & the Eunice Kennedy Shriver National Institute of Child Health and Human Development Early Child Care Research Network (2010). Instruction, teacher–student relations, and math achievement trajectories in elementary school. *Journal of Educational Psychology, 102,* 407–417.

Darling-Hammond, L., & Bransford, J. (Eds.). (2005). *Preparing teachers for a changing world: What teachers should learn and be able to do.* San Francisco, CA: Wiley.

Davis, H. A. (2003). Conceptualizing the role and influence of student–teacher relationships on children's social and cognitive development. *Educational Psychologist, 38,* 207–234.

Day, C., & Gu, Q. (2009). Veteran teachers: Commitment, resilience and quality retention. *Teachers and Teaching, 15,* 441–457.

Den Brok, P., van Tartwijk, J., Wubbels, T., & Veldman, I. (2010). The differential effect of the teacher–student interpersonal relationship on student outcomes for students with differential ethnic backgrounds. *British Journal of Educational Psychology, 80,* 199–221.

Evertson, C. M., & Weinstein, C. S. (Eds.) (2006). *Handbook of classroom management: Research, practice, and contemporary issues.* Mahwah, NJ: Lawrence Erlbaum.

Finn, J. D. (1989). Withdrawing from school. *Review of Educational Research, 59,* 117–142.

Fives, H., Hamman, D., & Olivarez, A. (2007). Does burnout begin with student-teaching? Analyzing efficacy, burnout, and support during the student-teaching semester. *Teaching and Teacher Education, 23,* 916–934.

Fraser, B. J., & Fisher, D. L. (1982). Predicting students' outcomes from their perceptions of classroom psychosocial environment. *American Educational Research Journal, 19,* 498–518.

Frenzel, A. C., Goetz, T., Lüdtke, O., Pekrun, R., & Sutton, R. E. (2009). Emotional transmission in the classroom: Exploring the relationship between teacher and student enjoyment. *Journal of Educational Psychology, 101,* 705–716.

Frenzel, A. C., Goetz, T., Stephens, E. J., & Jacob, B. (2009). Antecedents and effects of teachers' emotional experiences: An integrated perspective and empirical test. In P. A. Schutz and M. Zembylas (Eds.), *Advances in teacher emotion research* (pp. 129–151). New York, NY: Springer.

Fulmer, S. M., & Turner, J. C. (2013). The perception and implementation of challenging instruction by middle school teachers: Overcoming pressures from students. *Elementary School Journal, 114,* 303–326.

Furrer, C., & Skinner, E. (2003). Sense of relatedness as a factor in children's academic engagement and performance. *Journal of Educational Psychology, 95,* 148–162.

Gay, G. (2000). *Culturally responsive teaching.* New York: Teachers College Press.

Gibbs, S., & Powell, B. (2011). Teacher efficacy and pupil behaviour: The structure of teachers' individual and collective beliefs and their relationship with numbers of pupils excluded from school. *British Journal of Educational Psychology, 82,* 564–584.

Goodenow, C. (1992). Strengthening the links between educational psychology and the study of social contexts. *Educational Psychologist, 27,* 177–196.

Goodenow, C. (1993). Classroom belonging among early adolescent students: Relationships to motivation and achievement. *Journal of Early Adolescence, 13,* 21–43.

Hamre, B. K., & Pianta, R. C. (2007). Learning opportunities in preschool and early elementary classrooms. In R. Pianta, M. Cox, & K. Snow (Eds.), *School readiness and the transition to kindergarten in the era of accountability* (pp. 49–84). Baltimore, MD: Brookes.

Hamre, B. K., Pianta, R. C., Downer, J. T., DeCoster, J., Mashburn, A. J., Jones, S. M., Brown, J. L., Cappella, E., Atkins, M., Rivers, S. E., Brackett, M. A., & Hamagami, A. (2013). Teaching through interactions: Testing a developmental framework of teacher effectiveness in over 4,000 classrooms. *The Elementary School Journal, 113,* 461–487.

Hargreaves, A., & Fullan, M. (2012). *Professional capital.* New York: Teachers College.

Huberman, M. (1989). The professional life cycle of teachers. *Teachers College Record, 91,* 31–57.

Jarodzka, H., van Gog, T., Dorr, M., Scheiter, K., & Gerjets, P. (2013). Learning to see: Guiding students' attention via a model's eye movements fosters learning. *Learning and Instruction, 25,* 62–70.

Jerome, E. M., Hamre, B. K., & Pianta, R. C. (2008). Teacher–child relationships from kindergarten to sixth grade: Early childhood predictors of teacher-perceived conflict and closeness. *Social Development, 18,* 915–945.

Juvonen, J. (2006). Sense of belonging, social bonds, and school functioning. In P. Alexander & P. Winne (Eds.), *Handbook of educational psychology* (2nd ed., pp. 655–674). Mahwah, NJ: Lawrence Erlbaum.

Katz, M. S., Noddings, N., & Strike, K. A. (Eds.) (1999). *Justice and caring: The search for common ground in education.* New York, NY: Teachers College Press.

Klassen, R. M., Al-Dhafri, S., Mansfield, C. F., Purwanto, E., Siu, A., Wong, M. W., & Woods-McConney, A. (2012a). Teachers' engagement at work: An international validation study. *Journal of Experimental Education, 80,* 1–20.

Klassen, R. M., & Chiu, M. M. (2010). Effects on teachers' self-efficacy and job satisfaction: Teacher gender, years of experience, and job stress. *Journal of Educational Psychology, 102,* 741–756.

Klassen, R. M., Perry, N. E., & Frenzel, A. C. (2012b). Teachers' relatedness with students: An underemphasized component of teachers' basic psychological needs. *Journal of Educational Psychology, 104,* 150–165.

Klassen, R. M., & Tze, V. M. C. (2014). Teachers' self-efficacy, personality, and teaching effectiveness: A meta-analysis. *Educational Research Review, 12,* 59–76.

Klassen, R. M., Tze, V. M. C., Betts, S., & Gordon, K. A. (2011). Teacher efficacy research 1998-2009: Signs of progress or unfulfilled promise? *Educational Psychology Review, 23,* 21–43.

Klassen, R. M., Yerdelen, S., & Durksen, T. L. (2013). Measuring teacher engagement: The development of the Engaged Teacher Scale (ETS). *Frontline Learning Research, 2,* 33–52.

Knoblauch, D., & Woolfolk Hoy, A. (2008). "Maybe I can teach *those* kids." The influence of contextual factors on student teachers' efficacy beliefs. *Teaching and Teacher Education, 24,* 166–179.

Kooij, D., de Lange, A., Jansen, P., & Dikkers, J. (2008). Older workers' motivation to continue to work: Five meanings of age. *Journal of Managerial Psychology, 23,* 364–394.

Kunter, M., Frenzel, A., Nagy, G., Baumert, J., & Pekrun, R. (2011). Teacher enthusiasm: Dimensionality and context specificity. *Contemporary Educational Psychology, 36,* 289–301.

Kyriacou, C. (1987). Teacher stress and burnout: An international review. *Educational Research, 29,* 146–152.

Kyriacou, C. (2001). Teacher stress: Directions for future research. *Educational Review, 53,* 27–35.

Ladd, G. W., Birch, S. H., & Buhs, E. S. (1999). Children's social and scholastic lives in kindergarten: Related spheres of influence? *Child Development, 70,* 1373–1400.

Malinen, O.-P., Savolainen, H., Engelbrecht, P., Xu, J., Nel, M., Nel, N., & Tlale, D. (2013). Exploring teacher self-efficacy for inclusive practices in three diverse countries. *Teaching and Teacher Education, 33,* 34–44.

Malmberg, L.-E., Hagger, H., & Webseter, S. (2014). Teachers' situation-specific mastery experiences: Teacher, student group and lesson effects. *European Journal of Psychology of Education, 29,* 429–451.

Menges, R. J., & Austin, A. E. (2001). Teaching in higher education. In V. Richardson (Ed.), *Handbook of research on teaching* (4th ed., pp. 1122–1156). Washington, DC: American Educational Research Association.

Midgley, C., Feldlaufer, H., & Eccles, J. S. (1989). Student/teacher relations and attitudes toward mathematics before and after the transition to junior high school. *Child Development, 60,* 981–992.

Moos, R. H., & Moos, B. S. (1978). Classroom social climate and student absences and grades. *Journal of Educational Psychology, 70,* 263–269.

Munby, H., Russell, T., & Martin, A. K. (2001). Teachers' knowledge and how it develops. In V. Richardson (Ed.), *Handbook of research on teaching* (4th ed., pp. 877–904). Washington, DC: American Educational Research Association.

Murdock, T. B., Anderman, L. H., & Hodge, S. A. (2000). Middle-grades predictors of students' motivation and behavior in high school. *Journal of Adolescent Research, 15,* 327–331.

Murdock, T. B., Miller, A., & Kohlhardt, J. (2004). Effects of classroom context variables on high school students' judgments of the acceptability and likelihood of cheating. *Journal of Educational Psychology, 96,* 765–777.

Nash-Wood, M. (2011). Are school zero-tolerance policies too harsh? *USA Today.* Retrieved from http://usatoday30.usatoday.com/news/nation/story/2011-12-04/zero-tolerance-policy/51632100/1 (accessed July 17, 2013).

Noddings, N. (1988). An ethic of caring and its implications for instructional arrangements. *American Journal of Education, 96*(2), 215–230.

Noddings, N. (1992). *The challenge to care in schools.* New York, NY: Teachers College Press.

Noddings, N. (2007). *When school reform goes wrong.* New York, NY: Teachers College Press.

Noddings, N. (2012). The caring relation in teaching. *Oxford Review of Education, 38*(6), 771–781.

Patrick, H., Anderman, L. H., Shalter, P. B., & Duffin, L. C. (2011). The role of educational psychology in teacher education: Three challenges for educational psychologists. *Educational Psychologist, 46*(2), 71–83.

Pianta, R. C., & Hamre, B. K. (2009). Conceptualization, measurement, and improvement of classroom processes: Standardized observation can leverage capacity. *Educational Researcher, 38,* 109–119.

Pianta, R. C., Hamre, B. K., & Mintz, S. L. (2012). *The CLASS: Secondary manual.* Charlottesville, VA: Teachstone.

Pianta, R. C., Steinberg, M. S., & Rollins, K. B. (1995). The first two years of school: Teacher–child relationships and deflections in children's classroom adjustment. *Development and Psychopathology, 7,* 295–312.

Pintrich, P. R. (2000). Educational psychology at the millennium: A look back and a look forward. *Educational Psychologist, 35,* 221–226.

Rich, B. L., Lepine, J. A., & Crawford, E. R. (2010). Job engagement: Antecedents and effects on job performance. *The Academy of Management Journal, 53,* 617–635.

Richardson, P. W., Watt, H. M. G., & Devos, C. (2013). Types of professional and emotional coping among beginning teachers. In M. Newberry, A. Gallant, & P. Riley (Eds.), *Advances in research on teaching* (pp. 229–253). Bingley, UK: Emerald.

Roorda, D. L., Koomen, H. M. Y., Spilt, J. L., & Oort, F. J. (2011). The influence of affective teacher–student relationships on students' school engagement and achievement: A meta-analytic approach. *Review of Educational Research, 81,* 493–529.

Ross, J. & Bruce, C. (2007). Professional development effects on teacher efficacy: Results of randomized field trial. *Journal of Educational Research, 101,* 50–60.

Rubinkam, M. (2013). Kids' recent school suspensions renew debate over zero tolerance policies. Retrieved from http://www.huffingtonpost.com/2013/02/19/kids-school-suspensions_n_2717996.html (accessed July 17, 2013).

Ryan, A. M., & Patrick, H. (2001). The classroom social environment and changes in adolescents' motivation and engagement during middle school. *American Educational Research Journal, 38,* 437–460.

Ryan, R. M., & Deci, E. L. (2000). Self-determination theory and the facilitation of intrinsic motivation, social development and well-being. *American Psychologist, 55,* 68–78.

Saft, E. W., & Pianta, R. C. (2001). Teachers' perceptions of their relationships with students: Relations with child and teacher characteristics. *School Psychology Quarterly, 16,* 125–141.

Schaufeli, W. B., Bakker, A. B., & Salanova, M. (2006). The measurement of work engagement with a short questionnaire. *Educational and Psychological Measurement, 66,* 701–716.

Schuell, T. J. (1996). Teaching and learning in a classroom context. In D. C. Berliner & R. C. Calfee (Eds.), *Handbook of educational psychology* (pp. 726–764). New York: Macmillan.

Schutz, P. A., & Pekrun, R. (Eds.). (2007). *Emotion in education.* Boston, MA: Elsevier.

Sørlie, M-A., & Torsheim, T. (2011). Multilevel analysis of the relationship between teacher collective efficacy and problem behaviour in school. *School Effectiveness and School Improvement: An International Journal of Research, Policy and Practice, 22,* 175–191.

Strati, A. D., & Schmidt, J. A. (2013). *Exploring the role of teacher challenge and support in high school students' engagement in general science classrooms.* Paper presented at the annual meeting of the American Educational Research Association, San Francisco, CA.

Sutton, R. E., & Harper, E. (2009). Teachers' emotion regulation. In L. J. Saha & A. G. Dworkin (Eds.), *International handbook of research on teachers and teaching* (pp. 389–401). New York: Springer.

Tan, X., Shiyko, M. P., Li, R., Li, Y., & Dierker, L. (2012). A time-varying effect model for intensive longitudinal data. *Psychological Methods, 17,* 61–77.

Tsouloupas, C. N., Carson, R. L., Matthews, R., Grawitch, M. J., & Barber, L. K. (2010). Exploring the association between teachers' perceived student misbehavior and emotional exhaustion: The importance of teacher efficacy beliefs and emotion regulation. *Educational Psychology, 30,* 173–189.

Turner, J. C., Gray, D. L., Anderman, L. H., Dawson, H.S., & Anderman, E. M. (2013). Getting to know my teacher: Does the relation between perceived mastery goal structures and perceived teacher support change across the school year? *Contemporary Educational Psychology, 38,* 316–327.

Tyler, K., M., Boykin, A. W., & Walton, T. R. (2006). Cultural considerations in teachers' perceptions of student classroom behavior and achievement. *Teaching and Teacher Education, 22,* 998–1005.

Veldman, I., van Tartwijk, J., Brekelmans, M., & Wubbels, T. (2013). Job satisfaction and teacher–student relationships across the teaching career: Four case studies. *Teaching and Teacher Education, 32,* 55–65.

Wentzel, K. R. (1997). Student motivation in middle school: The role of perceived pedagogical caring. *Journal of Educational Psychology, 89,* 411–419.

Wentzel, K. R. (1998). Social support and adjustment in middle school: The role of parents, teachers and peers. *Journal of Educational Psychology, 86,* 173–182.

Wentzel, K. R. (2010). Students' relationships with teachers. In J. L. Meece & J. S. Eccles (Eds.), *Handbook of research on schools, schooling, and human development* (pp. 75–91). New York: Routledge.

Wentzel, K. R., & Looney, L. (2007). Socialization in school settings. In J. E. Grusec & P. D. Hastings (Eds.), *Handbook of socialization: Theory and research* (pp. 382–403). New York: Guilford.

Williford, A. P., Maier, M. F., Downer, J. T., Pianta, T. C., & Howes, C. (2013). Understanding how children's engagement and teachers' interactions combine to predict school readiness. *Journal of Applied Developmental Psychology*, doi: 10.1016/j.appdev.2013.05.002.

Woolfolk Hoy, A., & Burke Spero, R. (2005). Changes in teacher efficacy during the early years of teaching: A comparison of four measures. *Teaching and Teacher Education, 21,* 343–356.

Wolters, C. A., & Daugherty, S. G. (2007). Goal structures and teachers' sense of efficacy: Their relation and association to teaching experience and academic level. *Journal of Educational Psychology, 99,* 181–193.

Woolfolk Hoy, A., Davis, H., & Pape, S J. (2006). Teacher knowledge and beliefs. In P. A. Alexander & P. H. Winne (Eds.), *Handbook of educational psychology* (2nd ed.) (pp. 715–737). Mahwah, NJ: Lawrence Erlbaum.

Wubbels, T., den Brok, P., Veldman, I., & van Tartwijk, J. (2006). Teacher interpersonal competence for Dutch multicultural classrooms. *Teachers and Teaching: Theory and Practice, 12*(4), 407–433.

# AFTERWORD I

# Perspectives on the Past, Present, and Future of Educational Psychology

FRANK FARLEY
Temple University

PATRICIA A. ALEXANDER
University of Maryland

EVA L. BAKER
University of California, Los Angeles

DAVID C. BERLINER
Arizona State University

ROBERT C. CALFEE
Stanford University

ERIK DE CORTE
University of Leuven, Belgium

JAMES G. GREENO
University of Pittsburgh

ANITA WOOLFOLK HOY
The Ohio State University

RICHARD E. MAYER
University of California, Santa Barbara

This final chapter in the Afterword section of the *Handbook* provides personal perspectives from national leaders in educational psychology on some of the major highlights of our history, the present status of the discipline, and prospects for the future. The chapter reports in brief essays those perspectives of eight leaders in educational psychology who were invited to contribute to this volume by the first author. The relative emphasis on the past, present, or future of our discipline was left up to each scholar. As will be seen, their views are sometimes similar and often different. Some are more positive, some more negative. One is a personal narrative.

In the first brief essay, Patricia A. Alexander looks at educational psychology as a discipline that influences or leads to other disciplines, a progenitor of developing fields, a contributor to the evolution of discipline. She argues that there is a long future for educational psychology in this strong role of disciplinary progenitor.

In the next essay, David C. Berliner advances the provocative argument that educational psychology is becoming increasingly irrelevant because of its spectacular successes as a trainer in high-quality research methodologies. He argues that this success has led other disciplines to become our equal in the research game; there has been a shift to other "go-to" disciplines such as anthropology or economics that embraced broader contexts for research and emerging mixed methods. Berliner suggests that these other methods are often seen as more relevant to actual education than many of the educational psychology approaches. He contends that educational psychology is not now the lead science in education research, and affirms that, in his view, multidisciplinary approaches and mixed methods are the directions to take going forward. He concludes, nevertheless, that there is still life left in the discipline: It "will not fade away."

Robert C. Calfee discusses three key events concerning the profound issues of learning and transfer as a focus for his essay; namely, the Common Core Standards for Literacy of 2010; a special session at the 2013 annual convention of the American Educational Research Association entitled "The Learning Sciences and Educational Entrepreneurship"; and finally, collaborations in teaching statics and the "freebody diagram" between Stanford University and University of California, Riverside. Calfee notes the common thread across these complex instructional programs where learning and transfer are essential. He concludes with a look ahead and his view that the Common Core Standards may revive investigations of learning and cognition *vis-à-vis* understanding an application.

Erik De Corte takes a look at what he perceives as a disconnect between the science of educational psychology on the one hand and the improvement of educational practice on the other. He lauds the accomplishments of educational psychology with respect to the former, and decries its failures regarding the latter. But to look for promise in the future, De Corte considers design-based research and argues that it may provide the needed bridge, the two-way traffic of research and use. Again, with an eye on the future, DeCorte briefly introduces neuroscience and education and the need going forward for interdisciplinary, neuroeducational studies, echoing some of the preceding chapters in this volume.

James G. Greeno focuses heavily on learning with historical perspectives on behavioristic versus cognitive science approaches. He touches on such significant concepts as schemata, noting especially the accomplishments of cognitive analyses. He notes that "the goal of providing conceptually meaningful instruction that is accessible to all students could be taken on successfully if society were sufficiently committed to it." Looking forward, he also describes briefly a recent line of "practical scientific work" called "activity systems" or "the situative program," antedating behaviorist or cognitive programs.

Anita Woolfolk Hoy considers particularly the teaching of educational psychology and reviews some history concerning the value of those teachings and their applications to schools. She raises the question of applied relevance of the field in the latter role, and notes the great improvements of the last few decades. However, Hoy points out that time and coursework given to educational psychology at universities have declined, and requirements of educational psychology in teacher education programs have been reduced. She states: "We must resist the accusation that we are irrelevant." Looking to the future, Hoy decries the sometimes balkanization she sees from different camps and worldviews, and strongly endorses the need for immediate application of our work. She concludes with some wise advice for current graduate students in educational psychology.

Richard E. Mayer defines educational psychology very succinctly as "the scientific study of how instruction affects learning." He then reviews the discipline's past as a science of learning, instruction, and assessment, arguing for its strong success in all these efforts. In discussing the present state of educational psychology, Mayer emphasizes the practical value of contemporary basic research, including for online and multimedia instruction. Turning to the future, he references challenges from the left (e.g., radical social constructivism) and the right (misinterpretation of cognitive neuroscience). The future will need to incorporate both theoretical and practical goals, writes Mayer, who concludes that, "Educational psychology's future is bright to the extent that it can continue to focus on basic research on practical educational problems."

Eva L. Baker's essay is a first-person, autobiographical account of her astounding career as a leading educational psychologist. It is particularly motivational for students who might be contemplating a career in this wonderful field. She is a model of ethical, entrepreneurial, scholarly, organizational, and motivated accomplishment, achieving levels as high as one can achieve. The history of Baker's experience reflects the major changes in ideas and practices as educational psychology has evolved.

Some of the more frequent themes emerging from the foregoing essays are the following:

a. the relationship of the science of educational psychology to the practical use of the research;
b. the evolving status of educational psychology in relation to other disciplines in the study of education. The issue of the relevance of educational psychology;
c. the value of proven instructional and learning techniques and concepts in improving education;
d. the central contributions of cognitive theory to education;
e. changes in the methodologies being used in the science of educational psychology;
f. the powerful role of transfer in learning and instruction research—transfer between contexts, tasks, and between the present and the future.

Although differences exist among the authors in their relative emphasis on the themes just listed, there is some common ground in the essays. Most of the authors agreed on the following three perspectives: (a) major contributions within educational psychology have evolved with the shift from behavioral approaches to cognitive psychology; (b) educational psychology is a multidisciplinary field covering several subject matters and other fields; and (c) educational psychology is still relevant to education. Despite these advances, some authors felt for various reasons that the field might be becoming irrelevant. Decades ago, educational psychology was thriving as it developed a solid scientific basis for its research; however, other cognate disciplines have become increasingly based in scientific principles, and added importance has been given to emerging qualitative and mixed-method approaches that will need full incorporation into educational psychology. Finally, two authors discussed the Common Core Standards and neuroscience as being important topics for educational psychology today.

To summarize, these essayists' delineations of issues related to the *past* included: the nature of the science in our field; the multidisciplinarity of educational psychology; the transition from behavioral to cognitive theories; the importance of transfer of learning; and the role of effective instructional and learning strategies. Their depiction of issues related to the *present* included: the effectiveness of transfer of learning; the connection of research to practice; educational psychology's status as a multidisciplinary field; and addressing the Common Core Standards. The issues they raised as *future* concerns included: the field remaining multidisciplinary; continuing to connect research to practice; and addressing relevant developments in neuroscience.

## Educational Psychology as Disciplinary Progenitor

### Patricia A. Alexander

> If species are only well-marked varieties, of which the characters have become in a high degree permanent, we can understand this fact; for they have already varied since they branched off from a common progenitor in certain characters, by which they have come to be specifically distinct from each other; and therefore these same characters would be more likely still to be variable than the generic characters which have been inherited without change for an enormous period. Charles Darwin (1859), *On the Origin of Species*, pp. 473–474

In pondering the past, present, and future of educational psychology, I was drawn to Darwin's notion of the "common progenitor." This was not simply by chance, given that the writings of Darwin and his cousin, Francis Galton, proved highly influential to the thinking of forefathers of educational psychology, including William James and John Dewey. As suggested by this allusion to progenitors, to truly grasp the history of educational psychology we must appreciate its disciplinary wellspring, philosophy, and the characteristics that our field still shares with its "mother" discipline. Moreover, to understand educational psychology's place in the world today, we must recognize that it has itself become the progenitor for many now well-established and vibrant disciplines— from developmental and social psychology to school and counseling psychology. How educational psychology has fared with each new branching tells us much about what has remained genetically dominant within our field and what features or characteristics have become more recessive over time. Further, in contemplating educational psychology's future, we must ponder what recent branchings have emerged and whether those new offshoots pose any serious threat to the health and well-being of educational psychology.

***Our philosophical roots.*** I have long argued that we cannot appreciate who we are as educational psychologists if we do not understand the influence that our disciplinary progenitor, philosophy, has wielded and continues to wield. As the chapter in this volume by Bredo points out (Chapter 1), our philosophical DNA is unavoidable, even if the passage of time has obscured this reality. Recognition of this fact was why I authored a special issue of *Educational Psychologist* (2003) entitled "Rediscovering the Philosophical Roots of Educational Psychology," with impressive contributions from educational psychologists like Frank Pajares (2003)

and P. Karen Murphy (2003), as well as recognized philosophers like John McDermott (2003) and Jerry Rosiek (2003). As I wrote in the preface to that issue:

> By coming home to philosophy, we can potentially infuse new ideas and alternative perspectives into ongoing educational research and practice. By coming home, we can reconsider the obvious merits of explicit philosophical inquiries, such as the study of epistemology, ontology, or axiology. In addition, we can glimpse the philosophical shading cast over mainstream educational psychology topics—from self-concept to achievement and from interest to perception. (Alexander, 2003, p. 129)

***Disciplinary branching.*** Almost as soon as educational psychology as a field took root at the dawning of the twentieth century, it spawned new offshoots that today stand as recognized domains of inquiry in their own right. For example, the child study movement sparked by G. Stanley Hall was a catalyst for the emergent field of developmental psychology, while the writings of William James on the I-self and me-self were significant in the formation of the contemporary fields of clinical and counseling psychology. Even after all these years, we can still see certain prominent features that genetically link these various disciplines to educational psychology, including a shared interest in human learning and development, individual differences, and assessment.

Nonetheless, as Alexander, Murphy, and Greene (2012) have argued, each disciplinary spawning comes with certain costs and benefits that must be understood. Using the metaphor of giving birth, these researchers—who interestingly represent three generations of educational psychologists— contended that "disciplinary birthing" is "neither painless nor without postpartum complications" (p. 7). To date, educational psychology, while serving as the disciplinary progenitor for a number of recognized domains and disciplines, has managed to maintain its genetic integrity. That is, educational psychology has retained enough of its core disciplinary substance to stay viable and relevant even within an increasingly multidisciplinary and interdisciplinary academic world.

***Evolutionary future.*** But what will become of educational psychology in the decades to come? That is the perplexing and potentially troubling question that we must ask. Forces within and without give us reason to pause (Alexander et al., 2012). For one, our credibility to speak to educational policies and practices has long been a point of contention, and remains so in a climate where empirical evidence does not always seem to inform educational policy or instructional practice. As David Berliner (2006; also in this chapter) has so eloquently argued, part of the fault lies with us and with our failure to communicate well with educational and policy communities. Whatever the causes, it remains imperative that educational psychology does not lose the tendrils that bind it to educational policy and practice and that provide essential sustenance.

Yet, some of the concern for the future resides in the world beyond the classroom, where the evidence and justification for actions are often elusive or too frequently based on speculation, mythology, or unfounded beliefs (Alexander & the Disciplined Reading and Learning Research Laboratory [DRLRL], 2012; Murphy, Alexander, & Muis, 2012). Certainly, a dearth of thinking critically and analytically would be a problem at any time or in any place. But, especially when we consider the digital lives of today's learners and the informational deluge that confronts them, the ability to ponder, weigh, and justify—epistemic competence (Alexander & the DRLRL, 2012)—seems even more of an imperative (Murphy & Alexander, 2013). What role educational psychology will play in understanding learning and development in this new century is still unfolding, although promising trends are emerging.

***Final thoughts.***  So, educational psychology's roots are strong and reach back well over 100 years. At present, the knowledge, procedures, and insights afforded by that century-plus of theoretical and empirical work are still clearly evident not only in the features of discipline-specific inquiry, but also in the characteristics and contributions of many related fields to which educational psychology was a disciplinary progenitor.

It is my contention that educational psychology as a disciplinary progenitor will continue to thrive for many decades to come and that its core genetic makeup will remain strong and sustainable. We can only guess what new branches may appear on the horizon, but they will inevitably be able to trace themselves back to their disciplinary progenitor, educational psychology. Speaking precisely to this issue in relation to such interdisciplinary movements as neuroscience and learning sciences, Alexander et al. (2012, p. 25) wrote:

> It remains unclear as to the degree that educational psychologists, long devoted to human learning, will be central players in such interdisciplinary confederations. From our perspective, it would be hard to fathom that such enterprises could be sustained were they to overlook the centuries of expertise on human learning represented within the field of educational psychology.

I still hold to that judgment. To my way of thinking, as long as there is concern for human learning and development, as long as there is an appreciation for individual differences and the need to assess and address such differences, and as long as there are those invested in the study of knowledge, motivation, and emotions, educational psychology will exist in some form. Such is the process of disciplinary evolution.

## Thoughts on Educational Psychology

### David C. Berliner

I believe that educational psychology is now almost irrelevant as a field of study for a most unusual reason; namely, because it was a spectacular success. It was so remarkably influential, particularly in colleges of education, that it now has almost put itself out of business.

Educational psychology's father, E. L. Thorndike, and his heirs ruled schools of education for decades. They understood tests and measures, and were students of learning theory. Because of that they were the first to provide the growing numbers of schools of education both rigorous methods and an empirically validated theory of learning. That is, educational psychology sought to provide a scientific basis for the vast enterprise that was education. It fought a battle for the souls of schools of education, trying to wrest the art of teaching and the haphazard forms of learning from philosophers and other humanists, and from Christian educators who often ran America's schools and schools of education in the late nineteenth century. The battle ended about 1912 (Berliner, 1993). Thorndike won; Dewey and James lost; and while scientifically unsupported beliefs about education did not lose completely, they were finally challenged. Our field, educational psychology, ushered in the era of the scientific study of education. So educational psychology flourished. School subjects such as reading and mathematics were studied more by psychologists than by reading and mathematics educators. The fields of curriculum studies, physical education, music, and art were each influenced by educational psychologists, as we asserted that the use of our science was the best way to improve education.

Along the way we trained reading and mathematics educators, as well as those in other educational specialties, in both our educational psychology methods and our habits of mind. And towards the end of the twentieth century, they, in turn, were training the next generation of educationists in research methods peculiar to their own fields. The result of our success as the "scientists" in educational matters is that the research in reading, mathematics, science, physical education, the study of teaching, computer-assisted learning, and so many other educational specialties grew to be of extremely high quality. This is a tribute to our influence on all of education, but particularly on our colleagues in other departments in America's colleges of education.

A side effect of the tremendous growth in high-quality research in education is the marginalization of educational psychology as "the" foundational discipline for advanced study in education. Once upon a time, just a few decades ago, a Ph.D. degree in many educational specialties required that an educational psychologist be on the candidates' committee to insure "scientific quality." That day is gone. Research traditions of high quality are well established in reading, mathematics, physical education, science, and so forth. Our field is no longer unique, and thus it is no longer as prestigious in colleges of education as it once was.

But there is both a second and third reason for a reduction in the influence of educational psychology. Those reasons grew out of the rise of alternative social scientific fields of study, and a rebellion against the rigid psychometric and statistical methods promoted by our educational psychology brethren. Towards the end of the twentieth century, as educational psychology was slowly changing from its root paradigm as a behavioral science to its new paradigm (an embrace of the cognitive sciences), rebellions over methods used for the study of education became apparent.

As I witnessed it in the workplaces I inhabited, the disciplinary fight for dominance as the "go-to" science for the study of education changed from educational psychology to anthropology, first; and then to economics, later. The great influence of anthropological ways of thinking about culture, norms, social groupings, hierarchies, dominance, family structures, childrearing, and so forth seemed to have explanatory powers that were at least as great as were those emanating from educational psychology. In part that was because we educational psychologists discovered that the findings we had assumed would transfer from classroom to classroom or school to school often did not. We needed ways of describing contexts, for which psychology seemed less adequate. Anthropology appeared to do that better. Anthropology had different beliefs about the way the world worked and different methods for studying that world. For example, psychology was primarily focused on the individual, but anthropology was primarily focused on the social group. This made education a natural setting for anthropologists to do research.

Not long after that disciplinary rival took root in schools of education, the business community began to dominate American politics and media. The rise of corporate influences on the Western world brought to education new interests in economics, another social science competing for research dollars and the hearts and minds of doctoral candidates. Our society was also slowly reducing its funding for public schools, in part because of a reduction in the taxes paid by both individuals and corporations. Thus econometric analyses were thought appropriate to help in either justifying or reducing the billions of dollars that were spent annually for education. For educational psychology, that meant that decisions about whether a program such as early-childhood education had effects no longer relied solely on the outcomes we educational psychologists valued. These were often tests we constructed and questionnaires we designed. Instead, for the economists, looking at effects meant measuring such things as returns to society of income earned, grades of schooling completed, incarceration avoided, health attained, and other measures that were much more the province of economics and sociology, but not mainstream educational psychology. So our discipline of educational psychology was no longer the most acceptable arbiter for declaring programs successes or failures, as had once been the case. The result was a loss in status for our field.

Finally, while the quantitative requirements of economics majors were similar enough to those required of educational psychologists, the methodology of anthropology was not. In alliance with the humanists in schools of education, who survived the 50 years or so of dominance by educational psychology, anthropologists mounted challenges against the methods most frequently used by our discipline. A leading educational psychologist labeled these "The Paradigm Wars" (Gage, 1989). Anthropologists were much more at home with studies of groups—a family, a tribe, an occupation, a school. They often studied these groups with methods that were emic. These are methods for obtaining information from inside the group studied, as in participant observer work or fieldwork, taking months or years of observation. Psychology generally preferred

methods that were etic—the observations of an outsider—data thought to be more "objective," more "scientific." In the zeitgeist affecting the educational research community during the last few decades of the twentieth century, the pendulum swung, and emic methods gained currency. Thus, in educational research, what we now call qualitative methods, including story and narrative, grew to be honored as legitimate ways of knowing. And the influence of educational psychology waned because of that. We now seem to have some stasis. Even diehard methodological purists in educational psychology now seem to believe that "mixed methods" may yield more interpretable and actionable knowledge than either quantitative or qualitative methods alone. But that kind of tolerance did not come quickly or without rancor, and over that time period the field of educational psychology suffered.

In sum, I believe that three influences on educational psychology had negative effects on the way our field is perceived. One is our spectacular success in training other educational scholars to do high-quality research, thus reducing our influence in schools of education and their research programs. This revolution was also accompanied by a change in the qualifications of those who received funding from government agencies and foundations. Given the reward structure of universities, our reputation was damaged. The second negative influence on us was the rise of other social sciences as credible ways of studying educational phenomena, a change that I think was quite appropriate. Finally, the rise of alternative methods for the study of education took away some of the methodological monopoly that was held by educational psychologists in so many of America's schools of education. In my estimation, we no longer are the most important science for the study of education, and our status is certainly less than it was.

But we educational psychologists should remember that schools are sites, and education is an enterprise, a task in which individuals and societies choose to engage. To understand the complex sites in which the many forms of the educational enterprise take place might, as several chapters in this volume attest, require multidisciplinary research approaches and mixed methodologies. So psychologists who are well trained in the learning sciences and in psychometrics will always be needed to better understand how schools work and how the educational enterprise might be improved. Educational psychology will not fade away. We have ideas, research findings, and methods that can contribute to the study and improvement of education. But in the future, educational psychologists will have to share the investigative tasks with other social sciences and humanistic fields of study. While the changes I have discussed may have diminished the discipline of educational psychology, the object of our studies, the educational enterprise, is likely to be better illuminated.

## Back to the Future: Learning and Transfer Redux

### Robert C. Calfee

Three events during the past few years, each related to learning and transfer, provide the setting for this note. They led me to reminisce about my early years as a psychologist, and to wonder about the current status of research on learning and transfer; where is this work when we need it? Here are the three events:

a. the release in June 2010 of the *Common Core Standards for Literacy* (National Governors' Association & Council of Chief State School Officers (NGA/CCSSO), 2010), which lay out a remarkable vision for American schools, ensuring that high-school graduates are college-, career-, and citizen-ready;

b. a session on *The Learning Sciences and Educational Entrepreneur-ship,* sponsored by Kaplan Inc. during the 2013 American Educational Research Association convention (https://kapx.kaplan.com/events/learning-science-ed-entrepreneurship/);

c. collaborations with colleagues in engineering schools at Stanford and University of California, Riverside, around statics and the *freebody diagram* (Lee, DeSilva, Peterson, Calfee, & Stahovich, 2008).

The common theme of the three events is the design of complex instructional programs, in which a lot has to be learned and transfer is essential. As I thought about my assignment for this note—"reflect on the discipline and projections for the future"—I recalled my early years at the University of California, Los Angeles and Stanford during the late 1950s and early 1960s, and memories of Skinner, Hull and Spence, Tolman, and Gagné, so well captured by Bower and Hilgard (1981). A highlight of this period was Estes' (1950) paper, "A statistical theory of learning," which initiated a line of thinking that lasted almost half a century (Atkinson, Bower, & Crothers, 1965), when Bower (1994) wrote that the ideas have been assimilated by information-processing models and the cognitive revolution. By 1980, books on "learning theories" had almost vanished (but cf. Olson & Hergenbahn, 2012; Schunk, 2011); the term is not in the index of either the first or second editions of this *Handbook*.

Statistical learning theory had its origins in stimulus–response associationism; Estes was a Skinner student. Associative learning emphasized the role of practice with feedback. Estes' model assumed that each item in a list of paired associates was represented by a large population of stimulus elements, from which a sample was drawn at the beginning of each trial, which determined the probability that the subject made one or another response; the subject was then given the correct response, all of the elements in the sample were connected or "conditioned" to the reinforced response at the end of the trial, and then returned to the population. The mathematical machine generated the exponential curve that is typical of many learning curves: large initial improvements, with steady but diminishing changes over successive trials. Every blow of the hammer produces an increment of improvement, as Ebbinghaus reported in 1885 (see Ebbinghaus, 1913).

Estes applied the stimulus-sampling model in a broad spectrum of experimental settings. The logical clarity and empirical power of the model attracted the attention of Patrick Suppes, Director of Stanford's Institute for Mathematical Studies in the Social Sciences, which emerged in the 1960s as a magnet, attracting scholars like Atkinson, Bower, Luce, and Estes to the Institute's "summer institutes." In 1961, Bower proposed the all-or-none (AON) model as a dramatic alternative to the incremental model, demonstrated how to evaluate it, and pointed out the importance of attention to individual learning trajectories. In the AON model, each item was represented by a single "element," which could be linked to the correct response in a single "insightful" trial, a mnemonic moment. Bower showed that the model provided an equally good account of paired-associate learning curves. Estes, skeptical of Bower's findings, investigated a broad array of laboratory learning outcomes, and became a believer (Estes, 1964). Practice made neither perfect nor permanent, but instead provided opportunities for a connection to occur. In one of the final episodes of this story, Atkinson proposed the "random-trials incremental" (RTI) model (Atkinson & Crothers, 1964), where, on each trial, the learner might "grab an incremental insight." The RTI model gave a better account of learning data than either the incremental or AON models, but the story came to an end at this point.

Meanwhile, the Stanford Institute moved into the educational arena, featuring computer-assisted projects in reading (Atkinson) and mathematics (Suppes), along with logic and Russian (Suppes). This work was guided by objectives-based models of instructional design—define specific outcomes, present instructional opportunities, assess the outcomes, and proceed to mastery. The cognitive revolution flourished, featuring computer simulations of human thinking and problem solving. *Learning Sciences* emerged in the early 1990s as an outgrowth of the revolution, with calls for a richer and more diverse playing field for the study of complex human activities, a broader scope of ideas, methods, and applications. Ann Brown, Robbie Case, and John Bransford, among others, many grounded in experimental psychology, entered the increasingly tumultuous classroom arena.

Transfer is largely missing from the preceding account. I will now backtrack for a closer look at the *three events* and *three models*, which I will relate to recent developments in transfer, and then venture *a glance into the future*, which seems quite promising for our understanding of learning and transfer.

The first event, the *Common Core Literacy Standards*, differs in several ways from current practice (Calfee & Wilson, in press): (a) they present language and literacy as an integrated system that serves to amplify intellectual potential (Martinez, 2013); (b) they call for students to perform research projects in academic disciplines during the high-school years; (c) they depart from the objectives-based models of the past half-century, relying instead on holistic and contextually rich environments for promoting student achievement; and (d) they propose that all students meet these high expectations through the professional efforts of classroom teachers. For the Standards, learning is all about transfer—about outcomes stretching far beyond the 13 years of schooling.

The second event, the *Learning Science* symposium (Kaplan Higher Education Corporation, 2013), puzzled me. Learning was presented as a commodity to be developed, marketed, funded by venture capital, and so on. Following the symposium, I mulled over the question of what the participants meant by "learning"? How was it to be conceptualized, defined, measured, described? It was clearly something other than "change in behavior" or "standardized test scores" from earlier times. Technology was an important feature (see Chapter 2 in this volume). As an academic domain, Learning Sciences traces back to an international conference in 1991, where it emerged as an interdisciplinary enterprise focused on the study of teaching and learning in formal and informal settings (Sawyer, 2006). But it is not indexed in *How People Learn* (Bransford, Brown, & Cocking, 2000), nor in the previous two *Handbooks*. Neither is mathematical learning theory mentioned in Sawyer's (2006) handbook on the learning sciences.

The third event was my involvement with statics, an introductory course in engineering mechanics. Several years ago I was approached by an instructor for assistance in evaluating a project designed to enhance learning in his introductory course. Statics, the analysis of forces at work on a system in equilibrium (nothing is moving), is required for the engineering degree. The *freebody diagram*, a key concept in this analysis, is a drawing that abstracts the elements in a physical system, specifying the magnitude and direction of all forces. In physics, a prerequisite for statics, students investigate force in simple settings, blocks and inclined planes and cylinders. In engineering, the problems are messy: a front-loader about to dump a load of gravel while perched at a 25-degree angle over a ditch. The first task is to sketch the freebody diagram for the problem, then Newton's laws of motion are applied to fill slots in the equilibrium equations, after which calculators make quick work of the numbers.

The challenge in sketching a freebody diagram is primarily perceptual—abstracting from a complex image the key elements in relation to one another, in a way that highlights the "force fields." Students are eager to get to the mathematics, which they know well, and which require little transfer. Linear algebra takes a while to "learn," but once acquired, equations look remarkably similar across contexts. Drawing freebody diagrams is partly an art form, and depends on perceptual transfer, on "seeing" structural similarities across a wide range of situations. Note: *force is invisible!* In fact, it is not directly accessible to *any* of the senses. Of course, lots of "things" are unobservable, abstractions such as *love* and *fear*, phenomena such as *light* and *sound waves*, and "beneath-the-surface" entities such as nerves and glands (cf. Achieve, 2013; National Research Council, 2011). In the case of force, Newton's three laws of motion provide lenses for those who learn how to use them.

***Learning is invisible.*** So is transfer. Both can be operationalized, which means that we have proxies, but these are not really lenses. Following the example of Newton's laws, what about exploring the potential of learning models? For example, the incremental model included machinery for handling response probability and latency, and also covered simple transfer situations. Most investigations dealt with simple situations where these indices captured the significant outcomes. Models can also be used to assess the incrementality

of the learning process. For example, Bower's (1961) *backward learning curve* provides a way to distinguish between the incremental and AON models. The technique is rather clever. On each trial, the outcome is classified as Correct or Error, producing a sequence of Cs and Es. If learning is incremental, then any "slice" of a learning curve will reflect an incremental pattern. If learning is AON, then the CE sequence will be completely random up to the critical point where the AON connection takes place, after which performance will be perfect (or nearly so). The backward learning curve is generated by finding the point at which learning occurred (several correct responses in a row), and then analyzing the probability of a correct response before the AON connection. In a final development in this story, Atkinson's *RTI model* combined these two processes. Each trial provides an opportunity for the learner to make an incremental improvement in performance, yielding a stepwise learning curve. Both the AON and RTI models provide techniques for "seeing" certain aspects of learning, and for measuring rate parameters.

Much more can be gained from applying learning models. Suppose, in the spirit of the learning sciences, we dress up these models in more qualitative, cognitive garb. Table A.1 provides a snapshot of qualitative differences between *learning by doing* and *learning by knowing*. I created this table in the 1980s as part of a professional development program showing teachers the relevance of cognitive psychology to educational practice (Calfee, 1981). For most teachers, the topic of learning models was new, and for some teachers, the idea of rapid insightful learning was rather intriguing.

Barebones mathematical models, even when clothed in qualitative garb, can be rather boring to teachers attending after-school workshops, unless they can see connections to practice. The incremental model is well suited to rote-learning situations, where understanding is minimal, where context is not a serious consideration, and where the emphasis is on rapid and somewhat mindless responses. Learning to touch-type or strip an AK-47 exemplify a training scenario that typifies gradual improvement through practice with feedback. Elementary teachers do not deal with either touch-typing or AK-47s, but they do handle a lot of rote-learning situations, especially in areas like phonics and vocabulary, where a frequent frustration is the lack of transfer. Most frequently the concern is that learning does not last—"I taught them the /AI/ vowel digraph last week, and half had forgotten it by Monday." But transfer is also a problem. "I told them that the rule for vowel digraphs is that 'when two vowels go walking,

**Table A.1    Portraits of Learning by Doing (Incremental) and Learning by Knowing (All-or-None)**

| Doing—Incremental | Knowing—All-or-None |
| --- | --- |
| Repeated trials—rote exercises | Often the result of instruction |
| Takes time—mistakes and practice with feedback | Instantaneous "aha!" metacognitive |
| Over trials, schemata are organized | Information is organized and coherent |
| Provides a foundation for gaining knowledge | Can serve to guide practice |

the first does the talking.' This morning we started work on /EE/ and /IE/, and it was like they had never learned /AI/!"

Transfer during incremental learning often seems quite limited, but the potential is greater in AON learning. In rote learning, the task consists of a large collection of isolated objectives. AON (and RTI) learning works for big-picture items–but the learner needs to understand the big picture, the gestalt. To illustrate, here is an anecdote from a rafting trip on the Colorado several years ago. Passengers were encouraged to take over the oars for the smaller rapids, and I volunteered several times. The river is smooth just before plunging into the surging rapid. Instructions are to "ferry angle" the raft before into the rapid, and then pull hard to the right or left midway through. I did as instructed, with no understanding and little effect. My big picture was a mess. The goal was to keep the raft moving in the current as the river made a turn below the rapids, but my timing was always off. Following a spectacular rapid midway through the trip, we pulled on to the beach, and the boat people gathered for a powwow. Peering over their shoulders, I saw that they had drawn a map in the sand and were moving a model raft around the map. They were discussing changes they needed to make in the ferry angle. I asked my boat person for an explanation, and she described how, by placing the raft at the proper angle before entering a rapid, the force of the current could be used to turn the boat at a critical moment. A flash of insight—it was all about inertia! The next time I volunteered, I knew how to angle the raft, and "saw" what was happening in the rapid with new clarity. I missed the critical instant and lost control, I had learned a "piece" of the puzzle, and could see what was happening in the turmoil with new clarity.

Understanding turns out to be critical in the generation of transfer during learning. In a comprehensive and cogent review of the topic, Day and Goldstone (2012) note the essentiality of transfer ("education is fundamentally about acquiring knowledge to be used outside of the classroom"; p. 153), next present the "frustrating and contentious" state of affairs with regard to the topic ("researchers . . . argue that meaningful transfer seldom if ever actually occurs"; p. 153), and then offer a promising proposal about "the role of perceptual processes and perceptual representations in knowledge transfer" (p. 153). Underlying structural similarity between the conditions of initial learning and transfer is the primary basis for *meaningful* transfer, but surface resemblances and contextual variations have the major influence on behavior (p. 155). Skilled chess players can see the "game" on a chess board, whereas novices see the pieces, and respond accordingly. Emphasizing and explaining the importance of transfer to students (and teachers) can promote transfer, especially when part of the bargain is that the learner take responsibility (p. 155), and sees the task as *preparation for the future* (p. 165). Finally, fostering the construction of spatial representations to support verbal relations can be especially powerful for transferable learning (pp. 167–171).

These ideas are rich and well developed, and merit careful reading. An important piece is missing, however—an account of how learning processes operate to promote transfer. Metacognition and self-explanation are mentioned in the review, but as add-ons. Expertise also appears throughout the review in relation to transfer, but with little connection to the underlying cognitive processes. What might be going on here? One possibility is that transferable learning calls for the development of progressions toward big-picture expertise rather than the mastery of isolated, piecemeal objectives. It is in this spirit that the Standards call for "staying on a topic within a grade and across grades" (NGA/CCSSO, 2010, p. 33). Science offers numerous instances in which individuals carry around contradictory views of a phenomenon—preconceptions versus school knowledge—based on piecemeal knowledge. Harvard graduates discussing the seasons or Duckworth's accounts of teachers explaining the phases of the moon (Duckworth, 2006) illustrate the compartmentalization of learning that confound transfer theorists. There is also the lack of transfer of thematic issues in literary works to social behavior. Children (and adults) are totally beguiled by the portrayal of the complexities of friendship in *Charlotte's Web*, yet fail to see the parallel in their own lives.

These issues are coming to a head in the *Common Core Standards for Literacy*, in the challenges of deciding what they mean and how they should be implemented. During the past 3 years, a view of the *Standards* has emerged in which they are viewed as slight revisions of objectives-based learning, which I translate as rote, incremental learning of short-term outcomes, providing little chance for transfer to the larger goals of "college- and career-ready" (Calfee & Wilson, in press). Current plans emphasize *close reading of complex texts*, while downplaying students' engagement in research projects of increasing depth and complexity. One would think that the *Standards* would have been grounded in the rich traditions of scholarship and empirical studies of learning and thinking, the voices from the varied domains that constitute the "master science" of education (Wittrock & Farley, 1989a). As things now stand, these voices are muted—there is no reference to the previous editions of this *Handbook*, nor even to the monumental *How People Learn* (Bransford, Brown, & Cocking, 2000). Educational psychology has much to offer the field of educational practice; we also have a big job in making our contributions better known and more fully employed.

## Two Faces of Educational Psychology: Knowledge Advancement Disconnected from Educational Practice

### Erik De Corte

Due perhaps to my basic training as an elementary-school teacher, the choices of my research topics have always been guided by two objectives: contributing to the advancement of our scientific knowledge about the processes and outcomes of learning and teaching in schools, and at the same time contributing to the research-based improvement of educational practices. The tension between both objectives has continuously been a challenge for me personally, but the history of educational psychology shows that the field as a whole has been struggling with the problem of reconciling both objectives since its origin in the early years of the twentieth century. And today reducing and overcoming what David Berliner (2008) has called "the great disconnect" between research and classroom practice still constitutes one of the major missions of educational psychology.

In her 1994 Presidential Address to the Annual Meeting of the American Educational Research Association, the late Ann Brown confirmed this disconnect: "Enormous advances have been made in this century in our understanding of learning and development. School practices in the main have not changed to reflect these advances" (1994, p. 4; see also Weinert & De Corte, 1996). But in this statement she also argued—rightly— that educational psychology has achieved substantial progress in the twentieth century in advancing our knowledge of learning. This progress is well documented in a series of major books published over the past decades, starting in 1996 with the first volume of this *Handbook* (Berliner & Calfee, 1996), the *International Encyclopedia of Developmental and Instructional Psychology* (De Corte & Weinert, 1996), the second edition of this *Handbook* (Alexander & Winne, 2006), *The Cambridge Handbook of the Learning Sciences* (Sawyer, 2006); and, in 2011, by the *Handbook of Research on Learning and Instruction* (Mayer & Alexander, 2011). The progressive broadening and deepening of our insight in the processes and outcomes of learning and teaching, and in the multiple variables that influence them, have been fostered by important paradigm shifts during the twentieth century in the general views of cognition and learning. We have gone from behaviorism to the cognitive, information-processing view to constructivism and socio-constructivism (De Corte, 2010; see also Greeno, Collins, & Resnick, 1996; see other chapters in this present volume). As a result of these developments, there is now a rather broad consensus about the following principles of learning in schools presented and discussed, for instance, in a booklet in the "Educational Practices Series" of the International Academy of Education, entitled *How Children Learn* (Vosniadou, 2001; also available in Spanish, Chinese, Greek, Korean, Polish, and Portuguese on the website of the International Bureau of Education): (a) active involvement; (b) social participation; (c) meaningful activities; (d) relating new information to prior knowledge; (e) being strategic; (f) engaging in self-regulation and being reflective; (g) restructuring prior knowledge; (h) aiming towards understanding rather than memorization; (i) helping students learn to transfer; (j) taking time to practice; (k) accommodating developmental and individual differences; and (l) creating motivated learners. A similar list of principles has been published by the American Psychological Association (Learner-Centered Principles Work Group of the APA Board of Educational Affairs, 1997).

Apart from this overall shift in the conception of learning, substantial progress has been made over the past 25 years in our knowledge and understanding of important learning-related phenomena. Major examples in this respect are conceptual change, self-regulated learning, and transfer. Conceptual change research was initially focused on science, investigating how science concepts are acquired and explaining students' difficulties in learning advanced and counterintuitive concepts (see Chapter 18, this volume; Vosniadou, 2008).

An important development of the past 10 years is the expansion of this domain by applying the conceptual change approach to other subject matter domains, first to mathematics and more recently to the social and behavioral sciences. Self-regulation refers to the active involvement of learners in their own learning by setting goals, organizing and monitoring their cognitive activities and motivation, and reflecting on their learning processes (as discussed in several chapters in this volume). Although research on self-regulation began only about 25 years ago, a substantial amount of research-based knowledge has been acquired, showing the importance of self-regulation skills for productive learning, and—very importantly—that self-regulation can be enhanced in students through appropriate guidance and instruction (e.g., Zimmerman & Schunk, 2011).

In contrast to conceptual change and self-regulation, as Calfee noted above, transfer is an old-timer in educational psychology. It was studied already in the early twentieth century, for instance by Thorndike. This is not surprising. Indeed, throughout history, educators have always attempted to equip their students with knowledge and skills that they can apply beyond the initial learning situation. However, the study of transfer has over the past 15 years been revitalized through the emergence of new perspectives that are more in line with the now prevailing view of learning, described above (Goldstone & Day, 2012). For instance, one such alternative perspective emphasizes the preparation for future learning as the major aspect of transfer (Bransford & Schwartz, 1999).

I would add to this selective and thus incomplete short list of success stories one other productive accomplishment of educational psychology over the past two decades, namely the important and expanding research on the learning and teaching of subject matter domains, especially mathematics, science, and reading and writing (Mayer & Alexander, 2011; see other relevant chapters in this volume). This development was facilitated by the advent of the information-processing approach. Indeed, psychologists became interested in studying the knowledge structures and processes underlying tasks and problems similar to those involved in school curricula. And the rise of the socio-constructivist perspective that stresses the importance of context, and especially social interaction, stimulated interest in studying learning in the complex reality of classrooms (Greeno et al., 1996). But Berliner stated in 2008: "Toward the end of the twentieth century, learning in real-world contexts began to be studied more earnestly, but, sadly, such research still appears not to be affecting practice very much" (p. 306). In other words, notwithstanding the enormous progress with regard to the first objective of educational psychology, namely the advancement in our knowledge of the processes of learning and instruction, the field has so far largely failed in pursuing and achieving the second objective, i.e., the innovation and improvement of educational practices. Therefore, as already said above, bridging the gap between theory/research and classroom practices constitutes one of the major challenges that lies ahead of us.

A representative illustration of the research–practice disconnect relates to what Salomon and Ben-Zvi (2006) have called "the difficult marriage between education and technology." Whereas an enormous amount of studies on the impact of information and communications technology (ICT) on learning have accumulated, the technology has so far not met the high expectations raised in the 1980s concerning its positive influence on educational practice (Hattie, 2009; Lehtinen, 2010). A major reason for this failure is that the technology has been mainly introduced as an add-on to an otherwise unchanged classroom setting. As argued by Salomon and Ben-Zvi (2006), ICT can only contribute to education if it is embedded as a tool beside other resources in powerful learning environments based on the new perspectives on learning and teaching.

Although Pat Alexander (2004) is to some degree right that "educational practice has not been particularly open to the recent advances of educational psychology" (p. 153), it would be unfair to blame the practitioners for what is to a large degree our failure, because we were unable to communicate with educational professionals in such a way that the relevant outcomes of research become palatable, accessible, and usable for teachers. Moreover, there is today research evidence showing that integrating new ideas about learning and teaching in curricula and textbooks does not at all guarantee that they are appropriately implemented in classroom practice (Depaepe, De Corte, & Verschaffel, 2007). Taking this into account, one possible way to contribute to overcoming the "great disconnect" consists in the further elaboration and wide application of a method of inquiry that was introduced in 1992 by the late Ann Brown (1992) and Alan Collins (1992), and has since raised increasing interest in educational research, namely design-based research (DBR) (Anderson & Shattuck, 2012).

In terms of Stokes' (1997) quadrant model of scientific inquiry, DBR can correctly be situated in Pasteur's quadrant that represents use-inspired basic research: it aims at the simultaneous pursuit of the advancement of our understanding of the processes of learning and instruction on the one hand, and the innovation and improvement of classroom practices on the other hand (De Corte, in press). In that perspective a key feature of a DBR consists in the *theory-driven* creation of an educational intervention or learning environment: designing the intervention draws upon the available evidence-informed knowledge about productive learning and effective teaching that derives from multiple disciplines. But, as pointed out by Penuel and Frank in this volume (see Chapter 2), a DBR is also *theory-oriented*: it is anticipated that the implementation and evaluation of the intervention will contribute to the continuous development and elaboration of theory. Because DBR has been criticized for lack of rigor, especially the confounding of variables and the lack of randomization, design experiments should as much as possible approach the rigor of randomized classroom trials. And to increase the likelihood that DBRs can result in principles and artifacts that lead to the innovation and improvement of classroom practices, the design of interventions should involve an interactive collaboration among researchers and practitioners, in which the interventions are implemented and evaluated in regular classroom contexts. However, guaranteeing as much as possible the "high-fidelity" implementation in classrooms of models of productive learning environments

that result from DBR will require substantial investment in initial training and professional development of teachers and school leaders. The latter is a crucial, indispensable condition to have a reasonable chance of being successful.

Another provocative domain of research lies at the interface of cognitive neuroscience and education (see Chapter 5, this volume). There is no doubt that by providing detailed data on brain activity, neuroscience can contribute to a more precise description and better understanding of the cognitive processes that take place during thinking and learning. One important challenge for the near future is to start interdisciplinary, neuroeducational research (Howard-Jones, 2010) aimed at portraying the effects of instruction on brain activity. But the road from research, to applications of neuroscience, to educational practice seems to be still quite long and methodologically rocky. Of immediate importance is to expel resistant neuromyths.

A final positive comment is that over the past 30 years the "Atlantic gap" has progressively been bridged. Especially since the foundation of the European Association for Research on Learning and Instruction in 1985, productive exchanges and interactions between North American and European instructional psychologists have increased substantially. There is no doubt that the field can in the future benefit from further intensification of those interactions in the format of more exchanges among scholars and cooperative research projects.

## Learning and Understanding about Learning with Understanding

### James G. Greeno

My perspective on educational psychology focuses on learning, especially when learners advance their understanding of explanatory concepts and principles.

A major accomplishment in recent decades is the development of a set of concepts and methods for representing what students can learn in order to know and understand in subject matter domains. By the 1960s, educational psychologists had worked out ways to formulate behavioral objectives and prerequisites systematically (e.g., Gagné, 1965); by the 1970s, this scientific resource was used to construct sequences of instruction called mastery learning that were quite successful in empirical trials (especially by Bloom, 1976). This development, itself an impressive scientific accomplishment, has yet to be exploited significantly in the educational system, although if it were, it could result in substantial progress toward removing the achievement gap between groups of students according to the assessments of their learning that are feasible with current testing methods (see also Calfee's section in this chapter).

One reason for not advocating a wholesale adoption of the methods of behavioristic mastery learning is that we know, scientifically, about aspects of learning that many people value and that are lacking when instruction is designed to only produce acquisition of skills. Therefore, we know better than to be satisfied with mastery of skills, characterized as behaviors, as a sufficient set of aims for the education of young people in our society.

One of the kinds of learning outcomes treated shallowly in behavioristic programs is conceptual understanding. Research on learning has advanced significantly in developing theoretical concepts and empirical methods that can be used to study and represent cognitive structures and processes of conceptual understanding. Cognitive science research developed a concept of *schemata,* a theoretical workhorse that can be used to represent hypotheses about information patterns that students can acquire and to provide hypotheses about what constitutes conceptual understanding and strategic reasoning. This idea, developed in the theory of problem solving (Newell & Simon, 1972) and in the theory of text comprehension (Kintsch & van Dijk, 1978), can be used to formulate definite hypotheses about understanding and aims for instruction. The aim of learning with understanding has a longer history, including discussions by Charles Judd (e.g., 1936), and empirical studies by William Brownell (e.g., 1935) in educational psychology, and by other psychologists such as George Katona (1940) and Max Wertheimer (1959). The value added by cognitive-science concepts and methods is the support they can give to formulating hypotheses about learning, problem solving, and understanding with greater specificity than the earlier behaviorist and associationist theories could support.

I count the ability to formulate cognitive analyses of understanding and cognitive objectives of instruction as a major scientific accomplishment and advance in educational psychology. This achievement, as significant as it is, is incomplete. Theoretically, analyses of information structures aimed at representing knowledge for understanding and problem solving in specific domains provide important theoretical insights and guidance for instruction and assessment that focus on quite specific topics in specific domains. (Examples include Hunt and Minstrell's (1996) analysis of facets of knowledge and understanding in high-school physics.) Recently an effort to develop a more general theoretical framework has made significant progress (Koedinger, Corbett, & Perfetti, 2012). The capability, provided by the cognitive program, to analyze and represent objectives and outcomes of instruction on specific topics and sequences of topics in domains, is being deployed in several programs of instructional research and development, to good effect. As these programs continue to develop, it will become increasingly feasible for schools to provide instruction that is accessible to all of their students in which they can not only gain the skills needed to perform successfully on assessments of their behavioral capabilities, but also achieve meaningful understanding of concepts and principles of the domains of school learning.

We can imagine a program to improve instruction and assessment that could be informed by the results of cognitive analyses of information structures and processes involved in performing tasks in all subjects that could be effective in making conceptual understanding and proficient skills available for all students to learn. Most of the analyses that would be needed for such a program would have to be conducted; however, the body of analytical work that we have provides an impressive collection of examples, sufficient as a proof of the concept. Even so, the goal of providing conceptually meaningful instruction that is accessible to all students could be taken on successfully if the society were sufficiently committed to it to provide the support needed to conduct the analyses and develop the needed curriculum materials and assessments and to support teachers in developing the understanding and capabilities that they would need.

While I believe that the progress that has been made in cognitive analyses and conceptualizations is already a major advance of educational psychology, and that its current and prospective development portends very strong scientific and practical educational value, I also believe that there is another line of fundamental and practical scientific work that will extend the value of that program at least as strongly as it has extended and will continue to extend the behaviorist program. This program investigates, designs, develops, and studies learning and resources at the level of activity systems that can include multiple individual persons along with the material and informational resources with which they interact. (The term "activity systems" comes from Engeström, 1999.) In this program, sometimes called the situative program (Greeno, 2011), activity is understood as participation in practices that the participating members have in common with others in communities of practice. Learning by an individual is understood as improvement in one's abilities to participate in the practices of the system, and learning by an activity system is understood as change in its practices in a way that makes it more effective in achieving valued functions. The development of this program of theoretical and empirical research, design, development, and evaluation is in an earlier stage than either the behaviorist or cognitive programs, so it remains to be seen whether its advancement will provide the same kind of strong accomplishment.

## The Most Important Course You Will Take

### Anita Woolfolk Hoy

In reflecting on the field of educational psychology past, I speak only of the areas of educational psychology that connect most directly to teaching and teachers—the realm that has been my world for the past 45 years. In looking to the future, I am quite speculative and selective. But in my perspective on educational psychology past and future, I maintain, as I have since the early 1970s—*this is the most important course you will take* if you want to teach.

***Four-plus decades of education psychology.*** The educational psychology of my graduate school days was filled with attention to developmental theorists such as Piaget and Kohlberg; learning theories put forward by Skinner, Bruner, and Ausubel; the humanistic psychology of Carl Rogers; research on teaching described by Wittrock, Rosenshine, and Gage; and explanations of assessment and intelligence by Anastasi, Bloom, and Wechsler. I taught an undergraduate course in educational psychology using the Personalized System of Instruction—the Keller Plan. In the field, the debates were between behavioral and cognitive explanations of learning and language, nature versus nurture in the origins of intelligence, and discovery versus exposition in teaching. *Education and Ecstasy* (Leonard, 1968) was a popular book that challenged traditional views of schooling. In some ways, the players and the positions were more defined and clear cut. This is oversimplifying, but there was an either–or character to many of the discussions.

In my early years as a professor, the great excitement for me and for many in the field was the Invisible College for Research on Teaching. There was such a sense of discovery and purpose as the results of many large, well-designed studies converged on a base of knowledge for teaching. The meetings of the Invisible College right before the American Educational Research Association (AERA) every year were engrossing. Many of the attendees left exhausted but sure that nothing we would hear at AERA would top the presentations and discussions of the 2 days at the Invisible College. The notion of knowing something valuable and true about teaching was exhilarating.

But the times, they were a-changin', to quote Bob Dylan. New methodologies drawn from anthropology, sociolinguistics, and literature led to views that challenged the coalescing research on teaching. What began as paradigm expansion seemed to become, as Gage (1989) described, "paradigm wars." Unfortunately, it seemed that some of the fallout from those wars was to question the value of educational psychology in teacher preparation. As Richard Mayer—and before him, John Carroll and Jere Brophy—and now, with the present chapter, David Berliner, have noted, educational psychology often has been dismissed as *irrelevant*. In 1963, Carroll described educational psychology as "a discipline with a large, but by no means wholly realized potential for effective application, and we shall continue to teach educational psychology to teachers with a mixture of pious optimism and subdued embarrassment" (p. 119). Brophy called for research in educational psychology "that has immediate practical application" (Brophy, 1974, p. 46). He argued "the problem is not quality; it is relevance. By and large, we simply are not studying problems that are related to the needs of the classroom teacher" (Brophy, 1974, p. 48).

Progress was rapid in the next decades. Thirty years after he questioned the potential of educational psychology for effective application, Carroll was ready to claim that, "no longer must we be embarrassed about our potential contribution to educational practice; indeed, we should be openly forthright about the usefulness and validity of our claims" (Carroll, 1993, p. 90). Mayer (1992) agreed that educational psychology had met the challenge of relevance in research because cognitive research had turned to the study of subject matter knowledge and learning—topics that had been removed from texts for teachers by about 1956. Brophy's call for research with immediate implications was heard. We need only look at the contents of the *Educational Psychologist* to trace the move toward relevance in the foci of our field from 1980 to the present.

I began a list of topics deeply relevant for educators from that journal, but when the number exceeded 30, I realized there is not space here to cite them all. Just a few examples are teaching, assessment, and grading of all school subjects, including the use of a range of technologies, class organizations, and homework; adapting instruction for students with many different needs and talents; motivation and self-regulation in teaching and learning; fostering student resilience, well-being, and physical health; relationships among students, teachers, and families; culture and language in classrooms; and school reform. Clearly, throughout all these decades, educational psychologists addressed critical and perennial questions for practitioners.

### Where are we headed and what challenges do we face?

First, as educational psychologists, we must be clear about who we are and why we matter. Our task in teacher education is daunting. It is difficult for 19-year-olds who have little experience with children or teaching, adolescents who are still developing themselves, to gain a sophisticated understanding of the development and learning of children across years and different cultural contexts—but that is our challenge as educational psychology teachers. Unfortunately, around the country, teacher education programs are more likely to decrease than expand courses, and time for the study of educational psychology has dwindled. Over the years, many state or university certification agencies decided our expertise was not needed in the preparation of teachers. Educational psychologists have responded with arguments for the value of our field (Anderson et al., 1995; Berliner, 1992; Blumenfeld & Anderson, 1996; Blumenfeld, Hicks, & Krajcik, 1996; McInerney, 2006; Patrick, Anderman, Bruening, & Duffin, 2011; Peterson, Clark, & Dickson, 1990; Woolfolk Hoy, 1996, 2000). In fact, the American Psychological Association currently is circulating yet another task force report on the value of educational psychology in teacher education (Worrell, 2013).

In teacher education, we perennially walk a line between being appreciated as a necessary and valuable part of teacher preparation and being appropriated into existing methods and foundations courses, then abandoned because the other courses "cover that" (Woolfolk Hoy, 2000). It is true that everyone in education has an interest in and something to say about teaching and learning, but educational psychology has been systematically studying these processes for at least two centuries; it is important for prospective and practicing teachers to have access to the knowledge gained in our long and successful enterprise. Beyond the design of teacher education programs, we seldom are consulted when our own universities make most decisions about teaching and learning programs and procedures. We must resist the accusation that we are irrelevant in all these arenas.

As we move forward in our research, what challenges will we face? Collaboration and multidisciplinary work are useful and encouraged by educational institutions as well as funding agencies. But when we collaborate with people in other fields we should not lose our identity or forget our shared knowledge. We must avoid knowing too little about too much—mistaking scattered superficiality for multidisciplinary. Also, we have to resist splintering into camps that spend most of their energy attacking the worldviews of the other camps. And at every point we need to remember Jere Brophy's encouragement to devote a good portion of our research into work that has immediate application—that is relevant to the practical and predictable problems and tasks of learning and teaching. Eric Anderman (2011) updated this call for educational psychologists "to engage in specific types of outreach activities so that our research can truly impact policy and practice" (p. 185). As ever, we must make a compelling case for the value of solid, but evolving, theories as the bases for thinking about and intervening in schooling, always keeping culture and context in mind.

Another challenge will be to integrate social, motivational, relational, and contextual perspectives with classic concerns about cognition, learning, and development. In the face of too many claims and "guidelines" for teachers about constructivist and brain-friendly teaching, educational psychology needs to appropriately incorporate sociocultural and neuroscience research—in fact, all relevant insights from the learning sciences. We must continue to examine how biological, psychological, and social/cultural/historical contexts work together in individuals and in classrooms. And because educational psychologists often explore learning in groups, we must continue to develop rigorous methods for studying composites—small groups, classrooms, and schools. Many of the chapters in this volume attest to these principles.

Finally, I have been thinking lately about advice I would give current educational psychology graduate students: I would ask them to spend time in schools with teachers and students, learn to develop funding sources, master their research methods, and get at least a working understanding of alternative methods. I would encourage them to find a mentor—not necessarily at their home institution, to write every day, and learn to use technology to support their teaching and connections to their own future students.

## The Past, Present, and Future of Educational Psychology

### Richard E. Mayer

Educational psychology is the scientific study of how instruction affects learning (Mayer, 2008). Thus, educational psychology seeks to understand how instructional manipulations by the instructor affect changes in knowledge created in the learner. For more than 100 years, beginning with the work of E. L. Thorndike, educational psychologists have been grappling with how to improve education based on scientific evidence rather than on opinions, fads, and ideologies (Mayer, 2003). In this short comment, I examine the past, present, and future of the field of educational psychology.

***Educational psychology's past.***   Since its inception in the early 1900s, educational psychology has made monumental contributions to the science of learning, the science of instruction, and the science of assessment.

The *science of learning* is the scientific study of how people learn (Mayer, 2011). Psychologists initially conceptualized the goal of the science of learning as the establishment of general laws of learning, based largely on rigorous experiments involving how rats and pigeons learn in contrived environments or how humans memorize word lists. In contrast, one of educational psychology's lasting contributions to the science of learning is the development of psychologies of subject matter (Mayer, 2004)—that is, focusing on how people learn and think in subject areas. Instead of asking about how people learn in general, educational psychologists asked about how people learn in specific school subjects such as reading, writing, mathematics, science, and history. This more contextualized (or domain-specific) approach has been enormously successful, compared to the now discredited approach of seeking general laws of learning, and represents one of educational psychology's major contributions to both psychology and education.

The *science of instruction* is the scientific study of how to help people learn (Mayer, 2011). Educators originally took a practical approach by studying which instructional methods worked, without much regard to theoretical underpinnings (Mayer, 1992). The result was a fragmented collection of teaching dos and don'ts that lacked consistency or rationale. In contrast, educational psychologists have been successful in pinpointing effective instructional methods and learning strategies that can greatly improve learning. Some consistently effective instructional methods include appropriate use of feedback, visualizations, and examples, whereas some consistently effective learning strategies include summarizing, self-explanation, and self-testing (Dunlosky, Rawson, Marsh, Nathan, & Willingham, 2013; Hattie, 2009; Mayer & Alexander, 2011).

The *science of assessment* is concerned with the scientific study of how to determine what people know (Mayer, 2011; Pellegrino, Chudowsky, & Glaser, 2001). Early attempts by learning psychologists to measure learning focused on measuring the rate or speed of responding by lab animals, based on the idea that learning involved strengthening and weakening of associations (Mayer, 1992). Subsequent attempts by learning psychologists focused on counting the number of items recalled from a rote list, based on the idea that learning involved adding elements to memory that varied in trace strength (Mayer, 1992). Once educational psychologists focused on meaningful learning of authentic academic content, assessments of learning outcomes shifted from focusing solely on retention to include measures of transfer (Anderson et al., 2001; Mayer & Wittrock, 2006). Developing useful measures of understanding (based on transfer rather than solely on retention) represents an important contribution of educational psychology to the science of assessment.

***Educational psychology's present.***   By taking a rigorous, scientific approach to the challenges raised by educators, educational psychologists are making monumental progress in understanding how learning, instruction, and assessment work. An example of this progress is the increasingly practical value of basic research on effective instructional techniques, including research-based guidelines for multi-media and online instruction (Clark & Mayer, 2011; O'Neil, 2005), an Association for Psychological Science task force report on 25 research-based principles of instructional design (Halpern, Graesser, & Hakel, 2007), an Institute of Educational Sciences practice guide on effective study techniques (Pashler et al., 2007), and a recent review of research-based learning techniques in *Psychological Science in the Public Interest* (Dunlosky et al., 2013).

***Educational psychology's future.*** Educational psychology faces a future in which it is challenged on the left by ideologies (such as radical social constructivism and the forces of postmodern relativism) and on the right by reductionism (such as the misinterpretation of cognitive neuroscience as replacing rather than supplementing our field). Educational psychologists of the future need to make sure that neither popular ideologies of the day nor misapplications of brain science can deter our field.

Being an educational psychologist in the future will involve moving between disciplinary boundaries in which our field is viewed as too theoretical by some educators and as too practical by some psychologists. As Stokes (1997) has nicely explained, we work in a field that has both practical and theoretical goals that mutually reinforce one another. To lose either goal would result in a future in which we focus on theory at the expense of practice or practice at the expense of theory. Educational psychology's future is bright to the extent that it can continue to focus on basic research on practical educational problems.

## Reflections on Educational Psychology

### *Eva L. Baker*

It's a scary thing to look back at one's career, as I have been asked to do. I found that I have imposed a sweet logic to explain the shifts made and values kept, although retrospect makes the role of chance more than obvious. Perhaps serendipity and reactiveness may apply to the path of psychology over the years.

I began intending to be a novelist, and as a graduate student in English, investigated teaching only as a survival mechanism. I found my way into the Education School at the University of California, Los Angeles (UCLA) to pursue a teaching credential, and as an unparalleled test taker, I was offered the job of reading exams for classes I had not yet taken. Apparently, standards in the School were not as high as they are now. Upon admission, I traipsed into Jim Popham's class, perhaps his first year at UCLA, and liked what seemed at first to be icy clarity, an approach never available in the critical analyses of literary forms. So I embraced empiricism; first, for teaching, as I became a teaching assistant for a behaviorally oriented methods course, and then in the psychology of learning through my multiyear-long work with A. A. Lumsdaine. Lumsdaine was a man so committed to experimentally controlled studies of human performance that he disdained (although himself a

statistician and social psychologist) the use of fancy analyses or, forbid the thought, non-experimental studies. This was the era of Benjamin Bloom, Ralph Tyler, Campbell, and Stanley, and, most important to my life over the years, Robert Glaser. The field was contending at once with six major shifts, how to: (a) preserve the theoretical orientation of psychology; (b) make psychology practical and useful in educational settings; (c) transfer from a behavioral to a cognitive model; (d) understand automation and technology; (e) invent a new model of assessment, i.e., criterion-referenced; (f) legitimate research and evaluation that was qualitative and interpretative as opposed to principle-driven; and (g) understand "third-force" psychology. All of this intellectual grappling was taking place in the complex foment of social revolution, civil rights, and the Vietnam War, women's rights, and a creeping anti-intellectualism that flourishes today.

Glaser himself was struggling with at least five of those seven issues, and as luck would have it, he was a co-author with Lumsdaine and a consultant to Popham, so I saw a lot of him. Glaser had a profound piece, written while I was just beginning UCLA as an undergraduate, in *Teaching Machines and Programmed Learning* (1965), the most inappropriately named volume ever. In it, Glaser discussed approaches advocated by Ramo and Skinner, including specifying the domain of learning, determining the best methods by evaluating outcomes, providing good feedback, and having a mechanism to record and transfer the types of prior learning and success each student has before entering any new instructional environment. He ended by saying he hoped the field of applied psychology would not take another 35 years (or to 1995) to achieve these goals. Clearly, he was an optimist. So was I, as I learned from my mentors that ideas could work, change performance, be documented and transferred. But this took far more time than I anticipated. Unfortunately, the rest of the world was and is focused on processes—reasons why not rather than why (paraphrasing Robert Kennedy).

My early work was focused on teaching teachers instructional principles that had a scientific pedigree, whether from Skinner, Pressey, Guthrie, or Thorndike. I believed that if they used them, they would improve important educational outcomes for students. Practice, feedback, step size, and a focus on goals were the core. These ideas would augment their personal attributes, their interest in students, and their interpersonal skills. My dissertation study judged teacher performance by student outcomes, albeit in a known domain with high cognitive demands, and not on a standardized test battery.

Despite my optimism, not much changed in real classroom learning, and I recognized that behaviorists, myself included, focused on too molecular a level of outcomes. Jumping ahead 40 or so years, it is a little ironic that we are back to decomposing large domains or constructs into micro levels of behavior, such as clicks and gazes. To understand important goals, we look at elements in ontologies or the targets of data-mining efforts. Psychometricians also build models of validity and growth for complex cognitive outcomes, starting with the smallest levels of behavior and combining them ultimately into domains, constructs, and real performance, instead of just test performance.

I became very despondent at the lack of positive findings for instructional interventions that I thought should have worked in experiments. I had begun to do my work in schools rather than in short, lab-like settings. Schools were noisy and not well-controlled contexts, then as now. So I asked a reasonable question: maybe the dependent measures, i.e., standardized tests at the time, were not the problem; rather it was the interventions. Elegant studies by Cronbach and Snow made the point better, as they searched for aptitude–treatment interactions (ATI), and found that general outcome measures typically were not sensitive to interventions, and were influenced more by student background variables. Perhaps this is still the case.

Just about 7 years after I joined UCLA as a faculty member, I was appointed by John Goodlad, as Director of the Center for the Study of Evaluation (CSE). CSE was principally focused on Marv Alkin's evaluation theory and the conduct of evaluations, and I began by doing evaluations and elaborating on formative evaluation of instruction. CSE had a beginning presence in the achievement-testing area, and I believed that I could make some use of my English background and administrative "power" by pushing the team to study writing assessment. Much writing assessment at the time depended on multiple-choice proxies. Others had idiosyncratic and not well-developed scoring approaches that made everyone think that writing or any open-ended product or performance was soft and subjective.

A systematic set of studies of writing and assessment across levels from elementary school through the university led to investigations of complex thinking, resource use, rater training, and validity. This work jibed nicely with the cognitive revolution in education. When we pushed ourselves into writing about content, such as American history, chemistry, or mathematics, we were helping to invent the structure of performance assessments, using some of the methods gleaned from the study of expertise. So this is one area where I have continued to engage, in particular, given both Lumsdaine's and Glaser's commitment to technology. I have moved from only school-based assessments of the sort now under development by the Consortia assessing the new *Common Core State Standards* to deep engagement in the world of technology and assessment through technology.

Probably 5 years after I became CSE Director, I began a long connection with research and development in the military. I was engaged in the mid-1980s in studies of intelligent games, intelligent tutoring systems, and other artificial intelligence interventions. Here developments in cognitive science were central and this domain influenced our team's additional studies in problem solving, metacognition, teamwork, and decision making. In most technology, our role began as evaluators, developing first reasonable outcome measures, validating them, and finding a way to document the effects or lack thereof of the systems. Eventually, I began to be part of the design of systems, rather than simply their evaluation, first through the structure of formative evaluation or formative assessment, and then as a developer. Our current work

in games and simulations lasting over the last 8 years or so and continuing forward is a good illustration of the transition. Another note from the past is that the search continues to find methods to personalize again learning for different learners.

A side effect of my activities, first in evaluation, then in performance assessment, and the focus on validity, was a move into the public policy arena, where I have played occasionally useful and often symbolic roles in helping the United States (and some few other countries) to improve their education and assessment processes. Psychology too became a player in public policy, but may recently have experienced harder times as the politics of education shifted to methods to be used immediately to improve educational quality, instead of midterm or more basic research. Ironically, the emphasis on short-term quality has had little yield, like corporate research and development.

At one level, I can see that there are nice connections as I progressed from intellectual emphasis to emphasis and almost always carried with me my previous interests. On the other hand, I see now a lack of flexibility for psychological scientists of the learning and instruction persuasion, at least in government funding. I miss and am trying to recreate the years at the CSE, which became the National Center for Research on Evaluation, Standards, and Student Testing (CRESST), where we could find the best scholars in the world and let them think up ideas that might be useful in the longer run. As an example, we were dealing with measuring learnable cognitive processes in the 1970s and 1980s, investigating how to measure almost the very same list just reified by a recent report of the National Research Council (2011).

So what happened? I was very young, and one of the few women around, and as a consequence I was given many opportunities usually held for more august scholars. I liked being the youngest in the room, liked the power it gave me, and tried not to waste opportunities. Looking back personally, I have been able, for the most part, to set my own goals and have been lucky to have had wonderful people to guide me, to work with, and to take ideas, change them, and make them real. I have had an innovative life, not by any external judgment, but by my own lights. Now I am the oldest in the room, not the power position, but happy most often to be involved. Were I to do it over again, I would take more time to play with my children.

## Conclusion

### Frank Farley

Many of the reflections on the past, present, and future of educational psychology expressed by the essayists in this chapter are in accord with a volume of a quarter of a century ago sponsored by the American Psychological Association Division of Educational Psychology and edited by Wittrock and Farley (1989a). That work projected many of the recent developments in the field discussed by our essayists, themselves scholars who have often been instrumental in these developments. In outlining essential competencies of educational psychologists and a model curriculum, Wittrock and

Farley (1989b) proposed as necessary "for the further development of educational psychology as a discipline" many of the topics emphasized in this chapter. They included such topics as "cognition and instruction; motivation and emotion; human development; individual differences; . . . technology, learning and instruction; . . . measurement; research methods (quantitative and qualitative) and statistical analyses of data (including the powerful new multivariate techniques)." Notably, other chapters in the present volume have these emphases as well.

As the overall editor of this chapter, I have, of course, reflected myself on the question of our past, present, and future that I posed to the eight essayists. Clearly the central emergence of cognitive psychology was absorbed by educational psychology but also influenced by educational psychology (see Farley, 2010). Education became historically a major venue for developing, testing, and applying cognitive paradigms. Where the present status is concerned, the discipline is strong, but in my view some storm clouds are gathering.

The quality of the science in psychology and education needs serious evaluation at the present, and projecting the future (Farley, Jennings, & Smith-Dyer, 2011; Makel & Plucker, 2014; Mervis, 2014; Nosek, Spies, & Motyl, 2012; Spelman, 2012). Research in the broad domain of psychology seldom is subjected to direct replication, replicability being widely seen as a gold standard in science; participant samples are usually relatively small, convenience samples; overgeneralizations are often made based upon limited and special samples; conditions of testing, and of conducting studies, are often divorced from the real world and conducted under contrived conditions; confirmation bias and other biases may be at work; tests and measures used may be poorly validated; the "file drawer effect" and the bias toward publication of statistically significant results over null results may be an impediment to valid causal inference, among other issues of scientific quality. The widespread embrace of complex statistical analyses in educational psychology (see any recent major journal in the discipline), such as structural equation modeling, hierarchical linear modeling, growth curve modeling, and big data, where the conclusions drawn are often abstract and far removed from an actual child or proximal behavior, are not helpful for Ms. Brown in her fourth-grade classroom. This remove from actual behavior concerns me. This issue of the usability of research has also been raised by some of the essayists herein.

There are evolving areas of scholarship that bear on education and psychology, such as online learning, games, and educational technology generally, where many different scholarly disciplines are increasingly involved. Maintaining educational psychology's identity as the main home where education and psychology meet may become increasingly difficult. This writer and most of the essayists above are optimistic about educational psychology's future. The very fact of the current debates over the quality of psychological research is healthy, so that future research and application can be improved as needed. Bringing psychology to bear on education will not cease, and educational psychology will be significantly involved in the evolution of learning and teaching in the decades ahead.

## References

Achieve. (2013). *Next generation science standards.* Washington, DC: Achieve.

Alexander, P. A. (Ed.). (2003). Rediscovering the philosophical roots of educational psychology. (Special issue.) *Educational Psychologist, 38*(3).

Alexander, P. A. (2004). In the year 2020: Envisioning the possibilities for educational psychology. *Educational Psychologist, 39,* 149–156.

Alexander, P. A., & the Disciplined Reading and Learning Research Laboratory. (2012). Reading into the future: Competence for the 21st century. *Educational Psychologist, 47*(4), 1–22.

Alexander, P. A., Murphy, P. K., & Greene, J. A. (2012). Projecting educational psychology's future from its past and present: A trend analysis. In K. R. Harris, S. Graham, & T. Urdan (Eds.), *Educational psychology handbook: Vol. 1. Theories, constructs, and critical issues* (pp. 3–32). Washington, DC: American Psychological Association.

Alexander, P. A., & Winne, P. H. (Eds.) (2006). *Handbook of educational psychology* (2nd ed.). Mahwah, NJ: Lawrence Erlbaum Associates.

Anderman, E. M. (2011). Educational psychology in the twenty-first century: Challenges for our community. *Educational Psychologist, 46,* 185–196.

Anderson, L. M., Blumenfeld, P., Pintrich, P. R., Clark, C. M., Marx, R. W., & Peterson, P. (1995). Educational psychology for teachers: Reforming our courses, rethinking our roles. *Educational Psychologist, 30,* 143–157.

Anderson, L., Krathwohl, D. R., Airasian, P. W., Cruikshank, K. A., Mayer, R. E., Pintrich, P. R., Raths, J., & Wittrock, M. C. (2001). *A taxonomy for learning, teaching, and assessing.* New York: Longman.

Anderson, T. & Shattuck, J. (2012). Design-based research: A decade of progress in educational research? *Educational Researcher, 41*(1), 16–25.

Atkinson, R. C., Bower, G. H., & Crothers, E. H. (1965). *An introduction to mathematical learning theory.* New York: Wiley.

Atkinson, R. C., & Crothers, E. J. (1964). A comparison of paired-associated learning models having different acquisition and retention axioms. *Journal of Mathematical Psychology, 1,* 285–315.

Berliner, D. C. (1992). Telling the stories of educational psychology. *Educational Psychologist, 27,* 143–161.

Berliner, D. C. (1993). The science of psychology and the practice of schooling: The one hundred year journey of educational psychology from interest, to disdain, to respect for practice. In T. K. Fagan & G. R. VandenBos (Eds.), *Exploring applied psychology: Origins and critical analysis: Master lecturers, 1992.* Washington, DC: American Psychological Association.

Berliner, D. C. (2006). Educational psychology: Searching for essence throughout a century of influence. In P. A. Alexander & P. H. Winne (Eds.), *Handbook of educational psychology* (2nd ed., pp. 3–27). Mahwah, NJ: Erlbaum.

Berliner, D. C. (2008). Research, policy, and practice: The great disconnect. In S. D. Lapan & M. T. Quartaroli (Eds.), *Research essentials: An introduction to designs and practices* (pp. 295–325). Hoboken, NJ: Jossey-Bass.

Berliner, D. C., & Calfee, R. C. (Eds.) (1996). *Handbook of educational psychology.* New York: Macmillan.

Bloom, B. (1976). *Human characteristics and school learning.* New York: McGraw-Hill.

Blumenfeld, P. & Anderson, L. (Eds.). (1996). Special issue: Teacher education and educational psychology. *Educational Psychologist, 31,* 1–4.

Blumenfeld, P. C., Hicks, L., & Krajcik, J. S. (1996). Teaching educational psychology through instructional planning. *Educational Psychologist, 31,* 51–61.

Bower, G. H. (1961). Application of an all-or-none model to paired-associate learning. *Psychometrika, 26,* 255–276.

Bower, G. H. (1994). A turning point in mathematical learning theory. *Psychological Review, 101*(2), 290–300.

Bower, G. H., & Hilgard, E. R. (1981). *Theories of learning,* 5th ed. Englewood Cliffs, NJ: Prentice-Hall.

Bransford, J. D., Brown, A. L., & Cocking, R. R. (Eds.). (2000). *How people learn*. Washington, DC: National Academy Press.

Bransford, J. D., & Schwartz, D. L. (1999). Rethinking transfer: A simple proposal with multiple implications. In A. Iran-Nejad, & P. D. Pearson (Eds.), *Review of research in education: Vol. 24* (pp. 61–100). Washington, DC: American Educational Research Association.

Brophy, J. E. (1974). Some good five-cent cigars. *Educational Psychologist, 11*, 46–51.

Brown, A. (1992). Design experiments: Theoretical and methodological challenges in creating complex interventions in classroom settings. *Journal of the Learning Sciences, 2*, 141–178.

Brown, A. (1994). The advancement of learning. *Educational Researcher, 28*(8), 4–12.

Brownell, W. A. (1935). Psychological considerations in the learning and teaching of arithmetic. In *The teaching of arithmetic: Tenth yearbook of the National Council of Teachers of Mathematics*. New York: Columbia University Press.

Calfee, R. C. (1981). Cognitive psychology and educational practice. In D. C. Berliner (Ed.), *Review of research in education* (pp. 3–74). Washington, DC: American Educational Research Association.

Calfee, R. C., & Wilson, K. M. (in press). *Assessing the Common Core Standards: American schools in 2020 and how they got there*. New York: Guilford Press.

Carroll, J. B. (1963). The place of education psychology in the study of education. In J. Walton, & J. L. Kuethe (Eds.), *The discipline of education* (pp. 101–119). Madison, WI: University of Wisconsin Press.

Carroll, J. B. (1993). Education psychology in the 21st century. *Educational Psychologist, 28*, 89–96.

Clark, R. C., & Mayer, R. E. (2011). *E-learning and the science of instruction* (3rd ed.). San Francisco: Pfeiffer.

Collins, A. (1992). Toward a design science of education. In E. Scanlon & T. O'Shea (Eds.), *New directions in educational technology* (pp. 15–22). Berlin: Springer.

Darwin, C. R. (1859). *On the origin of species by means of natural selection, or the preservation of favoured races in the struggle for life*. London: John Murray.

Day, S. B., & Goldstone, R. L. (2012). The import of knowledge export: Connecting findings and theories of transfer of learning. *Educational Psychologist, 47*(3), 153–176.

De Corte, E. (2010). Historical developments in the understanding of learning. In H. Dumont, D. Istance, & F. Benavides (Eds.), *The nature of learning. Using research to inspire practice* (pp. 35–67). Paris: OECD Publishing.

De Corte, E. (in press). Design experiments. In D. C. Phillips (Ed.), *Encyclopedia of educational theory and philosophy*. Thousand Oaks, CA: Sage Publications.

De Corte, E., & Weinert, F. E. (Eds.). (1996). *International encyclopedia of developmental and instructional psychology*. Oxford, UK: Elsevier Science.

Depaepe, F., De Corte, E., & Verschaffel, L. (2007). Unravelling the culture of the mathematics classroom: A videobased study in sixth grade. *International Journal of Educational Research, 46*, 266–279.

Duckworth, E. (2006). *The having of wonderful ideas: And other essays on teaching and learning* (3rd ed.). New York: Teachers College Press.

Dunlosky, J., Rawson, K. A., Marsh, E. J., Nathan, M. J., & Willingham, D. T. (2013). Improving students' learning with effective learning techniques: Promising directions from cognitive and educational psychology. *Psychological Science in the Public Interest, 14*(1), 1–58.

Ebbinghaus, H. (1913). *Memory: A contribution to experimental psychology* (trans. H. A. Ruger). New York: Teachers College Press (originally published in 1885).

Engeström, Y. (1999). Activity theory and individual and social transformation. In Y. Engeström, R. Miettinen, & R. L. Punamaki (Eds.), *Perspectives on activity theory* (pp. 19–38). Cambridge, England: Cambridge University Press.

Estes, W. (1950). Toward a statistical theory of learning. *Psychological Review, 57*(2), 94–107.

Estes, W. K. (1964). All-or-none processes in learning and retention. *American Psychologist, 19,* 16–25.

Farley, F. (Ed.). (2010). Special section: The contributions of M.C. Wittrock—A scientific, professional, and personal appreciation. *Educational Psychologist, 45*(1), 37–70.

Farley, F., Jennings, H., & Smith-Dyer, T. (2011). *Examining psychological science: Some inconvenient truths in the new monastic order.* Paper presented at the American Psychological Association Annual Meeting, Washington, DC.

Gage, N. L. (1989). The paradigm wars and their aftermath: A "historical" sketch of research on teaching since 1989. *Educational Researcher, 18* (7), 4–10.

Gagné, R. (1965). *The conditions of learning.* New York: Holt, Rinehart & Winston.

Glaser, R. (Ed.). (1965). *Teaching machines and programmed learning II: Data and directions.* Washington, DC: National Education Association.

Goldstone, R. L., & Day, S. B. (Eds.). (2012). New conceptualizations of transfer of learning (Special issue). *Educational Psychologist, 47,* 149–258.

Greeno, J. G. (2011). A situative perspective on cognition and learning in interaction. In T. Koschmann (Ed.), *Theories of learning and studies of instructional practice* (pp. 41–72). New York: Springer.

Greeno, J. G., Collins, A. M., & Resnick, L. B. (1996). Cognition and learning. In D. C. Berliner & R. C. Calfee (Eds.), *Handbook of educational psychology* (pp. 15–46). New York: Macmillan.

Halpern, D. F., Graesser, A., & Hakel, M. (2007). *25 learning principles to guide pedagogy and the design of learning environments.* Washington, DC: Association for Psychological Science Task Force on Lifelong Learning at Work and at Home.

Hattie, J. J. (2009). *Visible learning: A synthesis of over 800 meta-analyses relating to achievement.* New York: Routledge.

Howard-Jones, P. (2010). *Introducing neuroeducational research. Neuroscience, education and the brain from contexts to practice.* London: Routledge.

Hunt, E., & Minstrell, J. (1996). Effective instruction in science and mathematics: Psychological principles and social constraints. *Issues in Education: Contributions from Educational Psychology, 2,* 123–162.

Judd, C. H. (1936). *Education as cultivation of the higher mental processes.* New York: Macmillan.

Kaplan Higher Education Corporation. (2013). *Learning science and educational entrepreneurship.* Retrieved from https://kapx.kaplan.com/events/learning-science-ed-entrepreneurship/ (accessed February 20, 2015).

Katona, G. (1940). *Organizing and memorizing: Studies in the psychology of learning and teaching.* New York: Columbia University Press.

Kintsch, W., & van Dijk, T. A. (1978). Toward a model of text comprehension and production. *Psychological Review, 85,* 363–394.

Koedinger, K. R., Corbett, A. C., & Perfetti, C. (2012). The knowledge-learning-instruction (KLI) framework: Bridging the science–practice chasm to enhance robust student learning. *Cognitive Science, 36,* 757–798.

Learner-Centered Principles Work Group of the APA Board of Educational Affairs. (1997). *Learner-centered psychological principles: A framework for school reform and redesign.* Washington, DC: American Psychological Association.

Lee, W., DeSilva, R., Peterson, E. J., Calfee, R. C., & Stahovich, T. F. (2008). Newton's pen: A pen-based tutoring system for statics. *Computers & Graphics, 32*(5), 511–524.

Lehtinen, E. (2010). Potential of teaching and learning supported by ICT for the acquisition of deep conceptual knowledge and the development of wisdom. In E. De Corte & J. E. Fenstad (Eds.), *From information to knowledge; from knowledge to wisdom: Challenges and changes facing higher education in the digital age* (pp. 79–88). London: Portland Press.

Leonard, G. (1968). *Education and ecstasy.* New York: Delacorte Press.

Makel, M. C., & Plucker, J. A. (2014). Facts are more important than novelty: Replication in the education sciences. *Educational Researcher, 43*(6), 304–316.

Martinez, M. E. (2013). *Future bright: A transforming vision of human intelligence.* New York: Oxford University Press.

Mayer, R. E. (1992). Cognition and instruction: On their historic meeting within educational psychology. *Journal of Educational Psychology, 84,* 405–412.

Mayer, R. E. (2003). E. L. Thorndike's enduring contributions to educational psychology. In B. J. Zimmerman & D. H. Schunk (Eds.), *Educational psychology: A century of contributions* (pp. 113–154). Washington, DC: American Psychology Association.

Mayer, R. E. (2004). Teaching of subject matter. In S. T. Fiske (Ed.), *Annual review of psychology* (Vol. 55, pp. 715–744). Palo Alto, CA: Annual Reviews.

Mayer, R. E. (2008). *Learning and instruction* (2nd ed.). Upper Saddle River, NJ: Pearson.

Mayer, R. E. (2011). *Applying the science of learning.* Upper Saddle River, NJ: Pearson.

Mayer, R. E., & Alexander, P. A. (2011). *Handbook of research on learning and instruction.* New York: Routledge.

Mayer, R. E., & Wittrock, M. C. (2006). Problem solving. In P. Alexander, P. Winne, & G. Phye (Eds.), *Handbook of educational psychology* (pp. 287–303). Mahwah. NJ: Erlbaum.

McDermott, J. J. (2003). Hast any philosophy in thee, shepherd? *Educational Psychologist, 38*(3), 133–136.

McInerney, D. M. (2006). Educational psychology—theory, research, and teaching: A 25-year retrospective. In K. Wheldall (Ed.), *Developments in educational psychology: How far have we come in 25 years?* (pp. 13–27). New York: Routledge.

Mervis, J. (2014). Why null results rarely see the light of day. *Science, 345*, 992.

Murphy, P. K. (2003). The philosophy in thee: Tracing philosophical influences in educational psychology. *Educational Psychologist, 38*(3), 137–145.

Murphy, P. K., & Alexander, P. A. (2013). Situating text, talk, and transfer in conceptual change: Concluding thoughts. In S. Vosniadou (Ed.), *International handbook of research on conceptual change* (2nd ed., pp. 603–621). New York: Routledge.

Murphy, P. K., Alexander, P. A., & Muis, K. R. (2012). Knowledge and knowing: The journey from philosophy and psychology to human learning. In K. R. Harris, S. Graham, & T. Urdan (Eds.), *Educational psychology handbook: Vol. 1. Theories, constructs, and critical issues* (pp. 189–226). Washington, DC: American Psychological Association.

National Governors' Association (NGA) & Council of Chief State School Officers (CCSSO). (2010). *Common Core Standards for English language, arts & literacy in history/social studies, science, and technical subjects.* Washington, DC: National Governors' Association (NGA) & Council of Chief State School Officers (CCSSO).

National Research Council. (2011). *A framework for science education.* Washington, DC: National Research Council.

Newell, A., & Simon, H. A. (1972). *Human problem solving.* Englewood Cliffs, NJ: Prentice Hall.

Nosek, B. A., Spies, J. R., & Motyl, M. (2012). Scientific utopia: II. Restructuring incentives and practices to promote truth over publishability. *Perspectives in Psychological Science, 7*, 615–631.

Olson, M. H., & Hergenbahn, B. R. (2012). *Introduction to theories of learning* (9th ed.). New York: Pearson.

O'Neil, H. F. (Ed.). (2005). *What works in distance learning: Guidelines.* Greenwich, CT: Information Age Publishing.

Pajares, F. (2003). In search of psychology's philosophical center. *Educational Psychologist, 38*(3), 177–181.

Pashler, H., Bain, P., Bottage, B., Graesser, A., Koedinger, K., McDaniel, M., & Metcalfe, J. (2007). *Organizing instruction and study to improve student*

*learning.* Washington, DC: National Center for Educational Research, Institute of Educational Sciences, U.S. Department of Education.

Patrick, H., Anderman, L. H., Bruening, P. S., & Duffin, L. C. (2011). The role of educational psychology in teacher education: Three challenges for educational psychologists. *Educational Psychologist, 46,* 71–83.

Pellegrino, J. W., Chudowsky, N., & Glaser, R. (2001). *Knowing what students know.* Washington, DC: National Academy Press.

Peterson, P. L., Clark, D. M., & Dickson, W. P. (1990). Educational psychology as a foundation in teacher education: Reforming an old notion. *Teachers College Record, 91*, 322–346.

Rosiek, J. (2003). A qualitative research methodology psychology can call its own: Dewey's call for qualitative experimentalism. *Educational Psychologist, 38*(3), 165–175.

Salomon, G., & Ben-Zvi, D. (2006). The difficult marriage between education and technology: Is the marriage doomed? In L. Verschaffel, F. Dochy, M. Boekaerts, & S. Vosniadou (Eds.), *Instructional psychology: Past, present and future trends. Sixteen essays in honour of Erik De Corte.* Oxford, UK: Elsevier.

Sawyer, R. K. (Ed.) (2006). *The Cambridge handbook of the learning sciences.* Cambridge, MA: Cambridge University Press.

Schunk, D. H. (2011). *Learning theories: An educational perspective.* New York: Pearson.

Spelman, B.A. (2012). Introduction to the special issue: Data, data, everywhere . . . especially in my file drawer. *Perspectives in Psychological Science, 7*, 58–59.

Stokes, D. E. (1997). *Pasteur's quadrant: Basic science and technological innovation.* Washington, DC: Brookings Institution Press.

Vosniadou, S. (2001). *How children learn.* (Educational Practices Series, 7). Geneva: International Bureau of Education.

Vosniadou, S. (Ed.). (2008). *International handbook of research on conceptual change.* New York: Routledge.

Weinert, F. E., & De Corte, E. (1996). Translating research into practice. In E. De Corte & F. E. Weinert (Eds.), *International encyclopedia of developmental and instructional psychology* (pp. 43–50). Oxford, UK: Elsevier Science.

Wertheimer, M. (1959). *Productive thinking* (enlarged edition). New York: Harper & Row. (Original work published 1945.)

Wittrock, M. C., & Farley, F. (Eds.) (1989a). *The future of educational psychology.* Hillsdale, NJ: Lawrence Erlbaum Associates.

Wittrock, M. C., & Farley, F. (1989b). Toward a blueprint for educational psychology. In M. C. Wittrock, & F. Farley (Eds.), *The future of educational psychology* (pp. 193–199). Hillsdale, NJ: Lawrence Erlbaum Associates.

Woolfolk Hoy, A. (1996). Teaching educational psychology: Texts in context. *Educational Psychologist, 31*, 41–49.

Woolfolk Hoy, A. (2000). Educational psychology in teacher education. *Educational Psychologist, 35*, 257–270.

Worrell, F. C. (2013). *Applying psychological science to using data for continuous teacher preparation program improvement: Draft report of a board of educational affairs task force.* Washington DC: American Psychological Association.

Zimmerman, B. J., & Schunk, D. H. (Eds.). (2011). *Handbook of self-regulation of learning and performance.* New York: Routledge.

# AFTERWORD II

# On Impact Beyond the Field

*Eric M. Anderman*
The Ohio State University

*Lyn Corno*
Teachers College, Columbia University

After completing a project of this scope and breadth, editors can pause to reassess their approach, strategies, and decisions. We have each previously engaged in large projects of this nature, and on occasion during this one, expressed the feeling that we might have been better off doing some things differently. Nevertheless, having now had the opportunity to see the entirety of the volume completed, we are most pleased with the results. Our authors worked diligently to meet our goals, producing chapters that acknowledge successes of years past at the same time that they look toward the future.

As fields of inquiry move forward, inevitably there is tension between what researchers *want* and what they *need* to study. Establishing a balance between our intrinsic interests and external demands is challenging but important. The work in this volume makes clear that for the educational psychology community, it is particularly essential to respond to larger-scale changes in education policies that affect learners of all ages. Policies evolve continuously, of course, and at multiple levels. Those charged with the education of children, adolescents, and adults must operate within the constraints of local, national, and international policies that take many forms. Some policies are legislated, some are enforced locally, and some reach the stature of national standards, but they all remain present and in need of attention from our field, certainly in the near future.

To give just a few examples, in the United States over the past decade there have been extraordinarily significant changes in educational standards (e.g., the "Common Core"), in the use of technology in learning environments, and in the nature of schools (e.g., the roles of charter schools and for-profit education). Because these radical policy shifts continue to occur in education, educational psychologists have come to recognize that we do not operate in a vacuum (e.g., E. Anderman, 2011; Patrick, Anderman, Bruening, & Duffin, 2011). As the prominent authors of the first section of this

Afterword make clear, if our field is going to thrive, we must continue to acknowledge our place within the larger social context of education, and do a better job of using our past discoveries as guides to its future. We sincerely hope that the chapters in this book are helpful to educational psychologists on this more extended journey. Ultimately, whether we refer to ourselves as educational psychologists, learning scientists, educational researchers (or any of a host of other territorial monikers), we all seek to improve learning across the lifespan and over diverse contexts.

A consistent problem that educational psychologists lament is the fact that, while there actually is methodologically rigorous research with consistent findings that can be used to inform educational practice productively, that research is not shared often among practitioners, for a variety of reasons. Change is not equivalent to implementation. The knowledge provided by each chapter in this volume can potentially inform educational practice; the challenge is to move this information from our bookshelves into the policy domain. These chapters contain updated, state-of-the-art information about research-based practices related to a host of recurring policy issues; how will readers use them?

In this vein, there are a few developments worth mentioning that are discussed by our authors in different research domains within the field. One area that has seen incredible growth since the publication of the second edition of this *Handbook* is the use of technology in education. The chapters by Mishra and his colleagues on educational psychology within the digitally networked world (Chapter 3), and by Natriello on networked learning (Chapter 25), directly address the impact of the digital world on our work. Several other chapters also examine the roles of technology in specific areas of educational psychology. For example, Hmelo-Silver and Chinn discuss aspects of technology as they relate to group collaboration (Chapter 26). In addition, Barron and

Bell discuss the role played by computer-based learning environments beyond school (Chapter 24). Finally, chapters by Penuel and Frank (Chapter 2) and by Mandinach and Lash (Chapter 29) review recent developments in data mining and learning analytics, which have tremendous implications for the study and assessment of learning. These are just a few examples, but the theme of technology resurfaces continuously throughout many of the chapters in this volume, providing suggestions for ways that practitioners and administrators in education might improve their work.

Another issue that consistently arises and often is addressed in education policy is literacy instruction, including when, how, and where to teach it. The chapters by Bailey (Chapter 15) and by Wilkinson and Gaffney (Chapter 17), in particular, provide updated summaries of scholarship that can immediately inform practice. O'Brien and Rogers (Chapter 23) take on the social dimensions of literacy acquisition to illustrate how sometimes theory can be a useful guide to practical change. Still other salient developments include the explosion of science, technology, engineering, and mathematics (STEM) programs internationally, and the globally diverse student populations present in today's schools. Chapters in this *Handbook* that should be useful reading for those involved in STEM education are those by Sinatra and Seyranian (Chapter 18) and Tabak (Chapter 20, which also discusses the role of the internet in science learning), among others. Our authors are likewise eloquent on ways that practitioners can better understand and capitalize on the growing diversity in schooling (e.g., see chapters by Nasir, Rowley, and Perez (Chapter 14); Ford (Chapter 27); and Anderman and Klassen (Chapter 30).

Finally, the complicated problem of dropping out of school continues to loom. Dropping out of high school in today's milieu is something rooted in as many external issues that confront students as it is in their internal motivations. As a result, the numerous policies implemented to address early exit have met with little success. And yet, several chapters in this volume inform important practices that can be implemented in a timely manner to prevent student dropout. These include the chapter on motivation by Linnenbrink-Garcia and Patall (Chapter 7); the chapter on volition by Oettingen, Schrage, and Gollwitzer (Chapter 8); the chapter on emotion by Boekaerts and Pekrun (Chapter 6); and the chapter on motivational interventions by Hulleman and Barron (Chapter 12).

In closing, we say once again that the authors writing in this *Handbook* represent the wisdom of our long history of research in educational psychology, as well as its newer and emerging innovations. Reading and editing these chapters has been rewarding labor for both of us, providing a reminder of why we went to graduate school to study educational psychology. If this book could serve as a valued resource for practitioners and policy makers as well as scholars, then that would be a gratifying outcome indeed.

## References

Anderman, E. M. (2011). Educational psychology in the twenty-first century: Challenges for our community. *Educational Psychologist, 46*(3), 185–196.

Patrick, H., Anderman, L. H., Bruening, P. S., & Duffin, L. C. (2011). The role of educational psychology in teacher education: Three challenges for educational psychologists. *Educational Psychologist, 46*(2), 71–83.

# Contributor Bios

**Patricia A. Alexander** is the Jean Mullan Professor of Literacy and Distinguished Scholar-Teacher in the Department of Human Development and Quantitative Methodology at the University of Maryland (UMD). She also directs the Disciplined Reading and Learning Research Laboratory at UMD. Her programs of research, which relate broadly to human learning and academic development, include studies of epistemic beliefs, expertise development, learning in academic domains, and learning from text both online and offline.

**Eric M. Anderman** is a Professor of Educational Psychology in the College of Education and Human Ecology at The Ohio State University. His research examines motivation during adolescence, with particular foci on academic cheating, changes in motivation across school transitions, and engagement in risky behaviors. He is a Fellow of the American Educational Research Association (AERA) and the American Psychological Association Division 15, and is a former President of Division 15 and former Chair of the AERA Motivation in Education special-interest group. He served as Associate Editor for the *Journal of Educational Psychology*, and is currently editor of *Theory into Practice*.

**Lynley H. Anderman** is a Professor of Educational Psychology in the College of Education and Human Ecology at The Ohio State University. She conducts research on student motivation in school settings, with a particular focus on students' perceptions of the social interpersonal climate of classrooms and schools, and malleable factors in instructional climates. She has served as Executive Editor for the *Journal of Experimental Education*, Associate Editor for *Theory into Practice*, and on several editorial boards. She is a Fellow of the American Psychological Association Division 15. She holds a Ph.D. from the Combined Program in Education and Psychology at the University of Michigan.

**Alison L. Bailey** is Professor of Human Development and Psychology at the University of California, Los Angeles. A graduate of Harvard University, Bailey is a developmental psycholinguist working on issues germane to children's linguistic, social, and educational development. She has published widely in these areas and authored commercial assessments of early language and literacy development as well as analytical tools for language and literacy characterization. She is also a Faculty Research Partner at the National Center for Research on Evaluation, Standards, and Student Testing, and serves on the technical advisory boards of a number of states and consortia.

**Eva L. Baker** is Distinguished Professor of Education in the University of California, Los Angeles Graduate School of Education and Information Studies and Co-Director of the National Center for Research on Evaluation, Standards, and Student Testing. Baker initiated and served as president of the World Education Research Association, following her tenure as president of the American Educational Research Association (AERA). She was president of the Educational Psychology Division of the American Psychological Association, where she is a fellow, a status also held in the American Psychological Society and AERA. She was Chair of the Board on Testing and Assessment of the National Research Council and Co-Chair of the Joint Committee on the Revision of the *Standards for Educational and Psychological Testing* (1999). She has membership in the National Academy of Education.

**Brigid Barron** is an Associate Professor at the School of Education at Stanford, is a faculty co-lead of the Learning in Informal and Formal Environments (LIFE) center, and directs the Youth Learning Across Boundaries (YouthLAB) research group (http://www. stanford.edu/group/youthlab). She takes an ecological approach to understanding social processes of learning in and out of school with a focus on how digital technologies can serve as catalysts for collaborative learning. She has developed methods to document the evolution of interest-based learning, mapping children's activities to reveal the networks of partners and resources that have supported expertise development. A special focus of this work is articulating relationships between learner pathways, the development of interests, personal social networks, and designed catalysts for learning.

**Kenn E. Barron** is a professor of psychology at James Madison University and a faculty affiliate in the Center for Faculty Innovation. Kenn also co-coordinates the Motivation Research Institute at James Madison. In 2012, he was named a fellow of the American Psychological Association and one of Princeton Review's Top 300 Professors in America. He received his Ph.D. in social and personality psychology from the University of Wisconsin-Madison.

**Philip Bell** is a Professor of Education at the University of Washington Seattle and holds the Shauna C. Larson Chair in Learning Sciences. He pursues a cognitive and cultural program of research about how people learn about science and technology in ways that are personally consequential to them both in and out of school. His current work involves design-based research on novel learning experiences and resources that promote educational equity as well as broad-scale design-based implementation research conducted through collaborative partnerships of researchers and practitioners. He serves as the Executive Director of the Institute for Science and Math Education at the University of Washington that conducts equity-focused research and development projects in science, technology, engineering, and mathematics education.

**David C. Berliner** is Regents' Professor Emeritus at the Mary Lou Fulton Teachers College at Arizona State University. He is a former president of Division 15 and the American Educational Research Association (AERA). He is a fellow of the National Academy of Education and the International Academy of Education. He has been honored with the Brock award, the AERA award for distinguished contributions to education, the E. L. Thorndike award from the American Psychological Association for lifetime achievements, and the National Education Association Friend of Education award for his work on behalf of the education profession. Berliner has authored more than 200 published articles, chapters, and books.

**Angela Bermudez** is a researcher at the Center for Applied Ethics in Deusto University (Bilbao, Spain). Her current research investigates the processes and mechanisms by which history education in different countries fosters or hinders a critical understanding of political violence. She obtained her doctorate from the Harvard Graduate School of Education in 2008. Prior to that, she worked in Colombia, where she conducted research and developed curriculum guidelines, teaching resources, and assessment tools for social studies and civic education. She also worked in several teacher professional development programs, and taught history and democracy to high-school students.

**Monique Boekaerts** is currently an emeritus full professor at Leiden University. She built up a national and international reputation for the development and application of her dual-processing self-regulation model. She is an expert in motivation, emotion, and self-regulation. For many years she was the principal investigator of the Platform for School Innovation in Secondary Vocational Education in the Netherlands. Boekaerts is a founding member of the European Association of Learning and Instruction (EARLI). She served as the president of EARLI (1999–2001), Educational, Instructional and School Psychology of the International Association for Analytical Psychology (1998–2002), and the International Academy of Education (2006–2012).

**Eric Bredo** is Professor at the Ontario Institute for Studies in Education, University of Toronto. Much of his work in recent years relates classical philosophical pragmatism to contemporary thought in psychology, sociology, and education. He has held positions at the University of Illinois, Virginia Tech, and the University of Virginia. He received an MS in Engineering Economic Systems, an MA in sociology, and a Ph.D. in sociology of education from Stanford University.

**Robert C. Calfee** passed away during the production of this *Handbook*. He was a cognitive psychologist known for his research on the effects of schooling on the intellectual potential of individuals and groups. His interests focused on assessment of beginning literacy skills and the broader reach of the school as a literate environment. At the time of this writing, he was Professor Emeritus at Stanford University and the University of California, Riverside.

**Mario Carretero** is Professor of Cognitive Psychology at Autonoma University Madrid (Spain). He currently investigates history learning processes, mainly related to historical narratives as cultural tools constructing national identity and patriotism. He holds a Ph.D. in Developmental Psychology from Complutense University (Madrid). He has been invited researcher at Harvard and Stanford University and received the Guggenheim Fellowship.

**Clark A. Chinn** is a professor of educational psychology at Rutgers, the State University of New Jersey. He received his Ph.D. from the University of Illinois at Urbana-Champaign in 1997. His research focuses on reasoning and argumentation, epistemic practices and epistemic cognition, conceptual change, and collaborative learning. He has worked extensively with model-based inquiry in middle-school science classes, designing learning environments and investigating how these environments promote conceptual change and growth in reasoning. He is currently the Editor of the journal *Educational Psychologist*.

**Sherice N. Clarke** is a Postdoctoral Research Associate at the University of Pittsburgh's Learning Research and Development Center. Her research examines learning through engaging in dialogue. She examines the ways in which social processes interface with and impact learning processes in dialogue. She holds an MEd and Ph.D. in education from the University of Edinburgh.

**Lyn Corno** was formerly Professor of Education and Psychology, Teachers College, Columbia University. Currently she is Co-Editor of *Teachers College Record* and a member of the Teachers College EdLab, a collective conducting technology-oriented research and design studies. She has been President of Division 15 of the American Psychological Association, Chair of the Visiting Panel for Research at Educational Testing Service, and Chair of the Board for the National Society for the Study of Education. She has also been Editor of the *American Educational Research Journal* and *Educational Psychologist*. She is author, co-author, or editor of several scholarly books, including *Remaking the Concept of Aptitude: Extending the Legacy of Richard E. Snow* (2002).

**Erik De Corte** is Emeritus Professor of Educational Psychology and former director (and co-founder) of the Centre for Instructional Psychology and Technology at the Faculty of Psychology and Educational Sciences of the University of Leuven, Belgium. His research concentrated on different aspects of mathematics learning and teaching using a broad-spectrum approach, i.e., the concurrent application of a variety of complementary data-gathering and data-analysis techniques. Currently he serves as the chair of the Higher Education, Research and Culture in European Society (HERCULES) Expert Group of the Academia Europaea.

**Frank Farley** is L. H. Carnell Professor, Temple University. He is former President of the American Psychological Association (APA) and its Divisions 1, 10, 15, 32, 46, and 52 and current President of Division 48; former President of the American Educational Research Association (AERA), International Council of Psychologists. He is Fellow of the American Association for the Advancement of Science, New York Academy of Sciences, American Psychological Association, AERA, Psychonomics Society, and the Association for Psychological Science, among other societies. He is recipient of the E. L. Thorndike Award for Career Achievement in Educational Psychology. As a public intellectual he averages 100 or so media engagements a year. His scholarship covers education, personality, motivation, risk taking, heroism, crime, and violence.

**Donna Y. Ford** holds a joint appointment in the Department of Special Education and Department of Teaching and Learning at Vanderbilt University. She earned her Doctor of Philosophy degree in Urban Education (educational psychology) from Cleveland State University. She conducts research primarily in gifted education and multicultural/urban education. Specifically, her work focuses on the achievement gap; recruiting and retaining culturally different students in gifted education; multicultural curriculum and instruction; culturally competent teacher training and development; African American identity; and African American family involvement. She consults with school districts, and educational and legal organizations on topics such as underrepresentation in gifted education and advanced placement classes, multicultural/urban education and counseling, and closing the achievement gap. She has written several books, and

numerous articles and book chapters, and received several awards for her work in gifted education and urban education.

**Kenneth A. Frank** is a professor of Measurement and Quantitative Methods in the College of Education and Professor of Fisheries and Wildlife in the College of Agriculture at Michigan State University. His research interests include the study of schools as social organizations and the social embeddedness of natural resource use. His substantive areas are linked to several methodological interests: social network analysis, causal inference, and multilevel models.

**Janet S. Gaffney** is a Professor of Educational Psychology-Literacy at the University of Auckland and Professor Emeritus at the University of Illinois at Urbana-Champaign. Her research foci are literacy learning and leading in a coherent approach to teacher revitalization in which children's learning is the centripetal force that drives decisions and actions. She earned her Ph.D. in Special Education from Arizona State University.

**Robert Goldstone** is Chancellor's Professor in the Department of Psychological and Brain Sciences and Program in Cognitive Science at Indiana University. His research interests include concept learning and representation, perceptual learning, educational applications of cognitive science, decision making, collective behavior, and computational modeling of human cognition. He holds a Ph.D. in Psychology from University of Michigan.

**Peter M. Gollwitzer** is a Professor of Psychology at the Psychology Department of New York University and the University of Konstanz/Germany. Throughout his academic career, he has developed various models of action control: the Theory of Symbolic Self-Completion (with Robert A. Wicklund), the Mindset Model of Action Phases (with Heinz Heckhausen), the Auto-Motive Model of Automatic Goal Striving (with John A. Bargh), and the Theory of Intentional Action Control (that makes a distinction between goal intentions and implementation intentions). In all of these models various mechanisms of behavior change are delineated and respective moderators and mediators are distilled.

**Christine Greenhow** is an assistant professor of educational psychology and educational technology at the College of Education at Michigan State University. She holds undergraduate degrees in English and government from Dartmouth College, a master's in education from Boston College, and a doctorate in technology, innovation, and education from Harvard University. Her work explores learning and teaching in social media contexts, the design of networked learning environments, such as open source social networking applications for education, and a framework for social scholarship, or the integration of social media into novice and expert scholars' everyday work for potentially transformative practices.

**James G. Greeno** is an Adjunct Professor of Education at the School of Education at the University of Pittsburgh and an Emeritus Professor of Education of Stanford University. At Pitt he is a member of the Learning Science and Policy program. He has conducted empirical and theoretical research about learning and problem solving that is conceptually meaningful, using mathematical models, computational simulations, and discourse analysis. He is a member of the Society of Experimental Psychologists and is a retired member of the National Academy of Education.

**Helen Haste** is Visiting Professor in Education at Harvard Graduate School of Education and Emeritus Professor of Psychology at the University of Bath, UK. Her work is on moral and political development and action, peace movements, gender politics, and political engagement of young people. She has written extensively on the intersection of cultural discourses and narratives, the negotiation and social construction of meaning, and how the individual's thinking is generated in interaction with these. She has also explored these ideas in relation to science and society. Haste was President of the International Society of Political Psychology in 2002. She is a Fellow of the British Psychological Society, the British Academy of Social Sciences and the Royal Society of Arts.

**Cindy E. Hmelo-Silver** is Director of the Center for Research on Learning and Technology and Professor of Learning Sciences at Indiana University. She received her Ph.D. from Vanderbilt University in 1994. Her research focuses on learning in complex domains, computer-supported collaborative learning, and technology support for problem-based learning. She has worked with populations ranging from middle-school students to pre-service teachers to medical students. She has edited several books on collaborative learning and is past editor-in-chief of the *Journal of the Learning Sciences*. She is currently past-president of the International Society of Learning Sciences.

**Chris S. Hulleman** is a research associate professor at the Center for Advanced Study of Teaching and Learning in the Curry School of Education at the University of Virginia and a fellow of the Carnegie Foundation for the Advancement of Teaching. Chris also co-coordinates the Motivation Research Institute and is an affiliated faculty member in the Department of Psychology at James Madison University. He received his Ph.D. in social and personality psychology from the University of Wisconsin-Madison.

**Kimberly Reynolds Kelly** is Assistant Professor of Human Development at California State University Long Beach (CSULB). She received her Ph.D. in Education from the University of California, Los Angeles in 2011. Her research focuses on child discourse development, interactive and socioemotional origins of child linguistic and cognitive outcomes, parent–child interactions during autobiographical narrative conversations, and narrative measures of attachment. She is faculty advisor for the Human Development Student Association at CSULB.

**Robert M. Klassen** is Professor and Chair of the Psychology in Education Research Centre at the University of York in the United Kingdom. His research background is in motivation and engagement in school settings, but recently he has been focusing on applying educational psychology research to the problem of teacher selection. He has served as Associate Editor for the *Journal of Educational Psychology* and the *British Journal of Educational Psychology*, and on numerous editorial boards. He was awarded the American Psychological Association Division 15 Richard Snow Award in 2012 and the Paul Pintrich Award in 2004. He holds a Ph.D. in Educational Psychology from Simon Fraser University.

**Matthew J. Koehler** is professor of educational psychology and educational technology at the College of Education at Michigan State University. He holds undergraduate degrees in mathematics and computer science, a master's degree in computer science, and a Ph.D. in Educational Psychology. His work explores the pedagogical affordances (and constraints) of newer technologies for learning, specifically in the context of the professional development of teachers, and the design of technology-rich and innovative learning environments for adults and children. His work with teachers and technology has led to the development (in collaboration with Dr. Punya Mishra) of the Technological Pedagogical Content Knowledge framework.

**Patrick C. Kyllonen** is the Director of the Center for Academic and Workforce Readiness and Success (CAWRS) in the Research Division at Educational Testing Service in Princeton, New Jersey. CAWRS conducts research on and develops innovative assessments for skills that are important for success in K-12, higher education, and the workforce but that are not typically measured with conventional standardized tests. The work includes assessing non-cognitive skills on large-scale domestic and international achievement surveys, such as the Programme for International Student Assessment (PISA). He received his Ph.D. at Stanford University under the supervision of Richard Snow and Lee Cronbach.

**Andrea A. Lash** is a Senior Research Scientist at WestEd. As Co-Director of the Nevada Education Research Alliance of the Western Regional Educational Laboratory, she is working to build research collaborations with Nevada's school districts, institutes of higher education, and the state department of education, with the goals of improving students' chances of graduating from high school and the graduates' chances of being prepared for postsecondary education. She holds an MS in statistics and a Ph.D. in educational psychology from Stanford University.

**Lisa Linnenbrink-Garcia** is an associate professor of Educational Psychology in the Department of

Counseling, Educational Psychology, and Special Education at Michigan State University. She received her Ph.D. in Education and Psychology from the University of Michigan, Ann Arbor. Her research focuses on the development of achievement motivation in school settings and the interplay among motivation, emotions, and learning, especially in science and mathematics.

**Ellen B. Mandinach** is a senior research scientist and the director of the Data for Decisions Initiative at WestEd. She is an expert on data-driven decision making at classroom, school, district, and state levels. She is focusing on the development and measurement of a new construct, data literacy for teachers. She served as the president of the Division of Educational Psychology of the American Psychological Association. She holds a Ph.D. in educational psychology from Stanford University.

**Richard E. Mayer** is Professor of Psychology at the University of California, Santa Barbara, where he has served since 1975. His research interests are in applying the science of learning to education, with current projects on multimedia learning, computer-supported learning, and computer games for learning. He served as President of Division 15 (Educational Psychology) of the American Psychological Association and Vice President of the American Educational Research Association for Division C (Learning and Instruction). He is the winner of the Thorndike Award for career achievement in educational psychology, the Scribner Award for outstanding research in learning and instruction, and the American Psychological Association's Distinguished Contribution of Applications of Psychology to Education and Training Award.

**Punya Mishra** is professor of educational psychology and educational technology at the College of Education at Michigan State University. He co-directs the Master's Program in Educational Technology and is former chair of the Innovation and Technology Committee of the American Association of Colleges of Teacher Education. He holds an undergraduate degree in engineering, master's degrees in visual and mass communication, and a Ph.D. in Educational Psychology. He has worked extensively in the area of technology integration in teacher education which led to the development (in collaboration with Dr. M. J. Koehler) of the Technological Pedagogical Content Knowledge framework. His current research focuses on transdisciplinary creativity and the role that digital technologies can play in fostering creativity in teaching and learning.

**Chauncey Monte-Sano** is an Associate Professor of Educational Studies at the University of Michigan. Her research examines how history students learn to reason with evidence in writing, and how their teachers learn to teach such historical thinking. She has won research grants from the Institute of Education Sciences and the Spencer Foundation, as well as awards from the National Council of the Social Studies, American

Historical Association, and Division K of the American Educational Research Association. She holds a Ph.D. in curriculum and teacher education from Stanford University.

**Benjamin Nagengast** is a Professor of Educational Psychology at the Hector Research Institute of Education Sciences and Psychology at the University of Tübingen, Germany. His methodological research interests include latent variable models, causal inference, and multilevel modeling. Substantively, he is interested in individual and institutional factors shaping motivation and academic self-concept, educational effectiveness, and the impact of educational interventions. He is the deputy director of the Graduate School on Learning, Educational Achievement, and Life Course Development, which is funded by the excellence initiative of the German federal and state governments. Nagengast holds a Ph.D. in Psychology from the University of Jena, Germany.

**Na'ilah Suad Nasir** is the H. Michael and Jeanne Williams Chair of African American Studies, and holds the Birgeneau Chair in Educational Disparities in the Graduate School of Education at the University of California, Berkeley. Her program of research focuses on issues of race, culture, and schooling. She is the author of *Racialized Identities: Race and Achievement for African-American Youth*, published by Stanford University Press.

**Gary Natriello** is the Ruth L. Gottesman Professor of Educational Research and Professor of Sociology and Education in the Programs in Cognitive Studies and Developmental Psychology in the Department of Human Development at Teachers College, Columbia University. Professor Natriello is the Director of the Teachers College EdLab, a design and development unit devoted to creating new educational possibilities for the information age. He is the executive editor of the *Teachers College Record* and the Director of the Gottesman Libraries at Teachers College. Professor Natriello's research interests include school organization, evaluation, at-risk youth, and the sociology of online learning. He holds an A.B. (English) from Princeton University, an A.M. (sociology) from Stanford University, and a Ph.D. (sociology of education) from Stanford University. He has also been a postdoctoral fellow in the National Institute of Mental Health Program in Structurally Induced Social Problems and Mental Health in the Department of Sociology at Johns Hopkins University.

**David O'Brien** is Professor of Literacy Education at the University of Minnesota, Twin Cities. His research is in the area of adolescent literacy, including disciplinary literacy, digital literacies, reading at middle- and high-school levels, and teacher education related to the literacy practices of adolescent learners. His most recent projects include research on the motivation and engagement of "struggling" and disengaged students using digital media and studying the relation between the affordances of multimodal literacy environments and learning in the disciplines.

**Gabriele Oettingen** is a Professor of Psychology at New York University and the University of Hamburg/Germany. In her research, she is exploring how conscious and non-conscious processes interact in influencing people's control of thought, feelings, and action. She distinguishes between self-regulatory processes involving fantasies versus expectations, and their differential short-term and long-term influences on information processing, effort, and successful performance. She also created the model of mental contrasting that specifies which conscious and non-conscious processes corroborate in turning wishes and fantasies into binding goals and plans, and eventually goal attainment. Her recent research uses insights from research on mental contrasting to develop powerful time and cost-effective behavior change interventions; this research is linked to implementation intention theory as proposed by Peter Gollwitzer.

**Anna Osipova** is an Adjunct Assistant Professor within the Division of Special Education and Counseling at the California State University, Los Angeles (CSULA). Her research focuses on atypical first- and second-language acquisition and development, as well as issues in literacy and academic language development for students with learning disabilities and English Language Learners. She holds two MA degrees (Teaching English as a Second Language and Special Education), and is a doctoral candidate in the joint special education program at CSULA and the University of California, Los Angeles.

**Erika A. Patall** is an assistant professor of Educational Psychology at The University of Texas at Austin. She received her Ph.D. in social psychology at Duke University. Her research focuses on the determinants, development, and corollaries of motivation, particularly in school contexts. She is also interested in the development and use of meta-analytic methods in social science and education policy relevant research.

**Reinhard Pekrun** holds the Research Chair for Personality and Educational Psychology at the University of Munich. He is a pioneer in research on emotions in education and the originator of the Control-Value Theory of Achievement Emotions. Pekrun is a Fellow of the International Academy of Education and of the American Educational Research Association. He served as President of the Stress and Anxiety Research Society, as senior editor of *Anxiety, Stress and Coping*, as Vice-President for Research at the University of Munich, and as a member of expert groups in educational evaluation, such as the Organisation for Economic Cooperation Development Programme for International Student Assessment (PISA).

**William R. Penuel** is a professor of educational psychology and learning sciences in the School of Education at the University of Colorado Boulder. His research focuses on teacher learning and organizational processes that shape the implementation of educational policies, school curricula, and after-school programs.

**William Perez** is an Associate Professor of Education at Claremont Graduate University. His research focuses on immigrant adolescent psychosocial development (e.g., ethnic identity, acculturation), academic achievement, achievement motivation, and higher-education access. His most recent work focuses on undocumented students and Mexican indigenous immigrant adolescents in the United States.

**Arthur E. Poropat** worked in organizational development and workplace learning prior to his academic career in the Griffith Business School and the School of Applied Psychology at Griffith University. This background prompted his interest in factors contributing to individual learning and work performance, and later recognition of parallels in the links between personality and academic performance. Exploration of these links led to consideration of interpersonal relationships, and the consequences of varying the perspective of personality assessments between self and others. His current interests are focused on interpersonal understandings of both personality and various types of performance, with the aim of developing integrated models that can be applied in organizational and educational practice.

**Abby Reisman** is an Assistant Professor of Teacher Education at the University of Pennsylvania's Graduate School of Education. She received her Ph.D. from Stanford University, where she directed the Reading Like a Historian Project in San Francisco, a history curriculum intervention in urban high schools. Reisman's work focuses on the pragmatics of translating text-based historical inquiry into classroom instruction with struggling readers. Her research interests include curriculum design, teacher education, pedagogy, and high-leverage instructional practices.

**Lauren B. Resnick** is a Distinguished University Professor of Psychology and Cognitive Science and senior research scientist at the University of Pittsburgh's Learning Research and Development Center. Her recent work focuses on the nature and development of thinking abilities, and the role of talk and discourse in learning. She has served as president of the Division of Educational Psychology of the American Psychological Association and as president of the American Educational Research Association and is an elected member of the National Academy of Arts and Sciences and National Academy of Education. She holds an Ed.D. in education from Harvard University.

**Bethany Rittle-Johnson** is an Associate Professor of Psychology at Peabody College, Vanderbilt University. Her research focuses on learning of key concepts and problem-solving procedures in mathematics, with an emphasis on experiences that promote learning. She conducts this research in both laboratory and classroom contexts to better understand learning processes. She received her Ph.D. in Developmental Psychology from Carnegie Mellon University.

**Theresa Rogers** is a Professor in the Department of Language and Literacy at the University of British Columbia. She holds a Ph.D. from the University of Illinois and an M.Ed. from Harvard University. Her current research focuses on the integration of arts, media, and critical literacy practices among adolescents and adults. She has served on the editorial boards of *Reading Research Quarterly* and the *American Educational Research Association Journal* and is currently a co-editor of the *Journal of Literacy Research*. She has also served as a board member of the Literacy Research Association.

**Carolyn Penstein Rosé** is Associate Professor of Language Technologies and Human–Computer Interaction. Her work focuses on understanding the social and pragmatic nature of conversation, and using this understanding to build computational systems that can improve the efficacy of conversation between people, and between people and computers. She is president elect of the International Society of the Learning Sciences. She holds an M.S. in Computational Linguistics and a Ph.D. in Language and Informational Technologies from Carnegie Mellon University.

**Cary J. Roseth** is an associate professor of educational psychology and co-director of the educational psychology and educational technology doctoral program at Michigan State University. He received his Ph.D. in educational psychology from the University of Minnesota in 2006, before which he worked for 9 years as a high-school teacher, administrator, and coach. His research focuses on how the presence of others—and especially peers—affects academic achievement, motivation, and social behaviors.

**Stephanie J. Rowley** is a Professor of Psychology at the University of Michigan. She studies the ways in which parents academically socialize children and the roles of race and gender in those strategies. Professor Rowley also serves on the executive committee of the Center for the Study of Black Youth in Context.

**Jana Schrage** is a research scientist at the University of Hamburg (Germany). Her research interest is in motivation, self-regulation, and conflict resolution. She focuses on how people can effectively self-regulate their conciliatory behavior and reconcile in the aftermath of interpersonal conflicts. She holds a Ph.D. in psychology from the University of Hamburg.

**Daniel L. Schwartz** taught secondary English, Math, and Science in Los Angeles Unified School District and Yukon Koyukuk School District before taking a Ph.D. in Human Learning at Columbia University. He works at the intersection of cognitive science, computer science, and education, by examining cognition and instruction in individual, cross-cultural, and technological settings. He is the Nomellini-Olivier Professor of Educational Technology at Stanford's Graduate School of Education.

**Viviane Seyranian** is an Assistant Professor of Social Psychology at California State Polytechnic University, Pomona. Her research focuses on social influence processes, social identity, and attitudinal and behavior change. Many of her research projects apply social psychological theories and insights to address social problems, particularly in the realm of environmental issues and the encouragement of interest and learning in science, technology, engineering, and mathematics. Her research has been funded by the Haynes Foundation, the Bill and Melinda Gates Foundation, the University of Southern California, and Claremont Graduate University. She earned her Ph.D. and M.A. in social psychology from Claremont Graduate University and completed a postdoctoral fellowship at the University of Southern California under the advisement of Gale Sinatra.

**Gale M. Sinatra** is a Professor of Psychology and Education at the Rossier School of Education at the University of Southern California and head of the Motivated Change Research Laboratory (MCRL). Her research focuses on understanding the cognitive, affective, and motivational processes that lead to successful learning. More specifically, she and her colleagues in the MCRL explore the role of motivation and emotion in teaching and learning about controversial topics such as climate change and evolution. She holds a Ph.D. in Psychology from the University of Massachusetts, Amherst.

**Jon R. Star** is an Associate Professor of Education at the Graduate School of Education, Harvard University. His research focuses on the teaching and learning of mathematics at all grade levels, but with particular emphasis on middle- and high-school students' learning of algebra. Star is a former middle-school and high-school mathematics teacher; he is also an experienced teacher of in-service and pre-service mathematics teachers. Star received his Ph.D. in Education and Psychology from the University of Michigan.

**H. Lee Swanson** is a distinguished professor in educational psychology and holds the Peloy Endowed Chair at the University of California-Riverside. He received his Ph.D. from the University of New Mexico and completed his postdoctoral studies at the University of California, Los Angeles. His current research focuses on the relationship between cognition and academic difficulties in children with learning disabilities. He is currently editor of the *Journal of Learning Disabilities*.

**Iris Tabak** is co-editor of the *Journal of the Learning Sciences*. She is a senior lecturer and chair of Curriculum and Instruction in the Education Department at Ben-Gurion University of the Negev, Israel. She investigates domain-specific dimensions of complex reasoning, as well as the design of material, computational, and social supports for such reasoning. She served as the president of the International Society of the Learning Sciences. She holds a B.S.E. in computer engineering from the University of Michigan, and a Ph.D. in learning sciences from Northwestern University.

**Ulrich Trautwein** is a Professor of Education Sciences at the Hector Research Institute of Education Sciences and Psychology at the University of Tübingen, Germany. His main research interests include the effects of different learning environments on self-concept, interest, and personality development, the role of self-related cognitions in students' homework behavior, and educational transitions. Trautwein directs two longitudinal large-scale school achievement studies and a number of large-scale intervention projects. He is also the director of the Graduate School on Learning, Educational Achievement, and Life Course Development (LEAD), which is funded by the excellence initiative of the German federal and state governments.

**Ellen L. Usher** is an associate professor of educational psychology at the University of Kentucky. She received her Ph.D. in educational studies from Emory University in 2007, before which she taught elementary and middle school. Her research has focused on the sources and effects of personal efficacy beliefs. She is the director of the P20 Motivation and Learning Lab.

**Ian A. G. Wilkinson** is Professor in the Department of Teaching and Learning at The Ohio State University. His research focuses on school and classroom contexts for literacy learning and the cognitive consequences for students. He is currently conducting research on the impact of classroom discussion on students' reading comprehension and the implications for professional development of teachers. He served as Co-editor of *Reading Research Quarterly* from 2006 to 2012. He holds a Ph.D. in Educational Psychology from the University of Illinois at Urbana-Champaign.

**Anita Woolfolk Hoy** is Professor Emeritus of educational psychology and philosophy at The Ohio State University, Columbus, Ohio, where she studied the role of educational psychology in the preparation of teachers as well as teachers' thinking and beliefs, particularly the meaning and measure of teachers' sense of efficacy. Her text, *Educational Psychology* (Pearson) is moving into its 13th edition and has been translated into over a dozen languages. In addition, her *Child and Adolescent Development* (Pearson) book with Nancy Perry is in its second edition.

# Author Index

Note: The following abbreviations have been used – $f$ = figure; $n$ = note; $t$ = table

# Subject Index

Note: The following abbreviations have been used – $f$ = figure; $n$ = note; $t$ =table